EIGHTH EDITION

ADULT DEVELOPMENT AND AGING

JOHN C. CAVANAUGH
Consortium of Universities of the Washington Metropolitan Area

FREDDA BLANCHARD-FIELDS

Australia • Brazil • Canada • Mexico • Singapore • United Kingdom • United States

Adult Development and Aging, Eighth Edition

John C. Cavanaugh and Fredda Blanchard-Fields

Product Director: Marta Lee-Perriard

Product Team Manager: Star Burruto

Product Manager: Andrew Ginsberg

Content Developer: Nedah Rose

Product Assistant: Leah Jenson

Digital Content Specialist: Allison Marion

Content Project Manager: Ruth Sakata Corley

Production and Composition Service: SPi Global

Intellectual Property Analyst: Deanna Ettinger

Intellectual Property Project Manager: Reba Frederics

Illustrator: Lisa Torri

Art Director: Vernon Boes

Text and Cover Designer: Liz Harasymczuk

Cover Image: Rob Marmion/Shutterstock.com, Diego Cervo/Shutterstock.com, KoBoZaa/Shutterstock.com, arek_malang/Shutterstock.com, ESB Professional/Shutterstock.com, Martin Novak/Shutterstock.com, A and N photography/Shutterstock.com, Blend Images/Shutterstock.com, Blend Images – John Lund/Sam Diephuis/Brand X Pictures/Getty Images

Compositor: SPi Global

© 2019, 2015 Cengage Learning, Inc.

Unless otherwise noted, all content is © Cengage.

ALL RIGHTS RESERVED. No part of this work covered by the copyright herein may be reproduced or distributed in any form or by any means, except as permitted by U.S. copyright law, without the prior written permission of the copyright owner.

For product information and technology assistance, contact us at
Cengage Customer & Sales Support, 1-800-354-9706.

For permission to use material from this text or product, submit all requests online at **www.cengage.com/permissions.**
Further permissions questions can be e-mailed to
permissionrequest@cengage.com.

Library of Congress Control Number: 2017950380

Student Edition:
ISBN: 978-1-337-55908-9

Loose-leaf Edition:
ISBN: 978-1-337-56352-9

Cengage
200 Pier 4 Boulevard
Boston, MA 02210
USA

Cengage is a leading provider of customized learning solutions with employees residing in nearly 40 different countries and sales in more than 125 countries around the world. Find your local representative at **www.cengage.com.**

To learn more about Cengage platforms and services, visit **www.cengage.com.**

Printed in Mexico
Print Number: 06   Print Year: 2021

In memory of Fredda Blanchard-Fields, friend and collaborator,
who dedicated her life to educating students.
To Chris

Brief Contents

1. Studying Adult Development and Aging 1
2. Neuroscience as a Basis for Adult Development and Aging 29
3. Physical Changes 56
4. Longevity, Health, and Functioning 90
5. Where People Live: Person–Environment Interactions 126
6. Attention and Memory 157
7. Intelligence, Reasoning, Creativity, and Wisdom 185
8. Social Cognition 215
9. Personality 243
10. Clinical Assessment, Mental Health, and Mental Disorders 270
11. Relationships 307
12. Work, Leisure, and Retirement 339
13. Dying and Bereavement 371
14. Healthy Aging 401

Contents

CHAPTER 1
Studying Adult Development and Aging   1

1.1 Perspectives on Adult Development and Aging   3
DISCOVERING DEVELOPMENT Myths and Stereotypes About Aging   3
The Life-Span Perspective   4
The Demographics of Aging   4

1.2 Issues in Studying Adult Development and Aging   7
The Forces of Development   8
Interrelations Among the Forces: Developmental Influences   9
Culture and Ethnicity   9
The Meaning of Age   10
Core Issues in Development   11

REAL PEOPLE Pope Francis Sets Many New Examples   12

CURRENT CONTROVERSIES Does Personality in Young Adulthood Determine Personality in Old Age?   13

1.3 Research Methods   15
Measurement in Adult Development and Aging Research   15
General Designs for Research   16
Designs for Studying Development   17
Integrating Findings from Different Studies   21
Conducting Research Ethically   21

HOW DO WE KNOW? Conflicts Between Cross-Sectional and Longitudinal Data   22

Social Policy Implications   24

Summary   25
Review Questions   27
Integrating Concepts in Development   27
Key Terms   27

CHAPTER 2
Neuroscience as a Basis for Adult Development and Aging   29

2.1 The Neuroscience Approach   31
Neuroimaging Techniques   31
Neuroscience Perspectives   32

DISCOVERING DEVELOPMENT What Do People Believe About Brain Fitness?   33

2.2 Neuroscience and Adult Development and Aging   33
How Is the Brain Organized?   34
What Age-Related Changes Occur in Neurons?   35
What Age-Related Changes Occur in Neurotransmitters?   35
What Age-Related Changes Occur in Brain Structures?   36
What Do Structural Brain Changes Mean? The Theory of Mind   37

HOW DO WE KNOW? The Aging Emotional Brain   38

2.3 Making Sense of Neuroscience Research: Explaining Changes in Brain-Behavior Relations   42
The Parieto-Frontal Integration Theory   43
Can Older Adults Compensate for Changes in the Brain?   44
Theories of Brain-Behavior Changes Across Adulthood   45

REAL PEOPLE Oliver Sacks, Brain Mapper   45

2.4 Plasticity and the Aging Brain   48
What Is Brain Plasticity?   49
Exercise and Brain Aging   49

CURRENT CONTROVERSIES Are Neural Stem Cells the Solution to Brain Aging?   50

Nutrition and Brain Aging   50
Social Policy Implications   51

Summary   52
Review Questions   53
Integrating Concepts in Development   54
Key Terms   54

CHAPTER 3
Physical Changes   56

3.1 Why Do We Age? Biological Theories of Aging   57
Metabolic Theories   58

DISCOVERING DEVELOPMENT Why Do Most People Think We Age?   58

Cellular Theories   58

Genetic Programming Theories 60
Implications of the Developmental Forces 60

3.2 Appearance and Mobility 61
Changes in Skin, Hair, and Voice 61
Changes in Body Build 62
Changes in Mobility 63
Psychological Implications 66

3.3 Sensory Systems 67
Vision 68
Hearing 69

HOW DO WE KNOW? Hearing and Quality of Life Among Community-Dwelling Older Adults 71

Somesthesia and Balance 72
Taste and Smell 73

3.4 Vital Functions 75
Cardiovascular System 75

REAL PEOPLE Donna Arnett's Recovery from Stroke 78

Respiratory System 79

3.5 The Reproductive System 80
Female Reproductive System 80

CURRENT CONTROVERSIES Menopausal Hormone Therapy 81

Male Reproductive System 82
Psychological Implications 82

3.6 The Autonomic Nervous System 83
Autonomic Nervous System 83
Psychological Implications 84
Social Policy Implications 85

Summary 86
Review Questions 88
Integrating Concepts in Development 88
Key Terms 89

CHAPTER 4
Longevity, Health, and Functioning 90

4.1 How Long Will We Live? 91

DISCOVERING DEVELOPMENT Take the Longevity Test 92

Average and Maximum Longevity 92
Genetic and Environmental Factors in Average Longevity 94
Ethnic Differences in Average Longevity 95
Gender Differences in Average Longevity 95
International Differences in Average Longevity 96

4.2 Health and Illness 97
Defining Health and Illness 97
Quality of Life 98
Changes in the Immune System 98
Chronic and Acute Diseases 100
The Role of Stress 101

HOW DO WE KNOW? Negative Life Events and Mastery 104

4.3 Common Chronic Conditions and Their Management 105
General Issues in Chronic Conditions 105
Common Chronic Conditions 106

REAL PEOPLE The "Angelina Jolie Effect" 109

CURRENT CONTROVERSIES The Prostate Cancer Dilemma 111

Managing Pain 112

4.4 Pharmacology and Medication Adherence 113
Patterns of Medication Use 113
Developmental Changes in How Medications Work 114
Medication Side Effects and Interactions 114
Adherence to Medication Regimens 115

4.5 Functional Health and Disability 116
A Model of Disability in Late Life 116
Determining Functional Health Status 119
What Causes Functional Limitations and Disability in Older Adults? 120

Social Policy Implications 121

Summary 121
Review Questions 123
Integrating Concepts In Development 124
Key Terms 124

CHAPTER 5
Where People Live: Person–Environment Interactions 126

5.1 Describing Person–Environment Interactions 128
Competence and Environmental Press 128

DISCOVERING DEVELOPMENT What's Your Adaptation Level? 130

Preventive and Corrective Proactivity Model 130
Stress and Coping Framework 132
Common Theoretical Themes and Everyday Competence 132

5.2 The Ecology of Aging: Community Options 133

REAL PEOPLE Designing for a Reimagined Aging 134

    Aging in Place 135
    Deciding on the Best Option 136
    Home Modification 136
    Adult Day Care 138
    Congregate Housing 138
    Assisted Living 139

5.3 Living in Nursing Homes 140

    Long-Term Care in Nursing Homes 142

CURRENT CONTROVERSIES Financing Long-Term Care 142

    Who Is Likely to Live in Nursing Homes? 143
    Characteristics of Nursing Homes 143
    Special Care Units 144
    Can a Nursing Home Be a Home? 145
    Communicating with Residents 146

HOW DO WE KNOW? Identifying Different Types of Elderspeak in Singapore 147

    Decision-Making Capacity and Individual Choices 150
    New Directions for Nursing Homes 151

Social Policy Implications 152

Summary 153
Review Questions 155
Integrating Concepts in Development 155
Key Terms 155

CHAPTER 6
Attention and Memory 157

6.1 Information Processing and Attention 159

    Information-Processing Model 159
    Attention: The Basics 160
    Speed of Processing 160
    Processing Resources 160

DISCOVERING DEVELOPMENT How Good Are Your Notes? 161

    Automatic and Effortful Processing 162

6.2 Memory Processes 162

    Working Memory 162
    Implicit Versus Explicit Memory 163
    Long-Term Memory 164
    Age Differences in Encoding Versus Retrieval 165

6.3 Memory in Context 166

    Prospective Memory 167

HOW DO WE KNOW? Failing to Remember I Did What I Was Supposed to Do 168

    Source Memory and Processing of Misinformation 170
    Factors That Preserve Memory 171
    Training Memory Skills 172

REAL PEOPLE The Yoda of Memory Training 172

6.4 Self-Evaluations of Memory Abilities 175

    Aspects of Memory Self-Evaluations 175
    Age Differences in Metamemory and Memory Monitoring 175

6.5 Clinical Issues and Memory Testing 177

    Normal Versus Abnormal Memory Aging 177
    Memory and Physical and Mental Health 178

CURRENT CONTROVERSIES Concussions and Athletes 178

    Memory and Nutrition 180

Social Policy Implications 180

Summary 180
Review Questions 182
Integrating Concepts in Development 183
Key Terms 183

CHAPTER 7
Intelligence, Reasoning, Creativity, and Wisdom 185

7.1 Defining Intelligence 187

    Intelligence in Everyday Life 187
    The Big Picture: A Life-Span View 187
    Research Approaches to Intelligence 189

DISCOVERING DEVELOPMENT How Do People Show Intelligence? 189

7.2 Developmental Trends in Psychometric Intelligence 190

    The Measurement of Intelligence 190
    Primary and Secondary Mental Abilities 191
    Fluid and Crystallized Intelligence 192
    Neuroscience Research and Intelligence in Young and Middle Adulthood 193
    Moderators of Intellectual Change 194
    Modifying Primary Abilities 196

HOW DO WE KNOW? Think Fast, Feel Fine, Live Long 197

7.3 Qualitative Differences in Adults' Thinking 199

    Piaget's Theory 199
    Going Beyond Formal Operations: Thinking in Adulthood 201

REAL PEOPLE Feeling the Bern 203
   Integrating Emotion and Logic 203

7.4 Everyday Reasoning and Problem Solving 204
   Decision Making 205
   Problem Solving 205
   Expertise 207
   Creativity and Wisdom 208

CURRENT CONTROVERSIES Does Creativity Exist? 210

Social Policy Implications 211

Summary 211
Review Questions 213
Integrating Concepts in Development 213
Key Terms 214

CHAPTER 8
Social Cognition 215

8.1 Stereotypes and Aging 217
   Content of Stereotypes 217
   Age Stereotypes and Perceived Competence 218
   Activation of Stereotypes 218
   Stereotype Threat 220

CURRENT CONTROVERSIES Are Stereotypes of Aging Associated with Lower Cognitive Performance? 220

8.2 Social Knowledge Structures and Beliefs 221
   Understanding Age Differences in Social Beliefs 222
   Self-Perception and Social Beliefs 222

HOW DO WE KNOW? Age Differences in Self-Perception 223

8.3 Social Judgment Processes 224
   Emotional Intelligence 224
   Impression Formation 224

REAL PEOPLE Impressions of Hillary Clinton and Donald Trump 225
   Knowledge Accessibility and Social Judgments 227
   A Processing Capacity Explanation for Age Differences in Social Judgments 228
   Attributional Biases 229

8.4 Motivation and Social Processing Goals 231
   Personal Goals 231
   Emotion as a Processing Goal 232
   Cognitive Style as a Processing Goal 233

8.5 Personal Control 234
   Multidimensionality of Personal Control 234

DISCOVERING DEVELOPMENT How Much Control Do You Have Over Your Cognitive Functioning? 234
   Control Strategies 235
   Some Criticisms Regarding Primary Control 236

8.6 Social Situations and Social Competence 236
   Collaborative Cognition 237
   Social Context of Memory 238

Social Policy Implications 238

Summary 239
Review Questions 240
Integrating Concepts in Development 241
Key Terms 242

CHAPTER 9
Personality 243

9.1 Dispositional Traits Across Adulthood 245
   The Case for Stability: The Five-Factor Model 246
   What Happens to Dispositional Traits Across Adulthood? 247
   Conclusions About Dispositional Traits 249

CURRENT CONTROVERSIES Intraindividual Change and the Stability of Traits 249

9.2 Personal Concerns and Qualitative Stages in Adulthood 250
   What's Different About Personal Concerns? 251
   Jung's Theory 251
   Erikson's Stages of Psychosocial Development 252

REAL PEOPLE What Will History Say About You? 256
   Theories Based on Life Transitions 256
   Conclusions About Personal Concerns 257

9.3 Life Narratives, Identity, and the Self 258

DISCOVERING DEVELOPMENT Who Do You Want to Be When You "Grow Up"? 258
   McAdams's Life-Story Model 259
   Whitbourne's Identity Theory 259
   Six Foci Model of Adult Personality 260
   Self-Concept and Well-Being 261
   Possible Selves 262

HOW DO WE KNOW? Possible Selves and Pursuing Social Goals 263
   Religiosity and Spiritual Support 264
   Conclusions About Narratives, Identity, and the Self 265

Social Policy Implications 265

Summary 266
Review Questions 268
Integrating Concepts in Development 268
Key Terms 268

CHAPTER 10
Clinical Assessment, Mental Health, and Mental Disorders 270

REAL PEOPLE Pat Summitt, Winningest College Basketball Coach of All Time 272

10.1 Mental Health and the Adult Life Course 273
Defining Mental Health and Psychopathology 273
A Multidimensional Life-Span Approach to Psychopathology 274
Ethnicity, Gender, Aging, and Mental Health 275

10.2 Developmental Issues in Assessment and Therapy 276
Areas of Multidimensional Assessment 276
Factors Influencing Assessment 277
Assessment Methods 278
Developmental Issues in Therapy 278

10.3 The Big Three: Depression, Delirium, and Dementia 279
Depression 279
Delirium 285
Dementia 285

CURRENT CONTROVERSIES Diagnostic Criteria for Alzheimer's Disease 290

HOW DO WE KNOW? Training Persons with Dementia to Be Group Activity Leaders 294

10.4 Other Mental Disorders and Concerns 298
Anxiety Disorders 298
Psychotic Disorders 299
Alcohol Use Disorder 300

DISCOVERING DEVELOPMENT What Substance Abuse Treatment Options Are Available in Your Area? 302

Social Policy Implications 302

Summary 303
Review Questions 305
Integrating Concepts in Development 305
Key Terms 306

CHAPTER 11
Relationships 307

11.1 Relationship Types and Issues 308
Friendships 308

REAL PEOPLE The Dornenburg Sisters 310

Love Relationships 311

HOW DO WE KNOW? Patterns and Universals of Romantic Attachment Around the World 313
Violence in Relationships 314

11.2 Lifestyles and Love Relationships 316
Singlehood 316
Cohabitation 317
LGBTQ Relationships 318
Marriage 318
Divorce 322
Remarriage 324
Widowhood 325

DISCOVERING DEVELOPMENT What Is It Like to Lose a Spouse/Partner? 326

11.3 Family Dynamics and the Life Course 326
The Parental Role 326
Midlife Issues: Adult Children and Caring for Aging Parents 330

CURRENT CONTROVERSIES Paid Family Leave 330
Grandparenthood 332
Social Policy Implications 334

Summary 335
Review Questions 337
Integrating Concepts in Development 337
Key Terms 337

CHAPTER 12
Work, Leisure, and Retirement 339

12.1 Occupational Selection and Development 340
The Meaning of Work 340
Occupational Choice Revisited 341
Occupational Development 342
Job Satisfaction 344

12.2 Gender, Ethnicity, and Discrimination Issues 346
Gender Differences in Occupational Selection 346
Women and Occupational Development 347
Ethnicity and Occupational Development 349
Bias and Discrimination 349

CURRENT CONTROVERSIES Helping Women Lean In? 350

12.3 Occupational Transitions 351
Retraining Workers 352
Occupational Insecurity 352
Coping with Unemployment 353

DISCOVERING DEVELOPMENT What Unemployment Benefits Are Available in Your Area? 353

12.4 Work and Family 355
  The Dependent Care Dilemma 355
  Juggling Multiple Roles 356

12.5 Leisure Activities 359
  Types of Leisure Activities 359
  Developmental Changes in Leisure 360

HOW DO WE KNOW? Long-Term Effects of Leisure Activities 360

  Consequences of Leisure Activities 361

12.6 Retirement and Work in Late Life 362
  What Does Being Retired Mean? 362
  Why Do People Retire? 363
  Adjustment to Retirement 363
  Employment and Volunteering 364

REAL PEOPLE Retiring to the Peace Corps 365

Social Policy Implications 366

Summary 367
Review Questions 369
Integrating Concepts in Development 369
Key Terms 370

CHAPTER 13
Dying and Bereavement 371

13.1 Definitions and Ethical Issues 373
  Sociocultural Definitions of Death 373
  Legal and Medical Definitions 374
  Ethical Issues 374

CURRENT CONTROVERSIES The Brittany Maynard Case 376

13.2 Thinking About Death: Personal Aspects 377
  A Life-Course Approach to Dying 378

DISCOVERING DEVELOPMENT A Self-Reflective Exercise on Death 378

REAL PEOPLE Randy Pausch's Last Lecture 378
  Dealing with One's Own Death 379
  Death Anxiety 380

13.3 End-of-Life Issues 382
  Creating a Final Scenario 382
  The Hospice Option 383
  Making Your End-of-Life Intentions Known 385

13.4 Surviving the Loss: The Grieving Process 386
  The Grief Process 387
  Typical Grief Reactions 388
  Coping with Grief 389

HOW DO WE KNOW? Grief Processing and Avoidance in the United States and China 390

  Ambiguous Loss 392
  Complicated or Prolonged Grief Disorder 393
  Adult Developmental Aspects of Grief 393
  Conclusion 395

Social Policy Implications 396

Summary 397
Review Questions 398
Integrating Concepts in Development 399
Key Terms 399

CHAPTER 14
Healthy Aging 401

14.1 Demographic Trends and Social Policy 402
  Demographic Trends: 2030 403
  Social Security and Medicare 404

CURRENT CONTROVERSIES What to Do About Social Security and Medicare 407

14.2 Healthy Aging: Living Well in Later Life 408
  What Is Healthy Aging? 408

DISCOVERING DEVELOPMENT What Is Living Well? 408

  Health Promotion and Quality of Life 409
  Using Technology to Maintain and Enhance Competence 410
  Health Promotion and Disease Prevention 412
  Lifestyle Factors 414

14.3 Epilogue 418

Summary 419
Review Questions 419
Integrating Concepts in Development 420
Key Terms 420

References 421
Name Index 461
Glossary/Subject Index 468

Preface

People's experiences growing older in the 21st century differ dramatically from their parents' and grandparents' experience. The complex issues confronting individuals and societies are the reason a solid grounding in research and theory about adult development and aging is essential even for understanding news events. The healthcare debates, for example, bring many issues to the forefront, including Medicare, end-of-life issues, and longevity and the possibility of significant intergenerational policy issues. Other news stories about genetic breakthroughs, stem cell research, brain-imaging techniques, and the latest breakthroughs in treating dementia happen regularly. To understand why these issues are so critical, one must understand aging in a broader, rapidly changing context. That is why *Adult Development and Aging* is now in its eighth edition.

The next few decades of this century will witness a fundamental change in the face of the population—literally. Along with many countries in the industrialized world, the United States will experience an explosive growth in the older adult population due to the continued aging of the baby-boom generation. Additionally, the proportion of older adults who are African American, Latino, Asian American, and Native American will increase rapidly. To deal with these changes, new approaches need to be created through the combined efforts of people in many occupations—academics, gerontologists, social workers, healthcare professionals, financial experts, marketing professionals, teachers, factory workers, technologists, government workers, human service providers, and nutritionists, to mention just a few. Every reader of this book, regardless of his or her area of expertise, needs to understand older adults to master the art of living.

This eighth edition of *Adult Development and Aging* continues to provide in-depth coverage of the major issues in the psychology of adult development and aging. The eighth edition adds numerous topics and provides expanded coverage of many of the ones discussed in earlier editions.

Chapter-by-Chapter Additions and Enhancements to *Adult Development and Aging*, Eighth Edition

Chapter 1
- Rewritten section on the demographics of aging
- New *Real People* feature highlighting Pope Francis

Chapter 2
- Addition of the disconnected brain hypothesis related to cognitive decline
- Fuller discussion of structural brain changes and their relation to behavioral change with age
- More specific information about brain structures and cognition
- Added concept of Theory of Mind
- New *Real People* feature highlighting Oliver Sacks
- Added discussion of the PASA model of brain function changes with age
- Update to the STAC theory of cognitive aging to STAC-r

Chapter 3
- New discussion of forms of age-related macular degeneration
- New *How Do We Know?* feature on hearing loss and quality of life
- New *Real People* feature highlighting Donna Arnett's recovery from stroke
- Added note that vaping may lead to respiratory disease
- Added mention of soy, yoga, and pharmacogenomics as approaches to addressing menopausal symptoms
- Added discussion of the Kronos Early Estrogen Prevention Study (KEEPS)

Chapter 4
- Additional information on genetics of health and genomic-based interventions throughout
- Longevity data on OECD countries
- Stronger emphasis on distinction between health-related and non-health-related aspects of quality of life
- Additional information about genetics and cancer, including *PALB2* as a genetic factor in breast cancer
- New *Real People* feature about Angelina Jolie and breast cancer risk
- Addition of the hierarchy of loss in the disability and frailty section

Chapter 5
- Revised *Discovering Development* feature on adaptation level
- More discussion regarding Accessory Dwelling Units
- New *Real People* feature highlighting Matthias Hollwich, an architect
- Expanded discussion about assisted living
- New discussion of the *MESSAGE Communication Strategies in Dementia* training program
- Expanded discussion about Eden Alternative, Green House Project, Pioneer Network

Chapter 6
- New *Real People* feature about Harry Lorayne
- Chapter reorganization to include memory training in Memory in Context section
- Considerably more information about neurological development, and neuroimaging and neuroscience research

Chapter 7
- New *How Do We Know?* feature on longitudinal data on the relations among intelligence, health, and survival
- New *Real People* feature on Bernie Sanders and the 2016 election
- New *Current Controversies* feature on whether creativity actually exists
- Discussion of the Openness-Fluid-Crystallized-Intelligence (OFCI) model
- Discussion added of terminal decline
- Revised *Social Policy* feature regarding misleading claims of cognitive training programs

Chapter 8
- Discussion of the serious negative effects of believing negative stereotypes about aging
- Revised section on stereotypes and competence
- New discussion of Implicit Association Test and imagined intergroup contact intervention strategy
- New *Real People* feature on Hillary Clinton and Donald Trump
- New discussion of emotional intelligence
- Discussion of the Strength and Vulnerability Integration (SAVI) model of emotional experience across adulthood

Chapter 9
- *Current Controversies* feature rewritten
- New discussion of the TESSERA model of personality in adulthood
- New *Real People* feature on each person's legacy
- New section on the Six Foci Model of Adult Personality
- New *How Do We Know?* feature on possible selves and social goal pursuit

Chapter 10
- New *Real People* feature on Pat Summitt (Tennessee women's basketball coach)
- Discussion of culturally based norms for mental health assessment
- Role of microglial cells in depression pointed out
- New section on dementia with Lewy bodies and its relation to Parkinson's disease
- New discussion on Alcohol Abuse Disorder from DSM-5

Chapter 11
- Discussion of Social Baseline Theory to explain how the brain activity reveals how people seek social relationships to mitigate risk
- New *Real People* feature on the Dornenburg sisters
- Revised discussion of financial exploitation and the role of financial institutions in preventing it
- Inclusion of millennial generation lifestyles, including their likely much lower rates of marriage and likelihood of being less well-off than their parents
- Rewritten discussion of LGBTQ adults
- New *Discovering Development* feature on the experience of losing a spouse/partner
- New *Current Controversies* feature on paid family leave

Chapter 12
- New chapter introduction focusing on the shift to the "gig economy" and its impact on the meaning of work
- Differentiation of mentoring and coaching
- Mention of burnout effects on the brain
- Reduced redundancy in parenting and work–family conflict sections

- New *How Do We Know?* feature on the long-term health effects of leisure activities
- New *Real People* feature on David and Champa Jarmul, Peace Corps volunteers

Chapter 13
- Table with most frequent causes of death by age
- Discussion of updated brain death criteria and implementation issues
- New *Current Controversies* featuring the Brittany Maynard case
- Discussion of death doulas
- New *Real People* feature with focus on Randy Pausch's last lecture
- Discussion of the Model of Adaptive Grieving Dynamics
- Discussion of disenfranchised grief
- Added discussion of ambiguous grief

Chapter 14
- New chapter title
- Chapter restructured to focus on social issues and the healthy aging framework
- Revised discussions of Social Security and Medicare based on recent political activity
- Discussion of salutogenesis added as an important framework for promoting wellness

Writing Style

Although *Adult Development and Aging, Eighth Edition* covers complex issues and difficult topics, we use clear, concise, and understandable language. All terms were examined to ensure their use is essential; otherwise, they were eliminated.

The text is aimed at upper-division undergraduate students. Although it will be helpful if students completed an introductory psychology or life-span human development course, the text does not assume this background.

Instructional Aids

The many pedagogical aids in previous editions have been retained and enhanced in the eighth edition.

- *Learning Aids in the Chapter Text*. Each chapter begins with a chapter outline. At the start of each new section, learning objectives are presented. These objectives are keyed to each primary subsection that follows, and they direct the students' attention to the main points to be discussed. At the conclusion of each major section are concept checks, one for each primary subsection, that help students spot-check their learning. Key terms are defined in context; the term itself is printed in boldface, with the sentence containing the term's definition in italic.
- *End-of-Chapter Learning Aids*. At the end of each chapter are summaries, organized by major sections and primary subsection heads. This approach helps students match the chapter outline with the summary. Numerous review questions, also organized around major sections and primary subsections, are provided to assist students in identifying major points. Integrative questions are included as a way for students to link concepts across sections within and across chapters. Key terms with definitions are listed.
- *Boxes*. Four types of boxes are included. Those titled *How Do We Know?* draw attention to specific research studies that were discussed briefly in the main body of the text. Details about the study's design, participants, and outcomes are presented as a way for students to connect the information about these issues in Chapter 1 with specific research throughout the text. *Current Controversies* boxes raise controversial and provocative issues about topics discussed in the chapter. These boxes get students to think about the implications of research or policy issues and may be used effectively as points of departure for class discussions. *Discovering Development* boxes give students a way to see developmental principles and concepts in the "real world" as well as some suggestions on how to find others. *Real People* provides actual examples of aspects of aging and how people chose to handle them. These boxes provide a starting point for applied projects in either individual or group settings, and help students understand how development is shaped by the interaction of biological, psychological, sociocultural, and life-cycle forces.

MindTap

MindTap® Psychology for Cavanaugh/Blanchard-Fields' *Adult Development and Aging*, 8th Edition is the digital learning solution that powers students from memorization to mastery. It gives you complete control of your course—to provide engaging content, to challenge every individual, and to build their confidence. Empower students to accelerate their progress with MindTap.

With MindTap you can:

- Integrate your own content into the MindTap Reader using your own documents or pulling from sources like RSS feeds, YouTube videos, websites, Googledocs, and more.
- Use powerful analytics and reports that provide a snapshot of class progress, time in course, engagement, and completion.

In addition to the benefits of the platform, MindTap for *Adult Development and Aging* includes:

- Formative assessments at the conclusion of each chapter.
- Investigate Development enables students to observe, evaluate, and make decisions about human development so they see the implications of research on a personal level. Students interact with simulated case studies of milestones in a person's development, observing and analyzing audio-visual cues, consulting research, and making decisions. Instead of rote memorization of isolated concepts, Investigate Development compels students to think critically about research and brings human development to life.

Instructor Companion Site

Everything you need for your course in one place! This collection of book-specific lecture and class tools is available online via www.cengage.com/login. Access and download an instructor's manual, test bank, and PowerPoint slides.

Cengage Learning Testing Powered by Cognero

The Test Bank is also available through Cognero, a flexible, online system that allows you to author, edit, and manage test bank content as well as create multiple test versions in an instant. You can deliver tests from your school's learning management system, your classroom, or wherever you want.

Acknowledgments

As usual, it takes many people to produce a textbook; such is the case with the eighth edition. The editorial group at Cengage is excellent.

Thanks to Andrew Ginsberg, Product Manager; Nedah Rose, Content Developer, for taking the reins and guiding the eighth edition; Ruth Sakata-Corley, Content Production Manager; and Vernon Boes, Art Director, for their work in bringing this edition to life. Thanks to Phil Scott for his work as Project Manager.

Finally to a group too often overlooked—the sales representatives. Without you, none of this would have any payoff. You are an extension of us and the whole Cengage editorial and production team. What a great group of hard-working folks you are!

Thanks to you all. Live long and prosper!

John C. Cavanaugh

About the Author

John C. Cavanaugh is President and CEO of the Consortium of Universities of the Washington Metropolitan Area. Previously, he was Chancellor of the Pennsylvania State System of Higher Education and President of the University of West Florida. A researcher and teacher of adult development and aging for more three decades, he has published more than 80 articles and chapters and authored, coauthored, or coedited 19 books on aging, information technology, and higher education policy. He is a Past President of Division 20 (Adult Development and Aging) of the American Psychological Association (APA) and is a Fellow of APA (Divisions 1, 2, 3, and 20) and the Gerontological Society of America, and a Charter Fellow of the Association for Psychological Science. He has held numerous leadership positions in these associations, including Chair of the Committee on Aging for APA. He has served on numerous state and national committees for aging-related and higher education organizations. John is a devoted fan of *Star Trek* and a serious traveler, photographer, backpacker, cook, and chocoholic. He is married to Dr. Christine K. Cavanaugh.

1 | Studying Adult Development and Aging

CHAPTER OUTLINE

1.1 Perspectives on Adult Development and Aging
DISCOVERING DEVELOPMENT Myths and Stereotypes about Aging
The Life-Span Perspective
The Demographics of Aging

1.2 Issues in Studying Adult Development and Aging
The Forces of Development
Interrelations Among the Forces: Developmental Influences
Culture and Ethnicity
The Meaning of Age
REAL PEOPLE Pope Francis Sets Many New Examples
Core Issues in Development
CURRENT CONTROVERSIES Does Personality in Young Adulthood Determine Personality in Old Age?

1.3 Research Methods
Measurement in Adult Development and Aging Research
General Designs for Research
Designs for Studying Development
HOW DO WE KNOW? Conflicts Between Cross-Sectional and Longitudinal Data
Integrating Findings from Different Studies
Conducting Research Ethically

Social Policy Implications

Summary
Review Questions
Integrating Concepts in Development
Key Terms

Although tired and a bit unsteady, Diana Nyad got out of the water and walked under her own power onto the beach at Key West, Florida. At age 64, she had just become the first person ever to swim the 110 miles from Havana, Cuba, to Key West, Florida, without the protection of a shark cage. Her feat, completed on September 2, 2013, after more than 50 hours of open water swimming, is just one more in a growing list of accomplishments by people at a point in life once thought to be a time of serious decline in abilities. No more.

It is definitely a time of changing perceptions of and opportunities for older adults. Consider that at the time of the Democratic and Republican national conventions in 2016, three of the final five major contenders in their respective parties were at least 68 years old (Hillary Clinton, Donald Trump, and Bernie Sanders). Jorge Mario Bergoglio was 76 when he became Pope Francis. Janet Yellen became Chair of the Federal Reserve at 67. The 14th Dalai Lama still inspired people in his 80s. John Lewis continued to work for social justice in his 70s. Ennio Morricone won an Oscar for best music score at age 87, topping the previous record held by Christopher Plummer, who won for best supporting actor at age 82. And Mick Jagger still wowed audiences when he passed age 70.

From athletes to politicians to people in everyday life, boundaries once thought fixed are being pushed every day.

Diana Nyad, Hillary Clinton, and Pope Francis are great examples of how older adults are being looked at differently today. They demonstrate that adults are capable of doing things thought unimaginable or inappropriate not very long ago. They also illustrate how the normal changes people experience as they age vary across individuals and why we need to rethink common stereotypes about age.

There is also an entire generation poised to redefine what growing older really means. The baby-boom generation, consisting of people born between 1946 and 1964, are on average the healthiest and most active generation to reach old age in history. They are not content with playing traditional roles assigned to older adults and are doing their best to change the way older adults are perceived and treated.

In this chapter, we examine a seemingly simple question: Who are older people? We will see that the answer is more complicated than you might think. We also consider the ways in which gerontologists study adults and how adults develop. ■

U.S. long-distance swimmer Diana Nyad is pictured before attempting to swim to Florida from Havana August 31, 2013.

Jorge Mario Bergoglio was elected as Pope Francis at age 76.

Mick Jagger shows that 70-somethings can still rock.

1.1 Perspectives on Adult Development and Aging

LEARNING OBJECTIVES
- What is gerontology? How does ageism relate to stereotypes of aging?
- What is the life-span perspective?
- What are the characteristics of the older adult population?
- How are they likely to change?

Roberto's great-grandmother Maria is 89 years old. Maria tells Roberto that when she was a young girl in El Paso, there were very few older women in either her family or the neighborhood. Roberto knows there are many older people, mostly women, in his own neighborhood, and wonders when and why this changed over her lifetime.

Before you read any more, take a minute and think about your own grandparents or great-grandparents. How would you and other people describe them? Do you want to be like them when you are their age?

We are all headed toward old age. How do you want to be thought of and treated when you get there? Do you look forward to becoming old, or are you afraid about what may lie ahead? Most of us want to enjoy a long life like Maria's but don't think much about growing old in our daily lives.

Reading this book will give you the basic facts about growing older. You will learn how to organize these facts by putting them into two contexts: the bio-psychosocial framework and the life-span approach. By the time you are finished, you should have a new, different way of thinking about aging.

You already enjoy a major advantage compared with Maria. She and other people her age did not have the opportunity as young students to learn much about what is typical and what is not typical about aging. Until the last few decades, very little information was available about old age, which people generally thought to be characterized only by decline. **Gerontology**, *the scientific study of aging from maturity through old age, has changed our understanding of aging and the aging process.* As you can imagine from reading about famous older adults at the beginning of the chapter, and as you will see throughout this book, aging reflects the individual differences you have come to expect across people as they change over time.

Still, many myths about old people persist. *These myths of aging lead to negative stereotypes of older people, which may result in* **ageism**, *a form of discrimination*

DISCOVERING DEVELOPMENT
Myths and Stereotypes About Aging

We are surrounded by misconceptions of older adults. We have all seen cartoons making jokes about older adults whose memories are poor or whose physical abilities have declined. Most damaging are the ideas portrayed in the media that older adults are incapable of leading productive lives and making a difference. For example, many greeting cards portray older people as having little memory, no teeth, and no desire for sex. As a way to discover something about development, try to find several examples of myths or stereotypes about aging. Look at those greeting cards, cartoons, advertisements, YouTube videos, articles in popular magazines, television shows, and music. Gather as many as you can, and then check them against the research on the topic discussed in this text. By the end of the course, see how many myths and stereotypes you can show to be wrong.

against older adults based on their age. Ageism has its foundations in myths and beliefs people take for granted, as well as in intergenerational relations (Nelson, 2016; North & Fiske, 2012, 2016). It may be as blatant as believing that all old people are senile and are incapable of making decisions about their lives. It may occur when people are impatient with older adults in a grocery store checkout line. Or it may be as subtle as dismissing an older person's physical complaints with the question "What do you expect for someone your age?" As you will learn by doing the activities in the Discovering Development feature, such stereotypes surround us.

This book rebuts these erroneous ideas, but it does not replace them with idealized views of adulthood and old age. Rather, it paints an accurate picture of what it means to grow old today, recognizing that development across adulthood brings growth and opportunities as well as loss and decline. To begin, we consider the life-span perspective, which helps place adult development and aging into the context of the whole human experience. Afterward, we consider the fundamental developmental forces, controversies, and models that form the foundation for studying adult development and aging. In particular, we examine the biological, psychological, sociocultural, and life-cycle forces, and the nature–nurture and continuity–discontinuity controversies. We consider some basic definitions of age, and you will see that it can be viewed in many different ways. Finally, by examining various research methods we show how the information presented in this book was obtained.

The Life-Span Perspective

Imagine trying to understand, without knowing anything about his or her life, what your best friend is like. We cannot understand adults' experiences without appreciating what came before in childhood and adolescence. Placing adulthood in this broader context is what the life-span perspective is all about. *The* **life-span perspective** *divides human development into two phases: an early phase (childhood and adolescence) and a later phase (young adulthood, middle age, and old age).* The early phase is characterized by rapid age-related increases in people's size and abilities. During the later phase, changes in size are slow, but abilities continue to develop as people continue adapting to the environment (Baltes, Lindenberger, & Staudinger, 2006).

Viewed from the life-span perspective, adult development and aging are complex phenomena that cannot be understood within the scope of a single disciplinary approach. Understanding how adults change requires input from a wide variety of perspectives. Moreover, aging is a lifelong process, meaning that human development never stops.

One of the most important perspectives on life-span development is that of Paul Baltes (1987; Baltes et al., 2006), who identified four key features of the life-span perspective:

1. *Multidirectionality:* Development involves both growth and decline; as people grow in one area, they may lose in another and at different rates. For example, people's vocabulary ability tends to increase throughout life, but reaction time tends to slow down.
2. *Plasticity:* One's capacity is not predetermined or set in concrete. Many skills can be trained or improved with practice, even in late life. There are limits to the degree of potential improvement, however, as described in later chapters.
3. *Historical context:* Each of us develops within a particular set of circumstances determined by the historical time in which we are born and the culture in which we grow up. Maria's experiences, described in the vignette, were shaped by living in the 20th century in a Chicano neighborhood in southwest Texas.
4. *Multiple causation:* How people develop results from a wide variety of forces, which we consider later in this chapter. You will see that development is shaped by biological, psychological, sociocultural, and life-cycle forces.

The life-span perspective emphasizes that human development takes a lifetime to complete. It sets the stage for understanding the many influences we experience and points out that no one part of life is any more or less important than another.

Basing their theories on these principles, Baltes et al. (2006) argue that life-span development consists of the dynamic interactions among growth, maintenance, and loss regulation. In their view, three factors are critical:

1. As people age, they begin to focus on or select those abilities deemed essential for functioning.
2. People then optimize their behavior by focusing on this more limited set of abilities.
3. Finally, people learn to compensate for declines by designing workaround strategies.

Taken together, this Selective Optimization with Compensation (SOC) approach explains how people shift more and more resources to maintain function and deal with biologically related losses as we grow old, leaving fewer resources to be devoted to continued growth. As we see throughout this book, this shift in resources has profound implications for experiencing aging and for pointing out ways to age successfully.

The Demographics of Aging

There have never been as many older adults alive as there are now, so you see many more older people than your great-grandparents (or even your parents) did when they were your age. The proportion of older adults in the population of developed countries has increased tremendously, mainly due to better health care over the past century (e.g., the elimination or prevention of previously fatal acute diseases, especially during childhood, better treatment for chronic diseases) and to lowering women's mortality rate during childbirth.

People who study population trends, called, **demographers***, use a graphic technique called a* **population pyramid** *to illustrate these changes.* Figure 1.1 shows average population pyramids for the most developed and least developed countries around the world. Let's consider developed countries first (they're down the left side of the figure). Notice the shape of the population pyramid in 1950, shown in the

1.1 Perspectives on Adult Development and Aging 5

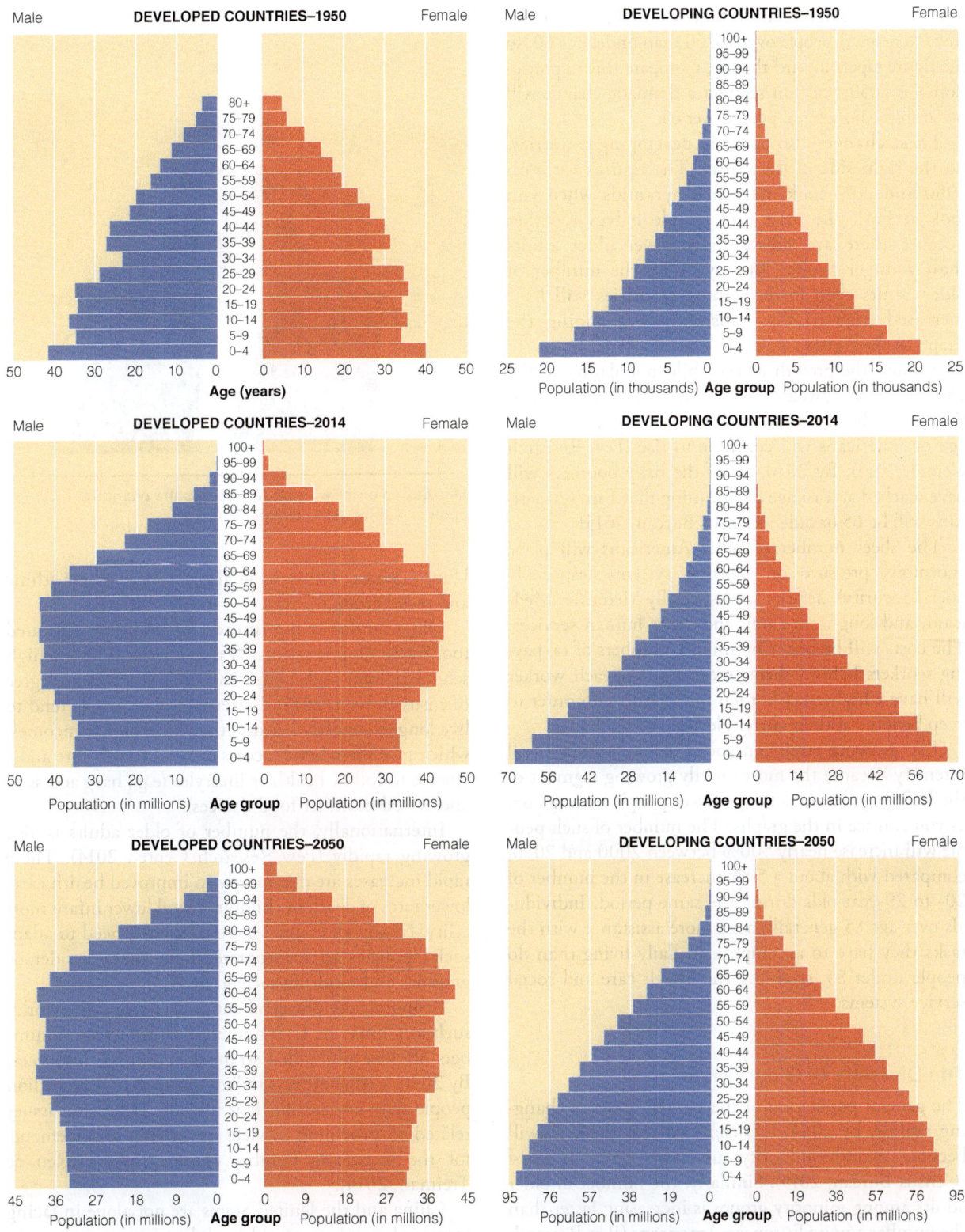

FIGURE 1.1 Population pyramids for developed and developing countries 1950–2050.
Source: From International programs: International database, by U.S. Census Bureau. Copyright © U.S. Census Bureau. Retrieved from www.census.gov/population/international/data/idb/ (1950 developed countries). Remaining data extracted from census data tables. See Kail and Cavanaugh, *Essentials of Human Development*, 2nd ed., p. 369.

top panel of the figure. In the middle of the 20th century, there were fewer people over age 60 than under age 60; so the figure tapers toward the top. Compare this to projections for 2050; you can see that a dramatic change will occur in the number of people over 65.

These changes also occur in developing countries, on the right side of the figure. The figures for both 1950 and 2015 look more like pyramids when you look at both the male and female halves together because there are substantially fewer older adults than younger people. But by 2050, the number of older adults even in developing countries will have increased dramatically, substantially changing the shape of the figure.

Because the growth of the child population in the United States slowed in the 20th century and essentially stops by the middle of this century, the average age of Americans will continue to rise (Pew Research Center, 2015). By 2030, all of the baby boomers will have reached at least age 65, meaning that 1 in 5 Americans will be 65 or older (Census Bureau, 2015).

The sheer number of older Americans will place enormous pressure on pension systems (especially Social Security), health care (especially Medicare, Medicaid, and long-term care), and other human services. The costs will be borne by smaller numbers of taxpaying workers behind them, meaning that each worker will have a higher tax burden in the future in order to keep benefits at their current levels.

The growing strain on social service systems will intensify because the most rapidly growing segment of the U.S. population is the group of people over age 85, as you can see in the graphs. The number of such people will increase nearly 500% between 2000 and 2050, compared with about a 50% increase in the number of 20- to 29-year-olds during the same period. Individuals over age 85 generally need more assistance with the tasks they have to accomplish in daily living than do people under 85, straining the health care and social service systems.

The Diversity of Older Adults

The general population of the United States is changing rapidly. By 2044, it is expected that the U.S. will become majority-minority, up from 38% in 2014 (Census Bureau, 2015). Similarly, the number of older adults among minority groups is increasing faster than the number among European Americans (Pew Research Center, 2014). In terms of gender, as you can see in the graphs, older women outnumber older men in the

This Latina older woman represents the changing face of older adults in the United States.

United States. This is true also for each major ethnic and racial group.

Older adults in the future will be better educated too. By 2030, it is estimated that 85% will have a high school diploma and about 75% will have a college degree (Census Bureau, 2015). Better-educated people tend to live longer—mostly because they have higher incomes, which give them better access to good health care and a chance to follow healthier lifestyles (e.g., have access to and afford healthier food choices).

Internationally, the number of older adults is also growing rapidly (Pew Research Center, 2014). These rapid increases are due mostly to improved health care, lower rates of death in childbirth, and lower infant mortality. Nearly all countries are facing the need to adapt social policies to incorporate these changing demographics and resulting societal needs.

Economically powerful countries around the world, such as China, are trying to cope with increased numbers of older adults that strain the country's resources. By 2040, China expects to have more than 300 million people over age 60. So it is already addressing issues related to providing services and living arrangements for the increasing number of older adults (Ren & Treiman, 2014).

China and the United States are not alone in facing increased numbers of older adults. As you can see in Figure 1.2, the population of many countries will include substantially more older adults over the next few

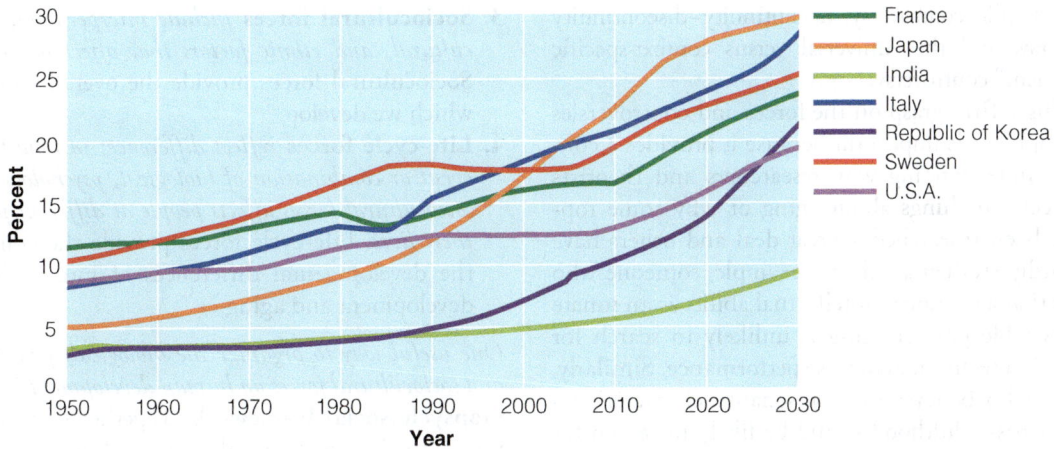

FIGURE 1.2 The proportion of older adults (65 years and older) is increasing in many countries and will continue to do so.
Source: United Nations, Statistics Bureau, Ministry of Public Management, Home Affairs, Post and Telecommunications, Ministry of Health, Labour, and Welfare. See Kail and Cavanaugh, *Essentials of Human Development*, 2nd ed., p. 370.

decades. All of these countries will need to deal with an increased demand for services to older adults and, in some cases, competing demands with children and younger and middle-aged adults for limited resources.

Adult Development in Action

If you were a staff member for your congressional representative, what would you advise with respect to economic and social policy given the demographic changes in the U.S. population?

1.2 Issues in Studying Adult Development and Aging

LEARNING OBJECTIVES

- What four main forces shape development?
- What are normative age-graded influences, normative history-graded influences, and nonnormative influences?
- How do culture and ethnicity influence aging?
- What is the meaning of age?
- What are the nature–nurture, stability–change, continuity–discontinuity, and the "universal versus context-specific development" controversies?

Levar Johnson smiled broadly as he held his newborn granddaughter for the first time. So many thoughts rushed into his mind. He could only imagine the kinds of things Devonna would experience growing up. He hoped that she would have a good neighborhood in which to play and explore her world. He hoped that she inherited the family genes for good health. He wondered how Devonna's life growing up as an African American in the United States would be different from his experiences.

Like many grandparents, Levar wonders what the future holds for his granddaughter. The questions he considers are interesting in their own right, but they are important for another reason: They get to the heart of general issues of human development that have intrigued philosophers and scientists for centuries. You have probably asked these or similar questions yourself. How do some people manage to remain thin, whereas other people seem to gain weight merely by looking at food? Why do some people remain very active and mentally well into later life? How does growing up in a Spanish-speaking culture affect one's views of family caregiving? Answering these questions requires us to consider the various forces that shape us as we mature. Developmentalists place special emphasis on four forces: biological, psychological, sociocultural, and life cycle. These forces direct our development much as an artist's hands direct the course of a painting or sculpture.

Following from the forces that shape adult development and aging are questions such as: What is the relative importance of genetics and environment on people's behavior? Do people change gradually, or do they change more abruptly? Do all people change in the same way? These questions reflect controversies that historically underlie the study of human development (Newman & Newman, 2016): the nature–nurture controversy, the change–stability controversy, the continuity–discontinuity controversy, and the "universal versus context-specific development" controversy.

Having a firm grasp on the forces and controversies of development is important because it provides a context for understanding why researchers and theorists believe certain things about aging or why some topics have been researched a great deal and others have been hardly studied at all. For example, someone who believes that a decline in intellectual ability is an innate and inevitable part of aging is unlikely to search for intervention techniques to raise performance. Similarly, someone who believes that personality characteristics change across adulthood would be likely to search for life transitions.

The Forces of Development

Hair color, remembering, personality, activity levels—Why do adults differ so much on these and other things? The answer lies in understanding the basic forces that shape us and how they interact. Developmentalists typically consider four interactive forces (shown in Figure 1.3):

1. **Biological forces** *include all genetic and health-related factors that affect development.* Examples of biological forces include menopause, facial wrinkling, and changes in the major organ systems.
2. **Psychological forces** *include all internal perceptual, cognitive, emotional, and personality factors that affect development.* Collectively, psychological forces provide the characteristics we notice about people that make them individuals.
3. **Sociocultural forces** *include interpersonal, societal, cultural, and ethnic factors that affect development.* Sociocultural forces provide the overall contexts in which we develop.
4. **Life-cycle forces** *reflect differences in how the same event or combination of biological, psychological, and sociocultural forces affects people at different points in their lives.* Life-cycle forces provide the context for the developmental differences of interest in adult development and aging.

One useful way to organize the biological, psychological, and sociocultural forces on human development is with the **biopsychosocial framework**. Together with life-cycle forces, the biopsychosocial framework provides a complete overview of the shapers of human development. Each of us is a product of a unique combination of these forces. Even identical twins growing up in the same family eventually have their own unique friends, partners, occupations, and so on because they each experience the combination of forces differently.

To see why all these forces are important, imagine that we want to know how people feel about forgetting. We would need to consider biological factors, such as whether the forgetting was caused by an underlying disease. We would want to know about such psychological factors as what the person's memory ability has been throughout his or her life and about his or her beliefs about what happens to memory with increasing age. We would need to know about sociocultural factors, such as the influence of social stereotypes about forgetting on actual memory performance. Finally, we would need to know about the age of the person when a forgetting experience occurs. Focusing on only one (or even

FIGURE 1.3 The biopsychosocial framework shows that human development results from interacting forces.

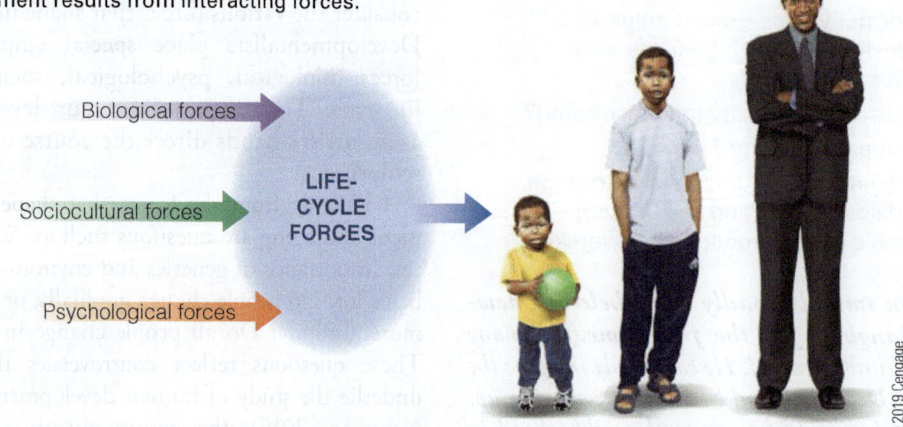

two or three) of the forces would provide an incomplete view of how the person feels. The biopsychosocial framework, along with life-cycle forces, will provide a way to understand all the developmental outcomes you will encounter in this text.

Interrelations Among the Forces: Developmental Influences

All the forces we have discussed combine to create people's developmental experiences. One way to consider these combinations is to consider the degree to which they are common or unique to people of specific ages. An important concept in this approach is cohort. A **cohort** *is a group of people born at the same point in time or within a specific time span.* So everyone born in 1995 would be the 1995 cohort; similarly, those born between 1946 and 1964 represent the baby-boom cohort. Based on this notion of cohort, Baltes (1987; Baltes et al., 2006) identified three sets of influences that interact to produce developmental change over the life span: normative age-graded influences, normative history-graded influences, and nonnormative influences.

Normative age-graded influences *are experiences caused by biological, psychological, and sociocultural forces that occur to most people of a particular age.* Some of these, such as puberty, menarche, and menopause, are biological. These normative biological events usually indicate a major change in a person's life; for example, menopause is an indicator that a woman can no longer bear children without medical intervention. Normative psychological events include focusing on certain concerns at different points in adulthood, such as a middle-aged person's concern with socializing the younger generation. Other normative age-graded influences involve sociocultural forces, such as the time when first marriage occurs and the age at which someone retires. Normative age-graded influences typically correspond to major time-marked events, which are often ritualized. For example, many younger adults formally celebrate turning 21 as the official transition to adulthood, getting married typically is surrounded with much celebration, and retirement often begins with a party celebrating the end of employment. These events provide the most convenient way to judge where we are on our social clock.

Normative history-graded influences *are events that most people in a specific culture experience at the same time.* These events may be biological (such as epidemics), psychological (such as particular stereotypes), or sociocultural (such as changing attitudes toward sexuality). Normative history-graded influences often give a generation its unique identity, such as the baby-boom generation, generation X (people born roughly between 1965 and 1975), and the millennial generation (sometimes called the echo boomers or generation Y, born roughly between the early 1980s and 2000 or so). Normative history-graded influences can have a profound effect across all generations. For example, the attacks on the World Trade Center on September 11, 2001, fundamentally changed attitudes about safety and security that had been held for decades.

Nonnormative influences *are random or rare events that may be important for a specific individual but are not experienced by most people.* These may be favorable events, such as winning the lottery or an election, or unfavorable ones, such as an accident or layoff. The unpredictability of these events makes them unique. Such events can turn one's life upside down overnight.

Life-cycle forces are especially key in understanding the importance of normative age-graded, normative history-graded, and nonnormative influences. For example, history-graded influences may produce generational differences and conflict; parents' and grandparents' experiences as young adults in the 1960s and 1970s (before AIDS, smartphones, and global terrorism) may have little to do with the complex issues faced by today's young adults. In turn, these interactions have important implications for understanding differences that appear to be age related. That is, differences may be explained in terms of different life experiences (normative history-graded influences) rather than as an integral part of aging itself (normative age-graded influences). We will return to this issue when we discuss age, cohort, and time-of-measurement effects in research on adult development and aging.

Culture and Ethnicity

Culture and ethnicity jointly provide status, social settings, living conditions, and personal experiences for people of all ages, and they influence and are influenced by biological, psychological, and life-cycle developmental forces. Culture can be defined as shared basic value orientations, norms, beliefs, and customary habits and ways of living. Culture provides the basic worldview of a society in that it gives it the basic explanations about the meanings and goals of everyday life (Matsumoto & Juang, 2017). Culture is such a powerful influence because it connects to biological forces through family lineage, which is sometimes the way in which members of a particular culture are defined. Psychologically, culture shapes people's core beliefs; in some cases this can result in ethnocentrism, or the belief that one's own culture is superior to others. Being socialized as a child within a culture usually has a more profound effect on a person than when one adopts a culture later in life, resulting in significant life-cycle timing effects. Culture is extremely important in gerontology because how people define basic concepts such as *person*, *age*, and *life course* varies a great deal across cultures.

Equally important is the concept of ethnicity, which is an individual and collective sense of identity based on historical and cultural group membership and related behaviors and beliefs (Matsumoto & Juang, 2017). Compared with culture, ethnic group identities have both solid and fluid properties, reflecting the fact that there are both unchanging and situation-specific aspects to ethnic identity (Jaspal, 2015; Jaspal & Cinnirella, 2012). An example of these properties is that the terms referring to an ethnic group can change over time; for example, the terms *colored people*, *Negroes*, *black Americans*, and *African Americans* have all been used to describe Americans of African ancestry. Ethnic identity is first influenced by biology through one's parents. However, how one incorporates ethnic identity depends on numerous psychological factors as well as age.

Both culture and ethnicity are key dimensions along which adults vary. However, we know very little about how culture or ethnicity affects how people experience old age. Throughout the rest of this book, we explore areas in which culture and ethnicity have been studied systematically. Unfortunately, most research focuses only on European Americans. Given the demographic trends discussed earlier, this focus must change so we can understand the experience of growing older in the United States in the next few decades.

The Meaning of Age

When you are asked the question "How old are you?" what crosses your mind? Is it the number of years since the day of your birth? Is it how old you feel at that time? Is it defined more in terms of where you are biologically, psychologically, or socially than in terms of calendar time? You may not have thought about it, but age is not a simple construct (and in the case of the !Kung people living in the Kalahari Desert in southwest Africa, it has no meaning at all).

Likewise, aging is not a single process. Rather, it consists of at least three distinct processes: primary, secondary, and tertiary aging (Birren & Cunningham, 1985). **Primary aging** is *normal, disease-free development during adulthood*. Changes in biological, psychological, sociocultural, or life-cycle processes in primary aging are an inevitable part of the developmental process; examples include menopause, decline in reaction time, and the loss of family and friends. Most of the information in this book represents primary aging. **Secondary aging** is *developmental changes that are related to disease, lifestyle, and other environmentally induced changes that are not inevitable (e.g., pollution)*. The progressive loss of intellectual abilities in Alzheimer's disease and related forms of dementia are examples of secondary aging. Finally, **tertiary aging** *is the rapid*

A new view of aging as one involving continued activity and engagement is becoming more widely accepted.

losses that occur shortly before death. An example of tertiary aging is a phenomenon known as terminal drop, in which intellectual abilities show a marked decline in the last few years before death.

Everyone does not grow old in the same way. Whereas most people tend to show usual patterns of aging that reflect the typical, or normative, changes with age, other people show highly successful aging in which few signs of change occur. For example, although most people tend to get chronic diseases as they get older, some people never do. What makes people who age successfully different? At this point, we do not know for sure. It may be a unique combination of genetics, optimal environment, flexibility in dealing with life situations, a strong sense of personal control, and maybe a bit of luck. For our present discussion, the main point to keep in mind is that everyone's experience of growing old is somewhat different. Although many people develop arthritis, how each person learns to cope is unique.

When most of us think about age, we usually think of how long we have been around since our birth; this way of defining age is known as chronological age. *Chronological age* is a shorthand way to index time and organize events and data by using a commonly understood standard: calendar time. Chronological age is not the only shorthand index variable used in adult development and aging. Gender, ethnicity, and socioeconomic status are others. No index variable itself actually causes behavior. In the case of gender, for example, it is not whether a person is male or female per se that determines how long he or she will live on average but rather the underlying forces, such as hormonal effects, that are the true causes. This point is often forgotten when age is the index variable, perhaps because it is so familiar to us and so widely used. However, age (or time) does not directly cause things to happen, either. Iron left out in the rain will rust, but rust is not caused simply by time. Rather, rust is a time-dependent process involving oxidation in which time is a measure of the rate at which rust is created. Similarly, human behavior is affected by experiences that occur with the passage of time, not by time itself. What we study in adult development and aging is the result of time- or age-dependent processes, not the result of age itself.

Whereas chronological age represents your age in elapsed time, *perceived age* refers to the age you think of yourself as. The saying "You're only as old as you feel" captures perceived age. Still another way of describing age is in terms of *biological age*, assessed by measuring the functioning of the various vital, or life-limiting, organ systems, such as the cardiovascular system.

Psychological age refers to the functional level of the psychological abilities people use to adapt to changing environmental demands. These abilities include memory, intelligence, feelings, motivation, and other skills that foster and maintain self-esteem and personal control.

Finally, *sociocultural age* refers to the specific set of roles individuals adopt in relation to other members of the society and culture to which they belong. Sociocultural age is judged on the basis of many behaviors and habits, such as style of dress, customs, language, and interpersonal style. Sociocultural age is especially important in understanding many of the family and work roles we adopt. When to get married, have children, make career moves, retire, and so on often are influenced by what we think our sociocultural age is. Such decisions also play a role in determining our self-esteem and other aspects of personality. Many of the most damaging stereotypes about aging (e.g., that older people should not have sex) are based on faulty assumptions about sociocultural age.

A good example of the complexities of age is the concept of emerging adulthood. *Some human developmentalists view the period from the late teens to the mid-to late 20s as* **emerging adulthood**, *a period when individuals are not adolescents but are not yet fully adults* (Arnett, 2016). Emerging adulthood is a time to explore careers, self-identity, and commitments. It is also a time when certain biological and physiological developmental trends peak, and brain development continues in different ways.

In sum, a person's age turns out to be quite complex. Think about yourself. You probably have days when even though the calendar says you're a certain age, your exploits the day before resulted in your feeling much younger at the time and much older the next morning. Or perhaps the other way around. How "old" anyone is can (and does) change from one moment to the next. A great example of these points can be seen in the life of Pope Francis, as discussed in the Real People feature.

Core Issues in Development

Is it your genes or experiences that determine how intelligent you are? If a young adult woman is outgoing, does this mean she will be outgoing in late life? If people change, is it more gradual or sporadic? Is aging the same around the world? These and similar questions have occupied some of the greatest Western philosophers in history: Plato, Aristotle, René Descartes, John Locke, and Ludwig Wittgenstein, among many

Real People
Pope Francis Sets Many New Examples

History was made on March 13, 2013. For the first time since the year 741, when Pope Gregory II from Syria died, the Roman Catholic Church elected a non-European as its leader. Jorge Mario Bergoglio, who took the name of Pope Francis, because the first South American (he is from Argentina) and first Jesuit to be elected pope. He was 76 years old. It is likely that the Catholic Church will never be the same.

Pope Francis set out immediately to change the dynamic of the role of the pope. He refused to wear the traditional red shoes or to live in the posh Vatican apartment. He used his long-lived experience to focus on what he saw as central traits: mercy, humility, and compassion.

He also defies our stereotype of an older person—he is always on the go, full of energy, with a very sharp wit and intellect.

Pope Francis set out quickly to establish his values as central to the way people should live, especially in terms of sustainability and in the need to provide adequate wages and living conditions for all. He has embraced all religions and has emphasized the need to treat all people with respect.

Pope Francis is certainly redefining what it means to be a church leader. He is also redefining what it means to be an older adult through his relentless schedule and activity in service of others.

---

others. Four main issues occupy most of the discussion: nature versus nurture, stability versus change, continuity versus discontinuity, and universal versus context-specific development. Because each of these issues cuts across the topics we discuss in this book, let's consider each briefly.

The Nature–Nurture Issue Think for a minute about a particular characteristic that you and several people in your family have, such as intelligence, good looks, or a friendly, outgoing personality.

Why is this trait so prevalent? Is it because you inherited the trait from your parents? Or is it because of where and how you and your parents were brought up? Answers to these questions illustrate different positions on the **nature–nurture issue**, *which involves the degree to which genetic or hereditary influences (nature) and experiential or environmental influences (nurture) determine the kind of person you are.* Scientists once hoped to answer these questions by identifying either heredity or environment as *the* cause of a particular aspect of development. The goal was to be able to say, for example, that intelligence was due to heredity or that personality was due to experience. Today, however, we know that virtually no features of life-span development are due exclusively to either heredity or environment. Instead, development is always shaped by both: Nature and nurture are mutually interactive influences.

For example, it is known that some forms of later-onset Alzheimer's disease are genetically linked. However, whether one actually gets Alzheimer's disease, and possibly even how the disease progresses, may be influenced by the environment. Specifically, an environmental trigger may be needed for the disease to occur. Moreover, evidence indicates that providing a supportive environment for people with Alzheimer's disease improves their performance on cognitive tasks (De Witt-Hoblit, Miller, & Camp, 2016).

So in order to understand a newborn's future we must simultaneously consider his or her inborn, hereditary characteristics and the environment. Both factors must be considered together to yield an adequate account of why we behave the way we do. To explain a person's behavior and discover where to focus intervention, we must look at the unique interaction for that person between nature and nurture.

The Stability–Change Issue Ask yourself the following question: Are you pretty much the same as you were 10 years ago, or are you different? How so? Depending on what aspects of yourself you considered, you may have concluded that you are pretty much the same (perhaps in terms of learning style) or that you are different (perhaps in some physical feature such as weight). *The* **stability–change issue** *concerns the degree to which people remain the same over time*, as discussed in the Current Controversies feature. Stability at some basic level is essential for us (and others) to recognize that one is the same individual as time goes on. But we also like to believe that our characteristics are not set in concrete, that we can change ourselves if we so desire. (Imagine not being able to do anything to rid yourself of some character defect.)

Although there is little controversy about whether children change in some ways from birth through age 18, there is much controversy about whether people also change across adulthood. Much of the controversy over stability and change across adulthood stems from how specific characteristics are defined and measured. How much we remain the same and how much we change, then, turns out to be a difficult issue to resolve in an objective way. For many gerontologists, whether stability or change is the rule depends on what personal aspect is being considered and what theoretical perspective one is adopting.

The Continuity–Discontinuity Controversy The third major issue in developmental psychology is a derivative of the stability–change controversy. *The* **continuity–discontinuity controversy** *concerns whether a particular developmental phenomenon represents a smooth progression over time (continuity) or a series of abrupt shifts (discontinuity).* Continuity approaches usually focus on the amount of a characteristic a person has, whereas discontinuity approaches usually focus on the kinds of characteristics a person has. Of course, on a day-to-day basis, behaviors often look nearly identical, or continuous. But when viewed over the course of many months or years, the same behaviors may have changed dramatically, reflecting discontinuous change. Throughout this book, you will find examples of developmental changes that appear to be more on the continuities side and ones that appear to be more on the discontinuities side.

An example of continuity is discussed in Chapter 6: reaction time. As people grow older, the speed with which they can respond slows down. But in Chapter 8 you will read about an example of discontinuity: How people approach problems, especially ones with complex and ambiguous features, undergoes fundamental shifts from young adulthood through middle age.

Within the discontinuity view lies the issue of how adaptable people are in situations as they age. Baltes and colleagues (1998; Baltes et al., 1999) use the term *plasticity* to describe this in relation to people's capacity. **Plasticity** *refers to the belief that capacity is not fixed but can be learned or improved with practice.* For example, people can learn ways to help themselves remember information, which in turn may help them deal with declining short-term memory ability with age. Although plasticity can be demonstrated in many arenas, there are limits to the degree of potential improvement, as we will see in later chapters.

CURRENT CONTROVERSIES
Does Personality in Young Adulthood Determine Personality in Old Age?

Lest you think the controversies underlying adult development and aging do not reflect ongoing debate, consider the case of personality in adulthood. Perhaps no other topic in gerontology has resulted in such heated debates as whether people's basic personality remains the same throughout adulthood or undergoes fundamental change. As we explore in detail in Chapter 9, numerous theories have been developed just to account for the data on this one topic.

Consider yourself and other adults you know. Is the person labeled "class clown" in high school likely to be as much of a fun-loving person 10, 20, or 30 years later? Will the shy person who would never ask anyone to dance be as withdrawn? Or will these people be hardly recognizable at their various class reunions? Probably in your experience you've encountered both outcomes; that is, some people seem to remain the same year after year, whereas some people seem to undergo tremendous change. Why is that?

For one thing, it depends on how specific you get in looking at aspects of a person's personality. In the case of a very specific trait, such as shyness, you will probably see overall stability across adulthood. But if you look at a more global aspect such as the degree to which a person is concerned with the next generation, then you are more likely to find change.

What does this mean? Certainly, it means you have to be very careful in making general statements about stability or change. It also means you have to be quite specific about what you are interested in measuring and at what level of complexity. We will encounter many more examples of both stability and change throughout the book that reflect both these needs.

Members of the !Kung tribe experience development in ways very different from the ways most Americans do.

The Universal Versus Context-Specific Development Controversy The **universal versus context-specific development controversy** *concerns whether there is just one path of development or several.* Consider the !Kung tribe, who live in the Kalahari Desert in southwest Africa (Lee, Hitchcock, & Biesele, 2002). If you were to ask an older !Kung "How old are you?" you would quickly learn that the question has no meaning. !Kung also do not keep track of the number of years they have been alive, the number of children they have, or how often they move. !Kung mothers can describe in detail each of their children's births, but they leave it to others to figure out how many children this adds up to. To the !Kung, age per se is unimportant; when asked to describe people who are "younger" or "older," they give the names of specific people. Social roles among the !Kung also do not differ by age; for example, women in their 20s and 60s all tend gardens, draw water from wells, and take care of children.

Life among !Kung adults contrasts sharply with life among adults in the United States, where age matters a great deal and social roles differ accordingly. Can one theory explain development in both groups? Maybe. Some theorists argue that such differences are more apparent than real and that development worldwide reflects one basic process for everyone. According to this view, differences in development are simply variations on a fundamental developmental process, much as Hershey, Chocolopolis, La Chatelaine, and Godiva chocolates are all products of the same basic manufacturing process.

The opposing view is that differences between people may not be just variations on a theme. Advocates of this view argue that adult development and aging are inextricably intertwined with the context in which they occur. A person's development is a product of complex interactions with the environment, and these interactions are not fundamentally the same in all environments. Each environment has its own set of unique procedures that shape development, just as the "recipes" for chocolates, computers, and pens have little in common.

The view adopted in this book is that adult development and aging must be understood within the contexts in which they occur. In some cases, this means that contexts are sufficiently similar that general trends can be identified. In others, such as the !Kung and U.S. societies, these differences prevent many general statements. In Levar's case with his granddaughter, it may be a blend of the two.

Adult Development in Action

How would understanding the forces and issues that shape human development help you be a better healthcare worker at a neighborhood clinic in a very diverse neighborhood?

1.3 Research Methods

LEARNING OBJECTIVES

- What approaches do scientists use to measure behavior in adult development and aging research?
- What are the general designs for doing research?
- What specific designs are unique to adult development and aging research?
- What ethical procedures must researchers follow?

Leah and Sarah are both 75 years old and are in fairly good health. They believe their memory is not as good as it once was, so they both use various memory aids: Leah tries to think of images in her mind to remember her grocery list, whereas Sarah writes them down. Leah and Sarah got into a discussion recently about which technique works better.

You might be asking yourself why you need to know about research methods when you could just Google the topic and find out all sorts of things about it. Here's why—there is good research and bad research and everything else in between. A web search does not help you tell the difference. The only way to differentiate good versus poor research is by knowing the principles of good research that results in trustworthy information.

Just as in any profession, gerontology has certain tools of the trade that are used to ensure good research. That's what we will be considering in this section—the tools that gerontologists have used for decades in discovering the secrets of adult development and aging.

This section is so important that if you have trouble understanding the information after reading it a few times, ask your instructor.

So suppose Leah and Sarah know that you're taking a course in adult development and aging, and they ask you to settle the matter. You know research could show whose approach is better under what circumstances, but how? Gerontologists must make several key decisions as they prepare to study any topic. They need to decide how to measure the topic of interest, they must design the study, they must choose a way to study development, and they must respect the rights of the people who will participate in the study.

What makes the study of adult development and aging different from other areas of social science is the need to consider multiple influences on behavior. Explanations of development entail consideration of all the forces we considered earlier. This makes research on adult development and aging more difficult, if for no other reason than it involves examining more variables.

Measurement in Adult Development and Aging Research

Researchers typically begin by deciding how to measure the topic of interest. For example, the first step toward resolving Leah and Sarah's discussion about remembering grocery items would be to decide how to measure remembering. Gerontologists usually use one of three approaches: observing systematically, using tasks to sample behavior, and asking people for self-reports. In addition, researchers need to be concerned with how representative the participants in the study are of the larger group of people in question.

Regardless of the kind of method chosen, researchers must show it is both reliable and valid. *The* **reliability** *of a measure is the extent to which it provides a consistent index of the behavior or topic of interest.* A measure of memory is reliable to the extent that it gives a consistent estimate of performance each time you administer it. All measures used in gerontological research must be shown to be reliable, or they cannot be used. *The* **validity** *of a measure is the extent to which it measures what researchers think it measures.* For example, a measure of memory is valid only if it can be shown to actually measure memory (and not vocabulary ability, for example). Validity often is established by showing that the measure in question is closely related to another measure known to be valid. Because it is possible to have a measure that is reliable but not valid (a ruler is a reliable measure of length but not a valid measure of memory), researchers must ensure that measures are both reliable and valid.

Systematic Observation As the name implies, **systematic observation** *involves watching people and carefully recording what they say or do.* Two forms of systematic observation are common. In naturalistic observation, people are observed as they behave spontaneously in some real-life situation. For example, Leah and Sarah could be observed in the grocery store purchasing their items as a way to test how well they remember.

Structured observations differ from naturalistic observations in that the researcher creates a setting that is particularly likely to elicit the behavior of interest. Structured observations are especially useful for studying behaviors that are difficult to observe naturally. For example, how people react to emergencies is hard to study naturally because emergencies generally are rare and unpredictable events. A researcher could stage an emergency and watch how people react. However, whether the behaviors observed in staged situations are the same as would happen naturally often is hard to determine, making it difficult to generalize from staged settings to the real world.

Sampling Behavior with Tasks When investigators can't observe a behavior directly, another popular alternative is to create tasks that are thought to sample the behavior of interest. For example, one way to test older adults' memory is to give them a grocery list to learn and remember. Likewise, police training includes putting the candidate in a building in which targets pop up that may be either criminals or innocent bystanders. This approach is popular with gerontological researchers because it is so convenient. The main question with this approach is its validity: Does the task provide a realistic sample of the behavior of interest? For example, asking people to learn grocery lists would have good validity to the extent it matched the kinds of lists they actually use.

Self-Reports The last approach, self-reports, is a special case of using tasks to sample people's behavior. **Self-reports** *are simply people's answers to questions about the topic of interest.* When questions are posed in written form, the verbal report is a questionnaire; when they are posed verbally, it is an interview. Either way, questions are created that probe different aspects of the topic of interest. For example, if you think imagery and lists are common ways people use to remember grocery items, you could devise a questionnaire and survey several people to find out.

Although self-reports are very convenient and provide information on the topic of interest, they are not always good measures of people's behavior, because they are inaccurate. Why? People may not remember accurately what they did in the past, or they may report what they think the researcher wants to hear.

Representative Sampling Researchers usually are interested in broad groups of people called populations. Examples of populations are all students taking a course on adult development and aging or all Asian American widows. Almost all studies include only a sample of people, which is a subset of the population. Researchers must be careful to ensure that their sample is truly representative of the population of interest. An unrepresentative sample can result in invalid research. For example, what would you think of a study of middle-aged parents if you learned that the sample consisted entirely of two-parent households? You would, quite correctly, decide that this sample is not representative of all middle-aged parents and question whether its results apply to single middle-aged parents.

As you read on, you'll soon discover that most of the research we consider in this text has been conducted on middle-class, well-educated European Americans. Are these samples representative of all people in the United States? In the world? Sometimes, but not always. Be careful not to assume that findings from this group apply to people of other groups. In addition, some developmental issues have not been studied in all ethnic groups and cultures. For example, the U.S. government does not always report statistics for all ethnic groups. To change this, some U.S. government agencies, such as the National Institutes of Health, now require samples to be representative. Thus, in the future we may gain a broader understanding of aging.

General Designs for Research

Having selected the way we want to measure the topic of interest, researchers must embed this measure in a research design that yields useful, relevant results. Gerontologists rely on primary designs in planning their work: experimental studies, correlational studies, and case studies. The specific design chosen for research depends in large part on the questions the researchers are trying to address.

Experimental Design To find out whether Leah's or Sarah's approach to remembering works better, we could gather groups of older adults and try the following. We could randomly assign the participants into three groups: those who are taught to use imagery, those who are taught to use lists, and those who are not taught to use anything. After giving all the groups time to learn the new technique (where appropriate), we could test each group on a new grocery list to see who does better.

What we have done is an example of an **experiment**, *which involves manipulating a key factor that the researcher believes is responsible for a particular behavior and randomly assigning participants to the experimental and control groups. In our case, the key variable being manipulated (termed the* **independent variable**) *is the instructions for how to study. In a study of memory, a typical behavior that is observed (termed the* **dependent variable**) *is the amount of information actually remembered.*

More generally, in an experiment the researcher is most interested in identifying differences between groups of people. One group, the experimental group, receives the manipulation; another group, the control group, does not. This sets up a situation in which the level of the key variable of interest differs across groups. In addition, the investigator exerts precise control over all important aspects of the study, including the variable of interest, the setting, and the participants. Because the key variable is systematically manipulated in an experiment, researchers can infer cause-and-effect relations about that variable. In our example, we can conclude that type of instruction (how people study) causes better or worse performance on a memory test. Discovering such cause-and-effect relations is important if we are to understand the underlying processes of adult development and aging.

Finally, we must note that age cannot be an independent variable, because we cannot manipulate it. Consequently, we cannot conduct true experiments to examine the effects of age on a particular person's behavior. At best, we can find age-related effects of an independent variable on dependent variables.

Correlational Design In a **correlational study**, *investigators examine relations between variables as they exist naturally in the world*. In the simplest correlational study, a researcher measures two variables, and then sees how they are related. Suppose we wanted to know whether the amount of time spent studying a grocery list such as one that Sarah might create was related to how many items people remember at the store. To find out, the researcher would measure two things for each person in the study: the length of study time and the number of items purchased correctly.

The results of a correlational study usually are measured by computing a correlation coefficient, abbreviated r. Correlations can range from -1.0 to 1.0, reflecting three different types of relations between study time and number of groceries remembered.

1. When $r = 0$, the two variables are unrelated: Study time has no relation to remembering groceries.
2. When $r > 0$, the variables are positively related: As study time increases (or decreases), the number of grocery items remembered also increases (or decreases).
3. When $r < 0$, the variables are inversely related: When study time increases (or decreases), the number of groceries remembered decreases (or increases).

Correlational studies do not give definitive information about cause-and-effect relations; for example, the correlation between study time and the number of groceries remembered does not mean that one variable caused the other, regardless of how large the relation was. However, correlational studies do provide important information about the strength of the relation between variables, which is reflected in the absolute value of the correlation coefficient. Moreover, because developmental researchers are interested in how variables are related to factors that are very difficult, if not impossible, to manipulate, correlational techniques are used a great deal. In fact, most developmental research is correlational at some level because age cannot be manipulated within an individual. This means we can describe a great many developmental phenomena, but we cannot explain very many of them.

Case Studies Sometimes researchers cannot obtain measures directly from people and are able only to watch them carefully. *In certain situations, researchers may be able to study a single individual in great detail in a* **case study**. This technique is especially useful when researchers want to investigate very rare phenomena, such as uncommon diseases or people with extremely high ability. Identifying new diseases, for example, begins with a case study of one individual who has a pattern of symptoms that is different from any known syndrome. Case studies are also very valuable for opening new areas of study, which can be followed by larger studies using other methods (e.g., experiments). However, their primary limitation is figuring out whether the information gleaned from one individual holds for others as well.

Designs for Studying Development

Once the general design is chosen, most gerontologists must decide how to measure possible changes or age differences that emerge as people develop. For example, if we want to know how people continue (or fail) to use imagery or lists in remembering grocery items as they get older, we will want to use a design that is particularly sensitive to developmental differences. Such designs are based on three key variables: age, cohort, and time of measurement. Once we have considered these, we will examine the specific designs for studying development.

Age, Cohort, and Time of Measurement Every study of adult development and aging is built on the combination of three building blocks: age, cohort, and time of measurement (Cavanaugh & Whitbourne, 2003).

Age effects *reflect differences caused by underlying processes, such as biological, psychological, or sociocultural changes*. Although usually represented in research by chronological age, age effects are inherent changes within the person and are not caused by the passage of time per se.

Cohort effects *are differences caused by experiences and circumstances unique to the generation to which one belongs*. In general, cohort effects correspond to the normative history-graded influences discussed earlier. However, defining a cohort may not be easy. Cohorts can be specific, as in all people born in one particular year, or general, such as the baby-boom cohort. As described earlier, each generation is exposed to different sets of historical and personal events (such as World War II, tablet computers, or opportunities to attend college). Later in this section we consider evidence of how profound cohort effects can be.

Time-of-measurement effects *reflect differences stemming from sociocultural, environmental, historical, or other events at the time the data are obtained from the participants.* For example, data about wage increases given in a particular year may be influenced by the economic conditions of that year. If the economy is in a serious recession, pay increases probably would be small. In contrast, if the economy is booming, pay increases could be large. Clearly, whether a study is conducted during a recession or a boom affects what is learned about pay changes. In short, the point in time in which a researcher decides to do research could lead him or her to different conclusions about the phenomenon being studied.

The three building-block variables (age, cohort, and time of measurement) can be represented in a single chart, such as the one shown in Table 1.1. Cohort is represented by the years in the first column, time of measurement is represented by the years across the top, and age is represented by the numbers in the individual cells. Note that age is computed by subtracting the cohort year from the time of measurement.

In conducting adult development and aging research, investigators have attempted to identify and separate the three effects. This has not been easy, because all three influences are interrelated. If one is interested in studying 40-year-olds, one must necessarily select the cohort that was born 40 years ago. In this case age and cohort are *confounded*, because one cannot know whether the behaviors observed occur because the participants are 40 years old or because of the specific life experiences they have had as a result of being born in a particular historical period. *In general,* **confounding** *is any situation in which one cannot determine which of two or more effects is responsible for the behaviors being observed.* Confounding of the three effects we are considering here is the most serious problem in adult development and aging research.

What distinguishes developmental researchers from their colleagues in other areas of psychology is a fundamental interest in understanding how people change. Developmental researchers must look at the ways in which people differ across time. Doing so necessarily requires that researchers understand the distinction between age change and age difference. An age change occurs in an individual's behavior over time. Leah's or Sarah's memory at age 75 may not be as good as it was at age 40. To discover an age change, one must examine the same person (in this case, Leah or Sarah) at more than one point in time. An age difference is obtained when at least two different people of different ages are compared. Leah and Sarah may not remember as many grocery items as a person of age 40. Even though we may be able to document substantial age differences, we cannot assume they imply an age change. We do not know whether Leah or Sarah has changed since she was 40, and of course we do not know whether the 40-year-old will be any different at age 75. In some cases, age differences reflect age changes; in other cases they do not.

If what we really want to understand in developmental research is age change (what happens as people grow older), we should design our research with this goal in mind. Moreover, different research questions necessitate different research designs. We next consider the most common ways in which researchers gather data about age differences and age changes: cross-sectional, longitudinal, time lag, and sequential designs.

Cross-Sectional Designs *In a* **cross-sectional study**, *developmental differences are identified by testing people of different ages at the same time.* Any single column in Table 1.2 represents a cross-sectional design. Cross-sectional designs allow researchers to examine age differences but not age change.

Cross-sectional research has several weaknesses. Because people are tested at only one point in their development, we learn nothing about the continuity of development. Consequently, we cannot tell whether someone who remembers grocery items well at age 50 (in 2000) is still able to do so at age 80 (in 2030),

TABLE 1.1 Three Basic Building Blocks of Developmental Research

| Cohort | Time of Measurement ||||
	2000	2010	2020	2030
1950	50	60	70	80
1960	40	50	60	70
1970	30	40	50	60
1980	20	30	40	50

Cohort is represented by the years in the first column, time of measurement by the years across the top, and age by the values in the cells.

TABLE 1.2 Cross-Sectional Design

Cohort	Time of Measurement			
	2000	2010	2020	2030
1950	**50**	60	70	80
1960	**40**	50	60	70
1970	**30**	40	50	60
1980	**20**	30	40	50

Cohort is represented by the years in the first column, time of measurement by the years across the top, and age by the values in the cells.

because the person would be tested at age 50 or 80, but not both. Cross-sectional studies also are affected by cohort effects, meaning that differences between age groups (cohorts) may result as easily from environmental events as from developmental processes. Why? Cross-sectional studies assume that when the older participants were younger, they resembled the people in the younger age groups in the study. This isn't always true, of course, which makes it difficult to know why age differences are found in a cross-sectional study. In short, age and cohort effects are confounded in cross-sectional research.

Despite the confounding of age and cohort and the limitation of being able to identify only age differences, cross-sectional designs dominate the research literature in gerontology. Why? The reason is a pragmatic one: Because all the measurements are obtained at one time, cross-sectional research can be conducted more quickly and inexpensively than research using other designs. In addition, one particular variation of cross-sectional designs is used the most: the extreme age groups design.

Suppose you want to investigate whether people's ability to remember items at the grocery store differs with age. Your first impulse may be to gather a group of younger adults and compare their performance with that of a group of older adults. Typically, such studies compare samples obtained in convenient ways; younger adults usually are college students, and older adults often are volunteers from senior centers or church groups.

Although the extreme age groups design is very common (most of the studies cited in this book used this design), it has several problems (Hertzog & Dixon, 1996). Three concerns are key. First, the samples are not representative, so we must be very careful not to read too much into the results; findings from studies on extreme age groups may not generalize to people other than ones like those who participated. Second, age should be treated as a continuous variable, not as a category ("young" and "old"). Viewing age as a continuous variable allows researchers to gain a better understanding of how age relates to any observed age differences. Finally, extreme age group designs assume the measures used mean the same thing across both age groups. Measures may tap somewhat different constructs, so the reliability and validity of each measure should be checked in each age group.

Despite the problems with cross-sectional designs in general and with extreme age groups designs in particular, they can provide useful information if used carefully. Most importantly, they can point out issues that may provide fruitful avenues for subsequent longitudinal or sequential studies, in which case we can uncover information about age changes.

Longitudinal Designs In a **longitudinal study**, *the same individuals are observed or tested repeatedly at different points in their lives.* As the name implies, a longitudinal study involves a lengthwise account of development and is the most direct way to watch growth occur. A longitudinal design is represented by any horizontal row in Table 1.3. A major advantage of longitudinal designs is that age changes are identified because we are studying the same people over time.

Usually the repeated testing of longitudinal studies extends over years, but not always. *In a* **microgenetic study**, *a special type of longitudinal design, participants are tested repeatedly over a span of days or weeks, typically with the aim of observing change directly as it occurs.* For example, researchers might test children every week, starting when they are 12 months old and continuing until 18 months. Microgenetic studies are particularly useful when investigators have hypotheses about a specific period when developmental change should occur, or in order to intensively document a behavior over time (Flynn, Pine, & Lewis, 2006).

TABLE 1.3 Longitudinal Design

Cohort	Time of Measurement			
	2000	2010	2020	2030
1950	50	60	70	80
1960	**40**	**50**	**60**	**70**
1970	30	40	50	60
1980	20	30	40	50

Cohort is represented by the years in the first column, time of measurement by the years across the top, and age by the values in the cells.

Microgenetic studies are particularly useful in tracking change as a result of intervention. For example, older adults could be given a series of measures of memory ability and then be interviewed about their use of memory strategies. A series of training sessions about how to improve memory could be introduced including additional memory tests and interviews, followed by a posttest to find out how well the participants learned the skills in which they were trained. The microgenetic method would look in detail at the performance of those who learned and improved after training, compared to those who did not, and search for differences in either the pattern of performance in the memory tests or in the details in the interviews for reasons why some people improved while others did not. This would provide a vivid portrait of change over the period of the intervention.

If age changes are found in longitudinal studies, can we say why they occurred? Because only one cohort is studied, cohort effects are eliminated as an explanation of change. However, the other two potential explanations, age and time of measurement, are confounded. For example, suppose we wanted to follow the 1990 cohort over time. If we wanted to test these individuals when they were 20 years old, we would have had to do so in 2010. Consequently, any changes we identify could result from changes in underlying processes or factors related to the time we choose to conduct our measurement. For instance, if we conducted a longitudinal study of salary growth, the amount of salary change in any comparison could stem from real change in the skills and worth of the person to the company or from the economic conditions of the times. In a longitudinal study we cannot tell which of these factors is more important.

Longitudinal studies have three additional potential problems. First, if the research measure requires some type of performance by the participants, we may have the problem of practice effects. Practice effects result from the fact that performance may improve over time simply because people are tested over and over again with the same measures.

Second, we may have a problem with participant dropout because it is difficult to keep a group of research participants intact over the course of a longitudinal study. Participants may move, lose interest, or die. Participant dropout can result in two different outcomes. We can end up with positive selective survival if the participants at the end of the study tend to be the ones who were initially higher on some variable (e.g., the surviving participants are the ones who were the healthiest at the beginning of the study). In contrast, we could have negative selective survival if the participants at the conclusion of the study were initially lower on an important variable (e.g., the surviving participants may have been those who were initially less healthy).

The third problem with longitudinal designs is that our ability to apply the results to other groups is limited. The difficulty is that only one cohort is followed. Whether the pattern of results that is observed in one cohort can be generalized to another cohort is questionable. Thus, researchers using longitudinal designs run the risk of uncovering a developmental process that is unique to that cohort.

Because longitudinal designs necessarily take more time and usually are expensive, they have not been used very often. However, researchers now recognize that we badly need to follow individuals over time to further our understanding of the aging process. Thus, longitudinal studies are becoming more common.

Sequential Designs Thus far, we have considered two developmental designs, each of which has problems involving the confounding of two effects. These effects are age and cohort in cross-sectional designs, and age and time of measurement in longitudinal designs. These confounds create difficulties in interpreting behavioral differences between and within individuals, as illustrated in the How Do We Know? feature. Some of these interpretive dilemmas can be alleviated by using more complex designs called sequential designs, which are shown in Table 1.4. Keep in mind, though, that sequential designs do not cure the confounding problems in the three basic designs.

Sequential designs *represent different combinations of cross-sectional or longitudinal studies.* In the table, a cross-sequential design consists of two or more cross-sectional studies conducted at two or more times of measurement. These multiple cross-sectional designs

TABLE 1.4 Sequential Design

Cohort	Time of Measurement			
	2000	2010	2020	2030
1950	50	60	70	80
1960	**40**	50	60	**70**
1970	30	**40**	50	60
1980	20	30	40	50

Cohort is represented by the years in the first column, time of measurement by the years across the top, and age by the values in the cells.

include the same age ranges; however, the participants are different in each wave of testing. For example, we might compare performances on intelligence tests for people between ages 20 and 50 in 1980 and then repeat the study in 1990 with a different group of people aged 30 to 60.

Table 1.4 also depicts the longitudinal sequential design. A longitudinal sequential design consists of two or more longitudinal designs that represent two or more cohorts. Each longitudinal design in the sequence begins with the same age range and follows people for the same length of time. For example, we may want to begin a longitudinal study of intellectual development with a group of 50-year-olds in 1980 using the 1930 cohort. We would then follow this cohort for a period of years. In 1990, we would begin a second longitudinal study on 50-year-olds, using the 1940 cohort, and follow them for the same length of time as we follow the first cohort. This design helps clarify whether the longitudinal effects found in a single longitudinal study are cohort-specific or are more general findings.

Although sequential designs are powerful and provide by far the richest source of information about developmental issues, few researchers use them, because they are costly. Trying to follow many people over long periods of time, generating new samples, and conducting complex data analyses are expensive and time consuming. Clearly, this type of commitment to one project is not possible for most researchers.

Integrating Findings from Different Studies

Several times in the past few pages, we've emphasized the value of using different methods to study the same phenomenon. The advantage of this approach is that conclusions are most convincing when the results are the same regardless of method.

In reality, though, findings are often inconsistent. Suppose, for example, many researchers find that people often share personal information with friends (e.g., through Facebook or Google+), some researchers find that people share occasionally with friends, and a few researchers find that people never share with friends. What results should we believe? What should we conclude? **Meta-analysis** *allows researchers to synthesize the results of many studies to estimate relations between variables* (Plonsky & Oswald, 2012). In conducting a meta-analysis, investigators find all studies published on a topic over a substantial period of time (e.g., 10 to 20 years), and then record and analyze the results and important methodological variables.

Thus, meta-analysis is a particularly powerful tool because it allows scientists to determine whether a finding generalizes across many studies that used different methods. In addition, meta-analysis can reveal the impact of those different methods on results.

Conducting Research Ethically

Choosing a good research design involves more than just selecting a particular method. Researchers must determine whether the methods they plan on using are ethical. That is, when designing a research study, investigators must do so in a way that does not violate the rights of people who participate. To verify that every research project has these protections, local panels of experts and community representatives review proposed studies before any data are collected. Only with the approval of this panel can scientists begin their study. If the review panel objects to some aspects of the proposed study, the researcher must revise those aspects and present them anew for the panel's approval. Likewise, each time a component of a study is changed, the review panel must be informed and give its approval.

To guide review panels, professional organizations (e.g., the American Psychological Association) and government agencies (e.g., the National Institutes of Health) have codes of conduct that specify the rights of research participants and procedures to protect these participants. The following essential guidelines are included in all of these codes:

- *Minimize risks to research participants.* Use methods that have the least potential for causing harm or stress for research participants. During the research, monitor the procedures to be sure to avoid any unforeseen stress or harm.
- *Describe the research to potential participants so they can determine whether they wish to participate.* Prospective participants must be told the purpose of the project, what they will be asked to do, whether there are any risks or potential harm, any benefits they may receive, that they are free to discontinue participation at any time without penalty, that they are entitled to a complete debriefing at the end of the project, and any other relevant information the review panel deems appropriate. After the study has been explained, participants sign a document that says they understand what they will do in the study. Special caution must be exercised in obtaining consent for the participation of children and

How Do We Know?
Conflicts Between Cross-Sectional and Longitudinal Data

Who was the investigator, and what was the aim of the study? In the 1950s, little information was available concerning longitudinal changes in adults' intellectual abilities. What there was showed a developmental pattern of relative stability or slight decline, quite different from the picture of substantial across-the-board decline obtained in cross-sectional studies. To provide a more thorough picture of intellectual change, K. Warner Schaie began the Seattle Longitudinal Study in 1956. The Seattle Longitudinal Study is widely regarded as one of the most extensive investigations in psychology of how adults develop and change across adulthood.

How did the investigator measure the topic of interest? Schaie used standardized tests of primary mental abilities to assess a wide range of abilities such as logical reasoning and spatial ability.

Who were the participants in the study? Over the course of the study, more than 5,000 individuals have been tested at eight testing cycles (1956, 1963, 1970, 1977, 1984, 1991, 1998, and 2005). The participants were representative of the upper 75% of the socioeconomic spectrum and were recruited through a very large health maintenance organization in Seattle. Extensions of the study include longitudinal data on second-generation family members and on the grandchildren of some of the original participants.

What was the design of the study? To provide a thorough view of intellectual change over time, Schaie invented a new type of design—the sequential design. Participants were tested every seven years. Like most longitudinal studies, Schaie's sequential study encountered selectivity effects—that is, people who return over the years for retesting tend to do better initially than those who fail to return (in other words, those who don't perform well initially tend to drop out of the study). However, an advantage of Schaie's sequential design is that by bringing in new groups of participants, he was able to estimate the importance of selection effects, a major improvement over previous research.

Were there ethical concerns with the study? The most serious issue in any study in which participants are followed over time is confidentiality. Because people's names must be retained for future contact, the researchers were very careful about keeping personal information secure.

What were the results? Among the many important findings from the study are differential changes in abilities over time and cohort effects. As you can see in Figure 1.4, scores on tests of primary mental abilities improve gradually until the late 30s or early 40s. Small declines begin in the 50s, increase as people age into their 60s, and become increasingly large in the 70s (Schaie & Zanjani, 2006).

Cohort differences were also found. Figure 1.5 shows that on some skills, such as inductive reasoning ability, but not others, more recently born younger and middle-aged cohorts performed better than cohorts born earlier. An example of the latter is that older cohorts outperformed younger ones on number skills (Schaie & Zanjani, 2006). These cohort effects probably reflect differences in educational experiences; younger groups' education emphasized

FIGURE 1.4
Longitudinal changes in intellectual functions from age 25 to 88.

Source: From "Intellectual Development Across Adulthood" by K. Warner Schaie and Faika A. K. Zanjani, in *Handbook of Adult Development and Learning*, ed. by C. Hoare, p. 102. Copyright © 2006 by Oxford University Press.

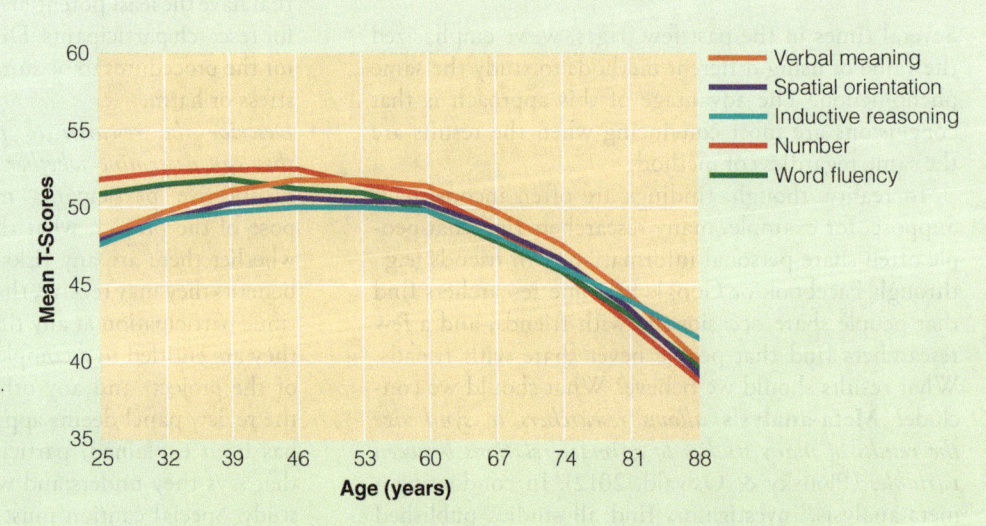

figuring things out on one's own, whereas older groups' education emphasized rote learning. Additionally, older groups did not have calculators or computers, so they had to do mathematical problems by hand.

Schaie uncovered many individual differences as well; some people showed developmental patterns closely approximating the overall trends, but others showed unusual patterns. For example, some individuals showed steady declines in most abilities beginning in their 40s and 50s; others showed declines in some abilities but not others; but some people showed little change in most abilities over a 14-year period. Such individual variation in developmental patterns means that average trends, like those depicted in the figures, must be interpreted cautiously; they reflect group averages and do not represent the patterns shown by each person in the group.

Another key finding is that how intellectual abilities are organized in people does not change over time (Schaie et al., 1998). This finding is important because it means that the tests, which presuppose a particular organizational structure of intellectual abilities, can be used across different ages. Additionally, Schaie (1994) identified several variables that appear to reduce the risk of cognitive decline in old age:

- Absence of cardiovascular and other chronic diseases
- Living in favorable environmental conditions (such as good housing)
- Remaining cognitively active through reading and lifelong learning
- Having a flexible personality style in middle age
- Being married to a person with high cognitive status
- Being satisfied with one's life achievements in middle age

What did the investigator conclude? Three points are clear. First, intellectual development during adulthood is marked by a gradual leveling off of gains, followed by a period of relative stability, and then a time of gradual decline in most abilities. Second, these trends vary from one cohort to another. Third, individual patterns of change vary considerably from person to person.

Overall, Schaie's findings indicate that intellectual development in adulthood is influenced by a wide variety of health, environmental, personality, and relationship factors. By attending to these influences throughout adulthood, we can at least stack the deck in favor of maintaining good intellectual functioning in late life.

What converging evidence would strengthen these conclusions? Although Schaie's study is one of the most comprehensive ever conducted, it is limited. Studying people who live in different locations around the world would provide evidence as to whether the results are limited geographically. Additional cross-cultural evidence comparing people with different economic backgrounds and differing access to health care would also provide insight into the effects of these variables on intellectual development.

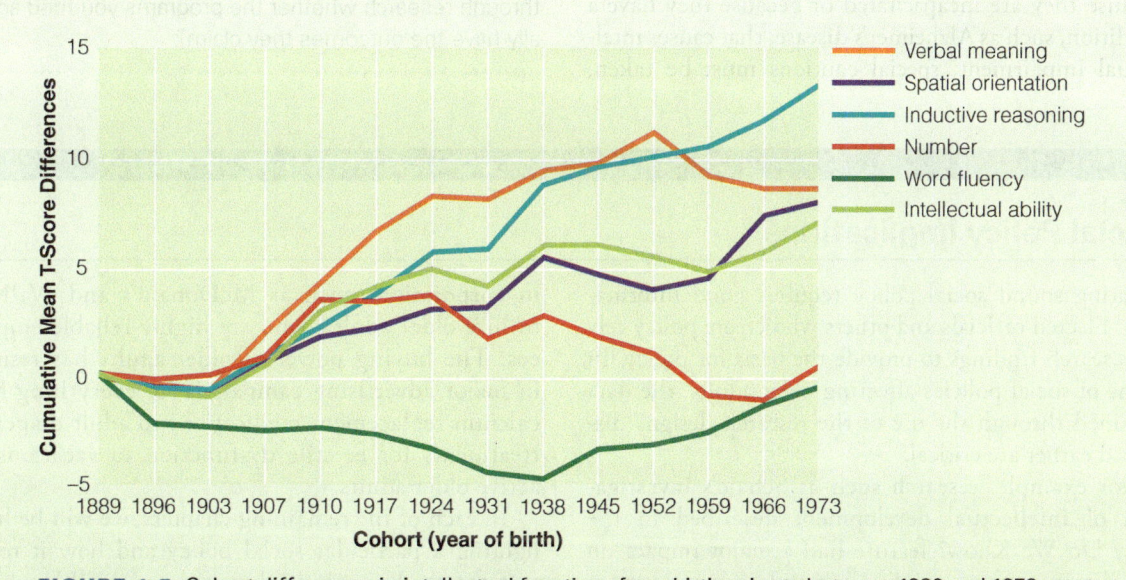

FIGURE 1.5 Cohort differences in intellectual functions from birth cohorts between 1889 and 1973.
Source: From "Intellectual Development Across Adulthood" by K. Warner Schaie and Faika A. K. Zanjani, in *Handbook of Adult Development and Learning*, ed. by C. Hoare, p. 106. Copyright © 2006 by Oxford University Press.

adolescents, as well as people who have conditions that affect intellectual functioning (e.g., Alzheimer's disease, severe head injury). In these cases, consent from a parent, legal guardian, or other responsible person, in addition to the agreement of the person him- or herself, is necessary for participation.
- *Avoid deception; if participants must be deceived, provide a thorough explanation of the true nature of the experiment as soon as possible.* Providing complete information about a study in advance sometimes biases or distorts a person's responses. Consequently, investigators may provide participants with partial information about the study or even mislead them about its true purpose. As soon as it is feasible—typically just after the experiment—any false information that was given to research participants must be corrected, and the reasons for the deception must be provided.
- *Results should be anonymous or confidential.* Research results should be anonymous, which means that people's data cannot be linked to their name. When anonymity is not possible, research results should be confidential, which means the identity of participants is known only to the investigator conducting the study.

The requirement for informed consent is very important. If prospective participants cannot complete the informed consent procedure themselves, perhaps because they are incapacitated or because they have a condition, such as Alzheimer's disease, that causes intellectual impairment, special cautions must be taken.

The Alzheimer's Association (2015), among other professional organizations, has published guidelines outlining some of these protections for persons whose cognitive capacity may be challenged. For example, when the participant cannot understand the consent process, someone else (usually a family member) must complete it. In addition, the researcher must describe the procedures to the participant and still obtain the participant's assent. However, this process is task specific; some cognitively impaired people, particularly early in the disease process, can respond appropriately to certain types of consent. And researchers can obtain advance consent for future participation when the cognitive impairment is more severe. In all cases, though, researchers must take extra precautions to be sensitive to these individuals; for example, if it becomes apparent that the participant does not like the procedures, the researcher must stop collecting data from that individual.

These ethical principles provide important protections for participants and investigators alike. By treating research participants with respect, investigators are in a better position to make important discoveries about adult development and aging.

Adult Development in Action

If you were responsible for making grants at your local United Way organization, how might you determine through research whether the programs you fund actually have the outcomes they claim?

Social Policy Implications

Creating sound social policy requires good information. Elected officials and others who create policy rely on research findings to provide the basis for policy. In terms of social policies affecting older adults, the data obtained through the use of the research designs discussed earlier are critical.

For example, research such as Schaie's investigation of intellectual development described in the How Do We Know? feature had a major impact on the elimination of nearly all mandatory retirement rules in the 1980s. Research on worker satisfaction and post-retirement lifestyles influenced decisions in corporations such as McDonald's and WalMart to hire older adults, who are highly reliable employees. The buying power of older adults has resulted in major advertising campaigns for everything from calcium replacement medications to adult diapers to treatments for erectile dysfunction to vacations for active older adults.

In each of the remaining chapters, we will be highlighting a particular social policy and how it relates to research. By making these ties, you will be able to understand better how research findings can be applied to address social issues.

SUMMARY

1.1 Perspectives on Adult Development and Aging

What is gerontology? How does ageism relate to stereotypes of aging?
- Gerontology is the study of aging from maturity through old age, as well as the study of older adults as a special group.
- Myths of aging lead to negative stereotypes of older people, which can result in ageism, a form of discrimination against older people simply because of their age.

What is the life-span perspective?
- The life-span perspective divides human development into two phases: an early phase (childhood and adolescence) and a later phase (young adulthood, middle age, and old age).
- There are four key features of the life-span perspective: multidirectionality, plasticity, historical context, and multiple causation.

What are the characteristics of the older adult population?
- The number of older adults in the United States and other industrialized countries is increasing rapidly because of better health care, including declines in mortality during childbirth. The large numbers of older adults have important implications for human services.
- The number of older Latino, Asian American, and Native American adults will increase much faster between now and 2050 than will the number of European American and African American older adults.
- Whether older adults reflect individualism or collectivism has implications for interventions.
- The increase in numbers of older adults is most rapid in developing countries.

1.2 Issues in Studying Adult Development and Aging

What four main forces shape development?
- Development is shaped by four forces. (1) Biological forces include all genetic and health-related factors. (2) Psychological forces include all internal perceptual, cognitive, emotional, and personality factors. (3) Sociocultural forces include interpersonal, societal, cultural, and ethnic factors. (4) Life-cycle forces reflect differences in how the same event or combination of biological, psychological, and sociocultural forces affects people at different points in their lives.

What are normative age-graded influences, normative history-graded influences, and nonnormative influences?
- Normative age-graded influences are life experiences that are highly related to chronological age. Normative history-graded influences are events that most people in a specific culture experience at the same time. Nonnormative influences are events that may be important for a specific individual but are not experienced by most people.

How do culture and ethnicity influence aging?
- Culture and ethnicity jointly provide status, social settings, living conditions, and personal experiences for people of all ages. Culture can be defined as shared basic value orientations, norms, beliefs, and customary habits and ways of living, and it provides the basic worldview of a society. Ethnicity is an individual and collective sense of identity based on historical and cultural group membership and related behaviors and beliefs.

What is the meaning of age?
- Three types of aging are distinguished. (1) Primary aging is normal, disease-free development during adulthood. (2) Secondary aging is developmental changes that are related to disease. (3) Tertiary aging is the rapid losses that occur shortly before death.
- Chronological age is a poor descriptor of time-dependent processes and serves only as a shorthand for the passage of calendar time. Time-dependent processes do not actually cause behavior.
- Perceived age is the age you think of yourself as being.
- Better definitions of age include biological age (where a person is relative to the maximum number of years he or she could live), psychological age (where a person is in terms of the abilities people use to adapt to changing environmental demands), and sociocultural age (where a person is in terms of the specific set of roles adopted in relation to other members of the society and culture).

What are the nature–nurture, stability–change, continuity–discontinuity, and the "universal versus context-specific development" issues?
- The nature–nurture issue concerns the extent to which inborn, hereditary characteristics (nature) and experiential, or environmental, influences (nurture) determine who we are. The focus on nature and nurture must be on how they interact.

- The stability–change issue concerns the degree to which people remain the same over time.
- The continuity–discontinuity issue concerns competing views of how to describe change: as a smooth progression over time (continuity) or as a series of abrupt shifts (discontinuity).
- The issue of universal versus context-specific development concerns whether there is only one pathway of development or several. This issue becomes especially important in interpreting cultural and ethnic group differences.

1.3 Research Methods

What approaches do scientists use to measure behavior in adult development and aging research?

- Measures used in research must be reliable (measure things consistently) and valid (measure what they are supposed to measure).
- Systematic observation involves watching people and carefully recording what they say or do. Two forms are common: naturalistic observation (observing people behaving spontaneously in a real-world setting) and structured observations (creating a setting that will elicit the behavior of interest).
- If behaviors are hard to observe directly, researchers often create tasks that sample the behavior of interest.
- Self-reports involve people's answers to questions presented in a questionnaire or interview about a topic of interest.
- Most research on adults has focused on middle-class, well-educated European Americans. This creates serious problems for understanding the development experiences of other groups of people.

What are the general designs for doing research?

- Experiments consist of manipulating one or more independent variables, measuring one or more dependent variables, and randomly assigning participants to the experimental and control groups. Experiments provide information about cause and effect.
- Correlational designs address relations between variables; they do not provide information about cause and effect but do provide information about the strength of the relation between the variables.
- Case studies are systematic investigations of individual people that provide detailed descriptions of people's behavior in everyday situations.

What specific designs are unique to adult development and aging research?

- Age effects reflect underlying biological, psychological, and sociocultural changes. Cohort effects are differences caused by experiences and circumstances unique to the generation to which one belongs. Time-of-measurement effects reflect influences of the specific historical time when one is obtaining information. Developmental research designs represent various combinations of age, cohort, and time-of-measurement effects. Confounding is any situation in which one cannot determine which of two or more effects is responsible for the behaviors being observed.
- Cross-sectional designs examine multiple cohorts and age groups at a single point in time. They can identify only age differences and confound age and cohort. The use of extreme age groups (young and older adults) is problematic in that the samples may not be representative, age should be treated as a continuous variable, and the measures may not be equivalent across age groups.
- Longitudinal designs examine one cohort over two or more times of measurement. They can identify age change but have several problems, including practice effects, dropout, and selective survival. Longitudinal designs confound age and time of measurement. Microgenetic studies are short-term longitudinal designs that measure behaviors very closely over relatively brief periods of time.
- Sequential designs involve more than one cross-sectional (cross-sequential) or longitudinal (longitudinal sequential) design. Although they are complex and expensive, they are important because they help disentangle age, cohort, and time-of-measurement effects.
- Meta-analyses examine the consistency of findings across many research studies.

What ethical procedures must researchers follow?

- Investigators must obtain informed consent from their participants before conducting research.

REVIEW QUESTIONS

1.1 Perspectives on Adult Development and Aging

- What are the premises of the life-span perspective?
- How are population demographics changing around the world, and what difference does it make?

1.2 Issues in Studying Adult Development and Aging

- What are the four basic forces in human development?
- What are the major characteristics of normative age-graded, normative history-graded, and non-normative influences?
- How do nature and nurture interact? What are culture and ethnicity? In what ways can age be defined? What are the advantages and disadvantages of each definition?
- What is the stability–change issue? What is the continuity–discontinuity issue? What kinds of theories derive from each view?
- What is the universal versus context-specific development issue, and how does it relate to sociocultural forces?

1.3 Research Methods

- What are the reliability and validity of a measure?
- What are the three main approaches scientists use to measure behavior in adult development and aging research? What are the strengths and weaknesses of each?
- How do we know whether a sample is representative?
- What is an experiment? What information does it provide?
- What is a correlational design? What information does it provide?
- What is a case study? What information does it provide?
- What are age, cohort, and time-of-measurement effects? How and why are they important for developmental research?
- What is a cross-sectional design? What are its advantages and disadvantages?
- What is a longitudinal design? What are its advantages and disadvantages?
- What differences are there between cross-sectional and longitudinal designs in terms of uncovering age differences and age changes?
- What are sequential designs? What different types are there? What are their advantages and disadvantages?
- What are the limitations of the extreme age groups design?
- What steps must researchers take to protect the rights of participants?

INTEGRATING CONCEPTS IN DEVELOPMENT

- Analyze each of the four major controversies in development in terms of the four developmental forces. What real-world examples can you think of that are examples of each combination of controversy and force?
- Using yourself as an example, figure out your age using chronological, perceived, biological, psychological, and sociocultural definitions. How do they differ? Why?
- Using the Leah and Sarah vignette as an example, design cross-sectional, longitudinal, and sequential studies of two different styles of caring for people with Alzheimer's disease. What will you learn from each of the studies?

KEY TERMS

age effects One of the three fundamental effects examined in developmental research, along with cohort and time-of-measurement effects, which reflects the influence of time-dependent processes on development.

ageism The untrue assumption that chronological age is the main determinant of human characteristics and that one age is better than another.

biological forces One of four basic forces of development that includes all genetic and health-related factors.

biopsychosocial framework Way of organizing the biological, psychological, and sociocultural forces on human development.

case study An intensive investigation of individual people.

cohort A group of people born at the same point in time or within a specific time span.

cohort effects One of the three basic influences examined in developmental research, along with age and time-of-measurement effects, which reflects differences caused by experiences and circumstances unique to the historical time in which one lives.

confounding Any situation in which one cannot determine which of two or more effects is responsible for the behaviors being observed.

continuity–discontinuity controversy The debate over whether a particular developmental phenomenon represents smooth progression over time (continuity) or a series of abrupt shifts (discontinuity).

correlational study An investigation in which the strength of association between variables is examined.

cross-sectional study A developmental research design in which people of different ages and cohorts are observed at one time of measurement to obtain information about age differences.

demographers People who study population trends.

dependent variable Behaviors or outcomes measured in an experiment.

emerging adulthood A period when individuals are not adolescents but are not yet fully adults.

experiment A study in which participants are randomly assigned to experimental and control groups and in which an independent variable is manipulated to observe its effects on a dependent variable so that cause-and-effect relations can be established.

gerontology The study of aging from maturity through old age.

independent variable The variable manipulated in an experiment.

life-cycle forces One of the four basic forces of development that reflects differences in how the same event or combination of biological, psychological, and sociocultural forces affects people at different points in their lives.

life-span perspective A view of the human life span that divides it into two phases: childhood/adolescence and young/middle/late adulthood.

longitudinal study A developmental research design that measures one cohort over two or more times of measurement to examine age changes.

meta-analysis A technique that allows researchers to synthesize the results of many studies to estimate relations between variables.

microgenetic study A special type of longitudinal design in which participants are tested repeatedly over a span of days or weeks, typically with the aim of observing change directly as it occurs.

nature–nurture issue A debate over the relative influence of genetics and the environment on development.

nonnormative influences Random events that are important to an individual but do not happen to most people.

normative age-graded influences Experiences caused by biological, psychological, and sociocultural forces that are closely related to a person's age.

normative history-graded influences Events that most people in a specific culture experience at the same time.

plasticity The belief that capacity is not fixed, but can be learned or improved with practice.

population pyramid Graphic technique for illustrating population trends.

primary aging The normal, disease-free development during adulthood.

psychological forces One of the four basic forces of development that includes all internal perceptual, cognitive, emotional, and personality factors.

reliability The ability of a measure to produce the same value when used repeatedly to measure the identical phenomenon over time.

secondary aging Developmental changes that are related to disease, lifestyle, and other environmental changes that are not inevitable.

self-reports People's answers to questions about a topic of interest.

sequential designs Types of developmental research designs involving combinations of cross-sectional and longitudinal designs.

sociocultural forces One of the four basic forces of development that include interpersonal, societal, cultural, and ethnic factors.

stability–change issue A debate over the degree to which people remain the same over time as opposed to being different.

systematic observation A type of measurement involving watching people and carefully recording what they say or do.

tertiary aging Rapid losses occurring shortly before death.

time-of-measurement effects One of the three fundamental effects examined in developmental research, along with age and cohort effects, which result from the time at which the data are collected.

universal versus context-specific development controversy A debate over whether there is a single pathway of development, or several.

validity The degree to which an instrument measures what it is supposed to measure.

2 Neuroscience as a Basis for Adult Development and Aging

CHAPTER OUTLINE

2.1 The Neuroscience Approach
Neuroimaging Techniques
Neuroscience Perspectives

DISCOVERING DEVELOPMENT What Do People Believe about Brain Fitness?

2.2 Neuroscience and Adult Development and Aging
How Is the Brain Organized?
What Age-Related Changes Occur in Neurons?
What Age-Related Changes Occur in Neurotransmitters?
What Age-Related Changes Occur in Brain Structures?
What Do Structural Brain Changes Mean? The Theory of Mind

HOW DO WE KNOW? The Aging Emotional Brain

2.3 Making Sense of Neuroscience Research: Explaining Changes in Brain-Behavior Relations
The Parieto-Frontal Integration Theory
Can Older Adults Compensate for Changes in the Brain?
Theories of Brain-Behavior Changes Across Adulthood

REAL PEOPLE Oliver Sacks, Brain Mapper

2.4 Plasticity and the Aging Brain
What Is Brain Plasticity?

CURRENT CONTROVERSIES Are Neural Stem Cells the Solution to Brain Aging?
Exercise and Brain Aging
Nutrition and Brain Aging

Social Policy Implications

Summary
Review Questions
Integrating Concepts in Development
Key Terms

You see and hear more and more advertisements and literature touting the importance of "brain fitness." In the grocery store and on television, marketers and self-help solicitors encourage people to eat the right "brain foods" filled with antioxidants. *They promise that these* **antioxidants** *will protect your cells from the harmful effect of* **free radicals**, *substances that can damage cells, including brain cells, and play a role in cancer and other diseases as we grow older.* Similarly, advertisements promote exercising your brain through mental aerobics such as playing chess, reading the newspaper, and attending plays. There is an entire industry of online and computerized brain-training games, such as Lumosity.com, supposedly aimed at delaying the onset of cognitive decline and prolonging cognitive vitality.

This relatively recent phenomenon has coincided with the rapid surge of research in **neuroscience** *or the study of the brain—in particular, plasticity of the aging brain.* Neuroscience enables us to observe, measure, and understand what is going on in a person's brain. Images such as the one shown in the figure below are one way that researchers and clinicians measure brain activity.

Our understanding of how the brain works is expanding exponentially. We now know through the Human Connectome Project that uses sophisticated studies of brain imagery and computer analyses that each hemisphere of the brain (that is, the left and right halves) contains at least 180 distinct functional areas that differ in their structure, function, and connections with other brain areas (Glasser et al., 2016). This is roughly double the number of specific areas we knew about previously.

Perhaps the most important insight from neuroscience research is the evidence that the brain can change for the better as we grow older. These findings send an intriguing message to our aging population. However, there is danger in this. As in any relatively new field, descriptions in the media, especially the Internet, may extend well beyond the actual scope of our scientific understanding of the brain.

In this chapter we explore our understanding of the aging brain by examining contemporary theories and recent empirical findings of neuroscience and aging. First, we briefly review the various neuroscience theories underlying and techniques used in studying the brain. Next, we focus on cognitive neuroscience and aging including age-related change in brain structures, neurochemical properties, and brain function. Two contemporary areas of research are explored, including cultural influences on brain aging, as well as neural plasticity in later adulthood. Finally, we explore more recent developments in the area of social neuroscience and aging—in particular, intriguing findings that reveal the neurological underpinnings of enhanced emotional processing in older adulthood in contrast to declines in cognitive processing such as the ability to control information in the conscious mind. ∎

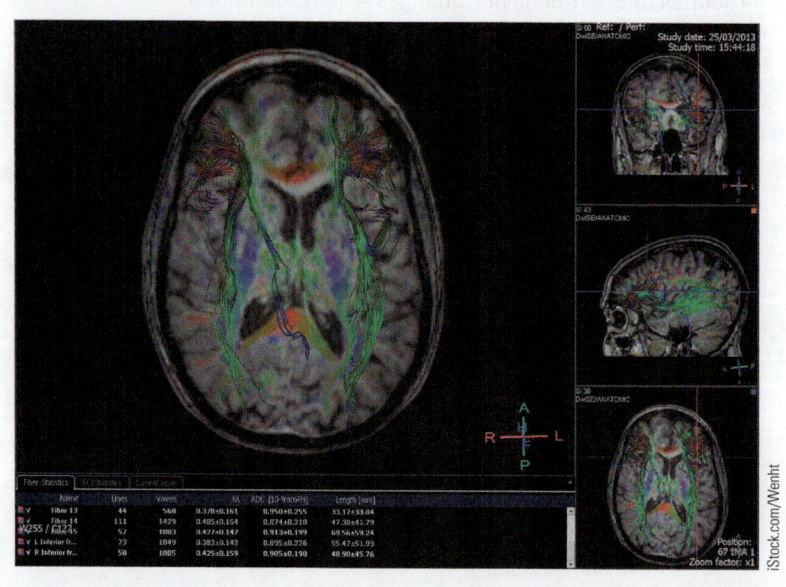

Images such as this help us understand how the brain operates.

2.1 The Neuroscience Approach

LEARNING OBJECTIVES
- What brain imaging techniques are used in neuroscience research?
- What are the main research methods used and issues studied in neuroscience research in adult development and aging?

At age 70, Margaret was having trouble moving the left side of her body. With the aid of accurate brain imaging techniques, she was diagnosed as having a tumor located at the front of the right motor cortex. (Because the brain is wired in general to control the side of the body opposite of the side of the brain in question, movement on one's left side is controlled by the right side of the brain in the area called the motor cortex.) With image-guided surgery, the tumor was removed, and Margaret recovered comfortably.

How did Margaret's physicians figure out what was wrong with her? We are learning a great deal about the relations between changes in the brain and changes in behavior through technological advances in noninvasive imaging and in assessing psychological functioning (Linden, 2016; Sugiura, 2016). **Neuroimaging** *is a set of techniques in which pictures of the brain are taken in various ways to provide understanding of both normal and abnormal cognitive aging.*

Neuroimaging Techniques

What neuroimaging does is allow us to see inside the brain of a living person to examine the various structures of the brain. Neuroimaging has revolutionized our understanding of the relations between the brain and our behavior, and it is responsible for an explosion of knowledge over the past few decades. Advances in neuroimaging have led to much of our understanding of such diseases as Alzheimer's disease (which we will consider in detail in Chapter 10) and to other key insights into age-related changes that occur to everyone and those changes that reflect disease or other abnormal changes.

But neuroimaging must be used carefully and ethically. For one thing, we are still figuring out which changes in the brain are normative and which ones are not. We need to know what a "healthy" brain looks like at different points in the human life span. So just because we observe a change does not mean anything in and of itself unless additional research is done to place it in context.

Two neuroimaging techniques are used most often:

1. **Structural neuroimaging** *provides highly detailed images of anatomical features in the brain.* The most commonly used are X-rays, computerized tomography (CT) scans, and magnetic resonance imaging (MRI). Images from structural neuroimaging techniques are like photographs in that they document what a specific brain structure looks like at a specific point in time. Structural neuroimaging is usually effective at identifying such things as bone fractures, tumors, and other conditions that cause structural damage in the brain, such as strokes.

2. **Functional neuroimaging** *provides an indication of brain activity but not high anatomical detail.* The most commonly used neuroimaging techniques are single photon emission computerized tomography (SPECT), positron emission tomography (PET), functional magnetic resonance imaging (fMRI), magnetoencephalography (or multichannel encephalography), and near infrared spectroscopic imaging (NIRSI). In general, fMRI is the most commonly used technique in cognitive neuroscience research (Poldrack, 2012). Functional neuroimaging provides researchers with information about what parts of the brain are active when people are doing specific tasks. A typical image will show different levels of brain activity as different colors; for example, red on an image might indicate high levels of brain activity in that region, whereas blue might indicate low levels of activity.

These techniques, coupled with tests of behavior such as specific cognitive processing tasks (e.g., recognizing which pictures you studied from a deck containing pictures you saw and pictures you did not), have shown quite convincingly that age-related brain changes are responsible for age-related changes in performance (Sugiura, 2016).

In Margaret's case, an MRI scan was conducted. This identified areas of the brain associated with specific functions. The scan produced an image showing the brain location of interest and the outline of a tumor in the area of the brain involved in controlling movement.

In addition to using MRIs to locate brain tumors, we are interested in how neuroimaging techniques advance our understanding of how the brain changes as we grow older. Do the changes reflect decline, stability, or perhaps improvement and compensation? Is there plasticity or growth in the aging brain? These are important questions that researchers in the field of contemporary neuroscience and aging are exploring.

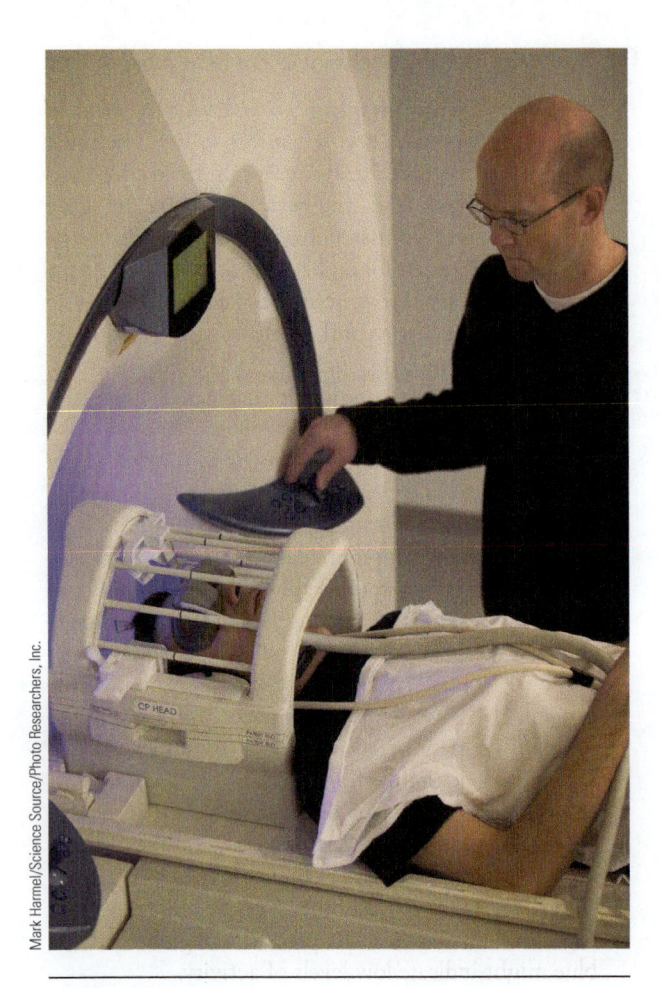

A research participant being readied for an fMRI neuroimaging study.

theories using cutting-edge methods. Furthermore, examination of the structure and function of the brain has become even more informative for cognitive aging research as the focus has shifted from describing brain activation patterns toward explaining them.

Neuroscience Perspectives

Researchers take three general methodological perspectives in tackling the neuroscience of aging: the neuropsychological, the neurocorrelational, and the activation imaging approach (Cabeza, 2004). *The* **neuropsychological approach** *compares brain functioning of healthy older adults with adults displaying various pathological disorders in the brain.* In this approach researchers are interested in whether patients of any age with damage in specific regions of the brain show similar cognitive deficits to those shown by healthy older adults. If this is the case, then researchers can conclude that decline in cognitive functioning as we grow older may be related to unfavorable changes in the same specific regions of the brain observed in the brain-damaged patients.

Let's suppose this type of comparison is made between healthy older adults and persons showing frontal lobe damage. People with brain damage in the frontal lobe display lower levels of dopamine (a chemical substance we will consider a bit later in detail), which results in a decrease in how quickly mental processing occurs, termed speed of processing. Interestingly, this same slowing resembles what is observed in healthy older adults.

Another important objective of research using this approach is to isolate the neural or brain mechanisms that are associated with both normal and pathological decline in cognitive functions. These findings stimulate development of theories by identifying influential factors that warrant theoretical explanation as to how and why these factors may cause cognitive decline as we age.

Just as we saw in Chapter 1 in relation to adult development and aging research in general, neuroscience researchers use certain research designs to study changes in brain structures and processes.

The **neuro-correlational approach** *attempts to relate measures of cognitive performance to measures of brain structure or functioning.* For example, a researcher may be interested in the correlation between cognitive behavior, such as the ability to remember information over short periods of time, and neural structural measures, such as the volume of the brain or activity in specific areas of the brain (Cabeza & Dennis, 2013; Sugiura, 2016). Instead of direct measures of brain structure or functioning, some researchers investigate

A neuroscientific approach to the study of aging has several advantages. For example, the neuroscience approach has resulted in the development of new, effective interventions that are enhancing the quality of life of older adults (e.g., Linden, 2016). Neuroscience research can even be applied to protecting older adults from financial exploitation through understanding the connection between cognitive decline and the ability to understand financial transactions (Marson, 2016).

These techniques and others can test models of cognitive aging. Neuroscience has become increasingly more relevant to cognitive aging research as the focus has expanded beyond studying pathologies of the aging brain, such as Alzheimer's or Parkinson's disease, toward investigating normative and healthy aging (Sugiura, 2016). In addition, neuroscientific data are more informative for models of cognitive aging and usher in increased progress in the field by testing established

the correlation between behavioral tests that are associated with the function of specific brain regions (e.g., tests of frontal lobe functioning). However, this approach is speculative, in that we cannot be certain whether the tests accurately reflect the actual anatomical and functional activity of the specific brain region under investigation.

The **activation imaging approach** *attempts to directly link functional brain activity with cognitive behavioral data.* This approach allows real-time investigation of changes in brain function as they affect cognitive performance in older adults. As you may have surmised, this approach relies on functional neuroimaging techniques, such as fMRI. For example, studies using this approach have found that younger adults' brains show unilateral activation (i.e., activation in only one hemisphere of the brain) when they perform specific cognitive tasks, but older adults' brains tend to show increased activation in both brain hemispheres when performing the same tasks (Grady, 2012). As we will discuss later, this difference in activation in younger and older adult brains may provide neurological evidence that older adults' brains compensate for age-related changes. **Compensatory changes** *are changes that allow older adults to adapt to the inevitable behavioral decline resulting from changes in specific areas of the brain.*

Overall, neuroscience has brought an important perspective to studying cognitive aging, influencing theories of adulthood in several ways (Johnson, 2016; Sugiura, 2016). First, theories of brain-behavior relations can be tested using these approaches. For instance, age-related changes in how we selectively direct our attention to specific characteristics of our environment can be validated by examining how age-related changes in performance are associated with both functional and structural changes in the brain. In other words, we can explain how changes in performance map to changes in the brain.

Second, research methods that focus on the age-related changes in the structure and functioning of the brain can help to explain why certain cognitive functions, such as well-practiced tasks, vocabulary, and wisdom, can be preserved into old age while other functions, such as processing speed, decline rapidly as people age. By carefully tracking which brain structures and functions change in which direction—or in some cases remain the same—we can differentiate and explain seemingly contradictory patterns of behavior over time.

As powerful and useful as they are, neuroscientific methods, such as PET scans, have limitations (Slough et al., 2016). Like any set of tools, neuroscience techniques

DISCOVERING DEVELOPMENT
What Do People Believe About Brain Fitness?

With all the hype about keeping your brain fit, what do people believe you have to do to accomplish this? To find out, ask some people of different ages these questions:

- What happens to the brain as we grow older?
- What do you think causes these changes?
- What do you think you can do to make sure that the brain stays fit as you grow older?

Compile the results from your interviews and compare them with what you discover in this chapter. To what extent do people's beliefs correspond to the scientific evidence? In which areas are they completely off base?

must be used appropriately and ethically. Nevertheless, advances in the field of neuroscience have had a major impact on our understanding of cognitive aging because they have revealed new findings that psychological theories have to account for and be consistent with.

Before we explore some of the scientific research on age-related changes in the brain, complete the Discovering Development exercise. Compare your findings with the evidence described in the text that follows. What similarities and differences are revealed?

Adult Development in Action

How would a physician decide whether to use structural neuroimaging or functional neuroimaging to aid in a clinical diagnosis?

2.2 Neuroscience and Adult Development and Aging

LEARNING OBJECTIVES
- How is the brain organized structurally?
- What are the basic changes in neurons as we age?
- What changes occur in neurotransmitters with age?
- What changes occur in brain structures with age?
- What do age-related structural brain changes mean for behavior?

Samuel is 73, and he is worried about contracting Alzheimer's disease. He remembers that his father became disoriented at this age and had trouble remembering things that he had just been told. How can Samuel find out if his brain is aging normally or pathologically? Psychological tests are somewhat predictive of disease—but not completely. This is a dilemma older adults are facing in our society today.

Much adult development and aging research has focused on cognitive aging, both normal and pathological. Historically, this research was based on behavioral data, which in turn gave rise to the classic theories of cognitive aging (see Chapter 6; Salthouse, 1996; Schaie, 1996). More recently, though, the availability of neuroscientific methods has stimulated research that allows us to study cognitive processes—and changes in these processes—in the living brain, using noninvasive brain imaging techniques discussed earlier. Knowing what is going on inside a living person's brain gives us enormous insights into both normative and nonnormative activity. For instance, brain activity involved in the identification of faces occurs in areas of the brain that are among the first affected by Alzheimer's disease (Saavedra, Iglesias, & Olivares, 2012; Yamasaki et al., 2016). So changes in brain activity in these regions may signal the onset of the disease before other, more obvious behavioral changes occur.

This is exactly the type of information in which Samuel, the man in the vignette, would be interested. To make these types of discoveries, we must first have a strong knowledge base of how the brain ages normally. Let's examine what the field of neuroscience and aging has contributed to our knowledge of the aging brain.

How Is the Brain Organized?

The human brain is an amazingly complex organ. It still remains more flexible and capable than any computer, handling billions of computations and providing us with the wide range of emotions we experience. Needless to say, the structure of such a complex organ is, well, complex. *At the most basic level, the brain is made up of cells called* **neurons**, an example of which is shown in Figure 2.1. *Key structural features of the neuron are the* **dendrites**, *which act like antennas to receive signals from other nearby neurons, the* **axon**, *which is part of the neuron containing the* **neurofibers**, *which are the structures that carry information inside the neuron from the dendrites to the* **terminal branches**, *which are the endpoints of the neuron. Neurons do not physically touch each other. In order for information to be passed from one neuron to another, the terminal branches release chemicals called* **neurotransmitters**, *that travel across the space between neurons, called the* **synapse**, *where they are received by the dendrites of the next neuron.*

Now that we know the basic building block of the brain, let's take a look at how the neurons themselves are organized into various brain structures. Figure 2.2 shows the major structures of the brain that are the focus of neuroscience research in adult development and aging. *The study of the structure of the brain, called* **neuroanatomy**, *is fundamental to neuroscience*. We will refer to a number of brain regions that exhibit age-related changes in both structure and function.

The **cerebral cortex** *is the outermost part of the brain. It consists of two hemispheres (left and right) that are connected by a thick bundle of neurons called the* **corpus callosum**. Most neuroscience research focuses on the cerebral cortex.

FIGURE 2.1 A typical neuron showing dendrites, axon, neurofibers, and terminal branches.

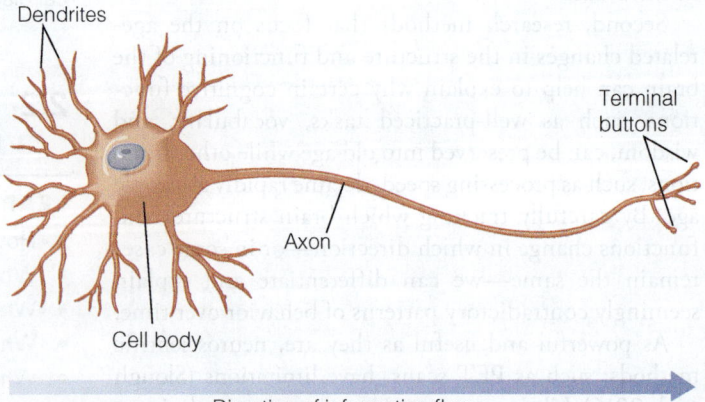

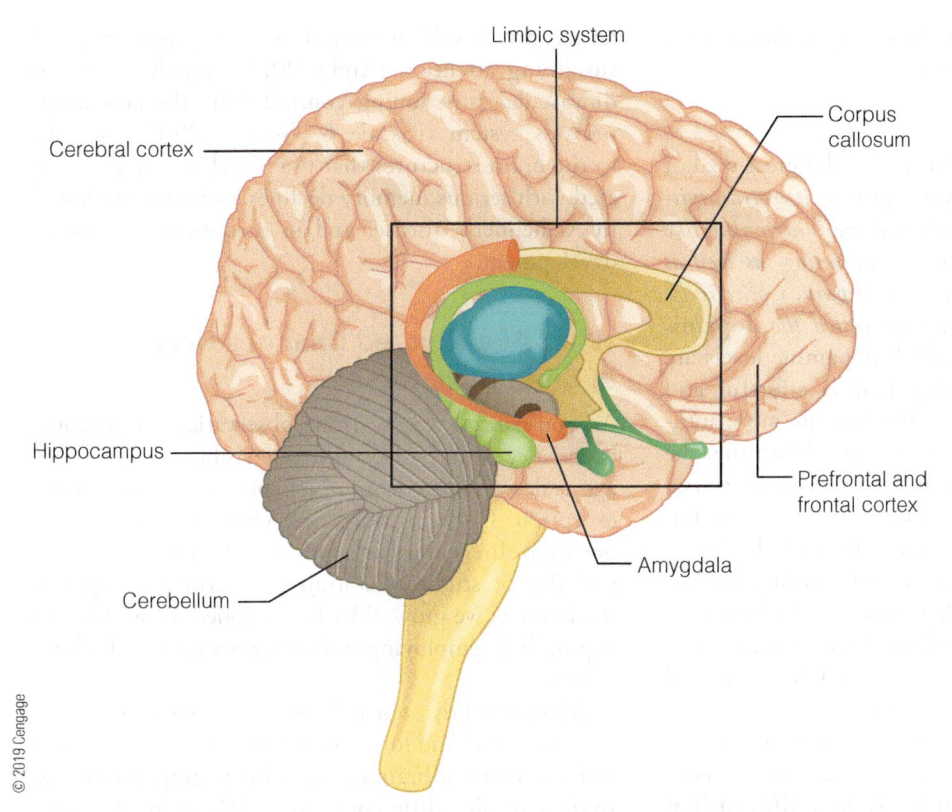

FIGURE 2.2 Major structures of the human brain showing cerebral cortex, corpus callosum, prefrontal and frontal cortex, cerebellum hippocampus, limbic system, and amygdala.

Each region of the brain has distinguishing features that relate to the specific functions those regions control. For example, in most people, language processing is associated primarily with the left hemisphere, whereas recognizing nonspeech sounds, emotions, and faces is associated with the right hemisphere. *The **prefrontal and frontal cortex** is intimately involved in higher-order executive functions such as the ability to make and carry out plans, switch between tasks, and maintain attention and focus, and connects with other key brain structures that are involved with emotion. In addition, the **cerebellum**, at the back of the brain, controls equilibrium and the coordination of fine motor movements, and may be involved in some cognitive functions. The **hippocampus**, located in the middle of the brain, is a key structure associated with memory. The **limbic system** is a set of brain structures involved with emotion, motivation, and long-term memory, among other functions. For adult development and aging research, the most important components of the limbic system include the **amygdala**, and the hippocampus.*

Details regarding both additional brain structures and the functional aspects of the various regions of the brain will be discussed more fully with respect to specific age-related changes.

What Age-Related Changes Occur in Neurons?

Several changes occur with age in neurons (Whalley, 2015). As we age, the number of neurons in the brain declines. Structural changes include decreases in the size and number of dendrites, the development of tangles in the fibers that make up the axon, and increases in the deposit of certain proteins. The number of potential connections also declines, as measured by the number of synapses among neurons.

Interestingly, these same changes occur but in much greater numbers in diseases such as Alzheimer's disease, leading some researchers to speculate that there may be a link between normal brain aging and pathological brain aging having to do with the speed and number of changes, not in the kind of changes that occur.

What Age-Related Changes Occur in Neurotransmitters?

As noted earlier, because neurons do not touch each other, much of the information transmission from one neuron to another occurs chemically via neurotransmitters. Advances have also been made in measuring changes in neurotransmitters in the aging brain. Let's explore some of the key findings.

Dopamine

One neurotransmitter that has received a great deal of attention is dopamine. **Dopamine** *is a neurotransmitter associated with higher-level cognitive functioning like inhibiting thoughts, attention, and planning, as well as emotion, movement, and pleasure and pain. Collectively, the neurons that use dopamine are called the* **dopaminergic system**. For example, high dopamine levels are linked to cognitive processing that is effortful and deliberate, but not to the processes that are more automatic and less effortful. To investigate dopamine, the majority of studies have used postmortem analyses (i.e., analyses during autopsies), results from neuropsychological tests, and simulated modeling and the imaging of dopamine activity. Researchers (Bäckman et al., 2010; Mather, 2016; Park & Festini, 2017) have concluded that there is clear evidence that effective functioning of the dopaminergic system declines in normal aging. Exactly what does this mean?

Declines in the dopaminergic system are related to declines in several different aspects of memory (Nevalainen et al., 2015; Yin & Wang, 2016), such as episodic (short-term) memory and memory for information acquired in tasks that must be performed quickly, and the amount of information that can be held in mind at any given moment (called working memory). As we shall see in Chapter 6, these are cognitive tasks that are effortful and not automatic. Fewer age differences are observed in more automatic tasks, like judging the familiarity of information. Overall, the studies using neuroscience methods to examine changes in the dopaminergic system with increasing age suggest that these changes play a role in cognitive aging.

Other Neurotransmitters

The neurotransmitter serotonin is involved in several types of brain processes, including memory, mood, appetite, and sleep. Abnormal processing of serotonin has been shown to be related to cognitive decline both in normal aging and in Alzheimer's disease, as well as other disorders such as schizophrenia (Rodriguez, Noristani, & Verkhratsky, 2012; Štrac, Pivac, & Mück-Šeler, 2016). Increasing the functional level of serotonin has beneficial effects (Štrac et al., 2016). In Chapter 10, we will return to the role of serotonin in mental disorders.

Another important neurotransmitter related to aging is acetylcholine. In the brain, acetylcholine has an important role in arousal, sensory perception, and sustaining attention (Ando, 2012) as well as in cardiovascular functioning controlled by the autonomic nervous system (Pascale & Govoni, 2016). Damage to the brain structures that use acetylcholine is associated with serious memory declines such as those found in Alzheimer's disease, and in cardiovascular disease development.

What Age-Related Changes Occur in Brain Structures?

As you already know from observation or personal experience, our bodies undergo visible changes with age as described in detail in Chapter 3. The brain is no exception. Documenting those changes, however, has not been direct until the past decade. As a result, the majority of studies examining structural changes in the brain as we grow older have applied a correlational approach by employing postmortem analyses of adults' brains.

More recently, researchers have been able to use cross-sectional and longitudinal designs to examine age differences in the brain using brain imaging techniques. In these studies, different regions of the brain are examined in terms of various structural changes and deficiencies, such as thinning and shrinkage in volume and density, and the declining health of the brain's white matter, termed white matter hyperintensities (WMH). **White matter** *refers to neurons that are covered by myelin that serve to transmit information from one part of the cerebral cortex to another or from the cerebral cortex to other parts of the brain.* **White matter hyperintensities** *are determined by the observation of high signal intensity or a bright spotty appearance on images, which indicate brain pathologies such as neural atrophy* (Habes et al., 2016).

Overall, postmortem and neuroimaging studies demonstrate that many changes occur with age. One important change is that the brain shrinks, or atrophies, by late life. However, atrophy is selective (Pini et al., 2016). For example, the prefrontal cortex, the hippocampus, and the cerebellum show profound atrophy. In contrast, the areas of the brain related to sensory functions, such as the visual cortex, show relatively little shrinkage. These differential patterns map to different rates of change in abilities, and can be used to track abnormal changes associated with disease.

The white matter area also shows deterioration with increasing age. *A neuroimaging method* called **diffusion tensor imaging (DTI)** *is a type of magnetic*

2.2 Neuroscience and Adult Development and Aging

resonance imaging that assesses the rate and direction that water diffuses through the white matter. This results in an index of the structural health of the white matter (Emsell, Van Hecke, & Tournier, 2016). By using DTI, studies examining WMH have demonstrated that deterioration of white matter may represent a cause of increased dysfunction in the prefrontal cortex in older adults. As we will see later, deterioration of the prefrontal cortex has very important implications for cognitive functioning in late adulthood. Of equal importance is the fact that WMH are linked to cerebrovascular diseases (e.g., stroke resulting from hypertension), which are preventable and can be treated through medication and changes in lifestyle. These results provide a key example of how DTI is used in diagnosing serious diseases in order to start treatment earlier that would occur otherwise.

What Do Structural Brain Changes Mean? The Theory of Mind

One of the most important abilities we have is to interpret one's own and other's mental and emotional states. *This ability, termed* **Theory of Mind (ToM),** *helps us understand that other people have beliefs, desires, ideas, feelings, intentions, and viewpoints that are different from our own.* One's ToM develops across the life span and is one benchmark by which to determine whether an individual has a developmental or cognitive impairment (Healey & Grossman, 2016; Lagattuta, Elrod, & Kramer, 2016; Rosi et al., 2016). Research indicates that ToM abilities increase during childhood and show age-related decline in adults over age 75. Let's take a closer look at the underlying changes in the brain that might explain the changes in later life.

Linking Structural Changes with Executive Functioning

Understanding how changes in brain structures affect behavior involves careful linking of specific brain structures to specific behaviors. First, it is necessary to carefully describe the target behavior. Second, careful documentation of structural changes in the brain is necessary. Third, the two sets of data need to be studied to establish the link.

Executive functioning is a good example, as its various aspects are well described. Among the most studied aspects of executive functioning are processes such as the ability to control what one is thinking about at any specific point in time, and the ability to focus on relevant information and eliminate the irrelevant information. Executive functioning failures in older adults can result in the erroneous selection of irrelevant information as relevant, the inability to divert attention away from irrelevant information to the task at hand, and inefficiency in switching tasks, among others, and mortality rates are higher in those showing the most decline (Baggetta & Alexander, 2016; Yaffe et al., 2016). For example, when older adults are reading an article that is filled with information some of which is true and some of which is false, even if they are told which information is false they still have a difficult time factoring out the false information in their understanding of the article.

Poor performance on executive functioning tasks has been linked to decreased volume of the prefrontal cortex (McEwen, Nasca, & Gray, 2016). Evidence also suggests that WMH in healthy older adults who show no signs of serious cognitive disease (such as Alzheimer's disease) have been linked to lower cognitive test scores and decreased executive functioning (Madden et al., 2012). Age-related decline in the functioning of blood vessels in the brain may affect white matter structures that underlie all the areas important to executive functioning. Whatever the cause, evidence is mounting that decline in executive functioning with age is related to the degeneration of connections among various regions of the brain (Fjell et al., 2017). This "disconnected brain" hypothesis is being used to explain much of cognitive decline in older adults.

Linking Structural Changes with Memory

A great deal of research has examined links between memory and specific structural changes in the brain (Jackson et al., 2016). For example, reductions in volume

Driving a car involves complex, higher-order cognitive skills that involve executive functioning.

in the hippocampus are related to memory decline, the prefrontal cortex and amygdala are connected to memory and emotion, and the atrophy of the temporal lobe has been connected to Alzheimer's disease.

Considerable research has focused on the central involvement of the hippocampus in memory (Jackson et al., 2016; Sheldon & Levine, 2016). Two lines of inquiry are used most. One involves the basic understanding of how the hippocampus is involved in memory. From this approach, we know, for example, that the hippocampus is intimately involved in various aspects of memory, such as autobiographical memory (remembering aspects of our lives; Sheldon & Levine, 2016) and recognizing patterns (Kirwan & Nash, 2016). The other approach involves examining changes to the hippocampus in diseases such as Alzheimer's disease (Lazarov & Hollandis, 2016) and chronic stress (McEwen et al., 2016) that show negative impacts on memory. Intriguingly, evidence is emerging that intellectual stimulation in earlier adulthood (e.g., reading) helps increase the size of the hippocampus, which may provide some protection against memory decline associated with certain diseases (Sumowski et al., 2016).

Research has also established that the temporal lobes communicate with the hippocampus, so are also involved in memory. For example, the temporal lobes are involved in incidental and intentional remembering (Wang & Giovanello, 2016), face/body recognition (Harry et al., 2016), language processing (Abutalebi & Green, 2016), and links between emotion and memory (Meletti, 2016).

In each of these cases, deterioration of the specific brain structure due to normative age-related processes, disease, or injury results in a significant deficit in memory and related cognitive abilities (Jackson et al., 2016). In order to understand how these complex systems work and are connected and integrated, we will focus on the case of memory and emotion as one key system that shows marked age-related changes.

Linking Structural Changes with Emotion

As we have just seen, the age-related changes observed in executive functioning and memory map onto age-related deterioration in specific brain structures. Let's now take a closer look at another very important aspect of the human experience—emotion—and see how structural brain changes affect it. To begin, let's consider an example of how neuroimaging research helps establish linkages between brain structures and behavior, in this case, emotion. An excellent example of how this research is done is a groundbreaking study by Winecoff and her colleagues (2011) described in the How Do We Know? feature.

How Do We Know?
The Aging Emotional Brain

Who were the investigators, and what was the aim of the study? Very little research has examined the specific underlying neural mechanisms of emotion. Winecoff and her colleagues (2011) decided to examine these mechanisms and discover whether they differed with age.

How did the investigators measure the topic of interest? Winecoff and her colleagues used a battery of tests to measure cognitive performance and emotional behavior. They tested participants' immediate recall, delayed recall, and recognition. They also administered a response-time test to measure psychomotor speed, and a digit-span test to measure working memory. (A digit-span test is one in which strings of random digits are presented and the participant has to remember them in order. The longest number of digits the person can remember is called the "digit-span.") The researchers also had participants complete three questionnaires to measure various types of emotions.

After these measures were obtained, participants were given the cognitive reappraisal task depicted in Figure 2.3. In brief, participants learned a reappraisal strategy that involved thinking of themselves as an emotionally detached and objective third party. During the training session, they told the experimenter how they were thinking about the image to ensure task compliance, but they were instructed not to speak during the scanning session. This instruction was given to ensure that the brain activity measured was related to thinking, and not to the brain activity necessary to move one's tongue and mouth during speech, for example. During the fMRI session, participants completed 60 positive image trials (30 "Experience" and 30 "Reappraise"), 60 negative image trials (30 "Experience" and 30 "Reappraise") trials, and 30 neutral image trials (all "Experience"). Within each condition, half of the images contained people, and the other half did not.

continued

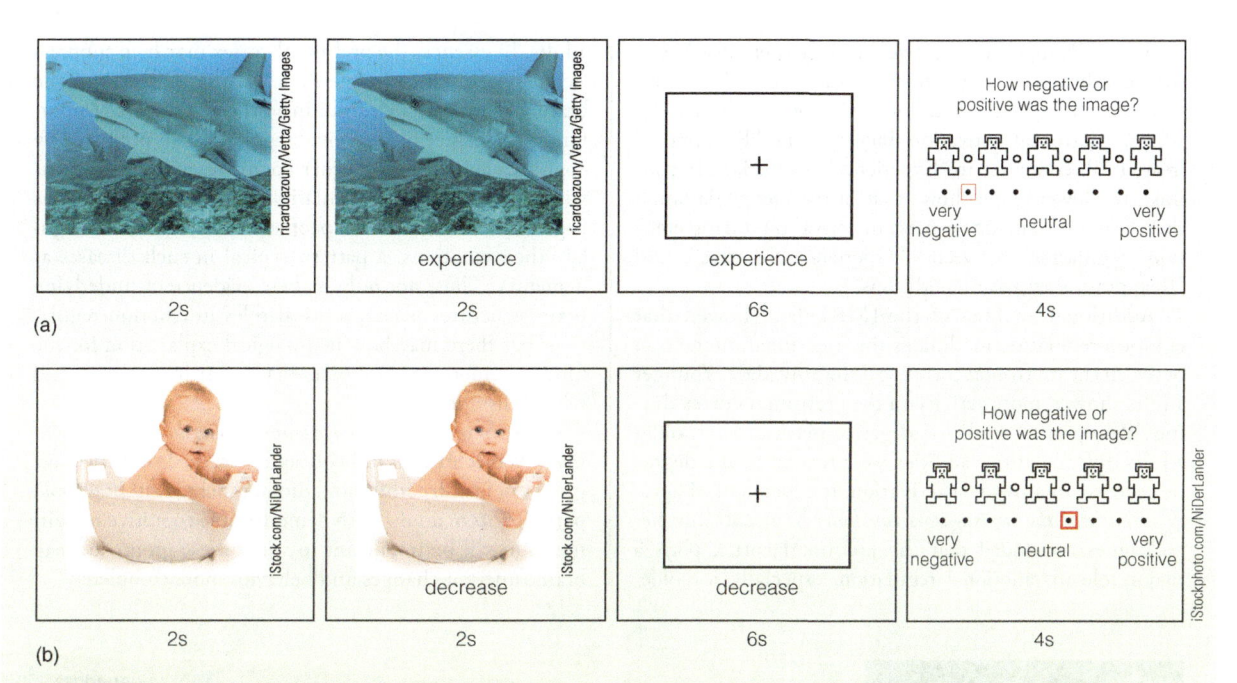

FIGURE 2.3 Cognitive reappraisal task. Participants were trained in the use of a reappraisal strategy for emotional regulation. (a) On "experience" trials, participants viewed an image and then received an instruction to experience naturally the emotions evoked by that image. The image then disappeared, but participants continued to experience their emotions throughout a 6-second delay period. At the end of the trial, the participants rated the perceived emotional valence of that image using an eight-item rating scale. (b) "Reappraise" trials had similar timing, except that the cue instructed participants to decrease their emotional response to the image by reappraising the image (e.g., distancing themselves from the scene). Shown are examples of images similar to those of the negative (a) and positive (b) images used in the study.

Source: Winecoff, A., LaBar, K. S., Madden, D. J., Cabeza, R., & Huettel, S. A. (2011). Cognitive and Neural Contributions to Emotion Regulation in Aging. *Social Cognitive and Affective Neuroscience, 6*. By permission of Oxford University Press.

The fMRI session provided images of ongoing brain activity.

Who were the participants in the study? The sample consisted of 22 younger adults (average age = 23 years, range = 19–33 years) and 20 older adults (average age = 69 years; range = 59–73 years). Participants were matched on demographic variables including education. Participants received the cognitive, memory, and emotion tests on one day, and the reappraisal task in the fMRI session on a second day. Participants were paid $55.

What was the design of the study? The study used a cross-sectional design, with testing of two age groups over two sessions.

Were there ethical concerns with the study? All participants provided written consent under a protocol approved by the Institutional Review Board of Duke University Medical Center.

What were the results? Younger and older adults performed the reappraisal tasks similarly; that is, in the reappraisal condition, positive images were reported as less positive and negative images were reported as less negative. However, older adults' reports of negative emotion were higher than those of younger adults in the negative reappraisal situation.

Examination of the fMRI results showed that reappraisals involved significant activation of specific areas in the prefrontal cortex for both positive and negative emotions. For both age groups, activity in the prefrontal area increased, and activity in the amygdala decreased during the reappraisal phase. These patterns are shown in Figure 2.4. As you can see in the top figure, certain areas in the prefrontal cortex showed a pattern of activation that followed participants' self-reports of emotion regulation. Shown here are activation patterns in the contrast between "Reappraise-Negative" and "Experience-Negative" conditions. The graph shows that for both positive and negative stimuli, and for both younger and older adults, prefrontal activation increased in "Reappraise" (reap) trials compared to "Experience" (exp) trials. In contrast, the lower graph shows that in the amygdala (amy) there was a systematic decrease in activation during emotion regulation between "Experience-Negative" and "Reappraise-Negative" conditions.

Additional analyses of the fMRI data showed that emotion regulation modulates the functional interaction between the prefrontal cortex and the amygdala. Younger adults showed more activity in the prefrontal cortex during "Reappraise" trials for negative pictures than older adults did. Cognitive abilities were related to the degree of decrease in amygdala activation, independent of age.

What did the investigators conclude? Winecoff and her colleagues concluded that the prefrontal cortex plays a major role in emotional regulation, especially for older adults. In essence, the prefrontal cortex may help suppress (regulate) emotions in the same way as that area of the brain is involved in inhibiting other behaviors. Importantly, the degree of emotional regulation was predicted by cognitive ability, with higher cognitive ability associated with higher emotional regulation. This may mean that as cognitive abilities decline, people may be less able to regulate their emotions, a pattern typical in such diseases as dementia. Thus, not only is there evidence of underlying brain structures playing critical roles in emotion regulation, but there may be a neurological explanation for the kinds of emotional outbursts that occur in dementia and related disorders.

What converging evidence would strengthen these conclusions? Winecoff and her colleagues studied only two age groups of healthy adults and did not include either old-old participants or adults with demonstrable cognitive impairment. It will be important to study these groups to map brain function changes and behavior more completely.

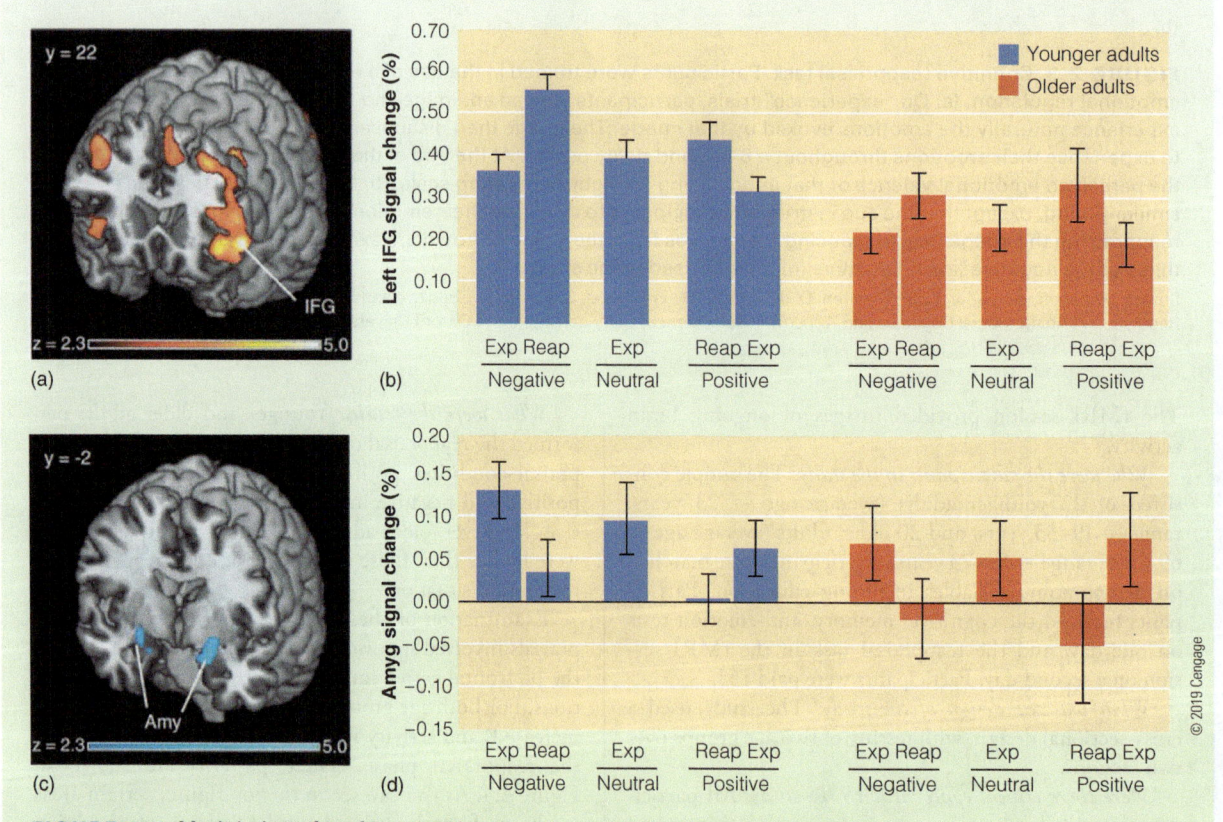

FIGURE 2.4 Modulation of prefrontal and amygdalar activation by emotion regulation.
Source: Winecoff, A., LaBar, K. S., Madden, D. J., Cabeza, R., & Huettel, S. A. (2011). Cognitive and Neural Contributions to Emotion Regulation in Aging. *Social Cognitive and Affective Neuroscience, 6*. By permission of Oxford University Press.

How does the way that the brain processes emotions change across adulthood? The quick answer is that it's complicated (Mather, 2016; Ziaei & Fisher, 2016). In general, research shows that adults of all ages report about the same range and experience of emotion. But there is also evidence that changes in brain activity in the prefrontal cortex and the amygdala with age may be related to a decrease in processing of negative emotional information and an increase in processing of positive emotional information. These differences tend to be interpreted as reflecting increased emotional regulation with age; in other words, older adults tend to be able to regulate their emotions better than younger adults. This may be due to a desire as people age to develop closer, more meaningful relationships that generate positive emotions, while avoiding people and situations that generate negative ones.

These results show that cognition and emotion interact. Kensinger and colleagues (Kensinger, 2012; Ford, Morris, & Kensinger, 2014) propose two distinct cognitive and neural processes that contribute to emotional processing and memory. The difference depends upon how emotionally arousing the information is. Processing of negative high-arousal information for memory is relatively automatic in nature and is linked to activation of the amygdala as it interacts with the hippocampus to support memory performance. For memory processing of negative low-arousal stimuli, more activation of the prefrontal cortex–hippocampus network is necessary.

Kensinger (2012) argues that whether emotional arousal enhances memory depends on the engagement in emotion-specific processes that are linked to these distinct neural processes. So when a person accurately remembers negative high-arousal items, this corresponds to increased activation of the amygdala and prefrontal cortex. Other studies support this conclusion. For instance, if the amygdala is damaged, individuals do not attend to arousing stimuli.

How do age-related structural and functional changes in the brain affect processing of emotion? The short answer is that it depends (Fossati, 2012; McEwen et al., 2016; Sugiura, 2016; Ziaei & Fisher, 2016). Older adults show more brain activity between the prefrontal cortex and the medial temporal lobe than younger adults do, regardless of whether the content is emotionally positive or negative. These increases in connections may be due to age-related changes that occur in the prefrontal cortex that make it necessary for older adults to use more connections to process the information (Waring, Addis, & Kensinger, 2013). When disorders such as mild cognitive impairment (MCI) occur, these connection patterns are disrupted and begin to show loss (Hampstead et al., 2016). We'll return to this need for and roles of extra connections a bit later when we consider whether older adults compensate for brain changes.

Linking Structural Changes with Social-Emotional Cognition

What happens in the brain when things get even more complicated, such as when we have to process complex situations that involve social judgments, when memory, emotion, and previously learned information come together? The story begins in the early 2000s, when researchers first outlined a social cognitive neuroscience approach to attributional inferences, or how people make causal judgments about why social situations occur (e.g., Lieberman et al., 2002). That work identified a social judgment process that involves a relatively automatic system in which people read cues in the environment quickly and easily, without deliberation, and then make social judgments.

For example, if someone is staggering down the hallway, we may automatically assume the person is intoxicated without taking into consideration many other factors that might cause someone to stagger (e.g., the person is injured or experiencing a medical emergency). In other words, we have a tendency to automatically put the person into a preexisting social category. We base this judgment on easily activated, well-practiced categories of information based on our past experiences and current goals, and we do this most prominently when the situation is ambiguous. In such situations, we are unlikely to consider alternative explanations.

What's intriguing is that researchers have presented compelling evidence that drawing these kinds of quick conclusions in ambiguous situations is probably a result of how our brains are wired. It turns out we have specialized areas in the brain, such as the orbitofrontal cortex, lateral temporal cortex, amygdala, and basal ganglia, that are associated with automatic social cognition (Platt, Seyfarth, & Cheyney, 2016; Ziaei & Fisher, 2016). We are thereby hard-wired to quick-process certain social cognitive information in particular ways, so attempting to do it in other ways takes tremendous focusing and effort.

Suppose we need to be more deliberate in our processing. Researchers also have identified another system that underlies this form of social cognitive judgments that employs symbolic logic and reflective awareness.

The neural basis of these more reflective judgments appears to reside in the prefrontal cortex, the anterior cingulate cortex, and the hippocampus (Lee & Siegle, 2012).

So how do these different brain pathways change with age, and what difference does that make? The brain structures involved in more automatic processing (e.g., the amygdala) show less age-related deterioration, whereas those involved in more reflective processing (e.g., the prefrontal cortex) show more severe deterioration. Based on these findings, we would expect that older adults might tend to rely more on automatic processes.

Complex Development in the Prefrontal Cortex

There is no question that neuroscience research points to the central role played by the prefrontal cortex in adult development and aging. This part of the brain is intimately involved in the most important aspects of thinking and reasoning, including executive functioning, memory, and emotion. So it is probably not surprising to discover that at a detailed level, age-related changes in the prefrontal cortex are complex.

The most important arena in this complex pattern is in the interface between emotion and memory. We have already seen that brain pathways involved in memory tend to deteriorate with age, whereas key pathways involved in emotion do not. How is this explained?

Let's start by focusing on a well-documented effect, the positivity effect. The **positivity effect** *refers to the fact that older adults are more motivated to derive emotional meaning from life and to maintain positive feelings* (Isaacowitz & Blanchard-Fields, 2012; Kensinger & Gutchess, 2017; Scheibe & Carstensen, 2010). As a result, older adults are more likely than younger adults to attend to the emotional meaning of information.

Some of the brain pathways for processing both positive and negative emotion are the same for all adults. Specifically, the common pathways in emotion processing for adults of all ages include the amygdala and the part of the prefrontal cortex right behind the eyes (the lateral orbitofrontal cortex). How active the amygdala is during emotion processing appears particularly important. In certain people who have intermittent explosive disorder (i.e., become extremely angry when shown angry faces, for instance), the amygdala shows hyperactivation (McCloskey et al., 2016), which may be the cause of the disorder.

Research also shows that in addition to some common brain areas that process all emotion, there are also some unique pathways. For instance, positive emotional processing occurs in the front section of the prefrontal cortex. For negative emotion processing, the temporal region is brought into action instead.

But there are some important age-related differences in brain pathways, too, that help us understand age-related differences in emotion-related behaviors. When older adults process information that is emotionally positive, they also show increased activity in the middle portion of the prefrontal cortex, the amygdala, and the cingulate cortex (a structure that forms a "collar" around the corpus callosum). Bringing additional areas of the brain into play during processing is an age-related phenomenon we will return to a bit later.

These age-related changes in how the brain processes positive and negative emotional information show both that there are probably underlying structural changes in the brain that result in age-related differences in behavior, and that these structural changes can be quite nuanced and complex. Additionally, neuroimaging research has drawn attention to the truly central and critical role played by the prefrontal cortex in understanding why people are the way they are and process information in the ways they do (Grady et al., 2016). Changes in how the prefrontal cortex is connected with other parts of the brain has important implications for behavior, as we will see at several other points in this book.

Adult Development in Action

You are a healthcare worker and a specialist in geriatric medicine. One of your clients shows significant declines in memory and executive functioning. What brain structures and processes might you want to examine closely for evidence of age-related change?

2.3 Making Sense of Neuroscience Research: Explaining Changes in Brain-Behavior Relations

LEARNING OBJECTIVES
- What is the Parieto-Frontal Integration Theory, and what does it explain?
- How do older adults attempt to compensate for age-related changes in the brain?
- What are the major differences among the HAROLD, CRUNCH, and STAC-r models of brain activation and aging?

Recently, Barbara read an article in a major newspaper describing research on brain aging. The article described in detail several aspects of negative changes in the brain that made her wonder about her own situation. Approaching 90, Barbara wondered whether all of the changes happening to her were negative.

We have considered evidence that structural and neurochemical changes occur in the brain as we grow older, and that these changes in the brain relate to changes in cognitive functioning. With that as background, let's now reconsider research that is based on functional brain imaging techniques, such as fMRI, that we noted earlier. Recall that the main point of functional brain imaging research is to establish how age-related deterioration in specific brain structures affects a person's ability to perform various tasks, measuring both at the same time.

A second aim of these types of studies, and the point of this section, is to identify patterns of how the brain is sometimes able to compensate for negative age-related changes by activating different or additional regions when tasks pose a distinct difficulty.

In other words, older and younger adults may differ in terms of which regions of the brain are used in order to perform cognitive tasks more effectively. On the one hand, these compensation strategies could result in roughly equivalent performance despite other differences across age. On the other hand, these compensation strategies could be ineffective and could reveal the neurological underpinnings of the cognitive decline observed in older adults. Which of these outcomes occurs not only has important consequences for performance on research tasks, but also in how well older adults might adapt to challenges in their daily lives.

The research we will consider in this section will provide insights into Barbara's concerns. Are older adults able to compensate for normative declines that occur?

The Parieto-Frontal Integration Theory

The typical finding is reduced brain activity in older as compared to younger adults in prefrontal and temporal areas that support cognitive functioning, such as memory (Sugiura, 2016). However, we also know that there is a marked increase in activity in specific areas of the prefrontal cortex and other brain regions during certain tasks, specifically memory for emotional material, in older adults as compared to younger adults (Grady, 2012; Grady et al., 2016). We will come back to this discrepancy a bit later.

There's more, though. Grady (2012) points out that reduced prefrontal recruitment in aging is context-dependent. That is, older adults sometimes show reduced activation or recruitment of the appropriate prefrontal regions, and sometimes show the same or more recruitment compared to younger adults depending on the tasks they are doing at the time (Gallen et al., 2016).

Given the pivotal role played by the prefrontal cortex in such a wide range of cognitive tasks, researchers are homing in on its role in explaining intelligence at a holistic level. Research now shows that the prefrontal cortex, along with the parietal lobe (an area of the brain at the top of the head), plays an important role in general intellectual abilities. Based on 37 studies using various types of neuroimaging techniques, Jung and Haier (2007) proposed the Parieto-Frontal Integration Theory. *The* **Parieto-Frontal Integration Theory (P-FIT)** *proposes that intelligence comes from a distributed and integrated network of neurons in the parietal and frontal areas of the brain.* Figure 2.5. Shows these key brain areas. In general, P-FIT accounts for individual differences in intelligence as having their origins in individual differences in brain structure and function. For example, research indicates that the P-FIT predicts a type of intelligence termed *fluid intelligence* (see Chapter 7) that includes such skills as spatial reasoning (Nikolaidis et al., 2017; Pineda-Pardo et al., 2016).

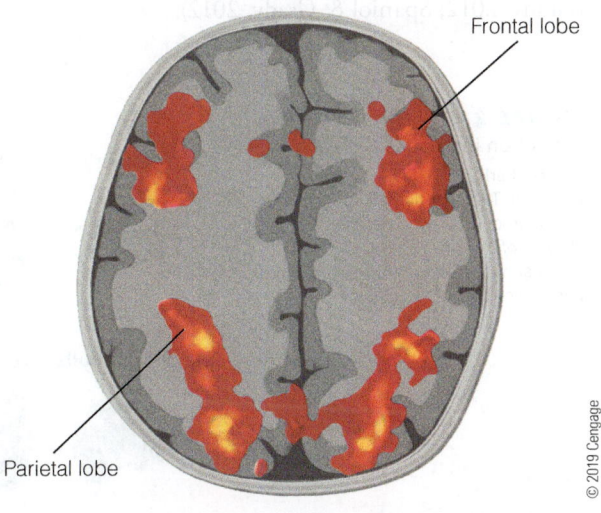

FIGURE 2.5 The P-FIT model indicates that integration of the parietal and frontal lobes underlies intelligence.

The P-FIT model is an example of theories based on neuroscience research, and has been tested and supported in several studies. It is clear that performance on specific measures of intelligence, including many of those that we will consider in detail in Chapter 7, as well as how efficiently such information is processed, are quite likely related to specific combinations of brain structures (Pineda-Pardo et al., 2016; Sugiura, 2016). Clearly, any impairment in frontal lobe processing creates serious challenges. Because such changes occur normatively with age, we would expect to find significant, predictable patterns of change in cognition. We will pursue this idea in detail in Chapters 6 and 7.

Given different patterns of brain activation across adulthood for certain tasks, the question arises whether these differences reflect adaptive behavior as people age. That's the issue we'll consider next.

Can Older Adults Compensate for Changes in the Brain?

We have seen that differences in brain activation have been documented between younger and older adults, and that these differences relate to differences in performance. There are additional, and interesting, nuances to these findings. For example, it turns out that it is not simply that older adults show reduced activation in regions associated with a particular cognitive task. Rather, studies focusing on verbal working memory and long-term memory show focal, unilateral activity in the left prefrontal region in younger adults but bilateral activation (i.e., in both the left and right prefrontal areas) in older adults when performing the same tasks (Grady, 2012; Spaniol & Grady, 2012).

These findings surprised researchers, and ushered in much discussion and research as to what this meant for the aging brain. Is the older brain working to compensate for deterioration in these focal regions related to the cognitive task? Is the older brain working harder and recruiting more brain structures, or is the bilateral activation merely the inefficient operation of poor inhibition of irrelevant information that turns the activation into interference of optimal functioning (Sugiura, 2016)?

The answer appears to be yes—older adults are compensating. Researchers concluded that this bilateral activation in older adults may serve a functional and supportive role in their cognitive functioning (Grady, 2012; Sugiura, 2016). Supportive evidence comes from the association between bilateral activation in older adults and higher performance, evidence not found in younger adults, across a number of tasks including category learning tasks, visual field tasks, and various memory tasks.

Figure 2.6 shows that there is greater prefrontal bilateral activity in older adults during working memory tasks than in younger adults. On the left side of the figure, you can see that there is left-lateralized prefrontal engagement in younger adults, whereas older adults also engage the right prefrontal areas. The right side demonstrates that younger adults and low-performing older adults show right-lateralized activation during a long-term memory task. Interestingly, high-performing older adults still show bilateral prefrontal engagement. It may be that high-functioning older adults are more adept at compensating for normative deterioration in the brain by utilizing other areas of the brain. Whether or not this is an accurate conclusion is still being debated.

To make matters even more interesting, there is emerging evidence that under some circumstances,

FIGURE 2.6 Prefrontal bilateral activation increases with age.
Source: Park, D. C., & Reuter-Lorenz, P. (2009). The adaptive brain: Aging and neurocognitive scaffolding. *Annual Review of Psychology, 60*, 173–196. www.annualreviews.org. Reprinted with permission.

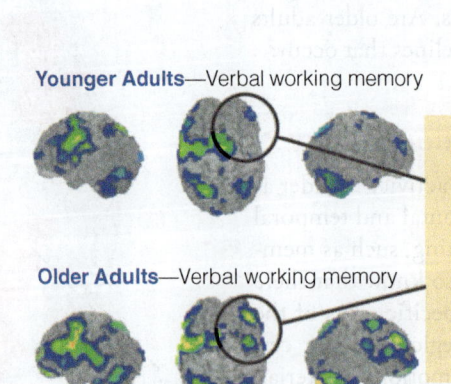

Younger Adults—Verbal working memory

Older Adults—Verbal working memory

More frontal bilateral activity in older adults during a verbal working memory task (left) and in older adults with higher performance in a long–term memory task (right)

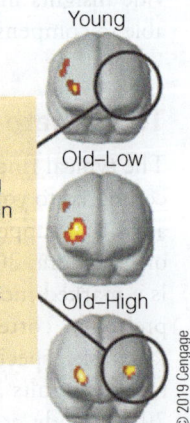

Young

Old–Low

Old–High

researchers fail to find evidence of either reduced specialization of functions in the brain or of compensation. When Campbell and colleagues (2016) separated the different processes needed to complete a task (e.g., attention, decision making), they found consistent patterns of brain activity in both younger and older adults. The question is whether these results are simply a matter of which task was examined or evidence that challenges the conventional view of broader activation as compensation in older adults.

Theories of Brain-Behavior Changes Across Adulthood

As we have seen, several studies have shown evidence for different patterns of brain activity in specific regions in older adults across numerous cognitive tasks, suggesting that the underlying brain changes are not overly specific to a narrow set of circumstances (e.g., Gallen et al., 2016; Grady, 2012; Grady et al., 2016; Sugiura, 2016). Additional age-related neural activation (especially in prefrontal areas) may be functional and adaptive for optimal performance as people grow older. Researchers now suggest that these activation patterns may reflect an adaptive brain that functionally reorganizes and compensates for age-related changes (Sugiura, 2016).

One way researchers study how brain activation patterns among key structures operate is to study them in people with known neurological disorders. A pioneer in this effort was Oliver Sacks, a neurologist who did much of his work in New York. The Real People feature describes some of his more noteworthy studies.

A number of models have been used to attempt to explain these findings. Four of the most prominent are

Real People
Oliver Sacks, Brain Mapper

It was the interesting cases that attracted intrigued Oliver Sacks, a man who the *New York Times* called "the poet laureate of contemporary medicine" (Marshall, 1986). One such case of a man who had visual agnosia (an inability to recognize visual objects due to damage in the parietal lobes) who mistook his wife for a hat. This recognition error became the title of one of his most popular books.

Sacks explored numerous aspects of brain-behavior relations in individuals who had brain disorders, such as Tourette syndrome, achromatopsia (total colorblindness), dementia, Parkinson's disease, and amyotrophic lateral sclerosis (Lou Gehrig's disease). His successful work with a group of survivors of the 1920s sleeping sickness *encephalitis lethargica* became the basis of the book and Oscar-nominated movie *Awakenings* that starred Robert DeNiro and Robin Williams.

But Sacks's interests were much broader, too. He looked at music and music therapy in his book *Musicophilia: Tales of Music and the Brain*. He wrote of his own personal experience with prosopagnosia (the inability to recognize faces) and ocular melanoma and his loss of stereoscopic vision as a result of the treatment.

When he was diagnosed with metastatic cancer in December 2014 (the melanoma tumor in his eye had spread to his liver and brain), he wrote a series of deeply personal articles that expressed his intent to "live in the richest, deepest, most productive way I can" (Sacks, 2015). When he died in 2015, the man who could not recognize his own face had become one of the most recognized medical researchers in history.

Oliver Sacks

the HAROLD model by Cabeza (2002), the CRUNCH model developed by Reuter-Lorenz and her colleagues (Reuter-Lorenz, 2002; Reuter-Lorenz & Mikels, 2006), the PASA model (Davis et al., 2008), and the STAC-r model (Park & Reuter-Lorenz, 2009). These models make a common assumption: The primary reason for greater activation in different brain regions, as well as for the different patterns within the prefrontal cortex, is the need for the recruitment of additional brain regions in order to successfully execute cognitive functions as one grows older.

The HAROLD Model

Numerous studies have documented the fact that younger adults show brain activation in one brain hemisphere when performing various cognitive tasks, but that older adults' brains tend to show increased activation in both brain hemispheres. Explaining this difference led to the development of the HAROLD model. *The* **HAROLD model** *stands for* **Hemispheric Asymmetry Reduction in OLDer adults**, *which explains the empirical findings of reduced lateralization in prefrontal lobe activity in older adults (that is, the reduced ability of older adults to separate cognitive processing in different parts of the prefrontal cortex)* (Cabeza, 2002; Collins & Mohr, 2013; Morcom & Johnson, 2015). It suggests that the purpose of the reduced lateralization with age is compensatory in nature; that is, older adults are recruiting additional neural units and using them to increase attentional resources, processing speed, or inhibitory control.

The HAROLD model has been supported by several studies that show how the brain creates and uses reserve abilities to lessen the impact of age-related changes in the brain (e.g., Cabeza & Dennis, 2013; Collins & Mohr, 2013; Morcom & Johnson, 2015). What remains to be established, though, is where the line should be drawn separating normal age-related changes that can be compensated and changes that are so extensive or are happening so rapidly that compensation does not work.

The CRUNCH Model

The **CRUNCH model** *stands for* **Compensation-Related Utilization of Neural Circuits Hypothesis**, *and describes how the aging brain adapts to neurological decline by recruiting additional neural circuits (in comparison to younger adults) to perform tasks adequately* (DeCarli et al., 2012; Reuter-Lorenz & Cappell, 2008). Like the HAROLD model, the CRUNCH model incorporates bilaterality of activation. But the CRUNCH model suggests this is not the only form of compensation. Two main mechanisms are suggested that the older brain uses to perform tasks: *more of the same and supplementary processes*. *More of the same* means that when task demands are increased, more activation can be found in the same brain region that is activated for processing easier tasks. This effect can be found in younger as well as older adults. However, in older adults, neural efficiency declines, so additional neuronal circuits are recruited earlier than they are in younger adults.

Supplementary processes take place when different brain regions are activated to compensate for lacking or insufficient processing resources. Reduced lateralization is one way of recruiting additional resources because both hemispheres are called into action rather than just one. In addition, however, compared to younger adults' brains older adults' brains also show overactivation in different brain regions. This happens when the activation level in older adults' brains occurs in the same regions as in younger adults' brains, but at a significantly higher level. These patterns suggest that compensation can take different forms in the aging brain.

The CRUNCH model also has considerable support (e.g., DeCarli et al., 2012; Gallen et al., 2016; Park & Festini, 2017). However, just as is true about the HAROLD model, the point at which compensation breaks down is not well established under the CRUNCH model.

The PASA Model

In general, neuroimaging data in cognitive aging research shows an age-related reduction in brain activity in parts of the back, or posterior, parts of the brain and increased activity in the front, or anterior, areas, especially the prefrontal cortex. *This* **posterior-anterior shift in aging (PASA)** *from occipital to frontal processing is thought to reflect age-related compensation* (Davis et al., 2008). The consistent finding of increased prefrontal activity with age is typically seen as evidence of compensatory processing activity by older adults (Kaufman, Keith, & Perlstein, 2016). However, some research does not support lower levels of processing in posterior areas of the brain with age, and questions whether this prefrontal activity indicates actual compensatory processing or something else (Wang & Giovanello, 2016).

The STAC-r Model

How do we explain the specific patterns of age-related changes in prefrontal activity and resolve interpretive dilemmas? To answer that question, Reuter-Lorenz

2.3 Making Sense of Neuroscience Research: Explaining Changes in Brain-Behavior Relations   47

and Park (2014) proposed the STAC-r model, shown in Figure 2.7. *The* **Scaffolding Theory of Cognitive Aging-Revised (STAC-r)** *model is based on the idea that age-related changes in one's ability to function reflect a life-long process of compensating for cognitive decline by recruiting additional brain areas, and takes life-course factors that enhance or deplete neural resources into account.* It is based on an earlier version (Park & Reuter-Lorenz, 2009) that did not include the life course variables.

As we will see especially in Chapters 6 and 7, aging is associated with both decline as well as preservation of various cognitive abilities. The STAC-r model explains neuroimaging studies that show selective changes in the aging brain that reflect neural decline as well as compensatory neural recruitment, especially in the prefrontal cortex. Taking this life-span view makes STAC-r unique among the models of cognitive aging based on neuroscience.

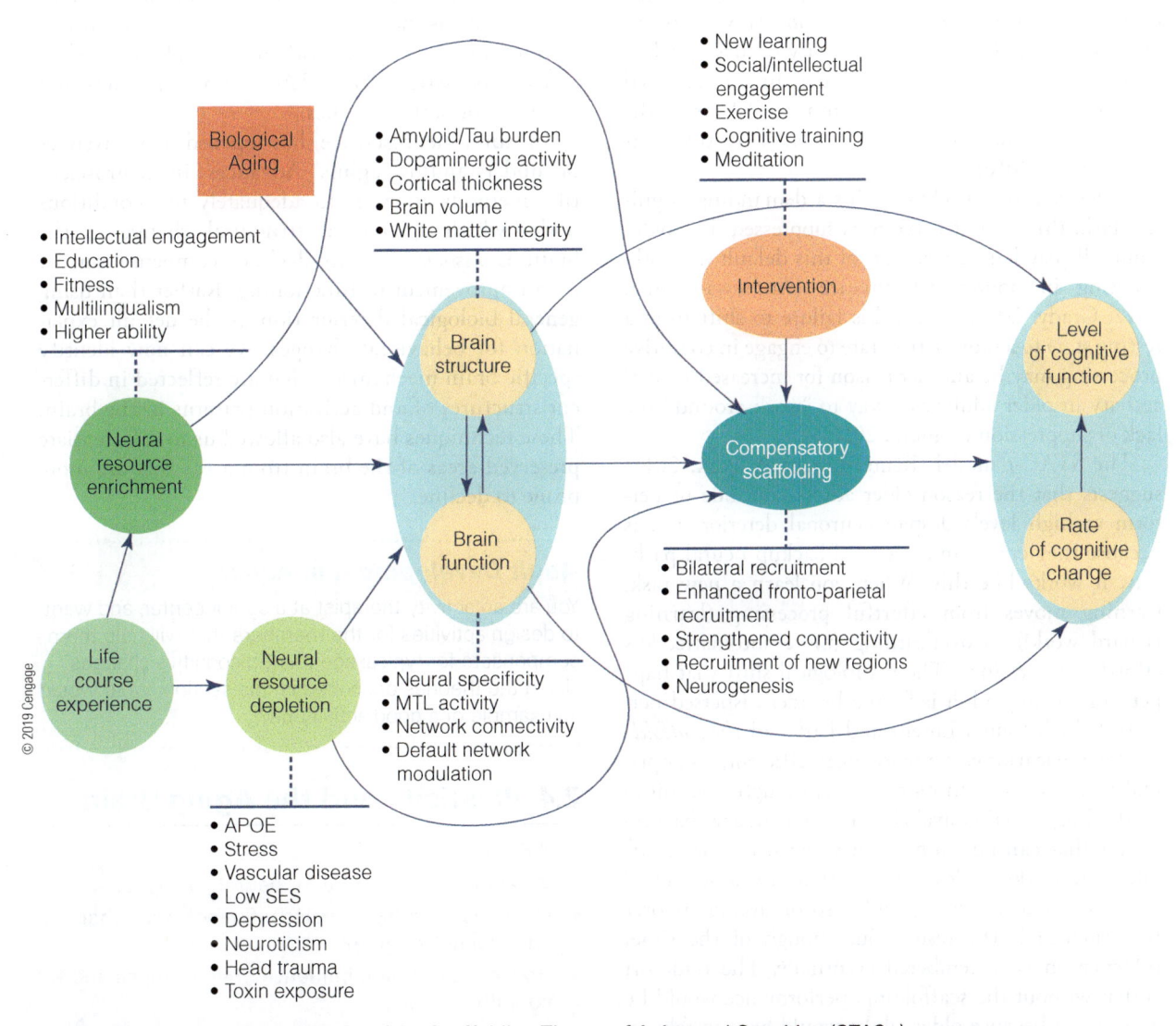

FIGURE 2.7 A Life Course Model of the Scaffolding Theory of Aging and Cognition (STAC-r)
Source: Reuter-Lorenz, P. A., & Park, D. C. (2014). How does it STAC up? Revisiting the scaffolding theory of aging and cognition. *Neuropsychology Review, 24*, 355–370. doi:10.1007/s11065-014-9270-9 (Figure 2).

From the perspective of the STAC-r model, what's the purpose of the compensation? For one thing, there is growing evidence that the increase in frontal activity in older adults may be a response to decreased efficiency of neural processing in the perceptual areas of the brain and normative neurophysiological deterioration (Reuter-Lorenz & Park, 2014).

There's another reason, too. Remember how the prefrontal region helps suppress irrelevant information that may interfere with the task one is actually performing? It turns out that older adults have trouble suppressing what's referred to as the default network of the brain. The **default network of the brain** *refers to regions of the brain that are most active when one is at rest.* One example of this would be the brain activity occurring when an individual lies quietly and is not directly engaged in a cognitive task (Andrews-Hanna, 2012) or in the spontaneous generation and evaluation of creative ideas (Beaty et al., 2016).

When a younger adult begins a demanding cognitive task, this default network is suppressed. But older adults display less suppression of this default network, resulting in poorer performance (Andrews-Hanna, 2012; Grady, 2012). Thus, this failure to shift from a resting state to a more active state to engage in cognitive processing may be another reason for increased frontal activity in older adults as a way to "work around" the lack of suppression (Sugiura, 2016).

The STAC-r model (Reuter-Lorenz & Park, 2014) suggests that the reason older adults continue to perform at high levels despite neuronal deterioration is because they create and rely on a backup neural pathway. It works like this. When you learn a new task, learning moves from effortful processing (learning is hard work!) to overlearning (more automatic, less effortful processing). The neurological shift that happens in a young adult is from a broader dispersed network (which Reuter-Lorenz and Park call *the scaffold*) used while learning to a more focal, efficient, and optimal neural circuit. In older adults, though, the initial scaffolding remains available as a secondary, backup circuit that can be counted on when necessary. Scaffolded networks are less efficient than the honed, focal ones they used as young adults, so on average poorer performance is the result. But enough of the time, information is remembered eventually. The trade-off is that without the scaffolding, performance would be even worse because older adults would have to rely on the more focal areas.

The elegance of the STAC-r model is that older adults' performance can be understood in terms of factors that impact decline and those that impact compensation. The first concept, *neural resource enrichment*, refers to any influence that serves to enhance brain structure or function. For example, as we will see in Chapter 14, remaining active is related to better cognitive functioning in middle- and old age. The second concept, *neural resource depletion*, refers to those influences on the brain that are harmful. For example, the APOE-4 gene puts one at much higher risk of Alzheimer's disease. As Reuter-Lorenz and Park (2014) argue, this integrative approach embraces a lifelong potential for plasticity and the ability to adapt to age-related changes.

Finally, the STAC-r model clearly indicates that Barbara's concerns, noted in the vignette that began this section, can be countered with evidence of both decline and compensation. The STAC-r model predicts and accounts for both outcomes.

In sum, neuroscience has opened new avenues of understanding aging. Advances in neuroscientific methods allow us to adequately test conditions under which age-related structural change in the brain is associated with decline, compensation, or even improvement in functioning. Rather than using general biological deterioration as the default explanation for behavioral changes, we can now identify specific brain mechanisms that are reflected in different structures of and activation patterns in the brain. These techniques have also allowed us to differentiate preserved areas of the brain from areas that are more prone to decline.

Adult Development in Action

You are an activity therapist at a senior center, and want to design activities for the members that will help them compensate for typical age-related cognitive changes. Using the theories described in this section, what would an example of a good activity be?

2.4 Plasticity and the Aging Brain

LEARNING OBJECTIVES

- What evidence is there for neural plasticity?
- How does aerobic exercise influence brain changes and cognitive aging?
- How does nutrition influence brain changes and cognitive activity?

Marisa has been playing incessantly with her latest Nintendo Wii video game. Her grandmother, Leticia, became captivated by her granddaughter's gaming and *asked her granddaughter to teach her how to do it. Marisa was delighted and helped her grandmother learn the game. After months of practice, Marisa noted that her grandmother seemed stronger in her normal physical activities and her perceptual skills seemed to have improved. In addition, Leticia and her granddaughter Marisa had more in common than ever before.*

There's an old saying that "You can't teach an old dog new tricks." Even if that's true for dogs, is it true for people? Neuroscience research helps provide some answers.

What Is Brain Plasticity?

As discussed earlier in this chapter, there are certain situations in which the brain itself compensates for age-related changes. As was noted then, compensation is based on the notion that there is plasticity in both brain changes and behavior across the adult life span. **Plasticity** *involves the changes in the structure and function of the brain as the result of interaction between the brain and the environment.* In other words, plasticity is the result of people and their brains living in the world and accumulating and learning from experiences over time. Leticia's observations of the positive changes that took place after she started playing the Wii video game are a good example of this plasticity.

Plasticity provides a way to understand compensatory changes in both the more observable behavior and the less observable (without neuroimaging, anyway) reorganization of neural circuitry in the brain. Many attempts have been made to assess the potential for plasticity in cognitive functioning by focusing on ways to improve cognitive performance through training (a good example of which would be Leticia's practice on the video game).

Baltes and colleagues' now classic research set the standard for documenting the range of plasticity in older adults' cognitive performance (e.g., Baltes & Kliegl, 1992; Willis, Blieszner, & Baltes, 1981). They found that whereas older adults are able to improve cognitive ability in memory tasks through tailored strategy training beyond the level of untrained younger adults, this is highly task-specific, and the ability-level gains are very narrow in focus.

Since these early findings, research has shown that basic cognitive processes affected by aging can indeed be improved through training, and that they transfer to multiple other kinds of functioning as long as the tasks share the same basic underlying functions (e.g., Dahlin, et al., 2008). Training has also been shown to increase the level of activity in the prefrontal cortex, and the strength of connections between the prefrontal and parietal cortex (Constantinidis & Klingberg, 2016).

From a neural plasticity perspective, research on neural stem cells has revealed compelling evidence that the brain is capable of new neurons and related cells when needed (Pardal & Barneo, 2016). **Neural stem cells** *(also known as neural progenitors or neural precursor cells) are cells in the brain and spinal cord (the central nervous system, CNS) that are thought to give rise to the broad array of specialized cells of the CNS, including both neurons and glial cells.* The discovery of neural stem cells proved wrong the long-standing belief that neurogenesis (i.e., the development of new neurons) dwindles away at the end of embryonic development. In practical terms, it means that you certainly *can* teach an old dog new tricks. Not only that, but neural stem cells are the focus of much research relating to potential cures for various brain diseases, such as Parkinson's disease (Zhu, Caldwell, & Song, 2016) and Alzheimer's disease (Hunsberger et al., 2016).

All of this research adds a new level of understanding to what happens to individuals as they grow older. For example, even though aging is associated with an overall decrease in the number of new neurons, this differs across regions of the brain and may be altered even at advanced ages.

The big question, of course, is whether the discovery of neural stem cells and the fact that neurons can regenerate even in late life means that neuroscience research could be used to cure brain diseases and essentially create "new brains" (Kazanis, 2012). Perhaps, that is likely many years from now. In the meantime, what we do know is that brain cells can regenerate, even in late life, under the right circumstances, and that the brain shows considerable plasticity to create ways for people to compensate with age-related declines in functioning. Still, this work is not without controversy, as discussed in the Current Controversies feature.

Exercise and Brain Aging

Some of the most compelling work that has moved beyond the mere documentation of plasticity to the actual improvement of cognitive skills and concomitant changes in the brain focuses on the influence of aerobic exercise. Overall, research shows clearly that brain plasticity is enhanced as a result of aerobic exercise (Nishijima, Torres-Aleman, & Soya, 2016; Thomas et al., 2012), and some studies have even shown that aerobic exercise

Current Controversies
Are Neural Stem Cells the Solution to Brain Aging?

Imagine if you could replace brain cells that had either died or had been damaged. That's the goal of researchers who study neural stem cells. Clearly, this research would fundamentally change our understanding of aging and of brain disease.

Research on the potential of neural stem cells took a major leap forward in 2007 with the founding of the New York Neural Stem Cell Institute. The Institute's mission is "to develop regenerative therapies for diseases of the central nervous system." Ongoing research programs include identifying potential uses of neural stem cells in treating such diseases as amyotrophic lateral sclerosis, Alzheimer's disease, brain injury and stroke, macular degeneration, multiple sclerosis, optic neuropathy, Parkinson's disease, retinitis pigmentosa, and spinal cord injury, among others.

The National Human Neural Stem Cell Resource supplies researchers with reliable sources of neural stem cells obtained from the post-natal, postmortem, human brain. They encourage research to study the cells "as potential transplantable tissue for addressing damage from stroke or brain injury, and for curing diseases."

These and other similar research centers play a critical role in brain research. Despite the great promise of this research to, for instance, offer potential cures for fatal and degenerative diseases, a basic question is whether it should be done at all. Several key ethical questions arise (Ramos-Zúñiga, 2015). This research requires that the human brain be used as an experimental object of study, and be manipulated in specific ways. Certainly, any such intervention, whether it is a treatment for a disease or a replacement of defective brain cells, requires the highest level of ethical principles. Perhaps the most difficult issue is that just because an intervention *can* be done, does not necessarily mean that it *should* be done.

As a result, researchers must go to great lengths to analyze the ethical implications of every research project involving neural stem cells, along with any potential clinical applications and outcomes. The usual medical standard of causing no harm is especially important in this research, as is a very careful assessment of the risk–benefit balance. But most important is keeping in the forefront of everything the fact that the research involves a human and a human brain.

---

can counter the declines in the hippocampus associated with Alzheimer's disease (Intlekofer & Cotman, 2013), although the precise mechanisms by which functions are preserved are not yet understood (Duzel, van Praag, & Sendtner, 2016).

An example of this line of research is a study by Erickson and his colleagues (2009). They were interested in learning whether aerobic exercise had any effect on the volume of the hippocampus, a key brain structure connected to memory. Erickson and colleagues had older adults exercise on a motorized treadmill, while their respiration, blood pressure, and heart rate were continuously monitored. Participants also completed a spatial memory task and had an MRI to measure hippocampal volume. They found that higher aerobic fitness levels were associated with the preservation of greater hippocampal volume, which in turn was the best predictor of how well participants performed on the spatial memory task.

We will return to the many benefits of exercise in Chapter 14. As a preview, the positive effects on the brain are only one reason to get up and move.

Nutrition and Brain Aging

We began this chapter with a consideration of "brain food" and the claims that certain foods result in benefits for the brain. Thanks to neuroimaging studies, researchers are beginning to understand the important relations between categories of nutrients and brain structures (Smith & Blumenthal, 2016).

For example, Bowman and colleagues (2012) identified three nutrient biomarker patterns associated with cognitive function and brain volume. Two patterns were associated with better cognitive functioning and greater brain volume: one higher in blood plasma levels of vitamins B (B1, B2, B6, folate, and B12), C, D, and E, and another high in blood plasma levels of omega-3 fatty acids (usually found in seafood). A third pattern characterized by high transfat was associated with less favorable cognitive function and less total cerebral brain volume.

More detailed analyses have examined two different omega-3 fatty acids: eicosapentaenoic acid (EPA) and docosahexaenoic acid (DHA). Samieri and colleagues (2012) showed that only the EPA type was associated with maintaining better neuronal structure in the right part of the amygdala, and that atrophy of this part of the amygdala was associated with significant declines in memory and increases in symptoms of depression. Some additional research indicates that DHA may slow the progression of Alzheimer's disease, but once the disease has developed the effect disappears (Cunnane et al., 2013).

Although researchers are only beginning to understand how nutrition affects brain structures, the findings to date clearly show that the effects could be substantial. As with exercise, we will return to the topic of nutrition and its effects on aging in Chapter 14.

Adult Development in Action

As the director of older adult services at a regional Area Office on Aging, you need to design websites about the benefits of exercise and good nutrition for older adults. What would the key information elements of the website be?

Aerobic exercise is good for maintaining brain health.

Social Policy Implications

The fact that the general view that the human brain gradually loses tissue from age 30 onward, and that those changes can mean poorer cognitive performance, combined with the projected rapid growth of an aging population present society with numerous public policy issues regarding the staggering costs of medical intervention and care for older adults. The good news is that advanced research in neuroscience tells us that this is an oversimplification of what really happens to the aging brain. Of importance to policy makers is that researchers are identifying ways in which such brain deterioration can be reduced or even reversed. In addition, researchers have identified areas of the brain that are relatively preserved and may even show growth. Thus, it is important for policy makers to obtain a more complete and accurate picture of aging. Why?

Research in neuroscience and aging is extremely important for a wide range of social policies from healthcare policies to laws pertaining to renewing drivers' licenses and the age at which people should be eligible for retirement benefits, among others. Federal agencies such as the National Institute on Aging have focused much of their efforts onto better ways to assess and understand changes in the brain. These efforts demand more multidisciplinary research.

A good example is the compelling research regarding the effects of aerobic exercise and diet on the aging brain and how well it functions. The old saying of "use-it-or-lose-it" appears to be true.

What's at stake regarding policy? We are now talking about extending the vitality of older adulthood. Evidence from neuroimaging research provides a platform from which new interventions might be developed to make this a reality. However, policy makers must continue to support neuroscience research in order to keep our knowledge moving forward.

SUMMARY

2.1 The Neuroscience Approach

What brain imaging techniques are used in neuroscience research?
- Structural neuroimaging such as computerized tomography (CT) and magnetic resonance imaging (MRI) provide highly detailed images of anatomical features in the brain.
- Functional neuroimaging such as single photon emission computerized tomography (SPECT), positron emission tomography (PET), functional magnetic resonance imaging (fMRI), magnetoencephalography, and near infrared spectroscopic imaging (NIRSI) provide an indication of brain activity but not high anatomical detail.

What are the main research methods used and issues studied in neuroscience research in adult development and aging?
- The neuropsychological approach compares brain-related psychological functioning of healthy older adults with adults displaying pathological disorders in the brain.
- The neuro-correlational approach links measures of behavioral performance to measures of neural structure or functioning.
- The activation imaging approach directly links functional brain activity with behavioral data.

2.2 Neuroscience and Adult Development and Aging

How is the brain organized structurally?
- The brain consists of neurons, which are comprised of dendrites, axons, neurofibers, and terminal branches. Neurons communicate across the space between neurons called the synapse via chemicals called neurotransmitters.
- Important structures in the brain for adult development and aging include the cerebral cortex, corpus callosum, prefrontal and frontal cortex, cerebellum, hippocampus, limbic system, and amygdala.

What are the basic changes in neurons as we age?
- Structural changes in the neuron include declines in number, decreases in size and number of dendrites, the development of tangles in neurofibers, and increases in deposits of certain proteins.

What changes occur in neurotransmitters with age?
- Important declines occur in the dopaminergic system (neurons that use dopamine) that are related to declines in memory, among others.
- Age-related changes in serotonin affect memory, mood, appetite, and sleep.
- Age-related changes in acetylcholine are related to arousal, sensory perception, and sustained attention.

What changes occur in brain structures with age?
- White matter (neurons covered by myelin) becomes thinner and shrinks, and does not function as well with age. White matter hyperintensities (WMH) are related to neural atrophy.
- Many areas of the brain show significant shrinkage with age.

What do age-related structural brain changes mean for behavior? The Theory of Mind
- The ability that helps us understand that other people have beliefs, desires, ideas, feelings, intentions, and viewpoints that are different from our own is termed Theory of Mind.
- Structural changes in the prefrontal cortex with age cause significant declines in executive functioning.
- Age-related structural changes in the prefrontal cortex and the hippocampus cause declines in memory function.
- Older and younger adults process emotional material differently. Older adults show increased activity in more areas of the prefrontal cortex.
- Brain structures involved in automatic processing (e.g., amygdala) show less change with age, whereas brain structures involved in more reflective processing (e.g., prefrontal cortex) show more change with age.
- The positivity effect refers to the fact that older adults are more motivated to derive emotional meaning from life and to maintain positive feelings. Older adults activate more brain structures when processing emotionally positive material.

2.3 Making Sense of Neuroscience Research: Explaining Changes in Brain-Behavior Relations

What is the Parieto-Frontal Integration Theory, and what does it explain?
- The Parieto-Frontal Integration Theory (P-FIT) proposes that intelligence comes from a distributed and integrated network of neurons in the parietal and frontal areas of the brain.

How do older adults attempt to compensate for age-related changes in the brain?
- Older adults compensate for brain changes by activating more areas of the brain than young adults when performing the same tasks.

What are the major differences among the HAROLD, CRUNCH, PASA, and STAC-r models of brain activation and aging?
- The Hemispheric Asymmetry Reduction in Older Adults (HAROLD) model explains the finding of the reduced ability of older adults in separating cognitive processing in different parts of the prefrontal cortex.
- The Compensation-Related Utilization of Neural Circuits Hypothesis (CRUNCH) model describes how the aging brain adapts to neurological decline by recruiting additional neural circuits (in comparison to younger adults) to perform tasks adequately. This model explains how older adults show overactivation of certain brain regions.
- The Posterior-Anterior Shift in Aging (PASA) model of cognitive aging reflects a decline in processing in the posterior (rear) areas of the brain to anterior (frontal) processing that is thought to reflect age-related compensation.
- The Scaffolding Theory of Cognitive Aging-revised (STAC-r) model is based on the idea that age-related changes in one's ability to function reflect a lifelong process of compensating for cognitive decline by recruiting additional brain areas. This explains how older adults build and rely on backup neural pathways. The model also accounts for life course influences.

2.4 Plasticity and the Aging Brain

What evidence is there for neural plasticity?
- Plasticity involves the changes in the structure and function of the brain as the result of interaction between the brain and the environment. Plasticity helps account for how older adults compensate for cognitive changes.
- Neural stem cells are cells that persist in the adult brain and can generate new neurons throughout the life span.

How does aerobic exercise influence brain changes and cognitive aging?
- Brain plasticity is enhanced through aerobic exercise.

How does nutrition influence brain changes and cognitive activity?
- Maintaining good levels of certain nutrients in blood plasma helps reduce the levels of brain structural changes and cognitive declines.

REVIEW QUESTIONS

2.1 The Neuroscience Approach
- Describe structural and functional neuroimaging techniques. How do they differ?
- Describe the various neuroscience methodological perspectives used to study the aging brain. What are their strengths and their limitations?
- How does the neuroscience level of examination contribute to our understanding of adult development and aging?

2.2 Neuroscience and Adult Development and Aging
- Describe the basic structures in the brain. What age-related changes are observed in neurons? What happens to dopamine functioning in the aging brain? What age-related changes occur in other neurotransmitters?
- What age-related changes occur in brain structures? What structures play major roles in the aging process?
- What are the differences in brain activation during cognitive tasks for younger and older adults? What key differences have been identified in activity in the prefrontal cortex between younger and older adults?
- What age-related differences have been documented in executive processing?
- What differences are there in memory with age as they relate to brain activation?
- How do younger and older adults process emotionally related material?

2.3 Making Sense of Neuroscience Research: Explaining Changes in Brain-Behavior Relations
- What does P-FIT explain?
- What evidence is there that older adults compensate for age-related changes in the brain?
- Compare and contrast the HAROLD, CRUNCH, and STAC-r theories

2.4 Plasticity and the Aging Brain
- What is neural plasticity? How might neural stem cells be used to increase neural plasticity?
- How does aerobic exercise affect age-related brain changes?
- How does nutrition affect age-related brain changes?

INTEGRATING CONCEPTS IN DEVELOPMENT

- Which of the theories of bilateral activation in older adults' brains makes the most sense to you? Why?
- What would you say about the stereotypes of aging now that you understand the plasticity of brain functioning?
- What does the work on brain plasticity imply for exercising the mind and body?
- How would you design a cognitive training program to take advantage of age-related changes in brain structures and plasticity?

KEY TERMS

activation imaging approach Attempts to directly link functional brain activity with cognitive behavioral data.

amygdala The region of the brain, located in the medial-temporal lobe, believed to play a key role in emotion.

antioxidants Compounds that protect cells from the harmful effects of free radicals.

axon A structure of the neuron that contains neurofibers.

cerebellum The part of the brain that is associated with motor functioning and balance equilibrium.

cerebral cortex The outermost part of the brain consisting of two hemispheres (left and right).

Compensation-Related Utilization of Neural Circuits Hypothesis (CRUNCH) model A model that describes how the aging brain adapts to neurological decline by recruiting additional neural circuits (in comparison to younger adults) to perform tasks adequately.

compensatory changes Changes that allow older adults to adapt to the inevitable behavioral decline resulting from changes in specific areas of the brain.

corpus callosum A thick bundle of neurons that connects the left and right hemispheres of the cerebral cortex.

default network of the brain The regions of the brain that are most active at rest.

dendrites A structural feature of a neuron that acts like antennas to receive signals from other nearby neurons.

diffusion tensor imaging (DTI) A type of magnetic resonance imaging that measures the diffusion of water molecules in tissue to study connections of neural pathways in the brain.

dopamine A neurotransmitter associated with higher-level cognitive functioning.

dopaminergic system Neuronal systems that use dopamine as their major neurotransmitter.

executive functions Include the ability to make and carry out plans, switch between tasks, and maintain attention and focus.

free radicals Substances that can damage cells, including brain cells, and play a role in cancer and other diseases as we grow older.

functional neuroimaging Provides an indication of brain activity but not high anatomical detail.

Hemispheric Asymmetry Reduction in OLDer adults (HAROLD) model A model that explains the empirical findings of reduced lateralization in prefrontal lobe activity in older adults (that is, the reduced ability of older adults to separate cognitive processing in different parts of the prefrontal cortex).

hippocampus Located in the medial-temporal lobe, this part of the brain plays a major role in memory and learning.

limbic system A set of brain structures involved with emotion, motivation, and long-term memory, among other functions.

neural stem cells (Also known as neural progenitors or neural precursor cells) are cells in the brain and spinal cord (the central nervous system, CNS) that are thought to give rise to the broad array of specialized cells of the CNS, including both neurons and glial cells.

neuro-correlational approach An approach that attempts to relate measures of cognitive performance to measures of brain structure or functioning.

neuroanatomy The study of the structure of the brain.

neurofibers Structures in the neuron that carry information inside the neuron from the dendrites to the terminal branches.

neuroimaging A set of techniques in which pictures of the brain are taken in various ways to provide understanding of both normal and abnormal cognitive aging.

neurons A brain cell.

neuropsychological approach Compares brain functioning of healthy older adults with adults displaying various pathological disorders in the brain.

neuroscience The study of the brain.

neurotransmitters Chemicals that carry information signals between neurons across the synapse.

Parieto-Frontal Integration Theory (P-FIT) A theory that proposes that intelligence comes from a distributed and integrated network of neurons in the parietal and frontal areas of the brain.

plasticity Involves the interaction between the brain and the environment and is mostly used to describe the effects of experience on the structure and functions of the neural system.

positivity effect When an individual remembers more positive information relative to negative information.

Posterior-Anterior Shift in Aging (PASA) model Model of cognitive aging reflecting from occipital to frontal processing that is thought to reflect age-related compensation.

prefrontal cortex Part of the frontal lobe that is involved in executive functioning.

Scaffolding Theory of Cognitive Aging-Revised (STAC-r) A model based on the idea that age-related changes in one's ability to function reflect a life-long process of compensating for cognitive decline by recruiting additional brain areas and takes life-course factors that enhance or deplete neural resources into account.

structural neuroimaging A set of techniques that provides highly detailed images of anatomical features in the brain.

synapse The gap between neurons across which neurotransmitters travel.

terminal branches The endpoints in a neuron that help transmit signals across the synapse.

Theory of Mind (ToM) The ability that helps us understand that other people have beliefs, desires, ideas, feelings, intentions, and viewpoints that are different from our own.

white matter Neurons that are covered by myelin that serve to transmit information from one part of the cerebral cortex to another or from the cerebral cortex to other parts of the brain.

white matter hyperintensities (WMH) Abnormalities in the brain often found in older adults; correlated with cognitive decline.

3 | Physical Changes

CHAPTER OUTLINE

3.1 Why Do We Age? Biological Theories of Aging
DISCOVERING DEVELOPMENT Why Do Most People Think We Age?
Metabolic Theories
Cellular Theories
Genetic Programming Theories
Implications of the Developmental Forces

3.2 Appearance and Mobility
Changes in Skin, Hair, and Voice
Changes in Body Build
Changes in Mobility
Psychological Implications

3.3 Sensory Systems
Vision
Hearing

HOW DO WE KNOW? Hearing and Quality of Life in Community-Dwelling Older Adults
Somesthesia and Balance
Taste and Smell

3.4 Vital Functions
Cardiovascular System

REAL PEOPLE Donna Arnett's Recovery from Stroke
Respiratory System

3.5 The Reproductive System
Female Reproductive System

CURRENT CONTROVERSIES Menopausal Hormone Therapy
Male Reproductive System
Psychological Implications

3.6 The Autonomic Nervous System
Autonomic Nervous System
Psychological Implications

Social Policy Implications

Summary
Review Questions
Integrating Concepts in Development
Key Terms

Could you run 135 miles through the desert and up mountains? That's the course for the Badwater® 135, held each July from its starting line in Death Valley, California. With extreme temperatures up to 130°F and 14,600 feet of ascent, ultramarathoners consider it "the world's toughest foot race."

In 2015, at age 70, Bob Becker of Ft. Lauderdale, Florida, finished the nonstop run in 41 hours, 30 minutes, and 21 seconds. But he wasn't done. He then climbed 11 miles up to the summit of Mt. Whitney, reversed course, and completed the 146-mile return to Death Valley. His round-trip of 292 miles took him only seven days, 8 hours, and 48 minutes. Not only was Bob the oldest person to complete the full circuit, but only the 29th person ever to do so.

Older adult ultramarathoners are shattering previous beliefs about physical performance and age. To be sure, athletic success is a combination of years of intense practice and excellent genes. But who would have thought Bob could do it?

Certainly, Bob performs well beyond the level that most of us could attain even at much younger ages. But each of us can attain impressive levels when we work at it. In this chapter, we will discover how physical abilities typically change across adulthood, and how such things as race times lengthen with age. ■

Bob Becker

3.1 Why Do We Age? Biological Theories of Aging

LEARNING OBJECTIVES
- How do metabolic theories explain aging?
- What are the major hypotheses in cellular theories of aging?
- How do genetic programming theories propose that we age?
- How do the basic developmental forces interact in biological and physiological aging?

Before he started selling his Lean Mean Grilling Machine, George Foreman was a champion boxer. In fact, at age 44 he became the oldest boxer ever to win the heavyweight championship. Foreman's success in the boxing ring came after a 10-year period when he did not fight and despite the belief that his career was finished.

Why is it that some people, like George Foreman and Dara Torres, who at age 41 became the oldest woman to win an Olympic gold medal in swimming, manage to stay competitive in their sports into middle age and others of us experience significant physical decline?

Why do we age at all? After all, some creatures, such as lobsters, do not age as humans do. (As far as scientists can tell, lobsters never show measurable signs of aging, such as changes in metabolism or declines in strength or health.) For millennia, scientists and philosophers have pondered this question. Their answers have spurred researchers to create a collection of theories based on basic biological and physiological processes. The search has included many hypotheses, such as metabolic rates and brain sizes, that haven't proved accurate. But as scientists continue unlocking the keys to our genetic code, hope is rising that we may eventually have an answer. To date, though, none of the more than 300 existing theories provides a complete explanation of all the normative changes humans experience (Yin, 2016).

Before we explore some of the partial explanations from scientific research, complete the Discovering Development exercise. Compare your results for this exercise with some of the theories described next. What similarities and differences did you uncover?

Metabolic Theories

One theory of aging that makes apparent commonsense postulates that organisms have only so much energy to expend in a lifetime. (Couch potatoes might like this theory and may use it as a reason why they are not physically active.) The basic idea is that the rate of a creature's metabolism is related to how long it lives (Barzilai et al., 2012).

Several changes in the way that hormones are produced and used in the human body have been associated with aging, but none have provided a definitive explanation.

Although some research indicates that significantly reducing the number of calories animals and people eat may increase longevity, research focusing on nonhuman primates shows that longer lives do not always result from restricting calories alone. For instance, research indicates that our circadian rhythms interact with caloric restriction in such a way that it matters when during the awake cycle feeding occurs and in what quantities and in what exactly is eaten for the caloric restriction benefits to be observed consistently (Chaudhari et al., 2017). Furthermore, the quality of life that would result for people on such a diet raises questions about how good a strategy calorie restriction is (Barzilai et al., 2012). That's because the caloric restrictions in this research tend to be extreme. Extrapolated to people, the restrictions could well cause a drop in humans' ability to engage in the kinds of activities we would consider important for a high quality of life.

Cellular Theories

A second family of ideas points to causes of aging at the cellular level. One notion focuses on the number of times cells can divide, which presumably limits the life span of a complex organism. Cells grown in laboratory culture dishes undergo only a fixed number of divisions before dying, with the number of possible divisions dropping depending on the age of the donor organism; this phenomenon is called the Hayflick limit, after its discoverer, Leonard Hayflick (Hayflick, 1996). For example, cells from human fetal tissue are capable of 40 to 60 divisions; cells from a human adult are capable of only about 20. It turns out that the Hayflick limit sets an upper bound on the number of cell divisions possible even in the absence of other factors, such as telomere damage, discussed next (Bernadotte, Mikhelson, & Spivak, 2016).

What causes cells to limit their number of divisions? *Evidence suggests that the tips of the chromosomes, called* **telomeres**, *play a major role in aging by adjusting the cell's response to stress and growth stimulation based on cell divisions and DNA damage, and by typically shortening with each cell replication* (Bernadotte et al., 2016). Healthy, normal telomeres help regulate the cell division and reproduction process.

An enzyme called **telomerase** *is needed in DNA replication to fully reproduce the telomeres when cells divide.* But telomerase normally is not present in somatic cells, so with each replication the telomeres become shorter. Eventually, the chromosomes become unstable and cannot replicate because the telomeres become too short. This process is depicted in Figure 3.1.

Some researchers believe that in some cases cancer cells proliferate so quickly because telomeres are not able to regulate cell growth and reproduction (Akincilar,

■ DISCOVERING DEVELOPMENT
Why Do Most People Think We Age?

What does the average person believe about how and why we age physiologically? To find out, list the various organ and body systems discussed in this chapter. Ask some people of different ages two sets of questions. First, ask them what they think happens to each system as people grow older. Then ask them what they think causes these changes. Compile the results from your interviews, share them with your classmates to create a larger database, and then compare them with what you discover in this chapter. To what extent were your interviewees correct in their descriptions? Where were they off base? Does any of the misinformation match up with the stereotypes of aging we considered in Chapter 1? Why do you think this might be the case? How accurate are people in describing aging?

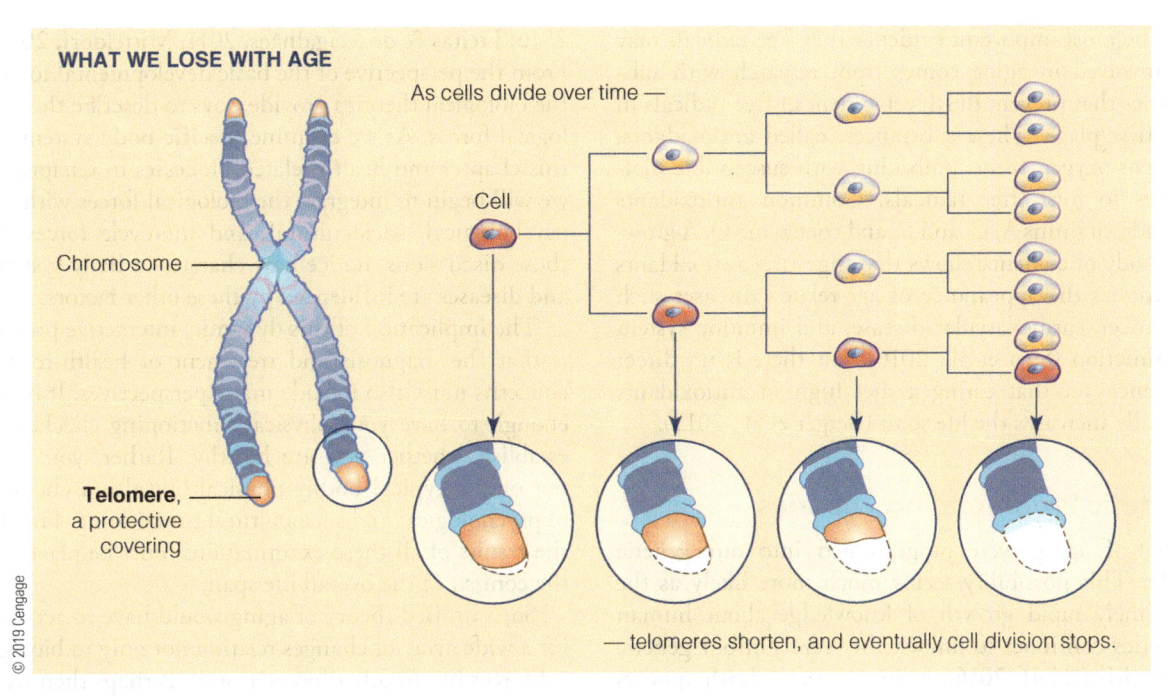

FIGURE 3.1 The process by which telomeres shorten as we age.
Source: telomeres-aging.com/images/shorteningdna.jpg.

Unal, & Tergaonkar, 2016). The culprit appears to be the production of telomerase, an enzyme that plays a major role in the reproduction of telomeres. Because at least 85% of human cancers are linked to the activation of telomerase and the unregulated reproduction of cells (Akincilar et al., 2016), current thinking is that effective cancer treatments may involve targeting telomerase production. Other research indicating the telomeres can be lengthened is promising (Epel, 2012; Spivak, Mikhelson, & Spivak, 2016).

Chronic stress may accelerate the changes that occur in telomeres and thereby shorten one's life span (Oliveira et al., 2016; Spivak et al., 2016). Research also shows that moderate levels of exercise may maintain telomere length or at least slow the rate at which telomeres shorten, which may help slow the aging process itself (Savela et al., 2013; Silva et al., 2016). However, the precise mechanisms for this process are not understood (Denham, O'Brien, & Charchar, 2016).

A second cellular theory is based on a process called **cross-linking**, *in which certain proteins in human cells interact randomly and produce molecules that are linked in such a way as to make the body stiffer* (Cavanaugh, 1999b). The proteins in question, which make up roughly one-third of the protein in the body, are called collagen. Collagen in soft body tissue acts much like reinforcing rods in concrete. The more cross-links there are, the stiffer the tissue. For example, leather tanning involves using chemicals that create many cross-links to make the leather stiff enough for use in shoes and other products. As we age, the number of cross-links increases. This process may explain why muscles, such as the heart, and arteries become stiffer with age. However, few scientific data demonstrate that cross-linking impedes metabolic processes or causes the formation of faulty molecules that would constitute a fundamental cause of aging (Hayflick, 1996). Thus, even though cross-linking occurs, it probably is not an adequate explanation of aging.

A third type of cellular theory proposes that aging is caused by unstable molecules called **free radicals**, *which are highly reactive chemicals produced randomly in normal metabolism* (Dutta et al., 2012). When these free radicals interact with nearby molecules, problems may result. For example, free radicals may cause cell damage to the heart by changing the oxygen levels in cells. There is also evidence that free radicals may have a role in the development of Alzheimer's disease (Wojtunik-Kulesza et al., 2016).

The most important evidence that free radicals may be involved in aging comes from research with substances that prevent the development of free radicals in the first place. These substances, called antioxidants, prevent oxygen from combining with susceptible molecules to form free radicals. Common antioxidants include vitamins A, C, and E, and coenzyme Q. A growing body of evidence shows that ingesting antioxidants postpones the appearance of age-related diseases such as cancer, cardiovascular disease, and immune system dysfunction (Suja et al., 2016), but there is no direct evidence yet that eating a diet high in antioxidants actually increases the life span (Berger et al., 2012).

Genetic Programming Theories

What if aging were programmed into our genetic code? This possibility seems much more likely as the extremely rapid growth of knowledge about human genetics continues to unlock the secrets of our genetic code (Mitteldorf, 2016). Even when cell death appears random, researchers believe that such losses may be part of a master genetic program that underlies the aging process (Freitas & de Magalhães, 2011; Mackenzie, 2012). Programmed cell death appears to be a function of physiological processes, the innate ability of cells to self-destruct, and the ability of dying cells to trigger key processes in other cells, all of which are also thought to be influenced by external environmental factors (Arbeev, Ukraintseva, & Yashin, 2016; Ukraintseva et al., 2016). At present, we do not know how this genetic self-destruct program is activated, nor do we understand how it works. Nevertheless, there is increasing evidence that many diseases associated with aging (such as Alzheimer's disease) have genetic aspects.

It is quite possible that the other explanations we have considered in this section and the changes we examine throughout this text are the result of a genetic program. We will consider many diseases throughout the text that have known genetic bases, such as Alzheimer's disease. As genetics research continues, it is likely that we will have some exciting answers to the question, Why do we age?

Implications of the Developmental Forces

Although scientists do not yet have one unified theory of biological and physiological aging, the picture is becoming clearer. We know that there are genetic components, that the body's chemistry lab sometimes produces incorrect products, and that errors occur in the operation and replication of DNA (Bernadotte et al., 2016; Freitas & de Magalhães, 2011; Mitteldorf, 2016). From the perspective of the basic developmental forces, the biological theories provide ways to describe the biological forces. As we examine specific body systems in this chapter and health-related processes in Chapter 4, we will begin to integrate the biological forces with the psychological, sociocultural, and life-cycle forces. In those discussions, notice how changes in body systems and diseases are influenced by these other factors.

The implication of this dynamic, interactive process is that the diagnosis and treatment of health-related concerns must also include many perspectives. It is not enough to have your physical functioning checked to establish whether you are healthy. Rather, you need not only a typical bodily physical but also a checkup of psychological and sociocultural functioning. Finally, the results of all these examinations must be placed in the context of the overall life span.

So, a unified theory of aging would have to account for a wide array of changes relating not only to biological forces but to other forces as well. Perhaps then we'll discover why George Foreman was still successful in the boxing ring, Dara Torres was winning in the pool, and Gunhild Swanson was running 100 miles when most of their peers got exhausted watching them on television.

Or we just might discover how to reverse or stop aging. The business of "antiaging medicine," products designed to stop or prevent aging, is booming. Although most researchers who specialize in studying the fundamental mechanisms of aging largely dismiss such efforts, not all do. For example, research on the Chinese herb Sanchi (or San Qi; *Panax notoginsengs*) shows promise in reducing wrinkles (Ling, Ning, & Hoon, 2016; Rattan et al., 2013). Healthy behaviors that delay the effects of aging are legitimate activities that have a research foundation; whether they should be called "antiaging" is another matter (Palmore, 2007). Exercise has been shown to delay many aspects of aging; cosmetic surgery aimed at making someone look younger does not and is likely more related to aging stereotypes than healthy lifestyles.

There are three general research-based approaches to the work aimed at slowing or reversing aging. First, the goal is to delay the chronic illnesses of old age. Second, there is research aimed at slowing the fundamental processes of aging so that the average life span is increased to over 110 years (from roughly 78 now). Third, some researchers seek to arrest or even reverse aging, perhaps by removing the damage inevitably caused by metabolic processes.

Research separating healthy behaviors from age denials is key (Palmore, 2007). Legitimate research sponsored by such agencies as the National Institutes of Health becomes confused with counterfeit antiaging interventions. If the legitimate research unlocks the secrets of aging, then a serious public discussion is needed to prepare society for the implications of a possible significant lengthening of the life span.

Adult Development in Action

If you were a geriatric nurse, what advice would you give to your patients about living longer based on existing biological theories of aging?

3.2 Appearance and Mobility

LEARNING OBJECTIVES

- How do our skin, hair, and voices change with age?
- What happens to our body build with age?
- What age-related changes occur in our ability to move around?

By all accounts, Kristina is extremely successful. She was a famous model in her late teens and 20s, and by the time she was 36 she had learned enough about the business to start her own multinational modeling agency. The other day Kristina was very upset when she looked in the mirror and saw a wrinkle. "Oh no," she exclaimed, "I can't be getting wrinkles! What am I going to do?"

Kristina's experience isn't unique. We all see the outward signs of aging first in the mirror: gray hair, wrinkled skin, and an expanding waistline or hips. These changes occur gradually and at different rates; some of us experience all the changes in young adulthood, whereas others don't have them until late middle or old age. How we perceive the person staring back at us in the mirror says a great deal about how we feel about aging; positive feelings about the signs of aging are related to positive self-esteem.

How easily we move our changing bodies in the physical environment is also a major component of adaptation and well-being in adulthood. If we cannot get around, we must depend on others, which lowers our self-esteem and sense of competence. Having a body that moves effectively also lets us enjoy physical activities such as walking, swimming, and skiing.

Changes in Skin, Hair, and Voice

When we, like Kristina, see the first visible signs of aging, it makes no difference that these changes are universal and inevitable. Nor does it matter that our wrinkles are caused by a combination of changes in the structure of the skin and its connective and supportive tissue and the cumulative effects of exposure to sunlight. As normal as the loss of hair pigmentation is, we may still want to hide the gray (Aldwin & Gilmer, 2013). What matters on that day is that we have seen our first wrinkle and gray hair.

Changes in the Skin

Why does our skin wrinkle? Wrinkling is actually a complex, four-step process (Blume-Peytavi et al., 2016; Robert, Labat-Robert, & Robert, 2012; Tobin, 2017). First, the outer layer of skin becomes thinner through cell loss, causing the skin to become more fragile. Second, the collagen fibers that make up the connective tissue lose much of their flexibility, making the skin less able to regain its shape after a pinch. Third, elastin fibers in the middle layer of skin lose their ability to keep the skin stretched out, resulting in sagging. Finally, the underlying layer of fat, which helps provide padding to smooth out the contours, diminishes.

It may surprise you to know that how quickly your face ages is largely under your control. Two major environmental causes of wrinkles are exposure to ultraviolet rays from the sun, which breaks down the skin's connective tissue, and smoking, which restricts the flow of blood to the skin around the lips. But diets poor in fresh fruits and vegetables, excessive alcohol, sweat, and repetitive facial expressions also help create wrinkles (American Academy of Dermatology, 2016; Tobin, 2017). Decades of research indicate the overall health benefits of sunscreens in preventing skin cancers and slowing skin aging significantly outweigh criticism that they also interfere with the formation of vitamin D by the skin (Nash & Tanner, 2016). In fact, the American Cancer Society (2016a) adopted a public messaging campaign originally developed in Australia in the early 1980s to remind people what to do—the Slip! Slop! Slap!® and Wrap campaign. It consists of:

- Slip on a shirt
- Slop on sunscreen
- Slap on a hat
- Wrap on sunglasses to protect your eyes and sensitive skin around them

Older adults' skin is naturally thinner and drier, giving it a leathery texture, making it less effective at regulating heat or cold, and making it more susceptible to cuts, bruises, and blisters. To counteract these problems, people should use skin moisturizers, vitamin E, and facial massages (Blume-Peytavi et al., 2016; Robert et al., 2012).

The coloring of light-skinned people undergoes additional changes with age. The number of pigment-containing cells in the outer layer decreases, and those that remain have less pigment, resulting in lighter skin. In addition, age spots (areas of dark pigmentation that look like freckles) and moles (pigmented outgrowths) appear more often (Tobin, 2017). Some of the blood vessels in the skin may become dilated and create small, irregular red lines. Varicose veins may appear as knotty, bluish irregularities in blood vessels, especially on the legs; various treatment methods are available (Aldwin & Gilmer, 2013; Dillavou et al., 2016).

Changes in the Hair

Gradual thinning and graying of the hair of both men and women occur inevitably with age, although there are large individual differences in the rate of these changes. Hair loss is caused by destruction of the germ centers that produce the hair follicles. Men usually do not lose facial hair as they age; you probably have seen many balding men with thick, bushy beards. In addition, men often develop bushy eyebrows and hair growth inside the ears. In contrast, women often develop patches of hair on the face, especially on the chin (Aldwin & Gilmer, 2013). This hair growth is related to the hormonal changes of the climacteric, discussed later in this chapter.

Graying of the hair is also a widespread experience of most people as they age, although when the change occurs is subject to wide individual differences. Graying results from a cessation of pigment production in the hair follicle. Research has uncovered a genetic basis for graying hair (Adhikari et al., 2016). Cultural variations are evident in whether people let their hair turn gray or whether they color it.

Changes in the Voice

The next time you're in a crowd of people of different ages, close your eyes and listen to the way they sound. You probably will be fairly accurate in guessing how old the speakers are just from the quality of the voices you hear. Younger adults' voices tend to be full and resonant, whereas older adults' voices tend to be thinner or weaker. Age-related changes in one's voice include lowering of pitch, increased breathlessness and trembling, slower and less precise pronunciation, and decreased volume (Whited et al., 2016). A longitudinal study of Japanese adults revealed that women have more changes in their fundamental frequency, and shimmer (i.e., frequent change from soft to loud volume) and glottal noise is characteristic of older voices (Kasuya et al., 2008). Some researchers report that these changes are due to changes in the larynx (voice box), the respiratory system, and the muscles controlling speech. However, other researchers contend that these changes result from poor health and are not part of normal aging.

Changes in Body Build

If you have been around the same older people, such as your grandparents, for many years, you undoubtedly have noticed that the way their bodies look changed over time. Two changes are especially visible: a decrease in height and fluctuations in weight. Height remains fairly stable until the 50s, and has been shown to be a good indicator of overall health (Perkins et al., 2016). However, between the mid-50s and mid-70s men lose about 1 inch and women lose about 2 inches in height on average (Havaldar, Pilli, & Putti, 2012).

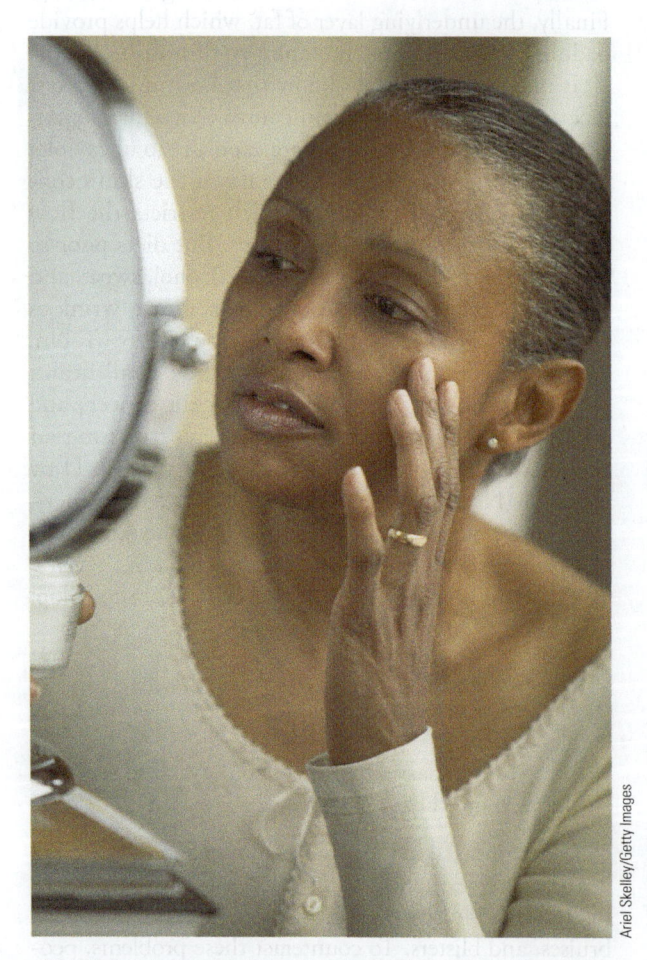

Getting gray hair and wrinkles is part of the normative aging process.

Height loss in later life usually is caused by compression of the spine from loss of bone strength (often from osteoporosis, a disease we will consider a bit later), changes in the discs between the vertebrae in the spine, and changes in posture. Importantly, height loss of more than 3 cm is associated with increased risk of dying from cardiovascular (Miedema et al., 2014; Perkins et al., 2016) and respiratory diseases (Masunari et al., 2012). We consider some specific aspects of changes in bone structure a bit later.

Weight gain in middle age followed by weight loss in later life is common. Typically, people gain weight between their 20s and their mid-50s but lose weight throughout old age. In part, the weight gain is caused by changes in body metabolism, which tends to slow down, and reduced levels of exercise, which in turn reduces the number of calories needed daily. Unfortunately, many people do not adjust their food intake to match these changes, and continue consuming the same number of calories. The result of these age-related changes is often noticed first when one's clothes become tighter fitting.

For men, weight gain tends to be around the abdomen, creating middle-aged "belly bulge." For women, weight gain tends to be around the hips, giving women a more "pear-shaped" figure. By late life, though, the body loses both muscle and bone, which weigh more than fat, in addition to some fat, resulting in overall weight loss (Yang, Bishai, & Harman, 2008). Research on the relationships among body weight, health, and survival shows that older adults who have normal body weight at age 65 have longer life expectancy and lower rates of disability than 65-year-olds in other weight categories. Additionally, greater weight loss per decade from middle age to late life increases the risk of mild cognitive impairment (Alhurani et al., 2016). Keeping your weight in the normal range for your height, then, may help you live healthier longer.

Changes in Mobility

Being able to get around on one's own is an important part of remaining independent. As you will see, we all experience some normative changes that can affect our ability to remain mobile, but most of these changes do not inevitably result in serious limitations.

Muscles and Balance

Although the amount of muscle tissue in our bodies declines with age, this loss is usually not noticeable in terms of strength and endurance up to age 70, as the loss is no more than 20% for most people up to that point. After that, however, the rate of loss increases. By age 80 the loss in strength is up to 40%, and it appears to be more severe in the legs than in the arms and hands. However, some people retain their strength well into old age (Seene & Kaasik, 2015; Seene, Kaasik, & Riso, 2012). Research evidence suggests that muscle endurance also diminishes with age but at a slower rate. Men and women show no differences in the rate of muscle change.

This loss of muscle strength is especially important in the lower body (El Haber et al., 2008). As lower body strength declines, the likelihood of balance problems and falls increases, as do problems with walking. Research evidence clearly indicates that resistance-type exercise can rebuild muscle fitness and mass, and may help delay these changes (Seene & Kaasik, 2015).

Bones

You have probably seen commercials and advertisements aimed mostly at women for products that help maintain bone mass. If you surmise that such products reflect a serious and real health concern, you are correct. Normal aging is accompanied by the loss of bone tissue throughout the body. Bone loss begins in the late 30s, accelerates in the 50s (particularly in women), and slows by the 70s (Havaldar et al., 2012). The gender difference in bone loss is important. Once the process begins, women lose bone mass approximately twice as fast as men on average. The difference results from two factors. First, women have less bone mass than men in young adulthood, meaning that they start out with less ability to withstand bone loss before it causes problems. Second, the depletion of estrogen after menopause speeds up bone loss.

What happens to aging bones? The process involves a loss of bone mass inside the bone, which makes bones more hollow. In addition, bones tend to become porous. The changes result from body weight, genetics, and lifestyle factors such as smoking, alcohol use, and diet (Havaldar et al., 2012). All these bone changes cause an age-related increase in the likelihood of fractures, because hollow, porous bones are easier to break. Furthermore, broken bones in older people present more serious problems than in younger adults, because they are more likely to be clean fractures that are difficult to heal. Younger adults' bones fracture in such a way that there are many cracks and splinters to aid in healing. This is analogous to the difference between breaking a young, green tree branch (which is harder to do) and snapping an old, dry twig.

Women are especially susceptible to severe bone degeneration, a disease called **osteoporosis**, *in which the severe loss of bone mass creates bones that resemble laced honeycombs.* You can see the result in Figure 3.2. Eventually, people with osteoporosis tend to develop a distinct curvature in their spines, as shown in Figure 3.3.

Osteoporosis is the leading cause of broken bones in older women (National Osteoporosis Foundation, 2016a). Although it is most common in older adults, osteoporosis can occur in people in their 50s.

Osteoporosis is more common in women than in men, largely because women have less bone mass in general, because some girls and women do not consume enough dietary calcium to build strong bones when they are younger (i.e., build bone mass), and because the decrease in estrogen following menopause greatly accelerates bone loss.

Osteoporosis is caused in part by having low bone mass at skeletal maturity (the point at which your bones reach peak development), deficiencies in calcium and vitamin D, estrogen depletion, and lack of weight-bearing exercise that builds up bone mass. Other risk factors include smoking; high-protein diets; and excessive intake of alcohol, caffeine, and sodium. Women who are being treated for asthma, cancer, rheumatoid arthritis, thyroid problems, or epilepsy are also at increased risk because the medications used can lead to the loss of bone mass.

The National Osteoporosis Foundation (2016b) recommends getting enough vitamin D and dietary calcium as ways to prevent osteoporosis. There is evidence that calcium supplements after menopause may slow the rate of bone loss and delay the onset of osteoporosis, but benefits appear to be greater when the supplements are provided before menopause. People should consume foods (such as milk, sardines, collard greens, broccoli, or kale) that are high in calcium and should also take calcium supplements if necessary. Recommended calcium intake for men and women of various ages are shown in Table 3.1. Although sunlight is a good source for vitamin D, due to the risk of skin cancer from overexposure to the sun, most people get their recommended amounts of vitamin D from dietary sources (National Osteoporosis Foundation, 2016c).

In terms of medication interventions, bisphosphonates are the most commonly used and are highly effective but can have serious side effects if used over a long period of time (Adler et al., 2016). Bisphosphonates slow the bone breakdown process by helping to maintain bone density during menopause. Research indicates that using bisphosphonates for up to five years appears relatively safe if followed by stopping the

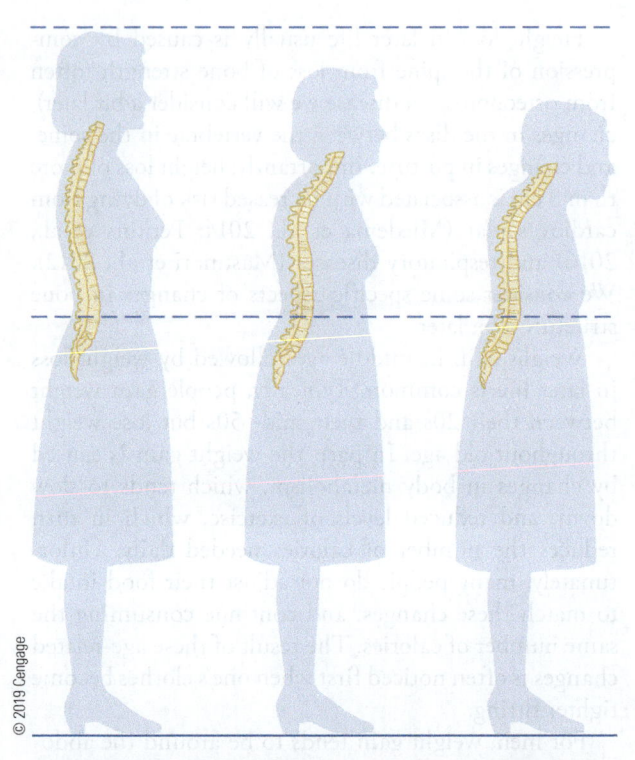

FIGURE 3.3 Changes in the curvature of the spine as a result of osteoporosis. These changes create the stooping posture common to older people with advanced osteoporosis.

Source: Reprinted with permission from Ebersole, P., & Hess, P. (1998). *Toward Healthy Aging*, 5th ed., (p. 395). St. Louis, MO: Mosby. With permission from Elsevier.

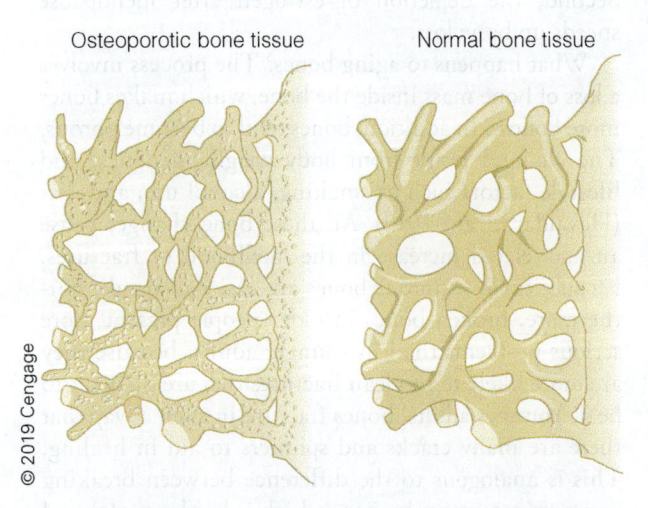

Osteoporotic bone tissue   Normal bone tissue

FIGURE 3.2 Osteoporotic and normal bone structures. Notice how much mass the osteoporotic bone has lost.

TABLE 3.1 Recommended Calcium and Vitamin D Intakes

Age	Calcium (Milligrams)	Vitamin D (International Units)
Infants		
Birth to 6 months	200	400
6 months to 1 year	260	400
Children and Young Adults		
1 to 3 years	700	600
4 to 8 years	1,000	600
9 to 13 years	1,300	600
14 to 18 years	1,300	600
Adult Women and Men		
19 to 30 years	1,000	400–800
31 to 50 years	1,000	400–800
51- to 70-year-old males	1,000	800–1,000
51- to 70-year-old females	1,200	800–1,000
Over 70 years	1,200	800–1,000

Source: National Osteoporosis Foundation (2016c). Calcium/Vitamin D. Retrieved from www.nof.org/patients/treatment/calciumvitamin-d/.

medication (called a "drug holiday"); there is evidence for protective effects lasting up to five years more. Periodic reevaluation of people taking medications to assess whether continued medication treatment is needed is crucial to appropriate and effective use of these drugs (Adler et al., 2016).

Lowering the risk of osteoporosis involves dietary, medication, and activity approaches (National Osteoporosis Foundation, 2016a, b). Some evidence also supports the view that taking supplemental magnesium, zinc, vitamin K, and special forms of fluoride may be effective. Estrogen replacement is effective in preventing women's bone loss after menopause but is controversial because of potential side effects (as discussed later). There is also evidence that regular weight-bearing exercise (e.g., weight lifting, jogging, or other exercise that forces you to work against gravity) is beneficial.

Joints

Many middle-aged and older adults have good reason to complain of aching joints. Beginning in the 20s, the protective cartilage in joints shows signs of deterioration, such as thinning and becoming cracked and frayed. Two types of arthritis can result: osteoarthritis and rheumatoid arthritis. These diseases are illustrated in Figure 3.4.

Over time and repeated use, the bones underneath the cartilage become damaged, which can result in **osteoarthritis**, *a disease marked by gradual onset and progression of pain and disability, with minor signs of inflammation* (National Institute of Arthritis and Musculoskeletal and Skin Diseases, 2014a). The disease usually becomes noticeable in late middle age or early old age, and it is especially common in people whose joints are subjected to routine overuse and abuse, such as athletes and manual laborers. Because it is caused by overuse and abuse of joints, osteoarthritis is considered a wear-and-tear disease. Pain from osteoarthritis typically is worse when the joint is used, but skin redness, heat, and swelling are minimal or absent. Osteoarthritis usually affects the hands, spine, hips, and knees, sparing the wrists, elbows, shoulders, and ankles. Effective management consists mainly of certain steroids and anti-inflammatory drugs, rest, nonstressful exercises that focus on range of motion, diet, and a variety of homeopathic remedies.

A second form of arthritis is **rheumatoid arthritis**, *a more destructive disease of the joints that also develops slowly and typically affects different joints and causes other types of pain and more inflammation than osteoarthritis* (National Institute of Arthritis and Musculoskeletal and Skin Diseases, 2014b). Most often, a pattern of morning stiffness and aching develops in the fingers, wrists, and ankles on both sides of the body. Joints appear swollen.

The American College of Rheumatology (Singh et al., 2016) has adopted guidelines for treating rheumatoid arthritis. The typical low-level therapy consists of aspirin or other nonsteroidal anti-inflammatory drugs, such as Advil or Aleve. Newer treatments include disease-modifying anti-rheumatic drugs (DMARDs) (such as hydroxycholorquine and methotrexate) that limit the damage occurring in the joints, glucocorticoids, and TNF-alpha inhibitors that act as an anti-inflammatory agent and have been shown to stop the disease's progression in some patients. Rest and passive range-of-motion exercises are also helpful.

Both osteoarthritis (Warner & Valdes, 2016) and rheumatoid arthritis (Yarwood, Huizinga, & Worthington, 2016) have genetic components. Although the exact nature of these inheritance factors are unknown, several potential locations have been identified as possible markers. Further advances in our knowledge of these genetic links could result in more effective and more individualized treatments.

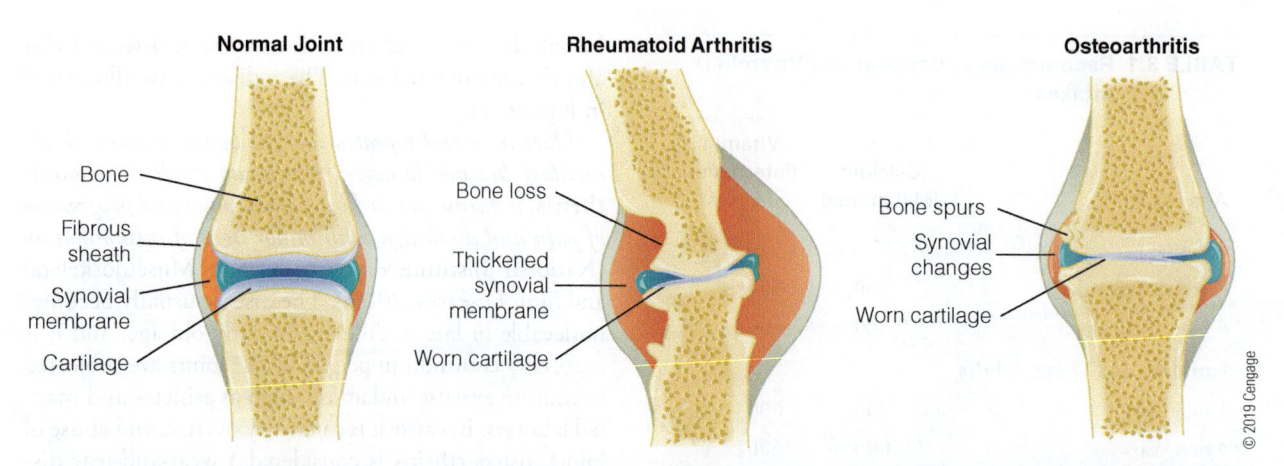

FIGURE 3.4 Rheumatoid arthritis versus osteoarthritis. Osteoarthritis, the most common form of arthritis, involves the wearing away of the cartilage that caps the bones in your joints. With rheumatoid arthritis, the synovial membrane that protects and lubricates joints becomes inflamed, causing pain and swelling. Joint erosion may follow.
Adapted from the MayoClinic.com article, "Arthritis," www.mayoclinic.com/health/arthritis/DS01122.

Surgical interventions may be an option if medications do not provide relief. For example, *arthroplasty*, or the total replacement of joints damaged by arthritis, continues to improve as new materials help artificial joints last longer. Hip and knee replacement surgery is becoming both more common and more effective as less invasive surgical techniques are developed that dramatically reduce recovery time. When joints become inflamed, surgeons may be able to remove enough affected tissue to provide relief. In some cases, cartilage may be transplanted into a damaged joint. These latter two approaches help patients avoid full joint replacement, generally viewed as the method of last resort.

Osteoporosis, osteoarthritis, and rheumatoid arthritis can appear similar and cause similar symptoms. As we have seen, though, they are different diseases requiring different treatment approaches. Comparisons among osteoporosis, osteoarthritis, and rheumatoid arthritis can be seen in Table 3.2.

Psychological Implications

The appearance of wrinkles, gray hair, fat, and the like can have major effects on a person's self-concept (Aldwin & Gilmer, 2013) and reflect ageism in society (Levy & Macdonald, 2016). Middle-aged adults may still think of themselves as productive members of society and rebel against being made invisible. Because U.S. society places high value on looking young, middle-aged and older adults, especially women, may be regarded as inferior on a number of dimensions, including intellectual ability. Consequently, women report engaging in "beauty work" (dyeing their hair, cosmetic surgery, and the like) to remain visible in society. In contrast, middle-aged men with some gray hair often are considered distinguished, more experienced, and more knowledgeable than their younger counterparts.

Given the social stereotypes we examined in Chapter 1, many women (and increasingly, some men) use any available means to compensate for these changes. Some age-related changes in facial appearance can be disguised with cosmetics. Hair dyes can restore color. Surgical procedures such as face-lifts can tighten sagging and wrinkled skin. But even plastic surgery only delays the inevitable; at some point everyone takes on a distinctly old appearance.

Losses in strength and endurance in old age have much the same psychological effects as changes in appearance (Aldwin & Gilmer, 2013). In particular, these changes tell the person that he or she is not as capable of adapting effectively to the environment. Loss of muscle coordination (which may lead to walking more slowly, for example) may not be inevitable, but it can prove embarrassing and stressful. In Chapter 4 we will examine the many benefits of exercise in addressing both the age-related changes noted here as well as other positive outcomes.

The changes in the joints, especially in arthritis, have profound psychological effects, including depression (Ryan, 2014). These changes can severely limit movement, thereby reducing independence and the ability to complete normal daily routines. Moreover, joint pain is very difficult to ignore or disguise, unlike changes in appearance. Consequently, the person who

TABLE 3.2 Similarities and Differences Among Osteoporosis, Osteoarthritis, and Rheumatoid Arthritis

	Osteoporosis	Osteoarthritis	Rheumatoid Arthritis
Risk Factors			
Age-related	x	x	
Menopause	x		
Family history	x	x	x
Use of certain medications such as glucocorticoids or seizure medications	x		
Calcium deficiency or inadequate vitamin D	x		
Inactivity	x		
Overuse of joints		x	
Smoking	x		
Excessive alcohol	x		
Anorexia nervosa	x		
Excessive weight		x	
Physical Effects			
Affects entire skeleton	x		
Affects joints		x	x
Is an autoimmune disease			x
Bony spurs		x	x
Enlarged or malformed joints		x	x
Height loss	x		

Source: National Institute of Arthritis and Musculoskeletal and Skin Diseases (2006), www.niams.nih.gov/Health_Info/Bone/Osteoporosis/Conditions_Behaviors/osteoporosis_arthritis.asp

can use cosmetics to hide changes in appearance cannot use the same approach to deal with constant pain in the joints. Older adults who suffer bone fractures face several other consequences in addition to discomfort. For example, a hip fracture may force hospitalization or even an extended stay in a rehabilitation facility. For all fractures, the recovery period is much longer than for a younger adult. In addition, older people who witness friends or relatives struggling during rehabilitation may reduce their own activities as a precaution.

Adult Development in Action

If you were a personal exercise trainer, what regimen would you recommend for your older clients to help them maintain maximum health?

3.3 Sensory Systems

LEARNING OBJECTIVES
- What age-related changes happen in vision?
- How does hearing change as people age?
- What age-related changes occur in people's senses of touch and balance?
- What happens to taste and smell with increasing age?

Bertha has attended Sunday services in her local AME (African Methodist Episcopal) church for 82 years. Over the past few years, though, she has experienced greater difficulty in keeping her balance as she walks down the steps from her row house to the sidewalk. Bertha is noticing that her balance problems occur even when she is walking on level ground. Bertha is concerned *that she will have to stop attending her beloved church because she is afraid of falling and breaking a bone.*

You have probably seen people like Bertha walking slowly and tentatively along the sidewalk. Why do older people have these problems more often? If you said it is because the sensory system directly related to maintaining balance, the vestibular system, and muscle strength decline with age, you would only be partly correct. It turns out that keeping one's balance is a complex process in which we integrate input from several sources, such as vision and touch, as well as bones and joints. In this section we examine the changes that occur in our sensory systems. These changes challenge our ability to interact with the world and communicate with others.

Vision

Have you ever watched middle-aged people try to read something that is right in front of them? If they do not already wear glasses or contact lenses, they typically move the material farther away so that they can see it clearly. This change in vision is one of the first noticeable signs of aging, along with the wrinkles and gray hair we considered earlier. A major study of 10 European countries revealed that because we rely extensively on sight in almost every aspect of our waking life, its normative, age-related changes have profound and pervasive effects on people's everyday lives, especially feelings of sadness and loss of enjoyment of life (Mojon-Azzi, Sousa-Poza, & Mojon, 2008).

How does eyesight change with age? The major changes are best understood by grouping them into two classes: changes in the structures of the eye, which begin in the 40s, and changes in the retina, which begin in the 50s (Alavi, 2016).

Structural Changes in the Eye

Two major kinds of age-related structural changes occur in the eye. One is a decrease in the amount of light that passes through the eye, resulting in the need for more light to do tasks such as reading (Alavi, 2016). As you might suspect, this change is one reason why older adults do not see as well in the dark, which may account in part for their reluctance to go places at night. One possible logical response to the need for more light would be to increase illumination levels in general. However, this solution does not work in all situations because we also become increasingly sensitive to glare. In addition, our ability to adjust to changes in illumination, called adaptation, declines. Going from outside into a darkened movie theater involves dark adaptation; going back outside involves light adaptation. Research indicates that the time it takes for both types of adaptation increases with age (Alavi, 2016). These changes are especially important for older drivers, who have more difficulty seeing after confronting the headlights of an oncoming car.

The other key structural changes involve the lens (Alavi, 2016). As we grow older, the lens becomes more yellow, causing poorer color discrimination in the green—blue—violet end of the spectrum. Also, the lens's ability to adjust and focus declines as the muscles around it stiffen. *This is what causes difficulty in seeing close objects clearly, called* **presbyopia**, *necessitating either longer arms or corrective lenses.* To complicate matters further, the time our eyes need to change focus from near to far (or vice versa) increases. This also poses a major problem in driving. Because drivers are constantly changing their focus from the instrument panel to other autos and signs on the highway, older drivers may miss important information because of their slower refocusing time.

Besides these normative structural changes, some people experience diseases caused by abnormal structural changes. *First, opaque spots called* **cataracts** *may develop on the lens, which limits the amount of light transmitted.* Cataracts are usually treated by laser surgical removal of the original lens and the insertion of corrective lenses.

Second, the fluid in the eye may not drain properly, causing very high pressure; this condition, called **glaucoma**, *can cause internal damage and progressive loss of vision.* Glaucoma, a fairly common disease in middle and late adulthood, is usually treated with eye drops.

Retinal Changes

The second major family of changes in vision result from changes in the retina (Alavi, 2016). The retina sits along approximately two-thirds of the interior of the eye. The specialized receptor cells in vision, the rods and the cones, are contained in the retina. They are most densely packed toward the rear and especially at the focal point of vision, a region called the macula. At the center of the macula is the fovea, where incoming light is focused for maximum acuity, as when you are reading.

With increasing age, the probability of degeneration of the macula increases (Alavi, 2016). Age-related macular degeneration (AMD) involves the progressive and irreversible destruction of receptors from any of a number of causes. This disease results in the loss of the ability to see details; for example, reading is extremely difficult, and television often is reduced to a blur. It is the leading cause of functional blindness in older adults. There are two forms of AMD: wet and dry. The wet form is usually treated by injection of drugs that stop the abnormal growth of blood vessels under the retina that cause the disease. Unfortunately, there is no effective treatment for the dry form, so physicians recommend a nutrient supplement as a preventive strategy (American Academy of Ophthalmology, 2016).

A second age-related retinal disease is a by-product of diabetes, a chronic disease described in detail in Chapter 4. Diabetes is accompanied by accelerated aging of the arteries, with blindness being one of the more serious side effects. Diabetic retinopathy, as this condition is called, can involve fluid retention in the macula, detachment of the retina, hemorrhage, and aneurysms, and is the most common cause of blindness among working-age people (National Eye Institute, 2015). Because it takes many years to develop, diabetic retinopathy is more common among people who developed diabetes early in life.

The combined effects of the structural changes in the eye reduces the ability to see detail and to discriminate different visual patterns, called acuity. Declines in visual acuity occur steadily between ages 20 and 60, with a more rapid decline thereafter. Loss of acuity is especially noticeable at low light levels (Alavi, 2016).

Psychological Effects of Visual Changes

Clearly, age-related changes in vision affect every aspect of older adults' daily lives and their well-being (Burton, Gibson, & Shaw, 2016; Mojon-Azzi et al., 2008). Imagine the problems people experience performing tasks that most young adults take for granted, such as reading a book, watching television, reading grocery labels, or driving a car. Fortunately, some of the universal changes, such as presbyopia, can be corrected easily through glasses or contacts. Laser surgery to correct cataracts is now routine. But treatment for other conditions, such as dry macular degeneration, remain elusive.

If you want to provide environmental support for older adults, taking their vision changes into account, you need to think through your intervention strategies carefully. For example, simply making the environment brighter may not be the answer. For increased illumination to be beneficial, surrounding surfaces must not increase glare. Using flat latex paint rather than glossy enamel and avoiding highly polished floors are two ways to make environments older adult friendly. There should be high contrast between the background and operational information on dials and controls, such as on stoves and radios. Older adults may also have trouble seeing some fine facial details, which may lead them to decrease their social contacts for fear of not recognizing someone.

Visual impairments with age change the relations between certain personality traits and emotion (Wahl, Heyl, & Schilling, 2012). For instance, the relationship between extraversion and positive emotions is stronger in people with few or no impairments than in people with impairments. Visual problems also increase vulnerability to falls because the person may be unable to see hazards in his or her path or to judge distance very well. Thus, part of Bertha's concern about falling may be caused by changes in her ability to tell where the next step is or to see hazards along the sidewalk.

Hearing

Experiencing hearing loss is one of the most well-known normative changes with age (Davis et al., 2016). A visit to any housing complex for older adults will easily verify this point; you will quickly notice that television sets and radios are turned up fairly loud in most of the apartments. Yet you don't have to be old to experience significant hearing problems. When he began to find it difficult to hear what was being said to him, President Bill Clinton obtained two hearing aids. He was 51 years old at the time, and he attributed his hearing loss to too many high school bands and rock concerts when he was young. His situation is far from unique. Among many other celebrities, Oscar winner Halle Berry and Stephen Colbert both have significant hearing loss.

Due to presbyopia, middle-aged adults typically have trouble reading without glasses.

Loud noise is the chief enemy of hearing at any age. You probably have seen people who work in noisy environments, such as construction workers and musicians during concerts, wearing protective headsets so that they are not exposed to loud noise over extended periods of time.

You don't need to be at a concert to damage your hearing, either. Using headphones or earbuds, especially at high volume, can cause the same serious damage and should be avoided (Jiang et al., 2016). It is especially easy to cause hearing loss with headphones or earbuds if you wear them while exercising; the increased blood flow to the ear during exercise makes hearing receptors more vulnerable to damage. Because young adults do not see their music listening behavior as a risk (Gilliver et al., 2012), hearing loss from this and other sources of loud noise is on the rise. In fact, a systematic review of research indicates that nearly 60% of adolescents and young adults listen to music on personal listening devices at levels that are unsafe, and significant losses in hearing ability result (Jiang et al., 2016). The worse news is that because of these behaviors, hearing loss is likely to increase among older adults in the future (Davis et al., 2016).

The cumulative effects of noise and normative age-related changes create the most common age-related hearing problem: reduced sensitivity to high-pitched tones, called **presbycusis**, *which occurs earlier and more severely than the loss of sensitivity to low-pitched tones* (Davis et al., 2016). Research indicates that by the late 70s, roughly half of older adults have presbycusis. Men typically have greater loss than women, but this may be because of differential exposure to noisy environments. Hearing loss usually is gradual at first but accelerates during the 40s, a pattern shown clearly in Figure 3.5.

FIGURE 3.5 Gender differences in hearing loss. Notice that the changes in men are greater.

Source: Ordy, J. M., Brizzee, K. R., Beavers, T. & Medart, P. (1979). Age differences in the functional and structural organization of the auditory system in man. In J. M. Ordy & K. R. Brizzee (eds.), *Sensory Systems and Communication in the Elderly.* New York, NY: Raven Press.

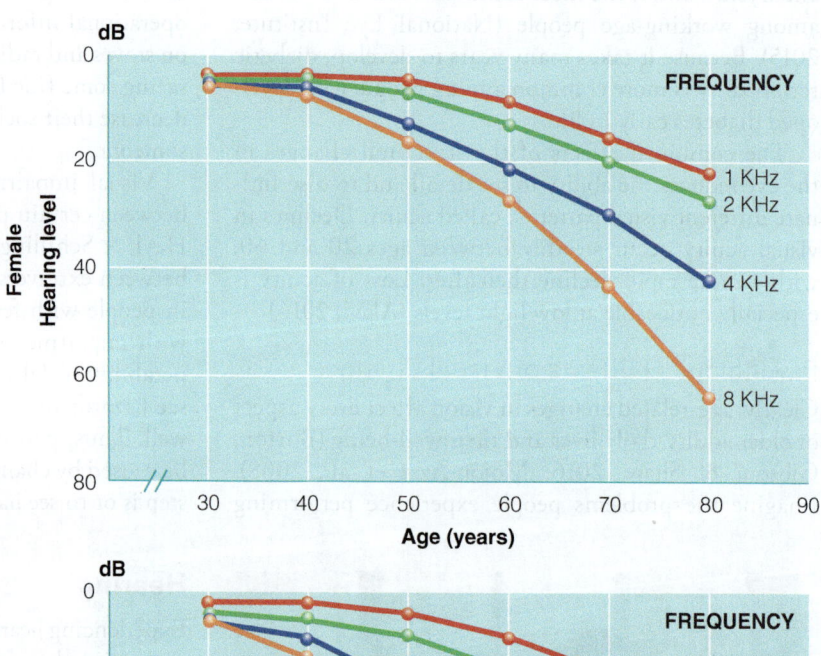

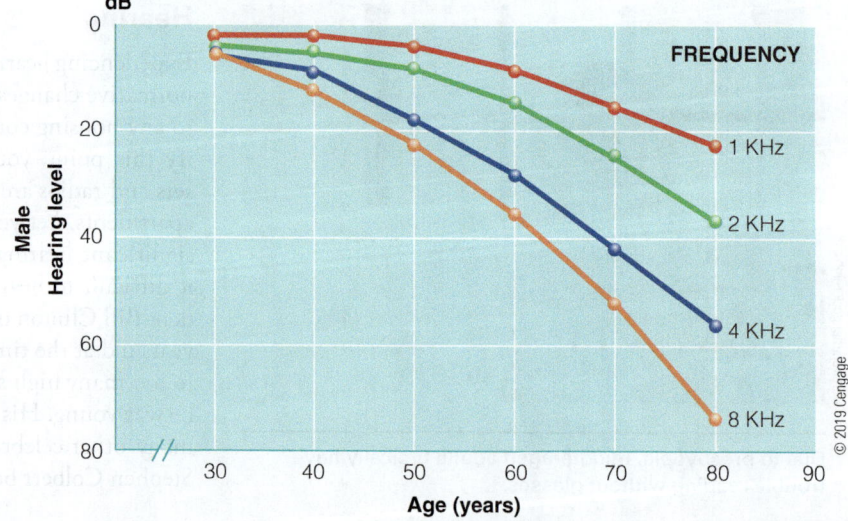

Presbycusis results from four types of changes in the inner ear (Nagaratnam, Nagaratnam & Cheuk, 2016): sensorineural, consisting of atrophy and degeneration of receptor cells or the auditory nerve, and is permanent; and conductive, consisting of obstruction of or damage to the vibrating structures in the outer or middle ear area. Knowing the cause of a person's presbycusis is important, because the different causes have different implications for treatment and for other aspects of hearing (Nagaratnam et al., 2016). Sensory presbycusis has little effect on other hearing abilities. Neural presbycusis seriously affects the ability to understand speech. Metabolic presbycusis produces severe loss of sensitivity to all pitches. Finally, mechanical presbycusis also produces loss across all pitches, but the loss is greatest for high pitches.

Because hearing plays a major role in social communication, its progressive loss could have an equally important effect on people's quality of life (Davis et al., 2016; Heyl & Wahl, 2012). Dalton and colleagues (2003) found that people with moderate to severe hearing loss were significantly more likely to have functional impairments with tasks in daily life (e.g., shopping). In addition, they were more likely to have decreased cognitive functioning. Clearly, significant hearing impairment can result in decreased quality of life (Cherko, Hickson, & Bhutta, 2016). The How Do We Know? feature explores this connection in more detail.

Loss of hearing in later life can also cause numerous adverse emotional reactions, such as loss of independence, social isolation, irritation, paranoia, and depression (Cherko et al., 2016). Much research indicates

How Do We Know?
Hearing and Quality of Life Among Community-Dwelling Older Adults

Who were the investigators, and what were the aims of the studies? As noted in the text, hearing loss can have a negative impact on people's quality of life. Because hearing loss is so widespread among older adults, Polku and colleagues (in press) wondered whether this impact is reflected in all aspects of quality of life (physical, psychological, social, and environmental) and whether it is related only to actual hearing impairment or also to one's perceived hearing loss.

How did the investigators measure the topic of interest? Each participant was given the 16-item Real-Life Environments assessment to measure perceived hearing ability. Higher scores indicate more hearing difficulties. People who had hearing aids gave two responses, one reflecting their hearing with, and the other without, their hearing aid. Additionally, participants were given a pure-tone audiometric hearing test to assess actual hearing ability. Finally, participants completed the 26-item World Health Organization Quality of Life Assessment short version. Higher scores on this scale reflect higher quality of life.

Who were the participants in the study? Participants were a random sample of 230 people drawn from the Life-Space Mobility in Old Age (LISPE) project in Finland. All participants were community dwelling, and were screened for chronic and neurological diseases. The average age of participants was 82 years, with 63% women and 18% stating that they owned a hearing aid.

What was the design of the studies? This study was a substudy of the larger LISPE project. The questionnaires were completed via mail.

Were there ethical concerns with the study? Participants in the study were provided with informed consent and were closely monitored throughout the study, so there were no ethical concerns.

What were the results? Results showed that perceived hearing problems in different real-life environments were negatively correlated with the different domains of quality of life. Interestingly, actual hearing ability as assessed with the audiometric test, was not associated with quality of life.

What did the investigators conclude? Polku and colleagues note two important conclusions from their research. First, physiologic hearing loss, assessed through the audiometric test, is not necessarily a good or accurate assessment of how people perceive their hearing problems and the impact these have on their daily lives. It is critical that both be assessed. Second, perceived hearing difficulties may be a reflection of the challenges posed by actual hearing loss in terms of how well people are able to cope or adapt with the decline. In this sense, the findings fit well with the competence-environmental press model discussed in Chapter 5. That is, if one has the ability and opportunity to compensate for a specific loss, then an individual is able to mitigate or even eliminate any negative effect that loss may have had on quality of life.

hearing loss per se does not cause social maladjustment or emotional disturbance. However, friends and relatives of an older person with undiagnosed or untreated hearing loss often attribute emotional changes to hearing loss, which strains the quality of interpersonal relationships (Li-Korotky, 2012). Thus, hearing loss may not directly affect older adults' self-concept or emotions, but it may negatively affect how they feel about interpersonal communication, especially between couples. Moreover, over 11% of adults with hearing loss report having experienced moderate to severe depression, double the rate of adults without hearing loss (Li et al., 2014). By understanding hearing loss problems and ways to overcome them, people who have no hearing loss can play a large part in minimizing the effects of hearing loss on the older people in their lives.

Fortunately, many people with hearing loss can be helped through two types of amplification systems and cochlear implants, described in Table 3.3. Analog hearing aids are the most common and least expensive, but they provide the lowest-quality sound. Digital hearing aids include microchips that can be programmed for different hearing situations. Cochlear implants do not amplify sound; rather, a microphone transmits sound to a receiver, which stimulates auditory nerve fibers directly. Although technology continues to improve, none of these devices can duplicate your original equipment, so be kind to your ears and keep the volume down on your headphones and earbuds.

Somesthesia and Balance

Imagine that you are locked in an embrace with a lover right now. Think about how good it feels when you are caressed lovingly, the tingly sensations you get. The way your lips feel during a passionate kiss.

You can thank your somesthetic system for that; without it, you probably wouldn't bother acting romantic. Remember Bertha, the older woman worried about falling? To maintain her balance and avoid falling, her somesthetic system integrates a great deal of information about her body position.

Somesthesia

As you've probably discovered, a lover's touch feels different on various parts of your body. That's because the distribution of touch receptors is not consistent throughout the body; the greatest concentrations are in the lips, tongue, and fingertips—as you likely already had figured out. Although it takes more pressure with age to feel a touch on the smooth (non-hairy) skin on the hand, such as the fingertips, touch sensitivity in the hair-covered parts of the body is maintained into later life (Tremblay & Master, 2016).

Older adults often report that they have more trouble regulating body temperature so that they feel comfortable (Guergova & Dufour, 2011). Changes in the perception of temperature are likely caused by aging of the skin and reduction in the number of temperature

TABLE 3.3 Helping People with Hearing Loss

Type of Device	How It Works
Analog hearing aid	Although there are various styles, the basic design is always the same. A mold is placed in the outer ear to pick up sound and send it through a tube to a microphone. The microphone sends the sound to an amplifier. The amplifier enhances the sound and sends it to the receiver. The receiver sends the amplified sound to the ear.
Digital hearing aid	These are similar to analog hearing aids, but digital aids use directional microphones to control the flow of sound. Compression technology allows the sound to be increased or decreased as it rises and falls naturally in the room. Microchips allow hearing aids to be programmed for different hearing situations. This technology also uses multiple channels to deliver sound with varying amplification characteristics.
Cochlear implant	The main difference between hearing aids and cochlear implants is that implants do not make the sound louder. Rather, the implant is a series of components. A microphone, usually mounted behind the ear on the scalp, picks up sound. The sound is digitized by microchips and turned into coded signals, which are broadcast via FM radio signals to electrodes that have been inserted into the inner ear during surgery. The electrodes stimulate the auditory nerve fibers directly.

receptors, as well as possible changes in the peripheral nerves. These changes are greater in the arms and legs. We will consider other aspects of temperature regulation later in this chapter in our discussion of the autonomic nervous system.

Sensations from the skin, internal organs, and joints serve critical functions. They keep us in contact with our environment, help us avoid falling, help us communicate, keep us safe, and factor into our perception of pain. In terms of self-esteem, how well our body is functioning tells us something about how well we are doing. Losing bodily sensations can have major implications; loss of sexual sensitivity and changes in the ability to regulate one's body temperature affect the quality of life. How a person views these changes is critical for maintaining self-esteem. We can help by providing supportive environments that lead to successful compensatory behaviors. Despite years of research, we do not understand how or even whether our ability to perceive these sensations changes with age. Part of the problem has to do with how such sensations, including pain, are measured and how individual differences in tolerance affects people's reports.

Balance

Bertha, the older woman we met in the vignette, is like many older adults—she is worried about losing her balance and falling. She has good reason to be concerned. Each year, about one-third of adults over age 65 fall (National Council on Aging, 2016). Falls are the leading cause of fatal injury and of nonfatal injuries requiring hospitalization in older adults.

Bertha (and each of us) gets information about balance mainly from the vestibular system, housed deep in the inner ear, but the eyes also provide important cues. The vestibular system is designed to respond to the forces of gravity as they act on the head and then to provide this information to the parts of the brain that initiate the appropriate movements so that we can maintain balance. The eyes send signals to the back of the brain (the occipital cortex) and provide visual cues about maintaining balance.

Importantly, changes in the brain are associated with falling. Changes in white matter in the frontal cortex and in the occipital cortex that occur with age have been shown to be related to difficulty in maintaining proper balance (van Impe et al., 2012). The importance of white matter in aging was discussed in Chapter 2. Similarly, lower amounts of gray matter at any age are associated with increased risk of falling, leading researchers to conclude that gray matter protects adults from falling (Boisgontier et al., 2016).

Dizziness (the vague feeling of being unsteady, floating, and light-headed) and vertigo (the sensation that one or one's surroundings are spinning) are common experiences for older adults. Although age-related structural changes in the vestibular system account for some of the problems, they do not entirely account for increases in dizziness and vertigo. Also, it takes older adults longer to integrate all the other sensory information coming to the brain to control posture (Aldwin & Gilmer, 2013). And dizziness can be a side effect of certain medications and physical illnesses.

Because of these changes, the likelihood of falling increases with age, especially after age 70 (National Council on Aging, 2016). However, the risk of falls can be reduced through several simple interventions. For example, environmental hazards such as loose rugs and slippery floors can be made safer.

Because fear of falling has a real basis, it is important that concerns not be taken lightly (Granacher, Muehlbauer, & Gruber, 2012). Careful assessment of balance is important in understanding the nature and precise source of older adults' problems. Indeed, balance training is the most common form of fall prevention intervention, and is reasonably effective (Criter & Honaker, 2016; Tsang & Fu, 2016). Such training can even be successful using virtual reality such as Wii Fit. People can also be trained to prevent falls through tai chi (Holmes et al., 2016; Li et al., 2008).

Taste and Smell

Taste

There is an expression "too old to cut the mustard," which dates to when people made mustard at home by grinding mustard seed and adding just the right amount of vinegar ("cutting the mustard") to balance the taste. If too much vinegar was added, the concoction tasted terrible, so the balance was critical. Many families found that older members tended to add too much vinegar.

Despite the everyday belief that taste ability changes with age, we do not have much data documenting what actually happens. We do know that the ability to detect different tastes declines gradually and that these declines vary a great deal from flavor to flavor and person to person (Doets & Kremer, 2016). Food preferences also change, influenced mainly by social and psychological factors, such as what others are eating and what is currently fashionable, making it difficult to draw firm conclusions about age-related change. Whatever age differences we observe are not caused by a decline in the sheer number of taste buds (Imoscopi et al., 2012). There is evidence that the ability to taste sour and bitter tastes changes most (thus, the trouble with cutting the mustard), but the physiological reasons for this are not yet understood due to the negative effects on taste from medications and chronic diseases (Sergi et al., 2017).

The influence of disease and medication, combined with the psycho-social aspects of eating, may underlie older adults' complaints about boring food, that in turn may underlie increased risk of malnutrition (Henkin, 2008). For instance, we are much more likely to eat a balanced diet and to enjoy our food when we feel well enough to cook, when we do not eat alone, and when we get a whiff of the enticing aromas from the kitchen. Speaking of enticing aromas…

Smell

"Those cookies smell delicious!" "Stop and smell the roses." "Ooh! What's that perfume you're wearing?" "Yuck! What's that smell?" There is a great deal of truth in the saying "The nose knows." Smell is a major part of our everyday lives. How something smells can alert us that dinner is cooking, warn of a gas leak or a fire, let us know that we are clean, or be sexually arousing. Many of our social interactions involve smell (or the lack of it). We spend billions of dollars making our bodies smell appealing to others. It is easy to see that any age-related change in sense of smell would have far-reaching consequences.

Researchers agree that the ability to detect odors remains fairly intact until the 60s, when it begins to decline, but there are wide variations across people and types of odors (Croy, Nordin, & Hummel, 2014). These variations could have important practical implications. A large survey conducted by the National Geographic Society indicated that older adults were not as able to identify particular odors as younger people. One of the odors tested was the substance added to natural gas that enables people to detect leaks—not being able to identify it is a potentially fatal problem.

Abnormal changes in the ability to smell are turning out to be important in the differential diagnosis of probable Alzheimer's disease, resulting in the development of several quick tests such as the Pocket Smell Test (Steffens & Potter, 2008). According to several studies, people with Alzheimer's disease can identify only 60% of the odors identified by age-matched control participants; in more advanced stages of the disease, this further declined to only 40% compared with controls. Further research suggests that a screening test using cinnamon, fish odor, and banana can successfully identify older adults with normal odor identification ability (Lötsch, Ultsch, & Hummel, 2016). These changes and an apparently easy screening test give clinicians important tools for diagnosing suspected cases of abnormal development, including dementia.

The major psychological consequences of changes in smell concern eating, safety, and pleasurable experiences. Odors play an important role in enjoying food and protecting us from harm. Socially, decreases in our ability to detect unpleasant odors may lead to embarrassing situations in which we are unaware that we have body odors or need to brush our teeth. Social interactions could suffer as a result of these problems. Smells also play a key role in remembering life experiences from the past. Who can forget the smell of cookies baking in Grandma's oven? Loss of odor cues may mean that our sense of the past suffers as well.

How food tastes is a complex interaction among smell, psychological, and social factors in addition to the basic ability to taste.

Adult Development in Action

If you were a consultant asked to design the optimal home environment for older adults, what specific design features would you include that would provide support for normative age-related sensory changes? (Keep your answer and refer to it in Chapter 5.)

3.4 Vital Functions

LEARNING OBJECTIVES

- What age-related changes occur in the cardiovascular system? What types of cardiovascular disease are common in adult development and aging? What are the psychological effects of age-related changes in the cardiovascular system?
- What structural and functional changes occur with age in the respiratory system? What are the most common types of respiratory diseases in older adults? What are the psychological effects of age-related changes in the respiratory system?

Steve is an active 73-year-old man who walks and plays golf regularly. He smoked earlier in his life, but he quit years ago. He also watches his diet to control fat intake. Steve recently experienced some chest pains and sweating but dismissed it as simply age related. After all, he thinks, I take care of myself. However, Steve's wife, Grace, is concerned he may have a more serious problem.

You gotta have heart. It's quite simple—You cannot live without your cardiovascular (heart and blood vessels) and your respiratory (lungs and air passageways) systems; that's why they are called vital functions. Each undergoes important normative changes with age that can affect the quality of life. In this section, we'll find out whether Grace has reason to worry about Steve's symptoms. We'll also discover why figuring out the pattern of age-related changes in the respiratory system is very difficult (here's a tip—it has to do with biological-psychological-environmental interactions).

Overall, the age-related changes in the cardiovascular and respiratory systems are excellent examples of how the forces of development interact. On the biological front, we know that some cardiovascular and respiratory diseases have important genetic links. Psychologically, certain personality traits have been linked with increased risk of disease. Socioculturally, some cardiovascular and respiratory diseases are clearly tied to lifestyle. The impact of both cardiovascular and respiratory diseases also differs as a function of age. Let's explore in more detail how these various forces come together.

Cardiovascular System

Tune into your pulse. The beating of your heart is the work of an amazing organ. In an average lifetime, the heart beats more than 3 billion times, pumping the equivalent of more than 900 million gallons of blood. Two important age-related structural changes in the heart are the accumulation of fat deposits and the stiffening of the heart muscle caused by tissue changes. By the late 40s and early 50s, the fat deposits in the lining around the heart may form a continuous sheet. Meanwhile, healthy muscle tissue is being replaced by connective tissue, which causes a thickening and stiffening of the heart muscle and valves. These changes reduce the amount of muscle tissue available to contract the heart. The net effect is that the remaining muscle must work harder. To top it off, the amount of blood that the heart can pump declines from roughly 5 liters per minute at age 20 to about 3.5 liters per minute at age 70 (National Institute on Aging, 2015a).

The most important age-related change in the circulatory system involves the stiffening (hardening) of the walls of the arteries. These changes are caused by calcification of the arterial walls and by replacement of elastic fibers with less elastic ones.

The combination of changes in the heart and the circulatory system results in a significant decrease in a person's ability to cope with physical exertion, especially aerobic exercise. By age 65, the average adult has experienced a 60 to 70% decline in the aerobic capacity since young adulthood. However, if you stay in good shape throughout adulthood, the decline is much less (National Institute on Aging, 2015a). This decline is one reason why older adults who are not in good physical shape are more likely to have heart attacks while performing moderately exerting tasks such as shoveling snow. The changes that occur with aging in the heart related to exercise are shown in Figure 3.6.

Cardiovascular Diseases

In the United States, more than 30% of the people currently have some form of cardiovascular disease; this rate may increase as the overall population continues to age (Mozaffarian et al., 2016). It is the leading cause of death in all ethnic groups in the United States and in many other countries. The incidence of cardiovascular disease increases dramatically with age, with the rates for men higher until age 75 for coronary heart disease and for women higher for stroke. The rate of cardiovascular disease in women increases after menopause, and converges with that of men over age 75. These are deadly statistics. One in every three deaths in the United States is caused by cardiovascular disease.

FIGURE 3.6 The Heart: Young and Old.

Source: National Institute on Aging. (2008). *Aging Hearts and Arteries: A Scientific Quest*. Design by Levine and Associates, Washington, DC. Retrieved from www.nia.nih.gov/health/publication/aging-hearts-and-arteries/preface.

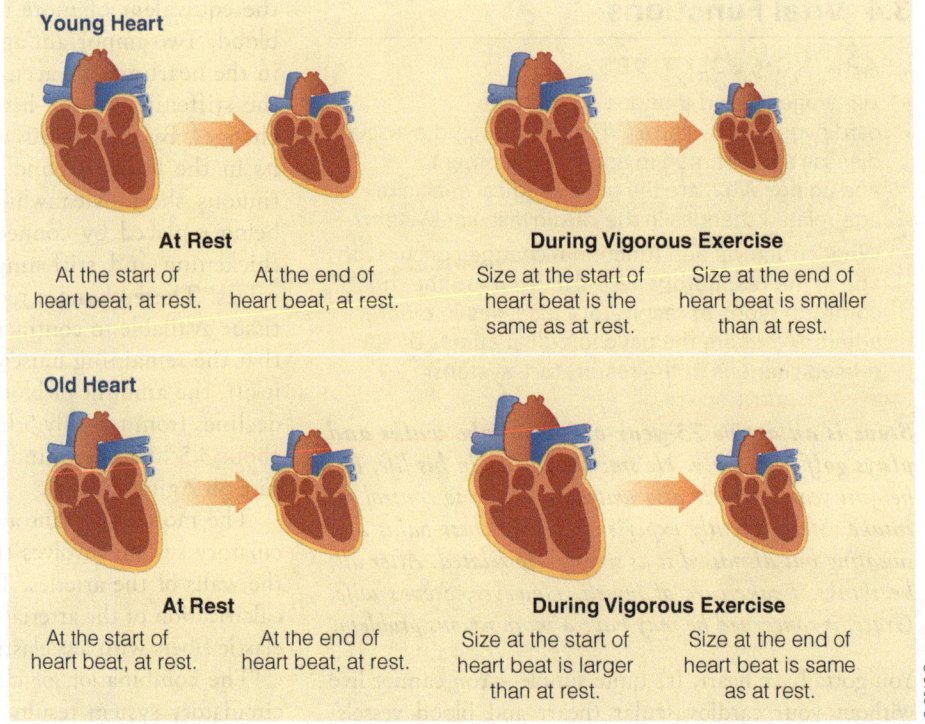

In terms of ethnic differences in various types of cardiovascular disease, African Americans, American Indians, and Native Hawaiians have the highest rates of hypertension (high blood pressure; we will consider this condition a bit later), and Asian Americans have the lowest rate of heart disease (Mozaffarian et al., 2016). In part these differences are due to genetics, and in part they are due to lifestyle and inadequate access to health care.

The good news is that rates of cardiovascular disease have been declining in the United States, especially among men, since the 1980s (Mozaffarian et al., 2016). In part this is due to lower rates of smoking and better nutrition. However, these declines may be deceiving, because key risk factors are actually increasing; for example, roughly two-thirds of adults are classified as overweight, and rates of diabetes are going up.

Several types of cardiovascular disease are noteworthy in relation to age. **Congestive heart failure** *occurs when cardiac output and the ability of the heart to contract severely decline, making the heart enlarge, pressure in the veins increase, and the body swell.* Congestive heart failure is the most common cause of hospitalization for people over age 65. **Angina pectoris** *occurs when the oxygen supply to the heart muscle becomes insufficient, resulting in chest pain.* Angina may feel like chest pressure, a burning pain, or a squeezing that radiates from the chest to the back, neck, and arms (Mayo Clinic, 2016a). In most cases the pain is induced by physical exertion and is relieved within 5 to 10 minutes by rest. The most common treatment of angina is nitroglycerine, although in some cases coronary arteries may need to be cleared through surgical procedures or replaced through coronary bypass surgery.

Heart attack, called **myocardial infarction (MI)**, *occurs when blood supply to the heart is severely reduced or cut off.* Mortality after a heart attack is much higher for older adults (Mozaffarian et al., 2016). The initial symptoms of an MI may be identical to those of angina but typically are more severe and prolonged; there may also be nausea, vomiting, numbness or severe weakness, back or jaw pain, and sweating, which Steve experienced in the vignette. Thus, Grace is right to be concerned about Steve's symptoms.

For both women and men, the most common symptom of MI is chest pain, but women are more likely to experience some of the other symptoms. Additionally, women can experience MI without chest pain or pressure (American Heart Association, 2016a). Treating heart attack victims of all ages includes careful evaluation and a prescribed rehabilitation program consisting of lifestyle changes in diet and exercise.

Atherosclerosis

Atherosclerosis *is an age-related disease caused by the buildup of fat deposits on and the calcification of the arterial walls* (National Heart, Lung and Blood Institute, 2015). A diagram depicting how atherosclerosis develops is shown in Figure 3.7. Much like sandbars in a river or mineral deposits in pipes, the fat deposits that develop inside arteries interfere with and restrict blood flow. These deposits begin very early in life and continue throughout the life span. Some amount of fat deposit inevitably occurs and is considered a normal part of aging. However, excess deposits may develop from poor nutrition, smoking, and other aspects of an unhealthy lifestyle.

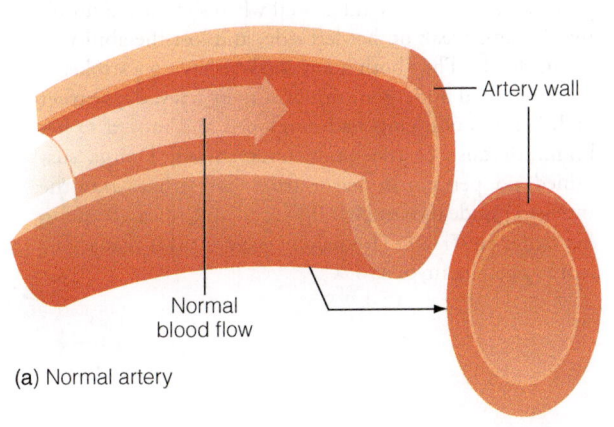

When severe atherosclerosis occurs in blood vessels that supply the brain, neurons may not receive proper nourishment, causing them to malfunction or die, a condition called cerebrovascular disease. *When the blood flow to a portion of the brain is completely cut off, a* **cerebrovascular accident (CVA)**, *or stroke, results.* Estimates are that someone in the United States dies from a CVA every four minutes, making stroke one of the most common forms of cardiovascular disease (Centers for Disease Control and Prevention, 2016a). Causes of CVAs include clots that block blood flow in an artery or the actual breaking of a blood vessel, which creates a cerebral hemorrhage.

The severity of a CVA and likelihood of recovery depend on the specific area of the brain involved, the extent of disruption in blood flow, and the duration of the disruption. Consequently, a CVA may affect such a small area that it goes almost unnoticed, or it may be so severe as to cause immediate death. Two common problems following a CVA are *aphasia* (problems with speech) and *hemiplegia* (paralysis on one side of the body).

The risk of a CVA increases with age, and is much more common among African Americans, American Indians, and Alaska Natives than for other groups (Centers for Disease Control and Prevention, 2016b). The higher risk among these three groups appears to be caused by a greater prevalence of hypertension in this population compounded by poorer quality and access to health care in general (Centers for Disease Control and Prevention, 2016a).

Treatment of CVA has advanced significantly. The most important advance is use of the clot-dissolving drug tissue plasminogen activator (tPA) to treat CVAs (American Stroke Association, 2016). Currently, tPA is the only approved treatment for CVAs caused by blood clots, which constitute 80% of all CVAs. Not every patient should receive tPA treatment, and tPA is effective only if given promptly, which is vitally important. So if you or a person you know thinks they are experiencing a CVA, get medical attention immediately, because tPA therapy must be started within 3 hours after the onset of a stroke to be most effective. A second treatment for stroke caused by a blood clot is surgical removal of the clot.

Recovery from CVA depends on the severity of the stroke, area and extent of the brain affected, and patient age. It can be a long, difficult process, as described in the Real People feature.

Besides blood clots, high blood pressure plays a major role in CVAs. (Do you know what yours is?) Blood pressure consists of measuring two types of

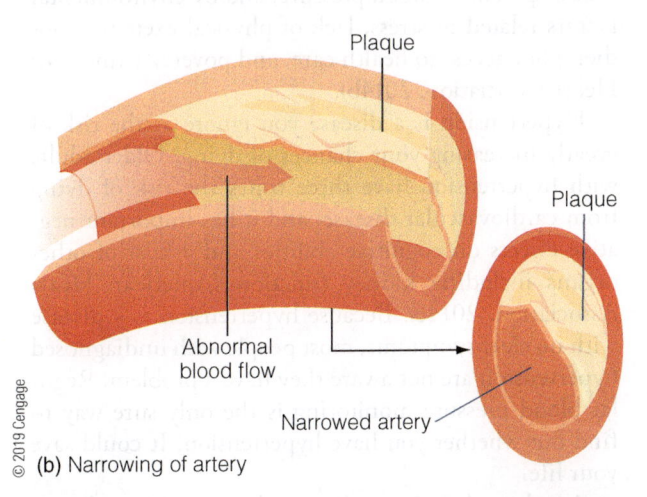

FIGURE 3.7 Normal artery and atherosclerosis. (A) shows a normal artery with normal blood flow. (B) shows an artery with plaque buildup.

Source: National Heart, Lung and Blood Institute (2011). Retrieved from www.nhlbi.nih.gov/health/health topics/topics/atherosclerosis/.

Real People
Donna Arnett's Recovery from Stroke

By all measures, Dr. Donna K. Arnett is highly successful. She serves as the dean of the College of Public Health at the University of Kentucky and was the first epidemiologist to be named president of the American Heart Association. She is an internationally recognized scholar on hypertension. Yet, Dr. Arnett came close to achieving none of this success. At age 27, she suffered a stroke.

As Donna herself describes it, one morning she woke at 5:30 a.m., and as usual let her dog, Nikki, out. After getting a cup of coffee, she went to call Nikki back. The words that came out were not what she intended to say. She felt "fuzzy," but nonetheless drove to work. When that feeling didn't improve, she went to her boss. Because she was a practicing nurse, Donna knew she had a serious problem, and her boss did as well when she started drooling, became weak on her left side, and lost the ability to speak clearly. They both knew she was having a stroke.

Arnett had undergone minor surgery a few days earlier and, it turns out, clots had developed and moved to her brain. Because of the quick intervention, Donna sustained no permanent harm from her stroke. But the intense episode did lead her into academic research and to her career in service. Donna's message to all is that stroke can happen to anyone.

Donna K. Arnett

---

pressure: the pressure during the heart's contraction phase when it is pumping blood through the body, called the *systolic pressure*, and the pressure during the heart's relaxation phase between beats, called the *diastolic pressure*. The systolic pressure is always given first. On average, a blood pressure of 120 over 80 mm Hg (millimeters of mercury, the scale on which the pressure is measured) or a bit lower is considered optimal for adults.

As we grow older, blood pressure tends to increase normally, mostly because of structural changes in the cardiovascular system. When blood pressure increases become severe, defined as 140 mm Hg or more systolic pressure (the top number in a blood pressure reading) or 90 mm Hg or more diastolic pressure (the lower number in the reading), the disease **hypertension** results (American Heart Association, 2014a). Nearly one-third of the population age 18 and older has some degree of hypertension. This rate is roughly the same for European Americans and Mexican Americans, but jumps to about 40% among African Americans. This difference may be caused by a genetic mutation affecting enzymes that help control blood pressure, and by environmental factors related to stress, lack of physical exercise, poor diet, poor access to health care, and poverty (American Heart Association, 2014b).

Hypertension is a disease you ignore at the risk of greatly increasing your chances of dying. Older adults with hypertension have three times the risk of dying from cardiovascular disease, and it has important negative effects on cognitive abilities and a host of other organs including kidney function (American Heart Association, 2014c). Because hypertension is a disease with no clear symptoms, most people with undiagnosed hypertension are not aware they have a problem. Regular blood pressure monitoring is the only sure way to find out whether you have hypertension. It could save your life.

Another chronic cardiovascular condition that is discussed less often is *hypotension,* or low blood pressure. Symptoms of hypotension include dizziness or light-headedness that is caused most commonly when you stand up quickly after lying down or sitting, or sometimes after eating (American Heart Association, 2014d). Hypotension often is related to anemia and is more common in older adults. Although hypotension per se is not a dangerous condition, the resulting dizziness and other symptoms can increase the likelihood of fainting and falls, which may result in more serious injury.

Respiratory System

You probably don't pay much attention to your breathing unless you're gasping for breath after exercise—or you're an older adult. Older adults tend to notice their breathing a great deal more. Why? With increasing age, the rib cage and the air passageways become stiffer, making it harder to breathe. The lungs change in appearance over time, going gradually from their youthful pinkish color to a dreary gray, caused mainly by breathing in carbon particles (from air pollution). The maximum amount of air we can take into the lungs in a single breath begins to decline in the 20s, decreasing by 40% by age 85. The rate at which we can exchange oxygen for carbon dioxide also drops significantly as the membranes of the air sacs in the lungs deteriorate. Even people who report no symptoms have more cysts and show several changes in the bronchial tubes (Copley, 2016).

One of the difficulties in understanding age-related changes in the respiratory system is that it is hard to know how much of the change is caused specifically by normative developmental factors and how much is caused by environmental factors. For example, it is difficult to determine how much age-related change in respiratory function is due to air pollution and how much is due to the processes underlying aging.

Respiratory Diseases

The most common and incapacitating respiratory disorder in older adults is **chronic obstructive pulmonary disease (COPD),** *a family of diseases that includes chronic bronchitis and emphysema.* COPD is the third-leading-cause of death in the United States. Over 11 million people have been diagnosed with COPD, but as many as 24 million may have it and not know it. Both the rates of COPD and deaths from it are higher in women than in men. Smoking is the most important cause of COPD, but secondhand smoke, air pollution, and industrial dusts and chemicals can also cause it (American Lung Association, 2016).

Emphysema *is the most serious type of COPD and is characterized by the destruction of the membranes around the air sacs in the lungs* (American Lung Association, 2016). This irreversible destruction creates holes in the lung, drastically reducing the ability to exchange oxygen and carbon dioxide. To make matters worse, the bronchial tubes collapse prematurely when the person exhales, thereby preventing the lungs from emptying completely. Emphysema is a very debilitating disease. In its later stages, even the smallest physical exertion causes a struggle for air. People with emphysema may have such poorly oxygenated blood that they become confused and disoriented. Most cases of emphysema are self-induced by smoking or other form of pollution; the remaining cases are caused by a genetic deficiency of a protein known as a 1-antitrypsin (WebMD, 2016). This protein, a natural lung protector, is made by the liver; when it is missing, emphysema is inevitable. Although some drugs are available to help ease breathing, lung transplantation remains a treatment of last resort for people with emphysema, especially in the genetic form of the disease.

Chronic bronchitis, another form of COPD, can occur at any age, but it is more common in people over age 45, especially among people who are exposed to high concentrations of dust, irritating fumes, and air pollution. Treatment usually consists of medication (called bronchodilators) to open bronchial passages and a change of work environment. Similarly, asthma is another very common respiratory disease that is increasing in prevalence. Treatment for asthma also involves the use of bronchodilators.

Researchers are gathering evidence that e-cigarettes can at least damage the lungs and possibly result in COPD (Ween et al., 2016). Far from being benign, vaping is turning out to be a harmful habit after all.

Overall, treatment for COPD needs to begin as soon as a problem is diagnosed. The most important step is to stop smoking if you are a smoker. In some cases, supplemental oxygen or glucocorticosteroid medications may provide some relief. The thing to remember, though, is that the damage caused by COPD is irreversible.

Adult Development In Action

If you ran a training program for personal exercise trainers, what age-related changes in vital functions would you emphasize?

3.5 The Reproductive System

LEARNING OBJECTIVES
- What reproductive changes occur in women?
- What reproductive changes occur in men?
- What are the psychological effects of reproductive changes?

Helen woke up in the middle of the night drenched in sweat. *She'd been feeling fine when she went to bed after her 48th birthday party, so she wasn't sure what was the matter. She thought she was too young to experience menopause. Helen wonders what other things she'll experience.*

As you probably surmised, Helen has begun going through "the change," a time of life that many women look forward to and just as many see as the beginning of old age. For women like Helen, "the change" is the defining physiological event in middle age. Men do not endure such sweeping biological changes, experiencing several gradual changes instead. Beyond the physiological effects, these changes related to reproduction have important psychological implications because many people use them as a trigger for redefining themselves. Let's see how the experience differs for women and men.

Female Reproductive System

As Helen is beginning to experience, the major reproductive change in women during adulthood is the loss of the natural ability to bear children. *As women enter midlife, they experience a major biological process, called the* **climacteric**, *during which they pass from their reproductive to nonreproductive years.* **Menopause** *is the point at which menstruation stops.*

The major reproductive change in women during adulthood is the loss of the natural ability to bear children. (Pregnancy and childbirth are still possible, though, through medical intervention.) This change begins in the 40s as menstrual cycles become irregular, and by age 50 to 55 it is usually complete (MedlinePlus, 2014). *This time of transition from regular menstruation to menopause is called* **perimenopause**, *and how long it lasts varies considerably.* The gradual loss and eventual end of monthly periods is accompanied by decreases in estrogen and progesterone levels, changes in the reproductive organs, and changes in sexual functioning.

A variety of physical and psychological symptoms may accompany perimenopause and menopause with decreases in hormonal levels (WomensHealth.gov, 2010): hot flashes, night sweats, headaches, sleep problems, mood changes, more urinary infections, pain during sex, difficulty concentrating, vaginal dryness, less interest in sex, and an increase in body fat around the waist. Many women report no symptoms at all, but most women experience at least some, and there are large differences across social, ethnic, and cultural groups in how they are expressed (Nosek, Kennedy, & Gudmundsdottir, 2012). For example, women in the Mayan culture of Mexico and Central America welcome menopause and its changes as a natural phenomenon and do not attach any stigma to aging (Mahady et al., 2008). In the United States, Latinas and African Americans, especially working-class women, tend to view menopause more positively, whereas European American women describe it more negatively (Dillaway et al., 2008). Women in South American countries report a variety of symptoms that impair quality of life, many of which persist five years beyond menopause (Blümel et al., 2012).

Several treatments have been researched to alleviate menopausal symptoms, including estrogen replacement therapy (discussed next), and nonpharmacological interventions such as diet, particularly soy (Schmidt et al., 2016), and yoga (Jorge et al., 2016). Because there appears to be a genetic component to the experience of symptoms that may also help explain the wide variations in experiences, an emergent treatment approach is pharmacogenomics, the tailoring of medical intervention to each individual's specific genetics (Moyer, Miller, & Faubion, 2016).

The decline in estrogen that women experience after menopause is a very big deal. Estrogen loss is related to numerous health conditions, including increased risk of osteoporosis, cardiovascular disease, stress urinary incontinence (involuntary loss of urine during physical stress, as when exercising, sneezing, or laughing), weight gain, and memory loss, in short, almost every major body system (Women's Health Research Institute, 2016). Consider just one negative effect—cardiovascular disease. At age 50 (prior to menopause) women have three times less risk of heart attacks than men on average. Ten years after menopause, when women are about 60, their risk equals that of men. Clearly, estrogen depletion has a negative effect on health.

In response to these increased risks and to the estrogen-related symptoms that women experience, one approach is the use of **menopausal hormone therapy (MHT)**: *women take low doses of estrogen, which is often combined with progestin (synthetic form of progesterone).* Hormone therapy is controversial and has been the focus of many research studies with conflicting results (North American Menopause Society, 2016). There appear to be both benefits and risks with MHT, as discussed in the Current Controversies Feature.

Women's genital organs undergo progressive change after menopause. The vaginal walls shrink and become thinner, the size of the vagina decreases, vaginal lubrication is reduced and delayed, and the external genitalia

CURRENT CONTROVERSIES
Menopausal Hormone Therapy

For many years, women have had the choice of taking medications to replace the female hormones that are no longer produced naturally by the body after menopause. Hormone therapy may involve taking estrogen alone or in combination with progesterone (or progestin in its synthetic form). Research on the effects of menopause hormone therapy have helped clarify the appropriate use of such medications.

Until about 2003, it was thought that menopausal hormone therapy (MHT) was beneficial for most women, and results from several studies were positive. But results from the Women's Health Initiative research in the United States and from the Million Women Study in the United Kingdom indicated that, for some types of MHT, there were several potentially serious side effects. As a result, physicians are now far more cautious in recommending MHT.

The Women's Health Initiative (WHI), begun in the United States in 1991, was a very large study (National Heart, Lung, and Blood Institute, 2010). The estrogen plus progestin trial used 0.625 milligram of estrogen taken daily plus 2.5 milligrams of medroxyprogesterone acetate (Prempro) taken daily. This combination was chosen because it is the mostly commonly prescribed form of the combined hormone therapy in the United States and, in several observational studies, had appeared to benefit women's health. The women in the WHI estrogen plus progestin study were aged 50 to 79 when they enrolled in the study between 1993 and 1998. The health of study participants was carefully monitored by an independent panel called the Data and Safety Monitoring Board (DSMB). The study was stopped in July 2002 because investigators discovered a significant increased risk for breast cancer and that overall the risks outnumbered the benefits. However, in addition to the increased risk of breast cancer, heart attack, stroke, and blood clots, MHT resulted in fewer hip fractures and lower rates of colorectal cancer.

The Million Women Study began in 1996 and includes 1 in 4 women over age 50 in the United Kingdom, the largest study of its kind ever conducted. Like the Women's Health Initiative, the study examines how MHT (both estrogen/progestin combinations and estrogen alone) affects breast cancer, cardiovascular disease, and other aspects of women's health. Results from this study confirmed the Women's Health Initiative outcome of increased risk for breast cancer associated with MHT.

A third important study is the Kronos Early Estrogen Prevention Study (KEEPS). In the primary study, 727 women were randomly assigned to three groups. One group received a dose of Premarin that was lower than in the WHI study, another group received a patch, and the third group received a placebo. Both treatment groups experienced a drop in menopausal symptoms. Most important, all three groups showed similar changes in cardiovascular function and no significant changes in biomarkers, no significant differences in breast cancer rates, or in rate of blood clots.

The combined results from the WHI, the Million Women Study, and the KEEPS led physicians to modify their recommendations regarding MHT (Moyer et al., 2016; North American Menopause Society, 2016; Women's Health Research Institute, 2016). Specifically, the joint recommendation of the American Society for Reproductive Medicine, The Endocrine Society, and the North American Menopause Society is that MHT is reasonably safe for healthy women under age 60 who have moderate to severe menopausal symptoms. Advances in genomics is likely to make MHT more precise because of the increasing ability to tailor the hormone therapy to each woman's own genetics (Moyer et al., 2016; Panay, 2016).

MHT is not recommend for women over age 60 or for those who have significant risk factors for side effects (e.g., blood clots). Additionally, women over age 60 who begin MHT are at increased risk for certain cancers.

In sum, women face difficult choices when deciding whether to use MHT as a means of com-batting certain menopausal symptoms and protecting themselves against other diseases. For example, MHT can help reduce hot flashes and night sweats, help reduce vaginal dryness and discomfort during sexual intercourse, slow bone loss, and perhaps ease mood swings. On the other hand, MHT can increase a woman's risk of blood clots, heart attack, stroke, breast cancer, and gallbladder disease.

The best course of action is to consult closely with one's physician to weigh the benefits and risks.

shrink somewhat. These changes have important effects on sexual activity, such as an increased possibility of painful intercourse and a longer time and more stimulation needed to reach orgasm. Failure to achieve orgasm is more common in midlife and beyond than in a woman's younger years. However, maintaining an active sex life throughout adulthood lowers the degree to which problems are encountered. Despite these changes, there is no physiological reason not to continue having an active and enjoyable sex life from middle age through late life. The vaginal dryness that occurs, for example, can be countered by using personal lubricants, such as *K-Y* or *Astroglide*.

Whether women continue to have an active sex life has a lot more to do with the availability of a suitable partner than a woman's desire for sexual relations. This is especially true for older women. The AARP *Modern Maturity* sexuality study (AARP, 1999), the *Sex in America* study (AARP, 2005), and the *Sex, Romance, and Relationships* (AARP, 2010) studies all found that older married women were far more likely to have an active sex life than unmarried women. The primary reason for the decline in women's sexual activity with age is the lack of a willing or appropriate partner, not a lack of physical ability or desire (AARP, 1999, 2005, 2010).

Male Reproductive System

Unlike women, men do not have a physiological (and cultural) event to mark reproductive changes, although there is a gradual decline in testosterone levels (Gunes et al., 2016) that can occur to a greater extent in men who are obese or have diabetes (Nigro & Christ-Crain, 2012). Men do not experience a complete loss of the ability to father children, as this varies widely from individual to individual, but men do experience a normative decline in the quantity of sperm (Gunes et al., 2016). However, even at age 80 a man is still half as fertile as he was at age 25 and is quite capable of fathering a child.

With increasing age the prostate gland enlarges, becomes stiffer, and may obstruct the urinary tract. Prostate cancer becomes a real threat during middle age; annual screenings are often recommended for men over age 50 (American Cancer Society, 2012a).

Men experience some physiological changes in sexual performance. By old age, men report less perceived demand to ejaculate, a need for longer time and more stimulation to achieve erection and orgasm, and a much longer resolution phase during which erection is impossible (Gunes et al., 2016). Older men also report more frequent failures to achieve orgasm and loss of erection during intercourse (AARP, 1999, 2005, 2010). However, the advent of Viagra, Cialis, and other medications to treat erectile dysfunction has provided older men with easy-to-use medical treatments and the possibility of an active sex life well into later life.

As with women, as long as men enjoy sex and have a willing partner, sexual activity is a lifelong option. Also as with women, the most important ingredient of sexual intimacy for men is a strong relationship with a partner (AARP, 1999, 2005, 2010). For example, married men in early middle age tend to have intercourse four to eight times per month, but this rate drops about 20% per decade. The loss of an available partner is a significant reason frequency of intercourse decreases with age. Still, late middle-aged and older people continue to enjoy themselves. Nearly three-quarters of people 57–64 had sex during the past year, as did over half of those 65–74 and over 25% of those 75–85 (Watson, 2013). Practicing safe sex is equally important for older adults, as sexually transmitted disease remains a major concern.

Psychological Implications

Older adults say that engaging in sexual behavior is an important aspect of human relationships throughout adulthood (AARP, 1999, 2005, 2010). Healthy adults at any age are capable of having and enjoying sexual relationships. Moreover, the desire to do so normally does not diminish. Unfortunately, one of the myths in our society is that older adults cannot and should not be sexual. Many young adults find it difficult to think about their grandparents having great sex.

Such stereotyping has important consequences. What do you think to yourself when we see an older couple being publicly affectionate? Can you envision your grandparents enjoying an active sex life? Many people feel that such behavior is cute. But observers tend not to refer to their own or their peers' relationships in this way. Many nursing homes and other institutions actively dissuade their residents from having sexual relationships and may even refuse to allow married couples to share the same room. Adult children may believe their widowed parent does not have the right to establish a new sexual relationship. The message we are sending is that sexual activity is fine for the young but not for the old. The major reason why older women do not engage in sexual relations is the lack of a socially sanctioned partner. It is not that they have lost interest; rather, they believe they are simply not permitted to express their sexuality any longer.

Adult Development in Action

As a gerontologist, what do you think should be done to create a more realistic view of reproductive changes and interest in sex across the adult lifespan?

3.6 The Autonomic Nervous System

LEARNING OBJECTIVES
- What major changes occur in the autonomic nervous system?
- What are the psychological effects of changes in the autonomic nervous system?

Jorge is an active 83-year-old former factory worker who lives with his wife, Olivia, in a crowded apartment in Los Angeles. Over the past few years, Jorge has had increasing difficulty handling the heat of southern California summers. Olivia has noticed that Jorge takes more naps during the day and sleeps poorly at night. Jorge and Olivia wonder whether there is something wrong with him.

As we saw in Chapter 2, our brains are the most complex structures yet discovered in the universe. Everything that makes us individuals is housed in the brain, and we are only now beginning to unlock its mysteries through the techniques described in Chapter 2.

In this section, we build in the changes we encountered in Chapter 2 and turn our attention to the autonomic nervous system. *The* **autonomic nervous system** *consists of the nerves in the body outside the brain and spinal column.* Jorge's experiences are related to changes in the autonomic nervous system; we'll discover whether Jorge's problems are normative.

Autonomic Nervous System

Do you feel hot or cold right now? Do your palms sweat when you get nervous? What happens when you get frightened? These and other regulation functions in your body are controlled by the autonomic nervous system. Fortunately, few changes occur in the autonomic nervous system as we age, but two changes do tend to get people's attention: body temperature control and sleep. Jorge, whom we met in the vignette, is experiencing both of these changes.

Regulating Body Temperature

Every year, newscasts around the world report that during very cold or very hot spells more older adults die than people in other age groups. Why does this happen?

We considered evidence earlier in this chapter that cold and warm temperature thresholds may change little with age. If older people can feel cold and warm stimuli placed against them about as well as people of other age groups, what accounts for these deaths?

It turns out that older adults have difficulty telling that their core body temperature is low (Blatteis, 2012). In other words, older people are much less likely to notice that they are cold. Regulating body temperature involves nearly all body systems, most of which undergo declines with age. Because some of them respond to training (e.g., fitness training can help with declines in the musculoskeletal system), some causes of the declines can be addressed. However, changes in the skin and metabolic systems are inevitable. To make matters worse, older adults also have slower vasoconstrictor response, which is the ability to raise core body temperature (i.e., warm up) when the body's peripheral temperature drops (Blatteis, 2012; Liao & Jan, 2016).

Similarly, older adults have trouble responding to high heat, because they do not sweat as much (Blatteis,

Older people are less able to regulate their core body temperature because they have more difficulty noticing they are too cold or too hot.

2012; Liao & Jan, 2016). Sweating decreases with age from the lower limbs up to the forehead, and is due to lower sweat production.

Taken together, the difficulties older adults have in regulating body temperature in extreme cold and heat are the primary reason why older adults are much more susceptible to hypothermia (body temperature below 95°F over a long period) and hyperthermia (body temperature above 98.6°F that cannot be relieved by sweating) (Blatteis, 2012; Liao & Jan, 2016). This is why social service agencies are especially mindful of older adults during major weather events.

Sleep and Aging

How did you sleep last night? If you are older, chances are that you had some trouble. In fact, sleep complaints and problems are common in older adults (Mattis & Sehgal, 2016). These complaints most often concern difficulty in falling asleep, frequent or prolonged awakenings during the night, early morning awakenings, and a feeling of not sleeping very well. Effects of poor sleep are experienced the next day; moodiness, poorer performance on tasks involving sustained concentration, fatigue, and lack of motivation are some of the telltale signs.

Nearly every aspect of sleep undergoes age-related changes (Mattis & Sehgal, 2016). It takes older adults longer to fall asleep, they are awake more at night, they are more easily awakened, and they experience major shifts in their sleep—wake cycles, called circadian rhythms. Across adulthood, circadian rhythms move from a two-phase pattern of sleep (awake during the day and asleep at night for most people) to a multiphase rhythm reminiscent of that of infants (daytime napping and shorter sleep cycles at night). These changes are related to the changes in regulating core body temperature discussed earlier. Other major causes of sleep disturbance include sleep apnea (stopping breathing for 5 to 10 seconds), periodic leg jerks, heartburn, frequent need to urinate, poor physical health, and depression.

Older adults try lots of things to help themselves, such as taking daytime naps, without success (Boswell, Thai, & Brown, 2015). As a result, many older adults are prescribed sleeping pills or hypnotic sedatives. But these medications must be used with great caution with older adults, and often do not help alleviate the problem in any case. Among the most effective treatments of sleep problems are increasing physical exercise, reducing caffeine intake, avoiding daytime naps, and making sure that the sleeping environment is as quiet and dark as possible (Boswell et al., 2015).

Some research has linked the need for sleep to the amount of brain activity devoted to learning that occurred prior to sleep (Cirelli, 2012). So one hypothesis is that sleep needs decrease with age in relation to decreased new learning that occurs with age. However, research specifically examining this hypothesis remains to be done.

Research evidence also points to difficulties in regulating the optimal body temperature for good sleep may also be part of the issue for older adults (Romeijn et al., 2012). Interestingly, this problem may in turn be related to changes in the frontal cortex, a key part of the brain that is involved in evaluating comfort. As we saw in Chapter 2, this part of the brain is involved in numerous age-related changes. Whether interventions that are aimed at helping insomniacs find their optimal body temperature for sleeping will work remains to be seen.

As we now know, Jorge's difficulty with heat and sleep reflect normative changes that occur with age. Olivia should be informed of these changes and encouraged to make sure Jorge drinks plenty of water and adopts good sleep habits.

Psychological Implications

Being able to maintain proper body temperature can literally be a matter of life and death. So the increased difficulty in doing that poses a real threat to older adults. Being in an environment that provides external means of temperature regulation (i.e., heating and air conditioning), and that has back-up systems in the event of emergency (e.g., generators in the event of power failures) are much more important for older adults.

Because thermoregulation involves so many of the body's systems, and because many of the age-related changes that occur are inevitable, it is important to focus on those systems that respond to intervention. By doing whatever is possible to keep those systems functioning as well as possible, people can lessen the overall problem of regulating body temperature.

A good night's sleep is also important for maintaining good overall health. Ensuring that the sleep environment is maximally conducive to sleeping and by providing whatever environmental supports possible, we can increase the odds of improving sleep.

Adult Development in Action

What would be the best questions to ask an older adult client if you, as a social worker, were establishing whether the client had any problems with tolerating heat/cold or sleeping?

Social Policy Implications

No one wants to fall and get hurt. That's true in any age group, but especially so with older adults, particularly older adults who live alone. The fear of falling is real, and even has been used as the basis for a famous television ad for an emergency alert system: An older woman is shown falling and saying, "I've fallen, and I can't get up." (Check out the original ad and the remixes on YouTube.)

Because of normative age-related changes in vision, hearing, balance, musculoskeletal changes, and other aspects of functioning, the risk of falling increases with age. As you can see in Figure 3.8, that increase is quite dramatic over age 75.

Falls can result in serious injuries or even death to older adults. People with osteoporosis are especially vulnerable to breaking their hip or pelvis, or may suffer a traumatic brain injury, any of which may necessitate a long rehabilitation. As a result, much attention has been paid to preventing falls. Some of these interventions are simple (such as removing loose floor rugs and ensuring that there is sufficient light and reduced glare). Others involve lifestyle changes or technology.

The Centers for Disease Control and Prevention (2016b) has translated the research findings about increased risk and consequences of falls in older adults and have created several suggestions on how to prevent them. Among their suggestions are:

- Get exercise to strengthen muscles. Programs such as tai chi and qigong, among others, are effective.
- Be careful of medication side effects. Some medications may cause dizziness or drowsiness, which can increase the risk for falling.
- Correct any visual impairments to the extent possible.
- Remove hazards at home. Remove clutter you can trip over (books, clothes, and other materials on the floor). Install handrails on stairways. Use nonslip mats and grab bars in showers and bath tubs.

The materials compiled by the Centers for Disease Control and Prevention include posters and brochures in English, Spanish, and Chinese, as well as more formal booklets for community-based programs. These recommendations, if followed, would result in a safer environment for older adults.

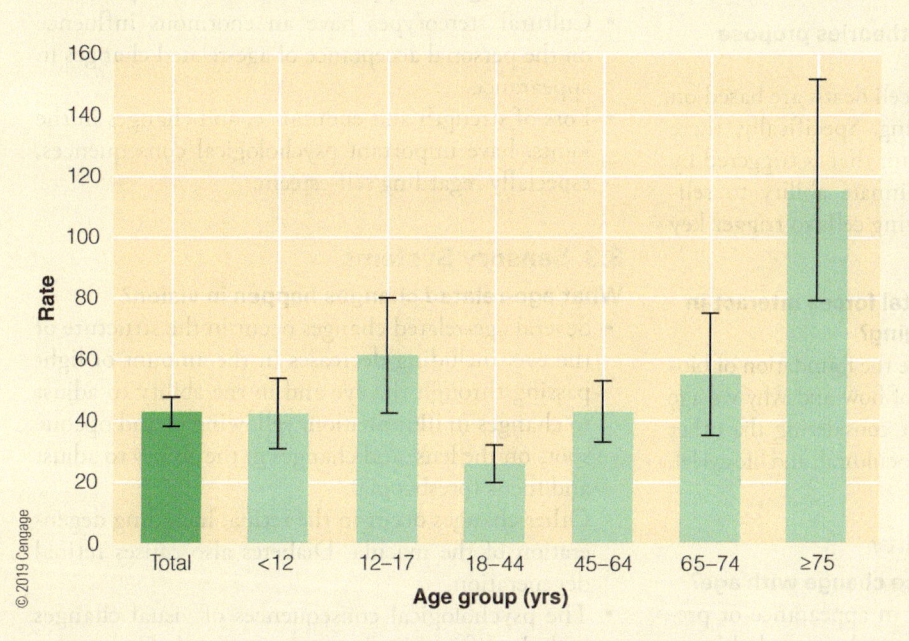

FIGURE 3.8 The figure shows the rate of nonfatal, medically consulted fall injury episodes, by age group, in the United States during 2010, according to the National Health Interview Survey. Rates increased with age for adults aged ≥ 18 years.

Source: Adams, P. F., Martinez, M. E., Vickerie, J. L., & Kirzinger, W. K. (2012). Summary health statistics for the U.S. population: National health interview survey, 2011. *Vital Health Statistics, 10(255)*. Retrieved from www.cdc.gov/nchs/data/series/sr_10/sr10_255.pdf.

SUMMARY

3.1 Why Do We Age? Biological Theories of Aging

How do metabolic theories explain aging?
- Metabolic theories are based on the idea that people are born with a limited amount of energy that can be expended at some rate unique to the individual.
- Research is mixed on whether eating fewer calories may be related to living longer.

What are the major hypotheses in cellular theories of aging?
- Cellular theories suggest that there is a limit on how often cells may divide before dying (called the Hayflick limit), which may partially explain aging. The shortening of telomeres may be the major factor.
- A second group of cellular theories relate to a process called cross-linking that results when certain proteins interact randomly and produce molecules that make the body stiffer. Cross-links interfere with metabolism.
- A third type of cellular theory proposes that free radicals, which are highly reactive chemicals produced randomly during normal cell metabolism, cause cell damage. There is some evidence that ingesting antioxidants may postpone the appearance of some age-related diseases.

How do genetic programming theories propose that we age?
- Theories about programmed cell death are based on genetic hypotheses about aging. Specifically, there appears to be a genetic program that is triggered by physiological processes, the innate ability to self-destruct, and the ability of dying cells to trigger key processes in other cells.

How do the basic developmental forces interact in biological and physiological aging?
- Although biological theories are the foundation of biological forces, the full picture of how and why we age cannot be understood without considering the other three forces (psychological, sociocultural, and life cycle).

3.2 Appearance and Mobility

How do our skin, hair, and voice change with age?
- Normative changes with age in appearance or presentation include wrinkles, gray hair, and thinner and weaker voice.
- Protecting the skin from overexposure to the sun is a key factor in both skin aging and preventing skin cancers.

What happens to our body build with age?
- Normative changes include decrease in height and increase in weight in midlife, followed by weight loss in late life.

What age-related changes occur in our ability to move around?
- The amount of muscle decreases with age, but strength and endurance change only slightly until age 70, when changes occur more rapidly.
- Loss of bone mass is normative; in severe cases, though, the disease osteoporosis may result, in which bones become brittle and honeycombed and break more easily.
- Calcium and vitamin D intake are factors in preventing osteoporosis.
- Osteoarthritis is a wear-and-tear disease of the bones underneath damaged cartilage marked by gradual onset and progression of pain and disability, with little inflammation.
- Rheumatoid arthritis is a more destructive disease of the joints that affects different joints than osteoarthritis, and involves more pain and inflammation.

What are the psychological implications of age-related changes in appearance and mobility?
- Cultural stereotypes have an enormous influence on the personal acceptance of age-related changes in appearance.
- Loss of strength and endurance, and changes in the joints, have important psychological consequences, especially regarding self-esteem.

3.3 Sensory Systems

What age-related changes happen in vision?
- Several age-related changes occur in the structure of the eye, including decreases in the amount of light passing through the eye and in the ability to adjust to changes in illumination, yellowing of and opaque spots on the lens, and changes in the ability to adjust and focus (presbyopia).
- Other changes occur in the retina, including degeneration of the macula. Diabetes also causes retinal degeneration.
- The psychological consequences of visual changes include difficulties in getting around. Compensation strategies must take several factors into account; for example, the need for more illumination must be weighed against increased susceptibility to glare.

How does hearing change as people age?
- Age-related declines in the ability to hear high-pitched tones (presbycusis) are normative.
- Exposure to noise speeds up and exacerbates hearing loss.
- Psychologically, hearing losses can reduce the ability to have satisfactory communication with others and lower quality of life.

What age-related changes occur in people's senses of touch and balance?
- Changes in sensitivity to touch, temperature, and pain are complex and not well understood; age-related trends are unclear in most cases.
- Dizziness and vertigo are common in older adults and increase with age, as do falls. Changes in balance may result in greater caution in older adults when walking. The fear and risk of falling can be reduced through various exercise and other intervention programs.

What happens to taste and smell with increasing age?
- Age-related changes in taste are minimal. Many older adults complain about boring food; however, these complaints appear to be largely unrelated to changes in taste ability. Medications can affect the ability to taste.
- The ability to detect odors declines rapidly after age 60 in most people. Changes in smell are primarily responsible for reported changes in food preference and enjoyment.
- Changes in the ability to detect certain odors appears to be diagnostic for dementia.

3.4 Vital Functions

What age-related changes occur in the cardiovascular system?
- Some fat deposits in and around the heart and inside arteries are a normal part of aging. Heart muscle gradually is replaced with stiffer connective tissue. The most important change in the circulatory system is the stiffening (hardening) of the walls of the arteries.
- Overall, men have a higher rate of cardiovascular disease than women, but women's risk equals men's by late life. Several diseases increase in frequency with age: congestive heart failure, angina pectoris, myocardial infarction, atherosclerosis (severe buildup of fat inside and the calcification of the arterial walls), cerebrovascular accidents (stroke), and hypertension (high blood pressure). Treatments for these diseases have improved, and overall rates have declined as fewer people smoke and more have stopped smoking.

What structural and functional changes occur with age in the respiratory system?
- The amount of air we can take into our lungs and our ability to exchange oxygen and carbon dioxide decrease with age. Declines in the maximum amount of air we can take in also occur.
- Chronic obstructive pulmonary disease (COPD), such as emphysema, increases with age. Emphysema is the most common form of age-related COPD; although most cases are caused by smoking, a few are caused by genetic factors. Chronic bronchitis also becomes more prevalent with age.

3.5 The Reproductive System

What reproductive changes occur in women?
- The transition from childbearing years to the cessation of ovulation is called the climacteric; menopause is the point at which menstruation stops. A variety of physical and psychological symptoms accompany menopause (e.g., hot flashes); however, women in different cultures report different experiences. Diet and certain exercise programs, such as yoga, have been shown to alleviate symptoms.
- Menopausal hormone therapy remains controversial because of conflicting results about its long-term effects.
- Additional normative changes include vaginal dryness and thinning of the vaginal walls.
- No changes occur in the desire to have sex; however, the availability of a suitable partner for women is a major barrier.

What reproductive changes occur in men?
- In men, sperm production declines gradually with age. Changes in the prostate gland occur and should be monitored through yearly examinations.
- Some changes in sexual performance, such as increased time to erection and ejaculation and increased refractory period, are typical.

What are the psychological implications of age-related changes in the reproductive system?
- Healthy adults of any age are capable of engaging in sexual activity, and the desire to do so does not diminish with age. However, societal stereotyping creates barriers to free expression of such feelings.

3.6 The Autonomic Nervous System

What major changes occur in the autonomic nervous system?

- Regulating body temperature becomes increasingly problematic with age. Older adults have difficulty telling when their core body temperature drops, and their vasoconstrictor response diminishes. When they become very hot, older adults are less likely than are younger adults to drink the water they need.
- Sleep patterns and circadian rhythms change with age. Older adults are more likely to compensate by taking daytime naps, which exacerbates the problem. Effective treatments include exercising, reducing caffeine, avoiding daytime naps, and making the sleep environment as quiet and dark as possible.

What are the psychological implications of changes in the brain?

- Maintaining body temperature is essential to good health. Getting good sleep is also important for good functioning.

REVIEW QUESTIONS

3.1 Why Do We Age? Biological Theories of Aging

- What biological theories have been proposed to explain aging? What are their similarities and differences?
- Why do some people argue that diets high in antioxidants can prolong life?
- What are some of the sociocultural forces that operate on the biological theories? What are some examples of these forces?

3.2 Appearance and Mobility

- What age-related changes occur in appearance?
- How does body build change with age?
- How do muscle and bone tissue change with age?

3.3 Sensory Systems

- What age-related changes occur in vision? What are the psychological effects of these changes?
- What age-related changes occur in hearing? What are the psychological effects of these changes?
- What age-related changes occur in somesthesia and balance?
- What age-related changes occur in taste and smell?

3.4 Vital Functions

- What changes occur with age in the cardiovascular system? What gender differences have been noted? Which cardiovascular diseases increase in frequency with age?
- What changes occur with age in the respiratory system? How are respiratory diseases related to age?

3.5 The Reproductive System

- What age-related nges occur in women's and men's reproductive ability?
- How does interest in sexual activity change with age? What constraints operate on men and women?

3.6 The Nervous System

- What changes occur in people's ability to regulate body temperature?
- How does sleep change with age?

INTEGRATING CONCEPTS IN DEVELOPMENT

- How do the various biological theories of aging match with the major age-related changes in body systems? Which theories do the best job? Why?
- Given what you now know about normative changes in appearance, what would you say about the stereotypes of aging you identified in the Discovering Development exercise you did in Chapter 1?
- Why do you think the rates of death from cardiovascular disease are so much higher in industrialized countries than elsewhere?
- How might the age-related changes in the respiratory system be linked with societal policies on the environment?

KEY TERMS

angina pectoris A painful condition caused by temporary constriction of blood flow to the heart.

atherosclerosis A process by which fat is deposited on the walls of arteries.

autonomic nervous system The nerves in the body outside the brain and spinal column.

cataracts Opaque spots on the lens of the eye.

cerebrovascular accident (CVA) An interruption of the blood flow in the brain.

chronic obstructive pulmonary disease (COPD) A family of age-related lung diseases that block the passage of air and cause abnormalities inside the lungs.

climacteric The transition during which a woman's reproductive capacity ends and ovulation stops.

congestive heart failure A condition occurring when cardiac output and the ability of the heart to contract severely decline, making the heart enlarge, increasing pressure to the veins, and making the body swell.

cross-linking Random interaction between proteins that produce molecules that make the body stiffer.

emphysema Most serious form of COPD characterized by the destruction of the membranes around the air sacs in the lungs.

free radicals Unstable chemicals produced randomly in normal metabolism that are thought to cause aging.

glaucoma A disease in the eye caused by improper drainage of fluid in the eye resulting in internal damage and progressive loss of vision.

hypertension A disease in which one's blood pressure is too high.

menopausal hormone therapy (MHT) Low doses of estrogen, which is often combined with progestin (synthetic form of progesterone) taken to counter the effects of declining estrogen levels.

menopause The cessation of the release of eggs by the ovaries.

myocardial infarction (MI) Also called heart attack, a result of a blockage in blood supply to the heart.

osteoarthritis A form of arthritis marked by gradual onset and progression of pain and swelling, caused primarily by overuse of a joint.

osteoporosis A degenerative bone disease more common in women in which bone tissue deteriorates severely to produce honeycomb-like bone tissue.

perimenopause The time of transition from regular menstruation to menopause.

presbycusis A normative age-related loss of the ability to hear high-pitched tones.

presbyopia The normative age-related loss of the ability to focus on nearby objects, usually resulting in the need for corrective lenses.

rheumatoid arthritis A destructive form of arthritis that develops slowly and involves different joints and more swelling than osteoarthritis.

telomerase An enzyme needed in DNA replication to fully reproduce the telomeres when cells divide.

telomeres, Tips of the chromosomes that shorten with each cell replication.

4 | Longevity, Health, and Functioning

CHAPTER OUTLINE

4.1 How Long Will We Live?
DISCOVERING DEVELOPMENT Take the Longevity Test
Average and Maximum Longevity
Genetic and Environmental Factors in Average Longevity
Ethnic Differences in Average Longevity
Gender Differences in Average Longevity
International Differences in Average Longevity

4.2 Health and Illness
Defining Health and Illness
Quality of Life
Changes in the Immune System
Chronic and Acute Diseases
The Role of Stress

HOW DO WE KNOW? Negative Life Events and Mastery

4.3 Common Chronic Conditions and Their Management
General Issues in Chronic Conditions
Common Chronic Conditions

REAL PEOPLE The "Angelina Jolie Effect"

CURRENT CONTROVERSIES The Prostate Cancer Dilemma

Managing Pain

4.4 Pharmacology and Medication Adherence
Patterns of Medication Use
Developmental Changes in How Medications Work
Medication Side Effects and Interactions
Adherence to Medication Regimens

4.5 Functional Health and Disability
A Model of Disability in Late Life
Determining Functional Health Status
What Causes Functional Limitations and Disability in Older Adults?

Social Policy Implications
Summary
Review Questions
Integrating Concepts in Development
Key Terms

Jeanne Calment was one of the most important people to ever live. Her amazing achievement was not made in sports, government, or any other profession. When she died on August 4, 1997, at age 122 years and 164 days, she set the world record for the longest verified human life span that still stands. Jeanne lived her entire life in Arles, France. During her lifetime, she met Vincent Van Gogh, experienced the invention of the lightbulb, automobiles, airplanes, space travel, computers, and all sorts of everyday conveniences. She survived two world wars. Longevity ran in her family: Her older brother, François, lived to the age of 97, her father to 93, and her mother to 86. Jeanne was extraordinarily healthy her whole life, rarely being ill. She was also active; she learned fencing when she was 85, and still rode a bicycle at age 100. She lived on her own until she was 110, when she moved to a nursing home. Her life was documented in the 1995 film *Beyond 120 Years with Jeanne Calment*. Shortly before her 121st birthday, Musicdisc released *Time's Mistress*, a CD of Jeanne speaking over a background of rap and hip-hop music.

Did you ever wonder how long you would like to live? Would you like to live to be as old as Jeanne Calment? Scientific advances are happening so quickly in our understanding of the factors that influence longevity, many scientists think that numerous, perhaps most people could live to 120 years or even beyond with the right interventions. Indeed, the February 23/March 2, 2015, double issue of *Time* magazine devoted its main feature to the possibility the baby on the front cover could live to 142 years (or longer). Let's take a closer look at what we know about human longevity. ■

Jeanne Calment lived more than 122 years.

4.1 How Long Will We Live?

LEARNING OBJECTIVES

- What is the average and the maximum longevity for humans?
- What genetic and environmental factors influence longevity?
- What ethnic factors influence average longevity?
- What factors create gender differences in average longevity

Susie is a 51-year-old Chinese American living in San Francisco. Susie's mother (age 76), father (age 77), and grandmother (age 103), who are all in excellent health, live with her and her husband. Susie knows that several of her other relatives have lived long lives, but she wonders whether this has any bearing on her own life expectancy.

As we saw in Chapter 1, many more people are living to old age today than ever before. Like Susie, people today have already seen far more older adults than their great-great-grandparents ever saw. The tremendous increase in the number of older adults has focused renewed interest in how long you may live. Susie's question about her own longevity exemplifies this interest. Knowing how long we are likely to live is important not only for us but also for government agencies, service programs, the business world, and insurance companies. Why?

The length of life has an enormous impact on just about every aspect of life, from decisions about government healthcare programs (e.g., how much money should Congress allocate to Medicare) to retirement policy (e.g., debates over the age at which people may collect maximum retirement benefits) to life insurance premiums (e.g., longer lives on average mean cheaper rates for young adults because they are now healthier for longer periods of their lives). Longer lives is also partly responsible for the increase in the average age of the American population increasing over the past few decades (lower rates of childbirth is another factor). The impact on everyday life of more longer-lived people will continue for the next several decades.

Life expectancy can be examined from the perspective of the basic developmental forces, because how long we live depends on complex interactions among biological, psychological, socioeconomic, and life-cycle forces. For example, some people, like Susie, have many relatives who live to very old age, whereas others have relatives who die young. Tendencies toward long lives (or short ones, for that matter) tend to run in families. As you will see, our "long-life genes" play a major role in governing how long we are likely to live.

But the world in which we live can affect how long we live, too. Environmental factors such as disease and toxic chemicals modify our genetic heritage and shorten our lifetime, sometimes drastically. By the same token, environmental factors such as access to high-quality medical care can sometimes offset genetic defects that would otherwise have caused early death, thereby increasing our longevity. In short, no single developmental force can account for the length of life. Let's begin by exploring the concept of longevity. To get started, complete the exercise in the Discovering Development feature and see how long you might live. When you have finished, continue reading to discover the research base behind the numbers.

DISCOVERING DEVELOPMENT
Take the Longevity Test

Did you ever speculate about how long you might live? Are you curious? If you'd like a preview of several of the key influences on how long we live, try completing the questions at www.livingto100.com. It is based on research from the New England Centenarian Study. Take notes about why you think each question is being asked. Once you're finished, submit your form. Take time to read about each of the topics, then read more about them in the text. How long will you live? Only time will tell!

Average and Maximum Longevity

How long you live, called longevity, is jointly determined by genetic and environmental factors. Researchers distinguish between two different types of longevity: average longevity and maximum longevity. **Average longevity** *is commonly called average life expectancy and refers to the age at which half of the individuals who are born in a particular year will have died.* Average longevity is affected by both genetic and environmental factors.

Average longevity can be computed for people at any age. The most common method is to compute average longevity at birth, which is the projected age at which half of the people born in a certain year will have died. This computation takes into account people who die at any age, from infancy onward. The current average longevity is about 79 years at birth for people in the United States (National Center for Health Statistics, 2016a). This means that of the people born in 2016, for example, half of them will still be alive when the group reaches age 79. When average longevity is computed at other points in the life span, the calculation is based on all the people who are alive at that age; people who died earlier are not included. For example, computing the average longevity for people currently 65 years old would provide a predicted age at which half of those people will have died. People who were born into the same birth cohort but who died before age 65 are not counted. Eliminating those who die at early ages from the computation of average longevity at a specific age makes projected average longevity at age 65 longer than it was at birth. In the United States, females currently aged 65 can expect to live on average about 20 more years; men about 18 more years (National Center for Health Statistics, 2016b).

For people in the United States, average longevity has been increasing steadily since 1900; recent estimates for longevity at birth, at age 65, and at age 75 are presented in Figure 4.1. Pay attention to some important aspects of the data. First, data were only collected and reported for certain racial/ethnic groups. Second, whereas data on life expectancy at birth has been collected for over a century, data on life expectancy at ages 65 and 75 have only been collected and reported more recently. These differences reflect changes in both research design and in an understanding that data need to be reported separately for various racial/ethnic groups.

Note in the figure that the most rapid increases in average longevity at birth occurred in the first half of the 20th century. These increases in average longevity were caused mostly by declines in infant mortality rates,

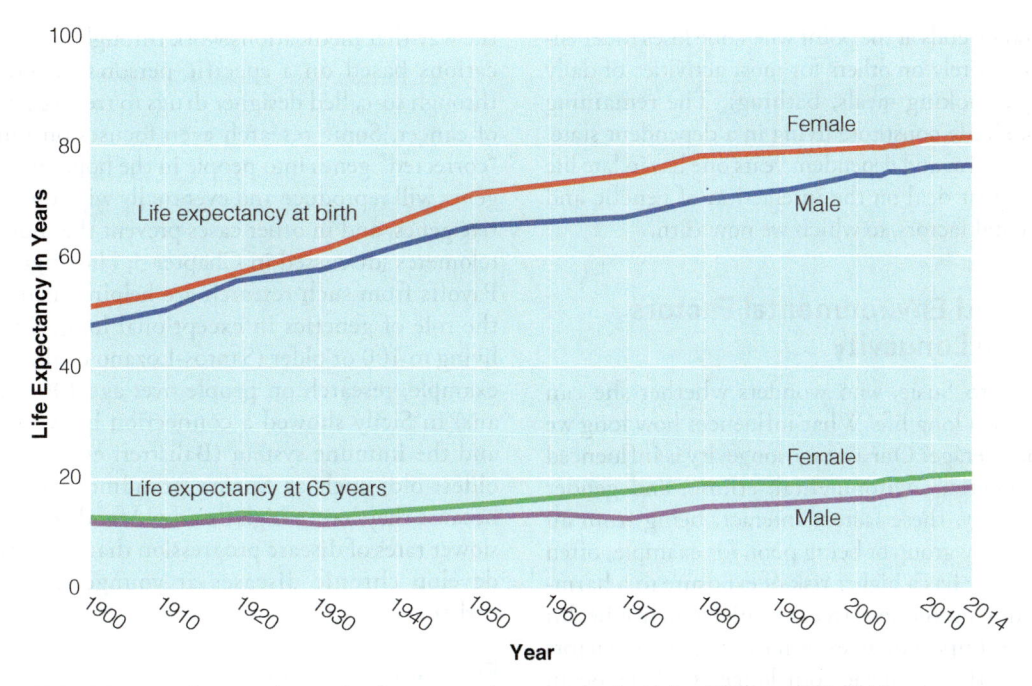

FIGURE 4.1 Average longevity for men and women in the United States 1900–2014.
Source: National Center for Health Statistics. (2016a). *Health, United States, 2015*. Retrieved from www.cdc.gov/nchs/data/hus/hus15.pdf.

brought about by eliminating diseases such as smallpox and polio, and through better health care. The decrease in the number of women who died during childbirth was especially important in raising average life expectancies for women. Advances in medical technology and improvements in health care mean that more people survive to old age, thereby increasing average longevity in the general population.

Note also that life expectancy at ages 65 and 75 have also increased over the time periods in which the data have been collected, and that they vary across racial/ethnic groups. These increases also reflect better health care and healthier life styles in general, but as we will see there are some other factors in play.

Maximum longevity *is the oldest age to which any individual of a species lives.* Although the biblical character Methuselah is said to have lived to the ripe old age of 969 years, modern scientists are more conservative in their estimates of a human's maximum longevity. Even if we were able to eliminate all diseases and other environmental influences, most researchers estimate the limit to be somewhere around 120 years because key body systems such as the cardiovascular system have limits on how long they can last (Hayflick, 1998).

Genetic theories also place the human limit around 120 years (Barja, 2008; Rattan, 2012). As we noted at the beginning of the chapter, the world record for longevity that can be verified by birth records is held by Jeanne Calment of France, who died in 1997 at age 122 years.

It remains to be seen whether maximum longevity will change as new technologies produce better artificial organs and health care. An important issue is whether extending the life span indefinitely would be a good idea. Because maximum longevity of different animal species varies widely (Barja, 2008; Rattan, 2012), scientists have tried to understand these differences by considering important biological functions that we considered in Chapter 3 when we examined biological theories of aging. But no one has figured out how to predict longevity. For example, why the giant tortoises of the Galapagos Islands typically live longer than we do remains a mystery.

Increasingly, researchers are differentiating between **active life expectancy** and **dependent life expectancy**; *the difference is between living to a healthy old age (active life expectancy) and simply living a long time (dependent life expectancy).* Said another way, it is the difference between adding years to life and adding life to years. One's active life expectancy ends at the point when one loses independence or must rely on others for most activities of daily living (e.g., cooking meals, bathing). The remaining years of one's life constitute living in a dependent state. How many active and dependent years one has in late life depends a great deal on the interaction of genetic and environmental factors, to which we now turn.

Genetic and Environmental Factors in Average Longevity

Let's return to Susie, who wonders whether she can expect to live a long life. What influences how long we will live on average? Our average longevity is influenced most by genetic, environmental, ethnic, and gender factors. Clearly, these factors interact; being from an ethnic minority group or being poor, for example, often means that one has a higher risk of exposure to a harmful environment and less access to high-quality health care. But it is important to examine each of these factors and see how they influence our longevity. Let's begin with genetic and environmental factors.

Genetic Factors

Living a long life has a clear, but complex, genetic link. We have known for a long time that a good way to have a greater chance of a long life is to come from a family with a history of long-lived individuals. Alexander Graham Bell (the same guy who received the credit for inventing the telephone) was one of the first people to demonstrate systematically the benefits of coming from a long-lived family. Bell considered 8,797 of William Hyde's descendants and found that children of parents who had lived beyond 80 survived about 20 years longer than children whose parents had both died before they were 60. Thus Susie's long-lived family sets the stage for Susie to enjoy a long life herself.

Similar research indicates that about 25% of the variation in human longevity is due to a person's genetics (Passarino, De Rango, & Montesanto, 2016). So it is the case that people like Susie who are born into families with many long-lived members tend also to have longer average longevity.

One exciting line of research, the Human Genome Project, completed in 2003, mapped all our genes. This research and its spinoffs in microbiology and behavior genetics are continuing to produce astounding results in terms of genetic linkages to disease and aging (you can track these through the main website of the Project).

Based on this gene mapping work, ongoing research is revolutionizing how we treat diseases by improving the way that medications work through tailoring medications based on a specific person's genes, such as through so-called designer drugs to treat specific forms of cancer. Some research even focuses on implanting "corrected" genes into people in the hope that the good genes will reproduce and eventually wipe out the defective genes, and in other cases prevent the shortening of telomeres (discussed in Chapter 3; Harrington, 2016). Payoffs from such research are helping us understand the role of genetics in exceptional longevity, such as living to 100 or older (Santos-Lozano et al., 2016). For example, research on people over age 100 (centenarians) in Sicily showed a connection between genetics and the immune system (Balistreri et al., 2012). The oldest-old, such as Suzie's grandmother, are hardy because they have a high threshold for disease and show slower rates of disease progression than their peers who develop chronic diseases at younger ages and die earlier.

Environmental Factors

Although genes are a major determinant of longevity, environmental factors also affect the life span, often in combination with genes (Passarino et al., 2016). Some environmental factors are more obvious; diseases, toxins, lifestyle, and social class are among the most important. Diseases, such as cardiovascular disease and Alzheimer's disease, and lifestyle issues, such as smoking and exercise, receive a great deal of attention from researchers. Environmental toxins, encountered mainly as air and water pollution, are a continuing problem. For example, toxins in fish, bacteria, and cancer-causing chemicals in drinking water, and airborne pollutants are major agents in shortening longevity.

Living in poverty shortens longevity. The impact of socioeconomic status on longevity results from reduced access to goods and services, especially medical care and diet, that characterizes most ethnic minority groups, the poor, and many older adults, as clearly demonstrated in a very large study (566,402 participants) of premature mortality in community dwelling adults (Doubeni et al., 2012). Most of these people have restricted access to good health care and cannot afford healthy food. For many living in urban areas, air pollution, poor drinking water, and lead poisoning from old water pipes are serious problems, but they simply cannot afford to move. Although longevity differences between high and low socioeconomic groups in the United States narrowed during the latter part of the 20th century, these improvements have stopped since 1990 due to continued differences in access to health care (Swanson & Sanford, 2012).

How environmental factors influence average life expectancy changes over time. For example, acquired immunodeficiency syndrome (AIDS; Kinsella & Phillips, 2005) and diseases from bushmeat-related activities (Kurpiers et al., 2016) have had a devastating effect on life expectancy in sub-Saharan Africa. In contrast, negative effects of cardiovascular diseases on average longevity are lessening as the rates of those diseases decline in many developed countries (National Center for Health Statistics, 2016a).

The sad part about most environmental factors is that human activity is responsible for most of them. Denying adequate health care to everyone, continuing to pollute our environment, and failing to address the underlying causes of poverty have undeniable consequences: These causes needlessly shorten lives and dramatically increase the cost of health care.

Ethnic Differences in Average Longevity

People in different ethnic groups do not have the same average longevity at birth. For example, although African Americans' average life expectancy at birth is about 4 years less for men and about 3 years less for women than it is for European Americans, by age 65 this gap has narrowed to about 2 and 1 years, respectively, for men and women. By age 85, African Americans tend to outlive European Americans. Why the shift over time?

Lower access to good-quality health care in general means that those African Americans who live to age 85 may be in better health on average than their European American counterparts. But this is just a guess, because Latinos have higher average life expectancies than European Americans and African Americans at all ages despite having, on average, less access to health care (National Center for Health Statistics, 2016a). The full explanation for these ethnic group differences remains to be discovered.

Gender Differences in Average Longevity

Have you ever visited a senior center or a nursing home? If so, you may have asked yourself, "Where are all the very old men?" The answer is that women live longer, on average, than do men. Women's average longevity is about 5 years more than men's at birth, narrowing to roughly 1 year by age 85 (National Center for Health Statistics, 2016a).

These differences are fairly typical of most industrialized countries but not of developing countries. In fact, the female advantage in average longevity in the United States became apparent only in the early 20th century (Hayflick, 1996). Why? Until then, so many women died in childbirth that their average longevity as a group was no more than that of men. Death in childbirth still partially explains the lack of a female advantage in developing countries today; however, another part of the difference in some countries results from infanticide of baby girls. In industrialized countries, socioeconomic factors such as access to health care and improved lifestyle factors also help account for the emergence of the female advantage.

Coming from a family with many long-lived members increases your chances of having a long life yourself.

Many ideas have been offered to explain the significant advantage women have over men in average longevity in industrialized countries, and that emerging in developing countries (Roy, Punhani, & Shi, 2012). Overall, men's rates of dying from the top 15 causes of death are significantly higher than women's at nearly every age, and men are also more susceptible to infectious diseases. These differences have led some to speculate that perhaps it is not just a gender-related biological difference at work in longevity, but a more complex interaction of lifestyle, improved health care, greater susceptibility in men of contracting certain fatal diseases and dying prematurely (e.g., in war or through accidents at work), and genetics.

Other researchers disagree; they argue that there are potential biological explanations. These include the fact that women have two X chromosomes, compared with one in men; men have a higher metabolic rate; women have a higher brain-to-body weight ratio; and women have lower testosterone levels. Some research points to older women's more effective natural killer (NK) cells, a key aspect of human immune systems as another reason (Al-Attar et al., 2016). (We consider the role of NK cells later in this chapter.) However, no single explanation has sufficient scientific support to explain why most women in industrialized countries can expect, on average, to outlive most men (Roy et al., 2012).

Despite their longer average longevity, women do not have all the advantages. Interestingly, older men who survive beyond age 90 are the hardiest segment of their birth cohort in terms of performance on cognitive tests (Perls & Terry, 2003). Between ages 65 and 89, women score higher on cognitive tests; beyond age 90, men do much better.

International Differences in Average Longevity

Countries around the world differ dramatically in how long their populations live on average. As you can see for countries in the Organisation for Economic Co-operation and Development (OECD) in Figure 4.2, the current

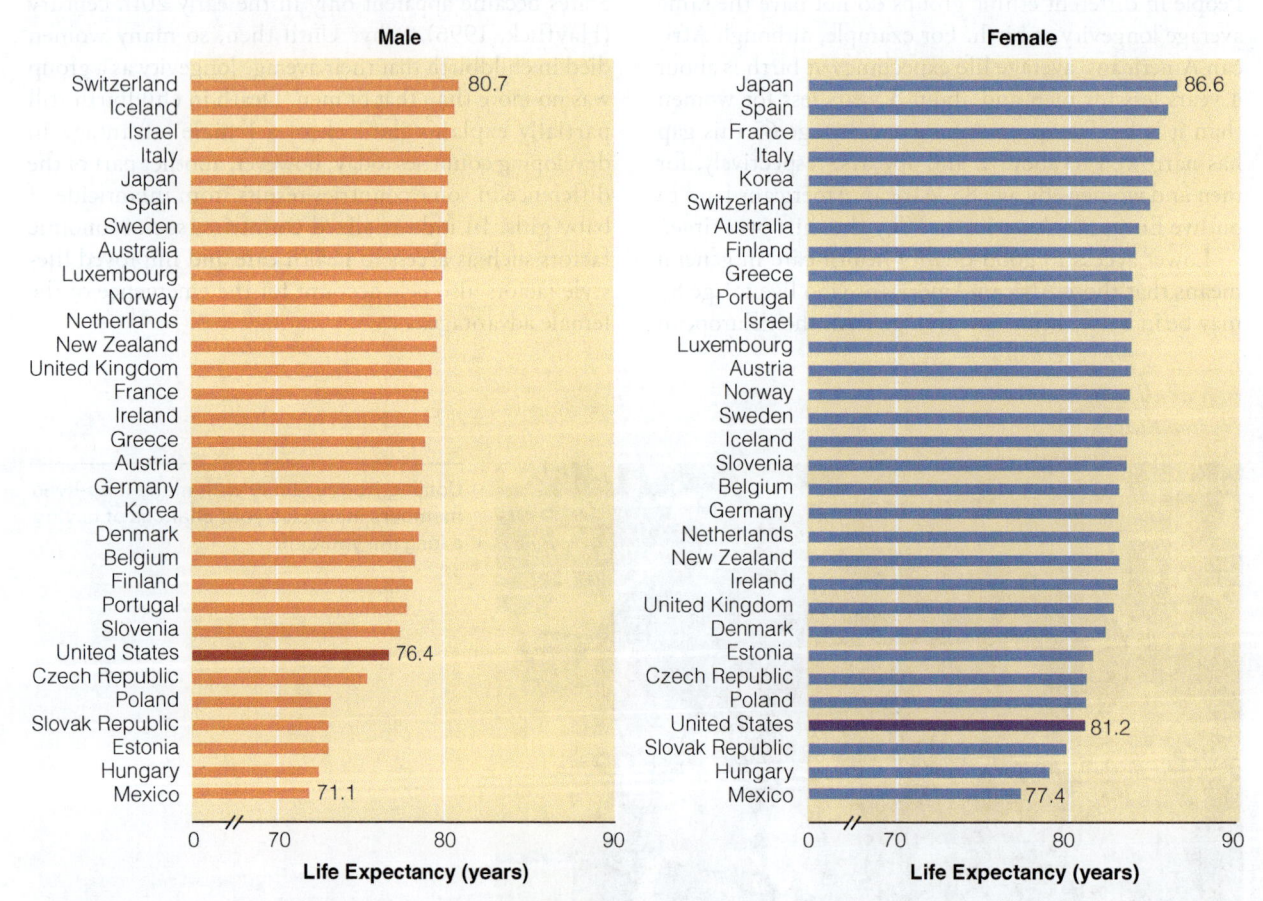

FIGURE 4.2 Life expectancy at birth, OECD countries, 2013.

Source: CDC/NCHS, Health, United States, 2015, Figure 1 and Tables 14 and 15. Data from the National Vital Statistics System (NVSS) and the Organisation for Economic Co-operation and Development (OECD).

range extends from 71.7 years in Mexico to over 82 years in Japan. In contrast, some developing countries, such as Sierra Leone in Africa, have an average longevity at birth of less than 40 years. Such a wide divergence in life expectancy reflects vast discrepancies in genetic, sociocultural and economic conditions, health care, disease, and the like across industrialized and developing nations. The differences also mean that populations in countries such as Sierra Leone are very much younger, on average, than they are in countries such as Japan or the United States.

Adult Development in Action

Suppose you are a financial planner for people who want to save for their retirement. Given what you have learned about longevity, how would you advise people in their 40s in terms of savings?

4.2 Health and Illness

LEARNING OBJECTIVES

- What are the key issues in defining health and illness?
- How is quality of life assessed?
- What normative age-related changes occur in the immune system?
- What are the developmental trends in chronic and acute diseases?
- What are the key issues in stress across adulthood?

Rosa is a 72-year-old immigrant from Mexico, living in a small apartment in a large city in the southwestern United States. For most of her life she has been very healthy, but lately she has noticed it is getting harder to get up every morning. In addition, when she gets a cold, she takes longer to recover than when she was younger. Rosa wonders whether these problems are typical or whether she is experiencing something unusual.

Each of us has had periods of health and of illness. Most people are like Rosa—healthy for nearly all our lives. In this section, we will tackle the difficult issue of defining health and illness. We will consider quality of life, an increasingly important notion as medical technology keeps people alive longer. We will see how the differences between acute and chronic disease become more important with age. Because our immune system plays such a central role in health and illness, we will examine key age-related changes in it. Finally, we will consider how stress can affect our health.

Defining Health and Illness

What does the term *health* mean to you? Total lack of disease? Complete physical, mental, and social well-being? Actually, scientists cannot agree on a comprehensive definition, largely because the term has been used in so many different contexts (Davies, 2007; Taylor, 2015). Many people now include biological, psychological, sociocultural, spiritual, and environmental components; as Davies (2007) puts it, health is an ongoing outcome from the processes of a life lived well.

The World Health Organization defines **health** *as a state of complete physical, mental, and social well-being, and not merely the absence of disease or infirmity.* **Illness** *is the presence of a physical or mental disease or impairment.*

Think for a moment about your health. How would you rate it? Although this question looks simple, how people answer it turns out to be predictive of illness and mortality in certain situations (Cristina et al., 2016; Longest & Thoits, 2012). Why? There are several possibilities (Idler & Benyamini, 1997; Wolinsky & Tierney, 1998). One is that self-rated health captures more aspects of health than other measures. A second possibility is that self-rated health reflects changes in respondents' health and life circumstances, experiences, and expectations. A third is that people's self-ratings affect their health-related behaviors, which in turn affect health outcomes. Finally, self-rated health may actually represent an assessment of people's internal and external resources that are available to support health. Research data support all these ideas; a review of more than 30 years of research has shown that self-ratings of health are very predictive of future health outcomes (Blazer, 2008).

When measured over time, self-ratings of health tend to fall into two general patterns: relatively stable over time and declining over time (Blazer, 2008). Within these general patterns are differences; for example, some people rate their health consistently good, whereas others rate it as consistently poor. Decline in self-rated health can be gradual or more sudden.

Among the oldest-old, self-rated health is a powerful predictor of mortality across cultures; for example, a two-year study in China showed that self-rated health still predicted mortality even after socioeconomic status and health conditions had been accounted for (Chen & Wu, 2008). Similar results were obtained for men in India (Hirve et al., 2012).

Not surprisingly, self-ratings of health reflect differences in socioeconomic background in terms of how healthy people say they are. For example, indigenous

Australians rate their health as significantly poorer than nonindigenous Australians, mainly due to differences in economic variables (e.g., access to health care) (Booth & Carroll, 2008). In the United States, African Americas are twice as likely, and Mexican Americans and Puerto Rican Americans three times more likely, to self-report their health as fair or poor than European Americans (Benjamins et al., 2012; Landrine et al., 2016).

Overall, given the strong relation between self-rated health and actual health-related outcomes, including one's own mortality, it should come as no surprise that researchers often include such measures in their studies of older adults. Such measures provide a good proxy (or stand-in) variable for health, avoiding a time-consuming (and possibly costly) assessment of health. This approach works most of the time. But as we have noted, we must keep in mind certain systematic differences across racial and ethnic groups that result from external factors such as discrimination and differential access to adequate health care.

Quality of Life

We'll bet if you asked most people what they want out of life, they would say something about a good quality of life. But what does that mean? Precise definitions are hard to find. Sometimes people find it easier to say what quality of life is not: being dependent on a respirator while in a permanent vegetative state is one common example. Researchers, though, like to be more specific. They tend to look at several specific aspects of quality of life: *health-related quality of life* and *non-health-related quality of life*. **Health-related quality of life** *includes all of the aspects of life that are affected by changes in one's health status.* **Non-health-related quality of life** *refers to things in the environment, such as entertainment, economic resources, arts, and so on that can affect our overall experience and enjoyment in life.*

Most research on quality of life has focused on two areas: quality of life in the context of specific diseases or conditions and quality of life relating to end-of-life issues. We briefly lay out the issues here. We will return to them as we discuss specific situations in this chapter and in Chapters 5 (interventions that increase quality of life) and 13 (end-of-life issues).

In many respects, quality of life is a subjective judgment that can be understood in the context of broader models of adult development and aging. One such model describes ways in which people select domains of relative strength, optimize their use of these strengths, and compensate for age-related changes (Baltes et al., 2006). In addition, one must also consider not only the physical health aspects but also mental health and the person's life situation in assessing quality of life (Brett et al., 2012). From this perspective, quality of life is a successful use of the selection, optimization, and compensation model (SOC) to manage one's life, resulting in successful aging. Applying this approach to research in health care, quality of life refers to people's perceptions of their position in life in context of their culture (Karim et al., 2008) and in relation to their goals, expectations, values, and concerns (Brett et al., 2012). This is especially important when studying cultures, such as Aboriginal populations in Australia, that have very different perspectives on defining concepts such as health (Kite & Davy, 2015).

In general, research on health-related quality of life addresses a critical question (Lawton et al., 1999): To what extent does distress from illness or side effects associated with treatment reduce a person's wish to live? Lawton and colleagues (1999) set the standard for answering this question by showing that it depends a great deal on a person's valuation of life, the degree to which a person is attached to his or her present life. How much one enjoys life, has hope about the future, and finds meaning in everyday events, for example, have a great deal of impact on how long that person would like to live. Assessing a person's valuation of life helps clinicians develop better strategies to maximize quality of life (Gitlin et al., 2016).

Narrowing the focus of the quality-of-life concept as it relates to specific conditions brings us to the domains of physical impairment or disability and of dementia. Quality of life in the former context includes issues of environmental design that improve people's functioning and well-being, such as bathrooms and facilities accessible to the handicapped, as we explore in Chapter 5 (Pynoos, Caraviello, & Cicero, 2010).

Quality of life is more difficult to assess in people with dementia and chronic diseases, although new assessment instruments have been developed (Gitlin et al., 2016; Karim et al., 2008; Skevington & McCrate, 2012). We consider this issue in more detail in Chapter 10 when we focus on Alzheimer's disease.

Changes in the Immune System

Every day, our bodies are threatened by invaders: bacterial, viral, and parasitic infections (as well as their toxic by-products), and abnormal cells such as precancerous and tumor cells. Fortunately for us, we have a highly advanced defense system that is constantly working to protect us against foreign invaders: the immune system.

The National Institutes of Health provides web-based overviews of how our immune system works; check them out to learn how sophisticated our defense system is.

Although our understanding of how our immune system works has advanced tremendously over the past decade or so, many details remain unknown. For instance, one great mystery is how the immune system learns to differentiate your own cells from invaders. Researchers think the mechanism involves recognizing certain substances, called *antigens*, on the surface of invading bacteria and cells that have been taken over by viruses. Regardless of how this actually happens, once the immune system has learned to recognize the invader, it creates a defense against it.

How does this defense system work? It's an amazing process that is based essentially on only three major types of cells that form an interacting network (Helbert, 2017): cell-mediated immunity (consisting of cells originating in the thymus gland, or *T-lymphocytes*), immunity based on the release of antibodies in the blood, such as those manufactured in bone marrow or acquired from immunization or previous infection (*B-lymphocytes*), and nonspecific immunity (*monocytes* and *polymorphonuclear neutrophil leukocytes*). Together, they work as specialized forces in the war against invaders.

The primary job of the T- and B-lymphocytes is to defend against malignant (cancerous) cells, viral infection, fungal infection, and some bacteria. Natural killer cells are another, special type of lymphocytes that monitor our bodies to prevent tumor growth. NK cells are our primary defense against cancer, although how this happens is not fully understood. NK cells also help fight viral infections and parasites. In addition, there are five major types of specialized antibodies called immunoglobulins (IgA, IgD, IgE, IgG, and IgM). For example, IgM includes the "first responders" in the immune system, IgE is involved in allergies and asthma, and IgG (also called g-globulin) helps fight hepatitis.

How does aging affect the immune system? Researchers are only beginning to understand this process, and there are large gaps in knowledge (Helbert, 2017). Moreover, the immune system is sensitive to a wide variety of lifestyle and environmental factors, such as diet, stress, exercise, and disease, making it very difficult to isolate changes caused by aging alone (Valiathan, Ashman, & Asthana, 2016).

Changes in health with age provide insights into immune functioning. Older adults are more susceptible to certain infections and have a much higher risk of cancer (both of which are discussed in more detail later in this chapter), so most researchers believe that the immune system changes with age. Indeed, although the number of NK cells appears to increase with age after midlife, they and several other aspects of the immune system decrease in effectiveness with age (Vicente et al., 2016). For one thing, older adults' immune systems take longer to build up defenses against specific diseases, even after an immunization injection. This is probably caused by the changing balance in T-lymphocytes, which decline later in life, and may partially explain why older adults need to be immunized earlier against specific diseases such as influenza.

Similarly, B-lymphocytes decrease in functioning. Research examining the administration of substances such as growth hormones to older adults to stimulate lymphocyte functioning indicates that some specific lymphocyte functioning returns to normal with treatment, and can regenerate the thymus gland, both of which are important in ensuring good immune system functioning (Hirokawa, Utsuyama, & Kikuchi, 2016). However, growth hormone deficiency, which happens naturally with aging, appears favorable for a longer life span. Clearly, use of growth hormone presents a trade-off of improved immune function versus longer life. This process for T- and B-lymphocytes is described in Figure 4.3.

Changes in immune system function have important implications (Helbert, 2017; Hirokawa et al., 2016; Vicente et al., 2016). Older adults become more prone to serious consequences from illnesses—such as those

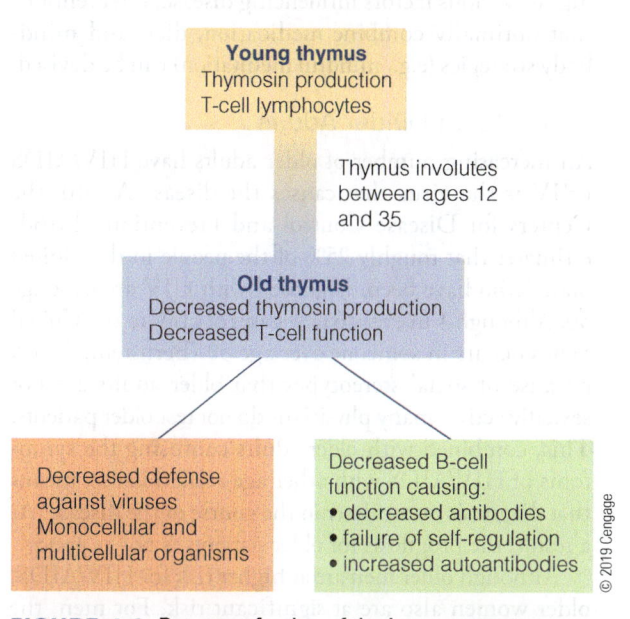

FIGURE 4.3 Process of aging of the immune system.
Source: Reprinted with permission from Ebersole, P., & Hess, P., *Toward Healthy Aging* (5th ed., p. 41). Copyright © 1998 Mosby St. Louis: with permission from Elsevier.

caused by viruses—that are easily defeated by younger adults. Older adults also benefit less from immunizations. In addition, various forms of leukemia, which are cancers of the immune cells, increase with age, along with other forms of cancer. *Finally, the immune system can begin attacking the body itself in a process called* **autoimmunity**. Autoimmunity results from an imbalance of B- and T-lymphocytes, giving rise to autoantibodies, and is responsible for several disorders, such as rheumatoid arthritis (Mälzer, Schulz, & Thiel, 2016).

A growing body of evidence is pointing to key connections between our immune system and our psychological state. Over 20 years of research shows how our psychological state, or a characteristic such as our attitude, creates neurological, hormonal, and behavioral responses that directly change the immune system and make us more likely to become ill. This is especially the case in terms of the negative effects of stress on our immune system (Reed & Raison, 2016).

From this discussion, it should be clear that the immune system is affected by many other body systems. **Psychoneuroimmunology** *is the study of the relations between psychological, neurological, and immunological systems that raise or lower our susceptibility to and ability to recover from disease.* Psychoneuroimmunology is increasingly being used as a framework to understand health outcomes and in predicting how people cope with and survive illness (Reed & Raison, 2016). By considering the various factors influencing disease, interventions that optimally combine medication, diet, and mind–body strategies (e.g., mindful meditation) can be devised.

HIV/AIDS and Older Adults

An increasing number of older adults have HIV/AIDS (HIV is the virus that causes the disease AIDS); the Centers for Disease Control and Prevention (2016d) estimates that roughly 25% of the people in the United States who have been diagnosed with HIV are over age 50. Although 1 in every 6 new cases of HIV in the United States occurs in someone over age 50 (Bernstein, 2016), because of social stereotypes that older adults are not sexually active, many physicians do not test older patients. This, combined with older adults confusing the symptoms of HIV/AIDS with other age-related issues, means that diagnosis occurs later in the course of the disease. As a result, the prognosis for older patients is not as good.

Although older men are at higher risk for HIV/AIDS, older women also are at significant risk. For men, the most common risk factor is homosexual or bisexual behavior. In contrast, HIV/AIDS usually is transmitted to older women through heterosexual contact with infected partners. Older adults may be more susceptible to HIV infection because of the changes in the immune system discussed earlier. For women, the thinning of the vaginal wall with age makes it more likely that it will tear, making it easier for the HIV to enter the bloodstream. Older adults are the least likely group to practice safe sex through such things as condom usage, which also raises the risk (Silva, 2016). Older African Americans are 12 times more likely than their European American counterparts to have HIV, and Latinos are five times more likely (Gay Men's Health Crisis, 2010).

Once they are infected, the progression from HIV-positive status to AIDS is more rapid among older adults due to the changes in the immune system with age described earlier (AIDS.gov, 2015). HIV/AIDS increases the likelihood of other related diseases, such as chronic inflammation. Once they are diagnosed with AIDS, older adults' remaining life span is significantly shorter than it is for newly diagnosed young adults, and mortality rates are higher.

Clearly, older adults need to be educated about their risk for HIV and AIDS, and about the continued need for condom use. Older adults who are reentering the dating scene may incorrectly think they are not at risk. However, ageism on the part of professionals, misconceptions about sexual activity among older adults, and older adults' lack of knowledge concerning HIV/AIDS are all barriers to proper education and screening (AIDS.gov, 2015; Silva, 2016). Because AIDS/HIV is not a major focus of media stories about older adult sexual activity, older adults may mistakenly believe they have nothing to worry about. They are less likely to raise the issue with a physician, less likely to be tested, and, if diagnosed, less likely to seek support groups. In short, we need to change outmoded beliefs about older adults and sexuality and focus on health and prevention.

Chronic and Acute Diseases

Rosa, the immigrant from Mexico, is typical of older adults: She is beginning to experience some recurring health difficulties and is finding out that she does not recover as quickly from even minor afflictions. You probably have had several encounters with illnesses that come on quickly, may range from mild to very severe, last a few days, and then go away. Illnesses such as influenza and strep throat are examples. You also may have experienced conditions that come on more slowly, last much longer, and have long-term consequences. Kidney disease, diabetes, and arthritis are examples. Your experiences reflect the difference between acute and chronic diseases.

Acute diseases *are conditions that develop over a short period of time and cause a rapid change in health.* We are all familiar with acute diseases, such as colds, influenza, and food poisoning. Most acute diseases are cured with medications (such as antibiotics for bacterial infections) or are monitored and allowed to run their course (the case with most viral infections). Acute diseases include such things as influenza, strep throat, and the common cold.

In contrast, **chronic diseases** *are conditions that last a longer period of time (at least 3 months) and may be accompanied by residual functional impairment that necessitates long-term management.* Chronic diseases include such things as cardiovascular disease, arthritis, and diabetes mellitus.

What do you think happens to the incidence of acute and chronic diseases as people age? If you say that as people get older the rates of acute diseases go down whereas the rates of chronic diseases go up, you are correct. Contrary to what many people believe, older adults have fewer colds, for example, than younger adults. That is because the human immune system learns from fighting invaders over the life span and creates increased aspects of immunity to different viruses, for instance. However, when they do get an acute disease, older adults tend to get sicker, recovery takes longer, and death from acute disease occurs more often (Centers for Disease Control and Prevention, 2015). Thus, although they get fewer acute infections, older people may actually spend more days feeling sick than their younger counterparts.

This is probably why many people mistakenly believe that the rates of acute disease increase with age. Because they have more problems fighting acute infections, older adults are more at risk from dying of an acute condition than are other adults. For example, the rate of respiratory infection is about the same for younger and older adults, but people over age 65 account for nearly all deaths from pneumonia and influenza. For these reasons, health professionals strongly recommend that older adults be vaccinated against pneumonia and influenza.

Until the 1990s, chronic disease was simply viewed as a part of aging. With the publication in 1991 of the historic document *Healthy People 2000: National Health Promotion and Disease Prevention* (U.S. Department of Health and Human Services, 1991), the view shifted dramatically to one that emphasized prevention and wellness. Chronic disease came to be viewed as *disease,* not part of the normative aging process. As we see a bit later in this chapter, advances in understanding the causes of chronic disease have resulted in better prevention in many cases, and better disease management in others.

The Role of Stress

You know what it feels like to be stressed. Whether it's from the upcoming exam in this course, the traffic jam you sat in on your way home yesterday, or the demands your children or your job place on you, stress seems to be everywhere.

There is plenty of scientific evidence that over the long term, stress is very bad for your health. But despite thousands of scientific studies that result in our certainty about what stress does to us, scientists still cannot agree on a formal definition of what stress is. What is clear is that stress involves both physiological and psychological aspects (Levy & Bavishi, in press).

The most widely applied approaches to stress involve: (a) focusing on the physiological responses the body makes through the nervous and endocrine systems; and (b) the idea that stress is what people define as stressful. Let's consider each in more detail.

Stress as a Physiological Response

There is widespread agreement across many research studies that people differ in their physiological responses to stress (Campbell & Ehlert, 2012; Laurent et al., 2016). Prolonged exposure to stress results in damaging influences from the sympathetic nervous system (which controls such things as heart rate, respiration, perspiration, blood flow, muscle strength, and mental activity) and a weakening of the immune system. As Cohen and colleagues (2012) discussed in their model of these effects, prolonged stress has a direct causative effect on susceptibility to a wide range of diseases, from the common cold to cardiovascular disease to cancer. At the cellular level, stress may play a role in shortening telomeres (see Chapter 3; Mathur et al., 2016).

Gender differences in physiological stress responses have also been documented. For example, there is some evidence that the hormone oxytocin plays a different role in women than in men. Oxytocin is the hormone important in women's reproductive activities and for establishing strong bonds with one's children (Kim, Strathearn, & Swain, 2016). Researchers speculate that when stressed, men opt for a "flight or fight" approach whereas women opt for a "tend and befriend" approach (Taylor, 2006). Fischer-Shofty, Levkovitz, and Shamay-Tsoory (2013) showed that oxytocin improves accurate perception of social interactions, but in different ways in men and women. In men, performance improved only for competition recognition, whereas in women it improved for kinship recognition.

The Stress and Coping Paradigm

Suppose you are stuck in a traffic jam. Depending on whether you are late for an important appointment or have plenty of time on your hands, you will probably feel very different about your situation. *The **stress and coping paradigm** views stress not as an environmental stimulus or as a response but as the interaction of a thinking person and an event* (Lazarus, 1984; Lazarus et al., 1985; Lazarus & Folkman, 1984). How we interpret an event such as being stuck in traffic is what matters, not the event itself or what we do in response to it. Put more formally, stress is "a particular relationship between the person and the environment that is appraised by the person as taxing or exceeding his or her resources and endangering his or her well-being" (Lazarus & Folkman, 1984, p. 19). Note that this definition states that stress is a transactional process between a person and the environment, that it takes into account personal resources, that the person's appraisal of the situation is key, and that unless the situation is considered to be threatening, challenging, or harmful, stress does not result. A diagram of the transactional model is shown in Figure 4.4.

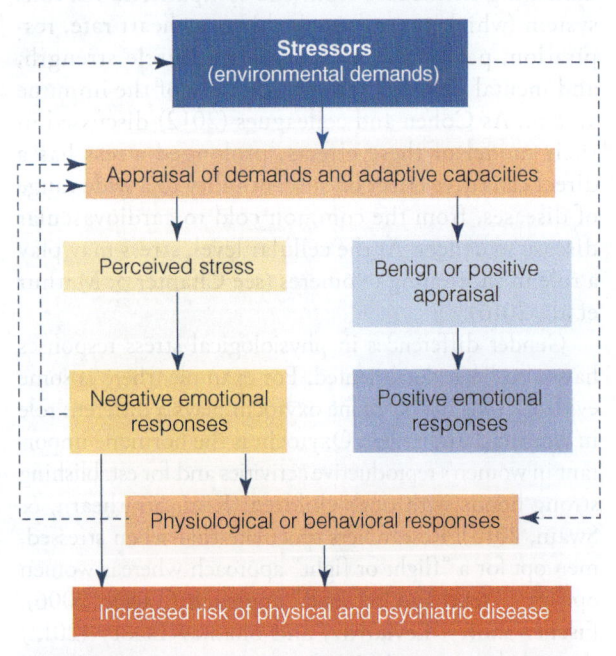

FIGURE 4.4 An example of a transactional model of stress.

Source: From Cohen, S., Kessler, R. & Gordon, L. (Eds.), *Measuring Stress: A Guide for Health and Social Scientists.* Copyright © 1995 by Oxford University Press. Used with permission from Oxford University Press.

Appraisal

Lazarus and Folkman (1984) describe three types of appraisals of stress. **Primary appraisal** *categorizes events into three groups based on the significance they have for our well-being: irrelevant, benign or positive, and stressful.* Primary appraisals filter the events we experience. Specifically, any event that is appraised as either irrelevant (things that do not affect us) or as benign or positive (things that are good or at least neutral) is not stressful. So, we literally decide which events are potentially stressful and which ones are not. This is an important point for two reasons. First, it means we can effectively sort out the events that may be problems and those that are not, allowing us to concentrate on dealing with life's difficulties more effectively. Second, it means that we could be wrong about our reading of an event. A situation that may appear at first blush to be irrelevant, for example, may actually be very important, or a situation deemed stressful initially may turn out not to be. Such mistakes in primary appraisal could set the stage for real (or imagined) crises later on.

If a person believes that an event is stressful, a second set of decisions, called secondary appraisal, is made. **Secondary appraisal** *evaluates our perceived ability to cope with harm, threat, or challenge.* Secondary appraisal is the equivalent of asking three questions: "What can I do?" "How likely is it that I can use one of my options successfully?" and "Will this option reduce my stress?" How we answer these questions sets the stage for addressing them effectively. For example, if you believe there is something you can do in a situation that will make a difference, then your perceived stress may be reduced, and you may be able to deal with the event successfully. In contrast, if you believe there is little that you can do to address the situation successfully or reduce your feelings of stress, then you may feel powerless and ineffective, even if others around you believe there are steps you could take.

Sometimes, you learn additional information or experience another situation that indicates you should reappraise the original event. **Reappraisal** *involves making a new primary or secondary appraisal resulting from changes in the situation.* For example, you may initially dismiss an accusation that your partner is cheating on you (i.e., make a primary appraisal that the event is irrelevant), but after being shown pictures of your partner in a romantic situation with another person, you reappraise the event as stressful. Reappraisal can either increase stress (if your partner had initially denied the encounter) or lower stress (if you discovered that the photographs were fakes).

The three types of appraisals demonstrate that determining whether an event is stressful is a dynamic process. Initial decisions about events may be upheld over time, or they may change in light of new information or personal experience. Different events may be appraised in the same way, and the same event may be appraised differently at any two points in time. This dynamic process helps explain why people react the way they do over the life span. For example, as our physiological abilities change with increasing age, we may have fewer physical resources to handle particular events. As a result, events that were appraised as not stressful in young adulthood may be appraised as stressful in late life.

Coping

During the secondary appraisal of an event labeled stressful in primary appraisal, we may believe there is something we can do to deal with the event effectively. *Collectively, these attempts to deal with stressful events are called* **coping**. Lazarus and Folkman (1984) view coping more formally as a complex, evolving process of dealing with stress that is learned. Much like appraisals, coping is seen as a dynamic, evolving process that is fine-tuned over time. Our first attempt might fail, but if we try again in a slightly different way we may succeed. Coping is learned, not automatic. That is why we often do not cope very well with stressful situations we are facing for the first time (such as the end of our first love relationship). The saying "practice makes perfect" applies to coping, too. Also, coping takes time and effort. Finally, coping entails only managing the situation; we need not overcome or control it. Indeed, many stressful events cannot be fixed or undone; many times the best we can do is to learn to live with the situation. It is in this sense that we may cope with the death of a spouse.

People cope in different ways. At a general level we can distinguish between problem-focused coping and emotion-focused coping. **Problem-focused coping** *involves attempts to tackle the problem head-on*. Taking medication to treat a disease and spending more time studying for an examination are examples of problem-focused coping with the stress of illness or failing a prior test. In general, problem-focused coping entails doing something directly about the problem at hand. **Emotion-focused coping** *involves dealing with one's feelings about the stressful event*. Allowing oneself to express anger or frustration over becoming ill or failing an exam is an example of this approach. The goal here is not necessarily to eliminate the problem, although this may happen. Rather, the purpose may be to help oneself deal with situations that are difficult or impossible to tackle head-on.

Several other behaviors can also be viewed in the context of coping. Many people use their relationship with God as the basis for their coping (Bade, 2012; Kinney et al., 2003). For believers, using religious coping strategies usually results in positives outcomes when faced with negative events.

How well we cope depends on several factors. For example, healthy, energetic people are better able to cope with an infection than frail, sick people. Psychologically, a positive attitude about oneself and one's abilities is also important. Good problem-solving skills put one at an advantage by creating several options with which to manage the stress. Social skills and social support are important in helping one solicit suggestions and assistance from others. Finally, financial resources are important; having the money to pay a mechanic to fix your car allows you to avoid the frustration of trying to do it yourself.

The most effective ways to deal with stress are through various relaxation techniques. Whether you prefer yoga, visualization, progressive muscle relaxation, meditation or contemplative prayer, massage, or just chilling does not really matter. All good relaxation methods have a similar effect in that they slow your pulse, lower blood pressure, slow your breathing, reduce tension, focus concentration, lower anger and fatigue, and boost confidence.

Keep in mind that the number of stressful events, per se, is less important than one's appraisal of them and whether the person has effective skills to deal with them. Of course, should the number of stressful issues exceed one's ability to cope, then the number of issues being confronted would be a key issue.

Aging and the Stress and Coping Paradigm

Two important age-related differences in the stress and coping paradigm are the sources of stress and the choice of coping strategies. In terms of stress, three national

Religiosity and spirituality are important aspects of a person's lifestyle that must be considered in holistic approaches to health and wellness.

surveys in the United States (in 1983, 2006, and 2009) showed that younger adults, and those with lower levels of education and income reported higher stress than older adults and those with higher levels of education and income (Cohen & Janicki-Deverts, 2012).

Age differences in coping strategies across the life span are consistent (Meléndez et al., 2012; Rubio et al., 2016). One key difference is that older adults are less likely to use active coping strategies and are more likely to use past experience, emotion-focused, and religious coping strategies.

We explore the relation between age and stress in more detail in the How Do We Know? feature. Cairney and Krause (2008) use data from a large Canadian longitudinal study to show that the experience of negative life events matters in the lives of older adults.

How Do We Know?
Negative Life Events and Mastery

Who were the investigators, and what was the aim of the study? How older adults cope with the effects of stressful events related to personal mastery (whether people feel in control of things in their life) is important in understanding how people manage their lives. John Cairney and Neal Krause (2008) decided to see if exposure to life events affects age-related decline in feelings of mastery. This is one of the few large-scale studies to examine this issue over time in the same participants.

How did the investigators measure the topic of interest? To get a broad assessment of the key variables, Cairney and Krause used several self-report measures. *Mastery* was measured by a seven-item self-report questionnaire that is widely used in this type of research (a sample item is "You have little control over the things that happen to you."). *Recent life events* were measured by the number of negative life events that the respondent or someone close to the respondent had experienced in the previous 12 months. *Physician contact* was measured by asking the respondent how many times he or she had seen or talked with a family physician or general practitioner in the past 12 months. *Physical health concerns* were measured by asking respondents about 21 chronic health conditions, and by asking about limitations in daily activities. *Social support* was measured by asking whether respondents had someone (a) to confide in, (b) to count on, (c) who could give them advice, and (d) who made them feel loved. *Socioeconomic measures* included the highest education level the respondent had obtained and a five-level measure of income adequacy.

Who were the participants in the study? The sample was drawn from the longitudinal biennial National Population Health Survey (NPHS) conducted by Statistics Canada. This telephone survey consists of a national probability sample of Canadian residents across all 10 provinces every 2 years beginning in 1994 (Wave 1). For Wave 1, of the 18,342 possible respondents aged 12 and over, 17,626 participated (96.1%); 16,291 were over age 18. After eliminating cases with missing data, the final sample consisted of 15,410 respondents. Wave 4 (in 2000) included the same set of measures as Wave 1 for mastery, allowing a comparison over time. Of the respondents who completed Wave 1, 1,840 died and 5,049 could not be relocated, declined to participate, or provided incomplete data in Wave 4. This left 9,521 respondents for this longitudinal study.

What was the design of the study? Cairney and Krause used a longitudinal design with two times of measurement: 1994 and 2000.

Were there ethical concerns in the study? Because people had the right not to participate, and data were not identifiable by individual and only reported in aggregate, there were no ethical concerns with the study.

What were the results? Because of the problems inherent in longitudinal designs (see Chapter 1), Cairney and Krause checked for systematic differences in participants in the Wave 1 and Wave 4 data. They found that men, those from higher income groups, those with only a high school education, older adults, and those with more physical disabilities or health problems were more likely to have died by Wave 4. Single individuals, those with lower income adequacy, with more physical disability, and with higher levels of social support were more likely to drop out by Wave 4.

An analysis of the effects of stress on perceived mastery was done by comparing outcomes at ages 25, 45, and 65. This analysis showed that at each time of measurement for people in all three age groups, exposure to more negative life events was associated with decline in mastery, with this outcome being strongest with the age 65 group. Looking at the data longitudinally, the effects of more negative life events over time was greatest for the group that was age 65 in Wave 1.

What did the investigators conclude? These findings show that experiencing negative life events is a major source of age-related declines in feelings of personal mastery. In turn, loss of personal mastery may explain why older adults are more vulnerable to the negative effects of stress.

Effects of Stress on Health

How does stress affect us? If the stress is short, such as being stuck in a traffic jam for an hour when we're already late in an otherwise relaxed day, the answer is that it probably will have little effect other than on our temper. But if the stress is continuous, or chronic, then the picture changes dramatically.

There is ample evidence that perceived stress is related to brain structures; for instance, the size of the hippocampus, a brain structure intimately involved in cognition (see Chapter 2) is smaller in people who report moderate to high levels of chronic stress (Lindgren, Bergdahl, & Nyberg, 2016). Likewise, chronic stress has been clearly shown to have very significant negative effects on health, including pervasive negative effects on the immune system that cause increased susceptibility to viral infections, increased risk of atherosclerosis and hypertension, and impaired memory and cognition, as well as psychopathology (Frank et al., 2016; Webster-Marketon & Glaser, 2008). Effects can last for decades; severe stress experienced in childhood has effects that last well into adulthood (Shonkoff et al., 2012).

Research indicates that different types of appraisals that are interpreted as stressful create different physiological outcomes (Frank et al., 2016; Webster-Marketon & Glaser, 2008). This may mean that how the body reacts to stress depends on the appraisal process; the reaction to different types of stress is not the same. In turn, this implies that changing people's appraisal may also be a way to lower the impact of stress on the body.

One of the most serious consequences of chronic stress is that it increases the level of LDL cholesterol, which has significant negative consequences (see Chapter 3; McKay, 2016). LDL cholesterol levels rise as a result of chronic stress for several reasons: people stop exercising, eat more unhealthy foods, and have higher levels of cortisol and adrenaline (which stimulate the production of triglycerides and free fatty acids, which in turn increase LDL cholesterol levels over time). High levels of LDL cholesterol are associated with cardiovascular disease and stroke (see Chapter 3).

Adult Development in Action

Design an education program for adults regarding health and the immune system, with special focus on stress and coping.

4.3 Common Chronic Conditions and Their Management

LEARNING OBJECTIVES
- What are the most important issues in chronic disease?
- What are some common chronic conditions across adulthood?
- How can people manage chronic conditions?

Moses is a 75-year-old African American man who worked as a lawyer all his life. Recently, he was diagnosed as having prostate cancer. Moses has heard about several treatment options, such as surgery and radiation therapy, and he is concerned about potential side effects, such as impotence. Moses wonders what he should do.

Every day, millions of older adults get up in the morning and face another day of dealing with chronic diseases such as diabetes and arthritis. Although medical advances are made every year, true cures for these conditions probably are not imminent. We considered some chronic diseases in Chapter 3 in the context of discussing age-related changes in major body systems; arthritis and cardiovascular disease were among them. In this section, we will consider other chronic conditions, such as diabetes and cancer. We will see that Moses's concern about how to deal with his prostate cancer is one facing many men. As Moses will discover, in many situations there is no clear-cut "right" way to proceed. We will also examine some ways to help alleviate the effects of some chronic conditions and consider some ways in which we may be able to prevent such diseases or at least reduce our chances of getting them.

General Issues in Chronic Conditions

Having a chronic disease does not mean that one immediately becomes incapacitated. Even though the type and severity of chronic conditions vary across people, most older adults manage to accomplish the necessary tasks of daily living despite having a chronic condition.

Chronic conditions can make life unpleasant and in some cases can increase susceptibility to other diseases. Understanding chronic conditions requires understanding how the four developmental forces interact. We saw in Chapter 3 that researchers are beginning to understand genetic connections with chronic conditions such as cardiovascular disease and cancer. Other biological aspects include the changes in physical systems with age, including the immune system, which can set the stage for chronic conditions. Key psychological aspects of chronic disease include the coping skills people bring to bear on their conditions; we consider some of these later in this chapter. Sociocultural factors include the lack of adequate health care, which creates barriers to treatment. The ethnic group differences in some chronic conditions, such as hypertension, are also important to keep in mind. Finally, life-cycle factors help us understand why reactions to the same chronic condition vary with the age of onset. Moreover, some conditions, such as rheumatoid arthritis, can occur at any point in adulthood, whereas others, such as prostate cancer, tend to occur mostly after midlife. As the number of older adults increases rapidly, so will the extent of chronic conditions as health problems. This will necessitate a fundamental change in health care, reflecting a shift from an acute care focus to one that focuses much more on managing chronic conditions.

Common Chronic Conditions

Roughly half of adults in the United States have a chronic health condition (National Center for Health Statistics, 2016a). Some of the most common, such as cardiovascular disease and arthritis, were considered in Chapter 3. We will consider three other common conditions, diabetes mellitus, cancer, and incontinence, in this section.

Diabetes Mellitus

The disease **diabetes mellitus** *occurs when the pancreas produces insufficient insulin.* The primary characteristic of diabetes mellitus is above-normal sugar (glucose) in the blood and urine caused by problems in metabolizing carbohydrates. People with diabetes mellitus can go into a coma if the level of sugar gets too high, and they may lapse into unconsciousness if it gets too low.

There are two general types of diabetes (American Diabetes Association, 2016a). **Type 1 diabetes** *usually develops earlier in life and requires the use of insulin, hence it is sometimes called insulin-dependent diabetes.* **Type 2 diabetes** *typically develops in adulthood and is often effectively managed through diet.* There are three groups of older adults with diabetes: those who develop diabetes as children, adolescents, or young adults; those who develop diabetes in late middle age and also typically develop cardiovascular problems; and those who develop diabetes in late life and usually show mild problems. This last group includes the majority of older adults with diabetes mellitus.

In adults, diabetes mellitus is often associated with obesity. The symptoms of diabetes seen in younger people (excessive thirst, increased appetite and urination, fatigue, weakness, weight loss, and impaired wound healing) may be far less prominent or absent in older adults. As a result, diabetes mellitus in older adults often is diagnosed during other medical procedures or screenings, such as regular annual examinations or hospitalizations for other conditions.

Overall, diabetes is more common among older adults and members of minority groups (National Center for Health Statistics, 2016a). For people with diabetes, the chronic effects of increased glucose levels may result in serious complications. The most common long-term effects include nerve damage, diabetic retinopathy (discussed in Chapter 3), kidney disorders, cerebrovascular accidents (CVAs), cognitive dysfunction, damage to the coronary arteries, skin problems, and poor circulation in the arms and legs, which may lead to gangrene. Diabetes also increases the chance of having a stroke or developing atherosclerosis and coronary heart disease.

Although it cannot be cured, diabetes can be managed effectively through a low-carbohydrate and low-calorie diet; exercise; proper care of skin, gums, teeth, and feet; and medication (insulin) (American Diabetes Association, 2016b). For older adults, it is important to address potential memory difficulties with the daily testing and management regimens. Following the appropriate management strategy is key to avoiding or minimizing the risk of the complications noted earlier. Education about diabetes mellitus is included in Medicare coverage, making it easier for older adults to learn how to manage the condition. Taking the appropriate steps to avoid diabetes in the first place is the best strategy, of course, so monitoring diet and weight are important aspects of an overall wellness-based life style.

Cancer

Cancer is the second leading cause of death in the United States, behind cardiovascular disease (National Center for Health Statistics, 2016a). However, it is likely that cancer will become the leading cause within the coming decade. Over the life span, American men have about a 42% chance and American women have about a 38% chance of developing some form of cancer. The risk of dying from cancer is slightly less than one in four for men and one in five for women (American Cancer Society, 2016b). The risk of getting cancer increases markedly with age, in part because of declines in the effectiveness of the immune system, in part because of the cumulative effects of environmental effects, in part because of changes in our genetic structures, and in part for reasons we do not yet understand. Because of the remarkable advances in interventions, especially those based on designer genetic treatments, death rates for most types of cancer have been falling since the 1990s.

Many forms of cancer are preventable (American Cancer Society, 2016c). For example, some forms of cancer, such as lung and colorectal cancer, are caused in large part by unhealthy lifestyles. Smoking causes more preventable health conditions than any other lifestyle issue. Most skin cancers can be prevented by limiting exposure to the sun's ultraviolet rays. Clearly, changes in lifestyle could significantly lower the occurrence of certain cancers.

The incidence and mortality rates of some common forms of cancer in men and women are shown in Table 4.1. Notice that prostate cancer is the most common form of cancer in men, and breast cancer is the most common form in women (American Cancer Society, 2016b).

Death rates from various forms of cancer differ: Lung cancer kills more than three times as many men as prostate cancer and considerably more women than breast cancer. Five-year survival rates for people aged 55 to 64 for various forms of cancer also differ dramatically. Whereas only 4% of patients with glioblastoma (a form of brain cancer) are still living 5 years after diagnosis, roughly 90% of female patients with stage 0, 1, or 2 breast cancer and nearly all men with prostate cancer are (American Cancer Society, 2016d, 2016e, 2016f).

Why older people have a much higher incidence of cancer is not understood fully. Part of the reason is the cumulative effect of poor health habits over a long period of time, such as cigarette smoking and poor diet. In addition, the cumulative effects of exposure to pollutants and cancer-causing chemicals are partly to blame. As noted earlier in this chapter, some researchers believe that normative age-related changes in the immune system, resulting in a decreased ability to

TABLE 4.1 Lifetime Risk of Developing or Dying from Selected Types of Cancer

Males	Risk of Developing		Risk of Dying From	
	%	1 in	%	1 in
All sites	42.05	2	22.62	4
Brain and nervous system	0.69	145	0.51	196
Colon and rectum	4.69	21	1.99	50
Lung and bronchus	7.19	14	6.33	16
Melanoma	2.62	38	0.43	233
Prostate	13.97	7	2.58	39
Testicles	0.38	263	0.02	5,000
Females				
All sites	37.58	3	19.13	5
Brain and nervous system	0.54	185	0.40	250
Breast	12.32	8	2.69	37
Colon and rectum	4.35	23	1.81	55
Lung and bronchus	6.04	17	4.89	20
Melanoma	1.63	61	0.21	476
Ovary	1.31	76	0.97	103

Source: American Cancer Society (2016). *Lifetime risk of developing or dying from cancer.* Retrieved from www.cancer.org/cancer/cancerbasics/lifetime-probability-of-developing-or-dying-from-cancer.

inhibit the growth of tumors, may also be responsible. And we noted in Chapter 3 that changes occur in the cells themselves that could also play a role.

Research in molecular biology and microbiology is increasingly pointing to genetic links, likely in combination with environmental factors (Battista et al., 2012). The National Cancer Institute initiated the Cancer Genome Anatomy Program (CGAP) that includes tools to find genes and how they are expressed, and it supports an online journal and other resources in order to genetics-based research on cancer.

Genetics-based research is responsible for tremendous advances in detecting and treating cancer. For example, three breast cancer susceptibility genes that have been identified are *BRCA1* on chromosome 17 and *BRCA2* on chromosome 13, as well as *PALB2*, which works in conjunction with *BRCA2*. These genes produce proteins that suppress tumors. These proteins help repair damaged DNA and help ensure the stability of the cell's genetic material. When either of these genes is mutated, or altered, such that its protein product either is not made or does not function correctly, DNA damage may not be repaired properly. As a result, cells are more likely to develop additional genetic alterations that can lead to cancer. That is why a woman who carries a mutation in *BRCA1*, *BRCA2*, or *PALB2* is at a greater risk of being diagnosed with breast or ovarian cancer at some point in her life.

Similarly, a potential susceptibility locus for prostate cancer has been identified on chromosome 1, called *HPC1*, which may account for about 1 in 500 cases of prostate cancer. An additional rare mutation of *HOXB13*, on chromosome 17, has also been identified.

Although routine genetic screening tests for breast and prostate cancer for the general population are not yet warranted, people who are at risk for the diseases may get screened. Should the results be positive for the mutations, a key question is what to do next. For women facing an increased risk of breast cancer, for instance, this may involve decisions about prophylactic mastectomy or other surgical procedures. The Real People feature explores how one famous woman, Angelina Jolie, made her decision.

Genetics is also providing much of the exciting new research on possible treatments by giving investigators new ways to fight the disease. Age-related tissue changes have been associated with the development of tumors, some of which become cancerous; these may be genetically linked as well. The discovery that the presence of telomerase causes cells to grow rapidly and without limits on the number of divisions they can undergo provides additional insights into how cancer develops (Harrington, 2016; see Chapter 3). What remains to be seen is how these genetic events interact with environmental factors, such as viruses or pollutants. Understanding this interaction process, predicted by the basic developmental forces, could explain why there are great differences among individuals in when and how cancer develops.

Additionally, genetics research has resulted in a therapeutic approach using monoclonal antibodies (mAbs) and adoptive cellular therapy to treat cancer by modulating the immune response (Khalil et al., 2016). These interventions work by targeting the specific genetic structures of tumors through targeted strengthening of the patient's own immune system. These interventions have shown dramatic results, including the remission of advanced stage tumors. It is highly likely that most future cancer treatments will be based on this approach.

Of course, prevention is the preferred way to address the problem of cancer. The appropriate use of screening techniques and preventive lifestyle changes can lower the rates of most cancers, as well as deaths. The American Cancer Society (2015a, 2015b) strongly recommends these steps for people of all ages, but older adults need to be especially aware of what to do. Table 4.2 on page 110 shows guidelines for the early detection of some common forms of cancer.

As Moses is learning, one of the biggest controversies in cancer prevention concerns screening and treatment for prostate cancer. The Current Controversies feature summarizes the issues: lack of data about the causes and the course of the disease and disagreement over treatment approaches. This controversy mirrors similar debates over the screening and treatment of breast cancer, contrasting the relative merits of regular screening mammography, and treatment approaches including radical mastectomy (removal of the breast and some surrounding tissue) versus lumpectomy (removal of the cancerous tumor only) and how chemotherapy, radiation, and drugs such as tamoxifen fit into the overall treatment approach. As with any healthcare decision, people with cancer need to become as educated as possible about the options.

Incontinence

For many people, the loss of the ability to control the elimination of urine and feces on an occasional or consistent basis, called **incontinence**, *is a source of great concern and embarrassment.* As you can imagine, incontinence can result in social isolation and lower quality of life if no steps are taken to address the problem.

Real People
The "Angelina Jolie Effect"

Angelina Jolie is one of the most famous actresses in the world. Because of her fame, many people watch her behavior carefully and base their own actions on what she does. In 2013, Angelina learned that she carried the BRCA1 gene, which, considered in the context of the rest of her family health history and other tests that detected protein abnormalities, gave her an estimated 87% risk of breast cancer and 50% chance of ovarian cancer. What she did next created both a media sensation and greatly increased awareness of the challenges and decisions that confront thousands of women each year.

Angelina decided to have a double mastectomy and reconstructive surgery, and subsequently had her ovaries and Fallopian tubes removed. After her mastectomies, she had reconstructive surgery using her own tissue. She decided to be public about her situation in order to raise awareness of breast cancer and ovarian cancer risks and the options women have. She wrote two op-eds in the *New York Times* (Jolie, 2013, 2015) to explain her decision making. Her decision, and her fame, made a very big difference.

It became clear that an "Angelina Jolie effect" resulted. Research in the United Kingdom indicates that following the announcement of her breast cancer risk and surgery in May 2013, referrals for genetic screening for breast cancer more than doubled (Evans et al., 2014). Such increases were found globally (Lebo et al., 2015). In general, women expressed increased knowledge of breast cancer screening, techniques of reconstructive surgery, and genetic testing and risk.

Angelina Jolie's public discussion of her learning of her cancer risk, how and why she made the decisions she did, and her recovery process caused controversy. Some argued that she should have monitored her health and not undergone surgery. Others argued that she provided additional support for the stereotype of female beauty. Still others thought her decision was a brave one. What is indisputable is that her fame raised the issues much higher in public awareness, resulting in many more women consulting their physicians about potential genetic risk and health screening. And that is a very good and important outcome.

Angelina Jolie

Urinary incontinence, the most common form, is a common occasional experience (National Center for Health Statistics, 2014). Among community-dwelling older adults, roughly 60% of women and 40% of men have ever experienced urinary or bowel leakage. Rates tend to increase with age.

Urinary incontinence occurs most often for four major reasons (Mayo Clinic, 2014). **Stress incontinence** *happens when pressure in the abdomen exceeds the ability to resist urinary flow.* This may occur when a person coughs, sneezes, exercises, or lifts a heavy object. **Urge incontinence** *usually is caused by a central nervous system*

TABLE 4.2 American Cancer Society Guidelines for the Early Detection of Cancer

	The American Cancer Society Recommends These Screening Guidelines for Most Adults
Breast cancer (Women)	• From ages 40 to 44, choose whether you want to get a mammogram to screen for breast cancer. • Between ages 45 and 54, get a mammogram every year. • For age 55 and over, either switch to every two years or continue annual mammograms for as long as you are healthy and expect to live at least 10 more years. • Be aware of the risks, benefits, limitations, and harms linked with breast cancer screening. • Women should know how their breasts normally look and feel and report any breast change promptly to their healthcare provider. Breast self-exam (BSE) is an option for women starting in their 20s. • If you are at increased risk for breast cancer due to family or personal history, consult your physician for the best screening plan for you.
Colorectal cancer and polyps	Beginning at age 50, both men and women should follow one of these testing schedules: **Tests that find polyps and cancer** • Flexible sigmoidoscopy every 5 years, or • Colonoscopy every 10 years, or • Double-contrast barium enema every 5 years, or • CT colonography (virtual colonoscopy) every 5 years **Tests that primarily find cancer** • Yearly fecal occult blood test (gFOBT), or • Yearly fecal immunochemical test (FIT) every year, or • Stool DNA test (sDNA)
Cervical cancer	• **Cervical cancer screening (testing) should begin at age 21**. Women under age 21 should *not* be tested. • **Women between ages 21 and 29** should have a Pap test every 3 years. Now there is also a test called the HPV test. HPV testing should *not* be used in this age group unless it is needed after an abnormal Pap test result. • **Women between the ages of 30 and 65** should have a Pap test plus an HPV test (called "co-testing") every 5 years. This is the preferred approach, but it is also OK to have a Pap test alone every 3 years. • **Women over age 65** who have had regular cervical cancer testing with normal results should *not* be tested for cervical cancer. Once testing is stopped, it should not be started again. Women with a history of a serious cervical pre-cancer should continue to be tested for at least 20 years after that diagnosis, even if testing continues past age 65. • **A woman who has had her uterus removed (and also her cervix)** for reasons not related to cervical cancer and who has no history of cervical cancer or serious pre-cancer should *not* be tested. • **A woman who has been vaccinated against HPV** should still follow the screening recommendations for her age group.
Lung cancer	The American Cancer Society does not recommend tests to screen for lung cancer in people who are at average risk of this disease. However, if you are between the ages of 55 and 74, are in otherwise average health but have smoked for many years AND either still smoke or only quit within the past 15 years, the ACS recommends consulting a healthcare provider about the best screening options for you.
Prostate cancer (Men)	At age 50, the ACS recommends that men make an informed decision with their physician about whether to be tested for prostate cancer. If you are African American or have a family history of prostate cancer, have this discussion at age 45.

Take control of your health, and reduce your cancer risk

- Stay away from all forms of tobacco.
- Stay at a healthy weight.
- Get moving with regular physical activity.
- Eat healthy with plenty of fruits and vegetables.
- Limit how much alcohol you drink to no more than one drink per day if you are a woman, and two drinks per day if you are a man.
- Protect your skin from the sun.
- Know yourself, your family history, and your risks.
- Have regular check-ups and cancer screening tests.
- For information on how to reduce your cancer risk and other questions about cancer, you can call 1-800-227-2345 or visit ACS online at www.cancer.org

Sources: www.cancer.org/acs/groups/content/@editorial/documents/document/acspc-035113.pdf; www.cancer.org/acs/groups/content/@editorial/documents/document/acspc-035114.pdf.

Current Controversies
The Prostate Cancer Dilemma

Roughly the size of a walnut and weighing about an ounce, the prostate gland is an unlikely candidate to create a major medical controversy. The prostate is located in men in front of the rectum and below the bladder, and wraps around the urethra (the tube carrying urine out through the penis). Its primary function is to produce fluid for semen, the liquid that transports sperm. In half of all men over age 60, the prostate tends to enlarge, which may produce such symptoms as difficulty in urinating and frequent nighttime urination.

Enlargement of the prostate can happen for three main reasons: prostatitis (an inflammation of the prostate that is usually caused by an infection), benign prostatic hyperplasia (BPH), and prostate cancer. BPH is a noncancerous enlargement of the prostate that affects the innermost part of the prostate first. This often results in urination problems as the prostate gradually squeezes the urethra, but it does not affect sexual functioning.

Prostate cancer is the second most common form of cancer in men (skin cancer is the most common). Prostate cancer often begins on the outer portion of the prostate, which seldom causes symptoms in the early stages. Each year, more than 180,000 men in the United States are diagnosed with prostate cancer; over 26,000 die (National Cancer Institute, 2016a). For reasons we do not yet understand, African American men such as Moses have a 40% higher chance of getting prostate cancer. In addition, a genetic link is clear: A man whose brother has prostate cancer is four times more likely to get prostate cancer than a man with no brothers having the disease. There is some evidence of links to several genes: *RNASEL, BRCA1, BRCA2, MSH2, MLH1,* and *HOXB13.* However, how these genetic mutations may work is not completely understood. Additionally, most prostate cancers occur in men with no apparent family history.

Much of the controversy surrounding prostate cancer relates to whether early detection reduces mortality from the disease. Research investigating whether screening for early detection of prostate cancer saved lives indicated that, overall, it did not, and may actually create problems such as unnecessary treatment because most forms of prostate cancer are very slow growing. This lack of data led the U.S. Preventive Services Task Force, the Canadian Task Force on the Periodic Health Examination, and others to recommend abandoning routine prostate cancer screening because of the cost and the uncertain benefits associated with it.

The American Cancer Society (ACS) and the National Comprehensive Cancer Network jointly created a guide to prostate cancer screening and treatment to help men negotiate the confusing state of affairs (American Cancer Society, 2016g; National Comprehensive Cancer Network, 2012). The background information provided by these organizations can help men decide what, if any, screening and treatment options are best for them.

The sharp division among medical experts highlights the relation between carefully conducted research and public health policy. At present, there has been insufficient

continued

comparison of various treatment options (which include surgery, radiation, hormones, and drugs), and we do not fully understand the natural course of prostate cancer in terms of which types of tumors grow rapidly or spread to other organs and the typical type that grows slowly and does not. Given that some of the side effects of surgery include urinary incontinence and impotence, and that some of the other therapies may produce other unpleasant effects, there is debate on whether the disease should be treated at all in most patients (National Cancer Institute, 2016b).

At present, men who experience prostate-related symptoms or who are concerned about prostate cancer are left to decide for themselves, in consultation with their physician, what to do. Many men opt for immediate treatment and learn how to live with any subsequent side effects. Support groups for men with prostate cancer are becoming more common, and many encourage the patient's partner to participate.

The controversy surrounding early screening and detection of prostate cancer is unlikely to subside soon because the necessary research concerning effective treatment and survival will take years to conduct. Until then, if you or someone you know is over 50 or is in a high-risk group, the decision still must be made. Talk at length with a physician who is up-to-date on the topic and educate yourself about the alternatives.

problem after a stroke or urinary tract infection. People feel the urge to urinate but cannot get to a toilet quickly enough. **Overflow incontinence** *results from improper contraction of the kidneys, causing the bladder to become overdistended.* Certain drugs, tumors, and prostate enlargement are common causes of overflow incontinence. **Functional incontinence** *occurs when the urinary tract is intact but because of physical disability or cognitive impairment the person is unaware of the need to urinate.* This is the most common form in people with dementia, Parkinson's disease, or arthritis.

Most types of incontinence can be alleviated with interventions. Among the most effective are behavioral interventions, which include diet changes, relearning to recognize the need to toilet, and pelvic floor muscle training for stress incontinence (Hsu, Suskind, & Huang, 2016). Certain medications and surgical intervention may be needed in some cases. Numerous products such as protective undergarments and padding also are available to help absorb leaks. All these options help alleviate the psychological and social effects of incontinence and help people live better lives (Markland et al., 2012).

Managing Pain

People do not like to be in pain, and they fear pain more than almost any other aspect of disease. Perhaps that is because pain is one of the most unpleasant aspects of many chronic diseases. Pain is disruptive, saps energy, negatively affects quality of life, and can lead to an ever-intensifying cycle of pain, anxiety, and anguish. Pain is also one of the most common complaints of older adults, affecting more than 40% of community-dwelling older adults on a regular basis (Jones et al, 2016; Shega et al., 2012). Pain for older adults does not necessarily reflect the same things as pain in younger adults; for older adults it is not only an indication that something is wrong, but can also be responsible for depression, sleep disorders, decreased social interaction, impaired mobility, and increased healthcare costs (Jones et al., 2016).

Unfortunately, many myths exist about pain in older adults, such as that older adults should simply accept the physical pain they experience as part of growing older. Failure to understand the real causes and nature of pain in older adults can lead to a failure to relieve it, and to appropriately and accurately diagnose any underlying conditions that cause it.

How do people manage pain? Perhaps the most important aspects are to understand that pain is not a necessary part of treatment, that people can control their pain, that no one approach is likely to be sufficient, and that asking for pain relief is to be expected. There are two general pain management techniques: pharmacological and nonpharmacological (Jones et al., 2016). These approaches often are used together for maximum pain relief.

Pharmacological approaches to pain management include nonnarcotic and narcotic medications. Nonnarcotic medications are best for mild to moderate pain, while narcotic medications are best for severe pain. Nonnarcotic medications include NSAIDs (nonsteroidal anti-inflammatory drugs), such as ibuprofen and acetaminophen, and are commonly used for conditions causing pain such as arthritis. However, these drugs must be used with caution because they may cause toxic side effects in older adults. Narcotic or opioid drugs that work well in older adults include morphine and codeine; other commonly used drugs, such as meperidine and pentazocine, should be avoided because of age-related changes in metabolism. Patients taking any of these medications must be monitored very closely, as there is a significant risk of addiction or abuse of these medications.

Nonpharmacological pain control includes a variety of approaches, all of which are effective with some people; the trick is to keep trying until the best approach is found. Common techniques include the following:

- Deep and superficial stimulation of the skin through therapeutic touch, massage, vibration, heat, cold, and various ointments
- Electrical stimulation over the pain site or to the spine
- Acupuncture and acupressure
- Biofeedback, in which a person learns to control and change the body processes responsible for the pain
- Distraction techniques such as soft music that draw a person's attention away from the pain
- Relaxation, meditation, and imagery approaches that rid the mind of tension and anxiety
- Hypnosis, either self-induced or induced by another person

The most important point is that pain is not a necessary part of growing old or having a disease. Pain relief is an important part of recovery and should be included in any treatment regimen for adults of all ages.

Adult Development in Action

Given the higher frequency of chronic disease with age, what issues would you, as a professional human resources expert, need to include in creating support programs for employees?

4.4 Pharmacology and Medication Adherence

LEARNING OBJECTIVES
- What are the developmental trends in using medication?
- How does aging affect the way the medications work?
- What are the consequences of medication interactions?
- What are the important medication adherence issues?

Lucy is an 80-year-old woman who has several chronic health problems. As a result, she takes 12 medications every day. She must follow the regimen very carefully; some of her medications must be taken with food, some on an empty stomach, and some at bedtime. Lucy's daughter is concerned that Lucy may experience serious problems if she fails to take her medications properly.

One of the most important health issues for older adults is the use of both prescription and over-the-counter medications. In fact, older adults take more medications on average than any other age group, roughly half of all drugs prescribed in the United States. When over-the-counter drugs are included, this translates into about six or seven medications per older adult; Lucy takes more than the average. Like Lucy, most people take these drugs to relieve pain or related problems resulting from chronic conditions.

Patterns of Medication Use

The explosion of new prescription and over-the-counter medications over the past few decades has created many options for physicians in treating disease, especially chronic conditions. Although advances in medication are highly desirable, there are hidden dangers for older adults (U.S. Food and Drug Administration, 2015).

Until the late 1990s, clinical trials of new medications were not required to include older adults. Thus, for many medications currently on the market, we do not know whether they are as effective for older adults as they are for younger or middle-aged adults. Equally important, because of normative changes in metabolism with age, the effective dosage of medications may change as people get older, which can mean a greater risk of overdose with potentially serious consequences, including death, or the need to increase the dose in order to get the desired effect. This lack of knowledge may result in physicians being more cautious in prescribing certain medications for older people.

In the United States, the cost of prescription drugs is both controversial and a barrier for many older adults with low incomes even with insurance through Medicare Part D because of premiums and co-payments. Additionally, figuring out which option is best can be quite complex, serving as a further barrier. (You can get much more information from the official Medicare prescription drug coverage website.)

The age-related increase in chronic disease typically results in related increases in the number of medications people take to help manage those diseases and help maintain health. When multiple medications are used, interaction effects must be carefully understood and monitored. As we will see, in many cases the need to take multiple medications results in complicated regimens that may also create memory challenges. Understanding how medications work and how these processes change with age is extremely important.

Developmental Changes in How Medications Work

When Lucy takes her medications every day, what happens? Understanding how medications work involves knowing the developmental changes in absorption, distribution, metabolism, and excretion of medications (Chisholm-Burns et al., 2016).

Absorption *is the time needed for one of Lucy's medications to enter the bloodstream.* For drugs taken orally, a key factor is the time it takes for the medication to go from the stomach to the small intestine, where maximum absorption occurs. This transfer may take longer than expected in older adults, resulting in too little or too much absorption, depending on the drug. For example, if a drug takes longer to transfer from the stomach to the small intestine in older adults, too little of the drug may be left to be effective. However, once in the small intestine, absorption does not appear to differ among older, middle-aged, or younger adults (Chisholm-Burns et al., 2016).

Once in the bloodstream, the medication is distributed throughout the body. How well distribution occurs depends on the adequacy of the cardiovascular system. Maximal effectiveness of a drug depends on the balance between the portions of the drug that bind with plasma protein and the portions that remain free. As we grow older, more portions of the drug remain free; this means that toxic levels of a drug can build up more easily in older adults. Similarly, drugs that are soluble in water or fat tissue can also build up more easily in older adults because of age-related decreases in total body water or possible increases in fat tissue.

Because the effective dosage of a drug depends critically on the amount of free drug in the body, the age changes just summarized mean that medical professionals must monitor drug levels very closely in order to avoid overdose or toxicity. Knowing the age, sex, weight, and other metabolic factors is key to ensuring that the effective dose of each medication is provided (Chisholm-Burns et al., 2016).

Getting rid of medications in the bloodstream is partly the job of the liver, a process called **drug metabolism**.
There is much evidence that this process is slower in older adults, meaning that drugs stay in the body longer as people grow older (Le Couteur, McLachan, & de Cabo, 2012). Slower drug metabolism can also create the potential for toxicity if the medication schedule does not take this into account.

Sometimes drugs are decomposed into other compounds to help eliminate them. **Drug excretion** *occurs mainly through the kidneys in urine, although some elimination occurs through feces, sweat, and saliva.* Changes in kidney function with age, related to lower total body water content, are common. This means that drugs often are not excreted as quickly by older adults, again setting the stage for possible toxic effects (Le Couteur et al., 2012).

What do these changes mean? Most important, there are multiple age-related changes in metabolism that affect how well medications are absorbed into and excreted from the body. Each of these changes has the potential for creating toxic side effects from levels of medications that are too high. For all these reasons, the dosage of a drug needed to get a desired effect may be different for older adults than for middle-aged or younger adults. In many cases, healthcare professionals recommend using one-third to one-half the usual adult dosage when the difference between the effective dosages and toxic dosages is small or there is a high rate of side effects (Le Couteur et al., 2012). In addition, because of age-related physiological changes, several drugs are not recommended for use by older adults. In general, a dosage strategy of "start low and go slow" is best.

Medication Side Effects and Interactions

Because of their high rate of medication use, older adults also have the highest risk of adverse drug effects (Le Couteur et al., 2012; Chisholm-Burns et al., 2016; U.S. Food and Drug Administration, 2015). In part, these problems result from physiological changes that occur with age in how drugs are absorbed into the body, how long they remain, and how well they work. For example, changes in the stomach may slow down the rate at which drugs enter the body, meaning that achieving the effective level of the drug in the body may take longer. Changes in liver and kidney functioning affect how rapidly the drug is removed and excreted from the body, meaning that levels of the drug may remain high for longer periods of time.

As we have seen, age-related increases in the frequency of chronic conditions means that older adults are likely to have more than one medical problem for which they take medications. In this regard, Lucy is fairly typical. *Treating multiple conditions results in* **polypharmacy**, *the use of multiple medications.* Polypharmacy is potentially dangerous because many drugs do not interact well; the action of some drugs is enhanced in combination with others, whereas other drugs may not work at all in combination. Drug interactions may create secondary medical problems that in turn need to be treated, and the primary condition may not be treated as effectively. Moreover, drug interactions can produce symptoms that appear to be caused by other diseases; in some cases they may cause confusion and memory loss that mimics Alzheimer's disease.

Healthcare professionals and family members need to monitor the situation closely. Lucy's daughter is correct in worrying about her mother taking her medications as prescribed. Analyzing a person's medication regimen, including both prescription and over-the-counter medications, and asking the patient or caregiver to describe how they are taken is important in diagnosing health problems. It is extremely important to know all of the medications, including diet supplements, a person is taking regardless of whether they are prescribed or not.

Given the high level of medication use among older adults, what can be done to minimize drug interaction effects? Healthcare professionals play a key role, but others also must be alert because older adults typically go to more than one physician. Accurate medication histories including all types of medicines are essential. If a problem is detected, then careful consideration of the risks and benefits of each medication is necessary, and alternative approaches to intervention, such as behavioral interventions, should be explored. The goal should be to use medications only when absolutely necessary, and to avoid creating additional problems through their use.

Adherence to Medication Regimens

For medications to be maximally effective, it is important that they be taken as directed. This means that there is a critical memory component to the safe and effective use of medications—one must remember to take them. This is much easier when one is taking only a few medications. However, as one is required to take more medications, keeping track of each becomes a more difficult memory challenge. A good example of having to keep track of six different medications, not uncommon among older adults, each of which has a different administration schedule, is presented in Table 4.3.

Medication adherence (taking medications correctly) becomes less likely the more drugs people take and the more complicated the regimens are. Combined with sensory, physical, and cognitive changes in older adults, medication adherence is a significant problem in this age group (Chisholm-Burns et al., 2016; Suchy, 2016). Prospective memory, remembering to take one's medication at a future time, is critical to good adherence to a medication regimen (Suchy, 2016; Zogg et al., 2012). The oldest old are especially at risk; the most common problem is that they simply forget to take the medication. (We consider ways to help people remember to take their medications in Chapter 7.) Yet adherence is crucial to treatment success. Christensen and Johnson (2002) present an interactive model that describes the context of patient adherence. This model is shown in Figure 4.5.

A related issue is whether there are age-related differences in the ability of people to notice and remember adverse side effects from medications. Evidence suggests

TABLE 4.3 Example of a Complex Medication Regimen

	Morning	Dinner	Bedtime
Large yellow pill	Take 1 each day with food		
Small blue pill	Take 1 every other day		
Small white pill	Take 2 per day for two days, then 1 per day; repeat		
Round pink tablet		Take 1 every other day	
Oval white pill			Take 2 each night with plenty of water
Small yellow pill			Take one per week

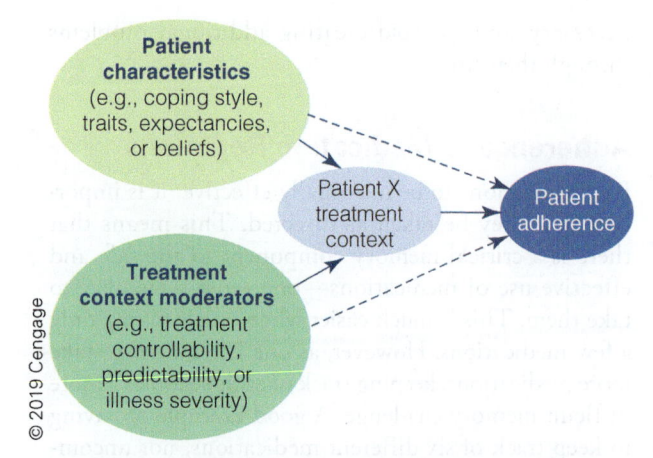

FIGURE 4.5 Conceptual representation of the patient-by-treatment context interactive framework. The dashed lines reflect the fact that research generally does not find that patient characteristics or contextual features have a significant effect on adherence.

that when older adults are told to remember side effects that range from mild to severe, they recall the severe ones as well as younger adults. However, when told that certain side effects are critical to remember, they are less likely to differentiate those from other familiar side effects than are younger adults, which may lead to a failure to contact their healthcare provider should those side effects occur (Friedman et al., 2015).

One way to support medication adherence is via technology. Smartphone apps are available that monitor medication schedules as well as several health indicators of compliance (Higgins, 2016). These apps are increasingly used as part of a comprehensive telemedicine health and wellness approach to ensure that medications are taken and other interventions and health monitoring are occurring as required.

The best approach, of course, is to keep the number of medications (and memory load) to a minimum. If the use of drugs is determined to be essential, then periodic reevaluations should be conducted and the medication discontinued when possible. In addition, the lowest effective dosage should be used. In general, medication use by older adults should get the same careful consideration as by any other age group.

Adult Development in Action

If you were a home health aide, what would you do to help your clients remember to take their medications? (Write down your answer and then see if you came up with similar ideas as you will read about in Chapter 7.)

4.5 Functional Health and Disability

LEARNING OBJECTIVES
- What factors are important to include in a model of disability in late life?
- What is functional health?
- What causes functional limitations and disability in older adults?

Brian is a 68-year-old former welder who retired 3 years ago. He and his wife, Dorothy, had planned to travel in their RV and see the country. But Brian's arthritis has been getting worse lately, and he is having increasing difficulty getting around and doing basic daily tasks. Brian and Dorothy wonder what the future holds for them.

Brian and Dorothy are not alone. Many couples plan to travel or to do other activities after they retire, only to find health issues complicating the situation. As the focus on health has shifted over the past several decades to chronic disease, researchers have increasingly focused on how well people can function in their daily lives. In this section, we examine how functional health is determined and how disability occurs.

A Model of Disability in Late Life

As we saw earlier in this chapter, one defining characteristic of a chronic condition is that it lasts a long time. This means that for most adults, the time between the onset of a chronic condition and death is long, measured in years and even decades. Chronic diseases typically involve some level of discomfort, and physical limitations are common, everyday issues for most people, as they are for Brian. Over the course of the disease, these problems usually increase, resulting in more efforts by patients and healthcare workers to try to slow the progress of the disease. In many cases, these efforts allow people to resume such activities as daily walks and shopping and to feel optimistic about the future (Verbrugge, 1994, 2005; Verbrugge, Brown, & Zajacova, 2017; Verbrugge & Jette, 1994). This is especially true for the oldest old (He & Larsen, 2014). Social context also matters for older adults, as disablement is associated with much higher loneliness, and positive marital relationships are associated with lower impairment (Warner & Adams, 2016).

In the context of chronic conditions, **disability** is the effects of chronic conditions on people's ability to engage in activities that are necessary, expected, and personally *desired in their society* (Verbrugge, 1994, 2005). When people are disabled as a result of a chronic condition, they have difficulty doing daily tasks, such as household chores, personal care, job duties, active recreation, socializing with friends and family, and errands. One of the most important research efforts related to health and aging is seeking to understand how disability results from chronic conditions and what might be done to help prevent it. For these reasons, it is important to understand the changing context of disability in the United States.

Researchers point out that as the age at which disablement occurs in late life gets closer to the end of life, these changes create what is called the compression of morbidity (Andersen et al., 2012; Lindley, 2012). **Compression of morbidity** *refers to the situation in which the average age when one becomes disabled for the first time is postponed, causing the time between the onset of disability and death to be compressed into a shorter period of time.* This implies that older adults in the United States are becoming disabled later in life than previously, and are disabled a shorter time before dying than in past generations. Actual evidence for this idea, though, is mixed, with several studies finding no evidence for the compression hypothesis (Beltrán-Sánchez, Jiménez, & Subramanian, 2016; Walter et al., 2016). The disagreement may be the result of better diagnosis of chronic disease earlier in adulthood, and advances in geroscience in terms of emerging understandings of disease and disability (Fried & Ferrucci, 2016).

Verbrugge and Jette (1994) originally proposed a comprehensive model of disability resulting from chronic conditions, a model that has greatly influenced research (see Figure 4.6). The model consists of four main parts. The main pathway emphasizes the relations between pathology (the chronic conditions a person has), impairments of organ systems (such as muscular degeneration), functional limitations in the ability to perform activities (such as restrictions in one's mobility), and disability.

The model also includes risk factors and two types of intervention strategies: environmental and health care (*extraindividual factors*) and behavioral and personality (*intraindividual factors*). **Risk factors** *are long-standing behaviors or conditions that increase one's chances of functional limitation or disability.* Examples of risk factors include low socioeconomic status, chronic health conditions, and health-related behaviors such as smoking. Extraindividual factors include interventions such as surgery, medication, social support services (e.g., Meals on Wheels), and physical environmental supports

Many people manage the pain of arthritis through medication.

(e.g., wheelchair ramps). The presence of these factors often helps people maintain their independence and may make the difference between living at home and living in a long-term care facility. Intraindividual factors include such things as beginning an exercise program, keeping a positive outlook, and taking advantage of transportation programs to increase mobility.

Extraindividual and intraindividual interventions are both aimed at reducing the restrictions and difficulties resulting from chronic conditions. Unfortunately, sometimes they do not work as intended and may even create problems of their own. For example, a prescribed medication may produce negative side effects that, instead of alleviating the condition, create a new problem. Or social service agencies may have inflexible policies about when a particular program is available, which may make it difficult for a person who needs the program to participate. *Such situations are called* **exacerbators**, *because they make the situation worse than it was originally.* Although they may be unintended, the results of exacerbators can be serious and necessitate additional forms of intervention.

EXTRAINDIVIDUAL FACTORS

Medical care and rehabilitation
Surgery, physical therapy, speech therapy, counseling, health education, job retraining, etc.

Medications and other therapeutic regimens
Drugs, recreational therapy, aquatic exercise, biofeedback, meditation, rest, energy conservation, etc.

External supports
Personal assistance, special equipment and devices, standby assistance and supervision, day care, respite care, Meals on Wheels, etc.

Built, physical, and social environment
Structural modifications at job and home, access to buildings and public transportation, improvement of air quality, reduction of noise and glare, health insurance and access to medical care, laws and regulations employment discrimination, etc.

THE MAIN PATHWAY

Pathology
Diagnoses of disease, injury, congenital or developmental condition

→

Impairments
Dysfunctions and structural abnormalities in specific body systems: musculoskeletal, cardiovascular, neurological, etc.

→

Functional limitations
Restrictions in basic physical and mental actions: ambulate, reach, stoop, climb stairs, produce intelligible speech, see standard print, etc.

→

Disability
Difficulty doing activities of daily life: job, household management, personal care, hobbies, active recreation, clubs, socializing with friends and kin, child care, errands, sleep, trips, etc.

RISK FACTORS
Predisposing characteristics: demographic, social, lifestyle, behavioral, psychological, environmental, biological

INTRAINDIVIDUAL FACTORS

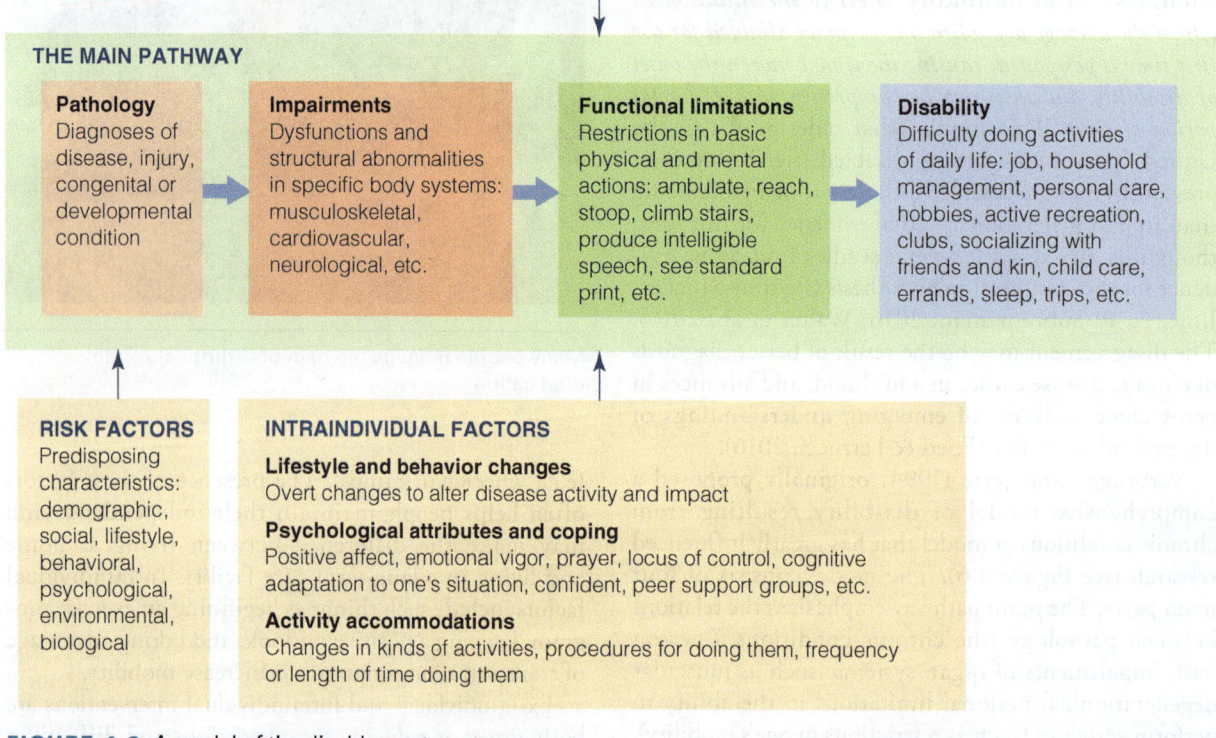

Lifestyle and behavior changes
Overt changes to alter disease activity and impact

Psychological attributes and coping
Positive affect, emotional vigor, prayer, locus of control, cognitive adaptation to one's situation, confident, peer support groups, etc.

Activity accommodations
Changes in kinds of activities, procedures for doing them, frequency or length of time doing them

FIGURE 4.6 A model of the disablement process.
Source: Verbrugge, L. M., & Jette, A. M. (1994). The disablement process. *Social Science and Medicine*, 38(4). Reprinted with permission.

One of the most important aspects of Verbrugge and Jette's (1994) model is the emphasis on the fit between the person and the environment, a topic we explore in detail in Chapter 5. When a person's needs are met by the environment, the person's quality of life and adaptation are optimal.

Verbrugge and Jette's model has been extended and validated in several ways. For example, the basic aspects of the model were extended to explain the disablement process in osteoarthritis (Wang, Chern, & Chiou, 2005). Femia, Zarit, and Johansson (2001) and Fauth and colleagues (2008) validated the model in research on older adults over age 79 in Sweden. Among the most important results were the mediating role of psychosocial factors such as mastery, depression, and loneliness on risk factors for disability; for example, higher feelings of mastery resulted in lower levels of disability. And the model is helping in the development of a new approach to classifying disability in China (Purser et al., 2012).

Determining Functional Health Status

How can we determine where a person can be categorized along Verbrugge and Jette's continuum? *The answer to this question describes a person's* **functional health status**, *that is, how well the person is functioning in daily life.* Determining functional health status requires very careful assessment. Research indicates that loss of function tends not to occur randomly, but rather follows certain sequences (Kingston et al., 2012; Levy et al., 2016; Wloch, Kuh, & Cooper, 2016). Generally, the first areas of difficulty involve tasks associated with strength, balance, and coordination, and the last with manual dexterity. *This sequence of loss of function is referred to as the* **hierarchy of loss**.

Most of the time, assessing functional health status is done for a very practical reason: to identify older adults who need help with everyday tasks. **Frail older adults** *are those who have physical disabilities, are very ill, and may have cognitive or psychological disorders and need assistance with everyday tasks.* They constitute a minority of older adults, but the size of this group increases a great deal with age.

Frail older adults are people whose competence is declining. However, they do not have one specific problem that differentiates them from their active, healthy counterparts. Some researchers zero in on the age-related loss of muscle mass and strength, called *sarcopenia* (Afilalo, 2016). Other researchers argue that frailty is the result of accumulated deficits in several functional areas (Rockwood, 2016). In either case, to identify the areas in which people experience limited functioning, researchers have developed observational and self-report techniques to measure how well people can accomplish daily tasks.

Everyday competence assessment consists of examining how well people can complete activities of daily living and instrumental activities of daily living, and whether they have other physical limitations (Verbrugge et al., 2017). **Activities of daily living (ADLs)** *include basic self-care tasks such as eating, bathing, toileting, walking, or dressing.* A person can be considered frail if he or she needs help with one or more of these tasks. **Instrumental activities of daily living (IADLs)** *are actions that entail some intellectual competence and planning.* Which activities constitute IADLs varies widely across cultures. For example, for most adults in Western culture, IADLs would include shopping for personal items, paying bills, making telephone calls, taking medications appropriately, and keeping appointments. In other cultures, IADLs might include caring for animal herds, making bread, threshing grain, and tending crops. *A third way of assessing competence is to focus on* **physical limitations (PLIM)**, *activities that reflect functional limitations such as walking a block or sitting for about two hours.*

As you can see in Figure 4.7, the number of difficulties with ADLs, IADLs, and PLIMs increases as men and women age (Verbrugge et al., 2017). Such limitations increase rapidly when the person nears death.

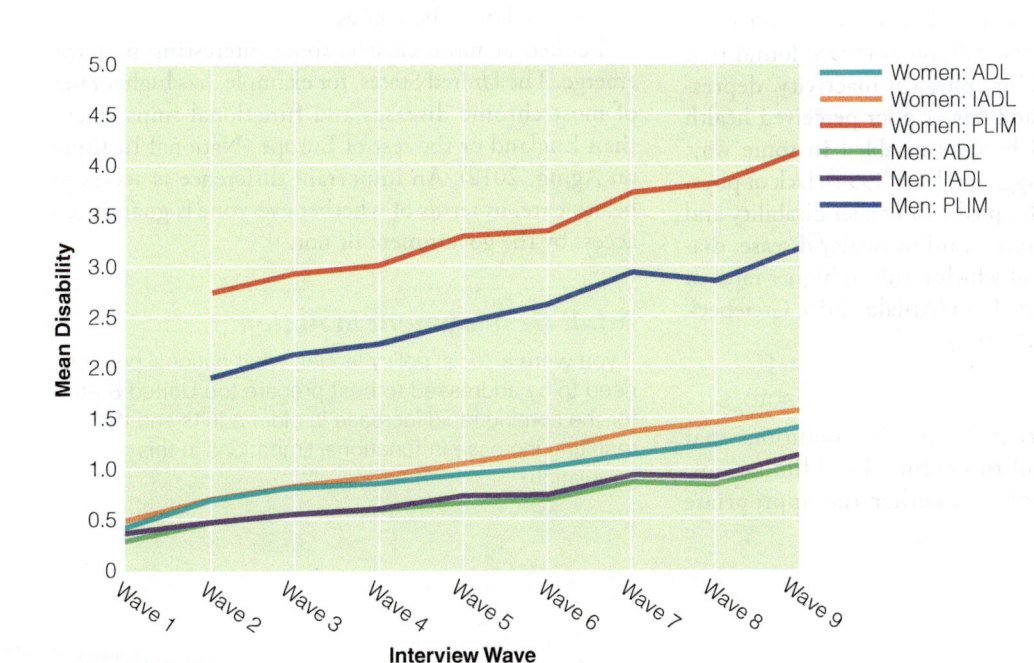

FIGURE 4.7 Mean disability of the AHEAD living cohort by gender, 1993–2010

Source: Verbrugge, L. M., Brown, D. C., Zajacova, A. (2017). Disability rises gradually for a cohort of older Americans, *Journals of Gerontology: Psychological Sciences, 72*, 151–161. doi: 10.1093/geronb/gbw002.

People who live longer show both fewer disabilities on average as well as slower increases in disability over time. By paying close attention to the number and extent of disabilities, healthcare professionals and family members may get advance warning of serious underlying problems.

In addition to basic assistance with ADLs, IADLs, and PLIMs, frail older adults have other needs. Research shows that these individuals are also more prone to depression and anxiety disorders (Kojima et al., 2016). Although frailty becomes more likely with increasing age, especially as a person approaches death, there are many ways to provide a supportive environment for frail older adults. We take a closer look at some of them in Chapter 5.

What Causes Functional Limitations and Disability in Older Adults?

As you were reading about the Verbrugge and Jette (1994) model, you may have been thinking about Brian's situation and those of other adults you know. If you and your classmates created a list of all the conditions you believe cause functional limitations and disabilities in older adults, the list undoubtedly would be long. (Try it and see for yourself.) But by strategically combining a large representative sample of conditions with sophisticated statistical analyses, this list can be shortened greatly. If these steps are taken, what conditions best predict future problems in functioning?

In a classic longitudinal study conducted over three decades, Strawbridge and colleagues (1998) found that smoking, heavy drinking, physical inactivity, depression, social isolation, and fair or poor perceived health predicted who would become disabled in some way. As predicted by Verbrugge and Jette (1994), lack of physical activity is a powerful predictor of later disability and with higher rates of cancer, cardiovascular disease, diabetes, and obesity, all of which result in higher rates of disability and premature death (Afilalo, 2016; Gretebeck et al., 2012; Rockwood, 2016).

How Important Are Socioeconomic Factors?

Once we have identified the specific conditions that are highly predictive of future functional limitations, an important question is whether the appropriate intervention and prevention programs should be targeted at particular groups of people. That is, would people who are well educated and have high incomes have the same rate of key chronic conditions as people in lower socioeconomic groups? If not, then people with different socioeconomic backgrounds have different needs.

Research indicates a fairly strong and consistent relationship between socioeconomic status and health-related quality of life. Across all racial and ethnic groups, more affluent older adults have lower levels of disability and higher health-related quality of life than individuals in lower socioeconomic groups (Gardiner, Mishra, & Dobson, 2016; National Center for Health Statistics, 2016a). A Canadian study showed that this difference appears to be set in early adulthood and maintained into late life (Ross et al., 2012).

How Does Disability in Older Adults Differ Globally?

Throughout this and previous chapters, we have encountered important differences between men and women and between various ethnic/racial and socioeconomic groups. Do these patterns hold globally?

Not surprisingly, the answer is "yes" (World Health Organization, 2012). As the number of older adults rises around the world, the number of people with disabilities or functional limitations does, too. Also, the rates of disabilities are higher in low-income countries and among women. Early detection and treatment of chronic disease can lower these rates.

Looked at more closely, some interesting patterns emerge. The United States, for example, has higher rates of most chronic diseases and functional impairment than England or the rest of Europe (National Institute on Aging, 2012). An important difference is access to health care, in terms of whether everyone is guaranteed access by the government or not.

Adult Development in Action

If you were a social policy leader, what national policies need to be addressed to best prepare the United States for the coming rapid increase in older adults and the resulting increase in functional limitations in this population?

Social Policy Implications

Two demographic trends will create the potential for significant worldwide change over the next few decades. First, increasing longevity in developed and emerging economy countries will result in many more older adults. This means that societies and governments will have increased pressure to provide services tailored to older adults. Such services are often much more expensive. For example, health care for older adults costs more because it involves treating more chronic diseases and more intensive intervention over time.

Second, the size of various generations will affect the scope of this change. For instance, the large baby-boom generation, combined with increased longevity, will make the issue of more older adults acute.

What does this mean? For the next few decades there will be increased emphasis on social policies and services that directly benefit older adults, and they are likely to demand them. While they have the numbers, and the concomitant political power, such policies are likely to be adopted, perhaps to the detriment of younger generations.

This changing political climate plays out in elections. You may remember that in the 2012 presidential election campaign there was great debate over changing the rules by which Medicare operates and in the 2016 campaign over the future of Social Security benefits. The commentary on both sides of the issue was loud, even from older adults who would not have been affected by any of the proposed changes.

As the baby boomers age and die, though, two further things will occur. First, there will be a tremendous transfer of wealth to a smaller generation (Gen-X), with the likely outcome of concentrating wealth in fewer hands. Second, policies generally favorable to older adults may get changed as the next large generation (the Millennials) enters middle age.

These shifts in policy could have major implications for everything from housing (e.g., more state and federal support for subsidized housing for older adults) to health care (e.g., substantially more expenditures for older adults' health care). If the policies change to reflect the demographic needs of the day, then such policies may need to be undone in the future, which is often politically difficult to accomplish. Close attention to all these issues is necessary for the best policies to be enacted.

So what do you think? What policies need to be changed? How?

SUMMARY

4.1 How Long Will We Live?

What is the average and maximum longevity for humans?
- Average longevity is the age at which half of the people born in a particular year will have died. Maximum longevity is the longest time a member of a species lives. Active longevity is the time during which people are independent. Dependent life expectancy is the time during which people rely on others for daily life tasks.
- Average longevity increased dramatically in the first half of the 20th century, but maximum longevity currently remains at about 120 years. The increase in average longevity resulted mainly from the elimination of many diseases and a reduction in deaths during childbirth.

What genetic and environmental factors influence longevity?
- Having long- or short-lived parents is a good predictor of your own longevity.
- Living in a polluted environment can dramatically shorten longevity; being in a committed relationship lengthens it. Environmental effects must be considered in combination with each other and with genetic influences.

What ethnic factors influence average longevity?
- Different ethnic groups in the United States have different average longevity. However, these differences result primarily from differences in nutrition, health care, stress, and socioeconomic status. In late life, people in some ethnic minority groups live longer than European Americans.

What factors create gender differences in average longevity?

- Women tend to live longer than men, partly because men are more susceptible to disease and environmental influences. Numerous hypotheses have been offered for this difference, but none have been supported strongly.

4.2 Health and Illness

What are the key issues in defining health and illness?

- Health is the absence of acute and chronic physical or mental disease and impairments. Illness is the presence of a physical or mental disease or impairment.
- Self-rated health is a good predictor of illness and mortality. However, gender and cultural differences have been found.

How is the quality of life assessed?

- Quality of life is a multidimensional concept that encompasses biological, psychological, and sociocultural domains at any point in the life cycle.
- In the context of health, people's valuation of life is a major factor in quality of life.

What normative age-related changes occur in the immune system?

- The immune system is composed of three major types of cells, which form a network of interacting parts: cell-mediated immunity (consisting of thymus-derived, or T-lymphocytes), humoral immunity (B-lymphocytes), and nonspecific immunity (monocytes and polymorphonuclear neutrophil leukocytes). Natural killer (NK) cells are also important components. How effective lymphocytes and NK cells fight invaders declines with age. Emerging treatments for diseases such as cancer are based in boosting natural immune functioning.
- The immune system can begin attacking itself, a condition called autoimmunity.
- Psychoneuroimmunology is the study of the relations between psychological, neurological, and immunological systems that raise or lower our susceptibility to and ability to recover from disease.
- HIV and AIDS are growing problems among older adults.

What are the developmental trends in chronic and acute diseases?

- Acute diseases are conditions that develop over a short period of time and cause a rapid change in health. Chronic diseases are conditions that last a longer period of time (at least 3 months) and may be accompanied by residual functional impairment that necessitates long-term management.
- The incidence of acute disease drops with age, but the effects of acute disease worsen. The incidence of chronic disease increases with age.

What are the key issues in stress across adulthood?

- The stress and coping paradigm views stress, not as an environmental stimulus or as a response, but as the interaction of a thinking person and an event.
- Primary appraisal categorizes events into three groups based on the significance they have for our well-being: irrelevant, benign or positive, and stressful. Secondary appraisal assesses our ability to cope with harm, threat, or challenge. Reappraisal involves making a new primary or secondary appraisal that results from changes in the situation.
- Attempts to deal with stressful events are called *coping*. Problem-focused coping and emotion-focused coping are two major categories. People also use religion as a source of coping. Relaxation techniques are very effective behavioral strategies to lower stress.
- There are developmental declines in the number of stressors and in the kinds of coping strategies people use.
- Stress has several negative consequences for health.

4.3 Common Chronic Conditions and Their Management

What are the most important issues in chronic disease?

- Chronic conditions are the interaction of biological, psychological, sociocultural, and life-cycle forces.
- Diabetes mellitus occurs when the pancreas produces insufficient insulin. Although it cannot be cured, late-onset diabetes it can be managed effectively. However, some serious problems, such as diabetic retinopathy, can result.
- Many forms of cancer are caused by lifestyle choices, but genetics also plays an important role. The risk of developing cancer increases markedly with age. Prostate and breast cancer involve difficult treatment choices.
- For many people, the inability to control the elimination of urine and feces on an occasional or consistent basis, called incontinence, is a source of great concern and embarrassment. Effective treatments are available.

How can people manage chronic conditions?
- Effective pain management can be achieved through pharmacological and nonpharmacological approaches. Pain is not a normal outcome of aging and is not to be dismissed.

4.4 Pharmacology and Medication Adherence

What are the developmental trends in using medication?
- Older adults use nearly half of all prescription and over-the-counter drugs. The average older adult takes six or seven medications per day. However, the general lack of older adults in clinical trials research means we may not know the precise effects of medications on them.
- The speed with which medications move from the stomach to the small intestine may slow with age. However, once drugs are in the small intestine, absorption rates are the same across adulthood. The distribution of medications in the bloodstream changes with age. The speed of drug metabolism in the liver slows with age. The rate at which drugs are excreted from the body slows with age.

What are the consequences of medication interactions?
- Older adults are more prone to harmful side effects of medications.
- Polypharmacy is a serious problem in older adults and may result in serious drug interactions.

What are the important medication adherence issues?
- Polypharmacy leads to lower rates of correct adherence to medication regimens.

4.5 Functional Health and Disability

What factors are important to include in a model of disability in late life?
- Disability is the effects of chronic conditions on people's ability to engage in activities in daily life.
- A model of disability includes pathology, impairments, functional limitations, risk factors, extraindividual factors, and intraindividual factors. This model includes all four main developmental forces.

What is functional health?
- Frail older adults are those who have physical disabilities, are very ill, or may have cognitive or psychological disorders and who need assistance with everyday tasks.
- Activities of daily living (ADLs) include basic self-care tasks such as eating, bathing, toileting, walking, and dressing.
- Instrumental activities of daily living (IADLs) are actions that entail some intellectual competence and planning.
- Physical limitations (PLIMs) involve limitations in performing higher level activities such as walking a block and sitting for at least 2 hours.
- Rates of problems with ADLs, IADLs, and PLIMs increase dramatically with age.

What causes functional limitations and disability in older adults?
- The chronic conditions that best predict future disability are arthritis and cerebrovascular disease. Other predictors include smoking, heavy drinking, physical inactivity, depression, social isolation, and fair or poor perceived health.
- Being wealthy helps increase average longevity but does not protect one from developing chronic conditions, meaning that such people may experience longer periods of disability late in life.
- Women's health generally is poorer across cultures, especially in developing countries.
- Ethnic group differences are also important. The validity of measures of functioning sometimes differs across ethnicity and gender.

REVIEW QUESTIONS

4.1 How Long Will We Live?
- What is the difference between average longevity and maximum longevity?
- What genetic and environmental factors influence average longevity?
- What ethnic and gender differences have been found?

4.2 Health and Illness
- How are the definitions of health and illness linked? How is quality of life defined generally, especially in relation to health?
- What are the major age-related changes in the immune system? How do they affect health and illness?

- What is the difference between acute and chronic diseases? How do the rates of each change with age?
- How does the stress and coping paradigm explain the experience of stress? What age-related changes occur in the process?

4.3 Common Chronic Conditions and Their Management

- What are the general issues to consider in managing chronic disease?
- What are some common chronic diseases experienced by older adults?
- What are examples of emerging treatment options for chronic diseases?
- How is pain managed?

4.4 Pharmacology and Medication Adherence

- What is the typical pattern of medication use in older adults?
- What changes occur with age that influence how well medications work?
- What are the major risks for side effects and drug interactions?
- How can adherence to medication regimens be improved?

4.5 Functional Health and Disability

- What are the key components in a model of disability in older adults?
- What are ADLs, IADLs, and PLIMs? How does the number of people needing assistance change with age?
- What conditions result in disability most often? How do socioeconomic status, ethnicity, and gender affect health and disability?

INTEGRATING CONCEPTS IN DEVELOPMENT

- What physiological changes described in Chapter 2 are important in understanding health?
- Based on information in Chapters 2 and 3, how might a primary prevention program be designed to prevent cardiovascular disease? (Compare your answer with the intervention types described in Chapter 5.)
- How do the ethnic differences in average longevity and in health relate to the diversity issues we examined in Chapter 1?

KEY TERMS

absorption The time needed for a medication to enter a patient's bloodstream.

active life expectancy The age to which one can expect to live independently.

activities of daily living (ADLs) Basic self-care tasks such as eating, bathing, toileting, walking, and dressing.

acute diseases Conditions that develop over a short period of time and cause a rapid change in health.

autoimmunity The process by which the immune system begins attacking the body.

average longevity The length of time it takes for half of all people born in a certain year to die.

chronic diseases Conditions that last a longer period of time (at least 3 months) and may be accompanied by residual functional impairment that necessitates long-term management.

compression of morbidity The situation in which the average age when one becomes disabled for the first time is postponed, causing the time between the onset of disability and death to be compressed into a shorter period of time.

coping In the stress and coping paradigm, any attempt to deal with stress.

dependent life expectancy The age to which one can expect to live with assistance.

diabetes mellitus A disease that occurs when the pancreas produces insufficient insulin.

disability The effects of chronic conditions on people's ability to engage in activities that are necessary, expected, and personally desired in their society.

drug excretion The process of eliminating medications, usually through the kidneys in urine, but also through sweat, feces, and saliva.

drug metabolism The process of getting rid of medications in the bloodstream, partly in the liver.

emotion-focused coping A style of coping that involves dealing with one's feelings about the stressful event.

exacerbators Situations that makes a situation worse than it was originally.

Key Terms

frail older adults Older adults who have physical disabilities, are very ill, and may have cognitive or psychological disorders and need assistance with everyday tasks.

functional health status How well a person is functioning in daily life.

functional incontinence A type of incontinence usually caused when the urinary tract is intact but due to physical disability or cognitive impairment the person is unaware of the need to urinate.

health The absence of acute and chronic physical or mental disease and impairments.

health-related quality of life Includes all of the aspects of life that are affected by changes in one's health status.

hierarchy of loss Sequence of the loss of functional abilities.

illness The presence of a physical or mental disease or impairment.

incontinence The loss of the ability to control the elimination of urine and feces on an occasional or consistent basis.

instrumental activities of daily living (IADLs) Actions that entail some intellectual competence and planning.

maximum longevity The maximum length of time an organism can live—roughly 120 years for humans.

non-health-related quality of life Refers to things in the environment, such as entertainment, economic resources, arts, and so on that can affect our overall experience and enjoyment in life.

overflow incontinence A type of incontinence usually caused by improper contraction of the kidneys, causing the bladder to become overdistended.

physical limitations (PLIM) Activities that reflect functional limitations such as walking a block or sitting for about two hours.

polypharmacy The use of multiple medications.

primary appraisal First step in the stress and coping paradigm in which events are categorized into three groups based on the significance they have for our well-being—irrelevant, benign or positive, and stressful.

problem-focused coping A style of coping that attempts to tackle a problem head-on.

psychoneuroimmunology The study of the relations between psychological, neurological, and immunological systems that raise or lower our susceptibility to and ability to recover from disease.

reappraisal In the stress and coping paradigm, this step involves making a new primary or secondary appraisal resulting from changes in the situation.

risk factors Long-standing behaviors or conditions that increase one's chances of functional limitation or disability.

secondary appraisal In the stress and coping paradigm, an assessment of our perceived ability to cope with harm, threat, or challenge.

stress and coping paradigm A model that views stress, not as an environmental stimulus or as a response, but as the interaction of a thinking person and an event.

stress incontinence A type of incontinence that happens when pressure in the abdomen exceeds the ability to resist urinary flow.

Type 1 diabetes A type of diabetes that tends to develop earlier in life and requires the use of insulin; also called insulin-dependent diabetes.

Type 2 diabetes A type of diabetes that tends to develop in adulthood and is effectively managed through diet.

urge incontinence A type of incontinence usually caused by a central nervous system problem after a stroke or urinary tract infection in which people feel the urge to urinate but cannot get to a toilet quickly enough.

5 | Where People Live: Person–Environment Interactions

CHAPTER OUTLINE

5.1 Describing Person–Environment Interactions
Competence and Environmental Press
DISCOVERING DEVELOPMENT What's Your Adaptation Level?
Preventive and Corrective Proactivity Model
Stress and Coping Framework
Common Theoretical Themes and Everyday Competence

5.2 The Ecology of Aging: Community Options
REAL PEOPLE Designing for a Reimagined Aging
Aging in Place
Deciding on the Best Option
Home Modification
Adult Day Care
Congregate Housing
Assisted Living

5.3 Living in Nursing Homes
Long-Term Care in Nursing Homes
CURRENT CONTROVERSIES Financing Long-Term Care
Who Is Likely to Live in Nursing Homes?
Characteristics of Nursing Homes
Special Care Units
Can a Nursing Home Be a Home?
Communicating with Residents
HOW DO WE KNOW? Identifying Different Types of Elderspeak in Singapore
Decision-Making Capacity and Individual Choices
New Directions for Nursing Homes

Social Policy Implications

Summary
Review Questions
Integrating Concepts in Development
Key Terms

CHAPTER 5   Where People Live: Person–Environment Interactions

You encounter them every day—devices such as grip bars in bathrooms, wider doorways, and ramps leading to building entrances. You may not pay much attention to them and even take them for granted, but these environmental modifications matter. They may mean the difference between living independently and living somewhere else. Supportive environments for adults, especially older adults with significant physical or cognitive impairment, are key to providing continuing quality of life.

Technology is also making it easier to be independent. Smart phones make it possible to create reminders for medications and appointments, and keep track of key health indicators. In development are a host of innovative devices, from companion robots to self-driving cars. Within a generation or so, we will have gone from very challenging situations for many older adults to having the option to age in place nearly anywhere.

All of these changes and innovation have resulted in research on how people deal with the settings where they reside, which in turn has revolutionized the way we design houses and care facilities. The rapidly increasing need for alternatives to traditional nursing homes has resulted in the creation of a wide range of options for families. These changes began with the simple observation that behavior is a function of the environment in which it occurs and the interaction with the individual's personal characteristics.

In this chapter, we explore how differences in the interaction between personal characteristics and the living environment can have profound effects on our behavior and feelings about ourselves. Several theoretical frameworks are described that help us understand how to interpret person–environment interactions in a developmental context. Next, we consider the ecology of aging and discover how people can age in place, along with the support systems that underpin that goal. We consider the role of adult day care and several housing options that help people stay in the community as much as possible. Because some people need intensive support, we take a close look at nursing homes. Sometimes we must consider the person separately from the environment, but keep in mind throughout the chapter that in the end it is the interaction of the two we want to understand.

Home adaptations help people age in place.

5.1 Describing Person–Environment Interactions

LEARNING OBJECTIVES
- What is the competence and environmental press model?
- What is the preventive and corrective proactivity model?
- What are the major aspects of stress and coping theory relating to person–environment interactions?
- What are the common themes in the theories of person–environment interactions?

Hank has lived in the same neighborhood all of his 75 years. He has lived alone for the past several months since his wife, Marilyn, had a stroke and was placed in a nursing home. Hank's oldest daughter expressed concern about her father and has been pressing him to move in with her. Hank is reluctant; he likes knowing his neighbors, shopping in familiar stores, and being able to do what he wants. He wonders how well he could adapt to living in a new neighborhood after all these years. He realizes it might be easier for him to cope if he lived with his daughter, but it's a tough decision.

To appreciate the roles different environments play in our lives, we need a framework for interpreting how people interact with them. Theories of person–environment interactions help us understand how people view their environments and how these views may change as people age. These views have been described since the 1930s and have significant impact on the study of adults (Pynoos et al., 2010; Scharlach & Lehning, 2016). We consider four that affect views of adult development and aging: competence and environmental press, congruence, stress and coping, and everyday competence.

All these theories can be traced to a common beginning. Kurt Lewin (1936) was the first psychologist to conceptualize person–environment interactions as an interactive relationship, which he represented in the equation: $B = f(P, E)$. *This relationship defining* **person–environment interactions** *means behavior (B) is a function of both the person (P) and the environment (E).* More recent theorists took Lewin's equation and described the components in the equation in more detail. Specifically, their speculations concern the characteristics of people and environments that combine to form behavior.

Most of these models emphasize the importance of people's perceptions of their environments. Although objective aspects of environments (i.e., crime, housing quality) are important, personal choice plays a major role. For example, many people deliberately choose to live in New York or Atlanta, even though certain crime rates in those cities are higher than in Selma or Walla Walla. The importance of personal perception in environments is similar to the role of personal perception in social cognition and in concepts such as personal control (see Chapter 9). As you will see, these ideas, especially the notion of personal control, are included in many approaches to understanding person–environment interactions.

Competence and Environmental Press

Understanding psychosocial aging requires attention to individuals' needs rather than treating all older adults alike. One method focuses on the relation between the person and the environment (Aldwin, 2015; Aldwin & Igarashi, 2012). The competence–environmental press approach is a good example of a theory incorporating elements of the biopsychosocial model into the person–environment relation (Lawton & Nahemow, 1973; Nahemow, 2000; Pynoos et al., 2010).

Competence *is defined as the upper limit of a person's ability to function in five domains: physical health, sensory-perceptual skills, motor skills, cognitive skills, and ego strength.* These domains are viewed as underlying all other abilities and reflect the biological and psychological forces. **Environmental press** *refers to the physical, interpersonal, or social demands that environments put on people.* Physical demands might include having to walk up three flights of stairs to your apartment. Interpersonal demands may require adjusting your behavior patterns to different types of people. Social demands involve dealing with laws or customs that place certain expectations on people. These aspects of the theory reflect biological, psychological, and social forces. Both competence and environmental press change as people move through the life span; what you are capable of doing as a 5-year-old differs from what you are capable of doing as a 25-, 45-, 65-, or 85-year-old. Similarly, the demands put on you by the environment change as you age. Thus, the competence–environmental press framework also reflects life-cycle factors.

The competence and environmental press model depicted in Figure 5.1 shows how the two are related. Low to high competence is represented on the vertical axis, and weak to strong environmental press is displayed on the horizontal axis. Points in the figure represent various combinations of the two. Most important, the shaded areas show adaptive behavior and positive affect can result from many different combinations of

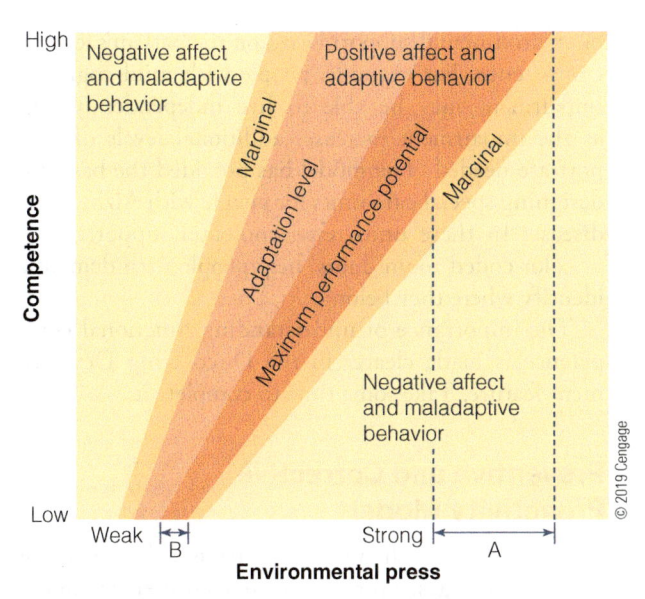

FIGURE 5.1 Behavioral and emotional outcomes of person–environment interactions are based on the competence and environmental press model. This figure indicates a person of high competence will show maximum performance over a larger range of environmental conditions than will a person with lower levels of competence. The range of optimal environments occurs at a higher level of environmental press (A) for the person with the most competence than it does for the person with the lowest level of competence (B).

Source: Lawton, M. P. & Nahemow, L. (1973). Ecology of the aging process. In C. Eisdorfer & M. P. Lawton (Eds.), *The Psychology of Adult Development and Aging*, p. 661.

competence and environmental press levels. **Adaptation level** *is the area where press level is average for a particular level of competence; this is where behavior and affect are normal. Slight increases in press tend to improve performance; this area on the figure is labeled the* **zone of maximum performance potential**. *Slight decreases in press create the* **zone of maximum comfort**, *in which people are able to live happily without worrying about environmental demands.* Combinations of competence and environmental press that fall within either of these two zones result in adaptive behavior and positive emotion that translate into a high quality of life.

As a person moves away from these areas, behavior becomes increasingly maladaptive and affect becomes negative. Notice that these outcomes can result from several different combinations and for different reasons. For example, too many environmental demands on a person with low competence and too few demands on a person with high competence both result in maladaptive behaviors and negative emotion.

What does this mean with regard to late life? Is aging merely an equation relating certain variables? The important thing to realize about the competence–environmental press model is that each person has the potential of being happily adapted to some living situations, but not to all. Whether people function well depends on if what they are able to do fits what the environment forces them to do. When their abilities match the demands, people adapt; when there is a mismatch, they don't. In this view, aging is more than an equation, because the best fit must be determined on an individual basis.

How do people deal with changes in their particular combinations of environmental press (such as adjusting to a new living situation) and competence (perhaps losing abilities due to illness)? People respond in two basic ways (Lawton, 1989; Nahemow, 2000). *When people choose new behaviors to meet new desires or needs, they exhibit* **proactivity** *and exert control over their lives. In contrast, when people allow the situation to dictate the options they have, they demonstrate* **docility** *and have little control.* Lawton (1989) argues that proactivity is more likely to occur in people with relatively high competence, and docility in people with relatively low competence.

The model has considerable research support. For example, the model accounts for why people choose the activities they do (Lawton, 1982), how well people adhere to medication regimens (LeRoux & Fisher, 2006), and how they adapt to changing housing needs over time (Granbom et al., 2016; Iwarsson, Slaug, & Fänge, 2012). This model helps us understand how well people adapt to various care settings (Golant, 2012; Scharlach & Lehning, 2016). In short, there is considerable merit to the view that aging is a complex interaction between a person's competence level and environmental press, mediated by choice. This model can be applied in many different settings.

Before leaving Lawton and Nahemow's model, we need to note an important implication for aging. To the extent people experience declines in competence (such as resulting from declines in health, sensory processes, motor skills, cognitive skills, or ego strength), they are less able to cope with environmental demands. That is why the interventions discussed at the beginning of the chapter, such as grab bars and smartphones, are important—they functionally increase competence. Interventions based on artificial intelligence, such as robots and self-driving cars, will do even more to increase functional competence and enable people to live in the community. City planners now incorporate aspects of the competence–environmental press model in designing housing and neighborhoods (Lewis & Groh, 2016).

Additionally, the competence and environmental press model has been the basis for evaluating and optimizing living situations with people who have severe cognitive impairments, such as those of Alzheimer's disease (Dalton, 2014). To manage severe cognitive impairment effectively, caregivers must identify the right level of environmental support based on the patient's level of competence. For example, people with mild cognitive impairment may be able to live independently, but as the impairment increases additional levels of support are needed. The model has provided the basis for designing special care units for people with Alzheimer's disease. In these units, environmental supports such as color-coded room doors, help people with dementia identify where they belong.

The importance of understanding functional competence is made clearer in the Discovering Development feature. Take some time to complete it.

DISCOVERING DEVELOPMENT
What's Your Adaptation Level?

Lawton and Nahemow's competence and environmental press model has wide applicability. The model provides an excellent introduction to the importance of considering people's capabilities and the demands that the environment places on them. To understand how the model works, consider yourself. Make a list of the different aspects of your life, such as school, family, social activities, work, and so forth. Think about each of these areas and rate yourself in terms of your abilities. For example, in the case of school, consider each course you are taking and rate how capable you are in each. Then consider the number and kinds of demands made on you in each area. For instance, think about the many demands put on you in each course.

Now look at how the rating of your competence intersects with the kinds and number of demands in each aspect of your life. Does it place you in the position of feeling bored? In this case, you would fall in the left side of Figure 5.1 because your level of competence is greater than that needed to deal with the demands being put on you. To make yourself feel less bored, you may want to increase those demands just enough to put you in the area of adaptation. Are you feeling stressed out and under pressure? Then you would fall on the right side of the graph because the demands on you outstrip your ability to deal with them given your level of competence. In this case, you would need to find ways to increase your competence through compensations, such as better study techniques if the high demands are in a course. Or, you could figure out a way to lower the demands, such as taking fewer classes. Feeling just about right? You've experienced your adaptation level.

Doing this analysis for the various aspects of your life will help you understand why you feel more competent in some areas than in others. It also shows the relative ease or difficulty in increasing your functional level of competence or in lowering the level of demands. Understanding how competence and demands work together provides insight into how well people can adapt to the situations in which they find themselves.

Preventive and Corrective Proactivity Model

Maintaining a high quality of life is a key goal for adults of all ages. From the competence-environmental press approach we saw proactivity, exerting control over one's life, is central to achieving that goal. Because proactivity is so important, Kahana and Kahana (2003; Midlarsky, Kahana, & Belser, 2015) built a model of successful aging on the core concept of proactivity. The model is shown in Figure 5.2.

The preventive and corrective proactivity (PCP) model explains how life stressors (such as life events, chronic illnesses) and lack of good congruence in person–environment interactions (Component B), especially when the person has nothing to help buffer or protect against these things, result in poor life outcomes (Component F). The helpful buffers include external resources (Component E) such as friends or home modifications, internal resources or dispositions (Component C) such as a positive outlook on life, and specific proactive behaviors (Component D), such as physical exercise, work to lower the negative impact of the stressors and prepare people to cope better in the future. In brief, the PCP model proposes proactive adaptations and helpful external resources reduce the effect of life stressors on quality-of-life outcomes.

What kinds of actions reflect proactive adaptations? Kahana, Kahana, and Zhang (2005) described two types of proactive adaptations: preventive and corrective. **Preventive adaptations** *are actions that avoid stressors and increase or build social resources*. An example of a preventive adaptation would be increasing one's social network by adding friends. **Corrective adaptations** *are actions taken in response to stressors and can be facilitated by internal and external resources*. An example of a corrective adaptation is changing one's diet after having a heart attack.

5.1 Describing Person–Environment Interactions

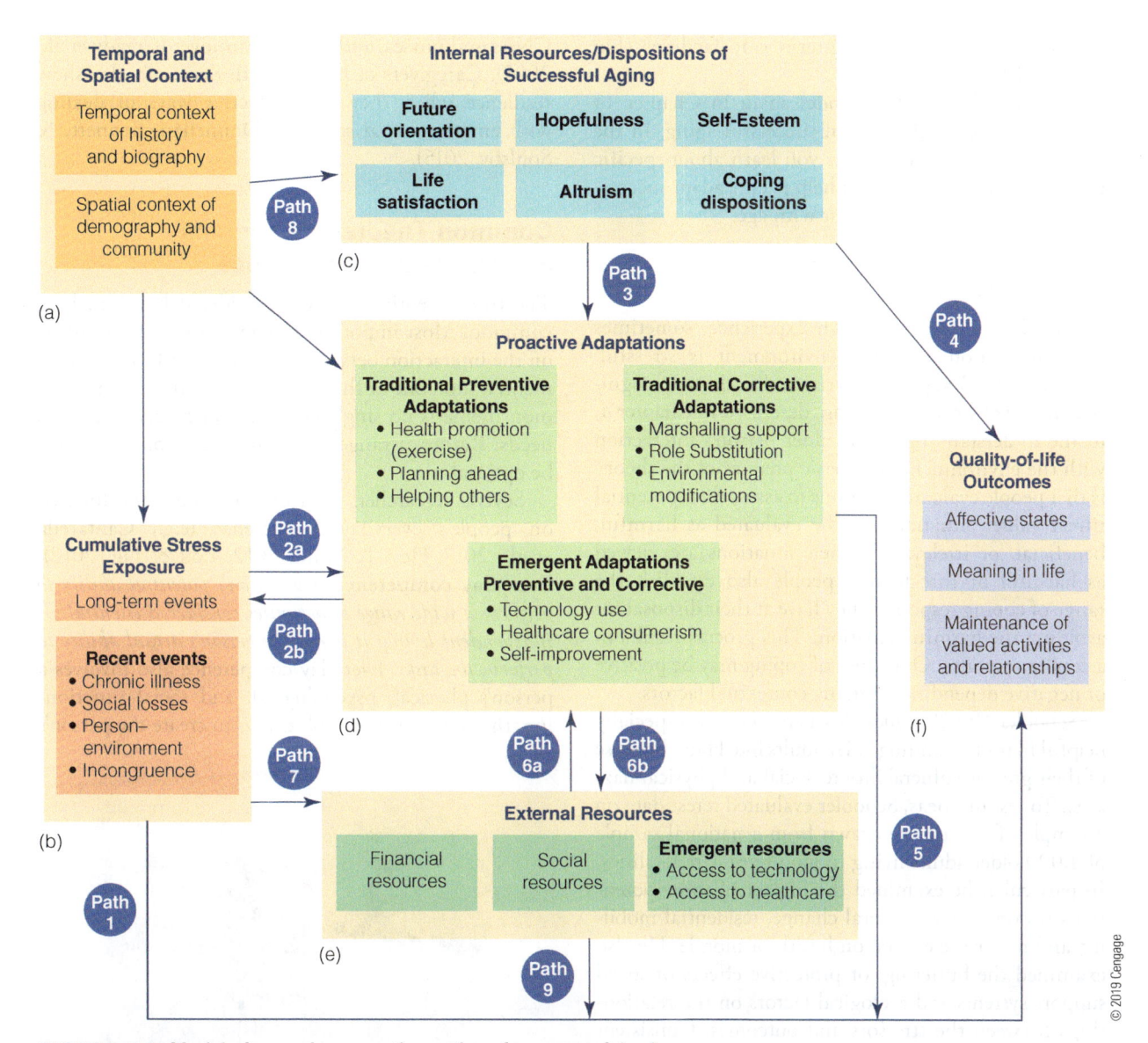

FIGURE 5.2 Model of emerging proactive options for successful aging.
Source: Kahana, E., Kahana, B., & Zhang, J. (2006). Motivational antecedents of preventive proactivity in late life: Linking future orientation and exercise. *Motivation and Emotion, 29*, 438–459 (Figure 1). doi: 10.1007/s11031-006-9012-2.

Older adults tend to engage in more corrective adaptations than preventive adaptations, at least initially. However, many actions that start as corrective adaptations turn into preventive adaptations. A great example of this is exercise. Many people begin an exercise program only after they are told to, perhaps as part of a recovery regimen after a health crisis. However, continued exercise becomes preventive by helping the person avoid future recurrences of the original health problem and avoid other problems altogether.

Research supports the importance of proactivity as described in the PCP model. Kahana, Kelley-Moore, & Kahana (2012) showed life stressors can still have a negative effect on quality-of-life outcomes four years after they occur, but proactive adaptations (such as exercise, planning ahead, and gathering support) significantly reduce this negative impact. Longitudinal research in China also showed the importance of proactivity and other external and internal resources in improving quality-of-life outcomes in the oldest old residents in the community and in long-term care facilities (Liu et al., 2012).

We consider the PCP model again in Chapter 14 when we focus specifically on successful aging. In the meantime, keep it in mind as you learn about specific behaviors and situations that help people adapt successfully to the changes that occur with age.

Stress and Coping Framework

As you know from your own experience, sometimes your interaction with the environment is stressful. Schooler (1982) applied Lazarus and Folkman's cognitive theory of stress and coping, described in Chapter 4, to the understanding of the older person's interaction with the environment. The basic premise of the theory is that people evaluate situations to assess their potential threat value. Situations can be evaluated as harmful, beneficial, or irrelevant. When situations are viewed as harmful or threatening, people also establish the range of coping responses they have at their disposal for avoiding the harmful situation. This process results in a coping response. Outcomes of coping may be positive or negative depending on many contextual factors.

Schooler (1982) argues this perspective is especially helpful in understanding older adults like Hank because of their greater vulnerability to social and physical hazards. To test his ideas, Schooler evaluated retest data on a sample of 521 people drawn from a national sample of 4,000 older adults living in long-term care facilities. In particular, he examined the impact of three potential stressors (environmental change, residential mobility, and major life events) on health or morale. He also examined the buffering, or protective effects of social support systems and ecological factors on the relationships between the stressors and outcomes. Consistent with the theory, Schooler showed the presence of social support systems affected the likelihood that particular situations would be defined as threatening. For example, living alone is more likely to be viewed as stressful when people have little social support than when they have many friends who live nearby.

Schooler's research provides an important theoretical addition because it deals with the relation between everyday environmental stressors and the adaptive response of community-dwelling individuals. His ideas have been extended to other contexts. When certified nurse aides (CNAs) working in nursing homes were provided with training and empowered as a way to deal with environmental stressors, the result was better care for residents, better cooperation between CNAs and nurses, and reduced turnover (Cready et al., 2008). Caregivers of persons with dementia also show resilience when they have effective ways of dealing with environmental stressors (Donnellan, Bennett, & Soulsby, 2015).

Common Theoretical Themes and Everyday Competence

The three theories we have considered have much in common. Most important, all agree the focus must be on the interaction between the person and the environment, not on one or the other. Another important common theme is no single environment meets everyone's needs. Rather, a range of potential environments may be optimal.

Several researchers built on these ideas and focused on people's everyday competence (e.g., Cantarella et al., 2017; Heyl & Wahl, 2012; Lou & Ng, 2012). **Everyday competence** *is a person's potential ability to perform a wide range of activities considered essential for independent living; it is not the person's actual ability to perform the tasks.* Everyday competence also involves a person's physical, psychological, and social functioning, that interact in complex ways to create the person's

Older adults' ability to perform typical daily activities is essential for assessing everyday competence.

day-to-day behavior. Lou and Ng (2012) showed cognitive competence, closeness to family, and relationship-based coping are helping Chinese older adults who live alone to deal effectively with loneliness. Additionally, an older person's competence in the psychological domain includes cognitive problem-solving abilities, beliefs about personal control and self-efficacy, and styles of coping (Diehl et al., 2005; Diehl, Hay, & Chui, 2012).

Although everyday competence is most often considered in the context of activities of daily living (ADLs) and instrumental activities of daily living (IADLs; see Chapter 4), it can also be considered more broadly. The reason is a behavior must not be viewed in isolation; behavior is expressed in a particular environmental context. In particular, researchers and clinicians need to be sensitive to cultural and contextual differences in everyday competence across different environments (Diehl et al., 2005, 2012).

Using these ideas, Willis (1991; Allaire, 2012; Allaire & Willis, 2006; Jones et al., 2013; Schaie & Willis, 1999) developed a model of everyday competence incorporating all the key ideas discussed earlier. Willis distinguishes between antecedents, components, mechanisms, and outcomes of everyday competence. Antecedents include both individual (e.g., health, cognition) and sociocultural (e.g., cultural stereotypes, social policy, healthcare policy) factors. These influence the intraindividual and contextual components, the particular domains and contexts of competence. Which components are most important or exert the most influence depends on the overall conditions under which the person lives. These elements of the model reflect the basic ideas in both the competence and environmental press model and the person–environment model we considered earlier. The mechanisms involve factors that moderate the way competence is actually expressed; such as whether one believes he or she is in control of the situation, influences how competent the person turns out to be. Finally, the model proposes the primary outcomes of everyday competence are psychological and physical well-being, two of the major components of successful aging.

Understanding the complexities of everyday competence is important as a basis for considering whether people, especially some older adults, are capable of making certain decisions for themselves. This issue often arises in terms of competence to make key health care and other decisions, a topic we consider in more detail later in this chapter. The model of everyday competence also points out the health outcomes of one episode of everyday competence are the antecedents of the next, illustrating how future competence is related to current competence. Research on cognitive training from this perspective shows that training on reasoning, maintained over time, can attenuate age-related change (Jones et al., 2013), and may last up to 10 years in certain areas, such as reasoning (Rebok et al., 2014). Finally, decline in older adults' ability to handle everyday problems predicts mortality, indicating everyday competence may be a reasonable indicator of health status (Allaire & Willis, 2006).

All of this research supports the idea that older adults can age in place to the extent their everyday competence permits. Aging in place requires whatever necessary services and supports an older adult needs to live in the community be provided or made available. This approach has been adopted by governments (e.g., Australia in relation to disability; Australian Government Department of Social Services, 2016), and is the goal for much of the smart technology available for older adults, such as cognitive wellness systems (Meza-Kubo & Morán, 2013). We consider aging in place in more detail in the next section.

Adult Development in Action

How would a thorough understanding of competence and environmental press influence your work as a housing planner for older adults?

5.2 The Ecology of Aging: Community Options

LEARNING OBJECTIVES

- What is aging in place? How do people decide the best option?
- How can a home be modified to provide a supportive environment?
- What options and services are provided in adult day care?
- What is congregate housing? What are the characteristics of assisted living?

Mark was diagnosed as having vascular dementia about six months ago. Because he now has difficulty in remembering to turn off his gas stove, his daughter and son-in-law think it may be best for him to move into an assisted living facility. They had Mark evaluated by his physician, who indicates she thinks for safety reasons assisted living is a good idea, especially because Mark's family lives several hundred miles away.

Most people go through young adulthood, middle age, and into later life performing routine daily tasks without much thought. As we grow older, the normative changes that occur often result in more challenges in dealing with environments that were once not a problem at all. Even our homes, formerly a comfortable supportive place, can present difficult challenges; the walk up the stairs to a bedroom may become an equivalent of climbing a mountain.

Mark is typical of a growing number of older adults in the United States and other countries—he experiences a significant decline in function, lives alone, and his adult child and family live in another city some distance away. As a result, he, like many older adults, needs a different living situation. He does not need full-time nursing care at this point, but does need a more supportive environment.

Changes in functional status and how these changes are helped or hurt by the environments we live in are an important aspect of the experience of growing older for many people. *These changes are studied in a field called the* **ecology of aging** *or environmental psychology, which seeks to understand the dynamic relations between older adults and the environments they inhabit* (Scheidt & Schwarz, 2010; Schwarz, 2013). It is important to understand how seemingly small changes in a person's environment can result in major changes in behavior, changes that can make the difference between a person being able to live independently or needing a more supportive situation.

In this section, we consider options for older adults that help them maintain as much independence as possible. First, we evaluate the concept of aging in place. Then we present three approaches to helping people live in the community as long as possible: home modification, and two living situations that provide various levels of support—congregate housing and assisted living. All of these approaches are making people rethink options for older adults not only in the United States, but also Canada, Europe, and Latin America (Sánchez-González & Rodríguez-Rodríguez, 2016).

To set the stage, meet Matthias Hollwich, an architect profiled in the Real People feature. Matthias is one of an emerging group of young architects who are focusing on designing spaces in which people can grow

Real People
Designing for a Reimagined Aging

Matthias Hollwich is an architect and cofounder of HWKN who thinks differently. He starts with the premise that society needs to reimagine how to serve the needs of older adults better, and that can only happen if we deliberately plan our own aging. For Hollwich, this means adopting a fundamentally different mindset about every aspect of our lives, from valuing growing old to strategically using smartphones as assistive devices to adapting living spaces as physical abilities change.

In his book *New Aging: Live Smarter Now to Live Better Forever* (Hollwich, 2016), Hollwich urges people to "love aging" and to adopt changes advocated by such organizations as Aging2.0, a global group that fosters technology-based products and services for older adults. In his architecture practice, Hollwich helps clients rethink and reframe physical space to be readily adaptable as individual needs and competencies change. In that way, he strives for optimal competency-press balance so that people can maintain their independence.

Hollwich and other architects like him are challenging traditional notions of interior design and the use of physical space. By designing space today that anticipates future needs, they hope to change minds about the process of aging and to provide much better places in which that process occurs.

Matthias Hollwich (on the right)

old. As described in the feature, what's different about his approach is that it integrates smart technology with the biopsychosocial approach with the rethinking of physical space. It's intriguing, and a great mindset to use throughout the rest of this chapter.

Aging in Place

Imagine you are an older adult who has difficulty cooking meals and getting around. If you had a choice of where you wanted to live, where would it be? Maybe some of your family members urge you to move to a place where your meals are provided and you can be driven where you need to go, while others suggest you to stay in your own place even though there will be challenges. What do you do?

Based on the competence–environmental press model described earlier, older adults have options (Sánchez-González & Rodríguez-Rodríguez, 2016; Scheidt & Schwarz, 2010; Schwarz, 2013). As the environment in which one lives becomes more restrictive, many older adults engage in selection and compensation to cope. They may select a different place to live or they may adapt their behaviors in order to compensate for their limitations, such as using microwaveable prepared foods instead of cooking meals from scratch. Using a cane or other device to assist in walking is another example of compensation.

The idea of aging in place reflects a balancing of environmental press and competence through selection and compensation. Being able to maintain one's independence in the community is often important for people, especially in terms of their self-esteem and ability to continue engaging in meaningful ways with friends, family, and others. This is important psychologically (Fields & Dabelko-Schoeny, 2016). Older adults who age in place form strong emotional and cognitive attachment with their residences that help transform a "house" into a "home." Having a "home" provides a strong source of self-identity. Additionally, they form strong emotional connections with their community to create a sense of place.

Throughout adulthood, people adapt to changes in the places where they live, sometimes severing connections with past settings (Rowles & Watkins, 2003; Wahl, 2015). Making a change in where people live, and having to psychologically disconnect with a place where they may have lived for many decades, can be difficult and traumatic. There is no question people develop attachments to place, deriving a major portion of their identity from it and feeling they own it.

Rowles (2006) discusses the process of how a place becomes a home. Because of the psychological connections, the sense that one is "at home" becomes a major concern in relocation, especially if the relocation involves giving up one's home. This attachment to place appears to be cross-cultural phenomenon (Felix et al., 2015). Later in this chapter, we consider how a nursing home might become a home, but for now the important idea is that a key factor is a sense of belonging.

Feeling one is "at home" is a major aspect of aging in place. Providing older adults a place to call their own that supports the development of the psychological attachments necessary to convert the place to a home is key for successful aging in place (Scheidt & Schwarz, 2010; Wahl, 2015). Aging in place provides a way for older adults to continue finding aspects of self-identity in where they live, and to take advantage of support systems that are established and familiar.

The growing understanding of the importance of aging in place has resulted in a rethinking of certain housing options that provide a way for frail older adults to stay in their communities. Such options are important for fragile older adults who are poor and cannot afford more expensive formal assisted living or nursing home facilities (discussed later). One alternative is cluster housing that combines the aging in place philosophy with supportive services (de Jong et al., 2012; Golant, 2008; Scharlach & Lehning, 2016).

There are several types of affordable cluster housing care (Golant, 2008; Scharlach & Lehning, 2016). A key feature of cluster housing is that it consists of residential-like settings that provide a range of care. Services might range from having only a case manager

Aging in place is a major goal for the majority of older adults.

to actually providing caregiving assistance (e.g., meals, housekeeping), transportation, or health care. The aging in place philosophy in these settings emphasizes individual choice on the part of residents in terms of what services to use. This approach is being adopted in other countries, such as the Netherlands (de Jong et al., 2012).

Although cluster housing and other approaches to aging in place make sense as lower-cost alternatives to nursing homes that keep people in their communities, affording them is often difficult. Unlike long-term care facilities, cluster housing developments are not covered by Medicaid or other insurance. Finding solutions to the funding issue will be an important aspect for keeping costs down and providing supporting environments for older adults who need support. For many, making modifications to their existing housing represents a more cost-effective option, and provides a research-based way to remain in a familiar environment. We consider this approach later in this section.

Deciding on the Best Option

One of the most difficult decisions individuals and families have to make is where an older member should live (Wahl, 2015). Such decisions are never easy and can be quite wrenching. Figuring out the optimal "fit" where the individual's competence and the environmental press are in the best balance rests on the ability of all concerned to be objective about the individual's competence and the ability of the lived-in environment to provide the level of support necessary. This balance requires a degree of honesty in communication with all family members that is sometimes challenging. It also requires an understanding of what the future likely holds in terms of functional changes (Koss & Ekerdt, in press).

There are several key decision points in addressing the issue of the optimal housing environment. First, it must be determined whether the individual has or will likely have significant cognitive or physical impairment requiring intervention or support. Next, an assessment of the ability of family members or friends to provide support or care must be made. Once that information is understood, a series of decisions can be made about the best way to provide the necessary environmental supports to create the optimal "fit." Assuming all information shows the need for some sort of intervention, the next critical decision is whether there is an option for providing that intervention in the current home situation or if other options need to be pursued. Later, we consider several living options for individuals needing support ranging from minor modifications of the present home to skilled care nursing homes.

Throughout this process, the individual in question needs to be an integral part of decision making to the extent possible. This is especially important when the outcome is likely to be a placement that involves moving from the person's current residence. The degree the person actually understands the options available, why the options are being pursued, and the long-term meaning of the decision being considered is an integral part of the person's right to determine his or her own life outcome (a point considered in more detail later).

Individuals and families facing these decisions should consult with the person's physician after a thorough diagnostic evaluation. Additionally, objective information about available housing options can be obtained from local senior centers, offices on aging, and other nonprofit service providers.

Home Modification

The competence–environmental press model provides two options for people who experience difficulties dealing with the tasks of daily life. On one hand, people can increase their competency and develop better or new skills for handling. To better remember where you put your car keys, you can learn a new memory strategy. On the other hand, people can lower the environmental press by modifying the environment to make the task easier; putting a hook for the car keys next to the door you exit so you see them on your way out.

These two options represent applications of theory to real-world settings that also apply to helping people deal with the challenges they face in handling tasks of daily living in their homes. When it comes to these kinds of issues, the most frequent solution involves modifying one's home (i.e., changing the environment) in order to create a new optimal balance or better "fit" between competence and environmental press (Scheidt & Schwarz, 2010; Scharlach & Lehning, 2016).

Many strategies are available for modifying a home to help a person accommodate changing competencies. Minor structural changes, such as installing assistive devices (e.g., hand rails in bathrooms and door handles that are easier to grip), are common strategies. In other cases, more extensive modifications may be needed to make a home fully accessible, such as widening doorways, lowering countertops, adding power stairlifts, and constructing ramps.

Although minor alterations can often be done at low cost, more extensive modifications needed by people with greater limitations may be unaffordable for low-income individuals. Even though the cost of such interventions is significantly lower than placement in long-term care facilities or assisted living, many people simply cannot afford them. As a result, many older adults with functional impairments experience a mismatch between their competency and their environment (Granbom et al., 2016; Iwarsson et al., 2012; Wahl, 2015).

Research indicates home modifications done to address difficulties with accomplishing ADLs typically reduce disability-related outcomes (Iwarsson et al., 2012; Wahl, 2015; Yuen & Vogtle, 2016). Although home modification can help reduce falls in older adults (Ripp, Jones, & Zhang, 2016), understanding the role of self-efficacy beliefs in falling is also an important factor to address in successful interventions to reduce falling (Dadgari et al., 2015).

An emerging approach to home modification is the accessory or auxiliary dwelling unit (ADU; AccessoryDwellings.org, 2016a). The ADU is a new spin on an old concept—create a separate living space either from existing spare space (e.g., a room over a garage) or a separate dwelling placed next to a family's main dwelling to give an older relative both privacy and proximity to family (Kunkle, 2012). To provide maximum support for older adults the dwelling contains a number of design modifications (e.g., lower counter heights) and especially the incorporation of "smart" devices that do everything from serving as a virtual companion to providing voice control over many household functions. A diagram of a typical stand-alone unit is shown in Figure 5.3.

The advantage to ADUs is that they can be as temporary or permanent as needed, and they provide both

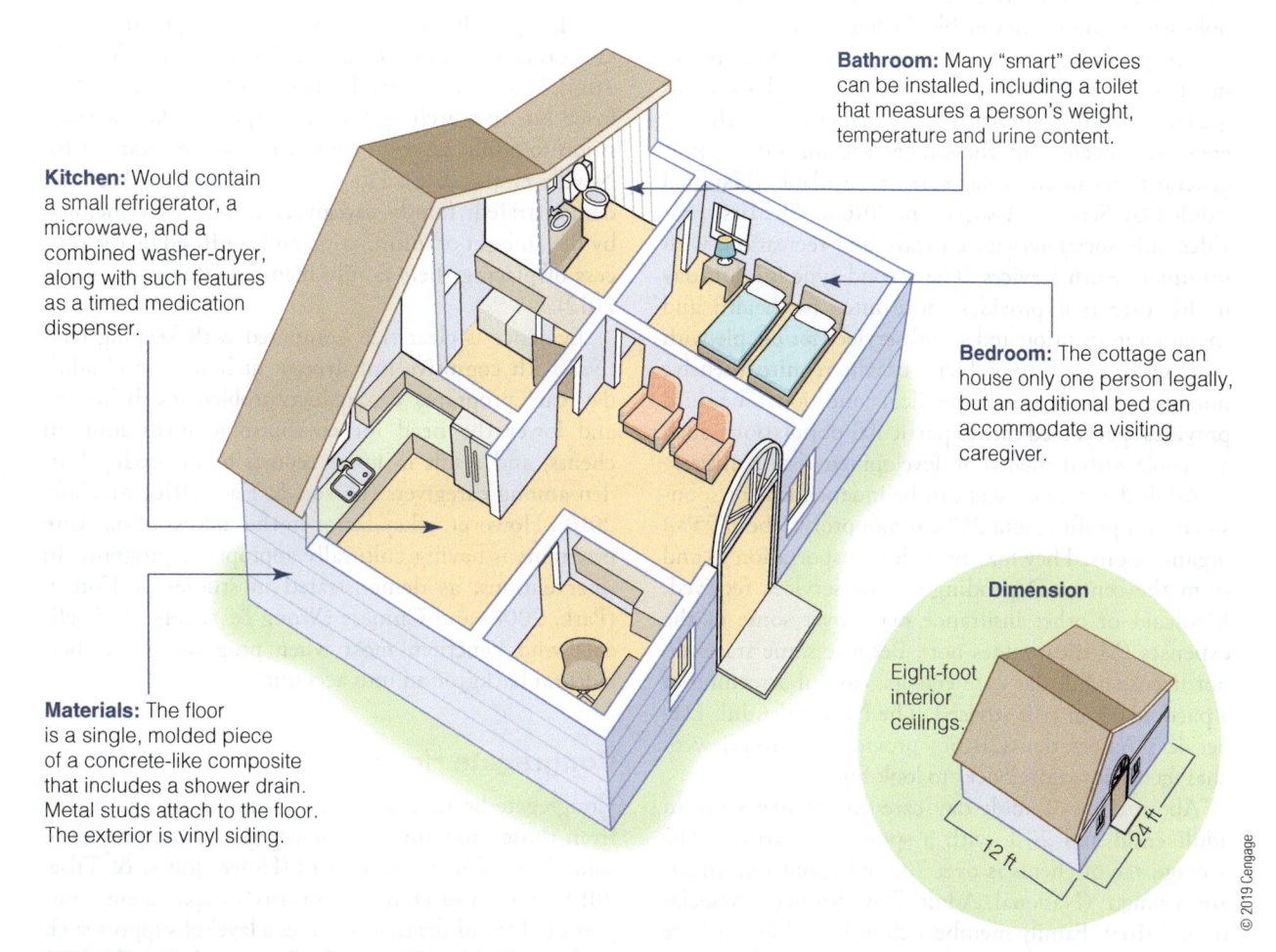

Kitchen: Would contain a small refrigerator, a microwave, and a combined washer-dryer, along with such features as a timed medication dispenser.

Bathroom: Many "smart" devices can be installed, including a toilet that measures a person's weight, temperature and urine content.

Bedroom: The cottage can house only one person legally, but an additional bed can accommodate a visiting caregiver.

Materials: The floor is a single, molded piece of a concrete-like composite that includes a shower drain. Metal studs attach to the floor. The exterior is vinyl siding.

Dimension

Eight-foot interior ceilings.

12 ft
24 ft

FIGURE 5.3 An example of an auxiliary dwelling unit.

independence and support for aging in place. As technology improves, it is likely solutions like ADUs will increase in popularity and decrease in cost. However, local building zoning codes vary a great deal, making ADUs an available option in only certain locations (AccessoryDwellings.org, 2016b). As the number of older adults increases rapidly, though, it is likely more communities will permit ADUs as a way to enable more older adults to age in place and to provide a much less expensive alternative than long-term care.

Adult Day Care

In some cases, older adults need more support than is possible with just home modification, but still do not need assistance on a full-time basis. For them, one possible option may be adult day care. **Adult day care** *is designed to provide support, companionship, and certain services during the day.* This situation arises most often when the primary caregiver is employed or has other obligations and is unavailable during the day.

The primary goal of adult day care is to delay placement into a more formal care setting. It achieves this goal by providing alternative care that enhances the client's self-esteem and encourages socialization. Three general types of adult day care are available (National Adult Day Services Association, 2016a). The first provides only social activities, meals, and recreation, with minimal health services. The second type is adult day health care that provides more intensive health and therapy intervention and social services for people with more serious medical problems or who require intensive nursing care for a specific medical condition. The third provides specialized care to particular populations, such as people with dementia or developmental disabilities.

Adult day care centers can be independent or sponsored by a profit (about 25%) or nonprofit (about 75%) organizations. They may provide transportation to and from the center. Depending on the services received, Medicaid or other insurance may cover some of the expenses (Medicare does not). Because some states do not license adult day care centers, careful screening of a particular center is advised. The National Adult Day Services Association (2016b) provides an overview of characteristics and services to look for.

About 35% of adult day care clients live with an adult child and 20% with a spouse or partner. The average age of clients is over 70, and about two-thirds are women (National Adult Day Services Association, 2016a). Family members choosing adult day care (and can afford it) typically do so because they need occasional assistance with caregiving, have safety concerns about the care recipient when the caregiver is not around, take increasing amounts of time off from work for caregiving, are experiencing problems in their relationship with the care recipient, or the care recipient could benefit from more contact with other older adults (MetLife, 2010). Most clients attend full-day programs and have significant physical impairment, chronic disease, or cognitive impairment.

For people with cognitive impairment, changes in routine can result in confusion or disruptive behavior. It is especially important for them, as it is for all older adults who may become adult day care clients, to inform them of this choice. A good strategy is to engage in a few trials to find out how well the person acclimates to the different surroundings and activities.

Research demonstrates adult day care is a viable and important option for caregivers. Caregivers are interested in programs that meet the needs of their loved ones and are generally satisfied with the services provided, especially in giving them time to pursue necessary other activities such as employment (Neville et al., 2015). Family members clearly seek what is best for their loved one in searching for and helping make the transition to adult day care centers (Larson & Kao, 2016; Neville et al., 2015). However, as a study in Australia demonstrated, family caregivers can be overwhelmed by the amount of information and confused by the process of placing their family member (Robinson et al., 2012).

Evidence is clear that compared with keeping relatives with cognitive impairment at home, good adult day care programs can reduce problematic behaviors and lower the need for psychotropic medication in clients, and result in lower reports of caregiving burden among caregivers (Larson & Kao, 2016; MetLife, 2010). However, a key factor in the success of day care programs is having culturally appropriate programs in interventions, as demonstrated in studies of Korean (Park, 2008) and Chinese (Wong & Yeung, 2015) clients who benefited most when programs took their cultural background into account.

Congregate Housing

Congregate housing includes a range of living options from those providing only housing to those providing some level of medical services (Howe, Jones, & Tilse, 2013). The most common form is an apartment complex of older adults that provides a level of support such as shared meals. Congregate housing is often the least expensive form of supported living for older adults, because the cost is typically subsidized by various government agencies and nonprofit organizations. Because of its relative affordability compared with skilled nursing care, it is an especially important option for older adults who need some support but not the level of care provided in skilled nursing care. However, there is a shortage of congregate housing in the United States.

Traditional congregate housing differs from assisted living in terms of the level of services provided. Although many traditional congregate housing complexes do not include individual kitchens and provide shared meals, the level of medical assistance, for example, is lower than in assisted living. Congregate housing facilities do not provide 24-hour medical services on site. Currently, newer congregate housing complexes are including higher levels of other service, so the distinction with assisted living is being blurred.

The service coordination provided in congregate living accomplishes several things: interface with housing officials, individual service plans for residents, coordination of shared activities (e.g., cleaning common spaces), and mediation of resident conflicts. Most congregate housing complexes require residents be capable of independent living and not require continual medical care, be medically stable, know where they are and oriented to time (e.g., know today's date and other key time-related information), show no evidence of disruptive behavior, be able to make independent decisions, and be able to follow any specific service plan developed for them. If at some point a resident no longer meets one of the criteria, he or she is usually required to move out.

The decision to move into congregate housing is usually done in conjunction with one's family, and is typically a response to a significant decline in functioning or other health-related problem (Koss & Ekerdt, in press). The best decisions about where one should live in late life are those that lead to outcomes that are congruent to the person's needs and goals, so congregate living can work for those seeking specific types of social engagement.

Assisted Living

Given that maintaining a sense of place, a home, is important to older adults, it should not come as a surprise that they prefer living options that foster that desire. That is how the option of assisted living came into being (Scheidt & Schwarz, 2010). **Assisted living facilities** are *housing options for older adults that provide a supportive living arrangement for people needing assistance with personal care (such as bathing or taking medications) but who are not so impaired physically or cognitively that they need 24-hour care.*

An ideal assisted living situation has three essential attributes (National Center for Assisted Living, 2016a; Scheidt & Schwarz, 2010). First, the physical environment where a person lives is designed to be as much like a single-family house as possible. That way, the setting has a residential appearance, a small scale, and personal privacy that includes at a minimum a private room and a full bath that is not shared with other residents unless the resident explicitly wishes. The public spaces in the facility are designed to provide indoor and outdoor access, which enhances a resident's autonomy and independence.

Second, the philosophy of care at an ideal assisted living facility emphasizes personal control, choice, dignity, and autonomy, and promotes a preferred lifestyle residents and their families consider to be a "normal," good quality of life. This philosophy is implemented by understanding residents' personal preferences and priorities, and allowing residents to exert control over their lives, schedules, and private dwellings.

Third, ideal assisted living facilities should meet residents' routine services and special needs. It is important to keep in mind that assisted living facilities foster residents' autonomy, so the levels of support provided are not meant to deal with high level, intensive nursing or other complex needs (Polivka & Rill, 2016; Thomas, Guihan, & Mambourg, 2011). However, assisted living facilities provide 24-hour supervision and assistance, help with ADLs, and meals in group dining rooms. Supports also tend to include transportation, socialization, and exercise and wellness programs.

Despite the fact assisted living facilities have existed for more than 20 years, there are serious gaps in service and in regulations (Polivka & Rill, 2016). For example, no national consensus or federal guidelines exist to govern the characteristics of the people who can and should be served in these facilities, the services provided, or minimum staffing standards. Despite the problems with precisely defining assisted living facilities, the number of them continues to grow. In the United States, there are over 30,000 assisted living facilities with over 1 million residents, and there is continued expectation for growth over the next few decades. One important reason for this growth is that assisted living offers a more cost-effective approach than long-term care facilities for those older adults who cannot live independently but do not need the level of nursing care provided in long-term care facilities.

To help families choose the best option, the National Center for Assisted Living (2016b) provides a *Consumer's Guide*. Before choosing an assisted living facility, you should consider several things:

- What are the resident's needs now, and what are they likely to be in the future? Will the facility meet those needs?
- Is the facility in a convenient location?
- What are the admission and retention policies?
- Does the facility permit residents to bring a few items from home?
- What level of support for personal care and what health services are provided?
- Does the facility provide a written statement of the philosophy of care and a statement of residents' rights?
- What do you notice on unannounced visits?
- How engaging and supportive are the staff? How is the food?
- What payment options are accepted by the facility?
- What social, recreational, and spiritual activities does the facility provide?
- What do other residents say about the facility?
- What types of training do staff receive and how frequently do they receive it?
- What information is contained in state licensing and accreditation reports?

The average annual cost of assisted living in the U.S. was nearly $45,000 in 2016, with an average cost increase of 2% per year (Genworth Financial, 2016). This is about half the cost of a nursing home. Medicare does not pay for either living costs or any of the services provided. In some cases, Medicaid or other specialized insurance may pay for services depending on the situation. Given that assisted living is usually less expensive than nursing homes, the lack of broad financial support for these programs means that the cost of care is not as low as it could be.

Research indicates that residents in assisted living facilities have higher well-being when the decision to live there was under their control and when the quality of relationships formed with co-residents is better (Street & Burge, 2012), and when they become attached to the place (Friesen et al., 2016). A key factor turns out to be how well the design of the facility, in combination with the services, optimizes the person–environment fit (discussed earlier in the chapter).

One of the main future challenges will be the blurring of current distinctions among congregate (independent) living, assisted living, and long-term care facilities into hybrids of these arrangements (Polivka & Rill, 2016; Scheidt & Schwarz, 2010; Schwarz, 2013). The hope is more stringent regulations will follow the blending of these forms of housing, and services will not destroy the special characteristics of assisted living. Another challenge, both now and in the future, is the cost of assisted living, which is already out of the reach of many elderly Americans and their families. Finally, researchers point to the need for updating our views of residential options for older adults (Granbom et al., 2016; Scharlach & Lehning, 2016). Because the future role of the government in providing funds for affordable shelter and care will continue to be limited, individuals and families will assume the largest financial burden of providing long-term care funds for their loved ones. Having access to the resources that this requires will be a major issue.

Adult Development in Action

As a gerontological social worker, what key factors would you consider when making recommendations about the best housing/living options for your older adult clients?

5.3 Living in Nursing Homes

LEARNING OBJECTIVES
- What are the major types of nursing homes?
- Who is most likely to live in nursing homes?
- What are the key characteristics of nursing homes?
- What are special care units?
- How can a nursing home be a home?
- How should people communicate with nursing home residents?
- How is decision-making capacity assessed?
- What are some new directions for nursing homes?

The last place Maria thought she would end up was a bed in one of the local nursing homes. "That's a place where old people go to die," she used to say. "It's not gonna be for me." But here she is. Maria, 84 and living alone, fell and broke her hip. She needs to stay for a few weeks while she recovers. She hates the food; "tasteless goo," she calls it. Her roommate, Arnetta, calls the place a "jail." Arnetta, 79 and essentially blind, has Alzheimer's disease.

Maria and Arnetta may be the kind of people you think of when you conjure up images of nursing homes. To be sure, you will probably find some people like them there. But for each Maria or Arnetta, there are many more that come to terms with their situation and struggle to make sense of their lives. Nursing homes are indeed places where people who have serious health problems go, and for many it is their final address. Yet if you visit a nursing home, you will find many inspiring people with interesting stories to tell.

Misconceptions about nursing homes are common. Contrary to what some people believe, less than 5% of older adults in the United States live in nursing homes on any given day (Centers for Medicare and Medicaid Services, 2016a). The percentage of people who live in a long-term care facility at any given point in time vary by age from about 17% for those aged 65–74 to over 40% for those over age 85 (Centers for Medicare and Medicaid Services, 2016a). Someone who turns 65 today has a nearly 70% chance of spending some time in a long-term care facility, with women requiring longer care (3.7 years on average) than men (2.2 years on average) (LongTermCare.gov, 2016). The gender difference is because older women take care of their husbands at home, but in turn need to relocate to a long-term care facility for their own care because their husbands are, on average, deceased.

Take a look at Figure 5.4, which depicts the percentage of minority older adults who reside in nursing homes. Note the regional differences, ranging from about 1% to nearly 87%. Increased numbers in some states largely reflect higher African American and Latino populations. Given the rapid increase in minority older adults, it is likely that these demographics will continue to change quickly over the coming decades. For now, a major limiting factor for more minority older adults' residence in nursing homes is cost.

Percent of minority nursing home residents, 2014

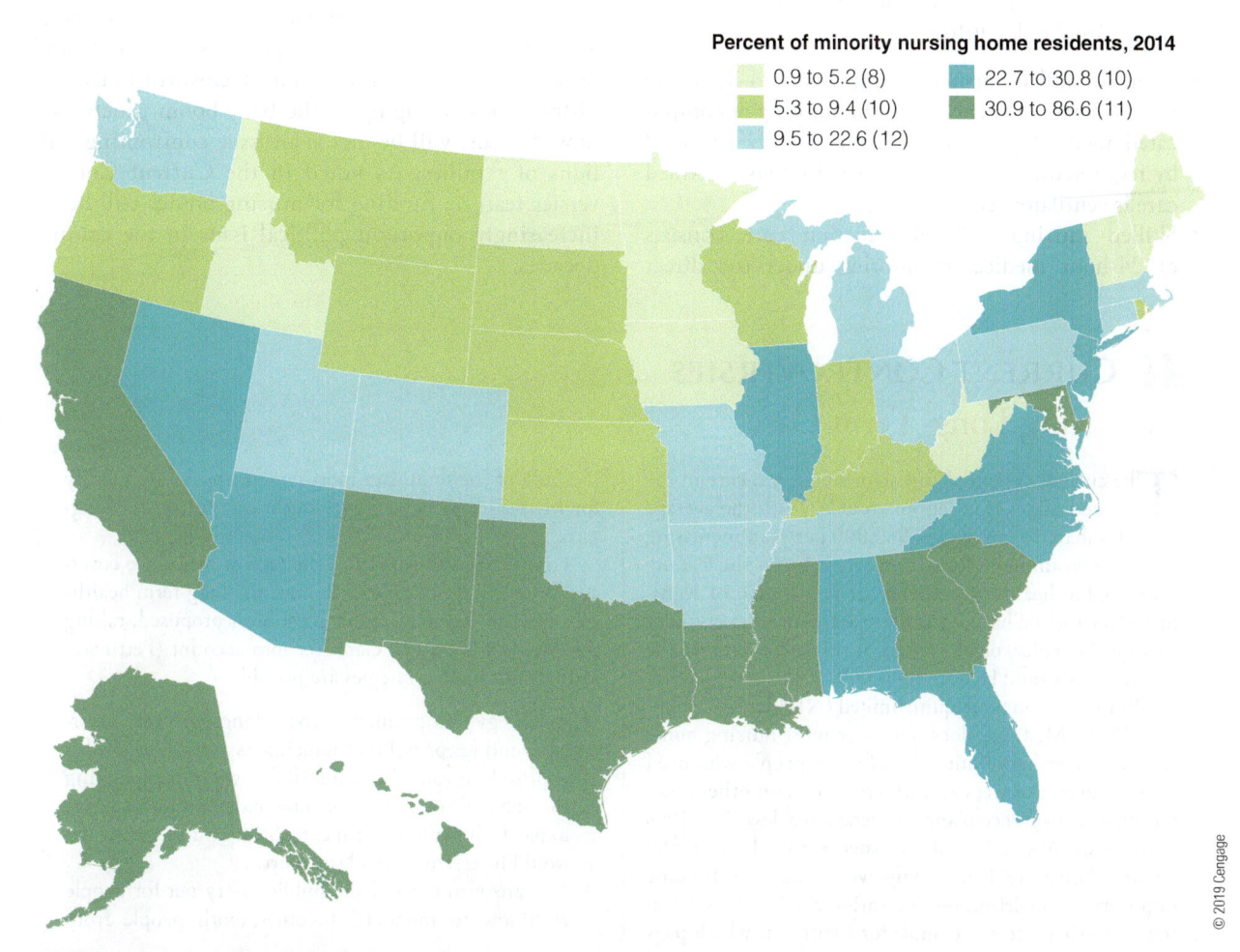

- 0.9 to 5.2 (8)
- 5.3 to 9.4 (10)
- 9.5 to 22.6 (12)
- 22.7 to 30.8 (10)
- 30.9 to 86.6 (11)

FIGURE 5.4 Percentage of minority residents of nursing homes, 2014.
Source: Centers for Medicare and Medicaid Services, *Nursing Home Data Compendium 2015 Edition*, p. 155.

Long-term care settings are different environments from those we have considered so far. The residents of such facilities differ in many respects from their community-dwelling counterparts. Likewise, the environment itself is dissimilar from neighborhood and community contexts. But because many aspects of the environment in these facilities are controlled, they offer a unique opportunity to examine person–environment interactions in more detail.

In this section we examine types of long-term care settings, the typical resident, the psychosocial environment, and residents' ability to make decisions for themselves.

Long-Term Care in Nursing Homes

Nursing homes house the largest number of older residents in long-term care facilities. They are governed by state and federal regulations that establish minimum standards of care. Four types of care are generally recognized (Brookdale, 2016):

- Intensive skilled nursing care consists of 24-hour care for residents needing constant monitoring or complicated medical procedures that is usually provided by registered nurses. An example of intensive skilled care is ventilator services.
- Skilled nursing and rehabilitation care consists of 24-hour medical monitoring under the direct supervision of a physician, with day-to-day services are provided by a registered nurse or licensed practical nurse. Although resident may stay for long periods, this level of care is often used for recovery from major illness (e.g., cerebrovascular accident), injury (e.g., broken pelvis), or surgery (e.g., hip replacement).
- Intermediate care may also 24-hour care including nursing supervision, but at a less intense level. Residents receiving this level of care usually have a long-term physical or emotional illness (e.g., dementia, severe mobility impairment). Such care may involve physical therapy, ongoing medication, and periodic medical monitoring.
- Custodial care includes all the nonmedical services a facility provides. Some residents may only need this level of care, which includes such things as feeding and assistance with ADLs.

The cost of nursing home care is high—an average of over $80,000 for a two-person shared room and over $91,000 for a private room (Genworth Financial, 2016). With the aging of the baby-boom generation, how this cost will be met is an issue confronting millions of families. As noted in the Current Controversies feature, funding for nursing homes will be an increasingly important political issue in the coming decades.

CURRENT CONTROVERSIES
Financing Long-Term Care

The current system of financing long-term care in the United States is in serious trouble. With the average cost of a shared room is over $80,000 per year, increasing roughly 4% annually, long-term care is by far the leading catastrophic healthcare expense. It is a source of legitimate fear for the havoc it can cause financially; consider that for the typical older woman, at current cost levels, the average cost would be over $200,000.

Payment options are quite limited (NIHSeniorHealth.gov, 2016). Medicare does not cover most nursing home care, but does have limited benefits for people who need skilled nursing services and who meet certain other criteria. Private insurance plans on average pay less than 10% of the costs. About 25% of the expense is paid directly by nursing home residents. Only when residents become impoverished (a definition that varies widely from state to state), do they become eligible for Medicaid, which pays the bulk of the total. But most Americans do not qualify for Medicaid, so must figure out a way to pay for long-term care themselves.

Given these expenses and the lack of insurance coverage, how will we be able to finance the long-term healthcare system? Several options have been proposed, taking the Affordable Health Care Act into account (Pettinato, 2013). Four main strategies are possible:

- A strategy that promotes private long-term care insurance and keeps public financing as a safety net. This approach spreads the financial risk without expanding the demands on federal or state budgets and taxpayers to pay fully for long-term care. Still, a public safety net would be essential as a last resort.
- A strategy to expand the public safety net for people with low to moderate incomes, with people from

continued

higher-income brackets expected to provide for themselves through private financing. This approach is a needs-tested model that targets the people with the greatest need and the fewest resources for government assistance.

- A strategy to establish public catastrophic long-term care insurance and support complementary private insurance to fill the gap along with the public safety net. This approach spreads the risk and the burden on a greater number of people, reducing the cost of private insurance, but still pricing it beyond the means of many older adults.
- A strategy to establish universal public long-term care insurance supplemented with private financing and a public safety net. This approach spreads the burden over the greatest number of people, thereby addressing the problem of affordability of private insurance.

Despite the wide range of options, many of them still place the burden on individuals to devise ways of financing their own care. Given the cost, and the fact that millions of Americans do not have access to either adequate health insurance or personal savings, large subsidies from the government will still be needed for long-term care regardless of what the private sector does.

Given that government subsidies for long-term care will be needed for the foreseeable future, the question becomes how to finance them. Under the current Medicaid system, older adults are not protected from becoming impoverished, and in essence are required to have few assets in order to qualify. With the aging of the baby-boom generation, many more people will spend down their assets to qualify, causing Medicaid costs to skyrocket. If we want to continue the program in its current form, additional revenues will be needed, either in the form of higher taxes or dramatic spending reductions in other areas of public budgets.

The questions facing us are whether we want to continue forcing older adults to become totally impoverished when they need long-term care, the government to continue subsidy programs, encourage those who can afford it to buy long-term care insurance, and if we are willing to pay higher taxes for better coverage. How we answer these questions will have a profound impact on the status of long-term care over the next few decades.

Who Is Likely to Live in Nursing Homes?

Who is the typical resident of a nursing home? She is over age 85, European American, recently admitted to a hospital, living in a retirement home rather than being a homeowner, is cognitively impaired, has problems with IADLs, is probably widowed or divorced, and has no siblings or children living nearby. Maria and Arnetta, whom we met in the vignette, reflect these characteristics. However, this profile is changing as more older adults of color become residents of long-term care facilities (Centers for Medicare and Medicaid Services, 2016a).

What are the health issues and functional impairments of typical nursing home residents? For the most part, the average nursing home resident has significant mental and physical problems. Nearly 65% of nursing home residents have significant impairments with at least 4 (of a possible 5) ADLs, and roughly 60% have moderate or severe cognitive impairment (Centers for Medicare and Medicaid Services, 2016a).

As you may surmise from the high level of impairment among nursing home residents, frail older people and their relatives do not see nursing homes as an option until other avenues have been explored. This may account for the numbers of truly impaired people who live in nursing homes; the kinds and number of problems make aging in place extremely difficult for them and their families, and also beyond the level of assistance provided by assisted living facilities. For these reasons, the decision to place a family member in a nursing home is a difficult one even when the family member in question has serious cognitive impairment (Koss & Ekerdt, in press; Lord et al., 2016). Placement decisions are often made quickly in reaction to a crisis, such as a person's impending discharge from a hospital or other health emergency. The decision tends to be made by spouses/partners or adult children, a finding generalized across ethnic groups such as European Americans, Mexican Americans, and Koreans, especially when there is evidence of cognitive impairment (Klug et al., 2012; Kwon & Tae, 2012; Ruiz et al., 2016).

Characteristics of Nursing Homes

Nursing homes vary a great deal in the amount and quality of care they provide. One useful way of evaluating them is by applying the competence–environmental press model. When applied to nursing homes, the goal is to find the optimal level of environmental support for people who have relatively low levels of competence.

Selecting a nursing home should be done carefully. The Centers for Medicare and Medicaid Services (2016b) provides a detailed *Five-Star Quality Rating*

System website that is a guide for choosing a nursing home based on several key quality factors. Among the most important things to consider are:

- Quality of life for residents (e.g., whether residents are well groomed, the food is tasty, and rooms contain comfortable furniture);
- Quality of care (whether staff respond quickly to calls, whether staff and family are involved in care decisions);
- Safety (whether there are enough staff, whether hallways are free of clutter); and
- Other issues (whether there are outdoor areas for residents to use).

These aspects of nursing homes reflect those dimensions considered by states in their inspections and licensing process.

Individuals and families should also keep several other things in mind:

- Skilled nursing care is usually available only for a short time following hospitalization, whereas custodial care may be an option for a much longer period. If a facility offers both types, it may or may not be possible to shift level of care without relocating to another room.
- Nursing homes that only take Medicaid residents may offer longer term but less-intensive care levels. Nursing homes that do not accept Medicaid may force the resident to leave when Medicare or private funds run out.
- Ensure the facility and its administrator are fully licensed, and a full array of staff training is available on such topics as recognizing abuse and neglect, how to deal with difficult residents, and how to investigate and report your complaints.
- Ensure the resident's care plan is put together by a team of professionals, and residents have choices, can exert some control over their routines and care, and have appropriate assistance with ADLs and IADLs.
- Ask questions about staff educational levels (including continuing education) and turnover.

Based on the various theories of person–environment interaction discussed earlier in this chapter, the best nursing homes use what researchers recommend—a "person-centered care" approach to nursing home policies (Morgan & Yoder, 2012). Although there is not yet complete consensus about the underlying characteristics of person-centered care (Sharma, Bamford, & Dodman, 2015), this approach is based on promoting residents' well-being through engaging them in shared decision making and participation in their care, and showing them respect. Person-centered planning focuses on the individual, and does not use a one-size-fits-all approach. An example of this approach includes such things as residents getting to decorate their own rooms, choosing what they want to eat from a buffet, and deciding whether they want to take a shower or a bath. Most important, this approach involves a team who knows and cares about the individual who work together with the person to create the best supportive environment possible.

Such policies are grounded in classic research showing that residents who have higher perceived personal control show significant improvement in well-being and activity level, and actually live longer (Langer & Rodin, 1976; Rodin & Langer, 1977). Nursing homes using the person-centered planning approach also note major decreases in the need for certain medications (e.g., sleep and antianxiety drugs) and soft restraints, as well as substantial declines in the number of residents who are incontinent (Wyatt, 2016). Feelings of self-efficacy are crucial to doing well and adjusting to life in a long-term care facility (Brandburg et al., 2013).

Today, person-centered care is considered a best practice in nursing homes (Sharma et al., 2015; Wyatt, 2016). Including nursing home residents in the planning of their own care represents a major shift in culture from previous models based on convenience for staff, and is an example of the application of research to practice.

Special Care Units

Most residents of nursing homes have cognitive impairment, and the majority of those individuals have dementia. Providing a supportive environment for people with moderate to severe dementia requires certain specialized design and intervention features. This need has resulted in the development of special care units in many nursing homes.

Well-designed special care units for people with dementia provide a supportive and therapeutic set of programs that help the person function at the highest level possible. Optimally, staff working in special care units receive specific training to work with persons with dementia. The best units have physical design elements that take functional limitations into account; for example, the hallways of some facilities are designed so if residents wander, they merely follow the interior halls or exterior path in a circle so they do not leave the building or the complex, and the decorating is done in a way to minimize confusion. Most facilities have residents with cognitive impairment wear wrist or ankle bands that trigger alarms if they wander beyond a certain point or exit the facility, another safe way to provide opportunities for residents to move about freely but safely. The best facilities also permit residents to bring a few personal items as reminders of their past in order to provide a more homelike environment. They also provide a private dining area in a family-like setting to minimize possible negative interactions between residents with dementia and residents without cognitive impairment.

Selecting the right special care unit for a person with dementia must be done carefully by the family with proper input from healthcare professionals, keeping in mind that such care units need to be grounded in basic principles of human rights (Charras, Eynard, & Viatour, 2016; Gillick, 2012). As noted in the competence–environmental press model, as competence declines the environment must provide more support for behavior to be optimized. So the special care unit must have the right level of environmental support at the placement, as well as the availability of additional levels of support when the person's competence level continues to decline. Memory aids should be built into the unit, such as color-coded halls. Staffing levels and training are key as is the range of intervention programs and activities available. Such programs should be research based, such as those based on the Montessori techniques discussed in Chapter 10.

The research-based staff training required at the best special care units includes several aspects of caring for older adults with moderate to severe cognitive impairment:

- Appropriate and effective communication techniques (as discussed later in this section);
- Behavioral management techniques to address aggressive or agitated behavior (a common symptom in dementia);
- Appropriate techniques for assisting with personal health and hygiene that protect residents' dignity;
- Appropriate methods for dealing with incontinence;
- Appropriate techniques for handling sexuality in persons with dementia;
- Effective techniques for controlling wandering (in addition to physical design aspects of the facility);
- Appropriate ways of supervising or assisting with eating;
- Appropriate techniques and interventions to address memory failure and disorientation;
- Appropriate techniques for assisting with mobility (e.g., walking, using a wheelchair).

Training in these areas will not guarantee high-quality care, but it increases the likelihood of it.

Research indicates that upon admission, residents of special care units are younger, more behaviorally impaired, and less likely to be minority than general nursing home residents when both exist in the same facility (e.g., Centers for Medicare and Medicaid Services, 2016a; Sengupta et al., 2012). Residents of special care units tend to have lower hospitalization rates, were less likely to have serious other health issues (e.g., be tube fed), and have family members who were satisfied with the quality of care than residents of non-special care units (Cadigan et al., 2012; Marquardt, Bueter, & Motzek, 2014). The increased quality of care residents of special care units receive is more the result of a difference in philosophy of care between nursing homes with and without special care units than it is due to the special care unit itself. The behavioral-based intervention preferred in well-designed special care units results in lower mortality and better functioning, all other factors held constant, and is also likely to be used throughout the nursing home, improving quality overall (Shum et al., 2016; Yu, 2016).

Can a Nursing Home Be a Home?

One key aspect of nursing homes has been largely overlooked: To what extent do residents consider a nursing home to be home? This gets to the heart of what makes people feel the place where they live is more than just a dwelling. On the surface, it appears nursing homes are

Nursing home residents benefit from social activities and interaction with residents and staff.

full of barriers to this feeling. After all, they may have regulations about the amount of furnishings and other personal effects residents may bring, and residents are in an environment with plenty of structural reminders that it is not a house in suburbia. Not having their own refrigerator, for example, means they can no longer invite friends over for a home-cooked meal. Thus, the culture of nursing homes make a difference in residents' experiences (Killett et al., 2016).

Can nursing home residents move beyond these barriers and reminders and achieve a sense of home? The answer is yes, but with some important qualifications. In a groundbreaking series of studies, Groger (1995, 2002) proposed a nursing home can indeed be perceived as a home. She interviewed older African American adults, some who lived in nursing homes and others who were home care clients, along with a sample of the nursing home residents' caregivers. Groger's analyses of her interviews revealed that nursing home residents can feel at home. The circumstances fostering this feeling include having the time to think about and participate in the placement decision, even if only minimally; having prior knowledge and positive experience with a specific facility; defining home predominantly in terms of family and social relationships rather than in terms of place, objects, or total autonomy; and being able to establish a kind of continuity between home and nursing home either through activities or similarities in living arrangements.

Groger (2002) points out that residents pull from their repertoire of coping strategies to help them come to terms with living in a nursing home. Groger (1995) also reports that getting nursing home residents to reminisce about home actually facilitates adjustment. Some residents concluded only after long and detailed reflection on their prior home that the nursing home was now home. In addition, it may be easier for nursing home residents to feel at home on some days than others and from one situation to another, depending on the events or stimuli at the time.

Helping nursing home residents feel at home is an important issue that must be explored in more detail. Perhaps having people think about what constitutes a home, before and after placement, may make the transition from community to the facility easier to face. For those needing the care provided in a nursing home, anything done to ease the transition is a major benefit. Assessing the degree to which residents feel at home is possible, and can be used to document functional changes after placement into a facility (Brandburg et al., 2013; Centers for Medicare and Medicaid Services, 2016b; Killett et al., 2016).

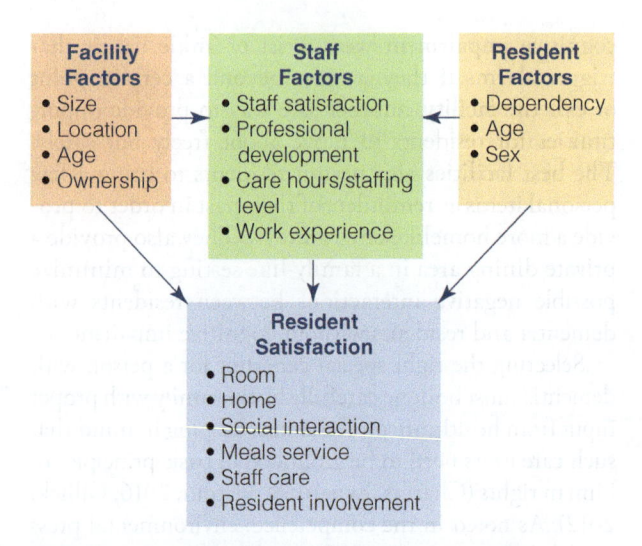

FIGURE 5.5 Major factors influencing resident satisfaction in nursing homes.
Source: Chou, S-C., Boldy, D. P., & Lee, A. H. (2003). Factors influencing residents' satisfaction in residential aged care. *The Gerontologist, 43*, 459–472, Copyright © Reprinted with permission from the Gerontological Society of America.

At a general level, nursing home residents' satisfaction relates to several key variables: facility, staff, and resident factors, as shown in Figure 5.5 (Chou et al., 2003). Research indicates that staff satisfaction plays a crucial role in nursing home residents' satisfaction. In contrast, providing more care does not (Chou et al., 2003). In addition, when residents have a voice in determining the quality of care, irrespective of their functional abilities, their quality of life improves (Killett et al., 2016; Sharma et al., 2015). As we will see next, how people communicate with residents is also key.

Communicating with Residents

Have you ever been to a nursing home? If so, you may experience difficulty talking with the residents at first, especially when interacting with residents who are cognitively impaired. Unfortunately, this uneasiness often results from people relying on stereotypes of older adults in general and nursing home residents in particular in speaking to them and results in inappropriate communication styles.

The communication style most people adopt is one in which younger adults over-accommodate their speech based on their stereotyped expectations of dependence and incompetence. This style is described as a general "communication predicament" of older adults (Ryan et al., 1986). Such speech conveys a sense of declining abilities, loss of control, and helplessness, which, if continued, may cause older adults to lose self-esteem and withdraw from social interactions. As time goes on, older adults who are talked to in this way may even begin behaving in ways that reinforce the stereotypes.

Inappropriate speech to older adults that is based on stereotypes of incompetence and dependence is called **patronizing speech**. Patronizing speech is slower speech marked by exaggerated intonation, higher pitch, increased volume, repetitions, tag and closed-end questions, and simplification of vocabulary and grammar. Speaking in this way can be conceptualized as "secondary baby talk," which is baby talk inappropriately used with adults (Mohlman et al., 2012). *Secondary baby talk, also called* **infantilization or elderspeak**, *also involves the unwarranted use of a person's first name, terms of endearment, simplified expressions, short imperatives, an assumption that the recipient has no memory, and cajoling as a way to demand compliance.* Elderspeak appears to be a cross-cultural problem, too (Cavallaro et al., 2016; Leeuwen, 2016).

In a classic study, Whitbourne, Culgin, and Cassidy (1995) established that infantilizing speech is viewed extremely negatively by some older adults. They found community-dwelling older adults rated infantilizing speech especially negatively and were particularly resentful of its intonation aspects as indicative of a lack of respect. Nursing home residents were less harsh in their judgments, giving support to the idea that being exposed to infantilizing speech lowers one's awareness of its demeaning qualities. Whitbourne and colleagues also found no evidence that infantilizing speech is high in nurturance, as some previous authors had suggested.

Residents with dementia tend to be more resistive to care when they are the targets of elderspeak, but show less resistance when elderspeak diminishes (Cavallaro et al., 2016; Williams et al., 2017). In younger adults, use of patronizing speech appears to be related to the amount of interaction they have had with unrelated older adults (i.e., older adults who are not their relatives), with more experience being related to lower use of patronizing speech (Hehman, Corpuz, & Bugental, 2012).

It turns out there may be different types of elderspeak, with different effects on the targets of the communications. In a study described in more detail in the How Do We Know? feature, Chee (2011), as part of the overall research of Cavallaro and colleagues (2016),

How Do We Know?
Identifying Different Types of Elderspeak in Singapore

Who were the investigators, and what was the aim of the study? Older adults who attend day services programs face many difficulties with the way people talk to (or about) them. The concept of patronizing speech, discussed in the text, captures the essence of the problem. Chee (2011) decided to establish the different kinds of patronizing speech used in such settings.

How did the investigator measure the topic of interest? Chee initially spent significant amounts of time at the adult day care center in Singapore to establish rapport with the clients. Data were gathered through observations and note taking during normal interactions between staff and clients. A coding system was developed to reflect different aspects of speech toward the older adult clients: (a) limited vocabulary, mirroring the limited vocabulary and sentence structure used when children are learning to speak; (b) infantilizing and over-parenting, when the staff member assumes the role of "parent" and treats the client as if he or she were the "child," an approach used most in conversations about toileting, displays of verbal affection, and reprimanding; and (c) repetition, which includes expansion, semantic elaboration, and comprehension checks.

Who were the participants in the study? Participants were 30 older adult clients (8 males, 22 females) with a variety of health conditions. Most of the clients were ethnic Chinese, but there were three ethnic Indians. Older adults' first languages varied, with most speaking Mandarin Chinese. For purposes of data analyses, clients were grouped into three clusters: those who were healthy and ambulatory, those who were healthy and wheelchair-bound, and those with dementia.

What was the design of the study? The design was naturalistic observation. Chee observed verbal communication interactions without participating herself.

Were there ethical concerns with the study? All participants were volunteers.

What were the results? Chee observed greater use of elderspeak with those clients who had greater physical or cognitive dependency on the caregiving staff. Thus, clients in wheelchairs and those with dementia were the targets of elderspeak more often than healthy clients.

continued

Although clients with dementia received all three types of elderspeak, they received the least reprimanding or domineering speech, perhaps because the staff perceived them as more in need of care. Clients in wheelchairs received nearly as much elderspeak as those with dementia. Female clients received more elderspeak than male clients.

More elderspeak occurred in situations in which clients were dependent on staff to help them perform some function, such as toileting or feeding. Situations in which clients were being encouraged to perform a task were also common ones in which elderspeak was used.

Clients did not appear to react strongly to elderspeak. Chee surmises that they either resigned themselves to it or chose not to respond.

What did the investigators conclude? Elderspeak occurs in a wide variety of interactions with clients in day services centers, but is related to level of physical or cognitive ability.

examined elderspeak in an eldercare facility in Singapore. She discovered there may be at least two types of elderspeak, what she terms "right" and "wrong." She also demonstrated elderspeak is a common approach used in a variety of settings, but that it is used toward older women most often.

Chee concluded elderspeak aimed at comprehension checking and encouragement, when no other elements of elderspeak are present, may enhance clients' performance. In contrast, other forms of elderspeak tended to result in poorer performance of the task at hand.

So how should people talk to older adults, especially those needing services or living in long-term care facilities? Ryan and her colleagues (1995) initially proposed the communication enhancement model as a framework for appropriate exchange. This model is based on a health promotion model that seeks opportunities for healthcare providers to optimize outcomes for older adults through more appropriate and effective communication. As you can see from Figure 5.6, this model emphasizes communication with older adults must be based on recognizing individualized cues, modifying

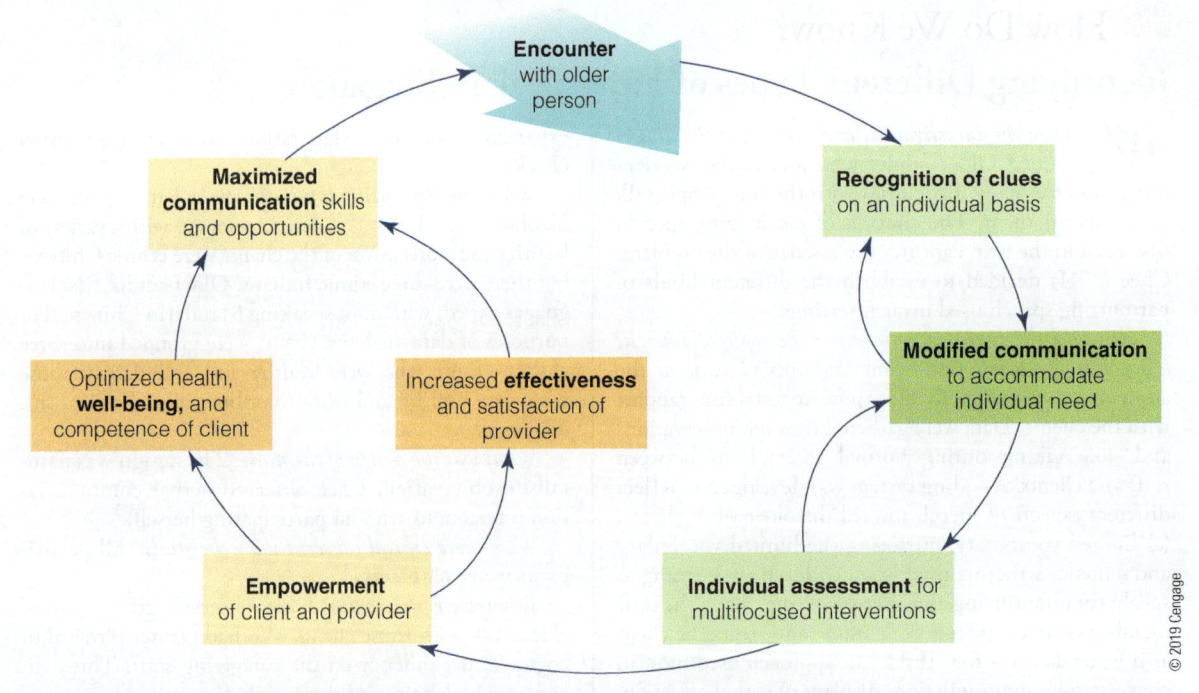

FIGURE 5.6 The communication enhancement model. Note that this model is dynamic in that there are opportunities to modify communication interactions and to have the outcomes of one interaction serve as input for another.

Source: Ryan, E. B., Meredith, S. D., MacLean, M. J., & Orange, J. B., (1995). Changing the way we talk with elders: Promoting health using the communication enhancement model. *International Journal of Aging and Human Development, 41,* 89–107. Reproduced by permission.

communication to suit individual needs and situations, appropriately assessing health and social problems, and empowering both older adults and healthcare providers.

Combining the communication enhancement model with the person-centered care model discussed earlier provides a way for paraprofessional staff in long-term care facilities to communicate more effectively with residents, including those living on dementia special care units (Passalacqua & Harwood, 2012; Savundranayagam, Sibalija, & Scotchmer, 2016). Such strategies are important if the culture in long-term care facilities is to change.

The University of Queensland (Australia) has developed the *MESSAGE Communication Strategies in Dementia* training program based on this approach. MESSAGE stands for:

- MAXIMIZE attention
- EXPRESSION and body language
- Keep it SIMPLE
- SUPPORT their conversation
- ASSIST with visual Aids
- GET their message
- ENCOURAGE and ENGAGE in communication

Research indicates that this training is effective and well-received by staff who care for individuals with dementia (Conway & Chenery, 2016).

In general, an approach to communication based on the communication enhancement model promotes mental, social, and physical well-being among older adults and counters the fostering of dependence that follows from the traditional medical model discussed earlier. When patronizing speech occurs in nursing homes, active steps should be taken to eliminate it (Cavallaro et al., 2016; Mohlman et al., 2012; Williams et al., in press). Most important, this research reminds us we must speak to all older adults in a way that conveys the respect they deserve.

So what should you do as a visitor? The first time most people visit a nursing home, they are ill-prepared to talk to family members who are frail, have trouble remembering, and cannot get around easily. The hardest part is trying to figure out what to say in order to avoid patronizing speech. However, visiting residents of nursing homes is a way to maintain social contacts and provide a meaningful activity. Even if the person you are visiting is frail, has a sensory impairment, or some other type of disability, visits can be uplifting. As noted earlier in the chapter, high-quality social contacts help older adults maintain their life satisfaction. Here are several suggestions for making visits more pleasant (Davis, 1985), along with guidance from the Gerontological Society of America (2012):

- Face older adults when you speak to them, with your lips at the same level as theirs.
- Ask open-ended questions and genuinely listen.
- Concentrate on the older adult's expertise and wisdom, as discussed in Chapter 7, by asking for advice on a life problem he or she knows a lot about, such as dealing with friends, cooking, or crafts.
- Ask questions about an older adult's living situation and social contacts.
- Allow the older person to exert control over the visit: where to go (even inside the facility), what to wear, what to eat (if choices are possible).
- Listen attentively, even if the older person is repetitive. Avoid being judgmental, be sympathetic to complaints, and acknowledge feelings.
- Talk about things the person likes to remember, such as raising children, military service, growing up, work, courtship, and so on.
- Do a joint activity, such as putting a jigsaw puzzle together, arranging a photograph album, or doing arts and crafts.
- Record your visit on audiotape or videotape. This is valuable for creating a family history you will be able to keep. The activity may facilitate a life review as well as provide an opportunity for the older person to leave something of value for future generations by describing important personal events and philosophies.
- Bring children when you visit, if possible. Grandchildren are especially important, because many older adults are happy to include them in conversations. Such visits also give children the opportunity to see their grandparents and learn about the diversity of older adults.
- Stimulate as many senses as possible. Wearing bright clothes, singing songs, reading books, and sharing foods (as long as they have been checked and approved with the staff) help to keep residents involved with their environment. Above all, though, hold the resident's hands. There's nothing like a friendly touch.

Always remember your visits may be the only way the residents have of maintaining social contacts with friends and family. By following these guidelines, you will be able to avoid difficulties and make your visits more pleasurable.

Decision-Making Capacity and Individual Choices

Providing high-quality care for nursing home residents means putting into practice the various competence-enhancing interventions we have discussed relating to personal control and communication. Doing so means residents participate in making decisions about their care. But how can we make sure residents understand what they are being asked to decide, especially when a majority of them have cognitive impairment?

The need to address this question became apparent in 1991 with the enactment of the Patient Self-Determination Act (PSDA). This law mandated all facilities receiving Medicare and Medicaid funds comply with five requirements regarding advance care planning, referred to as advance directives (American Bar Association, 2016):

- Providing written information to people at the time of their admission about their right to make medical treatment decisions and to formulate advance directives (i.e., decisions about life-sustaining treatments and who can make medical decisions for them if they are incapacitated);
- Maintaining written policies and procedures regarding advance directives;
- Documenting the completion of advance directives in the person's medical chart;
- Complying with state law regarding the implementation of advance directives; and
- Providing staff and community education about advance directives.

The PSDA mandates work well with most people. However, assessing a person's capacity to make medical decisions is a tremendous challenge for medical ethics (American Geriatrics Society Ethics Committee, 1996; Carney, 2016; Rich, 2013). In theory, advance directives enable people to choose the type of medical treatment they prefer in advance of a medical crisis (see Chapter 13). However, numerous studies show the theory does not hold up well in practice: Most people, especially older adults, see such planning as a family process, especially when competence is in question (Finucane, 2016). They may engage in informal advance care planning, preferring to allow family members to make decisions for them when the need arises and to give them and healthcare professionals leeway in interpreting advance directives even when they exist (Modra & Hilton, 2016). Thus, it is unlikely a person being admitted to a nursing home will have completed a formal advance directive before arriving.

Because placement in a nursing home is already stressful and likely to occur in the context of a medical crisis, the new resident may not understand the information presented as mandated by the PSDA. To make matters worse, if new residents are cognitively impaired, they may be thought to be unable to act in their own behalf in communicating treatment preferences and end-of-life wishes and understanding the consequences of their choices (Allen et al., 2003), although there still may be ways to assist them in expressing their preferences (Carney, 2016; Finucane, 2016). The degree to which cognitive impairment interferes with a person's ability to decide their treatment raises important ethical questions concerning whether physicians can trust any advance directive signed by such individuals after they move to a nursing home (Gillick, 2012; Rich, 2013).

Assessing a nursing home resident's ability to make medical treatment decisions can be conceptualized as a problem involving the fit between the original intent of the law and the resident's cognitive capacity (Kepple et al., 2015). Several researchers have tackled the problem of how to assess decision-making capacity with varying results. Most important, a careful assessment of the resident's capacity to understand treatment and intervention options is necessary (Carney, 2016).

Still, many problems remain. No uniform approach to determining residents' cognitive competence exists, although progress is being made through the establishment of guidelines (American Bar Association/American Psychological Association, 2005, 2006, 2008). One barrier to a common approach is that each state sets the criteria needed to demonstrate cognitive competence (which is usually approached from the opposite side—what it takes to establish incompetence). To complicate matters further, research also shows lack of agreement between what nursing home residents want and what their families think they would want, and this also varies with ethnicity (Connolly, Sampson, & Purandare, 2012; Winter & Parks, 2012). Resolving the problem involves using the various approaches we considered for determining person–environment interactions, combined with strong clinical assessment (see Chapter 10), in the context of specific treatment goals and maintaining quality of life. Clearly, creating an optimal solution takes an interdisciplinary team of professionals, residents, and family members working together.

One solution may be to assess key members of the family (who serve as proxies in completing the forms) as to their beliefs as well as careful observation of the resident's capacity by the staff. Healthcare staff also need to sit down with family members and talk with them directly about treatment options so better decisions are made (Lillyman & Bruce, 2017).

New Directions for Nursing Homes

Nursing homes are not static entities. New ways of approaching care continue to be developed. Three interesting new developments are the Eden Alternative, the Green House Project, and the Pioneer Network.

The Eden Alternative

Imagine an approach to caring for frail older adults starting from the premise that skilled care environments are habitats for people rather than facilities for the frail. Such an environment has the potential to address issues such as boredom, loneliness, and helplessness. The Eden Alternative takes this approach.

Founded in the early 1990s by Dr. Bill and Jude Meyers Thomas, the Eden Alternative approaches care from the perspective of protecting the dignity of each person. It is based on the following 10 principles (Eden Alternative, 2016):

1. The three plagues of loneliness, helplessness, and boredom account for the bulk of suffering among our elders.
2. An elder-centered community commits to creating a human habitat where life revolves around close and continuing contact with plants, animals, and children. It is these relationships that provide the young and old alike with a pathway to a life worth living.
3. Loving companionship is the antidote to loneliness. Elders deserve easy access to human and animal companionship.
4. An elder-centered community creates opportunity to give as well as receive care. This is the antidote to helplessness.
5. An elder-centered community imbues daily life with variety and spontaneity by creating an environment where unexpected and unpredictable interactions and happenings can take place. This is the antidote to boredom.
6. Meaningless activity corrodes the human spirit. The opportunity to do things that we find meaningful is essential to human health.
7. Medical treatment should be the servant of genuine human caring, never its master.
8. An elder-centered community honors its elders by deemphasizing top-down bureaucratic authority, seeking instead to place the maximum possible decision-making authority into the hands of the elders or into the hands of those closest to them.
9. Creating an elder-centered community is a never-ending process. Human growth must never be separated from human life.
10. Wise leadership is the lifeblood of any struggle against the three plagues. For it, there can be no substitute.

The Eden Alternative launched a culture change in nursing homes that improved residents' quality of life (Kapp, 2013; Zarit & Reamy, 2013) by blending person-centered care with relational care (care that takes unintended actions into account) (Rockwell, 2012). The main outcomes of this movement are resident-directed care and staff empowerment, which together result in significantly improved experiences for residents (Killett et al., 2016). Research also indicates the cultural changes resulting from the Eden Alternative are associated with less feelings of boredom and helplessness and improved quality of life (Bergman-Evans, 2004; Kapp, 2013). However, there is also evidence that staff may feel challenged to keep up with the consistent work assignments (Andersen & Spiers, 2015).

Green House Project

The Green House concept was created by Bill Thomas (founder of the Eden Alternative) in 2001, and is grounded in the Eden Alternative (Jenkins, 2016). It is a radical departure from the concept that skilled nursing care is best provided in large residential facilities. In contrast, a Green House aims to provide older adults

Alternatives to traditional nursing homes, such as The Green House Project shown here, provide a person-centered approach to care based on small communal living.

who need skilled nursing care a small, homelike environment that shifts the focus from a large facility to one that feels more like a home. Only 6 to 10 residents live in a dwelling that blends architecturally with houses in the neighborhood, making it much more homelike (Kapp, 2013; The Green House Project, 2016a; Zarit & Reamy, 2013).

The Green House concept emphasizes the importance of encouraging residents to participate in their care just as they did in their homes by helping with daily tasks such as cooking and gardening, assisted by specially trained staff (Johnson & Rhodes, 2007). By emphasizing participation in one's own care to the extent possible, personal dignity is maintained, and quality of life improved, a factor also true of traditional nursing homes (Bangerter et al., 2016). As a result, the Green House concept is spreading across the United States as a viable alternative to large nursing homes.

Research indicates that even though the Green House homes excluded residents from some decisions, they are the most consistent in creating a real home and in staff-related aspects of care, such as self-managed teams (Cohen et al., 2016). Green House homes lead to improvement in rehospitalization rates as well as other resident health indicators (Afendulis et al., 2016), and a reduction in overall annual Medicare Part A cost of roughly $7,700 per resident (Grabowski et al., 2016). Certainly, the Green House Project is having a positive effect on many dimensions of long-term care. Still, ensuring that the Green House culture is maintained takes a highly skilled staff and ongoing attention (Bowers et al., 2016).

The Pioneer Network

The Pioneer Network is also dedicated to changing the way older adults are treated in society, particularly in care facilities. The Pioneer Network focuses on changing the culture of aging in America regardless of where older adults live (Pioneer Network, 2016). Like the Eden Alternative and the Green House Project, the Pioneer Network focuses on respecting older adults and providing maximally supportive environments for them. Their values are also similar.

The Pioneer Network, as part of the larger cultural change in caring for older adults, advocates a major emphasis on making nursing homes resident-centered and more like a home, and works in cooperation with the Centers for Medicare and Medicaid Services, among others, to work for revisions in national nursing home regulations (Wyatt, 2016). This work is aimed at creating a new culture of aging.

What the Eden Alternative, the Green House concept, and the Pioneer Network have in common is a commitment to viewing older adults as worthwhile members of society regardless of their physical limitations. Treating all people with dignity is an important aspect in maintaining a person's quality of life. Everyone deserves that.

Adult Development in Action

As a nursing home administrator, what changes would you predict in resident demographics, nursing home design, and the types of services offered based on what you know about the aging population?

Social Policy Implications

One recurring theme in this chapter is the problem of financing healthcare interventions in later life for people in the United States. The Current Controversies feature raises several key points about the costs of nursing homes in the United States and the lack of ways to finance those costs. With the aging of the baby-boom generation, it is possible the coming wave of older adults will be unable to afford the level and quality of care they expect to receive.

The Commonwealth Fund (2015) compared costs of health care in 13 high-income countries (Australia, Canada, Denmark, France, Germany, Japan, Netherlands, New Zealand, Norway, Sweden, Switzerland, the United Kingdom, and the United States). The U.S. spends far more than any other country, driven largely by greater use of medical technology and higher prices, and not by more frequent physician visits or hospital admissions. Despite spending more, U.S. residents have poorer health outcomes, including shorter life expectancies and more chronic conditions.

International funding models for long-term care reflect a wide variety of approaches, including social insurance, universal coverage through public services, financial need-based systems, and hybrid approaches. Similarly, there is an equally wide array of ways for limiting expenses. Many countries provide services ranging from in-home care through skilled nursing care, and have formal evaluation procedures to determine the best approach to care for each individual.

It is clear there is an array of successful models of providing long-term care to older adults that range from those completely supported by taxes to those that combine public and private contributions. Each has advantages (and disadvantages) that could inform discussions in the United States. It is equally clear the current U.S. model is not sustainable financially, and without serious attention there will be major difficulties faced by the coming generation of aging baby boomers, as well as the generations that follow.

SUMMARY

5.1 Describing Person–Environment Interactions

What is the competence–environmental press model?
- Competence is the upper limit on one's capacity to function.
- Environmental press reflects the demands placed on a person.
- Lawton and Nahemow's model establishes points of balance between competence and environmental press, called adaptation levels. One implication of the model is the less competent a person is, the more impact the environment has.
- People can show proactivity (doing something to exert control over their lives) or docility (letting the situation determine their lives) depending on the interaction of competence and environmental press.

What is the proactive and corrective proactivity or PCP model?
- The PCP model explains how life stressors and lack of good congruence in person–environment interactions, especially when the person has nothing to help buffer or protect against these things, result in poor life outcomes.
- Preventive adaptations are actions that avoid stressors and increase or build social resources. Corrective adaptations are actions taken in response to stressors, and can be facilitated by internal and external resources.

What are the major aspects of stress and coping theory relating to person–environment interaction?
- Schooler applied Lazarus's model of stress and coping to person–environment interactions. Schooler claims older adults' adaptation depends on their perception of environmental stress and their attempts to cope. Social systems and institutions may buffer the effects of stress.

What are the common themes in the theories of person–environment interactions?
- All theories agree the focus must be on interactions between the person and the environment. No single environment meets everyone's needs.
- Everyday competence is a person's potential ability to perform a wide range of activities considered essential for independent living.
- Everyday competence forms the basis for deciding whether people are capable of making decisions for themselves.

5.2 The Ecology of Aging: Community Options

What is aging in place?
- The ecology of aging seeks to understand the dynamic relation between older adults and the environments they inhabit.
- Aging in place reflects the balance of environmental press and competence through selection and compensation. Feeling "at home" is a major aspect of aging in place. Aging in place has resulted in a rethinking of housing options for older adults.
- Throughout adulthood people compensate for change; aging in place represents a continuation of that process.

How do people decide the best option?
- The best placement options are based on whether a person has cognitive or physical impairment, the ability of family or friends to provide support, and whether intervention, if needed, can be provided in the current residence or a move is necessary.

How can a home be modified to provide a supportive environment?
- Modifying a home can be a simple process (such as adding handrails in a bathroom) or extensive (such as modifying doorways and entrances for wheelchair access).
- Home modifications are usually done to address difficulties with ADLs.
- An emerging approach to home modification is the accessory or auxiliary dwelling unit, which creates a separate living space from either existing or new space for older adults.

What options are provided in adult day care?
- Adult day care provides support, companionship, and certain types of services. Programs include social, health care, and specialized services.
- Introduction of adult day care needs to be done carefully with persons who have cognitive impairment.

What is congregate housing?
- Congregate housing includes a range of options that provide social support and meals but not ongoing medical care.

What are the characteristics of assisted living?
- Assisted living provides options for adults needing a supportive living environment, assistance with activities of daily living, and a modest level of medical care.
- Assisted living situations have three essential attributes: a homelike environment; the philosophy of care emphasizes personal control, choice, and dignity; and facilities meet residents' routine services and special needs.
- Research shows assisted living is especially helpful for frail older adults.

5.3 Living in Nursing Homes
- At any given time, only about 5% of older adults are in nursing homes. Such facilities are excellent examples of the importance of person–environment fit.

What are the major types of nursing homes?
- Distinctions are made among intensive skilled nursing care, skilled nursing and rehabilitation care, intermediate care, and custodial care.
- Costs of nursing home care are high, and only certain types of insurance cover part of the costs. Future funding is a major concern.

Who is likely to live in nursing homes?
- The typical resident is female, European American, very old, financially disadvantaged, widowed/divorced or living alone, has no children or family nearby, and has significant problems with activities of daily living. However, the number of minorities in nursing homes is increasing rapidly.
- Placement in nursing homes is seen as a last resort and is often based on the lack of other alternatives, lack of other caregivers, or policies governing the level of functioning needed to remain in one's present housing. It often occurs quickly in the context of a medical crisis.

What are the key characteristics of nursing homes?
- Selection of nursing homes must be done carefully and take the person's health conditions and financial situation into account. The U.S. government provides ratings systems.
- Person-centered planning is the best approach, especially for people who have cognitive impairment.

What are special care units?
- Special care units provide a supportive environment for people with specific problems such as dementia.
- Residents of special care units tend to be younger and more impaired than the rest of the nursing home residents.

Can a nursing home be a home?
- Residents of nursing homes can come to the conclusion that this can be home. Home is more than simply a place to live: Coming to the feeling that one is at home sometimes entails reflection on what one's previous home was like and recognizing a nursing home can have some of the same characteristics.

How should people communicate with nursing home residents?
- Inappropriate speech to older adults is based on stereotypes of dependence and lack of abilities. Patronizing and infantilizing speech are examples of demeaning speech, that are rated negatively by older adults. The communication enhancement model has been proposed as a framework for appropriate exchange. This model is based on a health promotion model that seeks opportunities for healthcare providers to optimize outcomes for older adults through more appropriate and effective communication. Similarly, the MESSAGE Communication Strategies in Dementia training program provides guidance for communication.

How is decision-making capacity assessed?
- The Patient Self-Determination Act (PSDA) requires people to complete advance directives when admitted to a healthcare facility. A major ethical issue concerns how to communicate this information to people with cognitive impairment in nursing homes.

What are some new directions for nursing homes?
- The Eden Alternative, the Green House concept, and the Pioneer Network have a commitment to viewing older adults as worthwhile members of society regardless of their physical limitations.

REVIEW QUESTIONS

5.1 Describing Person–Environment Interactions
- What are person–environment interactions? Describe Lawton and Nahemow's theory of environmental press. In their theory, what is adaptation level?
- Describe the preventive and corrective proactivity or PCP model.
- Describe the application of the stress and coping model to person–environment interactions. What kinds of things buffer stress?
- What are the common themes expressed by the various theories of person–environment interactions?
- What are the key components of everyday competence?

5.2 The Ecology of Aging: Community Options
- What is the ecology of aging?
- What is aging in place?
- What factors should people use to make decisions about the most supportive environment in which to live?
- How can homes be modified to support older adults? What is an auxiliary dwelling unit?
- What services are provided at adult day care centers?
- What is congregate housing? What services are provided at assisted living facilities?

5.3 Living in Nursing Homes
- How many older adults live in long-term care facilities at any given time?
- What types of nursing homes are there? Who is most likely to live in a nursing home? Why? How have the characteristics of nursing homes been studied?
- Why do special care units often reflect better placement for people with significant physical or cognitive impairment?
- How does a resident of a nursing home come to view it as a home?
- What are the characteristics of inappropriate speech aimed at older adults? What is an alternative approach?
- How does the Patient Self-Determination Act relate to residents' decision-making capacity?
- What do the Eden Alternative, the Green House concept, and the Pioneer Network have in common?

INTEGRATING CONCEPTS IN DEVELOPMENT

- What do the demographics about the aging of the population imply about the need for long-term care through the first few decades of the 21st century?
- How do the theories of person–environment interaction include the basic developmental forces?
- How might a better financing arrangement for alternative living environments be designed?

KEY TERMS

adaptation level In Lawton and Nahemow's model, the point at which competence and environmental press are in balance.

adult day care Designed to provide support, companionship, and certain services during the day.

assisted living facilities Housing options for older adults that provide a supportive living arrangement for people who need assistance with personal care (such as bathing or taking medications) but are not so impaired physically or cognitively they need 24-hour care.

competence In the Lawton and Nahemow model, the theoretical upper limit of a person's ability to function.

corrective adaptations Actions taken in response to stressors and can be facilitated by internal and external resources.

docility When people allow the situation to dictate the options they have and exert little control.

ecology of aging Also called environmental psychology, a field of study that seeks to understand the dynamic relations between older adults and the environments they inhabit.

environmental press In the Lawton and Nahemow model, the demands put on a person by the environment.

everyday competence A person's potential ability to perform a wide range of activities considered essential for independent living.

infantilization or elderspeak Also called secondary baby talk, a type of speech that involves the unwarranted use of a person's first name, terms of endearment, simplified expressions, short imperatives, an assumption that the recipient has no memory, and cajoling as a means of demanding compliance.

patronizing speech Inappropriate speech to older adults based on stereotypes of incompetence and dependence.

person–environment interactions The interface between people and the world they live in that forms the basis for development, meaning behavior is a function of both the person and the environment.

preventive adaptations Actions that avoid stressors and increase or build social resources.

proactivity When people choose new behaviors to meet new desires or needs and exert control over their lives.

zone of maximum comfort In competence–environmental press theory, the area where slight decreases in environmental press occur.

zone of maximum performance potential In competence–environmental press theory, the area where increases in press tend to improve performance.

6 Attention and Memory

CHAPTER OUTLINE

6.1 Information Processing and Attention
Information-Processing Model
Attention: The Basics
Speed of Processing
Processing Resources
DISCOVERING DEVELOPMENT How Good Are Your Notes?
Automatic and Effortful Processing

6.2 Memory Processes
Working Memory
Implicit Versus Explicit Memory
Long-Term Memory
Age Differences in Encoding Versus Retrieval

6.3 Memory in Context
Prospective Memory
HOW DO WE KNOW? Failing to Remember I Did What I Was Supposed to Do
Source Memory and Processing of Misinformation
Factors That Preserve Memory
Training Memory Skills
REAL PEOPLE: The Yoda of Memory Training

6.4 Self-Evaluations of Memory Abilities
Aspects of Memory Self-Evaluations
Age Differences in Metamemory and Memory Monitoring

6.5 Clinical Issues and Memory Testing
Normal Versus Abnormal Memory Aging
Memory and Physical and Mental Health
CURRENT CONTROVERSIES Concussions and Athletes
Memory and Nutrition

Social Policy Implications

Summary
Review Questions
Integrating Concepts in Development
Key Terms

157

Imagine waking up one day and having no memory of anything. You have no name, no past experiences, no knowledge base, no idea of what the things in the world are that you can see. Terror might be one reaction. Utter confusion might be another.

Memory is the most important cognitive ability we have. It gives us our identity through the recordings of our past. It gets us through our lives by enabling us to find our way home, to our job, our school, and to so many other places. It enables us to recognize ourselves and loved ones and friends (and to know who we have never met). It provides our vast repertoire of information about everything under the sun. Memory really is the core of our being.

Perhaps that is why we put so much value on maintaining a good memory in old age. In fact, the ability to remember is a common measure of how well we are doing in late life, because older adults are stereotyped as people whose memory is on the decline, people for whom forgetting is not to be taken lightly. Many people think forgetting to buy a loaf of bread when they are 25 is annoying but otherwise all right, but forgetting it when they are 70 is cause for concern ("Do I have Alzheimer's disease?"). We will see that forgetting is part of daily life, and the belief it only happens in late life or the fact that it happens in later life automatically means something is seriously awry is wrong. In fact, older adults are quite adept at using strategies in their everyday life contexts to remember what they need to know.

In this chapter, we focus on both attention and memory, since they go hand in hand. We examine how people process information from the world around them and make sense out of it. We then discover cognition is a highly dynamic thing; lower-order processes such as attention create and influence higher-order thought, and higher-order thought determines where we focus our attention. People need to notice things in order to build knowledge and remember, because what we already know shapes what we notice. Thus, current research emphasizes changes in the different qualitative ways we process information and the quantitative differences in the amount of processing that occurs as we grow older. This research proves the traditional stereotype about memory and aging is wrong.

An important aspect of this research is whether or not we observe age-related decline in cognitive processes such as memory and attention and depends on the type of task being administered or the context wherein the memory operates. Some tasks, such as memorizing long lists of unrelated words, show large declines in performance with age, whereas others, such as remembering emotionally charged or personally relevant information, show no decline, and at times, improvement with age.

These task-related differences bring us back to the life-span perspective. A key issue is the extent research on attention and memory reflects the everyday cognitive functioning of older adults. In other words, what are the practical implications of age-related changes in cognitive functioning in specific situations?

We use memory not only as an end, when the goal is what and how much we remember, but also as a means to an end. For example, we use memory as an end when we summarize the most recent episode of our favorite television show, tell other people about ourselves, or remember to make specific points in a discussion. In these situations we use memory, but the point is not just what or how much we remember. In these and many other situations, memory is also a means to facilitate social exchange, allow other people to get to know us, or give ourselves a shared past with others. We return to this idea when we examine cognition in context later in the chapter.

Throughout this chapter, we consider results from experiments with responses made by people using computers. Although there is substantial evidence for age differences in some of the ways young and older adults process information, part of the difference may be due to cohort effects (see Chapter 1). Specifically, older adults in general are much less used to working on computers than younger adults, making the task less familiar to older adults. Consequently, they may not perform up to their maximum. Whether this experiential difference accounts for part of the age differences researchers uncovered remains to be seen; however, given the research is cross-sectional, meaning that age and cohort effects are confounded (see Chapter 1), this explanation remains a possibility.

Memory provides the ability to recognize friends and to share common life experiences as part of defining our identities.

6.1 Information Processing and Attention

LEARNING OBJECTIVES
- What are the primary aspects of the information-processing model?
- What are the basic components of attention?
- How does speed of processing relate to cognitive aging?
- What types of processing resources relate to attention and memory?
- What is automatic and effortful processing?

Trey strolled into a car dealership and convinced the salesperson to let him take one of the sports cars on the lot for a spin around the block. When he climbed behind the wheel, his excitement almost got the better of him. As he started the engine and eased into first gear, he became filled with anxiety because he had never driven a powerful sports car before. He suddenly realized he must pay complete attention to what he was doing. Why? The car had—a clutch. He had not driven a car with manual transmission in a couple decades. Now he was faced with the need to filter out everything—people's conversations, the radio, and the sound of the wind whipping through his hair.

How can Trey filter everything out? More importantly, what abilities can he use to pay attention? If something happened on the road, how quickly could he respond? Would these abilities be any different in a younger adult than in an older adult? Have you ever had this experience? If so, how did you access this knowledge?

How do we learn, remember, and think about things? Psychologists do not know for sure. About the best they can do is create models or analogues of how they believe our cognitive processes work. In this section, we consider the most popular model: the information-processing model.

Information-Processing Model

The **information-processing model** *uses a computer metaphor to explain how people process stimuli.* As with a computer, information enters the system (people's brains) and is transformed, coded, and stored in various ways. Information enters storage temporarily, as in a computer's buffer, until it becomes stored more permanently, as on a computer storage device (USB, hard drive, cloud storage, etc.). At a later time, information can be retrieved in response to some cue, such as a command to open a file. Let's see how this works more formally.

The information-processing model is based on three long-held assumptions (Neisser, 1976): (1) People are active participants in the process; (2) both quantitative (how much information is remembered) and qualitative (what kinds of information are remembered) aspects of performance can be examined; and (3) information is processed through a series of processes. First, incoming information is transformed based on what a person already knows about it. The more one knows, the more easily the information is incorporated. Second, researchers look for age differences in both how much information is processed and what types of information are remembered best under various conditions. Third, researchers in adult development and aging focus on several specific aspects of information processing: early aspects, including a brief sensory memory and attention; and active processing that transfers information into a longer term store (e.g., long-term memory).

Using the information-processing model poses three fundamental questions for adult development and aging: (1) What areas of information processing show evidence of age differences (e.g., early stages of processing such as attention, working memory, long-term memory)? (2) How can we explain variability when we find age differences in information processing? (3) What are the practical implications of age-related changes in information processing?

Sensory Memory

All memories start as sensory stimuli—a song heard, a person seen, a hand felt. We need to experience these things for only a small fraction of a second in order to process the information. This ability is due to the earliest step in information processing, sensory memory, where new, incoming information is first registered. **Sensory memory** *is a brief and almost identical representation of the stimuli that exists in the observable environment.* Sensory memory takes in large amounts of information rapidly. It does not appear to have the limits other processes do when attentional focus is applied. This type of memory is as if the representation exists in your mind in the absence of the stimuli itself.

However, unless we pay attention to sensory information, the representation will be lost quickly. Try drawing either side of a U.S. penny in detail. (Those who are not from the United States can try drawing a common coin in their own country.) Most of us find this task difficult despite seeing the coins every day. Much detailed information about pennies has passed through our sensory memory repeatedly, but because we failed to pay attention, it was never processed to a longer lasting store. Importantly, age differences are not typically found in sensory memory (Mok et al., 2016; Nyberg et al., 2012; Park & Festini, 2017).

Attention: The Basics

Each of us have experienced being in a situation when our thoughts drift off and someone snaps at us, "Pay attention to me." We come back into focus, and realize we had not been paying attention.

But what exactly does it mean to "pay attention?" One way to look at it is to think of attention from a functional perspective (Bourke & Styles, 2017). From the functional perspective, attention is composed of separate dimensions serving different functions. The complex tasks we engage in when processing information usually require more than one attentional function. In Trey's case, he must selectively attend to or focus on the clutch, shifting gears, the road and its obstacles, and at the same time filter out distracting information. Changing focus from one function to another is how we control attention. In addition, attentional processes are influenced by our capacity to sustain attention, as well as the speed with which incoming information is processed.

In the brain, attentional control is linked to the integration of processing in the parietal and frontal lobes discussed in Chapter 2 (Ptak, 2012). As we know, parieto-frontal integration processes undergo significant change with age. Not surprisingly, then, age differences emerge in various aspects of attention. Let's consider these in more detail.

Speed of Processing

Imagine you are sitting quietly watching a video on your iPad. Suddenly, the fire alarm goes off. How quickly can you process this loud input?

That quick response refers to a notion in cognitive psychology known as speed of processing. **Speed of processing** *is how quickly and efficiently the early steps in information processing are completed.*

At one time, researchers believed decline in speed of processing explained the rest of age-related changes in cognitive functioning (e.g., Salthouse, 1996). After all, one belief about aging is that older people respond more slowly than young adults. However, this rather simple explanation fell out of favor because research shows whether or not you observe slowing depends on what

As adults grow older, how quickly and efficiently information processing occurs slows down.

the task is because all components of mental processing do not slow equivalently.

Evidence including neuroimaging studies indicates age-related slowing depends on what adults are being asked to do (e.g., choosing which response to make; Choi & Feng, 2016; Nyberg et al., 2012). Interestingly, the amount of beta-amyloid protein found in the central nervous system, a bio-marker linked with the possible subsequent development of dementia (see Chapter 10), has been shown to be related to the degree processing speed slows (Jagust, 2016; Rodrigue et al., 2012).

Processing Resources

Many theorists and researchers believe with increasing age comes a decline in the amount of cognitive "energy" one deploys on a task. This idea is described in terms of processing resources (Bourke & Styles, 2017). **Processing resources** *refers to the amount of attention one has to apply to a particular situation.*

The idea of a decline in general processing resources is appealing because it would account for poorer performance not only on attention but also on a host of other areas (Dirk & Schmiedek, 2012). However, there is a nagging problem about the processing resource construct: At this general level it has never been clearly defined and is too broad. Two more precise approaches to processing resources are inhibitory loss and attentional resources.

Inhibitory Loss

One popular hypothesis is older adults have reduced processing resources because they have difficulty inhibiting the processing of irrelevant information (Aslan et al., 2015; Murayama et al., 2014). Evidence indicates the oldest-old (people aged 85 or older) have more task-irrelevant thoughts during processing and have trouble keeping them out of their minds. This difference could explain why they tend to have trouble with changing and dividing their attention.

The inhibition idea has considerable support (Kimbler, Margrett, & Johnson, 2012). Not only do older adults have difficulty inhibiting irrelevant information in laboratory tasks, they also have difficulty in matters with respect to everyday problem-solving. Kimbler and colleagues (2012) showed emotionally supportive messages reduce distracting thoughts and improve performance on everyday tasks for middle-aged and older adults.

There are simple strategies to compensate for older adults' difficulties with inhibiting irrelevant information. For example, simply asking older adults to close their eyes or avert their gaze away from irrelevant information improves performance. Using this strategy, older adults were just as good as young adults in attending to auditory stimuli (Einstein, Earles, & Collins, 2002).

Finally, researchers are asking whether there is a beneficial effect for the lack of inhibition of information under the right circumstances. It turns out there is. When information that was initially distracting but later became relevant, older adults performed better than young adults (Lourenço & Maylor, 2015; Thomas & Hasher, 2012). In such cases, the inability to inhibit distracting information turned into an advantage as the nature of relevant information changed.

Once again, we embrace a life-span perspective: adult developmental changes in cognitive functioning are characterized by both gains and losses. It is important to consider inhibitory loss in both ways. Under certain conditions it can be a hindrance, and in others it can be helpful. It all depends on the situation (Murayama et al., 2014).

Attentional Resources

Another way of looking at processing resource issues is through the lens of attention. In particular, a key issue is how well adults can perform more than one task at a time. Such multitasking requires us to spread our attention across all the tasks. **Divided attention** concerns *how well people perform multiple tasks simultaneously.* Driving a car is a classic divided attention task—you pay attention to other cars, the gauges in your car, pedestrians along the side of the street, and perhaps your passengers as you have a conversation with them.

Although it is widely believed older adults have more trouble than younger adults at dividing attention, it turns out the age differences observed are due to older adults' difficulties with the individual tasks and not to spreading their attention across them per se (Horwood & Beanland, 2016; Rizzuto, Cherry, & LeDoux, 2012). Observations in the workplace show older workers are just as able to multitask but perform each task a bit more slowly than younger workers. However, when the tasks become complex, older adults encounter difficulties dividing their attention and their performance suffers as a result.

Age differences on divided-attention tasks can be minimized if older adults are given training, thereby reducing the demands on attention. Such training can even be through online computer games (Toril et al., 2016; van Muijden, Band, & Hommel, 2012). These results imply that older adults may be able to learn through experience how to divide their attention effectively between tasks. Check out this idea by completing the Discovering Development feature.

So, you may ask, when do older adults have difficulty performing multiple tasks simultaneously? You may have observed older adults having difficulty trying to remember something as they are walking down a staircase, or trying to simply walk and talk at the same time. Li and colleagues (Li et al., 2001) found older adults prioritize walking and maintaining balance at the expense of memory. In other words, older adults focused on the

■ DISCOVERING DEVELOPMENT
How Good Are Your Notes?

Divided attention tasks are encountered all the time. You are familiar with one of them—taking notes while listening to a lecture (either on video or live). An interesting developmental question is whether the quality of the notes differs with age. One way to find out informally is to compare the notes taken in the same class by younger and older students. If there are no older adults in your class, there may be some in other courses. Ask them if you can compare their notes with those of someone younger. What predictions would you make based on the research evidence you have read thus far? What role would practice play in these differences? Whose notes are actually better? Why do you think this is?

task most important to them: walking and balancing to prevent falls. This finding is supported by neurological research (Holtzer et al., 2016). Younger adults, on the other hand, optimized their memory performance and ignored walking and balancing.

Automatic and Effortful Processing

There are two other constructs that round out our understanding of attention and cognitive processing: automatic and effortful processing (Bourke & Styles, 2017). **Automatic processing** *places minimal demands on attentional capacity and gets information into the system largely without us being aware of it.* Some automatic processes appear to be "prewired" in the sense they require no attentional capacity and do not benefit from practice; others are learned through experience and practice. Additionally, the two processes are mediated through different brain systems (Jeon & Friederici, 2015). For example, those who have been driving a car for many years stop at a stop sign without really thinking about it. We will see that performance on tasks that depend on automatic processes do not demonstrate significant age differences.

In contrast, **effortful processing** *requires all of the available attentional capacity.* Most of the tasks involving deliberate memory, such as learning the words on a list, require effortful processing. In these cases, we are typically aware of what we are doing. When we first learn how to drive a car with a clutch, we are aware of the information we process (e.g., how much to let up on the clutch versus how hard to press the accelerator pedal). It is with effortful processing that age differences tend to emerge.

Finally, when considering attentional resources, it is extremely important to ask the question: Is attention a fixed capacity that decreases with age? Researchers observed decline in older adults' performance on laboratory tasks assessing memory. However, a different picture may emerge when we consider the functional capacity or resources necessary in specific task contexts can be modified depending on the relevance, accessibility of knowledge, and expertise related to the cognitive processes required (Hertzog, 2008). Under conditions where the task requirement is to simply have a familiarity with the information, there are no age differences. However, when there is effort and deliberate processing involved to remember the information, age differences emerge. Because age differences are sensitive to the conditions under which they are measured, the key question for researchers today is: When and under what circumstances will we observe age-related change in cognitive functioning, and when is that change problematic?

Adult Development in Action

If you are an employee at an Apple store who shows people how to use the new device they bought, what principles would you apply from this section when instructing older adults?

6.2 Memory Processes

LEARNING OBJECTIVES
- What is working memory?
- What age differences have been found in working memory?
- How does implicit memory and explicit memory differ across age?
- Within long-term memory, how does episodic and semantic memory performance differ across age?
- What age differences have been found in encoding versus retrieval?

Susan is a 75-year-old widow who feels she does not remember recent events, such as if she took her medicine, as well as she used to. She also occasionally forgets to turn off the gas on her stove and sometimes does not recognize her friend's voice on the phone. However, she has no trouble remembering things from her 20s. Susan wonders if this is normal or if she should be worried.

Memory researchers have long focused on three general steps in memory processing as potential sources of age differences: encoding, storage, and retrieval (Sternberg & Sternberg, 2017). **Encoding** *is the process of getting information into the memory system.* **Storage** *involves the manner in which information is represented and kept in memory. Getting information back out of memory is termed* **retrieval**. Because there is no evidence for age differences in how information is organized in storage, most research has examined encoding and retrieval as sources of age differences (Morcom, 2016).

Working Memory

Think about a time when you asked a friend for their mobile phone number so you could send them text messages. You don't have your phone or a pen and paper, and you don't have an app like Phoneswappr to help. So you work to keep the phone number in your mind until you can type it in.

To successfully complete the task, you have to use working memory. **Working memory** *is the active processes and structures involved in holding information in mind and simultaneously using that information, sometimes in conjunction with incoming information, to solve a problem, make a decision, or learn new information.*

Researchers typically consider working memory an umbrella term for many similar short-term holding and computational processes relating to a wide range of cognitive skills and knowledge domains (Sternberg & Sternberg, 2017). This places working memory right in the thick of things—it plays an active, critical, and central role in encoding, storage, and retrieval.

Recall that sensory memory has a large capacity to deal with incoming information. In contrast, researchers generally agree working memory has a relatively small capacity. This capacity limitation of working memory operates like a juggler who can only keep a small number of items in the air simultaneously.

Because working memory deals with information being processed right at this moment, it also acts as a kind of mental scratchpad. This means unless we take direct action to keep the information active, the page we are using will be used up quickly and tossed away. For this reason, we need to have some way to keep information in working memory. That process is known as rehearsal. **Rehearsal** *is the process that information is held in working memory, either by repeating items over and over or by making meaningful connections between the information in working memory and information already known.*

Most evidence indicates there is significant age-related decline in working memory (Heathcote, 2016), although the extent of the decline is still in doubt. These data are important because working memory is the key to understanding age differences in memory. The loss of some of the ability to hold items in working memory may limit older adults' overall cognitive functioning. If information becomes degraded or is only partially integrated into one's knowledge base due to problems in working memory, it will be difficult to remember it.

However, some evidence suggests age differences in working memory are not universal. Working memory performance appears to depend on the type of information being used and may vary across different tasks (Loaiza, Rhodes, & Anglin, 2015; McCabe & Loaiza, 2012). For example, age-related decline in spatial working memory tends to be greater than that in verbal working memory, although there is decline in both types of working memory (Oosterman et al., 2011). Greater prior knowledge in older adults appears to counterbalance declines in working memory in some situations (Loaiza et al., 2015).

Why does working memory ability decline with age? There are several reasons, including alertness at different times of the day, order of the tasks, and task interference (Rowe, 2011). Another idea is older adults have more trouble juggling all of the elements once they are accessed (McCabe & Loaiza, 2012).

Although the evidence for age-related decline in working memory is not entirely clear, there is compelling evidence for how age differences in working memory relate to performance on more complex cognitive tasks. For example, researchers have begun to show working memory may be key to understanding the age differences in recall performance (McCabe & Loaiza, 2012; Morcom, 2016).

Implicit Versus Explicit Memory

In addition to working memory, we can further divide memory systems into two other types: implicit memory and explicit memory. **Implicit memory** *(sometimes called procedural memory) involves retrieval of information without conscious or intentional recollection.* **Explicit memory** *(sometimes called declarative memory), is intentional and conscious remembering of information learned and remembered at a specific point in time.*

Implicit memory is much like getting into a routine—we do things from memory but we do not have to think about them. The exact way we brush our teeth tends not to be something we consciously think about at the time. We just remember how to do it. Whether age differences in implicit memory are observed depend on the specific kind of implicit memory task in question (Howard & Howard, 2012, 2013, 2016). Learning sequences of information tend to show age differences, whereas learning spatial context does not. Interestingly, some neuroscience imaging research shows the kind of overactivity in the frontal cortex in older adults that is typical in situations when older adults are compensating for declines (see Chapter 2 for more details). Additional neuroscience research reveals differences in how the prefrontal cortex, medial temporal lobe, and caudate communicate in older adults (Stillman et al., 2016).

By far, though, most research on memory aging focuses on explicit memory. In general, performance on explicit memory tasks declines with age, although there are many exceptions and qualifications to this conclusion (Light, 2012). This research typically concerns our next topic, long-term memory.

Long-Term Memory

When most people think about memory, they think about having to remember something over time, whether a few minutes or many days. Everyday life is full of examples—remembering routines, performing on an exam, summarizing a book or movie, and remembering an appointment. These types of situations constitute what memory researchers call long-term memory (Rutherford et al., 2012). **Long-term memory** *refers to the ability to remember rather extensive amounts of information from a few seconds to a few hours to decades.*

Memory researchers have created a wide variety of tasks requiring individuals to remember all sorts of information for varying lengths of time. Well over a century of research indicates long-term memory represents a relatively large-capacity store where information can be kept for long periods. Mounting evidence in cognitive neuroscience suggests long-term memory is not a unitary construct, but consists of distinct, functionally different multiple systems that are served by different brain structures (see Chapter 2). For example, Shimamura (2014) points to evidence indicating that memory for events involves interactions among prefrontal cortex, medial temporal lobe, and ventral posterior parietal cortex. From Chapter 2, we also know that the hippocampus and amygdala, among other structures, are involved in other aspects of memory. In short, because memory is such an important part of us, it involves numerous areas of our brain.

As we delve into the various aspects of long-term memory, let us focus first on the more deliberate and effortful systems of explicit long-term memory. Two important types of long-term memory are semantic and episodic memory. **Semantic memory** *concerns learning and remembering the meaning of words and concepts not tied to specific occurrences of events in time.* Examples of semantic memory include knowing the definitions of words in order to complete crossword puzzles, being able to translate this paragraph from English into French, and understanding what the instructor is saying in a lecture.

Episodic memory *is the general class of memory having to do with the conscious recollection of information from a specific event or point in time.* Examples of episodic memory include learning the material in this course so you will be able to reproduce it on an examination in the future, remembering what you did on your summer vacation last year, and memorizing a speech for a play.

Like implicit versus explicit memory, episodic and semantic memory appear to be impacted differently by aging (Morcom, 2016; Park & Festini, 2017; Shimamura, 2014). Episodic memory stays fairly stable until around 55–60 years of age and then shows a precipitous decline beginning around age 65. In contrast, semantic memory increases from 35–55 years of age and then levels off. Although semantic memory starts to decline at age 65, the decline is much less substantial than for episodic memory.

Semantic Memory

As indicated previously, semantic memory is relatively spared in normal aging. Evidence suggests there are no deficits in semantic memory processes such as language comprehension, the structure of knowledge, and the activation of general knowledge (Mohanty, Naveh-Benjamin, & Ratneshwar, 2016; Park & Festini, 2017). Semantic memory retrieval typically does not tax working memory, and thus older adults can draw upon experience in word meanings and/or general world knowledge (Loaiza et al., 2015). In addition, whereas retrieval of episodic memories is based on cues to the original experience, semantic memories are retrieved conceptually as part of our world knowledge. This connection between semantic memory and world knowledge will come up again in Chapter 7 when we consider certain types of intelligence show little, if any, decline with age.

However, research also shows age changes in semantic memory can happen if it becomes hard to access and retrieve. One reason for access problems is if the knowledge in semantic memory is not used on a regular basis (Hertzog et al., 2003). You may have experienced this already, if you learned another language in childhood but now have trouble with it if you didn't use it. You may even have the feeling that you should know the word in the other language, but you simply cannot remember it.

A second reason that age differences are sometimes found in semantic memory tasks is simple momentary retrieval failure for information that is otherwise accessible. A common example is when adults have a "tip-of-the-tongue" or "feeling-of-knowing" experience (Thomas, Lee, & Hughes, 2016). A feeling-of-knowing (FOK) experience is when you try to retrieve a name or word you are certain you know, but it is not quite accessible at the moment. Imagine you are at a party and see someone familiar; you "know" that person's name, but you simply cannot retrieve it. Another aspect of this FOK experience is you can retrieve partial information such as the number of syllables in that person's name, the initial sounds or letters.

Older adults not only experience more FOKs, but also report less partial information about the target, both in the laboratory and in everyday life (Facal et al., 2012). Such FOK problems indicate even highly familiar information can become more difficult to retrieve as we grow older.

Episodic Memory

Because episodic memory includes so many of the day-to-day activities adults perform, it has been the focus of more research than any other single topic in memory development (Light, 2012; Morcom, 2016; Park & Festini, 2017; Shimamura, 2014). Typically, researchers study episodic memory by having people learn information, such as a list of words, and then asking them to recall or recognize the items. In a **recall** test, *people are asked to remember information without hints or cues.* Everyday examples of recall include telling everything you can remember about a movie or taking an essay exam with no notes or access to materials. **Recognition**, on the other hand, *involves selecting previously learned information from among several items.* Everyday examples of recognition include taking multiple-choice tests and picking out the names of your high school friends from a complete list of your classmates.

Many factors influence adults' performance on episodic memory tests and whether age differences are found. Consider how the information to be learned is presented (organized with cues may be better than randomly), how fast it is presented (slower may be better), how familiar people are with the material (familiar may be better), and how the test is given (recognition is usually better) all make a difference.

The results from hundreds of studies point to several conclusions. Overall, older adults perform worse than younger adults on recall tests of episodic memory because they omit more information, include more intrusions, and repeat more previously recalled items (Light, 2012; Morcom, 2016; Park & Festini, 2017).

On recognition tests, differences between older and younger adults are reduced. However, in comparison with young adults, older adults are more likely to say they recognize items that were never-presented, especially if they share a conceptual meaning or perceptual resemblance to the items actually presented (Light, 2012; Park & Festini, 2017).

Numerous neuroimaging studies have examined the brain changes associated with episodic memory. It turns out that identifying where changes are most profound maps reasonably well to normative versus pathological memory aging. Specifically, a pattern of change that is located mainly in the prefrontal cortex is associated with normative aging, whereas significant damage to the hippocampus relative to the prefrontal cortex is indicative of Alzheimer's disease (Tromp et al., 2015). We will return to these differential findings in Chapter 10 when we examine Alzheimer's disease and other forms of dementia in more detail.

One thing that helps people remember information in episodic memory tests is using internal study strategies, such as rehearsal or organizing information into categories. Older adults tend to be less efficient at spontaneously using these strategies. But they can and do use them when instructed to do so, and show significant improvement in performance. Moreover, older and younger adults benefit similarly from strategy training (Brehmer et al., 2016). However, these improvements are not sufficient, in general, to eliminate age differences in recall, indicating age differences in recall of episodic information is caused more by retrieval problems than poor encoding during study (Hertzog et al., 2013).

Age differences between older and younger adults can be reduced (but not eliminated) in several other ways: allowing older adults to practice or perform a similar task before learning a new list; using material more familiar to older adults; and using compensatory strategies to help themselves remember (we will examine this later in the chapter).

Although it would be easy to conclude episodic memory does nothing but decline with age, that would be wrong. It turns out there is one episodic memory process relatively spared with age: autobiographical memory, that we will consider a bit later.

Age Differences in Encoding Versus Retrieval

As we saw earlier, encoding is the process of getting information into memory, and retrieval is the process of getting that information out. What key changes occur in these processes with age?

Encoding

Results from years of research suggest an age-related decrement in encoding processes (Craik & Rose, 2012). The most important reason for these changes is adults' spontaneous use of strategies during the learning of new information declines with age. *A **strategy** is anything people do to make the task easier and increase the efficiency of encoding or retrieval.*

Compared to younger adults, older adults tend not to behave as strategically when studying information to be remembered (Dunlosky, Bailey, & Hertzog, 2011). However, when instructed or taught to do so, older adults can use encoding strategies well. So, the age changes observed reflect more a decrease in the degree the strategies are used spontaneously, rather than a decrease in the ability to use strategies.

There is a neurological reason for these behavioral changes. Changes in the left lateral prefrontal cortex with age appears to underlie the encoding declines, because stimulation of this area during learning improves performance (Sandrini et al., 2016).

Certainly, if information does not get encoded well, it is less likely to be there or to be as accessible for remembering later. So, at least part of the reason older adults perform more poorly than younger adults on tests of memory recall is because of poorer encoding.

Retrieval

We have already seen that one of the most consistent research findings is that older adults do more poorly than younger adults at recalling information. Besides potential encoding difficulties, what else might account for this difference?

Research evidence clearly points to the fact older adults tend to spontaneously use fewer retrieval strategies (Hertzog et al., 2013; Light, 2012; Morcom, 2016; Park & Festini, 2017). Moreover, even when encoding strategies are provided, and the opportunity to apply them during recall is allowed, older adults still do worse.

Neuroscience Evidence

Cognitive neuroscience (discussed in Chapter 2) presents evidence suggesting age differences in encoding and retrieval. Neuroimaging studies indicate during encoding that several things change with age in how the brain works. We have already seen that older adults' prefrontal cortex shows overactivity, indicating the usual pattern of compensatory processes with age (see Chapter 2 for more details).

In terms of retrieval, neuroimaging studies show that another age-related difference is in how the prefrontal cortex and hippocampus work together (Giovanello & Schacter, 2012; Wang & Giovanello, 2016). In younger adults, activity in these areas depends on the extent the retrieval task requires relations to be made between the information being remembered, whereas activity in these regions in older adults stayed equivalent irrespective of relational processing.

Other research indicates age-related compensatory brain activity for retrieval, similar to that seen in other cognitive processing (Oedekoven et al., 2013). Specifically, younger adults have more extensive neural network connections in the parietal and frontal regions involved in retrieval than do older adults. However, older adults show higher levels of brain activity in these regions, indicating a likely compensatory strategy for less extensive networks.

Shimamura (2014) took all of these findings and proposed a theory explaining declines in encoding and retrieval in episodic memory as the result of changes in how certain areas of the brain communicate and interact. This theory proposes that the prefrontal cortex drives retrieval, which is facilitated by the medial temporal lobe. The parietal lobe is where information from these regions converges. As we know from Chapter 2, the integration processes in these brain regions undergoes significant change with age.

Overall, these data support the view, described in Chapter 2, that older adults process information in their brains differently than younger adults. These differences in part represent attempts at working around, or compensating for, the normal age-related changes occurring in information processing. In the area of memory, though, these compensation attempts are insufficient on their own, but with training they can mitigate some of the losses in performance.

In sum, the research on encoding and retrieval processes is important for two key reasons. First, it emphasizes age-related decrements in memory are complex; they are not due to changes in a single process. Second, memory intervention or training programs must consider both encoding and retrieval.

Adult Development in Action

Suppose you are a geriatric physician. Based on what you learned in this section, what would be a good way to test for normative age-related changes in memory?

6.3 Memory in Context

LEARNING OBJECTIVES

- What age differences are there in prospective memory?
- How does autobiographical memory change across adulthood?
- How does source memory and processing of misinformation change across adulthood?
- What are some factors that preserve memory as we grow older?

Tyler, an elderly man of 80, has exercised his memory abilities since he reached his 60th birthday. He made sure to read voraciously, do crossword puzzles religiously, and keep up on current events. At a recent family gathering, it was quite evident such behavior paid off. In a game of Jeopardy!, he was the ultimate winner. However, when his grandson told him nonstop about a car he wanted to buy, Tyler later had trouble recalling all of the details.

As noted at the beginning of this chapter, memory is so integral to our everyday life we often take it for granted. In the case of Tyler, using his memory of previously learned information proved extremely important in participating in family games. However, he still had trouble remembering the details of recently learned information. This difference in memory ability has been the focus of research on age differences and how memory operates in everyday life (Groome, 2016; Ossher, Flegal, & Lustig, 2013).

This research is extremely important for three reasons. First, it may shed some light that generalize findings based on laboratory tasks such as word-list recall. Second, new or alternative variables affecting performance could be uncovered, such as factors that enhance memory functioning in older adults could be identified. Third, research on everyday memory may force us to reconceptualize memory itself.

Prospective Memory

How well do you remember to do things such as pick up some vegetables on your way home? **Prospective memory** *involves remembering to remember something in the future, such as an action or event* (Dismukes, 2012). Everyday life is full of examples, such as remembering to pick up one's children after school and remembering you have a dinner date next Friday evening.

A theoretical model of how prospective memory works is shown in Figure 6.1 (Zogg et al., 2012). Note the process starts with the intention to remember something in the future and depends critically on monitoring both event and time cues. This distinction, first introduced by Einstein and McDaniel (1990), is critical for understanding why people do and do not perform the actual task they are attempting to remember to do.

In event-based tasks, an action is to be performed when a certain external event happens, such as getting your clothes out of the dryer when the timer rings. A time-based task involves performing an action after a fixed amount of time, such as remembering to take the cookies out of the oven after 12 minutes of baking.

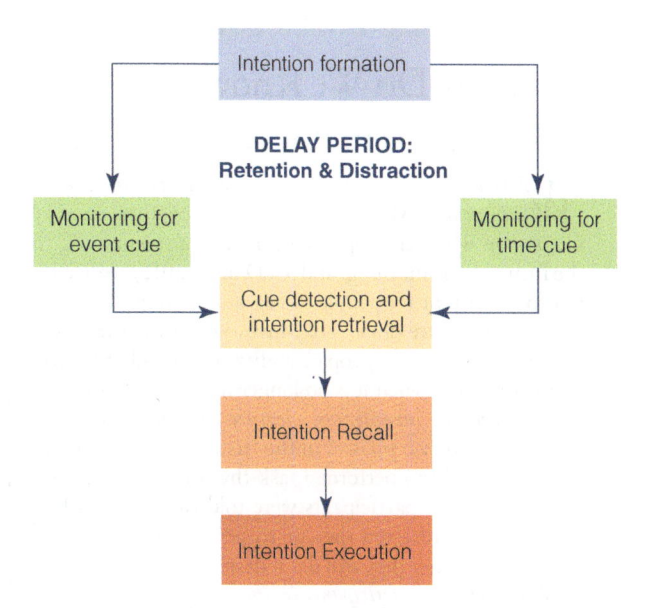

FIGURE 6.1 Conceptual model of the component processes of prospective memory.
Source: Zogg, J. B., Woods, S. P., Sauceda, J. A., Wiebe, J. S., & Simoni, J. M. (2012). The role of prospective memory in medication adherence: A review of an emerging literature. *Journal of Behavioral Medicine, 35*, 47–62. link.springer.com/article/10.1007/s10865-011-9341-9/fulltext.html#Sec1, Figure 1.

Researchers found time-based tasks showed more age differences as long as people used self-generated strategies to remember, as these tend to decline with age; the cues that typically accompany event-based tasks helped reduce or eliminate age differences (Kliegel et al., 2016). Adults of all ages benefit from the use of reminders, but older adults especially benefit from clear prioritization of tasks (i.e., ranking tasks from most to least important) (Kliegel et al., 2016).

Of course, it's clearly important to remember things one is supposed to do in the future. But once you have completed what you were supposed to do, it's equally important to remember *that fact*. Interestingly, little research has been done examining age differences in people's ability to determine that all of the tasks they are supposed to remember to complete have, in fact, been completed. One of these, showing important age differences, is described in the How Do We Know? feature.

Scullin et al.'s (2012) finding that older adults were more likely to continue to perform tasks even when they had been told it was no longer necessary has been supported by additional research (e.g., Anderson & Einstein, 2017). Forgetting that one has completed a task can have both innocuous and harmful consequences. Future research will likely focus on when such

How Do We Know?
Failing to Remember I Did What I Was Supposed to Do

Who were the investigators, and what was the aim of the study? Most research on prospective memory focuses on whether people remember to *do* something in the future. Scullin, Bugg, and McDaniel (2012) realized it is also important for people to *stop* doing something once all of the tasks are done. They investigated whether there are age differences in people's ability to remember to stop doing an action when it is no longer necessary to do it.

How did the investigators measure the topic of interest? The study had two phases. In the first, younger and older adults were told to perform a task that they subsequently did. In Phase 2, participants were told the task was finished, yet still received the cue to perform the task, and measured whether they still did it despite being told not to.

Who were the participants in the study? Younger adult university students (average age = 19 years) and community-dwelling older adults (average age = 75 years) participated.

What was the design of the study? The experiment was a 2×3 between-subjects design that included age group (younger or older) and condition (nonsalient-cue/task-match, salient-cue/task-match, or salient-cue/task-mismatch). The nonsalient-cue/task-match condition had a cue that did not signal the need to do the task. The salient-cue/task-match had a cue that was the signal to perform the task. The salient-cue/task-mismatch had the cue that formerly signaled the need to do the task, but no longer indicated that. Participants were randomly assigned to the three conditions.

Were there ethical concerns with the study? There were no ethical concerns because all of the participants were volunteers and had the experiment fully explained.

What were the results? In Phase 1, younger and older adults performed equivalently by correctly remembering to perform the task when cued. In Phase 2, though, older adults were more likely to continue attempting to perform the task when the cue occurred even though they had been told it was no longer necessary. Thus, older adults had more errors of commission.

What did the investigators conclude? Careful analyses of the results indicated older adults who made commission errors were less able to inhibit the task response than those who did not make commission errors. Inhibition is an important part of executive functioning, the higher-level cognitive processes that control decision-making (in this case the decision to complete the task). Additionally, older adults who made commission errors were more likely to get stuck making the task response in ways that implied they might have had trouble stopping even if they wanted to.

---

forgetting could be injurious, such as taking additional medication because one has forgotten that the dose has already been taken.

Autobiographical Memory

We noted earlier one main function of memory is to create one's sense of identity (Prebble, Addis, & Tippett, 2013). In other words, some of the information people learn and keep for a long time concerns information and events that happen to us. When we put all those incidents and information together, we create our autobiography. **Autobiographical memory** involves *remembering information and events from our own life.*

Testing autobiographical memory is tricky. To do it correctly requires having independent verification a remembered event actually happened in the way claimed. That's fine if there is a video of the event. But much of our lives are not on video, making it difficult to validate event recall. Plus, just because a person doesn't remember something could be due to memory failure, certainly, or because they deliberately choose not to report it, or they never actually learned it in the first place. Some ingenious researchers, though, managed to circumvent these problems and figured out how to study autobiographical memory.

Autobiographical memory is primarily a form of episodic memory, although it can also involve semantic memory. The episodic component of autobiographical memory is the recollection of temporal and spatial events from one's past (e.g., birthday parties, vacations, graduations). The semantic component consists of knowledge and facts of one's past (e.g., personal characteristics, knowledge that an event occurred) without having to remember exactly what or when things occurred.

Autobiographical memories change over time for all adults, with certain specific details (e.g., what objects are next to each other) being forgotten first, and other information (e.g., the main focus of the event) being remembered best (Talamini & Gorree, 2012). How this happens is in part a function of how the hippocampus processes memories (Sadeh et al., 2014). The number of autobiographical memories we remember in later life tends to overrepresent our young adulthood period, especially true of events involving social interaction (Fuentes & Desrocher, 2012).

As you may have experienced, details for autobiographical events change over time. For instance, shortly after not getting a job you wanted very much, your recollection of the event may be much more negative than it is years later after being in a different job you like quite a lot. You might think details for events would get fuzzier or fewer over time. For many events, that's true. But, surprisingly, that's not what always happens.

How memory for details of autobiographical events changes over time can only be studied when an independent record exists, made at the time the events happened. Biological/medical data, such as height or age at menarche (when a girl first menstruates) provide such a source. In a classic study, Casey and colleagues (1991) examined records available from the Harvard Longitudinal Studies of Child Health and Development on individuals from birth to age 50. Detailed information was collected over the years on such things as what childhood diseases the participants had, whether they smoked cigarettes, and what kinds and how much food they ate. At age 50, participants completed a lengthy questionnaire about these issues, and their responses were compared with similar reports made 10 and 20 years earlier, as well as with the official records. Casey and colleagues found half of the memories elicited at age 50 were more accurate than the memories for the same information elicited 10 years earlier at age 40. However, information about amounts of food consumed or individual episodes was not remembered well. Apparently, these events tend to get blended together and are not stored as separate incidents. Long-term accuracy for medical information has been validated by several other studies (e.g., Kyulo et al., 2012).

What distinguishes memorable events from those that aren't? What makes a moment we will remember the rest of our lives? Many people think highly traumatic or surprising and unexpected events are ones indelibly etched in our memories. Events such as September 11, 2001, or the unexpected death of a loved one are examples. *Researchers label memories for personally traumatic or unexpected events* **flashbulb memories**.

Flashbulb memories tend to feel real to people, who believe their recollections are highly accurate down to small details (Groome, 2016; Neisser, 2012). It is the case that people do tend to remember some details about major news events, such as the deaths of Michael Jackson and Osama Bin Laden (Demiray & Freund, 2015).

It turns out, though, when researchers compare what people claim they remember with independent records of actual events, the memories are often wrong. Many people feel absolutely certain they remember exact details of the events on September 11, 2001. President George Bush often related his detailed recollection of how and what he heard about the terrorist attacks. However, comparison with actual historical records indicate his memory was inaccurate in important ways concerning the details (Greenberg, 2004).

Nevertheless, people tend to get the gist of the story correct, and highly emotional events do tend to be remembered better than unemotional ones (Neisser, 2012). The errors and influences on autobiographical memory help explain why eyewitness testimony is often unreliable (Groome, 2016; Roediger, Wixted, & DeSoto, 2012).

Given autobiographical memory is the basis for identity, what events do people remember and when did they occur across the life span? What Susan experienced in the vignette, and as can be seen in Figure 6.2, is typical. For both younger and older adults, when asked to remember life events, vivid memories experienced earlier in life (between 10 and 30 years of age) are reported more often than those occurring during middle adulthood (between 30 and 50 years of age; Fitzgerald, 1999; Groome, 2016; Koppel & Berntsen, 2015). Events from less-remembered periods can be recalled if given additional context (such as news headlines from specific years) (Mace & Clevinger, 2013). Odors are especially powerful cues for early autobiographical memories (Willander & Larsson, 2006). It may be this earlier period of life contains more key events important in creating one's personal history (Koppel & Berntsen, 2015).

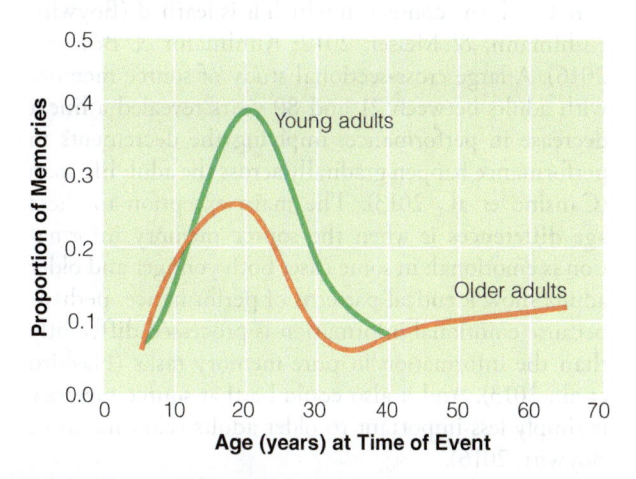

FIGURE 6.2 Both younger and older adults remember more life events from their teens and 20s than from any other period of life.

Source: Based on Fitzgerald, J. (1999). Autobiographical memory and social cognition. In T. M. Hess & F. Blanchard-Fields (Eds.), *Social Cognition and Aging*.

Source Memory and Processing of Misinformation

Why are some autobiographical memories that seem so vivid actually inaccurate at the detail level? Two main reasons have to do with how we remember the source of information and how susceptible we are to false information.

Source Memory

Think about a familiar event in your life. Now attempt to remember how you obtained your memory of it. Did you actually experience the event? Are you sure?

Source memory *refers to the ability to remember the source of a familiar event as well as the ability to determine if an event was imagined or actually experienced.* Remembering the source of information is important in many contexts. It is important for people to be able to discriminate whether they actually remembered to take medication or only thought about doing it. The ability to discriminate between these two events requires one to retrieve information about the context in which the event in question originally occurred. By reconstructing the original event accurately, the adults will remember whether they actually took the medication or not.

Research on age differences in source memory reveals older adults are less accurate at a number of source-memory tasks (Dulas & Duarte, 2012; Spaniol, 2016). The problem appears to be younger adults are better than older adults at connecting the item to be remembered with the context in which it is learned (Boywitt, Kuhlmann, & Meiser, 2012; Kuhlmann & Boywitt, 2016). A large cross-sectional study of source memory with adults between 21 and 80 years revealed a linear decrease in performance, implying the decrements in performance happen gradually across the adult life span (Cansino et al., 2013). The main exception to these age differences is when the source memory information is emotional; in some cases both younger and older adults show identical patterns of performance, perhaps because emotional information is processed differently than the information in pure memory tasks (Nashiro et al., 2013). And it also could be that source memory is simply less important to older adults (Kuhlmann & Boywitt, 2016).

Neuroimaging research indicates older adults show over-activation of areas in the prefrontal cortex when confronted with source memory tasks (Giovanello & Schacter, 2012; Spaniol, 2016; Wang & Giovanello, 2016), a pattern we saw in Chapter 2 reflecting compensatory behavior. Some research supports the notion the brain regions in which source memory is processed may even change with increasing age (Dulas & Duarte, 2012).

We can relate these findings to the role retrieval cues play in older adults' memory functioning. Naveh-Benjamin and colleagues (Old & Naveh-Benjamin, 2008; Smyth & Naveh-Benjamin, 2016) suggest contextual details can serve as retrieval cues, and without access to them older adults may have more difficulty in remembering events. Furthermore, episodic memory is more highly dependent upon contextual information that could explain why older adults have difficulties with that kind of task.

False Memory

At times in our lives, we may be repeatedly told stories about us by relatives or friends that we could not have personally experienced. However, if we hear them enough, we may start believing the events are real and falsely incorporate them into our autobiographical memory. **False memory** *is when one remembers items or events that did not occur.*

The focus in false memory research is on memory errors (Groome, 2016). One way to study false memory in the laboratory is to present participants with information (e.g., a list of related words, a video of an event) and test people's memory for both the information actually presented and information that was not (e.g., words related to those in the list but never studied, details that could plausibly have happened in the event but were not actually seen).

People tend to falsely recall and incorrectly recognize such plausible information and feel confident about it (Groome, 2016; Johnson et al., 2012). Important events may not be remembered at all, or may be remembered with the right kinds of cues. And, even highly emotional events can be accurate or highly inaccurate depending on the circumstances surrounding how they are remembered. Older adults tend to be more susceptible to these issues than younger adults (Colombel et al., 2016).

Once again, an explanation for this effect is older adults have more difficulty in correctly identifying information as false because they have trouble linking content information to its context, as noted earlier. Moreover, older adults have more difficulty separating misleading context from relevant context, that also explains why older adults are more susceptible to misleading information in general (Colombel et al., 2016; Jacoby et al., 2012).

Factors That Preserve Memory

As should be clear from research we just considered, older adults perform certain everyday memory tasks quite well. *These findings imply there may be specific factors that help preserve memory performance, termed* **cognitive reserve**. Let's investigate some of them.

Exercise

A major meta-analytic study showed conclusively physical fitness training improves cognitive performance in older adults regardless of the training method or the older adults' personal characteristics (Colcombe & Kramer, 2003).

Neuroscience research also clearly demonstrates regular exercise has a wide range of effects on the brain, such as increased neural plasticity (i.e., flexibility and adaptability of brain functioning), and can be viewed as an intervention alternative for diseases such as Parkinson's, Alzheimer's, and stroke, and may prevent some of the normative decline typically associated with aging (Marques-Aleixo et al., 2012). Additional evidence shows that exercise increases gray matter volume in the frontal, temporal, and parietal lobes, and in the hippocampus, thalamus, and basal ganglia, as well as reduced brain atrophy in other regions (Raji et al., 2016). In short, physical exercise is great for the aging brain, a point we will explore further in Chapter 14.

Multilingualism and Cognitive Functioning

In an intriguing study, Kavé and colleagues (2008) explored whether the number of languages a person speaks positively influences the cognitive state of older adults. In fact, older adults from 75 to 95 years of age who spoke four languages or more showed the best cognitive state. Neuroscience research on the benefits of bilingualism shows that it plays a large role in protecting older adults from cognitive decline, and that functional connectivity in the parietal-frontal control network is stronger (Bialystok, Craik, & Luk, 2012; Grady et al., 2015). These findings suggest speaking multiple languages might be a protective factor for maintaining our cognitive state as we age.

Semantic Memory in Service of Episodic Memory

Given that semantic memory is relatively unimpaired as we grow older (as discussed earlier), it may have an enhancement effect on episodic memory for older adults. Several studies show older adults perform better when they can use previously learned semantic information to support episodic knowledge (Badham, Estes, & Maylor, 2012; Badham et al., 2016; Badham & Maylor, 2016;). The more associations are made, the stronger the effect and the more performance is improved.

Negative Stereotypes and Memory Performance

Older adults may not perform at optimal levels because they are aware of and threatened by the typical belief that aging hampers memory ability (Hess et al., 2003; Lemaire, 2016). Specifically, negative or threatening stereotypes suppress older adults' controlled or conscious use of memory while increasing the likelihood they will use automatic response instead (Mazerolle et al., 2012; Popham & Hess, 2016). We will explore this psychosocial factor influencing cognition in Chapter 8.

Regular exercise has been shown to improve memory and overall cognitive functioning in older adults.

Training Memory Skills

The notion memory can be improved through acquiring skills and practicing them is old, dating back to prehistory (Yates, 1966). For example, the story related in *The Iliad* was told for generations through the use of mnemonic strategies before it was finally written down. Self-help books teach readers how to improve their own memory have also been around for a long time (e.g., Grey, 1756). Interestingly, the old how-to books taught techniques virtually identical with those advocated in more contemporary books such as those generated by Harry Lorayne, who is profiled in the Real People feature.

Training people how to remember information better, especially through the use of memory strategies, can be aimed at any adult. As you may have realized in our earlier discussion about memory strategies, most of the best strategies share several things in common. First, they require paying attention to the incoming information. Second, they rely on already-stored information to facilitate making new connections with the new material in semantic memory. Finally, in the process of encoding, strategies provide the basis for future retrieval cues. Additionally, putting training for memory strategies in the context of healthy life styles tends to enhance the positive outcomes. Research has generally shown well-designed memory training programs to be effective, and several studies show reasonably long-term positive effects (Brehmer et al., 2016; Jones et al., 2013; Miller et al., 2012; West & Strickland-Hughes, 2016). Memory improvement can also be an outcome of other forms of training that engage cognitive processes, such as training older adults to use iPads (Chan et al., 2016).

Memory aids or strategies can be organized into meaningful groups. Among the most useful of these

---

Real People
The Yoda of Memory Training

If you are like most people, you probably have trouble remembering the names of every person you meet. Not Harry Lorayne (born 1926). Harry was able to meet as many as 1,500 people for the first time, hear their name once, and remember each one perfectly. The book *Ageless Memory* (2008) is the culmination of his more than 40-year career training people how to remember information and dazzling audiences with his own abilities. Thousands of people bought his books and videos and attended his programs. *Time* Called him the "Yoda of memory training" (Kluger, 2000).

Why did Lorayne have such an impact?

Lorayne started his professional career as a table magician, but soon dazzled audiences by performing memory tricks, such as learning and remembering the names of everyone in the audience, which could be as many as 1,500 people. From there, he became a prolific and highly successful author of books on memory improvement and even opened a memory school. His *The Memory Book* was a New York Times bestseller.

The secret to Lorayn's success was grounded in very old mnemonic techniques that he adapted. Memory improvement was popular among the great Roman orators, for instance, so that they could remember speeches that sometimes lasted hours. Lorayne added a motivational framework to these tried-and-true strategies to create his unique blend of memory training programs.

As Lorayne grew older, he shifted his focus to demonstrating that older adults, with proper training and practice, could also improve their memory. Later in this chapter we will focus on research that shows the promise and challenges of this view. Still, there is no doubt that Harry Lorayne has had a major impact on the views people hold about memory. And don't you forget it!

Harry Lorayne.

classifications is Camp and colleagues' (1993) E-I-EI-O framework. The E-I-EI-O framework combines two types of memory, explicit memory and implicit memory, with two types of memory aids; external aids and internal aids. (The "O" is the reaction on the part of the learner when the strategy actually works.)

As discussed earlier, explicit memory involves the conscious and intentional recollection of information; remembering this definition on an exam is one example. Implicit memory involves effortless and unconscious recollection of information such as knowing stop signs are red octagons is usually not something people need to exert effort to remember when they see one on the road.

External aids *are memory aids that rely on environmental resources, such as notebooks or calendars.* **Internal aids** *are memory aids that rely on mental processes, such as imagery.* The Aha! or Oh! experience in the framework is the one that comes with suddenly remembering something. As you can see in Table 6.1, the E-I-E-I-O framework helps organize how different types of memory can be combined with different kinds of memory aids to provide a broad range of intervention options to help people remember.

We can use Camp and colleagues' approach to examine research on external and internal memory aids. In addition, we briefly review two alternatives, memory exercises and medications.

External Memory Aids

External memory aids are objects such as diaries, address books, calendars, notepads, microcomputers, and other devices commonly used to support memory in everyday situations like taking notes during a visit to the physician (McGuire et al., 2000; Mercer, 2016). Devices such as smartphones are increasingly being used to assist memory through various built—in functions and apps. Other tried-and-true methods include setting objects in obvious locations (e.g., positioning the kitchen wastebasket by the door to help you remember to take out the trash).

In general, explicit-external interventions, especially those involving technology-based devices, are the most frequently used, because they are easy to use, widely available, and work well with adults affected by a wide variety of physical or mental disorders (Mercer, 2016; Nyberg et al., 2012). Many of the apps on a smartphone are aimed at relieving us of memory burden (e.g., contacts, calendars, maps), and most social media use photos to help us link names and faces (presuming, of course, that the other user actually uses a self-photo). These explicit-external interventions have potential value for improving older adults' cognitive performance in real-world settings.

The problem of remembering one's complex medication schedule is best solved with an explicit-external intervention. The most common is a pillbox divided into compartments corresponding to days of the week and different times of the day, but smartphone apps can provide alarms with messages regarding what medication must be taken at that time. Memory interventions like this can help older adults maintain their independence. Nursing homes also use explicit-external interventions, such as bulletin boards with the date and weather conditions, to help residents keep in touch with current events.

Advocating the use of external aids in memory rehabilitation is becoming increasingly popular as well as extensively grounded in research. Camp, Zeisel, and Antenucci (2011) advocate external aids should be relied on alone or in combination with other techniques (e.g., Montessori methods) in working with people with dementia. Research also indicates for external cues to be most effective, they should (1) be given close to the time action is required, (2) be active rather than passive,

TABLE 6.1 The E-I-E-I-O Model of Memory Helps Categorize Different Types of Memory Aids

Type of Memory	Type of Memory Aid	
	External	Internal
Explicit	Appointment book	Mental imagery
	Grocery list	Rote rehearsal
Implicit	Color-coded maps	Spaced retrieval
	Sandpaper letters	Conditioning

© 2019 Cengage

Smartphones can serve as powerful external memory aids.

(3) be specific to the particular action, (4) be portable, (5) fit a wide range of situations, (6) store many cues for long periods, (7) be easy to use, and (8) not require a pen or pencil.

External-implicit combinations, more widely used with children, nevertheless have applicability with older adults in some situations. Many nursing homes use different color schemes to designate different wings or sections of the building. Because people process the color-coded aspects of the building automatically, the implicit nature of this external cue makes it ideal for people who may otherwise have difficulty learning and remembering new information.

Internal Memory Aids

Looking at Camp and colleagues' examples of internal memory aids may trigger some personal experiences. Many people use rote rehearsal in preparing for an examination (e.g., repeating Camp—E-I-E-I-O over and over), or use mental imagery in remembering the location of their car in a parking lot (we're parked near the light post with the giraffe sign).

Most research on memory training discussed earlier concerns improving people's use of these and other internal strategies that supply meaning and help organize incoming information. Classic examples of formal internal strategies include the method of loci (remembering items by mentally placing them in locations in a familiar environment), mental retracing (thinking about all the places you may have left your keys), turning letters into numbers, and forming acronyms out of initial letters (such as NASA from **N**ational **A**eronautic and **S**pace **A**dministration). Most memory improvement courses train people to become proficient at using one of these internal strategies.

Getting proficient at explicit-internal memory strategies is hard work. As noted earlier, explicit strategies require effortful processing that is more taxing on older adults. Thus, explicit memory intervention would most likely work best with older adults who are least likely to suffer memory failures or for young adults. In fact, healthy older adults are less willing to use effortful internal strategies. In addition, older adults with dementia are unlikely to benefit from these types of strategies (Camp et al., 2011). Thus, Camp argues older adults would benefit more from preserved implicit memory abilities.

One implicit-internal memory aid proven quite powerful is based on a technique called spaced retrieval. Camp and colleagues (Bourgeois et al., 2003; Camp, 2005; Hunter et al., 2012) relate even people with Alzheimer's disease can learn new things with this technique, a finding that has considerable support in other studies (e.g., Oren, Willerton, & Small, 2014). Spaced retrieval involves teaching persons with dementia or other serious cognitive impairment to remember new information by presenting to-be-remembered information (such as a person's name) and gradually increasing the time between retrieval attempts. This easy, almost magical technique has been used to teach names of staff members and other information, and it holds considerable potential for broad application. It is superior to other techniques (Haslam, Hodder, & Yates, 2011; Oren et al., 2014), and combining spaced retrieval with additional memory encoding aids helps even more (Kinsella et al., 2007).

Memory Drugs

The search for an effective medication that can improve memory, especially for people experiencing significant memory difficulties due to disease, has been intense for decades. It has met only with modest success.

To date, five medications have been approved by the U.S. Food and Drug Administration (FDA), all of which work through neurotransmitters (see Chapter 2). These are listed in Table 6.2. All of these medications have potentially serious side effects (e.g., nausea is a common one), and many people cannot tolerate them. Although they have been shown to have some effect in some people, they do not reverse the disease nor stop its ultimate progression.

As we will see in Chapter 10, much research on pharmacological interventions is also focusing on biomarkers of dementia, such as beta-amyloid protein (see also Chapter 2). Parallel work focuses on genomic approaches, which target suspected genetic mechanisms that cause the disease.

TABLE 6.2 Medications approved by the U.S. Food and Drug Administration for treatment of cognitive symptoms of Alzheimer's disease

Drug name	Brand name	Approved for
donepezil	Aricept	All stages
galantamine	Razadyne	Mild to moderate
memantine	Namenda	Moderate to severe
rivastigmine	Exelon	All stages
donepezil and memantine	Namzaric	Moderate to severe

Source: www.accessdata.fda.gov/scripts/cder/drugsatfda/index.cfm

Many medications, as well as general anesthesia used in surgery, have side effects that can cause serious and long-lasting memory problems. Medications commonly used to lower cholesterol (statins) can cause memory problems such as forgetfulness. Alcohol and many over-the-counter and prescription medications can create symptoms that mimic various types of memory problems caused by disease and cause diseases themselves (e.g., Wernicke-Korsakoff syndrome from chronic alcoholism). Clearly, if one is taking medications and experiencing memory difficulties, a thorough analysis of whether the medication is causing the side effect should be conducted.

Adult Development in Action

How might autobiographical memory be used in therapeutic settings?

6.4 Self-Evaluations of Memory Abilities

LEARNING OBJECTIVES
- What are the major types of memory self-evaluations?
- What age differences have been found in metamemory and memory monitoring?

Eugene just reached his 70th birthday. However, he is greatly concerned. He believed since he was young this is the age when memory really goes downhill. He has a great fear of losing his memory completely. He asks people to repeat things to him over and over for fear he will forget them. This fear takes a toll on his self-concept. He doesn't feel he has control over his life the way he used to.

How good is your memory? Do you forget where you put your keys? People's names? Or are you like the proverbial elephant who never forgets anything? Like most people, you probably tend to be your own harshest critic when it comes to evaluating your memory performance. We analyze, scrutinize, nitpick, and castigate ourselves for the times we forget; we rarely praise ourselves for all the things we do remember, and continue to be on guard for more memory slips. The self-evaluations we make about memory may affect our daily life in ways that traditionally were unrecognized. This is exactly what is happening to Eugene. His negative evaluations of his memory ability are creating much undue stress in his life.

The self-evaluations we make about memory are complex (Cavanaugh, 1996; Lucas et al., 2016; West & Strickland-Hughes, 2016). They are based not only on memory and performance per se but also on how we view ourselves in general, our theories about how memory works, what we remember from past evaluations, and our attributions and judgments of our effectiveness.

Aspects of Memory Self-Evaluations

Researchers of memory self-evaluation have focused primarily on two types of awareness about memory (Tauber & Dunlosky, 2016). *The first type involves knowledge about how memory works and what we believe to be true about it; this type of self-evaluation is referred to as* **metamemory**. For instance, we may know recall is typically harder than recognition memory. We may also know that using strategies during encoding and retrieval is often helpful, and that working memory is not limitless. We may also believe memory declines with age, appointments are easier to remember than names, and anxiety impairs performance. Metamemory has several related notions, including memory self-efficacy (the belief that I have the ability to learn and remember things), and memory self-evaluation (the personal inventory one does regarding memory ability). Metamemory is most often assessed with questionnaires asking about these various facts and beliefs.

The second type of self-evaluation, called **memory monitoring**, *refers to the awareness of what we are doing with our memory right now.* We can be aware of the process of remembering in many ways. At times we know how we study, search for some particular fact, or keep track of time for an appointment. At other times we ask ourselves questions while doing a memory task. For example, when faced with having to remember an important appointment later in the day, we may consciously ask ourselves whether the steps we have taken (e.g., making a note in our smartphone) are sufficient.

Age Differences in Metamemory and Memory Monitoring

Researchers explored age differences in metamemory mainly by using questionnaires, the most common, as well as judgments of confidence in one's ability or performance (see Castel, Middlebrooks, & McGillivray, 2016; Dunlosky, Mueller, & Thiede, 2016; Hertzog, 2016).

Questionnaires tap several dimensions of knowledge about memory and reflect the complexity memory itself. Older adults seem to know less than younger adults about the internal workings of memory and its capacity, view memory as less stable, expect memory will deteriorate with age, and perceive they have less direct control over memory (Castel et al., 2016; Hertzog, 2016; Hertzog & Dunlosky, 2011). Importantly, though, people with symptoms of depression tend to report poorer beliefs about memory, a key point we will examine later in this chapter and a key factor to consider in understanding the connections between memory beliefs and performance (Hülür et al., 2015).

Do these beliefs affect how well people actually remember information? Does what you believe about yourself matter?

The Role of Memory Self-Efficacy

Belief in one's ability to accomplish things is an old, pervasive theme in literature, religion, psychotherapy, and many other diverse arenas (Berry, 1989; Cavanaugh & Green, 1990). One of the most beloved children's books is *The Little Engine that Could*. The train engine keeps telling itself, "I think I can. I think I can." and, of course, it performs successfully.

As it applies to memory, belief in oneself is referred to as **memory self-efficacy**; *it is the belief one will be able to perform a specific task.* This is an important construct in understanding how memory changes with age (Berry, Cavanaugh, & West, 2016). Memory self-efficacy is an important type of memory belief distinct from general knowledge about memory; one may know a great deal about how memory works but still believe one's ability to perform in a specific situation is poor.

Memory self-efficacy emerged as one of the key aspects of metamemory because of its importance in accounting for performance in several different types of situations, as well as helping to explain how people make performance predictions in the absence of direct experience with tasks (Berry et al., 2016).

Overall, studies show older adults with lower memory self-efficacy perform worse on memory tasks. Longitudinal data from Australia show complicated patterns of interrelations in late life, but it is clear that knowledge about memory tasks is related to memory decline (Luszcz, Anstey, & Ghisletta, 2015). Older adults with low memory self-efficacy compensate for poor memory performance by using people for assistance and compensatory strategies to aid in their memory performance (de Frias et al., 2003; Lachman & Agrigoroaei, 2012). Interestingly, how old (or young) a person feels is related to memory performance; the younger one's subjective age, the better one's current performance and the slower one's decline is in immediate and delayed recall (Stephan et al., 2016).

Age Differences in Memory Monitoring

Memory monitoring involves knowing what you are doing with your memory right now. The ability to monitor one's memory per se does not appear to decline with age (Hertzog & Dunlosky, 2011). This is important, as memory monitoring may provide a basis for compensating for real age-related declines in episodic memory through the use of memory strategies.

Older adults who are better at monitoring are more likely to use effective strategies (Hertzog, Price, & Dunlosky, 2012), and apply strategies learned in training to other, appropriate situations (Hertzog & Dunlosky, 2012). Tapping into memory monitoring strategies may be an effective way to compensate for older adults' tendency to be more prone to false memories (Colombel et al., 2016; Shelton & Christopher, 2016).

Metamemory is important in understanding how people formulate predictions of how well they are likely to perform; monitoring and using data from one's performance may be more important for subsequent predictions on the same task. Both aspects are critical in stacking the deck in favor of successful memory strategy training, especially if the positive effects of training are to be maintained (West & Strickland-Hughes, 2016). The good news is evidence suggests in older adulthood, the ability to monitor multiple aspects of memory functioning is relatively spared (Hertzog & Dunlosky, 2011).

Memory monitoring is also a key aspect of prospective memory, an area we considered earlier in this chapter. In the present context, teaching older adults more effective memory monitoring strategies, such as imagining oneself completing the task in the future, improves prospective memory (Altgassen et al., 2015).

In short, building memory strategy interventions on skills that change little with age, such as metamemory and basic memory monitoring, can improve both performance and, by extension, quality of life.

Adult Development in Action

How might you use self-evaluations of memory in your job as a director of a senior center?

6.5 Clinical Issues and Memory Testing

LEARNING OBJECTIVES
- What is the difference between normal and abnormal memory aging?
- What are the connections between memory and physical and mental health?
- How is memory affected by nutrition?

Latarra's children are concerned. *Latarra is 80 and is becoming more and more forgetful. With the scare of Alzheimer's disease so salient in our society, they are concerned their mother is its next victim. What should they do? A friend tells them memory decline is normal with aging. But to ease their concerns they make an appointment for a clinical screening for their mother. This could reassure them it is only normal aging causing her forgetfulness, and not Alzheimer's disease.*

To this point we have been focusing on the changes that occur in normal memory with aging. But what about situations in which people have serious memory problems that interfere with their daily lives? How do we tell the difference between normal and abnormal memory changes?

These are two of the issues clinicians face. Latarra's children face this critical issue. Like Latarra's children, clinicians are often confronted with relatives of clients who complain of serious memory difficulties. Clinicians must differentiate the individuals who have no real reason to be concerned from those with some sort of disease. What criteria should be used to make this distinction? What diagnostic tests would be appropriate to evaluate adults of various ages?

Unfortunately, there are no easy answers to these questions. First, as we have seen, the exact nature of normative changes in memory with aging is not yet understood completely. This means we have few standards to compare for people who may have problems. Second, there are few comprehensive batteries of memory tests specifically designed to tap a wide variety of memory functions (Castro & Smith, 2015). Too often, clinicians are left with hit-or-miss approaches and have little choice but to piece together their own assessment battery based on their overall notion of the situation (Gould, Edelstein, & Gerolimatos, 2012; Stoner, O'Riley, & Edelstein, 2010).

As a result, clinicians approach memory assessment by focusing on several key questions: Has something gone wrong with memory? What makes the individual or the individual's family or friends believe that the problem goes beyond normative memory change with age? What is the prognosis if something serious is occurring? What can be done to help the client compensate or recover?

In this section we consider the efforts being made to bridge the gap between laboratory and clinic. We begin with a brief look at the distinction between normal and abnormal memory changes. Because abnormal memory changes could be the result of a psychological or physical condition, we consider links between memory and mental health. After that, we discuss how memory is affected by nutrition and drugs.

Normal Versus Abnormal Memory Aging

Throughout this chapter we have seen that many normative changes take place in memory as people grow old. Still, many aspects of memory functioning do not change, such as the ability to remember the gist of a story. Forgetting names or what one needs at the supermarket, though annoying, are normative changes of aging. However, some people experience far greater changes, such as forgetting where they live or their spouse's name. Where is the line dividing normative memory changes from abnormal ones?

From a functional perspective, one way to distinguish normal and abnormal changes is to ask whether the changes disrupt a person's ability to perform daily living tasks. The normative changes we encountered in this chapter usually do not interfere with a person's ability to function in everyday life. When problems appear, however, it would be appropriate to find out what is the matter. A person who repeatedly forgets to turn off the stove or how to get home is clearly experiencing changes affecting personal safety and interferes with his or her daily life. Such changes should be brought to the attention of a physician or psychologist.

As indicated in Chapter 2, recent advances in neuroscience, especially the study of brain–behavior relations through neuroimaging, led to an explosion in our knowledge of specific diseases and brain changes that can create abnormal memory performance. Such brain-imaging techniques also allow researchers to find tumors, strokes, and other types of damage or disease that could account for poorer-than-expected memory performance.

Neuroimaging mapping of the normative age-related changes in memory is not easy, mainly because numerous parts of the brain are involved in processing information that eventually ends up in memory (Husain & Schott, 2016; Sasson et al., 2012). We know from Chapter 2 that the prefrontal cortex, parietal region, temporal lobe, amygdala, and hippocampus are intimately involved in memory. There are also structural changes in the white and gray matter that occur in memory (Arvanitakis et al., 2016; Lee et al., 2016). The specific changes observed depend upon whether there is or is not a presence of disease, and in the latter case, which disease is occurring.

Some diseases, especially the dementias, are marked by massive changes in memory. For example, Alzheimer's disease involves the progressive destruction of memory beginning with recent memory and eventually including the most personal—self-identity. Wernicke-Korsakoff syndrome, which often accompanies long-term chronic alcoholism, involves major loss of recent memory and sometimes a total inability to form new memories after a certain point in time.

The most important point to keep in mind in assessment is that distinguishing between normal and abnormal memory aging, and in turn, between memory and other cognitive problems, is often difficult (Gould et al., 2012; Stoner et al., 2010). There is no magic number of times someone must forget something before getting concerned. Because serious memory problems can also be due to underlying mental or physical health problems, these must be thoroughly checked out in conjunction with obtaining a complete memory assessment. A good general rule, though, is this. Forgetting where you parked the car in a large parking lot is a typical memory problem. Forgetting that you drove is another matter.

Memory and Physical and Mental Health

Several psychological disorders involve distorted thought processes that sometimes result in serious memory problems. The two disorders that are the main focus of research are depression and dementia (see Chapter 10); but other diseases, such as chronic obstructive pulmonary disease (COPD, see Chapter 3) also cause memory impairment (Greenlund et al., 2016). In assessing memory function, it is very important to determine the cause of the impairment.

Damage to the brain resulting from physical or mental health disorders can result in profound decrements in different types of memory. For example, severe seizures in epilepsy can damage to the hippocampus. This usually makes it difficult for people to learn and remember new facts and events, typically resulting in serious disruption of everyday life. Damage to the medial temporal lobe usually results in severe impairment of long-term memory (Warren et al., 2012).

Occasionally, people temporarily experience a complete loss of memory and are disoriented in time, a condition known as **transient global amnesia (TGA)**. The condition is most common in middle-aged adults who experience a sudden blackout accompanied by repetitive questions. Episodes may last a few minutes or hours, with the only long-term effect a gap in memory. Currently, the cause is unknown, although neuroimaging studies have shown significant disruption of the hippocampus neural circuitry, especially that in the posterior medial network as a likely possibility (Park et al., 2016). TGA has been associated with migraines, temporal lobe epilepsy, a deficiency in a valve in the jugular vein, and especially transient ischemic attacks (TIAs) (Arena & Rabinstein, 2015).

Memory impairment as a result of concussion, or traumatic brain injury, is the focus of a great deal of research, especially following concussion injuries received playing sports. Research clearly indicates there are a variety of negative effects on cognitive functioning following concussion (White & Venkatesh, 2016). In the United States, roughly 1.7 million TBIs occur annually, resulting in 300,000 hospitalizations and 50,000 deaths (Sharp, Fleminger, & Powell, 2016). It is the most common cause of long-term disability and death among young adults. The effects of concussion and its relation to continuing to participate in sports is highly controversial, as discussed in the Current Controversies feature.

CURRENT CONTROVERSIES
Concussions and Athletes

Traumatic brain injury (TBI), such as concussion, can happen in just about any sport, as well as in combat injuries, exposure to explosions, automobile accidents, falls, or any other type of situation when one's head is hit hard. In essence, the brain slams against the skull, resulting in various levels of at least temporary damage and impairment. When you consider that on average 1.7 million Americans are treated for TBI each year, with many more untreated, it is clear that TBI is a major concern.

Two situations brought TBI to the forefront: war veterans and sports injuries (Finkbeiner et al., 2016; Schulz-Helk et al., 2016). Estimates are about 350,000 U.S. veterans have been diagnosed with TBI since 2000 (Defense and Veterans Brain Injury Center, 2016). Annual diagnoses continue to be high, largely because of better care in the field. Repeated TBI is a significant concern, as soldiers who have sustained a mild TBI are typically returned to duty within 7 to 10 days following a concussion. Regarding sports injuries, despite each state having legislation governing how soon athletes can return to playing after experiencing a concussion, there is little agreement on the diagnosis, treatment, and prognosis for patients.

There are several approaches to the diagnosis of concussion. In the United States, the American Congress of Rehabilitation Medicine established diagnostic criteria in 1993: any loss of consciousness, loss of memory before or after the event, and feeling disoriented. The American Academy of Neurology has also developed criteria for evaluating sports concussions, depending on whether there was loss of consciousness or amnesia. Globally, the Consensus Statement on Concussion in Sport, developed in Zurich in 2008, governs the decision-making process (McCrory et al., 2009). These criteria include the definition of concussion: Concussion is defined as a complex pathophysiological process affecting the brain, induced by traumatic biomechanical forces. Several common features can be described as follows:

- Caused either by a direct blow to the head, face, neck, or elsewhere on the body with an "impulsive" force transmitted to the head;
- Typically results in the rapid onset of short-lived impairment of neurologic function that resolves spontaneously;
- May result in neuropathological changes but the acute clinical symptoms largely reflect a functional disturbance rather than a structural injury;
- Results in a graded set of clinical symptoms that may or may not involve loss of consciousness. Resolution of the clinical and cognitive symptoms typically follow a sequential course; it is important to note in a small percentage of cases, post-concussive symptoms may be prolonged;
- No abnormality on standard structural neuroimaging.

The difficulty with all of these criteria is determining the seriousness of a TBI is often not easy. A significant percentage of people with a mild TBI based on the behavioral symptoms will show a significant lesion on a brain scan (Sharp, Fleminger, & Powell, 2016; White & Venkatesh, 2016). In contrast, individuals such as Natasha Richardson, who died after hitting her head in a fall on a ski slope in 2009, showed few immediate signs she was actually experiencing bleeding between her brain and her skull. Individuals who survive car accidents in which air bags deploy may be examined for injuries other than brain trauma, even though TBI may result.

Ignoring TBIs, especially repeated ones, can be deadly. A brain autopsy following the suicide at age 50 of former NFL player Dave Duerson in 2011 revealed he suffered from chronic traumatic encephalopathy (CTE), a form of dementia caused by repeated head trauma. Duerson suffered 10 known concussions and reported symptoms well after he retired from football. Other former NFL players who died relatively young have also had the disease, as have boxers and ice hockey and rugby players. Dr. Ann McKee, one of the global experts on CTE, has noted that we do not really know the extent of CTE among professional athletes who played contact sports (Smith, 2016).

Because of the concern over CTE, the National Institute of Neurological Disease and Stroke (NINDS) and the National Institute of Biomedical and Bioengineering established specific neuropathological criteria for the diagnosis of CTE (McKee et al., 2016). These criteria, established following the death of the individual, can now be used to definitively diagnose cases of CTE.

Clearly, there is more awareness of the problems associated with repeated TBI. Whether sports, or at least certain sports involving physical contact, should now be considered dangerous remains to be seen. What is certain, though, is the effects of repeated TBI last well into adulthood and can cause serious cognitive impairment, and perhaps death, at a relatively early age.

Former NFL standout Dave Duerson suffered brain injury from repeated concussions. His suicide helped launch studies of CTE in professional athletes.

Memory and Nutrition

Researchers and clinicians often overlook nutrition as a cause of memory failures in adulthood (Brown, 2017). Evidence points to several compounds in healthy diets essential for well-functioning memory. Considerable research indicates flavonoids, found in green tea and blueberries, among other foods, may reverse age-related deficits in spatial memory (Rendeiro, Rhodes, & Spencer, 2015). Dietary iron intake in midlife has also been associated with better verbal memory, even after other potential explanations for the data were taken into account (Rickard et al., 2012). Finally, several vitamins, especially B vitamins 6, 9 (folic acid), and 12, have been associated with memory and other cognitive functions (de Jager, 2012).

These data indicate it is important to consider older adults' diets when assessing their memory performance. What may appear to be serious decrements in functioning may, in fact, be induced by poor nutrition or specific medications. Too often, researchers and clinicians fail to inquire about eating habits. Adequate assessment is essential to avoid diagnostic errors.

Adult Development in Action

As a family member with older relatives living in your home, how can you help them maintain good memory?

Social Policy Implications

With the graying of America we will see more and more older adults with memory-related problems. Thus, one important implication of this demographic trend is to meet the needs of this growing issue. The number of outreach memory and aging centers is growing in the United States. Such centers attract individuals with any level of memory impairment. These outreach programs connect to local communities and provide educational and referral opportunities along with skill development and training and resource development. The centers are important because they can bridge the gap between research, education, and patient care. Many of these centers are interdisciplinary in nature and thus have the benefit of collaborations with researchers in aging, neurologists, neuropsychologists, nurses, and pharmacists. They serve as catalysts to facilitate interactions among local networks of researchers and other applied centers such as chapters of the Alzheimer's Disease Association to enhance education and information dissemination. Thus, the implications of memory and aging research are becoming more important in our society. With the aging of the baby boomers, the social implications of understanding the memory competencies of our newest older generation have only begun to become apparent.

A second area of policy need will be support of various memory health programs, such as nutrition, exercise, and other approaches that have demonstrated benefit in preventing memory loss. The techniques described in this chapter, particularly those developed and deployed in everyday memory settings, will be especially important.

We will return to this important topic in Chapter 10, in the context of dementia, and Chapter 14, in the context of healthy aging.

SUMMARY

6.1 Information Processing and Attention

What are the primary aspects of the information-processing model?

- The information-processing model is based on a computer metaphor and assumes an active participant, both quantitative and qualitative aspects of performance, and processing of information transformed through a series of systems.

- Sensory memory is the first level of processing incoming information from the environment. Sensory memory has a large capacity, but information only lasts there a short time.

What are the basic components of attention?

- From a functional perspective, attention consists of processing different aspects of stimuli.

How does speed of processing relate to cognitive aging?
- Speed of processing refers to how quickly and efficiently the early steps in information processing are performed. In general, older adults are slower.

What types of processing resources relate to attention and memory?
- Some researchers claim older adults have fewer processing resources than younger adults. However, this conclusion is suspect because processing resources is ill defined.
- Processing resources refers to the amount of attention one has to apply to a particular situation.
- Older adults have more difficulty filtering out or inhibiting irrelevant information (called inhibitory loss) than younger adults, but this may also have a beneficial effect under certain circumstances.
- Divided attention assesses attentional resources and involves doing more than one task that demands attention. Age differences in divided attention depend on the degree of task complexity and practice.

What are automatic and effortful processing?
- Automatic processing places minimal demands on attentional capacity whereas effortful processing requires all of the available attentional capacity. There are relatively no age differences in the former and pronounced age differences in the latter.

6.2 Memory Processes

What is working memory? What age differences have been found in working memory?
- Working memory refers to the processes and structures involved in holding information in mind and simultaneously using that information, sometimes in conjunction with incoming information, to solve a problem, make a decision, or learn. Information is kept active through rehearsal.
- In general, working memory capacity and rehearsal decline with age, although the extent of the decline is still in doubt. There is some evidence age differences in working memory are not universal.

How does implicit and explicit memory differ across age?
- Implicit memory involves retrieval of information without conscious or intentional recollection.
- Explicit memory is intentional and conscious remembering of information learned and remembered at a specific point in time.
- Older adults are generally better at implicit memory tasks than explicit memory tasks.

Within long-term memory, how does episodic and semantic memory performance differ across age?
- Long-term memory refers to the ability to remember extensive amounts of information from a few seconds to a few hours to decades.
- In episodic memory, age-related decrements are typically found on recall tests but not on recognition tests. Older adults tend not to use memory strategies spontaneously as often or as well as younger adults.
- Semantic memory concerns learning and remembering the meaning of words and concepts not tied to specific occurrences of events in time. Fewer age differences are found in semantic memory.

What age differences have been found in encoding versus retrieval?
- Age-related decrements in encoding may be due to decrements in rehearsal within working memory and being slower at making connections with incoming information. Older adults do not spontaneously organize incoming information as well as younger adults, but they can use organizational helps when told to do so. However, the benefits of this approach are short-lived.
- Although older adults tend not to use optimal encoding strategies, this does not account for poor memory performance. Age-related decline in retrieval is related to both poorer encoding to some degree as well as failure to use retrieval strategies. Older adults also have more tip-of-the-tongue experiences than younger adults.

6.3 Memory in Context

What age differences are there in prospective memory?
- Age differences are less likely on event-based prospective memory tasks than on time-based prospective memory tasks. How accurately prospective memory tasks are performed depends on the time of day. Processing speed may help explain these age differences.

How does autobiographical memory change across adulthood?
- Some aspects of autobiographical memory remain intact for many years whereas other aspects do not. More memories are present from young adulthood than later in life. Verification of autobiographical memories is often difficult.
- Older adults have fewer flashbulb memories and their impact is restricted to particular points in the life span.

How does source memory and processing misinformation change across adulthood?
- The ability to remember the source of a familiar event or whether the event was imagined or experienced declines with age.
- Older adults are more susceptible to false memories in that they remember items or events that did not occur under specific conditions of plausibility and are more likely to believe false information as true.

What are some factors that help preserve memory as we grow older?
- Exercise, multilingualism, use of semantic memory, and avoiding the application of memory stereotypes are all factors that can enhance memory in older adults and delay cognitive decline.

What are the major ways memory skills are trained? How effective are these methods?
- The E-I-E-I-O framework, based on explicit-implicit aspects of memory and external-internal types of strategies, is a useful way to organize memory training.
- Older adults can learn new internal memory strategies but, like all adults, usually abandon them over time.
- External-explicit strategies (such as lists and calendars) are common, but internal-implicit strategies are effective even with persons who have Alzheimer's disease.
- Use of memory enhancing drugs does not work over the long run.

6.4 Self-Evaluations of Memory Abilities

What are the major types of memory self-evaluations?
- There are two general categories of memory self-evaluations. Metamemory refers to knowledge about how memory works and what one believes to be true about it. Memory monitoring refers to the awareness of what we are doing with our memory right now.

What age differences have been found in metamemory and memory monitoring?
- Metamemory is typically assessed with questionnaires. Older adults seem to know less than younger adults about the workings of memory and its capacity, view memory as less stable, believe their memory will decline with age, and feel they have little control over these changes. Memory self-efficacy is an important predictor of performance in several settings.
- The ability to monitor one's performance on memory tasks does not usually decline with age. Memory monitoring may provide a basis for compensating for actual performance declines.

6.5 Clinical Issues

What is the difference between normal and abnormal memory aging?
- Whether memory changes affect daily functioning is one way to separate normal from abnormal aging. Brain-imaging techniques allow localization of problems with more precision.
- Some diseases are marked by severe memory impairments. However, in many cases, telling the difference between normal changes and those associated with disease or other abnormal events is difficult.
- Different areas of the brain control different aspects of memory.

What is the connection between memory and physical and mental health?
- Dementia (such as Alzheimer's disease) and severe depression both involve memory impairment. Other diseases and health conditions can also cause memory difficulties.
- Temporary global amnesia, more common in middle age than in younger or older adulthood, may be related to blood flow in the brain.
- Traumatic brain injury (TBI) can have serious consequences, as seen in the long-term potential damage from repeated concussions.

How is memory affected by nutrition?
- Flavonoids, iron, and B vitamins have all been shown to be related to memory functioning.

REVIEW QUESTIONS

6.1 Information Processing and Attention
- What is working memory? What is inhibition loss? What age differences have been found? What role do these processes play in understanding age differences in memory?
- What is episodic memory? What is semantic memory? How are they tested? What patterns of age differences have been found? What happens to the use of memory strategies with age?

- What is sensory memory? How do processing speed and processing resources affect older adults' information processing?
- In what way do older adults have difficulty filtering out information?
- How do automatic and effortful processing contribute to age differences in information processing?
- Why are attentional resources important to our understanding of age differences in memory?

6.2 Memory Processes
- What are working memory processes and how do they differ with increasing age?
- What is the difference between implicit and explicit memory? How do they change with age?
- Why are there age differences in episodic but not semantic memory?
- What are the relative contributions of encoding and retrieval in understanding age differences in memory?

6.3 Memory in Context
- What types of prospective memory have been distinguished? What age differences are there in prospective memory?
- What is autobiographical memory and how does it differ with age?

- How do source memory and processing of misinformation change with age?
- What are factors preventing decline in memory functioning? How do they work?
- What is the E-I-E-I-O framework? How does it help organize memory training programs?
- How much do older adults benefit from each of the major types of memory training programs?
- What kinds of memory interventions work over time?

6.4 Self-Evaluations of Memory Abilities
- What major types of self-evaluations have been described?
- What age differences are there in metamemory and memory self-efficacy?
- What age differences have been found in memory monitoring?

6.5 Clinical Issues
- What criteria are used to determine the difference between normal and abnormal changes in a person's memory?
- What physical and mental health conditions involve significant memory problems?
- What effect does nutrition have on memory?

INTEGRATING CONCEPTS IN DEVELOPMENT

- Based on material in Chapter 2 on cognitive neuroscience and the material in this chapter, what are the major factors involved in understanding age-related differences in memory?
- What aspects of neurological functioning would be important to consider in designing memory training programs?
- How could you design a good set of observations for family members to help them tell whether a relative's memory failures were normal or abnormal?
- Based on information in Chapters 3 and 4, what health-related behaviors might help preserve memory functioning?
- How would you design an informational brochure for older adults to maximize their ability to remember it?

KEY TERMS

autobiographical memory Remembering information and events from your own life.

automatic processing Processes that are fast, reliable, and insensitive to increased cognitive demands.

cognitive reserve Factors that provide flexibility in responding and adapting to changes in the environment.

divided attention The ability to pay attention and successfully perform more than one task at a time.

effortful processing It requires all of the available attentional capacity when processing information.

encoding The process of getting information into the memory system.

episodic memory The general class of memory having to do with the conscious recollection of information from a specific event or point in time.

explicit memory The conscious and intentional recollection of information.

external aids Memory aids that rely on environmental resources.

false memory When one remembers items or events that did not occur.

flashbulb memories Memories for personally traumatic or unexpected events.

implicit memory The effortless and unconscious recollection of information.

information-processing model The study of how people take in stimuli from their environment and transform them into memories; the approach is based on a computer metaphor.

internal aids Memory aids that rely on mental processes.

long-term memory The aspects of memory involved in remembering rather extensive amounts of information over relatively long periods of time.

memory monitoring The awareness of what we are doing in memory right now.

memory self-efficacy The belief in one's ability to perform a specific memory task.

metamemory Memory about how memory works and what one believes to be true about it.

processing resources The amount of attention one has to apply to a particular situation.

prospective memory Process involving remembering to remember something in the future.

recall Process of remembering information without the help of hints or cues.

recognition Process of remembering information by selecting previously learned information from among several items.

rehearsal Process by which information is held in working memory, either by repeating items over and over or by making meaningful connections between the information in working memory and information.

retrieval The process of getting information back out of memory.

semantic memory Learning and remembering the meaning of words and concepts that are not tied to specific occurrences of events in time.

sensory memory A very brief and almost identical representation of the stimuli that exists in the observable environment.

source memory The ability to remember the source of a familiar event as well as the ability to determine if an event was imagined or actually experienced.

speed of processing How quickly and efficiently the early steps in information processing are completed.

storage The manner in which information is represented and kept in memory.

strategies Various techniques that make learning or remembering easier and that increase the efficiency of storage.

transient global amnesia (TGA) Temporary experience of a complete memory loss and disorientation in time.

working memory Refers to the processes and structures involved in holding information in mind and simultaneously using that information, sometimes in conjunction with incoming information, to solve a problem, make a decision, or learn new information.

# 7 | Intelligence, Reasoning, Creativity, and Wisdom

CHAPTER OUTLINE

7.1 Defining Intelligence
Intelligence in Everyday Life
The Big Picture: A Life-Span View
Research Approaches to Intelligence
DISCOVERING DEVELOPMENT How Do People Show Intelligence?

7.2 Developmental Trends in Psychometric Intelligence
The Measurement of Intelligence
Primary and Secondary Mental Abilities
Fluid and Crystallized Intelligence
HOW DO WE KNOW? Think Fast, Feel Fine, Live Long
Neuroscience Research and Intelligence in Young and Middle Adulthood
Moderators of Intellectual Change
Modifying Primary Abilities

7.3 Qualitative Differences in Adults' Thinking
Piaget's Theory
Going Beyond Formal Operations: Thinking in Adulthood
REAL PEOPLE Feel the Bern
Integrating Emotion and Logic

7.4 Everyday Reasoning and Problem Solving
Decision Making
Problem Solving
Expertise
Creativity and Wisdom
CURRENT CONTROVERSIES Does Creativity Exist?

Social Policy Implications
Summary
Review Questions
Integrating Concepts in Development
Key Terms

185

The Dalai Lama, spiritual leader of the Tibetan people, was the recipient of the 1989 Nobel Peace Prize and is recognized as a leader in Buddhist philosophy, human rights, and global environmental problems. He reached this stature as a simple Buddhist monk, and claims he is "no more, no less." To the world, the Dalai Lama is recognized for his great wisdom and insight into the human condition. A sample of this wisdom is in his plea for "a new way of thinking . . . for responsible living and acting. If we maintain obsolete values and beliefs, a fragmented consciousness and a self-centered spirit, we will continue to hold to outdated goals and behaviors. Such an attitude by a large number of people would block the entire transition to an interdependent yet peaceful and cooperative global society." He also states as a Buddhist monk, he tries to develop compassion within, not simply as religious practice, but at a human level. To facilitate this, he "sometimes finds it helpful to imagine himself standing as a single individual on one side, facing a huge gathering of all other human beings on the other side. Then he asks himself, 'Whose interests are more important?' To him it is quite clear however important he feels he is, he is just one individual while others are infinite in number and importance."

Despite the Dalai Lama's and many other's long interest in wisdom, psychologists largely overlooked it for decades, perhaps because they were busy intensely studying a related topic— intelligence. Another reason for not researching wisdom was the widespread belief it would be a waste of time. At one time, researchers and theorists were convinced all intellectual abilities, wisdom included, inevitably declined as people aged, because of biological deterioration. For instance, Wechsler (1958) wrote "nearly all studies have shown that most human abilities decline progressively after reaching a peak somewhere between ages 18 and 25" (p. 135).

Controversy has raged for decades. Considering methodological comparisons between cross-sectional and longitudinal studies, Baltes and Schaie (1974) concluded "general intellectual decline is largely a myth" (p. 35). Botwinick (1977) countered with "decline in intellectual ability is clearly a part of the aging picture" (p. 580).

Who is right? Where do we stand now? Does intelligence decline, or is that a myth? Does wisdom come with age? Answering these questions will be our goal in this chapter. Such widely divergent conclusions about age-related changes in intelligence reflect different sets of assumptions about the nature of intelligence that are then translated into different theoretical and methodological approaches. We examine three avenues of research on intelligence and age: psychometric approach, life-span approach, and the cognitive-structural approach. Along the way we look at some attempts to modify intellectual abilities through training programs, but first we need to consider what intelligence is. ∎

The Dalai Lama

7.1 Defining Intelligence

LEARNING OBJECTIVES
- How do people define intelligence in everyday life?
- What are the major components of the life-span approach?
- What are the major research approaches for studying intelligence?

When Toni graduated from high school she decided to start her own pet-sitting business. She started small, but ultimately cornered the market in her city. *She lives a comfortable lifestyle. Her high school classmate Stacey went to college and majored in math. She pursued her doctorate and now lives a comfortable lifestyle as a university professor. In comparing Toni and Stacey on intellectual ability, who would come out on top?*

In terms of intelligence, the distinction between Toni and Stacey's success points to an important question to ask: What do we mean by intelligence? Is intelligence being able to learn new things quickly? Knowing a great deal of information? The ability to adapt to new situations or create new things or ideas? Or is intelligence the ability to make the most of what we have and to enjoy life? Intelligence encompasses all these abilities and more as we see in the different pathways Toni and Stacey took. It is all in the sense that people who stand out on these dimensions are often considered smart, or intelligent. It is more than just these abilities because intelligence also involves the qualitative aspects of thinking style, or how one approaches and conceptualizes problems.

Intelligence in Everyday Life

Robert Sternberg has argued for decades that intelligence involves more than just a particular fixed set of characteristics (Sternberg, 1985, 2016). One intriguing way he investigated intelligence was based on a list of behaviors that laypeople at a train station, supermarket, or college library reported to be distinctly characteristic of exceptionally intelligent, academically intelligent, everyday intelligent, or unintelligent people. This list of behaviors was given to experts in the field of intelligence and to a new set of laypeople. They were asked to rate either how distinctively characteristic each behavior was, or how important each behavior was in defining the four types of intelligent people. Ratings were analyzed separately for the experts and the laypeople (Sternberg, Jarvin, & Grigorenko, 2010).

There is extremely high agreement between experts and laypeople on ratings of the importance of particular behaviors in defining intelligence. The two groups agreed intelligence consisted of three major clusters of related abilities: problem-solving ability, verbal ability, and social competence. Problem-solving ability consists of behaviors such as reasoning logically, identifying connections among ideas, seeing all aspects of a problem, and making good decisions. Verbal ability comprises such things as speaking articulately, reading with high comprehension, and having a good vocabulary. Social competence includes behaviors such as accepting others for what they are, admitting mistakes, displaying interest in the world at large, and being on time for appointments.

In a classic study, Berg and Sternberg (1992) wanted to know how these conceptions of intelligence differed across the adult life span. To find out, people aged 22 to 85 were asked to rate 55 behaviors they viewed as characteristic of exceptionally intelligent 30-, 50-, or 70-year-olds. Behaviors such as motivation, intellectual effort, and reading were said to be important indicators of intelligence for people of all ages. Other behaviors were specific to particular points in the life span. For example, for a 30-year-old, planning for the future and being open-minded were listed most often. The intelligent 50- and 70-year-olds were described as acting responsibly, adjusting to life situations, being verbally fluent, and displaying wisdom.

The remarkable result from all of these studies was that people really have a consistent sense of what intelligent behavior looks like at different ages. Whether this consistency maps onto systematic psychological research is a question to which we now turn.

The Big Picture: A Life-Span View

One thing is clear about the ways people view intelligence—everyone has an idea of what intelligence is, and everyone considers it a complex construct. In the big picture, then, intelligence consists of many different skills. *Theories of intelligence, therefore, are* **multidimensional**; *that is, they specify many domains of intellectual abilities.* Although people disagree on the number of dimensions, they agree no single generic type of intelligence is responsible for all the mental activities we perform.

Baltes (1993; Baltes, Lindenberger, & Staudinger, 2006) took a broad view of intellectual development. The life-span concepts discussed in Chapter 1 including multidirectionality, plasticity, and interindividual variability play an important role in this conceptualization of intellectual change. Overall, this perspective asserts intellectual decline may be seen with age but stability and growth in mental functioning also can be seen across adulthood. The life-span perspective emphasizes the role of intelligence in human adaptation and daily activity.

The first concept, **multidirectionality**, *refers to the distinct patterns of change in abilities over the life span, with these patterns differing for different abilities.* For example, developmental functions for specific abilities differ, meaning the directional change in intelligence depends on the skills in question. As we will see later on, everyday knowledge accumulates over time and thus increases with age. However, basic cognitive mechanisms underlying key intellectual skills show more declines, especially into older age.

The term **plasticity** *refers to the range of functioning within an individual and the conditions under which a person's abilities can be modified within a specific age range.* Plasticity implies what may appear to be declines in some skills may in part represent a lack of practice in using them. Current studies examining brain plasticity and behavior find experience alters the brain across the life span (see Chapter 2). As we saw in Chapter 2, older adults activate areas in the brain that compensate for decline in their performance, resulting in better performance than would otherwise be the case. In other words, older adults activate new or additional areas in the brain to compensate for decline in other areas. Finally, the research on training cognitive abilities described later in this chapter supports this view because older adults who show decline in cognitive functioning can be trained to perform at a higher level.

The last concept, **interindividual variability**, *acknowledges adults differ in the direction of their intellectual development.* Schaie's (2008) sequential research indicates that within a given cohort or generation, some people show longitudinal decline in specific abilities, whereas other people show stability of functioning and display improvements in those same abilities. Consequently, a single representation of typical or average changes with age may not really represent how the various individuals in a group function.

Using these four concepts of multidimensionality, plasticity, multidirectionality, and interindividual variability, Baltes and his colleagues proposed the dual-component model of intellectual functioning (Baltes et al., 2006). Two interrelated types of developmental processes are postulated. *The first component, termed the* **mechanics of intelligence**, *concerns the neurophysiological architecture of the mind.* This architecture provides the foundational bases for cognitive abilities, including basic forms of thinking associated with information processing and problem solving such as attention, reasoning, spatial orientation, or perceptual speed. Intellectual change in this first component is greatest during childhood and adolescence, as we acquire the brain interconnections responsible for the requisite skills to handle complex cognitive tasks such as those encountered in school.

The second component, **pragmatic intelligence**, *concerns acquired bodies of knowledge available from and embedded within culture.* In other words, it includes everyday cognitive performance and human adaptation. Such abilities include verbal knowledge, wisdom, and practical problem solving. Pragmatic intellectual growth dominates adulthood.

These different trajectories of development are illustrated in Figure 7.1. As the figure suggests, different

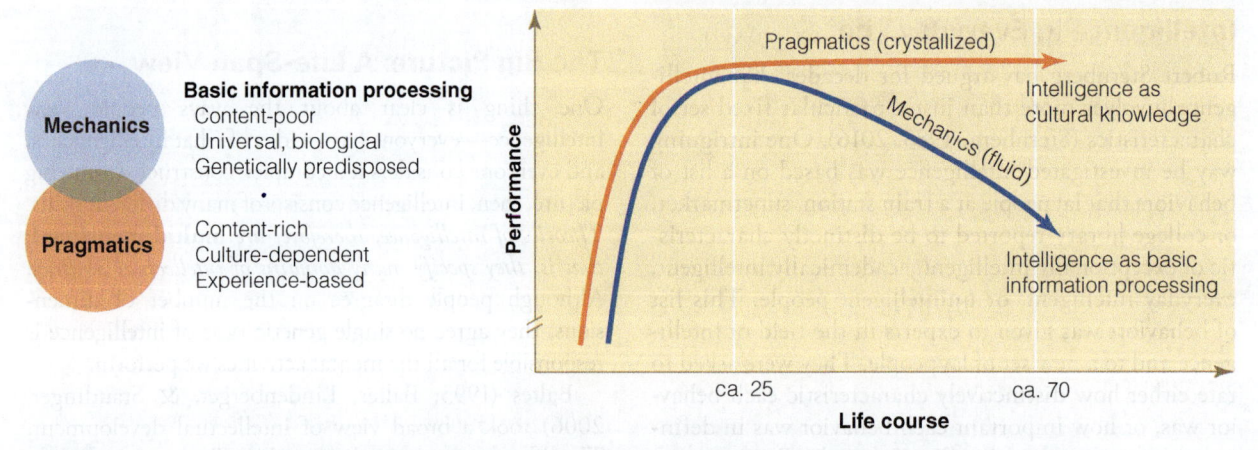

FIGURE 7.1 Life-span conceptualization of the mechanics and pragmatics of intelligence. The mechanics of intelligence correspond to fluid intelligence and the pragmatics to crystallized intelligence, as described later.
Source: Baltes, P. B. (1993). The aging mind: Potential and limits. *The Gerontologist, 33,* 580–594.

weightings of the forces of intelligence lead to specific predictions regarding the developmental pathway they take across the adult life span. The mechanics of intelligence are governed more by biological-genetic forces, so are subject to an overall downward trajectory across adulthood. However, the pragmatics of intelligence are governed more by environmental-cultural factors that accrue across adulthood, so an upward trajectory is maintained.

This broad view of intellectual development in adulthood provides the background for asking more specific questions about particular aspects of intelligence. As we will see, three primary research approaches have emerged.

Research Approaches to Intelligence

Sternberg's and Baltes' work point out that many different skills are involved in intelligence depending on one's point of view. Interestingly, the behaviors listed by Sternberg's participants and the organizational structure provided by Baltes fit nicely with the more formal attempts at defining intelligence we encounter later in this chapter. Researchers have studied these skills from many perspectives, depending on their theoretical orientation. For example, some investigators approach these skills from a statistical factor analysis approach and study them as separate pieces that can be added together to form intelligence. Others take a more holistic view and think of intelligence as a way or mode of thinking. These various theoretical orientations result in different means of studying intelligence.

Historically, psychological research on intelligence has focused on performance on standardized tests; this view represents the **psychometric approach**. For example, the problem-solving and verbal abilities in Sternberg and colleagues' study would be assessed by tests specifically designed to assess these skills. These tests focus on getting correct answers and tend to give less emphasis on the thought processes used to arrive at them. This is the approach you are likely to have experienced in school when you took standardized tests.

Other researchers focus on information-processing mechanisms reviewed in Chapter 6. This approach aims at a detailed analysis of aging-associated changes in components of cognitive mechanisms and their interactions, such as memory.

Finally, a number of researchers focus their efforts on reconceptualizing the meaning and measurement of intelligence by taking a cognitive-structural approach. *In the* **cognitive-structural approach** *researchers have been more concerned with the ways people conceptualize and solve problems than with scores on tests.* Such approaches to intelligence emphasize developmental changes in the modes and styles of thinking, and how these ways of thinking play out in everyday life.

In this chapter, we consider these approaches and the research they stimulated. We discover that each approach has its merits, and whether age-related changes in intelligence are found depends on how intelligence is defined and measured. Before you continue, complete the exercise in the Discovering Development feature. The information you uncover will be useful as you read the rest of the chapter.

DISCOVERING DEVELOPMENT
How Do People Show Intelligence?

Earlier in this section, we encountered Sternberg and colleagues' research on people's implicit theories of intelligence. However, that study only examined broad categories of behavior that could be considered intelligent. Moreover, it was not conducted in such a way as to permit comparisons with research-based approaches to intelligence.

You and your classmates could address these shortcomings in the following way. Ask adults of different ages what they think constitutes intelligent behavior, much the same as Sternberg and colleagues did. However, be careful to make sure people are specific about the abilities they nominate. In addition, ask them about what makes adults' thinking different from adolescents' thinking and whether they believe there might be different stages of adults' thinking. Again, try to get your respondents to be as specific as possible.

Collate all the data from the class. Look for common themes in specific abilities, as well as in the qualitative aspects of thinking. As you read the rest of the chapter, see to what extent your data parallels that from more formal investigations.

Adult Development in Action

If you were responsible for revising social policy regarding aging (say, criteria for living independently in the community), how would you approach that problem from the different perspectives of defining intelligence?

7.2 Developmental Trends in Psychometric Intelligence

LEARNING OBJECTIVES
- What is intelligence in adulthood?
- What are primary and secondary mental abilities?
- How do they change? What are fluid and crystallized intelligence? How do they change?
- How has neuroscience research furthered our understanding of intelligence in adulthood?

Ashley, a 35-year-old woman recently laid off from her job as an administrative assistant, slides into her seat on her first day of classes at the community college. She is clearly nervous. "I'm worried I won't be able to compete with these younger students, that I may not be smart enough," she sighs. "Guess we'll find out soon enough, though, huh?"

Many returning adult students like Ashley worry they may not be "smart enough" to keep up with 18- or 19-year-olds. You may have felt this way yourself. Are these fears realistic? Let's find out.

As seen earlier, people naturally view intelligence as consisting of many components. One traditional way to measure intelligence, then, is to focus on individuals' performances on various tests of these component intellectual abilities and how these performances are interrelated. This approach to intelligence has a long history; the ancient Chinese and Greeks used this method to select people for certain jobs, such as master horseman (Doyle, 1974; DuBois, 1968). Tests also served as the basis for Alfred Binet's (1903) pioneering work in developing standardized intelligence tests, as well as many modern theories of intelligence.

Because of this long history of research in psychometric intelligence, we probably know more about this area than any other area in cognitive aging except for episodic memory. Yet this still provided no sense of closure as to how intelligence changes with age. There is substantial agreement on descriptions of change in different intellectual abilities (as we discuss later) and agreement on the methodological issues needing to be addressed when studying intellectual change.

However, there is little consensus on the proper interpretation of the data. For example, what does it mean that changes in certain intellectual abilities are related to increasing age? Remember in Chapter 1 we noted age does not *cause* change, that the finding that

Cognitive abilities are assessed across the life span using standardized tests

age is *related to* decline in some intellectual abilities is not the same thing as "aging" per se. As we shall see, age-related intellectual change is also related to important variables such as health, activity level, and educational achievements. It is in this stew of complicated interrelationships that much of the controversy is still brewing.

The Measurement of Intelligence

Because the psychometric approach focuses on the interrelationships among intellectual abilities, the major goal has long been to describe the ways these relationships are organized (Sternberg, 1985). *This organization of interrelated intellectual abilities is termed the* **structure of intelligence**. The most common way

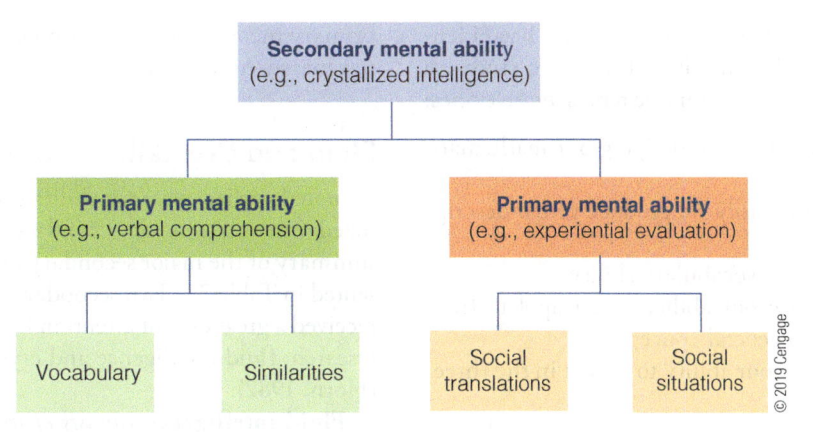

FIGURE 7.2 Secondary mental abilities reflect several primary mental abilities and their respective measurements. This figure shows those relations regarding crystallized intelligence.

to describe the structure of intelligence is to think of it as a five-level hierarchy, depicted in Figure 7.2 (Cunningham, 1987).

Each higher level of this hierarchy represents a higher level of organizing the components of the level below. The lowest level consists of individual test questions—the specific items people answer on an intelligence test. These items or questions can be organized into intelligence tests, which constitute the second level.

The third level reflects interrelationships among scores on intelligence tests that assess similar abilities; these clusters of abilities are called primary mental abilities. Continuing to move up the hierarchy, the interrelationships existing among the primary mental abilities produce the secondary mental abilities at the fourth level. Finally, general intelligence at the top refers to the interrelationships among the secondary mental abilities.

Keep in mind that each time we move up the hierarchy we move away from people's actual performance. Each level above the first represents a theoretical description of how things fit together. Thus, there are no tests of primary abilities per se; primary abilities represent theoretical relationships among tests, that in turn represent theoretical relationships among actual performances.

So exactly how do researchers construct this theoretical hierarchy? The structure of intelligence is uncovered through sophisticated statistical detective work using a technique called factor analysis. First, researchers obtain people's performances on many types of problems. Second, the results are examined to determine whether performance on one type of problem, such as filling in missing letters in a word, predicts performance on another type of problem, like unscrambling letters to form a word. *If the performance on one test is highly related to the performance on another, the abilities measured by the two tests are interrelated and are called a* **factor**.

Most psychometric theorists believe intelligence consists of several factors. However, we should note although factor analysis is a sophisticated statistical technique, it is not an exact technique. Thus, estimates of the exact number of factors vary from a few to over 100. Most researchers and theorists believe the number to be relatively small. We examine two factors: primary and secondary mental abilities.

Primary and Secondary Mental Abilities

Since the 1930s, researchers agreed intellectual abilities can be studied as groups of related skills (such as memory or spatial ability) organized into hypothetical constructs called **primary mental abilities**. *In turn, related groups of primary mental abilities can be clustered into a half dozen or so broader skills termed* **secondary mental abilities**.

Roughly 25 primary mental abilities have been identified (Horn, 1982). Because it is difficult to study all of them, researchers focused on five representative ones:

- *Number*: the basic skills underlying our mathematical reasoning
- *Word fluency*: how easily we produce verbal descriptions of things
- *Verbal meaning*: our vocabulary ability
- *Inductive reasoning*: our ability to extrapolate from particular facts to general concepts
- *Spatial orientation*: our ability to reason in the three-dimensional world

Even with a relatively small number of primary mental abilities, it is still hard to discuss intelligence by focusing on separate abilities. As a result, theories of intelligence emphasize clusters of related primary mental abilities as a framework for describing the structure of intelligence. Because they are one step removed from primary mental abilities, secondary mental abilities are not measured directly.

Fluid and Crystallized Intelligence

As noted earlier, primary abilities are themselves organized into clusters of secondary mental abilities. A summary of the major secondary mental abilities is presented in Table 7.1. Two secondary mental abilities have received a great deal of attention in adult developmental research: fluid intelligence and crystallized intelligence (Horn, 1982).

Fluid intelligence *consists of the abilities that make you a flexible and adaptive thinker, allow you to make inferences, and enable you to understand the relations among concepts*. It includes the abilities you need to understand and respond to any situation, but especially new ones: inductive reasoning, integration, abstract thinking, and the like (Horn, 1982). An example of a question that

TABLE 7.1 Descriptions of Major Secondary Mental Abilities

Crystallized Intelligence (Gc)
Crystallized intelligence reflects the breadth of knowledge and experience, understanding communications and social conventions, judgment, and reason. The components of Gc include the primary abilities of verbal comprehension, concept formation, logical reasoning, and general reasoning, among others. Tests of Gc include vocabulary (What does *timid* mean?) and analogies (Plato is to Kant as Shakespeare is to _____), among others. Gc is a rough estimate of the knowledge and sophistication that underlies the intelligence of a culture.

Fluid Intelligence (Gf)
Fluid intelligence reflects the abilities to see relationships among patterns, draw inferences from relationships, and comprehend the implications of relationships. The primary abilities underlying Gf include inductive reasoning, figural flexibility, and integration, among others. Tests of Gf include letter series (What comes next in the series *d f i m r x e*?), matrices (Identify the relationships among elements in a 2×2 matrix.), and shapes (From among a set of overlapping circles, squares, and triangles, choose a figure that enables you to place a dot inside a circle and triangle but outside of a square.) Gf provides a rough estimate of a person's problem solving and abstracting ability. It does not reflect cultural learning.

Visual Organization (Gv)
Visual organization reflects the underlying primary abilities visualization, spatial orientation, speed and flexibility of closure, among others. Gv is tested through holistic closure (Identify a figure that has missing parts.), form board (Put cutout parts together to create and match a specific figure.), and embedded figures (Find the duck in a complex visual image.). Gv differs from Gf in that Gv reflects relationships among visual patterns that are obvious, and not inferred (which would reflect Gf).

Auditory Organization (Ga)
Auditory organization reflects underlying primary abilities such as time tracking, auditory cognition of relations, and speech perception when the speech is degraded or distorted, among others. Tests of Ga include repeated tones (Identify the first occurrence of a tone that is played several times.), tonal series (Indicate which tone comes next in a specific series of tones.), and word identification in noise (Identify a specific word when it is embedded in a noisy background environment.), among others.

Short-Term Acquisition and Retrieval
This ability reflects the ability to be aware of and retain information long enough to do something with it. The underlying primary abilities all reflect aspects of short-term memory. Tests of Gstar include span memory (repeat increasingly long lists of numbers or words), associative memory (remember word pairs of related words), among others.

Long-Term Storage and Retrieval
This type of intelligence reflects the ability to store information and retrieve information that was acquired in the distant past.

Source: Horn, J. L. (1982). The aging of human abilities. In B. B. Wolman (Ed.), *Handbook of Developmental Psychology* (pp. 847–870). Englewood Cliffs, NJ: Prentice Hall. Reprinted with permission.

taps fluid abilities is the following: What letter comes next in the series *d f i m r x e*?[1]

Crystallized intelligence *is the knowledge you have acquired through life experience and education in a particular culture.* Crystallized intelligence includes your breadth of knowledge, comprehension of communication, judgment, and sophistication with information (Horn, 1982). Many popular television game shows (such as *Jeopardy* and *Wheel of Fortune*) are based on contestants' accumulated crystallized intelligence.

Developmentally, fluid and crystallized intelligence follow two different paths, as you can see in Figure 7.3. Notice that fluid intelligence declines throughout adulthood, whereas crystallized intelligence improves. Although we do not yet fully understand why fluid intelligence declines, it likely is related to underlying changes in the brain (see Chapter 2). In contrast, the increase in crystallized intelligence (at least until late life) indicates people continue adding knowledge every day.

What do these different developmental trends imply? First, they indicate that—although it continues through adulthood—performance or learning that depends on basic underlying skills becomes more difficult with age, whereas performance or learning that is based on what we already know continues to improve, at least until very late in life.

Second, intellectual development varies a great deal from one set of skills to another. Whereas individual differences in fluid intelligence remain relatively uniform over time, individual differences in crystallized intelligence increase with age, mainly because

maintaining crystallized intelligence depends on being in situations that require its use (Horn, 1982; Horn & Hofer, 1992). For example, few adults get much practice in solving complex letter series tasks such as the one at the top of the left-hand column, so individual differences tend to be minimal. But because people improve their vocabulary skills by reading and they vary considerably in how much they read, individual differences are likely to increase.

Neuroscience Research and Intelligence in Young and Middle Adulthood

As you might suspect from Chapters 2 and 6, considerable research shows specific areas in the brain are associated with intellectual abilities, and developmental changes in these areas are related to changes in performance. Remember from Chapter 2 that the Parieto-Frontal Integration Theory (P-FIT) proposes intelligence comes from a distributed and integrated network of neurons in the parietal and frontal lobes of the brain. In general, P-FIT accounts for individual differences in intelligence as having their origins in individual differences in brain structure and function. The P-FIT model has been tested in several studies. Results indicate support for the theory when measures of fluid and crystallized intelligence are related to brain structures (Basten, Hilger, & Fiebach, 2015; Brancucci, 2012; Pineda-Pardo et al., 2016). It is also clear performance on measures of specific abilities is likely related to specific combinations of brain structures (Di Domenico et al., 2015; Haier et al., 2010; Kievit et al., 2016; Pineda-Pardo et al., 2016).

A second theory of intelligence grounded in neuroscience evidence is based on how efficiently the

---

[1] The next letter is *m*. The rule is to increase the difference between adjacent letters in the series by one each time and use a continuous circle of the alphabet for counting. Thus, *f* is two letters from *d*, *i* is three letters from *f*, and *e* is seven letters from *x*.

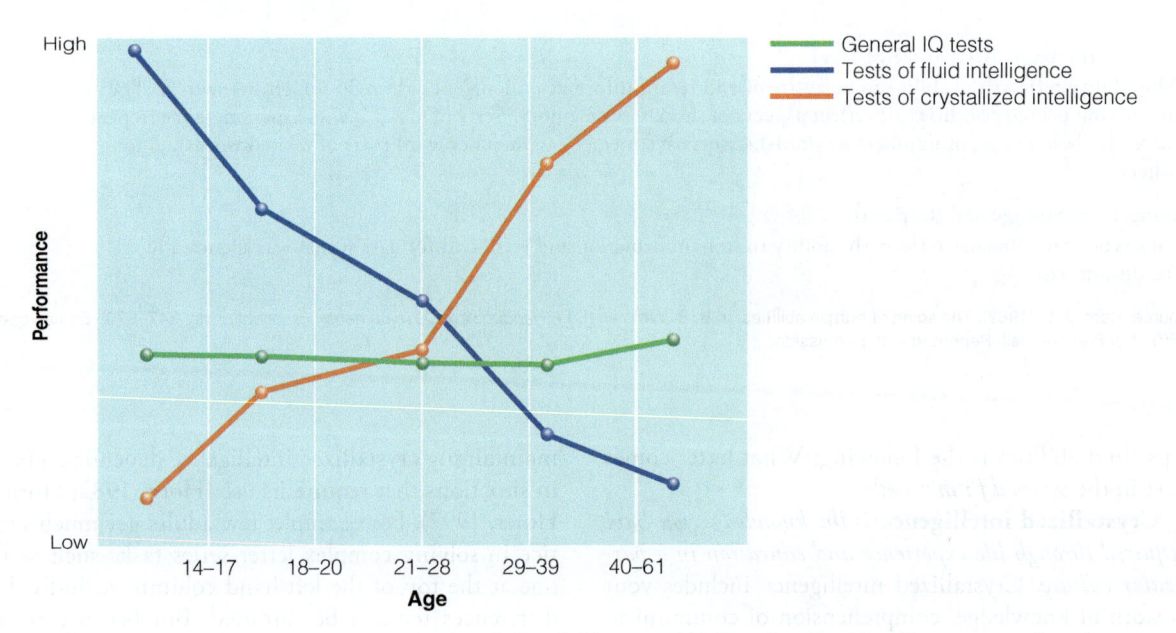

FIGURE 7.3 Performances on tests used to define fluid, crystallized, and general intelligence, as a function of age.
Source: Horn, J. L. (1970). Organization of data on life-span development of human abilities. In L. R. Goulet & P. B. Baltes (Eds.), *Life-span Development Psychology: Research and Theory* (p. 463). Copyright © 1970 by Academic Press, reproduced by permission of the publisher.

brain works (Brancucci, 2012; Di Domenico et al., 2015; Kievit et al., 2016; Langer et al., 2012). *The **neural efficiency hypothesis**, states intelligent people process information more efficiently, showing weaker neural activations in a smaller number of areas than less intelligent people.* Research evidence is mounting that this idea holds merit: with greater intelligence does come demonstrably increased efficiency in neural processing (e.g., Kievit et al., 2016; Langer et al., 2012; Lipp et al., 2012; Pineda-Pardo et al., 2016). However, how this neural efficiency develops is not yet known, nor are its developmental pathways understood.

It is clear neuroscience and related research on intelligence will continue to provide many insights into the bases for both the development of fluid and crystallized intelligence as well as provide an understanding of individual differences in each. As neuroimaging and other techniques continue to improve, it is likely that our understanding of both the brain structure–intelligence relations as well as their development will improve.

Moderators of Intellectual Change

Based on the research we considered thus far, two different developmental trends emerge: we see gains in experience-based processes but losses in information-processing abilities. The continued growth in some areas is viewed as a product of lifelong learning. The losses are viewed as an inevitable result of the decline of physiological processes with age.

A number of researchers, though, emphasize individual differences in the rate of change in intellectual aging (Baltes et al., 2006; Schaie, 2008). These researchers do not deny that some adults show intellectual decline. Based on large individual differences in intellectual performance over time, they simply suggest these decrements may not happen to everyone to the same extent. They argue many reasons besides age explain performance differences. In this section, we explore some of the social and physiological factors proposed as modifiers of intellectual development. These include cohort differences, education level, social variables, personality, health and lifestyle, and relevancy and appropriateness of tasks.

Cohort Differences

Do the differences in intellectual performance obtained in some situations reflect true age-related change or mainly cohort, or generational, differences? This question gets right to the heart of the debate over interpreting developmental research on intelligence (Salthouse, 2014). On one hand, dozens of cross-sectional studies document significant differences in intellectual performance with age. On the other hand, several longitudinal investigations show either no decrement or even an increase in performance (Hertzog, Dixon et al., 2003; Schaie, 2005, 2008, 2011; Zelinski et al., 2009).

The way to resolve the discrepancy between the two approaches involves comparing data collected over long periods of time from several samples of people born in the same cohort but tested for the first time at different ages and analyzed simultaneously in both cross-sectional and longitudinal designs as discussed in Chapter 1 (Salthouse, 2014). When this is done, the results indicate part of the apparent decline with age in performance on intelligence tests may reflect generational differences rather than age differences (Salthouse, 2014; Schaie, 2005, 2011). These trends reflect better education opportunities, healthier lifestyles, better nutrition, and improved health care.

The complex pattern of cohort differences indicates interpreting data from cross-sectional studies is difficult. Recall from Chapter 1 cross-sectional studies confound age and cohort; and because there are both age- and cohort-related changes in intellectual abilities, drawing any meaningful conclusions is nearly impossible. Schaie (2005, 2008, 2011) argues the trends that indicate a leveling off of cohort differences may come to a halt in the 21st century. This conclusion is supported by a study of 531 adult parent–offspring pairs indicating generational (cohort) improvements were becoming smaller for more recently born pairs (Schaie et al., 1992).

Information Processing

A number of researchers suggests general processing constraints that occur with aging (discussed in Chapter 6) may help identify mechanisms underlying decline in fluid intelligence abilities with age (Baltes et al., 2006; Kyllonen, 2015; Paccagnella, 2016; Zimprich & Martin, 2002, 2009). For example, evidence suggests perceptual speed accounts for much of the age-related decline in both fluid and crystallized mental abilities. Similarly, working memory decline with increasing age accounts for poor performance on the part of older adults when the tasks involve coordinating both new incoming information and stored information such as those found in the fluid and/or mechanic component of intelligence. Finally, evidence suggests the inability to inhibit actions and thoughts or to avoid interference typically found in older adults may also account for efficient functioning in fluid and/or mechanic abilities.

Social and Lifestyle Variables

Numerous social and lifestyle variables have been identified as important correlates of intellectual functioning. Think for a minute about the kind of job you currently have or would like to get. What kind of intellectual skills does it demand? What similarities or differences are there between your chosen job (e.g., school counselor) and a different one (say, accountant)?

An interesting line of research concerns how the differences in cognitive skills needed in different occupations make a difference in intellectual development (Bowlus, Mori, & Robinson, 2016; de Grip et al., 2008). To the extent a job requires you to use certain cognitive abilities a great deal, you may be less likely to show declines in them as you age.

Other social demographic variables implicated in slower rates of intellectual decline include a higher socioeconomic status, exposure to stimulating environments, the utilization of cultural and educational resources throughout adulthood, and not feeling lonely (Schaie, 2008). For example, research examining social relationships suggests that having poor social relationships is associated with more rapid cognitive decline

People in cognitively demanding jobs may be less likely to show noticeable declines in cognitive functioning with increasing age.

(Kuiper et al., 2016) and for having a mental health problem later in life (Coyle & Dugan, 2012; Feng & Astell-Burt, 2016).

Finally, although research suggests education and lifestyle factors are a predictor of intellectual functioning, it is still a matter of debate whether it helps slow cognitive change in late life (Hertzog et al., 2009; Opdebeeck, Martyr, & Clare, 2016; Zahodne et al., 2011).

Personality

Several aspects of personality have been proposed as important for understanding intellectual change. Similar to research we examined in Chapter 6 on memory, one of these aspects concerns self-efficacy (Hayslip & Cooper, 2012; Šatienė, 2015). Older adults perceive what they do to help maintain their intellectual abilities can make a difference. Specifically, high initial levels of fluid abilities and a high sense of internal control led to positive changes in people's perceptions of their abilities; low initial levels led to decreases in perceptions of ability and behavior (Lachman & Andreoletti, 2006).

Positive beliefs and attitudes also have important indirect effects on cognitive enrichment. This indirect effect is reflected in the influence of these beliefs and attitudes on desirable behaviors such as exercise and mental stimulation known to be associated with enrichment effects on intelligence (Hertzog et al., 2009). Research indicates people with flexible attitudes at midlife tend to experience less decline in intellectual competence than people who are more rigid in middle age (Lachman, 2004; Willis & Boron, 2008).

Related to this idea connecting flexibility and intellectual competence is emerging evidence that being open to experiences, a key personality trait we will examine more closely in Chapter 9, helps buffer declines in fluid intelligence because people who are more open receive more environmental stimulation, which in turn helps develop crystallized intelligence (Ziegler et al., 2015). Ziegler and colleagues (2015) propose this as the Openness-Fluid-Crystallized-Intelligence (OFCI) model.

In Chapter 8, we will consider the concept of *emotional intelligence* and see how people use their knowledge of their own and others' emotions to guide their thinking and behavior.

Health

The most obvious relationship between health and intelligence concerns the functioning of the brain itself. We noted in Chapter 2 several normative changes in brain structure with age affect functioning. We also noted in Chapter 6 how brain injuries, nutrition, and other factors can also affect functioning. Diseases such as dementia wreak havoc in the brain, and others, such as cardiovascular disease, cancer, and diabetes, can have serious negative effects directly and indirectly through medication side effects.

Cardiovascular disease and its implications for intellectual functioning have been studied extensively. These diseases are linked to a pattern of cognitive impairment that looks like what is typically observed in "normal" cognitive aging. Some researchers suggest the effects of age on intelligence and cognition are related at least in part to vascular disease that selectively affects the prefrontal cortex (Spiro & Brady, 2008).

As we note in Chapters 3, 6, and 14, physical exercise has considerable benefit. In this context, exercise helps maintain cognitive fitness as well as slow down cognitive decline once it has begun (Amoyal & Fallon, 2012; Law et al., 2014). This alone should be enough reason to get up and get moving!

The relation between health and intellectual functioning is perhaps no clearer than in the concept of *terminal decline* (Cowl, 2016). **Terminal decline** *is the gradual decline in cognitive function that occurs relatively near death.* Even in the absence of dementia and other major physical and mental health factors, decline in intellectual abilities is a significant predictor of mortality (Connors et al., 2015). Yet, establishing broad connections between cognitive decline and death does not answer the next question of what, specifically, is going on? Answering that question was the aim of the research conducted by Aichele, Rabbitt, and Ghisletta (2016) that is highlighted in the How Do We Know? feature.

Modifying Primary Abilities

As you have seen, older adults do not perform as well on tests of some primary abilities as younger adults, even after taking the moderators of performance into account (Schaie, 2005). In considering these results, investigators began asking whether there was a way to slow down or even reverse the declines. There has been much research examining the effects of lifestyle, health, and personality, among other variables, on intelligence.

Pursuing this issue further, we need to ask several questions regarding training. Are the age-related differences remaining after cohort and other effects are removed permanent, or might these differences be reduced or even eliminated if older adults are given

How Do We Know?
Think Fast, Feel Fine, Live Long

Who was the investigator and what was the aim of the study? Much research shows a relation between cognitive ability and the risk of dying. However, this connection is complicated because differences in cognitive ability and the risk of dying are both related to various physiological conditions, functional ability, psychological factors, and social support. To begin to unravel these complex relations, Stephen Aichele, Patrick Rabbitt, and Paolo Ghisletta (2016) examined a large set of health, well-being, and cognitive variables over a long period of time.

How did the investigator measure the topic of interest? Five areas of cognitive abilities were assessed: fluid intelligence (logic, arithmetic, number series, and verbal and visual object comparisons), crystallized intelligence (two vocabulary tests), verbal memory (free recall, cumulative recall, and delayed recall), visuospatial memory (picture recognition, memory for objects, and recall of shapes and their locations), and processing speed (visual search, alphabet coding, and semantic reasoning). Participants gave subjective ratings of their general health status, the number of prescribed medications they took daily, sleep patterns, number of hobbies, hours per month in which they engaged in 14 different activities (e.g., housework, driving, exercise), degree of difficulty encountered in 12 different daily life activities (e.g., climbing stairs, cooking), and number of weekly social interactions. Medical status was also assessed through a comprehensive checklist of 195 total medical and psychiatric behaviors and symptoms. Mortality was measured through publicly available death records.

Who were the participants in the study? Data came from 6,203 participants in the Manchester Longitudinal Study of Cognition (MLSC) in the United Kingdom. At the time of their initial assessment, participants ranged in age from 41 to 96. All participants were screened for severe visual or auditory handicaps; those with difficulties corrected by eyeglasses or hearing aids were allowed to participate. Information about participant mortality between 1983 (the beginning of the study) and 2012 (the most recent update on survival) was obtained through public records.

What was the design of the study? The study began in 1983. The cognitive assessments were administered four times, with each testing four years apart. Participants were followed over a 29-year span (1983–2012) in terms of their survival. Thus, the study was a longitudinal design.

Were there ethical concerns with the study? Participants were volunteers and were provided informed consent, so there were no ethical concerns. Mortality data were collected through public death records.

What were the results? The primary data analyses focused on predictors of mortality risk. In all, 65 predictor variables were considered: demographic variables (8), tobacco and alcohol use (5), slope and intercept of cognitive abilities (10), slope and intercept of daily life measures (16), and slope and intercept of health data (26). Two sets of survival analyses were conducted. Results showed that being female, having better subjective health, and smaller declines in processing speed with age were most strongly related to lower mortality risk. More years smoking was the strongest prediction of high mortality risk.

What did the investigators conclude? Aichele, Rabbitt, and Ghisletta examined more variables in relation to mortality risk over a longer period of time than had ever been done previously. After carefully examining 65 predictors over 29 years, they showed that two psychological factors, subjective ratings of health and processing speed, were better indicators of mortality outcomes in middle-aged and older adults than almost any other predictors examined. Because both can be measured easily and are valid across cultures, Aichele and colleagues argue that they might form the basis of easy screening measures for increased mortality risk.

---

appropriate training? Can we really modify adults' intelligence? This again addresses the important issue of plasticity in intellectual functioning, one of the lifespan tenets discussed in Chapter 1.

The most common training research focuses on those intellectual abilities that constitute primary mental abilities, especially those clustered into fluid intelligence. These are the intellectual abilities, such as speed of processing, most likely to decline with age. It turns out that middle-aged and older adults can be successfully taught to increase their speed of processing, and this training transfers to tasks not included in the training sessions (Cândea et al., 2015; Simpson et al., 2012).

Two large-scale projects examined training of primary abilities over extended periods of time. These projects adopt the view that aging in healthy adults has great potential for cognitive growth (Looi et al., 2016; Lövdén et al., 2012) and associated positive structural changes in the brain (Walhovd et al., 2016), with the research largely being conducted within the Selective Optimization with Compensation (SOC) framework described in Chapter 1. Let's see what researchers discovered in Project ACTIVE.

Project ACTIVE

Sherry Willis has revolutionized our understanding of how far researchers can go to investigate the impact of training primary mental abilities. She designed a longitudinal research project named Advanced Cognitive Training for Independent and Vital Elderly (ACTIVE) to provide answers to key questions about whether the age-related changes observed in intelligence research were inevitable or could be modified through training (Rebok et al., 2014; Schaie & Willis, 2015; Willis & Schaie, 2009).

Begun in the mid-1990s, the ACTIVE study was a multicenter, randomized, controlled clinical research project that investigates the long-term effectiveness of cognitive training on enhancing mental abilities (memory, reasoning, and attention) and preserving instrumental activities of daily living (managing finances, taking medication, using the telephone, and driving) in older adults. Six centers across the eastern United States enrolled nearly 3,000 people initially. Participants underwent detailed assessments of mental and functional ability on multiple occasions over several years of follow-up. The design of Project ACTIVE is shown in Figure 7.4.

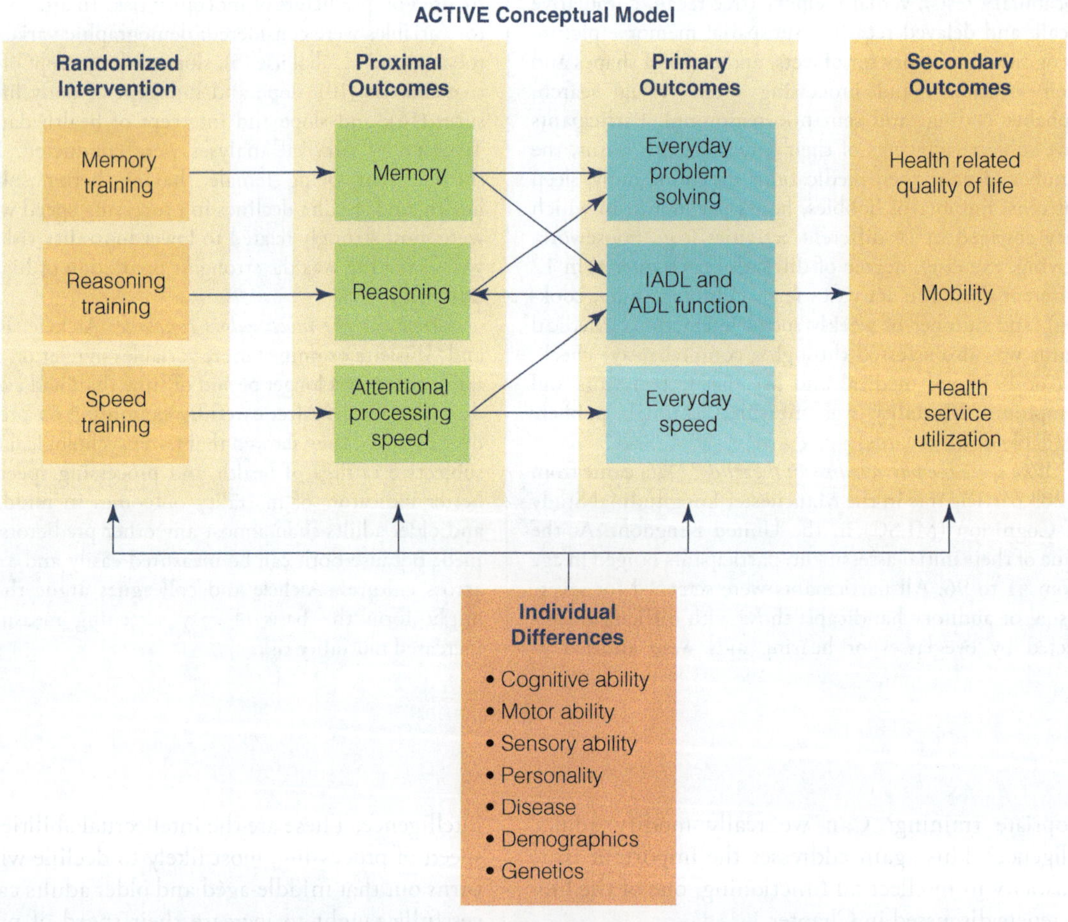

ACTIVE Conceptual Model

Randomized Intervention
- Memory training
- Reasoning training
- Speed training

Proximal Outcomes
- Memory
- Reasoning
- Attentional processing speed

Primary Outcomes
- Everyday problem solving
- IADL and ADL function
- Everyday speed

Secondary Outcomes
- Health related quality of life
- Mobility
- Health service utilization

Individual Differences
- Cognitive ability
- Motor ability
- Sensory ability
- Personality
- Disease
- Demographics
- Genetics

FIGURE 7.4 Experts in any field handle tasks in those fields differently than novices.
Source: Unverzagt, F. W., Smith, D. M., Rebok, G. W., Marsiske, M., Morris, J. N., Jones, R. et al. (2009). The Indiana Alzheimer Disease Center's Symposium on Mild Cognitive Impairment. Cognitive training in older adults: Lessons from the ACTIVE Study. *Current Alzheimer Research, 6,* 375–383. Retrieved from www.ncbi.nlm.nih.gov/pmc/articles/PMC2729785/figure/F1/.

The ACTIVE project findings show cognitive training interventions improved mental abilities and daily functioning in older independent living adults, with strong evidence that the improvements lasted at least 10 years (Rebok et al., 2014). These findings were especially the case for training in reasoning and processing speed; memory training did not have the same effects, particularly when participants showed signs of even mild cognitive impairment.

The results from Project ACTIVE allow us to conclude declines in fluid abilities may be reversible and preventable to some extent. Perhaps the best news is the training effects are relatively enduring.

What can we conclude from these findings? First, there is strong evidence in the normal course of development that no one is too old to benefit from training, and training reduces the rates of decline for those fluid abilities examined. Second, transfer of training occurs, but evidence is lacking that it occurs across a wide range of materials unless training involves executive functioning and working memory, when the effects generalize to many different tasks (Rebok et al., 2014).

Adult Development in Action

If you were a director of a human resources department, how would the research on intelligence across adulthood influence your decisions about employee training programs?

7.3 Qualitative Differences in Adults' Thinking

LEARNING OBJECTIVES
- What are the main points in Piaget's theory of cognitive development?
- What evidence is there for continued cognitive development beyond formal operations?
- What is the role of both emotion and cognition in cognitive maturity?

Eddie, a student at a local university, thought the test he had just taken in his math course was unfair because the instructors simply marked the answers to complex problems right or wrong. He complained he deserved partial credit for knowing how to set up the problem and being able to figure out some of the steps.

Although Eddie did not know it, his argument parallels one in the intelligence literature—the debate on whether we should pay attention mainly to whether an answer is right or wrong or to how the person reasons the problem through. The psychometric approach we considered earlier does not focus on the thinking processes underlying intelligence; rather, psychometrics concentrates on interrelationships among answers to test questions. In contrast, cognitive-structural approaches focus on the ways in which people think; whether a particular answer is right or wrong is not important.

We will consider two theories that represent cognitive-structural approaches. First, we examine Piaget's theory as a foundation for this approach. Second, we explore the discussions concerning possible extensions of it, postformal theory. Both these approaches postulate intellectual changes are mainly qualitative, even though they differ on many points.

Piaget's Theory

According to Piaget (1970, 1980), intellectual development is adaptation through activity. We create the ways our knowledge is organized and, ultimately, how we think. Piaget believed development of intelligence stems from the emergence of increasingly complex cognitive structures. He organized his ideas into a theory of cognitive development that changed the way psychologists conceptualize intellectual development.

Basic Concepts

For Piaget, thought is governed by the principles of adaptation and organization. Adaptation is the process of adjusting thinking to the environment. Just as animals living in a forest feed differently from the way animals living in a desert feed, how we think changes from one developmental context to another. Adaptation occurs through organization; that is, how the organism is put together. Each component part has its own specialized function that is coordinated into the whole. In Piaget's theory, the organization of thought is reflected in cognitive structures that change over the life span. Cognitive structures determine how we think. It is the change in cognitive structures, the change in the fundamental ways we think, Piaget tried to describe.

What processes underlie intellectual adaptation? Piaget defined two: assimilation and accommodation. **Assimilation** *is the use of currently available knowledge to make sense out of incoming information.* It is the application of cognitive structures to the world of experience that makes the world understandable. A child who knows only the word *dog* may use it for every animal she encounters. So, when the child sees a cat and calls it a dog, she is using available knowledge, the word *dog*, to make sense out of the world—in this case the cat walking across the living room. The process of assimilation sometimes leads to considerable distortion of incoming information, because we may have to force-fit it into our knowledge base. This is apparent in our tendency to forget information about a person that violates a stereotype.

Accommodation *involves changing one's thought to make it a better approximation of the world of experience.* The child in our example who thought cats were dogs eventually learns cats are cats. When this happens, she accommodated her knowledge to incorporate a new category of animal.

The processes of assimilation and accommodation serve to link the structure of thought to observable behavior. Piaget believed most changes during development involved cognitive structures. His research led him to conclude there were four structures (i.e., four stages) in the development of mature thought: sensorimotor, preoperational, concrete operational, and formal operational. We consider the major characteristics of each stage briefly. Because we are most interested in Piaget's description of adult thought, we emphasize that.

Sensorimotor Period

In this first stage of cognitive development, intelligence is seen in infants' actions. Babies and infants gain knowledge by using their sensory and motor skills, beginning with basic reflexes (sucking and grasping) and eventually moving to purposeful, planned sequences of behavior (such as looking for a hidden toy). The most important thing infants learn during the sensorimotor period is that objects continue to exist even when they are out of sight; this ability is called object permanence.

Preoperational Period

Young children's thinking is best described as egocentric. This means young children believe all people and all inanimate objects experience the world just as they do. Young children believe dolls feel pain. Although young children can sometimes reason through situations, their thinking is not based on logic. A young child may believe his father's shaving causes the tap water to be turned on, because the two events always happen together.

Concrete Operational Period

Logical reasoning emerges in the concrete operational period. Children become capable of classifying objects into groups, such as fruits or vegetables, based on a logical principle; mentally reversing a series of events; realizing when changes occur in one perceptual dimension and they are compensated for in another, no net change occurs (termed conservation); and understanding the concept of transitivity (for instance, if A > B and B > C, then A > C). However, children are still unable to deal with abstract concepts such as love; to children love is a set of concrete actions and not an ill-defined abstract concept.

Formal Operational Period

For Piaget, the acquisition of formal operational thought during adolescence marks the end of cognitive development. Because he argues formal operational thinking characterizes adult thought, we will consider this level in some detail. Piaget and other commentators (e.g., Lemieux, 2012) agree on four aspects of formal operational thought:

1. it takes a hypothesis-testing approach (termed hypothetico-deductive) to problem solving;
2. thinking is done in one framework at a time;
3. the goal is to arrive at one correct solution; and
4. it is unconstrained by reality.

Piaget describes the essence of formal operational thought as a way of conceiving abstract concepts and thinking about them in a systematic, step-by-step way. Formal operational thought is governed by a generalized logical structure that provides solutions to problems people have never seen and may never encounter. Hypothetico-deductive thought is similar to using the scientific method; it involves forming a hypothesis and testing it until the hypothesis is either confirmed or rejected. Just as scientists are systematic in testing experimental hypotheses, formal operational thinking allows people to approach problem solving in a logical, methodical way.

Consider the situation when your car breaks down. When you take it for repairs, the mechanic forms hypotheses about what may be wrong based on a description of the trouble. The mechanic then begins to test each hypothesis systematically. The compression of each cylinder may be checked, one cylinder at a time. This ability to hold other factors constant while testing a particular component is one of the hallmarks of formal operational thought. By isolating potential causes of the problem, the mechanic efficiently arrives at a correct solution.

When we use hypothetico-deductive thought, we do so to arrive at one unambiguous solution to the problem. Formal operational thought is aimed at resolving ambiguity; one and only one answer is the goal. When more than one solution occurs, there is a feeling of uneasiness and people begin a search for clarification. This situation can be observed in high school classes when students press their teacher to identify the right theory (from among several equally good ones) or the right way to view a social issue (such as abortion). Moreover, when people arrive at an answer, they are quite certain about it because it was arrived at through the use of logic. When answers are checked, the same logic and assumptions are typically used, that sometimes means the same mistake is made several times in a row. For example, a person may repeat a simple subtraction error time after time when trying to figure out why his or her checkbook failed to balance.

Formal operational thinking knows no constraints (Piaget, 1970, 1980). It can be applied just as easily to real or imaginary situations. It is not bound by the limits of reality (Labouvie-Vief, 1980). Whether one can implement a solution is irrelevant; what matters is one can think about it. This is how people arrive at solutions to disarmament, for example, such as getting rid of all nuclear warheads tomorrow. To the formal operational thinker, that this solution is logistically impossible is no excuse. The lack of reality constraints is not all bad, however. Reasoning from a "Why not?" perspective may lead to the discovery of completely new ways to approach a problem or the invention of new solutions.

One serious problem for Piaget's theory is many adults apparently do not attain formal operations. Piaget (1972) himself admitted formal operations were probably not universal but tended to appear only in those areas in which individuals were highly trained or specialized. This inspired a number of researchers to look beyond formal operations in determining pathways of adult cognitive development.

Going Beyond Formal Operations: Thinking in Adulthood

Suppose you are faced with the following dilemma: You are a member of your college's or university's student judicial board and are currently hearing a case involving plagiarism. The student handbook states plagiarism is a serious offense resulting in expulsion. The student accused of plagiarizing a paper admits copying from Wikipedia but says she has never been told she needed to use a formal citation and quotation marks. Do you vote to expel the student?

When this and similar problems are presented to older adolescents and young adults, interesting differences emerge. Adolescents tend to approach the problem in formal-operational terms and point out the student handbook is clear and the student ignored it, concluding the student should be expelled. Formal-operational thinkers are certain such solutions are right because they are based on their own experience and are logically driven.

But many adults are reluctant to draw conclusions based on the limited information in the problem, especially when the problem can be interpreted in different ways (Commons, 2016). They point out there is much about the student we don't know: Has she ever been taught the proper procedure for using sources? Was the faculty member clear about what plagiarism is? For adults, the problem is more ambiguous. Adults may eventually decide the student is (or is not) expelled, but they do so only after considering aspects of the situation that go well beyond the information given in the problem.

Based on numerous investigations, researchers concluded this different type of thinking represents a qualitative change beyond formal operations (King & Kitchener, 2015; Lemieux, 2012; Sinnott, 2014). **Postformal thought** *is characterized by recognition that truth (the correct answer) may vary from situation to situation, solutions must be realistic to be reasonable, ambiguity and contradiction are the rule rather than the exception, and emotion and subjective factors usually play a role in thinking.* In general, the research evidence indicates post formal thinking has its origins in young adulthood (King & Kitchener, 2015; Sinnott, 2014).

Several research-based descriptions of the development of thinking in adulthood have been offered. *One of the best is the description of the development of* **reflective judgment**, *a way adults reason through*

When confronted with real-world dilemmas, young adults think differently about them than adolescents do.

dilemmas involving current affairs, religion, science, personal relationships, and the like. Based on decades of longitudinal and cross-sectional research, King and Kitchener (2002, 2015) refined descriptions and identified a systematic progression of reflective judgment in young adulthood. A summary of these stages is shown in Table 7.2.

The first three stages in the model represent prereflective thought. People in these stages typically do not acknowledge and may not even perceive that knowledge is uncertain. Consequently, they do not understand some problems exist when there is not a clear and absolutely correct answer. A student pressuring her instructor for the "right" theory to explain human development reflects this stage. She is also likely to hold firm positions on controversial issues and does so without acknowledging other people's ability to reach a different (but nevertheless equally logical) position.

About halfway through the developmental progression, students think differently. In Stages 4 and 5, students are likely to say nothing can be known for certain and to change their conclusions based on the situation and the evidence. At this point, students argue knowledge is quite subjective. They are also less persuasive with their positions on controversial issues: "Each person is entitled to his or her own view; I cannot force my opinions on anyone else." Kitchener and King refer to thinking in these stages as "quasi-reflective" thinking.

As they continue their development into Stages 6 and 7, individuals begin to show true reflective judgment, understanding that people construct knowledge using evidence and argument after careful analysis of the problem or situation. They once again hold firm convictions but reach them only after careful consideration of several points of view. They also realize they must continually reevaluate their beliefs in view of new evidence.

Evidence of different stages of postformal thinking can be seen in everyday contexts. One especially good one is election campaigns. The Real People feature discusses how this was evident in the 2016 U.S. presidential election.

Even though people are able to think at complex levels, do they? Not usually (King & Kitchener, 2004, 2015). Why? Mostly because the environment does not provide the supports necessary for using one's highest-level thinking, especially for issues concerning knowledge and experience you already have. People may not always purchase the product with the least impact on the environment, such as a fully electric car, even though philosophically they are strong environmentalists, because recharging stations are currently not widely available. However, if pushed and if given the necessary supports (e.g., easily available charging stations), people demonstrate a level of thinking and performance far higher than they typically show on a daily basis.

TABLE 7.2 Description of the Stages of Reflective Judgment

Prereflective Reasoning (Stages 1–3): Belief that "knowledge is gained through the word of an authority figure or through firsthand observation, rather than, for example, through the evaluation of evidence. [People who hold these assumptions] believe that what they know is absolutely correct, and that they know with complete certainty. People who hold these assumptions treat all problems as though they were well-structured" (King & Kitchener, 2004, p. 39). *Example statements typical of Stages 1–3:* "I know it because I see it." "If it's on Fox News it must be true."

Quasi-Reflective Reasoning (Stages 4 and 5): Recognition "that knowledge—or more accurately, knowledge claims—contain elements of uncertainty, which [people who hold these assumptions] attribute to missing information or to methods of obtaining the evidence. Although they use evidence, they do not understand how evidence entails a conclusion (especially in light of the acknowledged uncertainty), and thus tend to view judgments as highly idiosyncratic" (King & Kitchener, 2004, p. 40). *Example statements typical of stages 4 and 5:* "I would believe in climate change if I could see the proof; how can you be sure the scientists aren't just making up the data?"

Reflective Reasoning (Stages 6 and 7): People who hold these assumptions accept "that knowledge claims cannot be made with certainty, but [they] are not immobilized by it; rather, [they] make judgments that are 'most reasonable' and about which they are 'relatively certain,' based on their evaluation of available data. They believe they must actively construct their decisions, and that knowledge claims must be evaluated in relationship to the context in which they were generated to determine their validity. They also readily admit their willingness to reevaluate the adequacy of their judgments as new data or new methodologies become available" (King & Kitchener, 2004, p. 40). *Example statements typical of stages 6 and 7:* "It is difficult to be certain about things in life, but you can draw your own conclusions about them based on how well an argument is put together based on the data used to support it."

Real People
Feeling the Bern

The 2016 U.S. presidential election cycle was different in many ways, not the least of which was that the final two major candidates included the first woman and the first businessman without government or military experience, who were the least well-liked candidates since polling began. But one candidate in the Democratic primaries, Senator Bernie Sanders (I-VT), created quite a stir for another reason.

Senator Sanders built his campaign on a number of premises relating to social justice and income inequality. He expressed sharp criticism of Wall Street and the overall "rigged system" that infects the government. Though these positions were ones he had long held, they resonated particularly with emerging and young adult voters, most of whom were not yet born when Sanders espoused them during his initial campaign for mayor of Burlington, Vermont, in 1980.

The various stages of reflective judgment could be seen in the Sanders supporters. Some argued that "the Bern's" positions were the only correct positions, and these voters subsequently refused to consider either the Clinton-Kaine or the Trump-Pence tickets. Others strongly believed that Sanders's positions were right, but they were willing to see good points in either of the other candidates' positions and supported them to effect at least some level of change.

Political campaigns are usually made up of a spectrum of supporters. Some are true believers who will not compromise because they believe they have found Truth. Others are ones who weigh the pros and cons and come to a decision based on the preponderance of evidence. Getting various supporters to talk about their decisions will likely reveal where they are along the developmental spectrum. It certainly did in 2016.

U.S. Senator Bernie Sanders (D)-VT

Integrating Emotion and Logic

In addition to an increased understanding there is more than one "right" answer, adult thinking is characterized by the integration of emotion with logic (Labouvie-Vief, 2015). Labouvie-Vief (2015; Labouvie-Vief, Grühn, & Mouras, 2009) describes this emotional development as paralleling intellectual development, demonstrating both gains and losses with increasing age. These parallel processes create tension, resulting in the cognitive-emotional integration and interplay that middle-aged and older adults use when confronted with real-life problems.

As they mature, adults tend to make decisions and analyze problems not so much on logical grounds as on pragmatic and emotional grounds. Rules and norms are viewed as relative, not absolute. Mature thinkers realize thinking is an inherently social enterprise that demands making compromises with other people and tolerating contradiction and ambiguity. Such shifts mean one's sense of self also undergoes a fundamental change.

A good example of this developmental shift is the difference between how late adolescents or young adults view an emotionally charged issue—such as unethical behavior at work—compared to the views of middle-aged adults. Younger people may view such behavior as completely inexcusable, with firing of the employee an inescapable outcome. Middle-aged adults may take contextual factors into account and consider what factors may have forced the person to engage in the behavior. Some might argue this is because the topic is too emotionally charged for adolescents to deal with intellectually whereas young adults are better able to incorporate emotion into their thinking.

The integration of emotion with logic in adulthood provides the basis for decision making in the personal and sometimes difficult arenas of love and work that we examine in detail in Chapters 11 and 12, respectively. In the present context, integration sets the stage for envisioning one's future life, a topic we take up later in this chapter.

As people grow older, two things happen in terms of the integration of emotion and thought (Labouvie-Vief, 2015). First, the rich emotional experience people have accumulated can be brought to bear on tasks that are not too difficult in terms of cognitive demands, meaning that in these situations older adults have an easier time than younger adults at integrating emotions and thought. In contrast, when the demands of the task are great, the arousal that is created narrows their ability to bring emotions to bear.

Neuroimaging Evidence

Evidence from neuroimaging research indicates emotion and logic processing is indeed integrated in adults (Gu et al., 2013). This integration occurs in the prefrontal cortex and the anterior insula (an area of the brain deep inside the cortex). Additional research reviewed in Chapter 2 indicates the amygdala is also involved in processing emotion, and this information is also integrated with thought.

Evidence of certain neural pathways in the brain associated with cognition-emotion integration can be used as a baseline for understanding what happens when the neural connections are altered or absent. Evidence is now clear that these interconnections are different in some forms of mental disorders (Anticevic, Repovs, & Barch, 2012; Hamilton, Hiatt Racer, & Newman, 2015). This means intellectual and emotion processing share common brain pathways in healthy adults, but use various other pathways in adults who experience mental disorders.

The integration of emotion with logic that happens in adulthood provides the basis for decision making in the personal and sometimes difficult arenas of love and work that we examine in detail in Chapters 11 and 12, respectively. It also provides the basis for broader perspectives about life, and the ability to see points of view different from one's own.

Adult Development in Action

For what types of jobs would an assessment of psychometric intelligence be more appropriate than of reflective judgment? What about the other way around?

7.4 Everyday Reasoning and Problem Solving

LEARNING OBJECTIVES

- What are the characteristics of older adults' decision making?
- What are optimally exercised abilities and unexercised abilities? What age differences have been found in practical problem solving?
- What is expertise and how does experience factor in?
- What are creativity and wisdom, and how do they relate to age and life experience?

Kim is a 75-year-old grandmother visiting her 14-year-old grandson. When he asks her to help with his algebra homework, she declines, stating she just did not have enough schooling to understand it. However, when he has trouble communicating with his parents, Kim can give him excellent advice on how to understand things from both their perspective and his. He ends up getting what he wanted and is delighted to know he can always go to his grandma for advice.

So far, our consideration of intellectual abilities includes examinations of how people's performance on standardized tests and their modes of thinking differ with age. But what we have not considered in detail is how people actually use their intellectual abilities and demonstrate characteristics we associate with intelligent people: solving problems, making decisions, gaining expertise, and becoming wise. This contrast in intellectual abilities is illustrated in Kim's lack of algebraic skills, yet wisdom in her interpersonal skills and the conduct of life. What we discovered in this chapter to this point is people's crystallized intelligence, reflecting life experience, continues to grow (or at least not decline) until later in life, and one hallmark of adults' thinking is the integration of emotion and logic. One might expect, then, the ability to make decisions and solve real-life problems would not decline until late adulthood, that expertise would increase and wisdom would be related to age. Are these expectations correct? Let's find out.

As we discussed, there are many age-related declines in basic cognitive and sensory mechanisms. We also learned there are age-related increases in experience that continues to build semantic memory and crystallized intelligence, as well as postformal thinking. Given these two perspectives on aging, an important distinction must be made. Although there are various age-related declines in the structure and processes of cognitive functioning, it is also important to consider the functional context of everyday behavior that is cognitively demanding. Thus, even though older adults may experience decline in memory, they may have appropriate skills and knowledge adequate for tasks in their daily lives. In other words, we cannot necessarily take information we learn in laboratory experiments on cognitive and intellectual aging and easily apply it to everyday life. Let's explore this distinction first in the area of everyday decision making.

Decision Making

At first glance, the research on decision making suggests older adults make less effective decisions (Besedeš et al., 2012; Strough, de Bruin, & Peters, 2015). For example, older adults use less optimal strategies when deciding what options to select to best meet their needs. When decision making involves a high degree of working memory capacity (e.g., a lot of information must be held in memory simultaneously in order to make quick decisions), older adults do not perform as well (see Chapter 6 regarding working memory). However, many everyday decision-making situations do not necessarily reflect the firm time constraints and cognitive demands studied in typical laboratory research. Additionally, older adults may not be as motivated to do well in artificial situations. Let's examine these factors to see the difference that makes in the presence or absence of age differences.

A common everyday decision-making situation involves choosing one best option from a number of choices. These range from assessing automobiles for future purchase (Lambert-Pandraud, Laurent, & Lapersonne, 2005) and treatment decisions for breast cancer (Meyer et al., 2007), to retirement and financial planning (Hershey, Austin, & Gutierrez, 2015). Findings are quite comparable. Older adults search for less information in order to arrive at a decision, require less information to arrive at a decision, tend to avoid risk, and rely on easily accessible information (Shivapour et al., 2012). These tendencies can result in the financial exploitation of older adults (Lichtenberg, 2016).

When decision making taps into relevant experience or knowledge, older adults tend to be just as effective or better in making decisions as younger adults. Experience and knowledge tend to make older adults less susceptible to irrational biases in their decision making in comparison to younger adults (Hess, Queen, & Ennis, 2013; Zaval et al., 2015).

One key to understanding when age-related declines in decision making are and are not present is understanding how decision making relates to fluid and crystallized intelligence. That is, to the extent that decision making relies heavily on such things as speedy mental processing, then age differences are likely. On the other hand, when decision making can be more reflective and relies on acquired knowledge and experience, age differences are much less likely (Zaval et al., 2015). Additionally, it may be when decisions are personally relevant it bolsters older adults' attentional focus on important cues resulting in efficient decisions (Hess et al., 2012; Meyer et al., 2007; Zaval et al., 2015).

Emotion also plays an important role in age differences in decision making. Negative emotions such as anger and fear can sometimes be evoked when making a decision. Health-related decisions are particularly distasteful because they can involve threat, and are high in personal relevance and in importance to the individual (Löckenhoff & Carstensen, 2007). In support of the idea older adults are motivated to reduce the experience of negativity and enhance the experience of positivity (Carstensen & Mikels, 2005), research shows older adults focused more on positive information when making a health decision (English & Carstensen, 2016; Löckenhoff & Carstensen, 2007). Interestingly, older adults focus more on positive information than younger adults do when making a decision only when they were asked to explicitly evaluate their options before making a choice (Glass & Osman, 2017; Kim et al., 2008) If not asked to do so, there are no age differences in decision making.

Going one step further, Kim and colleagues (2008) asked participants how satisfied they were with their decisions. For the older adult group asked to evaluate their options, their focus on the positive and satisfaction with their decisions remained high over two weeks. In other words, older adults' high level of satisfaction with their decisions increased and persisted over two weeks by simply asking them to spend a few minutes evaluating their options. This did not happen for younger adults. Kim et al. (2008) note that advertisements or interventions having a positive impact on one age group may have a completely different impact on another.

Problem Solving

One of the most important ways people use their intellectual abilities is to solve problems. Think for a minute about everyday life and the number of problem-solving situations you encounter in school, on the job, in relationships, driving a car, and so forth. Each of these settings requires you to analyze complex situations quickly, to apply knowledge, and to create solutions, sometimes in a matter of seconds.

Some people tend to be better at dealing with certain problems more than with others. Why is that? One possible explanation has to do with the kinds of abilities we use regularly versus the abilities we use only occasionally. Nancy Denney proposed a more formal version of this explanation that we consider next.

Denney's Model of Unexercised and Optimally Exercised Abilities

Denney (1984) postulates intellectual abilities relating to problem solving follow two types of developmental functions. One of these functions represents unexercised or unpracticed ability, and the other represents optimally trained or optimally exercised ability. **Unexercised ability** *is the ability a normal, healthy adult would exhibit without practice or training.* Fluid intelligence is thought to be an example of untrained ability, because by definition, it does not depend on experience and is unlikely to be formally trained (Horn & Hofer, 1992). **Optimally exercised ability** *is the ability a normal, healthy adult would demonstrate under the best conditions of training or practice.* Crystallized intelligence is an example of optimally exercised ability, because the component skills (such as vocabulary ability) are used daily.

Denney argues the overall developmental course of both abilities is the same: They tend to increase until late adolescence or early adulthood and slowly decline thereafter. At all age levels there is a difference in favor of optimally exercised ability, although this difference is less in early childhood and old age. As the developmental trends move away from the hypothetical ideal, Denney argues the gains seen in training programs will increase. As we noted earlier in our discussion of attempts to train fluid intelligence, it appears this increase occurs.

Practical Problem Solving

Denney's model spurred considerable interest in how people solve practical problems. Based on the model, adults should perform better on practical problems than on abstract ones like those typically used on standardized intelligence tests. Tests of practical problem solving would use situations such as the following (Denney, Pearce, & Palmer, 1982): "Let's say that a middle-aged woman is frying chicken in her home when, all of a sudden, a grease fire breaks out on top of the stove. Flames begin to shoot up. What should she do?" (p. 116).

One way to assess practical problem solving in more focused terms is to create measures with clearly identifiable dimensions that relate to specific types of problems (Allaire, 2012; Gamaldo & Allaire, 2016). This is what Diehl, Willis, and Schaie (1995) did by creating the Observed Tasks of Daily Living (OTDL) measure. The OTDL consists of three dimensions that reflect three specific problems in everyday life: food preparation, medication intake, and telephone use. Each of these dimensions also reflects important aspects of assessing whether people can live independently, a topic we explored in Chapter 5. Diehl et al. showed performance on the OTDL is directly influenced by age, fluid intelligence, and crystallized intelligence and indirectly by perceptual speed, memory, and several aspects of health. These results provide important links between practical problem solving and basic elements of psychometric intelligence and information processing. Additional research indicates basic measures of inductive reasoning, domain-specific knowledge, memory, working memory, cognitive strategies, and motivation were related to everyday assessments of each of these abilities (Allaire, 2012; Frank et al., 2016; Gamaldo & Allaire, 2016; Thornton & Dumke, 2005). Allaire and Marsiske (1999, 2002) conclude everyday problems reflecting well-structured challenges from activities of daily living show a strong relationship to traditional psychometric abilities.

The search for relations between psychometric intelligence and practical problem-solving abilities is only one way to examine the broader linkages with intellectual functioning. It focuses on the degree of how everyday problem solving is a manifestation of underlying intellectual abilities (Berg, 2008). However, recall postformal thinking is grounded in the ways people conceptualize situations. Indeed, much of the research that led to the discovery of postformal thought involved presenting adults with lifelike problems. This approach enlarges the scope of what we consider everyday problem solving to include not just cognitive abilities, but also social, motivational, and cultural factors influencing how we solve problems (Berg, 2008; Zaval et al., 2015).

Another important factor that influences the way we solve everyday problems is the context in which the problem occurs. Do we use the same approach when solving a family conflict between two siblings as we do when solving a conflict over the leading role in a project at work? The answer is no. Interestingly, however, age differences reveal younger adults are more likely to use a similar strategy across problem-solving contexts: self-action in order to fix the problem. Older adults, on the other hand, are more likely to vary their strategy given the problem-solving context. In interpersonal conflict problems (e.g., family conflict) they use more emotion-regulating strategies (i.e., managing their emotions) whereas in instrumental situations (e.g., dealing with defective merchandise) they use self-action strategies (return the product) (Blanchard-Fields, Chen, & Herbert, 1997). As we grow older and accumulate more everyday experience, we become more sensitive to the problem context and use strategies accordingly.

There are also individual differences in the way the same problem situation is interpreted. How individuals represent problems differs and could vary across the life span as developmental life goals change (Berg et al., 1998). Berg and colleagues (Berg et al., 1998; Strough, Berg, & Sansone, 1996) find there are age differences in how individuals define their own everyday problems. Overall, middle-aged older adults define problems more in terms of interpersonal goals (e.g., getting along with a person or spending more time with an individual), whereas adolescents and young adults focused more on competence goals (e.g., losing weight or studying for an exam). Furthermore, problem-solving strategies fit the problem definitions. Older adults defined problems more in terms of interpersonal concerns and subsequently reported strategies such as regulating others or including others, whereas competence goals resulted in strategies that involved more self-action. Along these lines Artistico, Cervone, and Pezzuti (2003) found older adults were more confident and generated more effective solutions to problems typical of the life stage of older adults. Finally, Blanchard-Fields, Mienaltowski, and Seay (2007) found older adults were rated as more effective in their everyday problem-solving strategy use than younger adults across all types of problem situations.

What can we conclude from the research on practical problem solving? First, practical problem-solving abilities are multidimensional and may not interrelate strongly with each other. Second, the developmental functions of these abilities are complex and may differ across abilities. Third, the relations between practical problem-solving abilities and psychometric intelligence are equally complex. Finally, the close connection between solving practical problems and emotion and motivation may prove fruitful in furthering our understanding of individual differences in abilities. In short, solving practical problems offers an excellent way to discover how all the topics we have considered in this chapter come together to produce behavior in everyday life.

Expertise

We saw earlier in this chapter aspects of intelligence grounded in experience (crystallized intelligence) tend to improve throughout most of adulthood. In a real-world experiential perspective, each of us becomes an expert at something important to us, such as our work, interpersonal relationships, cooking, sports, or auto repair. In this sense, an expert is someone who is much better at a task than people who have not put much effort into it. We tend to become selective experts in some areas while remaining amateurs or novices at others.

What makes experts better than novices? It's how experts handle the problem (Ericsson & Towne, 2010; Hambrick et al., 2016). For novices, the goal for accomplishing the activity is to reach as rapidly as possible a satisfactory performance level that is stable and "autonomous." In contrast, experts build up a wealth of knowledge about alternative ways of solving problems or making decisions. These well-developed knowledge structures are the major difference between experts and novices, and they enable experts to bypass steps needed by novices (Chi, 2006).

Experts don't always follow the rules as novices do; they are more flexible, creative, and curious; and they have superior strategies grounded on superior knowledge for accomplishing a task (Ericsson & Towne, 2010). Even though experts may be slower in terms of raw speed because they spend more time planning, their ability to skip steps puts them at a decided advantage. In a way, this represents "the triumph of knowledge over reasoning" (Charness & Bosman, 1990).

What happens to expertise over the adult life span? Research evidence indicates expert performance tends to peak by middle age and drops off slightly after that (Masunaga & Horn, 2001). However, the declines in expert performance are not nearly as great as they are for the abilities of information processing, memory, and fluid intelligence that underlie expertise, and expertise may sometimes compensate for declines in underlying cognitive abilities (Masunaga & Horn, 2001; Taylor et al., 2005).

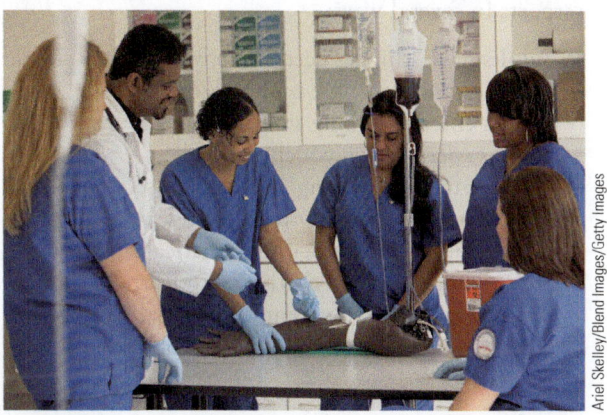

Experts in any field handle tasks in those fields differently than novices.

Such compensation is seen in expert judgments about such things as how long certain figure skating maneuvers will take. Older people who were experts were as good as younger adults who were still skating at predicting the amount of time skating moves take (Diersch et al., 2012). Thus, it appears knowledge based on experience is an important component of expertise. Indeed, researchers argue that people become "experts by experience" (Tolkko, 2016). But how do people keep acquiring knowledge? That's achieved through lifelong learning.

Lifelong Learning

Many people work in occupations where information and technology change rapidly. To keep up with these changes, many organizations and professions now emphasize the importance of learning how to learn, rather than learning specific content that may become outdated in a couple of years. For most people, a college education will probably not be the last educational experience they have in their careers. Workers in many professions—such as medicine, nursing, social work, psychology, auto mechanics, and teaching—are now required to obtain continuing education credits to stay current in their fields. Online learning has made lifelong learning more accessible to professionals and interested adults alike (Council for Adult and Experiential Learning, 2016).

Lifelong learning is gaining acceptance as the best way to approach the need for keeping active cognitively, and is viewed as critical part of aging globally (Formosa, 2014; Swindell, 2012), but should lifelong learning be approached as merely an extension of earlier educational experiences? Knowles, Holton, and Swanson (2015) argue teaching aimed at children and youth differs from teaching aimed at adults. Adult learners differ from their younger counterparts in several ways:

- Adults have a higher need to know why they should learn something before undertaking it.
- Adults enter a learning situation with more and different experience on which to build.
- Adults are most willing to learn those things they believe are necessary to deal with real-world problems rather than abstract, hypothetical situations.
- Most adults are more motivated to learn by internal factors (such as self-esteem or personal satisfaction) than by external factors (such as a job promotion or pay raise).

Lifelong learning is becoming increasingly important, but educators need to keep in mind learning styles change as people age. Effective lifelong learning requires smart decisions about how to keep knowledge updated and what approach works best among the many different learning options available (Knowles et al., 2015).

Creativity and Wisdom

Two additional aspects of cognition are important when viewed within an adult development context: creativity and wisdom. Each has been the focus of age-related stereotypes: creativity is assumed to be a function of young people, whereas wisdom is assumed to be the province of older adults. Let's see whether these views are accurate.

Creativity

What makes a person creative? Is it exceptional productivity? Does creativity mean having a career marked by precocity and longevity?

Researchers define creativity in adults as the ability to produce work that is novel, high in demand, and task appropriate (Kaufman, 2016; Simonton, in press). Creative output, in terms of the number of creative ideas a person has or the major contributions a person makes, varies across the adult life span and disciplines (Franses, 2016; Jones, 2010; Kaufman, 2016; Kozbelt & Durmysheva, 2007; Simonton, 2012). When considered as a function of age, the overall number of creative contributions a person makes tends to increase through one's 30s, peak in the late 30s to early 40s, and decline thereafter. A typical life-span trend is shown for painters and composers in Figure 7.5.

The age-related decline from midlife on does *not* mean people stop being creative altogether, just that they produce fewer creative ideas than when they were younger (Damian & Simonton, 2015). For example, the age when people made major creative contributions, such as research that resulted in winning the Nobel Prize, increased throughout the 20th century (Jones, 2010). And because creativity results from the interaction of cognitive abilities, personality, and developmental forces, all of these continue to operate throughout people's lives.

Exciting neuroimaging research is supporting previous research that one's most innovative contribution tends to happen most often during the 30s or 40s, as well as showing that creative people's brains are different. This research shows white-matter brain structures that connect brain regions in very different locations, and coordinate the cognitive control of information among them, are related to creativity and are more

When We Peak

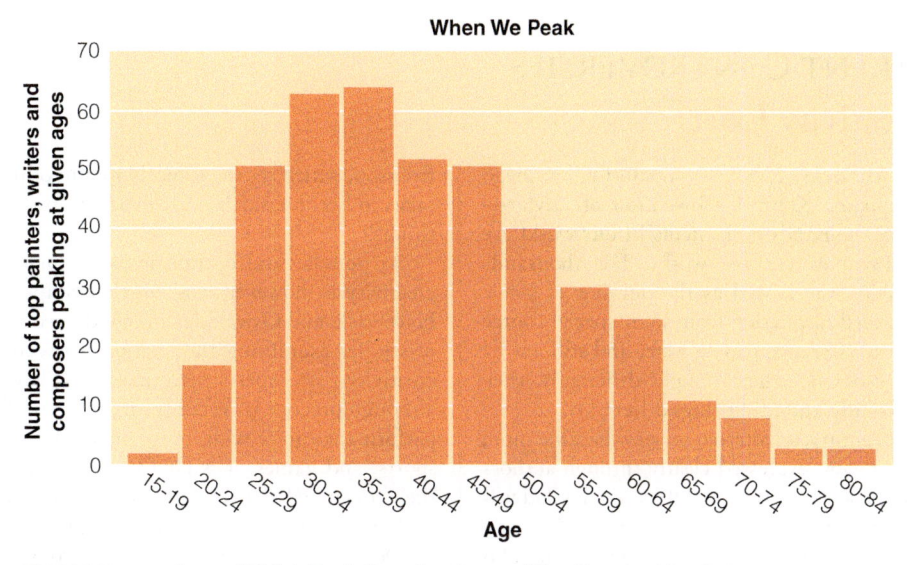

FIGURE 7.5 Age at Which Peak Creative Output Was Reached for Painters, Writers, and Composers
Source: img.washingtonpost.com/wp-apps/imrs.php?src=https://img.washingtonpost.com/blogs/wonkblog/files/2016/06/creative_age.png&w=1484.

apparent in creative people (Heilman, 2016; Zhu et al., 2016b). Such research has also linked certain brain pathways to actual everyday creative behavior.

As an example of such focused research, additional neuroimaging studies show different areas of the prefrontal and parietal areas are responsible for different aspects of creative thinking (Abraham et al., 2012). This research supports the belief creativity involves connecting disparate ideas in new ways, as different areas of the brain are responsible for processing different kinds of information. Because white matter tends to change with age, this finding also suggests there are underlying brain maturation reasons why innovative thinking tends to occur most often during late young adulthood and early middle age.

Building upon neuroimaging research, Jung, Flores, and Hunter (2016) developed the Hunter Imagination Questionnaire (HIQ) designed to assess imagination over time in a naturalistic way. Scores on the HIQ have been shown to be related to a wide array of brain volume in areas such as the hippocampus, areas of the frontal lobe, and other brain regions. It will likely be the case that such measures will continue to be refined, and may eventually show utility in helping to identify both high levels of creativity and potential early signs of brain disorders.

Even with this evidence, though, a nagging question remains for many researchers and theorists (e.g., Ericsson, 2014; Gladwell, 2008): Is what the typical person calls *creativity* nothing more than a high level of expertise that is honed after years of practice? The Current Controversies feature explores this question.

Wisdom

For thousands of years, cultures around the world greatly admired people who were wise. Based on years of research using in-depth think-aloud interviews with young, middle-aged, and older adults about normal and unusual problems people face, Baltes and colleagues (Ardelt, 2010; Baltes & Staudinger, 2000; Scheibe, Kunzmann, & Baltes, 2007) describe four characteristics of wisdom:

- Wisdom deals with important or difficult matters of life and the human condition.
- Wisdom is truly "superior" knowledge, judgment, and advice.
- Wisdom is knowledge with extraordinary scope, depth, and balance that is applicable to specific situations.
- Wisdom, when used, is well intended and combines mind and virtue (character).

Researchers used this framework to discover that people who are wise are experts in the basic issues in life (Ardelt, 2010; Baltes & Staudinger, 2000). Wise people know a great deal about how to conduct life, how to interpret life events, and what life means. Kunz (2007) refers to this as the strengths, knowledge, and understanding learned only by living through the earlier stages of life.

Current Controversies
Does Creativity Exist?

Lin-Manuel Miranda's *Hamilton*, a painting by Diego Rivera, Stephanie Kowalek's invention of Kevlar—these and many thousands more items in our world are generally described as creative works. For thousands of years, creativity was viewed as the purview of a few people who received inspiration from some special source (Simonton, 2006). Creative people were, and still are by many, seen as different—they thought differently, they felt things differently, they did things differently.

By the 20th century, an alternative view became more prominent. That view, expressed clearly through authors and researchers such as Ericsson (2014) and Gladwell (2008), sees creativity as not something special but as a trainable skill that is essentially achievable by anyone who puts in the time and practice. From this perspective, what people call creative output is little more than the next logical step in an ongoing process that is the result of expertise, and that is largely predictable. In his book *Outliers*, Gladwell (2008) made this quite prescriptive with his famous "10,000-Hour Rule," derived from research by Ericsson, which set the typical amount of practice time it takes to become sufficiently expert to produce "creative" things.

As popular and optimistic as the practice notion of creativity is, however, it is not that simple. Macnamara, Hambrick, and Oswald (2014) conducted a meta-analysis of studies examining the relation between practice and creativity or expert performance. They found that although practice is certainly an important factor in such performance in a wide range of fields, such as music, sports, and games, it is far from the only factor. Thus, they concluded that practice, while important, does not explain creative or highly expert output.

Does creativity exist? It seems to come down to this. Until we have a fuller understanding of what happens cognitively when a person puts many, often disparate ideas together in a novel way, we are left without a good alternative explanation. Something about that outcome is different. You cannot simply practice and make it happen.

Research studies indicate that, contrary to what many people expect, there is no association between age and wisdom (Ardelt, 2010; Baltes & Staudinger, 2000). In fact, the framework on wisdom discussed above has been applied to emerging adults (Booker & Dunsmore, 2016). As envisioned by Baltes and colleagues, whether a person is wise depends on whether he or she has extensive life experience with the type of problem given and has the requisite cognitive abilities and personality. Thus, wisdom could be related to crystallized intelligence, knowledge that builds over time and through experience (Ardelt, 2010).

Culture matters, though, in understanding wisdom. For instance, younger and middle-aged Japanese adults use more wisdom-related reasoning strategies (e.g., recognition of multiple perspectives, the limits of personal knowledge, and the importance of compromise) in resolving social conflicts than younger or middle-aged Americans (Grossman et al., 2012). However, older adults in both cultures used similar wisdom-related strategies.

It also turns out that people are more likely to show "wise thinking" in situatoins in which they are not personally involved (Grossman, 2017). When one is personally invested in the situation, it is difficult to take a neutral and more unemotional approach that fosters wisdom, Because self-focused situations inhibit wise thinking, it may be better to consult a neutral person or do whatever is possible to adopt a dispassionate mind-set.

So what specific factors help one become wise? Baltes (1993) identified three factors: (1) *general personal conditions* such as mental ability; (2) *specific expertise conditions* such as mentoring or practice; and (3) *facilitative life contexts* such as education or leadership experience. Personal growth during adulthood, reflecting Erikson's concepts of generativity and integrity also fosters the process, as do facing and dealing with life crises (Ardelt, 2010). All of these factors take time. Thus, although growing old is no guarantee of wisdom, it does provide the time, if used well, to create a supportive context for developing wisdom.

Becoming wise is one thing; having one's wisdom recognized is another. Interestingly, peer ratings of wisdom are better indicators of wisdom than self-ratings (Redzanowski & Glück, 2013). It appears people draw from a wide array of examples of wisdom (Westrate, Ferrari, & Ardelt, 2016) and are better at recognizing wisdom in others than they are in themselves. Perhaps it is better that way.

Interestingly, there is a debate over whether with wisdom comes happiness. There is research evidence that wise people are happier, have better mental health, are humble, and better quality of life (Bergsma & Ardelt, 2012; Etezadi & Pushkar, 2013; Krause, 2016; Thomas et al., 2017). Wise people tend to have higher levels of perceived control over their lives and use problem-focused and positive reappraisal coping strategies more often than people who are not wise. On the other hand, some evidence indicates the attainment of wisdom brings increased distress (Staudinger & Glück, 2011). Perhaps because with the experience that brings wisdom comes an understanding that life does not always work out the way one would like.

Adult Development in Action

If you were the director of a senior center, how would you capitalize on the wisdom of your members?

Social Policy Implications

In the section on training, evidence suggests a cognitively enriched lifestyle can positively influence intellectual change as we grow older. This suggests there is promise in developing long-term cognitive enrichment programs to reduce morbidity and dependence in older adults. For example, it may be the case we can defer the need for assisted living, improve well-being, and reduce healthcare costs. Projects aimed at training intellectual abilities in older adult populations thus have important public policy implications in terms of funding priorities and reducing the burden on public funding for disabilities in senior citizens. The long-term goals of projects such as ACTIVE is to reduce public health problems associated with the increasing need for more formal care and hospitalization along with the loss of independence in the growing number of American senior citizens.

People's concern over normative changes in cognitive abilities with age have fueled the development of popular interventions that claim to delay or prevent these changes. However, close scrutiny of the claims reveals that at least some overstate the case. For example, in 2016 one popular program, Lumosity, was found guilty in a U.S. District Court of making false claims. The Federal Trade Commission found that Lumosity's marketing "preyed on consumers' fears about age-related cognitive decline, suggesting their games could stave off memory loss, dementia, and even Alzheimer's disease."

To protect people from misleading claims and ineffective products, it will be critical for federal policy to be based on peer-reviewed, rigorous research examining the short- and long-term effects of well-designed cognitive training programs. As we have seen, such research indicates that getting these outcomes is both difficult and the result of complex sets of factors.

SUMMARY

7.1 Defining Intelligence

How Do People Define Intelligence In Everyday Life?
- Experts and laypeople agree intelligence consists of problem-solving ability, verbal ability, and social competence. Motivation, exertion of effort, and reading are important behaviors for people of all ages; however, some age-related behaviors are also apparent.

What are the major components of the life-span approach?
- The life-span view emphasizes there is some intellectual decline with age, primarily in the mechanics, but there is also stability and growth, primarily in the pragmatics. Four points are central. Plasticity concerns the range within one's abilities are modifiable. Multidimensionality concerns the many abilities that underlie intelligence. Multidirectionality concerns the many possible ways individuals may develop. Interindividual variability acknowledges people differ from each other.

What are the major research approaches for studying intelligence?
- Three main approaches are used to study intelligence. The psychometric approach focuses on performance on standardized tests. The cognitive-structural

approach emphasizes the quality and style of thought. The information-processing approach emphasis basic cognitive mechanisms.

7.2 Developmental Trends in Psychometric Intelligence

What is intelligence in adulthood?
- Intellectual abilities fall into various related abilities that form the structure of intelligence.
- Intelligence in adulthood focuses on how it operates in everyday life.

What are primary mental abilities and how do they change across adulthood?
- Primary abilities comprise the several independent abilities that form factors on standardized intelligence tests. The five that have been studied most are number, word fluency, verbal meaning, inductive reasoning, and spatial orientation.
- Primary mental abilities show normative declines with age that may affect performance in everyday life after around age 60, although declines tend to be small until the mid-70s. However, with individual differences, few people decline equally in all areas.

What are fluid and crystallized intelligence? How do they change?
- Fluid intelligence involves innate abilities that make people flexible and adaptive thinkers and underlie the acquisition of knowledge and experience. Fluid intelligence normally declines with age. Crystallized intelligence is knowledge acquired through life experience and education. Crystallized intelligence does not normally decline with age until late life. As age increases, individual differences remain stable with fluid intelligence but increase with crystallized intelligence.
- Age-related declines in fluid abilities have been shown to be moderated by cohort, education, social variables, personality, health, lifestyle, and task familiarity. Cohort effects and familiarity have been studied most. Cohort differences are complex and depend on the specific ability. Age differences in performance on familiar tasks are similar to those on standardized tests. Although taking both into account reduces age differences, they are not eliminated.
- Several studies show that fluid intelligence abilities improve after direct training and after anxiety reduction. Improvements in performance match or exceed individuals' level of decline. Training effects appear to last for several years regardless of the nature of the training, but generalization of training to new tasks is rare.

7.3 Qualitative Differences in Adults' Thinking

What are the main points in Piaget's theory of cognitive development?
- Key concepts in Piaget's theory include adaptation to the environment, organization of thought, and the structure of thought. The processes of thought are assimilation (using previously learned knowledge to make sense of incoming information) and accommodation (making the knowledge base conform to the environment). According to Piaget, thought develops through four stages: sensorimotor, preoperations, concrete operations, and formal operations.

What evidence is there for continued cognitive development beyond formal operations?
- Considerable evidence shows the style of thinking changes across adulthood. The development of reflective judgment in young adulthood occurs as a result of seven stages. Other research identified a progression from absolutist thinking to relativistic thinking to dialectical thinking. A key characteristic of postformal thought is the integration of emotion and logic. Much of this research is based on people's solutions to real-world problems. Although there have been suggestions that women's ways of knowing differ from men's, research evidence does not provide strong support for this view.

7.4 Everyday Reasoning and Problem Solving

What are the characteristics of older adults' decision making?
- Older adults make decisions in a qualitatively different way from younger adults. They tend to search for less information, require less information, and rely on preexisting knowledge structures in making everyday decisions. Older adults perform more poorly when asked to create or invent new decision rules, in unfamiliar situations, and when the decision task requires high cognitive load.

What age differences are found in practical problem solving?
- In Denney's model, both unexercised and optimally exercised abilities increase through early adulthood and slowly decline thereafter. Performance on practical problem solving increases through middle age. Research indicates sound measures of practical problem solving can be constructed, but these measures do not tend to relate to each other, indicating problem solving is multidimensional. The emotional

salience of problems is an important feature that influences problem-solving style with older adults performing better when problems involve interpersonal and emotional features.

What is the role of experience in expertise and problem solving?

- Older adults can often compensate for declines in some abilities by becoming experts that allows them to anticipate what is going to be required on a task. Knowledge encapsulation occurs with age, when the processes of thinking become connected with the products of thinking. Encapsulated knowledge cannot be decomposed and studied component by component.

What is wisdom and how does it relate to age and life experience?

- Wisdom involves four general characteristics: it deals with important matters of life; consists of superior knowledge, judgment, and advice; is knowledge of exceptional depth; and is well intentioned. Five specific behavioral criteria are used to judge wisdom: expertise, broad abilities, understanding how life problems change, fitting the response with the problem, and realizing life problems are often ambiguous. Wisdom also entails integrating thought and emotion to show empathy or compassion. Wisdom may be more strongly related to experience than age.

REVIEW QUESTIONS

7.1 Defining Intelligence

- How do laypeople and researchers define intelligence?
- What are the two main ways intelligence has been studied? Define each.

7.2 Developmental Trends in Psychometric Intelligence

- What are primary mental abilities? Which ones have been studied most? How do they change with age?
- Define fluid and crystallized intelligence. How does each change with age?
- What factors moderate age changes in fluid intelligence? What role does cohort play? What role do health and lifestyle play?
- What benefits do older people get from intervention programs aimed at improving fluid abilities? What training approaches have been used? How well do trained skills generalize?
- Are there any limitations on the extent that older adults can improve their cognitive performance?

7.3 Qualitative Differences in Adults' Thinking

- What are the key concepts in Piaget's theory?
- What stages of cognitive development did Piaget identify? Do adults use formal operations?

- What is reflective judgment? What are the stages in its development? What are absolutist, relativistic, and dialectical thinking?
- How do emotion and logic become integrated?
- What evidence is there for gender differences in postformal thinking?

7.4 Everyday Reasoning and Problem Solving

- How do older adults differ from younger adults in everyday decision making?
- What are unexercised and optimally exercised abilities? How do their developmental paths differ from each other?
- What are the developmental trends in solving practical problems? How does emotional salience of problems influence problem-solving style?
- What is an expert? How is expertise related to age?
- What is knowledge encapsulation?
- What criteria are used to define wisdom? How is wisdom related to age?

INTEGRATING CONCEPTS IN DEVELOPMENT

- How are the primary and secondary mental abilities related to the aspects of information processing considered in Chapters 6 and 7?
- What do you think an integrated theory linking postformal thinking, practical problem solving, expertise, and wisdom would look like?
- What aspects of secondary mental abilities do you think would be most closely linked to expertise? Why?
- How does effective social cognitive functioning considered in Chapter 9 relate to wisdom-related behaviors?

KEY TERMS

accommodation Changing one's thought to better approximate the world of experience.

assimilation Using currently available knowledge to make sense out of incoming information.

cognitive-structural approach An approach to intelligence that emphasizes the ways people conceptualize problems and focuses on modes or styles of thinking.

crystallized intelligence Knowledge acquired through life experience and education in a particular culture.

factor The interrelations among performances on similar tests of psychometric intelligence.

fluid intelligence Abilities that make one a flexible and adaptive thinker, that allow one to draw inferences, and allow one to understand the relations among concepts independent of acquired knowledge and experience.

interindividual variability An acknowledgment adults differ in the direction of their intellectual development.

mechanics of intelligence The aspect of intelligence that concerns the neurophysiological architecture of the mind.

multidimensional The notion intelligence consists of many dimensions.

multidirectionality The distinct patterns of change in abilities over the life span, with these patterns being different for different abilities.

neural efficiency hypothesis States intelligent people process information more efficiently, showing weaker neural activations in a smaller number of areas than less intelligent people.

optimally exercised ability The ability a normal, healthy adult would demonstrate under the best conditions of training or practice.

plasticity The range of functioning within an individual and the conditions under which a person's abilities can be modified within a specific age range.

postformal thought Thinking characterized by a recognition that truth varies across situations, solutions must be realistic to be reasonable, ambiguity and contradiction are the rule rather than the exception, and emotion and subjective factors play a role in thinking.

pragmatic intelligence The component of intelligence that concerns acquired bodies of knowledge available from and embedded within culture.

primary mental abilities Independent abilities within psychometric intelligence based on different combinations of standardized intelligence tests.

psychometric approach An approach to intelligence involving defining it as performance on standardized tests.

reflective judgment Thinking that involves how people reason through dilemmas involving current affairs, religion, science, and the like.

secondary mental abilities Broad-ranging skills composed of several primary mental abilities.

structure of intelligence The organization of interrelated intellectual abilities.

terminal decline The gradual decline in cognitive function that occurs relatively near death.

unexercised ability The ability a normal, healthy adult would exhibit without practice or training.

8 Social Cognition

CHAPTER OUTLINE

8.1 Stereotypes and Aging
Content of Stereotypes
Age Stereotypes and Perceived Competence
Activation of Stereotypes
Stereotype Threat

CURRENT CONTROVERSIES Are Stereotypes of Aging Associated with Lower Cognitive Performance?

8.2 Social Knowledge Structures and Beliefs
Understanding Age Differences in Social Beliefs
Self-Perception and Social Beliefs

HOW DO WE KNOW? Age Differences in Self-Perception

8.3 Social Judgment Processes
Emotional Intelligence
Impression Formation

REAL PEOPLE Impressions of Hillary Clinton and Donald Trump
Knowledge Accessibility and Social Judgments
A Processing Capacity Explanation for Age Differences in Social Judgments
Attributional Biases

8.4 Motivation and Social Processing Goals
Personal Goals
Emotion as a Processing Goal
Cognitive Style as a Processing Goal

8.5 Personal Control
Multidimensionality of Personal Control

DISCOVERING DEVELOPMENT How Much Control Do You Have over Your Cognitive Functioning?
Control Strategies
Some Criticisms Regarding Primary Control

8.6 Social Situations and Social Competence
Collaborative Cognition
Social Context of Memory

Social Policy Implications
Summary
Review Questions
Integrating Concepts in Development
Key Terms

When, on Thanksgiving Day 1993, a prominent Democrat married a prominent Republican, both of whom were the top consultants to the competing presidential candidates the previous year, people had difficulty making sense of it. Many thought the marriage of Mary Matalin (George H. W. Bush's political director) and James Carville (Bill Clinton's campaign strategist) was doomed because they were political "opposites." But the two of them did not. They saw their passion for politics as a core similarity, and, more than 25 years later, are still married and consulting for different political parties (you may have seen them on various news networks).

Marriages between seeming opposites are not rare, at least if you're considering political persuasion—about 30 percent of married couples are of "mixed" political party affiliation (Hersh & Ghitza, 2016). The public wonderment at the Matalin–Carville relationship, especially the longevity of their marriage, illustrates how people try to make sense of other people's behavior. Just as James and Mary are viewed through the stereotypes of political affiliation—incorrectly as it relates to their marriage—all of us use social cognition as a way to make sense of the people and the world around us.

In this chapter, we consider how the social context is involved in our cognitive processes. We take a closer look at how our basic cognitive abilities influence our social cognitive processing. We examine how our past experiences and beliefs influence our social judgment processes such as how people make impressions and explain behavior (causal attributions). Finally, we examine four aspects of social cognition: the role of motivation and emotion as processing goals, the way stereotypes affect how we judge older adults' behavior, the amount of personal control people feel they have, and how cognition is affected when we communicate with others in a social context.

First we need to highlight the importance of social-contextual aspects of cognition in terms of stereotypes. We are confronted with images of older adults all the time through cartoons, advertisements for medical products, jokes on greeting cards, and art. Many of these images are negative (e.g., older adults are terribly forgetful, slow, and easily confused) but some are positive (e.g., older adults are wise). The impact of these stereotypes on our lives is more pervasive than you may think. We'll explore some of these influences.

Additionally, social cognition research raised some important issues for aging research such as how our life experiences and emotions, as well as changes in our pragmatic knowledge, social expertise, and values, influence how we think and remember. To address these issues, we must consider both the basic cognitive architecture of the aging adult (identified in Chapters 6 and 7) and the functional architecture of everyday cognition (discussed in Chapter 7). Even if basic cognitive mechanisms decline (such as episodic memory recall or speed of processing) older adults still have the social knowledge and skills that allow them to function effectively. In fact, by taking into consideration social and emotional factors, researchers find older adults' cognitive functioning often remains intact and may even improve across the life span (Blanchard-Fields, Horhota, & Mienaltowski, 2008; see Chapters 6 and 7). This approach reinforces the perspective of this textbook that views effective development as a lifelong adaptive process. ■

James Carville and Mary Matalin

8.1 Stereotypes and Aging

LEARNING OBJECTIVES
- How does the content of stereotypes about aging differ across adulthood?
- How do younger and older adults perceive the competence of the elderly?
- How do stereotypes about aging unconsciously guide our behavior?

Mark, a 70-year-old man, was getting ready to go home from a poker game at his friend's house. However, he could not find his keys. Down the street, Guy, a 20-year-old college student, was ready to pick up his girlfriend and he could not find his keys. Each of their respective friends at the two social events had different perceptions of Mark and Guy. Mark's friends started to worry whether Mark was becoming senile, speculating it might be all downhill from now on. They wondered whether this was serious enough to call the doctor. However, Guy's friends attributed his forgetfulness to being busy, under a lot of stress, and nervous about his upcoming date.

What accounts for these different explanations of losing one's keys for Mark and Guy? An explanation for the attributions Mark's friends made involves the negative stereotype of aging that older adults are slow-thinking and incompetent. Negative stereotypes of aging are extremely pervasive throughout our culture. Just peruse your local greeting card store and you will find humorous birthday cards capitalizing on our negative expectations about aging. Jokes abound about the older adult who keeps losing his or her memory. This captures all our negative stereotypes about memory and aging.

In contrast, the same behavior in a young adult holds very different meaning for most people; stress, preoccupation, lack of attention, and other explanations are used. Rarely is the cause attributed to a young adult's declining cognitive ability.

Fortunately, positive expectations about aging coexist with the negative ones, and stereotypes can be changed (Chonody, 2015; Wurtele & Maruyama, 2013). Older adults are subjected to conflicting stereotypes. On the one hand, older adults are seen as grouchy, forgetful, and losing physical stamina and sexual abilities. On the other hand, older adults are seen as wise, generous, and responsible. The important question researchers ask is what effect stereotypes have on our social judgments and our behavior toward others, such as those in Mark's situation.

Content of Stereotypes

Stereotypes *are a special type of social knowledge structure or social belief. They represent socially shared beliefs about characteristics and behaviors of a particular social group.* We all have stereotypes of groups of people and beliefs about how they will act in certain situations, such as "Older adults are more rigid in their point of view" or "Older adults talk on and on about their past."

These beliefs affect how we interpret new information. In other words, we use stereotypes to help us process information when engaged in social interactions. Just as with the literature on impression formation discussed earlier, we use stereotypes to size up people when we first meet them. This categorizing helps us understand why they behave the way they do and guides us in our behavior toward other people. Remember, stereotypes are not inherently negative in their effect. However, too often they are applied in ways that underestimate the potential of the person we are observing. This becomes more evident as we explore age-related stereotypes.

Much research has examined adult developmental changes in the content and structure of stereotypes, particularly when emerging adults are given the opportunity to actually interact with older adults (e.g., Hayslip et al., 2013; Obhi & Woodhead, 2016). From a developmental perspective, a key question is whether changes in the nature and strength of our stereotypes as we grow older are typical, or must rely on intentional intervention. Overall, the consensus is growing that adults of all ages have access to and use multiple stereotypes of older adults and that specific interventions are often necessary to change them (Truxillo et al., 2012; Truxillo, Cadiz, & Hammer, 2015).

There are also age differences in how people perceive older adults and in the complexity of age stereotype beliefs. For example, the ability to estimate the age of someone by seeing their face decreases with age, but older adults are better with their age group than are younger adults at judging older faces (Voelkle et al., 2012). Other studies show older adults identify more subcategories that fit under the superordinate category "older adult" than do younger and middle-aged adults (Hayslip et al., 2013). Overall, these findings suggest as we grow older, our ideas and age stereotypes become more elaborate and rich as we integrate our life experiences into our beliefs about aging (Baltes et al., 2006; O'Brien & Hummert, 2006).

Beyond the complexity of stereotypes, are there age differences in how negatively or positively people view older adults? Research indicates older adults in general have a more positive view of aging in comparison to younger adults (Wentura & Brandtstädter, 2003), a finding that holds cross-culturally, such as in Brazil (de Paula Couto & Koller, 2012).

But what if people believe the negative stereotypes and incorporate them into their personal belief structures about themselves? The outcomes are clear, and definitely not good. Much research indicates that believing negative stereotypes about age is a direct threat to cognitive performance and physical well-being, and may exacerbate actual deterioration of key brain structures such as the hippocampus (Levy et al., 2016; Nelson, 2016). Specifically, believing aging stereotypes to be true reduces the will to live, impairs memory, reduces health promotion behaviors, lengthens the time it takes to recover from illness, increases cardiovascular reactivity to stress, and decreases longevity. Clearly, much work needs to be done to fight stereotypes and help individuals from believing them.

Age Stereotypes and Perceived Competence

Stereotypes are not simply reflected in our perceptions of what we think are the general representative personality traits or characteristics of older adults. We also make appraisals or attributions of older adults' competence when we observe them perform tasks, and we assess whether we can count on them to perform important tasks. No area is more susceptible to negative stereotyped attributions of aging than memory competence, as the vignette at the beginning of the section shows. As we discussed in Chapter 6, people of all ages believe memory declines with age and we have less and less control over current and future memory functioning as we grow older.

The interesting question is, how does this strong belief in age-related loss of memory affect our attributions (explanations) about older adults' competencies? In an elegant and classic series of studies, Joan Erber (e.g., Erber & Prager, 1999) found an age-based double standard in judging the competence of old versus young adults. *The* **age-based double standard** *is operating when an individual attributes an older person's failure in memory as more serious than a memory failure observed in a young adult.* So if an older woman cannot find her keys, this is seen as a much more serious memory problem (e.g., possibly attributed to senility) than if a younger woman cannot find her keys. The age-based double standard is most evident when younger people are judging the memory failure.

In contrast, when older people observe the same memory failure, they tend to judge both young and old targets of the story more equally. In fact, most of the time older adults are more lenient toward memory failures in older adults. However, in other types of competence judgments, older adults also display the age-based double standard. When assessing the *cause* of a memory failure, both younger and older people felt the failure was due to greater mental difficulty in the case of an older adult, whereas for younger adults participants attributed it to a lack of effort or attention (Erber, Szuchman, & Rothberg, 1990).

The research on the age-based double standard parallels work examining other aspects of aging stereotypes focused on competence. For example, considerable research indicates that older adults are stereotyped as warm and incompetent, based on perceptions of them as noncompetitive and low status (Cuddy, Norton, & Fiske, 2005). Such stereotypes are found across a wide range of cultures, and reflect consistently held views that older adults are incompetent. When put into practice in societies, these views result in a general social exclusion of older adults (Cuddy et al., 2005; Fiske & Taylor, 2013; Levy & Macdonald, 2016).

The widely held stereotypes of older adults as incompetent do not reflect the reality of a much more complicated picture, as we saw in Chapters 6 and 7. The social marginalization and the very serious individual effects that result from believing negative stereotypes have major consequences for societies that are aging, which nearly all economically developed and many emerging countries are (Levy & Macdonald, 2016; Nelson, 2016). We will revisit these negative outcomes in Chapter 14 when we explore broader societal issues; for now, we will focus more on how stereotypes operate in various ways.

Activation of Stereotypes

From the preceding review of research we know stereotypes of older adults exist regarding personality traits and perceptions of competence. They also influence our judgments about how capable older adults will be in memory-demanding situations. However, it is not enough to know the stereotypes exist; we need to know under what conditions they are activated, and if activated, how they affect our behavior and social judgments. How do negative stereotypes of older adults influence our behaviors (e.g., talking down to older adults as if they were children) and attitudes (Hehman, Corpuz, & Bugental, 2012)? Considerable research in social cognition focuses on stereotype activation as a relatively unconscious and automatic process that guides our behavior and social judgments in a wide variety of settings (e.g., Kunda & Spencer, 2003; Loe, Sherry, & Chartier, 2016).

Social psychologists suggest the reason stereotypes are automatically activated is they become overlearned and thus are spontaneously activated when we encounter a member or members of a stereotyped group, such as African Americans or Muslims (Proctor, 2016; Stojnov, 2013). *The activation of strong stereotypes, called* **implicit stereotyping**, *is not only automatic but also unconscious.* Thus they usually influence our behavior without our being aware of it.

The effects of such implicit stereotyping are illustrated in a clever and classic study conducted by John Bargh and colleagues (Bargh, Chen, & Burrows, 1996). They demonstrated if you subliminally (outside of conscious awareness) prime young people with the image of an elderly person, the young people's actual behavior is influenced in an age-related manner (where *age-related* refers to the target person's age). In this case, the implicitly primed young adults walked down the hall more slowly after the experiment than did young adults who were not primed with the elderly image. This is a powerful demonstration of how our unconscious stereotypes of aging can influence our behavior.

Measuring implicit aging stereotyping is a challenge because by definition it is inaccessible. However, research using a technique called the Implicit Association Test (IAT; Crisp & Turner, 2012; Hummert et al., 2002; Teiga-Mocigemba, Klauer, & Sherman, 2010) overcame this challenge. Let's consider how the IAT works when applied to aging (e.g., Crisp & Turner, 2012). Individuals are asked to categorize photographs of faces by indicating as fast as they can whether the photo is a younger or older person. They are asked to press a button with their right hand to indicate young and with their left hand to indicate old. Then they categorize other photographs as pleasant or unpleasant with the right hand indicating pleasant and the left hand indicating unpleasant. Next is the two-part test of implicit aging stereotypes. Part one consists of a combination of the young-old and pleasant-unpleasant categorization task using the same hands as just indicated. In this test, the right hand is associated with both young and pleasant, whereas the left hand is associated with both old and unpleasant. The second part reverses the hands for young-old. Now the right hand is associated with old and the left hand is associated with young. The right hand is still associated with pleasant, and the left hand with unpleasant. The logic is this: If you have a negative implicit stereotype regarding aging, you will be much slower in your response during the second test. It becomes difficult to use your right hand to indicate old because it is also associated with pleasant. This difficulty slows your response down.

Using this methodology, researchers (e.g., Crisp & Turner, 2012; Hummert et al., 2002) found people of all ages were faster to respond to young-pleasant and old-unpleasant trials than to old-pleasant and young-unpleasant trials. Furthermore, all individuals had implicit age attitudes that strongly favored the young over the old.

Based on these and related results, Crisp and Turner (2009) created an intervention strategy to help people change their implicit stereotypes—the imagined intergroup contact. The strategy is deceptively simple: imagine yourself having a positive interaction with a member

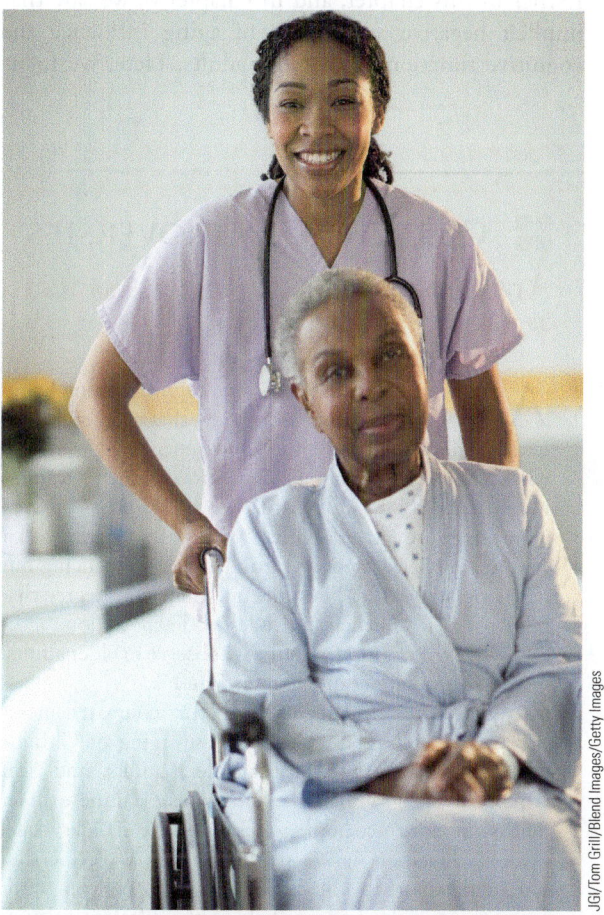

Implicit stereotyping of people, such as of older adults, can have a profound effect on people's behavior.

of a group about whom you hold negative stereotypes. There's more to it in actual practice, but essentially it is a focused, guided imagination strategy. Does it work?

A meta-analysis of the research using the imagined intergroup contact strategy focused on four indicators: attitudes, emotions, intentions, and behaviors (Miles & Crisp, 2014). The results showed significantly reduced bias across all four indicators. Two other findings were interesting: the more participants were asked to elaborate on the context in which their imagined interaction took place, the stronger the results, and the effects overall were greater for children than for adults. The findings show clearly that even though we are unaware of them, implicit stereotypes can be changed if we see ourselves having different kinds of interactions with the target groups, though the elder we get, the more work this takes.

Stereotype Threat

Earlier in this chapter, and in Chapter 6, we saw that implicit negative stereotypes of aging influence the cognitive functioning of older adults. Here, we focus on the process by which this works: stereotype threat. **Stereotype threat** *is an evoked fear of being judged in accordance with a negative stereotype about a group to which you belong*. For example, if you are a member of a socially stigmatized group such as Latinos or Muslims, you are vulnerable to cues in your environment that activate stereotype threat about academic ability. In turn, you may perform more poorly on a task associated with that stereotype regardless of high competence in academic settings.

Substantial attention has focused on understanding the harmful effects of negative aging stereotypes on memory performance in older adults (Levy et al., 2012, 2016). Does that mean that older adults belong to a stigmatized group that is vulnerable to stereotype threat? Data indicate that the answer is yes (also see Chapter 6). The studies examining stereotype threat used techniques similar to those used in stereotype activation: assessing implicit stereotyping. Becca Levy's nearly two decades of research has caused some controversy in this area. Read the Current Controversies feature. What do you think?

CURRENT CONTROVERSIES

Are Stereotypes of Aging Associated with Lower Cognitive Performance?

A major controversial issue in the cognitive aging literature is whether living in a society that equates old age with memory decline, senility, and dependency produces what Langer (1989) calls a "premature cognitive commitment" early in life. As children, we acquire ideas of what it means to be old, ideas that are usually negative, that become implicit stereotypes guiding and influencing our behavior later in life. Thus, the question is the degree that negative societal beliefs, attitudes, and expectations actually create the cognitive decline we observe in older adults, which we read about in Chapters 6 and 7.

When Levy and Langer (1994) first compared memory performance and attitudes about aging of Chinese older adults, hearing American older adults, and deaf American older adults, they found the Chinese older adults outperformed both groups of American older adults on several memory tasks. In addition, the deaf American older adults outperformed their hearing American counterparts. Attitudes on aging held by the different cultures were related to memory performance (Chinese had more positive attitudes, whereas Americans had more negative attitudes). Levy and Langer concluded negative stereotypes in American culture accounted for this difference.

However, there were several concerns with this correlational study. Does enhanced memory performance lead to more positive attitudes, or do positive attitudes lead to enhanced memory performance? Are there educational differences between the two cultural groups? Are the memory tests really the same given that they had to be translated into Chinese?

To further test this notion, Levy (1996) subliminally primed younger and older adults with negative stereotypes of an older adult (e.g., the word *senile*) or positive stereotypes (e.g., the word *wise*). She found when older adults were primed with negative aging stereotypes, their performance was worse on memory tests than older adults primed with positive stereotypes. Other researchers consistently confirmed this result (e.g., Bouazzaoui et al., 2016; Stein, Blanchard-Fields, & Hertzog, 2002; von Hippel & Henry, 2012).

Levy's most important and controversial finding goes well beyond results from laboratory task results in a one-time testing experience. She and her colleagues (Levy et al., 2012; see also Levy et al., 2016) showed adults over age 60 with more negative age stereotypes demonstrated over 30% greater decline in memory performance over 38 years than those with fewer negative age stereotypes.

It is intriguing and intuitive to believe a self-fulfilling prophecy operates with respect to older adults' memory performance. If society portrays older adults as declining in cognitive capacity and you are socialized to believe so at a young age, and if you believe these stereotypes, then it makes sense this will influence your memory performance as an older adult. Related evidence shows clearly that holding such stereotypes does have very serious negative effects on health, brain structures, and other aspects of behavior, as noted earlier in this chapter.

All in all, negative stereotypes of aging exist. They have an effect on cognitive performance. Thus, although you may not be able to eliminate the decline in performance, interventions for improving attitudes and outlook on aging have the potential to improve the quality of performance relative to one's own level of functioning (Calamia et al., 2016; Cherry et al., 2013, 2014).

There is also evidence middle-aged adults are susceptible to negative age stereotypes (O'Brien & Hummert, 2006; Weiss, in press). Middle-aged adults who identified with older adulthood showed poorer memory performance if they were told their performance would be compared with other older adults. Middle-aged adults with more youthful identities did not show differences in memory performance regardless of whether they were told they would be compared to younger or older individuals. Additionally, people who believe that aging is fixed and inevitable show poorer memory performance.

Although most of the research in this area focused on the detrimental effects of negative stereotypes, some evidence also exists for the beneficial effects of positive stereotypes on older adults' cognitive performance. Compared to Italians who live in Milan, those who live on Sardinia hold more positive attitudes about memory aging and perform better on memory tasks (Cavallini et al., 2013). Positive aging stereotypes are also good for your health and social life. Several studies have found better health indicators in those with positive views (e.g., Ayalon, 2016; Levy, Slade, & Kasl, 2002; Nelson, 2016). Positive views are also related to having more new friends later in life (Menkin et al., in press).

The preponderance of research evidence clearly indicates that what you believe is true about aging has very important consequences for what you actually experience. Believing that aging is inevitable and pretty much all decline results in decrements in cognitive performance, health, and social interactions. Believing that aging involves positive changes results in just the opposite, or at least a decrease in the speed and amount of decline. Which way you go is up to you.

Adult Development in Action

How would knowledge about the effects of negative stereotypes on older adult's cognition affect your approach to assessing them in a healthcare setting?

8.2 Social Knowledge Structures and Beliefs

LEARNING OBJECTIVES

- What are social knowledge structures?
- What are social beliefs, and how do they change with age?
- What are self-perceptions of aging, and what influences them across adulthood?

Anna is going on her first date since the death of her husband one year ago. She is 62 years old and was married for 30 years, so she is extremely nervous about what to do and how to act. When she meets her date, Eric, at a nice Italian restaurant, he asks if afterward they could go to a late movie. Although Anna is nervous, she makes it through the date with few problems. To her delight, how she needs to act and what she should do came back to her without an ounce of effort.

Anna found out firsthand that a well-learned social script or social knowledge, such as how to behave on a date, remains easily accessible even though it may not have been actively invoked in many years. These experiences have been likened to riding a bicycle—once you learn, you never really forget. It's this uncanny ability to remember social scripts and how they drive behavior that greatly interests social cognitive researchers.

Social knowledge structures and social beliefs are defined in terms of how we represent and interpret the behavior of others in a social situation (Frith & Frith, 2012; Molenberghs et al., 2016). They come in many different forms. We have scripted knowledge structures regarding everyday activities such as what people should do when they go to a physician's office or a restaurant. We are socialized to adhere to and believe in social rules, or how to behave in specific social situations, such as how a husband should act toward his partner.

Understanding Age Differences in Social Beliefs

Two interesting developmental questions arise with respect to social knowledge structures. First, does the content of our social knowledge and beliefs change as we grow older? And second, do our knowledge structures and beliefs affect our social judgments, memory, problem solving, and more like stereotypes do?

There are many types of belief systems that differ in content across age groups and also influence behavior. Understanding age differences in social belief systems has three important aspects (Blanchard-Fields & Hertzog, 2000; Blanchard-Fields et al., 2012; Blanchard-Fields & Horhota, 2006). First, we examine the specific content of social beliefs (i.e., the particular beliefs and knowledge individuals hold about rules, norms, and patterns of social behavior). Second, we consider the strength of these beliefs to know under what conditions they may influence behavior. Third, we need to know the likelihood these beliefs are automatically activated when a person is confronted with a situation when these beliefs are being violated or questioned. If these three aspects of the belief system are understood, it is possible to explain when and why age differences occur in social judgments.

Older adults may hold different beliefs than other age groups (e.g., different rules for appropriate social behavior). Such differences usually stem from cohort differences (see Chapter 1). For instance, Anna's beliefs about appropriate behavior on a date may differ from her granddaughter's. How strongly individuals hold these beliefs may vary as a function of how particular generations were socialized. Although some younger and older generations may both believe people should not live together before marriage, the oldest generation may be more adamant and rigid about this belief. However, evidence of age differences in the content of social beliefs does not provide a sufficient basis for understanding age differences in how and when such beliefs are activated and how they influence behavior.

Social cognition researchers argue there are individual differences in the strength of social representations of rules, beliefs, and attitudes linked to specific situations (Frith & Frith, 2012). Such representations can be both cognitive (how we conceptualize the situation) and emotional (how we react to the situation). When encountering a specific situation, the individual's belief system predictably triggers an emotional reaction and related goals tied to the content of that situation. This in turn drives social judgments.

Let's take the rule "You should never live with a romantic partner before you are married." If you were socialized from childhood to believe in this rule, you would negatively evaluate anyone violating it. If you were told Allen was putting pressure on Joan to live with him before they were married, and they subsequently broke up, you might have a negative emotional response and blame Allen for the breakup of the relationship because he was lobbying for cohabitation.

In a series of classic studies exploring social beliefs, age differences were found in the types of social rules related to marriage evoked in different types of situations (Blanchard-Fields, 1996, 1999). In the present context, these findings indicate the influence of cohort effects on how different generations were socialized with respect to important social rules, such as in marriage. The oldest generation was socialized differently from the current younger adult generation as to what is appropriate behavior.

In summary, how social rules are invoked in making social judgments is a complex process. To some extent, the process reflects generational differences, and it reflects life experience. How these judgments influence our judgments about personal responsibility for behavior is a topic we turn to next.

Self-Perception and Social Beliefs

An important facet for understanding the impact of social beliefs on people is to understand how we form impressions of ourselves. It's our personal answer to the question, "How old do you feel?" that creates our self-perception of aging. **Self-perception of aging** refers to *individuals' perceptions of their own age and aging.*

Researchers have been curious about how people see themselves on this dimension for many years. In Chapter 14, how we view ourselves is an important predictor of whether we age successfully (or not). We have already seen that holding positive views, or self-perceptions, are

How Do We Know?
Age Differences in Self-Perception

Who were the investigators and what was the aim of the study? Kotter-Grühn and Hess (2012) knew people's self-perceptions are important predictors of well-being and health. They wanted to find out what the specific indicators of self-perceptions of aging across adulthood are, and whether specific stereotypes about aging influenced self-perceptions.

How did the investigators measure the topic of interest? Personal satisfaction with aging was measured through a well-researched scale, the Philadelphia Geriatric Center Morale Scale. Respondents also indicated their "felt age," "desired age," and "perceived age." Physical health was assessed by a health survey. Age-related stereotypes were activated through a priming approach of rating faces described with either positive, negative, or neutral terms.

Who were the participants in the study? 183 adults aged 18–92 years volunteered to participate. There were 60 younger adults, 62 middle-aged adults, and 61 older adults. Overall, participants averaged over 14 years of education, and were paid $15/hour.

Were there ethical concerns with the study? Because the study used volunteers and were provided informed consent, there were no ethical concerns.

What were the results? As participant age increased, participants increasingly indicated they felt, wanted to be, and believed they looked proportionally younger than their actual age. Younger adults wanted to be about 4% older than they actually were, and older adults wanted to be about 33% younger than they were.

Following the priming task, older adults were the only age group to feel older regardless of whether the priming was positive or negative. For desired age, participants in all age groups who were in bad health reported they wanted to be a younger age after experiencing the negative priming task (but no change otherwise). For perceived age, all participants in poor health reported themselves as looking older after receiving the negative priming task.

All adults reported being relatively satisfied with their aging process.

What did the investigators conclude? Kotter-Grühn and Hess concluded that people's perceptions of their own aging are not made more positive by presenting them with positive images of aging. Actually, the opposite effect occurred for younger and middle-aged adults in good health—when given positive stereotypes, those groups reported feeling *older* than before the priming task. Their conclusion was negative images of aging have more powerful effects than positive ones in determining self-perceptions of aging.

---

correlated with many good outcomes, such as better well-being, better health, and longer life (Nelson, 2016).

There are two major frameworks to explain how this influence works. **Labeling theory** *argues when we confront an age-related stereotype, older adults are more likely to integrate it into their self-perception.* Research on impression formation and priming of stereotypes supports this view. **Resilience theory** *argues confronting a negative stereotype results in a rejection of that view in favor of a more positive self-perception.* This view comes from people's tendency to want to distance themselves from the negative stereotype. Research shows older adults dissociate themselves from their age group when negative stereotypes become relevant to them (e.g., Weiss, in press; Weiss & Lang, 2012; Weiss et al., 2016).

A good example of this line of research is highlighted in the How Do We Know? feature. Kotter-Grühn and Hess (2012) studied how negative views of aging were or were not assimilated into adults' views of themselves. Read the feature and discover how this process works.

What's so different about self-perceptions of age and aging is it is one of the few areas we go from looking at old people and aging as something that happens to someone else rather than something happening to us (Kornadt & Rothermund, 2012; Kornadt et al., in press). Research on how we incorporate societal views of age and aging indicate the extent to which that happens depends critically on our own old age and aging in specific domains of life (e.g., health).

Adult Development in Action

If you are a taking a poll on attitudes toward specific social issues, how would you design the survey to uncover the reasons for any age differences that were found?

8.3 Social Judgment Processes

LEARNING OBJECTIVES

- What is emotional intelligence and how does it development across adulthood?
- What is the negativity bias in impression formation, and how does it influence older adults' thinking?
- Are there age differences in accessibility of social information?
- How does processing context influence social judgments?
- To what extent do processing capacity limitations influence social judgments in older adults?

Alexandra and Klaus were taking care of their grandchildren for the weekend. They took them to the zoo for an outing. When they passed the gift shop, the children would not stop whining that they wanted a present. This frustrated Alexandra and Klaus, and they both tried to come up with an explanation for this distressing behavior. At first, they were worried because it seemed the behavior of their grandchildren indicated they were, in essence, selfish children. But on further reflection, they considered other factors. The parents always bought the children a gift at the zoo, and so the children naturally expected it to happen again. The grandparents felt better about the situation after considering the parents' role in it and bought the gifts for the children.

In this situation, Alexandra and Klaus were making important social judgments. They carefully analyzed the situation to understand their grandchildren's behavior by focusing on all the factors involved in it. Alexandra and Klaus show how we can correct our initial assessments of others if we take the time to reflect about all of the extenuating circumstances.

But what would have happened if they did not have the time to think about it, and instead had multiple distractions, such as dealing with the emotional outbursts of their grandchildren as well as their own emotional reactions? Their judgments could also have been influenced by strong beliefs about how children should behave in a social situation such as this one.

We consider the influence of both of these factors on making social judgments: the role played by cognitive capacity, or having enough time and making the effort to reflect on a situation, and social knowledge and beliefs. However, first let us explore emotional intelligence and how it develops.

Emotional Intelligence

The social cognition perspective provides a way of examining how basic cognitive abilities operate in social situations. The basic goal of the social cognition approach is to understand how people make sense of themselves, others, and events in everyday life (Fiske & Taylor, 2013; Frith & Frith, 2012; Kornadt et al., in press; Weiss, in press).

A key ability in social contexts is *emotional intelligence* (Goleman, 1995; Salovey & Mayer, 1990). **Emotional intelligence (EI)** *refers to people's ability to recognize their own and others' emotions, to correctly identify and appropriately tell the difference between emotions, and use this information to guide their thinking and behavior.* Emotional intelligence consists of two aspects. First, EI can be viewed as a trait that reflects a person's self-perceived dispositions and abilities. Second, EI can be viewed as an ability that reflects the person's success at processing emotional information and using it appropriately in social contexts. EI has been applied to a wide variety of situations, from everyday social cognition and problem solving to bullying to business to leadership. Although still controversial (Hunt & Fitzgerald, 2013, 2014), EI has been mapped onto brain structures (Barbey, Colom, & Grafman, 2014; Operskalski et al., 2015).

Research indicates that emotional intelligence increases with age (Chen, Peng, & Fang, 2016; Mankus, Boden, & Thompson, 2016), though there is some evidence that the specific ability to perceive others' emotions in the work context declines late in life (Doerwald et al., 2016). An important finding is that older adults' increased emotional intelligence may be a source of their higher subjective well-being (Chen et al., 2016).

EI may well be an underlying factor in the social cognitive situations we will now consider. Keep in mind that variations in a person's ability to sort out the emotional information available in any given social situation may play an important role in how they behave.

Impression Formation

When people meet each other, we tend to immediately come to conclusions about them on many dimensions. Researchers (e.g., Adams et al., 2012; Kotter-Grühn, 2016; Leshikar, Cassidy, & Gutchess, 2016) examine age differences in social judgments by examining impression formation. **Impression formation** *is the way we form and revise first impressions about others.* Researchers examine how people use diagnostic trait

Real People
Impressions of Hillary Clinton and Donald Trump

Managing the impressions people have of political candidates is extremely important for their respective campaigns. The U.S. presidential election of 2016 posed unique challenges on this front for several reasons.

Hillary Clinton

The two major party candidates established several "firsts." Hillary Rodham Clinton was the first woman nominee of any major political party for the presidency. She was also the first spouse of a former U.S. president to gain the nomination. Donald J. Trump was the first person who had not held any elected or appointed public office nor served in the military to be nominated, and was the first businessman to go straight from business to the nomination. He was also the first reality-TV star to be nominated.

Donald Trump

Additional challenges to impression formation and management came from both candidates' extremely high unfavorable ratings in national polls—over 60% of the people polled held unfavorable opinions of them.

Observers of the election could easily see the effects of impression formation processes in how voters talked about each candidate. Given that both Clinton and Trump had been public figures for decades, the first impressions people formed years earlier became very hard to change.

With hindsight, and with your knowledge of impression formation, how would you have advised the Clinton and Trump campaigns?

---

information (aspects about people that appear critical or unique) in making initial impressions of an individual, and how this process varies with age.

A common way of studying impression formation is to have two groups of adults presented with information about a person, either through descriptions or inferences. One group gets positive information first, such as evidence of honesty. The other group is presented with negative information first, such as incidents of dishonest behavior. Each group then subsequently gets the opposite information about the person (e.g., the group that got positive information first then gets negative information).

What happens to people's first impressions as a function of age is a well-established finding. As you can see from Figure 8.1, in a study that helped create this area of research focus, Hess and Pullen (1994) found all study participants modified their impressions. When new negative information was presented after the initial positive portrayal of the target person, older adults modified their impression of the target from positive to negative. Interestingly, however, they modified their first impression *less* when the negative portrayal was followed by positive information. Older adults make impressions influenced by all the information they receive.

In contrast, younger adults did not show this pattern. Instead, they were more concerned with making sure the new information was consistent with their initial impressions. To do so, they modified their impressions to correspond with the new information regardless of whether it was positive or negative. Younger adults, then, make their impression based on the most recent information they have.

Why do younger and older adults differ? Hess and Pullen suggest older adults may rely more on life experiences and social rules of behavior when making their interpretations, whereas younger adults may be more concerned with situational consistency of the new information presented. They also suggest older adults may be more subject to a negativity bias in impression formation. **Negativity bias** *occurs when people allow their initial negative impressions to stand despite subsequent positive information because negative information was more striking to them and thus affected them more strongly.*

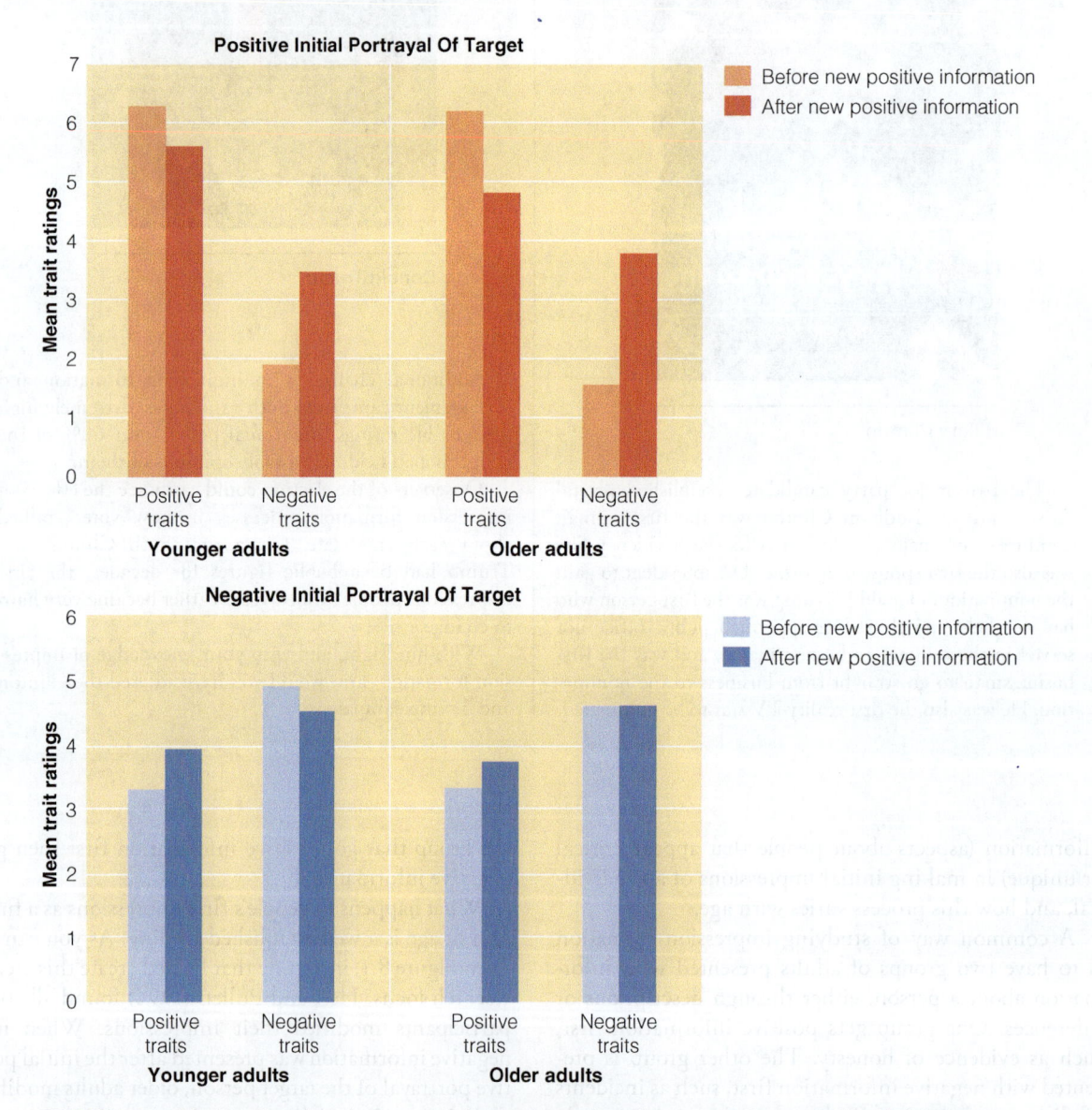

FIGURE 8.1 Mean trait ratings before and after presentation of new negative or positive information.
Source: A modified graph of the Hess, T. M., & Pullen, S. M. (1994). Adult age differences in impression change processes. *Psychology and Aging, 9,* p. 239.

This bias corresponds well with other studies demonstrating older adults pay attention to and seek out emotional information more than younger people do (Isaacowitz & Blanchard-Fields, 2012; Kalokerinos, von Hippel, & Henry, 2015). We discuss this further later in the chapter. This bias suggests decline in cognitive functioning limits the ability of older adults to override the impact of their initial impressions, a result supported by neuroimaging research (Leshikar et al., 2016).

Further evidence shows the social judgments older adults make appear to be more sensitive to the diagnosticity of the available information (Hess, 2006). If young adults receive new information about a person that contradicts their original impression, they are likely to adjust the initial impression. However, older adults are more selective in the information they choose to use in forming their judgments. They focus more on the relevant details to make those judgments, and change their initial impression only if the new information is *diagnostic*, that is, relevant and informative (Hess & Emery, 2012; Hess et al., 2005). It appears for older adults to invest information-processing resources in making a judgment, they need to be invested in the social situation that the judgment is made.

In some situations, older adults may be at a disadvantage when processing social information. Researchers have found although younger and older adults can process social information similarly, older adults are at a disadvantage when the social context is cognitively demanding (Hess & Emery, 2012; Kalokerinos et al., 2015). A cognitively demanding situation is similar to Alexandra and Klaus's situation in which they were trying to understand their grandchildren's behavior under conditions of time pressure and multiple distractions. Researchers find when older adults take their time to make a social judgment, they process information similarly to younger adults and take into consideration all of the relevant information. However, when given a time limit, they have difficulty remembering the information they need to make their social judgments (Coats & Blanchard-Fields, 2013; Ybarra & Park, 2002; Ybarra et al., 2011).

In the next section, we examine processes involved in accessing knowledge used to make social judgments.

Knowledge Accessibility and Social Judgments

Although we make judgments about people upon initial meeting and novel situations all the time, we tend not to be aware of exactly how those judgments are made.

When we are faced with new situations, we draw on our previous experiences stored in memory, in other words, our **social knowledge**.

The stored knowledge about previous situations that might be similar and how easily we can retrieve it, affects what types of social judgments we make and how we behave in social situations. If you are arriving on your first day of work, for example, in order to act appropriately you draw on social knowledge that tells you "how to behave in a job setting." This process includes having available stored representations of the social world or memories of past events, how to apply those memories to various situations, and easy access to the memories.

We draw on implicit theories of personality (our personal theories of how personality works) to make judgments. For example, how a supervisor should behave at work. If the supervisor's behavior is inconsistent with our implicit theory of how he or she should act, this affects the impression we form of the supervisor. If a supervisor dresses in shorts and a torn T-shirt and makes not-so-casual references about the wild party he attended last night at which everyone became highly intoxicated, this may violate our implicit theory that supervisors should dress and act professionally. Research supports that implicit personality theories we have about people, in general, influence the impressions we form about specific individuals (Kalokerinos et al., 2015; Uleman & Kressel, 2013; Uleman & Saribay, 2012).

However, the fact social information in memory is available does not necessarily imply it is always easy to access. The degree to which information in memory is easily accessible and remembered (see Chapter 6) determines the extent that information will guide social judgments and/or behavior. Easy access to information will be influenced by several variables. First, accessibility depends on the strength of the information stored in memory. If you have extensive past experience with people who are aggressive, retrieving and applying the specific personality trait "aggressive," will be a highly accessible social knowledge structure representing features of this particular personality trait (e.g., dominance in social situations, highly competitive, and so on). Thus, you would judge a person as "aggressive" by interpreting the collection of behaviors you associate with "aggressive" as clearly diagnostic of aggressiveness.

In contrast, the personality trait construct "aggressive" would not be easily accessible for people who have little or no experience with aggressive people because the trait of aggressiveness may not have been retrieved often. These people would be likely to interpret the behavior differently (Uleman & Kressel, 2013; Uleman & Saribay, 2012). They may see the dominant or aggressive behavior a person exhibits as indicative of positive leadership.

Age differences in the accessibility of social knowledge influence social judgments across adulthood. First, as we saw in the case of impression formation, older adults rely on easily accessible social knowledge structures such as the initial impression made about an individual. Second, *age differences in knowledge accessibility also depend on the extent people rely on* **source judgments**, *in other words, when they try to determine the source of a particular piece of information.* Suppose you and a friend were introduced to two new people last week. Jane is an athlete and Sereatha is a bookworm. Sereatha revealed to you she loves to play tennis. Today, your friend asks you whether it was Jane or Sereatha that loves to play tennis. This is a source judgment.

Mather and colleagues (Barber et al., 2016; Mather, 2012, 2016; Nashiro et al., 2013) found when making source judgments, older adults rely more on easily accessible knowledge than younger adults. In the example of meeting Jane and Sereatha, older adults would be more likely to erroneously remember Jane loves to play tennis, as they would rely on an easily accessible stereotype the athlete is more likely to love tennis than the bookworm.

Finally, older adults are more susceptible to social judgment biases because they have trouble distinguishing between true and false information (see Chapter 6; Wang & Chen, 2006). In studies by Chen and colleagues, older adults were instructed to disregard false information (printed in red) and pay attention to true information (printed in black) when reading criminal reports. The older adults had difficulty in doing so, and the false information (e.g., information exacerbating the nature of the crime) biased their judgments about how dangerous the criminal was and this affected their determination of the criminal's prison sentence.

Neuroimaging research indicates damage to or age-related changes in certain parts of the prefrontal cortex may be responsible for increased susceptibility to false information (Asp et al., 2012; Parris, 2016). We saw in Chapter 2 that this region of the brain is central to a host of complex cognitive and emotional processing. Therefore, there may be an age-related neurological reason why older adults are more likely to believe misleading information, such as that used in advertising or political campaigns.

A Processing Capacity Explanation for Age Differences in Social Judgments

Based on the research discussed so far, it appears processing resource limitations play an important role in understanding how older adults process and access social information. In fact, social cognitive researchers have long used information-processing models to describe how individuals make social judgments. In one of the best-known models, Gilbert and Malone (1995) established the ability to make unbiased social judgments depends on the cognitive demand accompanying those judgments. We all make snap initial judgments, but then we reconsider and evaluate possible extenuating circumstances to revise those judgments. This revision takes processing resources, and if we are busy thinking about something else we may not be able to revise our initial judgments.

As we consider in more depth in the section on causal attributions, Blanchard-Fields and colleagues (Blanchard-Fields & Beatty, 2005; Blanchard-Fields et al., 2012) found older adults consistently hold to their initial judgments or conclusions of why negative events occur more often than younger adults. They appear not to adjust their initial judgments by considering other factors, as Alexandra and Klaus were able to do when they revised their interpretation of their grandchildren's behavior.

Because older adults typically exhibit lower levels of cognitive processing resources (see Chapter 6), it is possible this decline in resource capacity might impact social judgment processes. In the case of impression formation, older adults may have limited cognitive resources to process detailed information presented after the initial impression is formed. Use of such information overworks processing resources. Similarly, source judgments and selectively attending to only true information also places demands on one's cognitive resources.

If processing resource capacity is the major factor explaining social judgment biases, then it should affect all types of situations older people encounter. However, it also may be that to the extent social information is accessible, it operates independently of a processing resource limitation to influence social judgments directly.

Attributional Biases

Consider the following scenario:

Erin is cleaning up after her infant son who spilled his dinner all over the table and floor. At the same time, she is listening on the phone to her coworker, Brittany, describing how anxious she was when she gave the marketing presentation in front of their new clients that day. Brittany is also describing how her supervisor told her the company depended on this presentation to obtain a contract from the new clients. After the phone call, Erin reflected on Brittany's situation. She decided Brittany is an anxious person and should work on reducing her anxiety in these types of situations.

Erin was interested in what caused Brittany's anxiety when presenting information at work. Was it something about Brittany, such as being an anxious person? Or was it because of the pressure placed on Brittany by her supervisor or even to luck?

Answers to these questions provide insights into particular types of social judgments people make to explain their behavior that are referred to as causal attributions. **Causal attributions** *are explanations of why behaviors occur*. There are two main types of attributions: dispositional and situational. A **dispositional attribution** *is a causal attribution that concludes the cause resides within the actor*. Erin's explanation that "Brittany is just an anxious person" would be a dispositional attribution of why Brittany is nervous. A **situational attribution** *is an explanation that the cause resides outside the actor*. An explanation such as, "Brittany is succumbing to pressures from her supervisor and that's why she's nervous" would be a situational attribution.

In this section, we explore if there are age differences in the tendency to rely more on dispositional attributions, situational attributions, or on a combination of both when making causal attributions.

One line of research on attributions and aging concerns attributional judgments made about the aging population, usually involving competence in some domain such as memory. In such situations, attributions about older persons' successes and failures are compared to similar successes and failures of younger adults. Such attributions go hand-in-hand with the stereotyping of older adults; for example, older adults' memory failures are given more dispositional attributions whereas younger adults' memory failures are given situational attributions.

A second focus of attribution and aging research examines changes in the nature of attributional processes, per se, in an adult developmental context. Thus, the question can be asked whether findings typically discovered in social psychological attribution theory and research hold true beyond the college years (Blanchard-Fields et al., 2008).

For many years, we have known emerging adults have a tendency to draw inferences about older people's dispositions from behavior that can be fully explained through situational factors, called **correspondence bias** (Gilbert & Malone, 1995). Ignoring critical situational information in determining the cause of another person's behavior can have important consequences in both individual and societal contexts.

Suppose you tried to approach your psychology professor yesterday. She did not acknowledge you were there but kept walking with her face buried in a manuscript. You might decide because your professor ignored your question, she is arrogant (a dispositional attribution). At the same time, you may have ignored important situational information, such as she was talking on her smartphone at the time. Thus you did not consider all the pertinent information to make a more accurate judgment. This type of finding has been primarily documented with emerging adults. However, it may be the case the life experience accumulated by middle-aged and older adults causes them to reach different conclusions because they have learned to consider equally both types of information in explaining why things happen the way they do.

In a series of creative investigations, Blanchard-Fields (Blanchard-Fields & Beatty, 2005; Blanchard-Fields & Horhota, 2005; Blanchard-Fields et al., 2007; Blanchard-Fields et al., 2012) studied the differences in causal attributions across the adult life span. Blanchard-Fields presented participants with different situations having positive or negative outcomes and asked them to decide whether something about the main character in the story (dispositional attributions), the situation (situational attributions), or a combination of both (interactive attributions) was responsible for the event. The vignettes represented situations such as that described earlier where Allen was pressuring Joan to live with him before marriage, Joan protested but Allen continued to pressure her, and the relationship ended up falling apart.

When the target events were ambiguous as to what was the specific cause of the outcome, as with Allen and Joan, all adults tended to make interactive attributions, but older adults did so at a higher rate. However, as can be seen from Figure 8.2, older adults paradoxically also blamed the main character more (dispositional attributions) than younger groups, especially in negative relationship situations.

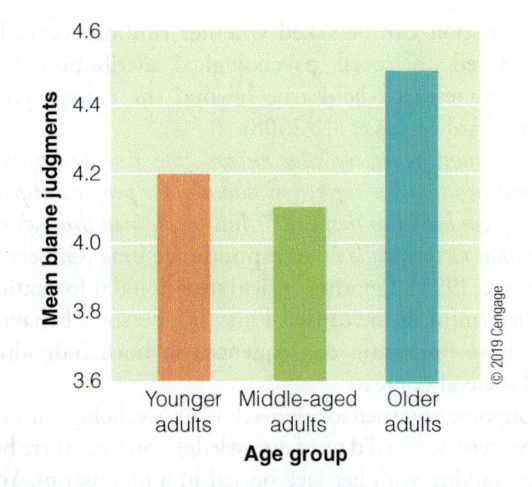

FIGURE 8.2 Dispositional attributions as a function of age.

In her research, Blanchard-Fields took a sociocultural perspective in explaining why older adults were more predisposed to making dispositional attributions and engaged in less postformal/dialectical reasoning in negative relationship situations. She notes the correspondence bias in older adults only occurred in negative relationship situations. In this case, older adults appeared to apply specific social rules about relationships in making their attributional judgments, apparently because of their stage in life and the cohort in which they were socialized (such as the rule "Marriage comes before career"). In these situations, strong beliefs about how one should act in relationship situations appeared to be violated for the older adults, particularly older women. Therefore, these women made snap judgments about the main character that violated their strong beliefs and did not feel it was necessary to engage in conscious, deliberate analyses. They *knew* the character was wrong, as in the husband who chose to work long hours and not spend time with his family.

The interesting question arises, however, as to whether these attributional biases in older adults are truly due to activated belief systems that strongly impact their judgments or whether the older adults are deficient in conducting a causal analysis. This deficiency could take the form of limited cognitive resources that might prevent them from processing all details of the situation (e.g., extenuating situational circumstances). The vignette involving Erin shows how, on the one hand, we can rely on our experience as older adults to guide us through uncomfortable situations; but on the other hand, a reduction in our capacity does not allow us to consider all the relevant information in this case to make an accurate judgment about Brittany's behavior.

Earlier we questioned whether a processing resource hypothesis was the best explanation of social judgment biases. Again, this is particularly important because in Blanchard-Fields's attribution studies, the dispositional bias was only found for older adults when they were presented with negative relationship situations. Researchers have found everyday reasoning biases in older adults occur not because of declining cognitive ability, but because older adults are more likely than younger adults to base their judgments on their own beliefs (Blanchard-Fields et al., 2012; Horhota, Mienaltowski, & Chen, 2014).

These findings indicate the explanations people create to account for behavior vary depending on the type of situation (e.g., relationship or achievement situations), the age of the person, and whether strong social beliefs have been violated by a person in the situation. What is also important is the sociocultural context in which people are socialized, since this appears to create different social rules that are then used to make causal attributions. Additional research supports this idea.

Blanchard-Fields and colleagues (2007) examined causal attributions in younger and older Chinese adults in comparison to younger and older American adults. Interestingly, they found older Americans showed a greater correspondence bias than younger Americans. However, both younger and older Chinese performed similarly and showed less correspondence bias. Older Americans may focus their attributions on the individual due to a lifelong experience of an individualistic orientation.

In order to adjust this initial judgment, the contextual information must be made salient to them in a socially meaningful manner. Support for this idea comes from studies showing when there is a plausible motivation for the target's behavior; older adults can correct their judgments to be less biased than in a standard attitude attribution paradigm (Blanchard-Fields & Horhota, 2005). Additionally, mindfulness training has been shown to reduce correspondence bias in emerging adults (Hopthrow et al., 2017).

For older Americans to correct their attributions, the constraint needs to provide a meaningful reason why a person would contradict his or her own beliefs. For Chinese older adults, the meaningful nature of the situation does not need to be emphasized because to them situational influences and constraints represent a naturally occurring manner to approach any judgment situation and they have a lifelong experience of a collectivist orientation. More research is needed to shed additional light on how these age differences are created and under what circumstances they appear.

Adult Development in Action

How might older adults' impression formation behavior be important to you as a political candidate?

8.4 Motivation and Social Processing Goals

LEARNING OBJECTIVES

- How do goals influence the way we process information, and how does this change with age?
- How do emotions influence the way we process information, and how does this change with age?
- How does a need for closure influence the way we process information, and how does it change with age?

Tracy and Eric are visiting their children and grandchildren on Cape Cod. All are having a good time until their son, Eddie, brings up the hot topic of a recent presidential decision. The debate between family members regarding the decision becomes heated. Tracy and Eric are concerned about the negative feelings generated in the debate and encourage everyone to change the topic. However, the brothers and sisters are more interested in settling the issue now rather than later. Tracy and Eric cannot handle the negative energy and retire to bed early.

Why did Tracy and Eric focus on the emotional side of the problem (the increase in negative feelings), whereas the siblings focused on the more instrumental side of the problem (e.g., whom to vote for)?

The different foci of Tracy and Eric in contrast to the children resulted in different problem-solving strategies. Much like the research on social rules and social judgments, there is a growing area of research suggesting change in the relative importance of social goals and motivation across the life span profoundly influence how we interpret and use social information or direct attention and effort to certain aspects of the problem situation (Hess, 2006).

Goals change with age as a function of experience and time left in the life span. This can influence the degree we observe age differences in social cognitive functioning, such as the desire to focus on preserving ones' resources or eliminating negative affect in problem situations. Let's explore these further.

Personal Goals

Personal goals play a major role in creating direction in our lives. They consist of underlying motivations for our behavior and how we perceive our own ever-changing environment. Across the life span, personal goals change to match our needs, with young adults striving mainly for achievement, like completing a college degree or starting a career, and middle-aged and older adults seeking a balance between functioning independently and sharing their lives with others (e.g., children, spouses).

Selective optimization with compensation (SOC; see Chapter 1) is an important theoretical model that suggests development occurs as we continuously update our personal goals to match our appraisal of available resources to obtain those goals (Baltes et al., 2006). We choose manageable goals based on our interests as well as physical and cognitive strengths and limitations. As we grow older our limitations become more salient and require us to reevaluate our interests. Therefore, in older adulthood, research suggests interests shift toward physical health and socio-emotional domains (Carstensen & Mikels, 2005; Isaacowitz & Blanchard-Fields, 2012).

This shift in priorities means goals for the same event may be perceived differently by older and younger adults. An example of the shift in goal selection can be seen in research that examines how younger and older adults prioritize how they want to perform in a dual-task situation. In a classic study, younger and older adults were asked to memorize a list of words while simultaneously maintaining their balance as they walked through an obstacle course (Li et al., 2001). Although age differences in performing two tasks at the same time were more costly for the memory task than the walking task, older adults chose to forgo aids to improve their memory (e.g., a list) and instead chose to use aids designed to optimize walking performance (e.g., a handrail). When deciding which was more important to them, memory performance versus balance, older adults displayed a preference for their physical safety even if it meant they would perform badly on a cognitive test. From this example, we see life-span shifts in personal goals can be both helpful and harmful.

Goal selection requires we thoughtfully choose where we invest our resources. In the laboratory, younger adults are primarily motivated to achieve maximum performance on any cognitive task presented to them. Older adults take a different perspective. They prefer to maintain steady performance by optimizing their current resources rather than risking loss with an unknown strategy (Baltes & Rudolph, 2012; Ebner, Freund, & Baltes, 2006; Napolitano & Freund, 2016).

Thus, although older adults are less willing than younger adults to invest energy into improving their cognitive performance, their strategy choice is more optimal for them because they are more interested in retaining their autonomy by maintaining abilities at their current level. Although this does not directly translate into cognitive gains, it does help older adults optimize their cognitive performance in those domains they prioritize in their lives (Baltes & Rudolph, 2012; Riediger, Freund, & Baltes, 2005). Although we cannot compensate for all of the resource limitations that come with advancing age, we can invest the resources we have into goals that maximize an independent lifestyle and a positive sense of well-being.

Along these lines, recent work by Carstensen and her colleagues suggests the pursuit of emotionally gratifying situations becomes a primary motivation that substantially influences cognition in the latter half of the life span (Carstensen & Mikels, 2005; Reed & Carstensen, 2012). We therefore turn to the impact of emotional processing goals on cognition.

Emotion as a Processing Goal

Emotional goals become increasingly important and salient as we grow older (Carstensen & Fried, 2012). It is primarily a motivational model that posits the degree an individual construes time as limited or expansive that leads to the ranking of emotional or knowledge-seeking goals as higher in priority, respectively. Thus, given limited time left in the life span, older adults may be more motivated to emphasize emotional goals and aspects of life. We examine this motivational factor in the context of maintaining and choosing intimate relationships in Chapter 10. However, it also can be applied in the context of social information processing.

A growing number of studies suggest older adults avoid negative information and focus more on positive information when making decisions and judgments and when remembering events, a phenomenon called the **positivity effect** (Carstensen & Fried, 2012; Carstensen, Mikels, & Mather, 2006; English & Carstensen, 2016). For example, older adults remember positive images more than negative ones, whereas younger adults remember both positive and negative images equally well (Isaacowitz & Blanchard-Fields, 2012; Reed & Carstensen, 2012). When examining what types of stimuli younger and older adults initially attend to, older adults allocate less attention to negative stimuli (e.g., angry faces) than younger adults do. Older adults also remember more positive information when recalling their own autobiographical information and remember the positive aspects of their decisions more than the negative ones.

An alternative perspective proposes focusing on negative information is adaptive because it signals danger and vulnerability and thus is important for survival. This emphasis on negativity has been found in both the social and cognitive neuroscience literature for many years (e.g., Lane & Nadel, 2000; Rozin & Royzman, 2001). Within the social cognitive aging literature, some studies demonstrate older adults spend more time viewing negative stimuli (Charles et al., 2003) and display a negativity effect (Thomas & Hasher, 2006; Wood & Kisley, 2006).

Emotional goals appear to help older adults because they create a supportive context for their cognitive functioning. In Chapter 6, we discussed the fact older adults create more false memories than younger adults

Older adults tend to remember more positive than negative information, such as good traits of their spouse or partner rather than negative ones.

do. Research on the interface between emotions and cognition suggest the distinctiveness of emotions helps older adults reduce the number of false memories produced (Mitchell, 2016; Sakaki, Niki, & Mather, 2012).

However, it is important to recognize there are times when emotions may impede information processing. For example, highly arousing situations require a great amount of executive control processing (discussed in Chapter 6) that may lead older adults to be poorer at remembering and processing information (Kensinger & Corkin, 2004; Reed & Carstensen, 2012; Shors & Millon, 2016). In addition, a focus on only positive information can interfere with decision making by leading older adults to miss out on important negative information necessary to make a quality decision (Reed & Carstensen, 2012).

As we have seen, emotion plays an increasingly important role as we grow older, and the brain mechanisms that underlie emotion change a bit and become more central. The power of the positivity effect also means that people intentionally use thoughts and behaviors to avoid negative emotional experiences.

Research shows that it takes a lifetime to master this ability to focus on positive experiences. The aging process itself, accompanied as it is by an increased focus on time left to live rather than time lived to date, may hold a key to understanding how this happens. Charles and Luong (2013; Piazza, Charles, & Luong, 2015) developed the Strength and Vulnerability Integration (SAVI) model to explain it.

The SAVI model is based on the normative aging process in which physiological vulnerabilities that occur with increasing age make regulating high levels of emotional arousal harder. So, when older adults experience high levels of distress, the usual advantage they have in regulating emotion is interfered with (and even reversed). This results in older adults paying a higher price for sustained negative emotional arousal. Such experiences push them to focus on the positive.

The SAVI model, then, can explain the seemingly contradictory findings that some older adults have higher well-being whereas others personify the stereotype of "grumpy older people" (Charles & Luong, 2013). It all comes down to how sustained emotional experiences are processed.

Cognitive Style as a Processing Goal

Another type of motivational goal that influences our thinking comes from our **cognitive style**, *or how we approach solving problems.* Examples include a need for closure and the inability to tolerate ambiguous situations. For example, people with a high need for closure prefer order and predictability, are uncomfortable with ambiguity, are closed-minded, and prefer quick and decisive answers (Bar-Tal, Shrira, & Keinan, 2013).

A question is whether cognitive resources or need for closure are implicated in biased judgments. As discussed earlier, situations that require substantial cognitive resources (i.e., require a lot of effort in cognitive processing such as processing information under time pressure) result in an increase in inaccuracies and biases in how we represent social information. However, biased judgments can also be caused by motivational differences such as an increase in need for closure. In fact, research using Need for Closure assessments suggests a high need for closure and/or structure is related to attributional biases, the tendency to make stereotyped judgments, formation of spontaneous trait inferences, and the tendency to assimilate judgments to primed constructs (e.g., Bar-Tal et al., 2013).

It may also be the case limited cognitive resources and motivational differences are both age-related and influence social judgments in interaction with each other (English & Carstensen, 2016; Stanley & Isaacowitz, 2012). Researchers argue changes in resources with aging (as in the declines in working memory noted in Chapter 6) may lead to an increase in a need for closure with age. This leads to biases in the way older adults process social information.

Research documents that a high need for closure does not influence susceptibility to emotional priming influences on neutral stimuli of young and middle-aged adults. However, priming effects increased with higher need for structure in older adults. In other words, older adults with a high need for closure could not inhibit the effects of an emotional prime (e.g., a subliminally presented negative word) on their subsequent behavior (e.g., whether they liked or disliked an abstract figure). Because of age-related changes in personal resources (social and cognitive), motivational factors such as coming to quick and decisive answers to conserve resources become important to older adults.

Adult Development in Action

If you were designing an advertisement for adults of different ages, how would you approach the suggestion to use emotion in the ad?

8.5 Personal Control

LEARNING OBJECTIVES
- What is the multidimensionality of personal control?
- How do assimilation and accommodation influence behavior?
- What is primary and secondary control? What is the primacy of primary control over secondary control?

Daniel did not perform as well as he thought he would on his psychology exam. He then had the unhappy task of determining why he did poorly. Was it his fault? Was the exam too picky? To add insult to injury, Daniel needed to raise his grades to maintain his scholarship grant. He decided the exam was too picky. This helped Daniel motivate himself to study for his next exams.

How Daniel answered such questions sheds light on how we tend to explain, or attribute our behavior, as in the earlier discussion of causal attributions. Among the most important ways we analyze the cause of events is in terms of who or what is in control in a specific situation. **Personal control** *is the degree one believes one's performance in a situation depends on something that one personally does.* A high sense of personal control implies a belief that performance is up to you, whereas a low sense of personal control implies your performance is under the influence of forces other than your own.

Personal control has become an extremely important idea in a wide variety of settings because of the way it guides behavior and relates to well-being (Brandtstädter, 1997; Curtis, Huxhold, & Windsor, in press; Lachman, 2006). Personal control is thought to play a central role in physical health (see Chapter 4), in adjustment to and survival in different care settings (see Chapter 5), in memory performance (see Chapter 6), in intelligence (see Chapter 7), and in mental health (see Chapter 10).

Multidimensionality of Personal Control

The general consensus about personal control is that it is multidimensional (Lachman, Rosnick, & Röcke, 2009). Specifically, one's sense of control depends on which domain, such as intelligence or health, is being assessed. Lachman and colleagues (2009) found interesting changes in control beliefs depending on the domain being examined. They found no changes in a sense of control over one's health up to the early 70s. However, when older adults transition from the early 70s to the mid-70s and 80s, their sense of control over their health declines. This makes sense given the oldest-old experience accumulated losses in their reserve capacity to function. This shift may actually be very adaptive. Chipperfield and colleagues (2016) found that feelings of personal control can be maladaptive when it leads to a sense of invincibility even in the face of poor health. Such beliefs can result in the failure to seek medical help when it is actually needed.

The same is true in an academic context such as college, where attributions of control are particularly important in determining the causes of success and failure in school. It would be interesting to explore the notion of control in regard to class performance among older and younger students. The exercise in the Discovering Development feature examines this question.

In sum, researchers find that, in general, maintaining a sense of control throughout adulthood is linked to better quality of social relationships, better health, and

DISCOVERING DEVELOPMENT
How Much Control Do You Have Over Your Cognitive Functioning?

As you progress through college, you are concerned with your grade point average, how much you will learn relative to your profession of choice, and your performance on exams. The more control you perceive you have over the situation, the more confident you feel. There are two types of control attributions you can make. For one, you can make an "entity" attribution about your performance in school. This means you attribute control to your innate ability to perform. Or you can hold a "skill" perspective. With this perspective you now attribute control over your performance in terms of how much effort you exert, such as how much you study for an exam.

Are there age differences in these control beliefs? To find out, talk to students at your university who range from first-year students to seniors and also in age. Be sure to include older students who have come back to school. Find out what they believe is the major cause of their successes and failures in school. Bring your results to class and pool them. See if there are college-level differences and/or age differences in perceptions of control over academic performance. Compare your findings to age differences reported in the text.

higher cognitive functioning. They suggest a sense of control may operate as a protective factor for one's well-being in the face of declining health and other losses associated with the oldest-old.

Control Strategies

The research just reviewed primarily examined control-related beliefs such as the belief that control is in one's own hands or in the hands of others. Building on these ideas, a number of theoretical approaches and research have examined control-related strategies.

Brandtstädter (1999) first proposed the preservation and stabilization of a positive view of the self and personal development in later life involve three interdependent processes. *First, people engage in* **assimilative activities** *that prevent or alleviate losses in domains that are personally relevant for self-esteem and identity.* People may use memory aids more if having a good memory is an important aspect of self-esteem and identity. *Second, people make* **accommodations** *and readjust their goals and aspirations as a way to lessen or neutralize the effects of negative self-evaluations in key domains.* If a person notices the time it takes to walk a mile at a brisk pace increased, then the target time can be increased to help lessen the impact of feelings of failure. *Third, people use* **immunizing mechanisms** *that alter the effects of self-discrepant evidence.* In this case, a person who is confronted with evidence his or her memory performance has declined can look for alternative explanations or simply deny the evidence.

Taking a similar approach, Heckhausen, Wrosch, and Schulz (2010; Barlow et al., 2017) view control as a motivational system that regulates individuals' abilities to control important outcomes over the life span. These researchers define control-related strategies in terms of primary control and secondary control.

Primary control strategies *involve bringing the environment in line with one's desires and goals.* Much like in Brandtstädter's assimilative activities, action is directed toward changing the external world. So, for example, if you lost your job, and thus your income, primary control strategies would entail an active search for another job (changing the environment so you once again have a steady income).

Secondary control strategies *involve bringing oneself in line with the environment.* Much like Brandtstädter's accommodative activities, it typically involves cognitive activities directed at the self. Secondary control strategies could involve appraising the situation in terms of how you really did not enjoy that particular job.

An important part of this theoretical perspective is that primary control has functional primacy over secondary control. In other words, primary control lets people shape their environment to fit their goals and developmental potential. Thus, primary control has more adaptive value to the individual. The major function of secondary control is to minimize losses or expand levels of primary control.

This relation is depicted in Figure 8.3. Notice that primary control striving is always high across the life span, but the capacity to achieve primary control peaks in midlife. As people continue to age, secondary control striving continues to increase, eventually approaching primary control striving.

Heckhausen and colleagues (2010; Barlow et al., 2017) believe this has important implications for aging. They find in childhood much development is directed at expanding the child's primary control potential, and they predict stability in primary control striving through most of adult life. However, as we enter old age, the maintenance of primary control increasingly depends on secondary control processes. This is because of threats to primary control as a function of biological decline that occurs as we grow older. Thus secondary control increases with age. Research confirms this prediction (Pfeiffer, 2013).

A particularly important question is how control strategies and beliefs affect emotional well-being. Research suggests control beliefs are important contributors to both positive and negative well-being. If

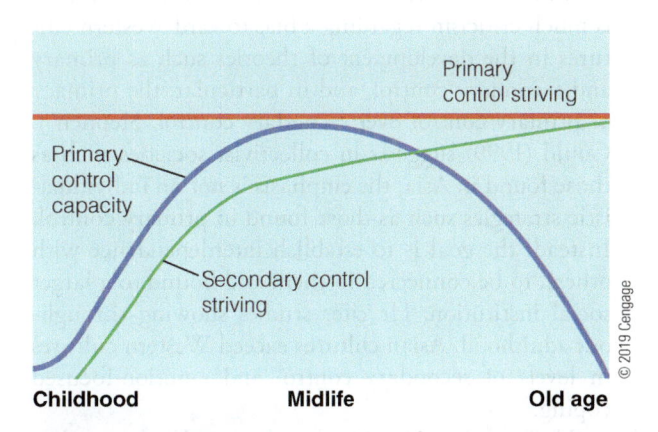

FIGURE 8.3 Hypothetical life-span trajectories for primary control potential and primary and secondary control striving.

Source: Heckhausen, J., Wrosch, C., & Schulz, R. (2010). A motivational theory of life-span development. *Psychological Review, 117*(1), 32–60 (at p. 36). doi:10.1037/ a0017668; www.ncbi.nlm.nih.gov/pmc/articles/PMC2820305/figure/F1/.

someone perceives he or she has control over desirable outcomes, this control is associated with high emotional well-being (Barlow et al., 2017; Heckhausen et al., 2010; Pfeiffer, 2013). However, how adaptive control beliefs relate to well-being varies with life stage. For young and middle-aged adults, a strong sense of control relates to how we compensate for failure, for example, "We can overcome this momentary failure." Older adults focus a sense of control on how to master everyday demands (Barlow et al., 2017; Heckhausen et al., 2010). Finally, for all age groups, planning for the future enhances one's sense of perceived control, and this in turn relates to high life satisfaction (Lachman et al., 2009).

Some Criticisms Regarding Primary Control

The notions of increases in accommodative strategies (Brandtstädter, 1999) and secondary strategies (Barlow et al., 2017; Heckhausen et al., 2010) in older age are not without its criticisms. Carstensen and Freund (1994; Freund & Ritter, 2009) question whether losses people experience, though real, actually threaten the self. In addition, these authors argue age-related changes in goals could also be the result of natural movement through the life cycle, not simply of coping with blocked goals.

Criticisms also can be launched against these approaches to control by considering the globalization of so many aspects of our functioning. From a sociocultural perspective (e.g., cross-cultural research), there is much criticism regarding a bias toward Western cultures in the development of theories such as primary and secondary control, and in particular, the primacy of primary control over secondary control. Stephen J. Gould (1999) suggests in collectivist societies such as those found in Asia, the emphasis is not on individualistic strategies such as those found in primary control. Instead, the goal is to establish interdependence with others, to be connected to them and bound to a larger social institution. He cites studies showing throughout adulthood, Asian cultures exceed Western cultures in levels of secondary control and emotion-focused coping.

Thus, one's sense of personal control is a complex, multidimensional aspect of personality. Consequently, general normative age-related trends might not be found. Rather, changes in personal control may well depend on one's experiences in different domains and the culture one grows up in, and may differ widely from one domain to another.

Adult Development in Action

As a professional working with older adults, how would you combine your knowledge of the effects of stereotyping with your knowledge of the importance of personal control beliefs to create an intervention program?

8.6 Social Situations and Social Competence

LEARNING OBJECTIVES
- What is the social facilitation of cognitive functioning?
- What is collaborative cognition, and does it facilitate memory in older adults?
- How does the social context influence memory performance in older adults?

Brandon and Stephanie's granddaughter asked them what happened when they first met. Stephanie recalled they met at a social gathering for Vietnam War soldiers but couldn't remember the name of the person who introduced them; she could only describe him as tall and dark-haired. However, this cued Brandon; he remembered the man's name was Tucker. This back-and-forth remembering continued until, to their own amazement, they successfully reconstructed the whole gathering. Their granddaughter was delighted and complimented them on their good memories.

When we typically think about the memories of older adults, we don't usually think of these kinds of successes. Brandon and Stephanie's reliance on each other to remember a past event shows how our social cognitive processes serve adaptive functions. In fact, there is a growing interest in how the social context can compensate for memory loss and facilitate memory performance. In this section, we examine two approaches to this issue: collaborative cognition and facilitative social contexts.

Similar to practical intelligence, wisdom, and everyday problem solving discussed in Chapter 7, the social cognition perspective offers us an enriched understanding of social competence in older adulthood. We are interested in how changes in social cognitive functioning both reflect the changing life contexts of the individual and affect adaptation to these changing contexts. In the previous sections, we primarily focused on how developmental changes in representations of self or other (such as social beliefs and self-beliefs) influence social cognitive processes such as making attributional judgments. In this section we focus on social cognition as it relates to the dynamic interplay between self, others, and context. A less researched but extremely important domain of social cognition and aging is how the particular types of social settings where we communicate with others influence our cognitive processing. This relates to a different aspect of social cognition and aging research: the social facilitation of cognitive functioning.

Collaborative Cognition

There has been a recent focus in the social cognition and aging literature to examine cognition in social contexts, that is, how cognition works when we are interacting with others. This can be seen in work on the benefits and costs of collaborative cognition on cognitive performance (e.g., memory and problem solving) (Bietti & Sutton, 2015; Dixon, 2011; Meade, Nokes, & Morrow, 2009). **Collaborative cognition** *occurs when two or more people work together to solve a cognitive task.*

Research shows collaborative cognition enhances adults' performance on a variety of memory and problem-solving tasks, thus serving an important adaptive function (Brennan & Ens, 2015). Following the old saying "Two heads are better than one," researchers are interested in examining how this type of collaborative context could mitigate deficits in memory we typically see when assessing older adults in the laboratory (see Chapter 6).

Research shows older adults can collaborate on story recall as well as problem-solving performance and their performance is better than the average performance of older adults in individual settings (Dixon, 2011). Memory knowledge and performance is also enhanced (Michaelian & Arango-Muñoz, 2016). In other words, cognitive performance improves with a collaborative context. On a recall task, by using a cognitive style together that minimizes working memory demands, older married couples performed just as well as younger couples. It is rare to find older adults' cognitive performance equal to that of younger adults.

How does this work? Bietti and Sutton (2015) describe a succession of processes that occur as the time scale increases and the memory goes from personal to cultural: (a) faster, lower-level coordination processes of behavioral matching and interactional synchrony occurring at short timescale; (b) mid-range collaborative processes which re-evoke past experiences in groups, unfolding at longer timescales; (c) cooperative processes involved in the transmission of memories over even longer periods; and (d) cultural processes and practices operating within distributed sociocognitive networks over evolutionary and historical time frames. Thus, collaborative cognition can occur from the small scale of two people (e.g., a couple remembering a movie they saw together) up through entire societies (e.g., societal remembering of a major historical event such as 9/11).

There is evidence of the positive outcomes of collaboration when older adults tackle everyday problem-solving tasks such as errand running and planning a vacation (Allaire, 2012). Interestingly, older adults prefer to collaborate in their problem solving when they perceive deficiencies in their own functioning but prefer to work alone when they feel competent in the area (Strough & Margrett, 2002; Strough, Cheng, & Swenson, 2002). Collaborators of all ages report the benefits include optimizing the decision, enhancing the relationship, and compensating for individual weaknesses (Dixon, 2011; Dixon et al., 2013; Kimbler et al., 2012). However, collaboration is not without its costs, such as selfishness, withholding of one's honest opinion, and not meeting the other partner's needs.

Older adults tend to use compensatory strategies for declining memories by jointly remembering events with others.

Because collaborative cognition is such a common experience and likely to be grounded in the nuances of the relationship people develop over time, it will be a rich area to learn more about the developmental trajectory of memory across adulthood. Most people do remembering in collaborative situations multiple times a day, whether with a spouse or partner or with other family or friends. As we will see in Chapter 11, the quality of the relationship where this cognitive activity occurs probably has important influences on actual performance. Whether this is true, though, awaits more research.

Social Context of Memory

Another approach to identifying conditions when social facilitation of cognition in older adults occurs is in examining contextual variables that influence memory performance. Adams argues memory performance is influenced when the task approximates a real-world learning and social memory experience (Adams et al., 2002). Others have pointed out that prior knowledge (Stein-Morrow & Miller, 2009) and how and how often memories are practiced together (Coman & Hirst, 2012) also influence performance. In this case, what happens to memory performance when the assessment situation approximates the kinds of memory demands that naturally occur in a real-life situation?

A typical and relevant cognitive task for older adults is to transmit sociocultural information to younger generations (Birditt et al., 2012; Quéniart & Charpentier, 2013). In this context, the older adult would be motivated to communicate effectively.

A storytelling situation is a good example. This kind of context is different from the traditional laboratory context, when the demand is to reproduce as much of the content of a text as possible. Adams et al. (2002) found when they placed older adults in a storytelling situation where they were asked to learn and retell a story from memory to a young child, their retellings of the story contained more detail and were more fluent than those of younger adults. Perhaps this superior performance stems from increased motivation in a social context where their concerns were directed at producing an interesting and coherent story for the child. This is a demonstration of how the social-communicative context or experience enhances what is most salient to the individual. Again, this finding illustrates the importance of taking into consideration the social context of a task situation when examining change in cognitive functioning as we grow older.

Adult Development in Action

How might the research on collaborative cognition be used in therapeutic situations you might design if you were working in a long-term care facility?

Social Policy Implications

The research on social cognition and aging further accentuates why it is important to consider social factors to explain cognitive functioning in older adulthood. Factors such as the social context we communicate in, the emotions we feel, and the strength of our beliefs and values drive our decisions and social judgments in important ways. Thus, it is important not to limit explanations of changes in thinking and decision making to cognitive processing variables.

Important social factors influence how and when an individual attends to specific information and when this information influences social cognitive functioning. These factors include those we discussed earlier: motivational goals, cognitive style, attitudes, and values. By not considering these factors, we run the risk of underestimating the competence of older adults. By considering these factors, we can explore the conditions under which older adults flourish and the conditions on which we need to focus aid and attention.

This has important policy implications with respect to how we treat older adults in the workforce, establishing health policies, and enhancing the treatment of our older adult population. We can be optimistic about the future promise of research on aging and social cognition for identifying and probing such important social components of information processing. To summarize, by looking at cognition in a social context we get a more complete picture of how cognition operates in an everyday social environment.

SUMMARY

8.1 Stereotypes and Aging

How does the content of stereotypes about aging differ across adulthood?
- The content of stereotypes varies by age: older adults include more positive stereotypes along with negative ones.
- Stereotypes can be changed, even by imagining positive interactions with a negatively perceived group.

How do younger and older adults perceive the competence of the elderly?
- An age-based double standard operates when judging older adults' failures in memory.
- Younger adults rate older adults as more responsible despite their own memory failures.

How do stereotypes about aging unconsciously guide our behavior?
- Automatically activated negative stereotypes about aging guide behavior beyond the individual's awareness.
- Implicit negative stereotypes decrease cognitive performance, health, social interactions, and change the way we communicate with older adults.
- Positive implicit stereotypes maintain or improve cognitive performance, health, and social networks. They are also associated with greater longevity.

What are the ways the positive and negative aging stereotypes influence older adults' behavior?
- Stereotypic beliefs have a negative impact on the cognitive performance of older adults.
- Stereotypic beliefs influence older adults' health and physical behavior.

8.2 Social Knowledge Structures and Beliefs

What are social knowledge structures?
- To understand age differences in social beliefs, we must first examine content differences.
- Second, we must assess the strength of the beliefs.
- Third, we need to know the likelihood beliefs will affect behavior.

What are social beliefs, and how do they change with age?
- Age differences in social beliefs can be attributed to generational differences and life-stage differences.

What are self-perceptions of aging, and what influences them across adulthood?
- Labeling theory (the incorporation of negative stereotypes) and resilience theory (distancing from negative stereotypes) both operate to create self-perceptions of aging.

8.3 Social Judgment Processes

What is emotional intelligence and how does it develop across adulthood?
- Emotional intelligence (EI) refers to people's ability to recognize their own and others' emotions, to correctly identify and appropriately tell the difference between emotions, and use this information to guide their thinking and behavior.
- EI tends to increase across adulthood and plays an important role in determining how people read social situations and decide what to do.

What is the negativity bias in impression formation, and how does it influence older adults' thinking?
- When forming an initial impression, older adults rely heavily on preexisting social structures.
- Older adults weigh negative information more heavily in their social judgments than do younger adults.
- Older adults use less detailed information in forming impressions than do younger adults.

Are there age differences in accessibility of social information?
- Social knowledge structures must be available to guide behavior.
- Social information must be easily accessible to guide behavior.
- Accessibility depends on the strength of the information stored in memory.
- How the situation is framed influences what types of social knowledge will be accessed.

How does processing context influence social judgments?
- Age-related changes in processing capacity influence social judgments.
- Stages of processing suggest we make initial snap judgments and later correct or adjust them based on more reflective thinking.

To what extent do processing capacity limitations influence social judgments in older adults?
- Older adults tend to make more snap judgments because of processing resource limitations.

How do causal attributions and the correspondence bias change with age?
- Older adults display a dispositional bias when confronted with negative relationship situations.
- Older adults display more interactive attributions in negative relationship situations.

- The dispositional bias on the part of older adults can be attributed to both processing resource limitations and differences in social knowledge that influence their attributional judgments.
- Older adults display a higher level of social expertise than younger adults do when forming impressions.

8.4 Motivation and Social Processing Goals

How do goals influence the way we process information, and how does this change with age?
- Life-span shifts in goal orientation show interests shift toward physical health and socio-emotional domains increase with age.
- The SAVI model accounts for older adults' higher well-being as well as instances of difficulty handling negative emotions.

How do emotions influence the way we process information, and how does this change with age?
- Older adults tend to focus their processing on positive emotional information more than negative information.

How does a need for closure influence the way we process information, and how does it change with age?
- Need for closure is a need for a quick and decisive answer with little tolerance for ambiguity.
- Older adults' social judgment biases are predicted by the degree they need quick and decisive closure. This is not so for younger age groups.

8.5 Personal Control

What is personal control, and what age differences exist in this area?
- Personal control is the degree that one believes performance depends on something one does.
- Age differences in the degree of personal control depend on the domain being studied. Some evidence suggests people develop several strategies concerning personal control to protect a positive self-image.

What is the multidimensionality of personal control?
- Older adults perceive less control over specific domains of functioning such as intellectual changes with aging.

- Perceived control over health remains stable until it declines in old age.
- Older adults perceive less control over social issues and personal appearance.

How do assimilation and accommodation influence behavior?
- Assimilative strategies prevent losses important to self-esteem.
- Accommodative strategies readjust goals.
- Immunizing mechanisms alter the effects of self-discrepant information.

What is primary and secondary control?
- Primary control helps change the environment to match one's goals.
- Secondary control reappraises the environment in light of one's decline in functioning.

What is the primacy of primary control over secondary control?
- Primary control has functional primacy over secondary control.
- Cross-cultural perspectives challenge the notion of primacy of primary control.

8.6 Social Situations and Social Competence

What is the social facilitation of cognitive functioning?
- Particular types of social settings where we communicate with others, influence our cognitive processing.

What is collaborative cognition, and does it facilitate memory in older adults?
- Collaborating with others in recollection helps facilitate memory in older adults.
- Collaborating with others enhances problem solving in older adults.

How does the social context influence memory performance in older adults?
- The social context can serve a facilitative function in older adults' memory performance.

REVIEW QUESTIONS

8.1 Stereotypes and Aging
- What are stereotypes? How is the content of stereotypes similar across age groups?
- How does the content of stereotypes differ across age groups?
- What is the age-based double standard of perceived competence in younger and older adults?

- What do older and younger adults perceive as the cause of memory failure in older individuals?
- How does perceived competence influence the way tasks are assigned to older and younger targets?
- What other factors besides competence are taken into consideration when judging older adults' future performance?

- What evidence supports the notion that stereotypes can be automatically activated out of conscious awareness?
- What is implicit stereotyping? Under what conditions are stereotypes activated? How do negative stereotypes of aging influence young adults' behavior?

8.2 Social Knowledge Structures and Beliefs
- What three important factors need to be considered to understand implicit social beliefs?
- Describe evidence for age differences in the content of social beliefs.
- What are labeling theory and resilience theory? What influences self-perceptions of aging across adulthood?

8.3 Social Judgment Processes
- What is emotional intelligence? How does it develop across adulthood?
- What are the stages in attributional processing? What is the negativity bias, and what are the age differences in its impact?
- Describe the age differences in the extent that trait information is used in forming an impression.
- How does processing capacity affect social cognitive processing?
- What influences the accessibility of social information?
- What is the status of processing resource limitations as an explanation for social judgment biases?
- What are causal attributions? What is a correspondence bias? Are there age differences in the correspondence bias? If so, under what conditions?
- What accounts for the age differences in the correspondence bias?

8.4 Motivation and Social Processing Goals
- How do personal goals influence behavior? To what extent are there age differences in emotion as a processing goal in social cognitive functioning?
- What is need for closure? How does need for closure influence the processing of social information?
- Are there age differences in the degree to which need for closure influences social information processing?

8.5 Personal Control
- What evidence is there of age differences in personal control beliefs?
- In what domains do older adults exhibit low perceived control, and in what domains do they exhibit higher levels of perceived control?
- How are assimilative and accommodative strategies adaptive in older adults' functioning?
- Why is primary control viewed as having more functional primacy than secondary control?
- What cross-cultural evidence challenges the notion of primary control as functionally more important?
- How does personal control influence older adults' emotional well-being?

8.6 Social Situations and Social Competence
- What is collaborative cognition? What evidence suggests collaborative cognition compensates for memory failures in older adults?
- How does collaborative cognition facilitate problem-solving behavior?
- How do marital relationships influence collaborative cognition?
- How does a storytelling context influence age differences in memory for stories?
- What does it mean to say the social context facilitates cognitive performance?

INTEGRATING CONCEPTS IN DEVELOPMENT

- To what degree are declines in processing resource capacity discussed in Chapter 6 as ubiquitous in their effects on social cognitive processes?
- What relations can be found among dispositional traits, personal concerns, and life narratives?
- How does emotion as a processing goal relate to socio-emotional selectivity theory in Chapter 10?
- How does social cognition relate to postformal thought as discussed in Chapter 7?
- How does personal control relate to concepts such as memory self-efficacy discussed in Chapter 6?

KEY TERMS

accommodations Readjustments of goals and aspirations as a way to lessen or neutralize the effects of negative self-evaluations in key domains.

age-based double standard When an individual attributes an older person's failure in memory as more serious than a memory failure observed in a young adult.

assimilative activities Exercises that prevent or alleviate losses in domains that are personally relevant for self-esteem and identity.

causal attributions Explanations people construct to explain their behavior, that can be situational, dispositional, or interactive.

cognitive style A traitlike pattern of behavior one uses when approaching a problem-solving situation.

collaborative cognition Cognitive performance that results from the interaction of two or more individuals.

correspondence bias The tendency to draw inferences about older people's dispositions from behavior that can be fully explained through situational factors.

dispositional attribution An explanation for someone's behavior that resides within the actor.

emotional intelligence People's ability to recognize their own and others' emotions, to correctly identify and appropriately tell the difference between emotions, and use this information to guide their thinking and behavior.

immunizing mechanisms Control strategies that alter the effects of self-discrepant evidence.

implicit stereotyping Stereotyped beliefs that affect your judgments of individuals without your being aware of it (i.e., the process is unconscious).

impression formation The way people combine the components of another person's personality and come up with an integrated perception of the person.

labeling theory Argues that when we confront an age-related stereotype, older adults are more likely to integrate it into their self-perception.

negativity bias Weighing negative information more heavily than positive information in a social judgment.

personal control The belief that what one does has an influence on the outcome of an event.

positivity effect The tendency to attend to and process positive information over negative information.

primary control The act of bringing the environment into line with one's own desires and goals, similar to Brandtstädter's assimilative activities.

resilience theory Argues that confronting a negative stereotype results in a rejection of that view in favor of a more positive self-perception.

secondary control The act of bringing oneself in line with the environment, similar to Brandtstädter's accommodative activities.

self-perception of aging Refers to individuals' perceptions of their own age and aging.

situational attribution An explanation for someone's behavior that is external to the actor.

social knowledge A cognitive structure that represents one's general knowledge about a given social concept or domain.

source judgments Process of accessing knowledge wherein one attempts to determine where one obtained a particular piece of information.

stereotypes Beliefs about characteristics, attributes, and behaviors of members of certain groups.

stereotype threat An evoked fear of being judged in accordance with a negative stereotype about a group to which an individual belongs.

9 | Personality

CHAPTER OUTLINE

9.1 Dispositional Traits Across Adulthood
The Case for Stability: The Five-Factor Model
What Happens to Dispositional Traits Across Adulthood?
Conclusions About Dispositional Traits
CURRENT CONTROVERSIES Intraindividual Change and the Stability of Traits

9.2 Personal Concerns and Qualitative Stages in Adulthood
What's Different About Personal Concerns?
Jung's Theory
Erikson's Stages of Psychosocial Development
REAL PEOPLE What Will History Say About You?
Theories Based on Life Transitions
Conclusions About Personal Concerns

9.3 Life Narratives, Identity, and the Self
DISCOVERING DEVELOPMENT Who Do You Want to Be When You "Grow Up"?
McAdams's Life-Story Model
Whitbourne's Identity Theory
Six Foci Model of Adult Personality
Self-Concept and Well-Being
Possible Selves
HOW DO WE KNOW? Possible Selves and Pursuing Personal Goals
Religiosity and Spiritual Support
Conclusions About Narratives, Identity, and the Self

Social Policy Implications

Summary
Review Questions
Integrating Concepts in Development
Key Terms

Maya Angelou (1969) perhaps said it best: "There is no agony like bearing an untold story inside of you." True to her conviction, she spent a lifetime writing her story in numerous books, poems, and other literary works. She described an incredible developmental path of oppression, hatred, and hurt that ultimately resulted in self-awareness, understanding, and compassion. For example, in her later years she realized in confronting the atrocities of the world that if she accepted the fact of evil, she also had to accept the fact of good, thereby providing her with as little fear as possible for the anticipation of death. Another example involves integrating spirituality into her self-perception. Author Ken Kelley once asked her how spirituality fits into a way of life. She answered, "There is something more, the spirit, or the soul. I think that that quality encourages our courtesy, and care, and our minds. And mercy, and identity" (Kelley, 1995).

Maya Angelou's writings reflect some of the key issues involved in personality development we will examine in this chapter. First, we consider whether personality changes or remains stable across adulthood. We examine this from two perspectives: a trait perspective, as well as personal concerns perspective. Then we discuss how we construct life narratives and our identity and self.

One of the oldest debates in psychology concerns whether personality development continues across the life span. From the earliest days, prominent people argued both sides. William James and Sigmund Freud believed personality was set by the time we reach adulthood. In contrast, Carl Jung asserted personality was continually shaped throughout our lives.

Although we still have these two theoretical camps, one arguing for stability and the other for change, there is a movement in the field to reconcile these differences. Although the data can be viewed as contradictory, results often depend on what specific measures researchers use and the aspect of personality investigated.

Why is the area of personality controversial? The answer lies in how we use personality in daily life. At one level we all believe and base our interactions with people on the presumption their personality remains relatively constant over time. Imagine the chaos that would result if every week or so everyone woke up with a brand new personality: The once easy-going husband is now a real tyrant, trusted friends become completely unpredictable, and our patterns of social interaction are in shambles. Clearly, to survive in day-to-day life we must rely on consistency of personality. Abrupt changes are usually taken as indications that something is seriously wrong.

Still, we also believe people can change, especially with respect to undesirable aspects of their personalities. Picture what it would be like if we could never overcome shyness; if anxiety was a lifelong, incurable curse; or if our idiosyncratic tendencies causing others to tear their hair out could not be eliminated. The assumption of the modifiability of personality is strong indeed. The existence of psychotherapy is a formal verification of that assumption.

So in important ways, our personal theories of personality incorporate both stability and change. Is it any wonder, then, formal psychological theories of personality do the same? Let's see how those views are described.

Levels of Analysis and Personality Research

Sorting out the various approaches to personality helps us understand what aspects of personality the various researchers describe. Drawing on the work of several theorists and

Maya Angelou

researchers, McAdams (1999) describes three parallel levels of personality structure and function, each containing a wide range of personality constructs: dispositional traits, personal concerns, and life narrative.

- **Dispositional traits** *consist of aspects of personality consistent across different contexts and can be compared across a group along a continuum representing high and low degrees of the characteristic.* Dispositional traits are the level of personality most people think of first, and they include commonly used descriptors such as shy, talkative, authoritarian, and the like.
- **Personal concerns** *consist of things important to people, their goals, and their major concerns in life.* Personal concerns are usually described in motivational, developmental, or strategic terms; they reflect the stage of life a person is in at the time.
- **Life narrative** *consists of the aspects of personality pulling everything together, those integrative aspects that give a person an identity or sense of self.* The creation of one's identity is the goal of this level.

In an extension of McAdams's model of personality, Karen Hooker (Bolkan & Hooker, 2012; Hooker & McAdams, 2003; Ko, Mejía, & Hooker, 2014) added three processes that act in tandem with the three structural components of personality proposed by McAdams. **State processes** *act with dispositional traits to create transient, short-term changes in emotion, mood, hunger, anxiety, and so on.* Personal concerns act in tandem with self-regulatory processes that include such processes as primary and secondary control (discussed in Chapter 8). **Cognitive processes** *act jointly with life narratives to create natural interactions that occur between a storyteller and listener, processes central in organizing life stories.*

Finally, as one moves from examining dispositional traits to personal concerns to life narrative (and their corresponding processes), it becomes more likely observable change will take place (Debast et al., 2014; Graham & Lachman, 2012; Schultz & Schultz, 2017). In a sense, the level of dispositional traits can be viewed as the "raw stuff" of personality, whereas each successive level must be constructed to a greater extent. In the following sections, we use McAdams's levels to organize our discussion of adulthood personality. Let's begin with the "raw stuff" and see how dispositional traits are structured in adulthood. ∎

9.1 Dispositional Traits Across Adulthood

LEARNING OBJECTIVES
- What is the five-factor model of dispositional traits?
- What happens to dispositional traits across adulthood?
- What can we conclude from theory and research on dispositional traits?

Abby was attending her high school reunion. She hadn't seen her friend Michelle in 20 years. Abby remembered that in high school Michelle was always surrounded by a group of people. She always walked up to people and initiated conversations, was at ease with strangers, pleasant, and often described as the "life of the party." Abby wondered if Michelle would be the same outgoing person she was in high school.

Many of us eventually attend a high school reunion. It is amusing, so it is said, to see how our classmates changed over the years. In addition to noticing gray or missing hair and a few wrinkles, we should pay attention to personality characteristics. The questions that surfaced for Abby are similar to the ones we generate ourselves. For example, will Katy be the same outgoing person she was as captain of the cheerleaders? Will Ted still be as concerned about social issues at 68 as he was at 18?

To learn as much about our friends as possible we could make careful observations of our classmates' personalities over the course of several reunions. Then, at the gathering marking 60 years since graduation, we could examine the trends we observed. Did our classmates' personalities change substantially or did they remain essentially the same as they were 60 years earlier?

How we think these questions will be answered provides clues to our personal biases concerning personality stability or change across adulthood. As we will see, biases about continuity and discontinuity are more obvious in personality research than in any other area of adult development.

In addition to considering the old debate of whether Michelle's personality characteristics remained stable or have changed, Abby's description of Michelle suggests Michelle is an outgoing, or extroverted, person. How did Abby arrive at this judgment? She probably combined several aspects of Michelle's behavior into a concept that describes her rather concisely. What we have done is use the notion of a personality trait. Extending this same reasoning to many areas of behavior is the basis for trait theories of personality. More formally, people's characteristic behaviors can be understood through attributes that reflect underlying dispositional traits that are relatively enduring aspects of personality. We use the basic tenets of trait theory when we describe ourselves and others with such terms as calm, aggressive, independent, friendly, and so on.

Three assumptions are made about traits (Costa & McCrae, 2011). First, traits are based on comparisons of individuals, because there are no absolute quantitative standards for concepts such as friendliness. Second, the qualities or behaviors making up a particular trait must be distinctive enough to avoid confusion. Imagine the chaos if friendliness and aggressiveness had many behaviors in common and others were vastly different! Finally, the traits attributed to a specific person are assumed to be stable characteristics. We normally assume people who are friendly in several situations are going to be friendly the next time we see them.

These three assumptions are all captured in the classic definition of a trait: "*A* **trait** *is any distinguishable, relatively enduring way that one individual differs from others*" (Guilford, 1959, p. 6). Based on this definition, **trait theories** *assume little change in personality occurs across adulthood.*

Most trait theories have several common guiding principles. An important one for this discussion concerns the structure of traits. Like it does for intelligence (see Chapter 7), structure concerns the way traits are organized within the individual. This organization is usually inferred from the pattern of related and unrelated personality characteristics, and is generally expressed in terms of dimensions. Personality structures can be examined over time to see whether they change with age.

The Case for Stability: The Five-Factor Model

Although many trait theories of personality have been proposed over the years, few have been concerned with or have been based on adults of different ages. A major exception to this is the five-factor model proposed by Costa and McCrae (1994; Costa & McCrae, 2011; McCrae, 2016; McCrae & Costa, 2003). Their model is strongly grounded in cross-sectional, longitudinal, and sequential research. *The* **five-factor model** *consists of five independent dimensions of personality: neuroticism, extraversion, openness to experience, agreeableness, and conscientiousness.*

The first three dimensions of Costa and McCrae's model—neuroticism, extraversion, and openness to experience—have been the ones most heavily researched. Each of these dimensions is represented by six facets reflecting the main characteristics associated with it. The remaining two dimensions were added to the original three in the late 1980s to account for more data and to bring the theory closer to other trait theories. Let's consider each of the five dimensions briefly.

- **Neuroticism.** The six facets of neuroticism are anxiety, hostility, self-consciousness, depression, impulsiveness, and vulnerability. Anxiety and hostility form underlying traits for two fundamental emotions: fear and anger. Although we all experience these emotions at times, the frequency and intensity with which they are felt vary from one person to another. People who are high in trait anxiety are nervous, high-strung, tense, worried, and pessimistic. Besides being prone to anger, hostile people are irritable and tend to be hard to get along with.

    The traits of self-consciousness and depression relate to the emotions shame and sorrow. Being high in self-consciousness is associated with being sensitive to criticism, teasing, and feelings of inferiority. Trait depression involves feelings of sadness, hopelessness, loneliness, guilt, and low self-worth.

    The final two facets of neuroticism—impulsiveness and vulnerability—are most often manifested as behaviors rather than as emotions. Impulsiveness is the tendency to give in to temptation and desires because of a lack of willpower and self-control. Consequently, impulsive people often do things in excess, such as overeating and overspending, and they are more likely to smoke, gamble, and use drugs. Vulnerability involves a lowered capability to deal effectively with stress. Vulnerable people tend to panic in a crisis or emergency and highly dependent on others for help. Costa and McCrae (1998, 2011; McCrae & Costa, 2003) note that, in general, people high in neuroticism tend to be high in each of the traits involved. High neuroticism typically results in violent and negative emotions that interfere with people's ability to handle problems or to get along with other people.

We can see how this cluster of traits operates. A person gets anxious and embarrassed in a social situation such as a class reunion; the frustration in dealing with others makes the person hostile, leading to excessive drinking at the party, and may result in subsequent depression for making a fool of oneself, and so on.

- **Extraversion.** The six facets of extraversion can be grouped into three interpersonal traits (warmth, gregariousness, and assertiveness) and three temperamental traits (activity, excitement seeking, and positive emotions). Warmth, or attachment, is a friendly, compassionate, intimately involved style of interacting with other people. Warmth and gregariousness (a desire to be with other people) make up what is sometimes called sociability. Gregarious people thrive on crowds; the more social interaction the better. Assertive people make natural leaders, take charge easily, make up their own minds, and readily express their thoughts and feelings.

  Temperamentally, extraverts like to keep busy; they are the people who seem to have endless energy, talk fast, and want to be on the go. They prefer to be in stimulating, exciting environments and often go searching for a challenging situation. This active, exciting lifestyle is evident in the extravert's positive emotion; these people are walking examples of zest, delight, and fun.

  An interesting aspect of extraversion is that this dimension relates well to occupational interests and values. People high in extraversion tend to have people-oriented jobs, such as social work, business administration, and sales. They value humanitarian goals and a person-oriented use of power. People low in extraversion tend to prefer task-oriented jobs, such as architecture or accounting.

- **Openness to Experience.** The six facets of openness to experience represent six different areas. In the area of fantasy, openness means having a vivid imagination and active dream life. In aesthetics, openness is seen in the appreciation of art and beauty, sensitivity to pure experience for its own sake. When open to action, people exhibit a willingness to try something new such as a new kind of cuisine, movie, or a travel destination. People who are open to ideas and values are curious and value knowledge for the sake of knowing. Open people also tend to be open-minded in their values, often admitting what may be right for one person may not be right for everyone. This outlook is a direct outgrowth of individuals' willingness to think of different possibilities in addition to their tendency to empathize with others in different circumstances. Open people also experience their own feelings strongly and see them as a major source of meaning in life.

  Not surprisingly, openness to experience is also related to occupational choice. Open people are likely to be found in occupations that place a high value on thinking theoretically or philosophically and less emphasis on economic values. They are typically intelligent and tend to subject themselves to stressful situations. Occupations such as psychologist or minister, for example, appeal to open people.

- **Agreeableness.** The easiest way to understand the agreeableness dimension is to consider the traits characterizing antagonism. Antagonistic people tend to set themselves against others; they are skeptical, mistrustful, callous, unsympathetic, stubborn, and rude; and they have a defective sense of attachment. Antagonism may be manifested in ways other than overt hostility. Some antagonistic people are skillful manipulators or aggressive go-getters with little patience.

  Scoring high on agreeableness, the opposite of antagonism, may not always be adaptive either, however. These people may tend to be overly dependent and self-effacing, traits that often prove annoying to others.

- **Conscientiousness.** Scoring high on conscientiousness indicates one is hardworking, ambitious, energetic, scrupulous, and persevering. Such people have a strong desire to make something of themselves. People at the opposite end of this scale tend to be negligent, lazy, disorganized, late, aimless, and not persistent.

What Happens to Dispositional Traits Across Adulthood?

Costa and McCrae investigated whether the traits that make up their model remain stable across adulthood (e.g., Costa & McCrae, 1988, 1994, 1997, 2011; McCrae & Costa, 2003). They suggest personality traits stop changing by age 30, after which they appear to be "set in plaster" (Costa & McCrae, 1994, p. 21). The data from the Costa, McCrae, and colleagues' studies came from the Baltimore Longitudinal Study of Aging for the 114 men who took the Guilford-Zimmerman Temperament Survey (GZTS) on three occasions, with each of the two follow-up tests about six years apart.

What Costa and colleagues found was surprising. Even over a 12-year period, the 10 traits measured by the GZTS remained highly stable; the correlations ranged from .68 to .85. In much of personality research we might expect to find this degree of stability over a week or two, but to see it over 12 years is noteworthy.

We would normally be skeptical of such consistency over a long period. But similar findings were obtained in other studies. In a longitudinal study of 60-, 80-, and 100-year-olds, Martin, Long, and Poon (2002) found stability higher for those in their 70s and 80s than for centenarians. However, some interesting changes did occur in the very old. There was an increase in suspiciousness and sensitivity that could be explained by increased wariness of victimization in older adulthood.

Stability was also observed in longitudinal data conducted over various lengths of time, from a 7-year period (Mõttus, Johnson, & Deary, 2012; Roberts & DelVecchio, 2000) to as long as a 30-year span (Leon et al., 1979). According to this evidence, it appears individuals change little in self-reported personality traits over periods of up to 30 years long and over the age range of 20 to 90 years of age.

However, there is evidence both stability and change can be detected in personality trait development across the adult life span (Allemand, Zimprich, & Hendriks, 2008; Caspi, Roberts, & Shiner, 2005; Debast et al., 2014; Mõttus et al., 2012; Schultz & Schultz, 2017). These findings came about because of advances in statistical techniques in teasing apart longitudinal and cross-sectional data (see Chapter 1). Researchers find the way people differ in their personality becomes more pronounced with older age. For example, researchers find extraversion and openness decrease with age whereas agreeableness increases with age. Conscientious appears to peak in middle age. Most interestingly, neuroticism often disappears or is much less apparent in late life. Such changes are found in studies that examine larger populations across a larger age range (e.g., 16 to mid-80s) and greater geographical regions (e.g., United States and Great Britain).

Will you recognize your classmates at a reunion many years from now by their personalities?

Ursula Staudinger and colleagues have a perspective that reconciles both stability and change in personality traits (Mühlig-Versen, Bowen, & Staudinger, 2012; Staudinger, 2015). They suggest personality takes on two forms: adjustment and growth. **Personality adjustment** *involves developmental changes in terms of their adaptive value and functionality, such as functioning effectively within society, and how personality contributes to everyday life running smoothly.* **Personality growth** *refers to ideal end states such as increased self-transcendence, wisdom, and integrity.* Examples of this will be discussed later and includes Erikson's theory.

Both of these personality dimensions interact because growth cannot occur without adjustment. However, Staudinger (2015) argues while growth in terms of ideal end states does not necessarily occur in everyone, since it is less easily acquired, strategies for adjustment develops across the latter half of the life span. This framework can be used to interpret stability and change in the Big Five personality factors.

First, the consensus regarding change in the Big Five with increasing age is the absence of neuroticism and the presence of agreeableness and conscientiousness. These three traits are associated with personality adjustment, especially in terms of becoming emotionally less volatile and more attuned to social demands and social roles (Mühlig-Versen et al., 2012; Staudinger, 2015). These characteristics allow older adults to maintain and regain levels of well-being in the face of loss, threats, and challenges; common occurrences in late life.

Studies also show a decrease in openness to new experiences with increasing age (e.g., Graham & Lachman, 2012; Helson et al., 2002; Roberts et al., 2006; Srivastava et al., 2003). Staudinger argues openness to experience is related to personal maturity because it is highly correlated with ego development, wisdom, and emotional complexity. **Ego development** *refers to fundamental changes in the ways our thoughts, values, morals, and goals are organized. Transitions from one stage to another depend on both internal biological changes and external social changes to which the person must adapt.* Evidence suggests these three aspects of personality (ego level, wisdom, and emotional complexity) do not increase with age and may show decline (Grühn et al., 2013; Mühlig-Versen et al., 2012; Staudinger, Dörner, & Mickler, 2005; Staudinger, 2015). Staudinger concludes personal growth in adulthood appears to be rare rather than normative.

To summarize, there appears to be increases in adjustment aspects of personality with increasing age, and it could be normative. At the same time, however, the basic indicators of personality growth tend to show stability or decline. You might ask, what's going on?

The most likely answer is personality growth or change across adulthood does not normally occur unless there are special circumstances and with an environmental push for it to occur. Thus, the personality-related adjustment grows in adulthood does so in response to ever-changing developmental challenges and tasks, such as establishing a career, marriage, and family.

Conclusions About Dispositional Traits

What can we conclude about the development of dispositional traits across adulthood? The evidence shows that personality traits as a whole remain mostly stable throughout adulthood when data are averaged across many different kinds of people. However, if we ask about specific aspects of personality in specific kinds of people, we are more likely to find evidence of both change and stability.

A reasonable resolution to the trait debate is to understand the answer to the basic question depends on how the data are analyzed (Helson et al., 2002; Hill et al., 2012; Mõttus et al., 2012; Mroczek & Spiro, 2003; Staudinger, 2015). Mroczek and colleagues challenge the conclusions drawn from the typical longitudinal studies on stability and change in personality by examining personality across the adult life span at the level of the individual. We describe this challenge in more detail in the Current Controversies feature.

The analytic approach discussed in the Current Controversies feature allows a more detailed answer to questions of stability and change. Based upon a detailed analysis of individual patterns of personality stability and change, Wrzus and Roberts (2017) propose a model that accounts for both developmental patterns. The **Tri**ggering situations, **E**xpectancy, **S**tates/**S**tate **E**xpressions, and **Rea**ctions (TESSERA) model, shown in Figure 9.1, describes a process by which long-term personality development is the product of repeated short-term, situational processes. These short-term processes repeat and create a feedback loop. These processes in turn can result in changes in personality characteristics and behavior over time, showing up eventually as changes in personality. That these short-term processes differ across people is why some people show changes in personality traits and others do not. It can also explain why the life narratives of people also differ, a topic we will explore later in this chapter.

■ CURRENT CONTROVERSIES

Intraindividual Change and the Stability of Traits

When is a person's personality "set?" That deceptively straightforward question continues to challenge social scientists, neuroscientists, and philosophers alike. We have seen evidence supporting the view that personality is set certainly by early adulthood. And we have seen evidence that in some specific areas it may never be fully "set." Why can't we just leave the matter as one that may be irresolvable and move on?

Personality traits are important predictors of mental and physical health as well as psychological well-being. As a result, whether personality is "set" or not has important implications for life outcomes. Specifically, if personality is "set," then a person would have a very difficult time moving from, say, a low sense of well-being to a more positive sense.

This is why the ongoing debate over how to analyze longitudinal data on personality across adulthood matters. Typically, stability and change are examined through average (mean) level comparisons over time. In other words, does the mean level of a particular personality trait such as extraversion in a target group of people at one age remain stable for them at another point in time (say 10 years later) or does it change?

There is a problem with this usual approach, though. Several researchers (e.g., Hill et al., 2012; Mõttus et al., 2012; Mroczek & Spiro, 2003) suggest examining change in mean levels of a personality trait does not adequately address stability and change at the level of the individual. Statistically, a group mean hides the variations in and particular individual's data. A better approach is to examine what happens to each person in a longitudinal study and to map individual patterns of stability and change. This allows researchers to ask the questions, "Do some people remain stable whereas others change?" and, if there are people who change, "Do some people change more than others?"

Data addressing these questions indicate important individual differences in the extent people do or do not change. As noted in the text, this has resulted in new models of the development of personality traits across adulthood.

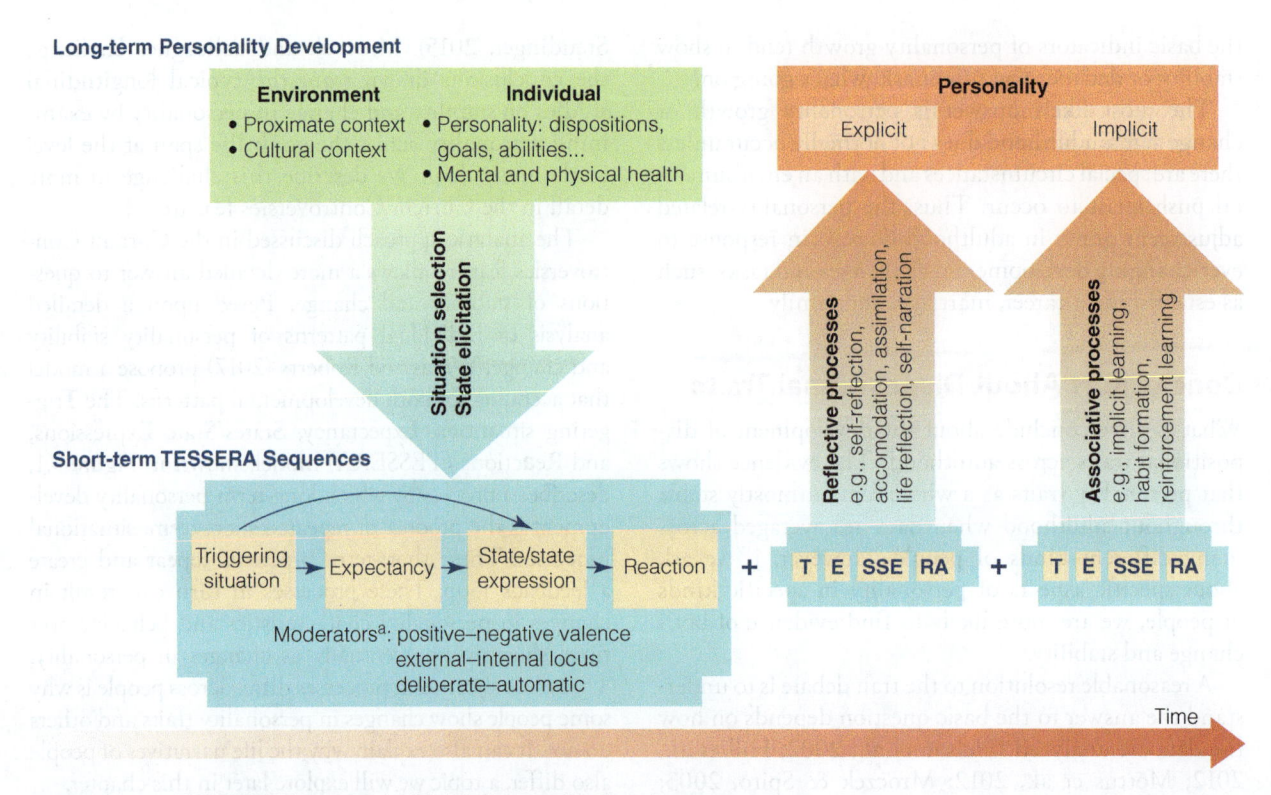

FIGURE 9.1 TESSERA Framework of Adult Personality Development
Source: Wrzus, C., & Roberts, B. W. (2017). Processes of personality development in adulthood: The TESSERA framework. *Personality and Social Psychology Review, 21*, 253–277. doi:10.1177/1088868316652279.

What about that high school reunion? On the basis of dispositional traits, then, we should have little difficulty knowing our high school classmates many years from now, even taking some degree of change into account.

Adult Development in Action

If you were a counselor, how would you use research on stability and dispositional traits to understand why it is difficult for people to change their behavior?

9.2 Personal Concerns and Qualitative Stages in Adulthood

LEARNING OBJECTIVES
- What are personal concerns?
- What are the main elements of Jung's theory?
- What are the stages in Erikson's theory? What types of clarifications and extensions of it have been offered? What research evidence is there to support his stages?
- What are the main points and problems with theories based on life transitions?
- What can we conclude about personal concerns?

Andy showed all the signs. He divorced his wife of nearly 20 years to enter into a relationship with a woman 15 years younger, sold his ordinary-looking mid-size sedan for a red sports car, and began working out regularly at the health club after years of being a couch potato. Andy claims he hasn't felt this good in years; he is happy to be making this change in middle age. All of Andy's friends agree: This is a clear case of midlife crisis—or is it?

Many people believe strongly middle age brings with it a normative crisis called the midlife crisis. There would appear to be lots of evidence to support this view, based on case studies like Andy's. But is everything as it seems? We'll find out in this section. First we consider the evidence people's priorities and personal concerns change throughout adulthood, requiring adults to reassess themselves from time to time. This alternative position to the five-factor model discussed earlier claims change is the rule during adulthood.

What does it mean to know another person well? McAdams and Olson (2010) believe to know another person well takes more than just knowing where he or she falls on the dimensions of dispositional traits. Rather, it means knowing what issues are important to a person, that is, what the person wants, how the individual goes about getting what he or she wants, what the person's plans are for the future, how the person interacts with others who provide key personal relationships, and so forth. In short, we need to know something about a person's personal concerns. Personal concerns reflect what people want during particular times of their lives and within specific domains; they are the strategies, plans, and defenses people use to get what they want and avoid getting what they don't.

What's Different About Personal Concerns?

Many researchers study personality in ways explicitly contextual, in contrast to work on dispositional traits that ignores context. This work emphasizes the importance of sociocultural influences on development that shape people's wants and behaviors (Hooker, 2015; Hooker & McAdams, 2003). This research shows, for example, that a person-centered approach focusing on personal control and social relationship quality is better than dispositional traits in understanding life satisfaction.

Focusing on personal concerns differs from research on dispositional traits (Hooker, 2015; Hooker & McAdams, 2003; McAdams & Olson, 2010). Most important, in this approach personality constructs are not reducible to traits. Rather, such personality needs to be viewed as conscious descriptions of what people are trying to accomplish during a given period of life and what goals and goal-based concerns they have.

As Cantor (1990) initially noted, these constructs speak directly to the question of what people actually do and the goals they set for themselves in life. For this reason, we would expect to see considerable change in personality across adulthood, given the importance of sociocultural influences and the changing nature of life tasks as people mature. Accompanying these goals and motivations that define personal concerns are the self-regulation processes implemented to effect change in personal concerns. The transition from primary control to secondary control or from assimilative to accommodative coping discussed in Chapter 8 enables people to recalibrate their goals and personal concerns

in later life. This process serves the important function of maintaining satisfaction and meaningfulness in life (Hooker, 2015; Hooker & McAdams, 2003; McAdams & Olson, 2010).

We will consider various person-centered approaches in this section and section 9.3. In this section, we focus on the idea that people's personality changes throughout the life span can be described as a series of qualitative stages that reflect the central concern of that period of life. Let's begin with Carl Jung's theory—the theory that started people thinking about personality change in midlife.

Jung's Theory

Jung represents a turning point in the history of psychoanalytic thought. Initially allied with Freud, he soon severed the tie and developed his own ideas that have elements of both Freudian theory and humanistic psychology. He was one of the first theorists to believe in personality development in adulthood; this marked a major break with Freudian thought, that argued personality development ended in adolescence.

Jung's theory emphasizes each aspect of a person's personality must be in balance with all the others. This means each part of the personality will be expressed in some way, whether through normal means, neurotic symptoms, or in dreams. Jung asserts the parts of the personality are organized in such a way as to produce two basic orientations of the ego. One of these orientations is concerned with the external world; Jung labels it extraversion. The opposite orientation, toward the inner world of subjective experiences, is labeled introversion. To be psychologically healthy, both of these orientations must be present, and they must be balanced. Individuals must deal with the external world effectively and also be able to evaluate their inner feelings and values. When people emphasize one orientation over another, they are classified as extraverts or introverts.

Jung advocates two important age-related trends in personality development. The first relates to the introversion–extraversion distinction. Young adults tend to be more extraverted than older adults, perhaps because of younger people's need to find a mate, have a career, and so forth. With increasing age, however, the need for balance creates a need to focus inward and explore personal feelings about aging and mortality (Cavanaugh, 2017). Thus, Jung argued with age comes an increase in introversion.

The second age-related trend in Jung's theory involves the feminine and masculine aspects of our personalities.

Each of us, according to Jung, has elements of both masculinity and femininity. In young adulthood, however, most of us express only one of them while working hard to suppress the other. In other words, young adults most often act in accordance with gender-role stereotypes appropriate to their culture. As they grow older, people begin to let out the suppressed parts of their personality. This means men begin to behave in ways that earlier in life they would have considered feminine, and women behave in ways that they formerly would have thought masculine. These changes achieve a better balance that allows men and women to deal more effectively with their individual needs rather than being driven by socially defined stereotypes. This balance, however, does not mean a reversal of sex roles. On the contrary, it represents the expression of aspects of ourselves that have been there all along but we have simply not allowed showing. We return to this issue at the end of the chapter when we consider gender-role development.

Jung's ideas that self and personality are organized by symbols and stories and the notion we transcend the dualities of femininity–masculinity and conscious–unconscious, among others, have now become active areas of research (Labouvie-Vief, 2015). However, as Labouvie-Vief points out, most empirical evidence suggests these reorganizations proposed by Jung are more indicative of advanced or exceptional development.

Jung stretched traditional psychoanalytic theory to new limits by postulating continued development across adulthood. Other theorists took Jung's lead and argued not only personality development occurred in adulthood but also it did so in an orderly, sequential fashion. We consider the sequences developed by Erik Erikson.

Erikson's Stages of Psychosocial Development

The best-known life-span theorist is Erik Erikson (1982), who called attention to cultural mechanisms involved in personality development. According to him, personality is determined by the interaction between an inner maturational plan and external societal demands. He proposes the life cycle has eight stages of development, summarized in Table 9.1. Erikson believed the sequence of stages is biologically fixed.

Each stage in Erikson's theory is marked by a struggle between two opposing tendencies and both are experienced by the person. The names of the stages reflect the issues that form the struggles. The struggles are resolved through an interactive process involving both the inner psychological and the outer social influences. Successful resolutions establish the basic areas of psychosocial strength; unsuccessful resolutions impair ego development in a particular area and adversely affect the resolution of future struggles. Thus each stage in Erikson's theory represents a kind of crisis.

The sequence of stages in Erikson's theory is based on the **epigenetic principle**, *meaning each psychosocial strength has its own special time of ascendancy, or period of particular importance.* The eight stages represent the order of this ascendancy. Because the stages extend across the whole

TABLE 9.1 Summary of Erikson's Theory of Psychosocial Development, with Important Relationships and Psychosocial Strengths Acquired at Each Stage

	Psychosocial Crisis	Significant Relations	Basic Strengths
1. Infancy	Basic trust versus basic mistrust	Maternal person	Hope
2. Early childhood	Autonomy versus shame and doubt	Paternal people	Will
3. Play age	Initiative versus guilt	Basic family	Purpose
4. School age	Industry versus inferiority	Neighborhood, school	Competence
5. Adolescence	Identity versus identity confusion	Peer groups and outgroups; models of leadership	Love
6. Young adulthood	Intimacy versus isolation	Partners in friendship, sex competition, cooperation	Love
7. Adulthood	Generativity versus stagnation	Divided labor and shared household	Care
8. Old age	Integrity versus despair	Humankind, "my kind"	Wisdom

Source: From *The Life Cycle Completed: A Review* by Erik H. Erikson. Copyright © 1982 by Rikan Enterprises, Ltd. Used by permission of W. W. Norton & Company.

life span, it takes a lifetime to acquire all of the psychosocial strengths. Moreover, Erikson realizes present and future behavior must have its roots in the past, because later stages build on the foundation laid in previous ones.

Erikson argues the basic aspect of a healthy personality is a sense of trust toward oneself and others. Thus the first stage in his theory involves trust versus mistrust, representing the conflict an infant faces in developing trust in a world it knows little about. With trust come feelings of security and comfort.

The second stage, autonomy versus shame and doubt, reflects children's budding understanding they are in charge of their own actions. This understanding changes them from totally reactive beings to ones who can act on the world intentionally. Their autonomy is threatened, however, by their inclinations to avoid responsibility for their actions and to go back to the security of the first stage.

In the third stage, the conflict is initiative versus guilt. Once children realize they can act on the world and are somebody, they begin to discover who they are. They take advantage of wider experience to explore the environment on their own, ask many questions about the world, and imagine possibilities about themselves.

The fourth stage is marked by children's increasing interests in interacting with peers, their need for acceptance, and their need to develop competencies. Erikson views these needs as representing industry versus inferiority, and is manifested behaviorally in children's desire to accomplish tasks by working hard. Failure to succeed in developing self-perceived competencies results in feelings of inferiority.

During adolescence, Erikson believes we deal with the issue of identity versus identity confusion. The choice we make—the identity we form—is not so much who we are but who we can become. The struggle in adolescence is choosing from among a multitude of possible selves the one we will become. Identity confusion results when we are torn over the possibilities. The struggle involves trying to balance our need to choose a possible self and the desire to try out many possible selves.

During young adulthood the major developmental task, achieving intimacy versus isolation, involves establishing a fully intimate relationship with another. Erikson (1968) argues intimacy means the sharing of all aspects of oneself without fearing the loss of identity. If intimacy is not achieved, isolation results. One way to assist the development of intimacy is to choose a mate who represents the ideal of all one's past experiences. The psychosocial strength that emerges from the intimacy–isolation struggle is love.

With the advent of middle age, the focus shifts from intimacy to concern for the next generation, expressed as generativity versus stagnation. The struggle occurs between a sense of generativity (the feeling people must maintain and perpetuate society) and a sense of stagnation (the feeling of self-absorption). Generativity is seen in such things as parenthood; teaching, like the man in the photograph; or providing goods and services for the benefit of society. If the challenge of generativity is accepted, the development of trust in the next generation is facilitated, and the psychosocial strength of care is obtained. We examine generativity in more detail a bit later in this chapter.

In old age, individuals must resolve the struggle between ego integrity and despair. This last stage begins with a growing awareness of the nearness of the end of life, but it is actually completed by only a small number of people (Erikson, 1982). According to Erikson (1982), this struggle comes about as older adults try to understand their lives in terms of the future of their family and community. Thoughts of a person's own death are balanced by the realization they live on through children, grandchildren, great-grandchildren, and the community as a whole. This realization produces what Erikson calls a "life-affirming involvement" in the present.

To achieve integrity, a person must come to terms with the choices and events that made his or her life unique. There must also be an acceptance of the fact one's life is drawing to a close. Research shows a connection between engaging in a life review and achieving integrity, so life review forms the basis for effective mental health interventions (Weiss, Westerhof, & Bohlmeijer, 2016; Westerhof, Bohlmeijer, & Webster, 2010).

Erikson's stage of integrity is achieved when older adults understand that they will live on through future generations of their family and community.

Who reaches integrity? Erikson (1982) emphasizes people who demonstrate integrity made many different choices and follow different lifestyles; the point is everyone has this opportunity to achieve integrity if they strive for it. Those who reach integrity become self-affirming and self-accepting; they judge their lives to have been worthwhile and good. They are glad to have lived the lives they did.

Clarifications and Expansions of Erikson's Theory

Erikson's theory made a major impact on thinking about life-span development. However, some aspects of his theory are unclear, poorly defined, or unspecified. Traditionally, these problems led critics to dismiss the theory as untestable and incomplete. However, the situation is changing. Other theorists tried to address these problems by identifying common themes, specifying underlying mental processes, and reinterpreting and integrating the theory with other ideas. These ideas are leading researchers to reassess the usefulness of Erikson's theory as a guide for research on adult personality development.

Logan (1986) points out Erikson's theory can be considered as a cycle that repeats: from basic trust to identity and from identity to integrity. In this approach the developmental progression is trust → achievement → wholeness. Throughout life we first establish we can trust other people and ourselves. Initially, trust involves learning about ourselves and others, represented by the first two stages (trust vs. mistrust and autonomy vs. shame and doubt). The recapitulation of this idea in the second cycle is seen in our struggle to find a person with whom we can form a close relationship yet not lose our own sense of self (intimacy vs. isolation).

In addition, Logan shows how achievement—our need to accomplish and to be recognized for it—is a theme throughout Erikson's theory. During childhood this idea is reflected in the two stages initiative versus guilt and industry versus inferiority, whereas in adulthood it is represented by generativity versus stagnation. Finally, Logan points out the issue of understanding ourselves as worthwhile and whole is first encountered during adolescence (identity vs. identity confusion) and is re-experienced during old age (integrity vs. despair). Logan's analysis emphasizes psychosocial development, although complicated on the surface, may actually reflect only a small number of issues. Moreover, he points out we do not come to a single resolution of these issues of trust, achievement, and wholeness. Rather, they are issues we struggle with our entire lives.

Slater (2003) expanded on Logan's reasoning, suggesting the central crisis of generativity versus stagnation includes struggles between pride and embarrassment, responsibility and ambivalence, career productivity and inadequacy, as well as parenthood and self-absorption. Each of these conflicts provides further knowledge about generativity as the intersection of society and the human life cycle.

Researchers focusing on emerging adulthood raised the possibility of an additional stage specific to this phase of life. Patterson (2012) speculates a fifth stage she labels incarnation versus impudence is needed between adolescence (identity vs. role confusion) and young adulthood (intimacy vs. isolation). For Patterson, this crisis is "resolved through experimental sexuality, temporal and spatial social and intimate relationships, interdependence and self-sufficiency and dependence and helplessness, and relativist and absolutist ideological experimentation."

Some critics argue Erikson's stage of generativity is much too broad to capture the essence of adulthood. Kotre (1999, 2005) contends adults experience many opportunities to express generativity that are not equivalent and do not lead to a general state. Rather, he sees generativity more as a set of impulses felt at different times and in different settings, such as at work or in grandparenting. More formally, Kotre describes five types of generativity: biological and parental generativity, that concerns raising children; technical generativity, relating to the passing of specific skills from one generation to another; cultural generativity, referring to being a mentor (discussed in more detail in Chapter 12); agentic generativity, the desire to be or to do something that transcends death; and communal generativity, manifesting as a person's participation in a mutual, interpersonal reality. Only rarely, Kotre contends, is there a continuous state of generativity in adulthood. He asserts the struggles identified by Erikson are not fought constantly; rather, they probably come and go. We examine this idea in more detail in the next section.

Research on Generativity

Perhaps the central period in adulthood from an Eriksonian perspective is the stage of generativity versus stagnation. One of the best empirically based efforts to describe generativity is McAdams's model (McAdams, 2001, 2015; McAdams & Guo, 2015) shown in Figure 9.2.

This multidimensional model shows how generativity results from the complex interconnections among societal and inner forces. The tension between creating a product or outcome that outlives oneself and selflessly

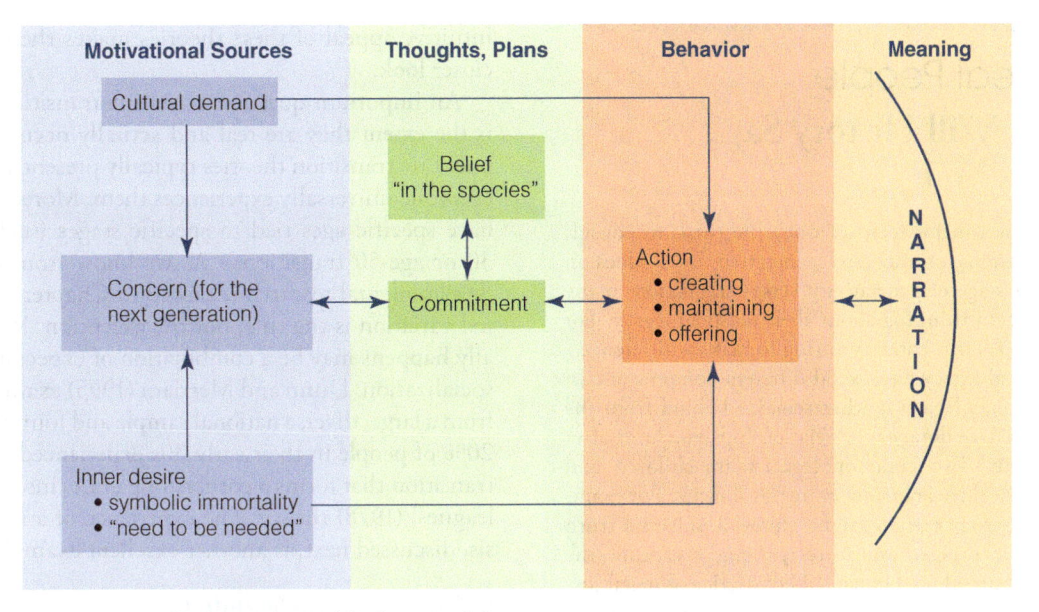

FIGURE 9.2 McAdams's model of generativity.
Source: McAdams, D. P., Hart, H. M., & Maruna, S. (1998). The anatomy of generativity. In D. P. McAdams & E. de St. Aubin (Eds.), *Generativity and Adult Development: How and Why We Care for the Next Generation* (p. 7). Washington, DC: American Psychological Association.

bestowing one's efforts as a gift to the next generation (reflecting a concern for what is good for society) results in a concern for the next generation and a belief in the goodness of the human enterprise. The positive resolution of this conflict finds middle-aged adults developing a generative commitment that produces generative actions. A person derives personal meaning from being generative by constructing a life story or narration that helps create the person's identity.

The components of McAdams's model relate differently to personality traits. Generative *concern* is a general personality tendency of interest in caring for younger individuals, and generative *action* is the actual behaviors that promote the well-being of the next generation. Generative concern relates to life satisfaction and overall happiness, whereas generative action does not. For example, new grandparents may derive satisfaction from their grandchildren and are greatly concerned with their well-being but have little desire to engage in the daily hassles of caring for them on a regular basis.

Although they can be expressed by adults of all ages, certain types of generativity are more common at some ages than others. Middle-aged and older adults show a greater preoccupation with generativity themes than do younger adults in their accounts of personally meaningful life experiences (McAdams, 2015; McAdams & Guo, 2015). Middle-aged adults make more generative commitments (e.g., "save enough money for my daughter to go to medical school"), reflecting a major difference in the inner and outer worlds of middle-aged and older adults as opposed to younger adults.

Similar research focusing specifically on middle-aged women yields comparable results. Hills (2013) argues leaving a legacy, a major example of generativity in practice, is a core concern in midlife, more so than at any other age. Schoklitsch & Bauman (2012) point out the capacity of generativity peaks during midlife, but people continue to accomplish generative tasks into late life (e.g., great-grandparenthood).

These data demonstrate the personal concerns of middle-aged adults are fundamentally different from those of younger adults. In fact, generativity may be a stronger predictor of emotional and physical well-being in midlife and old age (Gruenewald, Liao, & Seeman, 2012; McAdams & Guo, 2015; McAdams & Olson, 2010). Among women and men, generativity is associated with positive emotion and satisfaction with life and work, and predicts physical health. Considered together, these findings provide considerable support for Erikson's contention the central concerns for adults change with age. However, the data also indicate generativity is much more complex than Erikson originally proposed and, while peaking in middle age, may not diminish in late life.

Finally, an important aspect of generativity is leaving a personal legacy (Newton & Jones, 2016). This idea is explored in more detail in the Real People feature.

Real People
What Will History Say About You?

When a major focus of one's life turns to considerations of the next generation, as it does in Erikson's stage of generativity versus stagnation, many people begin thinking about their personal legacy. For most people, this entails wanting to make a difference.

Personal legacy has several different components. In general, one's legacy is what remains behind from the work you have done or the relationships you built after your death. Two common legacies are children and wealth, but there are many more possibilities. For example, an artistic creation might express a universal truth from your perspective. A recipe might capture the essence of an ethnic heritage. The practice of social justice can be passed to future generations as a way to help ensure people's fair treatment.

The point is that everyone, at one time or another, thinks about doing something that has an impact in such a way as to outlive them, and to provide a way to be remembered for having made a difference in people's lives.

What will be *your* legacy?

Theories Based on Life Transitions

Jung's belief in a midlife crisis and Erikson's belief personality development proceeds in stages laid the foundation for other theorists' efforts. For many laypeople, the idea adults go through an orderly sequence of stages that includes both crises and stability reflects their own experience. A universal assumption of these views is that people go through predictable age-related crises, often followed by periods of relative stability, creating a series of alternating periods of stability and change.

Compared with the theories we considered to this point, however, views based on life transitions are built on shakier ground. Some are based on small, highly selective samples (such as men who attended Harvard) or surveys completed by readers of particular magazines. This is in contrast to the large databases used to test the five-factor model. These theories are associated with psychometrically sound measures and are well researched. Thus, the research methods used in studies of life transitions are questionable. Still, the intuitive appeal of these theories makes them worth a closer look.

An important question about life transition theories is the extent they are real and actually occur to everyone. Life transition theories typically present stages as if everyone universally experiences them. Moreover, many have specific ages tied to specific stages (such as age-30 or age-50 transitions). As we know from cognitive developmental research reviewed in Chapter 7, individual variation is the rule, not the exception. What actually happens may be a combination of expectations and socialization. Dunn and Merriam (1995) examined data from a large, diverse national sample and found less than 20% of people in their early 30s experienced an age-30 transition that forms a cornerstone of Levinson and colleagues' (1978) theory. The experience of a midlife crisis, discussed next, is another excellent example.

In Search of the Midlife Crisis

Perhaps the most central idea in theories that consider the importance of life transitions is that middle-aged adults experience a personal crisis that results in major changes in how they view themselves. During a midlife crisis, people are supposed to take a good hard look at themselves and, they hope, attain a much better understanding of who they are. Difficult issues such as one's own mortality and inevitable aging are supposed to be faced. Behavioral changes are supposed to occur; we even have stereotypic images of the middle-aged male, like Andy, running off with a much younger female as a result of his midlife crisis. In support of this notion, Levinson and his colleagues (1978; Levinson & Levinson, 1996) write that middle-aged men in his study reported intense internal struggles much like depression.

However, far more research fails to document the existence, and more importantly, the universality of a particularly difficult time in midlife (Lachman, 2004). In fact, those who actually experience a crisis may be suffering from general problems of psychopathology (Goldstein, 2005; Labouvie-Vief & Diehl, 1999). Studies extending Levinson's theory to women have also failed to find strong evidence of a traumatic midlife crisis (Harris et al., 1986; Reinke et al., 1985; Roberts & Newton, 1987).

Researchers point out the idea of a midlife crisis became widely accepted as fact because of the mass media (Sterns & Huyck, 2001). People take it for granted they will go through a period of intense psychological turmoil in their 40s or 50s because the media told them they would.

The fact is that most people simply don't have a classic midlife crisis. The data suggest midlife is no more or no less traumatic for most people than any other period in life. Perhaps the most convincing support for this conclusion comes from research conducted by Farrell and Rosenberg (Rosenberg, Rosenberg, & Farrell, 1999). These investigators initially set out to prove the existence of a midlife crisis because they were firm believers in it. After extensive testing and interviewing, they emerged as nonbelievers.

However, there is evidence that people engage in self-reflection. Labouvie-Vief and colleagues (e.g., Grühn et al., 2013; Labouvie-Vief, 2015; Labouvie-Vief & Diehl, 1999; Labouvie-Vief et al., 2009) offer good evidence for a reorganization of self and values across the adult life span. They suggest the major dynamic that drives such changes may not be age dependent, but rather general cognitive changes. Cavanaugh's (2017) application of this same self-reflection to the personal spiritual realm agrees that cognitive development is key.

As discussed in Chapter 8, individuals in middle adulthood show the most complex understanding of self, emotions, and motivations. Cognitive complexity also is shown to be the strongest predictor of higher levels of complexity in general. From this approach, a midlife "crisis" may be the result of general gains in cognitive complexity from early to middle adulthood.

Abigail Stewart (Newton & Stewart, 2012; Peterson & Stewart, 1996; Torges, Stewart, & Duncan, 2008) found that women who have regrets about adopting traditional roles (e.g., wife/mother) but later pursue an education or career at midlife report higher well-being than either women who experience regret but do not make a change or women who never experienced regrets about their roles. *Stewart suggests rather than a midlife crisis, such an adjustment may be more appropriately considered a* **midlife correction**, *reevaluating one's roles and dreams and making the necessary corrections.*

Perhaps the best way to view midlife and beyond is as a time of both gains and losses (Lachman 2004; Robinson & Stell, 2015). That is, the changes people perceive in midlife and beyond can be viewed as representing both gains and losses. Competence, ability to handle stress, sense of personal control, purpose in life, and social responsibility are all at their peak, whereas physical abilities, such as women's ability to bear children, and physical appearance in men and women are examples of changes many view as negative. This gain–loss view emphasizes two things. First, the exact timing of change is not fixed but occurs over an extended period

Midlife is a time when one's sense of personal control and purpose peaks, and physical abilities begin to decline.

of time. Second, change can be both positive and negative at the same time. Thus, rather than seeing midlife as a time of crisis, one may want to view it as a period when several aspects of one's life acquire new meanings.

Finally, we cannot overlook examining midlife crises from a cross-cultural perspective (Tanner & Arnett, 2009). Research results suggest midlife crisis is a cultural invention (Menon, 2001; Menon and Shweder, 1998; Sterns & Huyck, 2001). For example, anthropological evidence suggests the concept of midlife itself is limited to adults studied in certain Western societies. In other cultures, transitions and crises are linked to role relations such as marriage and relocation into the spouse's family. Major transitions are defined by such events as children's marriages and mothers-in-law moving into the older adult role of observer (Menon, 2001; Tanner & Arnett, 2009). Again, this is a good reminder that cultural context plays an important role in adult development.

Conclusions About Personal Concerns

The theories and research evidence we considered show substantive change in adults' personal concerns as people age. This conclusion is in sharp contrast to the overall stability observed in dispositional traits. Taken together, the seemingly contradictory evidence supports the basic premises of the TESSERA framework we considered earlier—there is both stability and change in personality, with situational factors having a major role in determining which outcome occurs for which aspect of personality. Nest, we will consider another key facet of personality—how we conceive of ourselves.

Adult Development in Action

As a director of human resources at a major corporation, how would knowledge about generativity help you understand your middle-aged employees better?

9.3 Life Narratives, Identity, and the Self

LEARNING OBJECTIVES

- What are the main aspects of McAdams's life-story model?
- What are the main points of Whitbourne's identity theory?
- How does the Six Foci Model of adult personality account for development?
- How does self-concept come to take adult form? What is its development during adulthood?
- What are possible selves? Do they show differences during adulthood?
- What role does religion or spiritual support play in adult life?
- What conclusions can be drawn from research using life narratives?

Antje is a 19-year-old sophomore at a community college. She expects her study of early childhood education to be difficult but rewarding. She figures along the way she will meet a great guy she will marry soon after graduation. They will have two children before she turns 30. Antje sees herself getting a good job teaching preschool children and someday owning her own day care center.

Who are you? What kind of person are you trying to become? These are the kinds of questions Antje is trying to answer. Answering these questions requires concepts of personality going beyond dis-positional traits and personal concerns. The aspects of personality we discussed thus far are important, but they lack a sense of integration, unity, coherence, and overall purpose (Hooker, 2015; McAdams, 2015). For example, understanding a person's goals from the perspective of personal concerns does not reveal who a person is trying to be or become. What is lacking in other levels of analysis is a sense of the person's identity—a sense of self.

In contrast to Erikson's (1982) proposition that identity formation is the central task of adolescence, many researchers now believe identity and the creation of the self continue to develop throughout adulthood (e.g., Graham & Lachman, 2012; Grühn et al., 2013; Hooker, 2015; McAdams, 2015; Newton & Stewart, 2012). How adults continue constructing identity and the self relies on *life narratives*, or the internalized and evolving story that integrates a person's reconstructed past, perceived present, and anticipated future into a coherent and vitalizing life myth (Curtin & Stewart, 2012; Hooker, 2015; McAdams, 2015). Careful analysis of people's life narratives provides insight into their identity.

In this section, we consider three theories of identity. Dan McAdams is concerned with understanding how people see themselves and how they fit into the adult world. Susan Krauss Whitbourne investigated people's own conceptions of the life course and how they differ from age norms and the expectations for society as a whole. Karen Hooker and McAdams jointly describe an interactive approach to personality and identity development.

To round out our understanding of identity and the self, we also examine related constructs. Before beginning, though, take time to complete the exercise in the Discovering Development feature. This exercise will give you a sense of what a life narrative is and how it might be used to gain insight into identity and the sense of self.

DISCOVERING DEVELOPMENT
Who Do You Want to Be When You "Grow Up"?

From the time you were a child, people have posed this question to you. In childhood, you probably answered by indicating some specific career, such as firefighter or teacher. But now that you are an adult, the question takes on new meaning. Rather than simply a matter of picking a profession, the question goes much deeper to the kinds of values and the essence of the person you would like to become.

Take a few minutes and think about who you would like to be in another decade or two (or maybe even 50 years hence). What things will matter to you? What will you be doing? What experiences will you have had? What lies ahead?

This exercise can give you a sense of the way researchers try to understand people's sense of identity and self through the use of personal narrative. You might want to keep what you have written and check it when the appropriate number of years elapse.

McAdams's Life-Story Model

McAdams (2001, 2015) argues a person's sense of identity cannot be understood using the language of dispositional traits or personal concerns. Identity is not just a collection of traits, nor is it a collection of plans, strategies, or goals. Instead, it is based on a story of how the person came into being, where the person has been, where he or she is going, and who he or she will become, much like Antje's story. McAdams argues that people create a life story that is an internalized narrative with a beginning, middle, and an anticipated ending. The life story is created and revised throughout adulthood as people change and the changing environment places different demands on them.

McAdams's research indicates people in Western societies begin forming their life story during late adolescence and emerging adulthood, but its roots lie in one's earliest attachments in infancy. As in Erikson's theory, adolescence marks the full initiation into forming an identity, and thus, a coherent life story begins. In emerging adulthood it is continued and refined, and from midlife and beyond it is refashioned in the wake of major and minor life changes. Generativity marks the attempt to create an appealing story "ending" that will generate new beginnings for future generations.

Paramount in these life stories is the changing personal identity reflected in the emotions conveyed in the story (from tragedy to optimism or through comic and romantic descriptions). In addition, motivations change and are reflected in the person repeatedly trying to attain his or her goals over time. The two most common goal themes are agency (reflecting power, achievement, and autonomy) and communion (reflecting love, intimacy, and a sense of belonging). Finally, stories indicate one's beliefs and values, or the ideology a person uses to set the context for his or her actions.

Every life story contains episodes that provide insight into perceived change and continuity in life. People prove to themselves and others they have either changed or remained the same by pointing to specific events supporting the appropriate claim. The main characters, representing the roles we play, in our lives represent idealizations of the self, such as "the dutiful mother" or "the reliable worker." Integrating these various aspects of the self into a coherent whole is a major challenge of midlife and later adulthood. Finally, all life stories need an ending so the self can leave a legacy that creates new beginnings. Life stories in middle-aged and older adults have a clear quality of "giving birth to" a new generation, a notion essentially identical to generativity.

One of the more popular methods for examining the development of life stories is through autobiographical memory (Dunlop, Guo, & McAdams, 2016; Lilgendahl & McAdams, 2011; McLean, 2016; McLean & Pasupathi, 2012). When people tell their life stories to others, the stories are a joint product of the speaker and the audience, which includes other key people in a person's life, such as family (Pasupathi, 2013; McLean, 2016). This co-construction of identity is a good example of conversational remembering, much like collaborative cognition discussed in Chapter 8.

Overall, McAdams (2001, 2015) believes the model for change in identity over time is a process of fashioning and refashioning one's life story. This process appears to be strongly influenced by culture. At times, the reformulation may be at a conscious level, such as when people make explicit decisions about changing careers. At other times, the revision process is unconscious and implicit, growing out of everyday activities. The goal is to create a life story that is coherent, credible, open to new possibilities, richly differentiated, reconciling of opposite aspects of oneself, and integrated within one's sociocultural context.

Whitbourne's Identity Theory

Susan Krauss Whitbourne (e.g., 1986, 1987, 2010) understood that cognitive development plays a major role in how people their identities. *The result of this process is the* **life-span construct**, *the person's unified sense of the past, present, and future.*

The life-span construct has two structural components that in turn are the ways it is manifested. The first of these components is the *scenario*, consisting of expectations about the future that are often tied to achieving specific outcomes by a particular age. In short, a scenario is a GPS map for how we want our lives to unfold.

Whitbourne grounded her theory on a fascinating cross-sectional study of 94 adults ranging in age from 24 to 61 (Whitbourne, 1986). The subjects came from all walks of life and represented a wide range of occupations and life situations. Using data from detailed interviews, Whitbourne was able to identify what she believes is the process of adult identity development based on equilibrium between identity and experience. Her model is presented in Figure 9.3. As the figure shows, there is continuous feedback between identity and experience; this explains why we may evaluate ourselves positively at one point in time, yet appear defensive and self-protective at another.

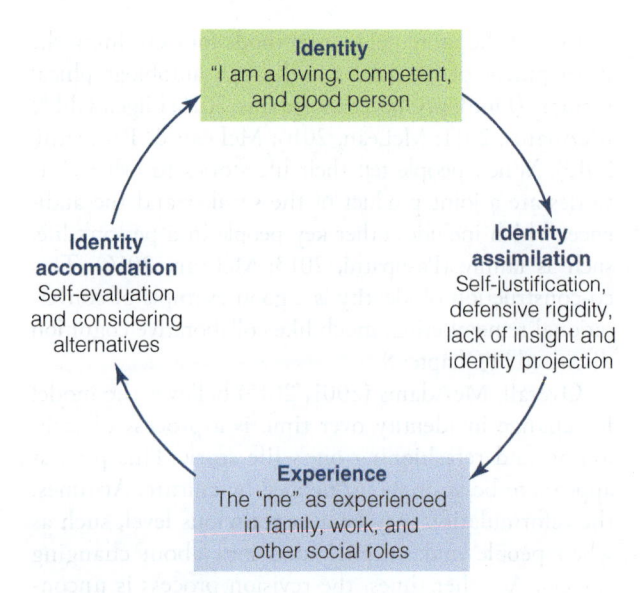

FIGURE 9.3 Whitbourne's model of adult identity processes.
Source: Whitbourne, S. K. (1986). The psychological construction of the life span. In J. E. Birren & K. W. Schaie (Eds.), *Handbook of the Psychology of Aging* (pp. 594-619). New York, NY: Van Nostrand Reinhold. All rights reserved. Reproduced by permission of the author.

As you can see, the processes of equilibrium are based on Piaget's concepts of assimilation and accommodation (see Chapter 7). Whitbourne explicitly attempted to integrate concepts from cognitive development with identity development to understand how identity is formed and revised across adulthood. The assimilation process involves using already existing aspects of identity to handle present situations. Overreliance on assimilation makes the person resistant to change. Accommodation, in contrast, reflects the willingness of the individual to let the situation determine what he or she will do. This often occurs when the person does not have a well-developed identity around a certain issue.

Although Whitbourne found evidence of life transitions, overall she found little evidence that these transitions occurred in a stagelike fashion or were tied to specific ages. Rather, she found people tend to go through transitions when they feel they needed to and to do so on their own time line. Her model has expanded to incorporate how people adapt more generally to middle age and the aging process (Whitbourne, 2010).

Several important ideas have emerged from Whitbourne's work. Most important, identity assimilation and identity accommodation change with age (Sneed & Whitbourne, 2003, 2005). Identity assimilation is higher in older adulthood and identity accommodation is higher in emerging adulthood. Furthermore, identity assimilation in older adulthood is associated with maintaining and enhancing positive self-regard through the minimization of negativity. In contrast, a changing identity (e.g., through accommodation) in older adulthood is associated more with poor psychological health. The ability to integrate age-related changes into one's identity and maintain a positive view of oneself is crucial to aging successfully (Whitbourne, 2010). This suggests people make behavioral adjustments to promote healthy adaptation to the aging process (see Chapter 3).

Six Foci Model of Adult Personality

It should be clear at this point that personality in adulthood is a pretty complicated matter. How each of us develops, indeed *whether* each of us experiences change in aspects of our personality, is a result of a complex set of forces. From this perspective, a more complete description of personality must include all of the forces discussed in Chapter 1, as well as cognitive development and underlying brain development.

This is what Hooker and McAdams (2003; Hooker, 2015; McAdams, 2015) have done in creating the Six Foci Model of Personality, depicted in Figure 9.4. The Six Foci Model integrates both the structures of personality (e.g., traits) and processes of personality within a levels-of-analysis framework. Let's take a closer look.

There are three levels of personality in the model. The first level is *traits*, the dispositional basis of personality.

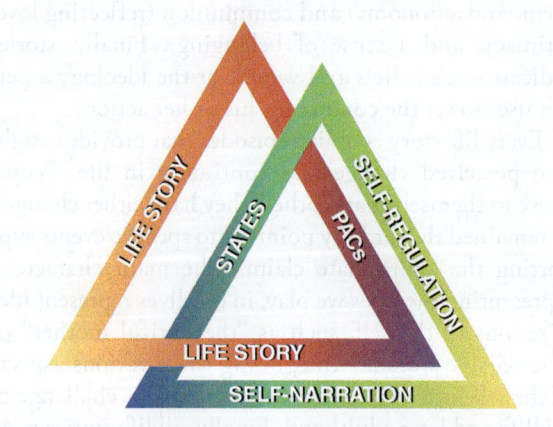

FIGURE 9.4 Six Foci Model of Adult Personality
Source: Hooker, K., & McAdams, D. P. (2003). Personality reconsidered: A new agenda for aging research. *Journal of Gerontology: Psychological Sciences, 58B*: 297. doi:10.1093/geronb/58.6.P296.

The corresponding process to trait is that of *states*, the intraindividual processes that offer the potential of change, and include such things as moods, fatigue, and anxiety.

The second level of personality structures refer to personal concerns and are called *personal action constructs (PACs)*. PACs include goals, motivation, developmental tasks, and reflect the "doing" of personality (Cantor, 1990). The parallel personality process to PACs is *self-regulatory processes*, such as self-efficacy and sense of control. Such self-regulatory processes place each PAC into specific domains, and result in differences across domains in whether personal goals are actually achieved.

Finally, the third structural level is the *life story* or scenario each person creates to provide meaning and purpose to one's life. The process counterpoint to the life story is *self-narration*, which reflects the changes one makes in telling one's life story depending on the audience.

Hooker and McAdams are clear that the levels and processes are not hierarchical; that is, they all operate simultaneously, and do not depend on each other. However, it is the case that life goals and life stories emerge later in development than do the other aspects.

What the Six Foci Model provides is a better framework in which to understand the complex ways that personality actually unfolds and operates. The model accounts for both stability and change, and explains the conditions under which each may occur. Interestingly, the model also implies that it is not until late life that personality is most fully developed.

Self-Concept and Well-Being

As we have seen, an important aspect of identity in adulthood is how one integrates various aspects of the self. Self-perceptions and how they differ with age have been examined in a wide variety of studies and are related to many behaviors. Changes in self-perceptions are often manifested in changed beliefs, concerns, and expectations. **Self-concept** *is the organized, coherent, integrated pattern of self-perceptions*. Self-concept includes the notions of self-esteem and self-image.

Kegan's Theory of Self-Concept

Kegan (1982, 1994, 2009) attempted to integrate the development of self-concept and cognitive development. He postulated six stages of the development of self, corresponding to stages of cognitive development described in Chapter 7. Kegan's first three stages—incorporative, impulsive, and imperial—correspond to Piaget's sensorimotor, preoperational, and concrete operational stages (see Chapter 7). During this time, he believes children move from knowing themselves on the basis of reflexes to knowing themselves through needs and interests.

He argues at the beginning of formal operational thought during early adolescence (see Chapter 7), a sense of interpersonal mutuality begins to develop; he terms this period the interpersonal stage. By late adolescence or young adulthood, people move to a mature sense of identity based on taking control of their own life and developing an ideology; Kegan calls this period the institutional stage.

Finally, with the acquisition of post-formal thought (see Chapter 7) comes an understanding that the self is a complex system that takes into account other people; Kegan terms this period the interindividual stage.

Kegan's work emphasizes that personality development does not occur in a vacuum. Rather, we must remember a person is a complex integrated whole. Consequently, an understanding of the development of self-concept or any other aspect of personality is enhanced by an understanding of how it relates to other dimensions of development.

Labouvie-Vief's Dynamic Integration Theory

The integration of cognitive and personality development has also been a major focus of Gisela Labouvie-Vief (1997, 2003, 2005, 2015). She argues the self is a product of the integration of emotion and cognition, topics we explored in Chapters 7 and 8.

For Labouvie-Vief, the integration of the optimization of happiness and the ability to tolerate tension and negativity is to maintain objectivity that creates a healthy self-concept in adulthood. She builds the case that the dynamic integration of this optimization and differentiation is what creates a healthy balance. The ability to accomplish this integration increases from young through middle adulthood, but decreases in late life.

This point was clearly demonstrated by Labouvie-Vief and colleagues (1995). Working within a cognitive-developmental framework, they documented age differences in self-representation in people ranging in age from 11 to 85 years. Specifically, they found mature adults move from representations of the self in young adulthood that are relatively poorly differentiated from others or from social conventions and expectations, to highly differentiated representations in middle age, to less differentiated representations in old age. An important finding was the degree of differentiation in self-representation was related to the level of cognitive development, thereby providing support for Kegan's position.

Other Research on Self-Concept

In addition to research integrating cognitive and emotional development, researchers also focused on other sources for creating the self across adulthood. In Chapter 8, we saw the incorporation of aging stereotypes strongly influences people's self-concept.

Some research documents how people organize the various facets of their self-concept. That research shows older adults compartmentalize the different aspects of self-concept (e.g., various positive and negative aspects) more than either younger or middle-aged adults (Ready, Carvalho, & Åkerstedt, 2012).

In general, research examining self-concept shows it is significantly related to a wide variety of variables such as health and longevity. Kotter-Grühn (2016) summarizes this work by concluding the self-concept does undergo some change across adulthood, but other aspects, such as self-perceptions of aging, remain fairly stable. We return to this issue in Chapter 14 when considering successful aging.

Well-Being and Emotion

How is your life going? Are you reasonably content, or do you think you could be doing better? Answers to these questions provide insight into your **subjective well-being**, *an evaluation of one's life associated with positive feelings*. Subjective well-being is usually assessed by measures of life satisfaction, happiness, and self-esteem (Oswald & Wu, 2010).

Overall, young-older adults are characterized by improved subjective well-being compared to earlier in adulthood (Charles & Carstensen, 2010). The differences in people's typical level of happiness across adulthood are illustrated in results from the United Kingdom, shown in Figure 9.5. These happiness-related factors hold across cultures as well; a study of Taiwanese and Tanzanian older adults showed similar predictors of successful aging (Hsu, 2005; Mwanyangala et al., 2010).

Emotion-focused research in neuroscience provides answers to the question of why subjective well-being tends to increase with age (Cacioppo et al., 2011; Mather, 2016). As discussed in Chapter 2, the amygdala helps regulate emotion and plays a major role in cognitive-affective processing. Evidence shows that age-related

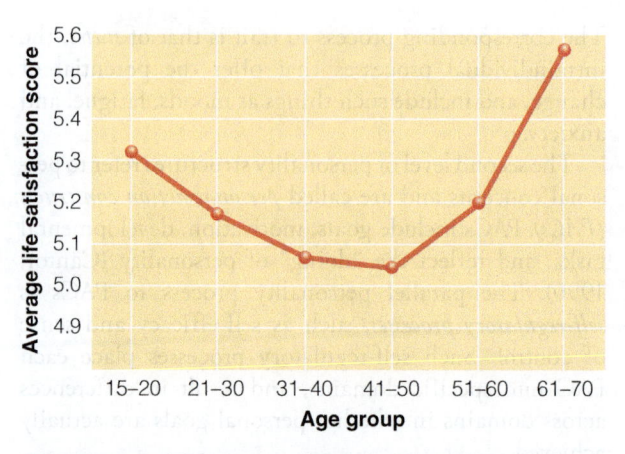

FIGURE 9.5 The pattern of a typical person's happiness through life in the United Kingdom.
Source: From *Happiness, Health, and Economics*, by A. Oswald. Copyright © Warwick University. imechanica.org/files/andrew_oswald_presentation_071129.pdf.

changes in how the amygdala functions plays a key role in understanding emotional regulation in older adults. Here's how. In young adults, arousal of the amygdala is associated with negative emotional arousal. When negative emotional arousal occurs, memory for events associated with the emotion are stronger. But the situation is different for older adults—both amygdala activation and emotional arousal are lower. That may be one reason why older adults experience less negative emotion, lower rates of depression, and better well-being (Cacioppo et al., 2011; Kensinger & Gutchess, 2017; Mather, 2016; Winecoff et al., 2011).

Possible Selves

When we are asked questions like, "What do you think you'll be like a few years from now?" it requires us to imagine ourselves in the future. When we speculate like this, we create a *possible self* (Markus & Nurius, 1986). **Possible selves** *represent what we could become, what we would like to become, and what we are afraid of becoming*. What we could or would like to become often reflects personal goals; we may see ourselves as leaders, as rich and famous, or in great physical shape. What we are afraid of becoming may show up in our fear of being alone, or overweight, or unsuccessful. Our possible selves are powerful motivators (Ko et al., 2014); indeed, how we behave is largely an effort to achieve or avoid these various possible selves and protect the current view of self (Baumeister, 2010).

In a rare set of similar studies conducted across time and research teams by Cross and Markus (1991) and Hooker and colleagues (Frazier et al., 2000, 2002; Hooker, 1999; Hooker et al., 1996; Morfei et al., 2001), people across the adult life span were asked to describe their hoped-for and feared-for possible selves. The responses were grouped into categories (e.g., family, personal, material, relationships, and occupation).

Several interesting age differences emerged. In terms of hoped-for selves, young adults listed family concerns—for instance, marrying the right person—as most important. In contrast, adults in their 30s listed family concerns last; their main issues involved personal concerns, such as being a more loving and caring person. By ages 40 to 59, family issues again became most common—such as being a parent who can "let go" of the children. Reaching and maintaining satisfactory performance in one's occupational career as well as accepting and adjusting to the physiological changes of middle age were important to this age group.

For adults over 60, researchers find personal issues are most prominent—like being active and healthy for at least another decade. The greatest amount of change occurred in the health domain, which predominated the hoped-for and feared-for selves. The health domain is the most sensitive and central to the self in the context of aging and people's possible self with regard to health is quite resilient in the face of health challenges in later life.

Overall, young adults have multiple possible selves and believe they can actually become the hoped-for self and successfully avoid the feared self. Their outlook tends to be quite positive (Remedios, Chasteen, & Packer, 2010). Life experience may dampen this outlook. By old age, both the number of possible selves and the strength of belief have decreased. Older adults are more likely to believe neither the hoped-for nor the feared-for self is under their personal control. These findings may reflect differences with age in personal motivation, beliefs in personal control, and the need to explore new options.

The emergence of online social media has created new opportunities for young adults to create possible selves (Lefkowitz, Vukman, & Loken, 2012). Such media present different ways for them to speculate about themselves to others.

The connection between possible selves and how we construct meaning in our lives is important. The link is through the process of setting personal goals that derive from the possible selves we envision. The details of this link are explored in the How Do We Know? feature.

How Do We Know?
Possible Selves and Pursuing Social Goals

Who were the investigators, and what was the aim of the study? As we have seen, personality development across adulthood involves the creation of life stories, which in turn involve setting and pursuing personal life goals. Han-Jung Ko, Shannon Mejía, and Karen Hooker (2014) wanted to understand one aspect of this process: how people make progress in achieving social goals that reflect their social possible selves over 100 days.

How did the investigators measure the topic of interest? Ko and colleagues used an initial questionnaire and 100 daily surveys. The initial survey focused on demographic information, a measure of hoped-for and feared social possible selves, the likelihood of each of the possible selves, and one social goal that was important to each participant that they intended to work on over the subsequent 100 days. The daily measures was an assessment of daily progress toward the selected social goal.

Who were the participants in the study? 105 adults between ages 52 and 88 (average age = 63) were recruited by emailing people on an existing list of potential research participants. 88% were women, 97% were European American, 93% said they were in good health, and 75% had earned at least a bachelor's degree.

Were there ethical concerns with the study? All participants were volunteers and provided written consent under a protocol approved by the Institutional Review Board.

What were the results? 22 participants only had hoped-for, 13 only had feared-for, and 15 had balanced social possible selves; the remaining 49 participants had possible selves in other domains, but not in the social domain. People with balanced social possible selves made better overall daily progress toward their social goal than any other group. Additionally, those with higher self-regulatory beliefs made better overall goal progress, as did people who showed greater consistency in day-to-day progress.

What did the investigators conclude? Making consistent progress from day-to-day toward a goal that personally matters appears to be the best way to achieve it. Additionally, hope, rather than fear, is the better motivator. The notion of keeping one's eyes on the prize is borne out in research, especially when the prize matters to the person.

Religiosity and Spiritual Support

When faced with the daily problems of living, how do older adults cope? Older adults in many countries use their religious faith and spirituality, more often than they use family or friends (Ai, Wink, & Ardelt, 2010; Ai et al., 2017). For some older adults, especially African Americans, a strong attachment to God is what they believe helps them deal with the challenges of life (Dilworth-Anderson, Boswell, & Cohen, 2007).

There is considerable evidence linking spirituality and health (Ai et al., 2010, 2017; Hayward et al., 2016; Krause, 2006; Park, 2007). In general, older adults who are more involved with and committed to their faith have better physical and mental health than older adults who are not religious. For example, older Mexican Americans who pray to the saints and the Virgin Mary on a regular basis tend to have greater optimism and better health (Krause & Bastida, 2011).

When asked to describe ways of dealing with problems in life that affect physical and mental health, many people list coping strategies associated with spirituality (Ai et al., 2010, 2017; White, Peters, & Schim, 2011). Of these, the most frequently used were placing trust in God, praying, and getting strength and help from God.

Researchers have increasingly focused on **spiritual support**—*meaning they seek pastoral care, participate in organized and nonorganized religious activities, and express faith in a God who cares for people—as a key factor in understanding how older adults cope.* Even when under high levels of stress people who rely on spiritual support report greater personal well-being (Ai et al., 2010, 2017; White et al., 2011). Krause and colleagues (2016; Krause, 2006) report feelings of self-worth are lowest in older adults who have very little religious commitment, a finding supported by cross-cultural research with Muslims, Hindus, and Sikhs (Mehta, 1997).

When people rely on spirituality to cope, how do they do it? Krause and colleagues (2000) found older adults reported turning problems over to God really was a three-step process: (1) differentiating between things that can and cannot be changed; (2) focusing one's own efforts on the parts of the problem that can be changed; and (3) emotionally disconnecting from those aspects of the problem that cannot be changed by focusing on the belief that God provides the best outcome possible for those. These findings show reliance on spiritual beliefs acts to help people focus their attention on parts of the problem that may be under their control.

Reliance on religion in times of stress appears to be especially important for many African Americans, who as a group are more intensely involved in religious activities (Taylor, Chatters, & Levin, 2004; Troutman, Nies, & Mavellia, 2011). They also are more likely to rely on God for support than are European Americans (Lee & Sharpe, 2007). Churches have historically offered considerable social support for the African American community, served an important function in advocating social justice, and ministers play a major role in providing support in times of personal need (Chatters et al., 2011).

Spiritual practice in all forms is evident throughout the latter half of the life span.

Similar effects of spirituality are observed in Asian and Asian American groups. The risk of dying in a given year among the old-old in China was found to be 21% lower among frequent religious participants compared to nonparticipants, after initial health condition was equated (Zeng, Gu, & George, 2011). Asian caregivers of dementia patients who are more religious report being able to handle the stresses and burden of caregiving better than nonreligious caregivers (Chan, 2010).

And neuroscience research shows there is a connection between certain practices and brain activity. There is evidence that people who practice meditation show more organized attention systems and less activity in areas of the brain that focus on the self (Atchley et al., 2016; Davidson, 2010; Lutz et al., 2009). Thus, neurological evidence indicates there may be changes in brain activity associated with spiritual practices that help people cope.

Healthcare and social service providers would be well advised to keep in mind the self-reported importance of spirituality in the lives of many older adults when designing interventions to help them adapt to life stressors. For example, older adults may be more willing to talk with their minister or rabbi about a personal problem than they would be to talk with a psychotherapist. Overall, many churches offer a wide range of programs to assist poor or homebound older adults in the community. Such programs may be more palatable to the people served than programs based in social service agencies. To be successful, service providers should try to view life as their clients see it.

Conclusions About Narratives, Identity, and the Self

We have seen to fully understand a person, we must consider how the individual integrates his or her life into a coherent structure. The life-narrative approach provides a way to learn how people accomplish this integration. The theoretical frameworks developed by McAdams and by Whitbourne offer excellent avenues for research. One of the most promising new areas of inquiry, possible selves, is already providing major insights into how people construct future elements of their life stories.

When combined with the data from the dispositional trait and personal concerns literatures, research findings on identity and the self, provide the capstone knowledge needed to understand what people are like. The complexity of personality is clear from this discussion; perhaps that is why it takes a lifetime to complete.

Adult Development in Action

If you were part of a multidisciplinary support team, how would you include spirituality as part of an overall plan to help your clients cope with life issues?

Social Policy Implications

Throughout this chapter, we emphasized that all aspects of personality interact in complex ways, and are inextricably linked to other aspects of development (e.g., cognitive development). What we have not examined is the extent to which external forces, such as public policy decisions at the societal level, can affect aspects of personality.

An intriguing analysis of this issue was done in Beijing by Sun and Xiao (2012). They examined the effects perceived fairness of certain social policies on social security and income distribution had on participants' well-being. Based on a survey of over 2100 residents of Beijing, they found perceived fairness of these policies were positively associated with well-being.

Similarly, Raju (2011) points out social policy in developing countries has a profound effect on the well-being of the rapidly increasing aging populations there. In the case of India, Raju argues healthcare policy in particular will be an important need to maximize the opportunity of people to age successfully.

These studies highlight an increasingly important consideration—that government policies can affect how people's experience of aging actually occurs. Positive government policies that provide the support and services necessary can improve well-being and the likelihood of people to age successfully. The reverse also appears to be true—that failure to enact such policies has a deleterious effect on people as they age.

continued

The 2016 U.S. presidential election included significant emphasis on social equity and fairness issues. Several of the major presidential candidates, such as Bernie Sanders, Donald Trump, and Hillary Clinton, connected the anger expressed by certain types of voters with inequity along various dimensions (e.g., income, power).

We will see in Chapter 14 the United States faces its own challenges with respect to ensuring that needed financial and health supports will be available through Social Security and Medicare. However, the baby boomers' overall lack of financial preparation for late life (e.g., lack of retirement savings) may mean their experience will not live up to their expectations. If that's true, then their well-being, along with the overall social mood of the country, may suffer.

SUMMARY

9.1 Dispositional Traits Across Adulthood

What is the five-factor model of dispositional traits?
- The five-factor model posits five dimensions of personality: neuroticism, extraversion, openness to experience, agreeableness, and conscientiousness. Each of these dimensions has several descriptors.
- Several longitudinal studies indicate personality traits show long-term stability.

What happens to dispositional traits across adulthood?
- Studies find evidence for change in Big Five factors such as neuroticism, agreeableness, conscientiousness, and extraversion. These are related to two dimensions of personality: adjustment and growth.
- Both stability and change characterize personality development in advanced old age.
- Several criticisms of the five-factor model have been made: The research may have methodological problems; dispositional traits do not describe the core aspects of human nature and do not provide good predictors of behavior; and dispositional traits do not consider the contextual aspects of development.
- An intraindividual perspective challenges stability by examining personality at the level of the individual.

What conclusions can we draw about dispositional traits?
- The bulk of the evidence suggests dispositional traits are relatively stable across adulthood, but there may be a few exceptions. Criticisms of the research point to the need for better statistical analyses and a determination of the role of life experiences.
- Stability in personality traits may be more evident later in the life span.
- The Triggering situations, Expectancy, States/State Expressions, and Reactions (TESSERA) framework provides a way to reconcile evidence of both stability and change in dispositional personality traits.

9.2 Personal Concerns and Qualitative Stages in Adulthood

What's different about personal concerns?
- Personal concerns take into account a person's developmental context and distinguish between "having" traits and "doing" everyday behaviors. Personal concerns entail descriptions of what people are trying to accomplish and the goals they create.

What are the main elements of Jung's theory?
- Jung emphasized various dimensions of personality (masculinity–femininity; extraversion–introversion). Jung argues people move toward integrating these dimensions as they age, with midlife being an especially important period.

What are the stages in Erikson's theory?
- The sequence of Erikson's stages is trust versus mistrust, autonomy versus shame and doubt, initiative versus guilt, industry versus inferiority, identity versus identity confusion, intimacy versus isolation, generativity versus stagnation, and ego integrity versus despair. Erikson's theory can be seen as a trust-achievement-wholeness cycle repeating twice, although the exact transition mechanisms have not been clearly defined.
- Generativity has received more attention than other adult stages. Research indicates generative concern

and generative action can be found in all age groups of adults, but they are particularly apparent among middle-aged adults.

What are the main points and problems with theories based on life transitions?
- In general, life transition theories postulate periods of transition that alternate with periods of stability. These theories tend to overestimate the commonality of age-linked transitions.
- Research evidence suggests crises tied to age 30 or the midlife crisis do not occur for most people. However, most middle-aged people do point to both gains and losses that could be viewed as change.
- A midlife correction may better characterize this transition for women.

What can we conclude about personal concerns?
- Theory and research both provide support for change in the personal concerns people report at various times in adulthood.

9.3 Life Narratives, Identity, and the Self

What are the main aspects of McAdams's life-story model?
- McAdams argues that people create a life story as an internalized narrative with a beginning, middle, and anticipated ending. An adult reformulates that life story throughout adulthood. The life story reflects emotions, motivations, beliefs, values, and goals to set the context for his or her behavior.

What are the main points of Whitbourne's identity theory?
- Whitbourne believes people have a life-span construct: a unified sense of their past, present, and future. The components of the life-span construct are the scenario (expectations of the future) and the life story (a personal narrative history). She integrates the concepts of assimilation and accommodation from Piaget's theory to explain how people's identity changes over time. Family and work are two major sources of identity.

How does the Six Foci Model of adult personality account for development?
- The Six Foci Model combines three structural and three process aspects of personality to provide a more complete explanation of development in adulthood.
- The structural-process pairs are: trait-state, personal action constructs-self-regulation, and life story-self-narration.

What is self-concept and how does it develop in adulthood?
- Self-concept is the organized, coherent, integrated pattern of self-perception. The events people experience help shape their self-concept. Self-presentation across adulthood is related to cognitive-developmental level. Self-concept tends to stay stable at the group mean level.

What are possible selves and how do they show differences during adulthood?
- People create possible selves by projecting themselves into the future and thinking about what they would like to become, what they could become, and what they are afraid of becoming.
- Age differences in these projections depend on the dimension examined. In hoped-for selves, young adults and middle-aged adults report family issues as most important, whereas 25- to 39-year-olds and older adults consider personal issues to be most important. However, all groups include physical aspects as part of their most feared possible selves.
- Although younger and middle-aged adults view themselves as improving, older adults view themselves as declining. The standards by which people judge themselves change over time.

What role does religion or spiritual support play in adult life?
- Older adults use religion and spiritual support more often than any other strategy to help them cope with problems in life. This provides a strong influence on identity. This is especially true for African American women, who are more active in their church groups and attend services more frequently. Other ethnic groups also gain important aspects of identity from religion.

What conclusions can we draw about narratives, identity, and the self?
- The life-narrative approach provides a way to learn how people integrate the various aspects of their personality. Possible selves, religiosity, and gender-role identity are important areas in need of additional research.

REVIEW QUESTIONS

9.1 Dispositional Traits Across Adulthood

- What is a dispositional trait? Describe Costa and McCrae's five-factor model of personality. What are the descriptors in each dimension? How do these dimensions change across adulthood?
- What evidence is there in other longitudinal research for change in personality traits in adulthood? Under what conditions is there stability or change?
- What are the specific criticisms raised concerning the five-factor model?
- What does most of the evidence say about the stability of dispositional traits across adulthood?
- What is the TESSERA framework?

9.2 Personal Concerns and Qualitative Stages in Adulthood

- What is meant by a personal concern? How does it differ from a dispositional trait?
- Describe Jung's theory. What important developmental changes did he describe?
- Describe Erikson's eight stages of psychosocial development. What cycles have been identified? How has his theory been clarified and expanded? What types of generativity have been proposed? What evidence is there for generativity? What modifications to Erikson's theory has this research suggested?
- What are the major assumptions of theories based on life transitions? What evidence is there a midlife crisis really exists? How can midlife be viewed from a gain–loss perspective?
- Overall, what evidence is there for change in personal concerns across adulthood?

9.3 Life Narratives, Identity, and the Self

- What are the basic tenets of McAdams's life-story theory? What are the seven elements of a life story?
- What is Whitbourne's life-span construct? How does it relate to a scenario and a life story? How did Whitbourne incorporate Piagetian concepts into her theory of identity?
- What is the Six Foci Model of personality development?
- What is self-concept? What shapes it? What are possible selves? What developmental trends have been found in possible selves?
- How are religiosity and spiritual support important aspects of identity in older adults?

INTEGRATING CONCEPTS IN DEVELOPMENT

- What relations can be found among dispositional traits, personal concerns, and life narratives?
- How does personality development reflect the four basic forces of development discussed in Chapter 1?
- How does cognitive development relate to personality change?
- How does personality change relate to stages in occupational transition?

KEY TERMS

cognitive processes A structural component of personality that acts jointly with life narratives to create natural interactions between a storyteller and listener, processes central in organizing life stories.

dispositional trait A relatively stable, enduring aspect of personality.

ego development The fundamental changes in the ways our thoughts, values, morals, and goals are organized. Transitions from one stage to another depend on both internal biological changes and external social changes to which the person must adapt.

epigenetic principle In Erikson's theory, the notion that development is guided by an underlying plan in which certain issues have their own particular times of importance.

five-factor model A model of dispositional traits with the dimensions of neuroticism, extraversion, openness to experience, agreeableness–antagonism, and conscientiousness–undirectedness.

life narrative The aspects of personality that pull everything together, those integrative aspects that give a person an identity or sense of self.

life-span construct In Whitbourne's theory of identity, the way people build a view of who they are.

midlife correction Reevaluating one's roles and dreams and making the necessary corrections.

personal concerns Things that are important to people, their goals, and their major concerns in life.

personality adjustment Involves developmental changes in terms of their adaptive value and functionality such as functioning effectively within society and how personality contributes to everyday life running smoothly.

personality growth Refers to ideal end states such as increased self-transcendence, wisdom, and integrity.

possible selves Aspects of the self-concept involving oneself in the future in both positive and negative ways.

self-concept The organized, coherent, integrated pattern of self-perceptions.

spiritual support Includes seeking pastoral care, participating in organized and nonorganized religious activities, and expressing faith in a God who cares for people as a key factor in understanding how older adults cope.

state processes A structural component of personality that acts with dispositional traits to create transient, short-term changes in emotion, mood, hunger, anxiety, and the like.

subjective well-being An evaluation of one's life that is associated with positive feelings.

trait Any distinguishable, relatively enduring way in which one individual differs from others.

trait theories of personality that assume little change occurs across adulthood.

10 | Clinical Assessment, Mental Health, and Mental Disorders

CHAPTER OUTLINE

10.1 Mental Health and the Adult Life Course
REAL PEOPLE Pat Summitt, Winningest College Basketball Coach of All Time
Defining Mental Health and Psychopathology
A Multidimensional Life-Span Approach to Psychopathology
Ethnicity, Gender, Aging, and Mental Health

10.2 Developmental Issues in Assessment and Therapy
Areas of Multidimensional Assessment
Factors Influencing Assessment
Assessment Methods
Developmental Issues in Therapy

10.3 The Big Three: Depression, Delirium, and Dementia
Depression
Delirium
Dementia

CURRENT CONTROVERSIES Diagnostic Criteria for Alzheimer's Disease
HOW DO WE KNOW? Training Persons with Dementia to Be Group Activity Leaders

10.4 Other Mental Disorders and Concerns
Anxiety Disorders
Psychotic Disorders
Alcohol Use Disorder

DISCOVERING DEVELOPMENT What Alcohol Use Disorder Treatment Options Are Available in Your Area?

Social Policy Implications

Summary
Review Questions
Integrating Concepts in Development
Key Terms

Although the incidence of many diseases often varies across socioeconomic class, dementia does not. It does not care whether you are rich and famous. As evidence, Malcolm Young (cofounder of AC/DC), Rosa Parks (civil rights leader), Ronald Reagan (40th president of the United States), Robin Williams (world famous comedian), and Pat Summitt (coach of the Lady Vols basketball team, the winningest coach in NCAA history who is highlighted in the Real People feature), along with 10 million more people globally each year, were all diagnosed with a form of dementia.

Malcolm Young

Ronald Reagan

Rosa Parks

Robin Williams

Real People
Pat Summitt, Winningest College Basketball Coach of All Time

Patricia "Pat" Summitt retired at age 59 from the University of Tennessee after having won 1,098 games as a college coach, more than any other coach of men's or women's basketball. She died on June 28, 2016, from early-onset Alzheimer's disease, the reason she had to retire. Of her many awards and achievements, including numerous basketball honors and the Presidential Medal of Freedom by President Barack Obama, perhaps the most remarkable is that in her 38 years of college coaching she never had a losing season.

Other coaches first noticed Pat's dementia because of uncharacteristic forgetting and other behavior. Three months after being diagnosed with early-onset Alzheimer's disease in 2011, she announced that the 2011–2012 season would be her last. As is typical of people with the early-onset form, Pat lived a bit more than four more years.

To honor Pat's legacy, the Pat Summitt Foundation and the Pat Summitt Alzheimer's Clinic at the University of Tennessee Medical Center are working to find a cure for the disease.

Pat Summitt

In this chapter, we consider situations in which the aging process goes wrong. Such problems happen to families every day across all demographic categories. It happened twice in John Cavanaugh's family (one of the authors of this book). Certainly, dementia is not part of normal aging, nor are the other conditions we consider.

This chapter is about the people who do not make it through adulthood and old age by only experiencing the normative physiological changes we considered in Chapters 3 and 4. A minority of adults develop mental health difficulties that cause them problems in their daily lives. We define mental health and how mental problems are assessed and treated. We focus on several specific problems, including depression, delirium, dementia, anxiety disorders, psychotic disorders, and substance abuse. As we consider different types of mental disorders, we note how each is diagnosed, the known causes, and effective treatments that are available.

10.1 Mental Health and the Adult Life Course

LEARNING OBJECTIVES
- How are mental health and psychopathology defined?
- What are the key dimensions used for categorizing psychopathology?
- Why are ethnicity and aging important variables to consider in understanding mental health?

Janet lives alone in a small apartment. *Lately, some of her neighbors have noticed she doesn't come to church services as regularly as she used to. Betty, her friend and neighbor, noticed Janet cries a lot when she's asked whether anything is wrong and at times seems confused. Betty knows several of Janet's friends died recently but still wonders whether something more serious is wrong with her.*

Situations like Janet's are common. Like Betty, we might think Janet is trying to deal with the loss of friends and is simply experiencing grief, but there may be something more serious; could Janet's confusion indicate a physical or mental health problem? Janet's situation points out the difficulty in knowing exactly where good mental health ends and mental illness or mental disorder begins. What distinguishes the study of mental disorders, or psychopathology, in adulthood and aging is not so much the content of the behavior as its context, that is, whether it interferes with daily functioning. To understand psychopathology as manifested in adults of different ages, we must see how it fits into the life-span developmental perspective outlined in Chapter 1.

Defining Mental Health and Psychopathology

The precise difference between mental health and mental disorder has never been clear (Segal, Qualls, & Smyer, 2011). Most scholars avoid the issue entirely or simply try to explain what mental health or psychopathology is not. How to tell the difference between normal or abnormal behavior is hard to define precisely because expectations and standards for behavior change over time, situations, and across age groups (Zarit & Zarit, 2007). Researchers and practitioners refer to Birren and Renner's (1980) classic argument that mentally healthy people have the following characteristics: a positive attitude toward self, an accurate perception of reality, a mastery of the environment, autonomy, personality balance, and growth and self-actualization. Thus, all these characteristics must be evaluated when determining the mental health status of an individual.

One could argue to the extent these characteristics are absent, mental disorder or psychopathology becomes more likely. In that case, we would consider behaviors that are harmful to individuals or others, lowers well-being, and perceived as distressing, disrupting, abnormal, or maladaptive. Although this approach is used frequently with younger or middle-aged adults, it presents problems when applied to older adults (Segal et al., 2011; Zarit & Zarit, 2007). Some behaviors considered abnormal under this definition may actually be adaptive under some circumstances for many older people (such as isolation, passivity, or aggressiveness).

Consequently, an approach to defining abnormal behavior that emphasizes considering behaviors in isolation and from the perspective of younger or middle-aged adults is inadequate for defining abnormal behaviors in older adults. Because of physical, financial, social, health, or other reasons, older adults do not always have the opportunity to master their environment. Depression or hostility may be an appropriate and justified response to such limitations. Moreover, such responses may help them deal with their situation more effectively and adaptively.

Statistics on the prevalence of various mental disorders as a function of age are difficult to obtain due to these definitional issues. Figure 10.1 compares common forms of mental disorder as a function of age from one of the few good investigations of this issue (Kessler et al., 2005). Further analyses of data from national surveys reveals older European Americans and Caribbean Blacks have a higher lifetime prevalence of major depressive disorder than do African Americans (Woodward et al., 2013). New soldiers in the U.S. Army were similar overall to the general population, except that they showed higher lifetime rates of posttraumatic stress, generalized anxiety, and conduct disorders (Rosellini et al., 2015).

The important point in differentiating mental health from psychopathology is that behaviors must be interpreted in context. We must consider what else is happening and how the behavior fits the situation in addition to such factors as age and other personal characteristics.

FIGURE 10.1 Lifetime prevalence of age-of-onset distribution of DSM-IV disorders in the National Comorbidity Survey Replication

Source: Kessler, R. C., Berglund, P., Demler, O., Jin, R., Merakangas, K., & Walters, E. (2005). *Arch Gen Psychiatry, 62*, 593-602. Copyright © 2005 by American Medical Association. All rights reserved.

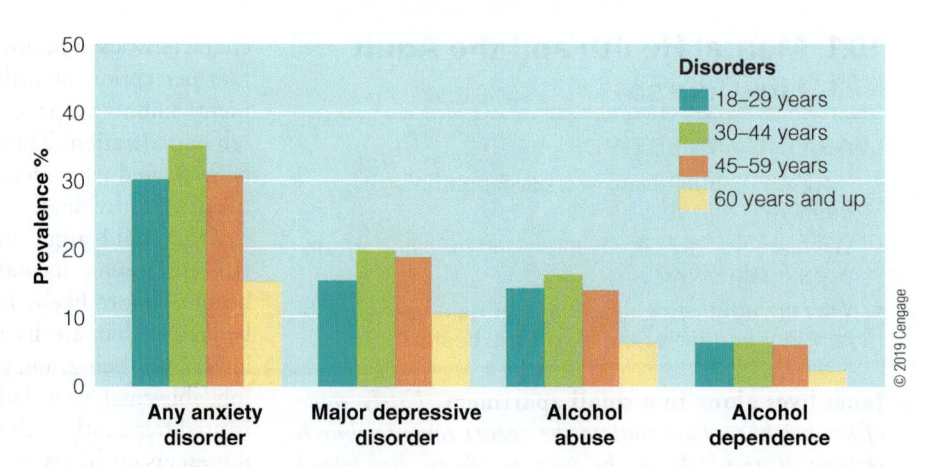

A Multidimensional Life-Span Approach to Psychopathology

Suppose two people, one young and one old, came into your clinic, each complaining about a lack of sleep, changes in appetite, a lack of energy, and feeling down. What would you say to them?

If you evaluate them in identical ways, you might be headed for trouble. As we saw in other chapters, older and younger adults may think or view themselves differently, so the meaning of their symptoms and complaints may also differ, even though they appear to be the same. This point is often overlooked (Segal et al., 2011). Some models of psychopathology assume the same underlying cause is responsible for maladaptive behavior regardless of age and symptoms of the mental disease are fairly constant across age. Although such models often are used in clinical diagnosis, they are inadequate for understanding psychopathology in old age. Viewing adults' behavior from a life-span developmental forces perspective makes a big difference in how we understand psychopathology. Let's see why.

Biological Forces

Various neurological changes, chronic diseases, functional limitations, and other ailments can change behavior. Changes in the structure and functioning of the brain can have important effects on behavior (Chapter 2). Because certain health problems increase with age (see Chapters 3 and 4) we must be more sensitive to them when dealing with older adults. In addition, genetic factors often underlie important problems in old age. For example, several forms of dementia have a genetic component.

Physical problems may provide clues about underlying psychological difficulties; for example, marked changes in appetite may be a symptom of depression. Moreover, physical problems may present themselves as psychological ones. Extreme irritability can be caused by thyroid problems, and memory loss can result from certain vitamin deficiencies. In any case, physical health and genetic factors are important dimensions to take into account in diagnosing psychopathology in adults and should be among the first avenues explored.

Psychological Forces

Psychological forces across adulthood are key to understanding psychopathology. As we saw in Chapters 6, 7, 8, and 9, several important changes in memory, intelligence, social cognition, and personality must be considered carefully in interpreting behavior. Normative changes with age in these arenas can mimic certain mental disorders; likewise, these changes make it more difficult to tell when an older adult has a given type of psychopathology.

In addition, the nature of a person's relationships with other people, especially family members and friends, is a basic dimension in understanding how psychopathology is manifested in adults of different ages. Important developmental differences occur in the interpersonal realm; younger adults are more likely to be expanding their network of friends, whereas older adults are more likely to be experiencing losses. Chapter 11 summarizes developmental changes in key relationships that may influence adults' interpretation of symptoms.

Sociocultural Forces

The social norms and cultural factors we all experience also play a key role in helping define psychopathology. They influence people's behaviors and affect our interpretation of them. An older person who lives alone may be highly suspicious of other people. To label her behavior "paranoid" may be inappropriate because her well-being may depend on maintaining a certain level of suspicion of others' motives toward her, for instance, regarding potential financial exploitation. Because customs differ across cultures, behaviors that may be normative in one culture may be viewed as indicating problems in another. In short, we must ask whether the behavior we see is appropriate for a person in a particular setting.

Life-Cycle Factors

How people behave at any point in adulthood is strongly affected by their past experiences and the issues they face. These life-cycle factors must be taken into account in evaluating adults' behaviors. A middle-aged woman who wants to go back to school may not have an adjustment disorder; she may simply want to develop a new aspect of herself. Some might interpret her behavior as an inability to cope with her current life situation when that is not the case at all; rather, she has a rational evaluation of her life and realizes she needs a degree to advance in her profession.

Likewise, an older man who provides vague answers to personal questions may not be resistant; he may simply be reflecting his generation's reluctance to disclose the inner self to a stranger. Most important, the meaning of particular symptoms change with age. Problems with early morning awakenings may indicate depression in a young adult but may simply be a result of normal aging in an older adult (see Chapter 3).

Ethnicity, Gender, Aging, and Mental Health

In neither the general nor specific ethnic populations do most people have mental disorders (Muntaner et al., 2013; Segal et al., 2011). However, social disparities such as differential access to health care can result in apparently different prevalence of mental disorders. That is because access to health care means many people are never evaluated by a mental healthcare professional. Poverty and social class are primary reasons for this (Muntaner et al., 2013).

Neither positive mental health nor psychopathology has been adequately defined in any group in a way that takes social context into account so as to be sensitive to contextual differences in ethnic communities. For example, although many explanations of deviant and antisocial behavior are grounded in the oppressive life conditions that characterize many ethnic communities, the conceptualization of positive mental health for older ethnic groups does not take into account the lifetime accumulation of such effects (Delgado, 2015; Jackson, Antonucci, & Gibson, 1995; Morrell, Echt, & Caramagno, 2008) nor the effects of a lifetime of inadequate access to health care (Miranda et al., 2008). However, such sensitivity to conditions does not preclude finding commonalities across ethnic groups; indeed, identifying such commonalities would be an excellent place to start.

What little data we have suggest both similarities and differences in the incidence of specific types of psychopathology across different ethnic groups at a general level. However, there are some differences within subgroups of ethnic groups. As noted earlier, Caribbean Blacks differ from African Americans in their prevalence of depression (Woodward et al., 2013).

People in different ethnic groups have different ways of describing how they feel, so they may describe symptoms of mental disorders differently. Such differences are amplified by ethnic and cultural differences in people's degree of comfort in revealing information about their inner self to strangers, even in a medical situation. Placed in a context of important differences in social stressors, physical health, and age, assessing mental health in older ethnic adults is a daunting task (Aldwin & Gilmer, 2013).

What can be done to determine the ways ethnicity influences mental health? Jackson et al. (1995) were among the first to argue researchers should adopt an ethnic research matrix that takes as its defining elements ethnicity, national origin, racial group membership, gender, social and economic statuses, age, acculturation, coping reactions, and mental health outcomes (e.g., psychopathology, positive adjustment). Only by adopting this comprehensive approach can we understand what, how, and when aspects of race, ethnicity, age, and the life course influence mental health.

Gender differences in prevalence of various mental disorders are well known and documented (Rosenfield & Mouzon, 2013; Smith, Mouzon, & Elliott, in press). A community study in Korea and a study of records in a day hospital in Italy found being female increased the risk of depressive symptoms (Luca et al., 2013; Oh et al., 2013). Males who are depressed are more likely to commit suicide than are women (Hawton et al., 2013).

Just as in the case of ethnicity, though, biases regarding gender and symptom interpretation may influence reported prevalence rates (Rosenfield & Mouzon, 2013). Thus, interpreting data regarding how many people of a specific background have a mental disorder must be done quite carefully, taking into account all of the aspects of the biopsychosocial model.

Adult Development in Action
As an elected official, how would you put the data about mental health and aging into social policy?

10.2 Developmental Issues in Assessment and Therapy

LEARNING OBJECTIVES
- What key areas are included in a multidimensional approach to assessment?
- What factors influence the assessment of adults?
- How are mental health issues assessed?
- What are some major considerations for therapy across adulthood?

Juan is a 70-year-old retired plumber living in California. Over the past year, his wife, Rocio, noticed Juan's memory isn't quite as sharp as it used to be; Juan also has less energy, stays home more, and does not show as much interest in playing dominos, a game at which he used to excel. Rocio wonders what might be wrong with Juan.

Many adults can relate to Rocio because they are concerned about someone they know. Whether the person is 25 or 85, it is important to be able to determine whether memory problems, energy loss, social withdrawal, or other areas of concern really indicate an underlying problem. As you might suspect, healthcare professionals should not use identical approaches to assess and treat adults of widely different ages. In this section, we consider how assessment methods and therapies must take developmental differences into account.

Areas of Multidimensional Assessment
What does it mean to assess someone's mental health status? Assessment makes it possible to describe the behavior or other characteristics of people in meaningful ways (Gould, Edelstein, & Gerolimatos, 2012; Groth-Marnat & Wright, 2016; Stoner, O'Riley, & Edelstein, 2010). Assessment is a formal process of measuring, understanding, and predicting behavior. It involves gathering medical, psychological, and sociocultural information about people through various means, such as interviews, observation, tests, and clinical interviews and examinations (Groth-Marnat & Wright, 2016).

As noted in Chapter 1, two central aspects of any assessment approach are reliability and validity. Without these psychometric properties, we cannot rely on any assessment approach to provide good information. In addition, any assessment method must be of practical use in determining the nature of the problem and choosing the appropriate treatment.

A multidimensional assessment approach is most effective (Gould et al., 2012; Groth-Marnat & Wright, 2016; Stoner et al., 2010). Multidimensional assessment is often done by a team of professionals; a physician may focus on physical health and medication regimen; a psychologist, cognitive, personality, and social functioning; a nurse, functional skills in daily life; and a social worker, the economic, social network, and environmental resources. Let's consider Juan's situation as an example.

A thorough assessment of Juan's physical health is essential, as it is for adults of all ages, especially for older adults. Many physical conditions can create (or hide) mental health problems, so it is important to identify any underlying issues. Laboratory tests can also be ordered to provide additional clues to the presence or even to the cause of the problem.

Establishing Juan's cognitive ability is also key. Complaints of cognitive problems increase across adulthood, so it is important to determine the extent abnormal changes in older people discriminate from normative change. Adults of all ages can be given intelligence tests, neuropsychological examinations, and mental status examinations. **Mental status exams** *are especially useful as quick screening measures of mental competence used to screen for cognitive impairment*; one commonly used instrument, the Mini Mental Status Exam (MMSE), is shown in Table 10.1. If Juan's score on these brief measures indicated potential problems, more complete follow-up assessments would be used. It is important to remember that scales such as the MMSE are only used for general screening and not for final diagnosis.

Psychological functioning is typically assessed through interviews, observation, and tests or questionnaires. Usually a clinician begins with an interview of Juan and brief screening instruments and follows up, if necessary, with more thorough personality inventories, tests, or more detailed interviews.

How well Juan functions in his daily life is also assessed carefully. Usually this entails determining whether he has difficulty with activities of daily living and instrumental activities of daily living (see Chapter 4). Also assessed is the person's decision-making capacity; each state has legal standards guiding the competency assessment.

10.2 Developmental Issues in Assessment and Therapy   277

TABLE 10.1 A Sampling of Questions from the Mini Mental Status Exam

Cognitive Area	Activity
Orientation to time	"What is the date?"
Registration stop	"Listen carefully. I am going to say three words. You say them back after I say them. Ready? Here they are … APPLE [pause], PENNY [pause], TABLE [pause]. Now repeat those words back to me." [Repeat up to 5 times, but score only the first trial.]
Naming	"What is this?" [Point to a pencil or pen.]
Reading stimulus form	"Please read this and do what it says." [Show examinee the words on the form.] CLOSE YOUR EYES

Source: Reproduced by special permission of the Publisher, Psychological Assessment Resources, Inc., 16204 North Florida Avenue, Lutz, Florida 33549, from the Mini Mental Status Examination, by Marshal Folstein and Susan Folstein. Copyright 1975, 1998, 2001 by Mini Mental LLC, Inc. Published 2001 by Psychological Assessment Resources, Inc. Further reproduction is prohibited without permission of PAR, Inc. The MMSE can be purchased from PAR, Inc., by calling (813) 968–3003.

In general, it is important to assess the broad array of support resources available to older adults (Chew-Graham & Ray, 2016; Randall et al., 2012). This includes social networks as well as other community resources.

Factors Influencing Assessment

Healthcare professionals' preconceived ideas about the people they assess may have negative effects on the assessment process (Chew-Graham & Ray, 2016; Gould et al., 2012). Two areas of concern are biases (negative or positive) and environmental conditions (where the assessment occurs, sensory or mobility problems, and health of the client).

Many types of bias have been documented as affecting the assessment process (Chew-Graham & Ray, 2016). Negative biases about people are widespread and include racial, ethnic, and age stereotypes. Clinicians may hold negative biases against younger adults of ethnic minorities and more readily "diagnose" problems that do not truly exist. Likewise, because of ageism, older adults may be "diagnosed" with untreatable problems such as Alzheimer's disease rather than treatable problems such as depression (see Chapter 1). In contrast, positive biases about certain people also work against accurate assessment. A belief that women do not abuse alcohol may result in a misdiagnosis; beliefs that older adults are "cute" may mitigate against accurate assessment of abilities. Clearly, the best defense against bias is for clinicians to be fully educated about their prospective clients.

The environmental conditions where the assessment occurs can also work against accurate outcomes. Clinicians do not always have the option of selecting an ideal environment; rather, assessments sometimes occur in hallways, with a bedridden patient, or in a

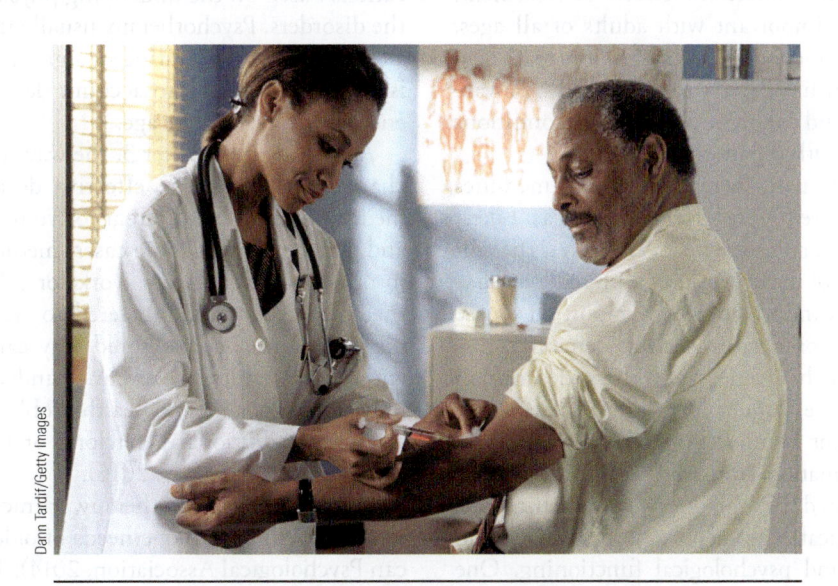

A thorough assessment of physical health is an essential part of a comprehensive assessment for depression or any mental health problem.

noisy emergency room. People with sensory or motor difficulties must be accommodated with alternative assessment formats. The patient's physical health may also complicate assessment; in cases with older adults, health issues can also create a negative bias so mental health issues may be overlooked when a health problem is discovered (Karel, Gatz, & Smyer, 2012; Smith & Smith, 2016).

Taken together, clinical assessment is an excellent example of how the forces of development come together. Only when all four forces are considered can mental health problems be assessed accurately.

Assessment Methods

How are adults assessed? In terms of cognitive, psychological, and social assessments, there are six primary methods (American Psychological Association, 2014; Edelstein & Kalish, 1999): interview, self-report, report by others, psychophysiological and neuroimaging assessment, direct observation, and performance-based assessment.

Clinical interviews are the most widely used assessment method (Groth-Marnat & Wright, 2016). They are useful because they provide both direct information in response to the questions and nonverbal information such as emotions. Interviews can be used to obtain historical information, determine appropriate follow-up procedures, build rapport with the client, obtain the client's informed consent to participate in the assessment, and evaluate the effects of treatment. All these tasks are important with adults of all ages. When interviewing older adults, though, it may be necessary to use somewhat shorter sessions, and be aware of sensory deficits and cognitive and medical conditions that may interfere with the interview.

Many commonly used formal assessment measures are presented in a self-report format, such as Likert scales. As noted in Chapter 1, a major concern is the reliability and validity of these measures with older adults.

Family members and friends are an important source of information. In some cases, such as dementia, discrepancies between the client's and others' description of the problem can be diagnostic. Such sources also are valuable if the client is unlikely or unable to tell the whole story. Information from these other key informants can be obtained through interviews or self-report.

Psychophysiological assessment examines the relation between physical and psychological functioning. One common psychophysiological measure is the electroencephalogram (EEG), which measures brain wave activity.

Other measures include heart rate, muscle activity, and skin temperature. Such measures provide a way to measure the body's reaction to certain stimuli, especially when the client gets anxious or fearful in response to them. Neuroimaging assessments, discussed in Chapter 2, may be used to help document the presence or absence of abnormalities in the brain.

In some cases it is possible to observe the client through systematic or naturalistic observation (see Chapter 1). Direct observation is especially useful when the problem involves specific behaviors, as in eating disorders. A variety of techniques exist for structuring observations, and they can be used in a wide array of settings, from homes to nursing homes.

Finally, performance-based assessment involves giving clients a specific task to perform. This approach underlies much cognitive and neuropsychological assessment. A person's memory is assessed by giving him or her a list of items to remember and then testing retention. Some neuropsychological tests involve drawing or copying pictures, or solving picture puzzles.

Developmental Issues in Therapy

Assuming Juan is assessed properly and found to have a mental disorder, what next? How can he be helped? Therapy for mental disorders generally involves two approaches (Chew-Graham & Ray, 2016; Segal et al., 2011): medical treatment and psychotherapy. Medical treatment most often involves the use of various medications based on the underlying physiological causes of the disorders. Psychotherapy usually involves talking to a clinician or participating in a group. In either case, it is essential to take into account developmental differences in people as they age.

As we saw in Chapter 3, the ways medications work change with age. The effective dosage of a specific medication may be different for younger, middle-aged, and older adults. In some cases, medications that work in one age group do not work for others. This means that medications administered to treat mental health disorders must be monitored very carefully, especially with older adults. Over- and under-medication not only can make a mental health problem worse, but may also cause additional behavioral or health difficulties (Chew-Graham & Ray, 2016).

In terms of psychotherapy, clinicians must adapt techniques to the unique needs of older adults (American Psychological Association, 2014). This has led some to propose a new, positive approach to geriatric psychiatry and geropsychology be adopted (Jeste & Palmer,

2013, 2015). This positive approach focuses "on recovery, promotion of successful ageing, neuroplasticity, prevention, and interventions to enhance positive psychological traits such as resilience, social engagement and wisdom" (Jeste & Palmer, 2013, p. 81).

Another major issue in psychotherapy is establishing whether a particular therapeutic approach is effective, based on research and clinical evidence. Major professional associations provide guidelines in their respective fields; the American Medical Association provides evidence-based approaches to medical therapy (American Medical Association, 2013), and the American Psychological Association developed a set of criteria for evidence-based psychotherapy (American Psychological Association, 2014; Goodheart, Kazdin, & Sternberg, 2006). The therapeutic approaches that meet the standard for adult therapy appear to be effective for a wide range of ages and are generally the therapies of choice. As we consider specific disorders, we focus on evidence-based approaches to therapy.

Adult Development in Action

What factors must be considered in conducting a thorough clinical assessment for mental disorders?

10.3 The Big Three: Depression, Delirium, and Dementia

LEARNING OBJECTIVES
- What are the most common characteristics of people with depression? How is depression diagnosed? What causes depression? What is the relation between suicide and age? How is depression treated?
- What is delirium? How is it assessed and treated? What is dementia? What are the major symptoms of Alzheimer's disease? How is it diagnosed?
- What causes it? What intervention options are there? What are some other major forms of dementia? What do family members caring for patients with dementia experience?

Ling has lived in the same neighborhood in New York for all of her 74 years. Her son, who visits her every week, started noticing Ling's memory problems have gotten much worse, her freezer is empty and her refrigerator has lots of moldy food. When he investigated further, he found her bank accounts were in disarray. Ling's son wonders what could be wrong with her.

Ling's behaviors certainly do not appear to be typical of older adults. Unfortunately, Ling is not alone in experiencing difficulties; many older adults have similar problems. In this section, we consider three of the most common difficulties: depression, delirium, and dementia. As we will see, both depression and delirium are treatable; the most common form of dementia, Alzheimer's disease, is not. The three conditions are connected by overlapping symptoms and the possibility that they may coexist. Let's consider each in detail.

Depression

Most people feel down or sad from time to time, perhaps in reaction to a problem at work or in one's relationships. But does this mean that most people are depressed? How is depression diagnosed? Are there age-related differences in the symptoms examined in diagnosis? How is depression treated?

First of all, let's dispense with a myth. Contrary to the popular belief most older adults are depressed, the rate of severe depression *declines* from young adulthood to old age for healthy people as shown in Figure 10.2 (National Institute of Mental Health, 2016a). However, this downward age trend does not hold in all cultures; depressive symptoms among Chinese older adults rose over a 24-year period (1987–2010, inclusive) (Shao et al., 2013). Averaged across age, U.S. data indicate different prevalence rates across different ethnic groups (National Institute of Mental Health, 2016a).

In the United States, the average age at diagnosis for depression is 32 (National Institute of Mental Health, 2016a). Being female, unmarried, widowed, or recently bereaved; experiencing stressful life events; and lacking an adequate social support network are more common among older adults with depression than younger adults (Segal et al., 2011). Less than 5% of older adults living in the community show signs of depression, but the percentage rises to over 13% among those who require home health care (National Institute of Mental Health, 2016a). Subgroups of older adults who are at greater risk include those with chronic illnesses (such as diabetes, cancer, heart disease, and Parkinson's disease; up to half may have major depression), nursing home residents, and family care providers.

Rates of clinical depression vary across ethnic groups, although correct diagnosis is frequently a problem with minorities due to inadequate access to physical and mental health care (Alegría et al., 2008; National Institute of Mental Health, 2016a). These issues also apply to immigrants (Ladin & Reinhold, 2013), who have higher rates of

12-month Prevalence of Major Depressive Episodes Among U.S. Adults (2015)

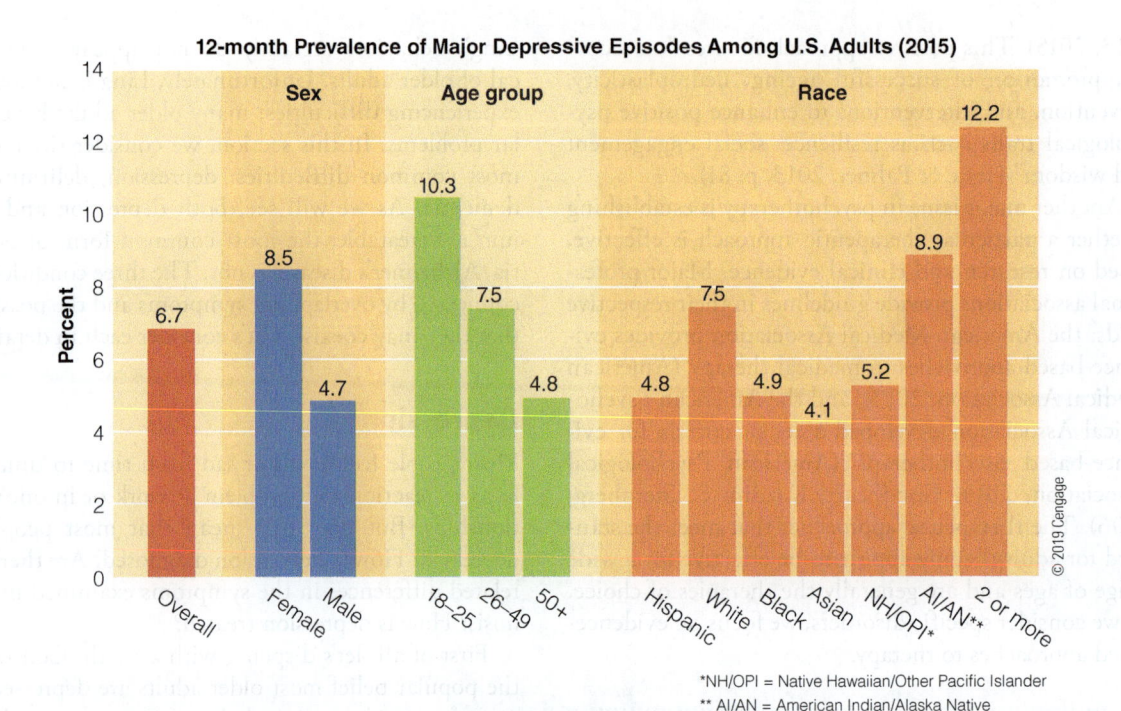

Category	Group	Percent
Overall	Overall	6.7
Sex	Female	8.5
Sex	Male	4.7
Age group	18–25	10.3
Age group	26–49	7.5
Age group	50+	4.8
Race	Hispanic	4.8
Race	White	7.5
Race	Black	4.9
Race	Asian	4.1
Race	NH/OPI*	5.2
Race	AI/AN**	8.9
Race	2 or more	12.2

*NH/OPI = Native Hawaiian/Other Pacific Islander
** AI/AN = American Indian/Alaska Native

FIGURE 10.2 Twelve-month prevalence of major depressive episode among U.S. adults (2014)
Source: National Institute of Mental Health (2013). 12-Month Prevalence of Major Depressive Episode Among U.S. Adults. Retrieved from www.nimh.nih.gov/health/statistics/prevalence/major-depression-among-adults.shtml.

depression, and to treatment disparities relating to minorities (Zurlo & Beach, 2013). Rates for depression tend to be higher in Latino older adults than for other groups of older adults (National Institute of Mental Health, 2012). Latinos who speak primarily Spanish or are foreign-born are especially likely to show depression (Mercado-Crespo et al., 2008). Older African Americans have lower rates of depression than European Americans (National Institute of Mental Health, 2016a). Clearly, the pattern of ethnic differences indicates the reasons for them are complex and not well understood.

Recognizing these differences, clinicians have developed culturally appropriate assessment and treatment guidelines (Kirmayer et al., 2015; Lewis-Fernández et al., 2015). Such guidelines take important contextual factors into account in the assessment process to help clinicians avoid making errors based simply on misunderstandings of culturally based behaviors.

General Symptoms and Characteristics of People with Depression

*The most prominent feature of clinical depression is **dysphoria**, that is, feeling down or blue.* You may be thinking that this sounds rather obvious. But there are important age differences in how dysphoria is expressed (Segal et al., 2011; NIHSeniorHealth, 2016a). Older adults may not talk about their feelings at all; they may have feelings that flow from life events such as bereavement that mimic depression, or may not label their down feelings as depression but rather as pessimism or helplessness (NIHSeniorHealth, 2016a; Zarit & Zarit, 2007). In addition, older adults are more likely to show signs of apathy, subdued self-deprecation, expressionlessness, and changes in arousal than are younger people (Segal et al., 2011). It is common for depressed older adults to withdraw, not speak to anyone, confine themselves to bed, and not take care of bodily functions. Younger adults may engage in some of these behaviors but do so to a much lesser extent. Thoughts about suicide are common, and may reflect a shutdown of a person's basic survival instinct.

The second major component of clinical depression is the accompanying physical symptoms (Chew-Graham & Ray, 2016). These include insomnia, changes in appetite, diffuse pain, troubled breathing, headaches, fatigue, and sensory loss. The presence of these physical symptoms in older adults must be evaluated carefully, though. As noted in Chapter 3, some sleep disturbances may reflect normative changes unrelated to depression; however, certain types of sleep disturbance, such as regular early morning awakening, are related to depression, even in older adults (Wiebe, Cassoff, & Gruber, 2012). There is evidence that changes in the prefrontal cortex and the regulatory processes underlying sleep may be responsible for the link between sleep disturbance and depression (Borbély et al., 2016); given that such changes occur with age, it may be one reason for the difficulty in understanding whether sleep disturbances are related to clinical depression in older adults.

Alternatively, physical symptoms may reflect an underlying physical disease that is manifested as depression. Indeed, many older adults admitted to the hospital with depressive symptoms turn out to have previously undiagnosed medical problems that are uncovered only after thorough examinations and evaluations (Chew-Graham & Ray, 2016). These underlying health problems that appear as depression include vitamin deficiencies (e.g., B_{12}), diabetes, cardiovascular disease, chronic pain, hypothyroidism, cancer, Cushing's syndrome, certain viruses, dementia, Parkinson's disease, rheumatoid arthritis, and medication interactions and side effects.

The third primary diagnostic characteristic is the duration: symptoms must last at least 2 weeks. This criterion is used to rule out the transient symptoms common to all adults, especially after a negative experience such as receiving a rejection letter from a potential employer or getting a speeding ticket.

Fourth, other causes for the observed symptoms must be ruled out (Chew-Graham & Ray, 2016). In addition to the diseases mentioned earlier, other health problems such as neurological disorders, metabolic conditions, alcoholism, or other forms of psychopathology can cause depressive symptoms. These causes influence appropriate diagnosis and treatment decisions.

Finally, the clinician must determine how patients' symptoms affect daily life. Can they carry out responsibilities at home? How well do they interact with other people? What about effects on work or school? Clinical depression involves significant impairment in daily living.

Assessment Scales

Numerous scales are used to assess depression, but because most were developed on younger and middle-aged adults, they are most appropriate for these age groups. The most important difficulty in using these scales with older adults is they all include several items assessing physical symptoms. The Beck Depression Inventory (Beck, 1967) contains items that focus on feelings and physical symptoms. Although the presence of such symptoms usually is indicative of depression in younger adults, as we noted earlier, such symptoms may not be related to depression at all in older adults.

Scales such as the Geriatric Depression Scale (Yesavage et al., 1983) aimed specifically at older adults have been developed. Physical symptoms are omitted, and the response format is easier for older adults to follow. This approach reduces the age-related symptom bias and scale response problems with other self-report scales measuring depressive symptoms. A third screening inventory, the Center for Epidemiologic Studies-Depression Scale (CES-D; Radloff, 1977) is also frequently used in research.

An important point to keep in mind about these scales is that the diagnosis of depression should never be made on the basis of a single scale. As we have seen, the symptoms observed in clinical depression could be indicative of other problems, and symptom patterns are complex. Only by assessing many aspects of physical and psychological functioning can a clinician make an accurate assessment.

Causes of Depression

Several biological and psychosocial theories about the causes of depression have been proposed (Segal et al., 2011). Biological theories focus most on genetic predisposition, brain changes, and changes in neurotransmitters (McKinney & Sibille, 2013; Moak, 2016). The genetic evidence is based on two sets of data: (a) several studies that show higher rates of depression in relatives of depressed people than would be expected given base rates in the population; and (b) genetically driven age-related changes in brain structures. The first type of genetic link is stronger in early-onset depression than in late-onset depression, whereas the second type of evidence is thought to underlie much of late-life onset.

There is substantial research evidence that major depressive disorder is linked to several physiological and genetic causes: imbalance in neurotransmitters such as low levels of serotonin and the action of brain-derived neurotrophic factor, the role of microglial cells in brain inflammation, and the role of the immune system (Ménard, Hodes, & Russo, 2016).

Low levels of serotonin are a likely result from high levels of stress experienced over a long period. The usual signs of low serotonin levels include waking up in the early morning (often around 4:00 a.m.), difficulty in concentrating and paying attention, feeling tired and listless, losing interest in activities such as sex or visiting friends, and racing of the mind with strong feelings of guilt and of reliving bad past experiences and creating negative thoughts. These effects of low serotonin are similar to those that characterize depression, which is why researchers believe that one possible cause is low serotonin.

Brain-derived neurotrophic factor (BDNF) is a compound found in blood serum, and its level is negatively correlated with the severity of depression (i.e., lower levels of BDNF are correlated with higher levels of depression). Research shows the use of antidepressant medication raises the level of BDNF.

Low levels of another neurotransmitter, norepinephrine, that regulates arousal and alertness, may be responsible for the feelings of fatigue associated with depression. These neurochemical links are the basis for the medications developed to treat depression we will consider a bit later.

Microglia are a widely distributed type of glial cell in the brain and are the main form of the brain's innate immunity. Their job is to react quickly to decrease inflammation and destroy invading pathogens before those pathogens destroy the brain. Under certain circumstances, neuroinflammation persists over time, causing cumulative damage. Such cumulative damage is thought to be one cause of both depression and Alzheimer's disease.

The psychological effects of loss are the most common basis for psychosocial theories of depression (Segal et al., 2011). Bereavement or other ways of losing a relationship is the type of loss that has received the most attention, but the loss of anything considered personally important could also be a trigger. Moreover, these losses may be real and irrevocable, threatened and potential, or imaginary and fantasized. The likelihood these losses will occur varies with age. Middle-aged adults are more likely to experience the loss of physical attractiveness, for example, whereas older adults are more likely to experience the loss of a loved one.

Cognitive-behavioral theories of depression adopt a different approach that emphasizes internal belief systems and focus on how people interpret uncontrollable events (Beck, 1967). The idea underlying this approach is that experiencing unpredictable and uncontrollable events instills a feeling of helplessness resulting in depression. In addition, perceiving the cause of negative events as some inherent aspect of the self that is permanent and pervasive also plays an important role in causing feelings of helplessness and hopelessness, as well as feelings of personal responsibility for the "fact" their life is in shambles. Importantly, people tend to ruminate on these negative ideas, often losing sleep doing so. Baddeley (2013) argues such negative self-thoughts and rumination are due to an inappropriate setting of the pleasurable experience detector in the brain, thus linking cognitive-behavior theory with biological theories of depression.

Treatment of Depression

As we have seen, depression is a complex problem that can result from a wide variety of causes. However, an extremely crucial point is most forms of depression benefit from intervention (Segal et al., 2011). Treatment of depression falls roughly into two categories: medical treatments and psychotherapy.

Medical treatments are typically used in cases of severe depression and involve mainly medication, but in some cases of long-term severe depression, these treatments include electroconvulsive therapy. For less severe forms of depression, and usually in conjunction with medication for severe depression, there are various forms of psychotherapy. A summary of the various treatment options is presented in Table 10.2.

Three families of medications are used to combat severe depression. Increasingly, these medications target specific neurotransmitter receptors rather than work by general action in the brain (Jainer et al., 2013). Each has potentially serious side effects (for a summary, see the Mayo Clinic's website on side effects of antidepressant medications where you can find up-to-date information).

The most common first-line medications used to treat depression target specific neurotransmitters and receptors. The most widely used is selective serotonin reuptake inhibitors (SSRIs; Jainer et al., 2013; National Institute of Mental Health, 2016b). SSRIs have the lowest overall rate of side effects of all antidepressants, although some side effects can be serious in some patients. SSRIs work by boosting the level of serotonin, a neurotransmitter involved in regulating moods that was discussed earlier.

Other types of first-line medications are serotonin and norepinephrine reuptake inhibitors (SNRIs), norepinephrine and dopamine reuptake inhibitors

TABLE 10.2 Summary of Depression Treatment Options

Antidepressant medications	Several options, including selective serotonin uptake inhibitors (SSRIs), tricyclics, MAO inhibitors, and others that have been shown to be effective in clinical trials research.	Adequate dosages, plasma levels, and treatment duration are essential to minimize response. Response may take 6–12 weeks, somewhat longer than in younger patients. Side effects may limit use.
Augmentation of antidepressants with lithium, thyroid medications, carbamazepine	Patients nonresponsive to several weeks of treatment with standard antidepressant medications may respond rapidly after these medications are added. Evidence is based on case series and reports.	May be useful in patients who are not responding or only partially responding to standard antidepressant medications. Constitutes acceptable clinical practice.
Electroconvulsive therapy	Clearly effective in severe depression, depression with melancholia, and depression with delusions, and when antidepressants are not fully effective. Sometimes combined with antidepressants.	In medication-resistant patients, acute response rate is approximately 50%. Relapse rate is high, necessitating attention to maintenance antidepressant treatment. Effects are more favorable with increasing age.
Psychotherapy	More effective treatment than waiting list, no treatment, or placebo; equivalent to antidepressant medications in geriatric outpatient populations generally, with major or minor depression. About half of studies are group interventions. Therapy orientations were cognitive, interpersonal, reminiscence, psychodynamic, and eclectic.	Studies have been in older outpatients who were not significantly suicidal and for whom hospitalization was not indicated. There is no evidence of efficacy in severe depression. Distribution of responses may be different from the response to medication.
Combined antidepressant medication and psychotherapy	Effective in outpatients using manual-based therapies; the relative contributions of each component are not well understood.	Combined therapy has not been adequately studied in older adults.

Source: U.S. Public Health Service (1993).

(NDRIs), combined reuptake inhibitors and receptor blockers, and tetracyclic antidepressants.

If the first-line medications do not work, the next most popular medications are the tricyclic antidepressants. These medications are most effective with younger and middle-aged people; in those age groups they work about 70% of the time. The main problem with tricyclic antidepressants in older adults is that they are more likely to have other medical conditions or to be taking other medications that preclude their use. People who are taking antihypertensive medications or who have any of a number of metabolic problems should not take the tricyclic antidepressants. Moreover, the risk of side effects beyond dry mouth, some of which can be severe, is much greater in older adults, although some of the newer tricyclics have significantly lower risk.

If none of these medications are effective, a third group of drugs that relieve depression is the monoamine oxidase (MAO) inhibitors, so named because they inhibit MAO, a substance that interferes with the transmission of signals between neurons. MAO inhibitors generally are less effective than the tricyclics and can produce deadly side effects. Specifically, they interact with foods that contain tyramine or dopamine—mainly cheddar cheese but also others, such as wine and chicken liver—to create dangerously and sometimes fatally high blood pressure. MAO inhibitors are used with extreme caution, usually only after SSRIs and HCAs have proved ineffective.

If periods of depression alternate with periods of mania or extremely high levels of activity, a diagnosis of bipolar disorder is made (American Psychiatric Association, 2013). Bipolar disorder is characterized by unpredictable, often explosive mood swings as the person cycles between extreme depression and extreme activity. The drug therapy of choice for bipolar disorder is lithium, although for some people valporic acid works better (Malhi et al., 2013; National Institute of Mental Health, 2016b). Lithium is effective in controlling the mood swings, although researchers do not completely understand why it works. The use of lithium must be monitored closely because the difference between an effective dosage and a toxic dosage is small. Because lithium is a salt, it raises blood pressure, making it dangerous for people who have hypertension or kidney disease. The effective dosage for lithium decreases with age; physicians unaware of this change run the risk of inducing an overdose, especially in older adults. Compliance is also a problem, because no improvement is seen for 4 to 10 days after the initial dose and because many people with bipolar disorder do not like having their moods controlled by medication.

Electroconvulsive therapy (ECT) is an effective treatment for severe depression, especially in people whose depression has lasted a long time, who are suicidal, who have serious physical problems caused by their depression, and who do not respond to medications (National Institute of Mental Health, 2016c). Unlike antidepressant medications, ECT has immediate effects. Usually only a few treatments are needed, in contrast to long-term maintenance schedules for drugs. But ECT may have some side effects that affect cognitive functioning. Memory of the ECT treatment itself is lost. Memory of other recent events is temporarily disrupted, but it usually returns within a week or two. ECT can be used safely and effectively with older adults (National Institute of Mental Health, 2016c).

In addition to ECT, there are other brain stimulation therapies for severe depression (National Institute of Mental Health, 2016d). These newer approaches include vagus nerve stimulation (VNS) and repetitive transcranial magnetic stimulation (rTMS). Although these methods are not yet commonly used, research has suggested they show promise.

Psychotherapy is a treatment approach based on the idea that talking to a therapist about one's problems can help. Often psychotherapy can be effective by itself in treating depression. In cases of severe depression, psychotherapy may be combined with drug therapy or ECT. *Two general approaches seem to work best for depression:* **behavior therapy**, *which focuses on attempts to alter current behavior without necessarily addressing underlying causes, and* **cognitive behavior therapy**, *which attempts to alter the ways people think.*

The fundamental idea in behavior therapy is that depressed people receive too few rewards or reinforcements from their environment (Lewinsohn, 1975). Thus, the goal of behavior therapy is to get them to increase the good things that happen to them. Often this can be accomplished by having people increase their activities; if they do more, the likelihood is more good things will happen. In addition, behavior therapy seeks to get people to decrease the number of negative thoughts they have because depressed people tend to look at the world pessimistically. They get little pleasure out of activities that nondepressed people enjoy a great deal: seeing a funny movie, playing a friendly game of volleyball, or being with a lover.

To get activity levels up and negative thoughts down, behavior therapists usually assign tasks that force clients to practice the principles they are learning during the therapy sessions. This may involve going out more to meet people, joining new clubs, or just learning how to enjoy life. Family members are instructed to ignore negative statements made by the depressed person and to reward positive self-statements with attention, praise, or even money.

Cognitive behavior therapy for depression is based on the idea that depression results from maladaptive beliefs or cognitions about oneself. From this perspective, a depressed person views the self as inadequate and unworthy, the world as insensitive and ungratifying, and the future as bleak and unpromising (Beck et al., 1979). In cognitive behavior therapy the person is taught how to recognize the thoughts that become so automatic and ingrained that other perspectives are not seen. Once this awareness has been achieved, the person learns how to evaluate the self, world, and future more realistically. These goals may be accomplished through homework assignments similar to those used in behavior therapy. These often involve reattributing the causes of events, examining the evidence before drawing conclusions, listing the pros and cons of maintaining an idea, and examining the consequences of that idea. Finally, people are taught to change the basic beliefs responsible for their negative thoughts. People who believe they have been failures all their lives or they are unlovable are taught how to use their newfound knowledge to achieve more realistic appraisals of themselves.

Cognitive behavior therapy is especially effective for older adults (Carr & McNulty, 2016; Jeste & Palmer, 2013). This is good news, because medications may not be as effective or as tolerated by older adults because of age-related changes in metabolism.

Delirium

Delirium *is characterized by confused thinking and reduced awareness of one's environment that develop rapidly* (Mayo Clinic, 2015b). The changes in cognition can include difficulties with attention, memory, orientation, and rambling speech. Delirium can also affect perception, the sleep–wake cycle, personality, and mood. The onset of delirium usually is rapid, and its course can vary a great deal over a day. Symptoms in older adults are generally more severe than in younger or middle-aged adults, and may go undetected. With older adults, clinicians recommend systematic screening with assessments such as the Confusion Assessment Method (Kuczmarska et al., 2016).

Delirium can be caused by any of a number of medical conditions (such as stroke, cardiovascular disease, and metabolic condition), dehydration, medication side effects, substance intoxication or withdrawal, exposure to toxins, sleep deprivation, fever, or any combination of factors (Mayo Clinic, 2015b). Because they take more medications on average than other age groups, older adults are particularly susceptible to delirium. However, delirium is often undiagnosed or misdiagnosed and symptoms are ascribed to other causes (Kuczmarska et al., 2016).

Once the presence of delirium and its likely cause have been identified, treatment focuses on removing the cause or mitigating its effects. In general, the most important aspect of diagnosis is differentiating delirium from depression and dementia.

About one-third of cases of delirium are preventable (Anand & MacLullich, 2013). If the cause of nonpreventable delirium can be identified and addressed, most cases of delirium can be cured. In some cases, however, delirium can be fatal or result in permanent brain damage.

Dementia

Probably no other condition associated with aging is more feared than the family of disorders known as dementia. In dementia individuals can literally lose their personal identity through the loss of autobiographical memory and the ability even to recognize one's spouse and children. Dementias serious enough to impair independent functioning affect nearly 48 million people globally (World Health Organization, 2015). The Alzheimer's Association (2016a) reports that dementia costs the United States roughly $236 billion annually, and 15 million caregivers provide well over 18 billion hours of unpaid care each year.

Despite the large numbers of people who have some form of dementia, it is the case that most older adults are not diagnosed with it. For many people, the fear of dementia is the most serious problem, leading them to consider every memory lapse a symptom. It is hard to know how many older adults have unstated fears about no longer being able to remember things in the same ways they did when they were younger; but as noted in Chapter 6, memory abilities show some normative changes with age. Consequently, what many people believe are signs they have dementia are actually normative indicators of aging.

The Family of Dementias

Dementia *is not a specific disease but rather a family of diseases characterized by cognitive and behavioral deficits involving some form of permanent damage to the brain.* About a dozen forms of dementia have been identified. Dementia involves severe cognitive and behavioral decline, is not caused by a rapid onset of a toxic substance or by acute infection, and gets worse over time (Alzheimer's Association, 2016b). For example, if delirium is present, dementia cannot be diagnosed.

We focus on several types of dementias that are irreversible and degenerative. The most common and widely known of these is Alzheimer's disease, but others are important as well: vascular dementia, Parkinson's disease, Huntington's disease, alcoholic dementia, Lewy body, and AIDS dementia complex.

Alzheimer's Disease

Alzheimer's disease *is the most common form of progressive, degenerative, and fatal dementia, accounting for between 60% and 80% of all cases of dementia*

(Alzheimer's Association, 2016c). New knowledge about Alzheimer's disease is discovered all the time, so it is important to monitor the research literature. However, because it is such a terrible disease, news of potential breakthroughs too often raises hope that does not pan out.

Nonetheless great progress has been made in diagnosing Alzheimer's disease, such that it is now possible for clinicians to make an accurate diagnosis following a very thorough battery of assessments (Alzheimer's Association, 2016c). The disease has several characteristics we will consider, both in terms of specific changes in the brain and behavioral symptoms.

Neurological Changes in Alzheimer's Disease. The changes in the brain that characterize Alzheimer's disease are microscopic. These changes are progressive, eventually causing so much brain destruction the person dies. The microscopic changes that define Alzheimer's disease are rapid cell death, neurofibrillary tangles, and neuritic plaques. Several changes in neurotransmitter levels also are observed, as is inflammation in brain structures. Rapid cell death occurs most in the hippocampus (a structure in the brain most closely involved in memory), the cortex (the outer layer of the brain where our higher-level cognitive abilities reside), and the basal forebrain (the lower portion of the front of the brain). This cell death occurs at a rate much greater and faster than what occurs in normative aging and results in dramatic brain shrinkage.

Each neuron has within it a set of tubules made of tau protein that act like railroad tracks to carry nutrients and information from the dendrites to the synapse. When too much phosphate binds with tau proteins, the aggregates cause the tubules to form neurofibrillary tangles (see Chapter 2) that are accumulations of pairs of neurofilaments that become wrapped around each other. When the neurofibers become twisted, these tangles interfere with the transmission of the nutrients and information and kill the neurons. Neurofibrillary tangles occur in several areas of the brain, and the number of tangles is directly related to the severity of symptoms, specifically the severity of memory impairment (National Institute on Aging, 2015b; Sala Frigerio & De Strooper, 2016). Figure 10.3 shows how this process works.

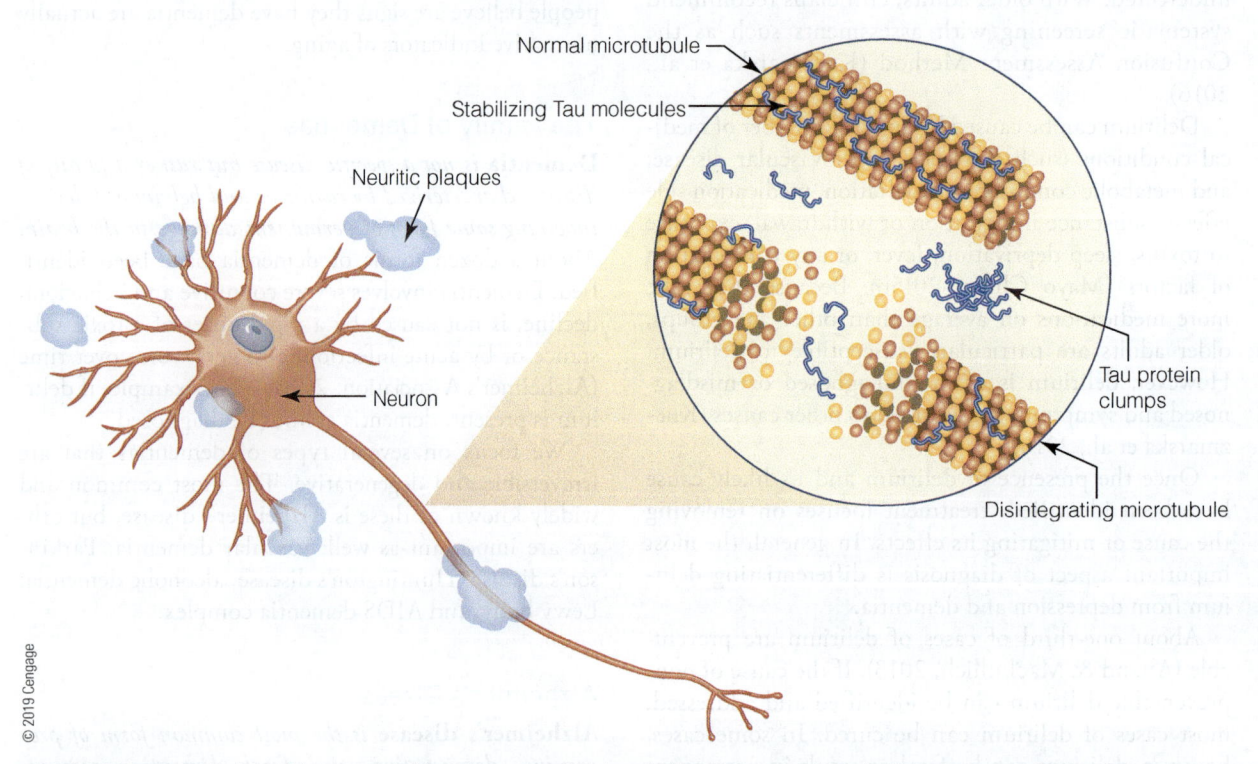

FIGURE 10.3 Action of beta-amyloid and tau proteins in relation to neurons. Each disrupts neurons, but in different ways.
Source: www.nytimes.com/interactive/2012/02/02/science/in-alzheimers-a-tangled-protein.html.

Neuritic or amyloid plaques (see Chapter 3) *are spherical structures consisting of a core of* **beta-amyloid**, *a protein, surrounded by degenerated fragments of dying or dead neurons.* The plaques are found in various parts of the brain, with the amount of beta-amyloid moderately related to the severity of the disease (National Institute on Aging, 2015b). A depiction of beta-amyloid plaques is also shown in Figure 10.3.

Considerable recent research has focused on beta-amyloid as a major factor in Alzheimer's disease, both in terms of the cause and possible avenues for treatment. The role of beta-amyloid is controversial, though. Some researchers view concentration of beta-amyloid as a biomarker of Alzheimer's disease (Sala Frigerio & De Strooper, 2016). Others consider it an early warning of potential cognitive decline, even in the absence of any behavioral symptoms (Gandy & DeKosky, 2013; Singh, Kaur et al., 2016). We will consider the controversy surrounding diagnostic categories related to Alzheimer's disease a bit later.

Although the structural changes occurring in the brains of people with Alzheimer's disease are substantial, we must use caution in assuming they represent qualitative differences from normal aging. They may not. As we saw in Chapter 3, all the changes seen in Alzheimer's disease, including the structural and neurotransmitter changes, are also found in normative aging. To be sure, the changes in Alzheimer's disease are much greater and, more importantly, happen much faster. But the important point is Alzheimer's disease may be merely an exaggeration of normal aging and not something qualitatively different from it.

Recent research also implicated certain neurochemicals as other possible causes of Alzheimer's disease. Increased levels of plasma homocysteine have been associated with the level of cognitive impairment observed in Alzheimer's disease and other forms of dementia (Ansari, 2016). Screening for these increased levels may improve diagnostic accuracy, and these levels are directly addressed by medication with memantine (discussed later) and B vitamins.

Symptoms and Diagnosis. The major symptoms of Alzheimer's disease are gradual changes in cognitive and related functioning in 10 areas (Alzheimer's Association, 2016d): memory loss that interferes with everyday life (e.g., asking the same question repeatedly due to failure to remember the answer), difficulty in dealing with everyday problems (e.g., trouble following a familiar recipe), difficulty completing familiar tasks (e.g., forgetting how to get to a familiar location), confusion with time or place, trouble understanding visual images (e.g., difficulty reading), new problems with words (e.g., trouble following or joining a conversation), misplacing things and having trouble retracing steps (which may result in accusations of stealing), poor judgment (e.g., giving large amounts of money to telemarketers), withdrawal from work or social activities, and changes in mood and personality.

These symptoms tend to be vague in the beginning, and mimic other psychological problems such as depression or stress reactions. An executive may not be managing as well as she once did and may be missing deadlines more often. Slowly, the symptoms get worse. For instance, an executive who could easily handle millions of dollars can no longer add two small numbers. A homemaker cannot set the table. A person who was previously outgoing is now quiet and withdrawn; a gentle person is now hostile and aggressive. Emotional problems become increasingly apparent, including depression, paranoia, and agitation, often accompanied by seemingly outlandish accusations of improper behavior with no real evidence (e.g., accusing a spouse of infidelity or relatives of stealing items).

One common problem exhibited by people with dementia is wandering. Wandering can become a serious problem, especially because the person may have no idea where he or she is or how to get home, thus posing a genuine safety concern. Neuroscience research indicates wandering likely results from damage to the specific parts of the brain that help us navigate through the world (the entorhinal cortex), an area usually damaged in the early stages of Alzheimer's disease (Igarashi, 2016; Jacobs & Lee, 2016).

As the disease progresses, the person likely becomes incontinent and more and more dependent on others for care, eventually becoming completely incapable of such simple tasks as dressing and eating. *In general, the symptoms associated with Alzheimer's disease are worse in the evening than in the morning, a phenomenon care providers call* **sundowning**.

The rate of deterioration in Alzheimer's disease varies widely from one person to the next (Gandy & DeKosky, 2013). Alzheimer's disease has an average duration of 9 years (but can range anywhere from 1 to over 20 years) from the onset of noticeable symptoms through death (Alzheimer's Association, 2016e). The early stage is marked especially by memory loss, disorientation to time and space, poor judgment, and personality changes. The middle stage is characterized by increased memory problems, increased difficulties with speech, restlessness, irritability, and loss of impulse control. People in the late stage of Alzheimer's disease experience incontinence of urine and feces, lose motor skills, have decreased appetite, have great difficulty with speech and language, may not recognize family members or oneself in a mirror, lose most if not all self-care abilities, and decreased ability to fight off infections. These stages are depicted in Figure 10.4.

Accurate early diagnosis of Alzheimer's disease depends on a thorough assessment of the number and severity of neurological and behavioral changes (Ismail et al., 2016). For an early diagnosis to be accurate, however, it must be comprehensive and broad. Figure 10.5 provides an overview of the process used to differentiate Alzheimer's disease from other conditions. Note a great deal of the diagnostic effort goes into ruling out other possible causes for the observed cognitive deficits: All possible treatable causes for the symptoms must be eliminated before a diagnosis of Alzheimer's disease can be made. Unfortunately, many clinicians do not conduct such thorough diagnoses; general practice physicians fail to accurately diagnose a significant number of cases of Alzheimer's disease (Skinner, Scott, & Martin, 2016). A common reason is the attitude on the part of some physicians that early diagnosis does more harm than good based on the mistaken belief patients and their families would prefer not to know or could not adequately deal with it; both are untrue.

As noted in the Current Controversies feature, there is considerable debate over the criteria that should be used to diagnose Alzheimer's disease, and whether there should be a diagnosis even before there are any measurable behavioral symptoms.

Earliest Alzheimer's
Changes may begin 20 years or more before diagnosis.

Mild to moderate Alzheimer's stages
Generally last from 2 to 10 years

Progression of Alzheimer's Through the Brain

Plaques and tangles (shown in the blue-shaded areas) tend to spread through the cortex in a predictable pattern as Alzheimer's disease progresses.
The rate of progression varies greatly. People with Alzheimer's live an average of eight years, but some people may survive up to 20 years. The course of the disease depends in part on age at diagnosis and whether a person has other health conditions.

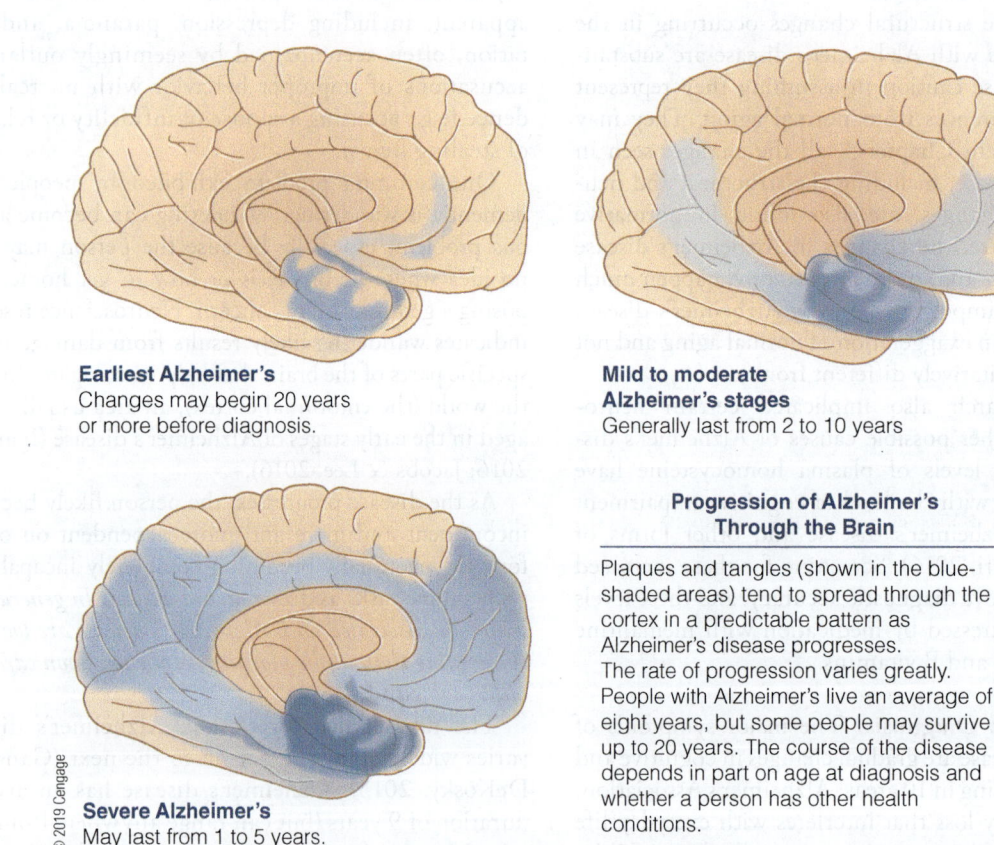

Severe Alzheimer's
May last from 1 to 5 years.

FIGURE 10.4 Progression of Alzheimer's disease through the brain
Source: Alzheimer's Association. (2016). *Progression through the brain*. Retrieved from www.alz.org/braintour/early_stage.asp (Slide 13).

FIGURE 10.5 Differential diagnosis in Alzheimer's disease algorithm.

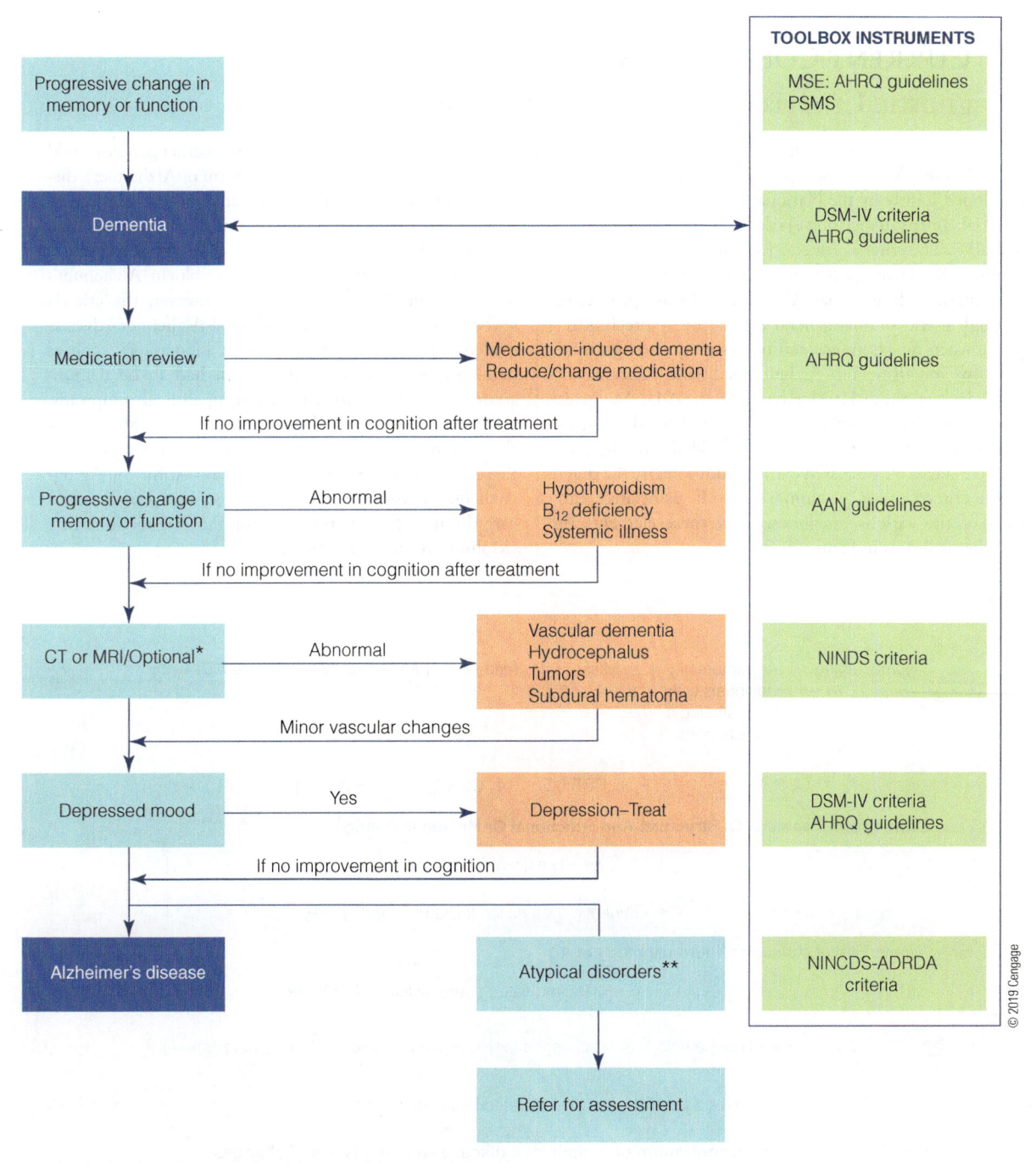

*It is required in patients with focal signs, rapid progression, and headache.

**This category will contain rare dementias (e.g., frontotemporal degenerations, Jakob-Creutzfeldt disease, Parkinson's disease [and other movement disorders that present with dementias]) that should be considered when unusual clinical features are present or a rapidly progressive course is noted.

Source: Alzheimer's Association online document. Retrieved from www.alz.org/medical/rtalgrthm.htm. Developed and endorsed by the TriAD Advisory Board. Copyright 1996 Pfizer Inc. and Esai Inc. with special thanks to J. L. Cummings. Algorithm reprinted from TriAD, Three for the Management of Alzheimer's Disease, with permission.

CURRENT CONTROVERSIES
Diagnostic Criteria for Alzheimer's Disease

The most commonly used diagnostic criteria for Alzheimer's disease were promulgated in 2011 and were developed jointly by the National Institute on Aging and the Alzheimer's Association (Jack et al., 2011; McKhann et al., 2011). The criteria created a firestorm (Jack et al., 2016; Molin & Rockwood, 2016). Research that was the basis for the criteria indicated that Alzheimer's disease progresses through a series of three general stages, from a "preclinical" phase when no symptoms can be detected, through mild cognitive impairment, to Alzheimer's disease (Albert et al., 2011; Jack et al., 2011; McKhann et al., 2011; Molin & Rockwood, 2016; Sperling et al., 2011). The Alzheimer's disease stage could, in turn, be subdivided into the progressive stages we discussed earlier. Additionally, the diagnostic criteria called for biomarkers to be associated with each of the various categories. How these elements fit together is shown in Figure 10.6.

What set off the controversy was whether people should be diagnosed with a "preclinical" form of Alzheimer's disease. Many clinicians objected to labeling individuals who had not shown any behavioral symptoms with a form of an incurable disease when many, perhaps most of them, would not subsequently develop full-blown Alzheimer's disease (Chiu & Brodaty, 2013). However, the criteria specified that to diagnose preclinical Alzheimer's disease evidence of the presence of specific biomarkers, such as beta-amyloid protein accumulation, had to be demonstrated. In individuals demonstrating clinical symptoms, biomarkers are also used to increase the probability that the symptoms are caused by Alzheimer's disease. Despite these arguments, though, the National Institute on Aging-Alzheimer's Association coalition does not actively advocate the use of biomarkers for routine diagnostic testing (Molin & Rockwood, 2016).

| Normal aging | Asymptomatic individuals with histopathologic AD changes | MCI | Mild AD | Moderate AD | Severe AD |

| CDR 0 | CDR 0.5 | CDR 1 | CDR 2 | CDR 3 |

Downstream Measures Of Structural And Functional Or Metabolic Change

← Brain structure (volumetric MRI) →

← Synaptic dysfunction (FDG-PET / fMRI) →

Biomarkers of Molecular Neuropathology of AD

← Tau-mediated neuronal injury (CSF) →

← Histopathological AD changes (amyloid plaques & neurofibrillary tangles) →

? Blood biomarkers and associated biochemical change

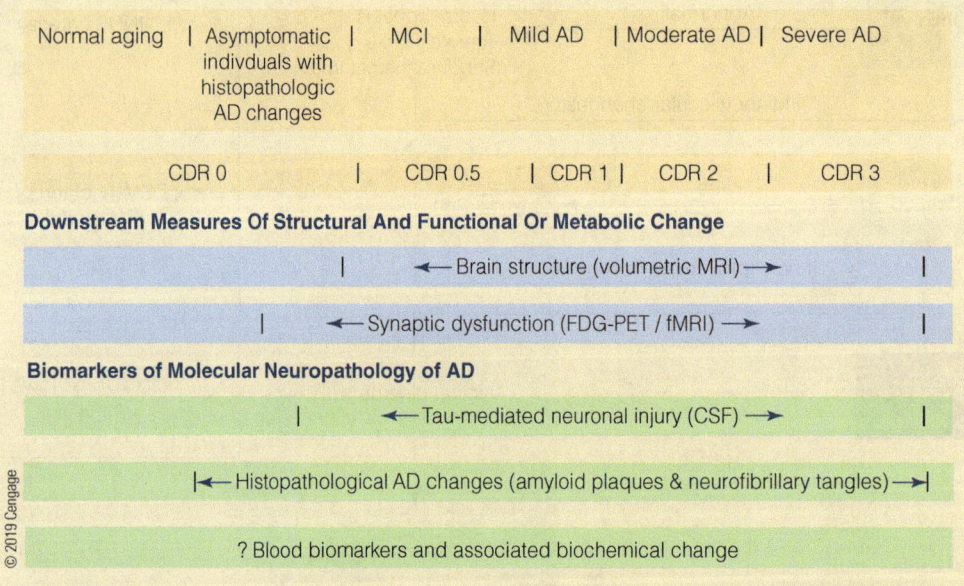

FIGURE 10.6 Clinical continuum of Alzheimer's disease showing types of changes over time. Blood biomarkers and associated biochemical changes are the focus of current research. AD = Alzheimer's disease; MCI = Mild Cognitive Impairment; CDR = Clinical Dementia Rating (a measure of severity of symptoms); FDGPET = Positron Emission Tomography scan using 18-FDG as the tracer molecule; fMRI = Functional Magnetic Resonance Imaging; CSF = cerebrospinal fluid.

Source: Chong, S., & Lee, T.-S. (2013). Predicting cognitive decline in Alzheimer's disease (AD): The role of clinical, cognitive characteristics and biomarkers. In I. Zerr (Ed.), *Understanding Alzheimer's disease* (pp. 375–408). Retrieved from www.intechopen.com/books/understanding-alzheimer-s-disease. doi: 10.5772/54289. Figure 1, p. 376.

One significant concern with the criteria is that many people who show high levels of beta-amyloid protein do not go on to develop Alzheimer's disease. This complicates the issue of whether to intervene during this preclinical stage in order to potentially "prevent" a disease that may never develop, or whether to run the risk of not intervening and having the person subsequently develop a devastating disease. At present, that leaves us in a quandary: The core criteria provide good diagnostic accuracy, but criteria incorporating biomarkers have not yet been validated.

Until we have definitive evidence of a specific set or pattern of biomarkers that inevitably result in the full clinical manifestation of Alzheimer's disease, though, whether we should identify those who may be "at risk" with a label of a disease will remain highly controversial.

Searching for a Cause

We do not know for certain what causes Alzheimer's disease. What we do know is that early-onset (before age 65) forms of Alzheimer's disease are mostly caused by single-gene mutations related to beta-amyloid protein production (Nicolas et al., 2016). Single-gene mutation forms of Alzheimer's disease usually involve mutations in the presenillin-1 (PSEN1), presenillin-2 (PSEN2), and amyloid (A4) precursor protein (APP) genes. The genetic inheritance aspect of early-onset Alzheimer's disease is a major concern of families.

Other genetic links to later-onset Alzheimer's disease involve the complex interaction of several genes, processes that are not yet well documented or understood. Several sites on various chromosomes have been tentatively identified as being potentially involved in the transmission of Alzheimer's disease, including chromosomes 1, 12, 14, 19, and 21. The most promising work noted links between the genetic markers and the production of beta-amyloid protein, the major component of neuritic plaques. Much of this research focuses on apolipoprotein ε4 (APOE-ε4), associated with chromosome 19, that may play a central role in creating neuritic plaques. People with the APOE-ε4 trait are more likely to get Alzheimer's disease than those with the more common APOE-ε3 trait (Di Battista, Heinsinger, & Rebeck, 2016). Additionally, a related mutation (TREM2) may be involved with APOE-ε4 by interfering with the brain's ability to contain inflammation (Jonsson et al., 2013; Sala Frigerio & De Strooper, 2016).

Interestingly, another version, APOE-ε2, seems to have the reverse effect from APOE-ε4: It decreases the risk of Alzheimer's disease (Liu et al., 2013). Despite the relation between APOE-ε4 and neuritic plaques, and between APOE-ε4 and beta-amyloid buildup, researchers have yet to establish strong relations directly between apolipoprotein ε and general cognitive functioning (Wu & Zhao, 2016).

A mutation on the ABCA7 gene has been identified that roughly doubles the chances for African Americans to get late-onset Alzheimer's disease (Cukier et al., 2016). This mutation creates overproduction of cholesterol and lipids, which in turn are known to be risks for cardiovascular disease and strokes, both of which have higher rates in African Americans.

Because researchers can identify definite biomarkers responsible for certain forms of early-onset Alzheimer's disease, they have been able to develop genetic screening tests to see whether people have the inheritance patterns (Nicolas et al., 2016). Although research shows no significant negative consequences to people when they know they have the marker for Alzheimer's disease or other forms of dementia or neurological disease (Paulsen et al., 2013), difficult choices may remain. Individuals who know they have the genes responsible for the disease may be faced with difficult decisions about having children and how to live out their lives. Genetic counseling programs that currently focus mostly on diseases of childhood would need to be expanded to help individuals face decisions about diseases occurring later in life. As research advances continue to improve our understanding of the causes of Alzheimer's disease, additional tests may be forthcoming. Helping people understand the true risks of developing (or, equally important, not developing) Alzheimer's disease will be an increasingly important focus of genetic counseling programs.

Much of the genetics and related biomarker research focuses on beta-amyloid and its proposed relation to Alzheimer's disease reviewed earlier. When viewed as a cause of Alzheimer's disease, researchers refer to the beta-amyloid cascade hypothesis as the process by which this occurs (Selkoe, 2016). *The* **beta-amyloid cascade hypothesis** *refers to the process by which beta-amyloid deposits create neuritic plaques, that in turn lead to neurofibrillary tangles, that cause neuronal death and, when this occurs severely enough, Alzheimer's disease.* As noted earlier, there is considerable evidence beta-amyloid is involved in Alzheimer's disease. Although there is insufficient evidence at this point to conclude it is the main cause, data are quite clear that it is at least an initiating factor (Selkoe, 2016).

One as yet unsolved mystery is why beta-amyloid deposits occur in the first place. An intriguing line of research is providing hints that beta-amyloid deposits linked with Alzheimer's disease could be caused by the brain's natural response to infection including ones that are too mild to cause symptoms (Kumar et al., 2016). The idea is that beta-amyloid is a natural antibiotic that protects the brain from infection. Kumar and colleagues' research shows that beta-amyloid deposits have actually trapped bacterial pathogens, so may reflect a natural immune response. The question being studied is whether this beta-amyloid response is to a true infection or is an abnormal response to a falsely perceived infection. Either way, this may open new avenues for research on treatments.

Other research regarding the cause(s) of Alzheimer's disease is focusing on the role of changes in the vascular system in the brain. Beason-Held and colleagues (2012) discovered increased blood flow in the frontal cortex, combined with decreased blood flow in the parietal and temporal lobes, resulted in significant cognitive impairment. Interestingly, the changes in blood flow occurred prior to measurable changes in cognitive functioning. Additionally, Hayakawa and colleagues (2015) reported that people whose blood pressure does not return to normal within 30 seconds of standing up have a higher rate of converting from mild cognitive impairment to dementia.

Other research focuses on different potential causes. De la Monte (2012) argues Alzheimer's disease is caused at least in part by impairment in the brain's ability to use glucose and produce energy. De la Monte found processed foods containing nitrites and high fat may exacerbate cognitive decline. Support for this idea comes from research showing that high blood sugar (glucose) levels are correlated with increased risk of Alzheimer's disease even in people without diabetes (Crane et al., 2013). These results go further than previous findings which show that diabetes is a risk factor for Alzheimer's disease (Vagelatos & Eslick, 2013).

Although much attention is focused on neuroinflammation related to the role of microglial cells discussed earlier, connecting it to forms of dementia has proven elusive (Stefaniak & O'Brien, 2016). To date, neuroimaging studies have been unable to associate neuroinflammation with a specific form of dementia or with specific patterns of neuroinflammation across individuals with the same type of dementia. Because the neuroinflammation hypothesis holds considerable promise, more research will be necessary to understand what role, if any, it plays in dementia.

Intervention Strategies: Medications

Alzheimer's disease is incurable. However, much research has been done to find medications to alleviate the cognitive deficits and behavioral problems that characterize the disease. The flurry of research on biomarkers, especially beta-amyloid and tau proteins, has led to research on potential medication treatments based on blocking their effects on the brain. No medications that prevent the buildup of either beta-amyloid or tau proteins are available yet, but there are expectations of a breakthrough (Godyń et al., 2016).

In the meantime, research also continues on various drugs that lessen the memory symptoms that occur in Alzheimer's disease. Currently, two groups of medications are approved by the Food and Drug Administration for use with Alzheimer's disease patients. Cholinesterase inhibitors (such as donepezil [Aricept®], galantamine [Razadyne®], and rivastigmine [Exelon®]) affect the levels of the neurotransmitter acetylcholine and are prescribed during the early and moderate stages. Memantine (Namenda®) regulates the activity of glutamate, and is generally prescribed during the moderate and severe stages. Unfortunately, none of the drugs actually stops disease progression.

Medications can also be prescribed to lessen behavioral symptoms, such as depression, irritability, anger, agitation, and sleep disturbances. These medications are essentially the same ones used to treat these problems in individuals who do not have dementia.

Intervention Strategies: Behavioral

To date, the most effective interventions for Alzheimer's disease are behavioral strategies; these approaches are recommended over medications because they give better and more effective outcomes (Barton et al., 2016). These strategies can be used from the time of initial diagnosis throughout the duration of the disease. Behavioral strategies range from simple interventions, such as large calendars to help with orientation to time, to the more complex, such as more elaborate memory interventions that we will consider a bit later. Because they are the approach of choice in such a wide variety of situations, we will consider a few as representative.

Behavioral interventions work best when they are based on a broad support network of relatives, medical personnel, and service providers. Of particular challenge to family members is that their responsibilities require changes in daily routines; people adjust to these roles at different rates.

Once they find themselves caring for a person with Alzheimer's disease, care providers must rethink many behaviors and situations they otherwise take for granted. Dressing, bathing, and grooming become more difficult or sometimes even aversive to the affected person. Using Velcro fasteners, joining the person during a bath or shower, and other such changes may be necessary. Nutritional needs must be monitored because people with dementia may forget they have just eaten or may forget to eat.

Sleeplessness can be addressed by establishing consistent bedtimes, giving warm milk before bedtime, and limiting caffeine intake. Wandering is especially troublesome because it is difficult to control; making sure the affected person has an identification bracelet with the nature of the problem on it and making the home more difficult to exit are two preventive steps.

Incontinence is an embarrassing issue for the person with dementia; using special undergarments or implementing any of a variety of behavioral interventions may help (Bochenska & Boller, 2016; Hsu, Suskind, & Huang, 2016). Incontinence is not necessarily related to Alzheimer's disease; stress incontinence, fairly common among older women, is unrelated to dementia.

Many care providers need to learn how to accomplish these tasks. Programs providing basic care information are available in multiple formats, including onsite face-to-face and online. A comparison of in-person and online formats in Hong Kong showed no differences in effectiveness (Lai et al., 2013). Burgio and colleagues (2003) showed such skills training is equally effective for European American and African American care providers, and reduces the number of problem behaviors the care providers must face from care recipients. Similarly, European American and Latino care providers both reported significant reductions in depressive symptoms, increased use of adaptive coping, and decreased use of negative coping strategies after training and practice in the use of specific cognitive and behavioral skills (Gallagher-Thompson et al., 2003). Additionally, home intervention strategies can result in care providers having more time to themselves and a decrease in the amount of assistance they need from external sources (Nichols et al., 2008).

One of the most difficult issues care providers face concerns taking tasks away from the affected person and restricting activity. For example, in many cases the person experiences problems handling finances. It is not uncommon for them to spend hundreds or even thousands of dollars on strange items, to leave the checkbook in disarray and bills unpaid, and to lose money. Although they can be given some money to keep, someone else must handle the day-to-day accounts. That transition may be traumatic, and the caregiver may be accused of trying to steal money.

Traveling alone is another difficult issue. Families of people with dementia who live in disparate parts of the country often do not recognize their loved one's deteriorating condition until a calamity occurs during travel by the affected person. Families should limit solo excursions to places within walking distance; all other trips should be made with at least one family member along. Related to this, driving is often a contentious

The WanderGuard® device on the woman's wrist keeps people who have dementia from wandering away and potentially getting lost or injured without using medication.

issue, especially if the person does not recognize his or her limitations. Once it is clear the patient cannot drive, the family must take whatever steps are necessary. In some cases, this entails simply taking the car keys, but in others it becomes necessary to disable the car. Suggesting the patient could be chauffeured is another alternative. In any case, care providers may be subjected to various sorts of accusations related to these issues.

How can family members and healthcare professionals deal with the behavioral and cognitive problems experienced by people with Alzheimer's disease? One successful approach for dealing with difficult behavior is a technique called *differential reinforcement of incompatible behavior* (DRI; Baker, Fairchild, & Seefeldt, 2015; Drossel, Fisher, & Mercer, 2011). In DRI, care providers reduce the incidence of difficult behavior by rewarding the person with Alzheimer's disease for engaging in appropriate behaviors that cannot be done at the same time as the problem behaviors. For example, a person who throws food during dinner could be rewarded for sitting quietly and eating. One major advantage of DRI for care providers is the technique can be used in the home and provides a good way to deal with troublesome behaviors. Most important, the DRI technique is easily learned, has no side effects, and can be as effective as or more effective than medical treatments.

Numerous effective behavioral and educational interventions have been developed to address the memory problems in early and middle-stage dementia. *One behavioral intervention involves using an implicit-internal memory intervention called* **spaced retrieval**. Developed by Camp and colleagues (e.g., Camp, 2001), spaced retrieval involves teaching persons with Alzheimer's disease to remember new information by gradually increasing the time between retrieval attempts (see Chapter 6 for more details). This easy, almost magical technique has been used to teach the names of staff members and other information; it holds considerable potential for broad application at home and in any residential care setting. It is easily taught to any care provider (Hunter et al., 2012). Research also shows combining spaced retrieval with additional memory-encoding aids helps even more (Kinsella et al., 2007; Oren, Willerton, & Small, 2014). Spaced retrieval also works in training nonmemory behaviors; it can be used with residents with dementia who have trouble swallowing to help them relearn how to swallow (Camp et al., 2012) and supporting people to eat (Leah, 2016).

In designing interventions for persons with Alzheimer's disease, the guiding principle should be optimizing the person's functioning. Regardless of the level of impairment, attempts should be made to help the person cope as well as possible with the symptoms. The key is helping all persons maintain their dignity as human beings. This can be achieved in creative ways, such as adapting the principles of Montessori methods of education to bring older adults with Alzheimer's disease together with preschool children so they perform tasks together (Malone & Camp, 2007). One example of this approach is discussed in the How Do We Know? feature.

How Do We Know?
Training Persons with Dementia to Be Group Activity Leaders

Who were the investigators, and what was the aim of the study? Dementia is marked by progressive and severe cognitive decline. But despite these losses, can people with dementia be trained to be group leaders? Most people might think the answer is "no," but Cameron Camp, Michael Skrajner, and Marty Kelly (2005) decided to find out by using a training technique based on the Montessori method.

How did the investigators measure the topic of interest? The Montessori method is based on self-paced learning and developmentally appropriate activities. As Camp and colleagues point out, many techniques used in rehabilitation (e.g., task breakdown, guided repetition, moving from simple to complex and concrete to abstract) and in intervention programs with people who have dementia (e.g., use of external cues and implicit memory) are consistent with the Montessori method.

For this study, a program was developed to train group leaders for Memory Bingo (see Camp, 1999a and 1999b, for details about this game). Group leaders learned what cards to pick for the game, where the answers were located on the card, where to "discard" the used (but not the winning) cards, and where to put the winning cards. Success in the program was measured by research staff raters, who made ratings of the type and quality of engagement in the task shown by the group leader.

Who were the participants in the study? Camp and colleagues tested four people who had been diagnosed as probably having dementia who were also residents of a special care unit of a nursing home.

What was the design of the study? The study used a longitudinal design so Camp and colleagues could track participants' performance over several weeks.

Were there ethical concerns with the study? Having persons with dementia as research participants raises important issues with informed consent. Because of their serious cognitive impairments, these individuals may not fully understand the procedures. Thus, family members such as a spouse or adult child caregiver are also asked to give informed consent. Additionally, researchers must pay careful attention to participants' emotions; if participants become agitated or frustrated, the training or testing session must be stopped. Camp and colleagues took all these precautions.

What were the results? Results showed at least partial adherence to the established game protocols was achieved at a high rate. Indeed, staff assistance was not required at all for most of the game sessions for any leader. All of the leaders said they enjoyed their role, and one recruited another resident to become a leader in the next phase of the project.

What did the investigators conclude? It appears persons with dementia can be taught to be group activity leaders through a procedure based on the Montessori Method. This is important as it provides a way for such individuals to become engaged in an activity and to be productive.

Although more work is needed to continue refining the technique, applications of the Montessori method offer a promising intervention approach for people with cognitive impairments.

The key conclusion is behavioral intervention strategies are powerful tools to assist care providers in helping people deal with Alzheimer's disease. Having essentially no side effects and being easy to learn how to administer, these strategies should be the first option tried.

Caring for Patients with Dementia at Home

Watching a loved one struggle with Alzheimer's disease can be both heartrending and uplifting for family members (O'Dell, 2007). Watching a spouse, parent, or sibling go from being an independent, mature adult to not remembering the names of family members is extremely difficult. But the unconditional love shown by family care providers and the opportunity for family members to develop closer relationships can be quite positive. In this section, we consider some of the key issues regarding caregiving for persons with dementia; we consider caregiving more generally in Chapter 11.

Most people with dementia (as well as other impairments) are cared for by their family members at home (Alzheimer's Association, 2016a). Roughly 16 million adults provide more than 18.1 billion hours of unpaid care relatives; it costs the typical family $5,000 per year to provide this care beyond an average of about $15,000 in lost income. When you consider that over 40% of care providers have household incomes of $50,000 or less, the costs represent a significant loss to the family.

One useful way to conceptualize family caregiving is as an unexpected career (Aneshensel et al., 1995). The caregiving career begins with the onset of the illness and moves through a number of separate steps. Note the process does not end with the placement of the affected family member in a nursing home, or even with that person's death. Rather, the career continues through the bereavement and social readjustment period, at which point one may continue with life. Observe the kind of caregiving changes, from the comprehensive caregiving that covers all aspects of the process, to sustained caregiving in the home and foreshortened caregiving in the nursing home, to withdrawal from caregiving.

Care providers are at greater risk for depression; estimates are that about 40% of family care providers suffer from depression (Alzheimer's Association, 2016a). It is important that care providers have access to the support they need. Whether support for care providers is provided in a traditional face-to-face setting or online does not appear to matter, as demonstrated in a study in the Netherlands (Blom et al., 2013) and a review of research in the U.S. (Eifert et al., 2016).

In addition to personal support for care providers, two other options for care providers that offer some relief for both the provider and the affected loved one are respite care and adult day care.

Respite care is designed to allow family members to get away from the caregiving situation for a time. It can consist of in-home care provided by professionals or temporary placement in a residential facility. In-home care is typically used to allow care providers to do errands or have a few hours free, whereas temporary residential placement is usually reserved for a more extended respite, such as a weekend. Research documents using respite care is a help to care providers (Hill, 2015; Roberto & Jarrott, 2008).

Adult day care provides placement and programing for frail older adults during the day. The goal of adult day care is to delay institutionalization, enhance self-esteem, and encourage socialization (National Adult Day Services Association, 2016a). Adult day care typically provides more intensive intervention than respite care.

This option is used most often by adult children who are employed. In general, adult day care is an effective approach for care providers (Roberto & Jarrott, 2008).

The demand for respite and adult day care far exceeds their availability, making them limited options. An additional problem is many insurance programs do not pay for these services, making them too expensive for care providers with limited finances. Clearly, with the increase in numbers of people who have dementia, ways to provide support for assistance to family care providers must be found.

Other Forms of Dementia

As we noted, dementia is a family of different diseases. We consider several of them briefly.

Vascular Dementia. Until it was discovered that Alzheimer's disease was not rare, most physicians and researchers believed most cases of dementia resulted from cerebral atherosclerosis and its consequent restriction of oxygen to the brain. As described in Chapter 3, atherosclerosis is a family of diseases that, if untreated, may result in heart attacks or strokes. For the present discussion it is the stroke, or cerebrovascular accident (CVA), that concerns us. CVAs (see Chapter 3) result from a disruption of the blood flow called an infarct that may be caused by a blockage or hemorrhage.

A large CVA usually produces rapid, severe cognitive decline, but this loss is almost always limited to specific abilities. This pattern differs from the classic, global, more gradual deterioration seen in Alzheimer's disease. *If a person experiences numerous small cerebral vascular accidents, a disease termed* **vascular dementia** *may result*. Vascular dementia is the second most common form of dementia after Alzheimer's disease. It may have a sudden onset after a CVA, and its progression is described as stepwise and highly variable across people, especially early in the disease. Again, this is in contrast to the similar cluster of cognitive problems shown by people with Alzheimer's disease.

Most people who have vascular dementia have a history of cerebrovascular or cardiovascular disease, and typical symptoms include hypertension, specific and extensive alterations on an MRI, and differential impairment on neuropsychological tests (a pattern of scores showing some functions intact and others significantly below average; Paul, Lane, & Jefferson, 2013). Individuals' specific symptom patterns may vary a great deal, depending on which specific areas of the brain are damaged. In some cases, vascular dementia has a much faster course than Alzheimer's disease, resulting in death an average of 2 to 3 years after onset; in others, the disease may progress much more slowly with idiosyncratic symptom patterns. It is fairly common for people to have vascular brain changes as well as show signs of other forms of dementia, such as Alzheimer's disease.

Dementia with Lewy Bodies. Dementia with Lewy bodies is the third most common form; this is the disease diagnosed in Robin Williams, the famous comedian. Dementia with Lewy bodies is an umbrella term for two related diseases, dementia with Lewy bodies and Parkinson's disease dementia. If the dementia occurs within about one year of the onset of Parkinson's disease, then dementia with Lewy bodies is diagnosed; if the dementia occurs well after the diagnosis of Parkinson's disease, the diagnosis is Parkinson's disease dementia.

The diagnosis of dementia with Lewy bodies depends on several specific things (Lewy Body Dementia Association, 2016). The hallmark Lewy bodies are abnormal accumulations of alpha-synuclein protein that develops inside neurons and cause progressive dementia. Three key behavioral symptoms are fluctuating cognition with significant variations in attention and alertness; recurring complex visual hallucinations; and spontaneous features of Parkinson's disease (discussed next).

Parkinson's Disease. Parkinson's disease is known primarily for its characteristic motor symptoms that are easily seen: very slow walking, difficulty getting into and out of chairs, and a slow hand tremor. Research indicates these problems are caused by a deterioration of neurons that produce the neurotransmitter dopamine. Dopamine is involved in transmitting messages between the brain structure called the substantia nigra and other parts of the brain to enable us to have smooth body movements. When roughly 60 to 80% of the dopamine-producing cells are damaged and do not produce enough dopamine, the motor symptoms of Parkinson's disease appear.

However, motor system changes may not be the most important symptom diagnostically. One prominent theory states the earliest indications of Parkinson's are found in a different part of the brain, the medulla and the olfactory bulb, which controls the sense of smell. According to this theory, Parkinson's only progresses to the substantia nigra and cortex over many years. In fact, there is evidence nonmotor symptoms such as a loss of the sense of smell, sleep disorders, and constipation may precede the motor features of the disease by several years (Lee et al., 2014).

Former boxing champion Muhammad Ali and actor Michael J. Fox are some of the more famous individuals who had or have Parkinson's disease. Roughly 1 million people in the United States live with Parkinson's disease (Parkinson's Disease Foundation, 2016a).

Symptoms are treated effectively with several medications (Parkinson's Disease Foundation, 2016b); the most popular are levodopa, which raises the functional level of dopamine in the brain; Sinemet® (a combination of levodopa and carbidopa), which gets more levodopa to the brain; and Stalevo® (a combination of Sinemet® and entacapone), that extends the effective dosage time of Sinemet®. Research indicates a device called a neurostimulator acts like a brain pacemaker by regulating brain activity when implanted deep inside the brain. This may prove effective in significantly reducing the tremors, shaking, rigidity, stiffness, and walking problems when medications are ineffective.

For reasons we do not yet understand, some people with Parkinson's disease also develop severe cognitive impairment and eventually dementia (Zheng et al., 2014). As noted earlier, Lewy bodies characterize dementia in Parkinson's disease; the key factor in the latter case is that the dementia component occurs later.

Huntington's Disease. Huntington's disease is a fatal autosomal dominant disorder (meaning that inheriting the gene from only one parent is necessary to have the disease) that usually begins between ages 30 and 45 (Huntington's Disease Society of America, 2016). The disease generally manifests itself through involuntary flicking movements of the arms and legs; the inability to sustain a motor act such as sticking out one's tongue; prominent psychiatric disturbances such as hallucinations, paranoia, and depression; and clear personality changes, such as swings from apathy to manic behavior.

Cognitive impairments typically do not appear until late in the disease. The onset of these symptoms is gradual. The course of Huntington's disease is progressive; patients ultimately lose the ability to care for themselves physically and mentally. Walking becomes impossible, swallowing is difficult, and cognitive loss becomes profound. Some people describe Huntington's disease as like having amyotrophic lateral sclerosis (ALS), Parkinson's disease, and Alzheimer's disease simultaneously (Huntington's Disease Society of America, 2016)

Huntington's disease affects the entire brain, but begins with degeneration of the caudate nucleus and the small-cell population, as well as with substantial decreases in the neurotransmitters g-aminobutyric acid (GABA) and substance P. A test is available to determine whether someone has the marker for the Huntington's disease gene (Huntington's Disease Society of America, 2016).

Alcohol-Related Dementia. Chronic alcohol abuse or dependence may result in cognitive decline, ranging from limited forms of amnesia or mild cognitive impairment to dementia (National Institute of Neurological Disorders and Stroke, 2016). The memory problems are caused by chronic and severe thiamine (vitamin B1) deficiency. B1 deficiency causes damage to the thalamus and hypothalamus, which results in the cognitive symptoms, along with vision problems, coma, hypothermia, low blood pressure, and lack of muscle coordination.

One key symptom of alcohol-related dementia is confabulation, when the person makes up apparently believable, but completely fictitious, stories that cover the gaps in memory. Other symptoms include personality changes (e.g., frustration, anger, suspicion, and jealousy), loss of problem-solving skills, communication problems (e.g., word-finding difficulty), and disorientation to time and place.

Early in the course of the disease, the memory problems may be reduced or reversed if the person stops drinking alcohol, eats a well-balanced diet, and is given vitamin replacements. Without treatment, symptoms continue to get worse and may result in death.

AIDS Dementia Complex. AIDS dementia complex (ADC), or HIV-associated encephalopathy, occurs primarily in persons with more advanced HIV infection (Manji, Jäger, & Winston, 2013; Tauber, Staszewski et al., 2016). The virus does not appear to directly invade nerve cells, but it jeopardizes their health and function. The resulting inflammation from glial cell action (as discussed earlier) may damage the brain and spinal cord and cause symptoms such as confusion and forgetfulness, behavioral changes (e.g., apathy, loss of spontaneity, depression, social withdrawal, and personality changes), severe headaches, progressive weakness, loss of sensation in the arms and legs, and stroke. Cognitive motor impairment or damage to the peripheral nerves is also common.

Research shows the HIV infection can significantly alter the size of certain brain structures involved in learning and information processing. Symptoms include encephalitis (inflammation of the brain), behavioral changes, and a gradual decline in cognitive function, including trouble with concentration, memory, and attention. Persons with ADC also show progressive slowing of motor function and loss of dexterity and coordination. When left untreated, ADC can be fatal. In the terminal phase of ADC, patients are bedridden, stare vacantly, and have minimal social and cognitive interaction.

Because HIV infection is largely preventable, ADC can be reduced through the practice of safe sex. Additionally, research shows aggressive treatment of HIV with antiretroviral medications can also dramatically reduce the risk of subsequently developing ADC (Manji et al., 2013).

Adult Development in Action

How are the key distinguishing features of depression, delirium, and dementia important to social workers?

10.4 Other Mental Disorders and Concerns

LEARNING OBJECTIVES
- What are the symptoms of anxiety disorders? How are they treated?
- What are the characteristics of people with psychotic disorders?
- What are the major issues involved with alcohol use disorder?

Daisy forces herself to do her daily routine. *She is shaky all the time because she just doesn't feel safe. She imagines all sorts of horrible things might happen to her. Her worst fear is no one would know if she were attacked or fell ill. So, she had a security company install multiple webcams around her house and in every room. She has called 911 several times, but the police never find anything amiss. She rarely goes out now and has convinced her son to bring her groceries and other supplies to her several times per week.*

Daisy's feelings indicate people have difficulties for many reasons. She is clearly afraid. One the one hand, it is possible that her fear could reflect a realistic assessment of her neighborhood. But her feelings could also be not based on an objective assessment of her situation. In this section, we examine three disorders that affective people across adulthood: anxiety disorders, psychotic disorders, and substance abuse.

Anxiety Disorders

Imagine you are about to give a speech before an audience of 500 people. In the last few minutes before your address, you begin to feel nervous, your heart starts to pound, and your palms get sweaty. These feelings, common even to veteran speakers, are similar to those experienced to a greater extent by people with anxiety disorders: a group of conditions based on fear or uneasiness.

Anxiety disorders include problems such as feelings of severe anxiety for no apparent reason, phobias with regard to specific things or places, and obsessive-compulsive disorders, when thoughts or actions are repeatedly performed (National Institute of Mental Health, 2016e, f; Segal et al., 2011). The prevalence of anxiety disorders in adults of all ages is about 18%, but the lifetime prevalence is about twice as high in young and middle-aged adults as it is in older adults. Overall, women are 60% more likely than men to experience an anxiety disorder over their lifetime (National Institute of Mental Health, 2016g).

Symptoms and Diagnosis of Anxiety Disorders

Common to all the anxiety disorders are physical changes that interfere with social functioning, personal relationships, or work. These physical changes include restlessness or feeling on edge, dry mouth, sweating, dizziness, upset stomach, diarrhea, insomnia, hyperventilation, chest pain, choking, frequent urination, headaches, and a sensation of a lump in the throat (Segal et al., 2011). These symptoms occur in adults of all ages, but they are particularly common in older adults because of loss of health, relocation stress, isolation, fear of losing control over their lives, or guilt resulting from feelings of hostility toward family and friends.

An important issue concerning anxiety disorders in older adults is anxiety may be an appropriate response to the situation (Carr & McNulty, 2016). Helplessness anxiety is generated by a potential or actual loss of control or mastery (Varkal et al, 2013). A study in Turkey showed older adults are anxious about their memory, reflecting at least in part a realistic assessment of normative, age-related decline.

In addition, a series of severe negative life experiences may result in a person's reaching the breaking point and appearing highly anxious. Many older adults who show symptoms of anxiety disorder have underlying health problems that may be responsible for the symptoms. In all cases the anxious behavior should be investigated first as an appropriate response that may not warrant medical intervention. The important point is to evaluate the older adult's behavior in context.

These issues make it difficult to diagnose anxiety disorders, especially in older adults (Carr & McNulty, 2016; Fitzwater, 2008; Segal et al., 2011). The problem is there usually is nothing specific a person can point to as the specific trigger or cause. In addition, anxiety in older adults often accompanies an underlying physical disorder or illness.

These secondary causes of anxiety must be disentangled from the anxiety symptoms so each may be dealt with appropriately. In short, the trick is to distinguish between the "worried" and the well. Zarit and Zarit (2007) report the key features of late-life anxiety disorder are distress and impairment, frequency and uncontrolled worry, muscle tension, and sleep disturbance.

Treating Anxiety Disorders. Anxiety disorders can be treated with medication and psychotherapy (Carr & McNulty, 2016; Chew-Graham & Ray, 2016; Segal et al., 2010). The most commonly used medications are benzodiazepine (e.g., Valium® and Librium®), paroxetine (an SSRI, e.g., Paxil®), buspirone, and beta-blockers. Though moderately effective, these drugs must be monitored carefully in older adults because the amount needed to treat the disorder is low and the potential for side effects is great. Obsessive-compulsive disorders are treated most often with serotonin reuptake inhibitors (SRIs) and selective serotonin reuptake inhibitors (SSRIs).

For older adults, the clear treatment of choice is psychotherapy, specifically cognitive behavioral or relaxation therapy, especially when anxiety disorders first occur in later life (Carr & McNulty, 2016; Hendriks et al., 2012). Relaxation therapy is exceptionally effective, easily learned, and presents a technique that is useful in many situations (e.g., falling asleep at night; Segal et al., 2011). The advantage of these psychotherapeutic techniques is they usually involve only a few sessions, have high rates of success, and offer clients procedures they can take with them.

Psychotic Disorders

Some forms of psychopathology, called psychoses, involve losing touch with reality and the disintegration of personality. Two behaviors that occur in these disorders are delusions, belief systems not based on reality, and hallucinations, distortions in perception. Daisy's fear that was described in the vignette is an example.

It is rare for older adults to develop new cases of psychotic disorders (Karim & Harrison, 2016; Salai, 2013). The behaviors present in psychotic disorders are commonly manifested as secondary problems caused by other disorders, such as delirium or dementia, or as side effects from medications. Thus, psychotic symptoms are an important aspect of the diagnosis of other disorders and can be managed in the same way.

Schizophrenia

Schizophrenia is characterized by the severe impairment of thought processes, including the content and style of thinking, distorted perceptions, loss of touch with reality, a distorted sense of self, and abnormal motor behavior (Karim & Harrison, 2016). People with schizophrenia may show these abnormal behaviors in several ways: loose associations (such as saying that they have a secret meeting with the president of the United States in the local bowling alley), hearing voices that tell them what to do, believing they can read other people's minds, believing their body is changing into something else, or having bizarre delusions (e.g., that they are Jesus or they are being spied on). In addition, people with schizophrenia tend to show little or highly inappropriate emotionality (e.g., showing no emotion at a truly tragic event, or laughing hysterically at the scene of a horrific accident). They are often confused about their own identity, have difficulty working toward a goal, and tend to withdraw from social contact.

A hallmark symptom of schizophrenia is delusions, or well-formed beliefs not based in reality. Most often, these delusions involve persecution ("People are out to get me"), which is what Daisy is experiencing.

The beliefs underlying delusions can result in anger, resentment, or even violent acts. Because people with psychoses are extremely suspicious and rarely seek help on their own, such people tend to come to the attention of authorities after having repeated run-ins with the police or neighbors, starting legal proceedings against others on mysterious grounds, or registering complaints about fictitious or distorted events.

The onset of schizophrenia occurs most often between ages 16 and 30, and much less often after age 40 (Clare & Giblin, 2008; Karim & Harrison, 2016). The symptoms of schizophrenia also differ by age; older adults show less thought disorder and less flattening of their emotions than do younger adults. Some researchers disagree, however, maintaining there are few differences with age in the numbers of people who experience schizophrenic symptoms and no differences in the nature of the symptoms. In any case, there is agreement that new cases of schizophrenia are rare in late life.

Longitudinal research indicates the natural course of schizophrenia is improvement over the adult life span (Salai, 2013; Segal et al., 2011). Studies show the first 10 years of the disorder are marked by cycles of remission and worsening, but symptoms generally lessen in more than half of people with schizophrenia in later life. This may be caused by a rebalancing of the neurotransmitters dopamine and acetylcholine that are heavily weighted toward dopamine in younger adults with schizophrenia. Additional rebalancing of other neurotransmitters may also play a role.

Treating Schizophrenia. Traditionally, treatment of schizophrenia has emphasized medication. Drug therapy consists of antipsychotics; medications believed to work on the dopamine system (see Chapter 2). Some of the more commonly used antipsychotics are haloperidol (Haldol®), chlorpromazine HCl (Thorazine®), and thioridazine HCl (Mellaril®). These medications must be used with extreme caution in adults of all ages because of the risk of serious toxic side effects, especially the loss of motor control. Despite these risks, antipsychotics often are used in nursing homes and other institutions as tranquilizing agents to control difficult patients.

In general, people with schizophrenia are difficult to treat with psychotherapy. The severe thought disturbances characteristic of schizophrenia make it difficult for therapists to work with such clients. Because of their extreme suspiciousness, paranoid people may be reluctant to cooperate in psychotherapy. However, there is evidence a comprehensive and integrated social rehabilitation program combined with healthcare management intervention can be effective (National Institute of Mental Health, 2016h; Pratt et al., 2008). The goals of therapy for such people tend to be adaptive rather than curative, helping these people adapt to daily living.

Alcohol Use Disorder

Although you might think substance abuse is primarily a problem of young and middle-aged adults, it's not—older adults also have the problem (National Institute on Alcohol Abuse and Alcoholism, 2016a). Because of the differences in the types of substances abused by younger and older adults (younger adults are more likely to abuse illegal drugs than are older adults), alcohol provides the best common basis for comparison.

What constitutes alcohol abuse disorder? **Alcohol use disorder (AUD)** *is a drinking pattern that results in significant and recurrent consequences that reflect loss of reliable control over alcohol use.* AUD is diagnosed whenever anyone meets any 2 of the 11 criteria listed in Table 10.3 during a 12-month period.

TABLE 10.3 Diagnosis of alcohol use disorder (AUD) based on DSM-5

Symptoms

In the past year, have you:

- Had times when you ended up drinking more, or longer, than you intended?
- More than once wanted to cut down or stop drinking, or tried to, but couldn't?
- Spent a lot of time drinking? Or being sick or getting over other aftereffects?
- Wanted a drink so badly you couldn't think of anything else?
- Found that drinking—or being sick from drinking—often interfered with taking care of your home or family? Or caused job troubles? Or school problems?
- Continued to drink even though it was causing trouble with your family or friends?
- Given up or cut back on activities that were important or interesting to you, or gave you pleasure, in order to drink?
- More than once gotten into situations while or after drinking that increased your chances of getting hurt (such as driving, swimming, using machinery, walking in a dangerous area, or having unsafe sex)?
- Continued to drink even though it was making you feel depressed or anxious or adding to another health problem? Or after having had a memory blackout?
- Had to drink much more than you once did to get the effect you want? Or found that your usual number of drinks had much less effect than before?
- Found that when the effects of alcohol were wearing off, you had withdrawal symptoms, such as trouble sleeping, shakiness, restlessness, nausea, sweating, a racing heart, or a seizure? Or sensed things that were not there?

Severity

The severity of the **AUD** is defined as:

- **Mild** The presence of 2 to 3 symptoms
- **Moderate** The presence of 4 to 5 symptoms
- **Severe** The presence of 6 or more symptoms

Source: Based on NIH Publication 13-7999. (2016). Alcohol Use Disorder: A Comparison Between DSM-IV and DSM-5. National Institutes of Health (NIH), National Institute on Alcohol Abuse and Alcoholism. Available at pubs.niaaa.nih.gov/publications/dsmfactsheet/dsmfact.pdf.

Roughly 17 million adults over age 18 in the United States are diagnosed with alcohol use disorder (National Institute on Alcohol Abuse and Alcoholism, 2016b). However, when data are examined more closely, there are gender and ethnic group differences in alcohol abuse. The percentage of men who abuse alcohol ranges from about two times (ages 18–29) to six times (ages 65 and over) higher than those for women. In fact, widowers over age 75 have the highest rate of AUD in the U.S. (National Council on Alcoholism and Drug Dependence, 2015). Native Americans have the highest rate of abuse, followed by European Americans, Latinos, African Americans, and Asian Americans.

Two patterns of onset are evident with older people with alcohol abuse disorder: early-onset in young adulthood or middle age with lifelong problem drinking, and late-onset problem drinking (Segal et al., 2011; Trevisan, 2014). People with an earlier onset alcohol use disorder have a more severe course of illness. This group makes up about two-thirds of the older adults with AUD. They are predominantly male, have more alcohol-related medical and mental health problems. They tend to be less well-adjusted and have more antisocial traits. Left untreated, alcohol dependency does not improve over time.

Patients with later-onset alcohol use disorder usually have fewer medical problems because of the shorter exposure to alcohol. They are more affluent, include more women, and are likely to begin their alcohol use after a stressful event, such as retirement, loss of a spouse, job, or home. Other risk factors for development of later life AUD include a personal and family history of alcohol abuse or dependence, chronic pain, predisposition to affective or anxiety disorders, and decreased alcohol metabolism.

Taking a life-span view of alcohol use disorder provides insights into important differences in drinking patterns and outcomes (National Institute on Alcohol Abuse and Alcoholism, 2016c). Young adults are more likely to binge drink, and consequently more likely to experience problems such as alcohol poisoning, drunk-driving offenses, and assaults. The earlier drinking begins, especially if it starts in adolescence, the more likely brain damage occurs and alcohol dependence develops. Young adult drinkers are less likely to feel the effects of alcohol, such as getting sleepy or losing motor coordination, that may result in their drinking more at one time ("binging"). However, young adults' cognitive performance is more impaired. Taken together, these effects create a dangerous situation—they do not feel the effects as easily, so tend to underestimate the degree they are impaired, and are worse at performing complex tasks such as driving, providing an explanation of why drunk driving is more prevalent among young adults.

Middle age is when the effects of continued alcohol dependence that began in young adulthood become evident. Diseases of the liver, pancreas, and various types of cancer and cardiovascular disease may occur. In part due to these health problems, middle-aged adults are the most likely group to seek treatment for their problem.

Drinking among older adults presents a more complicated picture. Even older adults who drink only modest amounts may experience dangerous interactions with medications they may be taking. Additionally, they metabolize alcohol much more slowly, meaning it remains in the bloodstream longer. As a result, older adults are at higher risk for abusing alcohol if they simply continue habits of drinking from earlier points in their lives, even if their consumption when they were younger was only moderate. Diagnosing alcohol dependence in older women can be especially difficult given the higher likelihood that they live alone.

Treatment for AUD in all age groups focuses on three goals (National Institute on Alcohol Abuse and Alcoholism, 2014; Segal et al., 2011): stabilization and reduction of substance consumption, treatment of coexisting problems, and arrangement of appropriate social interventions. Three main options for treatment are available: mutual-support groups, behavioral treatments, and medications.

Mutual-support groups are the most widely known, and include Alcoholics Anonymous (AA) and other 12-step groups. These groups provide peer support to help people stop abusing various drugs and alcohol. Behavioral treatments rely on individual or group counseling to stop or reduce drinking or drugging.

The U.S. Food and Drug Administration has approved three types of medications for use in treating alcohol use disorder (National Institute on Alcohol Abuse and Alcoholism, 2014):

- Disulfiram (Antabuse) is used to block alcohol metabolism, and causes very unpleasant symptoms such as nausea to help people stop drinking. Disulfiram has been used for nearly a century, but some people stop taking it to stop the unpleasant effects.
- Naltrexone reduces the pleasure received from drinking and reduces the cravings that compel chronic drinking by blocking the endorphin receptors in the brain. Research evidence is mostly positive on the effectiveness of naltrexone, especially when combined with other treatments.

- Acamprosate (Campral) reduces the unpleasant symptoms experienced from alcohol withdrawal by stabilizing the neurotransmitters in the brain. Research results on the effectiveness of acamprosate is mixed.

Perhaps the most important thing with people who have alcohol use disorder is to encourage them to get treatment. Unfortunately, only a minority of people who need such treatment actually get it at any age, but especially later in life. The Discovering Development feature focuses on finding out what options are available in your local area.

Adult Development in Action

Find out which treatment options for anxiety disorders, psychoses, and substance abuse are available in your region.

■ DISCOVERING DEVELOPMENT
What Substance Abuse Treatment Options Are Available in Your Area?

One of the most controversial topics regarding substance abuse is how to deal with people who have a problem such as alcohol use disorder. If they use illicit drugs, should they be treated or jailed? If treatment is the choice, should they be placed in inpatient facilities or in outpatient programs?

These decisions have become both political and sensitive. Many politicians built their careers on being perceived as "tough on drugs" and put offenders in jail. Budget pressures has also resulted in votes to reduce or eliminate treatment options for drug and alcohol offenders. The rise of health management organizations resulted in the near elimination of inpatient treatment facilities in favor of the less expensive outpatient programs and community treatment centers.

An enlightening exercise is to find out what treatment options are available in your area for people who have alcohol or other drug abuse problems. Find out whether there are any inpatient programs, which outpatient programs and community treatment centers are available, and how long one has to wait to receive treatment. Also, find out the costs of the various programs and whether health insurance policies cover the treatments.

Gather the information from several geographic regions, and compare program availability. Think about what you would do if you were poor and needed help in your area. What do you think should be done to address the problem?

Social Policy Implications

As we have seen, dementia, especially Alzheimer's disease, takes a devastating toll on the people who have a form of it as well as their family and friends. A significant problem facing the United States (as well as many other countries) is the prospect of a dramatic increase in the number of people with dementia over the next few decades with the continued aging of the baby boomers. The problem has many facets: the cost of caring for individuals with dementia, the lost income and productivity of family care providers, and the lack of prospects for effective treatment or cure in the near future.

From the current estimate of 5 million people in the United States with Alzheimer's disease, the number is expected to nearly triple by 2050 to about 14 million. That would mean that someone would be diagnosed with Alzheimer's disease in 2015 every 33 seconds (Alzheimer's Association, 2016a). The cost of care for these individuals will be staggering—roughly $1 trillion per year by 2050, or one of every three dollars spent in Medicare. The current model of funding cannot sustain this level of increase cost (discussed in Chapter 14).

Expecting family members to care for loved ones with dementia is not a good option either. Most adult child care providers and many spouse/partner care providers are still employed, and may not have employers that will provide flexible schedules or paid leave. Lost productivity to organizations due to parent/spouse/partner care is equivalent to billions of dollars each year. Many insurance plans do not cover behavioral or in-home care options. And very few employers provide paid leave for employees to care for older parents.

The social policy implications of the coming wave of people who will develop dementia are clear. First, research funding aimed at finding an effective way to prevent or cure dementia is essential. Second, redesigning healthcare plans and service delivery to include behavioral and in-home care along with other more cost-effective alternatives needs to be undertaken. Third, ways for employers to provide support for parent/spouse/partner care need to be found.

The increase in the number of people with dementia is only one major aspect of the coming healthcare crisis resulting from the aging of the baby boomers. We revisit this issue in more detail in Chapter 14.

SUMMARY

10.1 Mental Health and the Adult Life Course

How are mental health and psychopathology defined?
- Definitions of mental health must reflect appropriate age-related criteria.
- Behaviors must be interpreted in context. Mentally healthy people have positive attitudes, accurate perceptions, environmental mastery, autonomy, personality balance, and personal growth.

What key areas are included in a multidimensional approach to assessment?
- Considering key biological, psychological, sociocultural, and life-cycle factors is essential for accurate diagnosis of mental disorders.
- Diagnostic criteria must reflect age differences in symptomatology.

Why are ethnicity and aging important variables to consider in understanding mental health?
- Little research has been done to examine ethnic differences in the definition of mental health and psychopathology in older adults.
- There is some evidence of different incidence rates across groups.

10.2 Developmental Issues in Assessment and Therapy

What are the key dimensions used for categorizing psychopathology?
- Accurate assessment depends on measuring functioning across a spectrum of areas, including medical, psychological, and social.

What factors influence the assessment of adults?
- Negative and positive biases can influence the accuracy of assessment.
- The environmental conditions that the assessment is made can influence its accuracy.

How are mental health issues assessed?
- Six assessment techniques are used most: interview, self-report, report by others, psychophysiological assessment, direct observation, and performance-based assessment.

What are some major considerations for therapy across adulthood?
- The two main approaches are medical therapy (usually involving drugs) and psychotherapy.
- With psychotherapy, clinicians must be sensitive to changes in the primary developmental issues faced by adults of different ages.
- Clear criteria have been established for determining "well established" and "probably efficacious" psychotherapies.

10.3 The Big Three: Depression, Delirium, and Dementia

What are the most common characteristics of people with depression? How is depression diagnosed? What causes depression? What is the relation between suicide and age? How is depression treated?
- The prevalence of depression declines with age. Gender and ethnic differences in rates have been noted.
- Common features of depression include dysphoria, apathy, self-deprecation, expressionlessness, changes

in arousal, withdrawal, and several physical symptoms. In addition, the problems must last at least 2 weeks, not be caused by another disease, and negatively affect daily living. Clear age differences exist in the reporting of symptoms. Some assessment scales are not sensitive to age differences in symptoms.
- Possible biological causes of severe depression are neurotransmitter imbalance, abnormal brain functioning, or physical illness. Loss is the main psychosocial cause of depression. Internal belief systems also are important.
- Three families of drugs (SSRIs, HCAs, and MAO inhibitors), electroconvulsive therapy, and various forms of psychotherapy are all used to treat depression. Older adults benefit most from behavior and cognitive therapies.

What is delirium? How is it assessed and treated?
- Delirium is characterized by a disturbance of consciousness and a change in cognition that develop over a short period of time.
- Delirium can be caused by a number of medical conditions, medication side effects, substance intoxication or withdrawal, exposure to toxins, or any combination of factors. Older adults are especially susceptible to delirium.
- Most cases of delirium are cured, but some may be fatal.

What is dementia? What are the major symptoms of Alzheimer's disease? How is it diagnosed? What causes it? What intervention options are there? What are some other major forms of dementia? What do family members caring for patients with dementia experience?
- Dementia is a family of disorders. Most older adults do not have dementia, but rates increase significantly with age.
- Alzheimer's disease is a progressive, fatal disease diagnosed at autopsy through neurological changes that include neurofibrillary tangles and neuritic plaques.
- Major symptoms of Alzheimer's disease include gradual and eventually pervasive memory loss, emotional changes, and eventual loss of motor functions.
- Diagnosis of Alzheimer's disease consists of ruling out all other possible causes of the symptoms. This involves thorough physical, neurological, and neuropsychological exams.
- Current research suggests Alzheimer's disease may be genetic, perhaps with an autosomal dominant inheritance pattern, although other hypotheses have been proposed. Much research focuses on beta-amyloid and tau proteins.
- Although no cure for Alzheimer's disease is available, interventions to relieve symptoms are advisable and possible, including various drug and behavioral interventions. Dealing with declining functioning is especially difficult. Respite and adult day care are two options for care providers.
- Vascular dementia is caused by several small strokes. Changes in behavior depend on where in the brain the strokes occur.
- Characteristic symptoms of Parkinson's disease include tremor and problems with walking, along with decreases in the ability to smell. Treatment is done with drugs. Some people with Parkinson's disease develop dementia.
- Huntington's disease is a genetic disorder that usually begins in middle age with motor and behavioral problems.
- Alcoholic dementia (Wernicke-Korsakoff syndrome) is caused by a thiamine deficiency.
- AIDS dementia complex results from a by-product of HIV. Symptoms include a range of cognitive and motor impairments.

10.4 Other Mental Disorders and Concerns

What are the symptoms of anxiety disorders? How are they treated?
- Anxiety disorders include panic, phobia, and obsessive–compulsive problems. Symptoms include a variety of physical changes that interfere with normal functioning. Context is important in understanding symptoms. Both drugs and psychotherapy are used to treat anxiety disorders.

What are the characteristics of people with psychotic disorders?
- Psychotic disorders involve personality disintegration and loss of touch with reality. One major form is schizophrenia; hallucinations and delusions are the primary symptoms.
- Schizophrenia is a severe thought disorder with an onset usually before age 45, but it can begin in late life.

People with early-onset schizophrenia often improve over time as neurotransmitters become more balanced. Treatment usually consists of drugs; psychotherapy alone is not often effective.

What are the major issues involved with alcohol use disorder?
- With the exception of alcohol, the substances most likely to be abused vary with age; younger adults are more likely to abuse illicit substances, whereas older adults are more likely to abuse prescription and over-the-counter medications.
- Alcohol use disorder declines with age from its highest rates in young adulthood. Older adults take longer to withdraw, but similar therapies are effective in all age groups.

REVIEW QUESTIONS

10.1 Mental Health and the Adult Life Course
- How do definitions of mental health vary with age?
- What are the implications of adopting a multidimensional model for interpreting and diagnosing mental disorders?
- Why are ethnicity and gender important considerations in understanding mental health?

10.2 Developmental Issues in Assessment and Therapy
- What is multidimensional assessment? How is it done?
- What major factors affect the accuracy of clinical assessment?
- How do the developmental forces influence assessment?
- What are the main developmental issues clinicians must consider in selecting therapy?

10.3 The Big Three: Depression, Delirium, and Dementia
- How does the rate of depression vary with age, gender, and ethnicity?
- What symptoms are associated with depression? How do they vary with age?
- What biological causes of depression have been proposed? How are they related to therapy?
- How is loss associated with depression? What treatments for depression have been developed? How well do they work with older adults?
- What is delirium? What causes it? Why are older adults more susceptible?
- What is Alzheimer's disease? How is it diagnosed? What causes Alzheimer's disease? What interventions are available?
- What other types of dementia have been identified? What are their characteristics?

10.4 Other Mental Disorders and Concerns
- What symptoms are associated with anxiety disorders? How are anxiety disorders treated?
- What are psychoses? What are their major symptoms? What treatments are most effective for schizophrenia?
- What is alcohol use disorder? What specific aspects differ with age?

INTEGRATING CONCEPTS IN DEVELOPMENT

- Why is it so difficult to diagnose mental disorders in older adults? What concepts from Chapters 3 and 4 provide major reasons?
- Why do you think people with Alzheimer's disease might experience hallucinations and delusions?
- Why is there a connection between depression and dementia?
- What would studying people with Alzheimer's disease tell us about normal memory changes with age?

KEY TERMS

alcohol use disorder (AUD) A drinking pattern that results in significant and recurrent consequences that reflect loss of reliable control over alcohol use.

Alzheimer's disease An irreversible form of dementia characterized by progressive declines in cognitive and bodily functions, eventually resulting in death; it accounts for about 70% of all cases of dementia.

behavior therapy A type of psychotherapy that focuses on and attempts to alter current behavior. Underlying causes of the problem may not be addressed.

beta-amyloid A type of protein involved in the formation of neuritic plaques both in normal aging and in Alzheimer's disease.

beta-amyloid cascade hypothesis The process that beta-amyloid deposits create neuritic plaques, that in turn lead to neurofibrillary tangles, that cause neuronal death and, when this occurs severely enough, Alzheimer's disease.

cognitive behavior therapy A type of psychotherapy aimed at altering the way people think as a cure for some forms of psychopathology, especially depression. delirium A disorder characterized by a disturbance of consciousness and a change in cognition that develop over a short period of time.

dementia A family of diseases characterized by cognitive decline. Alzheimer's disease is the most common form.

dysphoria Feeling down or blue, marked by extreme sadness; the major symptom of depression.

mental status exam A short screening test that assesses mental competence, usually used as a brief indicator of dementia or other serious cognitive impairment.

spaced retrieval A behavioral, implicit-internal memory intervention used in early- and middle-stage dementia.

sundowning The phenomenon when people with Alzheimer's disease show an increase in symptoms later in the day.

vascular dementia A form of dementia caused by a series of small strokes.

11 Relationships

CHAPTER OUTLINE

11.1 Relationship Types and Issues
Friendships
REAL PEOPLE The Dornenburg Sisters
Love Relationships
HOW DO WE KNOW? Patterns and Universals of Romantic Attachment Around the World
Violence in Relationships

11.2 Lifestyles and Love Relationships
Singlehood
Cohabitation
LGBTQ Relationships
Marriage
Divorce
Remarriage
Widowhood
DISCOVERING DEVELOPMENT What Is It Like to Lose a Spouse/Partner?

11.3 Family Dynamics and the Life Course
The Parental Role
Midlife Issues: Adult Children and Caring for Aging Parents
CURRENT CONTROVERSIES Paid Family Leave
Grandparenthood

Social Policy Implications
Summary
Review Questions
Integrating Concepts in Development
Key Terms

Barack and Michelle Obama are, by nearly every measure, a successful couple. First elected president at age 47, Barack Obama completed two terms with the full support of his wife, Michelle, who herself is a successful professional. Their relationship provides them the grounding necessary to be there for each other. And they would be the first to say that neither of them could have achieved what they have without the help of many friends.

Barack's and Michelle's experiences reflect some of the key aspects of relationships we examine in this chapter. First, we consider friendships and love relationships and how they change across adulthood. Because love relationships usually involve a couple, we will explore how two people find and commit to each other. Because most long-term committed relationships involve marriage, we will consider the forces that lead people to marry and how marriages develop. We also consider singlehood, cohabitation, divorce, remarriage, and widowhood. Finally, we take up some of the important roles associated with personal relationships, including parenting, family roles, and grandparenting. ∎

President Barack and Michelle Obama

11.1 Relationship Types and Issues

LEARNING OBJECTIVES
- What role do friends play across adulthood?
- What characterizes love relationships? How do they vary across cultures?
- What are abusive relationships? What characterizes elder abuse, neglect, and exploitation?

Jamal and Kahlid have known each other all their lives. *They grew up together in New York, attended the same schools, and even married sisters. Their business careers took them in different directions, but they and their families always got together on major holidays. Now as older men, they feel a special bond; many of their other friends have died.*

Having other people in our lives we can count on is essential to our well-being. Just imagine how difficult life would be if you were totally alone, without even a Facebook "friend" to communicate with. In this section, we consider the different types of relationships we have with other people and learn how these relationships help—and sometimes hurt us.

Friendships

Jamal and Kahlid remind us some of the most important people in our lives are our friends. They are often the people to whom we are closest and are there when we need someone to lean on.

What is an adult friend? Someone who is there when you need to share? Someone who is not afraid to tell you the truth? Someone you have fun with? Friends, of course, are all of these and more. Researchers define *friendship* as a mutual relationship in which those involved influence one another's behaviors and beliefs, and define friendship quality as the satisfaction derived from the relationship (Blieszner, 2014; Blieszner & Roberto, 2012; Hall, 2016).

Friends are a source of support throughout adulthood (Arnett, 2013; Nehamas, 2016). Friendships are predominantly based on feelings and grounded in reciprocity and choice. Friendships are different from love relationships mainly because friendships are less emotionally intense and usually do not involve sex (Nehamas, 2016). Having good friendships boosts self-esteem, especially early in emerging adulthood (Miething et al., 2016), and happiness across adulthood (Adams & Taylor, 2015; Demir, Orthel-Clark et al., 2015; Fiori & Denckla, 2015). Friendships also help us become socialized into new roles throughout adulthood.

Friendship in Adulthood

From a developmental perspective, adult friendships can be viewed as having identifiable stages (Levinger, 1980, 1983): Acquaintanceship, Buildup, Continuation, Deterioration, and Ending. This ABCDE model describes the stages of friendships and how they change. Whether a friendship develops from Acquaintanceship to Buildup depends on where the individuals fall on several dimensions, such as the basis of the attraction, what each person knows about the other, how good the communication is between the partners, the perceived importance of the friendship, and so on. Although many friendships reach the Deterioration stage, whether a friendship ultimately ends depends heavily on the availability of alternative relationships. If potential friends appear, old friendships may end; if not, they may continue even though they are no longer considered important by either person.

Longitudinal research shows how friendships change across adulthood, some in ways that are predictable and others not. As you probably have experienced, life transitions (e.g., going away to college, getting married) usually result in fewer friends and less contact with the friends you keep (Blieszner, 2014; Blieszner & Roberto, 2012). People tend to have more friends and acquaintances during young adulthood than at any subsequent period (Demir, Orthel-Clark et al., 2015). Friendships are important throughout adulthood, in part because a person's life satisfaction is strongly related to the quantity and quality of contacts with friend. College students with strong friendship networks adjust better to stressful life events whether those networks are face-to-face (e.g., Brissette, Scheier, & Carver, 2002) or through online social networks (Antheunis, 2016; DeAndrea et al., 2012).

The importance of maintaining contacts with friends cuts across ethnic lines as well. People who have friendships that cross ethnic groups have more positive attitudes toward people with different backgrounds (Aberson, Shoemaker, & Tomolillo, 2004), including Facebook networks (Schwab & Greitemeyer, 2015). Thus, regardless of one's background, friendships play a major role in determining how much we enjoy life.

The quality and purpose of late-life friendships are particularly important (Adams & Taylor, 2015; Blieszner, 2014; Schulz & Morycz, 2013). Having friends provides a buffer against the losses of roles and status that accompany old age, such as retirement or the death of a loved one, and can increase people's happiness and self-esteem (Adams & Taylor, 2015; Schulz & Morycz, 2013). People who live alone especially benefit from friends in the neighborhood (Bromell & Cagney, 2013).

Why does friendship have such positive benefits for us? Although scientists do not know for certain, they are gaining insights through neuroscience research. Coan and colleagues (Beckes & Coan, 2013; Beckes, Coan, & Hasselmo, 2013; Coan, 2008; Coan & Sbarra, 2015) propose Social Baseline Theory, a perspective that integrates the study of social relationships with principles of attachment, behavioral ecology, cognitive neuroscience, and perception science. Social Baseline Theory suggests the human brain expects access to social relationships that mitigate risk and diminish the level of effort needed to meet a variety of goals by incorporating relational partners into neural representations of the self.

When people are faced with threatening situations, their brains process the situation differently when faced alone compared to with a close friend. Specifically, neuroimaging definitively shows the parts of the brain that respond to threat operate when facing threat alone but do not operate when facing the same threat with a close friend. A close friendship literally changes the way the brain functions, resulting in our perception of feeling safer and the trials we face are more manageable with friends than without them.

Patterns of friendship among older adults tend to mirror those in young adulthood (Adams & Taylor, 2015; Bleiszner, 2014). Older women have more numerous and intimate friendships than older men do. Men's friendships, like women's, evolve over time and become important sources of support in late life (Adams & Taylor, 2015). Three broad themes characterize both traditional (e.g., face-to-face) and new forms (e.g., online) of adult friendships (de Vries, 1996; Ridings & Gefen, 2004):

- The affective or emotional basis of friendship refers to self-disclosure and expressions of intimacy, appreciation, affection, and support, and all are based on trust, loyalty, and commitment.
- The shared or communal nature of friendship reflects how friends participate in or support activities of mutual interest.
- The sociability and compatibility dimension represents how our friends keep us entertained and are sources of amusement, fun, and recreation.

In the case of online friendships (e.g., through social media), trust develops on the basis of four sources: (1) reputation; (2) performance, or what users do online; (3) precommitment, through personal self-disclosure; and (4) situational factors, especially the premium placed on intimacy and the relationship (Håkansson & Witmer, 2015; Henderson & Gilding, 2004). Online social network friendships develop much like face-to-face ones in that the more time people spend online with friends the more likely they are to self-disclose (Chang & Hsiao, 2014). Online environments are more conducive to people who are lonely (Blachnio et al., 2016), which makes them potentially important for older adults (Cotten, Anderson, & McCullough, 2013; Quinn, 2016).

A special type of friendship exists with one's siblings, who are the friends people typically have the longest and that share the closest bonds; the importance of these relationships varies with age (Carr & Moorman, 2011; Merz & De Jong Gierveld, 2016; Moorman & Greenfield, 2010). The centrality of siblings in later life depends on several things, such as proximity, health, prior relationship, and degree of relatedness (full, step-, or half-siblings). No clear pattern of emotional closeness emerges when viewing sibling relationships on the basis of gender. The Real People feature examines an increasing common pattern of sibling relationship in later life—after years of separate lives, older siblings decide to live together.

Developmental Aspects of Friendships and Socioemotional Selectivity

Why are friends important to older adults? Some researchers believe one reason may be older adults' not wanting to become burdens to their families (Adams & Taylor, 2015; Blieszner & Roberto, 2012; Moorman & Greenfield, 2010). As a result, friends help each other remain independent by providing transportation, checking on neighbors, and doing errands.

Older adults tend to have fewer relationships with people in general and develop fewer new relationships than people do in midlife and particularly in young adulthood (Adams & Taylor, 2015; Carr & Moorman, 2011). Carstensen and colleagues (Carstensen, 2006; Charles & Carstensen, 2010; English & Carstensen, 2016; Reed & Carstensen, 2012) have shown the changes in social behavior seen in late life reflect a more complicated and important process. *They propose*

■ Real People
The Dornenburg Sisters

Noreen and Mary Dornenburg describe their lives simply—they grew up, grew apart, and grew close (Ansberry, 2016). Much of their lives were like most siblings, in that they had a very close relationship while growing up together and then did their own thing once they became adults. An experiment of living together when they were in their 30s failed after six months. Their six-year age difference meant that they had not lived together since Noreen was 18 and Mary was 12, after which Noreen went to college.

But things changed as they grew older. After their father died and their mother became legally blind, the sisters decided to give it another try. They found a three-story house, with Noreen (by then a faculty member who taught philosophy and business ethics) taking the third floor, Mary (who ran a picture framing business) the second, and their mother the first.

At first, Mary was her mother's primary caregiver. With time, though, they figured out that Noreen was actually better at it, as she was calmer in a crisis. And they became much closer as adult friends.

After their mother died in 2013 at age 97, the sisters, by then both well into their 60s, decided to keep the house and live together. They have agreed on the division of labor around the house, as well as other chores. They both describe how they adjusted to each other's quirks (e.g., Mary now closes open drawers, and Noreen kept some of her art off the wall). They describe it as "like being married" in that they pick their fights carefully and do their best to get along. It works well for them. And, increasingly, it's working for many older siblings.

a life-span theory of **socioemotional selectivity**, *that argues social contact is motivated by a variety of goals, including information seeking, self-concept, and emotional regulation.*

Each of these goals is differentially salient at different points of the adult life span and results in different social behaviors. When information seeking is the goal, such as when a person is exploring the world trying to figure out how he or she fits, what others are like, and so forth, meeting many new people is an essential part of the process. However, when emotional regulation is the goal, people become highly selective in their choice of social partners and nearly always prefer people who are familiar to them.

Carstensen and colleagues believe information seeking is the predominant goal for young adults, emotional regulation is the major goal for older people, and both goals are in balance in midlife. Their research supports this view; people become increasingly selective in whom they choose to have contact with. Additionally, evidence suggests that there is an increase with age in emotional competency (e.g., Doerwald et al., 2016; Magai, 2008). Older adults appear to orient more toward emotional aspects of life and personal relationships as they grow older, and emotional expression and experience become more complex and nuanced. Carstensen's theory provides a complete explanation of why older adults tend not to replace, to any great extent, the relationships they lose: Older adults are more selective and have fewer opportunities to make new friends, especially in view of the emotional bonds involved in friendships.

Men's, Women's, and Cross-Sex Friendships

Men's and women's friendships tend to differ in adulthood, reflecting continuity in the learned behaviors from childhood (Levine, 2009). Four characteristics of same-sex friends do not appear to differ between men and women and are similar across cultures and age groups: geographic proximity, similarity of interests and values, inclusion, and symmetrical reciprocity (Hall, 2016). Three characteristics that distinguish female same-sex friendships from males' same-sex friendships are communion and self-disclosure, greater effort and expectations from friends in general, and a greater risk of corumination (extensively discussing and re-visiting problems, and focusing on negative feelings) (Hall, 2016). In contrast, men base friendships on shared activities or interests.

What about friendships between men and women? These friendships are mainly a product of the 20th century (Weger, 2016) and have a beneficial effect, especially for men (Piquet, 2007). Cross-sex friendships help men have lower levels of dating anxiety and higher capacity for intimacy. These patterns hold across ethnic groups, too. Cross-sex friendships can also prove troublesome because of misperceptions. Some research shows men overestimate and women underestimate their friends' sexual interest in them (Koenig, Kirkpatrick, & Ketelaar, 2007). Maintaining cross-sex friendships once individuals enter into exclusive dating relationships, marriage, or committed relationships is difficult, and often results in one partner feeling jealous (Williams, 2005).

Love Relationships

Love is one of those things we feel but cannot fully describe. (Test yourself: Can you explain fully what you mean when you look at someone special and say, "I love you"?) One way researchers try to understand love is to think about what components are essential. In an interesting series of studies, Sternberg (2006a) found love has three basic components: (1) *passion*, an intense physiological desire for someone; (2) *intimacy*, the feeling that you can share all your thoughts and actions with another; and (3) *commitment*, the willingness to stay with a person through good and bad times. Ideally, a true love relationship has all three components; when couples have equivalent amounts and types of love, they tend to be happier, even as the balance among these components shifts over time.

Love Through Adulthood

The different combinations of love help us understand how relationships develop (Sternberg, 2006a). Research shows the development of romantic relationships in emerging adulthood is a complex process influenced by relationships in childhood and adolescence (Collins & van Dulmen, 2006; Oudekerk et al., 2015). Early in a romantic relationship, passion is usually high whereas intimacy and commitment tend to be low. This is infatuation: an intense, physically based relationship when the two people have a high risk of misunderstanding and jealousy. Indeed, it is sometimes difficult to establish the boundaries between casual sex and hook-ups and dating in young adulthood (Giordano et al., 2012).

Infatuation is short-lived. As passion fades, either a relationship acquires emotional intimacy or it is likely to end. Trust, honesty, openness, and acceptance must be a part of any strong relationship; when they are present, romantic love develops.

This pattern is a good thing. Research shows people who select a partner for a more permanent relationship (e.g., marriage) during the height of infatuation are more likely to divorce (Hansen, 2006). If the couple spends more time and works at their relationship, they may become committed to each other.

Campbell and Kaufman (2015) surveyed 1,529 people across the United States to better understand the connections among love, personality, and creativity. They found that as the length of the relationship increases, intimacy and passion decrease but intimacy and commitment increase. This and related research indicate that good relationships tend to deepen as time goes on, even if intense physical passion decreases.

Falling in Love

In his book *The Prophet*, Kahlil Gibran (1923) points out love is two-sided: Just as it can give you great ecstasy, so can it cause you great pain. Yet most of us are willing to take the risk. As you may have experienced, taking the risk is fun (at times) and difficult (at other times).

The best explanation of the process is the theory of **assortative mating**, *that states people find partners based on their similarity to each other.* Assortative mating occurs along many dimensions, including education, religious beliefs, physical traits, age, socioeconomic status, intelligence, and political ideology, among others (Horwitz et al., 2016). Such nonrandom mating occurs most often in Western societies that allow people to have more control over their own dating and pairing behaviors. Common activities are one basis for identifying potential mates, except, that is, in speed dating situations. In that case, it comes down to physical attractiveness (Luo & Zhang, 2009).

People meet people in all sorts of places, both face-to-face and virtually. Does how people meet influence the likelihood they will "click" on particular dimensions and form a couple? Kalmijn and Flap (2001) found that it does. Using data from more than 1,500 couples, they found meeting at school, for example, was most likely to result in *homogamy*—the degree to which people are similar. Not surprisingly, the pool of available people to meet is strongly shaped by the opportunities available, that in turn constrain the type of people one is likely to meet.

Speed dating provides a way to meet several people in a short period of time. Speed dating is practiced most by young adults (Fein & Schneider, 2013; Whitty & Buchanan, 2009). The rules governing partner selection during a speed-dating session seem quite similar to traditional dating: physically attractive people, outgoing and self-assured people, and moderately self-focused people are selected more often and their dates are rated as smoother (Herrenbrueck et al., 2016).

The popularity of online dating means an increasing number of people meet this way (Fein & Schneider, 2013; Lomanowska & Guitton, 2016; Whitty & Buchanan, 2009). Surveys indicate nearly 1 in every 5 couples in the United States meet online (compared with 1 in 10 in Australia, and 1 in 20 in Spain and the United Kingdom; Dutton et al., 2009). Emerging research indicates virtual dating sites offer both problems and possibilities, especially in terms of the accuracy of personal descriptions. As in the offline world, physical attractiveness strongly influences initial selections online (Sritharan et al., 2010), especially on sites such as Tinder and Grindr (Sumter, Vandenbosch, & Ligtenberg, 2017). Over a third of couples who marry first met online, often via online dating sites (M. D. Johnson, 2016).

One increasing trend among emerging adults is the hookup culture of casual sex, often without even knowing the name of one's sexual partner (Garcia et al., 2013; Kratzer & Stevens Aubrey, 2016). Research indicates both men and women are interested in having hookup sex, but also prefer a more romantic relationship over the long run. However, the perception there are no strings attached to hookup sex appear wrong, as nearly three-fourths of both men and women eventually expressed some level of regret at having hookup sex.

How does couple-forming behavior compare cross-culturally? As described in the How Do We Know? feature, Schmitt and his team of colleagues (2004) studied 62 cultural regions. They showed secure romantic attachment was the norm in nearly 80% of cultures and "preoccupied" romantic attachment was particularly common in East Asian cultures. In general, multicultural studies show there are global patterns in mate selection and romantic relationships. The romantic attachment profiles of individual nations were correlated with sociocultural indicators in ways that supported evolutionary theories of romantic attachment and basic human-mating strategies.

How Do We Know?
Patterns and Universals of Romantic Attachment Around the World

Who were the investigators and what was the aim of the study? One's attachment style may have a major influence on how one forms romantic relationships. In order to test this hypothesis, David Schmitt (2004) assembled a large international team of researchers.

How did the investigators measure the topic of interest? Great care was taken to ensure equivalent translation of the survey across the 62 cultural regions included. The survey was a two-dimension four-category measure of adult romantic attachment (the Relationship Questionnaire) that measured models of self and others relative to each other: secure romantic attachment (high scores indicate positive models of self and others), dismissing romantic attachment (high scores indicate a positive model of self and a negative model of others), preoccupied romantic attachment (high scores indicate a negative model of self and a positive model of others), and fearful romantic attachment (high scores indicate negative models of self and others). An overall score of model of self is computed by adding together the secure and dismissing scores and subtracting the combination of preoccupied and fearful scores. The overall model of others score is computed by adding together the secure and preoccupied scores and subtracting the combination of dismissing and fearful scores.

Additionally, there were measures of self-esteem, personality traits, and sociocultural correlates of romantic attachment (e.g., fertility rate, national profiles of individualism versus collectivism).

Who were the participants in the study? A total of 17,804 people (7,432 men and 10,372 women) from 62 cultural regions around the world took part in the study. Such large and diverse samples are unusual in developmental research.

What was the design of the study? Data for this cross-sectional, nonexperimental study were gathered by research teams in each country. The principal researchers asked the research collaborators to administer a nine-page survey to the participants that took 20 minutes to complete.

Were there ethical concerns with the study? Because the study involved volunteers, there were no ethical concerns. However, ensuring all participants' rights were protected was a challenge because of the number of countries and cultures involved.

What were the results? The researchers first demonstrated the model of self and others measures were valid across cultural regions, that provided general support for the independence of measures (i.e., they measure different things). Specific analyses showed 79% of the cultural groups studied demonstrated secure romantic attachments, but North American cultures tended to be dismissive and East Asian cultures tended to be high on preoccupied romantic attachment. These patterns are shown in Figure 11.1. Note all the cultural regions except East Asia showed the pattern of model of self scores higher than model of others scores.

What did the investigators conclude? Overall, Schmitt and colleagues concluded although the same attachment pattern holds across most cultures, no one pattern holds across all of them. East Asian cultures in particular tend to fit a pattern in which people report others do not get as emotionally close as the respondent would like, and respondents find it difficult to trust others or to depend on them.

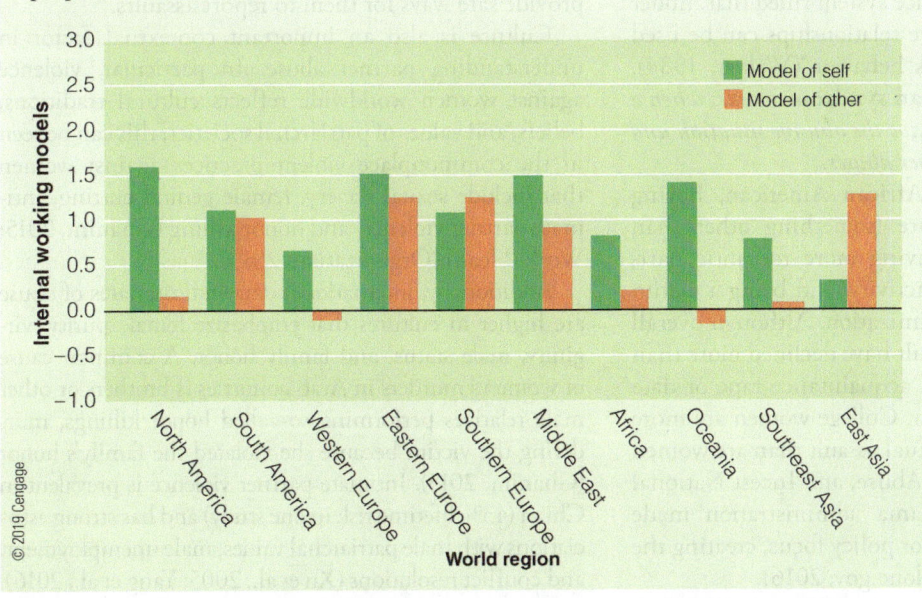

FIGURE 11.1 In research across 10 global regions, note that only in East Asian cultures were the "model of others" scores higher than the "model of self" scores.
Source: Data from Schmitt et al. (2004).

Culture is a powerful force in shaping mate selection choices. Specifically, across 48 different cultures globally, people from cultures that have good health care, education, and resources, and permit young adults to choose their own mates tend to develop more secure romantic attachments than do people from cultures without these characteristics (Schmitt et al., 2004).

Love styles within European cultures also predict relationship satisfaction (Rohmann, Führer, & Bierhoff, 2016). Cultural norms are sometimes highly resistant to change. Loyalty of the individual to the family is an important value in India, so despite many changes in mate selection, about 95% of marriages in India are carefully arranged to ensure an appropriate mate is selected (Dommaraju, 2010).

Similarly, Islamic societies use matchmaking as a way to preserve family consistency and continuity and ensure couples follow the prohibition on premarital relationships between men and women (Adler, 2001). Matchmaking in these societies occurs both through family connections and personal advertisements in newspapers. To keep up with the Internet age, Muslim matchmaking has gone online, too (Lo & Aziz, 2009).

Violence in Relationships

Up to this point, we have been considering relationships that are healthy and positive. Sadly, this is not always the case. *Sometimes relationships become violent; one person becomes aggressive toward the partner, creating an* **abusive relationship**. Such relationships have received increasing attention since the early 1980s, when the U.S. criminal justice system ruled that, under some circumstances, abusive relationships can be used as an explanation for one's behavior (Walker, 1984). *For example,* **battered woman syndrome** *occurs when a woman believes she cannot leave the abusive situation and may even go so far as to kill her abuser.*

Being female, Latina, African American, having an atypical family structure (something other than two biological parents), having more romantic partners, early onset of sexual activity, and being a victim of child abuse predicts victimization. Although overall national rates of sexual assault have declined more than 60% since the early 1990s, acquaintance rape or date rape is still a major problem. College women are more likely to be the victim of sexual assault than are women in other age groups (Rape, Abuse, and Incest National Network, 2016). The Obama administration made campus sexual assault a major policy focus, creating the *Not Alone* campaign (NotAlone.gov, 2016).

What range of aggressive behaviors occurs in abusive relationships? What causes such abuse? Based on considerable research of abusive partners, O'Leary (1993) proposed a continuum of aggressive behaviors toward a partner, and progresses as follows: verbally aggressive behaviors, physically aggressive behaviors, severe physically aggressive behaviors, and murder (see Table 11.1). The causes of the abuse also vary with the type of abusive behavior being expressed.

Two points about the continuum should be noted. First, there may be fundamental differences in the types of aggression independent of level of severity. Overall, each year about 5 million women and 3 million men experience partner-related physical assaults and rape in the United States (Rape, Abuse, and Incest National Network, 2016); worldwide, between 10 and 69% of women report being physically assaulted or raped, making it one of the priority areas for the World Health Organization (World Health Organization, 2013).

The second point, depicted in the table, is the suspected underlying causes of aggressive behaviors differ as the type of aggressive behaviors change (O'Leary, 1993; Sugimoto-Matsuda & Guerrero, 2016). Although anger and hostility in the perpetrator are associated with various forms of physical abuse, especially in young adulthood, the exact nature of this relationship remains elusive (Giordano et al., 2016).

Heterosexual men and members of the LGBTQ community are also the victims of violence from intimate partners, though at a reporting rate lower that of women (Rape, Abuse and Incest National Network, 2016). All victims need to be supported and provided avenues that provide safe ways for them to report assaults.

Culture is also an important contextual factor in understanding partner abuse. In particular, violence against women worldwide reflects cultural traditions, beliefs, and values of patriarchal societies; this can be seen in the commonplace violent practices against women that include sexual slavery, female genital cutting, intimate partner violence, and honor killing (Ghanim, 2015; World Health Organization, 2013).

Additionally, international data indicate rates of abuse are higher in cultures that emphasize female purity, virginity, male status, and family honor. A common cause of women's murders in Arab countries is brothers or other male relatives performing so-called honor killings, murdering the victim because she violated the family's honor (Ghanim, 2015). Intimate partner violence is prevalent in China (43% lifetime risk in one study) and has strong associations with male patriarchal values, male unemployment, and conflict resolutions (Xu et al., 2005; Yang et al., 2016).

TABLE 11.1 Continuum of Progressive Behaviors in Abusive Relationships

Verbal aggression →	Physical aggression →	Severe aggression →	Murder
Insults	Pushing	Beating	
Yelling	Slapping	Punching	
Name-calling	Shoving	Hitting with object	

Causes

Need to control* ──▶
Misuse of power* ───▶
Jealousy* ──▶
Marital discord ──▶

　　　　　　　　　　Accept violence as a means of control ─────────▶
　　　　　　　　　　Modeling of physical aggression ───────────────▶
　　　　　　　　　　Abused as a child ───────────────────────────▶
　　　　　　　　　　Aggressive personality styles ──────────────────▶
　　　　　　　　　　Alcohol abuse ───────────────────────────────▶

　　　　　　　　　　　　　　　　　　　　Personality disorders ────────▶
　　　　　　　　　　　　　　　　　　　　Emotional lability ───────────▶
　　　　　　　　　　　　　　　　　　　　Poor self-esteem ────────────▶

Contributing factors

Job stresses
unemployment

Note: Need to control and other variables on the left are associated with all forms of aggression; acceptance of violence and other variables in the middle are associated with physical aggression, severe aggression, and murder. Personality disorders and the variables on the right are associated with severe aggression and murder.

* More relevant for males than for females.

Source: O'Leary, K.D. (1993). Through a psychological lens: Personality traits, personality disorders, and levels of violence. In R. J. Gelles & D. R. Loseke (Eds.), *Current Controversies on Family Violence* (pp. 7–30). Copyright © 1993 by Sage Publications. Reprinted by permission of the publisher.

Alarmed by the seriousness of abuse, many communities established shelters for people who experience abuse. However, the legal system in many localities is still not set up to deal with domestic violence; for example, women in some locations cannot sue their husbands for assault, and restraining orders all too often offer little real protection from additional violence. Much remains to be done to protect people from the fear and the reality of abuse.

Elder Abuse, Neglect, and Exploitation

Although elder abuse, neglect, and exploitation are difficult to define precisely, several categories are commonly used (National Center for State Courts, 2016):

- *Physical abuse*: the use of physical force that may result in bodily injury, physical pain, or impairment
- *Sexual abuse*: nonconsensual sexual contact of any kind
- *Emotional or psychological abuse*: infliction of anguish, pain, or distress
- *Financial or material exploitation*: the illegal or improper use of an older adult's funds, property, or assets
- *Abandonment*: the desertion of an older adult by an individual who had physical custody or otherwise assumed responsibility for providing care for the older adult
- *Neglect*: refusal or failure to fulfill any part of a person's obligation or duties to an older adult

- *Self-neglect*: the behaviors of an older person that threaten his or her own health or safety, excluding those conscious and voluntary decisions by a mentally competent and healthy adult

Researchers estimate perhaps 1 in 10 older adults is at risk for some type of abuse, neglect, or exploitation (Roberto, 2016). A continuing problem in this field is the lack of clear definitions across states, embarrassment on the part of victims that dramatically lowers reporting, and a general lack of services. Unfortunately, only a small proportion of these cases are actually reported to authorities; of the ones that are, neglect is the most common type. Financial exploitation, particularly through electronic means, costs older adults billions of dollars annually (DeLiema, Yon, & Wilber, 2016). Researchers and policy makers argue that prevention of financial exploitation can be greatly assisted by banks and other financial institutions, who can monitor account activity and question unusual withdrawals (Lichtenberg, 2016).

If you suspect an older adult is a victim of elder abuse, neglect, or exploitation, the best thing to do is to contact your local adult protective services office and report it.

Adult Development in Action

As a couples therapist, what do you need to know about global friendship and mating patterns?

11.2 Lifestyles and Love Relationships

LEARNING OBJECTIVES
- What are the challenges and advantages of being single?
- Why do people cohabit?
- What are LGBTQ relationships like?
- What is marriage like across adulthood?
- Why do people divorce?
- Why do people remarry?
- What are the experiences of widows and widowers?

Bobbie and Jack were high school sweethearts who married a few years after World War II. *Despite many trials in their relationship, they have remained firmly committed to each other for more than 60 years. Not only are they still in love, but they are best friends. In looking back, they note that once their children moved away they grew closer again. Bobbie and Jack wonder whether this is typical.*

Bobbie and Jack show us forging relationships is only part of the picture in understanding how adults live their lives with other people. For most, one relationship becomes special and results in commitment, typically through marriage. Putting relationships in context is the goal of this section as we explore the major lifestyles of adults. First, we consider people who never get married. Next, we look at those who cohabit and those who are in same-sex relationships. We also consider couples who get married and those who divorce and remarry. Finally, we discuss people who are widowed.

Singlehood

Adult men and women are single—defined as not living with an intimate partner—at multiple points in their lives: before marriage or other long-term commitment, following divorce, and in widowhood are common examples. In this section, we focus most on young adult singles; elsewhere we return to singlehood in the context of divorce or the death of a spouse/partner.

What's it like to be a single young adult in the United States? It's tougher than you might think. Several researchers (e.g., Budgeon, 2016; Casper et al., 2016; DePaulo, 2006) point out numerous stereotypes and biases against single people, especially women. For example, married people are perceived as kinder and more giving, and public policy also tends to favor married individuals. Additionally, research indicates that rental agents and certain housing programs prefer married couples over singles (Goodsell, 2013; Morris, Sinclair, & DePaulo, 2007).

Many women and men remain single as young adults to focus on establishing their careers rather than marriage or relationships that most do later. Others report they simply did not meet "the right person" or prefer singlehood, a factor especially important among strongly religious groups (Engelberg, 2016; Ibrahim & Hassan, 2009). However, the pressure to marry is especially strong for women (Budgeon, 2016).

Men remain single a bit longer in young adulthood because they marry about two years later on average than women (Census Bureau, 2016). Fewer men than women remain unmarried throughout adulthood, though, mainly because men find partners more easily as they select from a larger age range of unmarried women.

Ethnic differences in singlehood reflect differences in age at marriage as well as social factors. Nearly twice as many African Americans are single during young adulthood as European Americans, and more are choosing to remain so (Census Bureau, 2010. Singlehood is also increasing among Latinos, in part because the average age of Latinos in the United States is lower than other ethnic groups (e.g., 28 for Latinos versus 42 for white non-Hispanic) and in part because of poor economic opportunities for many Latinos (Pew Research Center, 2015).

The millennial generation is also changing the assumptions about singlehood. The Urban Institute projects that the percentage of millennials who will remain single until at least age 40 may be as high as 30%, higher than any previous generation (Martin, Astone, & Peters, 2014). However, also likely are millennials who decide to live with a partner and forego the legality of marriage.

Globally, the meanings and implications of remaining single are often tied to strongly held cultural and religious beliefs. Muslim women who remain single in Malaysia speak in terms of *jodoh* (the soul mate one finds through fate at a time appointed by God) as a reason; they believe God simply has not decided to have them meet their mate at this time (Ibrahim & Hassan, 2009). But because the role of Malaysian women is to marry, they also understand their marginalized position in society through their singlehood. In Southeast Asia, the number of single adults has increased steadily as education levels rose over the past several decades (Hull, 2009). However, family systems in these cultures have not yet adapted to these changing lifestyle patterns (Jones, 2010).

An important distinction is between adults who are temporarily single (i.e., those who are single only until they find a suitable marriage partner) and those who choose to remain single. For most singles, the decision to never marry is a gradual one. This transition is represented by a change in self-attributed status that occurs over time and is associated with a cultural timetable for marriage. It marks the experience of "becoming single" that occurs when an individual identifies more with singlehood than with marriage (Davies, 2003). Choosing to remain single can also reflect an economic-based decision, especially for millennials, who are less likely to think they are better off than their parents as their own parents and grandparents thought at the same age (Kalish, 2016).

Cohabitation

Being unmarried does not necessarily mean living alone. *People in committed, intimate, sexual relationships but who are not married may decide living together, or* **cohabitation**, *provides a way to share daily life.* Cohabitation is becoming an increasingly popular lifestyle choice in the United States as well as in Canada, Europe, Australia, and elsewhere, especially among millennials and older adults (Luxenberg, 2014; Martin et al., 2014).

In the United States, evidence clearly indicates that cohabitation is common and has increased over the past several decades (Copen et al., 2013). For example, roughly half of all women cohabit with, rather than marry, a partner as a first committed relationship. Such cohabitation patterns range from about 70% for women with less than a high school diploma to about half of women with a baccalaureate degree or higher, and are longest for Latina women (33 months on average) and shortest for European American women (19 months on average). Cohabitations rates for adults 50 years of age and older have more than doubled since 2000.

The global picture differs by culture (Popenoe, 2009; Therborn, 2010). In most European, South American, and Caribbean countries, cohabitation is a common alternative to marriage for young adults. Cohabitation is extremely common in the Netherlands, Norway, and Sweden, where this lifestyle is part of the culture; 99% of married couples in Sweden lived together before they married and nearly one in four couples are not legally married. Decisions to marry in these countries are typically made to legalize the relationship after children are born—in contrast to Americans, who marry to confirm their love and commitment to each other.

Interestingly, having cohabitated does not seem to make marriages any better; in fact, under certain circumstances it may do more harm than good, resulting in lower quality marriages (M. D. Johnson, 2016). These findings reflect two underlying issues that can cause problems (M. D. Johnson, 2016): couples who have children while cohabiting, especially for European American women (as compared with African American and Latina women; Tach & Halpern-Meekin, 2009), and couples who are using cohabitation to test their relationship and keep separate finances (Addo, 2017).

Essentially, the happiest cohabiting couples are those that look very much like happily married couples: they share financial responsibilities and child care. Longitudinal studies find few differences in couples' behavior after living together for many years regardless of whether they married without cohabiting, cohabited then married, or simply cohabited (Stafford, Kline, & Rankin, 2004). Additionally, many countries extend the same rights and benefits to cohabiting couples as they do to married couples, and have done so for many years. Argentina provides pension rights to cohabiting partners, Canada extends insurance benefits, and

Australia has laws governing the disposition of property when cohabiting couples sever their relationship (Neft & Levine, 1997).

LGBTQ Relationships

The current generation of older adults in the LGBTQ community have largely experienced oppression and discrimination their entire adult lives (Robinson-Wood & Weber, 2016). This is especially true for those who also have low income and people of color. However, social attitudes toward the LGBTQ community in general and to older adults in particular have changed and continue to change rapidly, especially in view of the legal support for same-sex marriage (King, 2016).

For the most part, the relationships of gay and lesbian couples have many similarities to those of heterosexual couples (Kurdek, 2004). Most gay and lesbian couples are in dual-earner relationships, much like the majority of married heterosexual couples, and are likely to share household chores. However, gay and lesbian couples differ from heterosexual couples in the degree to which both partners are similar on demographic characteristics such as race, age, and education; gay and lesbian couples tend to be more dissimilar, except regarding education (Ciscato, Galichon, & Gousse, 2015).

King (2016) argues that the experiences of older lesbian, gay, and bisexual adults cannot be put into neat categories, even generational ones. Rather, King emphasizes that the LGB community is at least as diverse as the heterosexual community, and needs to be understood as such.

With the advent of legalized same-sex marriage, numerous issues that heterosexual married couples have long taken for granted are being confronted in the LGBTQ community, including end-of-life issues and legal matters regarding caregiving (Godfrey, 2016; Orel & Coon, 2016). Changes to state laws will continue as reforms and revisions continue to keep pace with change.

When compared to LGB individuals living with partners, LGB individuals living alone or with others (but not in a relationship with them) reported higher degrees of loneliness (Kim & Fredriksen-Goldsen, 2016). This finding parallels that in heterosexual individuals in similar living arrangements, and highlights the fact that there are many similarities in personal outcomes across various gender identity groups.

Little research has been conducted examining the development of transgender and gender nonconforming (TGNC) individuals across adulthood (Witten, 2016). One detailed examination of experiences of TGNC adults over age 50 found that many barriers to accessing key services such as health care and social services exist, largely due to anti-TGNC prejudice, discrimination, and lack of appropriate and adequate training of professionals (Porter et al., 2016). Additionally, research indicates that transgender older adults experience social isolation more than most other groups (Harley, Gassaway, & Dunkley, 2016).

As we explore marriage in the next section, keep in mind that although most of the research has been conducted with heterosexual couples, key findings regarding what matters most in relationship satisfaction, decisions about parenting, and caring for a spouse/partner hold for LGBTQ individuals who are married or in long-term committed relationships.

Marriage

Most adults want their love relationships to result in marriage. However, U.S. residents are in less of a hurry to achieve this goal; the median age at first marriage for adults in the United States has been rising for several decades. As shown in Figure 11.2, between 1970 and 2015, the median age for first marriage rose almost 7 years for both men and women (Census Bureau, 2016).

Research indicates committed gay and lesbian couples have most of the same characteristics as committed heterosexual couples.

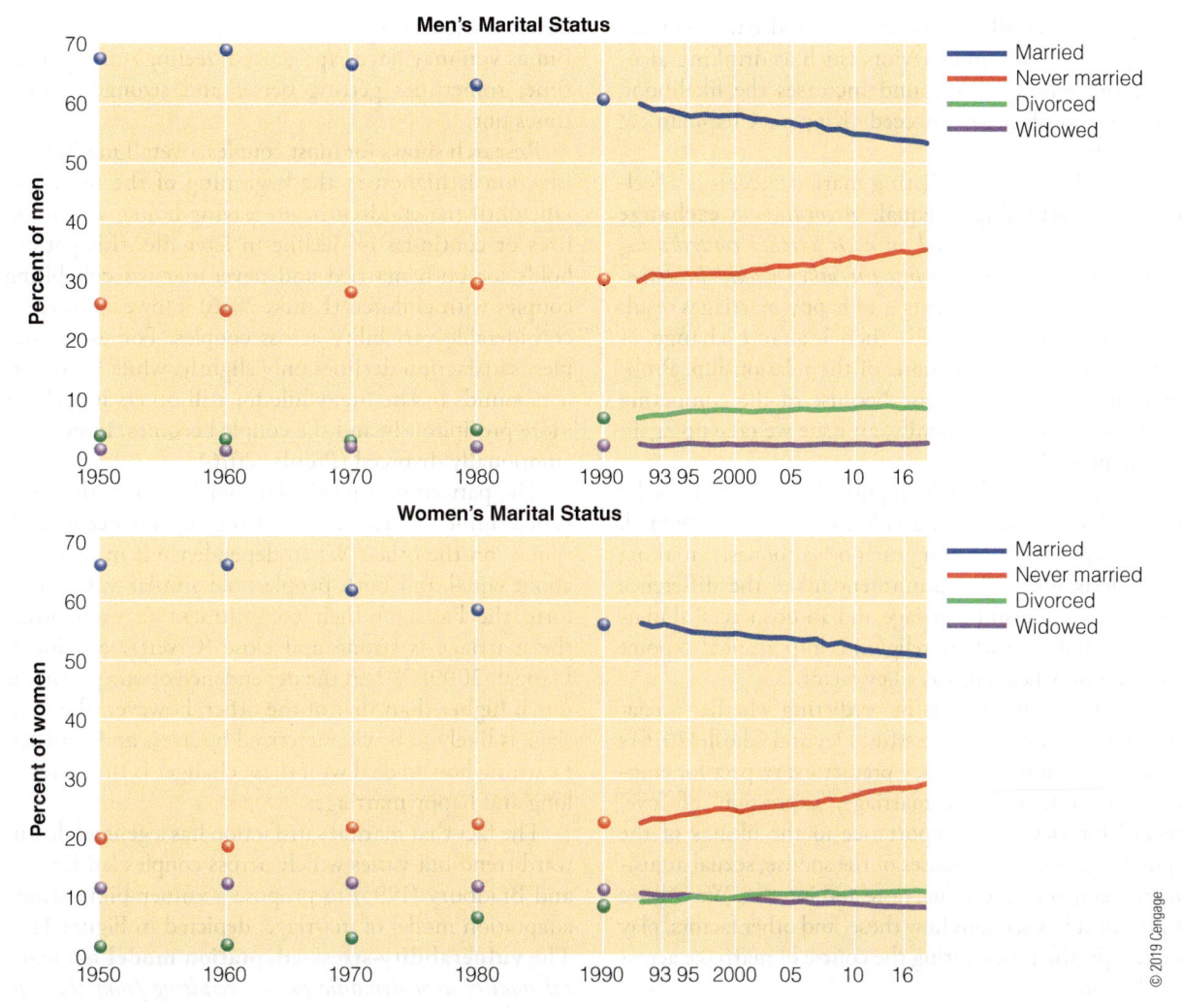

FIGURE 11.2 Note the median age at first marriage has been increasing for many years during the 20th and early 21st centuries.

Source: U.S Census Bureau, Current Population Survey, Annual Social and Economic Supplements, 1947–2012. Data for years prior to 1947 are from decennial censuses. Retrieved from www.census.gov/hhes/families/data/marital.html.

What Is a Successful Marriage and What Predicts It?

You undoubtedly know couples who appear to have a successful marriage. But what does that mean, really? Minnotte (2010) differentiates **marital success**, *an umbrella term referring to any marital outcome (such as divorce rate)*, **marital quality**, *a subjective evaluation of the couple's relationship on a number of different dimensions*, **marital adjustment**, *the degree spouses accommodate each other over a certain period of time*, and **marital satisfaction**, *a global assessment of one's marriage*. Each of these provides a unique insight into the workings of a marriage.

Marriages, like other relationships, differ from one another, but some important predictors of future success can be identified. One key factor is age. In general, the younger the partners are, the lower the odds the marriage will last—especially when the people are in their teens or early 20s (Census Bureau, 2013). Other reasons that increase or decrease the likelihood a marriage will last include financial security and pregnancy at the time of the marriage.

A second important predictor of successful marriage is **homogamy**, *or the similarity of values and interests a couple shares*. As we saw in relation to choosing a mate, the extent the partners share similar age, values, goals, attitudes (especially the desire for children), socioeconomic status, certain behaviors (such as drinking alcohol), and ethnic background increases the likelihood their relationship will succeed (Kippen, Chapman, & Yu, 2009).

A third factor in predicting marital success is a feeling the relationship is equal. *According to* **exchange theory**, *marriage is based on each partner contributing something to the relationship the other would be hard-pressed to provide.* Satisfying and happy marriages result when both partners perceive there is a fair exchange, or equity, in all the dimensions of the relationship. Problems achieving equity arise because of the competing demands of work and family, an issue we take up again in Chapter 12.

Cross-cultural research supports these factors. Couples in the United States and Iran (Asoodeh et al., 2010; Hall, 2006) say trust, consulting each other, honesty, making joint decisions, and commitment make the difference between a successful marriage and an unsuccessful marriage. Couples for whom religion is important also point to commonly held faith as a key factor.

So what really matters in predicting whether a relationship is likely to be successful? Dey and Ghosh (2016)'s findings point to several key predictors: respect for emotion, attitude towards marriage, expression of love, regard for views and importance to the likings of the spouse, ignoring weaknesses of the spouse, sexual adjustment, temperament, value, taste and interest. We will see in the next few sections how these, and other factors, play out at specific times during the course of marriage across adulthood.

Do Married Couples Stay Happy?

Few sights are happier than a couple on their wedding day. The beliefs people bring into a marriage influence how satisfied they will be as the marriage develops. But as you may have experienced, feelings change over time, sometimes getting better and stronger, sometimes not.

Research shows for most couples, overall marital satisfaction is highest at the beginning of the marriage, falls until the children begin leaving home, and stabilizes or continues to decline in later life; this pattern holds for both married and never-married cohabiting couples with children (Kulik, 2016). However, there is considerable variability across couples. For some couples, satisfaction declines only slightly, while for others it rebounds in late life, while for still others it declines more precipitously and the couple becomes, in essence, emotionally divorced (Proulx, 2016).

The pattern of a particular marriage over the years is determined by the nature of the dependence of each spouse on the other. When dependence is mutual and about equal and both people hold similar values that form the basis for their commitment to each other, the marriage is strong and close (Givertz, Segrin, & Hanzal, 2009). When the dependence of one partner is much higher than that of the other, however, the marriage is likely to be characterized by stress and conflict. Learning how to deal with these changes is the secret to long and happy marriages.

The fact that marital satisfaction has a general downward trend but varies widely across couples led Karney and Bradbury (1995) to propose a vulnerability-stress-adaptation model of marriage, depicted in Figure 11.3. The **vulnerability-stress-adaptation model** *sees marital quality as a dynamic process resulting from the couple's ability to handle stressful events in the context of their particular vulnerabilities and resources.* As a couple's ability to adapt to stressful situations gets better over time, the quality of the marriage will probably improve.

FIGURE 11.3 The vulnerability-stress-adaptation model shows how adapting to vulnerabilities and stress can result in either adaptation or dissolution of the marriage.

Source: From Karney, B. R. *Keeping marriages healthy, and why it's so difficult.* Retrieved from www.apa.org/science/about/psa/2010/02/sci-brief.aspx.

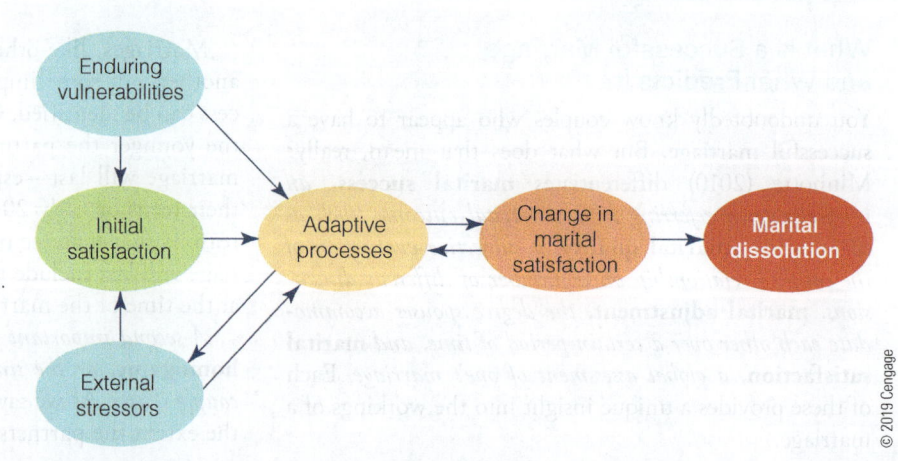

Enduring vulnerabilities → Adaptive processes
Initial satisfaction → Adaptive processes
External stressors → Adaptive processes
Adaptive processes → Change in marital satisfaction → Marital dissolution

How well couples adapt to various stresses on the relationship determines whether the marriage continues or they get divorced. Let's see how this works over time.

Setting the Stage: The Early Years of Marriage

Marriages are most intense in their early days. Discussing financial matters honestly is key since many newly married couples experience their first serious marital stresses around money issues (Parkman, 2007). How tough issues early in the marriage are handled sets the stage for the years ahead.

Early in a marriage, couples tend to have global adoration for their spouse regarding the spouse's qualities (Karney & Crown, 2007; Seychell, 2016). For wives, but not for husbands, more accurate specific perceptions of what their spouses are really like were associated with more supportive behaviors, feelings of control in the marriage, and a decreased risk of divorce. Couples who are happiest in the early stage of their marriage focus on the good aspects, not the annoyances; nit-picking and nagging do not bode well for long-term wedded bliss (Seychell, 2016).

As time goes on and stresses increase, marital satisfaction declines (Kulik, 2016). For many couples, the primary reason for this drop is having children. It's not just a matter of having a child. The temperament of the child matters, with fussier babies creating more marital problems (Greving, 2007; Meijer & van den Wittenboer, 2007). Parenthood also means having substantially less time to devote to the marriage.

However, using the birth of a child as the explanation for the drop in marital satisfaction is much too simplistic, because child-free couples also experience a decline in marital satisfaction (Kulik, 2016). Longitudinal research indicates disillusionment—as demonstrated by a decline in feeling in love, in demonstrations of affection, and in the feeling that one's spouse is responsive, as well as an increase in feelings of ambivalence—and other personality characteristics such as narcissism are key predictors of marital dissatisfaction (Lavner, Lamkin et al., 2016).

During the early years of their marriage, many couples may spend significant amounts of time apart, especially in the military (Fincham & Beach, 2010). Spouses that serve in combat areas on active duty assignment who suffer from post-traumatic stress disorder (PTSD) are particularly vulnerable, since they are at greater risk for other spouse-directed aggression.

What the nondeployed spouse believes turns out to be important. If the nondeployed spouse believes the deployment will have negative effects on the marriage, then problems are much more likely. In contrast, if the nondeployed spouse believes such challenges make the relationship stronger, then they typically can do so (Lewis, Lamson, & White, 2016; Renshaw, Rodrigues, & Jones, 2008). Research indicates the effects of deployment may be greater on wives than on husbands; divorce rates for women service members who are deployed is higher than for their male counterparts (Karney & Crown, 2007).

Marriage at Midlife

For most couples, marital satisfaction improves after the children leave, a state called the empty nest. Midlife brings both challenges and opportunities for marriages (Karasu & Karasu, 2005). Some use the launching of children to rediscover each other, and marital satisfaction rebounds.

For some middle-aged couples, however, marital satisfaction continues to be low. *They may have grown apart but continue to live together, a situation sometimes referred to as* **married singles** (Lamanna, Riedmann, & Stewart, 2015). In essence, they become emotionally divorced and live more as housemates than as a married couple; for these couples, spending more time together is not a welcome change. Research shows marital dissatisfaction in midlife is a process that develops over a long period of time and is not spontaneous (Jackson et al., 2014; Rokach, Cohen, & Dreman, 2004). Later in this chapter we explore the squeeze many midlife couples feel as they continue to provide support for (grown) children and assume more support and care providing responsibility for aging parents (Boyczuk & Fletcher, 2016; Igarashi et al., 2013).

Older Couples

Marital satisfaction in long-term marriages—that is, marriages of 40 years or more—is a complex issue. In general, marital satisfaction among older couples increases shortly after retirement but then decreases with health problems and advancing age, and is directly related to the level of perceived support each partner receives (Landis et al., 2013; Proulx, 2016). The level of satisfaction in these marriages appears to be unrelated to the amount of past or present sexual interest or sexual activity, but it is positively related to the degree of social engagement such as interaction with friends (Bennett, 2005). In keeping with the married-singles concept, many older couples have simply developed detached, contented styles (Connidis, 2001; Lamanna et al., 2015; Proulx, 2016).

Older married couples show several specific characteristics (O'Rourke & Cappeliez, 2005). Many older couples show a selective memory regarding the occurrence of negative events and perceptions of their partner. Older couples have a reduced potential for marital conflict and a greater potential for pleasure; they are more likely to be similar in terms of mental and physical health, and show fewer gender differences in sources of pleasure. This is especially true if the couple has developed strong dyadic coping strategies, that is, coping strategies that rely on the interconnectedness of the couple (Berg et al., 2016). In short, older married couples develop adaptive ways to avoid conflict and grow more alike. In general, marital satisfaction among older couples remains high until health problems begin to interfere with the relationship (Connidis, 2001).

Being married in late life has several benefits. A study of 9,333 European Americans, African Americans, and Latino Americans showed marriage helps people deal better with chronic illness, functional problems, and disabilities (Pienta, Hayward, & Jenkins, 2000). Although the division of household chores becomes more egalitarian after the husband retires than it was when the husband was employed, irrespective of whether the wife was working outside the home, women still do more than half of the work (Kulik, 2011).

Caring for a Spouse/Partner

When couples pledge their love to each other "in sickness and in health," most envision the sickness part to be no worse than an illness lasting a few weeks. That may be the case for many couples, but for some the illness they experience severely tests their pledge.

Francine and Ron are one such couple. After 42 years of mainly good times together, Ron was diagnosed as having Alzheimer's disease. When first contacted by staff at the local chapter of a caregiver support organization, Francine had cared for Ron for 6 years. "At times it's very hard, especially when he looks at me and doesn't have any idea who I am. Imagine, after all these years, not to recognize me. But I love him, and I know that he would do the same for me. But, to be perfectly honest, we're not the same couple we once were. We're just not as close; I guess we really can't be."

Francine and Ron are typical of couples in which one partner cares for the other. Caring for a chronically ill partner presents different challenges than caring for a chronically ill parent. The partner caregiver assumes the new role after decades of shared responsibilities. Often without warning, the division of labor that worked for years must be readjusted, and new household skills must be learned. Such change inevitably puts considerable stress on the relationship (Haley, 2013). This is especially true when one's spouse/partner has a debilitating chronic disease.

Studies of spousal caregivers of persons with Alzheimer's disease show marital satisfaction is much lower than for healthy couples (Cavanaugh & Kinney, 1994; Haley, 2013; Kulik, 2016; Proulx, 2016). Spousal caregivers report a loss of companionship, intimacy, and emotional support over the course of caregiving, but also that they derive more rewards than adult child caregivers (Raschick & Ingersoll-Dayton, 2004; Revenson et al., 2016). Marital satisfaction is an important predictor of spousal caregivers' reports of depressive symptoms; the better the perceived quality of the marriage, the fewer symptoms caregivers report (Kinney & Cavanaugh, 1993), a finding that holds across European American and minority spousal caregivers (Chiao, Wu, Hsiao, 2015; Parker, 2008).

Most partner caregivers adopt the caregiver role out of necessity, not choice. Although evidence about the mediating role of caregivers' appraisal of stressors is unclear, interventions that improve the functional level of the ill partner, or that provide better coping strategies, generally improve the caregiving partner's situation (Revenson et al., 2016; Van Den Wijngaart, Vernooij-Dassen, & Felling, 2007).

The importance of feeling competent as a partner caregiver fits with the docility component of the competence–environmental press model presented in Chapter 5. Caregivers attempt to balance their perceived competence with the environmental demands of caregiving. Perceived competence allows them to be proactive rather than merely reactive (and docile), that gives them a better chance to optimize their situation.

Even in the best of committed relationships, providing full-time care for a partner is both stressful and rewarding in terms of the marital relationship (Haley, 2013; Revenson et al., 2016). Coping with a wife who may not remember her husband's name, acts strangely, and has a chronic and fatal disease presents serious challenges even to the happiest of couples. Yet even in that situation, because of the nature of the relationship before the onset of disease in his wife, the caregiving husband may experience no change in marital happiness (Proulx, 2016).

Divorce

Despite what couples pledge on their wedding day, many marriages do not last until death parts them; instead, marriages are dissolved through divorce.

Most couples enter marriage with the idea their relationship will be permanent. Rather than growing together, though, many couples grow apart.

Who Gets Divorced and Why?

Divorce in the United States is common, and the divorce rate is substantially higher than it is in many other countries around the world; as you can see in Figure 11.4, couples have roughly a 50–50 chance of remaining married for life. In contrast, the ratio of divorces to marriages in Japan, Israel, and Greece are substantially lower as are rates in Africa and Asia. Divorce rates in nearly every developed country increased over the past several decades, and tend to vary as a function of religion.

Of those marriages in the U.S. ending in divorce within 20 years, Asian American couples have the lowest risk and African Americans the highest. College-educated women have much lower divorce rates than women who have a high school or lower education (Wang, 2015).

Why people divorce has been the focus of much research. Divorce touches every aspect of relationships: emotional, psychological, social, economic, and more (Coates, 2017). Still, we can gain insight into who is most likely to divorce, and why they do.

Gottman and Levenson (2000; Gottman & Silver, 2015) developed two models that predicted divorce early (within the first 7 years of marriage) and later (when the first child reaches age 14) with 93% accuracy over the 14-year period of their study. Negative emotions displayed during conflict between the couple predicted early divorce, but not later divorce. In general, this reflects a destructive interaction pattern of demand-withdraw (Baucom et al., 2015; Christensen, 1990) in which, during conflict, one partner places a demand on the other, who then withdraws either emotionally or physically. In contrast, the lack of positive emotions in a discussion of events-of-the-day and during conflict predicted later divorce, but not early divorce. An example would be a wife talking excitedly about a project she had just been given at work and her husband showing disinterest. Such "unrequited" interest and excitement in discussions likely carries over to the rest of the relationship.

Gottman's and other similar (e.g., Baucom et al., 2015) research is important because it clearly shows how couples show emotion is critical to marital success. Couples who divorce earlier typically do so because of high levels of negative feelings such as contempt, criticism, defensiveness, and stonewalling experienced as a result of intense marital conflict. But for many couples, such intense conflict is generally absent. But the mere absence of conflict does not mean the marriage is full of positive feelings. Although the absence of intense conflict makes it easier to stay in a marriage longer, the lack of positive emotions eventually takes its toll and results in later divorce. For a marriage to last, people need to be

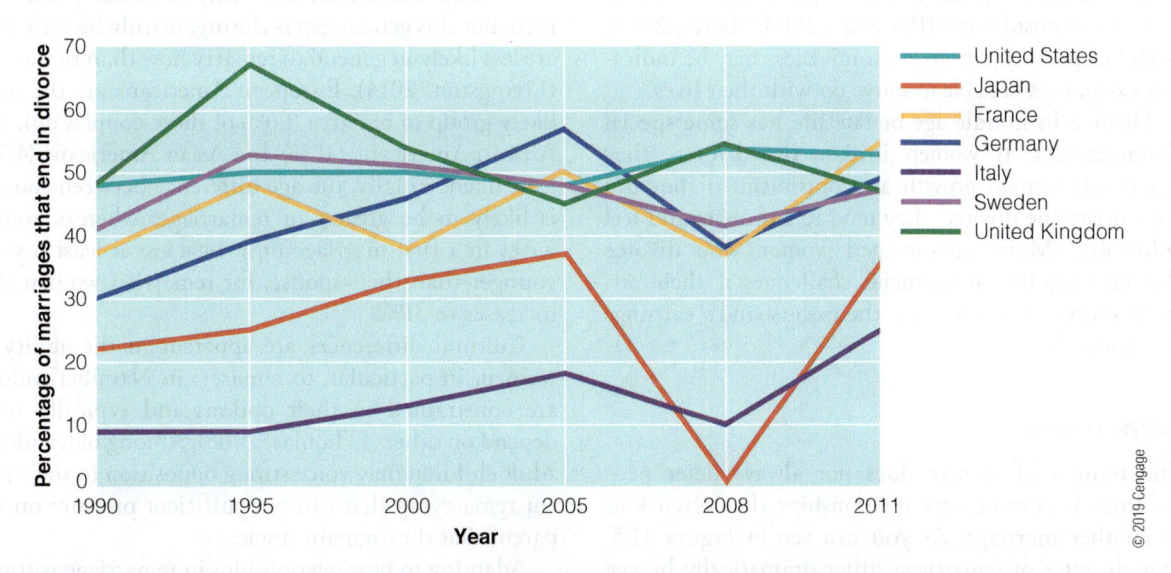

FIGURE 11.4 The United States has one of the highest divorce rates in the world.

Source: U.S. Bureau of Labor Statistics, updated and revised from "Families and Work in Transition in 12 Countries, 1980–2001," *Monthly Labor Review*, September 2003, with unpublished data. Retrieved from www.bls.gov/opub/mlr/2003/09/art1full.pdf.

told regularly they are loved and that what they do and feel really matters to their partner.

We must be cautious about applying Gottman's model to all married couples. Kim, Capaldi, and Crosby (2007) reported in lower-income high-risk couples, the variables Gottman says predict early divorce did not hold for that sample. The priority given to couples' communication as the source of marital satisfaction is not always apparent (Lavner, Karney, & Bradbury, 2016). For older, long-term married couples, the perception of the spouse's support is the most important predictor of remaining married (Landis et al., 2013).

Effects of Divorce on the Couple

Divorce takes a high toll on the couple. Unlike the situation when one's spouse dies, divorce often means the person's ex-spouse is present to provide a reminder of the failure. As a result, divorced people are typically unhappy in general, at least for a while. Especially because of the financial effects of divorce, the effects can even be traced to future generations due to long-term negative consequences on education and on quality of parenting (Amato & Cheadle, 2005; Friesen et al., in press). Divorced people suffer negative health consequences as well (Lamela, Figueiredo, & Bastos, 2016).

Divorced people sometimes find the transition difficult; researchers refer to these problems as "divorce hangover" (Walther, 1991). Divorce hangover reflects divorced partners' inability to let go, develop new friendships, or reorient themselves as single parents. Forgiving the ex-spouse is also important for eventual adjustment postdivorce (Rye et al., 2004; Sbarra, 2015). Both low preoccupation and forgiveness may be indicators ex-spouses are able to move on with their lives.

Divorce in middle age or late life has some special characteristics. If women initiate the divorce, they report self-focused growth and optimism; if they did not initiate the divorce, they tend to ruminate and feel vulnerable. Many middle-aged women who divorce also face significant financial challenges if their primary source of income was the ex-husband's earnings (Sakraida, 2005).

Remarriage

The trauma of divorce does not always deter people from beginning new relationships that often lead to another marriage. As you can see in Figure 11.5, though, rates of remarriage differ dramatically by age (Livingston, 2014). Additionally, the likelihood of ever remarrying has dropped in nearly all age groups since

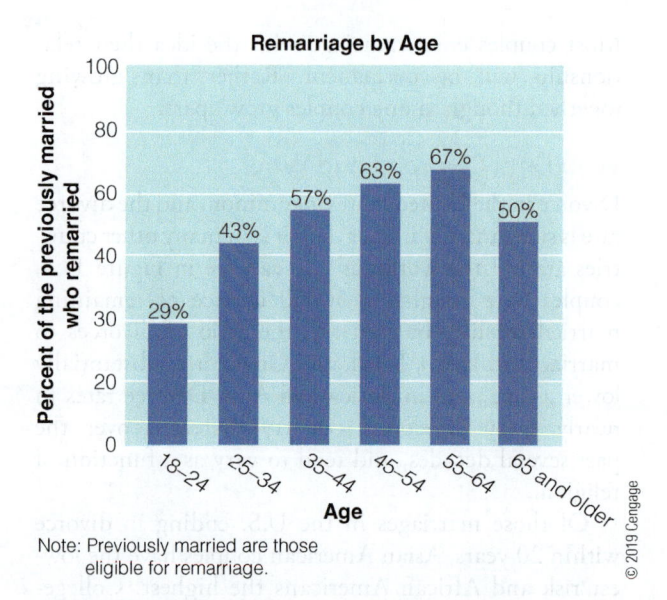

FIGURE 11.5 Remarriage as a function of age.
Source: Pew Research Center (2014). Retrieved from www.pewsocialtrends.org/2014/11/14/four-in-ten-couples-are-saying-i-do-again/st_2014-11-14_remarriage-06/.

the mid-20th century. For example, for those under age 35, remarriage declined from 72% in 1960 to 42% in 2013, from 76 to 57% in those 35–44, and from 69 to 63% in those 45–54. Interestingly, for those in older age groups, the trend is reversed: for those 55–64, remarriage increased from 55 to 67% and for those over 65, it increased from 34 to 50%.

Overall, women are less likely to remarry than are men, but this gender gap is closing, mainly because men are less likely in general to remarry now than in the past (Livingston, 2014). European Americans are the most likely group to remarry (60% of those couples do), and African Americans (48%) and Asian Americans (46%) least likely. Finally, the age difference between spouses is likely to be greater in remarriage: whereas among wives in a first marriage only 14% are at least 6 years younger than their spouse, for remarried women that increases to 31%.

Cultural differences are apparent in the ability of women, in particular, to remarry; in Namibia widows are constrained in their options and typically must depend on others (Thomas, 2008). Among older adults, adult children may voice strong opposition to their parent remarrying that can put sufficient pressure on the parent that they remain single.

Adapting to new relationships in remarriage is stressful. Partners may have unresolved issues from the previous marriage that may interfere with satisfaction with the new marriage (Faber, 2004; Gold, 2016; Martin-Uzzi & Duval-Tsioles, 2013). The challenges can include antagonism toward ex-spouses that interferes with child custody, differing loyalties among stepchildren, and financial difficulties. The effects of remarriage on children is complicated, at least for emerging adults (Collardeau & Ehrenberg, 2016; Gold, 2016). Parental divorce can have long-term consequences on children's attitudes toward marriage and divorce. The extent to which parental conflict was openly present and the religious affiliation of emerging adults influences their attitudes. For instance, those who were exposed to high levels of parental conflict have more positive views of divorce.

Remarriages tend to be less stable than first marriages, and have become less so since the 1990s (Council on Contemporary Families, 2015). The typical first marriage lasts 13 years, whereas the typical remarriage lasts 10. These differences do not reflect relationship quality, which is equivalent; rather, pressures from complex family relationships, lower commitment, and financial pressures take a higher toll on remarriages. Nevertheless, couples who are very committed to and work diligently at making the remarriage strong are usually successful.

Widowhood

Alma still feels the loss of her husband, Chuck. "There are lots of times when I feel him around. We were together for so long that you take it for granted that your husband is just there. And there are times when I just don't want to go on without him. But I suppose I'll get through it."

Like Alma and Chuck, virtually all older married couples see their marriages end legally because one partner dies. For most people, the death of a partner is one of the most traumatic events they experience, causing an increased risk of death among older European Americans (but not African Americans), an effect that lasts several years (Moorman & Greenfield, 2010). An extensive study of widowed adults in Scotland showed the increased likelihood of dying lasted for at least 10 years (Boyle, Feng, & Raab, 2011). Despite the stress of losing one's partner, most widowed older adults manage to cope reasonably well (Moorman & Greenfield, 2010).

The effects are broader than just mortality, though. Lucy Kalanithi (2016) described how her marriage vows to love, to honor, and to be loyal to her husband did not end with his death at age 37 from cancer. For her, marriage did not end with her transition to being a widow.

Women are much more likely to be widowed than are men. More than half of all women over age 65 are widows, but only 15% of men the same age are widowers. Women have longer life expectancies and typically marry men older than themselves. Consequently, the average married woman can expect to live at least 10 years as a widow.

The impact of widowhood goes well beyond the ending of a long-term partnership (Boyle et al., 2011; Brenn & Ytterstad, 2016; McCoyd & Walter, 2016). For example, there is evidence of increased mortality, especially within the first week of widowhood (Brenn & Ytterstad, 2016).

Loneliness is a major problem. Widowed people may be left alone by family and friends who do not know how to deal with a bereaved person. As a result, widows and widowers may lose not only a partner, but also those friends and family who feel uncomfortable with including a single person rather than a couple in social functions (McCoyd & Walter, 2016).

Feelings of loss do not dissipate quickly, as the case of Alma shows clearly. Men and women react differently to widowhood. In general, those who were most dependent on their partners during the marriage report the highest increase in self-esteem in widowhood because they have learned to do the tasks formerly done by their partners (Carr, 2004). Widowers may recover more slowly unless they have strong social support systems (Bennett, 2010). Widows often suffer more financially because survivor's benefits are usually only half of their husband's pensions (Weaver, 2010). For many women, widowhood results in difficult financial circumstances, particularly regarding medical expenses (McGarry & Schoeni, 2005).

For many reasons, including the need for companionship and financial security, some widowed people cohabit or remarry. A newer variation on re-partnering is "living alone together," an arrangement where two older adults form a romantic relationship but maintain separate living arrangements (Moorman & Greenfield, 2010). Re-partnering in widowhood can be difficult because of family objections (e.g., resistance from children), objective limitations (decreased mobility, poorer health, poorer finances), absence of incentives common to younger ages (desire for children), and social pressures to protect one's estate (Moorman & Greenfield, 2010).

In order to get a better sense of the experience of people who have lost a spouse or partner, complete the interviews described in the Discovering Development feature. What are the similarities and differences across age groups in their experiences?

DISCOVERING DEVELOPMENT
What Is It Like to Lose a Spouse/Partner?

You have read about the typically traumatic effects of losing a spouse/partner. As a way to more fully appreciate the full range of experiences and ways in which people cope, talk with several people of different ages who have lost a spouse/partner various lengths of time ago. With their permission, ask about their feelings and experiences immediately afterward, and after various lengths of time. How did their other family members react? Their friends? Their coworkers? What do they do to cope with their feelings? Do they still talk with their spouse/partner?

Compile your results and share them with others in your class (making sure to delete the names of the people you talked to and anyone they may have mentioned by name). How do the experiences stay similar across age? How do they differ? Why do you think that is? Share your ideas with others in your class.

Adult Development in Action

As a marital therapist, how would you use data on factors that predict divorce?

11.3 Family Dynamics and the Life Course

LEARNING OBJECTIVES

- What is it like to be a parent? What are the key issues across ethnic groups? What forms of parenting are there? How does parenting develop across adulthood?
- How do middle-aged adults interact with their children? How do they deal with the possibility of providing care to aging parents?
- How do grandparents interact with their grandchildren? What key issues are involved?

Susan is a 42-year-old married woman with two preadolescent children. *She is an only child. Her mother, Esther, is a 67-year-old widow and has been showing signs of dementia. Esther has little money and Susan's family is barely making ends meet. Susan knows her mother cannot live alone much longer, and she thinks she should have her move in with their family. Susan believes she has an obligation to provide care but also feels torn between her mother and her family and job. Susan wonders what to do.*

Susan's situation is far from unique. As more people live long lives, the need for families to deal with health problems in their older members is increasing. Many people like Susan also have to balance caring for aging parents with raising children at home. We'll see a bit later how the Susans of the world deal with being in the so-called sandwich generation.

In this section, we consider the dynamics of families, from deciding whether to have children through caring for aging parents and grandparenthood. As we do so, we must recognize the concept of "family" is undergoing change.

The Parental Role

The birth of a child transforms a couple (or a single parent) into a family. *The most common form of family in most Western societies is the* **nuclear family**, *consisting only of parent(s) and child(ren). However, the most common family form globally is the* **extended family**, *in which grandparents and other relatives live with parents and children.* Let's see how adding children to either family form matters.

Deciding Whether to Have Children

One of the biggest decisions couples (and many singles) make is whether to have children. Given this, you would think potential parents weigh the many benefits of child rearing with the many drawbacks. But you would be wrong—this is not what most people actually do.

Rijken (2009; Rijken & Knijn, 2009) reports potential parents actually don't think deliberately or deeply about when to have a child, and those who are career-oriented or like their freedom do not often deliberately postpone parenthood because of those factors. Rather, thoughts about having children are implicit and do not cross their minds until they are ready to begin thinking about having children.

Whether the pregnancy is planned or not (and more than half of all U.S. pregnancies are unplanned), a couple's first pregnancy is a milestone event in a relationship, with both benefits and stresses (Lavner & Bradbury, 2017; Meijer & van den Wittenboer, 2007). Parents largely agree children add affection, improve family ties, and give parents a feeling of immortality and sense of accomplishment. Most parents willingly sacrifice a great deal for their children and hope they grow up to be happy and successful. In this way, children bring happiness to their parents' relationship.

Nevertheless, finances are of great concern to most parents because children are expensive. How expensive? According to the U.S. Department of Agriculture (2017), a typical family who had a child in 2015 would spend about $284,570 for food, housing, and other necessities by the time the child is 18 years old, adjusting for inflation. College expenses would be additional. These costs do not differ significantly between two-parent and single-parent households but clearly are a bigger financial burden for single parents. Figure 11.6 shows the estimated costs by income level.

For many reasons that include personal choice, financial instability, and infertility, an increasing number of couples are child-free. Social attitudes in many countries (Austria, Germany, Great Britain, Ireland, Netherlands, and United States) are improving toward child-free couples (Blackstone & Stewart, 2016; Gubernskaya, 2010). Couples without children have some advantages: higher marital satisfaction, more freedom, and higher standards of living on average. Yet, they also must deal with societal expectations regarding having children and may feel defensive about their decision not to be a parent.

Today, parents in the United States typically have fewer children and have their first child later than in the past. The average age at the time of the birth of a woman's first child is nearly 26.3 (National Center for Health Statistics, 2016d). This average age has been increasing steadily since 1970 as a result of many women postponing having children because they marry later, they want to establish careers first, or they make a deliberate choice to delay childbearing.

Being older at the birth of one's first child is advantageous. Older mothers are more at ease being parents, spend more time with their babies, and are more affectionate, sensitive, and supportive to them (Berlin, Brady-Smith, and Brooks-Gunn, 2002; Camberis et al., 2016). The age of the father also makes a difference in how he interacts with children (Palkovitz & Palm, 2009). Compared to men who become fathers in their 20s, men who become fathers in their 30s are generally more invested in their paternal role and spend up to three times as much time caring for their preschool children as younger fathers do. Father involvement has increased significantly, due in part to social attitudes that support it (Fogarty & Evans, 2010).

Ethnic Diversity and Parenting

Ethnic background matters a great deal in terms of family structure and the parent–child relationship. African American husbands are more likely than their European American counterparts to help with household chores, regardless of their wives' employment status (Dixon, 2009). Overall, most African American parents provide a cohesive, loving environment that often exists within a context of strong religious beliefs (Anderson, 2007; Dixon, 2009), pride in cultural heritage, self-respect, and cooperation with the family (Coles, 2016).

As a result of several generations of oppression, many Native American parents have lost traditional cultural parenting skills: Children were valued, women were considered sacred and honored, and men cared for and provided for their families (Witko, 2006).

Nearly 25% of all children under 18 in the United States are Latino, and most are at least second generation (ChildStats.gov, 2016). Among two-parent families, Mexican American mothers and fathers both tend to adopt similar authoritative behaviors toward their preschool children (Gamble, Ramakumar, & Diaz, 2007).

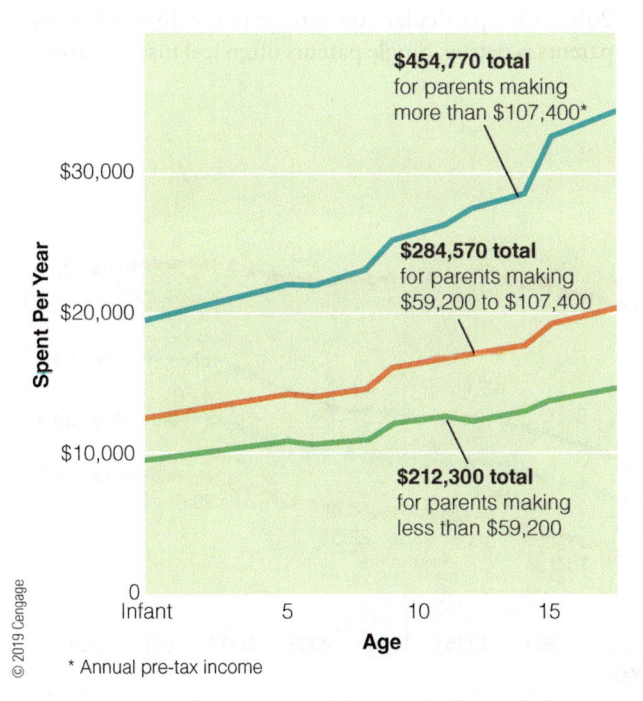

FIGURE 11.6 The cost of raising a child from birth to 18.
Source: USDA. (2017). *Expenditures on children by families, 2015.* p.19, Table 10. Retrieved from www.cnpp.usda.gov/sites/default/files/crc2015_March2017.pdf.

* Annual pre-tax income

Latino families demonstrate two key values: familism and the extended family. **Familism** *refers to the idea the well-being of the family takes precedence over the concerns of individual family members*. This value is a defining characteristic of Latino families; Brazilian and Mexican families consider familism a cultural strength (Carlo et al., 2007; Lucero-Liu, 2007). Indeed, familism accounts for the significantly higher trend for Latino college students to live at home (Desmond & López Turley, 2009). The extended family is also strong among Latino families and serves as the venue for a wide range of exchanges of goods and services, such as child care and financial support (Almeida et al., 2009).

Asian Americans also value familism (Meyer, 2007) and place an even higher value on extended family. Other key values include obtaining good grades in school, maintaining discipline, being concerned about what others think, and conformity. Asian American adolescents report high feelings of obligation to their families compared with European American adolescents (Kiang & Fuligni, 2009). In general, males enjoy higher status in traditional Asian families (Tsuno & Homma, 2009).

Raising multi-ethnic children presents challenges not experienced by parents of same-race children. Parents of biracial children report feeling discrimination, and they are targets of prejudicial behavior from others (Hubbard, 2010; Powell et al., 2016). These parents also worry their children may be rejected by members of both racial communities.

Single Parents

About 40% of births in the United States are to mothers who are not married, a rate that has declined 14% since peaking in 2008 (National Center for Health Statistics, 2016e). As can be seen in Figure 11.7, the percentage of births to nonmarried mothers differs considerably across race and ethnicity, from 72% among African Americans to 29.2% among European Americans. Among African American mothers, two-thirds of these mothers have no high school diploma, and evidence suggests that the education disadvantage significantly affects the child's future development (McLanahan & Jencks, 2015).

Single parents, regardless of gender, face considerable obstacles. Financially, they are usually much less well-off than their married counterparts. Integrating the roles of work and parenthood is more difficult. Single mothers are hardest hit, mainly because women typically are paid less than men.

Many divorced single parents report complex feelings such as frustration, failure, guilt, and a need to be overindulgent. Loneliness can be especially difficult to deal with (Anderson et al., 2004; Langlais, Anderson, & Greene, 2016). One particular concern for many divorced single parents is dating. Single parents often feel insecure about

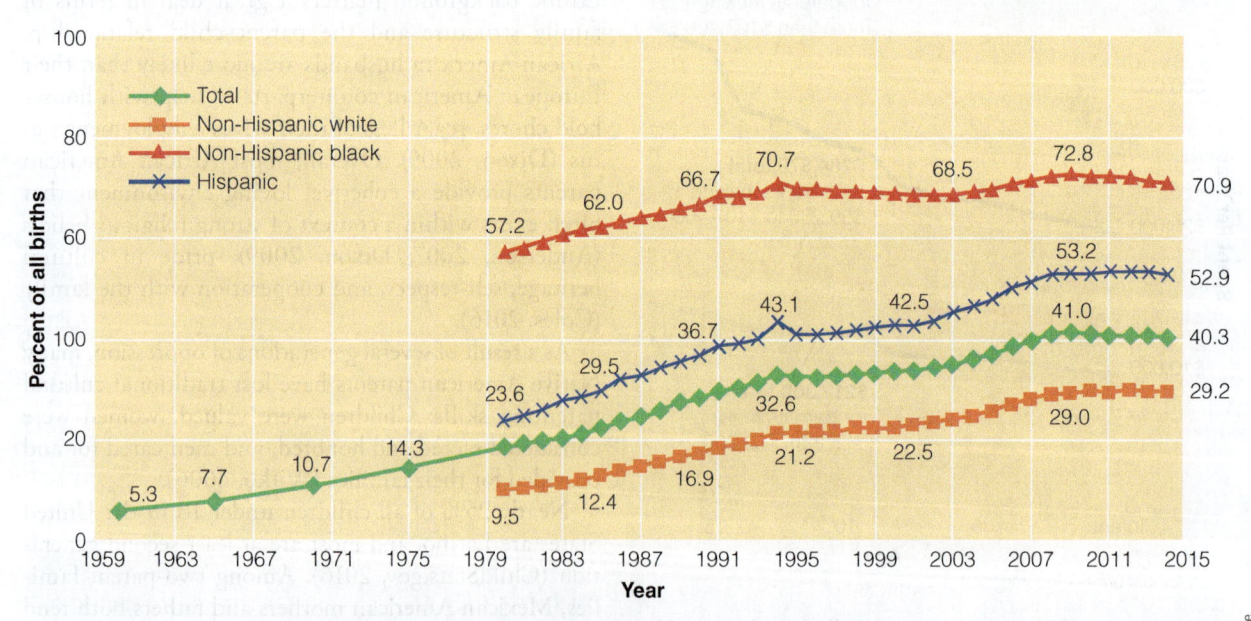

FIGURE 11.7 Percentage of all births that were to unmarried women, by race and Hispanic origin: selected years, 1960–2014.

Source: www.childtrends.org/wp-content/uploads/2015/03/75_Births_to_Unmarried_Women.pdf.

sexuality and how they should behave around their children in terms of having partners stay overnight (Langlais et al., 2016; Lampkin-Hunter, 2010).

Step-, Foster-, Adoptive, and Same-Sex Couple Parenting

Roughly one-third of North American couples become stepparents or foster or adoptive parents some time during their lives. In general, there are few differences among parents who have their own biological children or who become parents in some other way, but there are some unique challenges (Doss & Rhoades, 2017; Ganong & Coleman, 2017).

A big issue for foster parents, adoptive parents, and stepparents is how strongly the child will bond with them. Although infants less than 1 year old probably bond well, children who are old enough to have formed attachments with their biological parents may have competing loyalties. As a result, the dynamics in blended families can best be understood as a complex system (Dupuis, 2010). These problems are a major reason second marriages are at high risk for dissolution, as discussed later in this chapter. They are also a major reason why behavioral and emotional problems are more common among stepchildren (Ganong & Coleman, 2017).

Still, many stepparents and stepchildren ultimately develop good relationships with each other. Allowing stepchildren to develop a relationship with the stepparent at their own pace also helps. What style of stepparenting ultimately develops is influenced by the expectations of the stepparent, stepchild, spouse, and nonresidential parent (Ganong & Coleman, 2017).

Adoptive parents also contend with attachment to birth parents, but in different ways. Adopted children may wish to locate and meet their birth parents. Such searches can strain the relationships between these children and their adoptive parents, who may interpret these actions as a form of rejection (Curtis & Pearson, 2010).

Families with children adopted from another culture pose challenges of how to establish and maintain connection with the child's culture of origin (Yngvesson, 2010). For mothers of transracially adopted Chinese and Korean children, becoming connected to the appropriate Asian American community is a way to accomplish this (Johnston et al., 2007). Research in the Netherlands found children adopted from Columbia, Sri Lanka, and Korea into Dutch homes struggled with looking different, and many expressed desires to be white (Juffer, 2006). Canadian parents who adopted children from China took several different approaches to introducing their children to Chinese culture, from not at all ("my child is simply Canadian" to deliberately blending both cultures to leaving is up to the child (Bian, Blachford, & Durst, 2015).

Foster parents have the most tenuous relationship with their children because the bond can be broken for any of a number of reasons having nothing to do with the quality of the care being provided. Dealing with attachment is difficult; foster parents want to provide secure homes, but they may not have the children long enough to establish continuity. Furthermore, because many children in foster care have been unable to form attachments at all, they are less likely to form ones in the future because they believe they will inevitably be broken. Despite the challenges, placement in good foster care results in the development of attachment between foster parents and children who were placed out of institutional settings (Alper & Howe, 2015; Smyke et al., 2010).

Finally, many gay men and lesbian women also want to be parents. Although changes in laws regarding same-sex couples and parenting have changed in important ways, barriers remain (Frank, 2016). Some have biological children themselves, whereas others choose adoption or foster parenting. Same-sex couples make good parents; research over many years has clearly indicated that children reared by gay or lesbian parents do not experience any more problems than children reared by heterosexual parents and are as psychologically healthy as children of heterosexual parents (Bos et al., 2016; Frank, 2016). Evidence shows gay parents have more egalitarian sharing of child rearing than do fathers in heterosexual households (Biblarz & Savci, 2010).

Support for Parents

Having a child changes all aspects of couples' lives. Parenting is full of rewards, but it also takes a great deal of work. As we have seen, children place a great deal of stress on a relationship. Both motherhood and fatherhood require major commitment and cooperation.

Caring for young children may create disagreements over the division of labor, especially if both parents are employed outside the home (see Chapters 4 and 12). Even when mothers hold jobs (and roughly 70% of women with children under age 18 in the U.S. do), they still perform most of the child-rearing tasks. And when men take employment leave, although more likely to share tasks, they still do not spend more time with their children than fathers who do not take leave (Seward & Stanley-Stevens, 2014).

The United States is the only major industrialized country not to provide mandatory paid leave for new parents. Although some states and cities have passed laws requiring paid parental leave, most have not. The Current Controversies feature explores the issue of paid parental leave in more detail.

Midlife Issues: Adult Children and Caring for Aging Parents

Middle-aged family members, such as the current generation of baby boomers, serve as the links between their aging parents and their own maturing children (Deane et al., 2016; Fingerman et al., 2012; Hareven, 2001). *Middle-aged mothers (more than fathers) tend to take on this role of* **kinkeeper**, *the person who gathers family members together for celebrations and keeps them in touch with each other.*

Think about the major issues confronting a typical middle-aged couple: maintaining a good marriage, fulfilling parenting responsibilities, dealing with children who are becoming adults themselves, handling job pressures, and worrying about aging parents, just to name a few. Middle-aged adults truly have a lot to deal with every day in balancing their responsibilities to their children and their aging parents (Boyczuk & Fletcher, 2016). *Indeed, middle-aged adults are sometimes referred to as the* **sandwich generation** *because they are caught between the competing demands of two generations: their parents and their children.*

Letting Go: Middle-Aged Adults and Their Children

Sometime during middle age, most parents experience two positive developments with regard to their children (Buhl, 2008). Suddenly their children see them in a new light, and the children leave home.

The extent parents support and approve of their children's attempts at being independent matters. Most parents manage the transition successfully (Owen, 2005). That's not to say parents are heartless. When children leave home, emotional bonds are disrupted. Mothers in all ethnic groups report feeling sad at the time children leave, but have more positive feelings about the potential for growth in their relationships with their children (Feldman, 2010).

Still, parents provide considerable emotional support (by staying in touch) and financial help (such as paying college tuition, providing a free place to live until the child finds employment) when possible (Farris, 2016).

A positive experience with launching children is strongly influenced by the extent the parents perceive a job well done and their children have turned out well

CURRENT CONTROVERSIES
Paid Family Leave

Does your employer provide paid time off if you have a new child? In order to care for an ill child or older parent? If you have a serious illness or need to recover after surgery? If so, you are fortunate. One of the biggest needs for most employees is access to these types of benefits, especially employees in smaller organizations or employers that do not provide paid time off. In fact, the United States is the only industrialized country that does not either have a national government program or an employer mandate to provide such benefits (A Better Balance, 2016).

Currently, the federal Family and Medical Leave Act of 1993 (FMLA) is the only national program of its kind in the U.S. It requires employers to provide *unpaid* leave for up to 12 weeks for employees to care for a new child or seriously ill family member, to recover from one's own serious health condition, or to deal with certain obligations (including child care and related activities) arising from a spouse, parent, or child being on, or called to, active duty in the military. The FMLA also provides up to 26 weeks of unpaid leave per year for workers whose spouse, child, parent, or next of kin is a seriously ill or injured member of the armed services (A Better Balance, 2016).

However, due to the specific provisions that create coverage gaps in the law, roughly 40% of employees are not covered. And, the unpaid nature of the law means that only those who can afford to lose their income take it. To address these gaps and provide some income coverage, the Family Act was introduced in Congress in 2015. It would provide 12 weeks of paid leave for the situations covered in FMLA. It has yet to be enacted.

Fortunately, a few states have taken the lead to create *paid* family leave programs. For example, California, New Jersey, New York, and Rhode Island have different types of paid leave. Several other states are working to enact other versions. (Find out what the policy is in your home state.) Many advocates and employees agree that paid leave for family reasons is important. Many businesses do as well. As we have seen, the evidence is strong that being able to care for one's family or oneself improves well-being, and helps the employee be more productive. What do *you* think should be done?

(Farris, 2016; Mitchell, 2010). Children are regarded as successes when they meet parents' culturally based developmental expectations, and they are seen as "good kids" when there is agreement between parents and children in basic values.

Parents' satisfaction with the empty nest is sometimes short-lived. Roughly half of young adults in the United States return to their parents' home at least once after moving out (Farris, 2016). There is evidence these young adults, called "boomerang kids" (Farris, 2016; Mitchell, 2006), reflect a less permanent, more mobile contemporary society.

Why do children move back? A major impetus is the increased costs of living on their own when saddled with college debt, especially if the societal economic situation is bad and jobs are not available. This was especially true during the Great Recession of the late 2000s and early 2010s. It also reflects the different kind of relationship millennial adults have with their parents and a different attitude about living back at home (Farris, 2016).

Giving Back: Middle-Aged Adults and Their Aging Parents

Most middle-aged adults have parents who are in reasonably good health. But for nearly a quarter of adults, being a child of aging parents involves providing some level of care (Hyer, Mullen & Jackson, 2017). How adult children become care providers varies a great deal from person to person, but the job of caring for older parents usually falls to a daughter or a daughter-in-law (Barnett, 2013), and daughters also tend to coordinate care provided by multiple siblings (Friedman & Seltzer, 2010). In Japan, even though the oldest son is responsible for parental care, it is his wife who actually does the day-to-day caregiving for her own parents and her in-laws (Lee, 2010).

Most adult children feel a sense of responsibility, termed **filial obligation**, *to care for their parents if necessary.* Adult child care providers sometimes express the feeling they "owe it to Mom or Dad" to care for them; after all, their parents provided for them for many years, and now the shoe is on the other foot (Gans, 2007). Adult children often provide the majority of care when needed to their parents in all Western and non-Western cultures studied, but especially in Asian cultures (Barnett, 2013; Haley, 2013; Lai, 2010).

Roughly 50 million Americans provide unpaid care for older parents, in-laws, grandparents, and other older loved ones (National Alliance for Caregiving & AARP, 2015). The typical care provider is a middle-aged woman who is employed outside the home, has an average household income of under $46,000, and provides more than 20 hours per week of unpaid care. They expect to care for their loved one for about 10 years.

Stresses and Rewards of Providing Care

Providing care is a major source of both stress and reward. On the stress side, adult children and other family caregivers are especially vulnerable from two main sources (Pearlin et al., 1990):

- Adult children may have trouble coping with declines in their parents' functioning, especially those involving cognitive abilities and problematic behavior, and with work overload, burnout, and loss of the previous relationship with a parent.
- If the care situation is perceived as confining or seriously infringes on the adult child's other responsibilities (spouse, parent, employee, etc.), then the situation is likely to be perceived negatively, and that may lead to family or job conflicts, economic problems, loss of self-identity, and decreased competence.

When caring for an aging parent, even the most devoted adult child caregiver will at times feel depressed, resentful, angry, or guilty (Cavanaugh, 1999a; Haley, 2013; Hyer et al., 2017). Many middle-aged care providers are hard pressed financially: They may still be paying child care or college tuition expenses, perhaps trying to save adequately for their own retirement, and having to work more than one job to do it. Financial pressures are especially serious for those caring for parents with chronic conditions, such as Alzheimer's disease, that require services, such as adult day care, not adequately covered by medical insurance even if the older parent has supplemental coverage. In some cases, adult children may need to quit their jobs to provide care if adequate alternatives, such as adult day care, are unavailable or unaffordable, usually creating even more financial stress.

The stresses of caring for a parent mean the caregiver needs to carefully monitor his or her own health. Indeed, many professionals point out caring for the care provider is an important consideration to avoid care provider burnout (Ghosh, Capistrant, & Friedemann-Sánchez, 2017; Tamayo et al., 2010).

On the plus side, caring for an aging parent also has rewards. Caring for aging parents can bring parents and their adult children closer together and provide a way for adult children to feel they are giving back to their parents (Miller et al., 2008). Cross-cultural research examining Taiwanese (Lee, 2007) and Chinese (Zhan, 2006) participants confirms adults caring for aging parents can find the experience rewarding.

Cultural values enter into the care providing relationship in an indirect way (Mendez-Luck et al., 2016). Care providers in all cultures studied to date show a common set of outcomes: Care providers' stressors are appraised as burdensome, that creates negative health consequences for the care provider. However, cultural values influence the kinds of social support available to the care provider.

Things aren't always rosy from the parents' perspective, either. Independence and autonomy are important traditional values in some ethnic groups, and their loss is not taken lightly. Older adults in these groups are more likely to express the desire to pay a professional for assistance rather than ask a family member for help; they may find it demeaning to live with their children and express strong feelings about "not wanting to burden them" (Cahill et al., 2009). Most move in only as a last resort. Many adults who receive help with daily activities feel negatively about the situation, although cultural norms supporting the acceptance of help, such as in Japanese culture, significantly lessen those feelings (Park et al., 2013).

Determining whether older parents are satisfied with the help their children provide is a complex issue (Cahill et al., 2009; Park et al., 2013). Based on a critical review of the research, Newsom (1999) proposes a model of how certain aspects of care can produce negative perceptions of care directly or by affecting the interactions between care provider and care recipient (see Figure 11.8). The important thing to conclude from the model is even under the best circumstances, there is no guarantee the help adult children provide their parents will be well received. Misunderstandings can occur, and the frustration caregivers feel may be translated directly into negative interactions.

Grandparenthood

Becoming a grandparent takes some help. Being a parent yourself, of course, is a prerequisite. But it is your children's decisions and actions that determine whether you experience the transition to grandparenthood, making this role different from most others we experience throughout life.

Most people become grandparents in their 40s and 50s, though some are older, or perhaps as young as their late 20s or early 30s. For many middle-aged adults, becoming a grandparent is a peak experience (Gonyea, 2013; Hoffman, Kaneshiro, & Compton, 2012). Although most research on grandparenting has been conducted with respect to heterosexual grandparents, attention to lesbian, gay, and transgender grandparents is increasing as these family forms increase in society (Allen & Roberto, 2016; Orel & Fruhauf, 2013).

FIGURE 11.8 Whether a care recipient perceives care to be good depends on interactions with the care provider and whether those interactions are perceived negatively.

Source: From Newsom, J. T. (1999). Another side to caregiving: Negative reactions to being helped. *Current Directions in Psychological Science, 8,* 185. Reprinted by permission of Blackwell Publishing, Ltd.

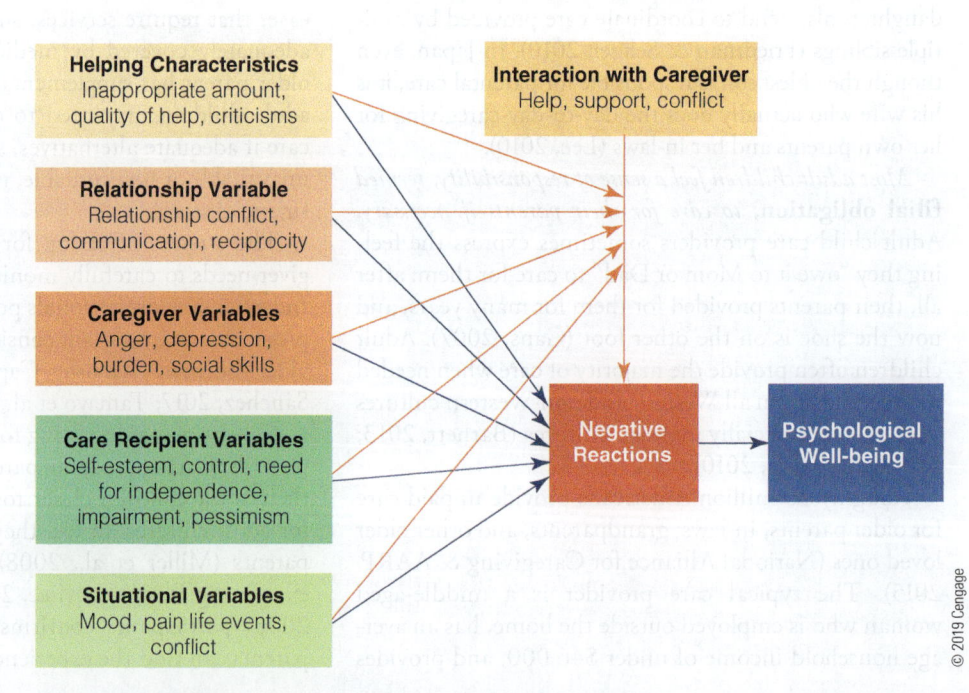

How Do Grandparents Interact with Grandchildren?

Grandparents have many different ways of interacting with their grandchildren. Categorizing these styles has been attempted over many decades (e.g., Neugarten & Weinstein, 1964), but none of these attempts has been particularly successful because grandparents use different styles with different grandchildren and styles change as grandparents and grandchildren age (Gonyea, 2013; Hoffman et al., 2012).

An alternative approach involves considering the many functions grandparents serve and the changing nature of families (Hills, 2010). The social dimension includes societal needs and expectations of what grandparents are to do, such as passing on family history to grandchildren. The personal dimension includes the personal satisfaction and individual needs fulfilled by being a grandparent. Many grandparents pass on skills—as well as religious, social, and vocational values (social dimension)—through storytelling and advice, and they may feel great pride and satisfaction (personal dimension) from working with grandchildren on joint projects.

Grandchildren give grandparents a great deal in return. Grandchildren keep grandparents in touch with youth and the latest trends. Sharing the excitement of surfing the web in school may be one way grandchildren keep grandparents on the technological forefront.

Being a Grandparent Is Meaningful

Being a grandparent really matters. Most grandparents derive multiple meanings, and they are linked with generativity (Gonyea, 2013; Hayslip & Blumenthal, 2016). For some, grandparenting is the most important thing in their lives. For others, meaning comes from being seen as wise, from spoiling grandchildren, from recalling the relationship they had with their own grandparents, or from taking pride in the fact they will be followed by not one but two generations.

Grandchildren also highly value their relationships with grandparents, even when they are young adults (Alley, 2004; Hayslip & Blumenthal, 2016). Grandparents are valued as role models as well as for their personalities, the activities they share, and the attention they show to grandchildren. Emerging adult grandchildren (ages 21–29) derive both stress and rewards from caring for grandparents, much the same way middle-aged adults do when they care for their aging parents (Fruhauf, 2007).

Ethnic Differences

How grandparents and grandchildren interact varies in different ethnic groups. Intergenerational relationships are especially important and historically have been a source of strength in African American families (Waites, 2009) and Latino families (Hayslip & Blumenthal, 2016). African American grandparents play an important role in many aspects of their grandchildren's lives, such as family storytelling (Fabius, 2016) and religious education (King et al., 2006; Lewis, Seponski, & Camp, 2011). African American grandfathers, in particular, tend to perceive grandparenthood as a central role to a greater degree than do European American grandfathers (Kivett, 1991). Latino American grandparents are more likely to participate in child rearing owing to a cultural core value of family (Burnette, 1999).

Native American grandparents are important in their grandchildren's lives, especially when the grandchildren live in urban settings and are reasonably close by (Limb, Shafer, & Sandoval, 2014). These grandparents provide

How grandparents and grandchildren interact varies across cultures.

grandchildren with a way to connect with their cultural heritage, and they are also likely to provide a great deal of care for their grandchildren (Mutchler, Baker, & Lee, 2007). Research also indicates Native American grandparents use their own experiences of cultural disruption to reinvest in their grandchildren to ensure the continuity of culture (Thompson, Cameron, & Fuller-Thompson, 2013). In general, Native American grandmothers take a more active role than do grandfathers and are more likely to pass on traditional rituals (Woodbridge, 2008).

Asian American grandparents, particularly if they are immigrants, serve as a primary source of traditional culture for their grandchildren (Yoon, 2005). When these grandparents become heavily involved in caring for their grandchildren, they especially want and need services that are culturally and linguistically appropriate.

When Grandparents Care for Grandchildren

Grandparenthood today is tougher than it used to be. Families are more mobile, and this means grandparents are more often separated from their grandchildren by geographical distance. Grandparents are more likely to have independent lives apart from their children and grandchildren. What being a grandparent entails in the 21st century is more ambiguous than it once was (Hayslip & Blumenthal, 2016; Hyer et al., 2017).

Perhaps the biggest change worldwide for grandparents is the increasing number serving as custodial parents or primary caregivers for their grandchildren (Choi, Sprang, & Eslinger, 2016). Estimates are that over 2.5 million grandparents provide basic needs (food, shelter, clothing) for one or more of their grandchildren (AARP, 2016). These situations are due to several factors (Choi et al., 2016): the most frequent is due to both parents being employed outside the home; when the parents are deceased, addicted, incarcerated, or unable to raise their children for some reason; or when discipline or behavior problems have been exhibited by the grandchild.

Because most grandparents in this situation do not have legal custody of their grandchild, problems and challenges such as dealing with schools and obtaining school or health records are frequent. Typically, social service workers must assist grandparents in navigating the many unresponsive policies and systems they encounter when trying to provide the best possible assistance to their grandchildren (Cox, 2007). Clearly, public policy changes are needed to address these issues, especially regarding grandparents' rights regarding schools and health care for their grandchildren (Ellis, 2010).

Raising grandchildren is not easy. Financial stress, cramped living space, and social isolation are only some of the issues facing custodial grandparents (Choi et al, 2016; Hayslip & Blumenthal, 2016). All of these stresses are also reported cross culturally; full-time custodial grandmothers in Kenya reported higher levels of stress than part-time caregivers (Oburu & Palmérus, 2005).

Even custodial grandparents raising grandchildren without these problems report more stress and role disruption than noncustodial grandparents, though most grandparents are resilient and manage to cope (Hayslip & Blumenthal, 2016; Hayslip, Davis, et al., 2013). Most custodial grandparents consider this situation to be better for their grandchild than any other alternative and report surprisingly few negative effects on their marriages.

Adult Development in Action

As a human resources director, what supports might you create to assist middle-aged adults handle family issues?

Social Policy Implications

As we saw earlier in this chapter, elder abuse and neglect is a major, underreported global problem. To help protect vulnerable older adults, the U.S. Congress passed and President Obama signed into law the Elder Justice Act in 2010 that was included as an amendment to the Patient Protection and Affordable Care Act. The Elder Justice Act provides federal resources to "prevent, protect, treat, understand, intervene in and, where appropriate, prosecute elder abuse, neglect and exploitation."

In brief, the law requires the Department of Health and Human Services to oversee the management of federal programs and resources for protecting older adults from abuse and neglect. Among the most important action steps in the law are:

- Establish the Elder Justice Coordinating Council
- Establish an Advisory Board on Elder Abuse
- Establish Elder Abuse, Neglect, and Exploitation Forensic Centers

- Enhance long-term care
- Fund state and local adult protective service offices
- Provide grants for long-term care ombudsmen programs and for evaluating programs
- Provide training
- Provide grants to state agencies to perform surveys of care and nursing facilities
- Require the U.S. Department of Justice to act to prevent elder abuse by creating elder justice programs; studying state laws and practices relating to elder abuse, neglect, and exploitation; training personnel; and ensuring enough resources are available for investigation and prosecution of perpetrators.

Unfortunately, Congress has never appropriately funded this law (National Adult Protective Services Association, 2016). Although the Violence Against Women Act that was reauthorized in 2013 authorizes $9 million per year to assist older women, that is a far cry from the nearly $200 million per year authorized in the Elder Justice Act, and even more inadequate given that victims of financial exploitation alone lose roughly $3 billion per year.

However, in 2016 the U.S. Department of Justice launched 10 regional elder justice task forces with a mandate to coordinate local and regional services to older adults living in the community or in other settings who are mistreated. The goal of these task forces is to ensure that older Americans are treated appropriately and are protected from abuse neglect, and exploitation.

The original Elder Justice Act expired in 2014. Legislation to reauthorize it awaits congressional action. Numerous national advocacy agencies, such as the Elder Justice Coalition, the National Adult Protective Services Association, and others, are dedicated to ensuring the Elder Justice Act gets reauthorized and receives the funding it deserves. Child abuse prevention has been funded for years. It is time to help older adults be equally protected.

SUMMARY

11.1 Relationship Types and Issues

What role do friends play across adulthood?
- People tend to have more friendships during young adulthood than during any other period. Friendships in old age are especially important for maintaining life satisfaction.
- Men have fewer close friends and base them on shared activities. Women have more close friends and base them on emotional sharing. Cross-gender friendships are difficult.

What characterizes love relationships? How do they vary across culture?
- Passion, intimacy, and commitment are the key components of love.
- The theory that does the best job explaining the process of forming love relationships is the theory of assortative mating.
- Selecting a mate works best when there are shared values, goals, and interests. There are cross-cultural differences in which specific aspects of these are most important.

What are abusive relationships? What characterizes elder abuse, neglect, or exploitation?
- Levels of aggressive behavior range from verbal aggression to physical aggression to murdering one's partner. People remain in abusive relationships for many reasons, including low self-esteem and the belief they cannot leave.
- Abuse, neglect, or exploitation of older adults is an increasing problem. Most perpetrators are spouses/partners or adult children. The causes are complex.

11.2 Lifestyles and Love Relationships

What are the challenges of being single?
- Most adults in their 20s are single. People remain single for many reasons; gender differences exist. Ethnic differences reflect differences in age at marriage and social factors.
- Singles recognize the pluses and minuses in the lifestyle. There are health and longevity consequences from remaining single for men but not for women.

Why do people cohabit?
- Cohabitation is on the increase globally.
- Three primary reasons for cohabiting are convenience (e.g., to share expenses), trial marriage, or substitute marriage.

What are LGBTQ relationships like?
- Gay and lesbian couples are similar to married heterosexual couples in terms of relationship issues. Lesbian couples tend to be more egalitarian.

What is marriage like across adulthood?
- The most important factors in creating stable marriages are maturity, similarity (called homogamy), and conflict resolution skills. Exchange theory is an important explanation of how people contribute to their relationships.
- For couples with children, marital satisfaction tends to decline until the children leave home, although individual differences are apparent, especially in long-term marriages.
- Most long-term marriages tend to be happy, and partners in them express fewer negative emotions.
- Caring for a spouse presents challenges. How well it works depends on the quality of the marriage. Most caregiving spouses provide care based on love.

Why do couples divorce?
- Currently, half of all new marriages end in divorce. Reasons for divorce include a lack of the qualities that make a strong marriage. Also, societal attitudes against divorce have eased and expectations about marriage have increased.
- Recovery from divorce is different for men and women. Men tend to have a tougher time in the short run. Women clearly have a harder time in the long run, often for financial reasons. Difficulties between divorced partners usually involve visitation and child support.

Why do people remarry?
- Most divorced couples remarry. Second marriages are especially vulnerable to stress if stepchildren are involved. Remarriage in later life tends to be happy, but may be resisted by adult children.

What are the experiences of widows and widowers?
- Widowhood is more common among women because they tend to marry men older than they are. Widowed men typically are older.
- Reactions to widowhood depend on the quality of the marriage. Men generally have problems in social relationships and in household tasks; women tend to have more financial problems.

11.3 Family Dynamics and the Life Course

What is it like to be a parent? What are the key issues across ethnic groups? What forms of parenting are there? How does parenting evolve across adulthood?
- Most couples choose to have children, although for many different reasons. The timing of parenthood determines in part how involved parents are in their families as opposed to their careers.
- Instilling cultural values in children is important for parents. In some cultures, familism changes the unit of analysis from the individual to the family.
- Single parents face many problems, especially if they are women and are divorced. The main problem is reduced financial resources. A major issue for adoptive parents, foster parents, and stepparents is how strongly the child will bond with them. Each of these relationships has special characteristics. Gay and lesbian parents also face numerous obstacles, but they usually are good parents.

How do middle-aged adults get along with their children? How do they deal with the possibility of providing care to aging parents?
- Most parents do not report severe negative emotions when their children leave. Difficulties emerge to the extent that children were a major source of a parent's identity. However, parents typically report distress if adult children move back.
- Middle-aged women often assume the role of kinkeeper to the family. Middle-aged parents may be squeezed by competing demands of their children, who want to gain independence, and their parents, who want to maintain independence; therefore, they are often called the sandwich generation.
- Most caregiving by adult children is done by daughters and daughters-in-law. Filial obligation, the sense of responsibility to care for older parents, is a major factor.
- Caring for aging parents can be highly stressful. Symptoms of depression, anxiety, and other problems are widespread. Financial pressures also are felt by most. Parents often have a difficult time in accepting the care. However, many caregivers also report feeling rewarded or uplifted for their efforts.

How do grandparents interact with their grandchildren? What key issues are involved?
- Being a grandparent is a meaningful role. Individual differences in interactive style are large.
- Ethnic differences in grandparenting are evident. Ethnic groups with strong family ties differ in style from groups who value individuality.
- Grandparents are increasingly being put in the position of raising their grandchildren. Reasons include incarceration and substance abuse by the parents.
- Great-grandparenthood is a role enjoyed by more people and reflects a sense of family renewal.

REVIEW QUESTIONS

11.1 Relationship Types and Issues
- How does the number and importance of friendships vary across adulthood?
- What gender differences are there in the number and type of friends?
- What are the components of love? What characteristics make the best matches between adults? How do these characteristics differ across cultures?
- What is elder abuse, neglect, or exploitation? Why is it underreported?

11.2 Lifestyles and Love Relationships
- How do adults who never marry deal with the need to have relationships?
- What are the relationship characteristics of gay and lesbian couples?
- What are the most important factors in creating stable marriages?
- What developmental trends are occurring in marital satisfaction? How do these trends relate to having children?
- What factors are responsible for the success of long-term marriages?
- What are the major reasons people get divorced? How are these reasons related to societal expectations about marriage and attitudes about divorce?
- What characteristics about remarriage make it similar to and different from first marriage? How does satisfaction in remarriage vary as a function of age?
- What are the characteristics of widowed people? How do men and women differ in their experience of widowhood?

11.3 Family Dynamics and the Life Course
- What ethnic differences are there in parenting? What is familism and how does it relate to parenting?
- What are the important issues in being an adoptive parent, foster parent, or stepparent? What special challenges are there for gay and lesbian parents?
- What impact do children leaving home have on parents? Why do adult children return?
- What are the important issues facing middle-aged adults who care for their parents?
- How do grandparents and grandchildren relate? How do these relationships change with the age of the grandchild?
- What ethnic differences have been noted in grandparenting?
- What are the important issues and meanings of being a great-grandparent?

INTEGRATING CONCEPTS IN DEVELOPMENT

- What components would a theory of adult relationships need to have?
- What are some examples of each of the four developmental forces as they influence adult relationships?
- What role do the changes in sexual functioning discussed in Chapter 3 have on love relationships?
- What key public policy issues are involved in the different types of adult relationships?

KEY TERMS

abusive relationship A relationship that one partner displays aggressive behavior toward the other partner.

assortative mating A theory that people find partners based on their similarity to each other.

battered woman syndrome A situation in which a woman believes she cannot leave an abusive relationship and where she may even go so far as to kill her abuser.

cohabitation Living with another person as part of a committed, intimate, sexual relationship.

exchange theory A theory of relationships based on the idea each partner contributes something to the relationship the other would be hard-pressed to provide.

extended family The most common family form globally in which grandparents and other relatives live with parents and children.

familism Refers to the idea the well-being of the family takes precedence over the concerns of individual family members.

filial obligation The feeling that, as an adult child, one must care for one's parents.

homogamy The notion similar interests and values are important in forming strong, lasting, interpersonal relationships.

kinkeeper The person who gathers family members together for celebrations and keeps them in touch with each other.

marital adjustment The degree spouses accommodate each other over a certain period of time.

marital quality The subjective evaluation of the couple's relationship on a number of different dimensions.

marital satisfaction A global assessment of one's marriage.

marital success An umbrella term referring to any marital outcome.

married singles Married couples who have grown apart but continue to live together.

nuclear family Form of family consisting only of parent(s) and child(ren).

sandwich generation Middle-aged adults caught between the competing demands of two generations: their parents and their children.

socioemotional selectivity A theory of relationships that argues social contact is motivated by a variety of goals, including information seeking, self-concept, and emotional regulation.

vulnerability-stress-adaptation model A model that sees marital quality as a dynamic process resulting from the couple's ability to handle stressful events in the context of their particular vulnerabilities and resources.

12 | Work, Leisure, and Retirement

CHAPTER OUTLINE

12.1 Occupational Selection and Development
The Meaning of Work
Occupational Choice Revisited
Occupational Development
Job Satisfaction

12.2 Gender, Ethnicity, and Discrimination Issues
Gender Differences in Occupational Selection
Women and Occupational Development
Ethnicity and Occupational Development
Bias and Discrimination

CURRENT CONTROVERSIES Helping Women Lean In?

12.3 Occupational Transitions
Retraining Workers
Occupational Insecurity
Coping with Unemployment

DISCOVERING DEVELOPMENT What Unemployment Benefits Are Available in Your Area?

12.4 Work and Family
The Dependent Care Dilemma
Juggling Multiple Roles

12.5 Leisure Activities
Types of Leisure Activities

HOW DO WE KNOW? Long-Term Effects of Leisure Activities
Developmental Changes in Leisure
Consequences of Leisure Activities

12.6 Retirement and Work in Late Life
What Does Being Retired Mean?
Why Do People Retire?
Adjustment to Retirement
Employment and Volunteering

REAL PEOPLE Retiring to the Peace Corps

Social Policy Implications
Summary
Review Questions
Integrating Concepts in Development
Key Terms

When you were young, you were undoubtedly asked, "What do you want to be when you grow up?" Now that we are "grown up," the question has changed to "What do you do?"

Work is a central aspect of life and a defining characteristic of who we are. For some, work is life; for all, our work is a prime source of identity in adulthood.

The world of work has changed dramatically over the past few decades in large part to the continuing replacement of jobs with technology (witness the new use of robots and iPads in restaurants instead of human servers, and the advent of driverless cars that could eliminate taxi and share-service drivers). The so-called gig economy, based on short-term contracts rather than long-term employment, is the fastest growing sector of the labor force (Intuit, 2016; Irwin, 2016). Employment as a series of short-term jobs largely eliminates the traditional employer–employee relationship, and mostly eliminates the availability of key benefits such as employer-paid health care, paid family leave, and retirement savings plans to workers. Intuit (2016) predicts that by 2020, 40% of all American workers will be in the gig economy and not employed in a traditional long-term way.

Aging baby boomers are also redefining work and retirement. The Great Recession of the late 2000s and early 2010s affected the workplace by forcing boomers who lost a significant part of their retirement savings to continue working, making it more difficult for younger adults to enter or advance in the workforce.

As a result, our understanding of what work is, what it means, and how people engage in it is undergoing fundamental change. We consider the complexities of the world of work throughout this chapter as we confront the reality of rapidly changing occupational conditions and opportunities, and how those are shaping adult development and aging, and raising issues about basic assumptions people have about retirement. ■

12.1 Occupational Selection and Development

LEARNING OBJECTIVES
- How do people view work? How do occupational priorities vary with age?
- How do people choose their occupations?
- What factors influence occupational development?
- What is the relationship between job satisfaction and age?

Monique, a 28-year-old senior communications major, wonders about careers. Should she enter the broadcast field as a behind-the-scenes producer, or would she be better suited as a public relations spokesperson? She thinks her outgoing personality is a factor she should consider in making this decision.

Choosing one's work is serious business. Like Monique, we try to select a field in which we are trained and maximizes the odds that we can meet our goal of doing meaningful work. You may be taking this course as part of your preparation for a career in human development, social services, psychology, nursing, allied, health, or other field, so in that sense it is career preparation. But work is more than that. Work is a source for friends and often for spouses/partners. People arrange personal activities around work schedules. Parents often choose childcare centers on the basis of proximity to where they work. People often choose where they live in terms of where they work.

We are socialized from childhood to think about careers.

The Meaning of Work

Studs Terkel, author of the fascinating classic book *Working* (1974), writes work is "a search for daily meaning as well as daily bread, for recognition as well as cash, for astonishment rather than torpor; in short, for a sort of life rather than a Monday through Friday sort of dying" (xiii). Kahlil Gibran (1923), in his mystical book *The Prophet*, put it this way: "Work is love made visible."

The meaning most of us derive from working includes both the money that can be exchanged for life's necessities (and perhaps a few luxuries) and the possibility of personal growth (Lips-Wiersma, Wright, & Dik, 2016; Rosso, Dekas, & Wrzesniewski, 2010). Schwartz (2015) says that the belief that people work only for a paycheck is wrong; most people want to do something meaningful with people who they respect and who respect them. To achieve that true goal, Schwartz says most people would even be willing to make less money.

The upshot is that the specific occupation a person holds appears to have no effect on his or her need to derive meaning from work. Finding meaning in one's work can mean the difference between feeling work is the source of one's life problems or a source of fulfillment and contentment (Grawitch, Barber, & Justice, 2010). Blue- and pink-collar workers tend to derive meaning most from finding unity with others and developing the inner self, whereas white-collar workers place more emphasis on expressing full potential.

Contemporary business theory supports the idea that meaning matters. *The concept called* **meaning-mission fit** *explains how corporate executives with a better alignment between their personal intentions and their firm's mission care more about their employees' happiness, job satisfaction, and emotional well-being* (Abbott, Gilbert, & Rosinski, 2013; Salomaa, 2014). Ensuring such fit is a major focus of talent management efforts in organizations.

Because work plays such a key role in providing meaning for people, an important question is how people select an occupation. Let's turn our attention to two theories explaining how and why people choose the occupations they do.

Occupational Choice Revisited

Decisions about what people want to do in the world of work do not initially happen in adulthood. Even by adolescence, there is evidence occupational preferences are related to their personalities. But what are people preparing for? Certainly, much has been written about the rapidly changing nature of work and how people cannot prepare for a stable career where a person works for the same organization throughout his or her working life (Fouad et al., 2016; Savickas, 2013).

Currently, it is more appropriate to consider careers as something people construct themselves rather than enter (Di Fabio, 2016; Hartung & Santilli, 2017; Savickas, 2013). **Career construction theory** *posits people build careers through their own actions that result from the interface of their own personal characteristics and the social context.* What people "do" in the world of work, then, results from how they adapt to their environment; that, in turn, is a result of bio-psychosocial processes grounded in the collection of experiences they have during their life.

In this regard, two specific theories about how people adapt themselves to their environment have influenced research. First, Holland's (1997) personality-type theory proposes people choose occupations to optimize the fit between their individual traits (such as personality, intelligence, skills, and abilities) and their occupational interests. Second, **social cognitive career theory (SCCT)** *proposes career choice is a result of the application of Bandura's social cognitive theory, especially the concept of self-efficacy.*

Holland categorizes occupations by the interpersonal settings that people must function and their associated lifestyles. He identifies six personality types that combine these factors: investigative, social, realistic, artistic, conventional, and enterprising, that he believes are optimally related to occupations.

How does Holland's theory help us understand the continued development of occupational interests in adulthood? Monique, the college senior in the vignette, found a good match between her outgoing nature and her major, communications. Indeed, college students of all ages prefer courses and majors that fit well with their own personalities. You are likely to be one of them. Later on, that translates into the tendency of people to choose occupations and careers they like.

Complementarily, social cognitive career theory proposes people's career choices are heavily influenced by their interests (Brown & Lent, 2016; Lent, 2013; Sheu et al., 2010). As depicted in Figure 12.1, SCCT has two versions. The simplest includes four main factors: Self-Efficacy (your belief in your ability), Outcome Expectations (what you think will happen in a specific situation), Interests (what you like), and Choice Goals (what you want to achieve). The more complex version also includes Supports (environmental things that help you) and Barriers (environmental things that block or frustrate you). Several studies show support for the six-variable version of the model (Brown & Lent, 2016; Sheu et al., 2010).

How well do these theories work in actual practice, particularly in the rapidly changing world in which we live and where people's careers are no longer stable? Certainly, the relations among occupation, personality,

FIGURE 12.1 The four-variable (paths 1–6) and six-variable (paths 1–13) versions of the Social Cognitive Career Theory interest and choice models.

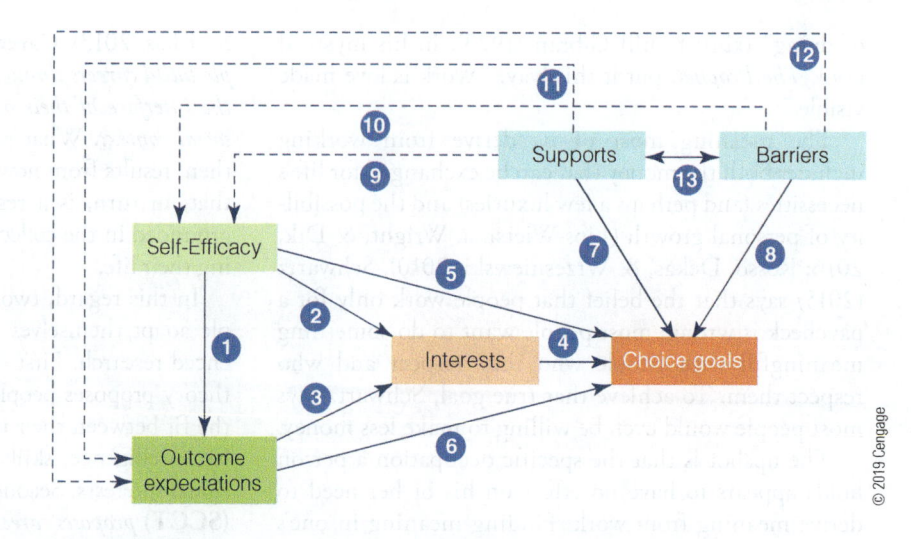

and demographic variables are complex (Brown & Lent, 2016; Hartung & Santilli, 2017). However, even given the lack of stable careers and the real need to change jobs frequently, there is still a strong tendency on people's part to find occupations in which they feel comfortable and they like (Brown & Lent, 2016; Hartung & Santilli, 2017). As we will see later, loss of self-efficacy through job loss and long-term unemployment provides support for the role the self-statements underling self-efficacy and SCCT are key.

SCCT has also been used as a framework for career counselors and coaches to help people identify and select both initial occupations and navigate later occupational changes. The goal is to have people understand the work world changes rapidly and they need to develop coping and compensatory strategies to deal with that fact.

Although people may have underlying tendencies relating to certain types of occupations, unless they believe they could be successful in those occupations and careers they are unlikely to choose them. These beliefs can be influenced by external factors. Occupational prestige and gender-related factors need to be taken into account (Deng, Armstrong, & Rounds, 2007).

Occupational Development

It is said that advancing through one's career is not just a function of being smart and doing what is a written requirement. It also depends on the socialization that occurs through learning the unwritten rules of an organization, in combination with one's own expectations of what the career should entail.

Occupational Expectations

Especially in adolescence, people begin to form opinions about what work in a particular occupation will be like, based on what they learn in school and from their parents, peers, other adults, and the media. These expectations influence what they want to become and when they hope to get there.

In adulthood, personal experiences affect people's opinions of themselves as they continue to refine and update their occupational expectations and development (Fouad, 2007; Fouad et al., 2016). This usually involves trying to achieve an occupational goal, monitoring progress toward it, and changing or even abandoning it as necessary. Modifying the goal happens for many reasons, such as realizing interests have changed, the occupation was not a good fit for them, they never got the chance to pursue the level of education necessary to achieve the goal, or because they lack certain essential skills and cannot acquire them. Still other people modify their goals because of age, race, or sex discrimination, a point we consider later in this chapter.

Research shows most people who know they have both the talent and the opportunity to achieve their occupational and career goals often attain them. When high school students identified as academically talented were asked about their career expectations and outcomes, it turned out that 10 and even 20 years later they had been surprisingly accurate (Perrone et al., 2010).

In general, research shows young adults modify their expectations at least once, usually on the basis of new information, especially about their academic ability. The connection between adolescent expectations and adult reality reinforces the developmental aspects of occupations and careers.

Many writers believe occupational expectations also vary by generation. Nowhere has this belief been stronger than in the supposed differences between the baby boom generation (born between 1946 and 1964) and the current millennial generation (born since 1983). What people in these generations, on average, expect in occupations appears to be different (Stewart et al., 2017). Millennials are more likely to change jobs more often than the older generations did, and are likely to view traditional organizations with more distrust and cynicism. Experts recommend that metrics used to evaluate job performance need to reflect these generational differences.

Contrary to most stereotypes, millennials are no more egotistical, and are just as happy and satisfied as young adults in every generation since the 1970s (Trzesniewski & Donnellan, 2010). However, millennials tend to have an inherent mistrust in organizations, prefer a culture focused on employee development, create information through interactive social media, are more globally aware and comfortable working with people from diverse socio-ethnic backgrounds, and do best in situations that value innovation through teamwork (Dannar, 2013; Stewart et al., 2017).

The importance of occupational expectations can be seen clearly in the transition from school to the workplace (Moen, 2016b; Moen & Roehling, 2005). The 21st-century workplace is not one where hard work and long hours necessarily lead to a stable career. *It can also be a place where you experience* **reality shock**, *a situation that what you learn in the classroom does not always transfer directly into the "real world" and does not represent all you need to know.* When reality shock sets in, things never seem to happen the way we expect. Reality shock befalls everyone. You can imagine how a new teacher feels when her long hours preparing a lesson result in students who act bored and unappreciative of her efforts.

Many professions, such as nursing and teaching, have gone to great lengths to alleviate reality shock (Hinton & Chirgwin, 2010; Shayshon & Popper-Giveon, in press). This problem is one best addressed through internship and practicum experiences for students under the careful guidance of experienced people in the field.

The Role of Mentors and Coaches

Entering an occupation involves more than the relatively short formal training a person receives. Instead, most people are oriented by a more experienced person who makes a specific effort to do this, taking on the role of a *mentor* or *coach*.

A **mentor** *is part teacher, sponsor, model, and counselor who facilitates on-the-job learning to help the new hire do the work required in his or her present role and to prepare for future career roles* (Volpe et al., 2016). *A* **developmental coach** *is an individual who helps a person focus on their goals, motivations, and aspirations to help them achieve focus and apply them appropriately* (Hunt & Weintraub, 2016). Mentoring and coaching are viewed as primary ways that organizations invest in developing their talent and future leadership (Smits & Bowden, 2013). Although mentors and coaches work with people at all career stages, mentoring is found most often with people new to a position, whereas coaching tends to focus on those with more experience.

The mentor helps a young worker avoid trouble and also provides invaluable information about the unwritten rules governing day-to-day activities in the workplace, and being sensitive to the employment situation (Smith, Howard, & Harrington, 2005). Good mentors make sure their protégés are noticed and receive credit from supervisors for good work. Thus, occupational success often depends on the quality of the mentor–protégé relationship and the protégé's perceptions of its importance (Eddleston, Baldridge, & Veiga, 2004).

What do mentors get from the relationship? Helping a younger employee learn the job is one way to achieve Erikson's phase of generativity (see Chapter 9; Marcia & Josselson, 2013).

Developmental coaching is a process that helps people make fundamental changes in their lives by focusing on general skill development and performance improvement (Volpe et al., 2016). It tends not to focus on specific aspects of a job; rather, the intent is more general improvement of one's overall career success. Thus, coaching complements mentoring and helps people develop all of the key aspects of themselves.

Women and minorities have an especially important need for both mentors and coaches (Hunt & Weintraub, 2016; Ortiz-Walters & Gilson, 2013; Pratt, 2010; Williams, Phillips, & Hall, 2014). When paired with mentors and coaches, women benefit by having higher expectations; mentored women also have better perceived career development (Schulz & Enslin, 2014). Latina nurses in the U.S. Army benefited from mentors in terms of staying in the military and getting better assignments (Aponte, 2007). It is also critical to adopt a culturally conscious model of mentoring and coaching in order to enhance the advantages of developing minority mentees (Campinha-Bacote, 2010). Culturally conscious mentoring and coaching involve understanding how an organization's and employee's cultures mutually affect employees, and explicitly building those assumptions, interrelationships, and behaviors into the mentoring or coaching situation.

Mentor-protégé relationships cut across all ages.

Despite the evidence that having a mentor or coach has many positive effects on one's occupational development, there is an important caveat; the quality of the mentor really matters (Tong & Kram, 2013; Volpe et al., 2016). Having a poor mentor or coach is worse than having no mentor at all. Consequently, people must be carefully matched. It is in the best interest of the organization to get the match correct. How can prospective matches happen more effectively? Some organizations have taken a page from dating and created speed mentoring as a way to create better matches (Berk, 2010; Cook, Bahn, & Menaker, 2010).

Job Satisfaction

What does it mean to be satisfied with one's job or occupation? **Job satisfaction** *is the positive feeling that results from an appraisal of one's work*. Research indicates job satisfaction is a multifaceted concept but certain characteristics—including hope, resilience, optimism, and self-efficacy—predict both job performance and job satisfaction (Luthans et al., 2007).

Satisfaction with some aspects of one's job increases gradually with age, and successful aging includes a workplace component (Robson et al., 2006). Why is this? Is it because people sort themselves out and end up in occupations they like? Is it because they simply learn to like the occupation they are in? What other factors matter?

So how does job satisfaction evolve over young and middle adulthood? You may be pleased to learn research shows, given sufficient time, most people eventually find a job where they are reasonably happy (Hom & Kinicki, 2001). Optimistically, this indicates there is a job out there, somewhere, where you will be happy. That's good, because research grounded in positive psychology theory indicates happiness fuels success (Achor, 2010).

It's also true job satisfaction does not increase in all areas and job types with age. White-collar professionals show an increase in job satisfaction with age, whereas those in blue-collar positions generally do not, and these findings hold with both men and women (Aasland, Rosta, & Nylenna, 2010). This is also true across cultures. A study of Filipino and Taiwanese workers in the long-term health care industry in Taiwan showed workers with 4 or 5 years' experience had lower job satisfaction than workers with less experience, but job satisfaction among older physicians in Norway increases over time (Aasland et al., 2010; Tu, 2006).

However, the changes in the labor market in terms of lower prospects of having a long career with one organization have begun to change the notion of job satisfaction (Bidwell, 2013; Böckerman et al., 2013). Specifically, the fact that companies may eliminate jobs and workers not based on performance but on stereotypes about older workers, for instance, makes it more difficult for employees to develop a sense of organizational commitment, thereby making the relationship between worker age and job satisfaction more complicated (Abrams, Swift, & Drury, 2016; Bayl-Smith & Griffin, 2014).

Also complicating traditional relations between job satisfaction and age is the fact that the type of job one has and the kinds of family responsibilities one has at different career stages—as well as the flexibility of work options such as telecommuting and family leave benefits to accommodate those responsibilities—influence the relationship between age and job satisfaction (Marsh & Musson, 2008). For instance, family caregiving responsibilities may collide with work demands, resulting in lower job satisfaction, especially if the employer has no flexible work options to accommodate the employee's needs (Paulson et al., 2016). This suggests the accumulation of experience, changing context, and the stage of one's career development all influence job satisfaction over time. The general increase in job satisfaction, then, may reflect the reality of workers figuring out how to manage their lives, understanding the limited alternative options they have, or taking advantage of alternative work assignments, such as telecommuting.

Alienation and Burnout

All jobs create a certain level of stress. For most workers, such negatives are merely annoyances. But, for others, extremely stressful situations on the job may result in alienation and burnout.

When workers feel what they are doing is meaningless and their efforts are devalued, or when they do not see the connection between what they do and the final product, a sense of **alienation** *is likely to result*. Terkel (1974) reported employees are most likely to feel alienated when they perform routine, repetitive actions. Alienation can also result from employees feeling abandoned by their employer, such as experiencing long periods without pay increases.

It is essential for companies to provide positive work environments to ensure the workforce remains stable and committed (Griffin et al., 2010). How can employers avoid alienating workers and improve organizational commitment? Research indicates that leaders who show trust and ethics are key (Bachman, 2017; Bligh, 2017), as is a perception among employees the employer deals with people fairly and impartially (Howard & Cordes, 2010). It is also helpful to involve employees in the decision-making process, create flexible work schedules, and institute employee development and enhancement programs.

Sometimes the pace and pressure of the occupation becomes more than a person can bear, resulting in **burnout**, *a depletion of a person's energy and motivation, the loss of occupational idealism, and the feeling that one is being exploited*. Burnout is a state of physical, emotional, and mental exhaustion that negatively affects self-esteem as a result of job stress (Shoji et al., 2016). Burnout is most common among people in the helping professions—such as police (McCarty & Skogan, 2013), teaching, social work, health care (Bermejo-Toro, Prieto-Ursúa, & Hernández, 2016; Shanafelt et al., 2016), and for those in the military (Simons et al., 2016). The tendency of organizations to keep employee numbers smaller during times of economic uncertainty adds to the workload for people on the job, increasing the risk of burnout (Bosco, di Masi, & Manuti, 2013).

First responders and people in helping professions must constantly deal with other people's complex problems, usually under time constraints. Dealing with these pressures every day, along with bureaucratic paperwork, may become too much for the worker to bear. Frustration builds, and disillusionment and exhaustion set in—burnout. Importantly, burnout negatively affects the quality of the services people are supposed to receive from the burned-out employee (Rowe & Sherlock, 2005).

Burnout has several bad effects on the brain (Michel, 2016). For instance, highly stressed workers are much less able to regulate negative emotions, resulting from weakened connections between the amygdala, anterior cingulate cortex, and prefrontal cortex (Golkar et al., 2014; Savic, Perski, & Osika, in press). Such structural changes probably underlie episodes of poorer judgment and emotional outbursts seen in highly stressed people.

We know burnout does not affect everyone in a particular profession. Why? Vallerand (2015) proposes the difference relates to people feeling different types of passion (obsessive and harmonious) toward their jobs. *A* **passion** *is a strong inclination toward an activity individuals like (or even love), they value (and thus find important), and where they invest time and energy* (Vallerand, 2015). Vallerand's (2015) Passion Model proposes people develop a passion toward enjoyable activities that are incorporated into identity.

Vallerand's model differentiates between two kinds of passion: obsessive and harmonious. A critical aspect of obsessive passion is the internal urge to engage in the passionate activity makes it difficult for the person to fully disengage from thoughts about the activity, leading to conflict with other activities in the person's life (Vallerand, 2015).

In contrast, harmonious passion results when individuals do not feel compelled to engage in the enjoyable activity; rather, they freely choose to do so, and it is in harmony with other aspects of the person's life (Vallerand, 2015).

Research in France and Canada indicate the Passion Model accurately predicts employees' feelings of burnout (Vallerand, 2008; Vallerand et al., 2010). As shown in Figure 12.2, obsessive passion predicts higher levels of conflict that, in turn, predicts higher levels of burnout. In contrast, harmonious passion predicts higher levels of satisfaction at work and predicts lower levels of burnout.

FIGURE 12.2 Model of the relations among passion, satisfaction at work, conflict, and burnout. Harmonious passion predicts higher levels of satisfaction at work that predict lower levels of burnout. In contrast, obsessive passion predicts higher levels of conflict, predicting higher levels of burnout.

Source: From Vallerand, R. J. et al. On the role of passion for work in burnout: A process model, *Journal of Personality*, 78.

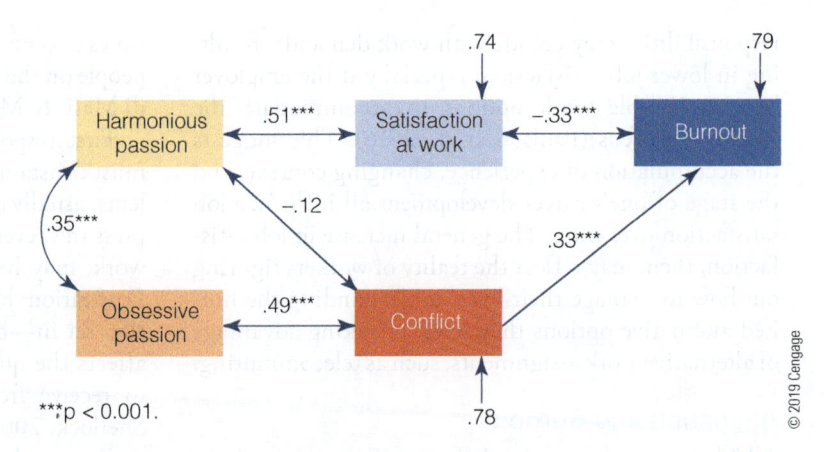

***$p < 0.001$.

The best ways to lower burnout are intervention programs that focus on both the organization and the employee (Awa, Plaumann, & Walter, 2010; Bagnall et al., 2016) and foster passion (Vallerand, 2015). At the organizational level, job restructuring and employee-provided programs are important. For employees, stress-reduction techniques, lowering other people's expectations, cognitive restructuring of the work situation, and finding alternative ways to enhance personal growth and identity are most effective (e.g., Allexandre et al., 2016).

Adult Development in Action

What would be the key aspects of creating an organization that fosters employee commitment and low levels of burnout?

12.2 Gender, Ethnicity, and Discrimination Issues

LEARNING OBJECTIVES

- How do women's and men's occupational selection differ? How are people viewed when they enter occupations not traditional for their gender?
- What factors are related to women's occupational development?
- What factors affect ethnic minority workers' occupational experiences and occupational development?
- What types of bias and discrimination hinder the occupational development of women and ethnic minority workers?

Janice, a 35-year-old African American manager at a business consulting firm, is concerned because her career is not progressing as rapidly as she had hoped. Janice works hard and receives excellent performance ratings every year. She noticed there are few women in upper management positions in her company. Janice wonders whether she will ever be promoted.

Occupational choice and development are not equally available to all, as Janice is experiencing. Gender, ethnicity, and age may create barriers to achieving one's occupational goals. Men and women in similar occupations may nonetheless have different life experiences and probably received different socialization as children and adolescents that made it easier or difficult for them to set their sights on a career. Bias and discrimination also create barriers to occupational success.

Gender Differences in Occupational Selection

About 58% of all women over age 16 in the United States participate in the labor force (down from its peak of 60% in 1999), and they represent roughly 47% of the total workforce (U.S. Department of Labor Women's Bureau, 2016a). Across ethnic groups, African American women participate the most (about 59%) and Latina women the least (about 56%). Compared to other countries, women in the United States tend to be employed at a higher rate (see Figure 12.3 for the U.S. rates). Still, structural barriers remain for women in the United States. Let's take a look at both traditional and nontraditional occupations for women.

What work people do has changed in many ways, not the least in terms of the gender breakdown of workers in specific jobs. A growing number of women work in occupations that have been traditionally male-dominated, such as construction and engineering. The U.S. Department of Labor (2016) categorizes women's nontraditional occupations as those in which women constitute 25% or less of the total number of people employed; the skilled trades (electricians, plumbers,

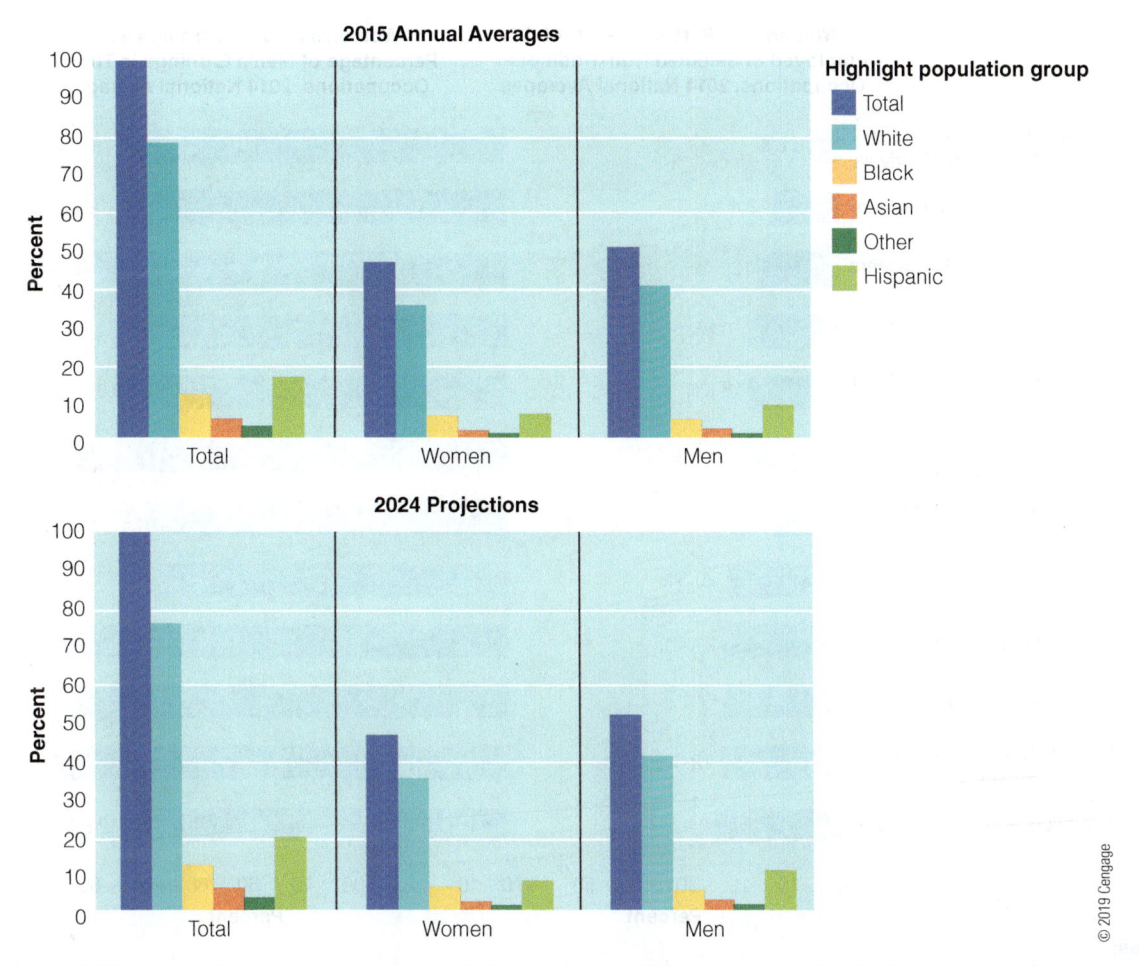

FIGURE 12.3 Labor force participation rate by sex, race, and Hispanic ethnicity: 2015 annual averages and 2024 projections.

Source: U.S. Department of Labor. (2016). *Latest annual data: Women of working age.* Retrieved from www.dol.gov/wb/stats/latest_annual_data.htm.

carpenters) still have among the lowest participation rates of women. Data for several occupations can be seen in Figure 12.4. Note the pay differentials between women and men; we will consider that a bit later.

Despite the efforts to counteract gender stereotyping of occupations, male-dominated occupations tend to pay more than women-dominated occupations (Price, 2016). Although the definition of nontraditional varies across cultures, women who choose nontraditional occupations and are successful in them are viewed negatively as compared with similarly successful men.

In patriarchal societies, both women and men gave higher "respectability" ratings to males than females in the same occupation (Sharma & Sharma, 2012). In the United States, research shows men prefer to date women who are in traditional occupations (Kapoor et al., 2010). Additionally, sexual objectification in the workplace, especially in nontraditional occupations, results in higher sexual harassment and worse work performance (Gervais et al., 2016).

Women and Occupational Development

The characteristics and aspirations of women who entered the workforce in the 1950s and those from the baby boomers (born between 1946 and 1964), Generation X (born between 1965 and 1982), and the millennials (born since 1983) are significantly different (Wegman et al., in press). The biggest difference across generations is the progressive increase in opportunities for employment choice.

In the 21st century, women entrepreneurs are starting small businesses but are disadvantaged in gaining access to capital (McLymont, 2016). As the millennial

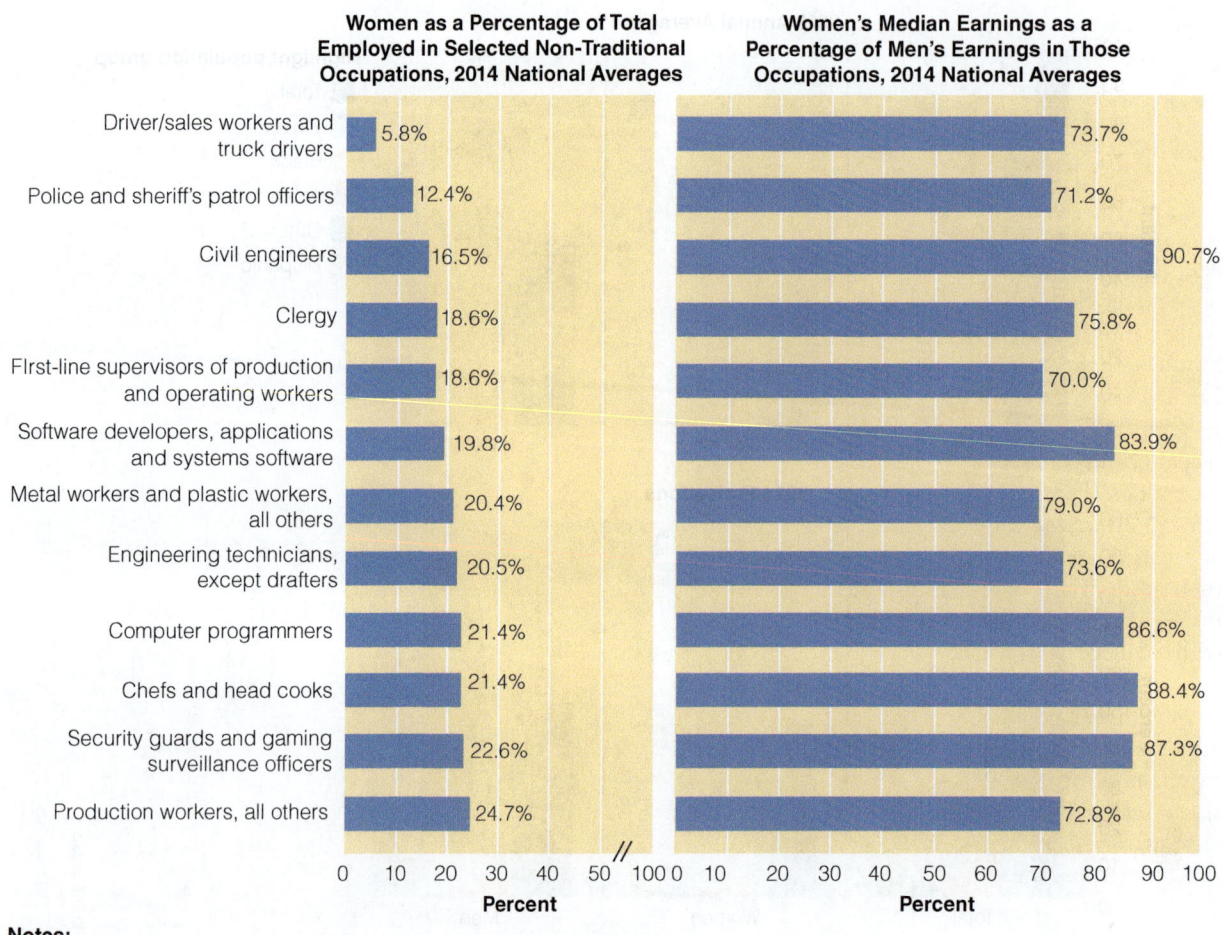

Women as a Percentage of Total Employed in Selected Non-Traditional Occupations, 2014 National Averages

Occupation	%
Driver/sales workers and truck drivers	5.8%
Police and sheriff's patrol officers	12.4%
Civil engineers	16.5%
Clergy	18.6%
First-line supervisors of production and operating workers	18.6%
Software developers, applications and systems software	19.8%
Metal workers and plastic workers, all others	20.4%
Engineering technicians, except drafters	20.5%
Computer programmers	21.4%
Chefs and head cooks	21.4%
Security guards and gaming surveillance officers	22.6%
Production workers, all others	24.7%

Women's Median Earnings as a Percentage of Men's Earnings in Those Occupations, 2014 National Averages

Occupation	%
Driver/sales workers and truck drivers	73.7%
Police and sheriff's patrol officers	71.2%
Civil engineers	90.7%
Clergy	75.8%
First-line supervisors of production and operating workers	70.0%
Software developers, applications and systems software	83.9%
Metal workers and plastic workers, all others	79.0%
Engineering technicians, except drafters	73.6%
Computer programmers	86.6%
Chefs and head cooks	88.4%
Security guards and gaming surveillance officers	87.3%
Production workers, all others	72.8%

Notes:
- Nontraditional or male-dominated occupations are those in which women represent 25 percent or less of total employed. Occupations include those with a sample size of at least 50,000 people employed.
- Median weekly earnings are 2014 annual averages based on full-time wage and salary workers only. http://www.bls.gov/cps/cpsaat39.htm

FIGURE 12.4 Women's nontraditional occupations and median weekly earnings, 2014 annual averages.
Source: Retrieved from www.dol.gov/wb/stats/Nontraditional%20Occupations.pdf.

generation heads into the workforce, it will be interesting to see whether their high degree of technological sophistication and broader experience and background in entrepreneurship will provide more occupational and career options (Wegman et al., in press).

In the corporate world, unsupportive or insensitive work environments, organizational politics, and the lack of occupational development opportunities are most important for women working full-time. Greater empowerment of women is an essential element in ensuring occupational development and remaining in their jobs (Cornwall, 2016). Female professionals leave their jobs for two main reasons. First, the organizations where women work are felt to idealize and reward masculine values of working—individuality, self-sufficiency, and individual contributions—while emphasizing tangible outputs, competitiveness, and rationality. Most women prefer organizations that highly value relationships, interdependence, and collaboration.

Second, women may feel disconnected from the workplace. By midcareer, women may conclude they must leave these unsupportive organizations in order to achieve satisfaction, growth, and development at work and rewarded for the relational skills they consider essential for success. As we see a bit later, whether women leave their careers or plateau before reaching their maximum potential level in the organization because of lack of support, discrimination, or personal choice is controversial.

Ethnicity and Occupational Development

Unfortunately, little research has been conducted from a developmental perspective related to occupational selection and development for people from ethnic minorities. Rather, most researchers focused on the limited opportunities ethnic minorities have and on the structural barriers, such as discrimination, they face.

Women do not differ significantly in terms of participation in nontraditional occupations across ethnic groups (Hegewisch & Hartman, 2014). However, African American women who choose nontraditional occupations tend to plan for more formal education than necessary to achieve their goal. This may actually make them overqualified for the jobs they get; a woman with a college degree may be working in a job that does not require that level of education.

Whether an organization is responsive to the needs of ethnic minorities makes a big difference for employees. Ethnic minority employees of a diverse organization in the several countries report more positive feelings about their workplace when they perceived their organizations as responsive and communicative in supportive and transparent ways (Boehm et al., 2014; Hofhuis, van der Rijt, & Vlug, 2016).

Bias and Discrimination

Since the 1960s, numerous laws have been enacted in the United States to prohibit various types of bias and discrimination in the workplace. Despite antidiscrimination laws, though, bias and discrimination still occur far too frequently. Let's consider some of the most common forms.

Gender Bias and the Glass Ceiling

More than half of all people employed in management, professional, and related occupations are women (U.S. Department of Labor Women's Bureau, 2016a). However, women are still underrepresented at the top. Janice's observation in the vignette that few women serve in the highest ranks of major corporations is accurate.

Why are there so few women in such positions? *The most important reason is* **gender discrimination**: *denying a job to someone solely on the basis of whether the person is a man or a woman*. Gender discrimination is still pervasive and gets worse the higher up the corporate ladder one looks (LeanIn.org, 2016).

Women themselves refer to a **glass ceiling**, *the level they may rise within an organization but beyond which they may not go*. The glass ceiling is a major barrier for women (LeanIn.org, 2016), and one of the most important sources of loss of women leaders (Heppner, 2013). Men are largely blind to the existence of the glass ceiling.

The glass ceiling is pervasive across higher management and professional workplace settings (Heppner, 2013; LeanIn.org, 2016). Despite decades of attention to the issue, little overall progress is being made in the number of women who lead major corporations or serve on their boards of directors (Cundiff & Stockdale, 2013; LeanIn.org, 2016). The glass ceiling has also been used to account for African American men's and Asian American men's lack of advancement in their careers as opposed to European American men (Cundiff & Stockdale, 2013; Hwang, 2007). It also provides a framework for understanding limitations to women's careers in many countries around the world such as South Africa (Kiaye & Singh, 2013).

Interestingly, a different trend emerges if one examines who is appointed to critical positions in organizations in times of crisis. Research shows that women are more likely put in leadership positions when a company is in crisis. *Consequently, women often confront a* **glass cliff** *where their leadership position is precarious*. Evidence shows companies are more likely to appoint a woman to their board of directors if their financial performance had been poor in the recent past, and women are more likely to be political candidates if the seat is a highly contested one (Ryan, Haslam, & Kulich, 2010; Ryan et al., 2016).

What can be done to eliminate the glass ceiling and the glass cliff? Kolb, Williams, and Frohlinger (2010) argue women can and must be assertive in getting their rightful place at the table by focusing on five key things: drilling deep into the organization so you can make informed decisions, getting critical support, getting the necessary resources, getting buy-in, and making a difference.

Much debate has erupted over the issue of women rising to the top. There is no doubt the glass ceiling and glass cliff exist. The controversy surrounds the extent women decide not to pursue or reluctance to pursue the top positions. As discussed in the Current Controversies feature, this debate is likely to rage for years.

CURRENT CONTROVERSIES
Helping Women Lean In?

Sheryl Sandberg is unquestionably successful. She has held the most important, powerful positions in the most recognizable technology companies in the world. When she published her book *Lean In: Women, Work, and the Will to Lead* in 2013, she set off a fierce debate. Sandberg claimed there is discrimination against women in the corporate world. She also argued an important reason women do not rise to the top more often is because of their own unintentional behavior that holds them back. She claimed women do not speak up enough, need to abandon the myth of "having it all," set boundaries, get a mentor, and not to "check out of work" when thinking about starting a family.

The national debate around these issues raised many issues: Sandberg's ability to afford to pay for support may make her points irrelevant for women who do not have those resources; she was "blaming the victim"; no one ever puts men in these situations of having to choose; and so on. When her husband died unexpectedly in 2015, she reassessed some of her arguments and acknowledged her privileged position. Still, she pushed hard on the issue of gender discrimination in the workplace, and founded LeanIn.org, an organization dedicated to helping women advance in their careers and to educate all in the overt and subtle ways gender discrimination operates.

Through LeanIn.org, Sheryl has also focused on documenting the problems and highlighting best practices in stopping gender discrimination. The report *Women in the Workplace 2016* provided rich data on numerous aspects of the problem.

Sheryl Sandberg has made gender discrimination an important focus of her life. She, and many others, are convinced that limits on women's careers will never be eliminated without a focused effort on everyone's part. Can gender discrimination be eliminated? Will women eventually be welcomed into every occupation? What do *you* think?

Equal Pay for Equal Work

In addition to discrimination in hiring and promotion, women are also subject to salary discrimination. According to the National Women's Law Center (2016), 98% of all occupations show a gender-based wage gap. Overall, the U.S. Department of Labor Women's Bureau (2016b) notes that women who work full-time earn about 79% of men's median annual earnings. As you can see in Figure 12.5, the wage gap depends on ethnicity and has been narrowing since the 1980s.

Many people have argued that there are legitimate reasons for the wage gap, such as women stepping out of their careers to raise children, or their taking lower-paying jobs in the first place. However, evidence of discrimination is apparent; for instance, research indicates that average earnings for individuals who undergo gender reassignment from male to female fall by about one-third (National Women's Law Center, 2016).

The Social Policy Implications feature at the end of the chapter discusses equal pay for equal work in more detail. In general, although few people disagree with the principle, eliminating the salary disparity between men and women has proven more difficult than many originally believed.

Sexual Harassment

Suppose you have been working hard on a paper for a course and think you've done a good job. When you receive an A for the paper, you are elated. When you discuss your paper (and your excitement) with your instructor, you receive a big hug. How do you feel? What if this situation involved a major project at work and the hug came from your boss? Your coworker? What if it were a kiss on your lips instead of a hug?

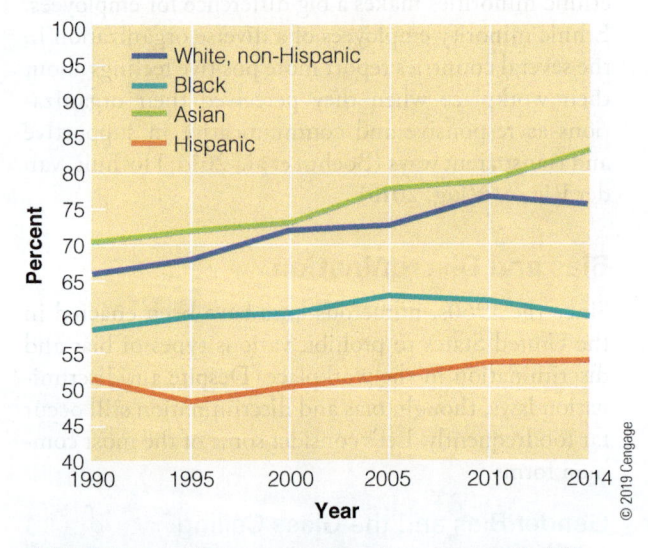

FIGURE 12.5 Women's earnings by race and ethnicity as a percentage of white, non-Hispanic men's earnings, March 1987–2014.

Source: Retrieved from www.dol.gov/wb/stats/earnings_race_ethnic_percent_white_nonhisp_mens_earn_87_14_txt.htm.

Whether such behavior is acceptable, or whether it constitutes sexual harassment, depends on many situational factors, including the setting, people involved, and the relationship between them.

How many people have been sexually harassed? That's a hard question to answer for several reasons: there is no universal definition of harassment, men and women have different perceptions, and many victims do not report it (Equal Employment Opportunity Commission, 2016a). Even given these difficulties, global research indicates between 40 and 50% of women in the European Union, and 30 to 40% of women in Asia-Pacific countries experience workplace sexual harassment (International Labour Organization, 2013). Complaints are filed most often by women, but about 17% of workplace cases are filed by men (Equal Employment Opportunity Commission, 2016b). Although the number of formal complaints in the United States is declining, it is unclear whether this is because of increased sensitivity and training by employers, reluctance of victims to report for fear of losing their jobs during economically difficult times, or both.

What are the effects of being sexually harassed? As you might expect, research evidence clearly shows negative job-related, psychological, and physical health outcomes (Holland & Cortina, 2016). These outcomes can affect people for many years after the harassment incident(s).

What can be done to provide people with safe work and learning environments, free from sexual harassment? Training in gender awareness is a common approach that often works, especially given that gender differences exist in perceptions of behavior. However, even very high profile cases of sexual harassment, such as those involving famous people (e.g., Bill Cosby) or well-known companies (e.g., Fox News) show that much remains to be done to eradicate sexual harassment.

Age Discrimination

Another structural barrier to occupational development is **age discrimination**, *that involves denying a job or promotion to someone solely on the basis of age.* The U.S. Age Discrimination in Employment Act of 1986 protects workers over age 40. A law that brought together all of the antidiscrimination legislation in the United Kingdom, the Equality Act of 2010 includes a prohibition against age discrimination, and more European countries are protecting middle-aged and older workers (Equality and Human Rights Commission, 2016; Lahey, 2010). These laws stipulate people must be hired based on their ability, not their age, and employers cannot segregate or classify workers or otherwise denote their status on the basis of age.

Employment prospects for middle-aged people around the world are lower than for their younger counterparts (Lahey, 2010; Vansteenkiste, Deschacht, & Sels, 2015). Age discrimination toward those over age 45 is common in Hong Kong (Cheung, Kam, & Ngan, 2011), resulting in longer periods of unemployment, early retirement, or negative attitudes.

Age discrimination is difficult to document, because employers can use such things as earnings history or other variable appear to be a deciding factor. Or they can attempt to get rid of older workers by using retirement incentives. Or supervisors can let their stereotypes about aging interfere with their assessment of the quality of older workers' performance. As noted by the Equal Employment Opportunity Commission (2016c), treating an older worker less favorably because of her or his age is illegal.

Adult Development in Action

What are the key factors that interfere with people's ability to create and manage their own careers?

12.3 Occupational Transitions

LEARNING OBJECTIVES
- Why do people change occupations?
- Is worrying about potential job loss a major source of stress?
- How does job loss affect the amount of stress experienced?

Fred has 32 years of service for an automobile manufacturer making pickup trucks. Over the years, more and more assembly-line jobs have been eliminated by new technology (including robots) and the export of manufacturing jobs to other countries. Although Fred has been assured his job is safe, he isn't so sure. He worries he could be laid off at any time.

In the past, people like Fred commonly chose an occupation during young adulthood and stayed in it throughout their working years. Today, however, not many people have that option. Corporations have restructured so often employees now assume occupational changes are part of the career process. Such corporate actions mean people's conceptions of work and career are in flux and losing one's job no longer has only negative meanings (Biggs et al., in press; Haworth & Lewis, 2005).

Several factors have been identified as important in determining who will remain in an occupation and who will change. Some factors—such as whether the person likes the occupation—lead to self-initiated occupation changes.

However, other factors—such as obsolete skills and larger economic trends—may cause forced occupational changes. Continued improvement of robots has caused some auto industry workers to lose their jobs; corporations send jobs overseas to increase profits; and economic recessions usually result in large-scale layoffs and high levels of unemployment.

Retraining Workers

When you are hired into a specific job, you are selected because your employer believes you offer the best fit between the abilities you already have and those needed to perform the job. As most people can attest, though, the skills needed to perform a job usually change over time. Such changes may be based in the introduction of new technology, additional responsibilities, or promotion.

Unless a person's skills are kept up-to-date, the outcome is likely to be either job loss or a career plateau (da Costa & Oliveira, 2016; Jiang, 2016). **Career plateauing** *occurs when there is a lack of challenge in one's job or promotional opportunity in the organization or when a person decides not to seek advancement.* Research in Canada (Foster, Lonial, & Shastri, 2011), Asia (Lee, 2003), and Australia (Rose & Gordon, 2010) shows feeling one's career has plateaued usually results in less organizational commitment, lower job satisfaction, and a greater tendency to leave. But attitudes can remain positive if it is only the lack of challenge and not a lack of promotion opportunity responsible for the plateauing (da Costa & Oliveira, 2016; Jiang, 2016).

In cases of job loss or a career plateau, retraining may be an appropriate response. Around the world, large numbers of employees participate each year in programs and courses offered by their employer or by a college or university and aimed at improving existing skills or adding new job skills. For midcareer employees, retraining might focus on how to advance in one's occupation or how to find new career opportunities—for example, through résumé preparation and career counseling. Increasingly, such programs are offered online to make them easier and more convenient for people to access. For people who were involuntarily separated from their employer, severance packages may provide a way to pay for these courses.

Alternatively, mid-career individuals may choose to change fields altogether. In this case, people may head back to college and earn a credential in a completely different field. Increasingly, middle-aged adults are seeking coaches to help them navigate through the decision to change careers (Stoltz, 2016).

The retraining of midcareer and older workers highlights the need for lifelong learning as a way to stay employable (Froehlich, Beausaert, & Segers, 2016). If corporations are to meet the challenges of a global economy, it is imperative they include retraining in their employee development programs. Such programs will improve people's chances of advancement in their chosen occupations and also assist people in making successful transitions from one occupation to another.

Occupational Insecurity

Over the past few decades, changing economic realities (e.g., increased competition in a global economy), changing demographics, continued advancements in technology, and a global recession forced many people out of their jobs. Heavy manufacturing and support businesses (such as the steel, oil, and automotive industries) and farming were the hardest-hit sectors during the 1970s and 1980s. The service sector (e.g., financial services) were hard hit during the Great Recession. No one is immune any more from layoff. The Great Recession that began in 2008 put many middle- and upper-level corporate executives out of work worldwide; previously, recession-driven layoffs hit lower-level employees harder.

As a result, many people feel insecure about their jobs much of the time. Economic downturns create significant levels of stress, especially when such downturns create massive job loss (Sinclair et al., 2010). Continued shifts from in-person retail to online retail result in nearly constant retrenchment in retail jobs. The advent of driverless cars even threatens the jobs of taxi, Uber, and Lyft drivers.

Like Fred, the autoworker in the vignette, many worried workers have numerous years of dedicated service to a company. Unfortunately, people who worry about their jobs tend to have poorer physical and psychological well-being (Gonza & Burger, in press; McKee-Ryan et al., 2005). Anxiety about one's job may result in negative attitudes about one's employer or even about work in general, and in turn may result in diminished desire to be successful. Whether there is an actual basis for people's feelings of job insecurity may not matter; sometimes what people *think* is true about their work situation is more important than what is actually the case. Just the possibility of losing one's job can negatively affect physical and psychological health.

So how does the possibility of losing one's job affect employees? Mantler and colleagues (2005) examined coping strategies for comparable samples of laid-off and employed high-technology workers. They found although unemployed participants reported higher levels of stress compared with employed participants, employment uncertainty mediated the association between employment status and perceived stress. That is, people who believe their job is in jeopardy—even if it is not—show levels of stress similar to unemployed participants.

This result is due to differences in coping strategies (see Chapter 4). There are several ways people deal with stress, and two of the more common are emotion-focused coping and problem-focused coping. Some people focus on how the stressful situation makes them feel, so they cope by making themselves feel better about it. Others focus on the problem itself and do something to solve it. People who used emotional avoidance as a strategy reported higher levels of stress, particularly when they were fairly certain of the outcome. Thus, even people whose jobs aren't really in jeopardy can report high levels of stress if they tend to use emotion-focused coping strategies.

Coping with Unemployment

Losing one's job can have enormous personal impact that can last a long time (Gonza & Burger, in press; McKee-Ryan et al., 2005; Norris, 2016). When the overall U.S. unemployment rates hit 10.6% in January 2010, millions of people could relate. Years later, the psychological impact remained (Gonza & Burger, in press), even for people who found other jobs. When unemployment lasts and reemployment does not occur soon, unemployed people commonly experience a wide variety of negative effects (Norris, 2016) that range from a decline in immune system functioning (Cohen et al., 2007) to decreases in well-being (Gonza & Burger, in press).

Coping with unemployment involves both financial and personal issues. As noted in the Discovering Development feature, the financial support people receive varies across states and situations. Unemployment compensation is typically much lower than one's original salary, often resulting in severe financial hardship and difficult choices for individuals. People risk losing their homes to foreclosure, for instance, as well as encountering difficulties with other everyday expenses.

DISCOVERING DEVELOPMENT
What Unemployment Benefits Are Available in Your Area?

When a person loses his or her job, there may be certain benefits available. Some of these are financial, such as weekly or monthly funds. Other benefits may be educational, such as job skills retraining. Find out what the range of benefits are in your area from government and private organization sources. See what programs are available at your local colleges and universities to help people who have lost their jobs. Pay special attention to the length of time benefits last, whether the amount of the benefit changes over time, and whether job retraining programs are required in order to collect benefits, and whether they are free or have tuition attached to them. Then compile the list and discuss it in class.

As part of your analysis, compute a budget for a family based on the projected unemployment benefit. Compute how long the typical family would be able to pay their bills.

Based on your analyses, what policy recommendations would you make regarding unemployment benefits?

In a comprehensive study of the effects of unemployment, McKee-Ryan and colleagues (2005) found several specific results from losing one's job. Unemployed workers had significantly lower mental health, life satisfaction, marital or family satisfaction, and subjective physical health (how they perceive their health to be) than their employed counterparts. With reemployment, these negative effects disappear. Figure 12.6 shows physical and psychological health following job displacement is influenced by several factors (McKee-Ryan et al., 2005).

The effects of job loss vary with age, gender, and education (Norris, 2016). In the United States, middle-aged men are more vulnerable to negative effects than older or younger men—largely because they have greater financial responsibilities than the other two groups and they derive more of their identity from work—but women report more negative effects over time (Bambra, 2010; Norris, 2016). Research in Spain indicates gender differences in responding to job loss are complexly related to family responsibilities and social class (Artazcoz et al., 2004). Specifically, to the extent work is viewed as your expected contribution to the family, losing one's job has a more substantial negative effect. Because this tends to be more the case for men than for women, it helps explain the gender differences. The higher one's education levels, the less stress one typically feels immediately after losing a job, probably because higher education level usually results in faster re-employment (Mandemakers & Monden, 2013).

Because unemployment rates are substantially higher for African Americans and Latinos than for European Americans (Bureau of Labor Statistics, 2016a), the effects of unemployment are experienced by a greater proportion of people in these groups. Economic consequences of unemployment are often especially difficult. Compared to European Americans, it usually takes minority workers significantly longer to find another job.

How long you are unemployed also affects how people react. People who are unemployed for at least a year perceive their mental health significantly more negatively than either employed people or those who have removed themselves from the labor force (e.g., have stopped looking for work). For example, suicide risk increases the longer unemployment lasts (Gunnell & Chang, 2016). Those who lost their jobs involuntarily feel a loss of control over their "work" environment and feel less demand placed on them. Importantly, a reasonable amount of "demand" is critical to maintaining good health, whereas too little demand lowers health.

Research also offers some advice for adults who are trying to manage occupational transitions (Ebberwein, 2001):

- Approach job loss with a healthy sense of urgency.
- Consider your next career move and what you must do to achieve it, even if there are no prospects for it in sight.
- Acknowledge and react to change as soon as it is evident.
- Be cautious of stopgap employment.
- Identify a realistic goal and then list the steps you must take to achieve it.

Additionally, the U.S. Department of Labor offers tips for job seekers, as do online services such as LinkedIn that also provides networking groups. These steps may not guarantee you will find a new job quickly, but they will help create a better sense that you are in control.

Adult Development in Action

How could the effects of losing a job be reduced?

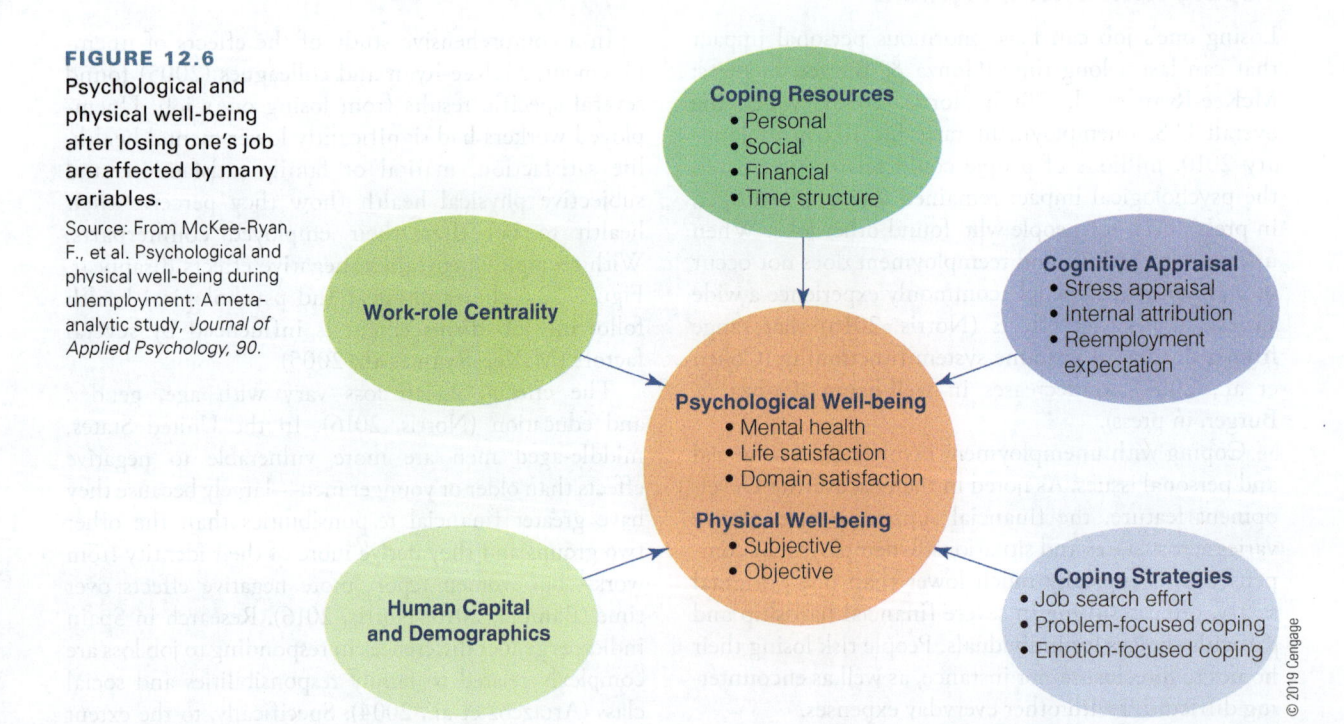

FIGURE 12.6
Psychological and physical well-being after losing one's job are affected by many variables.

Source: From McKee-Ryan, F., et al. Psychological and physical well-being during unemployment: A meta-analytic study, *Journal of Applied Psychology, 90.*

Coping Resources
- Personal
- Social
- Financial
- Time structure

Work-role Centrality

Human Capital and Demographics

Psychological Well-being
- Mental health
- Life satisfaction
- Domain satisfaction

Physical Well-being
- Subjective
- Objective

Cognitive Appraisal
- Stress appraisal
- Internal attribution
- Reemployment expectation

Coping Strategies
- Job search effort
- Problem-focused coping
- Emotion-focused coping

12.4 Work and Family

LEARNING OBJECTIVES

- What are the issues faced by employed people who care for dependents?
- How do partners view the division of household chores? What is work–family conflict, and how does it affect couples' lives?

Jennifer, a 38-year-old sales clerk at a department store, feels her husband, Bill, doesn't do his share of the housework or child care. Bill says real men don't do housework and he's really tired when he comes home from work. Jennifer thinks this isn't fair, especially because she works as many hours as her husband.

One of the most difficult challenges facing adults like Jennifer is trying to balance the demands of occupation with the demands of family. Over the past few decades, the rapid increase in the number of families where both parents are employed has fundamentally changed how we view the relationship between work and family. This can even mean taking a young child to work as a way to deal with the pushes and pulls of being an employed parent. In roughly half of married-couple families, both spouses are employed (Bureau of Labor Statistics, 2016b). Why? Families need the dual income to pay their bills and maintain a moderate standard of living, especially given the relatively flat incomes since the Great Recession.

We will see dual-earner couples with children experience both benefits and disadvantages. The stresses of living in this arrangement are substantial, and gender differences are clear—especially in the division of household chores.

The Dependent Care Dilemma

Many employed adults must also provide care for dependent children or parents. Deciding how to divide the chores is a major source of stress, as we will see.

Employed Caregivers

Many mothers have no option but to return to work after the birth of a child. In fact, about 64% of mothers with children under the age of 6 years, and roughly 75% of those with children between 6 and 17 years old are in the labor force (Bureau of Labor Statistics, 2016c).

Despite high participation rates, mothers grapple with the decision of whether they want to return to work. Surveys of mothers with preschool children reveal the motivation for returning to work tends to be related to financial need and how attached mothers are to their work. The amount of leave time a woman has matters; the passage of the Family and Medical Leave Act (FMLA) in 1993 entitled workers to take unpaid time off to care for their dependents with the right to return to their jobs. (It should be noted that the United States is the only developed country in the world that does not have a national mandatory paid family leave benefit.)

FMLA resulted in an increase in the number of women who returned to work at least part-time (Schott, 2010). Evidence from the few states with paid family leave show similar trends; for instance, mothers in California who take paid leave extend their time off roughly five weeks longer, and show more work hours during the second year of the child's life (Baum & Ruhm, 2016).

A concern for many women is whether stepping out of their occupations following childbirth will negatively affect their career paths. Indeed, evidence clearly indicates it does (Evertsson, Grunow, & Aisenbrey 2016; LeanIn.org, 2016). Women in the United States are punished, even for short leaves. In women-friendly countries such as Sweden, long leaves typically result in a negative effect on upward career movement, but with shorter leaves in Sweden and Germany no negative effects are observed. These universally negative impacts need to be taken into account as more U.S. states consider implementing paid family leave programs.

Often overlooked is the increasing number of workers who must also care for an aging parent or partner. As we saw in Chapter 11, providing this type of care takes a high toll through stress and has a generally negative impact on one's career.

Whether assistance is needed for one's children or parents, key factors in selecting an appropriate care site are quality of care, price, and hours of availability (Helpguide.org, 2016; National Association for the Education of Young Children, 2016). Depending on one's economic situation, it may not be possible to find affordable and quality care available when needed. In such cases, there may be no option but to drop out of the workforce or enlist the help of friends and family.

Dependent Care and Effects on Workers

Being responsible for dependent care has significant negative effects on caregivers. Whether responsible for the care of an older parent or a child, women and men report negative effects on their work, higher levels of stress, and problems with coping (Neal & Hammer, 2007). Roxburgh (2002) introduced the notion that parents of families dealing with time pressures feel much more stress; indeed, subsequent research clearly shows not only are stress levels higher, but "fast-forward families" also often deal with negative impacts on career advancement and physical and mental health consequences of this lifestyle (Ochs & Kremer-Sadlik, 2013). Unsurprisingly, women's careers are usually affected more negatively than men's.

How can these negative effects be lessened? When women's partners provide good support and women have average or high control over their jobs, employed mothers are significantly less distressed than employed nonmothers or mothers without support (Cram, Alkadry, & Tower, 2016). One of the most important factors in this outcome is the realization that it is impossible to "have it all" for either mothers or fathers (Cram et al., 2016; LeanIn.org, 2016).

Dependent Care and Employer Responses

Employed parents with small children or dependent spouses/partners or parents are confronted with the difficult prospect of leaving them in the care of others. This is especially problematic when the usual care arrangement is unavailable, such as due to weather-related closures of the care facility. *A growing need in the workplace is for* **backup care**, *that provides emergency care for dependent children or adults so the employee does not need to lose a day of work.* Does providing a workplace care center or backup care make a difference in terms of an employee's feelings about work, absenteeism, and productivity?

There is no simple answer. Making a childcare center available to employees does tend to reduce employee stress, but that does not necessarily reduce parents' work–family conflict or their absenteeism (Hipp, Morrissey, & Warner, in press). A "family-friendly" company must also pay attention to the attitudes of their employees and make sure the company provides broad-based support (Aryee et al., 2013; Hill et al., 2016). The keys are how supervisors act and the number and type of benefits the company provides. Cross-cultural research in Korea confirms having a family-friendly supervisor matters (Aryee et al., 2013). The most important single thing a company can do is allow the employee to leave work without penalty to tend to family needs (Lawton & Tulkin, 2010).

Research also indicates there may not be differences for either mothers or their infants between work-based and nonwork-based childcare centers in terms of the mothers' ease in transitioning back to work or the infants' ability to settle into day care (Hill et al., 2016; Hipp et al., 2016; Skouteris McNaught, & Dissanayake, 2007).

It will be interesting to watch how these issues—especially flexible schedules—play out in the United States, where such practices are not yet common. A global study of parental leave showed that the more generous the parental leave policies are, the lower the infant mortality rates would fall, clearly indicating parental leave policies are a good thing (Ferrarini & Norström, 2010).

Juggling Multiple Roles

When both members of a heterosexual couple with dependents are employed, who cleans the house, cooks the meals, and takes care of the children when they are ill? This question goes to the heart of the core dilemma of modern, dual-earner couples: How are household chores divided? How are work and family role conflicts handled?

Dividing Household Chores

Despite much media attention and claims of increased sharing in the duties, women still perform the lion's share of housework, regardless of employment status. As shown in Figure 12.7, this is true globally (OECD, 2016). This unequal division of labor causes the most arguments and the most unhappiness for dual-earner couples. This is the case with Jennifer and Bill, the couple in the vignette; Jennifer does most of the housework.

The additional burden women carry with respect to household chores, including child rearing, is still reflected in millennials, despite their endorsement of more gender-equal views on the matter. It appears that deeply held cultural beliefs about gender-based divisions of labor are difficult to change. There are indications, though, that change may be happening, slowly. The gap between women's and men's time spent on household chores and child rearing is narrowing.

Ethnic differences in the division of household labor are also apparent. In Mexican American families with husbands born in Mexico, men help more when family income is lower and their wives contribute a proportionately higher share of the household income (Pinto & Coltrane, 2009). Comparisons of Latino, African American, and European American men consistently show European American men help with the chores less than Latino or African American men (Omori & Smith, 2009).

12.4 Work and Family   357

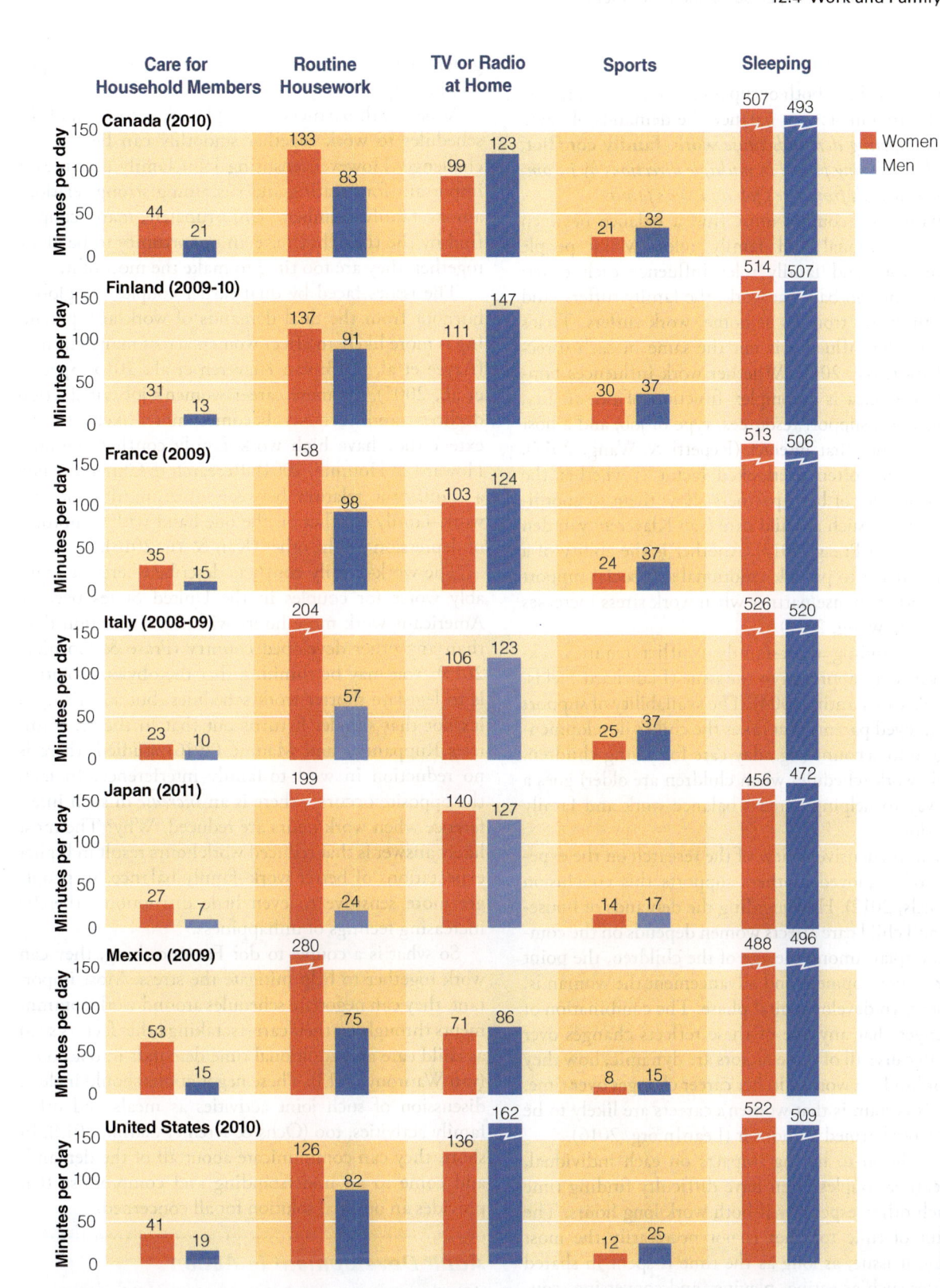

	Care for Household Members	Routine Housework	TV or Radio at Home	Sports	Sleeping
Canada (2010)	W 44, M 21	W 133, M 83	W 99, M 123	W 21, M 32	W 507, M 493
Finland (2009-10)	W 31, M 13	W 137, M 91	W 111, M 147	W 30, M 37	W 514, M 507
France (2009)	W 35, M 15	W 158, M 98	W 103, M 124	W 24, M 37	W 513, M 506
Italy (2008-09)	W 23, M 10	W 204, M 57	W 106, M 123	W 25, M 37	W 526, M 520
Japan (2011)	W 27, M 7	W 199, M 24	W 140, M 127	W 14, M 17	W 456, M 472
Mexico (2009)	W 53, M 15	W 280, M 75	W 71, M 86	W 8, M 15	W 488, M 496
United States (2010)	W 41, M 19	W 126, M 82	W 136, M 162	W 12, M 25	W 522, M 509

FIGURE 12.7 Time spent in unpaid work and leisure (minutes per day).

Source: OECD. (2016). *Balancing paid work, unpaid work and leisure.* Retrieved from www.oecd.org/gender/data/balancingpaidworkunpaidworkandleisure.htm.

Work–Family Conflict

When people have both occupations and children, they must figure out how to balance the demands of each. *These competing demands cause* **work–family conflict**, *the feeling of being pulled in multiple directions by incompatible demands from one's job and one's family.*

Dual-earner couples must find a balance between their occupational and family roles. Many people believe work and family roles influence each other: When things go badly at work, the family suffers, and when there are troubles at home, work suffers. That's true, but the influence is not the same in each direction (Andreassi, 2011). Whether work influences family or vice versa is a complex function of personality, coping skills, support resources, type of job, and a host of other issues that interact (Repetti & Wang, 2017). One key but often overlooked factor is whether the work schedules of both partners allow them to coordinate activities such as child care (van Klaveren, van den Brink, & van Praag, 2013). Another is the ability of a spouse/partner to provide emotional and social support for the other spouse/partner when work stress increases (Repetti & Wang, 2017).

Understanding work–family conflict requires taking a life-stage approach to the issue (Blanchard-Fields, Baldi, & Constantin, 2004). The availability of support for employed parents that takes the child's developmental age into account (e.g., day care for young children, flexible work schedules when children are older) goes a long way to helping parents balance work and family obligations.

A comprehensive review of the research on the experience of employed mothers supports this conclusion (Edwards, 2012). How juggling the demands of housework and child care affects women depends on the complex interplay among the age of the children, the point in career development and advancement the woman is, and her own developmental phase. The combination of challenges that any one of these reflects changes over time. Because all of these factors are dynamic, how they help or hinder a woman in her career changes over time. What is certain is that women's careers are likely to be irreparably harmed without it (LeanIn.org, 2016).

In addition to having impacts on each individual, dual-earner couples often have difficulty finding time for each other, especially if both work long hours. The amount of time together is not necessarily the most important issue; as long as the time is spent in shared activities such as eating, playing, and conversing, couples tend to be happy (Ochs & Kremer-Sadlik, 2013). Actively soliciting support from one's spouse/partner generally brings results that, in turn, result in happier relationships (Wang & Repetti, 2016).

When both partners are employed, getting all of the schedules to work together smoothly can be a major challenge. However, ensuring joint family activities is important for creating and sustaining strong relations among family members. Unfortunately, many couples find by the time they have an opportunity to be alone together, they are too tired to make the most of it.

The issues faced by dual-earner couples are global: burnout from the dual demands of work and parenting is more likely to affect women across many cultures (Aryee et al, 2013; van Klaveren et al., 2013; Spector et al., 2005). Japanese career women's job satisfaction declines, and turnover becomes more likely, to the extent they have high work–family conflict (Honda-Howard & Homma, 2001). Research in China revealed a significant relation between overcommitment and work–family conflict on the one hand with symptoms of depression on the other (Kan & Yu, 2016).

The work–family conflicts described here are arguably worse for couples in the United States because Americans work more hours with fewer vacation days than any other developed country (Frase & Gornick, 2013). You may be thinking that the obvious solution is to legislate shorter work schedules, but surprisingly, it's not that simple. It turns out that in the 32 countries Ruppanner and Maume (2016) studied, there is no reduction in work-to-family interference. In fact, the opposite occurs—there is an *increase* in such interference when work hours are reduced. Why? The most likely answer is that reduced work hours result in higher expectations of better work–family balance, so people get more sensitive to even little disruptions, thereby increasing feelings of unhappiness.

So what is a couple to do? For one thing, they can work together to help mitigate the stress. Most important, they can negotiate schedules around work commitments throughout their careers, taking other factors such as child care and additional time demands into account (van Wanrooy, 2013). These negotiations should include discussion of such joint activities as meals and other family activities, too (Ochs & Kremer-Sadlik, 2013). In short, they can communicate about all of the demands and come to an understanding and compromise that provides an optimal solution for all concerned.

Adult Development in Action

What are the stresses and ways to deal with stress facing dual-earner couples?

12.5 Leisure Activities

LEARNING OBJECTIVES

- What activities are leisure activities? How do people choose among them?
- What changes in leisure activities occur with age?
- What do people derive from leisure activities?

Claude is a 55-year-old electrician who has enjoyed outdoor activities his whole life. From the time he was a boy he fished the trout rivers and snow-skied in the mountains of Montana. Although he doesn't ski double black diamond runs any more, Claude still enjoys both sports every chance he gets.

Adults do not work every waking moment of their lives. As each of us knows, we need to disconnect from our smartphones, relax, and engage in leisure activities. Intuitively, leisure consists of activities not associated with work. **Leisure** *is discretionary activity that includes simple relaxation, activities for enjoyment, and creative pursuits.* Simply finding the time to fit leisure into an already busy schedule can be challenging. For too many people, leisure just becomes another scheduled component in our overall time management problem (Corbett & Hilty, 2006).

Types of Leisure Activities

Leisure can include virtually any activity. To organize the options, researchers classified leisure activities into several categories. Jopp and Hertzog (2010) developed an empirically based set of categories that includes a wide variety of activities: physical (e.g., lifting weights, backpacking, jogging), crafts (e.g., woodworking, household repairs), games (e.g., board/online games, puzzles, card games), watching TV, social-private (e.g., going out with a friend, visiting relatives, going out to dinner), social-public (e.g., attending a club meeting, volunteering), religious (e.g., attending a religious service, praying), travel (e.g., travel abroad, travel out of town), experiential (e.g., collect stamps, read for leisure, gardening, knitting), developmental (e.g., read as part of a job, study a foreign language, attend public lecture), and technology use (e.g., photography, use computer software, play an instrument).

More complete measures of leisure activities not only provide better understanding of how adults spend their time, but can help in clinical settings. Declines in the frequency of leisure activities is associated with depression (Schwerdtfeger & Friedrich-Mei, 2009), with lower well-being (Paggi, Jopp, & Hertzog, 2016), and with a later diagnosis of dementia (Hertzog et al., 2009). Monitoring changes in leisure activity levels during and after intervention programs can provide better outcomes assessments.

Given the wide range of options, how do people pick their leisure activities? Apparently, each of us has a leisure repertoire, a personal library of intrinsically motivated activities we do regularly and we take with us into retirement (Nimrod, 2007a, b). The activities in our repertoire are determined by two things: perceived competence (how good we think we are at the activity compared to other people our age) and psychological comfort (how well we meet our personal goals for performance). As you might expect, men and women differ in their views of leisure, as do people in different ethnic and age groups (van der Pas & Koopman-Boyden, 2010).

Personality factors are related to one's choice of leisure activities (Gaudron & Vautier, 2007), and it is possible to construct interest profiles that map individuals to specific types of leisure activities, and to each other (Leuty, Hansen, & Speaks, 2016). Other factors are important as well: income, health, abilities, transportation, education, and social characteristics. Some leisure activities, such as downhill skiing, are relatively expensive and require transportation and reasonably good health and physical coordination for maximum enjoyment. In contrast, reading requires minimal finances (if one uses a public library or other free sources) and is far less physically demanding.

The use of computer technology in leisure activities has increased dramatically. Most usage involves e-mail, Facebook, Twitter, or other social networking tools for such activities as keeping in touch with family and friends, pursuing hobbies, and lifelong learning. Multi-participant video streaming and multiplayer interactive

Leisure activities may involve creative pursuits.

computer gaming have also increased among adult players. All of these online activities provide opportunities to create virtual friendship networks that provide the same types of support as traditional face-to-face networks.

Developmental Changes in Leisure

Cross-sectional studies report age differences in leisure activities. Emerging adults participate in a greater range of activities than middle-aged adults. Furthermore, emerging adults prefer intense leisure activities that provide a "rush," such as rock climbing, whitewater kayaking, and hang gliding. In contrast, middle-aged adults focus more on home-based and family-oriented activities. In later middle age, they spend less of their leisure time in strenuous physical activities and more in sedentary activities such as reading and watching television and in moderately strenuous activities such as tennis and hiking (van der Pas & Koopman-Boyden, 2010).

Longitudinal studies of changes in individuals' leisure activities over time show considerable stability in leisure interests over reasonably long periods. Specifically, studies in the United States, Finland, Great Britain, and Japan show that level of activity in young adulthood predicts activity level later in life, and leisure physical activity in emerging adulthood bodes well for health later in life (Hillsdon et al., 2005; Lahti et al., 2016). Claude, the 55-year-old in the vignette who likes to fish and ski, is a good example of this overall trend. As Claude demonstrates, frequent participation in particular leisure activities earlier in life tends to continue into adulthood. Similar findings hold for the pre- and postretirement years. Apparently, one's preferences for certain types of leisure activities are established early in life; they tend to change over the life span primarily in terms of how physically intense they are. Explore these findings in more detail in the How Do We Know? feature.

How Do We Know?
Long-Term Effects of Leisure Activities

Who were the investigators and what was the aim of the study? It is well established that physical activity is related to better health at all ages in adulthood. However, much of the existing research has focused on more formal exercise programs, with much less attention paid to leisure forms of activity, and whether leisure-time physical activity during emerging adulthood is related to subsequent health and well-being in midlife. To answer these questions, Jouni Lahti and colleagues (2016) followed adults in Finland, Great Britain, and Japan.

How did the investigators measure the topic of interest? The investigators used the Short Form-36 (SF-36) health questionnaire to assess physical and mental health. The eight subscales of the SF-36 include physical functioning, role limitations due to physical problems, bodily pain, general health perceptions, mental health, role limitations due to emotional problems, social functioning, and vitality. Scores can range from 0 to 100. Low scores imply poor health functioning, whereas high scores imply good health functioning. The SF-36 has very good reliability and validity.

Who were the participants in the study? Participants in the study were prospective employee cohorts originally recruited for the Finnish HHS study (2000–2002 and 2007, N=5958), British WHII I study (1997–1999 and 2003–2004, N=4142) and Japanese Civil Servants Study (JACS) (1998–1999 and 2003, N=1768). Across the three study samples, participants ranged in age from 20 to 60.

What was the design of the study? The research used a longitudinal design. As noted in Chapter 1, the strength of longitudinal designs is being able to measure a behavior over time in the same individual; the confound is the age of the person at the time of measurement.

Were there ethical concerns with the study? All participants were informed of the nature of the larger study and had given their consent to participate.

What were the results? Leisure physical activity was associated with better subsequent physical health functioning in all three cohorts. However, results varied somewhat across country and gender. Differences were the clearest among Finnish women (inactive: 46.0, active vigorous: 49.5) and men (inactive: 47.8, active vigorous: 51.1) and British women (inactive: 47.3, active vigorous: 50.4). For mental health functioning, the differences were generally smaller and not clearly related to the intensity of physical activity.

What did the investigators conclude? Lahti and colleagues concluded that vigorous physical activity was associated with better subsequent physical health functioning in all three cohorts, although with some differences in magnitude across countries. For mental health functioning, the intensity of physical activity was less important. Promoting leisure-time physical activity may prove useful for the maintenance of health functioning among midlife employees.

Consequences of Leisure Activities

What do people gain from participating in leisure activities? Researchers have long known involvement in leisure activities is related to well-being (Paggi et al., 2016; Warr, Butcher, & Robertson, 2004). This relation holds in other countries, such as China, as well (Dai, Zhang, & Li, 2013). Research shows participating in leisure activities helps promote better mental health (e.g., Lahti et al., 2016). This is especially true for spouses who use family-based leisure as a means to cope during their spouse/partner's military deployment (Werner & Shannon, 2013), and buffers the effects of stress and negative life events. It even helps lower the risk of mortality (Talbot et al., 2007).

Studies show leisure activities provide an excellent forum for the interaction of the biopsychosocial forces discussed in Chapter 1 (Cheng & Pegg, 2016; Kleiber, 2013). Leisure activities are a good way to deal with stress, which—as we have seen in Chapter 4—has significant biological effects. This is especially true for unforeseen negative events, such as cancer (Chun et al., 2016). Psychologically, leisure activities have been well documented as one of the primary coping mechanisms people use, such as providing a sense of purpose in life (Chun et al., 2016; Patry, Blanchard, & Mask, 2007).

How people cope by using leisure varies across cultures depending on the various types of activities that are permissible and available. Likewise, leisure activities vary across social class; basketball is one activity that cuts across class because it is inexpensive, whereas downhill scuba diving is more associated with people who can afford to travel to diving resorts and pay the fees.

How do leisure activities provide protection against stress? Kleiber and colleagues (2002; Kleiber, 2013) offer four ways leisure activities serve as a buffer against negative life events:

- Leisure activities distract us from negative life events.
- Leisure activities generate optimism about the future because they are pleasant.
- Leisure activities connect us to our personal past by allowing us to participate in the same activities over much of our lives.
- Leisure activities can be used as vehicles for personal transformation.

Whether the negative life events we experience are personal, such as the loss of a loved one, or societal, such as a terrorist attack, leisure activities are a common and effective way to deal with them. They truly represent the confluence of biopsychosocial forces and are effective at any point in the life cycle.

Participating with others in leisure activities may also strengthen feelings of attachment to one's partner, friends, and family (Carnelley & Ruscher, 2000). Adults use leisure as a way to explore interpersonal relationships or to seek social approval. In fact, research indicates marital satisfaction is linked with leisure time; marital satisfaction is even helped when couples spend some leisure time with others in addition to spending it just as a couple (Zabriskie & Kay, 2013). But there's no doubt couples who play together are happier (Johnson, Zabriskie, & Hill, 2006).

There is a second sense of attachment that can develop as a result of leisure activities: place attachment. Place attachment occurs when people derive a deep sense of personal satisfaction and identity from a particular place (Di Masso, Dixon, & Hernández, 2017). Place attachment is an active process, bringing the individual a sense of belonging that might not be experienced elsewhere. As a result, place attachment generally drives people to return to the location over and over, and the meaning of being there continues to deepen over time.

What if leisure activities are pursued seriously? In some cases, people create leisure–family conflict by engaging in leisure activities to extremes (Heo et al., 2010). When things get serious, problems may occur. Only when there is support from others for such extreme involvement are problems avoided. For instance, professional quilters felt much more valued when family members were supportive (Stalp & Conti, 2011). As in most things, moderation in leisure activities is probably best, unless you know you have excellent support.

You have probably heard the saying "no vacation goes unpunished." It appears to be true, and the trouble is not just afterward. Research shows prevacation workload is associated with lower health and well-being for both men and women, and prevacation homeload (extra work that needs to be done at home) has the same negative effect for women (Nawijn, de Bloom, & Geurts, 2013).

Once on vacation, it matters what you do. If you detach from work, enjoy the activities during vacation, and engage in conversation with your partner, then the vacation can improve health and well-being, even after you return home (de Bloom, Geurts, & Kompier, 2012). Indeed, some have suggested that vacations and tourism be prescribed like a medication due to its positive benefits. However, workers report high postvacation workloads eliminate most of the positive effects of a vacation within about a week (de Bloom et al., 2010).

One frequently overlooked outcome of leisure activity is social acceptance. For persons with disabilities, this is a particularly important consideration (Choi, Johnson, & Kriewitz, 2013). There is a positive connection between frequency of leisure activities and positive identity, social acceptance, friendship development, and acceptance of differences. These findings highlight the importance of designing inclusive leisure activity programs.

Adult Development in Action

What effect does leisure have on adult development and aging?

12.6 Retirement and Work in Late Life

LEARNING OBJECTIVES
- What does being retired mean?
- Why do people retire?
- How satisfied are retired people?
- What employment and volunteer opportunities are there for older adults?

Marcus is a 77-year-old retired construction worker who labored hard all of his life. He managed to save a little money, but he and his wife live primarily off of his monthly Social Security checks. Though not rich, they have enough to pay the bills. Marcus is largely happy with retirement, and he stays in touch with his friends. He thinks maybe he's a little strange, though, since he has heard retirees are supposed to be isolated and lonely.

As a reader of this book, you're lucky. You take for granted that someday you will have the option of "retiring" from one lifestyle to another.

It wasn't always this way. Did you know that until 1934, when a railroad union sponsored a bill promoting mandatory retirement, and 1935, when Social Security was inaugurated, retirement was not even considered a possibility by most Americans like Marcus (McClinton, 2010; Sargent et al., 2013)? Only since World War II has there been a substantial number of retired people in the United States (McClinton, 2010).

Although we take retirement for granted, economic downturns have a major disruptive effect on people's retirement decisions and plans. New view of aging and increased health for the typical older adult has also had an effect on people's notions about retirement. These realities have, in turn, affected social policy. As more people retire and take advantage of longer lives, a significant social challenge is created regarding how to fund retiree benefits and how to support older adults who are still active (Monahan, 2017; Quinn & Cahill, 2016; Wise, 2017).

After having one or several careers across adulthood, many older adults find themselves questioning whether they want to continue in that line of work anymore, or find themselves being forced to go through that questioning because they lost their jobs. This period of questioning and potential exploration enables people to think about their options: retiring, looking for work in the same of a different field, volunteering, or some combination of all of these.

With the movement of the baby boom generation into old age, increasing numbers of these adults are redefining what "retirement" and "work" mean in late life. Realizing these generational shifts reflect important changes in how people view the latter part of one's working life, AARP created the *Life Reimagined*® tool that assists people in finding their path, including reawakening long-dormant interests.

As we consider retirement and other options in late life, keep in mind the world is changing, resulting in increased options and the likelihood more older adults will continue in the labor force by choice and necessity.

What Does Being Retired Mean?

Retirement means different things to men and women, and to people in different ethnic groups and careers (James, Matz-Costa, & Smyer, 2016; Loretto & Vickerstaff, 2013; Silver, 2016). It has also taken on new and different meanings since the beginning of the Great Recession in 2008 because of the abrupt change in people's planning and expectations as a result of the loss of savings or pensions (Quinn & Cahill, 2016; Sargent et al., 2013).

Part of the reason it is difficult to define retirement precisely is that the decision to retire involves the loss of occupational identity with no obvious replacement for that loss. Not having a specific job any more means we either put that aspect of our lives in the past tense—"I used to work as a manager at the Hilton"—or say nothing at all. Loss of this aspect of ourselves can be difficult to face, so some look for a label other than "retired" to describe themselves.

That's why researchers view retirement as another one of many transitions people experience in life (Kojola & Moen, 2016; Moen, 2016a; Sargent et al., 2013). This view makes retirement a complex process where people withdraw from full-time participation in an occupation (Moen, 2016a; Sargent et al., 2013), recognizing there are many pathways to this end (Kojola & Moen, 2016; Moen, 2016a; Sargent et al., 2013).

Why Do People Retire?

Provided they have good health, more workers retire by choice than for any other reason (Cohen-Mansfield & Regev, in press; Kojola & Moen, 2016), as long they feel financially secure after considering projected income from Social Security, pensions and other structured retirement programs, and personal savings (Quinn & Cahill, 2016). Of course, some people are forced to retire because of health problems or because they lose their jobs. As corporations downsize during economic downturns or after corporate mergers, some older workers accept buyout packages involving supplemental payments if they retire. Others are permanently furloughed, laid off, or dismissed.

The decision to retire is influenced by one's occupational history and goal expectations (Moen, 2016a; Sargent et al., 2013). Whether people perceive they will achieve their personal goals through work or retirement influences the decision to retire and its connection with health and disability.

The rude awakening many people received during the Great Recession was that the best made plans are only as good as external factors allow them to be, especially when it comes to financial savings and pensions. Many people lost much of their investment savings and home equity as the value of stocks plummeted, companies eliminated pension plans, and the housing market collapsed. Consequently, many people were forced to delay their retirement until they had the financial resources to do so, or to continue working part time when they had not planned to do so to supplement their income.

Income security is now at the forefront in retirement decisions (Monahan, 2017; Quinn & Cahill, 2016). Although 42% of respondents in one poll thought the ideal retirement age is between 60 and 65, only 29% thought they would actually be able to achieve that goal (Boschma, 2015). Indeed, 30% of respondents thought they would be unable to retire before age 70, if ever, mainly due to pessimism regarding financial security.

How much do you need to have in savings to be comfortable in retirement? A decent rule of thumb is to save enough to generate between 70% and 80% of your current income, and to plan for about 25 years in retirement. This figure takes into account typical living and medical expenses. The bottom line is longer life expectancies have added to the amount of money you will need in retirement—and that amount is usually much greater than people think.

Gender and Ethnic Differences

Women's experience of retiring can be quite different from men's (Loretto & Vickerstaff, 2013; Silver, 2016). Women's employment career may have developed differently, such as having starts and stops related to dependent care responsibilities, or may reflect later entry into the workforce. Because of the pay gap and possible interruptions in work history, many women have fewer financial resources for retirement.

For women who were never employed outside the home, the process of retirement is especially unclear (Loretto & Vickerstaff, 2013), even when such spouses are eligible for Social Security benefits. Because they were not paid for all of their work raising children and caring for the home, it is rare for them to have their own pensions or other sources of income in retirement beyond spousal survivor benefits. Additionally, the work they have always done in caring for the home continues, often nearly uninterrupted (Ciani, 2016).

There has not been much research examining the process of retirement as a function of ethnicity. African American and Latino older adults are likely to continue working beyond age 65, mainly due to greater financial vulnerability on average (Angel & Angel, 2015; Sullivan & Meschede, 2016; Troutman et al., 2011).

Adjustment to Retirement

How do people who go through the process of retirement adjust to it? Researchers agree on one point: New patterns of personal involvement must be developed in the context of changing roles and lifestyles in retirement (Ajrouch, Antonucci, & Webster, 2014; Potočnik, Tordera, & Peiró, 2013). People's adjustment to retirement evolves over time as a result of complex interrelations involving physical health, financial status, the degree to which their retirement was voluntary, and feelings of personal control (Moen, 2016a; Ng et al., 2016).

How do most people fare? As long as people have financial security, health, a supportive network of relatives and friends, and an internally driven sense of motivation, they report feeling good about being retired (Hershey & Henkens, 2014; Moen, 2016a; Ng et al., 2016; Potočnik et al., 2013). What motivates most people, though, is finding a sense of fulfillment in ways previously unavailable to them (James et al., 2016).

Many people think being retired has negative effects on health. Research findings show the relation between health and retirement is complex. On the one hand, there is no evidence voluntary retirement has immediate negative effects on health (Hershey & Henkens, 2014). In contrast, there is ample evidence being forced to retire is correlated with significantly poorer physical and mental health (Hershey & Henkens, 2014).

Employment and Volunteering

Retirement is an important life transition, one best understood through a life-course perspective that takes other aspects of one's life, such as one's marital relationship, into account (Moen, 2016a; Wickrama, O'Neal, & Lorenz, 2013). This life change means retirees must look for ways to adapt to new routines and patterns, while maintaining social integration and being active in various ways (e.g., friendship networks, community engagement).

Employment in Late Life

For an increasing number of people, especially for those whose retirement savings is insufficient, "retirement" involves working at least part-time. Employment for them is a financial necessity to make ends meet, especially for those whose entire income would consist only of Social Security benefits.

For others, the need to stay employed at least part-time represents a way to stay involved beyond an income supplement, and a way for employers to continue benefiting from employees' experience. For example, even in the rapidly changing knowledge industry, employment of workers over age 65 has been shown to benefit both older adults and companies (Bartkowiak, 2017).

As you can see in Figure 12.8, the percentage of adults age 65 and over who are in the workforce increased dramatically between 2000 and 2016, even as the overall percentage of Americans who were employed declined (DeSilver, 2016). Note also the trend has been consistently upward, indicating the forces keeping older adults in the labor force have been acting for many years.

Overall, labor force participation of older adults in the United States and other developed countries has been increasing most rapidly among women (DeSilver, 2016; Sterns & Chang, 2010). This is due mostly to more women being in the labor force across adulthood than in decades past, more older women being single, and greater financial need. The Great Recession exacerbated the need for older adults to work at least part-time to ensure greater financial security (Quinn & Cahill, 2016).

Older workers face many challenges, not the least of which are ageism and discrimination (Jackson, 2013). Employers may believe older workers are less capable, and there is evidence this translates into lower likelihood of getting a job interview compared to younger or middle-aged workers, all other things being equal (Abrams, Swift, & Drury, 2016). As we noted earlier in this chapter, despite the fact age discrimination laws in the United States protect people over age 40, such barriers are still widespread.

The relationship between age and job performance is extremely complex (Sterns & Chang, 2010). This is because it depends a great deal on the kind of job one is considering, such as one that involves a great deal of physical exertion or one involving a great deal of expertise and experience. In general, older workers show more reliability (e.g., showing up on time for work), organizational loyalty, and safety-related behavior.

How have companies adapted to having more older workers? One example is BMW, a company that changed a number of things in its automobile assembly plants to

FIGURE 12.8 Percentage of older Americans employed 2000–2016.

Source: DeSilver, D. (2016). More older Americans are working, and working more, than they used to. Retrieved from www.pewresearch.org/fact-tank/2016/06/20/more-older-americans-are-working-and-working-more-than-they-used-to/.

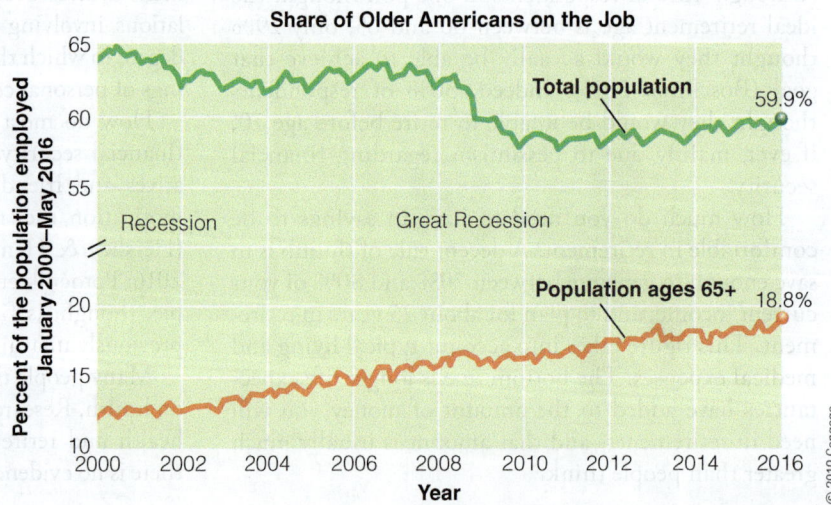

better meet the needs of older workers (de Pommereau, 2012). BMW provides physical trainers on the factory floor, has new, softer floors, offers chairs that rise up and down to make tasks easier, uses larger print fonts on computer screens, and provides special shoes.

The trend for companies to employ older workers, especially on a part-time basis, is likely to continue because it is a good option for companies (Beck, 2013; Coleman, 2015). Some companies find they need the expertise older workers bring, and the flexibility of older workers in terms of hours and the type of benefits they need (or do not need) often make it less expensive. Consequently, "retirement" is likely to continue to evolve as a concept, and likely to include some aspect of employment well into late life.

Coleman (2015) argues that the benefits of hiring and retaining older workers could make companies stronger and more successful. However, a change in approach will require overcoming stereotypes of aging, as well as balancing the need to provide opportunities for younger workers with the need to retain the experience and knowledge of older workers.

Volunteering

Healthy, active retired adults often find meaning and explore things they always wished they had had a chance to do by volunteering (Ajrouch et al., 2014; Kleiber, 2013). Older adults report they volunteer for many reasons that benefit their well-being (Ajrouch et al., 2015; Greenfield & Marks, 2005): to provide service to others, to maintain social interactions and improve their communities, and to keep active. Read the Real People feature to learn more about David Jarmul, the former head of communications at Duke University, who at age 63 headed with his wife Champa to Moldova as a Peace Corps volunteer.

Real People
Retiring to the Peace Corps

David Jarmul spent a long career in senior communications positions at the National Academy of Sciences, the Howard Hughes Medical Institute, and Duke University. He and his wife Champa could have enjoyed a relaxed retirement.

But that's not what they chose to do. Instead, they joined the Peace Corps and headed to Moldova, in Eastern Europe. They had a history with the Peace Corps—they met while David was a volunteer in Nepal, working at the same school where Champa was a teacher. They married in 1979.

It may surprise you to learn that David and Champa are not unusual. Although the majority of Peace Corps volunteers are emerging adults, adults over age 50 comprise more than 7% of all Peace Corps volunteers worldwide. Older adult volunteers like David and Champa are especially valued in countries that need particular expertise in business development and other technical fields that usually require greater levels of experience. Older volunteers may be at an advantage in those countries that are especially respectful of older adults.

Like David and Champa, many older Peace Corps volunteers are married couples, though widowed and single older adults are common. Volunteers come from every professional background imaginable, and from all parts of the United States.

The Peace Corps provides information for older adults interested in learning more. Some volunteers, such as David, keep their own blogs of their experience. David and Champa are just two examples of how more older adults are pushing the boundaries of expectations regarding life after retirement.

David and Champa Jarmul

Why do so many people volunteer? Several factors are responsible (Ajrouch et al., 2015; Tang, Morrow-Howell, & Choi, 2010): changing characteristics of social networks, developing a new aspect of the self, finding a personal sense of purpose, desire to share one's skills and expertise, a redefinition of the nature and merits of volunteer work, a more highly educated and healthy population of older adults, and greatly expanded opportunities for people to become involved in volunteer work that they enjoy. Research in New Zealand documents older adults who find volunteering enables them to give back to their local communities (Wiles & Jayasinha, 2013). Brown and colleagues (2011) argue volunteerism offers a way for society to tap into the vast resources older adults offer.

There is also evidence the expectations of people who volunteer in retirement are changing. Seaman (2012) notes women in the leading edge of the baby-boom generation are interested in volunteering for personal, rather than purely altruistic reasons and do so on their own terms. They are not as willing as volunteers were in previous generations to serve on time-consuming boards and to engage in fundraising. As a result, organizations that rely on volunteers need to be in touch with the concerns and motivations of their pool of volunteers.

The U.S. government has been tapping into this pool of talented volunteers since President John F. Kennedy's presidency, when the Senior Corps was created. As part of the Corporation for National and Community Service, the Senior Corps consists of three major programs: Foster grandparents, Retired Senior Volunteer Program (RSVP), and Senior Companions (Corporation for National and Community Service, 2016). These national programs have chapters across the country, and interested people aged 55 and over are encouraged to explore local opportunities. These and other programs provide organized ways to get and stay active and to find meaningful forms of engagement.

Adult Development in Action

What cognitive and physical factors influence the decision to retire?

Social Policy Implications

In the United States, the first law regarding pay equity was passed by Congress in 1963. Forty-six years later, in 2009, President Obama signed the Lilly Ledbetter Fair Pay Act, showing clearly that gender-based pay inequity still exists. Nearly a decade after this law was enacted, inequity remains (Lips, 2016).

Why? Consider this: Only one year out of college, a woman earns on average about $0.80 for every $1.00 a male college graduate earns. Over time, the difference gets bigger, not smaller. This is even after controlling for such important variables as occupation, hours worked, parenthood, and other factors associated with pay (Maatz & Hedgepath, 2013).

What if women choose a college major associated with high-paying jobs, such as those in science, technology, engineering, mathematics, and medicine (STEMM)? Will that help reduce the pay differential? No. Even after controlling for differences in academic field, women earn on average 11% less than men in first-year earnings after receiving their doctoral degree (Shen, 2016). Would choosing to enter a traditionally male-dominated major solve the problem? No. Women software developers, for example, earn only 81% of what their male counterparts earn.

A woman is also significantly disadvantaged when it comes to the division of labor at home if she is married to or living with a man (Shen, 2016). Despite decades of effort in getting men to do more of the housework and childcare tasks, little has changed in terms of the amount of time men actually spend on these tasks. In effect, this means women have two careers, one in the workplace and the other at home. If a college-educated woman stays at home to care for a child or parent, then her return to the workforce will be at a lower salary than it would have been otherwise.

Only through a concerted effort on the part of employers and policy makers can the gender-based pay gap be addressed. But more will be needed. Besides fairer pay rules and policies, we will also need a change in attitudes in the men who are the women's spouses and partners. They will need to step up and do an equal share of the work around the house and in child care. Because unless both aspects are addressed, the pay gap will never be closed.

SUMMARY

12.1 Occupational Selection and Development

How do people view work?
- Although most people work for money, other reasons are highly variable.

How do people choose their occupations?
- Holland's theory is based on the idea people choose occupations to optimize the fit between their individual traits and their occupational interests. Six personality types, representing different combinations of these, have been identified. Support for these types has been found in several studies.
- Social cognitive career theory emphasizes how people choose careers is also influenced by what they think they can do and how well they can do it, as well as how motivated they are to pursue a career.

What factors influence occupational development?
- Reality shock is the realization one's expectations about an occupation are different from what one actually experiences. Reality shock is common among young workers.
- Few differences exist across generations in terms of their occupational expectations.
- A mentor or developmental coach is a coworker who teaches a new employee the unwritten rules and fosters occupational development. Mentor–protégé relationships, like other relationships, develop through stages over time.

What is the relationship between job satisfaction and age?
- Older workers report higher job satisfaction than younger workers, but this may be partly due to self-selection; unhappy workers may quit. Other reasons include intrinsic satisfaction, good fit, lower importance of work, finding nonwork diversions, and lifecycle factors.
- Alienation and burnout are important considerations in understanding job satisfaction. Both involve significant stress for workers.
- Vallerand's Passion Model proposes people develop a passion toward enjoyable activities that are incorporated into identity. Obsessive passion happens when people experience an uncontrollable urge to engage in the activity; harmonious passion results when individuals freely accept the activity as important for them without any contingencies attached to it.

12.2 Gender, Ethnicity, and Discrimination Issues

How do women's and men's occupational selection differ? How are people viewed when they enter occupations that are not traditional for their gender?
- Boys and girls are socialized differently for work, and their occupational choices are affected as a result. Women choose nontraditional occupations for many reasons, including expectations and personal feelings. Women in such occupations are still viewed more negatively than men in the same occupations.

What factors are related to women's occupational development?
- Women leave well-paid occupations for many reasons, including family obligations and workplace environment. Women who continue to work full-time have adequate child care and look for ways to further their occupational development.
- The glass ceiling, which limits women's occupational attainment, and the glass cliff, which puts women leaders in a precarious position, affect how often women achieve top executive positions and how successful women leaders are.

What factors affect ethnic minority workers' occupational experiences and occupational development?
- Vocational identity and vocational goals vary in different ethnic groups. Whether an organization is sensitive to ethnicity issues is a strong predictor of satisfaction among ethnic minority employees.

What types of bias and discrimination hinder the occupational development of women and ethnic minority workers?
- Gender bias remains the chief barrier to women's occupational development. In many cases, this operates as a glass ceiling. Pay inequity is also a problem; women are often paid less than what men earn in similar jobs.
- Sexual harassment is a problem in the workplace. Current criteria for judging harassment are based on the "reasonable person" standard. Denying employment to anyone over 40 because of age is age discrimination.

12.3 Occupational Transitions

Why do people change occupations?
- Important reasons people change occupations include personality, obsolescence, and economic trends.
- To adapt to the effects of a global economy and gain a workforce, many corporations are providing retraining opportunities for workers. Retraining is especially important in cases of outdated skills and career plateauing.

Is worrying about potential job loss a major source of stress?
- Occupational insecurity is a growing problem. Fear that one may lose one's job is a better predictor of anxiety than the actual likelihood of job loss.

How does job loss affect the amount of stress experienced?
- Job loss is a traumatic event that can affect every aspect of a person's life. Degree of financial distress and the extent of attachment to the job are the best predictors of distress.

12.5 Work and Family

What are the issues faced by employed people who care for dependents?
- Caring for children or aging parents creates dilemmas for workers. Whether a woman returns to work after having a child depends largely on how attached she is to her work. Simply providing child care on-site does not always result in higher job satisfaction. A more important factor is the degree that supervisors are sympathetic.

How do partners view the division of household chores? What is work–family conflict? How does it affect couples' lives?
- Although women have reduced the amount of time they spend on household tasks over the past two decades, they still do most of the work. European American men are less likely than either African American or Latino American men to help with traditionally female household tasks.
- Flexible work schedules and the number of children are important factors in role conflict. Recent evidence shows work stress has a much greater impact on family life than family stress has on work performance. Some women pay a high personal price for having careers.

12.5 Leisure Activities

What activities are leisure activities?
- Leisure activities can be simple relaxation, activities for enjoyment, or creative pursuits. Views of leisure activities varies by gender, ethnicity, and age.

What changes in leisure activities occur with age?
- As people grow older, they tend to engage in leisure activities that are less strenuous and more family-oriented. Leisure preferences in adulthood reflect those earlier in life.

What do people derive from leisure activities?
- Leisure activities enhance well-being and can benefit all aspects of people's lives.

12.6 Retirement and Work in Late Life

What does being retired mean?
- Retirement is a complex process by which people withdraw from full-time employment. There is no adequate, single definition for all ethnic groups. People's decisions to retire involve several factors, including eligibility for certain social programs, and personal financial and health resources.

Why do people retire?
- People generally retire because they choose to, but many people are forced to retire because of job loss or serious health problems.

How satisfied are people with retirement?
- Retirement is an important life transition. Most people are satisfied with retirement. Many retired people maintain their health, friendship networks, and activity levels.

What employment and volunteer opportunities are there for older adults?
- Increasingly, people continue some level of participation in the labor force during retirement, usually for financial reasons. Labor force participation among older adults continues to increase. Volunteer work is another way of achieving this.

REVIEW QUESTIONS

12.1 Occupational Selection and Development

- What are occupational priorities and how do they change over time?
- How is work changing as a result of the global economy?
- Briefly describe social cognitive career theory (SCCT).
- How is reality shock a developmental concept? What is a mentor? What role does a mentor play in occupational development? How does the mentor–protégé relationship change over time?
- What is the developmental course of job satisfaction? What factors influence job satisfaction?
- What are alienation and burnout? How are they related to job satisfaction?
- Briefly describe Vallerand's Passion Model.

12.2 Gender, Ethnicity, and Discrimination Issues

- What gender differences have been identified relating to occupational choice? How are men and women socialized differently in ways that influence occupational opportunities?
- How are women in nontraditional occupations perceived?
- What are the major barriers to women's occupational development?
- What major barriers to occupational development are related to ethnicity?
- How are sex discrimination and the glass ceiling or glass cliff related?
- What are the structural barriers ethnic minorities face in occupational settings?
- How is sexual harassment defined?
- What is age discrimination and how does it operate?

12.3 Occupational Transitions

- What are the major reasons why people change occupations?
- Why is retraining workers important?
- What effects do people report after losing their jobs?

12.4 Work and Family

- What factors are important in dependent care for employees?
- How do dual-earner couples balance multiple roles and deal with role conflict?
- What important factors contribute to work-family conflict? What other occupational development effects occur?

12.5 Leisure Activities

- What are the major reasons people engage in leisure activities? What benefits occur?
- What kinds of leisure activities do people perform?
- How do leisure activities change over the life span?

12.6 Retirement and Work in Late Life

- In what ways can retirement be viewed? How may the definition of retirement change in the next several years?
- What are the main predictors of the decision to retire?
- How do people adjust to being retired?
- What factors influence decisions to continue working or volunteering in retirement?

INTEGRATING CONCEPTS IN DEVELOPMENT

- What roles do personal relationships play in one's work, leisure, and retirement?
- How do cognitive development and personality influence work roles?
- What implications are there for the removal of mandatory retirement in terms of normal cognitive changes with age?

KEY TERMS

age discrimination Denying a job or a promotion to a person solely on the basis of age.

alienation Situation in which workers feel what they are doing is meaningless and their efforts are devalued, or when they do not see the connection between what they do and the final product.

backup care Emergency care for dependent children or adults so the employee does not need to lose a day of work.

burnout The depletion of a person's energy and motivation, the loss of occupational idealism, and the feeling of being exploited.

career construction theory Posits people build careers through their own actions that result from the interface of their own personal characteristics and the social context.

career plateauing Situation occurring when there is a lack of challenge in the job or promotional opportunity in the organization or when a person decides not to seek advancement.

developmental coach Individual who helps a person focus on his or her goals, motivations, and aspirations to help the person achieve focus and apply them appropriately.

gender discrimination Denying a job to someone solely on the basis of whether the person is a man or a woman.

glass ceiling The level to which a woman may rise in an organization but beyond which she may not go.

glass cliff A situation in which a woman's leadership position in an organization is precarious.

job satisfaction The positive feeling that results from an appraisal of one' work.

leisure A discretionary activity that includes simple relaxation, activities for enjoyment, and creative pursuits.

meaning-mission fit Alignment between people's personal intentions and their company's mission.

mentor A person who is part teacher, sponsor, model, and counselor who facilitates on-the-job learning to help a new hire do the work required in his or her present role and to prepare for future roles.

passion A strong inclination toward an activity that individuals like (or even love), that they value (and thus find important), and in which they invest time and energy.

reality shock Situation in which what one learns in the classroom does not always transfer directly into the "real world" and does not represent all a person needs to know.

social cognitive career theory (SCCT) Proposes career choice is a result of the application of Bandura's social cognitive theory, especially the concept of self-efficacy.

work–family conflict The feeling of being pulled in multiple directions by incompatible demands from job and family.

13 | Dying and Bereavement

CHAPTER OUTLINE

13.1 Definitions and Ethical Issues
Sociocultural Definitions of Death
Legal and Medical Definitions
Ethical Issues
CURRENT CONTROVERSIES The Brittany Maynard Case

13.2 Thinking About Death: Personal Aspects
DISCOVERING DEVELOPMENT A Self-Reflective Exercise on Death
A Life-Course Approach to Dying
REAL PEOPLE Randy Pausch's Last Lecture
Dealing with One's Own Death
Death Anxiety

13.3 End-of-Life Issues
Creating a Final Scenario
The Hospice Option
Making Your End-of-Life Intentions Known

13.4 Surviving the Loss: The Grieving Process
The Grief Process
Typical Grief Reactions
Coping with Grief
HOW DO WE KNOW? Grief Processing and Avoidance in the United States and China
Ambiguous Loss
Complicated or Prolonged Grief Disorder
Adult Developmental Aspects of Grief
Conclusion

Social Policy Implications

Summary
Review Questions
Integrating Concepts in Development
Key Terms

When famous people such as Prince or Amy Winehouse die unexpectedly, people are confronted with the reality that death happens to everyone. Many of us die from the same conditions; the most likely ways people die are shown in Figure 13.1. But the plain truth is that each of us makes the transition from life to death.

We have a paradoxical relationship with death. Sometimes we are fascinated by it. As tourists, we visit places where famous people died or are buried. We watch as television newscasts show scenes of devastation in natural disasters and war. But when it comes to pondering our own death or that of people close to us, we experience difficulty. As French writer and reformer La Rochefoucauld wrote over 300 years ago, "looking into the sun is easier than contemplating our death." When death is personal, we become uneasy. Looking at the sun is hard indeed.

In this chapter we delve into thanatology. **Thanatology** is *the study of death, dying, grief, bereavement, and social attitudes toward these issues.* We first consider definitional and ethical issues surrounding death. Next, we look specifically at the process of dying. Dealing with grief is important for survivors, so we consider this topic in the third section. Finally, we examine how people view death at different points in the life span.

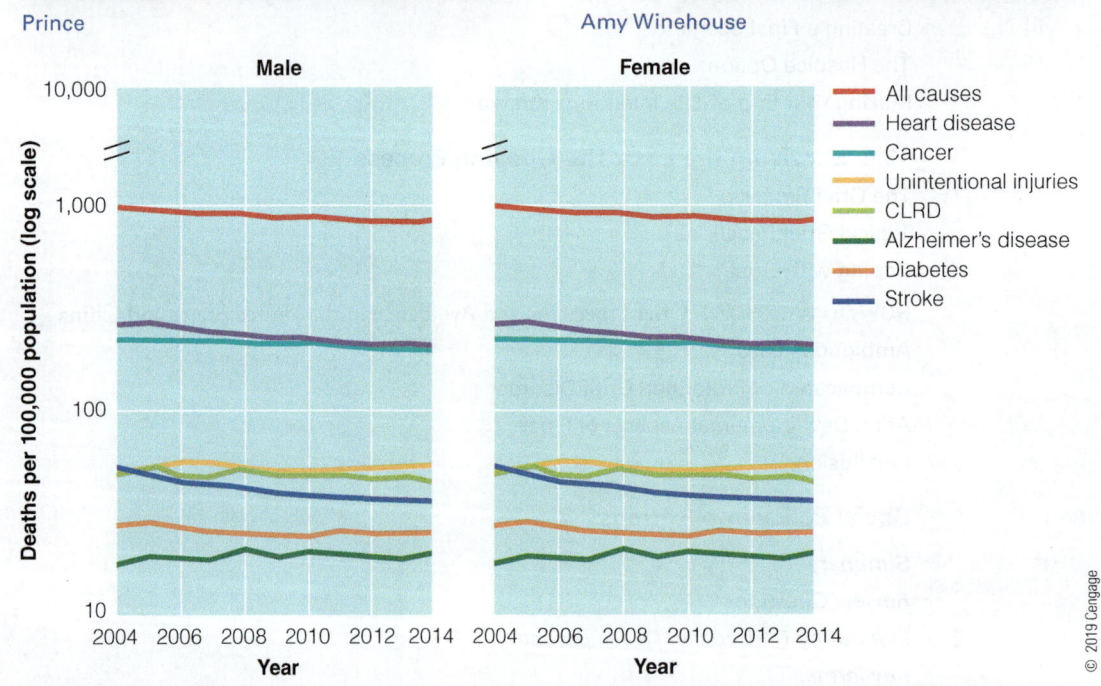

FIGURE 13.1 Age-adjusted death rates for selected causes of death for all ages, by sex: 2004–2014.

Source: National Center for Health Statistics. (2016). Health, United States, 2015. Figure 2. Retrieved from www.cdc.gov/nchs/data/hus/hus15.pdf.

13.1 Definitions and Ethical Issues

LEARNING OBJECTIVES
- How is death defined?
- What legal and medical criteria are used to determine when death occurs?
- What are the ethical dilemmas surrounding euthanasia?
- What issues surround the costs of life-sustaining care?

Ernesto and Paulina had been married 48 years when Ernesto developed terminal pancreatic cancer. Ernesto was suffering terrible pain and begged Paulina to make it stop. He said she would not let their pet suffer this way, so why let him? Paulina heard about "mercy killing" that involved administering high dosages of certain medications, but she believed this was the same as murder. Yet she could hardly bear to watch her beloved husband suffer. Paulina wondered what she should do.

When one first thinks about it, death seems a simple concept to define: It is the point when a person is no longer alive. Similarly, dying appears to be simply the process of making the transition from being alive to being dead. It all seems clear enough, doesn't it? But death and dying are actually far more complicated concepts.

As we will see, there are many cultural and religious differences in the definition of death and the customs surrounding it. The meaning of death depends on the observer's perspective as well as the specific medical and biological criteria one uses.

Sociocultural Definitions of Death

Although death is one of the few truly universal experiences, each culture has its own ways of thinking about, defining, and ritualizing it (Bustos, 2007; Gire, 2014; Penson, 2004). All cultures have their own views. Some cultures ritually pull their hair (Lewis, 2013). Melanesians have a term, *mate*, that includes the extremely sick, the very old, and the dead; the term *toa* refers to all other living people (Counts & Counts, 1985). Other cultures believe the life force leaves the body during sleep or illness, or involves reaching a certain age (Gire, 2014). Still other cultures view death as a transition to a different type of existence that still allows interaction with the living, and some believe that there is a circular pattern of multiple deaths and rebirths (Gire, 2014). In Ghana people are said to have a "peaceful" or "good" death if the dying person finished all business and made peace with others before death, and implies being at peace with his or her own death (van der Geest, 2004).

Mourning rituals, expressions of grief, and states of bereavement also vary in different cultures (Lee, 2010; Norton & Gino, 2014). Some cultures have formalized periods of time during which certain prayers or rituals are performed. After the death of a close relative, Orthodox Jews recite ritual prayers and cover all the mirrors in the house. The men slash their ties as a symbol of loss. In Papua New Guinea, there are accepted time periods for phases of grief (Hemer, 2010). The Muscogee Creek tribe's rituals include digging the grave by hand and giving a "farewell handshake" by throwing a handful of dirt into the grave before covering it (Walker & Balk, 2007). Ancestor worship, a deep respectful feeling toward individuals from whom a family is descended or who are important to them, is an important part of customs of death in many Asian cultures (Roszko, 2010). We must keep in mind the experiences of our culture or particular group may not generalize to other cultures or groups.

Death can be a truly cross-cultural experience. The international outpouring of grief over the death of world leaders such Nelson Mandela in 2013, the thousands killed in various terrorist attacks against the United States and other countries, and the hundreds of thousands killed in such natural disasters as the earthquake in Haiti in 2010 drew much attention to the ways the deaths of people we do not know personally can still affect us. It is at these times we realize death happens to us all and death can simultaneously be personal and public.

The symbols we use when people die, such as these elaborate caskets from Ghana, provide insights into how cultures think about death.

The many ways of viewing death can be seen in various funeral customs. You may have experienced a range of different types of funeral customs, from small, private services to elaborate rituals. Variations in the customs surrounding death are reflected in some of the most iconic structures on earth, such as the pyramids in Egypt, and some of the most beautiful, such as the Taj Mahal in India.

Legal and Medical Definitions

Sociocultural approaches help us understand the different ways people conceptualize and understand death; but they do not address a fundamental question: How do we determine someone has died? The medical and legal communities grappled with this question for centuries and continue to do so today. Let's see what the current answers are.

Determining when death occurs has always been subjective. *For hundreds of years, people accepted and applied the criteria that now define* **clinical death**: *lack of heartbeat and respiration.* Today, however, the definition used in most countries is **whole-brain death**. In 2010, the American Academy of Neurology proposed new guidelines for determining brain death (Wijdicks et al., 2010). The goal in this revision of the criteria was to provide guidelines that were based on research. According to the guidelines, there are three signs that a person's brain has permanently stopped functioning. First, the person is in a coma, and the cause of the coma is known. Second, all brainstem reflexes have permanently stopped working. Third, breathing has permanently stopped, so that a ventilator, or breathing machine, must be used to keep the body functioning.

The guidelines describe several complex steps physicians must follow to diagnose brain death. In some cases, this involves more than 25 specific tests. For example, the guidelines describe the best way to demonstrate absence of breathing. In contrast to previous guidelines, the current revision states that laboratory tests such as EEG or cerebral flow studies are not needed to determine brain death. The guidelines also make clear that this complex determination of brain death must be completed by a physician who has been trained in diagnosing brain death.

Although these criteria marked a significant advance over earlier definitions, they have still not been adopted at all hospitals in the United States (Greer et al., 2016). This means that somewhat different criteria for determining brain death are applied at different hospitals. This can result in misdiagnosis, delays in organ transplants, and emotionally-wrenching decisions for families (Kaplan, 2015).

Brain death is also controversial from some religious perspectives. For example, there is no general consensus whether brain death is accepted as true death under Islamic law (Al-Bar & Chamsi-Pasha, 2015; Miller, 2016). Roman Catholics focus on what they term "natural death" (Kassim & Alias, 2016). When these perspectives are considered, the determination of death can be difficult.

It is possible for a person's cortical functioning to cease while brainstem activity continues; this is a **persistent vegetative state**, *from which the person does not recover.* This condition can occur following disruption of the blood flow to the brain, a severe head injury, or a drug overdose. Persistent vegetative state allows for spontaneous heartbeat and respiration but not for consciousness. The whole-brain standard does not permit a declaration of death for someone who is in a persistent vegetative state. Because of conditions like persistent vegetative state, family members sometimes face difficult ethical decisions concerning care for the individual. These issues are the focus of the next section.

Ethical Issues

An ambulance screeches to a halt and emergency personnel rush a woman into the emergency room. As a result of an accident at a swimming pool, she has no pulse and no respiration. Working rapidly, the trauma team reestablishes a heartbeat through electric shock. A respirator is connected. An EEG and other tests reveal extensive and irreversible brain damage—she is in a persistent vegetative state. What should be done?

This is an example of the kinds of problems faced in the field of **bioethics**, *the study of the interface between human values and technological advances in health and life sciences.* Bioethics grew from two bases: respect for individual freedom and the impossibility of establishing any single version of morality by rational argument or common sense. Both of these factors are increasingly based on empirical evidence and cultural contexts (Priaulx, 2013; Sherwin, 2011). In practice, bioethics emphasizes the importance of individual choice and the minimization of harm over the maximization of good. That is, bioethics requires people to weigh how much the patient will benefit from a treatment relative to the amount of suffering he or she will endure as a result of the treatment. Examples of the tough choices required are those facing cancer patients about aggressive treatment for cancer that is quite likely to be fatal in any case and those facing family members about whether to turn off a life-support machine attached to their loved one.

In the arena of death and dying, the most important bioethical issue is **euthanasia**—*the practice of ending life for reasons of mercy.* The moral dilemma posed by euthanasia becomes apparent when trying to decide the circumstances a person's life should be ended, that implicitly forces one to place a value on the life of another (Bedir & Aksoy, 2011; Kassim & Alias, 2016; Munoz & Fox, 2013). It also makes us think about the difference between "killing" and "letting die" at the end of life (Dickens, Boyle, & Ganzini, 2008). In our society, this dilemma occurs most often when a person is being kept alive by machines or when someone is suffering from a terminal illness. This is the situation confronting Ernesto and Paulina in the opening vignette.

Euthanasia

Euthanasia can be carried out in two different ways: actively and passively (Moeller, Lewis, & Werth, 2010). **Active euthanasia** *involves the deliberate ending of someone's life, that may be based on a clear statement of the person's wishes or be a decision made by someone else who has the legal authority to do so.* Usually, this involves situations when people are in a persistent vegetative state or suffer from the end stages of a terminal disease. Examples of active euthanasia would be administering a drug overdose or ending a person's life through so-called mercy killing.

A second form of euthanasia, **passive euthanasia***, involves allowing a person to die by withholding available treatment.* A ventilator might be disconnected, chemotherapy might be withheld from a patient with terminal cancer, a surgical procedure might not be performed, or food could be withdrawn.

There is debate regarding the need to differentiate active and passive euthanasia (e.g., European Association of Palliative Care, 2011; Garrard & Wilkinson, 2005; Strinic, 2015). Some argue that any the single label "euthanasia" suffices; others prefer to distinguish between the traditional labels. The main point is that a decision to continue or terminate a person's life is made.

Most Americans favor such actions as disconnecting life support in situations involving patients in a persistent vegetative state, withholding treatment if the person agrees or is in the later stages of a terminal illness, and the concept of assisted death. But feelings also run strongly against such actions for religious or other reasons (Meilaender, 2013; Strinic, 2015). Even political debates incorporate the issue, as demonstrated in the summer of 2009 in the United States when opponents of President Obama's healthcare reform falsely claimed "death panels" would make decisions about terminating life support if the reform measure passed.

Globally, opinions about euthanasia vary (Bosshard & Materstvedt, 2011; Strinic, 2015). Western Europeans tend to view active euthanasia more positively based on less influence of religion and more social welfare services than residents of Eastern European and Islamic countries, who are more influenced by religious beliefs arguing against such practices (Baumann et al., 2011; Hains & Hulbert-Williams, 2013; Miller, 2016; Nayernouri, 2011).

Disconnecting a life support system is one thing; withholding nourishment from a terminally ill person is quite another issue for many people. Indeed, such cases often end up in court. The first high-profile legal case involving passive euthanasia in the United States was brought to the courts in 1990; the U.S. Supreme Court took up the case of Nancy Cruzan, whose family wanted to end her forced feeding. The court ruled that unless clear and incontrovertible evidence is presented to indicate that an individual desires to have nourishment stopped, such as through a healthcare power of attorney or living will, a third party (such as a parent or partner), cannot decide to terminate nourishment. We will consider later in this chapter how to ensure that one's wishes about these matters are expressed clearly.

Physician-Assisted Suicide

Taking one's own life through suicide has never been popular in the United States because of religious and other prohibitions. In other cultures, such as Japan, suicide is viewed as an honorable way to die under certain circumstances (Joiner, 2010).

Attitudes regarding suicide in certain situations are changing. *Much of this change concerns the topic of* **physician-assisted suicide***, in which physicians provide dying patients with a fatal dose of medication that the patient self-administers.* Most Americans, as do people in other countries, favor having a choice regarding assisted suicide if they should ever be diagnosed with a terminal disease. However, many oppose it on moral or religious grounds, irrespective of the wishes of the dying person.

In some cases this option has been put into law. Several countries—including Switzerland, Belgium, The Netherlands, and Colombia—have legalized physician-assisted suicide. Each of these laws sets clear guidelines for when this option is permitted. For example, in the

Netherlands, five criteria must be met before a terminally ill person can request physician-assisted suicide as an option:

1. The patient's condition is intolerable with no hope for improvement.
2. No relief is available.
3. The patient is competent.
4. The patient makes a request repeatedly over time.
5. Two physicians review the case and agree with the patient's request.

In the United States, voters in Oregon passed the Death with Dignity Act in 1994, the first physician-assisted suicide law in the country. Although the U.S. Supreme Court ruled in two cases in 1997 (*Vacco v. Quill* and *Washington v. Glucksberg*) there is no right to assisted suicide, the Court decided in 1998 not to overturn the Oregon law. As of 2016, physician-assisted suicide was also legal by state law in California, Vermont, and Washington, and by court decision in Montana. Several other states are considering legislation or have cases under court review.

In general, all of these laws permit people to obtain and use prescriptions for self-administered lethal doses of medication. The laws often require a physician to inform the person he or she is terminally ill and describe alternative options (e.g., hospice care, pain control). The person must be mentally competent and make multiple requests. Such provisions are included to ensure people making the request fully understand the issues and the request is not made hastily.

Available data indicate laws such as Oregon's have psychological benefits for patients, who value having autonomy in death as in life, especially in situations involving unbearable suffering (Hendry et al., 2013). Still, the idea of physicians helping people end their lives is a difficult topic for many.

A controversial case of assisted suicide involved Brittany Maynard, a 29-year old woman who had terminal brain cancer and committed suicide in 2014. As discussed in the Current Controversies feature, such cases reveal the difficult legal, medical, and ethical issues as well as the high degree of emotion surrounding the topic of euthanasia and death with dignity.

CURRENT CONTROVERSIES
The Brittany Maynard Case

On November 2, 2014, Brittany Maynard took a lethal dose of medication prescribed by her physician and ended her life. She was 29 years old, and had been suffering from terminal brain cancer, a diagnosis she received on New Year's Day 2014. She died in her bedroom, surrounded by loved ones (Bever, 2014a, b, c).

Brittany Maynard

Those are the bare facts of Brittany's case. The broader context and debate that her case created is more complicated. Rather than keep her situation private, Brittany went public, conducting several interviews with media and making her thoughts widely known. From there, debate raged.

Brittany's disease progressed rapidly. Nine days after her diagnosis, surgeons removed part of her brain and performed a partial resection of her temporal lobe to stop the tumor from growing. By April 2014, it was clear that this procedure did not work—the tumor was back, and it was more aggressive. Brittany was given about 6 months to live.

Because of her diagnosis, Brittany qualified for physician-assisted suicide under the Death with Dignity Act discussed earlier in the chapter. At the time, Brittany and her husband Dan Diaz lived in San Francisco. After carefully considering the various treatment options, which would not cure her, as well as hospice options, she made her decision. Because California does not have a death with dignity law, Brittany and her family moved to Portland, Oregon.

Brittany spent much of her remaining life working on behalf of the death with dignity movement, volunteering for Compassion & Choices. Because she was public and open about her dying process, her case has been a focal point for the right-to-die debate. Critics of death-with-dignity laws, such as National Right to Life, argue that terminal illness does not carry with it the "right" to be "assisted" in dying.

The Brittany Maynard case raises many serious personal, ethical, and moral issues. It also forces us to confront our anxieties about death, how we confront death as a society, and what we truly believe. Each of us must take the time to think through these issues, and make our desires known. What do *you* think about what Brittany chose?

There is no question the debate over physician-assisted suicide will continue. As the technology to keep people alive continues to improve, the ethical issues about active euthanasia in general and physician-assisted suicide in particular will continue to become more complex and will likely focus increasingly on quality of life and death with dignity (Gostin & Roberts, 2016).

The Price of Life-Sustaining Care

A growing debate in the United States, particularly in the aftermath of the Affordable Care Act passed in 2010, concerns the financial, personal, and moral costs of keeping people alive on life-support machines and continuing aggressive care when people have terminal conditions. Debate continues on whether secondary health conditions in terminally ill people should be treated. The argument is such care is expensive, these people will die soon anyway, and needlessly prolonging life is a burden on society.

However, many others argue all means possible should be used, whether for a premature infant or an older adult, to keep them alive despite the high cost and possible risk of negative side effects of the treatment or intervention. They argue life is precious, and humans should not "play God" and decide when it should end.

There is no question extraordinary interventions are expensive. Healthcare costs can soar during the last year of a person's life. Data indicate less than 7% of people who receive hospital care die each year, but account for nearly 25% of all Medicare expenditures (Adamy & McGinty, 2012). One example involves the continued use of chemotherapy for end-stage cancer patients; the higher costs of care given the evidence of limited benefit and potential harm of continued treatment are coming under increased scrutiny (Garrido et al., 2016). Expenditures for end-of-life care are typically less for those having advance directives (discussed later in this chapter) who receive palliative care.

The biggest challenge in confronting these differences in approach and cost is the difficulty in deciding when to treat or not treat a disease a person has. There are no easy answers. Witness the loud criticism when research evidence indicated various types of cancer screening (e.g., breast, prostate) should not be provided to everyone as early or as often as initially thought. Despite the lack of evidence to support and the cost of continuing traditional approaches, many patients and physicians do so anyway. Failure to base care on evidence has a price. Whether that is affordable in the long run seems unlikely.

Adult Development in Action

How should the biopsychosocial model influence political debates about dying and death?

13.2 Thinking About Death: Personal Aspects

LEARNING OBJECTIVES
- How do feelings about death change over adulthood?
- How do people deal with their own death?
- What is death anxiety, and how do people show it?

Jean is a 49-year-old woman whose parents have both died in the past three years. She now realizes she is the oldest living member of her family (she has two younger siblings). She started thinking about the fact that someday she too will die. Jean gets anxious when she thinks about her death, and tries to block it out of her mind.

Like Jean, most people are uncomfortable thinking about their own death, especially if they think it will be unpleasant. As one research participant put it,

"You are nuts if you aren't afraid of death" (Kalish & Reynolds, 1976). Still, death is a paradox, as we noted at the beginning of the chapter. That is, we are afraid of or anxious about death but we are drawn to it, sometimes in public ways. We examine this paradox at the personal level in this section. Specifically, we focus on two questions: How do people's feelings about death differ with age? What is it about death we fear or that makes us anxious?

Before proceeding, however, take a few minutes to complete the exercise in the Discovering Development feature.

A Life-Course Approach to Dying

Suppose you learned today you had only a few months to live. How would you feel about dying? That's what Randy Pausch, a professor at Carnegie Mellon University, faced when he was told he had had 3 to 6 months to live after his pancreatic cancer came back. What happened next, describe in the Real People feature, touched millions of people around the world.

DISCOVERING DEVELOPMENT
A Self-Reflective Exercise on Death

As we noted, thinking about death, especially one's own, is difficult. One common way to remember people is through an obituary, an experience we may have with hundreds of people we know but never our own. Here's a chance to think about one's own death from that perspective.

- In 200 words or less, write your own obituary. Be sure to include your age and cause of death. List your lifetime accomplishments. Don't forget to list your survivors.
- Think about all the things you will have done that are not listed in your obituary. List some of them.
- Think of all the friends you will have made and how you will have affected them.
- Would you make any changes in your obituary now?

Real People
Randy Pausch's Last Lecture

Randy Pausch was a famous computer scientist on the faculty at Carnegie Mellon University. He cofounded the Entertainment Technology Center there and invented a highly innovative way to teach computer programming, called Alice. But that's not what made him world-famous. He was a pioneer of virtual reality.

Randy Pausch

At the age of 46, Randy was told that his pancreatic cancer had recurred and that he had between 3 and 6 months to live. So instead of just getting depressed about it, he decided to give a lecture a month later about achieving one's childhood dreams. His lecture is both moving and funny. Rather than talking about dying, Randy focused on overcoming obstacles and seizing every moment of one's life because, as he put it, "time is all you have…and you may find one day that you have less than you think." He spoke of his love for his wife and three children. He had a birthday cake brought onto the stage for his wife. Randy lived several more months after his lecture, dying in July 2008 at age 47.

You can see Randy's lecture by searching YouTube. It was also published as a book. In a strange twist, the coauthor of the book, Jeff Zaslow, was himself killed in an automobile accident at age 53.

One never knows when one's life will end; it is said that the end comes like a thief in the night. But people such as Randy Pausch help us put our own death into perspective by reminding us what is important.

It probably doesn't surprise you to learn feelings about dying vary with age and cultures (Gire, 2014). Each person comes to terms with death in an individual and a family-based way, and together they co-create ways the patient meets his or her goals (Bergdahl et al., 2013; Carlander et al., 2011; Milligan et al., 2016).

Although not specifically addressed in research, the shift from formal operational thinking to post-formal thinking (see Chapter 7) could be important in young adults' contemplation of death. Presumably, this shift in cognitive development is accompanied by a lessening of the feeling of immortality in adolescence to one that integrates personal feelings and emotions with their thinking.

Midlife is the time when most people in developed countries confront the death of their parents. Until that point, people tend not to think much about their own death; the fact their parents are still alive buffers them from reality. After all, in the normal course of events, our parents are supposed to die before we do.

Once their parents die, people realize they are now the oldest generation of their family—the next in line to die. Reading the obituary pages, they are reminded of this, as the ages of many of the people who died get closer and closer to their own.

Probably as a result of this growing realization of their own mortality, middle-aged adults' sense of time undergoes a subtle yet profound change. It changes from an emphasis on how long they have already lived to how long they have left to live, a shift that increases into late life (Cicirelli, 2006; Maxfield et al., 2010). This may lead to occupational change or other redirection such as improving relationships that deteriorated over the years. It is also the case that certain strategies are used to deflect attention from or buffer the reality of death anxiety. For example, Yaakobi (2015) found that the desire to work serves as a death anxiety buffer for adults.

In general, older adults are less anxious about death and more accepting of it than any other age group. Still, because the discrepancy between desired and expected number of years left to live is greater for young-old than for mid-old adults, anxiety is higher for young-old adults (Cicirelli, 2006). In part, the greater overall acceptance of death results from the achievement of ego integrity, as described in Chapter 9. For other older adults, the joy of living is diminishing. More than any other group, they experienced loss of family and friends and have come to terms with their own mortality. Older adults have more chronic diseases (see Chapters 3 and 4) that are not likely to go away. They may feel their most important life tasks have been completed (Kastenbaum, 1999).

Understanding how adults deal with death, end-of-life issues, and grief can be approached from the perspective of attachment theory (Hales, 2016; Stroebe, Schut, & Stroebe, 2005). In this view, a person's reactions are a natural consequence of forming attachments and then losing them. We consider adult grief a bit later in the chapter.

Dealing with One's Own Death

Many authors have tried to describe the dying process, often using the metaphor of a trajectory that captures the duration of time between the onset of dying (e.g., from the diagnosis of a fatal disease) as well as death and the course of the dying process (D'Angelo et al., 2015; Field & Cassel, 2010). These dying trajectories vary a great deal across diseases, as illustrated in Figure 13.2. Some diseases, such as lung cancer, have a clear and rapid period of decline; this "terminal phase" is often used to determine eligibility for certain services (e.g., hospice, discussed later). Other diseases, such as congestive heart failure, have no clear terminal phase. The two approaches of describing the dying process we consider will try to account for both types of trajectories.

Kübler-Ross's Work

Elisabeth Kübler-Ross changed the way we approach dying. When she began her investigations into the dying process in the 1960s, such research was controversial; her physician colleagues initially were outraged and some even denied their patients were terminally ill. Still, she persisted. More than 200 interviews with terminally ill people convinced her most people experienced several emotional reactions. Using her experiences, she described five reactions that represented the ways people dealt with death: denial, anger, bargaining, depression, and acceptance (Kübler-Ross, 1969). Although they were first presented as a sequence, it was subsequently realized the emotions can overlap and be experienced in different order.

Although she believed these five stages represent the typical range of emotional development in the dying, Kübler-Ross's (1974) cautioned not everyone experiences all of them or progresses through them at the same rate or in the same order. Research supports the view her "stages" should not be viewed as a sequence (Charlton & Verghese, 2010; Parkes, 2013). In fact, we could actually harm dying people by considering these stages as fixed and universal. Individual differences are great.

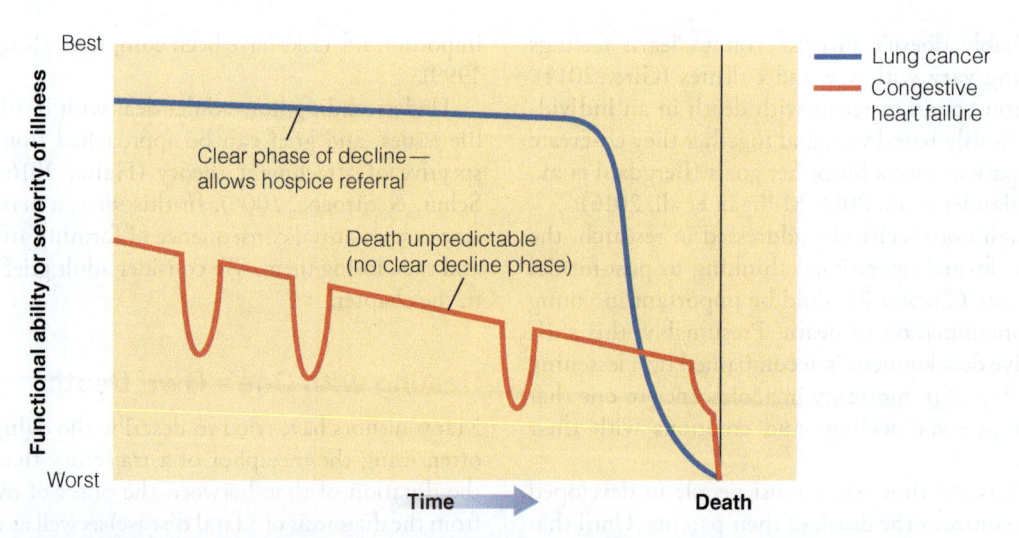

FIGURE 13.2 Some fatal diseases, such as lung cancer, have a clear decline phase, whereas others, such as congestive heart failure, do not.

Source: From Skolnick, A. A. (1998). MediCaring project to demonstrate and evaluate innovative end-of-life program for chronically ill. *Journal of the American Medical Association, 279*, 1511–1512. Reprinted with permission of the American Medical Association.© 2019 Cengage

Emotional responses may vary in intensity throughout the dying process. Thus, the goal in applying Kübler-Ross's ideas to real-world settings would be to help people achieve an appropriate death: one that meets the needs of the dying person, allowing him or her to work out each problem as it comes.

A Contextual Theory of Dying

Describing the process of dying is difficult. One reason for these problems is the realization there is no one right way to die, although there may be better or worse ways of coping (Corr, 2010a, b; Corr & Corr, 2013; Corr, Corr, & Nabe, 2008; Pope, 2017). Corr identified four dimensions of the issues or tasks a dying person faces from their perspective: bodily needs, psychological security, interpersonal attachments, and spiritual energy and hope. This holistic approach acknowledges individual differences and rejects broad generalizations. Corr's task work approach also recognizes the importance of the coping efforts of family members, friends, and caregivers as well as those of the dying person.

Kastenbaum and Thuell (1995) argue what is needed is an even broader contextual approach that takes a more inclusive view of the dying process. They point out theories must be able to handle people who have a wide variety of terminal illnesses and be sensitive to dying people's own perspectives and values related to death. The socio-environmental context where dying occurs often changes over time and must be recognized.

A person may begin the dying process living independently but end up in a long-term care facility. Such moves may have profound implications for how the person copes with dying. A contextual approach provides guidance for healthcare professionals and families for discussing how to protect the quality of life, provide better care, and prepare caregivers for dealing with the end of life. Such an approach would also provide research questions such as how does one's acceptance of dying change across various stages?

Although we do not yet have a comprehensive theory of dying, we examine people's experiences as a narrative that can be written from many points of view (e.g., the patient, family members, caregivers). What emerges would be a rich description of a dynamically changing, individual process.

Death Anxiety

We have seen how people view death varies with age. In the process, we encountered the notion of feeling anxious about death. **Death anxiety** *refers to people's anxiety or even fear of death and dying.* Death anxiety is tough to pin down; indeed, it is the ethereal, unknown nature of death, rather than something about it in particular, that makes us feel so uncomfortable. Because of this, we must look for indirect behavioral evidence to document death anxiety. Research findings suggest death anxiety is a complex, multidimensional construct.

For nearly three decades, researchers have applied terror management theory as a framework to study death anxiety (Burke, Martens, & Faucher, 2010; Park & Pyszczynski, 2016). **Terror management theory** *addresses the issue of why people engage in certain behaviors to achieve particular psychological states based on their deeply rooted concerns about mortality.* The theory proposes that ensuring the continuation of one's life is the primary motive underlying behavior and that all other motives can be traced to this basic one.

Additionally, some suggest older adults present an existential threat for the younger and middle-aged adults because they remind us all that death is inescapable, the body is fallible, and the bases that we may secure self-esteem (and manage death anxiety) are transitory (Martens, Goldenberg, & Greenberg, 2005). That may be why some people seek cosmetic surgery as a way to deal with their death anxiety (Tam, 2013). Thus, death anxiety is a reflection of one's concern over dying, an outcome that would violate the prime motive.

Neuroimaging research shows terror management theory provides a useful framework for studying brain activity related to death anxiety. Quirin and colleagues (2012) found brain activity in the right amygdala, left rostral anterior cingulate cortex, and right caudate nucleus was greater when male participants were answering questions about fear of death and dying than when they were answering questions about dental pain. Similarly, electrical activity in the brain indicates people defend themselves against emotions related to death (Klackl, Jonas, & Kronbichler, 2013). And younger adults show greater brain responses to death-related terms than do older adults, indicating a fundamental shift in how adults process death-related concepts with age (Bluntschli et al., in press). There is neurophysiological evidence that shows Jean's attempts to block thoughts of her own death in the opening vignette are common across people.

On the basis of several diverse studies using many different measures, researchers now conclude death anxiety consists of several components. Each of these components is most easily described with terms that reflect areas of great concern (anxiety) but that cannot be tied to any one specific focus. These components of death anxiety include pain, body malfunction, humiliation, rejection, nonbeing, punishment, interruption of goals, being destroyed, and negative impact on survivors (Power & Smith, 2008). To complicate matters further, each of these components can be assessed at any of three levels: public, private, and nonconscious. What we admit feeling about death in public may differ greatly from what we feel when we are alone with our own thoughts from what we may be unaware of that still influences our behavior. In short, the measurement of death anxiety is complex and researchers need to specify what aspects they are assessing.

Much research has been conducted to learn what demographic and personality variables are related to death anxiety. Although the results often are ambiguous, some patterns have emerged. Older adults tend to have lower death anxiety than younger adults, perhaps because of their tendency to engage in life review, have a different perspective about time, and their higher level of religious motivation (Henrie, 2010). Men show greater fear of the unknown than women, but women report more specific fear of the dying process (Cicirelli, 2001). Death anxiety varies across cultures in how it is (or is not) expressed (Park & Pyszczynski, 2016). In Taiwan, higher death anxiety among patients with cancer is associated with not having a purpose in life and level of fear of disease relapse (Tang et al., 2011).

Strange as it may seem, death anxiety may have a beneficial side. For one thing, being afraid to die means we often go to great lengths to make sure we stay alive, as argued by terror management theory (Burke et al., 2010; Park & Pyszczynski, 2016). Because staying alive ensures the continuation and socialization of the species, fear of death serves as a motivation to have children and raise them properly.

Learning to Deal with Death Anxiety

Although some degree of death anxiety may be appropriate, we must guard against letting it become powerful enough to interfere with normal daily routines. Several ways exist to help us in this endeavor. Perhaps the one most often used is to live life to the fullest. Kalish (1984, 1987) argues people who do this enjoy what they have; although they may still fear death and feel cheated, they have few regrets.

Koestenbaum (1976) proposes several exercises and questions to increase one's death awareness. Some of these are to write your own obituary (like you did earlier in this chapter) and to plan your own death and funeral services. You can also ask yourself: "What circumstances would help make my death acceptable?" "Is death the sort of thing that could happen to me right now?"

These questions serve as a basis for an increasingly popular way to reduce anxiety: death education. Most death education programs combine factual information about death with issues aimed at reducing anxiety and fear to increase sensitivity to others' feelings. These programs vary widely in orientation; they include such topics as philosophy, ethics, psychology, drama, religion, medicine, art, and many others. Additionally, they focus on death, the process of dying, grief and bereavement, or any combination of those. In general, death education programs help primarily by increasing our awareness of the complex emotions felt and expressed by dying people and their families. It is important to make education programs reflect the diverse backgrounds of the participants (Fowler, 2008).

Research shows participating in experiential workshops about death significantly lowers death anxiety in younger, middle-aged, and older adults and raises awareness about the importance of advance directives (Moeller et al., 2010).

Adult Development in Action

How might different approaches to lowering death anxiety be useful to you as a healthcare worker?

13.3 End-of-Life Issues

LEARNING OBJECTIVES
- What are end-of-life issues? What is a final scenario?
- What is hospice? How does hospice relate to end-of-life issues?
- How does one make end-of-life desires and decisions known?

Jean is a 72-year-old woman recently diagnosed with advanced colon cancer. She has vivid memories of her father dying a long, protracted death in great pain. Jean is afraid she will suffer the same fate. She heard the hospice in town emphasizes pain management and provides a lot of support for families. Jean wonders whether that is something she should explore in the time she has left.

When people think about how they would like to die, no one chooses a slow, painful process where medical intervention continues well beyond the point of increasing quality of life over quantity of life. However, medical intervention such as life support or cardiopulmonary resuscitation (CPR), are common, often required by law, even in situations in which people would prefer them not to be used. How can people make their wishes known about how they want to experience the end of their life known?

Creating a Final Scenario

When given the chance, many adults would like to discuss a variety of issues, collectively called **end-of-life issues**: *management of the final phase of life, after-death disposition of their body, memorial services, and distribution of assets* (Moeller et al., 2010). We are experiencing a major shift in how people handle end-of-life issues. Prior to the current generation of older adults, people rarely planned ahead for or made their wishes known about medical care they did or did not want. Now, people want to manage the final part of their lives by thinking through the choices between traditional care (e.g., provided by hospitals and nursing homes) and alternatives (such as hospices, that we discuss in the next section), completing advance directives (e.g., healthcare power of attorney, living will), resolving key personal relationships, and perhaps choosing the alternative of ending one's life prematurely through euthanasia.

Consider the issue of rituals surrounding the time immediately following death. What happens to one's body and how one is memorialized matters to most people. But decisions about these have to be made. Is a traditional burial preferred over cremation? A traditional funeral over a memorial service? Such choices often are based in people's religious beliefs and their desire for privacy for their families after they have died.

Making sure one's estate and personal effects are passed on appropriately often is overlooked. Making a will is especially important to ensure one's wishes are carried out. Providing for the informal distribution of personal effects also helps prevent disputes between family members.

Whether people choose to address these issues formally or informally, it is important they be given the opportunity to do so. In many cases, family members are reluctant to discuss these matters with the dying relative because of their own anxiety about death. *Making such choices known about how they do and do not want their lives to end constitutes a* **final scenario**.

One of the most difficult and important parts of a final scenario for most people is the process of separation from family and friends (Corr & Corr, 2013; Wanzer & Glenmullen, 2007). The final days, weeks, and months of life provide opportunities to affirm love, resolve conflicts, and provide peace to dying people. The failure to complete this process often leaves survivors feeling they did not achieve closure in the relationship, and can result in bitterness toward the deceased.

Healthcare workers realize the importance of giving dying patients the chance to create a final scenario and recognize the uniqueness of each person's final passage. A key part of their role is to ease this process through good communication with the family (Curtis et al., 2016; Wanzer & Glenmullen, 2007). Any given final scenario reflects the individual's personal past, that is the unique combination of the development forces the person experienced. Primary attention is paid to how people's total life experiences prepared them to face end-of-life issues (Curtis et al., 2016).

One's final scenario helps family and friends interpret one's death, especially when the scenario is constructed jointly, such as between spouses, and when communication is open and honest. The different perspectives of everyone involved are unlikely to converge without clear communication and discussion. Respecting each person's perspective is basic and greatly helps in creating a good final scenario.

Encouraging people to decide for themselves how the end of their lives should be handled helps people take control of their dying (Hains & Hulbert-Williams, 2013) and think through issues such as euthanasia are processed at the individual level (Feltz, 2015). Taking personal control over one's dying process is a trend occurring even in cultures such as Japan that traditionally defer to physician's opinions (Alden, Merz, & Akashi, 2012). The emergence of final scenarios as an important consideration fits well with the emphasis on addressing pain through palliative care, an approach underlying hospice.

The Hospice Option

As we have seen, most people would like to die at home among family and friends. An important barrier to this choice is the availability of support systems when the person has a terminal disease. Most people believe they have no choice but to go to a hospital or nursing home. However, another alternative exists. **Hospice** *is an approach to assist dying people emphasizing pain management, or palliative care, and death with dignity* (Knee, 2010; Winslow & Meldrum, 2013). The emphasis in a hospice is on the dying person's quality of life. This approach grows out of an important distinction between the prolongation of life and the prolongation of death, a distinction important to Jean, the woman we met in the vignette. In a hospice the concern is to make the person as peaceful and as comfortable as possible, not to delay an inevitable death. *An approach to care based on an ethic of controlling and relieving pain or other symptoms and not on attempting to cure disease is called* **palliative care** (Prince-Paul & Daly, 2016). Hospice is the leading provider of such care, but palliative care is also adopted in other settings.

Modern hospices are modeled after St. Christopher's Hospice in England, founded in 1967 by Dr. Cicely Saunders. Hospice services are requested only after the person or physician believes no treatment or cure is possible, making the hospice program markedly different from hospital or home care. The differences are evident in the principles that underlie hospice care (Knee, 2010):

- Clients and their families are viewed as a unit, clients should be kept free of pain, emotional and social impoverishment must be minimal;
- Clients must be encouraged to maintain competencies, conflict resolution and fulfillment of realistic desires must be assisted; and
- Clients must be free to begin or end relationships, an interdisciplinary team approach is used, and staff members must seek to alleviate pain and fear.

Two types of hospices exist: inpatient and outpatient. Inpatient hospices provide all care for clients; outpatient hospices provide services to clients who remain in their own homes. The outpatient variation, when a hospice nurse visits clients in their home, is becoming increasingly popular, largely because more clients can be served at a lower cost. Having hospice services available to people at home is a viable option for many people, especially in helping home-based caregivers cope with loss, but should be provided by specially-trained professionals (Newman, Thompson, & Chandler, 2013).

Hospices do not follow a hospital model of care. The role of the staff in a hospice is not so much to treat the client as it is just to be with the client. A client's dignity is always maintained; often more attention is paid to appearance and personal grooming than to medical tests. Hospice staff members also provide a great deal of support to the client's family.

Increasingly, this support includes different ways of being present to and with the person who is dying. Many hospices have the option for *death doulas* who help ease the passage through death. For some dying individuals, the doula may simply hold their hand; for others it may be through playing special music and sitting or meditating with them. The main role is to ensure that dying people are not alone, and that families, if present, have personal support.

Hospice and hospital patients differ in important ways (Knee, 2010). Hospice clients are more mobile, less anxious, and less depressed; spouses visit hospice clients more often and participate more in their care; and hospice staff members are perceived as more accessible. Research consistently shows significant improvements in clients' quality of life occur after hospice placement or beginning palliative care (Blackhall et al., 2016; Rocque & Cleary, 2013).

Although the hospice is a valuable alternative for many people, it may not be appropriate for everyone. Those who trust their physician regarding medical care options are more likely to select hospice than those who do not trust their physician, especially among African Americans, who as a group prefer more aggressive treatment options (Ludke & Smucker, 2007; Smith-Howell et al., 2016). Most people who select hospice suffer from cancer, AIDS, cardiovascular disease, pulmonary disease, or a progressive neurological condition such as dementia; two-thirds are over age 65; and most are in the last six months of life (Hospice Foundation of America, 2016a).

Needs expressed by staff, family, and clients differ (Hiatt et al., 2007). Staff and family members tend to emphasize pain management, whereas many clients want more attention paid to personal issues, such as spirituality and the process of dying. This difference means the staff and family members may need to ask clients more often what they need instead of making assumptions about what they need.

How do people decide among various care options, such as hospice, home health, or skilled care? Families should ask several key questions (Hospice Foundation of America, 2016b; Karp & Wood, 2012; Knee, 2010):

- *Is the person completely informed about the nature and prognosis of his or her condition?* Full knowledge and the ability to communicate with healthcare personnel are essential to understanding what hospice has to offer.
- *What options are available at this point in the progress of the person's disease?* Knowing about all available treatment options is critical. Exploring treatment options also requires healthcare professionals to be aware of the latest approaches and be willing to disclose them.
- *What are the person's expectations, fears, and hopes?* Some older adults, like Jean, remember or have heard stories about people who suffered greatly at the end of their lives. This can produce anxiety about one's own death. Similarly, fears of becoming dependent play an important role in a person's decision making. Discovering and discussing these anxieties helps clarify options.
- *How well do people in the person's social network communicate with each other?* Talking about death is taboo in many families. In others, intergenerational communication is difficult or impossible. Even in families with good communication, the pending death of a loved relative is difficult. As a result, the dying person may have difficulty expressing his or her wishes. The decision to explore the hospice option is best made when it is discussed openly.
- *Are family members available to participate actively in terminal care?* Hospice relies on family members to provide much of the care that is supplemented by professionals and volunteers. We saw in Chapter 11 being a primary caregiver can be highly stressful. Having a family member who is willing to accept this responsibility is essential for the hospice option to work.
- *Is a high-quality hospice care program available?* Hospice programs are not uniformly good. As with any healthcare provider, patients and family members must investigate the quality of local hospice programs before making a choice. The Hospice Foundation of America provides excellent material for evaluating a hospice.
- *Is hospice covered by insurance?* Hospice services are reimbursable under Medicare in most cases, but any additional expenses may or may not be covered under other forms of insurance.

Hospice provides an important end-of-life option for many terminally ill people and their families. Moreover, the supportive follow-up services they provide are often used by surviving family and friends. Most important, the success of the hospice option has had important influences on traditional health care. For example, the American Academy of Pain Medicine (2016) publishes official position papers regarding the appropriate use of medical and behavioral interventions to provide pain management. The Centers for Disease Control and Prevention (2016) also published guidelines for the appropriate use of opioids for pain management due to the risk of addiction from these medications.

Despite the importance of the hospice option for end-of-life decisions, terminally ill persons face the barriers of family reluctance to face the reality of terminal illness and participate in the decision-making process, and healthcare providers who hinder access to hospice care (Knee, 2010; Moon, 2017; Torres et al., 2016).

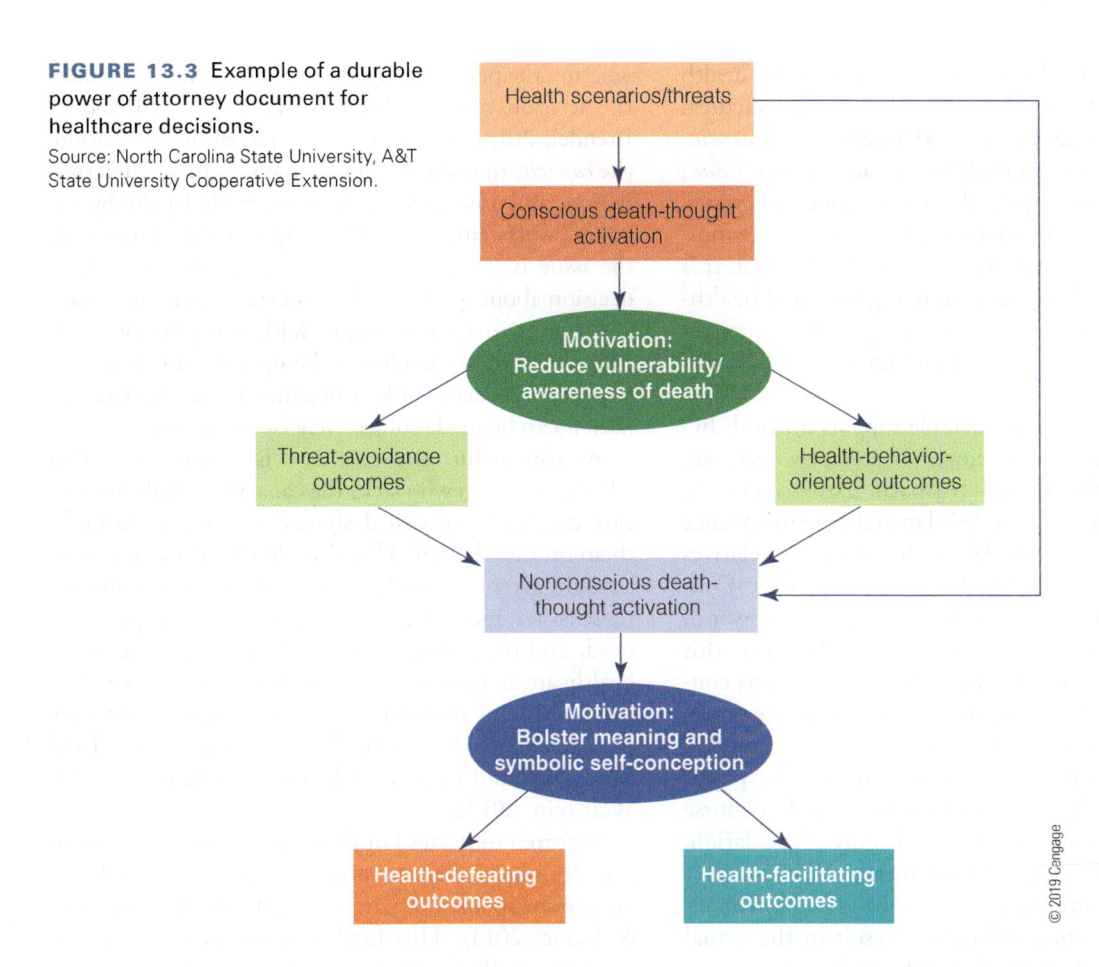

FIGURE 13.3 Example of a durable power of attorney document for healthcare decisions.

Source: North Carolina State University, A&T State University Cooperative Extension.

As the end of life approaches, the most important thing to keep in mind is that the dying person has the right to state-of-the-art approaches to treatment and pain management. Irrespective of the choice of traditional health care or hospice, the wishes of the dying person should be honored, and family members and primary care providers must participate.

Making Your End-of-Life Intentions Known

End-of-life realities raise complex legal, political, and ethical issues. In most jurisdictions, ending life through such means as euthanasia or assisted suicide is legal only when a person has made known his or her wishes concerning medical or other intervention. Unfortunately, many people fail to explicitly state their wishes, perhaps because it is difficult to think about such situations or because they do not know the options available to them. Without clear directions, though, medical personnel may be unable to take a patient's preferences into account. For instance, many states have laws requiring CPR or other attempts at resuscitation be used in the absence of clear evidence that the person does not want them used.

There are two ways to make one's intentions known. *In a* **living will**, *a person simply states his or her wishes about life support and other treatments. In a* **healthcare power of attorney**, *an individual appoints someone to act as his or her agent for healthcare decisions* (see Figure 13.3). A major purpose of both is to make one's wishes known about the use of life support interventions in the event the person is unconscious or otherwise incapable of expressing them, along with other related end-of-life issues such as organ transplantation and other healthcare options. Without them, the ethical considerations of life sustaining intervention for terminally ill patients is fraught with ethical dilemmas (Awadi & Mrayyan, 2016; Portnoy et al., 2015). A durable power of attorney for health care has an additional advantage: It names an individual who has the legal authority to speak and make decisions for the person if necessary.

A living will or a durable power of attorney for health care can be the basis for a "do not resuscitate" medical order. A **do not resuscitate (DNR) order** *means cardiopulmonary resuscitation (CPR) is not started should one's heart and breathing stop.* In the normal course of events, a medical team will immediately try to restore normal heartbeat and respiration. With a DNR order, this treatment is not done. As with living wills and healthcare power of attorney, it is extremely important to let all appropriate medical personnel know a DNR order is in effect.

Although there is considerable support for both living wills and healthcare power of attorney, there are several challenges as well (Alspach, 2016; Izumi & Son, 2016). States vary in their laws relating to advance directives. Many people fail to inform their relatives and physicians about their healthcare decisions. Others do not tell the person named in a durable power of attorney where the document is kept. Obviously, this puts relatives at a serious disadvantage if decisions concerning the use of life-support systems need to be made.

Fortunately, since 2016 Medicare covers advance care planning as a separate service provided by physicians and other healthcare professionals such as nurse practitioners (Henry J. Kaiser Family Foundation, 2016). This makes it easier for patients to discuss their wishes with a healthcare professional and to learn about options. Ideally, these discussions result in the actual documentation of a person's specific wishes.

Patient Self-Determination and Competency Evaluation

Making your decisions about health care known presumes that you are competent and able to make those decisions for yourself. To aid healthcare providers in this process, the Patient Self-Determination Act, passed in 1990, requires most healthcare facilities to provide information to patients in writing that they have the right to:

- Make their own healthcare decisions.
- Accept or refuse medical treatment.
- Make an advance healthcare directive.

Patients must be asked if they have an advance directive, and, if so, it must be included in the medical record. Staff at the healthcare facility must receive training about advance directives, and cannot make admissions or treatment decisions based on whether those directives exist.

One major concern regarding the appropriate implementation of the Patient Self-Determination Act is whether the person is cognitively or legally able to make the decisions about end-of-life care (Moye, Sabatino, & Brendel, 2013). There are two types of determination: the *capacity* to make decisions, that is a clinical determination, and a *competency* decision, made legally by the court (Wettstein, 2013). With capacity determinations, the issue is whether the individual is able to make a decision about specific tasks, and the abilities necessary are subject to measurement. With competency determinations, the individual is being judged either with respect to a specific task or in general, and the determination can be made subjectively by the court.

At this point, the case law is limited regarding whether a person who lacks the capacity to make healthcare decisions can still designate a surrogate to make them on their behalf. This situation is rather common, though, given the tendency for families to not discuss these issues, individual's reluctance to face the potential need, and the politicization of the conversation in the healthcare arena. Guidelines for professionals regarding the assessment of competence are available, and they provide insight into both the psychological and legal issues surrounding such evaluations (Moye et al., 2013; Wettstein, 2013).

Research indicates family members and other surrogate decision-makers are often wrong about what loved ones, even spouses or partners, really want (Moorman & Inoue, 2013). This further emphasizes the critical need, especially for couples, to discuss end-of-life issues ahead of time and ensure the appropriate advance directives are in place and key individuals are aware of them (Queen, Berg, & Lowrance, 2015).

Adult Development in Action

What steps are necessary to ensure that your advance directives about health care are followed?

13.4 Surviving The Loss: The Grieving Process

LEARNING OBJECTIVES

- How do people experience the grief process?
- What feelings do grieving people have?
- How do people cope with grief?
- What are the types of ambiguous loss?
- What is the difference between normal and complicated grief?
- What developmental aspects are important in understanding grief?

After 67 years of marriage, Bertha recently lost her husband. At 90, Bertha knew neither she nor her husband was likely to live much longer, but the death was a shock just the same. Bertha thinks about him much of the time and often finds herself making decisions on the basis of "what John would have done" in the same situation.

Each of us suffers many losses over a lifetime. Whenever we lose someone close to us through death or other separation, like Bertha we experience bereavement, grief, and mourning. **Bereavement** *is the state or condition caused by loss through death.* **Grief** *is the sorrow, hurt, anger, guilt, confusion, and other feelings that arise after suffering a loss.* **Mourning** *concerns the ways we express our grief.* You can tell people in some cultures are bereaved and in mourning because of the clothing they wear. Mourning is highly influenced by culture. For some, mourning may involve wearing black, attending funerals, and observing an official period of grief; for others, it means drinking, wearing white, and marrying the deceased spouse's sibling. Grief corresponds to the emotional reactions following loss, whereas mourning is the culturally approved behavioral manifestations of those feelings. Even though mourning rituals may be fairly standard within a culture, how people grieve varies, as we see next. We will also see how Bertha's reactions are fairly typical of most people.

The Grief Process

How do people grieve? What do they experience? Perhaps you already have a good idea about the answers to these questions from your own experience. If so, you already know the process of grieving is a complicated and personal one. Just as there is no right way to die, there is no right way to grieve. Recognizing there are plenty of individual differences, we consider these patterns in this section.

The grieving process is often described as reflecting many themes and issues people confront that may be expressed through rituals, both in-person and digital (Gamba, 2015; Norton & Gino, 2014). Like the process of dying, grieving does not have clearly demarcated stages through which we pass in a neat sequence, although there are certain issues people must face similar to those faced by dying people. When someone close to us dies, we must reorganize our lives, establish new patterns of behavior, and redefine relationships with family and friends. Indeed, Attig (1996) provided one of the best descriptions of grief when he wrote grief is the process by which we relearn the world.

Unlike bereavement, over which we have no control, grief is a process that involves choices in coping, from confronting the reality and emotions to using religion to ease one's pain (Cummings, 2015; Norton & Gino, 2014). From this perspective, grief is an active process when a person must do several things (Worden, 1991):

- *Acknowledge the reality of the loss.* We must overcome the temptation to deny the reality of our loss; we must fully and openly acknowledge it and realize it affects every aspect of our life.
- *Work through the emotional turmoil.* We must find effective ways to confront and express the complete range of emotions we feel after the loss and must not avoid or repress them.
- *Adjust to the environment where the deceased is absent.* We must define new patterns of living that adjust appropriately and meaningfully to the fact the deceased is not present.
- *Loosen ties to the deceased.* We must free ourselves from the bonds of the deceased in order to reengage with our social network. This means finding effective ways to say good-bye.

Grief is an active coping process (Bagbey Darian, 2014). In processing grief, survivors must come to terms with and integrate the physical world of things, places, and events as well as their spiritual place in the world; the interpersonal world of interactions with family and friends, the dead, and, in some cases, God; and aspects of our inner selves and our personal experiences. Bertha, the woman in the vignette, is in the middle of this process. Even the matter of deciding what to do with the deceased's personal effects can be part of this active coping process (Attig, 1996).

To make sense of grief, we need to keep several things in mind. First, grieving is a highly individual experience (Bagbey Darian, 2014; Cummings, 2015; Steck & Steck, 2016). A process that works well for one person may not be the best for someone else. Second, we must not underestimate the amount of time people need to deal with the various issues. To a casual observer, it may appear a survivor is "back to normal" after a few weeks (Harris, 2016). Actually, what may look like a return to normal activities may reflect bereaved people feeling social pressure to "get on with things." It takes most people much longer to resolve the complex emotional issues faced during bereavement. Researchers and therapists alike agree a person needs at least a year following the loss to begin recovery, and two years is not uncommon.

Finally, "recovery" may be a misleading term. It is probably more accurate to say we learn to live with our loss rather than we recover from it (Attig, 1996). The impact of the loss of a loved one lasts a long time, perhaps for the rest of one's life. Still, most people reach a point of moving on with their lives (Bagbey Darian, 2014; Bonanno, 2009; Harris, 2016).

Recognizing these aspects of grief makes it easier to know what to say and do for bereaved people. Among the most useful things are to simply to let the person know you are sorry for his or her loss, you are there for support, and mean what you say.

Risk Factors in Grief

Bereavement is a life experience most people have many times, and most people eventually handle it, often better than we might suspect (Bagbey Darian, 2014; Bonanno, 2009; Bonanno, Westphal, & Mancini, 2011; Cummings, 2015; Steck & Steck, 2016). However, there are some risk factors that make bereavement more difficult. Several of the more important are the mode of death, personal factors (e.g., personality, religiosity, age, gender, income), and interpersonal context (social support, kinship relationship).

Most people believe the circumstances of death affects the grief process. A person whose family member was killed in an automobile accident has a different situation to deal with than a person whose family member died after a long period of suffering with Alzheimer's disease. *It is believed when death is anticipated, people go through a period of* **anticipatory grief** *before the death that supposedly serves to buffer the impact of the loss when it does come and to facilitate recovery* (Shore et al., 2016). Indicators of anticipatory grief may appear as pre-loss grief, and as depression, anxiety, or pain.

The research evidence for whether anticipatory grief helps people cope with loss better is mixed. Anticipating the loss of a loved one from cancer or other terminal disease can provide a framework for understanding family members' reactions (Coombs, 2010; Shore et al., 2016). However, anticipatory grief does not appear to alleviate the outcome of the bereavement; in fact, it may even make it more difficult to reach a positive outcome (Nielsen et al., 2016).

The strength of attachment to the deceased person does make a difference in dealing with a sudden as opposed to an expected death. Attachment theory provides a framework for understanding different reactions (Hales, 2016; Stroebe & Archer, 2013). When the deceased person was one for whom the survivor had a strong and close attachment and the loss was sudden, the grief is greater. However, such secure attachment styles tend to result in less depression after the loss because of less guilt over unresolved issues (because there are fewer of them), things not provided (because more were likely provided), and so on.

Few studies of personal risk factors have been done, and few firm conclusions can be drawn. To date there are no consistent findings regarding personality traits that either help buffer people from the effects of bereavement or exacerbate them (Haley, 2013; Stroebe & Archer, 2013). Some evidence suggests church attendance or spirituality in general helps people to deal with bereavement and subsequent grief through the post-grief period (Gordon, 2013). There are, however, consistent findings regarding gender. Men and women differ in the ways they express emotions related to grief (Kersting & Nagl, 2016). Men have higher mortality rates following bereavement than women, who have higher rates of depression and complicated grief (discussed later in this section) than men, but the reasons for these differences are unclear (Kersting et al., 2011). Research also consistently shows older adults suffer the least health consequences following bereavement, with the impact perhaps being strongest for middle-aged adults, but strong social support networks, including virtual ones, lessen these effects to varying degrees (Chang et al., 2016; Papa & Litz, 2011).

Typical Grief Reactions

The feelings experienced during grieving are intense; these feelings not only make it difficult to cope but can also make a person question her or his own reactions. The feelings involved usually include sadness, denial, anger, loneliness, and guilt.

Many authors refer to the psychological side of coming to terms with bereavement as **grief work**. Whether the loss is ambiguous and lacking closure (e.g., waiting to learn the fate of a missing loved one) or certain (e.g., verification of death through a dead body), people need space and time to grieve (Berns, 2011; Harris, 2016). However, a major challenge in American society is that, as noted earlier, people feel pressured to "move on" quickly after a loss, especially if that loss is not of a spouse or child. That is not how people really feel or want to deal with their grief; they want the opportunity to work through their feelings on their own terms and timeline.

Muller and Thompson (2003) examined people's experience of grief in a detailed interview study and found five themes. *Coping* concerns what people do to deal with their loss in terms of what helps them. *Affect* refers to people's emotional reactions to the death of their loved one, such as certain topics that serve as emotional triggers for memories of their loved one. *Change* involves the ways survivors' lives change as a result of the loss; personal growth (e.g., "I didn't think I could deal with something that painful, but I did") is a common experience. *Narrative* relates to the stories survivors tell about their deceased loved one, that sometimes includes details about the process of the death. Finally, *relationship* reflects who the deceased person was and the nature of the ties between that person and the survivor. Collectively, these themes indicate the experience of grief is complex and involves dealing with one's feelings as a survivor as well as memories of the deceased person.

How people show their feelings of grief varies across ethnic and cultural groups (Bordere, 2016; Gire, 2014). For example, families in KwaZulu-Natal, South Africa, have a strong desire for closure and need for dealing with the "loneliness of grief" (Brysiewicz, 2008). In many cultures the bereaved construct a relationship with the person who died, but how this happens differs widely, from "ghosts" to appearances in dreams to connection through prayer and ancestor worship (Cacciatore & DeFrain, 2015). Differences in dealing with grief and bereavement can also be observed across different subgroups within ethnic groups. For instance, various Hispanic groups (e.g., Mexican, Puerto Rican, Central American) differ somewhat from each other in ritual practices (Schoulte, 2011).

In addition to psychological grief reactions, there are also physiological ones (McCoyd & Walter, 2016). Physical health may decline, illness may result, and use of healthcare services may increase. Some people report sleep disturbances as well as neurological and circulatory problems (Kowalski & Bondmass, 2008; Naef et al., 2013). Widowers in general report major disruptions in their daily routines (Naef et al., 2013).

In the time following the death of a loved one, dates having personal significance may reintroduce feelings of grief. Holidays such as Thanksgiving or birthdays that were spent with the deceased person may be difficult times. The actual anniversary of the death can be especially troublesome. The term **anniversary reaction** refers to *changes in behavior related to feelings of sadness on this date.* Personal experience and research show recurring feelings of sadness or other examples of the anniversary reaction are common in normal grief (DiBello, 2015; Holland & Neimeyer, 2010; Rostila et al., 2015). Such feelings also accompany remembrances of major catastrophes across cultures, such as Thais remembering the victims of a tsunami and major flood (Assanangkornchai et al., 2007).

Most research on how people react to the death of a loved one is cross-sectional. This work shows grief tends to peak within the first six months following the death of a loved one (Maciejewski et al., 2007), but may never fully go away, with effects on cognitive well-being being greater than for emotional well-being in general (Luhmann et al., 2012).

Research has been done to examine longitudinal effects of grief. Some widows show no sign of lessening of grief after 5 years (Kowalski & Bondmass, 2008). Rosenblatt (1996) reported people still felt the effects of the deaths of family members 50 years after the event. The depth of the emotions over the loss of loved ones sometimes never totally goes away, as people still cry and feel sad when discussing the loss despite the length of time that had passed. In general, though, people move on with their lives and deal with their feelings reasonably well (Bagbey Darian, 2014; Bonanno, 2009; Bonanno et al., 2011; Cummings, 2015; Steck & Steck, 2016).

Coping with Grief

Thus far, we considered the behaviors people show when they are dealing with grief. We have also seen these behaviors change over time. How does this happen? How can we explain the grieving process?

Numerous theories have been proposed to account for the grieving process, such as general life-event theories, psychodynamic, attachment, and cognitive process theories (Stroebe & Archer, 2013; Stroebe, Schut, & Boerner, 2010). All of these approaches to grief are based on more general theories that result in none of them providing an adequate explanation of the grieving process. Three integrative approaches have been proposed specific to the grief process: the four-component model, the dual process model of coping with bereavement, and the model of adaptive grieving dynamics.

The Four-Component Model

The **four-component model** *proposes understanding grief is based on four things: (1) the context of the loss, referring to the risk factors such as whether the death was expected; (2) continuation of subjective meaning associated with loss, ranging from evaluations of everyday concerns to major questions about the meaning of life; (3) changing representations of the lost relationship over time; and (4) the role of coping and emotion regulation processes that cover all* *coping strategies used to deal with grief* (Bonanno, 2009; Bonanno et al., 2011). The four-component model relies heavily on emotion theory, has much in common with the transactional model of stress, and has empirical support. According to the four-component model, dealing with grief is a complicated process only understood as a complex outcome that unfolds over time.

There are several important implications of this integrative approach. One of the most important in helping a grieving person involves helping her or him make meaning from the loss (Bratkovich, 2010; Wong, 2015). Second, this model implies encouraging people to express their grief may actually not be helpful. *An alternative view, called the* **grief work as rumination hypothesis**, *not only rejects the necessity of grief processing for recovery from loss but views extensive grief processing as a form of rumination that may actually increase distress* (Bonanno, Papa, & O'Neill, 2001). Although it may seem people who think obsessively about their loss or who ruminate about it are confronting the loss, rumination is actually considered a form of avoidance because the person is not dealing with his or her real feelings and moving on (Bui et al., 2015; Eisma et al., 2015; Robinaugh & McNally, 2013).

One prospective study shows, for instance, bereaved individuals who were not depressed prior to their spouse's death but then evidenced chronically elevated depression through the first year and a half of bereavement (i.e., a chronic grief pattern) also tended to report more frequently thinking about and talking about their recent loss at the 6-month point in bereavement (Bonanno, Wortman, & Neese, 2004). Thus, some bereaved individuals engage in minimal grief processing whereas others are predisposed toward more extensive grief processing. Furthermore, the individuals who engage in minimal grief processing will show a relatively favorable grief outcome, whereas those who are predisposed to more extensive grief processing tend toward ruminative preoccupation and, consequently, to a more prolonged grief course (Bonanno, 2009; Bonanno et al., 2011; Bui et al., 2015; Robinaugh & McNally, 2013).

In contrast to the traditional perspective that equates the absence of grief processing with grief avoidance, the grief work as rumination framework assumes resilient individuals are able to minimize processing of a loss through relatively automated processes, such as distraction or shifting attention toward more positive emotional experiences (Bonanno, 2009; Bonanno et al., 2011; Eisma et al., 2015). The grief work as rumination framework argues the deliberate avoidance or suppression of grief actually makes the experience of grief worse (Bonanno, 2009; Bonanno et al., 2011).

The How Do We Know? feature explores grief work regarding the loss of a spouse and the loss of a child in two cultures, the United States and China. As you read it, pay special attention to the question of whether encouraging people to express and deal with their grief is necessarily a good idea.

How Do We Know?
Grief Processing and Avoidance in the United States and China

Who were the investigators and what was the aim of the study? Bonanno and colleagues (2005) noted grief following the loss of a loved one often tends to be denied. However, research evidence related to positive benefits of resolving grief is largely lacking. Thus, whether unresolved grief is "bad" remains an open issue. Likewise, cross-cultural evidence is also lacking.

How did the investigators measure the topic of interest? Collaborative meetings between U.S. and Chinese researchers resulted in a 13-item grief processing scale and a 7-item grief avoidance scale, with both English and Mandarin Chinese versions. Self-reported psychological symptoms and physical health were also collected.

Who were the participants in the study? Adults under age 66 who had experienced the loss of either a spouse or child approximately 4 months prior to the start of data collection were asked to participate through solicitation letters. Participants were from either the metropolitan areas of Washington, D.C., or Nanjing, Jiangsu Province in China.

What was the design of the study? Two sets of measures were collected at approximately 4 months and 18 months after the loss.

Were there ethical concerns in the study? Because participation was voluntary, there were no ethical concerns.

What were the results? Consistent with the grief work as rumination view, scores on the two grief measures were uncorrelated. Overall, women tended to show more grief processing than men, and grief processing decreased over time. As you can see in Figure 13.4, Chinese participants reported more grief processing and grief avoidance than U.S. participants at the first time of measurement, but differences disappeared by the second measurement for grief processing.

What did the investigators conclude? Based on converging results from the United States and China, the researchers concluded the data supported the grief work as rumination view. The results support the notion excessive processing of grief may actually increase a bereaved person's stress and feelings of discomfort rather than being helpful. These findings contradict the idea people should be encouraged to work through their grief and doing so will always be helpful.

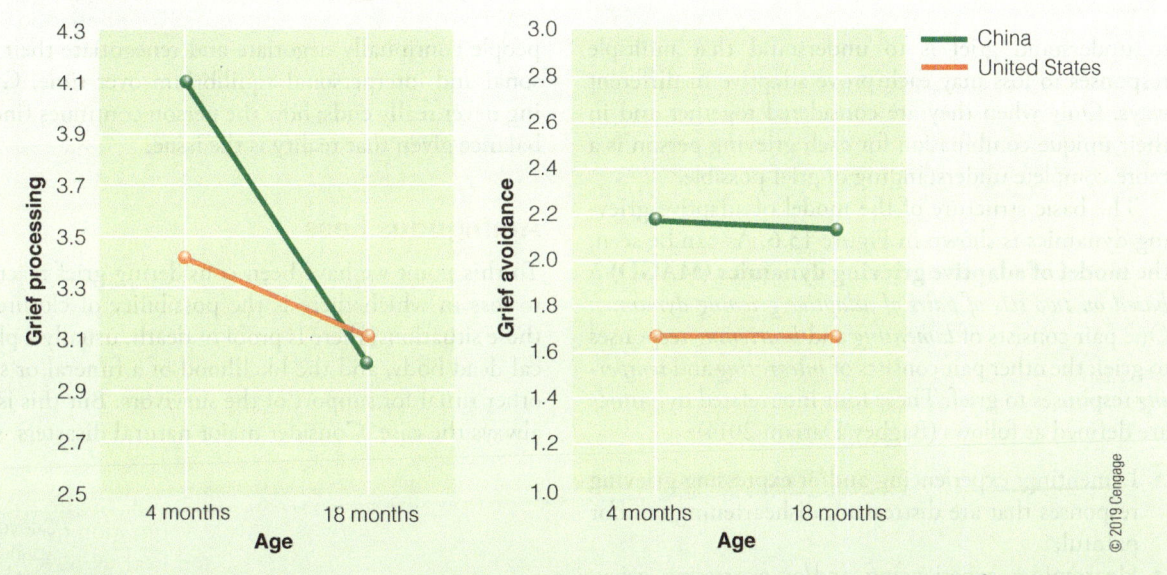

FIGURE 13.4 Grief processing and deliberate grief avoidance across time in China and the United States.
Source: From Bonanno et al. (2005), p. 92.

The Dual Process Model

The **dual process model (DPM)** *of coping with bereavement integrates existing ideas regarding stressors* (Stroebe & Archer, 2013; Utz & Pascoe, 2016). As shown in Figure 13.5, the DPM defines two broad types of stressors. *Loss-oriented stressors* concern the loss itself, such as the grief work that needs to be done. *Restoration-oriented stressors* are those that involve adapting to the survivor's new life situation, such as building new relationships and finding new activities. The DPM proposes dealing with these stressors is a dynamic process, as indicated by the lines connecting them in the figure. This is a distinguishing feature of DPM. It shows how bereaved people cycle back and forth between dealing mostly with grief and trying to move on with life. At times the emphasis will be on grief; at other times on moving forward.

The DPM captures well the process bereaved people themselves report—at times they are nearly overcome with grief, while at other times they handle life well. The DPM also helps us understand how, over time, people come to a balance between the long-term effects of bereavement and the need to live life. Understanding how people handle grief requires understanding of the various contexts in which people live and interact with others (Sandler, Wolchik, & Ayers, 2007; Sandler et al., 2013).

The Model of Adaptive Grieving Dynamics

For anyone who has experienced the loss of a loved one, grieving is an intense, personal, complicated process that does not follow a straight path through predictable stages (Bagbey Darian, 2014). Consequently,

FIGURE 13.5 The dual process model of coping with bereavement shows the relation between dealing with the stresses of the loss itself (loss-oriented) and moving on with one's life (restoration-oriented).

Source: Stroebe, M., & Schut, H. (2001). Models of coping with bereavement: A review. In M. S. Stroebe, R. O. Hansson, W. Stroebe, & H. Schut (Eds.), *Handbook of bereavement research: Consequences, coping, and care* (pp. 375-403). Washington, DC: American Psychological Association

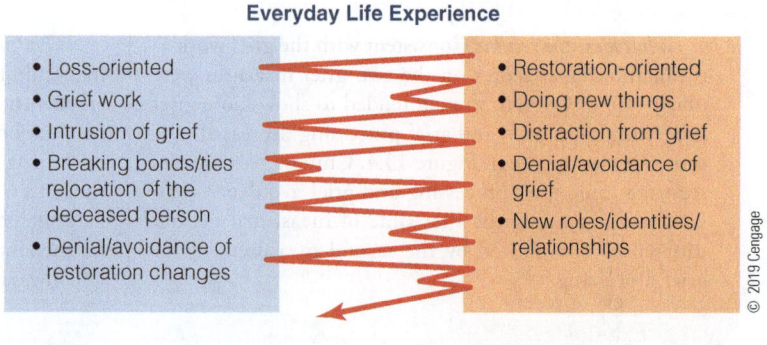

Everyday Life Experience

- Loss-oriented
- Grief work
- Intrusion of grief
- Breaking bonds/ties relocation of the deceased person
- Denial/avoidance of restoration changes

- Restoration-oriented
- Doing new things
- Distraction from grief
- Denial/avoidance of grief
- New roles/identities/relationships

to understand grief is to understand that multiple responses to loss may each prove adaptive in different ways. Only when they are considered together and in their unique combination for each grieving person is a more complete understanding of grief possible.

The basic structure of the model of adaptive grieving dynamics is shown in Figure 13.6. As can be seen, the **model of adaptive grieving dynamics (MAGD)** *is based on two sets of pairs of adaptive grieving dynamics.* One pair consists of *lamenting* and *heartening* responses to grief; the other pair consists of *integrating* and *tempering* responses to grief. These four interrelated dynamics are defined as follows (Bagbey Darian, 2014):

- Lamenting: experiencing and/or expressing grieving responses that are distressful, disheartening, and/or painful;
- Heartening: experiencing and/or expressing grieving responses that are gratifying, uplifting, and/or pleasurable;
- Integrating: assimilating internal and external changes catalyzed by a grief-inducing loss, and reconciling differences in past, present, and future realities in light of these changes; and
- Tempering: avoiding chronic attempts to integrate changed realities impacted by a grief-inducing loss that overwhelm a griever's and/or community's resources and capacities to integrate such changes.

Bagbey Darian (2014) argues that although the pairs of dynamics appear to be contradictory, in processing grief they actually work together. For instance, grieving people often experience both joy and sorrow simultaneously when remembering a loved one. This simultaneity of experience is a key difference between MAGD and the dual process model, as the dual process model argues that grieving people oscillate between loss-oriented tasks and restoration-oriented tasks.

According to the MAGD, the outcome of grief is not "working things through," or necessarily finding meaning in the loss. Rather, it aims at understanding how people continually negotiate and renegotiate their personal and interpersonal equilibrium over time. Grieving never really ends; how the person continues finding balance given that reality is the issue.

Ambiguous Loss

To this point we have been considering grief reactions to loss in which there is the possibility of closure. In these situations, there is proof of death, usually a physical dead body, and the likelihood of a funeral or some other ritual for support of the survivors. But this is not always the case. Consider major natural disasters, such

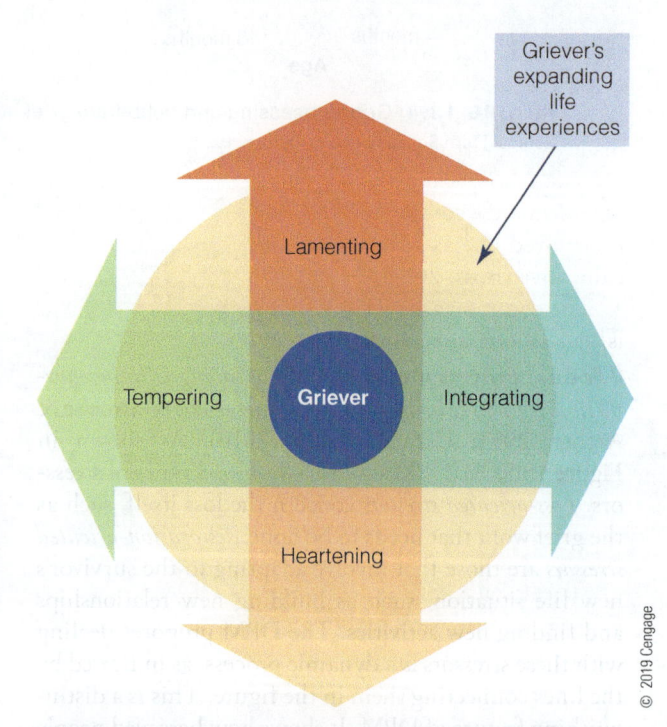

FIGURE 13.6 Model of Adaptive Grieving Dynamics
Source: Bagbey Darian, C. D. (2014). A new mourning: Synthesizing an interactive model of adaptive grieving dynamics. *Illness, Crisis & Loss*, 22(3), 195–235, at p.203. doi: 10.2190/IL.22.3.c

as tsunamis, or major explosions, accidents, or repressive governments who kidnap or otherwise make people "disappear." The tsunami in Japan in 2011 left thousands unaccounted for.

Boss (2015) coined the term *ambiguous loss* for these circumstances. **Ambiguous loss** *refers to situations of loss in which there is no resolution or closure*. Boss (2010, 2015) describes two types of ambiguous loss. The first type refers to a missing person who is physically absent but still very present psychologically to family and friends. Examples of this type include people missing after disasters, victims of kidnapping, and those never recovered from accidents.

The primary challenge for the families and friends of the missing is the unending pain of not knowing for certain what happened, where their loved one is at present, and their specific fate. It is this pain that terrorists rely on to inflict constant pain and suffering. Typical grief reactions are postponed indefinitely, making it essentially impossible for people to move on with their lives, sometimes for generations (Boss, 2015). What motivates these families and friends is hope for an eventual return of the loved one (Boss, 2015; Wayland et al., 2016).

A second type of ambiguous loss involves a loved one who is psychologically absent but who is still physically present. They are what people term "here but gone," as is the case in certain diseases such as dementia. Families caring for loved ones with Alzheimer's disease, for instance, report going through grieving as their loved one loses more and more of what makes them who they are, ultimately coming to a point at which they think of their loved one as "dead" even though they are physically alive (Boss, 2010).

The common aspect of both types of ambiguous loss is that as long as certainty is not reached, closure is not possible in the usual sense. Families and friends report feeling pressure to stop holding out hope, on one hand, or are accused of being cold on the other. Either way, ambiguous grief is especially difficult to deal with.

Complicated or Prolonged Grief Disorder

Not everyone is able to cope with grief well and begin rebuilding a life. Sometimes the feelings of hurt, loneliness, and guilt are so overwhelming they become the focus of the survivor's life to such an extent there is never any closure and the grief continues to interfere indefinitely with one's ability to function. *When this occurs, individuals are viewed as having* **complicated grief**, *which is characterized by persistent and intrusive feelings of grief lasting beyond the expected period of adaptation to loss, and is associated with separation distress and traumatic distress* (Arizmendi, Kaszniak, & O'Connor, 2016). *Symptoms of* **separation distress** *include preoccupation with the deceased to the point it interferes with everyday functioning, upsetting memories of the deceased, longing and searching for the deceased, and isolation following the loss. Symptoms of* **traumatic distress** *include feeling disbelief about the death, mistrust, anger, and detachment from others as a result of the death, feeling shocked by the death, and the experience of physical presence of the deceased.*

Complicated grief forms a separate set of symptoms from depression (Stroebe, Abakoumkin, & Stroebe, 2010). Individuals experiencing complicated grief report high levels of separation distress (such as yearning, pining, or longing for the deceased person), along with specific cognitive, emotional, or behavioral indicators (such as avoiding reminders of the deceased, diminished sense of self, difficulty in accepting the loss, feeling bitter or angry), as well as increased morbidity, increased smoking and substance abuse, and difficulties with family and other social relationships. Similar distinctions have been made between complicated or prolonged grief disorder and anxiety disorders.

Arizmendi and colleagues (2016) report that people who experience complicated grief process grief emotions differently. Specifically, they do not engage those areas of the brain that are typically involved in regulating emotions, supporting the idea that complicated grief involves avoidance and a disruption of emotion regulation.

The presence of complicated grief transcends culture. For example, Li & Prigerson (2016) validated a measure of complicated grief in a sample of Chinese adults. Likewise, complicated grief was validated in a sample of Spanish adults in terms of how they respond to emotion (Fernández-Alcántara et al., 2016).

Adult Developmental Aspects of Grief

Dealing with the loss of a loved one is never easy. How we deal with such losses as adults depends somewhat on the nature of the loss and our age and experience with death.

Special Challenges in Young Adulthood

Because young adults are just beginning to pursue the family, career, and personal goals they have set, they tend to be more intense in their feelings toward death.

When asked how they feel about death, young adults report a strong sense those who die at this point in their lives would be cheated out of their future (Attig, 1996). Complicated grief and mental health problems are relatively common (Bolton et al., 2016; Mash, Fullerton, & Ursano, 2013).

Wrenn (1999) relates one of the challenges faced by bereaved college students is learning "how to respond to people who ignore their grief, or who tell them they need to get on with life and it's not good for them to continue to grieve" (p. 134). College students have a need to express their grief like other bereaved people do, so providing them the opportunity to do so is crucial (Fajgenbaum, Chesson, & Lanzl, 2012; McCoyd & Walter, 2016).

Experiencing the loss of one's partner in young adulthood can be traumatic, not only because of the loss itself but also because such loss is unexpected. As Trish Straine, a 32-year-old widow whose husband was killed in the World Trade Center attack put it: "I suddenly thought, 'I'm a widow.' Then I said to myself, 'A widow? That's an older woman, who's dressed in black. It's certainly not a 32 -year-old like me'" (Lieber, 2001). One of the most difficult aspects for young widows and widowers is they must deal with both their own and their young children's grief and provide the support their children need and that can be extremely difficult. "Every time I look at my children, I'm reminded of Mark," said Stacey, a 35-year-old widow whose husband died of bone cancer. "And people don't want to hear you say you don't feel like moving on, even though there is great pressure from them to do that."

Becoming a widow as a young adult can be especially traumatic.

The death of a girlfriend or boyfriend in young adulthood is often unacknowledged as bereavement. Leichtentritt and colleagues (2013) found that girlfriends of soldiers killed in battle felt socially isolated and lonely in dealing with their loss. Clearly, this is a missed opportunity to be sensitive to people's loss and to provide support.

Death of One's Child

The death of one's child, for most parents, brings unimaginable grief (McCoyd & Walter, 2016; Stroebe et al., 2013). Because children are not supposed to die before their parents, it is as if the natural order of things has been violated, shaking parents to their core (Rubin & Malkinson, 2001). Mourning and relationship stress are always intense; some parents never recover or reconcile themselves to the death of their child and may terminate their relationship with each other, while others find solace and strength in each other (Albuquerque, Pereira, & Narciso, 2016). The intensity of feelings is due to the strong parent–child bond that begins before birth and lasts a lifetime (Maple et al., 2010; Rosenbaum, Smith, & Zollfrank, 2011).

Young parents who lose a child unexpectedly report high anxiety, a more negative view of the world, and much guilt, that results in a devastating experience (Seyda & Fitzsimons, 2010). The most overlooked losses of a child are those that happen through stillbirth, miscarriage, abortion, or neonatal death (Earle, Komaromy, & Layne, 2012; McCoyd & Walter, 2016). Attachment to the child begins before birth, especially for mothers, so the loss hurts deeply. For this reason, ritual is extremely important to acknowledge the death and validate parents' feelings of grief (Nuzum et al., 2015).

Yet parents who experience this type of loss are expected to recover quickly. The lived experience of parents tells a different story (Seyda & Fitzsimons, 2010). These parents talk about a life-changing event, and report a deep sense of loss and hurt, especially when others do not understand their feelings. Worst of all, if societal expectations for quick recovery are not met the parents may be subjected to unfeeling comments. As one mother notes, parents often just wish somebody would acknowledge the loss (Okonski, 1996).

The loss of a young adult child for a middle-aged parent is experienced differently but is equally devastating (Maple et al., 2013; Schneider, 2013). Complicated grief is more common among bereaved parents than in other groups, most likely due to the very different nature of the parent-child relationship (Zetumer et al., 2015).

Death of One's Parent

Most parents die after their children are grown. But whenever parental death occurs, it hurts. Losing a parent in adulthood is a rite of passage as one is transformed from being a "son" or "daughter" to being "without parents" (Abrams, 2013; McCoyd & Walter, 2016). We, the children, are now next in line.

The loss of a parent is significant. For young adult women transitioning to motherhood, losing their own mother during adolescence raises many feelings, such as deep loss at not being able to share their pregnancies with their mothers and fear of dying young themselves (Franceschi, 2005). Death of one's parent in adulthood has understandable effects on adult children, largely depending on the quality of the relationship with the deceased parent (Stokes, 2016).

The feelings accompanying the loss of an older parent reflect a sense of letting go, loss of a buffer against death, better acceptance of one's own eventual death, and a sense of relief the parent's suffering is over (Abrams, 2013; Igarashi et al., 2013; McCoyd & Walter, 2016). Yet, if the parent died from a cause, such as Alzheimer's disease, which involves the loss of the parent–child relationship along the way, then bodily death can feel like the second time the parent died (Shaw, 2007). Whether the adult child now tries to separate from the deceased parent's expectations or finds comfort in the memories, the impact of the loss is great.

Disenfranchised Grief

As we have noted repeatedly throughout this chapter, the experience of loss and the subsequent grief we feel is a highly personal matter. *Sometimes, a loss that appears insignificant to others is highly consequential to the person who suffers the loss; such situations give rise to* **disenfranchised grief**. A good example of disenfranchised grief is the loss of a pet. To most of the world, the loss is not a big deal—an animal has died. But to the person whose pet died, the loss may be very traumatic and result in social isolation in grief.

Disenfranchised grief stems from the social expectations we place on people to "move on" after loss (Harris, 2016). However, those expectations can result in failure to understand the personal impact that every loss has on someone and a failure to be empathetic to that person's experience. Such failure may also reflect certain stereotypes or bias regarding the value of various people's lives, such as drug addicts or very old people. In this context, it is good to keep in mind John Donne's passage from his *Devotions upon Emergent Occasions*, written in December 1623 as he recovered from a very serious illness:

> No man is an island,
> Entire of itself,
> Every man is a piece of the continent,
> A part of the main.
> If a clod be washed away by the sea,
> Europe is the less.
> As well as if a promontory were.
> As well as if a manor of thy friend's
> Or of thine own were:
> Any man's death diminishes me,
> Because I am involved in mankind,
> And therefore never send to know for whom the bell tolls;
> It tolls for thee.

Conclusion

Death is not as pleasant a topic as children's play or occupational development. It's not something we can go to college to master. What it represents to many people is the end of their existence, and that is a scary prospect. But because we all share in this fear at some level, each of us is equipped to provide support and comfort for grieving survivors.

Death is the last life-cycle force we encounter, the ultimate triumph of the biological forces that limit the length of life. Yet the same psychological and social forces so influential throughout life help us deal with death, either our own or someone else's. As we come to the end of our life journey, we understand death through an interaction of psychological forces—such as coping skills and intellectual and emotional understanding of death—and the sociocultural forces expressed in a particular society's traditions and rituals.

Learning about and dealing with death is clearly a developmental process across the life span that fits well in the biopsychosocial framework. Most apparent is that biological forces are essential to understanding death. The definition of death is based on whether certain biological functions are present; these same definitions create numerous ethical dilemmas that must be dealt with psychologically and socioculturally. Life-cycle forces also play a key role. We have seen, depending on a person's age, the concept of death has varied meanings beyond the mere cessation of life.

How a person's understanding of death develops is also the result of psychological forces. As the ability to think and reflect undergoes fundamental change, the view of death changes from a mostly magical approach to one that can be transcendent and transforming. As we have seen, people who face their own imminent death experience certain feelings. Having gained experience through the deaths of friends and relatives, a person's level of comfort with his or her own death may increase. Such personal experience may also come about by sharing the rituals defined through sociocultural forces. People observe how others deal with death and how the culture sets the tone and prescribes behavior for survivors. The combined action of forces also determines how they cope with the grief that accompanies the loss of someone close. Psychologically, confronting grief depends on many things, including the quality of the support system we have.

Thus, just as the beginning of life represents a complex interaction of biological, psychological, sociocultural, and life-cycle factors, so does death. What people believe about what follows after death is also an interaction of these factors. So, as we bring our study of human development to a close, we end where we began: What we experience in our lives cannot be understood from only a single perspective.

Adult Development in Action

How is grief a product of the biopsychosocial model? How would you use the biopsychosocial model to create a support group for bereaved people?

Social Policy Implications

As you probably surmised from the text, issues surrounding death and health care can be extremely controversial. Although the use of life-sustaining technologies (such as life support machines) is widespread, and courts have ensured individuals and designated others can make decisions about the extent and types of care received, the emotion attached to these events and decisions is high. Because most people do not spend time thinking about what they truly want and then making others, including their healthcare professionals, aware of those decisions, most are left trying to make them in the midst of a healthcare crisis. To make matters worse, if a person has not made any plans known, and is not in a condition to make them (e.g., is unconscious), steps may be taken that would not have been welcomed had those decisions been made an made known.

Arguably, two key events in the 21st century brought end-of-life decisions to the forefront of public discourse and social policy arena. The first was the Terri Schiavo case in 2005 that raised the issue of when life-sustaining intervention is allowed to end and who can make that decision when the patient had no advance directive. The second was the debate in 2009 in the midst of congressional consideration of the Affordable Care Act that raised the specter of "death panels."

The core social policy issues facing us today are those involving the extent individuals have to make their own decisions about care, even when that decision is contrary to medical advice; how to know whether that decision is made freely by a capable, competent person; whether physicians' declarations of brain death are accurate; and the extent a government itself has an interest in making the decision, even when it is contrary to an individual's or their family's wishes, especially if public funds are used in the care being provided or contemplated. These are quite complex issues that also extend into people's private belief structures, particularly religious/spiritual beliefs in matters of life and death.

Medically, the issues are complicated, too. To maximize the success of organ transplants, individuals may need to be kept on life support until the organs are ready to be taken. Is that ethical? Does that violate religious beliefs? Does the potential organ recipient have anything to say about the decision?

Now that physicians are provided reimbursement under certain conditions under medical insurance plans (e.g., Medicare) for taking the time to discuss end-of-life issues with their patients, it is possible these issues will get the attention they need and deserve. Hopefully, this will result in more people making their end-of-life wishes known in advance.

Clearly, more open discussion about end-of-life issues needs to be held and better policies more reflective of the reality of the complexity of the issues need to be created. With the aging of the baby-boom generation, more families than ever will be faced with having to decide whether they themselves, or a close family member, dies with dignity or has his or her life needlessly prolonged.

SUMMARY

13.1 Definitions and Ethical Issues

How is death defined?
- Death is a difficult concept to define precisely. Different cultures have different meanings and rituals surrounding death.

What legal and medical criteria are used to determine when death occurs?
- For many centuries, a clinical definition of death was used: the absence of a heartbeat and respiration. Currently, whole-brain death is the most widely used definition. It is based on several highly specific criteria that are assessed by trained healthcare professionals. The condition of persistent vegetative state often creates a complicated situation for determination of death.

What are the ethical dilemmas surrounding euthanasia?
- Two types of euthanasia are distinguished. Active euthanasia consists of deliberately ending someone's life, such as turning off a life-support system. Passive euthanasia is ending someone's life by withholding some type of intervention or treatment (e.g., by stopping nutrition). Physician-assisted suicide is a controversial issue and is being addressed in some states through laws. It is essential people make their wishes known through either a healthcare power of attorney or a living will.
- The personal and financial costs of prolonging life when the patient would have preferred another option are significant, as are the ethical issues regarding prolonging life without considering quality of life.

13.2 Thinking About Death: Personal Aspects

How do feelings about death change over adulthood?
- Cognitive developmental level is important for understanding how young adults view death, and the lessening of feelings of immortality.
- Middle-aged adults usually experience the death of their parents, and begin to confront their own mortality, undergoing a change in their sense of time lived and time until death.
- Older adults are less anxious about and more accepting of death.

How do people deal with their own death?
- Kübler-Ross's approach includes five stages: denial, anger, bargaining, depression, and acceptance. People may be in more than one stage at a time and do not necessarily go through them in order.
- A contextual theory of dying emphasizes the tasks a dying person must face. Four dimensions of these tasks have been identified: bodily needs, psychological security, interpersonal attachments, and spiritual energy and hope. A contextual theory incorporates differences in reasons people die and the places people die.

What is death anxiety, and how do people show it?
- Most people exhibit some degree of anxiety about death, even though it is difficult to define and measure. Terror management theory is a common frame for understanding death anxiety. Young adults show greater brain activity when exposed to death-related concepts than do older adults.
- The main ways death anxiety is shown are by avoiding death (e.g., refusing to go to funerals) and deliberately challenging it (e.g., engaging in dangerous sports). The many components of death anxiety affect many different aspects of behavior.
- Death education has been shown to be extremely effective in helping people deal with death anxiety.

13.3 End-of-Life Issues

How do people deal with end-of-life issues and create a final scenario?
- Managing the final aspects of life, after-death disposition of the body, memorial services, and distribution of assets are important end-of-life issues. Making choices about what people want and do not want done constitute making a final scenario. One of the most difficult parts of a final scenario is separation from family and friends. Jointly creating a final scenario among the dying person, family, and healthcare professionals is optimal.

What is hospice?
- The goal of a hospice is to maintain the quality of life and manage the pain of terminally ill patients. Hospice clients typically have cancer, AIDS, or a progressive neurological disorder. Family members tend to stay involved in the care of hospice clients. Pain management can also be achieved in ways other than through hospice.

How does one make one's end-of-life desires and decisions known?
- End-of-life decisions are made know most often through a living will, healthcare power of attorney, and specific medical requests such as a do not resuscitate order. It is important family and healthcare professionals are aware of these decisions. The

Patient Self-Determination Act requires healthcare facilities to inform patients of these rights, but must take the patient's competence to make decisions into account.

13.4 Surviving the Loss: The Grieving Process

How do people experience the grief process?

- Grief is an active process of coping with loss. Four aspects of grieving must be confronted: the reality of the loss, the emotional turmoil, adjusting to the environment, and loosening the ties with the deceased. When death is expected, survivors go through anticipatory grief; unexpected death is usually more difficult for people to handle.
- "Recovery" may be a misleading term, as the process of adjusting and readjusting to life following a loss never ends.
- The mode of death, personal factors, and extent of social support make a difference in dealing with grief.
- Anticipatory grief does not appear to make the grieving process any easier. However, the degree of attachment to the person who died does.

What feelings do grieving people have?

- Dealing with grief, called *grief work*, usually takes more time than society wants to allot. Grief is equally intense for both expected and unexpected death. Normal grief reactions include sorrow, sadness, denial, disbelief, guilt, and anniversary reactions.
- How people demonstrate grief varies across cultures.

How do people cope with grief?

- Three general approaches help explain how people cope with grief.
- The four-component model is based on the processes of: the context of the loss; continuation of subjective meaning of the loss; changing representations of the lost relationship over time; and the role of coping and emotion regulation processes. However, the grief work as rumination hypothesis rejects the need for grief as a basis for recovering form loss.
- The dual process model integrates existing ideas about stress into the context of loss and restoration. These stressors operate in a dynamic relation.

What are the types of ambiguous loss?

- Ambiguous loss refers to situations of loss in which there is no resolution or closure. There are two types of ambiguous loss. The first type refers to a missing person who is physically absent but still very present psychologically to family and friends. The second type refers to situations in which the loved one is psychologically absent but still physically present.

What is the difference between normal and complicated grief?

- Complicated grief involves symptoms of separation distress and traumatic distress. Separation distress is preoccupation with the deceased to the extent that it interferes with everyday functioning. Excessive guilt and self-blame are common manifestations of traumatic grief.

What developmental aspects are important in understanding grief?

- Young adults usually have intense feelings about death. Young adult spouses/partners are often more isolated and have more difficulty due to less social support. Boyfriends and girlfriends of people who die in young adulthood feel especially alone.
- The death of one's child is especially difficult to cope with. This is also true for loss due to miscarriage or stillbirth.
- The death of one's parent deprives an adult of many important things, and the feelings accompanying it are often complex.
- Disenfranchised grief, in which a loss is downplayed by others in a bereaved person's social network, is an important consideration in understanding grief.

REVIEW QUESTIONS

13.1 Definitions and Ethical Issues

- What is the most common legal definition of death?
- What are the criteria necessary for brain death?
- What is bioethics, and what kinds of issues does it deal with?
- What are the types of euthanasia? How do they differ?
- How do the personal and financial costs of life-sustaining treatment affect healthcare decisions?

13.2 Thinking About Death: Personal Aspects

- How do cognitive development and issues at midlife influence feelings about death?
- Describe Kübler-Ross's concepts of dying. How does it help explain people's processing of their own dying?
- What is necessary for creating a contextual theory of dying?

- What is death anxiety? What factors influence death anxiety? How does it relate to terror management theory?
- How do people demonstrate death anxiety?
- How do people learn to deal with death anxiety?

13.3 End-of-Life Issues
- What are end-of-life issues?
- How do people create a final scenario?
- What is a hospice? How does hospice care differ from hospital care?
- What are the major ways that people make known their end-of-life decisions?

13.4 Surviving the Loss: The Grieving Process
- What is meant by grief, bereavement, and mourning?
- What is the process of grief? What are the risk factors associated with grief?
- What are normal grief reactions and grief work?
- How does grief change over time?
- What is the four-component model of grief?
- What is the grief-work-as-rumination hypothesis?
- What is the dual process model of grief?
- What is the model of adaptive grieving dynamics?
- What are the two types of ambiguous loss?
- What is complicated grief?
- How do adults of different ages deal with different types of loss?

INTEGRATING CONCEPTS IN DEVELOPMENT

- What effect do you think being at different levels of cognitive development has on people's thinking about death?
- What parallels are there between the process of dying and the experience of grief? Why do you think they may be similar?
- How can we use the study of death, dying, bereavement, and grief to provide insights into the psychological development of people across adulthood?

KEY TERMS

active euthanasia The deliberate ending of someone's life.

ambiguous loss Refers to situations of loss in which there is no resolution or closure.

anniversary reaction Changes in behavior related to feelings of sadness on the anniversary date of a loss.

anticipatory grief Grief experienced during the period before an expected death occurs that supposedly serves to buffer the impact of the loss when it does come and to facilitate recovery.

bereavement The state or condition caused by loss through death.

bioethics Study of the interface between human values and technological advances in health and life sciences.

clinical death Lack of heartbeat and respiration.

complicated grief Expression of grief that is distinguished from depression and from normal grief in terms of separation distress and traumatic distress.

death anxiety People's anxiety or even fear of death and dying.

disenfranchised grief A loss that appears insignificant to others that is highly consequential to the person who suffers the loss.

do not resuscitate (DNR) order A medical order that means cardiopulmonary resuscitation (CPR) is not started should one's heart and breathing stop.

dual process model (DPM) View of coping with bereavement that integrates loss-oriented stressors and restoration-oriented stressors.

end-of-life issues Issues pertaining to the management of the final phase of life, after-death disposition of the body, memorial services, and distribution of assets.

euthanasia The practice of ending life for reasons of mercy.

final scenario Making choices known about how one does and does not want one's life to end.

four-component model Model of grief that understanding grief is based on (1) the context of the loss; (2) continuation of subjective meaning associated with loss; (3) changing representations of the lost relationship over time; and (4) the role of coping and emotion regulation processes.

grief The sorrow, hurt, anger, guilt, confusion, and other feelings that arise after suffering a loss.

grief work The psychological side of coming to terms with bereavement.

grief work as rumination hypothesis An approach that not only rejects the necessity of grief processing for recovery from loss but views extensive grief processing as a form of rumination that may actually increase distress.

healthcare power of attorney A document in which an individual appoints someone to act as his or her agent for healthcare decisions.

hospice An approach to assisting dying people that emphasizes pain management, or palliative care, and death with dignity.

living will A document in which a person states his or her wishes about life support and other treatments.

model of adaptive grieving dynamics (MAGD) A model of grief based on two pairs of adaptive grieving dynamics: lamenting/heartening, and integrating/tempering.

mourning The ways in which we express our grief.

palliative care Care that is focused on providing relief from pain and other symptoms of disease at any point during the disease process.

passive euthanasia Allowing a person to die by withholding available treatment.

persistent vegetative state Situation in which a person's cortical functioning ceases while brainstem activity continues.

physician-assisted suicide Process in which physicians provide dying patients with a fatal dose of medication the patient self-administers.

separation distress Expression of complicated or prolonged grief disorder that includes preoccupation with the deceased to the point it interferes with everyday functioning, upsetting memories of the deceased, longing and searching for the deceased, and isolation following the loss.

terror management theory Addresses the issue of why people engage in certain behaviors to achieve particular psychological states based on their deeply rooted concerns about mortality.

thanatology The study of death, dying, grief, bereavement, and social attitudes toward these issues.

traumatic distress Expression of complicated or prolonged grief disorder that includes feeling disbelief about the death, mistrust, anger, and detachment from others as a result of the death, feeling shocked by the death, and the experience of physical presence of the deceased.

whole-brain death Death that is declared only when the deceased meets certain criteria established revised in 2010.

14 | Healthy Aging

CHAPTER OUTLINE

14.1 Demographic Trends and Social Policy
Demographic Trends: 2030
Social Security and Medicare
CURRENT CONTROVERSIES What to Do About Social Security and Medicare

14.2 Healthy Aging: Living Well in Later Life
DISCOVERING DEVELOPMENT What Is Living Well?
What Is Healthy Aging?
Health Promotion and Quality of Life
Using Technology to Maintain and Enhance Competence
Health Promotion and Disease Prevention
Lifestyle Factors

14.3 Epilogue
Summary
Review Questions
Integrating Concepts in Development
Key Terms

Welcome to your future. In this epilogue, we take a different perspective on aging. What will be *our* experience of aging? What lessons can and will we learn based on what we know now about older adults and the process of aging? How will we apply those lessons to improve our own experience?

In this final chapter, we consider key steps in making our own aging the best experience possible. First, we look at what society must do to keep the social support programs we have come to rely on. Then we consider what each of us can do to keep ourselves in the best health possible to delay or even prevent some of the negative aspects of aging. We then take a closer look at how the baby boomers are changing everything from how older adults are viewed to the coming enormous pressure on governmental resources. We also look ahead a few decades to preview what may be in store for millennials when they reach late life.

Aging today and in the future is not what it was even a few years ago. Technological advances have and will continue to make commonplace what is only science fiction today. For example, aging in place will be the norm, as it is likely we will get our annual physical examination remotely, arrive by driverless car for classes or meetings led by someone's interactive holographic projection so they can literally be in multiple places simultaneously, and use robots at home for most routine chores. Medicine will make advances such as offering personalized genetic interventions that cure dementia and cancer, offering the possibility of much longer average life spans with improved quality of life. It is a future with many more support structures and systems for older adults. It will be an interesting experience, to say the least.

Throughout this book we made predictions about this future and guessed how older people may fare. Some of these predictions are not so happy; as many people live to an old age, there will be greater need for long-term care until cures for terminal, chronic diseases are discovered. Whether we will be able to afford to provide the optimal care for them is much in doubt. Other aspects of the future may be more positive; for instance, as many people live to older ages there will be a larger pool of older workers to balance the workforce. These predictions represent our best guess about what life will be like in the next few decades, based on what we know now and what is likely to happen if we continue down our current path.

We cannot always predict the path our lives will take.

The purpose of this chapter is to pull together several crucial issues facing gerontologists as we move through the 21st century and to illustrate how we can set the best stage for our own aging. This survey will not be exhaustive; rather, we focus on two aspects: points singled out for special concern and areas where major advances may have a dramatic impact on our own development.

14.1 Demographic Trends and Social Policy

LEARNING OBJECTIVES
- What key demographic changes will occur by 2030?
- What are the challenges facing Social Security and Medicare?

Nancy, a 35-year-old new employee at a marketing and public relations firm, was flipping through the company's benefits package. When it came to the retirement plan, she commented to the human resources person, "I guess I better pay attention. I don't think Social Security and Medicare will be there for me when the time comes. So, it will be very important for me to save as much as I can."

Nancy isn't alone. Many younger adults in the United States do not believe Social Security, Medicare, or other government programs will be in existence by the time they get old enough to qualify for them. Demographic and financial trends support this pessimistic view.

As we will show, the baby-boom generation, coupled with structural problems in Social Security and Medicare, give young adults good reasons to be concerned.

Demographic Trends: 2030

In Chapter 1, we noted several trends in the population of the United States and the rest of the world during the upcoming century. These trends are not likely to change in the foreseeable future. Changes in the composition of the older adult population contribute to potentially critical issues that will emerge over the next few decades. Keep in mind the baby boomers represent the largest generation ever to reach older adulthood. Generation X, the group right behind them, is much smaller. An even larger generation, the Millennials, will still be feeling the economic and other effects of aging boomers when they themselves grow older. One especially important effect concerns the potential for intergenerational conflict.

Because the resources and roles in a society are never divided equally among different age groups, the potential for conflict always exists. One well-known intergenerational conflict is between adolescents and their parents. Less well known is the potential for conflict between young/middle-aged adults and older adults. This type of conflict has not traditionally been a source of serious problems in society, for several reasons: Older adults made up a small proportion of the population, family ties between adult children and their parents worked against conflict, and middle-aged people were hesitant to withdraw support from programs for older adults. Despite these potent forces protecting against conflict, the situation is changing. The controversy over the rate of growth of Medicare and Social Security and the proportion they represent of the federal budget would have been unthinkable just a few years earlier.

To see more clearly how these changing demographics will have an enormous effect on society at large and on the programs that target older adults, let us project forward to the year 2030, when the last of the baby boomers reach age 65. Between now and 2030, the following changes will have set in:

- The proportion of older adults in the United States will nearly double.
- Older adults will be more educated, politically sophisticated, and organized than past generations. They will be familiar with life in a highly complex society where one must learn to deal with (and have little tolerance for) bureaucracies and they will be proficient users of the Internet and technology in general.
- Older adults will expect to keep their affluent lifestyle, Social Security benefits, Medicare/healthcare benefits, and other benefits accrued throughout their adult life. A comfortable retirement will be viewed as a right, not a privilege. However, they will not, on average, have the financial savings necessary to support those expectations.
- The dependency ratio will change. *The **dependency ratio** reflects the number of people under age 15 and over age 64 in a country.* The dependency ratio provides insight into the relative number of people who have to provide the financial support for others not as able to do so. The lower the number, the more workers are needed to pay taxes to provide the revenue for social support programs.

As shown in Figure 14.1, the overall global dependency ratio is about to shift dramatically as the population of older adults increases (He, Goodkind, & Kowal, 2016). This means there will be more older adults in more countries that will need to be supported through various programs. For the United States, this plays out most visibly in funding for Social Security and Medicare.

Let's consider one example—Social Security. The ratio of workers to retirees in the United States will fall

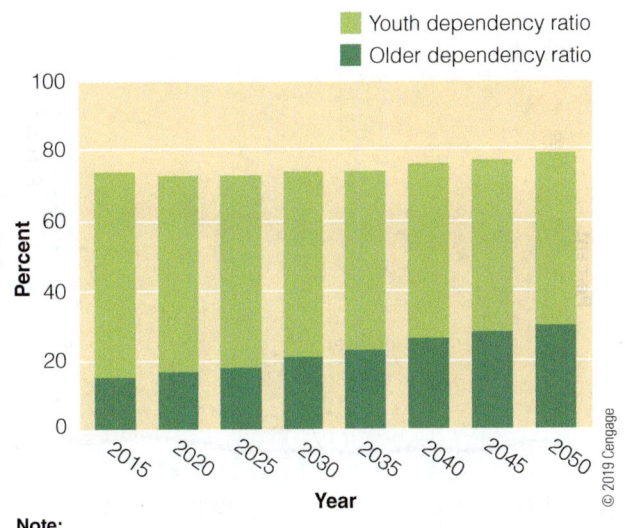

Note:
The older dependency ratio is the number of people aged 65 and over per 100 people aged 20 to 64. The youth dependency ratio is the number of people aged 0 to 19 per 100 people aged 20 to 64.

FIGURE 14.1 Dependency ratios for the world: 2015 to 2050

Source: He, W., Goodkind, D., & Kowal, P. (2016). *An aging world: 2015.* Retrieved from www.census.gov/content/dam/Census/library/publications/2016/demo/p95-16-1.pdf. Figure 3.8. p. 24.

from its current level of roughly 3:1 to 2:1 by 2030. This means to maintain the level of benefits in Social Security, the working members of society will have to pay significantly higher taxes than workers do now. This is because Social Security is a pay-as-you-go system; the money collected from workers today is used to pay current retirees, not to create a personal account that will support you when you retire. (Your taxes only support the people who are receiving Social Security payments *today*.) Whether policymakers will make the necessary changes to maintain benefits that citizens came to view as entitlements remains to be seen. We will take a closer look at both Social Security and Medicare later.

- The increase in divorce that has occurred over the past few decades may result in a lowered sense of obligation on the part of middle-aged adults toward parents or stepparents who were not involved in their upbringing, or who the adult child feels disrespected the other parent. Should this lowered sense of obligation result, it is likely fewer older adults will have family members available to care for them, placing a significantly greater burden on society.
- The rapid increase in the number of ethnic minority older adults compared to European American older adults will force a reconsideration of issues such as healthcare disparities and access to goods and services, on one hand, as well as provide a much richer and broader understanding of the aging process on the other hand.

No one knows for certain what society will be like by 2030. However, the changes we noted in demographic trends urge action now. Two areas facing the most challenge are Social Security and Medicare. Let's take a look at these to understand why they face trouble.

Social Security and Medicare

The dramatic improvements in the everyday lives of older adults in industrialized countries that began in the 20th century have continued and picked up pace in the 21st century. Unprecedented gains for the average older person have occurred in nearly every aspect of life, changing the way they are viewed and the roles they play in society (Giele, 2013; James et al., 2016; Johnson, 2016).

When it comes to income, though, those gains have stopped since the Great Recession (Federal Interagency Forum on Aging Related Statistics, 2016). As you can

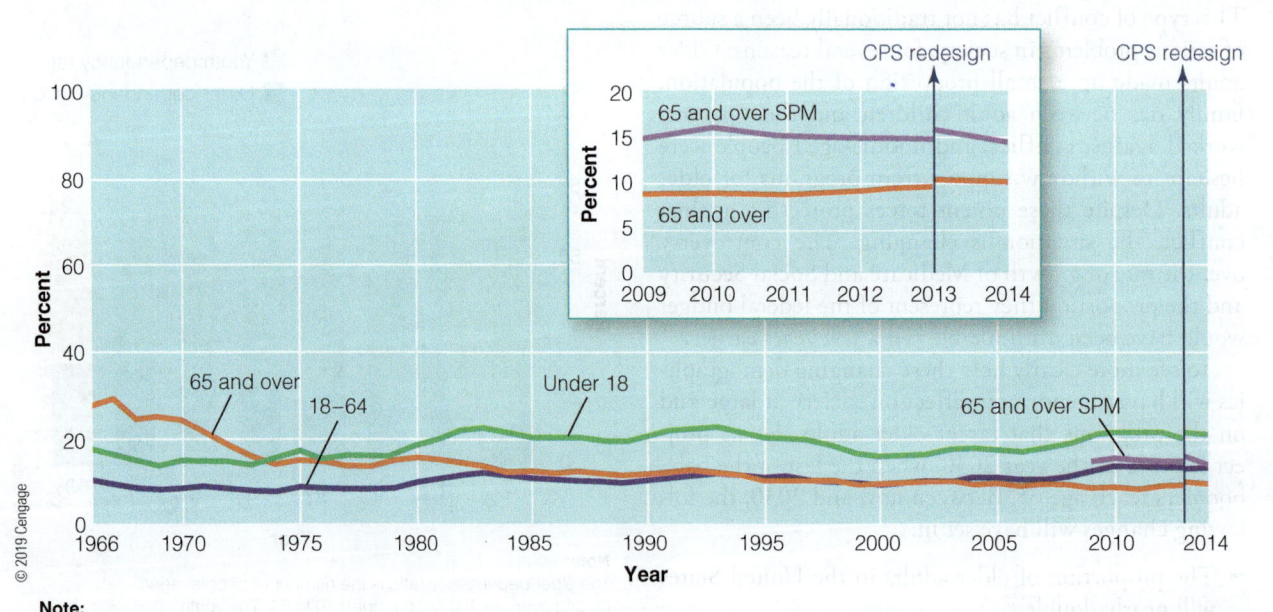

Note:
Poverty status in the Current Population Survey (CPS) is based on prior year income. The source of the 2013 estimates shown in this figure is the portion of the CPS Annual Social and Economic Supplement (ASEC) sample which received the redesigned income questions.

FIGURE 14.2 Poverty rate by age, by official poverty measure and by supplemental poverty measure, 1966–2014

Source: Federal Interagency Forum on Aging Related Statistics. (2016). *Older Americans 2016: Key indicators of well-being*, Retrieved from agingstats.gov/docs/LatestReport/OA2016.pdf. Indicator 7: Poverty, p. 12.

see in Figure 14.2, poverty rates for older adults in the United States declined fairly rapidly from the mid-1960s through the mid-1980s, and continued modest declines until the Great Recession in 2008. Since then, poverty rates as measured by traditional means or by the Supplemental Poverty Measure (SPM) that also includes assessments of people's savings and other resources, has remained mainly constant. Roughly 10% of older adults in the U.S. are under the traditional poverty definition of poverty (roughly $16,000 for a couple in 2016) and about 15% under the SPM definition that takes various savings and expenses into account.

Although things have improved in many respects for older adults, it is the case that many live on very limited resources. For instance, about half of all people on Medicare have incomes less than $23,500, which does not go very far (Cubanski, Casillas, & Damico, 2015). Compared to European Americans, poverty rates are three times higher for Latinos and two-and-one-half times higher for African Americans. Clearly, attention paid to income disparities must include older adults, and social policy needs to align with this reality.

The Political Landscape

Beginning in the 1970s, older adults began to be portrayed as scapegoats in the political debates concerning government resources. Part of the reason was due to the tremendous growth in the amount and proportion of federal dollars expended on benefits to them, such as through the increase of benefits paid from Social Security during the 1970s (Crown, 2001). At that time in history, older adults were also portrayed as highly politically active, fiscally conservative, and selfish (Fairlie, 1988; Gibbs, 1988; Smith, 1992). The healthcare reform debate of the early 1990s focused attention on the spiraling costs of care for older adults that were projected to bankrupt the federal budget if left uncontrolled (Binstock, 1999). This theme and warning continues today.

It was in this context the U.S. Congress began making substantive changes in the benefits for older adults on the grounds of intergenerational fairness. Beginning in 1983, Congress has made several changes in Social Security, Medicare, the Older Americans Act, and other programs and policies. Some of these changes reduced benefits to wealthy older adults and changed some eligibility rules (e.g., age at which one is eligible for full benefits), whereas others provided targeted benefits for poor older adults, all of which had an effect on how older adults are viewed from a financial cost perspective (Binstock, 1999; Polivka, 2010).

The aging of the baby boomers presents difficult and expensive problems (Elmendorf & Sheiner, 2016). One major reason the U.S. debt will likely increase from 75% of the gross domestic product (the value of all the goods and services produced in the United States) in 2016 to about 120% of GDP in 2040 is the cost of providing baby boomers with federal support programs for older adults. This growth in debt is not sustainable and will put younger generations at much greater financial risk.

Let's look at this another way. In fiscal year 2017, President Obama proposed federal spending of about $1.2 trillion on Social Security and $700 billion on Medicare, for a total of just under $2 trillion. These budget figures represent over 40% of the total federal budget (Social Security and Medicare Boards of Trustees, 2016). Given that these figures do not include a portion of Medicare or other federal programs that provide support to older adults along with others, you get the sense of urgency felt by elected officials.

Clearly, the political and social issues concerning benefits to older adults are quite complex. Driven by the eligibility of the first baby boomers for reduced Social Security benefits in 2008 and their eligibility for Medicare in 2011, the years through the early 2030s will see the impact of previous congressional inaction

The aging of the baby-boom generation will put severe strain on the federal budget in Social Security and Medicare.

and rapidly decreasing funds to use on discretionary programs such as education and infrastructure (e.g., mass transit, water pipes, power grids, etc.), and likely increased urgency to confront the issues as best as possible. There are no easy solutions, and it will be essential to discuss all aspects of the problem. Let's look more closely at Social Security and Medicare.

Social Security

Social Security had its beginnings in 1935 as an initiative by President Franklin Roosevelt to "frame a law which will give some measure of protection to the average citizen and to his family against the loss of a job and against poverty-ridden old age." Thus, Social Security was originally intended to provide a supplement to savings and other means of financial support.

Two key things have changed since then. First, the proportion of people who reach age 65 has increased significantly. In 1940, only about 54% of men and 61% of women reached age 65. Today, that has increased to about 75% of men and 85% of women. Since 1940, men collect payments about 3 years longer, and women collect about 5 years longer. Both trends increase the cost of the program.

Second, revisions to the original law have changed Social Security so it now represents the primary source of financial support after retirement for most U.S. citizens, and the only source for many (Polivka, 2010). Since the 1970s, more workers have been included in employer-sponsored defined contribution plans such as 401(k), 403(b), 457 plans, and mutual funds, as well as various types of individual retirement accounts (IRAs), but fewer defined benefit traditional pension plans (Polivka, 2010; Polivka & Luo, 2015). A key difference in these plans is defined contribution plans rely a great deal on employee participation (i.e., workers saving money for retirement) whereas traditional pension programs did not require employee participation as they provided a monthly income for life paid completely by the company.

On the face of it, this inclusion of various retirement plans, especially savings options, may permit more future retirees to use Social Security as the supplemental financial source it was intended to be, thereby shifting retirement financial planning responsibility to the individual (Henrikson, 2007). But that's not an accurate way of looking at it. What has actually happened is an erosion of the private retirement security system that guaranteed a certain income through company-provided pension plans (Polivka & Luo, 2015). Traditional pension plans were not subject to the ups and downs of the stock market like the typical contributory 401(k) or 403(b) plans are. Consequently, rather than lowering dependence on Social Security, the shift away from pensions to contributory plans is more likely to result in an increasing number of older adults relying on Social Security as their primary income source (Orlova, Rutledge, & Wu, 2015; Polivka & Luo, 2015).

The primary challenge facing Social Security is the aging of the baby boomers and the much smaller Generation X that immediately follows (National Academy of Social Insurance, 2016). That's why Nancy, the woman we met in the vignette, and other young and middle-aged adults are concerned. Because Social Security is funded by payroll taxes, the amount of money each worker must pay depends to a large extent on the ratio of the number of people paying Social Security taxes to the number of people collecting benefits. By 2030, this ratio will drop nearly in half; that is, by the time baby boomers have largely retired, there will only be two workers paying into Social Security to support every person collecting benefits, down from 3-to-1 today.

One point that confuses many people is the benefits received do not come from an "account" that reflects what you actually contributed over your employed career. Because Social Security is a revenue-in/payments-out model, people do not build up Social Security "savings." Rather, the money they pay in taxes today goes out as payments to those who are collecting benefits today. So the payments current workers receive in the future will actually be from the taxes paid by workers in the labor force at that future time. That's why the payee/recipient ratio matters—Social Security tax rates must inevitably go up or the benefits received must go down if there are fewer people paying to support an increasing number of recipients.

Over most of the history of Social Security, revenues were greater than payments because of the large number of people paying in compared to the lower number of people collecting benefits. Excess revenue was saved for the future. But that changed in 2010, when benefit payments first exceeded revenues, a situation that remains true today. The interest from those previous saved revenues in the Social Security Trust Fund is now being spent to make up the difference, and will keep the gap closed until around 2020. After that, the Trust Fund itself gets spent. By 2034, all of the Trust Fund assets will be gone. At that point, revenue from Social Security taxes would only cover about 75% of the benefits promised (Social Security and Medicare Boards of Trustees, 2016).

Despite knowing the fiscal realities for decades, Congress has not yet taken the actions necessary to ensure the long-term financial stability of Social Security.

Medicare

Over 55 million U.S. citizens depend on Medicare for their medical insurance (Kaiser Family Foundation, 2016). To be eligible, a person must meet one of the following criteria: be over age 65, be disabled, or have permanent kidney failure. Medicare consists of three parts (Centers for Medicare and Medicaid Services, 2016c): Part A covers inpatient hospital services, skilled nursing facilities, home health services, and hospice care; Part B covers the cost of physician services, outpatient hospital services, medical equipment and supplies, and other health services and supplies; and Part D provides some coverage for prescription medications. Expenses relating to most long-term care needs are funded by Medicaid, another major healthcare program funded by the U.S. government and aimed at people who are poor. Out-of-pocket expenses associated with co-payments and other charges are often paid by supplemental insurance policies, sometimes referred to as "Medigap" policies (Medicare.gov, 2016).

Like Social Security, Medicare is funded by a payroll tax. But unlike Social Security, where the income on which the tax is based has a cap, the tax supporting Medicare is paid on all of one's earnings. Still, the funding problems facing Medicare are arguably worse than those facing Social Security and are grounded in the aging of the baby-boom generation. In addition, Medicare costs have increased dramatically because of more rapid cost increases in health care. Expenditures will increase rapidly as the baby boomers increase the ranks of those covered (Social Security and Medicare Boards of Trustees, 2016).

Unlike Social Security, though, Medicare has been subjected to significant cuts in expenditures, typically through reduced payouts to healthcare providers. Additionally, projected Medicare costs over the next 75 years are much lower than they would have been prior to the passage of the Patient Protection and Affordable Care Act in 2010 due to the ways in which the insurance coverage is structured under both laws.

Taken together, the challenges facing society concerning older adults' financial security and health insurance coverage will continue to be major political and economic issues throughout the first half of the 21st century at least. There are no easy answers and many political challenges, but open discussion of the various arguments and the stark budget realities will be essential for creating the optimal solution. Public misperceptions of how the programs actually work, and the tough choices that must be faced are discussed in more detail in the Current Controversies feature.

■ CURRENT CONTROVERSIES

What to Do About Social Security and Medicare

As pointed out earlier in the chapter, the amount of benefits people collect in Social Security and Medicare is not directly connected to the amount they paid in taxes over their working careers. That's a point many people misunderstand—they think they get out what they have put in their personal account. As explained in the text, this misperception makes it very difficult to make changes in the benefits structure (the cost) of these programs.

The fact is, the average person collects substantially more in lifetime Medicare benefits than he or she paid in total taxes during their working career (Steuerle & Quakenbush, 2015). This imbalance (and misperception) is a major reason why restructuring the benefits or raising co-payments to control costs is so difficult to do, and why the current benefit structure is unsustainable.

There's another aspect to the problem. To keep Medicare Part B and Part D premiums affordable, the typical older Americans only pays about 25% of the actual cost through premiums, deductibles, and co-insurance (higher income people pay a larger share, up to 80%). Where does the rest of the money come from? General revenue in the national budget pays for the rest, and is why there is increasing pressure to cut reimbursements to healthcare providers under Medicare.

Similar analyses can be done for Social Security, but with a different outcome. Whereas nearly all Medicare recipients get much more out of the program than they paid in taxes, that's not true for many people regarding Social Security. Most people will pay more in taxes to support current beneficiaries (Steuerle & Quakenbush, 2015).

The biggest challenge is controlling the costs of Medicare given the arrival of the baby boomers as beneficiaries. But explaining this to those who are already receiving or are about to receive the benefit is a daunting task. That's why most proposals under discussion target individuals who are about 10 years away from receiving Medicare benefits.

The political debates around Social Security and Medicare will not end soon. What is clear, though, is the current financial model is unsustainable over the long run, and action, especially with respect to Medicare, is needed now.

Adult Development in Action

How are demographics affecting social policy in the United States?

14.2 Healthy Aging: Living Well in Later Life

LEARNING OBJECTIVES
- What is healthy aging?
- What are the key issues in health promotion and quality of life?
- How is technology used to maintain and enhance competence?
- What are the primary considerations in designing health promotion and disease prevention programs?
- What are the principal lifestyle factors that influence competence?

Jack heard about all the things available on the Web and that he was missing a great deal. So, after he purchased his first iPad at age 68, he began surfing. He never stopped. Now at age 73, he's a veteran with a wide array of apps and bookmarked sites, especially those relating to health issues. He also communicates by Facebook with his grandchildren and friends, and designed the electronic community newsletter.

Jack is like many older adults—better educated and more technologically sophisticated than their predecessors. The coming demographic changes in the United States and the rest of the world present a challenge for improving the kind of lives older adults live. For this reason, promoting wellness and healthy lifestyles in all living settings (community, long-term care, etc.) is regarded as one of the top healthcare priorities of the 21st century (Parrella & Vormittag, 2017). Remaining healthy is important for decelerating the rate of aging (Aldwin & Gilmer, 2013).

Before we plunge into an analysis of how to live well in later life, take a few minutes and reflect on the Discovering Development feature. What will constitute living well for you?

What Is Healthy Aging?

As you learned from completing the Discovering Development feature, what people list as criteria for living well have some commonalities as well as differences.

DISCOVERING DEVELOPMENT
What Is Living Well?

What does it mean to live well in later life? Take some time to think about this question for yourself. Develop a thorough list of everything it would take for you to say you will have aged as well as you could have when the time comes. Then ask this question to several people of different ages and backgrounds. Compare their answers. Do the criteria differ as a function of age or background characteristics (e.g., age, ethnicity, other experiences)? Discuss your findings with others in your class to see whether your results were typical.

Most people list something related to "being healthy" near the top. That notion of "being healthy" usually has lots of underlying meanings, some personal. Because it is so important to so many, it has become a focal point for theory and research about an appropriate goal for people to strive toward as they age.

As researchers and theorists have approached healthy aging, they have focused on optimizing the individual outcome of the interplay of biopsychosocial forces and the individual over a lifetime (Aldwin & Gilmer, 2013; Centers for Disease Control and Prevention, 2016e; Hostetler & Paterson, 2017; Samanta, 2017). **Healthy aging** *in this sense involves avoiding disease, being engaged with life, and maintaining high cognitive and physical functioning.* Healthy aging is both measurable (e.g., in terms of specific health metrics, cognitive performance, other specific behaviors) and subjective (e.g., well-being). It is reached when a person achieves his or her desired goals with dignity and as independently as possible.

The life-span perspective can be used to create a formal model for healthy aging. Heckhausen, Wrosch, & Schulz (2010; Barlow et al., 2017) developed a theory of life-span development based on motivation and control by applying core assumptions that recognize aging as a complex process that involves increasing specialization and is influenced by factors unrelated to age. The basic premises of healthy aging include keeping a balance between the various gains and losses that occur over time and minimizing the influence of factors unrelated to aging. In short, these premises involve paying attention to both internal and external factors impinging on the person. The antecedents include all the changes that happen to a person. The mechanisms in the model are the selection, optimization, and compensation processes that shape the course of development. Finally, the outcomes of the model denote that enhanced competence, quality of life, and future adaptation are the visible signs of healthy aging.

Using the SOC model, enhanced by Heckhausen and colleague's (2010; Barlow et al., 2017) notions of control and motivation, various types of interventions can be created to help people achieve healthy aging. In general, such interventions focus on the individual or on aspects of tasks and the physical and social environment that emphasize competence (Aldwin & Gilmer, 2013; Lindbergh, Dishman, & Miller, 2016; Thornton, Paterson, & Yeung, 2013). When designing interventions aimed primarily at the person, it is important to understand the target person's goals (rather than the goals of the researcher). For example, in teaching older adults how to use technology, it is essential to understand the kinds of concerns and fears older adults have and ensure the training program addresses them (Lesnoff-Caravaglia, 2010).

Performance on tests of everyday competence predicts longer term outcomes (Allaire & Willis, 2006; Lindbergh et al., 2016). Careful monitoring of competence can be an early indicator of problems, and appropriate interventions should be undertaken as soon as possible. Maintaining competence is an important element in determining quality of life, so which we now turn.

Health Promotion and Quality of Life

Few people disagree with the idea of living a healthy lifestyle. The difficult part is putting the idea into practice—ending unhealthy habits such as smoking and getting off the couch to exercise regularly are difficult. By and large, results from lifestyle changes take time to become apparent, which makes it tough to see the benefits of changing one's habits. Still, the data are quite clear that such changes do work, and improve overall quality of life.

Current models of behavioral change are complex and include not only behavioral, but also motivational, cognitive, social, and technology components (Aldwin & Gilmer, 2013; Manzoni et al., 2016; Skarin et al., 2017). The two that are the focus of most research are the self-efficacy model that emphasizes the role of goal setting and personal beliefs in the degree one influences the outcome, and the self-regulation model, that focuses on the person's motivation for change. All of these models increasingly rely on technology, such as virtual reality and apps.

There is insufficient research on health promotion programs designed specifically for older adults (Aldwin & Gilmer, 2013; Parrella & Vormittag, 2017). However, a few trends are apparent. First, although exercise is basic for good health, because older adults are more prone to injury, exercise programs for them need to take such issues into account and focus more on low-impact aerobic routines (e.g., walking, elliptical training, rowing, cycling). Second, health education programs are effective in minimizing the effects of emotional stress. Third, health screening programs effectively identifying serious chronic disease that can limit the quality of life, and can be addressed through behavioral interventions. Each of these areas within health promotion is most successful when ethnic differences are taken into account in designing the programs.

An increasingly important concept in the discussion of wellness is *salutogenesis*. **Salutogenesis** *is an approach that emphasizes factors that support and promote health, rather than factors that cause disease.* Introduced by Aaron Antonovsky (1979), salutogenesis has become a framework for creating wellness-based interventions in a wide range of settings, including school, work, and communities (Mittelmark & Bauer, 2017).

Mittelmark and Bauer (2017) point out that a salutogenesis framework emphasizes that life experiences help shape one's sense of coherence (a global orientation toward life). Life is more or less comprehensible, meaningful, and manageable. A strong sense of coherence helps one mobilize resources to cope with stressors and manage tension successfully. Through these resources, the sense of coherence helps determine one's movement along the Health-ease/Dis-ease continuum. In this way, salutogenesis is roughly equivalent to the sense of coherence.

Salutogenesis shifts people's lifestyle emphasis to positive aspects that improve their existence. In this way, applying salutogenesis to various settings such as work (Jenny et al., 2017) and communities (Vaandrager & Kennedy, 2017) puts the focus on positive steps that can be taken to improve employees' performance in a healthy, less-stressed way, or the resources residents have at their disposal to address needs in daily life.

People's state of health influences their **quality of life**, *that is, their well-being and life satisfaction.* Quality of life includes interpersonal relationships and social support, physical and mental health, environmental comfort, and many psychological constructs such as locus of control, emotions, usefulness, personality, and meaning in life (Aldwin & Gilmer, 2013). Quality of life is usually divided into environmental, physical, social, and psychological domains of well-being. Personal evaluation of these dimensions is critical to understanding how people view their situations. For instance, we considered quality of life at several points earlier in the text, such as in the context of deciding where to live in Chapter 5, and as a key factor in end-of-life decisions in Chapter 13.

In short, quality of life is a person's subjective assessment or value judgment of his or her own life (Aldwin & Gilmer, 2013). This subjective judgment may or may not correspond to the evaluation of others. And even though self- and other-perceived quality of life may diminish in late life, it may not seem like a loss for the older person. An older woman who has difficulty walking may feel happy simply to be alive, whereas another who is in objective good health may feel useless. Quality of life is best studied from the point of view of the person.

Using Technology to Maintain and Enhance Competence

We are very lucky to be living now. Like Jack, the man introduced in the vignette, increasing numbers of older adults are discovering that smartphones, tablets, and computers can be major assets. Many take advantage of the growing resources available on the Web, including sites dedicated specifically to older adults. E-mail, social networking, and video-calling enable people of all ages to stay in touch with friends and family, and the growing success of e-commerce makes it easier for people with limited time or mobility to purchase goods and services. Smartphones are being used in more

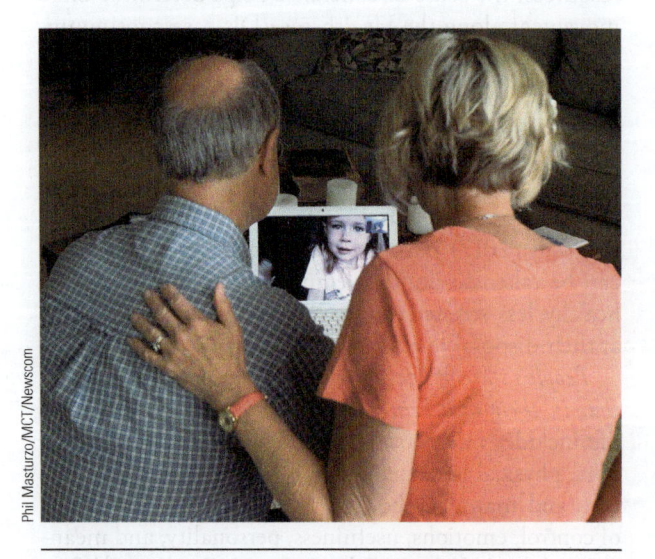

Older adults are increasingly using technology such as Skype or FaceTime to stay in touch with family.

telemedicine applications and settings, and the fully networked and interactive home environment will soon be taken for granted (Elshourbagy, 2017; Slaats, 2017).

The use of technology is one way to enhance the competence of older adults. In this section, we consider the general topic of how to maintain and enhance competence through a variety of interventions. How to grow old successfully is a topic of increasing concern in view of the demographic changes we considered earlier.

The life-span perspective we considered in Chapter 1 is an excellent starting point for understanding how to maintain and enhance people's competence. In this perspective, the changes that occur with age result from multiple biological, psychological, sociocultural, and life-cycle forces. Mastering tasks of daily living and more complex tasks (such as personal finances) contributes to a person's overall sense of competence even if the person has dementia (Dawadi & Cook, 2017; Gill et al., 2013). How can this sense be optimized for successful aging?

The answer lies again in applying three key adaptive mechanisms for aging: selection, optimization, and compensation (SOC) (Baltes et al., 2006). This framework addresses what Bieman-Copland, Ryan, and Cassano (2002) call the "social facilitation of the nonuse of competence": the phenomenon of older people intentionally or unintentionally failing to perform up to their true level of ability because of social stereotypes that operate to limit what older adults are expected to do. Instead of behaving at their true ability level, older adults behave in ways they believe typical or characteristic of their age group (Lang, 2004). This phenomenon is the basis for the communication patterns we considered in Chapter 5.

Technology provides powerful ways to achieve all of the aspects of the SOC model, but compensation is the most apparent. For instance, several options are available for visually or cognitively impaired adults to compensate for these challenges and find their way from place to place (Bosch & Gharaveis, 2017). Smartphone mapping apps provide voice directions for people to guide them to their destination and provide a means to maintaining independence. Similarly, other apps can provide ways for care providers to monitor wandering behavior (Gordijn & ten Have, 2016). Technology is also revolutionizing the approach to pain management (Bhattarai & Phillips, 2017) and in increasing adherence to various types of medical therapies, from medication adherence to rehabilitation (Mertens et al., 2017).

Perhaps the most anticipated goal for a technological boost to healthy aging is autonomous (so-called driverless) cars. Clearly, a fully autonomous vehicle would be a tremendous boost for aging in place (see Chapter 5) and personal independence.

The Society for Automotive Engineers (SAE) International (2014) developed definitions of the levels of automation for vehicles. As you can see in Figure 14.3, these definitions range from no automation to full automation. Many millions of dollars are being expended on research, the most optimistic estimate for autonomous cars being available for general purchase is the early 2020s (Ohnsman, 2016).

SAE Level	Name	Narrative Definition	Execution of Steering and Acceleration/ Deceleration	Monitoring of Driving Environment	Fallback Performance of Dynamic Driving Task	System Capability (Driving Modes)
Human driver monitors the driving environment						
0	No automation	The full-time performance by the human driver of all aspects of the dynamic driving task, even when enhanced by warning or intervention systems	Human driver	Human driver	Human driver	n/a
1	Driver assistance	The driving mode-specific execution by a driver assistance system of either steering or acceleration/deceleration using information about the driving environment and with the expectation that the human driver perform all remaining aspects of the dynamic driving task	Human driver and system	Human driver	Human driver	Some driving modes
2	Partial automation	The driving mode-specific execution by one or more driver assistance systems of both steering and acceleration/deceleration using information about the driving environment and with the expectation that the human driver perform all remaining aspects of the dynamic driving task	System	Human driver	Human driver	Some driving modes
Automated driving system ("system") monitors the driving environment						
3	Conditional automation	The driving mode-specific performance by an automated driving system of all aspects of the dynamic driving task with the expectation that the human driver will respond appropriately to a request to intervene	System	System	Human driver	Some driving modes
4	High automation	The driving mode-specific performance by an automated driving system of all aspects of the dynamic driving task, even if a human driver does not respond appropriately to a request to intervene	System	System	System	Some driving modes
5	Full automation	The full-time performance by an automated driving system of all aspects of the dynamic driving task under all roadway and environmental conditions that can be managed by a human driver	System	System	System	All driving modes

FIGURE 14.3 Summary of SAE International's levels of driving automation for on-road vehicles

Source: SAE International. (2014). *Taxonomy and definitions for terms related to on-road motor vehicle automated driving systems*. Retrieved from www.sae.org/misc/pdfs/automated_driving.pdf. Table, p. 2.

Health Promotion and Disease Prevention

Given that we have a framework for understanding healthy aging, along with a growing set of powerful, especially technology-based, tools, you're probably wondering how best to promote healthy aging for others as well as for yourself. You may not be surprised to learn there is no one set of steps or magic potion you can take to guarantee you will have healthy aging. But research using traditional methods as well as cutting-edge neuroimaging is showing there are some steps you can take to quality of life and the odds of aging well (Gatz, Smyer, & DiGilio, 2016; Stern, 2017).

As you can see in Table 14.1, most of the actions to achieve healthy aging are not complex. but they do capture the results of applying the model for maintaining and enhancing competence we examined at the beginning of the section. The key strategies are sound health habits; good habits of thought, including an optimistic outlook and interest in things; a social network; and sound economic habits.

These simple steps are difficult in practice, of course. To provide support, the U.S. Department of Health and Human Services created a national initiative to improve the health of all Americans through a coordinated and comprehensive emphasis on prevention. Updated every 10 years, the current version of this effort, the *Healthy People 2020* initiative, sets targets for a healthier population based on three broad goals: increase the length of healthy life, reduce health disparities among Americans, and achieve access to preventive services for all.

Similarly, the Centers for Disease Control and Prevention (2016e) established the *Healthy Aging* site. It also provides a wide array of lifestyle and other advice on how to live a healthy life as best as possible.

Challenges for achieving healthy aging through health promotion and disease prevention are still numerous. Many members of ethnic minority groups and the poor still have not seen significant improvements in their lives. With this in mind, there has been a deliberate shift from a focus only on prevention to one that also includes optimum health practices.

To help more people achieve the goal of healthy aging, the U.S. government allocates funds appropriated by the Older Americans Act through the Administration on Aging (AoA) to provide programs specifically aimed at improving the health of older adults. These funds support a wide variety of programs, including health risk assessments and screenings, nutrition screening and education, physical fitness, health promotion programs on chronic disabling conditions, home injury control services, counseling regarding social services, and follow-up health services.

One goal of these low-cost or free programs is to address the lack of awareness many people have about their own chronic health problems; the AoA estimates half of those with diabetes mellitus, more than half with hypertension, and 70% of those with high cholesterol levels are unaware they have serious conditions. Health promotion and disease prevention programs such as those sponsored by the AoA could reduce the cost of treating the diseases through earlier diagnosis and better prevention education. Getting people to participate and then engage in healthy behavior, though, remains elusive.

Issues in Prevention

In Chapter 4, we saw how Verbrugge and Jette's (1994) theoretical model offers a comprehensive account of disability resulting from chronic conditions and provides much guidance for research. Another benefit of the model is it also provides insight into ways to intervene so disability can be prevented or its progress slowed. Prevention efforts can be implemented in many ways, from providing flu vaccines to furnishing transportation to cultural events so otherwise homebound people can enjoy these activities.

Traditionally, three types of prevention discussed can be applied to aging: primary, secondary, and tertiary (Haber, 2013). Other researchers have introduced the concept of quaternary prevention (Jamoulle, 2015). A brief summary of these four levels of prevention is presented in Table 14.2.

Primary prevention *is any intervention that prevents a disease or condition from occurring.* Examples of primary prevention include immunizing against illnesses such as polio and influenza or controlling risk factors such as serum cholesterol levels and cigarette smoking in healthy people.

TABLE 14.1 Preventive Strategies for Maximizing Successful Aging

Adopt a healthy lifestyle. Make it part of your daily routine.

Stay active cognitively. Keep an optimistic outlook and maintain your interest in things.

Maintain a social network and stay engaged with others.

Maintain good economic habits to avoid financial dependency.

TABLE 14.2 Types of Prevention Interventions

Type of Prevention	Description	Examples
Primary	Any intervention that prevents a disease or condition from occurring	Immunizations against diseases, healthy diet
Secondary	Program instituted early after a condition has begun (but may not have been diagnosed) and before significant impairment has occurred	Cancer screening, other medical tests
Tertiary	Efforts to avoid the development of complications or secondary chronic conditions, manage the panic associated with the primary chronic condition, and sustain life	Moving a bedridden person to avoid sores, getting medical intervention, getting a patient out of bed to improve mobility after surgery
Quaternary	Effort specifically aimed at improving the functional capacities of people who have chronic conditions	Cognitive interventions for people with Alzheimer's disease, rehabilitation programs after surgery

Secondary prevention *is instituted early after a condition has begun (but may not yet have been diagnosed) and before significant impairments have occurred.* Examples of secondary intervention include cancer and cardiovascular disease screening and routine medical testing for other conditions. These steps help reduce the severity of the condition and may even reduce mortality from it. In terms of the main pathway in Verbrugge and Jette's (1994) model, secondary prevention occurs between pathology and impairments.

Tertiary prevention *involves efforts to avoid the development of complications or secondary chronic conditions, manage the pain associated with the primary chronic condition, and sustain life through medical intervention.* Some chronic conditions have a high risk of creating additional medical problems; for example, being bedridden as a result of a chronic disease often is associated with getting pneumonia. Tertiary prevention involves taking steps such as sitting the person up in bed to lower the risk of contracting additional diseases. In terms of the model, tertiary interventions are aimed at minimizing functional limitations and disability.

Tertiary prevention efforts do not usually focus on functioning or quality of life, but rather on avoiding additional medical problems and sustaining life (Haber, 2013). Consequently, the notion of quaternary prevention has been developed to address functional issues, especially the avoidance of overmedication (Jamoulle, 2015).

Quaternary prevention *efforts are specifically aimed at improving the functional capacities of people who have chronic conditions and avoiding overmedication.* Quaternary prevention strategies help healthcare professionals avoid unnecessary or excessive medical interventions, especially invasive ones. Some examples of quaternary prevention are cognitive interventions to help people with Alzheimer's disease remember things and occupational therapy to help people maintain their independence. It would also include palliative care (discussed in Chapter 13) and other nonmedical actions to improve quality of life.

Although most efforts with older adults to date have focused on primary prevention, increasing attention is being paid to secondary prevention through screening for early diagnosis of diseases such as cancer and cardiovascular disease (see Chapters 3 and 4).

Few systematic studies of the benefits and outcomes of tertiary and quaternary prevention efforts have been done with older adult participants, though. However, the number of such programs being conducted in local senior centers, healthcare facilities, and other settings is increasing steadily, with the focus of many of them on nutrition and exercise, as well as other behaviorally based strategies (Rippe, 2013, 2016).

The stakes are high. Because tertiary and quaternary prevention programs are aimed at maintaining functional abilities and minimizing disability, and at maintaining or improving quality of life, they offer effective, lower-cost alternatives for addressing the needs of older adults with chronic conditions. Lifestyle factors are the basis for these behavioral approaches that are clearly gaining favor in the healthcare professional community (Rippe, 2013, 2016). Achieving healthy aging requires more of these approaches. Let's take a closer look at these lifestyle factors.

Lifestyle Factors

Most attention in health promotion and disease prevention programs is on tackling a handful of behaviors that have tremendous payoff, such as keeping fit and eating properly. In turn, these programs educate adults about good healthcare practices and identify conditions such as hypertension, high cholesterol levels, and elevated blood sugar levels, which, if left untreated, can cause atherosclerosis, heart disease, strokes, diabetes mellitus, and other serious conditions.

Certain steps tend to underlie healthy aging. Chief among these is exercise, an almost magic preventive measure with numerous benefits. Let's see what several of them are.

Exercise is a major way to help delay or prevent chronic disease and promote a healthy late life.

Exercise

Since the ancient Greeks, physicians and researchers have known that exercise significantly slows the aging process. Indeed, evidence suggests a program of regular exercise, in conjunction with a healthy lifestyle, can slow the physiological aging process and improve the immune system (Bartlett & Huffman, 2017; Parrella & Vormittag, 2017). Being sedentary is absolutely hazardous to your health.

Adults benefit from **aerobic exercise**, *exercise that places moderate stress on the heart by maintaining a pulse rate between 60% and 90% of the person's maximum heart rate.* You can calculate your maximum heart rate by subtracting your age from 220. Thus, if you are 40 years old, your target range would be 108–162 beats per minute. The minimum time necessary for aerobic exercise to be of benefit depends on its intensity; at low heart rates, sessions may need to last an hour, whereas at high heart rates, 15 minutes may suffice. Examples of aerobic exercise include jogging, step aerobics, Zumba®, swimming, and cross-country skiing.

What happens when a person exercises aerobically (besides becoming tired and sweaty)? Physiologically, adults of all ages show improved cardiovascular functioning and maximum oxygen consumption; lower blood pressure; and better strength, endurance, flexibility, and coordination (Mayo Clinic, 2015a). Psychologically, people who exercise aerobically report lower levels of stress, better moods, and better cognitive functioning.

The best way to gain the benefits of aerobic exercise is to maintain physical fitness throughout the life span, beginning at least in middle age. The benefits of various forms of exercise are numerous and include lowering the risk of cardiovascular disease, osteoporosis (if the exercise is weight bearing), and a host of other conditions. The Mayo Clinic's *Healthy Lifestyle* Fitness websites provide an excellent place to start. In planning an exercise program, three points should be remembered. First, check with a physician before beginning an aerobic exercise program. Second, bear in mind that moderation is important. Third, just because you intend to exercise doesn't mean you will; you must take the necessary steps to turn your intention into action (Paech, Luszczynska, & Lippke, 2016; Schwarzer, 2008). If you do, and stick with it, you may feel much younger (Joyner & Barnes, 2013).

Without question, regular exercise is one of the two most important behaviors you can do to promote healthy living and good aging (not smoking is the other). In addition to the wide variety of positive effects on health (e.g., lower risk of cardiovascular disease, diabetes, hypertension), there is also substantial evidence exercise is also connected to less cortical atrophy, better brain function, and enhanced cognitive performance (Erickson, Gildengers, & Butters, 2013; Suo et al., 2016). Specifically, exercise has a positive effect on the prefrontal and hippocampal areas of the brain, increased gray matter, and reversed the progression of white matter hypersensitivities (a biomarker of cerebrovascular disease; see Chapter 2) and, as we have seen, is closely associated with memory and other cognitive functions.

Whether exercise can delay or prevent diseases associated with these brain structures, such as Alzheimer's disease, remains to be seen. But the evidence to date points in that direction (e.g., Suo et al., 2016), so researchers and clinicians are promoting exercise as a way to a healthy, better functioning brain in later life. A better functioning brain may well be related to the mood improvements seen as another positive benefit of exercise, as shown in Figure 14.4.

In summary, if you want to maximize the odds of healthy aging, exercise. Guidelines state about 150 minutes of moderate aerobic exercise weekly with additional whole-body strength training and balance work is sufficient to produce positive effects (Batt, Tanji, & Börjesson, 2013). When you are done your routine for the day, watch what you eat, as discussed next.

Nutrition

Once on a vacation trip, one of us (John Cavanaugh) took this photo outside a restaurant in Megalochori, Greece. It captures the essence of how you should approach diet as part of healthy aging.

"You are what you eat." Most people remember disagreements with parents (or now with their own children) about food. As adults, they may now realize those lima beans and other despised foods their parents urged them to eat really are healthy.

Experts agree nutrition directly affects one's mental, emotional, and physical functioning (Hammar & Östgren, 2013; McKee & Schüz, 2015). Diet has been linked to cancer, cardiovascular disease, diabetes, anemia, and digestive disorders. To stay maximally healthy, though, we must recognize that nutritional requirements and eating habits change across the life span. *This change is due mainly to differences in, or how much energy the body needs, termed* **metabolism**. Body metabolism and the digestive process slow down with age (Janssen, 2005).

The U.S. Department of Agriculture publishes dietary guidelines based on current research. In its *Dietary Guidelines for Americans 2015–2020* (Health.gov, 2015), the USDA recommends we eat a variety of nutrient-dense foods and beverages across the basic food groups. The general guidelines for adults can be seen in Figure 14.5.

As you can see, the USDA approaches nutrition from the perspective of ensuring people eat a healthy plate of food at each meal, and the contents of that plate be

The importance of diet is emphasized at this restaurant in Megalochori, Greece.

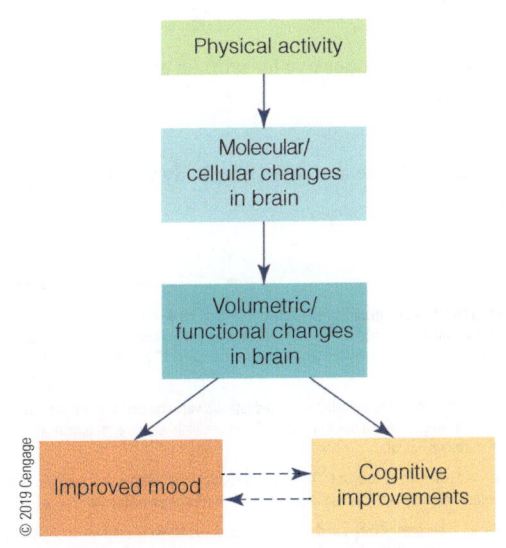

FIGURE 14.4 A schematic representation of the general path by which cognitive function and mood are improved by physical activity, it could be hypothesized that improvements in cognitive function mediate the improvements in mood or that improvements in mood mediate some of the improvements in cognitive function. The dotted lines represent these hypothesized paths.

Source: Erickson, K. I., Gildengers, A. G., & Butters, M. A. (2013). Physical activity and brain plasticity in late adulthood. *Dialogues in Clinical Neuroscience, 15*, 99–108. Open source. Retrieved from www.ncbi.nlm.nih.gov/pmc/articles/PMC3622473/. Image retrieved from www.ncbi.nlm.nih.gov/pmc/articles/PMC3622473/figure/DialoguesClinNeurosci-15-99-g001/.

Key Recommendations:

A healthy eating pattern accounts for all foods and beverages within an appropriate calorie level.

A healthy eating pattern includes:

- A variety of vegetables from all of the subgroups—dark green, red and orange, legumes (beans and peas), starchy, and other
- Fruits, especially whole fruits
- Grains, at least half of which are whole grains
- Fat-free or low-fat dairy, including milk, yogurt, cheese, and/or fortified soy beverages
- A variety of protein foods, including seafood, lean meats and poultry, eggs, legumes (beans and peas), and nuts, seeds, and soy products
- Oils

A healthy eating pattern limits:

- Saturated fats and *trans* fats, added sugars, and sodium

Calorie limits can help individuals achieve healthy eating patterns:

- Consume less than 10 percent of calories per day from added sugars[1]
- Consume less than 10 percent of calories per day from saturated fats[2]
- Consume less than 2,300 milligrams (mg) per day of sodium[3]
- If alcohol is consumed, it should be consumed in moderation—up to one drink per day for women and up to two drinks per day for men—and only by adults of legal drinking age.[4]

The importance of exercise:

The relationship between diet and physical activity contributes to calorie balance and managing body weight. As such, the *Dietary Guidelines* includes a Key Recommendation to:

- Meet the *Physical Activity Guidelines for Americans*.[5]

[1] The recommendation to limit intake of calories from added sugars to less than 10 percent per day is a target based on food pattern modeling and national data on intakes of calories from added sugars that demonstrate the public health need to limit calories from added sugars to meet food group and nutrient needs within calorie limits. The limit on calories from added sugars is not a Tolerable Upper Intake Level (UL) set by the Institute of Medicine (IOM). For most calorie levels, there are not enough calories available after meeting food group needs to consume 10 percent of calories from added sugars and 10 percent of calories from saturated fats and still stay within calorie limits.

[2] The recommendation to limit intake of calories from saturated fats to less than 10 percent per day is a target based on evidence that replacing saturated fats with unsaturated fats is associated with reduced risk of cardiovascular disease. The limit on calories from saturated fats is not a UL set by the IOM. For most calorie levels, there are not enough calories available after meeting food group needs to consume 10 percent of calories from added sugars and 10 percent of calories from saturated fats and still stay within calorie limits.

[3] The recommendation to limit intake of sodium to less than 2,300 mg per day is the UL for individuals ages 14 years and older set by the IOM. The recommendations for children younger than 14 years of age are the IOM age- and sex-appropriate ULs (see Appendix 7. Nutritional Goals for Age-Sex Groups Based on Dietary Reference Intakes and Dietary Guidelines Recommendations).

[4] It is not recommended that individuals begin drinking or drink more for any reason. The amount of alcohol and calories in beverages varies and should be accounted for within the limits of healthy eating patterns. Alcohol should be consumed only by adults of legal drinking age. There are many circumstances in which individuals should not drink, such as during pregnancy. See Appendix 9. Alcohol for additional information.

[5] U.S. Department of Health and Human Services. *2008 Physical Activity Guidelines for Americans*. Washington (DC): U.S. Department of Health and Human Services; 2008. ODPHP Publication No. U0036. Available at: www.health.gov/paguidelines. Accessed August 6, 2015.

FIGURE 14.5 Key Recommendations from Dietary Guidelines 2015–2020

Source: Retrieved from health.gov/dietaryguidelines/2015/resources/2015-2020_Dietary_Guidelines.pdf, p. xiii

appropriately balanced. Most important, we should choose foods that limit the intake of added sugar, saturated fats, sodium, and alcohol. And we need to keep our target calorie intake in mind. The full report contains much more detail about the specific foods that are best for you.

Of course, most people do not eat perfectly all the time. From time to time, each of craves something—whether a triple-dip cone of premium ice cream or really high-end chocolate. If you feel even a tiny bit guilty after you enjoy that splurge, you are among the people who have taken to heart (literally) the link between diet and cardiovascular disease. The American Heart Association (2016b) makes it clear foods high in saturated fat (such as our beloved ice cream) should be replaced with foods low in fat (such as fat-free frozen yogurt). Check out their website for the latest in advice on eating a heart-healthy diet.

Healthy aging and eating is also the focus of minority communities. For example, the American Heart Association has partnered with Native American tribes to create the *Seeds of Native Health* campaign for indigenous nutrition as a way to connect traditional native foods to healthy eating and healthy aging (American Heart Association, 2016c).

Much of the focus of the American Heart Association's various guidelines and initiatives is to lower the risk of cardiovascular disease. To achieve this goal, it is important to understand an important difference between two different types of lipoproteins reflected in different types of cholesterol. Lipoproteins are fatty chemicals attached to proteins carried in the blood. **Low-density lipoproteins (LDLs)** *cause fatty deposits to accumulate in arteries, impeding blood flow, whereas* **high-density lipoproteins (HDLs)** *help keep arteries clear and break down LDLs.* It is not so much the overall cholesterol number but the ratio of LDLs to HDLs that matters most in cholesterol screening. High levels of LDLs are a risk factor in cardiovascular disease, and high levels of HDLs are considered a protective factor. Reducing LDL levels is effective in diminishing the risk of cardiovascular disease in adults of all ages; in healthy adults, a high level of LDL (over 160 mg/dL) is associated with higher risk for cardiovascular disease (Mayo Clinic, 2016b). In contrast, higher levels of HDL are good (in healthy adults, levels at least above 40 mg/dL for men and 50 mg/dL for women). LDL levels can be lowered and HDL levels can be raised through various interventions such as exercise and a high-fiber diet. Weight control is also an important component.

If diet and exercise are not effective in lowering cholesterol, numerous medications exist for treating cholesterol problems. The most popular of these drugs are from a family of medications called *statins* (e.g., Lipitor, Crestor). These medications lower LDL and moderately increase HDL. Before prescribing statins, healthcare professionals also assess a person's risk of cardiovascular disease from family history and lifestyle, among other factors. If statins are prescribed, their potential side effects on liver functioning should be monitored, and patients should consult with their physicians on a regular basis.

Obesity is a serious and growing health problem related to diet. One good way to assess your own status is to compute your body mass index. **Body mass index (BMI)** *is a ratio of body weight and height and is related to total body fat.* You can compute BMI as follows:

$$BMI = w/h^2$$

where w = weight in kilograms (or weight in pounds divided by 2.2), and h = height in meters (or inches divided by 39.37).

The Centers for Disease Control and Prevention (2016d) defines healthy weight as having a BMI of less than 25. However, this calculation may overestimate body fat in muscular athletic people (e.g., professional athletes) and underestimate body fat in those who appear of normal weight but have little muscle mass.

Obesity is related to the risk of serious medical conditions and mortality: the higher one's BMI, the higher one's risk (Centers for Disease Control and Prevention, 2016d). Figure 14.6 shows the increased risk for several diseases and mortality associated with increased BMI (and obesity).

In the United States, obesity rates have increased very significantly since the 1970s. Today, nearly half of African Americans and over 40% of Latinos are obese (Centers for Disease Control and Prevention, 2016d). Across all racial and ethnic groups, more than one-third of older adults are obese. Reductions in these statistics is a primary focus of the federal government's nutrition and exercise guidelines.

Based on these data, you may want to lower your BMI if it's above 25. But be careful—lowering your BMI too much (below 18.5) may not be healthy either. Very low BMIs may indicate malnutrition, which is also related to increased mortality.

	BMI (Kg/m^2)	Obesity class	Men 102 cm (40 in) or less Women 88 cm (35 in) or less	Men > 102 cm (40 in) Women > 88 cm (35 in)
Underweight	<18.5		–	–
Normal	18.5–24.9		–	–
Overweight	25.0–29.9		Increased	High
Obesity	30.0–34.9	I	High	High
	35.9–39.9	II	Very high	Very high
Extreme obesity	40.0	III	Extremely high	Extremely high

FIGURE 14.6 Classification of overweight and obesity by BMI, waist circumference, and associate disease risks.
Source: Adapted from Centers for Disease Control and Prevention (2015). Retrieved from www.cdc.gov/healthyweight/assessing/.

Adult Development in Action

How could the information about exercise and nutrition in this section be combined with the health information in Chapters 3 and 4 to create an education program for adults?

14.3 Epilogue

Marie Chen just celebrated her 100th birthday. During the daylong festivities, many people asked her whether she believed she had a good life. She answered everyone the same way, telling them she had her health, enough money to live on, and her family. What more could she want?

Marie gives every sign of having achieved healthy aging. She's 100 years old, with a loving family, good enough health to live in the community, and enough income to pay her bills. But is there more to it than that?

In this book, you have seen a snapshot of what adult development and aging are like today. You learned about the complexities, myths, and realities of people's experience of growing old. But more than anything else, you have seen what we really know about the pioneers who blazed the trail ahead of us.

In a short time, it will be your turn to lead the journey. The decisions about social policy, about which interventions should be implemented and which ones should not, about how you will prepare for later life, and so many others, that you will make between now and then will have an enormous impact on those who will get there ahead of you: your parents, grandparents, and the people who taught and mentored you. These decisions will not be easy ones. But you have an advantage that the pioneers did not. You have the collected knowledge of gerontologists to apply in your decision making. With a continued concerted effort, you will be able to address the problems and meet the challenges that lie ahead. Then, when you yourself are old, you will be able to look back on your life and say, "I lived long—and I prospered."

Reaching the goal of healthy aging is often visible on the face of those who reach it.

SUMMARY

14.1 Demographic Trends and Social Policy

What key demographic changes will occur by 2030?

- The rapid increase in the number of older adults between now and 2030 means social policy must take the aging of the population into account. Changing demographics will affect every aspect of life in the United States and in most other countries, including health care and all social service programs.

What are the challenges facing Social Security and Medicare?

- Although designed as an income supplement, Social Security has become the primary source of retirement income for most U.S. citizens. The aging of the baby-boom generation will place considerable stress on the financing of the system.
- Medicare is the principal health insurance program for adults in the United States over age 65. Cost containment is a major concern, resulting in emphases on program redesign for long-term sustainability.

14.2 Healthy Aging: Living Well in Later Life

What is healthy aging?

- Healthy aging involves avoiding disease, being engaged with life, and maintaining high cognitive and physical functioning. The basic premises of healthy aging include keeping a balance between the various gains and losses that occur over time and minimizing the influence of factors unrelated to aging.

What are the key issues in health promotion and quality of life?

- Health promotion will become an increasingly important aspect of health care for older adults. Two models of behavioral change currently drive research: the self-efficacy model and the self-regulation model.
- Quality of life, a person's well-being and life satisfaction, is best studied from the perspective of the individual.

How is technology used to maintain and enhance competence?

- A useful framework for enhancing and maintaining competence is the selection, optimization, and compensation (SOC) model.
- The life-span approach provides a guide for designing competency-enhancing interventions.

What are the primary considerations in designing health promotion and disease prevention programs?

- Effective strategies for health promotion and disease prevention are adopting a healthy lifestyle, staying active cognitively, maintaining a social network, and preserving good economic habits.
- Four levels of prevention are: primary (preventing a disease or condition from occurring), secondary (intervening after a condition has occurred but before it causes impairment), tertiary (avoiding the development of complications), and quaternary (improving functional capacities in people with chronic conditions).

What are the principal lifestyle factors that influence competence?

- Maintaining a good exercise program and getting good nutrition are essential for delaying or preventing many negative aspects of physiological aging, especially chronic diseases.

REVIEW QUESTIONS

14.1 Demographic Trends and Social Policy

- What will the population of the United States look like in 2030?
- What social policy impact will these changes have?
- What pressures are there on Social Security and Medicare?

14.2 Healthy Aging: Living Well in Later Life

- What is meant by healthy aging?
- Why is health promotion likely to become increasingly important?
- What is meant by the term *quality of life?*
- What theoretical framework provides the best approach for enhancing competency?
- What are the four types of prevention strategies?
- Why are exercise and nutrition important for health promotion and disease prevention?

INTEGRATING CONCEPTS IN DEVELOPMENT

- Suppose you were brought in as a consultant on aging policy issues to your national government. Based on the demographic information in Chapter 1 and this chapter, what recommendations would you make?
- What trends in health care do you think will emerge based on information in this chapter and in Chapters 3, 4, and 10?
- How do you think older adults will define successful aging in the future?

KEY TERMS

aerobic exercise Exercise that places moderate stress on the heart by maintaining a pulse rate between 60% and 90% of the person's maximum heart rate.

body mass index (BMI) A ratio of body weight and height that is related to total body fat.

dependency ratio The ratio of the number of people under age 15 and over age 64 in a country to the number of people between 15 and 64.

healthy aging Involves avoiding disease, being engaged with life, and maintaining high cognitive and physical functioning.

high-density lipoproteins (HDLs) Help keep arteries clear and break down LDLs.

low-density lipoproteins (LDLs) Cause fatty deposits to accumulate in arteries, impeding blood flow.

metabolism How much energy the body needs.

primary prevention Any intervention that prevents a disease or condition from occurring.

quality of life A person's well-being and life satisfaction.

quaternary prevention Efforts specifically aimed at improving the functional capacities of people who have chronic conditions and avoiding overmedication.

salutogenesis An approach that emphasizes factors that support and promote health, rather than factors that cause disease.

secondary prevention Instituted early after a condition has begun (but may not yet have been diagnosed) and before significant impairments have occurred.

tertiary prevention Involves efforts to avoid the development of complications or secondary chronic conditions, manage the pain associated with the primary chronic condition, and sustain life through medical intervention.

References

A Better Balance. (2016). *The need for paid family leave*. Retrieved from www.abetterbalance.org/web/ourissues/familyleave.

AARP. (1999). *AARP/Modern maturity sexuality survey*. Retrieved from assets.aarp.org/rgcenter/health/mmsexsurvey.pdf.

AARP. (2005). *Sexuality at midlife and beyond: 2004 update of attitudes and behaviors*. Retrieved from assets.aarp.org/rgcenter/general/2004_sexuality.pdf.

AARP. (2010). *Sex, romance, and relationships: AARP survey of midlife and older adults*. Retrieved from assets.aarp.org/rgcenter/general/srr_09.pdf.

AARP. (2016). *About GrandFacts*. Retrieved from www.aarp.org/relationships/friends-family/grandfacts-sheets/.

Aasland, O. G., Rosta, J., & Nylenna, M. (2010). Healthcare reforms and job satisfaction among doctors in Norway. *Scandinavian Journal of Public Health, 38*, 253–258. doi:10.1177/1403494810364559

Abbott, G., Gilbert, K., & Rosinski, P. (2013). Cross-cultural working in coaching and mentoring. In J. Passmore, D. B. Peterson, & T. Freire (Eds.), *The Wiley-Blackwell handbook of coaching and mentoring* (pp. 483–500). Oxford, UK: Wiley-Blackwell.

Aberson, C. L., Shoemaker, C., & Tomolillo, C. (2004). Implicit bias and contact: The role of interethnic friendships. *Journal of Social Psychology, 144*, 335–347. doi:10.3200/SOCP.144.3.335-347

Abraham, A., Beudt, S., Ott, D. V. M., & von Cramon, D. Y. (2012). Creative cognition and the brain: Dissociations between frontal, parietal-temporal and basal ganglia groups. *Brain Research, 1482*, 55–70. doi:10.1016/j.bbr.2011.03.031

Abrams, D., Swift, H. J., & Drury, L. (2016). Old and unemployable? How age-based stereotypes affect willingness to hire job candidates. *Journal of Social Issues, 72*, 105–121. doi:10.1111/josi.12158

Abrams, R. (2013). *When parents die: Learning to live with the loss of a parent* (3rd ed.). New York: Routledge.

Abutalebi, J., & Green, D. W. (2016). Neuroimaging of language control in bilinguals: Neural adaptation and use. *Bilingualism: Language and Cognition, 19*, 689–698. doi:10.1017/S1366728916000225

Accessory Dwellings.org. (2016a) *Accessory dwellings*. Retrieved from accessorydwellings.org/what-adus-are-and-why-people-build-them/.

Accessory Dwellings.org. (2016b)*Accessory dwellings: What are the rules where I live?* Retrieved from accessorydwellings.org/adu-regulations-by-city/.

Achor, S. (2010). *The happiness advantage: The seven principles of positive psychology that fuel success and performance at work*. New York: Random House.

Adams, C., Smith, M. C., Pasupathi, M., & Vitolo, L. (2002). Social context effects on story recall in older and younger women: Does the listener make a difference? *Journals of Gerontology: Psychological Sciences, 57B*, P28–P40. doi:10.1093/ geronb/57.1. P28

Adams, R. B., Jr., Nelson, A. J., Soto, J. A., Hess, U., & Kleck, R. E. (2012). Emotion in the neutral face: A mechanism for impression formation? *Cognition and Emotion, 26*, 431–441. doi:10.1080/02699931.2012.666502

Adams, R. G., & Taylor, E. M. (2015). Friendship and happiness in the third age. In M. Demir (Ed.), *Friendship and happiness* (pp. 155–169). New York: Springer.

Adamy, J., & McGinty, T. (2012). *The crushing cost of care*. Retrieved from online.wsj.com/article/SB10001424052702304441404577483050976766184.html.

Addo, F. R. (2017). Financial integration and relationship transitions of young adult cohabiters. *Journal of Family and Economic Issues, 38*, 84–99. doi:10.1007/s10834-016-9490-7

Adhikari, K., Fontanil, T., Cal, S., Mendoza-Revilla, J., Fuentes-Guajardo, M., Chacón-Duque, J.-C. et al. (2016). A genome-wide association scan in admixed Latin Americans identifies loci influencing facial and scalp hair features. *Nature Communications, 7(Article no. 10815)*. Retrieved from www.nature.com/ncomms/2016/160301/ncomms10815/full/ncomms10815.html.

Adler, L. L. (2001). Women and gender roles. In L. L. Adler & U. P. Gielen (Eds.), *Cross-cultural topics on psychology* (2nd ed., pp. 103–114). Westport, CT: Praeger/Greenwood.

Adler, R. A., Fuleihan, G. E.-H., Bauer, D. C., Camacho, P. M., Clarke, B. L., Clines, G. A. et al. (2016). Managing osteoporosis in patients on long-term bisphosphonate treatment: Report of a task force of the American Society for Bone and Mineral Research. *Journal of Bone and Mineral Research, 31*, 16–35. doi:10.1002/jbmr.2708

Afendulis, C. C., Caudry, D. J., O'Malley, A. J., Kemper, P., Grabowski, D. C., & THRIVE Research Collaborative. (2016). Green House adoption and nursing home quality. *Health Services Research, 51*, 454– 474. doi:10.1111/1475-6773.12436

Afilalo, J. (2016). Conceptual models of frailty: The sarcopenia phenotype. *Canadian Journal of Cardiology, 32*, 1051–1055. doi:10.1016/j.cjca.2016.05.017

Ai, A. L., Wink, P., & Ardelt, M. (2010). Spirituality and aging: A journey for meaning through deep interconnection in humanity. In J. C. Cavanaugh & C. K. Cavanaugh (Eds.), *Aging in America: Vol. 3: Societal issues* (pp. 222–246). Santa Barbara, CA: Praeger Perspectives.

Ai, A. L., Wink, P., Gall, T. L., Dillon, M., & Tice, T. N. (2017). Assessing reverence in contexts: A positive emotion related to psychological functioning. *Journal of Humanistic Psychology, 57*, 64–97. doi:10.1177/0022167815586657

Aichele, S., Rabbitt, P., & Ghisletta, P. (2016). Think fast, feel fine, live long: A 29-year study of cognition, health, and survival in middle-aged and older adults. *Psychological Science, 27*, 518–529. doi:10.1177/0956797615626906

AIDS.gov. (2015). *Newly diagnosed: Older adults*. Retrieved from www.aids.gov/hiv-aids-basics/just-diagnosed-with-hiv-aids/overview/aging-population/.

Ajrouch, K. J., Antonucci, T. C., & Webster, N. J. (2014). Volunteerism: Social network dynamics and education. *Journal of Gerontology: Social Sciences, 71*, 309–319. doi:10.1093/geronb/gbu166

Akincilar, S. C., Unal, B., & Tergaonkar, V. (2016). Reactivation of telomerase in cancer. *Cellular and Molecular Life Sciences, 73*, 1659–1670. doi:10.1007/s00018-016-2146-9. Retrieved from link.springer.com/article/10.1007/s00018-016-2146-9.

Al-Attar, A., Presnell, S. R., Peterson, C. A., Thomas, D. T., & Lutz, C. T. (2016). The effect of sex on immune cells in healthy aging: Elderly women have more robust natural killer lymphocytes than do elderly men. *Mechanisms of Ageing and Development, 156*, 25–33. doi:10.1016/j.mad.2016.04.001

Alavi, M. V. (2016). Aging and vision. In C. B. Rickman, M. M. LaVail, R. E. Anderson, C. Grimm, J. Hollyfield, & J. Ash (Eds.), *Retinal degenerative diseases* (pp. 393–399). New York: Springer. doi:10.1007/978-3-319-17121-0_52

Al-Bar, M. A., & Chamsi-Pasha, H. (2015). Brain death. In M. A. Al-Bar & H. Chamsi-Pasha (Eds.), *Contemporary bioethics* (pp. 227–242). New York: Springer. doi:10.1007/978-3-319-18428-9_14

Albert, M. S., DeKosky, S. T., Dickson, D., Dubois, B., Feldman, H. A., Fox, N. C. et al. (2011). The diagnosis of mild cognitive impairment due to Alzheimer's disease: Recommendations from the National Institute on Aging—Alzheimer's Association workgroups on diagnostic guidelines for Alzheimer's disease. *Alzheimer's and Dementia: Journal of the Alzheimer's Assocation, 7*, 270–279. doi:10.1016/j.jalz.2011.03.008

Albuquerque, S., Pereira, M., & Narciso, I. (2016). Couple's relationship after the death of a child: A systematic review. *Journal of Child and Family Studies, 25*, 30–53. doi:10.1007/s10826-015-0219-2

Alden, D. L., Merz, M. Y., & Akashi, J. (2012). Young adult preference for physician decision-making style in Japan and the United States. *Asia-Pacific Journal of Public Health, 24*, 173–184. doi:10.1177/1010539510365098

Aldwin, C. M. (2015). How can developmental systems theories cope with free will? The importance of stress-related growth and mindfulness. *Research in Human development, 12*, 189–195. doi:10.1080/15427609.2015.1068042

Aldwin, C. M., & Gilmer, D. F. (2013). *Health, illness, and optimal aging: Biological and psychosocial perspectives* (2nd ed.). New York: Springer.

Aldwin, C., & Igarashi, H. (2012). An ecological model of resilience in late life. *Annual Review of Gerontology and Geriatrics, 32*, 115–130. doi:10.1891/0198-8794.32.115

Alegría, M., Chatterji, P., Wells, K., Cao, Z., Chen, C.-N., Takeuchi, D., Jackson, J., & Meng, X.-L. (2008). Disparity in depression treatment among racial and ethnic minority populations in the United States. *Psychiatric Services, 59*, 1264–1272. doi:10.1176/appi.ps.59.11.1264

Alhurani, R. E., Vassilaki, M., Aakre, J. A., Mielke, M. M., Kremers, W. K., Machulda, M. M. et al. (2016). Decline in weight and incident mild cognitive impairment: Mayo Clinic Study of Aging. *JAMA Neurology, 73*, 439–446. doi:10.1001/jamaneurol.2015.4756

Allaire, J. C. (2012). Everyday cognition. In S. K. Whitbourne & M. J. Sliwinski (Eds.), *The Wiley-Blackwell handbook of adult development and aging* (pp. 190–207). New York: Wiley. doi:10.1002/9781118392966.ch10

Allaire, J. C., & Marsiske, M. (1999). Everyday cognition: Age and intellectual ability correlates. *Psychology and Aging, 14*, 627–644. doi:10.1037/0882-7974.14.4.627

Allaire, J. C., & Marsiske, M. (2002). Well- and ill-defined measures of everyday cognition: Relationship to older adults' intellectual ability and functional status. *Psychology and Aging, 17*, 101–115. doi:10.1037/0882-7974.17.1.101

Allaire, J. C., & Willis, S. L. (2006). Competence in everyday activities as a predictor of cognitive risk and morbidity. *Aging,*

Neuropsychology, and Cognition, 13, 207–224. doi:10.1080/13825580490904228

Allemand, M., Zimprich, D., & Hendriks, A. A. J. (2008). Age differences in five personality domains across the life span. *Developmental Psychology, 44*(3), 758–770. doi:10.1037/0012-1649.44.3.758

Allen, K. R., & Roberto, K. A. (2016). Family relationships of older LGBT adults. In D. A Harley & P. B. Teaster (Eds.), *Handbook of LGBT elders* (pp. 43–64). New York: Springer.

Allen, R. S., DeLaine, S. R., Chaplin, W. F., Marson, D. C., Bourgeois, M. S., Kijkstra, K., & Burgio, L. D. (2003). Advance care planning in nursing homes: Correlates of capacity and possession of advance directives. *The Gerontologist, 43*, 309–317. doi:10.1093/geront/43.3.309

Allexandre, D., Bernstein, A. M., Walker, E., Hunter, J., Roizen, M. F., & Morledge, T. J. (2016). A web-based mindfulness stress management program in a corporate call center. *Journal of Occupational and Environmental Medicine, 58*, 254–264. doi:10.1097/JOM.0000000000000680

Alley, J. L. (2004). The potential meaning of the grandparent-grandchild relationship as perceived by young adults: An exploratory study. *Dissertation Abstracts International. Section B. Sciences and Engineering, 65*(3-B), 1536.

Almeida, J., Molnar, B. E., Kawachi, I., & Subramanian, S. V. (2009). Ethnicity and nativity status as determinants of perceived social support: Testing the concept of familism. *Social Science and Medicine, 68*, 1852–1858 doi:10.1016/j.socscimed.2009.02.029

Alper, J., & Howe, D. (Eds.). (2015). *Assessing adoptive and foster parents: Improving analysis and understanding of parenting capacity.* London, UK: Jessica Kingsley Publications.

Alspach, J. G. (2016). When it's your time, will it be your way? *Critical Care Nurse, 36*, 10–13. doi:10.4037/ccn2016452

Altgassen, M., Rendell, P. G., Bernhard, A., Henry, J. D., Bailey, P. E., Phillips, L. H. et al. (2015). Future thinking improves prospective memory performance and plan enactment in older adults. *The Quarterly Journal of Experimental Psychology, 68*, 192–204. doi:10.1080/17470218.2014.956127

Alzheimer's Association. (2015). *Protection of participants in research studies.* Retrieved from www.alz.org/documents_custom/statements/Protection_of_Participants_in_Research.pdf.

Alzheimer's Association. (2016a). *Quick facts.* Retrieved from www.alz.org/facts/overview.asp.

Alzheimer's Association. (2016b). *Alzheimer's and dementia basics.* Retrieved from www.alz.org/alzheimers_disease_what_is_alzheimers.asp.

Alzheimer's Association. (2016c). 2016 Alzheimer's disease facts and figures. *Alzheimer's and Dementia, 12*, 459–509. Retrieved from www.alz.org/documents_custom/2016-facts-and-figures.pdf.

Alzheimer's Association. (2016d). *10 early signs and symptoms of Alzheimer's.* Retrieved from alz.org/10-signs-symptoms-alzheimers-dementia.asp.

Alzheimer's Association. (2016e). *Stages of Alzheimer's.* Retrieved from www.alz.org/alzheimers_disease_stages_of_alzheimers.asp.

Amato, P. R., & Cheadle, J. (2005). The long reach of divorce: Divorce and child well-being across three generations. *Journal of Marriage & Family, 67*, 191–206. doi:10.1111/j.0022-2445.2005.00014.x

American Academy of Dermatology. (2016). *What causes our skin to age?* Retrieved from www.aad.org/public/skin-hair-nails/younger-skin.

American Academy of Ophthalmology. (2016). *Macular degeneration treatment: How is AMD treated?* Retrieved from www.aao.org/eye-health/diseases/amd-treatment.

American Academy of Pain Medicine. (2016) *Position statements to support your pain practice.* Retrieved from www.painmed.org/practicemanagement/position-statements/.

American Bar Association. (2016). *Health care advance directives: What Is the Patient Self-Determination Act?* Retrieved from www.americanbar.org/groups/public_education/resources/law_issues_for_consumers/patient_self_determination_act.html.

American Bar Association/American Psychological Association. (2005). *Assessment of older adults with diminished capacity: A handbook for lawyers.* Retrieved from www.apa.org/pi/aging/resources/guides/diminished-capacity.pdf.

American Bar Association/American Psychological Association. (2006). *Judicial determination of capacity of older adults in guardianship proceedings.* Retrieved from www.apa.org/pi/aging/resources/guides/judges-diminished.pdf.

American Bar Association/American Psychological Association. (2008). *Assessment of older adults with diminished capacity: A handbook for psychologists.* Retrieved from www.apa.org/pi/aging/programs/assessment/capacity-psychologist-handbook.pdf.

American Cancer Society. (2012). *Prostate cancer.* Retrieved from www.cancer.org/cancer/prostatecancer/index.

American Cancer Society. (2015a). *Women, help reduce your cancer risk and get your tests to find cancer early.* Retrieved from www.cancer.org/acs/groups/content/@editorial/documents/document/acspc-035113.pdf.

American Cancer Society. (2015b). *Men, reduce your cancer risk and get your tests to find cancer early.* Retrieved from www.cancer.org/acs/groups/content/@editorial/documents/document/acspc-035114.pdf.

American Cancer Society. (2016a). *American Cancer Society skin cancer prevention activities.* Retrieved from www.cancer.org/healthy/morewaysacshelpsyoustaywell/acs-skin-cancer-prevention-activities.

American Cancer Society. (2016b). Lifetime risk of developing or dying from cancer. Retrieved from www.cancer.org/cancer/cancerbasics/lifetime-probability-of-developing-or-dying-from-cancer.

American Cancer Society. (2016c). *Stay healthy.* Retrieved from www.cancer.org/healthy/index.

American Cancer Society. (2016d). *Survival rates for selected adult brain and spinal cord tumors.* Retrieved from www.cancer.org/cancer/braincnstumorsinadults/detailedguide/brain-and-spinal-cord-tumors-in-adults-survival-rates.

American Cancer Society. (2016e). *Survival rates for prostate cancer.* Retrieved from www.cancer.org/cancer/prostatecancer/detailedguide/prostate-cancer-survival-rates.

American Cancer Society. (2016f). *Breast cancer survival rates, by stage.* Retrieved from www.cancer.org/cancer/breastcancer/detailedguide/breast-cancer-survival-by-stage.

American Cancer Society. (2016g). *Prostate cancer.* Retrieved from www.cancer.org/cancer/prostatecancer/detailedguide/index.

American Diabetes Association. (2016a). *Diabetes basics.* Retrieved from www.diabetes.org/diabetes-basics/?loc=db-slabnav.

American Diabetes Association. (2016b). *Living with diabetes.* Retrieved from www.diabetes.org/living-with-diabetes/?loc=lwd-slabnav.

American Geriatrics Society Ethics Committee. (1996). Making treatment decisions for incapacitated older adults without advance directives. *Journal of the American Geriatrics Society, 44*, 986–987.

American Heart Association. (2014a). *Understanding blood pressure readings.* Retrieved from www.heart.org/HEARTORG/Conditions/HighBloodPressure/AboutHighBloodPressure/Understanding-Blood-Pressure-Readings_UCM_301764_Article.jsp#.VzHNQmP7048.

American Heart Association. (2014b). *High blood pressure.* Retrieved from www.heart.org/HEARTORG/Conditions/HighBloodPressure/High-Blood-Pressure-or-Hypertension_UCM_002020_SubHomePage.jsp.

American Heart Association. (2014c). *Why high blood pressure matters.* Retrieved from www.heart.org/HEARTORG/Conditions/HighBloodPressure/WhyBloodPressureMatters/Why-Blood-Pressure-Matters_UCM_002051_Article.jsp#.VzHO7GP7048.

American Heart Association. (2014d). *Low blood pressure.* Retrieved from www.heart.org/HEARTORG/Conditions/HighBloodPressure/AboutHighBloodPressure/Low-Blood-Pressure_UCM_301785_Article.jsp#.VzHPdmP7048.

American Heart Association. (2016a). *Heart attack symptoms in women.* Retrieved from www.heart.org/HEARTORG/Conditions/HeartAttack/WarningSignsofaHeartAttack/Heart-Attack-Symptoms-in-Women_UCM_436448_Article.jsp#.VzEgYWP7048.

American Heart Association. (2016b). *The American Heart Association's diet and lifestyle recommendations.* Retrieved from www.heart.org/HEARTORG/HealthyLiving/HealthyEating/Nutrition/The-American-Heart-Associations-Diet-and-Lifestyle-Recommendations_UCM_305855_Article.jsp#.V_jurPkrLIU.

American Heart Association. (2016c). *Seeds of native health: A campaign for indigenous nutrition.* Retrieved from seedsofnativehealth.org/fertile-ground-ii/.

American Lung Association. (2016). *COPD.* Retrieved from www.lung.org/lung-health-and-diseases/lung-disease-lookup/copd/.

American Medical Association. (2013). *PCPI™ Physician Consortium for Performance Improvement®.* Retrieved from www.ama-assn.org/ama/pub/physician-resources/physician-consortium-performance-improvement.page.

American Psychiatric Association. (2013). *Diagnostic and statistical manual of mental disorders: DSM-5™* (5th ed.). Arlington, VA: American Psychiatric Association.

American Psychological Association. (2014). Guidelines for psychological practice with older adults. *American Psychologist, 69*, 34–65. doi:10.1037/a0035063

American Stroke Association. (2016). *Stroke treatments.* Retrieved from www.strokeassociation.org/STROKEORG/AboutStroke/Treatment/Stroke-Treatments_UCM_310892_Article.jsp#.VzEmpWP7048.

Amoyal, N., & Fallon, E. (2012). Physical exercise and cognitive training clinical interventions used in slowing degeneration associated with mild cognitive impairment: A review of the recent literature. *Topics in Geriatric Rehabilitation, 28*, 208–216. doi:10.1097/TGR.0b013e31825fc8d3

Anand, A., & MacLullich, A. M. J. (2013). Delirium in hospitalized older adults. *Medicine, 41*, 39–42. doi:10.1016/j.mpmed.2012.10.011

Andersen, E., & Spiers, J. (2015). Alone in Eden: Care aides' perceptions of consistent assignments. *Western Journal of Nursing Research, 37*, 394–410 doi:10.1177/0193945914521903

Andersen, S. L., Sebastiani, P., Dworkis, D. A., Feldman, L., & Perls, T. T. (2012). Health span approximates life span among many supercentenarians: Compression of morbidity at the approximate limit of life span. *Journal of Gerontology: Biological Sciences, 67*A, 395–405. doi:10.1093/gerona/glr223

Anderson, E. R., Greene, S. M., Walker, L., Malerba, C., Forgatch, M. S., & DeGarmo, D. S. (2004). Ready to take a chance again: Transitions into dating among divorced parents. *Journal of*

Divorce & Remarriage, 40, 61–75. doi:10.1300/J087v40n03_04

Anderson, F. T., & Einstein, G. O. (2017). The fate of completed intentions. *Memory, 25*, 467–480. doi:10.1080/09658211.2016.1187756

Anderson, V. D. (2007). Religiosity as it shapes parenting processes in preadolescence: A contextualized process model. *Dissertation Abstracts International. Section B. Sciences and Engineering, 67* (9-B), 5439.

Ando, S. (2012). Neuronal dysfunction with aging and its amelioration. *Proceedings of the Japan Academy, Series B: Physical and Biological Sciences, 88*, 266–282. doi:10.2183/pjab.88.266

Andreassi, J. K. (2007). The role of personality and coping in work-family conflict: New directions. *Dissertation Abstracts International. Section A. Humanities and Social Sciences, 67*(8-A), 3053.

Andreassi, J. K. (2011). What the person brings to the table: Personality, coping, and work-family conflict. *Journal of Family Issues, 32*, 1474–1499. doi:10.1177/0192513X11401815

Andrews-Hanna, J. R. (2012). The brain's default network and its adaptive role in internal mentation. *The Neuroscientist, 18*, 251–270. doi:10.1177/1073858411403316

Aneshensel, C. S., Pearlin, L. I., Mullan, J. T., Zarit, S. H., & Whitlach, C. J. (1995). *Profiles in caregiving: The unexpected career*. San Diego, CA: Academic Press.

Angel, R. J., & Angel, J. L. (2015). *Latinos in an aging world: Social, psychological, and economic perspectives*. New York: Routledge.

Angelou, M. (1969). *I know why the caged bird sings*. New York: Random House.

Ansari, Z. (2016). Homocysteine and mild cognitive impairment: Are these the tools for early intervention in the dementia spectrum? *Journal of Nutrition, Health & Aging, 20*, 155–160. doi:10.1007/s12603-015-0576-y

Ansberry, C. (2016, June 16). Closer ties: Siblings matter more as we grow older. *Wall Street Journal*, D3. Retrieved from www.wsj.com/articles/two-sisters-close-again-after-decades-apart-1466004965.

Antheunis, M. L. (2016). Friendships and the internet. In C. R. Berger, M. E. Roloff, S. R. Wilson, J. P. Dillard, J. Caughlin, & D. Solomon (Eds), *The international encyclopedia of interpersonal communication*. New York: Wiley. doi:10.1002/9781118540190.wbeic261

Anticevic, A., Repovs, G., & Barch, D. M. (2012). Emotion effects on attention, amygdala activation, and functional capacity in schizophrenia. *Schizophrenia Bulletin, 38*, 967–980. doi:10.1093/schbul/sbq168

Antonovsky, A. (1979). *Health, stress, and coping*. San Francisco, CA: Jossey-Bass.

Aponte, M. (2007). Mentoring: Career advancement of Hispanic army nurses. *Dissertation Abstracts International. Section A. Humanities and Social Sciences, 68*(4-A), 1609.

Arbeev, K. G., Ukraintseva, S. V., & Yashin, A. I. (2016). Dynamics of biomarkers in relation to aging and mortality. *Mechanisms of Ageing and Development, 156*, 42–54. doi:10.1016/j.mad.2016.04.010

Ardelt, M. (2010). Age, experience, and the beginning of wisdom. In D. Dannefer & C. Phillipson (Eds.), *The SAGE handbook of social gerontology* (pp. 306–316). Thousand Oaks, CA: Sage Publications.

Arena, J. E., & Rabinstein, A. A. (2015). Transient global amnesia. *Mayo Clinic Proceedings, 90*, 264–272. doi:10.1016/j.mayocp.2014.12.001

Arizmendi, B., Kaszniak, A. W., & O'Connor, M.-F. (2016). Disrupted prefrontal activity during emotion processing in complicated grief: An fMRI investigation. *Neuroimage, 124 (Part A)*, 968–976. doi:10.1016/j.neuroimage.2015.09.054

Arndt, J., & Goldenberg, J. L. (2017). Where health and death intersect: Insights from a Terror Management Health Model. *Current Directions in Psychological Science, 26*, 126–131. doi:10.1177/0963721416689563

Arnett, J. J. (2013). *Adolescence and emerging adulthood: A cultural approach* (5th ed.). Upper Saddle River, NJ: Pearson.

Arnett, J. J. (2016). Introduction: Emerging adulthood theory and research: Where we are and where we should go. In J. J. Arnett (Ed.), *The Oxford handbook of emerging adulthood* (pp. 1–7). New York: Oxford University Press.

Artazcoz, L., Benach, J., Borrell, C., & Cortès, I. (2004). Unemployment and mental health: Understanding the interactions among gender, family roles, and social class. *American Journal of Public Health, 94*, 82–88. doi: 10.2105/AJPH.94.1.82

Artistico, D., Cervone, D., & Pezzuti, L. (2003). Perceived self-efficacy and everyday problem solving among young and older adults. *Psychology and Aging, 18*, 68–79. doi:10.1037/0882-7974.18.1.68

Arvanitakis, Z., Fleischman, D. A., Arfanakis, K., Leurgans, S. E., Barnes, L. L., & Bennett, D. A. (2016). Association of white matter hyperintensities and gray matter volume with cognition in older individuals without cognitive impairment. *Brain Structure and Function, 221*, 2135–2146. doi:10.1007/s00429-015-1034-7

Aryee, S., Chu, C. W. L., Kim, T.-Y., & Ryu, S. (2013). Family-supportive work environment and employee work behaviors: An investigation of mediating mechanisms. *Journal of Management, 39*, 792–813. doi:10.1177/0149206311435103

Aslan, A., Schlichting, A., John, T., & Bäuml, K.-H. T. (2015). The two faces of selective memory retrieval: Earlier decline of the beneficial than the detrimental effect with older age. *Psychology and Aging, 30*, 824–834. doi:10.1037/a0039874

Asoodeh, M. H., Khalili, S., Daneshpour, N., & Lavasani, M. G. (2010). Factors of successful marriage: Accounts from self-described happy couples. *Procedia Social and Behavioral Sciences, 5*, 2042–2046. doi:10.1016/j.sbspro.2010.07.410

Asp, E., Manzel, K., Koestner, B., Cole, C., Denburg, N. L., & Tranel, D. (2012). A neuropsychological test of belief and doubt: Damage to ventromedial prefrontal cortex increases credulity for misleading advertising. *Frontiers in Neuroscience, 6*. doi:10.3389/fnins.2012.00100

Assanangkornchai, S., Tangboonngam, S., Samangsri, N., & Edwards, J. G. (2007). A Thai community's anniversary reaction to a major catastrophe. *Stress and Health, 23*, 43–50. doi:10.1002/smi.1118

Atchley, R., Klee, D., Memmott, T., Goodrich, E., Wahbeh, H, & Oken, B. (2016). Event-related potential correlates of mindfulness meditation competence. *Neuroscience, 320*, 83–92. doi:10.1016/j.neuroscience.2016.01.051

Attig, T. (1996). *How we grieve: Relearning the world*. New York: Oxford University Press.

Australian Government Department of Social Services. (2016). *Ageing and aged care*. Retrieved from www.dss.gov.au/our-responsibilities/ageing-and-aged-care/aged-care-reform.

Awa, W. L., Plaumann, M., & Walter, U. (2010). Burnout prevention: A review of intervention programs. *Patient Education and Counseling, 78*, 184–190. doi:10.1016/j.pec.2009.04.008

Awadi, M. A., & Mrayyan, M. T. (2016). Opponents and proponents views regarding palliative sedation at end of life. *Journal of Palliative Care & Medicine, 6*, 242. doi:10.4172/2165-7386.1000242. Retrieved from www.omicsgroup.org/journals/opponents-and-proponents-views-regarding-palliative-sedation-at-end-oflife-2165-7386-1000242.php?aid=66887.

Ayalon, L. (2016). Satisfaction with aging results in reduced risk for falling. *International Psychogeriatrics, 28*, 741–747. doi:10.1017/S1041610215001969

Bachman, B. (2017). *Ethical leadership in organizations*. New York: Springer.

Bäckman, L., Lindenberger, U., Li, S.-C., & Nyberg, L. (2010). Linking cognitive aging to alterations in dopamine neurotransmitter functioning: Recent data and future avenues. *Neuroscience & Biobehavioral Reviews, 34*, 670–677. doi:10.1016/j.neubiorev.2009.12.008

Baddeley, A. (2013). Working memory and emotion: Ruminations on a theory of depression. *Review of General Psychology, 17*, 20–27. doi:10.1037/a0030029

Bade, M. K. (2012). *Personal growth in the midst of negative life experiences: The role of religious coping strategies and appraisals*. Dissertation submitted to Texas Tech University. Retrieved from repositories.ttu-ir.tdl.org/ttu-ir/handle/2346/10475.

Badham, S. P., Estes, Z., & Maylor, E. A. (2012). Integrative and semantic relations equally alleviate age-related associative memory deficits. *Psychology and Aging, 27*, 141–152. doi:10.1037/a0023924

Badham, S. R., & Maylor, E. A. (2016). Antimnemonic effects of schemas in young and older adults. *Aging, Neuropsychology, and Cognition: A Journal on Normal and Dysfunctional Development, 23*, 78–102. doi:10.1080/13825585.2015.1048774

Badham, S. R., Hay, M., Foxon, N., Kaur, K., & Maylor, E. A. (2016). When does prior knowledge disproportionately benefit older adults' memory? *Aging, Neuropsychology, and Cognition: A Journal on Normal and Dysfunctional Development, 23*, 338–365. doi:10.1080/1385585.2015.1099607

Bagbey Darian, C. D. (2014). A new mourning: Synthesizing an interactive model of adaptive grieving dynamics. *Illness, Crisis & Loss, 22*, 195–235. doi:10.2190/IL.22.3.c

Baggetta, P., & Alexander, P. A. (2016). Conceptualization and operationalization of executive function. *Mind, Brain, and Education, 10*, 10–33. doi:10.1111/mbe.12100

Bagnall, A.-M., Jones, R., Akter, H., & Woodall, J. (2016). *Interventions to prevent burnout in high risk individuals: Evidence review*. Retrieved from www.gov.uk/government/uploads/system/uploads/attachment_data/file/506777/25022016_Burnout_Rapid_Review_2015709.pdf.

Baker, J. C., Fairchild, K. M., & Seefeldt, D. A. (2015). Behavioral gerontology: Research and clinical considerations. In H. S. Roane, J. E. Ringdahl, & T. S. Falcomata (Eds.), *Clinical and organizational applications of applied behavior analysis* (pp. 425–450). San Diego, CA: Academic Press.

Balistreri, C. R., Candore, G., Accardi, G., Bova, M., Buffa, S., Bulati, M. et al. (2012). Genetics of longevity. Data from the studies on Sicilian centenarians. *Immunity and Ageing, 9*. Retrieved from www.biomedcentral.com/content.

Baltes, B. B., & Rudolph, C. W. (2012). Selective optimization with compensation. In M. Wang (Ed.), *The Oxford handbook of retirement* (pp. 88–101). New York: Oxford University Press.

Baltes, P. B. (1987). Theoretical propositions of life-span developmental psychology: On the dynamics between growth and decline. *Developmental Psychology, 23*, 611–626. doi:10.1037/0012-1649.23.5.611

Baltes, P. B. (1993). The aging mind: Potential and limits. *The Gerontologist, 33*, 580–594. doi:10.1093/geront/33.5.580

Baltes, P. B., & Kliegl, R. (1992). Further testing of limits of cognitive plasticity: Negative age differences in mnemonic skill are robust. *Developmental Psychology, 28*, 121–125. doi:10.1037/0012-1649.28.1.121

Baltes, P. B., & Schaie, K. W. (1974). Aging and IQ: The myth of the twilight years. *Psychology Today, 7,* 35–40.

Baltes, P. B., & Staudinger, U. M. (2000). Wisdom: A metaheuristic (pragmatic) to orchestrate mind and virtue toward excellence. *American Psychologist, 55,* 122–136. doi:10.1037/0003-066X.55.1.122

Baltes, P. B., Lindenberger, U., & Staudinger, U. M. (1998). Life-span theory in developmental psychology. In R. M. Lerner (Ed.), *Handbook of child psychology: Vol. 1. Theoretical models of human development* (5th ed., pp. 1029–1143). New York: Wiley.

Baltes, P. B., Lindenberger, U., & Staudinger, U. M. (2006). Life-span theory in developmental psychology. In R. M. Lerner & W. Damon (Eds.), *Handbook of child psychology: Vol. 1. Theoretical models of human development* (6th ed., pp. 569–664). Hoboken, NJ: Wiley.

Baltes, P. B., Staudinger, U. M., & Lindenberger, U. (1999). Life-span psychology: Theory and application to intellectual functioning. *Annual Review of Psychology, 50,* 471–507. doi:10.1146/annurev.psych.50.1.471

Bambra, C. (2010). Yesterday once more? Unemployment and health in the 21st century. *Journal of Epidemiology and Community Health, 64,* 213–215. doi: 10.1136/jech.2009.090621

Bangerter, L. R., Heid, A. R., Abbott, K., & Van Haitsma, K. (2016). Honoring the everyday preferences of nursing home residents: Perceived choice and satisfaction with care. *The Gerontologist, 56,* 702–713. doi:10.1093/geront/gnv697

Barber, S. J., Opitz, P. C., Martins, B., Sakaki, M., & Mather, M. (2016). Thinking about a limited future enhances the positivity of younger and older adults' recall: Support for socioemotional selectivity theory. *Memory and Cognition, 44,* 869–882. doi:10.3758/s13421-016-0612-0

Barbey, A. K., Colom, R., & Grafman, J. (2014). Distributed neural system for emotional intelligence revealed by lesion mapping. *Social Cognitive and Affective Neuroscience, 9,* 265–272. doi:10.1093/scan/nss124

Bargh, J. A., Chen, M., & Burrows, L. (1996). Automaticity of social behavior: Direct effects of trait construct and stereotype activation on action. *Journal of Personality and Social Psychology, 71,* 230–244. doi:10.1037/0022-3514.71.2.230

Barja, G. (2008). The gene cluster hypothesis of aging and longevity. *Biogerontology, 9,* 57–66. doi:10.1007/s10522-007-9115-5

Barlow, M., Wrosch, C., Heckhausen, J., & Schulz, R. (2017). Control strategies for managing physical health problems in old age: Evidence for the motivational theory of lifespan development. In: J. W. Reich & F. J. Infurna (Eds.), *Perceived control: Theory, research, and practice in the first 50 years* (pp. 281–308). New York: Oxford University Press. doi:10.1093/acprof:oso/9780190257040.003.0012

Barnett, A. E. (2013). Pathways of adult children providing care to older parents. *Journal of Marriage and the Family, 75,* 178–190. doi:10.1111/j.1741-3737.2012.01022.x

Bar-Tal, Y., Shrira, A., & Keinan, G. (2013). The effect of stress on cognitive structuring: A cognitive motivational model. *Personality and social Psychology Review, 17,* 87–99. doi:10.1177/1088868312461309

Bartkowiak, G. (2017). Best practices in the employment of knowledge workers 65 and over and the benefits of employing them (An empirical approach). In M. H. Bilgin, H. Danis, E. Demir, & U. Can (Eds.), *Financial environment and business development* (pp. 463–471). New York: Springer.

Bartlett, D. B., & Huffman, K. M. (2017). Lifetime interventions to improve immunesenescence. In V. Bueno, J. M. Lord, & T. A. Jackson (Eds.), *The ageing immune system and health* (pp. 161–176). New York: Springer.

Barton, C., Ketelle, R., Merrilees, J., & Miller, B. (2016). Non-pharmacological management of behavioral symptoms in frontotemporal and other dementias. *Current Neurology and Neuroscience Reports, 16,* 14. doi:10.1007/s11910-015-0618-1

Barzilai, N., Huffman, D. M., Muzumdar, R. H., & Bartke, A. (2012). The critical role of metabolic pathways in aging. *Diabetes, 61,* 1315–1322. doi:10.2337/db11-1300

Basten, U., Hilger, K., & Fiebach, C. J. (2015). Where smart brains are different: A quantitative meta-analysis of functional and structural brain imaging studies on intelligence. *Intelligence, 51,* 10–27. doi:10.1016/j.intell.2015.04.009

Batt, M. E., Tanji, J., & Börjesson, M. (2013). Exercise at 65 and beyond. *Sports Medicine, 43,* 525–530. doi:10.1007/s40279-013-0033-1

Battista, R. N., Blancquaert, I., Laberge, A.-M., van Schendel, N., & Leduc, N. (2012). Genetics in health care: An overview of current and emerging models. *Public Health Genomics, 15,* 34–45. doi:10.1159/000328846

Baucom, B. R., Dickenson, J. A., Atkins, D. C., Baucom, D. H., Fischer, M. S., Weusthoff, S. et al. (2015). The interpersonal process model of demand/withdraw behavior. *Journal of Family Psychology, 29,* 80–90. doi:10.1037/fam0000044

Baum, C. L., II, & Ruhm, C. J. (2016). The effects of paid family leave in California on labor market outcomes. *Journal of Policy Analysis and Management, 35,* 333–356. doi:10.1002/pam.21894

Baumann, A., Claudot, F., Audibert, G., Mertes, P.-M., & Puybasset, M. (2011). The ethical and legal aspects of palliative sedation in severely brain-injured patients: A French perspective. *Philosophy, Ethics, and Humanities in Medicine, 6.* Retrieved from preview.peh-med.com/content/pdf/1747-5341-6-4.pdf.

Baumeister, R.F. (2010). The self. In R. F. Baumeister & E. J. Finkel (Eds.), *Advanced social psychology: The state of the science* (pp. 139–175). New York: Oxford University Press.

Bayl-Smith, P. H., & Griffin, B. (2014). Age discrimination in the workplace: Identifying as a late career worker and its relationship with engagement and intended retirement age. *Journal of Applied Social Psychology, 44,* 588–599. doi:10.1111/jasp.12251

Beason-Held, L. L., Thambisetty, M., Deib, G., Sojkova, J., Landman, B. A., Zonderman, A. B. et al. (2012). Baseline cardiovascular risk predicts subsequent changes in resting brain function. *Stroke, 43,* 1542–1547. doi:10.1161/STROKEAHA.111.638437

Beaty, R. E., Benedek, M., Silvia, P. J., & Schacter, D. L. (2016). Creative cognition and brain network dynamics. *Trends in Cognitive Sciences, 20,* 87–95. doi:10.1016/j.tics.2015.10.004

Beck, A. T. (1967). *Depression: Clinical, experimental, and theoretical aspects.* New York: Harper & Row.

Beck, A. T., Rush, J., Shaw, B., & Emery, G. (1979). *Cognitive therapy of depression.* New York: Guilford.

Beck, V. (2013). Employers' use of older workers in the recession. *Employee Relations, 35,* 257–271. doi:10.1108/01425451311320468

Beckes, L., & Coan, J. A. (2013). Voodoo versus me-you correlations in relationship neuroscience. *Journal of Social and Personal Relationships, 30,* 189–197. doi:10.1177/0265407512454768

Beckes, L., Coan, J. A., & Hasselmo, K. (2013). Familiarity promotes the blurring of self and other in the neural perception of threat. *Social Cognitive and Affective Neuroscience, 8,* 670–677. doi:10.1093/scan/nss046

Bedir, A., & Aksoy, S. (2011). Brain death revisited: It is not 'complete death' according to Islamic sources. *Journal of Medical Ethics, 37,* 290–294. doi:10.1136/jme.2010.040238

Beltrán-Sánchez, H., Jiménez, M. P., & Subramanian, S. V. (2016). Assessing morbidity compression in two cohorts from the Health and Retirement Study. *Journal of Epidemiology & Community Health, 70,* 1011–1016. doi:10.1136/jech-2015-206722

Benjamins, M. R., Hirschman, J., Hirschtick, J., & Whitman, S. (2012). Exploring differences in self-rated health among Blacks, Whites, Mexicans, and Puerto Ricans. *Ethnicity and Health, 17,* 463–476. doi:10.1080/13557858.2012.654769

Bennett, K. M. (2005). Psychological wellbeing in later life: The longitudinal effects of marriage, widowhood and marital status change. *International Journal of Geriatric Psychiatry, 20,* 280–284. doi:10.1002/gps.1280

Bennett, K. M. (2010). How to achieve resilience as an older widower: Turning points or gradual change? *Ageing and Society, 30,* 369–382. doi:10.1017/S0144686X09990572

Berg, C. A. (2008). Everyday problem solving in context. In S. M. Hofer & D. F. Alwin (Eds.), *Handbook of cognitive aging: Interdisciplinary perspectives* (pp. 207–223). Greenwich, CT: Sage.

Berg, C. A., & Sternberg, R. J. (1992). Adults' conceptions of intelligence across the adult life span. *Psychology and Aging, 7,* 221–231. doi:10.1037/0882-7974.7.2.221

Berg, C. A., Sewell, K. K., Hughes Lansing, A. E., Wilson, S. J., & Brewer, C. (2016). A developmental perspective to dyadic coping across adulthood. In J. Bookwala (Ed.), *Couple relationships in the middle and later years: Their nature, complexity, and role in health and illness* (pp. 259–280). Washington, DC: American Psychological Association.

Berg, C. A., Strough, J., Calderone, K. S., Sansone, C., & Weir, C. (1998). The role of problem definitions in understanding age and context effects on strategies for solving every day problems. *Psychology and Aging, 13,* 29–44. doi:10.1037/0882-7974.13.1.29

Bergdahl, E., Benzein, E., Ternestedt, B.-M., Elmberger, E., & Andershed, B. (2013). Co-creating possibilities for patients in palliative care to reach vital goals—A multiple case study of home-care nursing encounters. *Nursing Inquiry, 20,* 341–351. doi:10.1111/nin.12022

Berger, R. G., Lunkenbein, S., Ströhle, A., & Hahn, A. (2012). Antioxidants in food: Mere myth or magic medicine? *Critical Reviews in Food Science and Nutrition, 52,* 162–171. doi:10.1080/10408398.2010.499481

Bergman-Evans, B. (2004). Beyond the basics: Effects of the Eden Alternative model on quality of life issues. *Journal of Gerontological Nursing, 30,* 27–34.

Bergsma, A., & Ardelt, M. (2012). Self-reported wisdom and happiness: An empirical investigation. *Journal of Happiness Studies, 13,* 481–499. doi:10.1007/s10902-011-9275-5

Berk, R. A. (2010). Where's the chemistry in mentor-mentee academic relationships? Try spend mentoring. *The International Journal of Mentoring and Coaching, 8,* 85–92. Retrieved from www.ronberk.com/articles/2010_mentor.pdf.

Berlin, L. J., Brady-Smith, C., & Brooks-Gunn, J. (2002). Links between childbearing age and observed maternal behaviors with 14-month-olds in the Early Head Start Research and Evaluation Project. *Infant Mental Health Journal, 23,* 104–129. doi:10.1002/imhj.10007

Bermejo-Toro, L., Prieto-Ursúa, M., & Hernández, V. (2016). Towards a model of teacher well-being: Personal and job resources involved in teacher burnout and engagement. *Educational Psychology, 36,* 481–501. doi:10.1080/01443410.2015.1005006

Bernadotte, A., Mikhelson, V. M., & Spivak, I. M. (2016). Markers of cellular senescence. Telomere shortening as a marker of cellular senescence. *Aging, 8*, 3–11. www.ncbi.nlm.nih.gov/pmc/articles/PMC4761709/.

Berns, N. (2011). *Closure: The rush to end grief and what it costs.* Philadelphia: Temple University Press.

Bernstein, L. (2016). *The graying of HIV: 1 in 6 new U.S. cases are people older than 50.* Retrieved from www.washingtonpost.com/national/health-science/the-graying-of-hiv-1-in-6-new-us-cases-are-people-older-than-50/2016/04/05/089cd9aa-f68a-11e5-8b23-538270a1ca31_story.html.

Berry, J. M. (1989). Cognitive efficacy across the life span: Introduction to the special series. *Developmental Psychology, 25*, 683–686.

Berry, J. M., Cavanaugh, J. C., & West, R. L. (2016). *Self-efficacy and human agency: Implications for aging well.* Unpublished manuscript, Department of Psychology, University of Richmond.

Berry, J. M., Cavanaugh, J. C., & West, R. L. (2016). *Self-efficacy and human agency: Implications for aging well.* Unpublished manuscript, Department of Psychology, University of Richmond.

Besedeš, T., Deck, C., Sarangi, S., & Shor, M. (2012). Age effects and heuristics in decision making. *The Review of Economics and Statistics, 94*, 580–595. doi:10.1162/REST_a_00174

Bever, L. (2014a). Cancer patient Brittany Maynard, 29, has scheduled her death for Nov. 1. *Washington Post.* Retrieved from wapo.st/10O22rQ.

Bever, L. (2014b). Brittany Maynard, as promised, ends her life at 29. *Washington Post.* Retrieved from wapo.st/1yPi6F0.

Bever, L. (2014c). How Brittany Maynard may change the right-do-die debate. *Washington Post.* Retrieved from wapo.st/1A3F9QR.

Bhattarai, P., & Phillips, J. L. (2017). The role of digital health technologies in management of pain in older people: an integrative review. *Archives of Gerontology and Geriatrics, 68*, 14–24. doi:10.1016/j.archger.2016.08.008

Bialystok, E., Craik, F. I. M., & Luk, G. (2012). Bilingualism: Consequences for mind and brain. *Trends in Cognitive Sciences, 16*, 240–250. doi:10.1016/j.tics.2012.03.001

Bian, F., Blachford, D., & Durst, D. (2015). The color purple: Perspectives of Canadian parents of adopted children from China. *Journal of Comparative Social Work, 10*(2). Retrieved from journal.uia.no/index.php/JCSW/article/view/345/289.

Biblarz, T. J., & Savci, E. (2010). Lesbian, gay, bisexual, and transgender families. *Journal of Marriage and Family, 72*, 480–497. doi:10.1111/j.1741-3737.2010.00714.x

Bidwell, M. (2013). What happened to long term employment? The role of worker power and environmental turbulence in explaining declines in worker tenure. *Organization Science, 24*, 1061–1082. doi:10.1287/orsc.1120.0816

Bieman-Copland, S., Ryan, E. B., & Cassano, J. (2002). Responding to the challenges of late life. In D. Pushkar, W. M. Bukowski, A. E. Schwartzman, D. M. Stack, & D. R. White (Eds.), *Improving competence across the lifespan* (pp. 141–157). New York: Springer.

Bietti, L. M., & Sutton, J. (2015). Interacting to remember at multiple timescales: Coordination, collaboration, cooperation and culture in joint remembering. *Interaction Studies, 16*, vii–xii. doi:10.1075/is.16.3.001int

Biggs, S., McGann, M., Bowman, D., & Kimberley, H. (2017). Work, health and the commodification of life's time: Reframing work-life balance and the promise of a long life. *Ageing and Society, 37*, 1458–1483. doi:10.1017/S0144686X16000404

Binet, A. (1903). *Etude expérimentale de l'intelligence.* Paris, France: Schleicher Frères & Cie.

Binstock, R. H. (1999). Public policy issues. In J. C. Cavanaugh & S. K. Whitbourne (Eds.), *Gerontology: Interdisciplinary perspectives* (pp. 414–447). New York: Oxford University Press.

Birditt, K. S., Tighe, L. A., Fingerman, K. L., & Zarit, S. H. (2012). Intergenerational relationship quality across three generations. *Journal of Gerontology: Psychological Sciences, 67*, 627–638. doi:10.1093/geronb/gbs050

Birren, J. E., & Cunningham, W. (1985). Research on the psychology of aging: Principles, concepts, and theory. In J. E. Birren & K. W. Schaie (Eds.), *Handbook of the psychology of aging* (2nd ed., pp. 3–34). New York: Van Nostrand Reinhold.

Birren, J. E., & Renner, V. J. (1980). Concepts and issues of mental health and aging. In J. E. Birren & R. B. Sloane (Eds.), *Handbook of mental health and aging* (pp. 3–33). Englewood Cliffs, NJ: Prentice Hall.

Blachnio, A., Przepiorka, A., Balakier, E., & Boruch, W. (2016). Who discloses the most on Facebook? *Computers in Human Behavior, 55 Part B*, 664–667. doi:10.1016/j.chb.2015.10.007

Blackhall, L. J., Read, P., Stukenborg, G., Dillon, P., Barclay, J., Romano, A. et al. (2016). CARE Track for advanced cancer: Impact and timing of an outpatient palliative clinic. *Journal of Palliative Medicine, 19*, 57–63. doi:10.1089/jpm.2015.0272

Blackstone, A., & Stewart, M. D. (2016). "There's more thinking to decide": How the childfree decide not to parent. *The Family Journal, 24*, 296–303. doi:10.1177/1066480716648676

Blanchard-Fields, F. (1996). Causal attributions across the adult life span: The influence of social schemas, life context, and domain specificity. *Applied Cognitive Psychology, 10* (Special Issue), 137–146. doi:10.1002/(SICI)1099-0720(199611)10:7<137::AID-ACP431>3.0.CO;2-Z

Blanchard-Fields, F. (1999). Social schematicity and causal attributions. In T. M. Hess & F. Blanchard-Fields (Eds.), *Social cognition and aging* (pp. 219–236). San Diego, CA: Academic Press.

Blanchard-Fields, F., & Beatty, C. (2005). Age differences in blame attributions: The role of relationship outcome ambiguity and personal identification. *Journals of Gerontology: Psychological Sciences, 60*, P19–P26. doi:10.1093/geronb/60.1.P19

Blanchard-Fields, F., & Hertzog, C. (2000). Age differences in schematicity. In U. von Hecker, S. Dutke, & G. Sedek (Eds.), *Processes of generative mental representation and psychological adaptation* (pp. 175–198). Dordrecht, The Netherlands: Kluwer.

Blanchard-Fields, F., & Horhota, M. (2006). How can the study of aging inform research on social cognition? *Social Cognition, 24*, 207–217. doi:10.1521/soco.2006.24.3.207

Blanchard-Fields, F., Baldi, R. A., & Constantin, L. P. (2004). *Interrole conflict across the adult lifespan: The role of parenting stage, career stages and quality of experiences.* Unpublished manuscript, School of Psychology, Georgia Institute of Technology.

Blanchard-Fields, F., Chen, Y., & Herbert, C. E. (1997). Interrole conflict as a function of life stage, gender, and gender-related personality attributes. *Sex Roles, 37*, 155–174. doi:10.1023/A:1025691626240

Blanchard-Fields, F., Hertzog, C., & Horhota, M. (2012). Violate my beliefs? Then you're to blame! Belief content as an explanation for causal attribution biases. *Psychology and Aging, 27*, 324–337. doi:10.1037/a0024423

Blanchard-Fields, F., Horhota, M., & Mienaltowski, A. (2008). Social context and cognition. In S. M. Hofer & D. F. Alwin (Eds.), *Handbook of cognitive aging: Interdisciplinary perspectives* (pp. 614–628). Greenwich, CT: Sage.

Blanchard-Fields, F., Mienaltowski, A., & Seay, R. (2007). Age differences in everyday problem-solving effectiveness: Older adults select more effective strategies for interpersonal problems. *Journals of Gerontology: Psychological Sciences, 62*, P61–P64. doi:10.1093/geronb/62.1.P61

Blatteis, C. M. (2012). Age-dependent changes in temperature regulation—A mini review. *Gerontology, 58*, 289–295. doi:10.1159/000333148

Blazer, D. G. (2008). How do you feel about…? Health outcomes in late life and self-perceptions of health and well-being. *The Gerontologist, 48*, 415–422. doi:10.1093/geront/48.4.415

Blieszner, R. (2014). The worth of friendship: Can friends keep us happy and healthy? *Generations, 38*, 24–30.

Blieszner, R., & Roberto, K. A. (2012). Partners and friends in adulthood. In S. K. Whitbourne & M. J. Sliwinski (Eds.), *The Wiley-Blackwell handbook of adulthood and aging* (pp. 381–398). Oxford, UK: Wiley-Blackwell.

Bligh, M. C. (2017). Leadership and trust. In J. Marques & S. Dhiman (Eds.), *Leadership today* (pp. 21–42). New York: Springer.

Blom, M. M., Bosmans, J. E., Cuijpers, P., Zarit, S. H., & Pot, A. M. (2013). Effectiveness and cost-effectiveness of an internet intervention for family caregivers of people with dementia: Design of a randomized controlled trial. *BMC Psychiatry, 13.* doi:10.1186/1471-244X-13-17. Retrieved from www.biomedcentral.com/1471-244X/13/17/.

Blümel, J. E., Chedraui, P., Baron, G., Belzares, E., Bencosme, A., Calle, A. et al. (2012). Menopausal symptoms appear before the menopause and persist 5 years beyond: A detailed analysis of a multinational study. *Climacteric, 15*, 542–551. doi:10.3109/13697137.2012.658462

Blume-Peytavi, U., Kottner, J., Sterry, W., Hodin, M. W., Griffiths, T. W., Watson, R. E. B. et al. (2016). Age-associated skin conditions and diseases: Current perspectives and future options. *The Gerontologist, 56*, S230–S242. doi:10.1093/geront/gnw003

Bluntschli, J. R., Maxfield, M. M., Grasso, R. L., & Kisley, M. A. (in press). The last word: A comparison of younger and older adults' brain responses to reminders of death. *Journals of Gerontology: Psychological Sciences and Social Sciences.* doi:10.1093/geronb/gbv115

Bochenska, K., & Boller, A.-M. (2016). Fecal incontinence: Epidemiology, impact, and treatment. *Clinics in Colon and Rectal Surgery, 29*, 264–270. doi:10.1055/s-0036-1584504

Böckerman, P., Ilmakunnas, P. Jokisaari, M., & Yuori, J. (2013). Who stays unwillingly in a job? A study based on a representative random sample of employees. *Economic and Industrial Democracy, 34*, 25–43. doi:10.1177/0143831X11429374

Boehm, S. A., Dwertmann, D. J. G., Kunze, F., Michaelis, B., Parks, K. M., & McDonald, D. P. (2014). Expanding insights on the diversity climate-performance link: The role of workgroup discrimination and group size. *Human Resource Management, 53*, 379–402. doi:10.1002/hrm.21589ER

Boisgontier, M. P., Cheval, B., van Ruitenbeek, P., Levin, O., Renaud, O., Chanal, J. et al. (2016). Whole-brain grey matter density predicts balance stability irrespective of age and protects older adults from falling. *Gait & Posture, 45*, 143–150. doi:10.1016/j.gaitpost.2016.01.019

Bolkan, C., & Hooker, K. (2012). Self-regulation and social cognition in adulthood. In S. K. Whitbourne & M. J. Sliwinski (Eds.), *The Wiley-Blackwell handbook of adulthood and aging* (pp. 355–380). Oxford, UK: Wiley-Blackwell.

Bolton, J. M., Au, W., Chateau, D., Walld, R., Leslie, W. D., Enns, J. et al. (2016). Bereavement after sibling death: A population-based longitudinal case-control study. *World Psychiatry, 15*, 59–66. doi:10.1002/wps.20293

Bonanno, G. A. (2009). *The other side of sadness: What the new science of bereavement tells us about life after loss.* New York: Basic Books.

Bonanno, G. A., Papa, A., & O'Neill, K. (2001). Loss and human resilience. *Applied and Preventive Psychology, 10*, 193–206. doi:10.1016/S0962-1849(01)80014-7

Bonanno, G. A., Papa, A., Lalande, K., Zhang, N., & Noll, J. G. (2005). Grief processing and deliberate grief avoidance: A prospective comparison of bereaved spouses and parents in the United States and the People's Republic of China. *Journal of Consulting and Clinical Psychology, 73*, 86–98. doi:10.1037/0022-006X.73.1.86

Bonanno, G. A., Westphal, M., & Mancini, A. D. (2011). Resilience to loss and trauma. *Annual Review of Clinical Psychology, 7*, 511–535. doi:10.1146/annurevclinpsy-032210-104526

Bonanno, G. A., Wortman, C. B., & Neese, R. M. (2004). Prospective patterns of resilience and maladjustment during widowhood. *Psychology and Aging, 19*, 260–271. doi:10.1037/0882-7974.19.2.260

Booker, J. A., & Dunsmore, J. C. (2016). Profiles of wisdom among emerging adults: Associations with empathy, gratitude, and forgiveness. *Journal of Positive Psychology, 11*, 315–325. doi:10.1080/17439760.2015.1081970

Booth, A. L., & Carroll, N. (2008). Economic status and the indigenous/non-indigenous health gap. *Economic Letters, 99*, 604–606. doi:10.1016/j.econlet.2007.10.005

Borbély, A. A., Daan, S., Wirz-Justice, A., & Deboer, T. (2016). The two-process model of sleep regulation: A reappraisal. *Journal of Sleep Research, 25*, 131–143. doi:10.1111/jsr.12371

Bordere, T. C. (2016). Social justice conceptualizations in grief and loss. In D. L. Harris & T. C. Bordere (Eds.), *Handbook of social justice in loss and grief: Exploring diversity, equity, and inclusion* (pp. 9–20). New York: Routledge.

Bos, H. M., Knox, J. R., van Rijn-van Gelderen, L., & Gartrell, N. K. (2016). Same-sex and different-sex parent households and child health outcomes: Findings from the National Survey of Children's Health. *Journal of Developmental & Behavioral Pediatrics, 37*, 179–187. doi:10.1097/DBP.0000000000000288

Bosch, S. J., & Gharaveis, A. (2017). Flying solo: A review of the literature on wayfinding for older adults experiencing visual or cognitive decline. *Applied Ergonomics, 58*, 327–333. doi:10.1016/j.apergo.2016.07.010

Boschma, J. (2015, June 23). When do Americans think they'll actually retire? *The Atlantic.* Retrieved from www.theatlantic.com/business/archive/2015/06/ideal-retirement-age-work/396464/.

Bosco, A., di Masi, M. N., & Manuti, A. (2013). Burnout internal factors—self-esteem and negative affectivity in the workplace: The mediation role of organizational identification in times of job uncertainty. In S. Bährer-Kohler (Ed.), *Burnout for experts* (pp. 145–158). New York: Springer.

Boss, P. (2010). The trauma and complicated grief of ambiguous loss. *Pastoral Psychology, 59*, 137–145. doi:10.1007/s11089-009-0264-0

Boss, P. (2015). Coping with the suffering of ambiguous loss. In R. E. Anderson (Ed.), *World suffering and quality of life* (pp. 125–134). New York: Springer. doi:10.1007/978-94-017-9670-5_10

Bosshard, G., & Materstvedt, L. J. (2011). Medical and societal issues in euthanasia and assisted suicide. In R. Chadwick, H. Ten Have, & E. M. Meslin (Eds.), *The SAGE handbook of health care ethics* (pp. 202–218). Thousand Oaks, CA: Sage Publications.

Boswell, J., Thai, J., & Brown, C. (2015). Older adults' sleep. In A. Green & C. Brown (Eds.), *An occupational therapist's guide to sleep and sleep problems* (pp. 185–206). Philadelphia: Jessica Kingsley Publishers.

Botwinick, J. (1977). Intellectual abilities. In J. E. Birren & K. W. Schaie (Eds.), *Handbook of the psychology of aging* (pp. 580–605). New York: Van Nostrand Reinhold.

Bouazzaoui, B., Follenfant, A., Ric, F., Fay, S., Croizet, J.-C., Atzeni, T. et al. (2016). Aging-related stereotypes in memory: When the beliefs come true. *Memory, 24*, 659–668. doi:10.1080/09658211.2015.1040802

Bourgeois, M. S., Camp, C., Rose, R., White, B., Malone, M., Carr, J., & Rovine, M. (2003). A comparison of training strategies to enhance use of external aids by persons with dementia. *Journal of Communication Disorders, 36*, 361–378. doi:10.1016/S0021-9924(03)00051-0

Bourke, P., & Styles, E. (2017). *The psychology of attention.* New York: Psychology Press.

Bowers, B., Nolet, K., Jacobson, and THRIVE Research Collaborative. (2016). Sustaining culture change: Experiences in the Green House model. *Health Services Research, 51*, 398–417. doi:10.1111/1475-6773.12428

Bowlus, A, J., Mori, H., & Robinson, C. (2016). *Ageing and the skill portfolio: Evidence from job based skill measures.* Retrieved from ir.lib.uwo.ca/cgi/viewcontent.cgi?article=1109&context=economicscibc.

Bowman, G. L., Silbert, L. C., Howieson, D., Dodge, H. H., Traber, M. G., Frei, B. et al. (2012). Nutrient bio-marker patterns, cognitive function, and MRI measures of brain aging. *Neurology, 78*, 241–249. doi:10.1212/WNL.0b013e318243598

Boyczuk, A. M., & Fletcher, P. C. (2016). The ebbs and flows: Stresses of sandwich generation caregivers. *Journal of Adult Development, 23*, 51–61. doi:10.1007/s10804-015-9221-6

Boyle, P. J., Feng, Z., & Raab, G. M. (2011). Does widowhood increase mortality risk? Testing for selection effects by comparing causes of spousal death. *Epidemiology, 22*, 1–5. doi:10.1097/EDE.0b013e3181fdcc0b

Boywitt, C. D., Kuhlmann, B. G., & Meiser, T. (2012). The role of source memory in older adults' recollective experience. *Psychology and Aging, 27*, 484–497. doi:10.1037/a0024729

Brancucci, A. (2012). Neural correlates of cognitive ability. *Journal of Neuroscience Research, 90*, 1299–1309. doi:10.1002/jnr.23045

Brandburg, G. L., Symes, L., Mastel-Smith, B., Hersch, G., & Walsh, T. (2013). Resident strategies for making a life in a nursing home: A qualitative study. *Journal of Advanced Nursing, 69*, 862–874. doi:10.1111/j.1365-2648.2012.06075.x

Brandtstädter, J. (1997). Action culture and development: Points of convergence. *Culture and Psychology, 3*, 335–352. doi:10.1177/1354067X9733007

Brandtstädter, J. (1999). Sources of resilience in the aging self. In T. M. Hess & F. Blanchard-Fields (Eds.), *Social cognition and aging* (pp. 123–141). San Diego, CA: Academic Press.

Bratkovich, K. L. (2010). *The relationship of attachment and spirituality with posttraumatic growth following a death for college students.* Doctoral dissertation submitted to the Department of Psychology at Oklahoma State University.

Brehmer, Y., Shing, Y. L., Heekeren, H. R., Lindenberger, U., & Bäckman, L. (2016). Training-induced changes in subsequent-memory effects: No major differences among children, younger adults, and older adults. *NeuroImage, 131*, 214–225. doi:10.1016/j.neuroimage.2015.11.074

Brenn, T., & Ytterstad, E. (2016). Increased risk of death immediately after losing a spouse: Cause-specific mortality following widowhood in Norway. *Preventive Medicine, 89*, 251–256. doi:10.1016/j.ypmed.2016.06.019

Brennan, A. A., & Enns, J. T. (2015). When two heads are better than one: Interactive versus independent benefits of collaborative cognition. *Psychonomic Bulletin & Review, 22*, 1076–1082. doi:10.3758/s13423-014-0765-4. Retrieved from link.springer.com/article/10.3758/s13423-014-0765-4.

Brett, C. E., Gow, A. J., Corley, J., Pattie, A., Starr, J. M., & Deary, I. J. (2012). Psychosocial factors and health as determinants of quality of life in community-dwelling older adults. *Quality of Life Research, 21*, 505–516. doi:10.1007/s11136-011-9951-2

Brissette, I., Scheier, M. F., & Carver, C. S. (2002). The role of optimism in social network development, coping, and psychological adjustment during a life transition. *Journal of Personality and Social Psychology, 82*, 102–111. doi:10.1037//0022-3514.82.1.102

Bromell, L., & Cagney, K. A. (2014). Companionship in the neighborhood context: Older adults' living arrangements and perceptions of social cohesion. *Research on Aging, 36*, 228–243. doi:10.1177/0164027512475096

Brookdale. (2016). *Levels of care offered at a skilled nursing center.* Retrieved from www.brookdale.com/resources/levels-care-offered-skilled-nursing-center/.

Brown, J. E. (2017). *Nutrition through the life cycle* (6th ed.). Boston: Cengage Learning.

Brown, J. W., Chen, S-l., Mefford, L., Brown, A., Callen, B., & McArthur, P. (2011). Becoming an older volunteer: A grounded theory study. *Nursing Research and Practice, 2011.* doi:10.1155/2011/361250. Retrieved from www.hindawi.com/journals/nrp/2011/361250.html.

Brown, S. D., & Lent, R. W. (2016). Vocational psychology: Agency, equity, and well-being. *Annual Review of Psychology, 67*, 541–565. doi:10.1146/annurev-psych-122414-033237

Brysiewicz, P. (2008). The lived experience of losing a loved one to a sudden death in KwaZulu-Natal, South Africa. *Journal of Clinical Nursing, 17*, 224–231. doi:10.1111/j.1365-2702.2007.01972.x

Budgeon, S. (2016). The 'problem' with single women: Choice, accountability and social change. *Journal of Social and Personal Relationships, 33*, 401–418. doi:10.1177/0265407515607647

Buhl, H. (2008). Development of a model describing individuated adult child-parent relationships. *International Journal of Behavioral Development, 32*, 381–389. doi:10.1177/0165025408093656

Bui, E., Mauro, C., Robinaugh, D. J., Skritskaya, N. A., Wang, Y., Gribbin, C. et al. (2015). The Structured Clinical Interview for Complicated Grief: Reliability, validity, and explanatory factor analysis. *Depression and Anxiety, 32*, 485–492. doi:10.1002/da.22385

Bureau of Labor Statistics. (2016a). *Unemployment rates by age, sex, race, and Hispanic or Latino ethnicity.* Retrieved from www.bls.gov/web/empsit/cpsee_e16.htm.

Bureau of Labor Statistics. (2016b). *Families by presence and relationship of employed members and family type, 2014–2015 annual averages.* Retrieved from www.bls.gov/news.release/famee.t02.htm.

Bureau of Labor Statistics. (2016c). *Employment characteristics of families—2015.* Retrieved from www.bls.gov/news.release/pdf/famee.pdf.

Burgio, L., Stevens, A. Guy, D., Roth, D. L., & Haley, W. E. (2003). Impact of two psychosocial interventions on white and African American family caregivers of individuals with dementia. *The Gerontologist, 43*, 568–579. doi:10.1093/geront/43.4.568

Burke, B. L., Martens, A., & Faucher, E. H. (2010). Two decades of terror management theory: A meta-analysis of mortality salience research. *Personality and Social Psychology Review, 14*, 155–195. doi:10.1177/1088868309352321

Burnette, D. (1999). Social relationships of Latino grandparent caregivers: A role theory perspective. *The Gerontologist, 39*, 49–58. doi:10.1093/geront/39.1.49

Burton, A. E., Gibson, J. M., & Shaw, R. L. (2016). How do older people with sight loss manage their general health? A qualitative study. *Disability and Rehabilitation, 38*, 2277–2285. doi:10.3109/09638288.2015.1123310

Bustos, M. L. C. (2007). La muerte en la cultura occidental: Antropología de la muerte [Death in Western culture: Anthropology of death]. *Revista Colombiana de Psiquiatria, 36*, 332–339. Retrieved from www.redalyc.org/articulo.oa?id=80636212.

Cabeza, R. (2002). Hemispheric asymmetry reduction in older adults: The HAROLD model. *Psychology and Aging, 17*, 85–100. doi:10.1037/0882-7974.17.1.85

Cabeza, R. (2004). Neuroscience frontiers in cognitive aging. In R. A. Dixon & L. G. Nilsson (Eds.), *New frontiers in cognitive aging* (pp. 179–196). New York: Oxford University Press.

Cabeza, R., & Dennis N A. (2013). Frontal lobes and aging: Deterioration and compensation. In D. T. Stuss & R. T. Knight (Eds.), *Principles of frontal lobe function* (2nd ed., pp. 628–652). New York: Oxford University Press. Retrieved from canlab.psych.psu.edu/compensationchapter_stussknightbook_cabezadennis_final.pdf.

Cacciatore, J., & DeFrain, J. (2015). *The world of bereavement*. New York: Springer.

Cacioppo, J. T., Berntson, G. G., Bechara, A., Tranel, D., & Hawkley, H. C. (2011). Could an aging brain contribute to subjective well-being? The value added by a social neuroscience perspective. In A. Todorov, S. Fiske, & D. Prentice (Eds.), *Social neuroscience: Toward understanding the underpinnings of the social mind* (pp. 249–262). New York: Oxford University Press.

Cadigan, R. O., Grabowski, D. C., Givens, J. L., & Mitchell, S. L. (2012). The quality of advanced dementia care in the nursing home: The role of special care units. *Medical Care, 50*, 856–862. doi:10.1097/MLR.0b013e31825dd713

Cahill, E., Lewis, L. M., Barg, F. K., & Bogner, H. R. (2009). "You don't want to burden them": Older adults' views on family involvement in care. *Journal of Family Nursing, 27*, 295–317. doi:10.1177/1074840709337247

Cairney, J., & Krause, N. (2008). Negative life events and age-related decline in mastery: Are older adults more vulnerable to the control-eroding effect of stress? *The Journals of Gerontology: Social Sciences, 63*, S162–S170.

Calamia, M., Reese-Melancon, C., Cherry, K. E., Hawley, K. S., & Jazwinski, S. M. (2016). The Knowledge of Memory Aging Questionnaire: Factor structure and correlates in a lifespan sample. *Yale Journal of Biology and Medicine, 89*, 91–96. Retrieved from www.ncbi.nlm.nih.gov/pmc/articles/PMC4797842/.

Camberis, A. L., McMahon, C. A., Gibson, F. L., & Bolvin, J. (2016). Maternal age, psychological maturity, parenting cognitions, and mother-infant interaction. *Infancy, 21*, 396–422. doi:10.1111/infa.12116

Camp, C. J. (1999a). Memory interventions for normal and pathological older adults. In R. Schulz, M. P. Lawton, & G. Maddox (Eds.), *Annual review of gerontology and geriatrics* (Vol. 18, pp. 155–189). New York: Springer.

Camp, C. J. (2001). From efficacy to effectiveness to diffusion: Making transitions in dementia intervention research. *Neuropsychological Rehabilitation, 11*, 495–517. doi:10.1080/09602010042000079

Camp, C. J. (2005). Spaced retrieval: A model for dissemination of a cognitive intervention for persons with dementia. In D. K. Attix & K. A. Velsh-Bohmer (Eds.), *Geriatric neuropsychology: Assessment and intervention* (pp. 275–292). New York: Guilford Press.

Camp, C. J. (Ed.). (1999b). *Montessori-based activities for persons with dementia* (Vol. 1). Beachwood, OH: Menorah Park Center for Senior Living.

Camp, C. J., Antenucci, V., Brush, J., & Slominski, T. (2012). Using spaced retrieval to effectively treat dysphagia in clients with dementia. *Perspectives on Swallowing and Swallowing Disorders (Dysphagia), 21*, 96–104. doi:10.1044/sasd21.3.96

Camp, C. J., Foss, J. W., Stevens, A. B., Reichard, C. C., McKitrick, L. A., & O'Hanlon, A. M. (1993). Memory training in normal and demented elderly populations: The E-I-E-I-O model. *Experimental Aging Research, 19*, 277–290. doi:10.1080/03610739308253938

Camp, C. J., Skrajner, M. J., & Kelly, M. (2005). Early stage dementia client as group leader. *Clinical Gerontologist, 28*, 81–85. doi: 10.1300/J018v28n04_06

Camp, C. J., Zeisel, J., & Antenucci, V. (2011). Implementing the "I'm Still Here"TM approach: Montessori-based methods for engaging persons with dementia. In P. E. Hartman-Stein & A. LaRue (Eds.), *Enhancing cognitive fitness in adults* (pp. 401–417). New York: Springer.

Campbell, J., & Ehlert, U. (2012). Acute psychosocial stress: Does the emotional stress response correspond with physiological responses? *Psychoneuroendocrinology, 37*, 1111–1134. doi: 10.1016/j.psyneuen.2011.12.010

Campbell, K., & Kaufman, J. (2017). Do you pursue your heart or your art? Creativity, personality, and love. *Journal of Family Issues, 38*, 287–311. doi:10.1177/0192513X15570318

Campbell, K. L., Samu, D., Davis, S. W., Geerlings, L., Mustafa, A., Tyler, L. K. et al. (2016). Robust resilience of the frontotemporal syntax system to aging. *The Journal of Neuroscience, 36*, 5214–5227. doi:10.1523/JNEUROSCI.4561-15.2016

Campinha-Bacote, J. (2010). A culturally conscious model of mentoring. *Nurse Educator, 35*, 130–135. doi: 10.1097/NNE.0b013e3181d950bf

Cândea, D. M., Cotet, C. D., Stefan, S., Valenas, S. P., & Szentagotai-Tatar, A. (2015). Computerized training for working memory in older adults: A review. *Transylvanian Journal of Psychology, 16*, 141–161.

Cansino, S., Estrada-Manilla, C., Hernández-Ramos, E., Martinez-Galindo, J. G., Torres-Trejo, F., Gómez-Fernández, T. et al. (2013). The rate of source memory decline across the adult life span. *Developmental Psychology, 49*, 973–985. doi: 10.1037/a0028894

Cantarella, A., Borella, E., Carretti, B., Kliegel, M., & de Beni, R. (2017). Benefits in tasks related to everyday life competencies after a working memory training in older adults. *International Journal of Geriatric Psychiatry, 32*, 86–93. doi:10.1002/gps.4448

Cantor, N. (1990). From thought to behavior: "Having" and "doing" in the study of personality and cognition. *American Psychologist, 45*, 735–750. doi: 10.1037/0003-066X.45.6.735

Carlander, I., Ternestedt, B.-M., Sahlberg-Blom, E., Hellström, I., & Sandberg, J. (2011). Being me and being us in a family living close to death at home. *Qualitative Health Research, 5*, 683–695. doi: 10.1177/1049732310396102

Carlo, G., Koller, S., Raffaelli, M., & de Guzman, M. R. T. (2007). Culture-related strengths among Latin American families: A case study of Brazil. *Marriage & Family Review, 41*, 335–360. doi: 10.1300/J002v41n03_06

Carnelley, K., & Ruscher, J. B. (2000). Adult attachment and exploratory behavior in leisure. *Journal of Social Behavior and Personality, 15*, 153–165. Retrieved from crawl.prod.proquest.com.s3.amazonaws.com/fpcache/cdd5594c53a7864881fb71e54a7422f1.pdf?AWSAccessKeyId=AKIAJF7V7KNV2KKY2NUQ&Expires=1476725696&Signature=EiFM036jVPsv4iNCNcf8At5HlAY%3D.

Carney, K. O. (2016). Capacity assessments. In S. K. Whitbourne (Ed.), *The encyclopedia of adulthood and aging* (pp. 141–145). Malden, MA: Wiley-Blackwell.

Carr, A., & McNulty, M. (2016). Cognitive behaviour therapy. In A. Carr & M. McNulty (Eds.), *The handbook of adult clinical psychology* (2nd ed.). Abingdon, UK: Routledge.

Carr, D. (2004). Gender, preloss marital dependence, and older adults' adjustment to widowhood. *Journal of Marriage and Family, 66*, 220–235. doi: 10.1111/j.0022-2445.2004.00016.x

Carr, D., & Moorman, S. M. (2011). Social relations and aging. In R. A. Settersten & J. L. Angel (Eds.), *Handbook of sociology of aging* (pp. 145–160). New York: Springer.

Carstensen, L. L. (2006). The influence of a sense of time on human development. *Science, 312*, 1913–1915. doi: 10.1126/science.1127488

Carstensen, L. L., & Freund, A. M. (1994). The resilience of the aging self. *Developmental Review, 14*, 81–92. doi: 10.1006/drev.1994.1004

Carstensen, L. L., & Fried, L. P. (2012). The meaning of old age. In J. Beard, S. Biggs, D. Bloom, L. Fried, P. Hogan, A., Kalache et al. (Eds.), *Global population ageing: Peril or promise?* (pp. 15–17). Harvard University Program on the Global Demography of Aging. Retrieved from mfile.narotama.ac.id/files/Jurnal/Jurnal%202012-2013/International%20Migration%20and%20Population%20Ageing.pdf#page=18.

Carstensen, L. L., & Mikels, J. A. (2005). At the intersection of emotion and cognition: Aging and the positivity effect. *Current Directions in Psychological Science, 14*, 117–121. doi: 10.1111/j.0963-7214.2005.00348

Carstensen, L. L., Mikels, J. A., & Mather, M. (2006). Aging and the intersection of cognition, motivation, and emotion. In J. E. Birren & K. W. Schaie (Eds.), *Handbook of the psychology of aging* (6th ed., pp. 343–362). Amsterdam, The Netherlands: Elsevier.

Casey, V. A., Dwyer, J. T., Coleman, K. A., Krall, E. A., Gardner, J., & Valadian, I. (1991). Accuracy of recall by middle-aged participants in a longitudinal study of their body size and indices of maturation earlier in life. *Annals of Human Biology, 18*, 155–166. doi: 10.1080/03014469100001492

Casper, W. J., Marquardt, D. J., Roberto, K. J., & Buss, C. (2016). The hidden family lives of single adults without dependent children. In T. D. Allen & L. T. Eby (Eds.), *The Oxford handbook of work and family* (pp. 182–195). New York: Oxford University Press.

Caspi, A., Roberts, B. W., & Shiner, R. (2005). Personality development. *Annual Review of Psychology, 56*, 453–484. doi:10.1146/annurev.psych.55.090902.141913

Castel, A. D., Middlebrooks, C. D., & McGillivray, S. (2016). Monitoring memory in old age: Impaired, spared, and aware. In J. Dunlosky & S. K. Tauber (Eds.), *The Oxford handbook of metamemory* (pp. 519–536). New York: Oxford University Press.

Castro, M., & Smith, G. E. (2015). Mild cognitive impairment and Alzheimer's disease. In P. A. Lichtenberg, B. T. Mast, B. D. Carpenter, & J. Loebach Wetherell (Eds.), *APA handbook of clinical geropsychology, Vol. 2: Assessment, treatment, and issues of later life* (pp. 173–207). Washington, DC: American Psychological Association.

Cavallaro, F., Seilhamer, M. F., Chee, Y. T. F., & Ng, B. C. (2016). Overaccommodation in a Singapore eldercare facility. *Journal of Multilingual and*

Multicultural Development, 37, 817–831. doi:10.1080/01434632.2016.1142553

Cavallini, E., Bottiroli, S., Fastame, M. C., & Hertzog, C. (2013). Age and subcultural differences on personal and general beliefs about memory. *Journal of Aging Studies, 27,* 71–81. doi: 10.1016/j.jaging.2012.11.002

Cavanaugh, J. C. (1996). Memory self-efficacy as a key to understanding memory change. In F. Blanchard-Fields & T. M. Hess (Eds.), *Perspectives on cognitive changes in adulthood and aging* (pp. 488–507). New York: McGraw-Hill.

Cavanaugh, J. C. (1999a). Caregiving to adults: A life event challenge. In I. H. Nordhus, G. R. VandenBos, S. Berg, & P. Fromholt (Eds.), *Clinical geropsychology* (pp. 131–135). Washington, DC: American Psychological Association.

Cavanaugh, J. C. (1999b). Theories of aging in the biological, behavioral, and social sciences. In J. C. Cavanaugh & S. K. Whitbourne (Eds.), *Gerontology: Interdisciplinary perspectives* (pp. 1–32). New York: Oxford University Press.

Cavanaugh, J. C. (2017). Spirituality as a framework for confronting life's existential questions. In J. D. Sinnott (Ed.), *Identity flexibility during adulthood: Perspectives on adult development.* New York: Springer.

Cavanaugh, J. C., & Green, E. E. (1990). I believe, therefore I can: Self-efficacy beliefs in memory aging. In E. A. Lovelace (Ed.), *Aging and cognition: Mental processes, self-awareness, and interventions* (pp. 189–230). Amsterdam, Netherlands: North-Holland.

Cavanaugh, J. C., & Kinney, J. M. (1994, July). *Marital satisfaction as an important contextual factor in spousal caregiving.* Paper presented at the 7th International Conference on Personal Relationships, Groningen, The Netherlands.

Cavanaugh, J. C., & Whitbourne, S. K. (2003). Research methods in adult development. In J. Demick & C. Andreoletti (Eds.), *Handbook of adult development* (pp. 85–100). New York: Kluwer Academic/Plenum.

Census Bureau. (2013). *American Community Survey on Marriage and Divorce.* Retrieved from www.census.gov/hhes/socdemo/marriage/data/acs/index.html.

Census Bureau. (2015). *New Census Bureau report analyzes U.S. population projections.* Retrieved from www.census.gov/newsroom/press-releases/2015/cb15-tps16.html.

Census Bureau. (2016). *Median age at first marriage: 1890 to present.* Retrieved from www.census.gov/hhes/families/files/graphics/MS-2.pdf.

Centers for Disease Control and Prevention. (2015). *National Health Interview Survey: 2014 data release.* Retrieved from www.cdc.gov/nchs/nhis/nhis_2014_data_release.htm.

Centers for Disease Control and Prevention. (2016a). *Stroke.* Retrieved from www.cdc.gov/stroke/.

Centers for Disease Control and Prevention. (2016b). *Preventing falls among older adults.* Retrieved from www.cdc.gov/Features/OlderAmericans/index.html.

Centers for Disease Control and Prevention. (2016c) *Guideline for prescribing opioids for chronic pain.* Retrieved from www.cdc.gov/drugoverdose/pdf/guidelines_factsheet-a.pdf.

Centers for Disease Control and Prevention. (2016d). *About adult BMI.* Retrieved from www.cdc.gov/healthyweight/assessing/bmi/adult_bmi/index.html.

Centers for Disease Control and Prevention. (2016e). *Adult obesity facts.* Retrieved from www.cdc.gov/obesity/data/adult.html.

Centers for Disease Control and Prevention. (2016f). *HIV among people aged 50 and over.* Retrieved from www.cdc.gov/hiv/group/age/olderamericans/index.html.

Centers for Disease Control and Prevention. (2016g). *Healthy aging.* Retrieved from www.cdc.gov/aging/index.html.

Centers for Medicare and Medicaid Services. (2016a). *Nursing home data compendium 2015.* Retrieved from www.cms.gov/Medicare/Provider-Enrollment-and-Certification/CertificationandComplianc/Downloads/nursinghomedatacompendium_508-2015.pdf.

Centers for Medicare and Medicaid Services. (2016b). *Five-Star Quality Rating System.* Retrieved from www.cms.gov/medicare/provider-enrollment-and-certification/certificationandcomplianc/fsqrs.html.

Centers for Medicare and Medicaid Services. (2016c). *Medicare program—General information.* Retrieved from www.cms.gov/Medicare/Medicare-General-Information/MedicareGenInfo/index.html.

Chan, M. Y., Haber, S., Drew, L. M., & Park, D. C. (2016). Training older adults to use table tcomputers: Does it enhance cognitive function? *The Gerontologist, 56,* 475–484. doi:10.1093/geront/gnu057

Chan, S. W-C. (2010). Family caregiving in dementia: The Asian perspective of a global problem. *Dementia and Geriatric Cognitive Disorders, 30,* 469–478. doi:10.1159/000322086

Chang, J. E. Sequeira, A., McCord, C. E., & Garney, W. R. (2016). Videoconference grief group counseling in rural Texas: Outcomes, challenges, and lessons learned. *Journal for Specialists in Group Work, 41,* 140–160. doi:10.1080/01933922.2016.114376

Chang, T.-S., & Hsiao, W.-H. (2014). Time spent on social networking sites: Understanding user behavior and social capital. *Systems Research and Behavioral Science, 31,* 102–114. doi:10.1002/ sres.2169

Charles, S. T., & Carstensen, L. L. (2010). Social and emotional aging. *Annual Review of Psychology, 61,* 383–409. doi:10.1146/annurev.psych.093008.100448

Charles, S. T., & Luong, G. (2013). Emotional experience across adulthood: The theoretical model of Strength and Vulnerability Integration. *Current Directions in Psychological Science, 22,* 443–448. doi:10.1177/0963721413497013

Charles, S. T., Mather, M., & Carstensen, L. L. (2003). Aging and emotional memory: The forgettable nature of negative images for older adults. *Journal of Experimental Psychology: General, 132,* 310–324. doi:10.1037/0096-3445.132.2.310

Charlton, B., & Verghese, A. (2010). Caring for Ivan Ilyich. *Journal of General Internal Medicine, 25,* 93–95. doi:10.1007/s11606-009-1177-4

Charness, N., & Bosman, E. A. (1990). Expertise and aging: Life in the lab. In T. M. Hess (Ed.), *Aging and cognition: Knowledge organization and utilization* (pp. 343–385). Amsterdam, Netherlands: North-Holland.

Charras, K., Eynard, C., & Viatour, G. (2016). Use of space and human rights: Planning dementia friendly settings. *Journal of Gerontological Social Work, 59,* 181–204. doi:10.1080/01634372.2016.1171268

Chatters, L. M., Taylor, R. J., Lincoln, K. D., Nguyen, A., & Joe, S. (2011). Church-based social support and suicidality among African Americans and black Caribbeans. *Archives of Suicide Research, 15:4,* 337–353. doi:10.1080/13811118.2011.615703

Chaudhari, A., Gupta, R., Makwana, K., & Kondratov, R. (2017). Circadian clocks, diets, and aging. *Nutrition and Healthy Aging, 4,* 101–112. Retrieved from content.iospress.com/articles/nutrition-and-healthy-aging/nha160006.

Chee, F. Y. T. (2011). *Elderspeak in Singapore: A case study.* Retrieved from dr.ntu.edu.sg/bitstream/handle/10220/7795/Felicia%20Chee.pdf?sequence=1.

Chen, J., & Wu, Z. (2008). Gender differences in the effects of self-rated health status on mortality among the oldest old in China. In Z. Yi, D. L. Poston, Jr., D. Asbaugh Vlosky, & D. Gu (Eds.), *Healthy longevity in China* (pp. 397–418). New York: Springer.

Chen, Y., Peng, Y., & Fang, P. (2016). Emotional intelligence mediates the relationship between age and subjective well-being. *International Journal of Aging and Human Development, 83,* 91–107. doi:10.1177/0091415016648705

Cheng, E., & Pegg, S. (2016). "If I'm not gardening, I'm not at my happiest": Exploring the positive subjective experiences derived from serious leisure gardening by older adults. *World Leisure Journal, 58,* 285–297. doi:10.1080/16078055.2016.1228219

Cherko, M., Hickson, L., & Bhutta, M. (2016). Auditory deprivation and health in the elderly. *Maturitas, 88,* 52–57. doi:10.1016/j.marturitas.2016.03.008

Cherry, K. E., Blanchard, B., Walker, E. J., Smitherman, E. A., & Lyon, B. A. (2014). Knowledge of memory aging across the lifespan. *The Journal of Genetic Psychology: Research and theory on Human Development, 175,* 547–553. doi:10.1080/00221325.2014.982069

Cherry, K. E., Brigman, S., Reese-Melancon, C., Burton-Chase, A., & Holland, K. (2013). Memory aging knowledge and memory self-appraisal in younger and older adults. *Educational Gerontology, 39,* 168–178. doi:10.1080/03601277.20 12.699838

Cheung, C. K., Kam, P. K., & Ngan, R. M. H. (2011). Age discrimination in the labour market from the perspectives of employers and older workers. *International Social Work, 54,* 118–136. doi:10.1177/0020872810372368

Chew-Graham, C. A., & Ray, M. (Eds.). (2016). *Mental health and older people: A guide for primary care practitioners.* New York: Springer.

Chi, M. T. H. (2006). Laboratory methods for assessing experts' and novices' knowledge. In K. A. Ericsson, N. Charness, P. J. Feltovich, & R. R. Hoffman (Eds.), *The Cambridge handbook of expertise and expert performance* (pp. 167–184). New York: Cambridge University Press.

Chiao, C.-Y., Wu, H.-S., & Hsiao, C.-Y. (2015). Caregiver burden for informal caregivers of patients with dementia: A systematic review. *International Nursing Review, 62,* 340–350. doi:10.1111/inr.12194

ChildStats.gov. (2016). *America's children in brief: Key national indicators of well-being, 2016.* Retrieved from www.childstats.gov/americaschildren/index.asp.

Chipperfield, J. G., Perry, R. P., Pekrun, R., Barchfield, P., Lang, F. R., & Hamm, J. M. (20176). The paradoxical role of perceived control in late life health behavior. *PloS one.* doi:10.1371/journal.pone.0148921. Retrieved from journals.plos.org/plosone/article?id=10.1371/journal.pone.0148921.

Chisholm-Burns, M. A., Schwinghammer, T. L., Wells, B. G., Malone, P. M., Kolesar, J. M., & DiPiro, J. T. (2016). *Pharmacotherapy principles and practice* (4th ed.). New York: McGraw-Hill Education.

Chiu, H. F. K., & Brodaty, H. (2013). Arguments against the biomarkerdriven diagnosis of AD. *International Psychogeriatrics, 25,* 177–181. doi: 10.1017/S1041610212002104

Choi, H. S., Johnson, B., & Kriewitz, K. (2013). Benefits of inclusion and segregation for individuals with disabilities in leisure. *International Journal on Disability and Human Development, 12,* 15–23. doi:10.1515/ ijdhd-2012-0120

Choi, H. S., & Feng, J. (2016). General slowing hypothesis. In S. K. Whitbourne (Ed.), *The encyclopedia of adulthood and aging* (Vol. 2, pp. 556–559). Malden, MA: Wiley. doi: 10.1002/9781118521373.wbeaa198

Choi, M., Sprang, G., & Eslinger, J. G. (2016). Grandparents raising grandchildren: A synthetic review and theoretical model for interventions. *Family & Community Health, 39,* 120–128. doi:10.1097/0000000000000097

Chonody, J. M. (2015). Addressing ageism in students: A systematic review of the pedagogical intervention literature. *Educational Gerontology, 41,* 859–887. doi:10.1080/03601277.2015.1059139

Chou, S.-C., Boldy, D. P., & Lee, A. H. (2003). Factors influencing residents' satisfaction in residential aged care. *The Gerontologist, 43,* 459–472. doi:10.1093/geront/43.4.459

Christensen, A. (1990). Gender and social structure in the demand/withdrawal pattern of marital conflict. *Journal of Personality and Social Psychology, 59,* 73–81. doi:10.1037/0022-3514.59.1.73

Christensen, A. J., & Johnson, J. A. (2002). Patient adherence with medical treatment regimens: An interactive approach. *Current Directions in Psychological Science, 11,* 94–97. doi:10.1111/1467-8721.00176

Chun, S., Heo, J., Lee, S., & Kim, J. (2016). Leisure-related predictors on a sense of purpose in life among older adults with cancer. *Activities, Adaptation & Aging, 40,* 266–280. doi:10.1080/01924788.2016.1199517

Ciani, E. (2016). Retirement, pension eligibility and home production. *Labour Economics, 38,* 106–120. doi:10.1016/j.labeco.2016.01.004

Cicirelli, V. G. (2001). Personal meaning of death in older adults and young adults in relation to their fears of death. *Death Studies, 25,* 663–683. doi:10.1080/713769896

Cicirelli, V. G. (2006). Fear of death in mid-old age. *Journals of Gerontology: Psychological Sciences, 61B,* P75–P81. Retrieved from psychsocgerontology.oxfordjournals.org/content/61/2/P75.full.

Cirelli, C. (2012). Brain plasticity, sleep and aging. *Gerontology, 58,* 441–445. doi:10.1159/000336149

Ciscato, E., Galichon, A., & Gousse, M. (2015). *Like attract like?* A structural comparison of monogamy across same-sex and different-sex households. *Social Science Research Network.* doi:10.2139/ssrn.2530724. Available at SSRN: ssrn.com/abstract=2530724.

Clare, L., & Giblin, S. (2008). Late onset psychosis. In R. Woods & L. Clare (Eds.), *Handbook of the clinical psychology of ageing* (2nd ed., pp. 133–144). New York: Wiley.

Coan, J. A. (2008). Toward a neuroscience of attachment. In J. Cassidy & P. R. Shaver (Eds.), *Handbook of attachment: Theory, research, and clinical implications* (2nd ed., pp. 241–265). New York: Guilford.

Coan, J. A., & Sbarra, D. A. (2015). Social baseline theory: The social regulation of risk and effort. *Current Opinion in Psychology, 1,* 87–91. doi:10.1016/j.copsyc.2014.12.021

Coates, B. A. (2017). *Divorce with decency* (5th ed.). Honolulu, HI: Latitude 20.

Coats, A. H., & Blanchard-Fields, F. (2013). Making judgments about other people: Impression formation and attributional processing in older adults. *International Journal of Ageing and Later Life, 8,* 97–110. Retrieved from www.ep.liu.se/ej/ijal/2013/v8/i1/12-199/ijal12-199.pdf.

Cohen, F., Kemeny, M. E., Zegans, L., Johnson, P., Kearney, K. A., & Sites, D. P. (2007). Immune function declines with unemployment and recovers after stressor termination. *Psychosomatic Medicine, 69,* 225–234. doi: 10.1097/PSY.0b013e31803139a6

Cohen, L. W., Zimmerman, S., Reed, D., Brown, P., Bowers, B. J., Nolet, K. et al. (2016). The green House model of nursing home care in design and implementation. *Health Services Research, 51,* 352–377. doi:10.1111/1475-6773.12418

Cohen, S., & Janicki-Deverts, D. (2012). Who's stressed? Distributions of psychological stress in the United States in probability samples from 1983, 2006, and 2009. *Journal of Applied Social Psychology, 42,* 1320–1334. doi:10.1111/j.1559-1816.2012.00900.x

Cohen, S., Janicki-Deverts, D., Doyle, W. J., Miller, G. E., Frank, E., Rabin, B. S. et al. (2012). Chronic stress, glucocorticoid receptor resistance, inflammation, and disease risk. *Proceedings of the National Academy of Sciences, 109,* 5995–5999. doi:10.1073/pnas.1118355109

Cohen-Mansfield, J., & Regev, I. (in press). Retirement preparation programs: An examination of retirement perceptions, self-mastery, and well-being. *Research on Social Work Practice.* doi:10.1177/1049731516645194

Colcombe, S., & Kramer, A. F. (2003). Fitness effects on the cognitive function of older adults: A meta-analytic study. *Psychological Science, 14,* 125–130. doi:10.1111/1467-9280.t01-1-01430

Coleman, J. (2015). *Unfinished work: The struggle to build an aging American workforce.* New York: Oxford University Press.

Coles, R. L. (2016). *Race and family: A structural approach* (2nd ed.). Lanham, MD: Rowman & Littlefield.

Collardeau, F., & Ehrenberg, M. (2016). Parental divorce and attitudes and feelings toward marriage and divorce in emerging adulthood: New insights from a multiway-frequency analysis. *Journal of European Psychology Students.* Retrieved from jeps.efpsa.org/articles/10.5334/jeps.341/.

Collins, K., & Mohr, C. (2013). Performance of younger and older adults in lateralized right and left hemisphere asymmetry tasks supports the HAROLD model. *Laterality, 18,* 491–512 doi:10.1080/1357650X.2012.724072

Collins, W. A., & van Dulmen, M. (2006). "The course of true love(s)...": Origins and pathways in the development of romantic relationships. In A. C. Crouter & A. Booth (Eds.), *Romance and sex in adolescence and emerging adulthood: Risks and opportunities* (pp. 63–86). Mahwah, NJ: Erlbaum.

Colombel, F., Tessoulin, M., Gilet, A.-L., & Corson, Y. (2016). False memories and normal aging: Links between inhibitory capacities and monitoring processes. *Psychology and Aging, 31,* 239–248. doi:10.1037/pag0000086

Coman, A., & Hirst, W. (2012). Cognition through a social network: The propagation of induced forgetting and practice effects. *Journal of Experimental Psychology: General, 141,* 321–336. doi:10.1037/a0025247

Commons, M. L. (2016). The fundamental issues with behavioral development. *Behavioral Development Bulletin, 21,* 1–12. doi:10.1037/bdb0000022

Connidis, I. A. (2001). *Family ties and aging.* Thousand Oaks, CA: Sage.

Connolly, A., Sampson, E. L., & Purandare, N. (2012). End-of-life care for people with dementia form ethnic minority groups: A systematic review. *Journal of the American Geriatrics Society, 60,* 351–360. doi:10.1111/j.1532-5415.2011.03754.x

Connors, M. H., Sachdev, P. S., Kochan, N. A., Xu, J., Draper, B., & Brodaty, H. (2015). Cognition and mortality in older people: The Sydney Memory and Aging Study. *Age and Ageing, 44,* 1049–1054. doi:10.1093/ageing/afv139

Constantinidis, C., & Klingberg, T. (2016). The neuroscience of working memory capacity and training. *Nature Reviews Neuroscience, 17,* 438–449. doi:10.1038/nrn.2016.43

Conway, E. R., & Chenery, H. J. (2016). Evaluating the MESSAGE Communication Strategies in Dementia training for use with community-based aged care staff working with people with dementia: A controlled pretest-post-test study. *Journal of Clinical Nursing, 25,* 1145–1155. doi:10.1111/jocn.13134

Cook, D. A., Bahn, R. S., & Menaker, R. (2010). Speed mentoring: An innovative method to facilitate mentoring relationships. *Medical Teacher, 32,* 692–694. doi:10.3109/01421591003686278

Coombs, M. A. (2010). The mourning that comes before: Can anticipatory grief theory inform family care in adult intensive care? *International Journal of Palliative Nursing, 16,* 580–584. doi:10.12968/ijpn.2010.16.12.580

Copen, C. E., Daniels, K., Mosher, W. D., & Division of Vital Statistics. (2013). *First premarital cohabitation in the United States: 2006–2010 National Survey of Family Growth.* Retrieved from www.cdc.gov/nchs/data/nhsr/nhsr064.pdf.

Copley, S. J. (2016). Morphology of the aging lung on computed tomography. *Journal of Thoracic Imaging, 31,* 140–150. doi:10.1097/RTI.0000000000000211

Corbett, B. A., & Hilty, D. M. (2006). Managing your time. In L. W. Roberts & D. M. Hilty (Eds.), *Handbook of career development in academic psychiatry and behavioral sciences* (pp. 83–91). Washington, DC: American Psychiatric Publishing.

Cornwall, A. (2016). Women's empowerment: What works? *Journal of International Development, 28,* 342–359. doi:10.1002/jid.3210

Corporation for National and Community Service (2016). *Senior Corps.* Retrieved from www.nationalservice.gov/programs/senior-corps.

Corr, C. A. (2010a). Children, development, and encounters with death, bereavement, and coping. In C. A. Corr & D. E. Balk (Eds.), *Children's encounters with death, bereavement, and coping* (pp. 3–19). New York: Springer.

Corr, C. A. (2010b). Children's emerging awareness and understandings of loss and death. In C. A. Corr & D. E. Balk (Eds.), *Children's encounters with death, bereavement, and coping* (pp. 21–37). New York: Springer.

Corr, C. A., & Corr, D. M. (2013). *Death and dying: Life and living* (7th ed.). Belmont, CA: Wadsworth.

Corr, C. A., Corr, D. M., & Nabe, C. M. (2008). *Death and dying: Life and living.* Belmont, CA: Wadsworth.

Costa, P. T., Jr., & McCrae, R. R. (1988). Personality in adulthood: A six-year longitudinal study of self-reports and spouse ratings on the NEO Personality Inventory. *Journal of Personality and Social Psychology, 54,* 853–863. doi:10.1037/0022-3514.54.5.853

Costa, P. T., Jr., & McCrae, R. R. (1994). Set like plaster? Evidence for the stability of adult personality. In T. F. Heatherton & J. L. Weinberger (Eds.), *Can personality change?* (pp. 21–40). Washington, DC: Academic Psychological Association.

Costa, P. T., Jr., & McCrae, R. R. (1997). Longitudinal stability of adult personality. In R. Hogan, J. Johnson, & S. Briggs (Eds.), *Handbook of personality psychology* (pp. 269–292). San Diego, CA: Academic Press.

Costa, P. T., Jr., & McCrae, R. R. (1998). Six approaches to the explication of facet-level traits examples from conscientiousness. *European Journal of Personality, 12,* 117–134. doi:10.1002/(SICI)10990984(199803/04)12:2<117::AID-PER295>3.0.CO;2-C

Costa, P. T., Jr., & McCrae, R. R. (2011). Five-factor theory, and interpersonal psychology. In L. M. Horowitz & S. Strack (Eds.), *Handbook of interpersonal psychology: Theory, research, assessment, and therapeutic interventions* (pp. 91–104). Hoboken, NJ: Wiley.

Cotton, S. R., Anderson, W. A., & McCullough, B. M. (2013). Impact of Internet use on loneliness and contact with others among older adults: Cross-sectional analysis. *Journal of Medical Internet Research, 15,* e39. doi:10.2196/jmir.2306. Retrieved from www.ncbi.nlm.nih.gov/pmc/articles/PMC3636305/.

Council for Adult and Experiential Learning. (2016). *Higher education.* Retrieved from www.cael.org/higher-education.

Council on Contemporary Families. (2015). *Remarriage in the United States: If at first they don't succeed, do most Americans "try, try again"?* Retrieved from contemporaryfamilies.org/remarriage-brief-report/.

Counts, D., & Counts, D. (Eds.). (1985). *Aging and its transformations: Moving toward death in Pacific societies*. Lanham, MD: University Press of America.

Cowl, A. (2016). Terminal decline. In S. K. Whitbourne (Ed.), *The encyclopedia of adulthood and aging* (Vol. 3, pp. 1398–1402). Malden, MA: Wiley.

Cox, C. B. (2007). Grandparent-headed families: Needs and implications for social work interventions and advocacy. *Families in Society, 88*, 561–566. doi:10.1606/1044-3894.3678

Coyle, C. E., & Dugan, E. (2012). Social isolation, loneliness, and health among older adults. *Journal of Aging and Health, 24*, 1346–1363. doi:10.1177/0898264312460275

Craik, F. I. M., & Rose, N. S. (2012). Memory encoding and aging: A neurocognitive approach. *Neuroscience and Biobehavioral Reviews, 36*, 1729–1739. doi:10.1016/j.neubiorev.2011.11.007

Cram, B., Alkadry, M. G., & Tower, L. E. (2016). Social costs: The career-family tradeoff. In M. L. Connerley & J. Wu (Eds.), *Handbook of well-being of working women* (pp. 473–487). New York: Springer.

Crane, P. K., Walker, R., Hubbard, R. A., Li, G., Nathan, D. M., Zhang, Z., Haneuse, S. et al. (2013). Glucose levels and risk of dementia. *New England Journal of Medicine, 369*, 540–548. doi:10.1056/NEJMoa1215740

Cready, C. M., Yeatts, D. E., Gosdin, M. M., & Potts, H. F. (2008). CNS empowerment: Effects on job performance and work attitudes. *Journal of Gerontological Nursing, 34*, 26–35. doi:10.3928/00989134-20080301-02

Crisp, R. J., & Turner, R. N. (2009). Can imagined interactions produce positive perceptions?: Reducing prejudice through simulated social contact. *American Psychologist, 64*, 231–240. doi:10.1037/a0014718

Crisp, R. J., & Turner, R. N. (2012). The imagined contact hypothesis. *Advances in Experimental Social Psychology, 46*, 125–182. doi:10.1016/B978-0-12-394281-4.00003-0

Cristina, T. J. N., Williams, J. A. S., Parkinson, L., Sibbritt, D. W., & Byles, J. E. (2016). Identification of diabetes, heart disease, hypertension and stroke in mid- and older-aged women: Comparing self-report and administrative hospital data records. *Geriatrics and Gerontology International, 16*, 95–102. doi:10.1111/ggi.12442

Criter, R. E., & Honaker, J. A. (2016). Identifying balance measures most likely to identify recent falls. *Journal of Geriatric Physical Therapy, 39*, 30–37. doi:10.1519/JPT.0000000000000039

Cross, S., & Markus, H. (1991). Possible selves across the lifespan. *Human Development, 34*, 230–255. doi:10.1159/000277058

Crown, W. (2001). Economic status of the elderly. In R. H. Binstock & L. K. George (Eds.), *Handbook of aging and the social sciences* (5th ed., pp. 352–368). San Diego, CA: Academic Press.

Croy, I., Nordin, S., & Hummel, T. (2014). Olfactory disorders and quality of life—An updated review. *Chemical Senses, 39*, 185–194. doi:10.1093/chemse/bjt072

Cubanski, J., Casillas, G., & Damico, A. (2015). *Poverty among seniors: An updated analysis of national and state poverty rates under the official and supplemental poverty measures*. Retrieved from files.kff.org/attachment/issue-brief-poverty-among-seniors-an-updated-analysis-of-national-and-state-level-poverty-rates-under-the-official-and-supplemental-poverty-measures.

Cuddy, A. J. C., Norton, M. I., & Fiske, S. T. (2005). The old stereotype: The pervasiveness and persistence of the elderly stereotype. *Journal of Social Issues, 61*, 267–285. doi:10.1111/j.1540-4560.2005.00405.x

Cukier, H. N., Kunkle, B. W., Vardarajan, B. N., Rolati, S., Hamilton-Nelson, K. L., Kohli, M. A. et al. (2016). ABCA7 frameshift deletion associated with Alzheimer disease in African Americans. *Neurology Genetics, 2*, e79. doi:10.1212/NXG.0000000000000079. Retrieved from ng.neurology.org/content/2/3/e79.full.

Cummings, K. (2015). *Coming to grips with loss: Normalizing the grief process*. Boston: Sense Publishers.

Cundiff, N. L., & Stockdale, M. S. (2013). Social psychological perspectives on discrimination against women leaders. In M. A. Paludi (Ed.), *Women and management: Global issues and promising solutions* (pp. 155–174). Santa Barbara, CA: ABC-CLIO.

Cunnane, S. C., Chouinard-Watkins, R., Castellano, C. A., & Barberger-Gateau, P. (2013). Docosahexaenoic acid homeostasis, brain aging and Alzheimer's disease: Can we reconcile the evidence? *Prostaglandins, Leukotrienes, and Essential Fatty Acids, 88*, 61–70. doi:10.1016/j.plefa.2012.04.006

Cunningham, W. R. (1987). Intellectual abilities and age. In K. W. Schaie (Ed.), *Annual review of gerontology and geriatrics* (Vol. 7, pp. 117–134). New York: Springer.

Curtin, N., & Stewart, A. J. (2012). Linking personal and social histories with collective identity narratives. In S. Wiley, G. Philogène, & T. A. Revenson (Eds.), *Social categories in everyday experience* (pp. 83–102). Washington, DC: American Psychological Association.

Curtis, J. R., Treece, P. D., Nielsen, E. L., Gold, J., Ciechanowski, P. S., Shannon, S. E. et al. (2016). Randomized trial of communication facilitators to reduce family distress and intensity of end-of-life care. *Respiratory and Critical Care Medicine, 193*, 154–162. doi:10.1164/rccm.201505-0900OC

Curtis, R. G., Huxhold, O., & Windsor, T. D. (in press). Perceived control and social activity in midlife and older age: A reciprocal association? Findings from the German Ageing Study. *Journals of Gerontology: Psychological Sciences*. doi:10.1093/geronb/gbw070

Curtis, R., & Pearson, F. (2010). Contact with birth parents: Differential psychological adjustment for adults adopted as infants. *Journal of Social Work, 10*, 347–367. doi:10.1177/1468017310369273

D'Angelo, D., Mastroianni, C., Hammer, J. M., Piredda, M., Vellone, E., Alvaro, R. et al. (2015). Continuity of care during end of life: An evolutionary concept analysis. *International Journal of Nursing Knowledge, 26*, 80–89. doi:10.1111/2047-3095.12041

da Costa, J. F., & Oliveira, T. C. (2016). Managing careers: Anchored, plateaued or drifting? In C. Machado & J. P. Davim (Eds.), *Organizational management* (pp. 31–62). New York: Springer.

Dadgari, A., Hamid, T. A., Hakim, M. N., Mousavi, S. A., Dadvar, L., Mohammadi, M. et al. (2015). The role of self-efficacy on fear of falls and fall among elderly community dwellers in Shahroud, Iran. *Nursing Practice Today, 2*, 112–120. Retrieved from npt.tums.ac.ir/index.php/npt/article/view/54/58.

Dahlin, E., Stigsdotter Neely, A., Larsson, A., Bäckman, L., & Nyberg, L. (2008). Transfer of learning after updating training mediated by the striatum. *Science, 320* (5882), 1510–1512. doi: 10.1126/science.1155466

Dai, B., Zhang, B., & Li, J. (2013). Protective factors for subjective well-being in Chinese older adults: the roles of resources and activity. *Journal of Happiness Studies, 14*, 1225–1239. doi:10.1007/s10902-012-9378-7

Dalton, C. (2014). Including smart architecture in environments for people with dementia. In J. van Hoof, G. Demiris, & E. J. M. Wouters (Eds.), *Handbook for smart homes, health care and well-being* (pp. 1–10). New York: Springer. doi:10.1007/978-3-319-0194-8_57-1

Dalton, D. S., Cruickshanks, K. J., Klein, B. E. K., Klein, R., Wiley, T. L., & Nondahl, D. M. (2003). The impact of hearing loss on quality of life in older adults. *The Gerontologist, 43*, 661–668. doi:10.1093/geront/43.5.661

Damian, R. I., & Simonton, D. K. (2015). Four psychological perspectives on creativity. *Emerging trends in the social and behavioral sciences: An interdisciplinary, searchable, and linkable resource.* doi:10.1002/9781118900772.etrds0134

Dannar, P. R. (2013). Millennials: What they offer our organizations and how leaders can make sure they deliver. *Journal of Values-Based Leadership, 6*, Article 3. Retrieved from scholar.valpo.edu/cgi/viewcontent.cgi?article=1073&context=jvbl.

Davidson, R. J. (2010). Empirical explorations of mindfulness: Conceptual and methodological conundrums. *Emotion, 10*, 8–11. doi:10.1037/a0018480

Davies, L. (2003). Singlehood: Transitions within a gendered world. *Canadian Journal on Aging, 22*, 343–352. doi:10.1017/S0714980800004219

Davies, P. G. (2007). Between health and illness. *Perspectives in Biology and Medicine, 50*, 444–452. doi:10.1353/pbm.2007.0026

Davis S. W., Dennis N. A., Daselaar S. M., Fleck M. S., & Cabeza R. (2008). Que PASA? The posterior-anterior shift in aging. *Cerebral Cortex, 18*, 1201–1209. doi:10.1093/cercor/bhm155

Davis, A., McMahon, C. M., Pichora-Fuller, K. M. Russ, S., Lin, F., Olusanya, B. O. et al. (2016). Aging and hearing health: The life-source approach. *The Gerontologist, 56*, S256–S267. doi:10.1093/geront/gnw033

Davis, B. W. (1985). *Visits to remember: A handbook for visitors of nursing home residents*. University Park, PA: Pennsylvania State University Cooperative Extension Service.

Dawadi, P. N., & Cook, D. J. (2017). Monitoring everyday abilities and cognitive health using pervasive technologies: Current state and prospect. In J. van Hoof, G. Demiris, & E. J. M. Wouters (Eds.), *Handbook of smart homes, health care and well-being* (pp. 365–385). New York: Springer.

de Bloom, J., Geurts, S. A. E., & Kompier, M. A. J. (2012). Effects of short vacations, vacation activities and experiences on employee health and well-being. *Stress and Health, 28*, 305–318. doi:10.1002/smi.1434

de Bloom, J., Geurts, S. A. E., Taris, T. W., Sonnentag, S., de Weerth, C., & Kompier, M. A. J. (2010). Effects of vacation from work on health and well-being: Lots of fun, quickly gone. *Work and Stress, 24*, 196–216. doi:10. 1080/02678373.2010.493385

de Frias, C. M., Dixon, R. A., & Bäckman, L. (2003). Use of memory compensation strategies is related to psychosocial and health indicators. *Journals of Gerontology: Psychological Sciences, 58B*, P12–P22. doi:10.1093/geronb/58.1.P12

de Grip, A., Bosma, H., Willems, D., & van Boxtel, M. (2008). Job-worker mismatch and cognitive decline. *Oxford Economic Papers, 60*, 237–253. doi:10.1093/oep/gpm023

De Jager, C. A. (2012). Vitamins and brain health. *Vitamin Trace Element, 1*, 3103. doi:10.4172/vte.100003103. Retrieved from omicsgroup.org/journals/VTE/VTE-1-e103.php.

de Jong, P., Rouwendal, J., van Hattum, P., & Brouwer, A. (2012). *Housing preferences of an ageing population: Investigation in the diversity among Dutch older adults*. Retrieved from arno.uvt.nl/show.cgi?fid=123055.

De la Monte, S. (2012). Brain insulin resistance and deficiency as therapeutic targets in Alzheimer's disease. *Current Alzheimer's Research, 9*, 35–66. doi:10.2174/156720512799015037

De Paula Couto, M. C. P., & Koller, S. H. (2012). Warmth and competence: Stereotypes of the elderly among young adults and older persons in Brazil. *International Perspectives in Psychology: Research, Practice, Consultation, 1,* 52–62. doi: 10.1037/a0027118

de Pommereau, I. (2012). *How BMW reinvents the factory for older workers.* Retrieved from www.csmonitor.com/World/Europe/2012/0902/How-BMW-reinvents-the-factory-for-older-workers.

de Vries, B. (1996). The understanding of friendship: An adult life course perspective. In C. Magai & S. H. McFadden (Eds.), *Handbook of emotion, adult development, and aging* (pp. 249–268). San Diego, CA: Academic Press.

De Witt-Hoblit, I., Miller, M. N., & Camp, C. J. (2016). Effects of sustained, coordinated activities programming in long-term care: The Memory in Rhythm® program. *Advances in Aging Research, 5.* doi:10.4236/aar.2016.51001. Retrieved from file.scirp.org/Html/1-2420185_63096.htm.

DeAndrea, D. C., Ellison, N. B., LaRose, R., Steinfield, C., & Fiore, A. (2012). Serious social media: On the use of social media for improving students' adjustment to college. *The Internet and Higher Education, 15,* 15–23. doi:10.1016/j.iheduc.2011.05.009

Deane, G., Spitze, G. Ward, R. A., & Zhuo, Y. (2016). Close to you? How parent-adult child contact is influenced by family patterns. *Journal of Gerontology: Social Sciences, 71,* 344–357. doi:10.1093/geronb/gbv036

Debast, I., van Alphen, S. P. J., Rossi, G., Tummers, J. H. A., Bolwerk, N., Derksen, J. J. L. et al. (2014). Personality traits and personality disorders in late middle and old age: Do they remain stable? A literature review. *Clinical Gerontologist, 37,* 253–271. doi:10/1080/07317115.2014.885917

DeCarli, C., Kawas, C., Morrison, J. H., Reuter-Lorenz, P., Sperling, R. A., & Wright, C. B. (2012). Session II: Mechanisms of age-related cognitive change and targets for intervention: Neural circuits, networks, and plasticity. *The Journal of Gerontology: Biological Sciences and Medical Sciences, 67,* 747–753. doi:10.1093/Gerona/gls111

Defense and Veterans Brain Injury Center. (2016). *DoD Worldwide numbers of rTBI.* Retrieved from dvbic.dcoe.mil/dod-worldwide-numbers-tbi.

Delgado, M. (2015). *Baby boomers of color: Implications for social work policy and practice.* New York: Columbia University Press.

DeLiema, M., Yon, Y., & Wilber, K. H. (2016). Tricks of the trade: Motivating sales agents to con older adults. *The Gerontologist, 56,* 335–344. doi:10.1093/geront/gnu039

Demir, M., Orthel-Clark, H., Özdemir, M., & Özdemir, S. B. (2015). Friendship and happiness among young adults. In M. Demir (Ed.), *Friendship and happiness* (pp. 117–135). New York: Springer.

Demiray, B., & Freund, A. M. (2015). Michael, Jackson, Bin Laden, and I: Functions of positive and negative, public and private flashbulb memories. *Memory, 23,* 487–506. doi:10.1080/09658211.2014.907428

Deng, C.-P., Armstrong, P. I., & Rounds, J. (2007). The fit of Holland's RIASEC model to US occupations. *Journal of Vocational Behavior, 71,* 1–22. doi:10.1016/j.jvb.2007.04.002

Denham, J., O'Brien, B. J., & Charchar, F. J. (2016). Telomere length maintenance and cardio-metabolic disease prevention through exercise training. *Sports Medicine, 46,* 1213–1237. doi:10.1007/s40279-016-0482-4

Denney, N. W. (1984). A model of cognitive development across the life span. *Developmental Review, 4,* 171–191. doi:10.1016/0273-2287(84)90006-6

Denney, N. W., Pearce, K, A., & Palmer, A. M. (1982). A developmental study of adults performance on traditional and practical problem-solving tasks. *Experimental Aging Research, 8,* 115–118. doi:10.1080/03610738208258407

DePaulo, B. M. (2006). *Singled out: How singles are stereotyped, stigmatized, and ignored, and still live happily ever after.* New York: St Martin's Press.

DeSilver, D. (2016). *More older Americans are working, and working more, than they used to.* Retrieved from www.pewresearch.org/fact-tank/2016/06/20/more-older-americans-are-working-and-working-more-than-they-used-to/.

Desmond, N., & López Turley, R. N. (2009). The role of familism in explaining the Hispanic-white college application gap. *Social Problems, 56,* 311–334. doi:10.1525/sp.2009.56.2.311

Dey, S., & Ghosh, J. (2016). Factors in the distribution of successful marriage. *International Journal of Social Sciences and Management, 3,* 60–64. doi:10.3126/ijssm.v3i1.14315

Di Domenico, S., Rodrigo, A. H., Ayaz, H., Fournier, M. A., & Ruocco, A. C. (2015). Decision-making conflict and the neural efficiency hypothesis of intelligence: A functional near-infrared spectroscopy investigation. *NeuroImage, 109,* 307–317. doi:10.1016/j.neuroimage.2015.01.039

Di Fabio, A. (2016). Life design and career counseling innovative outcomes. *The Career Development Quarterly, 64,* 35–48. doi:10.1002/cdq.12039

Di Masso, A., Dixon, J., & Hernández, B. (2017). Place attachment, sense of belonging and the micro-politics of place satisfaction. In G. Fleury-Bahi, E. Pol, & O. Navarro (Eds.), *Handbook of environmental psychology and quality of life research* (pp. 85–104). New York: Springer.

Di Bartista, A. M., Heinsinger, N. M., & Rebeck, G. W. (2016). Alzheimer's disease genetic risk factor APOE-ε4 also affects normal brain function. *Current Alzheimer Research, 13,* 1200–1207.

DiBello, K. K. (2015). Grief & depression at the end of life. *Nurse Practitioner, 40,* 22–28. doi:10.1097/01.NPR.0000463781.50345.95

Dickens, B. M., Boyle, J. M., Jr., & Ganzini, L. (2008). Euthanasia and assisted suicide. In P. A. Singer & A. M. Viens (Eds.), *The Cambridge textbook of bioethics* (pp. 72–77). New York: Cambridge University Press.

Diehl, M., Hay, E. L., & Chui, H. (2012). Personal risk and resilience factors in the context of daily stress. *Annual Review of Gerontology and Geriatrics, 32,* 251–274. doi:10.1891/0198-8794.32.251

Diehl, M., Hay, E. L., & Chui, H. (2012). Personal risk and resilience factors in the context of daily stress. *Annual Review of Gerontology and Geriatrics, 32,* 251–274. doi:10.1891/0198-8794.32.251

Diehl, M., Marsiske, M., Horgas, A. L., Rosenberg, A., Saczynski, J. S., & Willis, S. L. (2005). The Revised Observed Tasks of Daily Living: A performance-based assessment of everyday problem solving in older adults. *Journal of Applied Gerontology, 24,* 211–230. doi:10.1177/0733464804273772

Diehl, M., Marsiske, M., Horgas, A. L., Rosenberg, A., Saczynski, J. S., & Willis, S. L. (2005). The Revised Observed Tasks of Daily Living: A performance-based assessment of everyday problem solving in older adults. *Journal of Applied Gerontology, 24,* 211–230. doi:10.1177/0733464804273772

Diehl, M., Willis, S. L., & Schaie, K. W. (1995). Everyday problem solving in older adults: Observational assessment and cognitive correlates. *Psychology and Aging, 10,* 478–491. doi:10.1037/0882-7974.10.3.478

Diersch, N., Cross, E. S., Stadler, W., Schütz-Bosbach, S., & Rieger, M. (2012). Representing others' actions: The role of expertise in the aging mind. *Psychological Research, 76,* 525–541. doi:10.1007/s00426-011-0404-x

Dillavou, E. D., Harlander-Locke, M., Labropoulos, N., Elias, S., & Ozsvath, K. J. (2016). Current state of the treatment of perforating veins. *Journal of Vacular Surgery, 4,* 131–135. doi:10.1016/j.jvsv.2015.03.009

Dillaway, H., Byrnes, M., Miller, S., & Rehnan, S. (2008). Talking "among us": How women from different racial-ethnic groups define and discuss menopause. *Health Care for Women International, 29,* 766–781. doi:10.1080/07399330802179247

Dilworth-Anderson, P., Boswell, G., & Cohen, M. D. (2007). Spiritual and religious coping values and beliefs among African American caregivers: A qualitative study. *Journal of Applied Gerontology, 26,* 355–369. doi:10.1177/0733464807302669

Dirk, J., & Schmiedek, F. (2012). Processing speed. In S. K. Whitbourne & M. J. Sliwinski (Eds.), *The Wiley-Blackwell handbook of adulthood and aging* (pp. 133–153). Oxford, UK: Wiley-Blackwell.

Dismukes, R. K. (2012). Prospective memory in workplace and everyday situations. *Current Directions in Psychological Science, 21,* 215–220. doi:10.1177/0963721412447621

Dixon, P. (2009). Marriage among African Americans: What does the research reveal? *Journal of African American Studies, 13,* 29–46. doi:10.1007/s12111-008-9062-5

Dixon, R. A. (2011). Evaluating everyday competence in older adult couples: Epidemiological considerations. *Gerontology, 57,* 173–179. doi:10.1159/000320325

Dixon, R. A., McFall, G. P., Whitehead, B. P., & Dolcos, S. (2013). In R. M. Lerner, M. A. Easterbrooks, & J. Mistry (Eds.), *Handbook of psychology: Vol 6. Developmental psychology* (2nd ed., pp. 451–474). Hoboken, NJ: Wiley.

Doerwald, F., Scheibe, S., Zacher, H., & Van Yperen, N. W. (2016). Emotional competencies across adulthood: State of knowledge and implications for the work context. *Work, Aging and Retirement, 2,* 159–216. doi:10.1093/worker/waw013

Doerwald, F., Scheibe, S., Zacher, H., & Van Yperen, N. W. (2016). Emotional competencies across adulthood: State of knowledge and implications for the work context. *Work, Aging and Retirement, 2,* 159–216. doi:10.1093/worker/waw013

Doets, E. L., & Kremer, S. (2016). The silver sensory experience—A review of senior consumers' food perception, liking and intake. *Food Quality and Preference, 48B,* 316–332. doi:10.1016/j.foodqual.2015.08.010

Dommaraju, P. (2010). *The changing demography of marriage in India.* Podcast retrieved from ari.nus.edu.sg/Publication/Detail/1630.

Donnellan, W. J., Bennett, K. M., & Soulsby, L. K. (2015). What are the factors that facilitate or hinder resilience in older spousal dementia carers? A qualitative study. *Aging & Mental Health, 19,* 932–939. doi:10.1080/13607863.2014.977771

Doss, B. D., & Rhoades, G. K. (2017). The transition to parenthood: Impact on couples' romantic relationships. *Current Opinion in Psychology, 13,* 25–28. doi:10.1016/j.copsyc.2016.04.003

Doubeni, C. A., Schootman, M., Major, J. M., Torres Stone, R. A., Laiyemo, A. O., Park, Y. et al. (2012). Health status, neighborhood socioeconomic context, and premature mortality in the United States: The National Institutes of Health—AARP Diet and Health Study. *American Journal of Public Health, 102,* 680–688. doi:10.2105/AJPH.2011.300158

Doyle, K. O., Jr. (1974). Theory and practice of ability testing in ancient Greece. *Journal of the History of the Behavioral Sciences, 10,* 202–212. doi:10.1002/1520-6696(197404)10:2<202:AIDJHBS2300100208>3.0.CO;2-Q

Drossel, C., Fisher, J., & Mercer, V. (2011). A DBT training group for family caregivers of persons with dementia. *Behavior Therapy, 42,* 109–119. doi:10.1016/j.beth.2010.06.001

DuBois, P. H. (1968). A test-dominated society: China 1115 b.c.–1905 a.d. In J. L. Barnette (Ed.),

Readings in psychological tests and measurements (pp. 249–255). Homewood, IL: Dorsey Press.

Dulas, M. R., & Duarte, A. (2012). The effects of aging on material-independent and material-dependent neural correlates of source memory retrieval. *Cerebral Cortex, 22*, 37–50. doi:10.1093/cercor/bhr056

Dunlop, W. L., Guo, J., & McAdams, D. P. (2016). The autobiographical author through time: Examining the degree of stability and change in redemptive and contaminated personal narratives. *Social Psychological and Personality Science, 7*, 428–436. doi:10.1177/1948550616644654

Dunlosky, J., Bailey, H., & Hertzog, C. (2011). Memory enhancement strategies: What works best for obtaining memory goals? In P. E. Hartman-Stein & A. La Rue (Eds.), *Enhancing cognitive fitness in adults* (pp. 3–23). New York: Springer.

Dunlosky, J., Mueller, M. L., & Thiede, K. W. (2016). Methodology for investigating human metamemory: Problems and pitfalls. In J. Dunlosky & S. K. Tauber (Eds.), *The Oxford handbook of metamemory* (pp. 23–38). New York: Oxford University Press.

Dunn, T. R., & Merriam, S. B. (1995). Levinson's age thirty transition: Does it exist? *Journal of Adult Development, 2*, 113–124. doi:10.1007/BF02251259

Dupuis, S. (2010). Examining the blended family: The application of systems theory toward an understanding of the blended family system. *Journal of Couple and Relationship Therapy, 9*, 239–251. doi:10.1080/15332691.2 010.491784

Dutta, D., Calvani, R., Bernabei, R., Leeuwenburgh, C., & Marzetti, E. (2012). Contribution of impaired mitochondrial autophagy to cardiac aging: Mechanisms and therapeutic opportunities. *Circulation Research, 110*, 1125–1138. doi:10.1161/CIRCRESAHA.111.246108

Dutton, W. H., Helsper, E. J., Whitty, M. T., Li, N., Buckwalter, J. G., & Lee, E. (2009). The role of the Internet in reconfiguring marriages: A cross-national study. *Interpersona: An International Journal on Personal Relationships, 3*(Suppl. 2). Retrieved from abpri.files.wordpress.com/2010/12/interpersona-3-suppl-2_1.pdf.

Duzel, E., van Praag, H., & Sendtner, M. (2016). Can physical exercise in old age improve memory and hippocampal function? *Brain, 139*. doi:10.1093/brain/awv407. Retrieved from brain.oxfordjournals.org/content/brain/early/2016/02/11/brain.awv407.full.pdf.

Earle, S., Komaromy, C., & Layne, L. (Eds.). (2012). *Understanding reproductive loss: Perspectives on life, death and fertility*. Farnham, UK: Ashgate.

Ebberwein, C. A. (2001). Adaptability and the characteristics necessary for managing adult career transition: A qualitative investigation. *Dissertation Abstracts International. Section B. Sciences and Engineering, 62*(1-B), 545.

Ebner, N. C., Freund, A. M., & Baltes, P. B. (2006). Developmental changes in personal goal orientation from young to late adulthood: From striving for gains to maintenance and prevention of losses. *Psychology and Aging, 21*, 664–678. doi:10.1037/0882-7974.21.4.664

Eddleston, K. A., Baldridge, D. C., & Veiga, J. F. (2004). Toward modeling the predictors of managerial career success: Does gender matter? *Journal of Managerial Psychology, 19*, 360–385. doi:10.1108/02683940410537936

Edelstein, B., & Kalish, K. (1999). Clinical assessment of older adults. In J. C. Cavanaugh & S. K. Whitbourne (Eds.), *Gerontology: An interdisciplinary perspective* (pp. 269–304). New York: Oxford University Press.

Eden Alternative. (2016). *Mission, vision, values, principles*. Retrieved from www.edenalt.org/about-the-eden-alternative/mission-vision-values/.

Edwards, M. R. (2012). A temporal multifaceted adaptation approach to the experiences of employed mothers. *Marriage and Family Review, 48*, 732–768. doi:10.1080/01494929.20 12.700911

Eifert, E. K., Adams, R., Morrison, S., & Strack, R. (2016). Emerging trends in family caregiving using the life course perspective: Preparing health educators for an aging society. *American Journal of Health Education, 47*, 176–197. doi:10.1080/193250 37.2016.1158674

Einstein, G. O., & McDaniel, M. A. (1990). Normal aging and prospective memory. *Journal of Experimental Psychology: Learning, Memory, and Cognition, 16*, 717–726. doi:10.1037/0278-7394.16.4.717

Einstein, G. O., Earles, J. L., & Collins, H. M. (2002). Gaze aversion: Spared inhibition for visual distraction in older adults. *Journals of Gerontology: Psychological Sciences, 57B*, P65–P73. doi:10.1093/geronb/57.1.P65

Eisma, M. C., Schut, H. A. W., Stroebe, M. S., Voerman, K., van den Bout, J., Stroebe, W. et al. (2015). Psychopathology symptoms, rumination and autobiographical memory specificity: Do associations hold after bereavement? *Applied Cognitive Psychology, 29*, 478–484. doi:10.1002/acp.3120

El Haber, N., Erbas, B., Hill, K. D., & Wark, J. D. (2008). Relationship between age and measures of balance, strength, and gait: Linear and non-linear analyses. *Clinical Science, 114*, 719–727. doi:10.1042/ CS20070301

Ellis, J. W. (2010). Yours, mine, ours? Why the Texas legislature should simplify caretaker consent capabilities for minor children and the implications of the addition of Chapter 34 to the Texas Family Code. *Texas Tech Law Review, 42*, 987. Retrieved from papers.ssrn.com/sol3/papers.cfm?abstract_id=1811045.

Elmendorf, D., & Sheiner, L. (2016). *Federal budget policy with an aging population and persistently low interest rates*. Retrieved from www.brookings.edu/wp-content/uploads/2016/07/WP18-Elmendorf-Sheiner_Final-2.pdf.

Elshourbagy, S. A. M. (2017). Use of smart phones to improve the human factors engineering of people suffering from chronic diseases. In T. Z. Ahram & W. Karwowski (Eds.), *Advances in the human side of service engineering* (pp. 81–91). New York: Springer.

Emsell, L., Van Hecke, W., & Tournier, J.-D. (2016). Introduction to diffusion tensor imaging. In W. Van Hecke, L. Emsell, & S. Sunaert (Eds.), *Diffusion tensor imaging* (pp. 7–19). New York: Springer.

Engelberg, A. (2016). Religious Zionist singles: Caught between "family values" and "young adulthood." *Journal for the Scientific Study of Religion, 55*, 349–364. doi:10.1111/jssr.12259

English, T., & Carstensen L. L. (2016). Socioemotional selectivity theory. In N. A Pachana (Ed.), *Encyclopedia of geropsychology*. New York: Springer. doi:10.1007/978-287-080-3_110-1

English, T., & Carstensen, L. L. (2016). Socioemotional selectivity theory. In N. A. Prachana (Ed.), *Encyclopedia of geropsychology*. doi:10.1007/978-981-287-080-3_110-1

Epel, E. (2012). How "reversible" is telomeric aging? *Cancer Prevention Research, 5*, 1163–1168. doi:10.1158/1940-6207.CAPR-12-0370

Equal Employment Opportunity Commission. (2016a). *Sexual harassment*. Retrieved from www.eeoc.gov/laws/types/sexual_harassment.cfm.

Equal Employment Opportunity Commission. (2016b). *Charges alleging sexual harassment FY2010-FY2015*. Retrieved from www.eeoc.gov/eeoc/statistics/enforcement/sexual_harassment_new.cfm.

Equal Employment Opportunity Commission. (2016c). *Age discrimination*. Retrieved from www.eeoc.gov/laws/types/age.cfm.

Equality and Human Rights Commission. (2016). *What is the Equality Act?* Retrieved from www .equalityhumanrights.com/en/equality-act-2010/what-equality-act.

Erber, J. T., & Prager, I. G. (1999). Perceptions of forgetful young and older adults. In T. M. Hess & F. Blanchard-Fields (Eds.), *Social cognition and aging* (pp. 197–217). San Diego, CA: Academic Press.

Erber, J. T., Szuchman, L. T., & Rothberg, S. T. (1990). Everyday memory failure: Age differences in appraisal and attribution. *Psychology and Aging, 5*, 236–241. doi:10.1037/0882-7974.5.2.236

Erickson, K. I., Gildengers, A. G., & Butters, M. A. (2013). Physical activity and brain plasticity in late adulthood. *Dialogues in Clinical Neuroscience, 15*, 99–108. Retrieved from www.ncbi.nlm.nih.gov/pmc/articles/PMC3622473/.

Erickson, K. I., Prakash, R. S., Voss, M. W., Chaddock, L., Hu, L., Morris, K. S. et al. (2009). Aerobic fitness is associated with hippocampal volume in elderly humans. *Hippocampus, 19*, 1030–1039. doi:10.1002/hipo.20547

Ericsson, K. A. (2014). Creative genius: A view from the expert-performance approach. In D. K. Simonton (Ed.), *The Wiley-Blackwell handbook of genius* (pp. 321–349). Oxford, UK: Wiley-Blackwell.

Ericsson, K. A., & Towne, T. J. (2010). Expertise. *Wiley Interdisciplinary Reviews: Cognitive Science, 1*, 404–416. doi:10.1002/wcs.47

Erikson, E. H. (1968). *Identity: Youth and crisis*. New York: Norton.

Erikson, E. H. (1982). *The life cycle completed: Review*. New York: Norton.

Etezadi, S., & Pushkar, D. (2013). Why are wise people happier? An explanatory model of wisdom and emotional well-being in older adults. *Journal of Happiness Studies, 14*, 929–950. doi:10.1007/s10902-012-9362-2

European Association for Palliative Care. (2011). *The EAPC ethics task force on palliative care and euthanasia*. Retrieved from www.eapcnet.eu/Themes/Ethics/PCeuthanasiataskforce/tabid/232/Default.aspx.

Evans, D. G. R., Barwell, J., Eccles, D. M., Collins, A., Izatt, L., Jacobs, C. et al. (2014). The Angelina Jolie effect: How high celebrity profile can have a major impact on provision of cancer related services. *Breast Cancer Research, 16*, 442. doi:10.1186/s13058-014-0442-6. Retrieved from breast-cancer-research.biomedcentral.com/articles/10.1186/s13058-014-0442-6.

Evertsson, M., Grunow, D., & Aisenbrey, S. (2016). Work interruptions and young women's career prospects in Germany, Sweden, and the US. *Work, Employment and Society, 30*, 291–308. doi:10.1177/0950017015598283

Faber, A. J. (2004). Examining remarried couples through a Bowenian family systems lens. *Journal of Divorce & Remarriage, 40*, 121–133. doi:10.1300/J087v40n03_08

Fabius, C. D. (2016). Toward an integration of narrative identity, generativity, and storytelling in African American elders. *Journal of Black Studies, 47*, 423–434. doi:10.1177/0021934716638801

Facal, D., Juncos-Rabadán, O., Rodriguez, M. S., & Pereiro, A. X. (2012). Tip-of-the-tongue in aging: Influence of vocabulary, working memory and processing speed. *Aging Clinical Experimental Research, 24*, 647–656. doi:10.3275/8586

Fairlie, H. (1988). Talkin' bout my generation. *New Republic, 198*, 19–22.

Fajgenbaum, D., Chesson, B., & Lanzl, R. G. (2012). Building a network of grief support on college campuses: A national grassroots initiative. *Journal of College Student Psychotherapy, 26*, 99–120. doi:10.1 080/87568225.2012.659159

Farris, D. N. (2016). *Boomerang kids: The demography of previously launched adults*. New York: Springer.

Fauth, E. B., Zarit, S. H., & Malmberg, B. (2008). Mediating relationships within the Disablement Process model: A cross-sectional study of the oldest-old. *European Journal of Aging, 5,* 161–179. doi:10.1007/ s10433–008–0092-6

Federal Interagency Forum on Aging Related Statistics. (2016). *Older Americans 2016: Key indicators of well-being.* Retrieved from agingstats.gov/docs/LatestReport/OA2016.pdf.

Fein, E., & Schneider, S. (2013). *Not your mother's rules: the new secrets for dating.* New York: Grand Central Publishing.

Feldman, K. (2010). *Post parenthood redefined: Race, class, and family structure differences in the experience of launching children.* Doctoral dissertation completed at Case Western Reserve University. Retrieved from etd.ohiolink.edu/pg_10?0::NO:10:P10_ACCESSION_NUM:case1267730564.

Felix, E., De Haan, H., Vaandrager, L., & Koelen, M. (2015). Beyond thresholds: The everyday lived experience of the house by older people. *Journal of Housing for the Elderly, 29,* 329–347. doi:10.1080/0 27633893.2015.1055027

Feltz, A. (2015). Everyday attitudes about euthanasia and the slippery slope argument. In M. Cholbi & J. Varelius (Eds.), *New directions in the ethics of assisted suicide and euthanasia* (pp. 217–237). New York: Springer. doi:10.1007/978-3-319-22050-55_13

Femia, E. E., Zarit, S. H., & Johansson, B. (2001). The disablement process in very late life: A study of the oldest-old in Sweden. *Journals of Gerontology: Psychological Sciences,* 56B, P12–P23. doi:10.1093/geronb/56.1.P12

Feng, X., & Astell-Burt, T. (2016). What types of social interactions reduce the risk of psychological distress? Fixed effects longitudinal analysis of a cohort of 30,271 middle-to-older Australians. *Journal of Affective Disorders, 204,* 99–102. doi:10.1016/j.jad.2016.06.041

Fernández-Alcántara, M., Cruz-Quintana, Pérez-Marfil, M. N., Catena-Martinez, A., Pérez-Garcia, M., & Turnbull, O. H. (2016). Assessment of emotional and emotional recognition in complicated grief. *Frontiers in Psychology, 7.* doi:10.3389/fpsyg.2016.00126. Retrieved from www.ncbi.nlm.nih.gov/pmc/articles/PMC4751347/.

Ferrarini, T., & Norström, T. (2010). Family policy, economic development, and infant mortality: A longitudinal comparative analysis. *International Journal of Social Welfare, 19,* S89–S102. doi:10.1111/j.1468–2397.2010.00736.x

Field, M. J., & Cassel, C. K. (2010). Approaching death: Improving care at the end of life. In D. Meier, S. L. Isaacs, & R. G. Hughes (Eds.), *Palliative care: Transforming the care of serious illness* (pp. 79–91). San Francisco, CA: Jossey-Bass.

Fields, N. L., & Dabelko-Schoeny, H. (2016). Aging in place. In S. K. Whitbourne (Ed.), *Encyclopedia of adulthood and aging* (Vol. 1, pp. 51–55). Malden, MA: Wiley-Blackwell. doi:10.1002/9781118521373.wbeaa106

Fincham, F. D., & Beach, S. R. H. (2010). Marriage in the new millennium: A decade in review. *Journal of Marriage and Family, 72,* 630–649. doi:10.1111/j.1741-3737.2010.00722.x

Fingerman, K. L., Pillemer, K. A., Silverstein, M., & Suitor, J. J. (2012). The baby boomers' intergenerational relationships. *The Gerontologist, 52,* 199–209. doi:10.1093/geront/gnr139

Finkbeiner, N. W. B., Max, J. E., Longman, S., & Debert, C. (2016). Knowing what we don't know: Long-term psychiatric outcomes following adult concussion in sports. *The Canadian Journal of Psychiatry, 61,* 27–276. doi:10.1177/0706743716644953

Finucane, I. E. (2016). Social and ethical issues in home-based medical care. In J. L. Hayashi &

B. Leff (Eds.), *Geriatric home-based medical care* (pp. 237–249). New York: Springer. doi:10.1007/978-3-319-23365-9_11

Fiori, K. L., & Denckla, C. A. (2015). Friendship and happiness among middle-aged adults. In M. Demir (Ed.), *Friendship and happiness* (pp. 137–154). New York: Springer.

Fischer-Shofty, M., Levkovitz, Y., & Shamay-Tsoory, S. G. (2013). Oxytocin facilitates accurate perception of competition in men and kinship in women. *Social Cognitive and Affective Neuroscience.* doi:10.1093/scan/nsr100

Fiske, S. T., & Taylor, S. E. (2013). *Social cognition: From brains to culture* (2nd ed.). Thousand Oaks, CA: Sage Publications.

Fitzgerald, J. M. (1999) Autobiographical memory and social cognition: Development of the remembered self in adulthood. In T. M. Hess & F. Blanchard-Fields, *Social cognition in aging* (pp. 147–171). San Diego, CA: Academic Press.

Fitzwater, E. L. (2008). *Older adults and mental health: Part 2: Anxiety disorder.* Retrieved from www.netwellness.org/healthtopics/aging/anxietydisorder.cfm.

Fjell, A. M., Sneve, M. H., Grydeland, H., Storsve, A. B., & Walhovd, K. B. (2017). The disconnected brain and executive function decline in aging. *Cerebral Cortex, 27,* 2303–2317. doi:10.1093/cercor?bhw082

Flynn, E., Pine, K., & Lewis, C. (2006). The microgenetic method: Time for change? *The Psychologist, 19,* 152–155. Retrieved from www.thepsychologist.org.uk/archive/archive_home.cfm/volumeID_19-editionID_133-ArticleID_997-getfile_getPDF/thepsychologist/0306flyn.pdf.

Fogarty, K., & Evans, G. D. (2010). Being an involved father: What does it mean? Retrieved from edis.ifas.ufl.edu/he141.

Ford, J. H., Morris, J. A., & Kensinger, E. A. (2014). Neural recruitment and connectivity during emotional memory retrieval across the adult life span. *Neurobiology of Aging, 35,* 2770–2784. doi:10.1016/j.neurobiolaging.2014.05.029

Formosa, M. (2014). Four decades of universities of the Third Age: Past, present, future. *Ageing and Society, 34,* 42–66. doi:10.1017/S0144686X12000797

Fossati, P. (2012). Neural correlates of emotion processing: From emotional to social brain. *European Neuropsychopharmacology, 22* (Suppl. 3), S487–S491. doi:10.1016/j. euroneuro.2012.07.008

Foster, B. P., Lonial, S., & Shastri, T. (2011). Mentoring, career plateau tendencies, turnover intentions and implications for narrowing pay and position gaps due to gender—Structural equations modeling. *Journal of Applied Business Research, 27,* 71–84. Retrieved from www.journals.cluteonline.com/index.php/JABR/article/view/6467/6545.

Fouad, N. A. (2007). Work and vocational psychology: Theory, research, and applications. *Annual Review of Psychology, 58,* 543–564. doi:10.1146/annurev.psyc.58.110405.085713

Fouad, N., Ghosh, A., Chang, W.-h., Figueiredo, C., & Bachhuber, T. (2016). Career exploration among college students. *Journal of College Student Development, 57,* 460–464. doi:10.1353/csd.2016.0047

Fowler, L. R. (2008). "The wholeness of things": Infusing diversity and social justice into death education. *Omega: Journal of Death and Dying, 57,* 53–91. doi:10.2190/OM.57.1.d

Franceschi, K. A. (2005). The experience of the transition to motherhood in women who have suffered maternal loss in adolescence. *Dissertation Abstracts International: Section B: The Sciences and Engineering,* 65(8-B), 4282.

Frank, D. J., Jordano, M. L., Browne, K., & Touron, D. R. (2016). Older adults' use of retrieval strategies

in everyday life. *Gerontology, 62,* 624–635. doi:10.1159/000446277

Frank, M. G., Weber, M. D., Watkins, L. R., & Maier, S. F. (2016). Stress-induced neuroinflammatory priming: A liability factor in the etiology of psychiatric disorders. *Neurobiology of Stress, 66,* 82–90. doi:10.1016/j.ynstr.2015.12.004

Frank, N. (2016). Moving beyond anti-LGBT politics: Commentary on "Same-sex parent households and different-sex parent households and child health outcomes: Findings from the National Survey of Children's Health." *Journal of Developmental & Behavioral Pediatrics, 37,* 245–247. doi:10.1097/DBP.0000000000000295

Franses, P. H. (2016). When did classic composers make their best work? *Creativity Research Journal, 28,* 219–221. doi:10.1080/10400419.2016.1162489

Frase, P., & Gornick, J. C. (2013). The time divide in cross-national perspective: The work week, education and institutions that matter. *Social Forces, 91,* 697–724. doi:10.1093/sf/sos189

Frazier, L. D., Hooker, K., Johnson, P. M., & Kaus, C. R. (2000). Continuity and change in possible selves in later life: A 5-year longitudinal study. *Basic and Applied Social Psychology, 22,* 237–243. doi:10.1207/S15324834BASP2203_10

Frazier, L. D., Johnson, P. M., Gonzalez, G. K., & Kafka, C. L. (2002) Psychosocial influences on possible selves: A comparison of three cohorts of older adults. *International Journal of Behavioral Development, 26,* 308–317. doi:10.1080/01650250143000184

Freitas, A. A., & de Magalhães, J. P. (2011). A review and appraisal of the DNA damage theory of aging. *Mutation Research/Reviews in Mutation Research, 728,* 12–22. doi:10.1016/j.mrrev.2011.06.01

Freund, A. M., & Ritter, J. O. (2009). Midlife crisis: A debate. *Gerontology, 55,* 582–591. doi:10.1159/000227322

Fried, L. P., & Ferrucci, L. (2016). Etiological role of aging in chronic diseases: From epidemiological evidence to the new geroscience. In F. Sierra & R. Kohanski (Eds.), *Advances in geroscience* (pp. 37–51). New York: Springer.

Friedman, E. M., & Seltzer, J. A. (2010). *Providing for older parents: Is it a family affair?* California Center for Population Research paper #PWP-CCPR-2010-12. Retrieved from papers.ccpr.ucla.edu/papers/PWP-CCPR-2010-012/PWP-CCPR-2010-012.pdf.

Friedman, M. C., McGillivray, S., Murayama, K., & Castel, A. D. (2015). Memory for medication side effects in younger and older adults: The role of subjective and objective importance. *Cognitive Psychology, 43,* 206–215. doi:10.3758/s13421-014-0476-0

Friesen, M. D., Horwood, L. J., Fergusson, D. M., & Woodward, L. J. (2017). Exposure to parental separation in childhood and later parenting quality as an adult: Evidence from a 30-year longitudinal study. *Journal of Child Psychology and Psychiatry, 58,* 30–37. doi:10.1111/jcpp.12610

Friesen, S., Brémault-Phillips, S., Rudrum, L., & Rogers, L. G. (2016). Environmental design that supports health aging: Evaluating a new supportive living facility. *Journal of Housing for the Elderly, 30,* 18–34. doi:10.1080/02763893.2015 .1129380

Frith, C. D., & Frith, U. (2012). Mechanisms of social cognition. *Annual Review of Social Cognition, 63,* 287–313. doi:10.1146/annurevpsych-120710-100449

Froehlich, D. E., Beausaert, S., & Segers, M. (2016). Aging and the motivation to stay employable. *Journal of Managerial Psychology, 31,* 756–770. doi:10.1108/JMP-08-2014-0224

Fruhauf, C. A. (2007). Grandchildren's perceptions of caring for grandparents. *Dissertation Abstracts*

International. Section A. Humanities and Social Sciences, 68(3-A), 1120.

Fuentes, A., & Desrocher, M. (2012). Autobiographical memory in emerging adulthood: Relationship with self-concept clarity. *Journal of Adult Development, 19,* 28–39. doi:10.1007/s10804-011-9131-1

Gallagher-Thompson, D., Coon, D. W., Solano, N., Ambler, C., Rabinowitz, Y., & Thompson, L. W. (2003). Change in indices of distress among Latino and Anglo female caregivers of elderly relatives with dementia: Site-specific results from the REACH national collaborative study. *The Gerontologist, 43,* 580–591. doi:10.1093/geront/43.4.580

Gallen, C. L., Turner, G. R., Adnan, A., & D'Esposito, M. (2016). Reconfiguration of brain network architecture to support executive control in aging. *Neurobiology of Aging, 44,* 42–52. doi:10.1016/j.neurobiolaging.2016.04.003

Gamaldo, A. A., & Allaire, J. C. (2016). Daily fluctuations in everyday cognition: Is it meaningful? *Journal of Aging and Health, 28,* 834–849. doi:10.1177/0898264315611669

Gamba, F. (2015). *The digital age of grieving rituals: Mobility and the hybridization of memory. A project.* Retrieved from wp.lancs.ac.uk/futures-of-the-end-of-life/files/2015/11/Fiorenza-Gamba.pdf.

Gamble, W. C., Ramakumar, S., & Diaz, A. (2007). Maternal and paternal similarities and differences in parenting: An examination of Mexican-American parents of young children. *Early Childhood Research Quarterly, 22,* 72–88. doi:10.1016/j.ecresq.2006.11.004

Gandy, S., & DeKosky, S. T. (2013). Toward the treatment and prevention of Alzheimer's disease: Rational strategies and recent progress. *Annual Review of Medicine, 64,* 367–383. doi:10.1146/annurevmed-092611-084441

Ganong, L., & Coleman, M. (2017). *Stepfamily relationships: Development, dynamics, and interventions* (2nd ed.). New York: Springer.

Gans, D. (2007). Normative obligations and parental care in social context. *Dissertation Abstracts International. Section A. Humanities and Social Sciences, 68*(5-A), 2115.

Garcia, J. R., Reiber, C., Massey, S. G., & Merriwether, A. M. (2013). Sexual hook-up culture. *Monitor on Psychology, 44,* 60–67.

Gardiner, P. A., Mishra, G. D., & Dobson, A. J. (2016). The effect of socioeconomic status across adulthood on trajectories of frailty in older women. *Journal of the American Medical Directors Association, 17,* 372.e1-372.e3. doi:10.1016/j.jamda.2015.12.090

Garrard, E., & Wilkinson, S. (2005). Passive euthanasia. *Journal of Medical Ethics, 31,* 64–68. doi:10.1136/jme.2003.005777

Garrido, M. M., Prigerson, H. G., Bao, Y., & Maciejewski, P. K. (2016). Chemotherapy use in the months before death and estimated costs of care in the last week of life. *Journal of Pain and Symptom Management, 51,* 875–881. doi:10.1016/j.painsymman.2015.12.323

Gatz, M., Smyer, M. A., & DiGilio, D. A. (2016). Psychology's contribution to the well-being of older Americans. *American Psychologist, 71,* 257–267. doi:10.1037/a0040251

Gaudron, J.-P., & Vautier, S. (2007). Analyzing individual differences in vocational, leisure, and family interests: A multitrait-multimethod approach. *Journal of Vocational Behavior, 70,* 561–573. doi:10.1016/j.jvb.2007.01.004

Gay Men's Health Crisis. (2010). *Growing older with the epidemic: HIV and aging.* Retrieved from www.gmhc.org/files/editor/file/a_pa_aging10_emb2.pdf.

Genworth Financial. (2016). *Compare long term care costs across the United States.* Retrieved from www.genworth.com/corporate/about-genworth/industry-expertise/cost-of-care.html.

Gerontological Society of America. (2012). *Communicating with older adults: An evidence-based review of what really works.* Washington, DC: Author.

Gervais, S. J., Wiener, R. L., Allen, J., Farnum, K. S., & Kimble, K. (2016). Do you see what I see? The consequences of objectification in work settings for experiencers and third party predictors. *Analyses of Social Issues and Public Policy, 16,* 143–174. doi:10.1111/asap.12118

Ghanim, D. (2015). *The virginity trap in the Middle East.* New York: Springer.

Ghosh, S., Capistrant, B., & Friedemann-Sánchez, G. (2017). Who will care for the elder caregiver? Outlining theoretical approaches and future research questions. In T. Samanta (Ed.), *Cross-cultural and cross-disciplinary perspectives in social gerontology* (pp. 23–43). New York: Springer.

Gibbs, N. R. (1988). Grays on the go. *Time, 131* (8), 66–75.

Gibran, K. (1923). *The prophet.* New York: Knopf.

Giele, J. Z. (2013). *Family policy and the American safety net.* Thousand Oaks, CA: Sage Publications.

Gilbert, D. T., & Malone, P. S. (1995). The correspondence bias. *Psychological Bulletin, 117,* 21–38. doi:10.1037/0033-2909.117.1.21

Gill, D. P., Hubbard, R. A., Koepsell, T. D., Borrie, M. J., Petrella, R. J., Knopman, D. S. et al. (2013). Differences in rate of functional decline across three dementia types. *Alzheimer's & Dementia, 9 (Supplement),* S63–S71. doi:10.1016/j.jalz.2012.10.010

Gillick, M. R. (2012). Doing the right thing: A geriatrician's perspective on medical care for the person with advanced dementia. *The Journal of Law, Medicine and Ethics, 40,* 51–56. doi:10.1111/j.1748-720X.2012.00645.x

Gilliver, M., Carter, L., Macoun, D., Rosen, J., & Williams, W. (2012). Music to whose ears? The effect of social norms on young people's risk perceptions of hearing damage resulting from their music listening behavior. *Noise and Health, 14,* 47–51. Retrieved from www.noiseandhealth.org/article.asp?issn=1463-1741;year=2012;volume=14;issue=57;spage=47;epage=51;aulast=Gilliver.

Giordano, P. C., Copp, J. E., Longmore, M. A., & Manning, W. D. (2016). Anger, control, and intimate partner violence in young adulthood. *Journal of Family Violence, 31,* 1–13. doi:10.1007/s10896-015-9753-3

Giordano, P. C., Manning, W. D., Longmore, M. A., & Flanigan, C. M. (2012). Developmental shifts in the character of romantic and sexual relationships from adolescence to young adulthood. In A. Booth, S. L. Brown, N. S. Landale, W. D. Manning, & S. M. McHale (Eds.), *Early adulthood in a family context* (pp. 133–164). New York: Springer.

Giovanello, K. S., & Schacter, D. L. (2012). Reduced specificity of hippocampal and posterior ventrolateral prefrontal activity during relational retrieval in normal aging. *Journal of Cognitive Neuroscience, 24,* 159–170. doi:10.1162/jocn_a_00113

Gire, J. (2014). How death imitates life: Cultural influences on conceptions of death and dying. *Online Readings in Psychology and Culture, 6*(2). doi:10.9707/2307-0919.1120

Gitlin, L. N., Parisi, J., Huang, J., Winter, L., & Roth, D. L. (2016). Attachment to life: Psychometric analyses of the Valuation of Life Scale and differences among adults. *The gerontologist, 56,* e21-e31. doi:10.1093/geront/gnv696

Givertz, M., Segrin, C., & Hansal, A. (2009). The association between satisfaction and commitment differs across marital couple types. *Communication Research, 36,* 561–584. doi:10.1177/0093650209333035

Gladwell, M. (2008). *Outliers: The story of success.* New York: Little, Brown.

Glass, B. D., & Osman, M. (2017). Positive explorers: Modeling dynamic control in normal aging. *Aging, Neuropsychology, and Cognition: A Journal on Normal and Dysfunctional Development, 24,* 62–79. doi:10.1080/13825585.2016.1171290

Glasser, M. F., Coalson, T. S., Robinson, E. C., Hacker, C. D., Harwell, J., Yacoub, E. et al. (2016). A multi-modal parcellation of human cerebral cortex. *Nature, 536,* 171–178. doi:10.1038/nature18933

Godfrey, D. (2016). End-of-life issues for LGBT elders. In D. A. Harley & P. B. Teaster (Eds.), *Handbook of LGBT elders* (pp. 439–454). New York: Springer.

Godyn, J., Jonczyk, J., Panek, D., & Malawska, B. (2016). Therapeutic strategies for Alzheimers disease in clinical trials. *Pharmacological Reports, 68,* 127–138. doi:10.1016/j.pharep.2015.07.006

Golant, S. M. (2008). Affordable clustered housing-care: A category of long-term care options for the elderly poor. *Journal of Housing for the Elderly, 22,* 3–44. doi:10.1080/02763890802096906

Golant, S. M. (2012). Out of their residential comfort and mastery zones: toward a more relevant environmental gerontology. *Journal of Housing for the Elderly, 26,* 26–43. doi:10.1080/02763893.2012.655654

Gold, J. M. (2016). *Stepping in, stepping out: Creating stepfamily rhythm.* Alexandria, VA: American Counseling Association.

Goldstein, E. G. (2005). *When the bubble bursts: Clinical perspectives on midlife issues.* New York: Routledge.

Goleman, D. (1995). *Emotional intelligence.* New York: Bantam Books.

Golkar, A., Johansson, E., Kasahara, M., Osika, W., Perski, A., & Savic, I. (2014). The influence of work-related chronic stress on the regulation of emotion and on functional connectivity in the brain. *PLOS ONE 9:* e104550. doi:10.1371/journal.pone.0104550

Gonyea, J. G. (2013). Midlife, multigenerational bonds, and caregiving. In R. C. Talley & R. J. V. Montgomery (Eds.), *Caregiving across the lifespan* (pp. 105–130). New York: Springer.

Gonza, G., & Burger, A. (in press). Subjective well-being during the 2008 economic crisis: Identification of mediating and moderating factors. *Journal of Happiness Studies.* doi:10.1007/s10902-016-9797-y

Goodheart, C. D., Kazdin, A. E., & Sternberg, R. J. (Eds.). (2006). *Evidence-based psychotherapy: Where practice and research meet.* Washington, DC: American Psychological Association.

Goodsell, T. L. (2013). Familification: Family, neighborhood change, and housing policy. *Housing Studies, 28,* 845–868. doi:10.1080/02673037.2013.768334

Gordijn, B., & Have, H. (2016). Technology and dementia. *Medicine, Health Care and Philosophy, 19,* 339–340. doi:10.1007/s11019-016-9715-4

Gordon, T. A. (2013). Good grief: Exploring the dimensionality of grief experiences and social work support. *Journal of Social Work in End-of-Life and Palliative Care, 9,* 27–42. doi:10.1080/15524256.2012.758607

Gostin, L. O., & Roberts, A. E. (2016). Physician-assisted dying: A turning point? *JAMA, 315*(3), 249250. doi:10.1001/jama.2015.16586

Gottman, J. M., & Levenson, R. W. (2000). The timing of divorce: Predicting when a couple will divorce over a 14-year period. *Journal of Marriage and the Family, 62,* 737–745. doi:10.1111/j.1741-3737.2000.00737.x

Gottman, J. M., & Silver, N. (2015). *The seven principles for making marriage work* (Rev. ed) New York: Harmony Books.

Gould, C. E., Edelstein, B. A., & Gerolimatos, L. A. (2012). Assessment of older adults. In S.

K. Whitbourne & M. J. Sliwinski (Eds.), *The Wiley-Blackwell handbook of adulthood and aging* (pp. 331–354). Oxford, UK: Wiley-Blackwell. doi: 10.1002/9781118392966.ch17

Gould, S. J. (1999). A critique of Heckhausen and Schulz's (1995) life-span theory of control from a cross-cultural perspective. *Psychological Review, 106*, 597–604. doi: 10.1037/033-295X.106.3.597

Grabowski, D. C., Afendulis, C. C., Caudry, D. J., O'Malley, A. J., Kemper, P., & THRIVE Research Collaborative. (2016). The impact of Green House adoption on Medicare spending and utilization. *Health Services Research, 51*, 433–453. doi:10.1111/1475-6773.12438

Grady, C. (2012). The cognitive neuroscience of ageing. *Nature Reviews Neuroscience, 13*, 491–505. doi: 10.1038/nrn3256

Grady, C. L., Luk, G., Craik, F. I. M., & Bialystok, E. (2015). Brain network activity in monolingual and bilingual older adults. *Neuropsychologia, 66*, 170–181. doi:10.1016/j.neuropsychologia.2014.10.042

Grady, C., Sarral, S., Saverino, C., & Campbell, K. (2016). Age differences in the functional interactions among the default, frontoparietal control, and dorsal attention networks. *Neurobiology of Aging, 41*, 159–172. doi:10.1016/j.neurobiolaging.2016.02.020

Graham, E. K., & Lachman, M. E. (2012). Personality and aging. In S. K. Whitbourne & M. J. Sliwinski (Eds.), *The Wiley-Blackwell handbook of adulthood and aging* (pp. 254–272). Oxford, UK: Wiley-Blackwell.

Granacher, U., Muehlbauer, T., & Gruber, M. (2012). A qualitative review of balance and strength performance in healthy older adults: Impact for testing and training. *Journal of Aging Research*, 2012. doi:10.1155/2012/708905. Retrieved from www.hindawi.com/journals/jar/2012/708905/.

Granbom, M., Slaug, B., Löfqvist, C., Oswald, F., & Iwarsson, S. (2016). Community relocation in very old age: Changes in housing accessibility. *American Journal of Occupational Therapy, 70*, 7002270020p1-7002270020p9. doi:10.5014/ajot.2016.016147

Grawitch, M. J., Barber, L. K., & Justice, L. (2010). Rethinking the work-life interface: It's not about balance, it's about resource allocation. *Health and Well-Being, 2*, 127–159. doi:10.1111/j.1758-0854.2009.01023.x

Greenberg, D. L. (2004). President Bush's false [flashbulb] memory of 9/11/01. *Applied Cognitive Psychology, 18*, 363–370. doi:10.1002/acp.1016

Greenfield, E. A., & Marks, N. F. (2005). Formal volunteering as a protective factor for older adults' psychological well-being. *Journals of Gerontology: Social Sciences, 59*, S258–S264. doi:10.1093/geronb/59.5.S258

Greenlund, K. J., Liu, Y., Deokar, A. J., Wheaton, A. G., & Croft, J. B. (2016). Association of chronic obstructive pulmonary disease with increased confusion or memory loss and functional limitations among adults in 21 states, 2011 Behavioral Risk Factor Surveillance System. *Preventing Chronic Disease, 13*, E02. doi:10.5888/pcd13.150428 Retrieved from www.ncbi.nlm.nih.gov/pmc/articles/PMC4708003/.

Greer, D. M., Want, H. H., Robinson, J. D., Varelas, P. N., Henderson, G. V., & Wijdicks, E. F. M. (2016). Variability of brain death policies in the United States. *JAMA Neurology, 73*, 213–218. doi:10.1001/jamaneurol.2015.3943

Gretebeck, R. J., Ferraro, K. F., Black, D. R., Holland, K., & Gretebeck, K. A. (2012). Longitudinal change in physical activity and disability in adults. *American Journal of Health Behavior, 36*, 385–394. doi:10.5993/AJHB.36.3.9

Greving, K. A. (2007). Examining parents' marital satisfaction trajectories: Relations with children's temperament and family demographics. *Dissertation Abstracts International. Section A. Humanities and Social Sciences, 68*(4-A), 1676.

Grey, R. (1756). *Memoria technica* (4th ed.). London: Hinton.

Griffin, M. L., Hogan, N. L., Lambert, E. G., Tucker-Gail, K. A., & Baker, D. N. (2010). Job involvement, job stress, job satisfaction, and organizational commitment and the burnout of correctional staff. *Criminal Justice and Behavior, 37*, 239–255. doi: 10.1177/0093854809351682

Groger, L. (1995). A nursing home can be a home. *Journal of Aging Studies, 9*, 137–153. doi:10.1016/0890-4065(95)90008-X

Groger, L. (2002). Coming to terms: African-Americans' complex ways of coping with life in a nursing home. *The International Journal of Aging and Human Development, 55*, 183–205. doi:10.2190/MDLP-UDE7-P376-QXE3

Groome, D. (2016). Everyday memory. In D. Groome & M. W. Eysenck (Eds.), *An introduction to applied cognitive psychology* (2nd ed., pp. 153–173). New York: Routledge.

Grossman, I., Karasawa, M., Izumi, S., Na, J., Varnum, M. E. W., Kitayama, S. et al. (2012). Aging and wisdom: Culture matters. *Psychological Science, 23*, 1059–1066. doi: 10.1177/0956797612446025

Groth-Marnat, G., & Wright, A. J. (2016). *Handbook of psychological assessment* (6th ed.). Hoboken, NJ: Wiley.

Gruenewald, T. L., Liao, D. H., & Seeman, T. E. (2012). Contributing to others, contributing to oneself: Perceptions of generativity and health in later life. *Journal of Gerontology: Psychological Sciences, 67*, 660–665. doi:10.1093/geronb/gbs034

Grühn, D., Lumley, M. A., Diehl, M., Labouvie-Vief, G. (2013). Time-based indicators of emotional complexity: Interrelations and correlates. *Emotion, 13*, 226–237. doi:10.1037/a0030363

Gu, X., Liu, X., Van Dam, N. T., Hof, P. R., & Fan, J. (2013). Cognition-emotion integration in the anterior insular cortex. *Cerebral Cortex, 23*, 20–27. doi:10.1093/cercor/bhr367

Gubernskaya, Z. (2010). Changing attitudes toward marriage and children in six countries. *Sociological Perspectives, 53*, 179–200. doi:10.1525/sop.2010.53.2.179

Guergova, S., & Dufour, A. (2011). Thermal sensitivity in the elderly: A review. *Ageing Research Reviews, 10*, 80–92. doi:10.1016/j.arr.2010.04.009

Guilford, J. P. (1959). *Personality*. New York: McGraw-Hill.

Gunes, S., Hekim, G. N. T., Arslan, M. A., & Asci, R. (2016). Effects of aging on the male reproductive system. *Journal of Assisted Reproduction and Genetics, 33*, 441–454. doi:10.1007/s10815-016-0663-y

Gunnell, D., & Chang, S.-S. (2016). Economic recession, unemployment, and suicide. In R. C. O'Connor & J. Pirkis (Eds.), *The international handbook of suicide prevention* (2nd ed., pp. 284–300). Malden, MA: Wiley.

Haber, D. (2013). *Health promotion and aging: Practical applications for health professionals* (6th ed.). New York: Springer.

Habes, M., Erus, G., Toledo, J. B., Zhang, T., Bryan, N., Launer, L. J. et al. (2016). White matter hyperintensities and imaging patterns of brain ageing in the general population. *Brain: A Journal of Neurology, 139*, 1164–1179. doi:10.1093/brain/aww008

Haier, R. J., Schroeder, D. H., Tang, C., Head, K., & Colom, R. (2010). Gray matter correlates of cognitive ability tests used for vocational guidance. *BMC Research Notes, 3*. Retrieved from www.biomedcentral.com/1756-0500/3/206.

Hains, C.-A. M., & Hulbert-Williams, N. J. (2013). Attitudes toward euthanasia and physician-assisted suicide: A study of the multivariate effects of healthcare training, patient characteristics, religion and locus of control. *Journal of Medical Ethics, 39*, 713–716. doi:10.1136/medethics-2012-100729

Håkansson, P., & Witmer, H. (2015). Social media and trust: A systematic literature review. *Journal of Business and Economics, 6*, 517–524. doi:10.15341/jbe(2155-7950)/03.06.2015/010

Hales, S. (2016). Attachment and the end of life experience. In J. Hunter & R. Maunder (Eds.), *Improving patient treatment with attachment theory* (pp. 93–103). New York: Springer. doi:10.1007/978-3-319-233000-0_7

Haley, W. E. (2013). Family caregiving at the end-of-life: Current status and future directions. In R. C. Talley & R. J. V Montgomery (Eds.), *Caregiving across the lifespan* (pp. 157–175). New York: Springer.

Hall, J. A. (2016). Same-sex friendships. In C. R. Berger, M. E. Roloff, S. R. Wilson, J. P. Dillard, J. Caughlin, & D. Solomon (Eds), *The international encyclopedia of interpersonal communication*. New York: Wiley. doi:10.1002/9781118540190.wbeic138

Hall, S. S. (2006). Marital meaning: Exploring young adult's belief systems about marriage. *Journal of Family Issues, 27*, 1437–1458. doi:10.1177/0192513X06290036.

Hambrick, D. Z., Macnamara, B. N., Campitelli, G., Ullén, F., & Mosing, M. A. (2016). Chapter One—Beyond born versus made: A new look at expertise. *Psychology of Learning and Motivation, 64*, 1–55. doi:10.1016/bs.plm.2015.09.001

Hamilton, R. K. B., Hiatt Racer, K., & Newman, J. P. (2015). Impaired integration in psychopathology: A unified theory of psychopathic dysfunction. *Psychological Review, 122*, 770–791. doi:10.1037/a0039703

Hammar, M., & Östgren, C. J. (2013). Healthy aging and age-adjusted nutrition and physical fitness. *Best Practices and Research Clinical Obstetrics and Gynaecology, 27*, 741–752. doi:10.1016/j.bpobgyn.2013.01.004

Hampstead, B. M., Khoshnoodi, M., Yan, W., Deshpande, G., & Sathian, K. (2016). Patterns of effective connectivity during memory encoding and retrieval differ between patients with mild cognitive impairment and healthy older adults. *NeuroImage, 124 (Part A)*, 997–1008. doi:10.1016/j.neuroimage.2015.10.002

Hansen, S. R. (2006). Courtship duration as a correlate of marital satisfaction and stability. *Dissertation Abstracts International: Section B: The Sciences and Engineering, 67*(4-B4-B), 2279.

Hareven, T. K. (2001). Historical perspectives on aging and family relations. In R. H. Binstock & L. K. George (Eds.), *Handbook of aging and the social sciences* (5th ed., pp. 141–159). San Diego, CA: Academic Press.

Harley, D. A., Gassaway, L., & Dunkley, L. (2016). Isolation, socialization, recreation, and inclusion of LGBT elders. In D. A. Harley & P. B. Teaster (Eds.), *Handbook of LGBT elders* (pp. 563–581). New York: Springer.

Harrington, K. J. (2016). The biology of cancer. *Medicine, 44*, 1–5. doi:10.1016/j.mpmed.2015.10.005. Retrieved from www.medicinejournal.co.uk/article/S1357-3039(15)00270-4/pdf.

Harris, D. L. (2016). Social expectations of the bereaved. In D. L. Harris & T. C. Bordere (Eds.), *Handbook of social justice in loss and grief: Exploring diversity, equity, and inclusion* (pp. 165–174). New York: Routledge.

Harris, R. L., Ellicott, A. M., & Holmes, D. S. (1986). The timing of psychosocial transitions and changes in women's lives: An examination of women aged 45 to 60. *Journal of Personality and Social Psychology, 51*, 409–416. doi:10.1037/0022-3514.51.2.409

Harry, B. B., Umla-Runge, K., Lawrence, A. D., Graham, K. S., & Downing, P. E. (2016). Evidence for integrated visual face and body representations in the anterior temporal lobes. *Journal of Cognitive Neuroscience, 28*, 1178–1193. doi:10.1162/jocn_a_00966

Hart, W., Adams, J., & Tullett, A. (2016). "It's complicated"—Sex differences in perceptions of cross-sex friendships. *Journal of Social Psychology, 156*, 190–201. doi:10.1080/00224545.2015.1076762

Hartung, P. J., & Santilli, S. (2017). The theory and practice of career construction. In M. McMahon (Ed.), *Career counselling: Constructivist approaches* (2nd ed., pp. 174–184). Abingdon, UK: Routledge.

Haslam, C., Hodder, K. I., & Yates, P. J. (2011). Errorless learning and spaced retrieval: How do these methods fare in healthy and clinical populations? *Journal of Clinical and Experimental Neuropsychology, 33*, 1–16. doi:10.1080/13803395.2010.533155

Havaldar, R., Pilli, S. C., & Putti, B. B. (2012). Effects of ageing on bone mineral composition and bone strength. *IOSR Journal of Dental and Medical Sciences, 1*, 12–16. Retrieved from iosrjournals.org/iosr-jdms/papers/vol1-issue3/C0131216.pdf.

Haworth, J., & Lewis, S. (2005). Work, leisure and well-being. *British Journal of Guidance & Counselling, 33*, 67–78. doi:10.1080/03069880412 331335902

Hawton, K., Casañas i Comabella, C., Haw, C., & Saunders, K. (2013). Risk factors for suicide in individuals with depression: A systematic review. *Journal of Affective Disorders, 147*, 17–28. doi:10.1016/j.jad.2013.01.004

Hayakawa, T., McGarrigle, C. A., Coen, R. F., Soraghan, C. J., Foran, T., Lawlor, B. A. et al. (2015). Orthostatic blood pressure behavior in people with mild cognitive impairment predicts conversion to dementia. *Journal of the American Geriatrics Society, 63*, 1868–1873. doi:10.1111/jgs.13596

Hayflick, L. (1996). *How and why we age* (2nd ed.). New York: Ballantine.

Hayflick, L. (1998). How and why we age. *Experimental Gerontology, 33*, 639–653. doi:10.1016/jS0531-5565(98)00023-0

Hayslip Jr, B., & Blumenthal, H. (2016). Grandparenthood: A developmental perspective. In M. H. Meyer & E. A. Daniele (Eds.), *Gerontology: Changes, challenges, and solutions* (Vol. 1, pp. 271–298). Santa Barbara, CA: Praeger.

Hayslip, B., & Cooper, A. M. (2012). Subjective and objective intellectual change in older adults. *Educational Gerontology, 38*, 190–200. doi:10.1080/03601277.2010.532069

Hayslip, B., Jr., Caballero, D., Ward-Pinson, M., & Riddle, R. R. (2013). Sensitizing young adults to their biases about middle-aged and older persons: A pedagogical approach. *Educational Gerontology, 39*, 37–44. doi:10.1080/03601277.2012.660865

Hayslip, B., Jr., Davis, S. R., Neumann, C. S., Goodman, C., Smith, G. C., Maiden, R. J. et al. (2013). The role of resilience in mediating stressoroutcome relationships among grandparents raising their grandchildren. In B. Hayslip, Jr., & G. C. Smith (Eds.), *Resilient grandparent caregivers: A strengths-based perspective* (pp. 48–69). New York: Routledge.

Hayward, R. D., Krause, N., Ironson, G., Hill, P. C., & Emmons, R. (2016). Health and well-being among the non-religious: Atheists, agnostics, and no preference compared with the religious group members. *Journal of Religion and Health, 55*, 1024–1037. doi:10.1007/s10943-015-0179-2

He, W. L., Goodkind, D., & Kowal, P. (2016). *An aging world: 2015*. Retrieved from www.census.gov/content/dam/Census/library/publications/2016/demo/p95-16-1.pdf.

He, W. L., & Larsen, L. M. (2014). *Older Americans with a disability, 2008–2012 (American Community Survey Reports No. ACS-29)*. Washington, DC: U.S. Census Bureau. Retrieved from www.census.gov/content/dam/Census/library/publications/2014/acs/acs-29.pdf.

Healey, M. L., & Grossman, M. (2016). Social coordination in older adulthood: A dual-process model. *Experimental Aging Research, 42*, 112–127. doi:10.1080/0361073X.2015.1108691

Health.gov. (2015). *Dietary guidelines for Americans 2015–2020* (8th ed.). Retrieved from health.gov/dietaryguidelines/2015/resources/2015-2020_Dietary_Guidelines.pdf.

Heathcote, D. (2016). Working memory and performance limitations. In D. Groome & M. W. Eysenck (Eds.), *An introduction to applied cognitive psychology* (2nd ed., pp. 99–123). New York: Routledge.

Heckhausen, J., Wrosch, C., & Schulz, R. (2010). A motivational theory of life-span development. *Psychological Review, 117*, 32–60. doi:10.1037/a0017668

Hegewisch, A., & Hartman, H. (2014). *Occupational segregation and the gender wage gap: A job half done*. Retrieved from www.dol.gov/wb/resources/occupational_segregation_and_wage_gap.pdf.

Hehman, J. A., Corpuz, R., & Bugental, D. (2012). Patronizing speech to older adults. *Journal of Nonverbal Behavior, 36*, 249–261. doi:10.1007/s10919-012-0135-8

Heilman, K. M. (2016). Possible brain mechanisms of creativity. *Archives of Clinical Neuropsychology, 31*, 285–296. doi:10.1093/arclin/acw009

Helbert, M. (2017). *Immunology for medical students* (3rd ed.). Philadelphia: Elsevier.

Helpguide.org. (2016). *Adult day care services*. Retrieved from www.helpguide.org/articles/caregiving/adult-day-care-services.htm.

Helson, R., & Kwan, V. S.V. (2000). Personality change in adulthood: The big picture and processes in one longitudinal study. In S. E. Hampton (Ed.), *Advances in personality psychology* (Vol. 1, pp. 77–106). Hove, UK: Psychology Press.

Helson, R., Kwan, V. S. Y., John, O. P., & Jones, C. (2002). The growing evidence for personality change in adulthood: Findings from research with personality inventories. *Journal of Research in Personality, 36*, 287–306. doi:10.1016/S0092-6566(02)00010-7

Hemer, S. R. (2010). Grief as social experience: Death and bereavement in Lahir, Papua New Guinea. *TAJA: The Australian Journal of Anthropology, 21*, 281–297. doi:10.1111/j.1757-6547.2010.00097.x

Henderson, S., & Gilding, M. (2004). "I've never clicked this much with anyone in my life": Trust and hyperpersonal communication in online friendships. *New Media & Society, 6*, 487–506. doi:10.1177/146144804044331

Hendriks, G.-J., Keijsers, G. P. J., Kampman, M., Hoogduin, C. A. L., & Voshaar, R. C. O. (2012). Predictors of outcome of pharmacological and psychological treatment of late-life panic disorder with agoraphobia. *International Journal of Geriatric Psychiatry, 27*, 146–150. doi:10.1002/gps.2700

Hendry, M., Pasterfield, D., Lewis, R., Carter, B., Hodgson, D., & Wilkinson, C. (2013). Why do we want the right to die? A systematic review of the international literature on the views of patients, carers and the public on assisted dying. *Palliative Medicine, 27*, 13–26. doi:10.1177/0269216312463623

Henkin, R. I. (2008). Taste and appetite loss in the aged. *Perspectives on Gerontology, 13*, 20–32. doi:10.1044/gero13.1.20

Henrie, J. A. (2010). *Religiousness, future time perspective, and death anxiety among adults*. Dissertation submitted to West Virginia University.

Henrikson, C. R. (2007). Longevity's impact on retirement security. In M. Robinson, W. Novelli, C. Pearson, & L. Norris (Eds.), *Global health and global aging* (pp. 323–336). San Francisco, CA: Jossey-Bass.

Henry J. Kaiser Family Foundation. (2016). *10 FAQs: Medicare's role in end-of-life care*. Retrieved from kff.org/medicare/fact-sheet/10-faqs-medicares-role-in-end-of-life-care/.

Heo, J., Lee, Y., McCormick, B. P., & Pedersen, P. M. (2010). Daily experience of serious leisure, flow and subjective well-being of older adults. *Leisure Studies, 29*, 207–225. doi: 10.1080/02614360903434092

Heppner, R. S. (2013). *The lost leaders: How corporate America loses women leaders*. New York: Palgrave Macmillan.

Herrenbrueck, L., Xia, X., Eastwick, P., Finkel, E., & Hui, C. M. (2016). *Smart-dating in speed-dating: How a simple search model can explain matching decisions*. Retrieved from www.sfu.ca/econ-research/RePEc/sfu/sfudps/dp16-02.pdf.

Hersh, E. D., & Ghitza, Y. (2016). *Mixed partisan households and electoral participation in the United States*. Retrieved from www.eitanhersh.com/uploads/7/9/7/5/7975685/hersh_ghitza_mpsa.pdf.

Hershey, D. A., & Henkens, K. (2014). Impact of different types of retirement transitions on perceived satisfaction with life. *The Gerontologist, 54*, 232–244. doi: 10/1093/geront/gnt006

Hershey, D. A., Austin, J. T., & Gutierrez, H. C. (2015). Financial decision making across the adult life span: Dynamic cognitive capacities and real-world competence. In T. M. Hess, J. Strough, and C. E. Lockenhoff (Eds.), *Aging and decision making: Empirical and applied perspectives* (pp. 329–349). New York: Academic Press.

Hertzog, C. (2008). Theoretical approaches to the study of cognitive aging: An individual differences perspective. In S. M. Hofer & D. F. Alwin (Eds.), *Handbook of cognitive aging: Interdisciplinary perspectives* (pp. 34–49). Greenwich, CT: Sage.

Hertzog, C. (2016). Aging and metacognitive control. In J. Dunlosky & S. K. Tauber (Eds.), *The Oxford handbook of metamemory* (pp. 537–558). New York: Oxford University Press.

Hertzog, C., & Dixon, R. (1996). Methodological issues in research on cognition and aging. In F. Blanchard-Fields & T. Hess (Eds.), *Perspectives on cognitive change in adulthood and aging* (pp. 66–121). New York: McGraw-Hill.

Hertzog, C., & Dunlosky, J. (2011). Metacognition in later adulthood: Spared monitoring can benefit older adults' self-regulation. *Current Directions in Psychological Science, 20*, 167–173. doi:10.1177/0963721411409026

Hertzog, C., Dixon, R. A., Hultsch, D. F., & MacDonald, S. W. S. (2003). Latent change models of adult cognition: Are changes in processing speed and working memory associated with changes in episodic memory? *Psychology and Aging, 18*, 755–769. doi:10.1037/0882-7974.18.4.755

Hertzog, C., Fulton, E. K., Mandviwala, L., & Dunlosky, J. (2013). Older adults show deficits in retrieving and decoding associative mediators generated at study. *Developmental Psychology, 49*, 1127–1131. doi:10.1037/a0029414

Hertzog, C., Kramer, A. F., Wilson, R. S., & Lindenberger, U. (2009). Fit body, fit mind? *Scientific American Mind, 20*, 24–31. doi:10.1038/scientificamericanmind0709-24

Hertzog, C., Price, J., & Dunlosky, J. (2012). Age differences in the effects of experimenter-instructed versus self-generated strategy use. *Experimental Aging Research, 38*, 42–62. doi:10.1080/0361073X.2012.637005

Hess, T. M. (2006). Adaptive aspects of social cognitive functioning in adulthood: Age-related goal and knowledge influences. *Social Cognition, 24*, 279–309. doi:10.1521/soco.2006.24.3.279

Hess, T. M., & Emery, L. (2012). Memory in context: The impact of age-related goals on performance.

In M. Naveh-Benjamin & N. Ohta (Eds.), *Memory and aging: Current issues and future directions* (pp. 183–214). New York: Psychology Press.

Hess, T. M., & Pullen, S. M. (1994). Adult age differences in impression change processes. *Psychology and Aging, 9*, 237–250. doi:10.1037/0882-7974.9.2.237

Hess, T. M., Auman, C., Colcombe, S. J., & Rahhal, T. A. (2003). The impact of stereotype threat on age differences in memory. *Journals of Gerontology: Psychological Sciences, 58*, P3–P11. doi:10.1093/geronb/58.1.P3

Hess, T. M., Germain, C. M., Rosenberg, D. C., Leclerc, C. M., & Hodges, E. A. (2005). Aging-related selectivity and susceptibility to irrelevant affective information in the construction of attitudes. *Aging, Neuropsychology, and Cognition, 12*, 149–174. doi:10.1080/13825580590925170

Hess, T. M., Queen, T. L., & Ennis, G. E. (2013). Age and self-relevance effects on information search during decision making. *Journal of Gerontology: Psychological Sciences, 68*, 703–711. doi:10.1093/geronb/gbs108

Heyl, V., & Wahl, H.-W. (2012). Managing daily life with age-related sensory loss: Cognitive resources gain in importance. *Psychology and Aging, 27*, 510–521. doi:10.1037/a0025471

Hiatt, K., Stelle, C., Mulsow, M., & Scott, J. P. (2007). The importance of perspective: Evaluation of hospice care from multiple stakeholders. *American Journal of Hospice & Palliative Medicine, 24*, 376–382. doi:10.1177/1049909107300760

Higgins, J. P. (2016). Smartphone applications for patients' health and fitness. *The American Journal of Medicine, 129*, 11–19. doi:10.1016/j.amjmed.2015.05.038

Hill, P. L., Turiano, N. A., Mroczek, D. K., & Roberts, B. W. (2012). Examining concurrent and longitudinal relations between personality traits and social well-being in adulthood. *Social Psychological and Personality Science, 3*, 698–705. doi:10.1177/1948550611433888

Hill, R. T., Thomas, C., English, L., & Callaway, K. (2016). The importance and impact of child care on a woman's transition to motherhood. In C. Spitzmueller & R. A. Matthews (Eds.), *Research perspectives on work and the transition to motherhood* (pp. 241–265). New York: Springer.

Hill, T. J. (2015). *Family caregiving in aging populations*. New York: Palgrave MacMillan.

Hills, L. (2013). Why legacy matters more in midlife. *Lasting female educational leadership: Leadership legacies of women leaders* (pp. 15–26). New York: Springer.

Hills, W. E. (2010). Grandparenting roles in the evolving American family. In D. Wiseman (Ed.), *The American family: Understanding its changing dynamics and place in society* (pp. 65–78.) Springfield, IL: Charles C. Thomas.

Hillsdon, M., Brunner, E., Guralnik, J., & Marmot, M. (2005). Prospective study of physical activity and physical function in early old age. *American Journal of Preventive Medicine, 28*, 245–250. doi:10.1016/j.amepre.2004.12.008

Hinton, A., & Chirgwin, S. (2010). Nursing education: Reducing reality shock for graduate indigenous nurses—It's all about time. *Australian Journal of Advanced Nursing, 28*, 60–66. Retrieved from search.informit.com.au/documentSummary;dn=053211061337305;res=IELHEA.

Hipp, L., Morrissey, T. W., & Warner, M. E. (2017). Who participates and who benefits from employer-provided child-care assistance? *Journal of Marriage and Family, 79*, 614–635. doi:10.1111/momf.12359

Hirokawa, K., Utsuyama, M., & Kikuchi, Y. (2016). Trade off situation between thymus and growth hormone: Age-related decline of growth hormone is a cause of thymic involution but favorable for elongation of lifespan. *Biogerontology, 17*, 55–59. doi:10.1007/s10522-015-9590-z

Hirve, S., Juvekar, S., Sambhudas, S., Lele, P., Blomstedt, Y., Wall, S. et al. (2012). Does self-rated health predict death in adults aged 50 years and above in India? Evidence from a rural population under health and demographic surveillance. *International Journal of Epidemiology, 41*, 1719–1727. doi:10.1093/ije/dys163

Hoffman, E., Kaneshiro, S., & Compton, W. C. (2012). Peak-experiences among Americans in midlife. *Journal of Humanistic Psychology, 52*, 479–503. doi:10.1177/0022167811433851

Hofhuis, J., van der Rijt, P. G. A., & Vlug, M. (2016). Diversity climate enhances work outcomes through trust and openness in workgroup communication. *SpringerPlus, 5*, 714. doi:s40064-016-2499-4

Holland, J. M. (1997). *Making vocational choices: A theory of vocational personalities and work environments* (3rd ed.). Baltimore, MD: Johns Hopkins University Press.

Holland, J. M., & Neimeyer, R. A. (2010). An examination of stage theory of grief among individuals bereaved by natural and violent causes: A meaning-oriented contribution. *OMEGA: Journal of Death and Dying, 61*, 103–120. doi:10.2190/OM.61.2.b

Holland, K. J., & Cortina, L. M. (2016). Sexual harassment: Undermining the wellbeing of working women. In M. L. Connerley & J. Wu (eds.), *Handbook on well-being of working women* (pp. 83–101). New York: Springer.

Hollwich, M. (2016). *New aging: Living smarter now to live better forever*. New York: Penguin Books.

Holmes, M. I., Manor, B., Hsieh, W-h., Hu, K., Lipsitz, L. A., Li, L. et al. (2016). Tai Chi training reduced coupling between respiration and posture control. *Neuroscience Letters, 610*, 60–65. doi:10.1016/j.neulet.2015.10.053

Holtzer, R., Verghese, J., Allali, G., Izzetoglu, M., Wang, C., & Mahoney, J. R. (2016). Neurological gait abnormalities moderate the functional brain signature of the posture first hypothesis. *Brain Topography, 29*, 334–343. doi:10.1007/s10548-015-0465-z

Hom, P. W., & Kinicki, A. J. (2001). Toward a greater understanding of how dissatisfaction drives employee turnover. *Academy of Management Journal, 44*, 975–987. doi:10.2307/3069441

Honda-Howard, M., & Homma, M. (2001). Job satisfaction of Japanese career women and its influence on turnover intention. *Asian Journal of Social Psychology, 4*, 23–38. doi:10.1111/1467-839X.00073

Hooker, K. (1999). Possible selves in adulthood. In T. M. Hess & F. Blanchard-Fields (Eds.), *Social cognition and aging* (pp. 97–122). San Diego, CA: Academic Press.

Hooker, K. (2015). Towards a new synthesis for development in adulthood. *Research in Human Development, 12*, 229–236. doi:10.1080/15427609.2015.1068036

Hooker, K., & McAdams, D. P. (2003). Personality reconsidered: A new agenda for aging research. *Journal of Gerontology: Psychological Sciences, 58*, P296–P304. doi:10.1093/geronb/58.6.P296

Hooker, K., Fiese, B. H., Jenkins, L., Morfei, M. Z., & Schwagler, J. (1996). Possible selves among parents of infants and preschoolers. *Developmental Psychology, 32*, 542–550. doi:10.1037/0012-1649.32.3.542

Hopthrow, T., Hooper, N., Mahmood, L., Meier, B. P., & Weger, U. (2017). Mindfulness reduces the correspondence bias. *Quarterly Journal of Experimental Psychology, 70*, 351–360. doi:10.1080/17470218.2016.1149498

Horhota, M., Mienaltowski, A., & Chen, Y. (2014). Causal attributions across the adult lifespan. In P. Verhaeghen & C. Hertzog (Eds.), *The Oxford handbook of emotion, social cognition, and problem solving in adulthood* (pp. 288–301). New York: Oxford University Press.

Horn, J. L. (1982). The aging of human abilities. In B. B. Wolman (Ed.), *Handbook of developmental psychology* (pp. 847–870). Englewood Cliffs, NJ: Prentice Hall.

Horn, J. L., & Hofer, S. M. (1992). Major abilities and development in the adult period. In R. J. Sternberg & C. A. Berg (Eds.), *Intellectual development* (pp. 44–99). Cambridge, UK: Cambridge University Press.

Horwitz, B. N., Reynolds, C. A., Walum, H., Ganiban, J., Spotts, E. L., Reiss, D. et al. (2016). Understanding the role of mate selection processes in couples' pair-bonding behavior. *Behavior Genetics, 46*, 143–149. doi:10.1007/s10519-015-9766-y

Horwood, S., & Beanland, V. (2016). Inattentional blindness in older adults: Effects of attentional set and to-be-ignored distractors. *Attention, Perception, & Psychophysics, 78*, 818–828. doi:10.3758/s13414-015-1057-4

Hospice Foundation of America. (2016a). *What is hospice?* Retrieved from hospicefoundation.org/End-of-Life-Support-and-Resources/Coping-with-Terminal-Illness/Hospice-Services.

Hospice Foundation of America. (2016b). *A caregiver's guide to the dying process*. Retrieved from hospicefoundation.org/hfa/media/Files/Hospice_TheDyingProcess_Docutech-READERSPREADS.pdf.

Hostetler, A. J., & Paterson, S. E. (2017). Toward a community psychology of aging: A lifespan perspective. In M. A. Bond, I. Serrano-Garcia, C. B. Keys, & M. Shinn (Eds.), *APA handbook of community psychology: Methods for community research and action for diverse groups and issues* (Vol. s, pp. 605–622). Washington, DC: American Psychological Association.

Howard, D. V., & Howard, J. H., Jr. (2012). Dissociable forms of implicit learning in aging. In M. Naveh-Benjamin & N. Ohta (Eds.), *Memory and aging: Current issues and future directions* (pp. 125–151). New York: Psychology Press.

Howard, D. V., & Howard, J. H., Jr. (2016). Implicit learning and memory. In S. K. Whitbourne (Ed.), *The encyclopedia of adulthood and aging* (pp. 631–635). Malden, MA: Wiley.

Howard, J. H., Jr., & Howard, D. V. (2013, November 7). Aging mind and brain: Is Implicit learning spared in healthy aging? *Frontiers in Psychology*. doi:10.3389/fpsyg.2013.00817. Retrieved from journal.frontiersin.org/article/10.3389/fpsyg.2013.00817/full.

Howard, L. W., & Cordes, C. L. (2010). Flight from unfairness: Effects of perceived injustice on emotional exhaustion and employee withdrawal. *Journal of Business and Psychology, 25*, 409–428. doi:10.1007/s10869-010-9158-5

Howe, A. L., Jones, A. E., & Tilse, C. (2013). What's in a name? Similarities and differences in international terms and meanings for older peoples' housing with services. *Ageing and Society, 33*, 547–578. doi:10.1017/S0144686X12000086

Hsu, A., Suskind, A. M., & Huang, A. J. (2016). Urinary incontinence among older adults. In L. A. Lindquist (Ed.), *New directions in geriatric medicine* (pp. 49–69). New York: Springer. doi:10.1007/978-3-319-28137-7_4

Hsu, H.-C. (2005). Gender disparity of successful aging in Taiwan. *Women and Health, 42*, 1–21. doi:10.1300/J013v42n01_01

Hubbard, R. R. (2010). *Afro-German biracial identity development*. Retrieved from digarchive.library.vcu.edu/bitstream/10156/2804/1/Afro-German%20HEMBAGI%20%28F3%29.pdf.

Hull, T. H. (2009). *Fertility prospects in south-eastern Asia: Report of the United Nations Expert Group Meeting on Recent and Future Trends in Fertility.* Retrieved from www.un.org/esa/population/meetings/EGM-Fertility2009/P14_Hull.pdf.

Hülür, G., Hertzog, C., Pearman, A. M., & Gerstof, D. (2015). Correlates and moderators of change in subjective memory and memory performance: Findings from the Health and Retirement Study. *Gerontology, 61,* 232–240. doi:10.1159/000369010

Hummert, M. L., Garstka, T. A., O'Brien, L. T., Greenwald, A. G., & Mellott, D. S. (2002). Using the implicit association test to measure age differences in implicit social cognitions. *Psychology and Aging, 17,* 482–495. doi:10.1037/0882-7974.17.3.482

Hunsberger, J. G., Rao, M., Kurtzberg, J., Bulte, J. W. M., Atala, A., LaFerla, F. M. et al. (2016). Accelerating stem cell trials for Alzheimer's disease. *The Lancet Neurology, 15,* 219–230. doi:10.1016/S1474-4422(15)00332-4

Hunt, J. B., & Fitzgerald, M. (2013). The relationship between emotional intelligence and transformational leadership: An investigation and review of competing claims in the literature. *American International Journal of Social Science, 2,* 30–38. Retrieved from www.researchgate.net/profile/James_Hunt11/publication/264311660_The_Relationship_between_Emotional_Intelligence_and_Transformational_Leadership_An_Investigation_and_Review_of_Competing_Claims_in_the_Literature/links/56b15d5408ae795dd5c505a0.pdf.

Hunt, J. B., & Fitzgerald, M. (2014). An evidence-based assessment of the relationship between emotional intelligence and transformational leadership. *International Journal of Arts and Commerce, 3,* 85–100. Retrieved from www.researchgate.net/profile/James_Hunt11/publication/292802393_An_Evidence-based_Assessment_of_the_Relationship_Between_Emotional_Intelligence_and_Transformational_Leadership/links/56b16e2208ae56d7b06a0f5c.pdf.

Hunt, J. M., & Weintraub, J. R. (2016). *The coaching manager: Developing top talent* (3rd ed.). Thousand Oaks, CA: Sage Publications.

Hunter, C. E. A., Ward, L., & Camp, C. J. (2012). Transitioning spaced retrieval training to care staff in an Australian residential aged care setting for older adults with dementia: A case study approach. *Clinical Gerontologist, 35,* 1–14. doi:10.1080/07317115.2011.626513

Hunter, C. E. A., Ward, L., & Camp, C. J. (2012). Transitioning spaced retrieval training to care staff in an Australian residential aged care setting for older adults with dementia: A case study approach. *Clinical Gerontologist, 35,* 1–14. doi:10.1080/07317115.2011.626513

Huntington's Disease Society of America. (2016). *What is Huntington's disease?* Retrieved from hdsa.org/what-is-hd/.

Husain, M., & Schott, J. M. (2016). *Oxford textbook of cognitive neurology and dementia.* New York: Oxford University Press.

Hwang, M. J. (2007). Asian social workers' perceptions of glass ceiling, organizational fairness and career prospects. *Journal of Social Service Research, 33,* 13–24. doi:10.1300/J079v33n04_02

Hyer, L., Mullen, C. M., & Jackson, K. (2017). The unfolding of unique problems in later life families. In G. L. Welch & A. W. Harrist (Eds.), *Family resilience and chronic illness: Interdisciplinary and translational perspectives* (pp. 197–224). New York: Springer.

Ibrahim, R., & Hassan, Z. (2009). Understanding singlehood from the experiences of never-married Malay Muslim women in Malaysia: Some preliminary findings. *European Journal of Social Sciences, 8,* 395–405. Retrieved from server1.docfoc.us/uploads/Z2016/01/12/w29wSDYY47/40f707fa034e0fea7894a419dea90541.pdf.

Idler, E. L., & Benyamini, Y. (1997). Self-rated health and mortality: A review of twenty-seven community studies. *Journal of Health and Social Behavior, 38,* 21–37. doi:10.2307/2955359

Igarashi, H., Hooker, K. Coehlo, D. P., & Manoogian, M. M. (2013). "My nest is full:" Intergenerational relationships at midlife. *Journal of Aging Studies, 27,* 102–112. doi:10.1016/j. jaging.2012.12.004

Igarashi, K. M. (2016). The entorhinal map of space. *Brain Research, 1637,* 177–187. doi:10.1016/j.brainres.2015.10.041

Imoscopi, A., Inelmen, E. M., Sergi, G., Miotto, F., & Manzato, E. (2012). Taste loss in the elderly: Epidemiology, causes and consequences. *Aging Clinical and Experimental Research, 24,* 570–579. doi:10.3275/8520

International Labour Organization. (2013). *When work becomes a sexual battleground.* Retrieved from ilo.ch/global/about-the-ilo/newsroom/features/WCMS_205996/lang--en/index.htm.

Intlekofer, K. A., & Cotman, C. W. (2013). Exercise counteracts declining hippocampal function in aging and Alzheimer's disease. *Neurobiology of Disease, 57,* 47–55. doi:10.1016/j. nbd.2012.06.011

Intuit. (2016). *Intuit 2020 report: Twenty trends that will shape the next decade.* Retrieved from http-download.intuit.com/http.intuit/CMO/intuit/futureofsmallbusiness/intuit_2020_report.pdf.

Irwin, N. (2016, March 31). With "gigs" instead of jobs, workers bear new burdens. *New York Times.* Retrieved from www.nytimes.com/2016/03/31/upshot/contractors-and-temps-accounted-for-all-of-the-growth-in-employment-in-the-last-decade.html.

Isaacowitz, D. M., & Blanchard-Fields, F. (2012). Linking process and outcome in the study of emotion and aging. *Perspectives on Psychological Science, 7,* 3–16. doi:10.1177/1745691611424750

Isaacowitz, D. M., & Blanchard-Fields, F. (2012). Linking process and outcome in the study of emotion and aging. *Perspectives on Psychological Science, 7,* 3–16. doi:10.1177/1745691611424750

Ismail, Z., Smith, E. E., Geda, Y., Sultzer, D., Brodaty, H., Smith, G. et al. (2016). Neuropsychiatric symptoms as early manifestations of emergent dementia: Provisional diagnostic criteria for mild behavioral impairment. *Alzheimer's & Dementia, 12,* 195–202. doi:10.1016/j.jalz.2015.05.107

Iwarsson, S., Slaug, B., & Fänge, A. M. (2012). The Housing Enabler Screening Tool: Feasibility and interrater agreement in a real estate company practice context. *Journal of Applied Gerontology, 31,* 641–660. doi:10.1177/0733464810397354

Izumi, S., & Son, C. V. (2016). "I didn't know he was dying": Missed opportunities for making end-of-life decisions for older family members. *Journal of Hospice & Palliative Nursing, 18,* 74–81. doi:10.1097/0000000000000215

Jack, C. R., Jr., Albert, M. A., Knopman, D. S., McKhann, G. M., Sperling, R. A., Carrillo, M. C. et al. (2011). Introduction to the recommendations from the National Institute on Aging—Alzheimer's Association workgroups on diagnostic guidelines for Alzheimer's disease. *Alzheimer's and Dementia: Journal of the Alzheimer's Assocation, 7,* 257–262. doi:10.1016/j.jalz.2011.03.004

Jack, C. R., Jr., Knopman, D. S., Chételat, G., Dickson, D., Fagan, A. M., Frisoni, G. B. et al. (2016). Suspected non-Alzheimer disease pathophysiology—Concept and controversy. *Nature Reviews Neurology, 12,* 117–124. doi:10.1038/nrneurol.2015.251

Jackson, J. B., Miller, R. B., Oka, M., & Henry, R. G. (2014). Gender differences in marital satisfaction: A meta-analysis. *Journal of Marriage and Family, 76,* 105–129. doi:10.1111/jomf.12077

Jackson, J. S., Antonucci, T. C., & Gibson, R. C. (1995). Ethnic and cultural factors in research on aging and mental health: A life-course perspective. In D. K. Padgett (Ed.), *Handbook on ethnicity, aging, and mental health* (pp. 22–46). Westport, CT: Greenwood.

Jackson, M. A. (2013). Counseling older workers confronting ageist stereotypes and discrimination. In P. Brownell & J. J. Kelly (Eds.), *Ageism and mistreatment of older workers* (pp. 135–144). New York: Springer.

Jackson, P. A., Chiba, A. A., Berman, R. F., & Ragozzino, M. E. (2016). *The neurological basis of memory.* New York: Springer.

Jacobs, J., & Lee, S. A. (2016). Spatial cognition: Grid cells support imagined navigation. *Current Biology, 26,* R277–R279. doi:10.1016/j.cub.2016.02.032

Jacoby, L. L., Rogers, C. S., Bishara, A. J., & Shimizu, Y. (2012). Mistaking the recent past for the present: False seeing by older adults. *Psychology and Aging, 27,* 22–32. doi:10.1037/a0025924

Jagust, W. (2016). Is amyloid-β harmful to the brain? Insights from human imaging studies. *Brain, 139,* 23–30. doi:10.1093/brain/awv326

Jainer, A. K., Kamatchi, R., Marzanski, M., & Somashekar, B. (2013). Current advances in the treatment of major depression: Shift towards receptor specific drugs. In R. Woolfolk & L. Allen (Eds.), *Mental disorders: Theoretical and empirical perspectives* (pp. 269–288). doi: 10.5772/46217. Retrieved from cdn.intechopen.com/pdfs/41703/InTech-Current_advances_in_the_treatment_of_major_depression_shift_towards_receptor_specific_drugs.pdf.

James, J. B., Matz-Costa, C., & Smyer, M. A. (2016). Retirement security: It's not just about the money. *American Psychologist, 71,* 334–344. doi:10.1037/a0040220

Jamoulle, M. (2015). Quaternary prevention: An answer of family doctors to overmedicalization. *International Journal of Health Policy and Management, 4,* 61–64. doi: 10.15171/ijhpm.2015.24.

Janssen I, R. R. (2005). Linking age-related changes in skeletal muscle mass and composition with metabolism and disease. *Journal of Nutrition, Health and Aging, 9,* 408–419. Retrieved from www.researchgate.net/profile/Ian_Janssen/publication/7375203_Linking_age-related_changes_in_skeletal_muscle_mass_and_composition_with_metabolism_and_disease/links/00b7d535a3066571fa000000.pdf.

Jaspal, R. (2015). Migration and identity processes among first-generation British South Asians. *South Asian Diaspora, 7,* 79–96. doi:10.1080/19438192.2015.1007634

Jaspal, R., & Cinnirella, M. (2012). The construction of ethnic identity: Insights from identity process theory. *Ethnicities, 12,* 503–530. doi:10.1177/1468796811432689

Jenkins, J. A. (2016). *Disrupt aging: A bold new path to living your best life at every age.* New York: PublicAffairs Publishing.

Jenny, G. J., Bauer, G. F., Vinje, H. F., Vogt, K., & Torp, S. (2017). The application of salutogenesis to work. In M. B. Mittelmark, S. Sagy, M. Eriksson, G. F. Bauer, J. M. Pelikan, B. Lindström et al. (Eds.), *The handbook of salutogenesis* (pp. 197–210). New York: Springer.

Jeon, H.-A., & Friederici, A. D. (2015). Degree of automaticity and the prefrontal cortex. *Trends in Cognitive Sciences, 19,* 244–250. doi: 10.1016/j.tics.2015.03.003

Jeste, D. V., & Palmer, B. W. (2013). A call for a new positive psychiatry of ageing. *British Journal of Psychiatry, 202,* 81–83. doi:10.1192/bjp. bp.112.110643.

Jeste, D. V., & Palmer, B. W. (2015). Introduction: What is positive psychiatry? In D. V. Jeste & B. W. Palmer (Eds.), *Positive psychiatry: A clinical handbook* (pp. 1–16). Washington, DC: American Psychiatric Publishing.

Jiang, W., Zhao, F., Guderley, N., & Manchaiah, V. (2016). Daily music exposure dose and hearing problems using personal listening devices in adolescents and young adults: A systematic review. *International Journal of Audiology, 55*, 197–205. doi: 10.3109/14992027.2015.1122237

Jiang, Z. (2016). The relationship between career adaptability and job content plateau: The mediating roles of fit perceptions. *Journal of Vocational Behavior, 95*, 1–10. doi:10.1016/j.jvb.2016.06.001

Johnson, H. A., Zabriskie, R. B., & Hill, B. (2006). The contribution of couple leisure involvement, leisure time, and leisure satisfaction to marital satisfaction. *Marriage & Family Review, 40*, 69–91. doi:10.1300/J002v40n01_05

Johnson, M. D. (2016). Online dating. In M. D. Johnson (Ed.), *Great myths of intimate relationships: Dating, sex, and marriage* (pp. 52–70). New York: Wiley.

Johnson, M. K. (2016). Cognitive neuroscience: Applied cognitive psychology. *Journal of Applied Research in Memory and Cognition, 5*, 110–120. doi:10.1016/j.jarmac.2016.02.003

Johnson, M. K., Raye, C. L., Mitchell, K. J., & Ankudowich, E. (2012). The cognitive neuroscience of true and false memories. *Nebraska Symposium on Motivation, 58*, 15–52. doi:10.1007/978-1-4614-1195-6_2

Johnson, M. M., & Rhodes, R. (2007). Institutionalization: A theory of human behavior and the social environment. *Advances in Social Work, 8*, 219–236. Retrieved from journals.iupui.edu/index.php/advancesinsocialwork/article/view/143/144.

Johnson, R. W. (2016). Cumulative advantage and retirement security: What does the future hold? *Public Policy and Aging Report, 26*, 63–67. doi:10.1093/ppar/prw003

Johnston, K. E., Swim, J. K., Saltsman, B. M., Deater-Deckard, K., & Petrill, S. A. (2007). Mothers' racial, ethnic, and cultural socialization of transracially adopted Asian children. *Family Relations, 56*, 390–402. doi:10.1111/j.1741-3729.2007.00468.x

Joiner, T. (2010). *Myths about suicide.* Cambridge, MA: Harvard University Press.

Jolie, A. (2013). *My medical choice.* Retrieved from www.nytimes.com/2013/05/14/opinion/my-medical-choice.html.

Jolie, A. (2015). *Diary of a surgery.* Retrieved from mobile.nytimes.com/2015/03/24/opinion/angelina-jolie-pitt-diary-of-a-surgery.html?referrer=&_r=0.

Jones, B. F. (2010). Age and great invention. *Review of Economics and Statistics, 92*, 1–14. Retrieved from www.mitpressjournals.org/doi/pdfplus/10.1162/rest.2009.11724.

Jones, M. R., Ehrhardt, K. P., Ripoll, J. G., Sharma, B., Padnos, I. W., Kaye, R. J. et al. (2016). Pain in the elderly. *Current Pain and Headache Reports, 20*, 23. doi:10.1007/s11916-016-0551-2

Jones, R. N., Marsiske, M., Ball, K., Rebok, G., Willis, S. L., Morris, J. N. et al. (2013). The ACTIVE cognitive training interventions and trajectories of performance among older adults. *Journal of Aging and Health, 25*(suppl.), 186S-208S. doi:10.1177/0898264312461938

Jonsson, T., Stefansson, H., Steinberg, S., Jonsdottir, I., Jonsson, P. V., Snaedal, J. et al. (2013). Variant of *TREM2* associated with the risk of Alzheimer's disease. *New England Journal of Medicine, 368*, 107–116. doi:10.1056/NEJMoa1211103

Jopp, D. S., & Hertzog, C. (2010). Assessing adult leisure activities: An extension of a self-report activity questionnaire. *Psychological Assessment, 22*, 108–120. doi:10.1037/a0017662

Jorge, M. P., Santaella, D. F., Pontes, I. M. O., Shiramizu, V. K. M., Nascimento, E. B., Cabral, A. et al. (2016). Hatha yoga practice decreases menopause symptoms and improves quality of life: A randomized controlled trial. *Complementary Therapies in Medicine, 26*, 128–135. doi:10.1016/j.ctim.2016.03.014

Joyner, M. J., & Barnes, J. N. (2013). I am 80 going on 18: Exercise and the fountain of youth. *Journal of Applied Physiology, 114*, 1–2. doi:10.1152/japplphysiol.01313.2012

Juffer, F. (2006). Children's awareness of adoption and their problem behavior in families with 7-year-old internationally adopted children. *Adoption Quarterly, 9*, 1–22. doi:10.1300/ J145v09n02_01

Jung, R. E., Flores, R. A., & Hunter, D. (2016). A new measure of imagination ability: Anatomical brain imaging correlates. *Frontiers in Psychology, 7*, 496. doi:10.3389/fpsyq.2016.00496 Available at www.ncbi.nlm.nih.gov/pmc/articles/PMC4834344/.

Jung, R. E., & Haier, R. J. (2007). The parieto-frontal integration theory (P-FIT) of intelligence: Converging neuroimaging evidence. *Behavioral and Brain Sciences, 30*, 135–154. doi:10.1017/S0140525X07001185

Kahana, E., & Kahana, B. (2003). Patient proactivity enhancing doctor-patient-family communication in cancer prevention and care among the aged. *Patient Education and Counseling, 50*, 67–73. doi:10.1016/S0738-3991(03)00083-1

Kahana, E., Kahana, B., & Zhang, J. (2005). Motivational antecedents of preventive proactivity in late life: Linking future orientation and exercise. *Motivation and Emotion, 29*, 438–459 (Figure 1). doi:10.1007/s11031-006-9012-2. Retrieved from www.springerlink.com/content/61304201gm163778//fulltext.html#Fig1.

Kahana, E., Kelley-Moore, J., & Kahana, B. (2012). Proactive aging: A longitudinal study of stress, resources, and well-being in late life. *Aging and Mental Health, 16*, 438–451. doi:10.1080/13607863.20 11.644519

Kaiser Family Foundation. (2016). *Total number of Medicare beneficiaries.* Retrieved from kff.org/medicare/state-indicator/total-medicare-beneficiaries/?currentTimeframe=0&sortModel=%7B%22colId%22:%22Location%22,%22sort%22:%22asc%22%7D.

Kalanithi, L. (2016). *My marriage didn't end when I became a widow.* Retrieved from opinionator.blogs.nytimes.com/2016/01/06/my-marriage-didnt-end-when-i-became-a-widow/.

Kalish, E. (2016). *Millennials are the least wealthy, but most optimistic, generation.* Retrieved from www.urban.org/research/publication/millennials-are-least-wealthy-most-optimistic-generation.

Kalish, R. A. (1984). *Death, grief, and caring relationships* (2nd ed.). Pacific Grove, CA: Brooks/Cole.

Kalish, R. A. (1987). Death and dying . In P. Silverman (Ed.), *The elderly as modern pioneers* (pp. 320–334). Bloomington: Indiana University Press.

Kalish, R. A., & Reynolds, D. (1976). *Death and ethnicity: A psychocultural study.* Los Angeles: University of Southern California Press.

Kalmijn, M., & Flap, H. (2001). Assortative meeting and mating: Unintended consequences of organized settings for partner choices. *Social Forces, 79*, 1289–1312. doi:10.1353/sof.2001.0044

Kalokerinos, E. K., von Hippel, W., & Henry, J. D. (2015). Social cognition and aging. In N. A. Pachana (Ed.), *Encyclopedia of geropsychology.* New York: Springer. doi:10.1007/978-981-287-080-3_2-1

Kan, D., & Yu, X. (2016). Occupational stress, work-family conflict and depressive symptoms among Chinese bank employees: The role of psychological capital. *International Journal of Environmental Research and Public Health, 13*, 134. doi:10.3390/ijerp13010134

Kaplan, S. (2015). When are you dead? It may depend on which hospital makes the call. *Washington Post.* Retrieved from www.washingtonpost.com/news/morning-mix/wp/2015/12/29/when-are-you-dead-it-may-depend-on-which-hospital-makes-the-call/.

Kapoor, U., Pfost, K. S., House, A. E., & Pierson, E. (2010). Relation of success and nontraditional career choice to selection for dating and friendship. *Psychological Reports, 107*, 177–184. doi:10.2466/07.17.PR0.107.4.177-184

Kapp, M. B. (2013). Nursing home culture change: Legal apprehensions and opportunities. *The Gerontologist, 53*(5), 718–726. doi:10.1093/geront/gns131

Karasu, S. R., & Karasu, T. B. (2005). *The art of marriage maintenance.* Lanham, MD: Jason Aronson.

Karel, M. J., Gatz, M., & Smyer, M. A. (2012). Aging and mental health in the decade ahead: What psychologists need to know. *American Psychologist, 67*, 184–198. doi:10.1037/a0025393

Karim, S. S., Ramanna, G., Petit, T., Doward, L., & Burns, A. (2008). Development of the Dementia Quality of Life questionnaire (D-QOL): UK version. *Aging and Mental Health, 12*, 144–148. doi:10.1080/13607860701616341

Karney, B. R. (2010). *Keeping marriages healthy, and why it's so difficult.* Retrieved from www.apa.org/science/about/psa/2010/02/sci-brief.aspx.

Karim, S., & Harrison, K. (2016). Psychosis in the elderly. In C. A. Chew-Graham & M. Ray (Eds.), *Mental health and older people* (pp. 181–194). New York: Springer.

Karney, B. R., & Bradbury, T. N. (1995). The longitudinal course of marital quality and stability: A review of theory, method, and research. *Psychological Bulletin, 118*, 3–34. doi:10.1037/0033-2909.1881.1.3

Karney, B. R., & Crown, J. S. (2007). *Families under stress: An assessment of data, theory, and research on marriage and divorce in the military* (MG-599-OSD). Santa Monica, CA: RAND Corporation.

Karp, N., & Wood, E. (2012). Choosing home for someone else: Guardian residential decision-making. *Utah Law Review, 2012*, 1445–1490. Retrieved from epubs.utah.edu/index.php/ulr/article/view/837/646.

Kassim, P. N. J., & Alias, F. (2016). Religious, ethical and legal considerations in end-of-life issues: Fundamental requisites for medical decision making. *Journal of Religion and Health, 55*, 119–134. doi:10.1007/210943-014-9995-z

Kastenbaum, R. (1999). Dying and bereavement. In J. C. Cavanaugh & S. K.Whitbourne (Eds.), *Gerontology: An interdisciplinary perspective.* New York: Oxford University Press.

Kastenbaum, R., & Thuell, S. (1995). Cookies baking, coffee brewing: Toward a contextual theory of dying. *Omega: The Journal of Death and Dying, 31*, 175–187. doi:10.2190/ LQPX-71DE-V5AA-EPFT

Kasuya, H., Yoshida, H., Mori, H., & Kido, H. (2008). A longitudinal study of vocal aging: Changes in F0, jitter, shimmer, and glottal noise. *Journal of the Acoustical Society of America, 123*, 3428–3428. doi:10.1121/1.2934194

Kaufman, D. A. S., Keith, C. M., & Perlstein, W. M. (2016). Orbitofrontal cortex and early processing of visual novelty in healthy aging. *Frontiers in Aging Neuroscience, 8*, 101. doi:10.3389/fnagi.2016.00101. Retrieved from www.ncbi.nlm.nih.gov/pmc/articles/PMC4852196/.

Kaufman, J. C. (2016). *Creativity 101* (2nd ed.). New York: Springer.

Kavé, G., Eyal, N., Shorek, A., Cohen-Mansfield, J. (2008). Multilingualism and cognitive state in the oldest old. *Psychology and Aging, 23*, 70–78. doi:10.1037/0882-7974.23.1.70

Kazanis, I. (2012). Can adult neural stem cells create new brains? Plasticity in the adult mammalian neurogenic niches: Realities and expectations in the era of regenerative biology. *Neuroscientist, 18*, 15–27. doi:10.1177/1073858410390379

Kegan, R. (1982). *The evolving self*. Cambridge, MA: Harvard University Press.

Kegan, R. (1994). *In over our heads: The mental demands of modern life*. Cambridge. MA: Harvard University Press.

Kegan, R. (2009). A constructive-developmental approach to trans-formative learning. In K. Illeris (Ed.), *Contemporary theories of learning: Learning theorists … in their own words* (pp. 35–52). New York: Routledge.

Kelley, K. (1995, May/June). Visions: Maya Angelou. *Mother Jones*,. Retrieved from www.motherjones.com/media/1995/05/visions-maya-angelou.

Kensinger, E. A. (2012). Emotion-memory interactions in older adulthood. In M. Naveh-Benjamin & N. Ohta (Eds.), *Memory and aging: Current issues and future directions* (pp. 215–244). New York: Psychology Press.

Kensinger, E. A., & Corkin, S. (2004). The effects of emotional content and aging on false memories. *Cognitive, Affective and Behavioral Neuroscience, 4*, 1–9. doi:10.3758/CABN.4.1.1

Kensinger, E. A., & Gutchess, A. H. (2017). Cognitive aging in a social and affective context: Advances over the past 50 years. *Journal of Gerontology: Psychological Sciences, 72*, 61–70. doi:10.1093/geronb/gbw056

Kepple, A. L., Azzam, P. N., Gopalan, P., & Arnold, R. M. (2015). Decision-making capacity at the end of life. *Progress in Palliative Care: Science and the Art of Caring, 23*, 133–136. doi:10.1179/1743291X14Y.0000000109

Kersting, A., & Nagl, M. (2016). Grief after perinatal loss. In A. Milunsky & J. M. Milunsky (Eds.), *Genetic disorders and the fetus: Diagnosis, prevention, and treatment* (Vol. 7, pp. 1048–1062). Hoboken, NJ: Wiley. doi:10.1002/9781118981559.ch31

Kersting, A., Brähler, E., Glaesmer, H., & Wagner, B. (2011). Prevalence of complicated grief in a representative population-based sample. *Journal of Affective Disorders, 131*, 339–343. doi:10.1016/j.jad.2010.11.032

Kessler, R. C., Berglund, P., Demler, O., Jin, R., Merakangas, K. R., & Walters, E. E. (2005). Lifetime prevalence and age-of-onset distributions of DSM-IV disorders in the National Comorbidity Survey Replication. *Archives of General Psychiatry, 62*, 593–602. doi:10.1001/archpsyc.62.6.593

Khalil, D. N., Smith, E. L., Brentjens, R. J., & Wolchok, J. D. (2016). The future of cancer treatment: Immunomodulation, CARs, and combination immunotherapy. *Nature Reviews Clinical Oncology, 13*, 273–290. doi:10.1038/nrclinonc.2016.25 Retrieved from www.nature.com/nrclinonc/journal/v13/n5/abs/nrclinonc.2016.25.html.

Kiang, L., & Fuligni, A. J. (2009). Ethnic identity and family processes among adolescents from Latin American, Asian, and European backgrounds. *Journal of Youth and Adolescence, 38*, 228–241. doi:10.1007/s10964-008-9353-0

Kiaye, R. E., & Singh, A. M. (2013). The glass ceiling: A perspective of women working in Durban. *Gender in Management: An International Journal, 28*, 28–42. doi:10.1108/17542411311301556

Kievit, R. A., Scholte, H. S., Waldorp, L. J., & Borsboom, D. (2016). Inter- and intra-individual differences in fluid reasoning show distinct cortical responses. *bioRxiv*. doi:10.1101/039412 Retrieved from biorxiv.org/content/biorxiv/early/2016/02/10/039412.full.pdf.

Killett, A., Burns, D., Kelly, F., Brooker, D., Bowes, A., La Fontaine, J. et al. (2016). Digging deep: How organizational culture affects care home residents' experiences. *Ageing and Society, 36*, 160–188. doi:10.1017/S0144686X14001111

Killett, A., Burns, D., Kelly, F., Brooker, D., Bowes, A., & La Fontaine, J. (2016). Digging deep: How organisational culture affects care home residents' experiences. *Ageing & Society, 36*, 160–188. doi:10.1017/S0144686X14001111

Kim, H. K., Capaldi, D. M., & Crosby, L. (2007). Generalizability of Gottman and Colleagues' affective process models of couples' relationship outcomes. *Journal of Marriage and Family, 69*, 55–72. doi:10.1111/j.1741-3737.2006.00343.x

Kim, H.-J., & Fredriksen-Goldsen, K. I. (2016). Living arrangement and loneliness among lesbian, gay, and bisexual older adults. *The Gerontologist, 56*, 548–558. doi:10.1093/geront/gnu083

Kim, P., Strathearn, L., & Swain, J. E. (2016). The maternal brain and its plasticity in humans. *Hormones and Behavior, 77*, 113–123. doi:10.1016/j.yhbeh.2015.08.001

Kim, S., Healey, M. K., Goldstein, D., Hasher, L., & Wiprzycka, U. J. (2008). Age differences in choice satisfaction: A positivity effect in decision making. *Psychology and Aging, 23*, 33–38. doi:10.1037/0882-7974.23.1.33

Kimbler, K. J., Margrett, J. A., & Johnson, T. L. (2012). The role of supportive messages and distracting thoughts on everyday problem-solving performance. *Experimental Aging Research, 38*, 537–558. doi:10.1080/0361073X.2012.726158

King, A. (2016). *Older lesbian, gay, and bisexual adults: Identities, intersections, and institutions*. New York: Routledge.

King, P. M., & Kitchener, K. S. (2002). The reflective judgment model: Twenty years of research on epistemic cognition. In B. K. Hofer & P. R. Pintrich (Eds.), *Personal epistemology: The psychology of beliefs about knowledge and knowing* (pp. 37–61). Mahwah, NJ: Erlbaum.

King, P. M., & Kitchener, K. S. (2004). Reflective judgment: Theory and research on the development of epistemic assumptions through adulthood. *Educational Psychologist, 39*, 5–18. doi:10.1207/s15326985ep3901_2

King, P. M., & Kitchener, K. S. (2015). Cognitive development in the emerging adult: The emergence of complex cognitive skills. In J. J. Arnett (Ed.), *The Oxford handbook of emerging adulthood* (pp. 105–125). New York: Oxford University Press.

King, S. V., Burgess, E. O., Akinyela, M., Counts-Spriggs, M., & Parker, N. (2006). The religious dimensions of the grandparent role in three-generation African American households. *Journal of Religion, Spirituality & Aging, 19*, 75–96. doi:10.1300/J496v19n01_06

Kingston, A., Collerton, J., Davies, K., Bond, J., Robinson, L., & Jagger, C. (2012). Losing the ability to activities of daily living in the oldest old: A hierarchic disability scale from the Newcastle 85+ study. *PLOS ONE, 7*, e31665. doi:10.1371/journal.pone.0031665

Kinney, J. M., & Cavanaugh, J. C. (1993, November). *Until death do us part: Striving to find meaning while caring for a spouse with dementia*. Paper presented at the meeting of the Gerontological Society of America, New Orleans.

Kinney, J. M., Ishler, K. J., Pargament, K. I., & Cavanaugh, J. C. (2003). Coping with the uncontrollable: The use of general and religious coping by caregivers to spouses with dementia. *Journal of Religious Gerontology, 14*, 171–188. doi:10.1300/ J078v14n02_06

Kinsella, G. J., Ong, B., Storey, E., Wallace, J., & Hester, R. (2007). Elaborated spaced-retrieval and prospective memory in mild Alzheimer's disease. *Neuropsychological Rehabilitation, 17*, 688–706. doi:10.1080/09602010600892824

Kinsella, K., & Phillips, D. R. (2005).Global aging: The challenge of success. *Population Bulletin, 60*. Retrieved from www.prb.org/pdf05/60.1GlobalAging.pdf.

Kippen, R., Chapman, B., & Yu, P. (2009). *What's love got to do with it? Homogamy and dyadic approaches to understanding marital instability*. Retrieved from www.cbe.anu.edu.au/researchpapers/cepr/DP631.pdf.

Kirmayer, L. J., Rousseau, C., Eric Jarvis, G., & Guzder, J. (2015). The cultural context of clinical assessment. In A. Tasman, J. Kay, J. A.Lieberman, M. B. First, & M. B. Riba (Eds.), *Psychiatry* (4th ed., pp. 56–70). Chichester, UK: Wiley.

Kirwan, C. B., & Nash, M. I. (2016). Resolving interference: The role of the human hippocampus in pattern separation. In P. A. Jackson, A. A., Chiba, R. F. Berman, & M. E. Ragozzino (Eds.), *The neurological basis of memory* (pp. 151–173). New York: Springer. doi:10.1007/978-3-319-15759-7_7

Kite, E., & Davy, C. (2015). Using Indigenist and Indigenous methodologies to connect to deeper understandings of Aboriginal and Torres Strait Islander peoples' quality of life. *Health Promotion Journal of Australia, 26*, 191–194. doi:10.1071/HE15064

Kivett, V. R. (1991). Centrality of the grandfather role among older rural black and white men. *Journal of Gerontology: Social Sciences, 46*, S250–S258. doi:10.1093/ geronb/46.5.S250

Klackl, J., Jonas, E., & Kronbichler, M. (2013). Existential neuroscience: Neurophysiological correlates of proximal defenses against death-related thoughts. *Social Cognitive and Affective Neuroscience, 8*, 333–340. doi:10.1093/scan/nss003

Kleiber, D. A. (2013). Redeeming leisure in later life. In T. Freire (Ed.), *Positive leisure science* (pp. 21–38). New York: Springer.

Kleiber, D. A., Hutchinson, S. L., & Williams, R. (2002). Leisure as a resource in transcending negative life events: Self-protection, self-restoration, and personal transformation. *Leisure Sciences, 24*, 219–235. doi:10.1080/01490400252900167

Kliegel, M., Ballhausen, N., Hering, A., Ihle, A., Schnitzspahn, K. M., & Zuber, S. (2016). Prospective memory in older adults: Where we are now and what is next. *Gerontology, 62*, 459–466. doi:10.1159/000443698

Klug, M. G., Volkov, B., Muus, K., & Halaas, G. W. (2012). Deciding when to put grandma in the nursing home: Measuring inclinations to place persons with dementia. *American Journal of Alzheimer's Disease and Other Dementias, 27*, 223–227. doi:10.1177/1533317512449729

Kluger, J. (2000). How to improve it: The battle to save your memory. *Time, 155*(24), 46.

Knee, D. O. (2010). Hospice care for the aging population in the United States. In J. C. Cavanaugh & C. K. Cavanaugh (Eds.), *Aging in America: Vol. 3: Societal issues* (pp. 203–221). Santa Barbara, CA: Praeger Perspectives.

Knowles, M. S., Holton, E. F., III, & Swanson, R. A. (2015). *The adult learner* (8th ed.). New York: Routledge.

Ko, H.-J., Mejia, S., & Hooker, K. (2014). Social possible selves, self-regulation, and social goal progress in older adulthood. *International Journal of Behavioral Development, 38*, 219–227. doi: 10.1177/0165025413512063

Koenig, B. L., Kirkpatrick, L. A., & Ketelaar, T. (2007). Misperception of sexual and romantic interests in opposite-sex friendships: Four hypotheses. *Personal Relationships, 14*, 411–429. doi:10.1111/j.1475-6811.2007.00163.x

Koestenbaum, P. (1976). *Is there an answer to death?* Englewood Cliffs, NJ: Prentice Hall.

Kojima, G., Iliffe, S., Jivraj, S., & Walters, K. (2016). Association between frailty and quality of life among community-dwelling older people: A systematic review and meta-analysis. *Journal of Epidemiology & Community Health, 70*, 716–721. doi:10.1136/jech-2015-206717

Kojola, E., & Moen, P. (2016). No more lock-step retirement: Boomers' shifting meanings of work and retirement. *Journal of Aging Studies, 36*, 59–70. doi:10.1016/j.jaging.2015.12.003

Kolb, D. M., Williams, J., & Frohlinger, C. (2010). *Her place at the table: A woman's guide to negotiating five key challenges to leadership success*. San Francisco, CA: Jossey-Bass.

Koppel, J., & Berntsen, D. (2015). The peaks of life: The differential temporal locations of the reminiscence bump across disparate cueing methods. *Journal of Applied Research in Memory and Cognition, 4*, 66–80. doi:10.1016/j.jarmac.2014.11.004

Kornadt, A. E., & Rothermund, K. (2012). Internalization of age stereotypes into the self-concept via future self-views: A general model and domain-specific differences. *Psychology and Aging, 27*, 164–172. doi:10.1037/a0025110

Kornadt, A. E., Hess, T. M., Voss, P., & Rothermund, K. (in press). Subjective age across the life span: A differentiated, longitudinal approach. *Journal of Gerontology: Psychological Sciences*. doi:10.1093/geronb/gbw072

Koss, C., & Ekerdt, D. J. (in press). Residential reasoning and the tug of the Fourth Age. *The Gerontologist*. doi:10.1093/geront/gnw010

Kotre, J. N. (1999). *Make it count: How to generate a legacy that gives meaning to your life*. New York: Free Press.

Kotre, J. N. (2005, September). Generativity: Reshaping the past into the future. *Science and Theology News*, 42–43. Retrieved from www.johnkotre.com/images/generativity_s_t_news_2005.pdf.

Kotter-Grühn, D. (2016). Aging self. In S. K.Whitbourne (Ed.), *The encyclopedia of adulthood and aging* (pp. 55–59). Malden, MA: Wiley.

Kotter-Grühn, D., & Hess, T. M. (2012). The impact of age stereotypes on self-perceptions of aging across the adult lifespan. *Journal of Gerontology: Psychological Sciences, 67*, 563–571. doi:10.1093/geronb/gbr153

Kowalski, S. D., & Bondmass, M. D. (2008). Physiological and psychological symptoms of grief in widows. *Research in Nursing & Health, 31*, 23–30. doi:10.1002/nur.20228

Kozbelt, A., & Durmysheva, Y. (2007). Lifespan creativity in a non-Western artistic tradition: A study of Japanese Ukiyo-e printmakers. *International Journal of Aging & Human Development, 65*, 23–51. doi:10.2190/166N-6470-1325-T341

Kratzer, J. M. W., & Stevens Aubrey, J. (2016). Is the actual ideal?: A content analysis of college students' descriptions of ideal and actual hookups. *Sexuality and Culture, 20*, 236–254. doi:10.1007/s12119-015-9318-x

Krause, N. (2006). Religion and health in late life. In J. E. Birren & K. W.Schaie (Eds.), *Handbook of the psychology of aging* (6th ed., pp. 499–518). Amsterdam, The Netherlands: Elsevier.

Krause, N. (2016). Assessing the relationships among wisdom, humility, and life satisfaction. *Journal of Adult Development, 23*, 140–149. doi:10.1007/s10804-016-9230-0

Krause, N., & Bastida, E. (2011). Prayer to the saints or the Virgin and health among older Mexican Americans. *Hispanic Journal of Behavioral Sciences, 33*, 71–87. doi:10.1177/0739986310393628

Krause, N., Morgan, D., Chatters, L., & Meltzer, T. (2000). Using focus groups to explore the nature of prayer in late life. *Journal of Aging Studies, 14*, 191–212. doi:10.1016/ S0890-4065(00)80011-0

Kübler-Ross, E. (1969). *On death and dying*. New York: Macmillan.

Kübler-Ross, E. (1974). *Questions and answers on death and dying*. New York: Macmillan.

Kuczmarska, A., Ngo, L. H., Guess, J., O'Connor, M. A., Branford-White, L., Palihnich, K. et al. (2016). Detection of delirium in hospitalized older general medicine patients: A comparison of the 3D-CAM and CAM-ICU. *Journal of General Internal Medicine, 31*, 297–303. doi:10.1007/s11606-015-3514-0

Kuhlmann, B. G., & Boywitt, C. D. (2016). Aging, source memory, and the experience of "remembering." *Aging, Neuropsychology, and Cognition: A Journal on Normal and Dysfunctional Development, 23*, 477–498. doi:10.1080/13825585.2015.1120270

Kuiper, J., Zuidersma, M., Zuidema, S. U., Burgerhof, J. G. M., Stolk, R. P., Voshaar, R. C. O. et al. (2016). Social relationships and cognitive decline: A systematic review and meta-analysis of longitudinal cohort studies. *International Journal of Epidemiology, 45*, 1169–1206. doi:10.1093/ije/dyw089

Kulik, L. (2011). Developments in spousal power relations: Are we moving toward equality? *Marriage and Family Review, 47*, 419–435. doi:10.1 080/01494929.2011.619297

Kulik, L. (2016). Long-term marriages. In S. K. Whitbourne (Ed.), *The encyclopedia of adulthood and aging* (pp. 820–823). New York: Wiley.

Kumar, D. K. V., Choi, S. H., Washicosky, K. J., Eimer, W. A., Tucker, S., Ghofrani, J. et al. (2016). Amyloid-β peptide protects against microbial infection in mouse and worm models of Alzheimer's disease. *Science Translational Medicine, 8*, 340ra72. doi:10.1126/scitranslmed.aaf1059

Kunda, Z., & Spencer, S. J. (2003). When do stereotypes come to mind and when do they color judgment? A goal-based theoretical framework for stereotype activation and application. *Psychological Bulletin, 129*, 522–544. doi:10.1037/0033-2909.129.4.522

Kunkle, F. (2012). Pioneering the granny pod: Fairfax County family adapts to high-tech dwelling that could change elder care. *Washington Post*. Retrieved from www.washingtonpost.com/local/dc-politics/pioneering-the-granny-po-fairfax-county-family-adapts-to-high-tech-dwelling-that-could-changeelder-care/2012/11/25/4d9ccb44-1e18-11e2-ba31-3083ca97c314_story.html?hpid=z3.

Kunz, J. A. (2007). Older adult development. In J. A. Kunz & F. G. Soltys (Eds.), *Transformational reminiscence: Life story work* (pp. 19–39). New York: Springer.

Kurdek, L. A. (2004). Are gay and lesbian cohabiting couples really different from heterosexual married couples? *Journal of Marriage and Family, 66*, 880–900. doi:10.1111/j.0022-2445.2004.00060.x

Kurpiers, L. A., Schulte-Herbrüggen, Ejotre, I., & Reeder, D. M. (2016). Bushemat and emerging infectious diseases: Lessons from Africa. In F. M. Angelici (Ed.), *Problematic Wildlife* (pp. 507–551). New York: Springer. doi:10.1007/978-3-319-22246-2_24

Kwon, S., & Tae, Y.-S. (2012). Nursing home placement: The process of decision making and adaptation among adult children caregivers of demented parents in Korea. *Asian Nursing Research, 6*, 143–151. doi:10.1016/j.anr.2012.10.006

Kyllonen, P. C. (2015). Human cognitive abilities. In L. Corno & E. M. Anderman (Eds.), *Handbook of educational psychology* (3rd ed., pp. 121–134). New York: Routledge.

Kyulo, N. L., Knutsen, S. F., Tonstad, S., Fraser, G. E., & Singh, P. N. (2012). Validation of recall of body weight over a 26-year period in cohort members of the Adventist health Study 2. *Annals of Epidemiology, 22*, 744–746. doi:10.1016/j.annepidem.2012.06.106

Labouvie-Vief, G. (1980). Beyond formal operations: Uses and limits of pure logic in life-span development. *Human Development, 23*, 141–161. doi:10.1159/000272546

Labouvie-Vief, G. (1997). Cognitive-emotional integration in adulthood. In K. W. Schaie & M. P. Lawton (Eds.), *Annual review of gerontology and geriatrics: Focus on emotion and adult development* (Vol. 17. pp. 206–237). New York: Springer.

Labouvie-Vief, G. (2003). Dynamic integration: Affect, cognition, and the self in adulthood. *Current Directions in Psychological Science, 12*, 201–206. doi:10.1046/j.0963-7214.2003.01262.x

Labouvie-Vief, G. (2005). Self-with-other representations and the organization of the self. *Journal of Research in Personality, 39*, 185–205. doi:10.1016/j.jrp.2004.09.007

Labouvie-Vief, G. (2015). *Integrating emotions and cognition throughout the lifespan*. New York: Springer.

Labouvie-Vief, G., & Diehl, M. (1999). Self and personality development. In J. C.Cavanaugh & S. K. Whitbourne (Eds.), *Gerontology: An interdisciplinary perspective* (pp. 238–268). New York: Oxford University Press.

Labouvie-Vief, G., Chiodo, L. M., Goguen, L. A., Diehl, M., & Orwoll, L. (1995). Representations of self across the life span. *Psychology and Aging, 10*, 404–415. doi:10.1037/0882-7974.10.3.404

Labouvie-Vief, G., Grühn, D., & Mouras, H. (2009). Dynamic emotion-cognition interactions in development: Arousal, stress, and the processing of affect. In H. B. Bosworth & C. Hertzog (Eds.), *Aging and cognition: Research methodologies and empirical advances* (pp. 181–196). Washington, DC: American Psychological Association.

Lachman, M. E. (2004). Development in midlife. *Annual Review of Psychology, 55*, 305–331. doi:10.1146/ annurev.psych.55.090902.141521

Lachman, M. E. (2006). Perceived control over aging-related declines: Adaptive beliefs and behaviors. *Current Directions in Psychological Science, 15*(6), 282–286. doi:10.1111/j.1467-8721.2006.00453.x

Lachman, M. E., & Agrigoroaei, S. (2012). Low perceived control as a risk factor for episodic memory: The mediational role of anxiety and task interference. *Memory and Cognition, 40*, 287–296. doi:10.3758/s13421-011-0140-x

Lachman, M. E., & Andreoletti, C. (2006). Strategy use mediates the relationship between control beliefs and memory performance for middle-aged and older adults. *Journals of Gerontology: Psychological Sciences, 61*, P88–P94. Retrieved from psychsocgerontology.oxfordjournals.org/content/61/2/P88.full.

Lachman, M. E., Rosnick, C., & Röcke, C. (2009) The rise and fall of control beliefs in adulthood: Cognitive and biopsychosocial antecedents of stability and change over nine years. In H. Bosworth & C. Hertzog (Eds.), *Aging and cognition: Research methodologies and empirical advances* (pp. 143–160) Washington, DC: American Psychological Association.

Ladin, K., & Reinhold, S. (2013). Mental health of aging immigrants and native-born men across 11 European countries. *Journal of Gerontology: Social Sciences, 68*, 298–309. doi:10.1093/geronb/gbs163

Lagattuta, K. H., Elrod, N. M., & Kramer, H. J. (2016). How do thoughts, emotions and decisions align? A new way to examine theory of mind during middle childhood and beyond. *Journal of Experimental Child Psychology, 149*, 116–133. doi:10.1016/j.jecp.2016.01.013

Lahey, J. N. (2010). International comparison of age discrimination laws. *Research on Aging, 32*, 679–697. doi:10.1177/0164027510379348

Lahti, J., Sabia, S., Singh-Manoux, A., Kivimäki, M., Tatsuse, T., Yamada, M. et al. (2016). Leisure time physical activity and subsequent physical and mental health functioning among midlife Finnish, British, and Japanese employees: A follow-up study in three occupational cohorts. *BMJ Open, 6*, e009788. doi:10.1136/bmjopen-2015-009788

Lai, C. K. Y., Wong, L. F., Liu, K.-H., Lui, W., Chan, M. F., & Yap, L. S. Y. (2013). Online and onsite training for family caregivers of people with dementia: Results form a pilot study. *International Journal of Geriatric Psychiatry, 28*, 107–108. doi:10.1002/gps.3798

Lai, D. W. L. (2010). Filial piety, caregiving appraisal, and caregiving burden. *Research on Aging, 32*, 200–223. doi:10.1177/0164027509351475

Lamanna, M. A., Riedmann, A., & Stewart, S. D. (2015). *Marriages, families, and relationships: Making choices in a diverse society* (12th ed.). Stamford, CT: Cengage Learning.

Lambert-Pandraud, E., Laurent, G., & Lapersonne, E. (2005). Repeat purchasing of new automobiles by older consumers: Empirical evidence and interpretations. *Journal of Marketing, 69*, 97–113. doi: 1509/ jmkg.69.2.97.60757

Lamela, D., Figueiredo, B., Bastos, A., & Feinberg, M. (2016). Typologies of post-divorce coparenting and parental well-being, parenting quality and children's psychological adjustment. *Child Psychiatry & Human Development, 47*, 716–728. doi:10.1007/s10578-015-0604-5

Lampkin-Hunter, T. (2010). *Single parenting*. Bloomington, IN: Xlibris.

Landis, M., Peter-Wright, M., Martin, M., & Bodenmann, G. (2013). Dyadic coping and marital satisfaction of older spouses in long-term marriages. *GeroPsych: The Journal of Gerontopsychology and Geriatric Psychiatry, 26*, 39–47. doi:10.1024/1662-9647/a000077

Landrine, H., Corral, I., Hall, M. B., Bess, J. J., & Efird, J. (2016). Self-rated health, objective health, and racial discrimination among African-Americans: Explaining inconsistent findings and testing health pessimism. *Journal of Health Psychology, 21*, 2514–2524. doi:10.1177/1359105315580465

Lane, R. D., & Nadel, L. (Eds.). (2000). *Cognitive neuroscience of emotion*. New York: Oxford University Press.

Lang, F. R. (2004). Social motivation across the life span. In F. R. Land & K. L. Fingerman (Eds.), *Growing together: Personal relationships across the life span* (pp. 341–367). New York: Cambridge University Press.

Langer, E. J. (1989). *Mindfulness*. Reading, MA: Addison-Wesley.

Langer, E. J., & Rodin, J. (1976). The effects of choice and enhanced personal responsibility for the aged: A field experiment in an institutional setting. *Journal of Personality and Social Psychology, 34*, 191–198.

Langer, N., Pedroni, A., Gianotti, L. R. R., Hänggi, J., Knoch, D., & Jäncke, L. (2012). Functional brain network efficiency predicts intelligence. *Human Brain Mapping, 33*, 1393–1406. doi:10.1002/hbm.21297

Langlais, M. R., Anderson, E. R., & Greene, S. M. (2016). Consequences of dating for post-divorce maternal well-being. *Journal of Marriage and Family, 78*, 1032–1046. doi:10.1111/jomf.12319

Larson, C., & Kao, H. (2016). Caregiving. In J. L. Hayashi & B. Leff (Eds.), *Geriatric home-based medical care* (pp. 269–290). New York: Springer. doi:10.1007/978-3-319-23365-9_13

Laurent, H. K., Lucas, T., Pierce, J., Goetz, S., & Granger, D. A. (2016). Coordination of cortisol response to social evaluative threat with autonomic and inflammatory response s is moderated by stress appraisals and affect. *Biological Psychology, 118*, 17–24. doi:10.1016/j.biopsycho.2016.04.066

Lavner, J. A., & Bradbury, T. N. (2017). Protecting relationships from stress. *Current Opinion in Psychology, 13*, 11–14. doi:10.1016/j.copsyc.2016.03.003

Lavner, J. A., Karney, B. R., & Bradbury, T. N. (2016). Does couples' communication predict marital satisfaction, or does marital satisfaction predict communication? *Journal of Marriage and Family, 78*, 680–694. doi:10.1111/jomf.12301

Lavner, J. A., Lamkin, J., Miller, J. D., Campbell, W. K., & Karney, B. R. (2016). Narcissism and newlywed marriage: Partner characteristics and marital trajectories. *Personality Disorders: Theory, Research, and Treatment, 7*, 169–179. doi:10.1037/per0000137

Law, L. L. F., Barnett, F., Yau, M. K., & Gray, M. A. (2014). Effects of combined cognitive and exercise interventions on cognition in older adults with and without cognitive impairment: A systematic review. *Ageing Research Reviews, 15*, 61–75. doi:10.1016/j.arr.2014.02.008

Lawton, L. E., & Tulkin, D. O. (2010). Work-family balance, family structure and family-friendly employer programs. Paper presented at the annual meeting of the Population Association of America, Dallas, Texas. Retrieved from paa2010.princeton.edu/download.aspx?submissionId=100573.

Lawton, M. P. (1982). Competence, environmental press, and the adaptation of old people. In M. P. Lawton, P. G. Windley, & T. O. Byerts (Eds.), *Aging and the environment: Theoretical approaches* (pp. 33–59). New York: Springer.

Lawton, M. P. (1989). Environmental proactivity in older people. In V. L. Bengtson & K. W. Schaie (Eds.), *The course of later life: Research and reflections* (pp. 15–23). New York: Springer.

Lawton, M. P., & Nahemow, L. (1973). Ecology of the aging process. In C. Eisdorfer & M. P. Lawton (Eds.), *The psychology of adult development and aging* (pp. 619–674). Washington, DC: American Psychological Association.

Lawton, M. P., Moss, M., Hoffman, C., Grant, R., Have, T. T., & Kleban, M. H. (1999). Health, valuation of life, and the wish to live. *The Gerontologist, 39*, 406–416. doi:10.1093/geront/39.4.406

Lazarov, O., & Hollandis, C. (2016). Hippocampal neurogenesis: Learning to remember. *Progress in Neurobiology, 138–140*, 1–18. doi:10.1016/j.pneurobio.2015.12.006

Lazarus, R. S. (1984). Puzzles in the study of daily hassles. *Journal of Behavioral Medicine, 7*, 375–389. doi:10.1007/BF00845271

Lazarus, R. S., & Folkman, S. (1984). *Stress, appraisal, and coping*. New York: Springer.

Lazarus, R. S., DeLongis, A., Folkman, S., & Gruen, R. (1985). Stress and adaptational outcomes: The problem of confounded measures. *American Psychologist, 40*, 770–779. 10.1037/0003-066X.40.7.770

Le Couteur, D. G., McLachlan, A. J., & de Cabo, R. (2012). Aging, drugs, and drug metabolism. *Journal of Gerontology: Medical Sciences, 67*A, 137–139. doi:10.1093/Gerona/glr084

Leah, V. (2016). Supporting people with dementia to eat. *Nursing Older People, 28*, 33–39. doi:10.7748/nop.2016.e811

LeanIn.org. (2016). *Women in the workplace 2016*. Retrieved from womenintheworkplace.com.

Lebo, P. B., Quehenberger, F., Kamolz, L.-P., & Lumenta, D. B. (2015). The Angelina Jolie effect revisited: Exploring a media-related impact on public awareness. *Cancer, 121*, 3959–3964. doi:10.1002/cncr.29461

Lee, E.-K. O., & Sharpe, T. (2007). Understanding religious/spiritual coping and support resources among African American older adults: A mixed-method approach. *Journal of Religion, Spirituality & Aging, 19*, 55–75. doi:10.1300/J496v19n03_05

Lee, E.-Y., Eslinger, P. J., Du, G., Kong, L., Lewis, M. M., & Huang, X. (2014). Olfactory-related cortical atrophy is associated with olfactory dysfunction in Parkinson's disease. *Movement Disorders, 29*, 1205–1208. doi:10.1002/mds.25829

Lee, K. H., & Siegle, G. J. (2012). Common and distinct brain networks underlying explicit emotional evaluation: A meta-analytic study. *Social Cognitive and Affective Neuroscience, 7*, 521–534. doi:10.1093/scan/nsp001

Lee, K. S. (2010). Gender, care work, and the complexity of family membership in Japan. *Gender & Society, 24*, 647–671. doi:10.1177/0891243210382903

Lee, M.-D. (2007). Correlates of consequences of intergenerational caregiving in Taiwan. *Journal of Advanced Nursing, 59*, 47–56. doi:10.1111/j.1365-2648.2007.04274.x

Lee, P. C. B. (2003). Going beyond career plateau: Using professional plateau to account for work outcomes. *Journal of Management Development, 22*, 538–551. doi: 10.1108/02621710310478503

Lee, R. E., Hitchcock, R., & Biesele, M. (2002). Foragers to first peoples: The Kalahari San today. *Cultural Survival Quarterly, 26*, 8.

Lee, T.-Y. (2010). The loss and grief in immigration: Pastoral care for immigrants. *Pastoral Psychology, 59*, 159–169. doi:10.1007/s11089-009-0261-3

Lee, Y.-M., Ha, J.-K., Park, J.-M., Lee, B.-D., Moon, E., Chung, Y-I. et al. (2016). Impact of apolipoprotein E4 polymorphism on the gray matter volume and the white matter integrity in subjective memory impairment without white matter hyperintensities: Voxel-based morphometry and tract-based spatial statistics study under 3-Tesla MRI. *Journal of NeuroImaging, 26*, 144–149. doi:10.1111/jon.12207

Leeuwen, K. van. (2016). *Treating grandparents as grandchildren: An overview of elderspeak and the perception of elderspeak in Dutch nursing home*. Unpublished bachelor's thesis, Faculty of Humanities, University of Leiden. Retrieved from openaccess.leidenuniv.nl/handle/1887/37514.

Lefkowitz, E. S., Vukman, S. N., & Loken, E. (2012). Young adults in a wireless world. In A. Booth, S. L. Brown, N. S. Landale, W. D. Manning, & S. M. McHale (Eds.), *Early adulthood in a family context* (pp. 45–56). New York: Springer.

Leichtentritt, R. D., Leichtentritt, J., Barzlal, Y., & Pedatsur-Sukenik, N. (2013). Unanticipated death of a partner: The loss experience of bereaved girlfriends of fallen Israeli soldiers. *Death Studies, 37*, 803–829. doi:10.1080/07481187.2012.699907

Lemaire, P. (2016). *Cognitive aging: The role of strategies*. New York: Routledge.

Lemieux, A. (2012). Post-formal thought in gerontagogy or beyond Piaget. *Journal of Behavioral and Brain Science, 2*, 399–406. doi:10.4236/ jbbs.2012.23046

Lent, R. W. (2013). Career-life preparedness: Revisiting career planning and adjustment in the new workplace. *Career Development Quarterly, 61*, 2–14. doi:10.1002/j.2161-0045.2013.00031.x

Leon, G. R., Gillum, B., Gillum, R., & Gouze, M. (1979).Personality stability and change over a 30-year period: Middle to old age. *Journal of Consulting and Clinical Psychology, 47*, 517–524. doi:10.1037/0022-006X.47.3.517

LeRoux, H., & Fisher, J. E. (2006). Strategies for enhancing medication adherence in the elderly. In W. T. O'Donohue & E. R.Levensky (Eds.), *Promoting treatment adherence: A practical handbook for health care providers* (pp. 353–362). Thousand Oaks, CA: Sage.

Leshikar, E. D., Cassidy, B. S., & Gutchess, A. H. (2016). *Cognitive, Affective, & Behavioral*

Neuroscience, 16, 302–314. doi:10.3758/s13415-015-1-0390-3

Lesnoff-Caravaglia, G. (2010). Technology and aging: The herald of a new age. In J. C. Cavanaugh & C. K. Cavanaugh (Eds.), *Aging in America: Volume 3: Societal issues* (pp. 247–277). Santa Barbara, CA: ABC-CLIO.

Leuty, M. E., Hansen, J.-I. C., & Speaks, S. Z. (2016). Vocational and leisure interests: A profile-level approach to examining interests. *Journal of Career Assessment, 24*, 215–239. doi:10.1177/1069072715580321

Levine, I. S. (2009). *Best friends forever: Surviving a breakup with your best friend*. New York: Penguin.

Levinger, G. (1980). Toward the analysis of close relationships. *Journal of Experimental Social Psychology, 16*, 510–544. doi:10.1016/0022-1031(80)90056-6

Levinger, G. (1983). Development and change. In H. H. Kelley, E.Berscheid, A. Christensen, J. H. Harvey, T. L. Hutson, G. Levinger et al. (Eds.), Close relationships (pp. 315–359). New York: Freeman.

Levinson, D. J., Darrow, C., Kline, E., Levinson, M., & McKee, B. (1978). *The seasons of a man's life*. New York: Knopf.

Levinson, D. J., & Levinson, J. D. (1996). *The seasons of a woman's life*. New York: Knopf.

Levy, B. (1996). Improving memory in old age through implicit stereotyping. *Journal of Personality and Social Psychology, 71*, 1092–1107. doi:10.1037/0022-3514.71.6.1092

Levy, B. R., & Bavishi, A. (in press). Survival advantage mechanism: Inflammation as a mediator of positive self-perceptions of aging on longevity. *Journals of Gerontology: Psychological Sciences*. doi:10.1093/geronb/gbw035

Levy, B. R., Ferrucci, L., Zonderman, A. B., Slade, M. D., Troncoso, J., & Resnick, S. M. (2016). A culture-brain link: Negative age stereotypes predict Alzheimer's disease biomarkers. *Psychology and Aging, 31*, 82–88. doi:10.1037/pag0000062

Levy, B. R., Slade, M. D., & Kasl, S. V. (2002). Longitudinal benefit of positive self-perceptions of aging on functional health. *Journals of Gerontology: Psychological Sciences, 57*B, P409–P417. doi:10.1093/geronb/57.5.P409

Levy, B. R., Zonderman, A. B., Slade, M. D., & Ferrucci, L. (2012). Memory shaped by age stereotypes over time. *Journal of Gerontology: Psychological Sciences, 67*, 432–436. doi:10.1093/geronb/gbr120

Levy, B., & Langer, E. (1994). Aging free from negative stereotypes: Successful memory in China and among the American deaf. *Journal of Personality and Social Psychology, 66*, 989–997. doi:10.1037/0022-3514.66.6.989

Levy, C. R., Zargoush, M., Williams, A. E., Williams, A. R., Giang, P. Wojtusiak, J. et al. (2016). Sequence of functional loss and recovery in nursing homes. *The Gerontologist, 56*, 52–61. doi:10.1093/geront/gnv099

Levy, S. R., & Macdonald, J. L. (2016). Progress on understanding ageism. *Journal of Social Issues, 72*, 5–25. doi:10.1111/josi.12153. Retrieved from onlinelibrary.wiley.com/doi/10.1111/josi.12153/full.

Lewin, K. (1936). *Principles of topological psychology*. New York: McGraw-Hill.

Lewinsohn, P. M. (1975). The behavioral study and treatment of depression. In M. Hersen, R. M. Eisler, & P. M. Miller (Eds.), *Progress in behavior modification* (Vol. *1*, pp. 19–64). New York: Academic Press.

Lewis, D. C., Seponski, D. M., & Camp, T. G. (2011). Religious and spiritual values transactions: A constant-comparison analysis of grandmothers and adult-granddaughters. *Journal of Religion, Spirituality & Aging, 23*, 184–205. doi:10.1080/15528030.2011.533407

Lewis, J. L., & Groh, A. (2016). It's about the people...: Seniors' perspectives on age-friendly communities. In T. Moulaert & S. Garon (Eds.), *Age-friendly communities in international comparison* (pp. 81–98). New York: Springer. doi:10.1007/978-3-319-24031-2_6

Lewis, J. R. (2013). Hair-pulling, culture, and unmourned death. *International Journal of Psychoanalytic Self Psychology, 8*, 202–217. doi:10.1080/1 5551024.2013.768749

Lewis, M., Lamson, A., & White, M. (2016). The state of dyadic methodology: An analysis of the literature on interventions for military couples. *Journal of Couple & Relationship Therapy, 15*, 135–157. doi:10.1080/15332691.2015.1106998

Lewis-Fernández, R., Aggarwal, N. K., Hinton, L., Hinton, D. E., & Kirmayer, L. J. (2015). *DSM-5®: Handbook on the cultural formulation interview*. Washington, DC: American Psychiatric Publishing.

Lewy Body Dementia Association. (2016). *Lewy body dementia symptoms and diagnostic criteria*. Retrieved from www.lbda.org/content/symptoms.

Li, C. M., Zhang, X., Hoffman, H. J., Cotch, M. F., Themann, C. L., & Wilson, M. R. (2014). Hearing impairment associated with depression in US adults, National Health and Nutrition Examination Survey, 2005–2010. *JAMA Otolaryngology—Head & Neck Surgery, 140*, 293–302. doi:10.1001/jamaoto.2014.42

Li, F., Harmer, P., Glasgow, R., Mack, K. A., Sleet, D., Fisher, K. J., Kohn, M. A., Millet, L. M., Mead, J., Xu, J., Lin, M.-L., Yang, T., Sutton, B., & Tompkins, Y. (2008). Translation of an effective tai chi intervention into a community-based falls-prevention program. *American Journal of Public Health, 98*, 1195–1198. Retrieved from ajph.aphapublications.org/doi/pdf/10.2105/AJPH.2007.120402.

Li, J., & Prigerson, H. G. (2016). Assessment and associated features of prolonged grief disorder among Chinese bereaved individuals. *Comprehensive Psychiatry, 66*, 9–16. doi:10.1016/j.comppsych.2015.12.001

Li, K. Z. H., Lindenberger, U., Freund, A. M., & Baltes, P. B. (2001). Walking while memorizing: Age-related differences in compensatory behavior. *Psychological Science, 12*, 230–237. doi:10.1111/1467-9280.00341

Liao, F., & Jan, Y.-K. (2016). Using modified entropy to characterize aging-associated microvascular dysfunction. *Frontiers in Physiology, 7*, 126. doi:10.3389/fphys.2016.00126. Retrieved from www.ncbi.nlm.nih.gov/pmc/articles/PMC4828462/.

Lichtenberg, P. (2016). Financial exploitation, financial capacity, and Alzheimer's disease. *American Psychologist, 71*, 312–320. doi:10.1037/a0040192

Lichtenberg, P. A. (*2016*). New approaches to preventing financial exploitation: A focus on the banks. *Public Policy & Aging Report, 26*, 15–17. doi:10.1093/ppar/prv032

Lieber, J. (2001, October 10). Widows of tower disaster cope, but with quiet fury. *USA Today*, pp. A1–A2.

Lieberman, M. D., Gaunt, R., Gilbert, D. T., & Trope, Y. (2002). Reflexion and reflection: A social cognitive neuroscience approach to attributional inference. *Advances in Experimental Social Psychology, 34*, 199–249. doi:10.1016/S0065-2601(02) 80006-5

Light, L. L. (2012). Dual-process theories of memory in old age: An update. In M. Naveh-Benjamin & N. Ohta (Eds.), *Memory and aging: Current issues and future directions* (pp. 97–124). New York: Psychology Press.

Li-Korotky, H.-S. (2012). Age-related hearing loss: Quality of care for quality of life. *The Gerontologist, 52*, 265–271. doi:10.1093/geront/gnr159

Lilgendahl, J. P., & McAdams, D. P. (2011). Constructing stories of self-growth: How individual differences in patterns of autobiographical reasoning relate to well-being in midlife. *Journal of Personality, 79*, 391–428. doi:10.1111/j.1467-6494.2010.00688.x

Lillyman, S., & Bruce, M. (2017). Palliative care for people with dementia: A literature review. *International Journal of Palliative Nursing, 22*, 76–81. doi:10.12968/ijpn.2016.22.2.76

Limb, G. E., Shafer, K., & Sandoval, K. (2014). The impact of kin support on urban American Indian families. *Child & Family Social Work, 19*, 423–442. doi:10.1111/cfs.12041

Lindbergh, C. A., Dishman, R. K., & Miller, L. S. (2016). Functional disability I mild cognitive impairment: A systematic review and meta-analysis. *Neuropsychology Review, 26*, 129–159. doi:10.1007/s11065-016-9321-5

Linden, D. E. J. (2016). *Neuroimaging and neurophysiology in psychiatry*. Oxford, UK: Oxford University Press.

Lindgren, L., Bergdahl, J., & Nyberg, L. (2016). Longitudinal evidence for smaller hippocampus volume as a vulnerability factor for perceived stress. *Cerebral Cortex, 26*, 3527–3533. doi:10.1093/cercor/bhw154

Lindley, R. I. (2012). Drug trials for older people. *Journal of Gerontology: Biological Sciences, 67*A, 152–157. doi:10.1093/gerona/glr065

Ling, K. H., Ning, W. H., & Hoon, T. C. (2016). *Ginseng and ginseng products 101: What are you buying?* Singapore: World Scientific.

Lipp, I., Benedek, M., Fink, A., Koschutnig, K., Reishofer, G., Bergner, S. et al. (2012). Investigating neural efficiency in the visuo-spatial Domain: An fMRI Study. *PLOS ONE, 7*, e51316. doi:10.1371/journal. pone.0051316. Retrieved from www.plosone.org/article/info%3Adoi%2F10.1371%2Fjournal.pone.0051316.

Lips, H. M. (2016). The gender pay gap and the wellbeing of working women. In M. L. Connerley & J. Wu (Eds.), *Handbook on well-being of working women* (pp. 141–157). New York: Springer.

Lips-Wiersma, M., Wright, S., & Dik. B. (2016). Meaningful work: Differences among blue-, pink-, and white-collar occupations. *Career Development International, 21*, 534–551. doi:10.1108/DCI-04-2016-0052

Liu, C.-C., Kanekiyo, T., Xu, H., & Bu, G. (2013). Apolipoprotein E and Alzheimer's disease: Risk, mechanisms and therapy. *Nature Reviews Neurology, 9*, 106–118. doi:10.1038/ nrneurol.2012.263

Liu, G., Dupre, M. E., Gu, D., Mair, C. A., & Chen, F. (2012). Psychological well-being of the institutionalized and community-residing oldest old in China: The role of children. *Social Science and Medicine, 75*, 1874–1882. doi:10.1016/j.socscimed.2012.07.019

Livingston, G. (2014). *Four-in-ten couples are saying "I do," again*. Retrieved from www.pewsocialtrends.org/2014/11/14/four-in-ten-couples-are-saying-i-do-again/.

Lo, M., & Aziz, T. (2009). Muslim marriage goes online: The use of Internet matchmaking by American Muslims. *Journal of Religion and Popular Culture, 2*(3). doi:10.3138/jrpc.21.3.005

Loaiza, V., Rhodes, M. G., & Anglin, J. (2015). The influence of age-related differences in prior knowledge and attentional refreshing opportunities on episodic memory. *Journal of Gerontology: Psychological Sciences, 70*, 729–736. doi:10.1093/geronb/gbt119

Löckenhoff, C. E., & Carstensen, L. L. (2007). Aging, emotion, and health-related decision strategies: Motivational manipulations can reduce age differences. *Psychology and Aging, 22*, 134–146. doi:10.1037/0882-7974.22.1.134

Loe, M., Sherry, A., & Chartier, E. (2016). Ageism: Stereotypes, causes, effect, and countermovements. In M. H. Meyer & E. A. Daniele (Eds.), *Gerontology: Changes, challenges, and solutions* (Vol. 1, pp. 57–82). Santa Barbara, CA: ABC-CLIO.

Logan, R. D. (1986). A reconceptualization of Erikson's theory: The repetition of existential and instrumental themes. *Human Development, 29,* 125–136. doi:10.1159/000273036

Lomanowska, A. M., & Guitton, M. J. (2016). Online intimacy and well-being in the digital age. *Internet Interventions, 4* (Part2), 138–144. doi:10.1016/j.invent.2016.06.005. Retrieved from www.sciencedirect.com/science/article/pii/S2214782916300021.

Longest, K. C., & Thoits, P. A. (2012). Gender, the stress approach, and health: A configurational approach. *Society and Mental Health, 2,* 187–206. doi:10.1177/2156869312451151

LongTermCare.gov. (2016). *How much care will you need?* Retrieved from longtermcare.gov/the-basics/how-much-care-will-you-need/.

Looi, C. Y., Duta, M., Brem, A.-K., Huber, S., Nuerk, H.-C., & Kadosh, R. C. (2016). Combining brain stimulation and video game to promote long-term transfer of learning and cognitive enhancement. *Scientific Reports, 6,* 22003. doi:10.1038/srep22003

Lord, K., Livingston, G., Robertson, S., & Cooper, C. (2016). How people with dementia and their families decide about moving to a care home and support their needs: Development of a decision aid, a qualitative study. *BMC Geriatrics, 16,* 68. doi:10.1186/s12877-016-0242-1. Retrieved from bmcgeriatr.biomedcentral.com/articles/10.1186/s12877-016-0242-1.

Loretto, W., & Vickerstaff, S. (2013). The domestic and gendered context for retirement. *Human Relations, 66,* 65–86. doi:10.1177/0018726712455832

Lötsch, J., Ultsch, A., & Hummel, T. (2016). How many and which odor identification items are needed to establish normal olfactory function? *Chemical Senses, 41,* 339–344. doi:10.1093/chemse/bjw006

Lou, V. W. Q., & Ng, J. W. (2012). Chinese older adults' resilience to the loneliness of living alone: A qualitative study. *Aging and Mental Health, 16,* 1039–1046. doi:10.1080/1360786 3.2012.692764

Lourenço, J. S., & Maylor, E. A. (2015). When distraction holds relevance: A prospective memory benefit for older adults. *International Journal of Environmental Research and Public Health, 12,* 6523–6541. doi:10.3390/ijerph120606523

Lövdén, M., Brehmer, Y., Li, S.-C., & Lindenberger, U. (2012, May 15). Training-induced compensation versus magnification of individual differences in memory performance. *Frontiers in Human Neuroscience.* doi:10.3389/fnhum.2012.00141. Retrieved from journal.frontiersin.org/article/10.3389/fnhum.2012.00141/full.

Luca, M., Prossimo, G., Messina, V., Luca, A., Romeo, S., & Calandra, C. (2013). Epidemiology and treatment of mood disorders in a day hospital setting from 1996 to 2007: An Italian study. *Neuropsychiatric Disease and Treatment, 9,* 169–176. doi:10.2147/NDT.S39227

Lucas, H. D., Monti, J. M., McAuley, E., Watson, P. D., Kramer, A. F., & Cohen, N. J. (2016). Relational memory and self-efficacy measures reveal distinct profiles of subjective memory concerns in older adults. *Neuropsychology, 30,* 568–578. doi:10.1037/neu0000275

Lucero-Liu, A. A. (2007). Exploring intersections in the intimate lives of Mexican origin women. *Dissertation Abstracts International. Section A. Humanities and Social Sciences, 68*(3-A), 1175.

Ludke, R. L., & Smucker, D. R. (2007). Racial differences in the willingness to use hospice services. *Journal of Palliative Medicine, 10,* 1329–1337. doi:10.1089/jpm.2007.0077

Luhmann, M., Hofmann, W., Eid, M., & Lucas, R. E. (2012). Subjective well-being and adaptation to life events: A meta-analysis. *Journal of Personality and Social Psychology, 102,* 592–615. doi:10.1037/a0025948

Luo, S., & Zhang, G. (2009). What leads to romantic attraction: Similarity, reciprocity, security, or beauty? Evidence from a speed-dating study. *Journal of Personality, 77,* 933–964. doi:10.1111/j.1467-6494.2009.00570.x

Luszcz, M. A., Anstey, K. J., & Ghisletta, P. (2015). Subjective beliefs, memory and functional health: Change and associations over 12 years in the Australian Longitudinal Study of Ageing. *Gerontology, 61,* 241–250. doi:10.1159/000369800

Luthans, F., Avolio, B. J., Avey, J. B., & Norman, S. M. (*2007*). Positive psychological capital: Measurement and relationship with performance and satisfaction. *Personnel Psychology, 60,* 541–572. doi:10.1111/j.1744-6570.2007.00083.x

Lutz, A., Slagter, H. A., Rawlings, N. B., Francis, A. D., Greischar, L. L., & Davidson, R. J. (2009). Mental training enhances attentional stability: Neural and behavioral evidence. *The Journal of Neuroscience, 29,* 13418–13427. doi:10.1523/JNEUROSCI.1614-09.2009

Luxenberg, S. (2014, April 25).Welcoming love at an older age, but not necessarily marriage. *New York Times.* Retrieved from www.nytimes.com/2014/04/26/your-money/welcoming-love-at-an-older-age-but-not-necessarily-marriage.html?_r=0.

Maatz, L., & Hedgepath, A. (2013). *Women and work: 50 years of change since the American Women Report.* Retrieved from www.dol.gov/wb/resources/women_and_work.pdf.

Mace, J. H., & Clevinger, A. M. (2013). Priming voluntary autobiographical memories: Implications for the organization of autobiographical memory and voluntary recall processes. *Memory, 21,* 524–536. doi:10. 1080/09658211.2012.744422

Maciejewski, P. K., Zhang, B., Block, S. D., & Prigerson, H. G. (2007). An empirical examination of the stage theory of grief. *JAMA, 297,* 716–723. doi:10.1001/jama.297.7.716

Mackenzie, P. (2012). Normal changes of ageing. *InnovAiT.* doi:10.1093/ innovait/ins099.

Macnamara, B. N., Hambrick, D. Z., & Oswald, F. L. (2014). Deliberate practice and performance in music, games, sports, education, and professions: A meta-analysis. *Psychological Science, 25,* 1608–1618. doi: 10.1177/0956797614535810

Madden, D. J., Bennett, I. J., Burzynska, A., Potter, G. G., Chen, N-K., & Song, A. W. (2012). Diffusion tensor imaging of cerebral white matter integrity in cognitive aging. *Biochemica et Biophysica Acta (BBA)—Molecular Basis of Disease, 1822,* 386–400. doi:10.1016/j.bbadis.2011.08.003

Magai, C. (2008). Long-lived emotions: A life course perspective on emotional development. In M. Lewis, J. M. Haviland-Jones, & L. F. Barrett (Eds.), *Handbook of emotions* (3rd ed., pp. 376–392). New York: Guilford.

Mahady, G. B., Locklear, T. D., Doyle, B. J., Huang, Y., Perez, A. L., & Caceres, A. (2008). Menopause, a universal female experience: Lessons from Mexico and Central America. *Current Women's Health Reviews, 4,* 3–8. doi:10.2174/157340408783572033

Malhi, G. S., Tanious, M., Das, P., Coulston, C. M., & Berk, M. (2013). Potential mechanisms of action of lithium in bipolar disorder. *CNS Drugs, 27,* 135–153. doi:10.1007/s40263—13-0039-0

Malone, M. L., & Camp, C. J. (2007). Montessori-Based Dementia Programming®: Providing tools for engagement. *Dementia: The International Journal of Social Research and Practice, 6,* 150–157. doi:10.1177/1471301207079099

Mälzer, J. N., Schulz, A. R., & Thiel, A. (2016). Environmental influences on the immune system: The aging immune system. In C. Esser (Ed.), *Environmental influences on the immune system* (pp. 55–76). New York: Springer. doi:10.1007/978-3-7091-1890-0_3

Mandemakers, J. J., & Monden, C. W. S. (2013). Does the effect of job loss on psychological distress differ by educational level? *Work, Employment and Society, 27,* 73–93. doi: 10.1177/0950017012460312

Manji, H., Jäger, H. R., & Winston, A. (2013). HIV, dementia and antiretroviral drugs: 30 years of an epidemic. *Journal of Neurology, Neurosurgery, and Psychiatry, 84,* 1126–1137. doi:10.1136/jnnp-2012-304022

Mankus, A. M., Boden, M. T., & Thompson, R. J. (2016). Sources of variation in emotional awareness: Age, gender, and socioeconomic status. *Personality and Individual Differences, 89,* 28–33. doi:10.1016/j.paid.2015.09.043

Mantler, J., Matejicek, A., Matheson, K., & Anisman, H. (2005). Coping with employment uncertainty: A comparison of employed and unemployed workers. *Journal of Occupational Health Psychology, 10,* 200–209. doi:10.1037/1076-8998.10.3.200

Manzoni, G. M., Cesa, G. L., Bacchetta, M., Castelnuovo, G., Conti, S., Gaggioli, A. et al. (2016). Virtual reality-enhanced cognitive-behavioral therapy for morbid obesity: A randomized controlled study with 1 year follow-up. *Cyberpsychology, Behavior, and Social Networking, 19,* 134–140. doi:10.1089/cyber.2015.0208

Maple, M., Edwards, H., Plummer, D., & Minichiello, V. (2010). Silenced voices: Hearing the stories of parents bereaved through the suicide death of a young adult child. *Health and Social Care in the Community, 18,* 241–248. doi:10.1111/j.1365-2524.2009.00886.x

Maple, M., Edwards, H. E., Minichiello, V., & Plummer, D. (2013). Still part of the family: The importance of physical, emotional and spiritual memorial places and spaces for parents bereaved through the suicide death of their son or daughter. *Mortality, 18,* 54–71. doi:10.1080/13576275.2012.755158

Marcia, J., & Josselson, R. (2013). Eriksonian personality research and its implications for psychotherapy. *Journal of Personality, 81,* 617–629. doi:10.1111/jopy.12014

Markland, A. D., Vaughan, C. P., Johnson, T. M., Burgio, K. L., & Goode, P. S. (2012). Incontinence. *The Medical Clinics of North America, 95,* 539–554. doi:10.1016/j. mcna.2011.02.006

Markus, H., & Nurius, P. (1986). Possible selves. *American Psychologist, 41,* 954–969. doi:10.1037/0003-066X.41.9.954

Marquardt, G., Bueter, K., & Motzek, T. (2014). Impact of the design of the built environment on people with dementia: An evidence-based review. *Health Environments Research & Design Journal, 8,* 127–157. doi:10.1177/193758671400800111

Marques-Aleixo, I., Oliveira, P. J., Moreira, P. I., Magalhães, J., & Ascensão, A. (2012). Physical exercise as a possible strategy for brain protection: Evidence from mitochondrial-mediated mechanisms. *Progress in Neurobiology, 99,* 149–162. doi:10.1016/j.pneurobio.2012.08.002

Marsh, K., & Musson, G. (*2008*). Men at work and at home: Managing emotion in telework. *Gender, Work & Organization, 15,* 31–48. doi:10.111 1/j.1468-0432.2007

Marshall, J. C. (1986, March 2). In the region of lost minds. *New York Times,* C7. Retrieved from https://www.nytimes.com/books/98/12/06/specials/sacks-mistook.html.

Marson, D. (2016). Commentary: A role for neuroscience in preventing financial elder abuse. *Public Policy & Aging Report, 26,* 12–14. doi:10.1093/ppar/prv033

Martens, A., Goldenberg, J. L., & Greenberg, J. (2005). A terror management perspective on ageism. *Journal of Social Issues, 61*, 223–239. doi:10.1111/j.1540-4560.2005.00403.x

Mathur, M. B., Epel, E., Kind, S., Manisha, D., Parks, C. G., Sandler, D. P. et al. (2016). Perceived stress and telomere length: A systematic review, meta-analysis, and methodologic considerations for advancing the field. *Brain, Behavior, and Immunity, 54*, 158–169. doi:10.1016/j.bbi.2016.02.002

Martin, M., Long, M. V., & Poon, L. W. (2002). Age changes and differences in personality traits and states of the old and very old. *Journals of Gerontology: Psychological Sciences, 57B*, P144–P152. doi:10.1093/ geronb/57.2.P144

Martin, S. P., Astone, N. M., & Peters, H. E. (2014). *Fewer marriages, more divergence: Marriage projections for millennials to age 40*. Retrieved from www.urban.org/research/publication/fewer-marriages-more-divergence-marriage-projections-millennials-age-40/view/full_report.

Martin-Uzzi, M., & Duval-Tsioles, D. (2013). The experience of remarried couples in blended families. *Journal of Divorce & Remarriage, 54*, 43–57. doi:10.1080/10502556.2012.743828

Mash, H. B. H., Fullerton, C. S., & Ursano, R. J. (2013). Complicated grief and bereavement in young adults following close friend and sibling loss. *Depression and Anxiety, 30*(12), 1202–1210. doi:10.1002/da.22068

Masunaga, H., & Horn, J. (2001). Expertise and age-related changes in components of intelligence. *Psychology and Aging, 16*, 293–311. doi:10.1037/0882-7974.16.2.293

Masunari, N., Fujiwara, S., Kasagi, F., Takahashi, I., Yamada, M., & Nakamura, T. (2012). Height loss starting in middle age predicts increased mortality in the elderly. *Journal of Bone and Mineral Research, 27*, 138–145. doi:10.1002/jbmr.513

Mather, M. (2012). The emotion paradox in the aging brain. *Annals of the New York Academy of Sciences, 1251*, 33–49. doi:10.1111/j.1749-6632.2012.06471.x

Mather, M. (2016). The affective neuroscience of aging. *Annual Review of Psychology, 67*, 213–238. doi:10.1146/annurev-psych-122414-033540

Matsumoto, D., & Juang, L. (2017). *Culture and psychology* (6th ed.). Stamford, CT: Cengage Learning.

Mattis, J., & Sehgal, A. (2016). Circadian rhythms, sleep, and disorders of aging. *Trends in Endocrinology & Metabolism, 27*, 192–203. doi:10.1016/j.tem.2016.02.003

Maxfield, M., Solomon, S., Pyszczynski, T., & Greenberg, J. (2010). Mortality salience effects on the life expectancy estimates of older adults as a function of neuroticism. *Journal of Aging Research*. doi:10.4061/2010/260123. Retrieved from www.hindawi.com/journals/jar/2010/260123/.

Mayo Clinic. (2014). *Urinary incontinence*. Retrieved from www.mayoclinic.org/diseases-conditions/urinary-incontinence/basics/causes/con-20037883.

Mayo Clinic. (2015a). *Aerobic exercise*. Retrieved from www.mayoclinic.org/healthy-lifestyle/fitness/basics/aerobic-exercise/hlv-20049447.

Mayo Clinic. (2015b). *Delirium*. Retrieved from www.mayoclinic.org/diseases-conditions/delirium/basics/definition/con-20033982.

Mayo Clinic. (2016a). *Angina*. Retrieved from www.mayoclinic.org/diseases-conditions/angina/basics/definition/con-20031194.

Mayo Clinic. (2016b). *Managing your cholesterol*. Retrieved from www.mayoclinic.org/cholesterol-site/scs-20089333.

Mazerolle, M., Régner, I., Morisset, P., Rigalleau, F., & Huguet, P. (2012). Stereotype threat strengthens automatic recall and undermines controlled processes in older adults. *Psychological Science, 23*, 723–727. doi:10.1177/0956797612437607

McAdams, D. P. (2001). The psychology of life stories. *Review of General Psychology, 5*, 100–122. doi:10.1037/1089-2680.5.2.100

McAdams, D. P. (2015). *The art and science of personality development*. New York: Guilford.

McAdams, D. P., & Guo, J. (2015). Narrating the generative life. *Psychological Science, 26*, 475–483. doi:10.1177/0956797614568318

McAdams, D. P., & Olson, B. D. (2010). Personality development: Continuity and change over the life course. *Annual Review of Psychology, 61*, 517–542. doi:10.1146/annurev.psych.093008.100507

McCabe, D. P., & Loaiza, V. M. (2012). Working memory. In S. K. Whitbourne & M. J. Sliwinski (Eds.), *The Wiley-Blackwell handbook of adulthood and aging* (pp. 154–173). Oxford, UK: Wiley-Blackwell.

McCarty, W. P., & Skogan, W. G. (2013). Job-related burnout among civilian and sworn police personnel. *Police Quarterly, 16*, 66–84. doi:10.1177/1098611112457357

McClinton, B. E. (2010). *Preparing for the third age: A retirement planning course outline for lifelong learning programs*. Master's thesis from California State University, Long Beach. Retrieved from gradworks.umi.com/1486345.pdf.

McCloskey, M. S., Phan, K. L., Angstadt, M., Fettich, K. C., Keedy, S., & Coccaro, E. F. (2016). Amygdala hyperactivation to angry faces in intermittent explosive disorder. *Journal of Psychiatric Research, 79*, 34–41. doi:10.1016/j.jpsychires.2016.04.006

McCoyd, J. L. M., & Walter, C. A. (2016). *Grief and loss across the lifespan: A biopsychosocial perspective* (2nd ed.). New York: Springer.

McCrae, R. R. (2016). Integrating trait and process approaches to personality: A sketch of an agenda. In U. Kumar (Ed.), *The Wiley handbook of personality assessment* (pp. 3–18). Malden, MA: Wiley.

McCrae, R. R., & Costa, P. T. Jr. (1994). The stability of personality: Observation and evaluations. *Current Directions in Psychological Sciences, 3*, 173–175. doi:10.1111/1467-8721. ep10770693

McCrae, R. R., & Costa, P. T. Jr. (2003). *Personality in adulthood: A five-factor theory perspective* (2nd ed.). New York: Guilford.

McCrory, P., Meeuwisse, W., Johnston, K., Dvorak, J., Aubry, M., Molloy, M. et al. (2009). Consensus statement on concussion in sport: The 3rd International Conference on Concussion in Sport held in Zurich, November 2008. *British Journal of Sports Medicine, 43*, i76-i84. Retrieved from bjsm.bmj.com/content/43/Suppl_1/i76.full.

McEwen, B. S., Nasca, C., & Gray, J. D. (2016). Stress effects on neuronal structure: Hippocampus, amygdala, and prefrontal cortex. *Neuropsychopharmacology, 41*, 3–23. doi:10.1038/npp.2015.171

McGarry, K., & Schoeni, R. F. (2005). Widow(er) poverty and out-of-pocket medical expenditures near the end of life. *Journal of Gerontology: Social Sciences, 60*, S160–S168. doi:10.1093/ geronb/60.3.S160

McGuire, L. C., Morian, A., Codding, R., & Smyer, M. A. (2000). Older adults' memory for medical information: Influence of elderspeak and note taking. *International Journal of Rehabilitation and Health, 5*, 117–128. doi:10.1023/A:1012906222395

McKay, B. (2016, February 9). A cholesterol conundrum. *Wall Street Journal*, D1–D2.

McKee, A. C., Cairns, N. J., Dickson, D. W., Folkerth, R. D., Keene, C. D., Litvan, I. et al. (2016). The first NINDS/NIBIB consensus meeting to define neuropathological criteria for the diagnosis of chronic traumatic encephalopathy. *Acta Neuropathologica, 131*, 75–86. doi:10.1007/s00401-015-1515-z

McKee, K. J., & Schüz, B. (2015). *Psychosocial factors in healthy aging. Psychology & Health, 30*, 607–626. doi:10.1080/08870446.2015.1026905

McKee-Ryan, F., Song, Z., Wanberg, C. R., & Kinicki, A. J. (2005). Psychological and physical well-being during unemployment: A meta-analytic study. *Journal of Applied Psychology, 90*, 53–76. doi:10.1037/0021-9010.90.1.53

McKhann, G. M., Knopman, D. S., Chertkow, H., Hyman, B. T., Jack, C. R., Jr., Kawas, C. H. et al. (2011). The diagnosis of dementia due to Alzheimer's disease: Recommendations from the National Institute on Aging—Alzheimer's Association workgroups on diagnostic guidelines for Alzheimer's disease. *Alzheimer's and Dementia: Journal of the Alzheimer's Association, 7*, 263–269. doi:10.1016/j.jalz.2011.03.005

McKinney, B. C., & Sibille, E. (2013). The age-by-disease interaction hypothesis of late-life depression. *American Journal of Geriatric Psychiatry, 21*, 418–432. doi:10.1016/j.jagp.2013.01.053

McLanahan, S., & Jencks, C. (2015). Was Moynihan rights? What happens to children of unmarried mothers. *Education Next, 15*, 14–21.

McLean, K. C. (2016). *The co-authored self: Family stories and the construction of personal identity*. New York: Oxford University Press.

McLean, K. C., & Pasupathi, M. (2012). Processes of identity development: Where I am and how I got there. *Identity, 12*, 8–28. doi:10.1080/15283 488.2011.632363

McLymont, R. (2016, Spring). State of women-owned businesses. *The Network Journal*, 18–19.

Meade, M. L., Nokes, T. J., & Morrow, D. G. (2009). Expertise promotes facilitation on a collaborative memory task. *Memory, 17*, 39–48. doi:10.1080/09658210802524240

Medicare.gov. (2016). *What's Medicare supplemental insurance (Medigap)?* Retrieved from www.medicare.gov/supplement-other-insurance/medigap/whats-medigap.html.

MedlinePlus. (2014). *Aging changes in the female reproductive system*. Retrieved from www.nlm.nih.gov/medlineplus/ency/article/004016.htm.

Mehta, K. K. (1997). The impact of religious beliefs and practices on aging: A cross-cultural comparison. *Journal of Aging Studies, 11*, 101–114. doi:10.1016/ S0890-4065(97)90015-3

Meijer A. M., & van den Wittenboer, G. L. H. (2007). Contribution of infants' sleep and crying to marital relationship of first-time parent couples in the 1st year after childbirth. *Journal of Family Psychology, 21*, 49–57. doi:10.1037/0893-3200.21.1.49

Meilaender, G. (2013). *Bioethics: A primer for Christians* (3rd ed.). Grand Rapids, MI: Eerdmans Publishing.

Meléndez, J. C., Mayordomo, T., Sancho, P., & Tomás, J. M. (2012). Coping strategies: Gender differences and development throughout life span. *The Spanish Journal of Psychology, 15*, 1089–1098.

Meletti, S. (2016). Emotion regulation. In M. Mula (Ed.), *Neuropsychiatric symptoms of epilepsy* (pp. 177–193). New York: Springer.

Ménard, C., Hodes, G. E., & Russo, S. J. (2016). Pathogenesis of depression: Insights from human and rodent studies. *Neuroscience, 321*, 138–162. doi:10.1016/j.neuroscience.2015.05.053

Mendez-Luck, C. A., Geldhof, G. J., Anthony, K. P., Steers, W. N., Mangione, C. M., & Hays, R. D. (2016). Orientation to the caregiver role among Latinas of Mexican origin. *The Gerontologist, 56*, e99–e108. doi:10.1093/geront/gnw087

Menkin, J. A., Robles, T. F., Gruenewald, T. L., Tanner, E. K., & Seeman, T. E. (in press). Positive expectations regarding aging linked to more new friends in later life. *Journal of Gerontology: Social Sciences*. doi:10.1093/geronb/gbv118

Menon, U. (2001). Middle adulthood in cultural perspective: The imagined and the experienced in three cultures. In M. E. Lachman (Ed.), *Handbook of midlife development* (pp. 40–74). New York: Wiley.

Menon, U., & Shweder, R. A. (1998). The return of the "White man's burden": The moral discourse of anthropology and the domestic life of Hindu women. In R. A. Shweder (Ed.), *Welcome to the middle age (and other cultural fictions)* (pp. 139–188). Chicago: University of Chicago Press.

Mercado-Crespo, M. C., Arroyo, L. E., Rios-Ellis, B., D'Anna, L. H., Londoño, C., Núñez, L., Salazar, J., D'Oliveira, V., & Millar, C. (2008). *Latinos and depression: Findings from a community-based mental health promotion effort.* Paper presented at the annual meeting of the American Public Health Association, San Diego, CA.

Mercer, T. (2016). Technology-assisted memory. In A. Attrill & C. Fullwood (Eds.), *Applied cyberpsychology* (pp. 74–88). New York: Springer. doi:10.1057/9781137517036_5

Mertens, A., Becker, S., Theis, S., Rasche, P., Wille, M., Bröhl, C. et al. (2017). Mobile technology improves therapy-adherence rates in elderly patients undergoing rehabilitation—A crossover design study. In V. G. Duffy & N. Lightner (Eds.), *Advances in human factors and ergonomics in healthcare* (pp. 295–308). New York: Springer.

Merz, E.-M., & De Jong Gierveld, J. (2016). Childhood memories, family ties, sibling support and loneliness in ever-widowed older adults: Quantitative and qualitative results. *Ageing and Society, 36*, 534–561. doi:10.1017/S0144686X14001329

MetLife. (2010). *The MetLife national study of adult day services: Providing support to individuals and their family caregivers.* Retrieved from www.metlife.com/assets/cao/mmi/publications/studies/2010/mmiadult-day-services.pdf.

Meyer, B. J. F., Talbot, A. P., & Ranalli, C. (2007). Why older adults make more immediate treatment decisions about cancer than younger adults. *Psychology and Aging, 22*, 505–524. doi:10.1037/0882-7974.22.3.505

Meyer, J. F. (2007). Confucian "familism" in America. In D. S. Browning & D. A. Clairmont (Eds.), *American religions and the family: How faith traditions cope with modernization and democracy* (pp. 168–184). New York: Columbia University Press.

Meza-Kubo, V., & Morán, A. L. (2013). UCSA: A design framework for usable cognitive systems for the worried well. *Personal and Ubiquitous Computing, 17*, 1135–1145. doi:10.1007/s00779-012-0554-x

Michaelian, K., & Arango-Muñoz, S. (2016). *Collaborative memory knowledge: A distributed reliabilist perspective.* Retrieved from phil-mem.org/preprints/distributed-reliabilism.pdf.

Michel, A. (2016, February). Burnout and the brain. *Observer, 29.* Retrieved from www.psychologicalscience.org/index.php/publications/observer/2016/february-16/burnout-and-the-brain.html.

Midlarsky, E., Kahana, E., & Belser, A. (2015). Prosocial behavior in late life. In D. A Schroeder & W. G. Graziano (Eds.), *The Oxford handbook of prosocial behavior* (pp. 415–432). New York: Oxford University Press.

Miedema, M. D., Petrone, A. B., Arnett, D. K., Dodson, J. A., Carr, J. J., Pankow, J. S. et al. (2014). Adult height and prevalence of coronary artery calcium: The National Heart, Lung, and Blood Institute Family Heart Study. *Circulation: Cardiovascular Imaging, 7*, 52–57. doi:10.1161/CIRCIMAGING.113.000681

Miething, A., Almquist, Y. B., Rostila, M., Edling, C., & Rydgren, J. (2016). Friendship networks and psychological well-being from late adolescence to young adulthood: A gender-specific structural equation modeling approach. *BMC Psychology, 4*, 34. doi:10.1186/s40359-016-0143-2. Retrieved from bmcpsychology.biomedcentral.com/articles/10.1186/s40359-016-0143-2.

Miles, E., & Crisp, R. J. (2014). A meta-analytic test of the imagined contact hypothesis. *Group Processes & Intergroup Relations, 17*, 3–26. doi:10.1177/1368430213510573

Miller, A. C. (2016). Opinions on the legitimacy of brain death among Sunni and Shi'a scholars. *Journal of Religion and Health, 55*, 394–402. doi:10.1007/s10943-015-0157-8

Miller, K. I., Shoemaker, M. M., Willyard, J., & Addison, P. (2008). Providing care for elderly parents: A structurational approach to family caregiver identity. *Journal of Family Communication, 8*, 19–43. doi:10.1080/15267430701389947

Miller, K. J., Siddarth, P., Gaines, J. M., Parish, J. M., Ercoli, L. M., Marx, K. et al. (2012). The Memory Fitness Program: Cognitive effects of a healthy aging intervention. *American Journal of Geriatric Psychiatry, 20*, 514–523. doi:10.1097/JGP.0b013e3318227f821

Milligan, C., Turner, M., Blake, S., Brearley, S., Seamark, D., Thomas, C. et al. (2016). Unpacking the impact of older adults' home death on family care-givers' experiences of home. *Health & Place, 38*, 103–111. doi:10.1016/j.healthplace.2016.01.005

Minnotte, K. L. (2015). *Methodologies of assessing marital success.* Retrieved from workfamily.sas.upenn.edu/wfrn-repo/object/w2yp4p7if8lm7q4k.

Miranda, J., McGuire, T. G., Williams, D. R., & Wang, P. (2008). Mental health in the context of health disparities. *American Journal of Psychiatry, 165*, 1102–1108. doi:10.1176/appi.ajp.2008.08030333

Mitchell, B. A. (2006). *The boomerang age: Transitions to adulthood in families.* New Brunswick, NJ: Aldine Transaction.

Mitchell, B. A. (2010). Happiness in midlife parental roles: A contextual mixed methods analysis. *Family Relations, 59*, 326–339. doi:10.1111/j.1741-3729.2010.00605.x

Mitchell, K. J. (2016). The cognitive neuroscience of source monitoring. In J. Dunlosky & S. K. Tauber (Eds.), *The Oxford handbook of metamemory* (pp. 425–450). New York: Oxford University Press.

Mitteldorf, J. (2016). An epigenetic clock controls aging. *Biogerontology, 17*, 257–265. doi:10.1007/s10522-015-9617-5

Mittelmark, M. B., & Bauer, G. F. (2017). The meanings of salutogenesis. In M. B. Mittelmark, S. Sagy, M. Eriksson, G. F. Bauer, J. M. Pelikan, B. Lindström et al. (Eds.), *The handbook of salutogenesis* (pp. 7–13). New York: Springer.

Moak, G. S. (2016). *Beat depression to stay healthier and live longer: A guide for older adults and their families.* Lanham, MD: Rowman & Littlefield.

Modra, L., & Hilton, A. (2016). Ethical issues in resuscitation and intensive care medicine. *Anaesthesia & Intensive Care Medicine, 17*, 35–37. doi:10.1016/j.mpaic.2015.10.006

Moeller, J. R., Lewis, M. M., & Werth, J. L., Jr. (2010). End of life issues. In J. C. Cavanaugh & C. K. Cavanaugh (Eds.), *Aging in America: Vol. 1: Psychological aspects* (pp. 202–231). Santa Barbara, CA: Praeger Perspectives.

Moen, P. (2016a). *Encore adulthood: Boomers on the edge of risk, renewal, & purpose.* New York: Oxford University Press.

Moen, P. (2016b). Work over the gendered life course. In M. J. Shanahan, J. T. Mortimer, & M. K. Johnson (Eds.), *Handbook of the life course* (pp. 249–275). New York: Springer.

Moen, P., & Roehling, P. (2005). *The career mystique: Cracks in the American dream.* Oxford, UK: Rowman & Littlefield.

Mohanty, P., Naveh-Benjamin, M., & Ratneshwar, S. (2016). Beneficial effects of semantic memory support on older adults' episodic memory: Differential patterns of support of item and associative information. *Psychology and Aging, 31*, 25–36. doi:10.1037/pag0000059

Mohlman, J., Sirota, K. G., Papp, L. A., Staples, A. M., King, A., & Gorenstein, E. E. (2012). Clinical interviewing with older adults. *Cognitive and Behavioral Practice, 19*, 89–100. doi:10.1016/j.cbpra.2010.10.001

Mojon-Azzi, S. M., Sousa-Poza, A., & Mojon, D. S. (2008). Impact of low vision on well-being in 10 European countries. *Ophthalmologica, 222*, 205–212. doi:10.1159/000126085

Mok, R. M., Myers, N. E., Wallis, G., & Nobre, A. C. (2016). Behavioral and neural markers of flexible attention over working memory in aging. *Cerebral Cortex, 26*, 1831–1842. doi:10.1093/cercor/bhw011

Molenberghs, P., Johnson, H., Henry, J. D., & Mattingley, J. B. (2016). Unertanding the minds of others: A neuroimaging meta-analysis. *Neuroscience and Biobehavioral Reviews, 65*, 276–291. doi:10.1016/j.neurobiorev.2016.03.020

Molin, P., & Rockwood, K. (2016). The new criteria for Alzheimer's disease—Implications for geriatricians. *Canadian Geriatrics Journal, 19*, 66–73. doi:10.5770/cgj.19.207

Monahan, A. (2017). When a promise is not a promise: Chicago-style pensions. *UCLA Law Review, 64.* Available at SSRN: ssrn.com/abstract=2777736.

Moon, P. J., (2017). Hospice admission assessment: A narrative view. *American Journal of Hospice & Palliative Care, 34*, 201–204. doi:10.1177/1049909115624375

Moorman, S. M., & Greenfield, E. A. (2010). Personal relationships in later life. In J. C. Cavanaugh & C. K. Cavanaugh (Eds.), *Aging in America: Vol. 3: Societal Issues* (pp. 20–52). Santa Barbara, CA: ABC-CLIO.

Moorman, S. M., & Inoue, M. (2013). Persistent problems in end-of-life planning among young- and middle-aged American couples. *Journal of Gerontology: Social Sciences, 68*, 97–106. doi:10.1093/geronb/gbs103

Morcom, A. M. (2016). Mind over memory: Cuing the aging brain. *Current Directions in Psychological Science, 25*, 143–150. doi:10.1177/0963721416645536

Morcom, A. M., & Johnson, W. (2015). Neural reorganization and compensation in aging. *Journal of Cognitive Neuroscience, 27*, 1275–1285. doi:10.1162/jocn_a_00783

Morfei, M. Z., Hooker, K., Fiese, B. H., & Cordeiro, A. M. (2001). Continuity and change in parenting possible selves: A longitudinal follow-up. *Basic and Applied Social Psychology, 23*, 217–223. doi:10.1207/153248301750433777

Morgan, S., & Yoder, L. H. (2012). A concept analysis of person-centered care. *Journal of Holistic Nursing, 30*, 6–15. doi:10.1177/0898010111412189

Morrell, R. W., Echt, K. V., & Caramagno, J. (2008). *Older adults, race/ethnicity, and mental health disparities: A consumer focused research agenda.* Human Resources Research Organization. Retrieved from www.tapartnership.org/docs/researchAgendaOnAgeAndMHDisparities.pdf.

Morris, W. L., Sinclair, S., & DePaulo, B. M. (2007). No shelter for singles: The perceived legitimacy of marital status discrimination. *Group Processes & Intergroup Relation, 10*, 457–470. doi:10.1177/1368430207081535

Mõttus, R., Johnson, W., & Deary, I. J. (2012). Personality traits in old age: Measurement and rank-order stability and some mean-level change. *Psychology and Aging, 27*(1), 243–249. doi:10.1037/a0023690

Moye, J., Sabatino, C. P., & Brendel, R. W. (2013). Evaluation of the capacity to appoint a health-care proxy. *American Journal of Geriatric Psychiatry, 21*, 326–336. doi:10.1016/j.jagp.2012.09.001

Moyer, A. M., Miller, V. M., & Faubion, S. S. (2016). Could personalized management of menopause based on genomics become a reality? *Future Medicine, 17*, 659–662. doi:10.2217/pgs.16.17

Mozaffarian, D., Benjamin, E. J., Go, A. S., Arnett, D. K., Blaha, M. J., Cushman, M. et al. (2016). Heart disease and stroke statistics—2016 Update. *Circulation, 133*, e38–e360. doi:10.1161/CIR.0000000000000350. Retrieved from circ.ahajournals.org/content/early/2015/12/16/CIR.0000000000000350.

Mroczek, D. K., & Spiro, A. (2003). Modeling intraindividual change in personality traits: Findings from the normative aging study. *Journals of Gerontology: Psychological Sciences, 58B*, P153–P165. doi:10.1093/geronb/58.3.P153

Mühlig-Versen, A., Bowen, C. E., & Staudinger, U. M. (2012). Personality plasticity in later adulthood: Contextual and personal resources are needed to increase openness to new experiences. *Psychology and Aging, 27*, 855–866. doi:10.1037/a0029357

Muller, E. D., & Thompson, C. L. (2003). The experience of grief after bereavement: A phenomenological study with implications for mental health counseling. *Journal of Mental Health Counseling, 25*, 183–203. Retrieved from search.proquest.com/openview/d6eac397e4b2ac0d492d49986fe5368b/1?pq-origsite=gscholar.

Munoz, R. T., & Fox, M. D. (2013). Legal aspects of brain death and organ donorship. In D. Novitzky & D. K. C. Cooper (Eds.), *The brain-dead organ donor* (pp. 21–35). New York: Springer.

Muntaner, C., Ng, E., Vanroelen, C., Christ, S., & Eaton, W. W. (2013). Social stratification, social closure, and social class as determinants of mental health disparities. In C. S. Aneshensel, J. C. Phelan, & A. Bieman (Eds.), *Handbook of the sociology of mental health* (pp. 206–227). New York: Springer.

Murayama, K., Toshiya, B., Storm, D., & Benjamin, C. (2014). Forgetting as a consequence of retrieval: A meta-analytic review of retrieval-induced forgetting. *Psychological Bulletin, 140*, 1383–1409. doi:10.1037/a0037505

Mutchler, J. E., Baker, L. A., & Lee, S. A. (2007). Grandparents responsible for grandchildren in Native-American families. *Social Science Quarterly, 88*, 990–1009. doi:10.1111/j.1540-6237.2007.00514.x

Mwanyangala, M. A., Mayombana, C., Urassa, H., Charles, J., Mahutanga, C., Abdullah, S. et al. (2010). Health status and quality of life among older adults in rural Tanzania. *Global Health Action, 3*. Retrieved from journals.sfu.ca/coaction/index.php/gha/article/viewArticle/2142/6055.

Naef, R., Ward, R., Mahrer-Imhof, R., & Grande, G. (2013). Characteristics of the bereavement experience of older persons after spousal loss: An integrative review. *International Journal of Nursing Studies, 50*, 1108–1121. doi:10.1016/j.ijnurstu.2012.11.026

Nagaratnam, N., Nagaratnam, K., & Cheuk, G. (2016). Ear-related problems in the elderly. In N. Nagaratnam, K. Nagaratnam, & G. Cheuk (Eds.), *Diseases in the elderly* (pp. 357–371). New York: Springer. doi:10.1007/978-3-319-25787-7_17

Nahemow, L. (2000). The ecological theory of aging: Powell Lawton's legacy. In R. L. Rubinstein & M. Moss (Eds.), *The many dimensions of aging* (pp. 22–40). New York: Springer.

Napolitano, C. M., & Freund, A. M. (2016). On the use and usefulness of backup plans. *Perspectives on Psychological Science, 11*, 56–73. doi:10.1177/1745691615596991

Nash, J. F., & Tanner, P. R. (2016). The controversy of sunscreen product exposure: Too little, too much, or just right. In S. Q. Wang & H. W. Lin (Eds.), *Principles and practice of photoprotection* (pp. 125–139). New York: Springer. doi:10.1007/978-3-319-29382-0_8

Nashiro, K., Sakaki, M., Huffman, D., & Mather, M. (2013). Both younger and older adults have difficulty updating emotional memories. *Journal of Gerontology: Psychological Sciences, 68*, 224–227. doi:10.1093/geronb/gbs039

National Academy of Social Insurance. (2016). *Social Security benefits, finances, and policy options: A primer.* Retrieved from www.nasi.org/socialsecurityprimer.

National Adult Day Services Association. (2016a). *About adult day services.* Retrieved from www.nadsa.org/learn-more/about-adult-day-services/.

National Adult Day Services Association. (2016b). *Choosing a center.* Retrieved from www.nadsa.org/consumers/choosing-a-center/.

National Adult Protective Services Association. (2016). *Elder Justice Act.* Retrieved from www.napsa-now.org/policy-advocacy/eja-implementation/.

National Alliance for Caregiving and AARP. (2015). *Caregiving in the U.S.: 2015 report.* Retrieved from www.caregiving.org/wp-content/uploads/2015/05/2015_CaregivingintheUS_Final-Report-June-4_WEB.pdf.

National Association for the Education of Young Children. (2016). *What to look for in a program.* Retrieved from families.naeyc.org/what-to-look-for-in-a-program.

National Cancer Institute. (2016a). *SEER Stat Fact Sheets: Prostate Cancer.* Retrieved from seer.cancer.gov/statfacts/html/prost.html.

National Cancer Institute. (2016b). *Prostate cancer—Health professional version.* Retrieved from www.cancer.gov/types/prostate/hp.

National Center for Assisted Living. (2016a). *What is assisted living?* Retrieved from www.ahcancal.org/ncal/about/assistedliving/Pages/What-is-Assisted-Living.aspx.

National Center for Assisted Living. (2016b). *Choosing an assisted living residence: A consumer's guide.* Retrieved from: www.ahcancal.org/ncal/resources/Documents/Choosing%20An%20Assisted%20Living%20Residence%202013.pdf.

National Center for Health Statistics. (2014). *Prevalence of incontinence among older Americans.* Retrieved from www.cdc.gov/nchs/data/series/sr_03/sr03_036.pdf.

National Center for Health Statistics. (2016a). *Health, United States, 2015.* Retrieved from www.cdc.gov/nchs/data/hus/hus15.pdf.

National Center for Health Statistics. (2016b). *Changes in life expectancy by race and Hispanic origin in the United States, 2013–2014.* Retrieved from www.cdc.gov/nchs/products/databriefs/db244.htm.

National Center for Health Statistics. (2016c). *Marriage and divorce.* Retrieved from www.cdc.gov/nchs/fastats/marriage-divorce.htm.

National Center for Health Statistics. (2016d). *Mean age of mothers is on the rise: United States 2000–2014.* Retrieved from www.cdc.gov/nchs/products/databriefs/db232.htm.

National Center for Health Statistics. (2016e). *Unmarried childbearing.* Retrieved from www.cdc.gov/nchs/fastats/unmarried-childbearing.htm.

National Center for State Courts. (2016). *Elder abuse resource guide.* Retrieved from www.ncsc.org/Topics/Children-Families-and-Elders/Elder-Abuse/Resource-Guide.aspx.

National Comprehensive Cancer Network. (2012). *NCCN guidelines for patients: Prostate cancer.* Retrieved from www.nccn.org/patients/patient_guidelines/prostate/files/assets/seo/toc.html.

National Council on Aging. (2016). *Falls prevention facts.* Retrieved from www.ncoa.org/news/resources-for-reporters/get-the-facts/falls-prevention-facts/.

National Council on Alcoholism and Drug Dependence. (2015). *Alcohol, drug dependence, and seniors.* Retrieved from www.ncadd.org/about-addiction/seniors/alcohol-drug-dependence-and-seniors.

National Eye Institute. (2015). *Facts about diabetic eye disease.* Retrieved from nei.nih.gov/health/diabetic/retinopathy.

National Heart, Lung, and Blood Institute. (2010). *Women's Health Initiative.* Retrieved from www.nhlbi.nih.gov/whi/.

National Heart, Lung, and Blood Institute. (2015). *What is atherosclerosis?* Retrieved from www.nhlbi.nih.gov/health/health-topics/topics/atherosclerosis.

National Institute of Arthritis and Musculoskeletal and Skin Diseases. (2014a). *What is osteoarthritis?* Retrieved from www.niams.nih.gov/Health_Info/Osteoarthritis/osteoarthritis_ff.asp>.

National Institute of Arthritis and Musculoskeletal and Skin Diseases. (2014b). *What is rheumatoid arthritis?* Retrieved from www.niams.nih.gov/Health_Info/Rheumatic_Disease/rheumatoid_arthritis_ff.pdf.

National Institute of Mental Health. (2012). *Ethnic disparities persist in depression diagnosis and treatment among older Americans.* Retrieved from www.nimh.nih.gov/science-news/2012/ethnic-disparities-persist-in-depression-diagnosis-and-treatment-among-older-americans.shtm.

National Institute of Mental Health. (2016a). *Major depression among adults.* Retrieved from www.nimh.nih.gov/health/statistics/prevalence/major-depression-among-adults.shtml.

National Institute of Mental Health. (2016b). *Mental health medications.* Retrieved from www.nimh.nih.gov/health/topics/mental-health-medications/index.shtml#part_149856.

National Institute of Mental Health. (2016c). *Electroconvulsive therapy lifts depression, sustains remission in older adults.* Retrieved from www.nimh.nih.gov/news/science-news/2016/electroconvulsive-therapy-lifts-depression-sustains-remission-in-older-adults.shtml.

National Institute of Mental Health. (2016d). *Brain stimulation therapies.* Retrieved from www.nimh.nih.gov/health/topics/brain-stimulation-therapies/brain-stimulation-therapies.shtml.

National Institute of Mental Health. (2016e). *Anxiety disorders.* Retrieved from www.nimh.nih.gov/health/topics/anxiety-disorders/index.shtml.

National Institute of Mental Health. (2016f). *Obsessive-compulsive disorder.* Retrieved from www.nimh.nih.gov/health/topics/obsessive-compulsive-disorder-ocd/index.shtml.

National Institute of Mental Health. (2016g). *Any anxiety disorder among adults.* Retrieved from www.nimh.nih.gov/health/statistics/prevalence/any-anxiety-disorder-among-adults.shtml.

National Institute of Mental Health. (2016h). *What is coordinated specialty care (CSC)?* Retrieved from www.nimh.nih.gov/health/topics/schizophrenia/raise/what-is-coordinated-specialty-care-csc.shtml.

National Institute of Mental Health. (2016i). *Post-traumatic stress disorder.* Retrieved from www.nimh.nih.gov/health/topics/post-traumatic-stress-disorder-ptsd/index.shtml.

National Institute of Neurological Disorders and Stroke. (2016). *NINDS Wernicke-Korsakoff syndrome information page.* www.ninds.nih.gov/disorders/wernicke_korsakoff/wernicke-korsakoff.htm.

National Institute on Aging. (2012) *Longer lives and disability.* Retrieved from www.nia.nih.gov/research/publication/global-health-and-aging/longer-lives-and-disability.

National Institute on Aging. (2015a). *Aging hearts and arteries: A scientific quest.* Retrieved from d2cauhfh6h4x0p.cloudfront.net/s3fs-public/hearts_and_arteries.pdf.

National Institute on Aging. (2015b). *Alzheimer's disease: Unraveling the mystery. The hallmarks of AD.* Retrieved from www.nia.nih.gov/alzheimers/publication/part-2-what-happens-brain-ad/hallmarks-ad.

National Institute on Alcohol Abuse and Alcoholism. (2014). *Treatment of alcohol problems: Finding and getting help.* Retrieved from pubs.niaaa.nih.gov/publications/Treatment/treatment.htm.

National Institute on Alcohol Abuse and Alcoholism. (2016a). *Older adults.* Retrieved from www.niaaa.nih.gov/alcohol-health/special-populations-co-occurring-disorders/older-adults.

National Institute on Alcohol Abuse and Alcoholism. (2016b). *Alcohol use disorder.* Retrieved from www.niaaa.nih.gov/alcohol-health/overview-alcohol-consumption/alcohol-use-disorders.

National Institute on Alcohol Abuse and Alcoholism. (2016c). *Alcohol use in older people.* Retrieved from www.nia.nih.gov/health/publication/alcohol-use-older-people.

National Osteoporosis Foundation. (2016a). *Bone health basics: Get the facts.* Retrieved from www.nof.org/prevention/general-facts/.

National Osteoporosis Foundation. (2016b). *Food and your bones: Osteoporosis nutrition guidelines.* Retrieved from www.nof.org/patients/treatment/nutrition/.

National Osteoporosis Foundation. (2016c). *Calcium/Vitamin D.* Retrieved from www.nof.org/patients/treatment/calciumvitamin-d/.

National Women's Law Center. (2016). *The wage gap: The who, how, why, and what to do.* Retrieved from nwlc.org/resources/the-wage-gap-the-who-how-why-and-what-to-do/.

Nawijn, J., De Bloom, J., & Geurts, S. (2013). Pre-vacation time: Blessing or burden? *Leisure Sciences, 35,* 33–44. doi:10.1080/01490400.2013.739875

Nayernouri, T. (2011). Euthanasia, terminal illness and quality of life. *Archives of Iranian Medicine, 14,* 54–55. Retrieved from sid.ir/En/VEWSSID/J_pdf/86920110109.pdf.

Neal, M. B., & Hammer, L. B. (2007). *Working couples caring for children and aging parents: Effects on work and well-being.* Mahwah, NJ: Erlbaum.

Neft, N., & Levine, A. D. (1997). *Where women stand: An international report on the status of women in over 140 countries, 1997–1998.* New York: Random House.

Nehamas, A. (2016). *On friendship.* New York: Basic Books.

Neisser, U. (1976). *Cognition and reality.* San Francisco, CA: W. H. Freeman.

Neisser, U. (2012). Flashbulb memories. In S. R. R. Schmidt (Ed.), *Extraordinary memories for exceptional events* (pp. 45–66). New York: Psychology Press.

Nelson, T. D. (2016). Promoting healthy aging by confronting ageism. *American Psychologist, 71,* 276–282. doi: 10.1037/a0040221

Nelson, T. D. (2016). The age of ageism. *Journal of Social Issues, 72,* 191–198. doi:10.1111/josi.12162

Neugarten, B. L., & Weinstein, K. K. (1964). The changing American grandparent. *Journal of Marriage and Family, 26,* 299–304. doi:10.2307/349727

Nevalainen, N., Riklund, K., Andersson, M., Axelsson, J., Ögren, M., Lövden, M. et al. (2015). COBRA: A prospective multimodal imaging study of dopamine, brain structure and function, and cognition. *Brain Research, 1612,* 83–103. doi:10.1016/j.brainres.2014.09.010

Neville, C., Beattie, E., Fielding, E., & MacAndrew, M. (2015). Literature review: Use of respite by carers of people with dementia. *Health and Social Care in the Community, 23,* 51–63. doi:10.1111/hsc.12095

Newman, A., Thompson, J., & Chandler, E. M. (2013). Continuous care: A home hospice benefit. *Clinical Journal of Oncology Nursing, 17,* 19–20. doi:10.1188/13.CJON.19-20

Newman, B. M., & Newman, P. R. (2016). *Theories of human development* (2nd ed.). New York: Psychology Press.

Newsom, J. T. (1999). Another side to caregiving: Negative reactions to being helped. *Current Directions in Psychological Science, 8,* 183–187. doi:10.1111/1467-8721.00043

Newton, N. J., & Jones, B. K. (2016). Passing on: Personal attributes associated with midlife expressions of intended legacies. *Developmental Psychology, 52,* 341–353. doi:10.1037/a0039905

Newton, N. J., & Stewart, A. J. (2012). Personality development in adulthood. In S. K. Whitbourne & M. J. Sliwinski (Eds.), *The Wiley-Blackwell handbook of adulthood and aging* (pp. 209–235). Oxford, UK: Wiley-Blackwell.

Ng, R., Allore, H. G., Monin, J. K., & Levy, B. R. (2016). Retirement as meaningful: Positive retirement stereotypes associated with longevity. *Journal of Social Issues, 72,* 69–85. doi:10.1111/josi.12156

Nichols, L. O., Chang, C., Lummus, A., Burns, R., Martindale-Adams, J., Graney, M. J., Coon, D. W., & Czaja, S. (2008). The cost-effectiveness of a behavioral intervention with caregivers of patients with Alzheimer's disease. *Journal of the American Geriatrics Society, 56,* 413–420. doi:10.1111/j.1532-5415.2007.01569.x

Nicolas, G., Wallon, D., Charbonnier, C., Quenez, O., Rousseau, S., Richard, A.-C. et al. (2016). Screening of dementia genes by whole-exome sequencing in early-onset Alzheimer disease: Input and lessons. *European Journal of Human Genetics, 24,* 710–716. doi:10.1038/ejhg.2015.173

Nielsen, M. K., Neergaard, M. A., Jensen, A. B., Bro, F., & Guldin, M.-B. (2016). Do we need to change our understanding of anticipatory grief in caregivers? A systematic review of caregiver studies during end-of-life caregiving and bereavement. *Clinical Psychology Review, 44,* 75–93. doi:10.1016/j.cpr.2016.01.002

Nigro, N., & Christ-Crain, M. (2012). Testosterone treatment in the aging male: Myth or reality? *Swiss Medical Weekly.* doi:10.4414/ smw.2012.13539. Retrieved from www.smw.ch/content/smw-2012-13539/.

NIHSeniorHealth.gov. (2016a). *Depression.* Retrieved from nihseniorhealth.gov/depression/aboutdepression/01.html.

NIHSeniorHealth.gov. (2016b). *Paying for long-term care.* Retrieved from nihseniorhealth.gov/longtermcare/payingforlongtermcare/01.html.

Nikolaidis, A., Baniqued, P. L., Kranz, M. B., Scavuzzo, C. J., Barbey, A. K., Kramer, A. F. et al. (2017). Multivariate associations of fluid intelligence and NAA. *Cerebral Cortex, 27,* 2607–2616. doi:10.1093/cercor/bhw070. Retrieved from academic.oup.com/cercor/article/doi/10.1093/cercor/bhw070/3056296/Multivariate-Associations-of-Fluid-Intelligence.

Nimrod, G. (2007a). Retirees' leisure: Activities, benefits, and their contribution to life satisfaction. *Leisure Studies, 26,* 65–80. doi:10.1080/02614360500333937

Nimrod, G. (2007b). Expanding, reducing, concentrating and diffusing: Post retirement leisure behavior and life satisfaction. *Leisure Sciences, 29,* 91–111. doi:10.1080/01490400600983446

Nishijima, T., Torres-Aleman, I., & Soya, H. (2016). Exercise and cerebrovascular plasticity. In K. Masamoto, H. Hirase, & K. Yamada (Eds.), *New horizons in neurovascular coupling: A bridge between brain circulation and neural plasticity* (pp. 243–268). San Diego, CA: Elsevier.

Norris, D. R. (2016). *Job loss, identity, and mental health.* New Brunswick, NJ: Rutgers University Press.

North American Menopause Society. (2016). *The experts do agree about hormone therapy.* Retrieved from www.menopause.org/for-women/menopauseflashes/menopause-symptoms-and-treatments/the-experts-do-agree-about-hormone-therapy.

North, M. S., & Fiske, S. T. (2012). An inconvenienced youth? Ageism and its potential intergenerational roots. *Psychological Bulletin, 138,* 982–997. doi:10.1037/a0027843

North, M. S., & Fiske, S. T. (2016). Resource scarcity and prescriptive attitudes generate subtle, intergenerational older-worker exclusion. *Journal of Social Issues, 72,* 122–145. doi:10.1111/josi.12159

Norton, M. I., & Gino, F. (2014). Rituals alleviate grieving for loved ones, lovers, and lotteries. *Journal of Experimental Psychology: General, 143,* 266–272. doi:10.1037/a0031772

Nosek, M., Kennedy, H. P., & Gudmundsdottir, M. (2012). Distress during the menopause transition: A rich contextual analysis of midlife women's narratives. *Sage Open, 2.* doi:10.1177/2158244012455178

NotAlone.gov. (2016). *Not alone: Together against sexual assault.* Retrieved from www.notalone.gov/.

Nuzum, D., Meaney, S., O'Donoghue, K., & Morris, H. (2015). The spiritual and theological issues raised in stillbirth for healthcare chaplains. *Journal of Pastoral Care & Counseling, 69,* 163–170. doi:10.1177/1542305015602714

Nyberg, L., Lövdén, M., Riklund, K., Lindenberger, U., & Bäckman, L. (2012). Memory aging and brain maintenance. *Trends in Cognitive Sciences, 16,* 292–306. doi:10.1016/j.tics.2012.04.005

O'Brien, L. T., & Hummert, M. L. (2006). Memory performance of late middle-aged adults: Contrasting self-stereotyping and stereotype threat accounts of assimilation to age stereotypes. *Social Cognition, 24,* 338–358. doi:10.1521/soco.2006.24.3.338

O'Dell, C. D. (2007). *Mothering mother: A daughter's humorous and heartbreaking memoir.* Largo, FL: Kunati, Inc.

O'Leary, K. D. (1993). Through a psychological lens: Personality traits, personality disorders, and levels of violence. In R. J. Gelles & D. R. Loseke (Eds.), *Current controversies on family violence* (pp. 7–30). Newbury Park, CA: Sage.

O'Rourke, N., & Cappeliez, P. (2005). Marital satisfaction and self-deception: Reconstruction of relationship histories among older adults. *Social Behavior and Personality, 33,* 273–282. doi:10.2224/sbp.2005.33.3.273

Obhi, H. K., & Woodhead, E. L. (2016). Attitudes and experiences with older adults: A case for service learning for undergraduates. *Gerontology and Geriatrics Education, 37,* 108–122. doi:10.1080/02701960.2015.1079704

Oburu, P. O., & Palmérus, K. (2005). Stress-related factors among primary and part-time caregiving grandmothers of Kenyan grandchildren. *International Journal of Aging & Human Development, 60,* 273–282. doi:10.2190/XLQ2-UJEMTAQR-4944

Ochs, E., & Kremer-Sadlik, T. (2013). *Fast-forward family: Home, work, and relationships in middle-class America.* Berkeley, CA: University of California Press.

OECD. (2016). *Balancing paid work, unpaid work and leisure.* Retrieved from www.oecd.org/gender/data/balancingpaidworkunpaidworkandleisure.htm.

Oedekoven, C. S. H., Jansen, A., Kircher, T. T., & Leube, D. T. (2013). Age-related changes in parietal lobe activation during an episodic memory retrieval task. *Journal of Neural Transmission, 120,* 799–806. doi:10.1007/s00702-012-0904-x

Oh, D. H., Kim, S. A., Lee, H. Y., Seo, J. Y., Choi, B.-Y., & Nam, J. H. (2013). Prevalence and correlates of depressive symptoms in Korean adults: Results of a 2009 Korean community health survey. *Journal of Korean Medical Science, 28,* 128–135. doi:10.3346/jkms.2013.28.1.128

Ohnsman, A. (2016, September 28). Warning: Driverless cars are father than they appear. *Forbes,*. Retrieved from http://www.forbes.com/sites/alanohnsman/2016/09/28/warning-driverless-cars-are-farther-than-they-appear/#63ffb7117dee.

Okonski, B. (1996, May 6). Just say something. *Newsweek, 14.*

Old, S., & Naveh-Benjamin, M. (2008). Memory for people and their actions: Further evidence for an age-related associative deficit. *Psychology and Aging, 23,* 467–472. doi:10.1037/0882-7974.23.2.467

Oliveira, B. S., Zunzunegui, M. V., Quinlan, J., Fahmi, H., Tu, M. T., & Guerra, R. O. (2016). Systematic review of the association between chronic social stress and telomere length: A life course perspective. *Aging Research Reviews, 26,* 37–52. doi:10.1016/j.arr.2015.12.006

Omori, M., & Smith, D. T. (2009). The impact of occupational status on household chore hours among dual earner couples. *Sociation Today, 7.* Retrieved from www.ncsociology.org/sociationtoday/v71/chore.htm.

Oosterman, J. M., Morel, S., Meijer, L., Buvens, C., Kessels, R. P. C., & Postma, A. (2011). Differential age effects on spatial and visual working memory. *International Journal of Aging and Human Development, 73,* 195–208. doi:10.2190/AG.73.3.a

Opdebeeck, C., Martyr, A., & Clare, L. (2016). Cognitive reserve and cognitive function in healthy older people: A meta-analysis. *Aging, Neuropsychology, and Cognition: A Journal on Normal and Dysfunctional Development, 23,* 40–60. doi:10.1080/13825585.2015.1041450

Operskalski, J. T., Paul, E. J., Colom, R., Barbey, A. K., & Grafman, J. (2015). Lesion mapping the four-factor structure of emotional intelligence. *Frontiers in Human Neuroscience, 9,* 649. doi:10.3389/fnhum.2015.00649

Orel, N. A., & Coon, D. W. (2016). The challenges of change: How can we meet the care needs of the ever-evolving LGBT family? *Generations, 40,* 41–45.

Orel, N. A., & Fruhauf, C. A. (2013). Lesbian, gay, bisexual, and transgender grandparents. In A. E. Goldberg & K. R. Allen (Eds.), *LGBT-parent families* (pp. 177–192). New York: Springer.

Oren, S., Willerton, C., & Small, J. (2014). Effects of spaced retrieval training on semantic memory in Alzheimer's disease: A systematic review. *Journal of Speech, Language, and Hearing Research, 57,* 247–270. doi:10.1044/1092-4388(2013/12-0352)

Oren, S., Willerton, C., & Small, J. (2014). Effects of spaced retrieval training on semantic memory in Alzheimer's disease: A systematic review. *Journal of Speech, Language, and Hearing Research, 57,* 247–270. doi:10.1044/1092-4388(2013/12-0352)

Orlova, N. S., Rutledge, M. S., & Wu, A. Y. (2015). *The transition from defined benefit to defined contribution pensions: Does it influence elderly poverty?* Retrieved from crr.bc.edu/working-papers/the-transition-from-defined-benefit-to-defined-contribution-pensions-does-it-influence-elderly-poverty/.

Ortiz-Walters, R., & Gilson, L. L. (2013). Mentoring programs for under-represented groups. In J. Passmore, D. B. Peterson, & T. Freire (Eds.), *The Wiley-Blackwell handbook of coaching and mentoring* (pp. 266–282). Oxford, UK: Wiley-Blackwell.

Ossher, L., Flegal, K. E., & Lustig, C. (2013). Everyday memory errors in older adults. *Aging, Neuropsychology, and Cognition, 20,* 220–242. doi:10.1 080/13825585.2012.690365

Oswald, A. J., & Wu, S. (2010). Objective confirmation of subjective measures of human well-being: Evidence from the USA. *Science, 327,* 576–579. doi:10.1126/science.1180606

Oudekerk, B. A., Allen, J. P., Hessel, E. T., & Molloy, L. E. (2015). The cascading development of autonomy and relatedness from adolescence to adulthood. *Child Development, 86,* 472–485. doi:10.1111/cdev.12313

Owen, C. J. (2005). The empty nest transition: The relationship between attachment style and women's use of this period as a time for growth and change. *Dissertation Abstracts International. Section B. Sciences and Engineering, 65*(7-B), 3747.

Paccagnella, M. (2016). Age, ageing and skills: Results from the Survey of Adult Skills. *OECD Working Papers, No. 132.* doi:10.1787/5jm0q1n38lvc-en

Paech, J., Luszczynska, A., & Lippke, S. (2016). A rolling stone gathers no mosss—The long way from good intentions to physical activity mediated by planning, social support, and self-regulation. *Frontiers in Psychology, 7,* 1024. doi:10.3389/fpsyg.2016.01024

Paggi, M. E., Jopp, D., & Hertzog, C. (2016). The importance of leisure activities in the relationship between physical health and well-being in a life span sample. *Gerontology, 62,* 450–458. doi:10.1159/000444415

Palkovitz, R., & Palm, G. (2009). Transitions within fathering. *Fathering, 7,* 3–22. doi:10.3149/fth.0701.3

Palmore, E. B. (2007). Healthy behaviors or age denials? *Educational Gerontology, 33,* 1087–1097. doi:10.1080/03601270701700706

Panay, N. (2016). Body identical hormone replacement: The way forward? In A. R. Genazzani & B. C. Tarlatzis (Eds.), *Frontiers in gynecological endocrinology* (pp. 203–208). New York: Springer. doi:10.1007/978-3-319-23865-4_24

Papa, A., & Litz, B. (2011). Grief. In W. T. O'Donohue & C. Draper (Eds.), *Stepped care and e-health: Practical applications to behavioral disorders* (pp. 223–245). New York: Springer.

Pardal, R., & Barneo, J. L. (2016). Mature neurons modulate neurogenesis through chemical signals acting on neural stem cells. *Development, Growth & Differentiation, 58,* 456–462. doi: 10.1111/dgd.12283

Park D. C., & Reuter-Lorenz, P. (2009). The adaptive brain: Aging and neurocognitive scaffolding. *Annual Review of Psychology, 60,* 173–196. doi:10.1146/annurev. psych.59.103006.093656. Retrieved from www.ncbi.nlm.nih.gov/pmc/articles/PMC3359129/.

Park, C. L. (2007). Religiousness/spirituality and health: A meaning systems perspective. *Journal of Behavioral Medicine, 30,* 319–328. doi:10.1007/s10865-007-9111-x

Park, D. C., & Festini, S. B. (2017). Theories of memory and aging: A look at the past and a glimpse of the future. *Journal of Gerontology: Psychological Sciences, 72,* 82–90. doi:10.1093/geronb/gbw066

Park, J., Kitayama, S., Karasawa, M., Curhan, K., Markus, H. R., Kawakami, N. et al. (2013). Clarifying the links between social support and health: Culture, stress, and neuroticism matter. *Journal of Health Psychology, 18,* 226–235. doi:10.1177/1359105312439731

Park, Y. C., & Pyszczynski, T. (2016). Cultural universals and differences in dealing with death. In L. A. Harvell & G. S. Nisbett (Eds.), *Denying death: An interdisciplinary approach to terror management theory* (pp. 193–214). New York: Routledge.

Park, Y. H., Jeong, H.-Y., Jang, J.-W., Park, S. Y., Lim, J.-S., Kim, J.-Y. et al. (2016). Disruption of the posterior medial network during the acute stage of transient global amnesia. *Clinical EEG and Neuroscience, 47,* 69–74. doi:10.1177/1550059414543684

Park, Y.-H. (2008). Day healthcare services for family caregivers of older people with stroke: Needs and satisfaction. *Journal of Advanced Nursing, 61,* 619–630. doi:10.1111/j.1365-2648.2007.04545.x

Parker, L. D. (2008). A study about older African American spousal caregivers of persons with Alzheimer's disease. *Dissertation Abstracts International: Section B: The Sciences and Engineering, 68*(10-B), 6589.

Parkes, C. M. (2013). Elisabeth Kübler-Ross, *On death and dying:* A reappraisal. *Mortality, 18,* 94–97. doi:10.1 080/13576275.2012.758629

Parkinson's Disease Foundation. (2016a). *What is Parkinson's disease?* Retrieved from www.pdf.org/about_pd.

Parkinson's Disease Foundation. (2016b). *Prescription medications.* Retrieved from www.pdf.org/parkinson_prescription_meds.

Parkman, A. M. (2007). *Smart marriage: Using your (business) head as well as your heart to find wedded bliss.* Westport, CT: Praeger.

Parrella, N., & Vormittag, K. (2017). Health promotion and wellness. In A. A.,Paulman & L. S. Nasir (Eds.), *Family medicine* (pp. 99–111). New York: Springer.

Parris, B. A. (2016). The prefrontal cortex and suggestion: Hypnosis vs. placebo effects. *Frontiers in Psychology, 7,* 415. doi:10.3389/fpsyg.2016.00415. Retrieved from www.ncbi.nlm.nih.gov/pmc/articles/PMC4812013/.

Pasccle, A., & Govoni, S. (2016). Cerebral aging: Implications for the heart autonomic nervous system regulation. In E. Gronda, E. Vanoli, & A. Costea (Eds.), *Heart failure management: The neural pathways* (pp. 115–127). New York: Springer. doi:10.1007/978-3-319-24993-3_9

Passalacqua, S. A., & Harwood, J. (2012). VIPS communications skill straining for paraprofessional dementia caregivers: an intervention to increase person-centered dementia care. *Clinical Gerontologist, 35,* 425–445. doi:10.1080/07317115.2012.702655

Passarino, G., De Rango, F., & Montesanto, A. (2016). Human longevity: Genetics or lifestyle? It takes two to tango. *Immunity & Ageing, 13,* 12. doi:10.1186/s12979-016-0066-z. Retrieved from immunityageing.biomedcentral.com/articles/10.1186/s12979-016-0066-z.

Pasupathi, M. (2013). Making meaning for the good life: A commentary on the special issue. *Memory, 21,* 143–149. doi:10.1080/09658211.20 12.744843

Patry, D. A., Blanchard, C. M., & Mask, L. (2007). Measuring university students' regulatory leisure coping styles: Planned breathers or avoidance? *Leisure Sciences, 29,* 247–265. doi:10.1080/01490400701257963

Patterson, A. V. (2012). *Emerging adulthood as a unique stage in Erikson's psychosocial development theory: Incarnation v. impudence.* Dissertation submitted to the Graduate School of the University of Texas at Arlington. Retrieved from dspace.uta.edu/bitstream/handle/10106/11059/Patterson_uta_2502D_11766.pdf?sequence=1.

Paul, R., Lane, E., & Jefferson, A. (2013). Vascular cognitive impairment. In L. D. Ravdin & H. L. Katzen (Eds.), *Handbook of the neuropsychology of aging and dementia* (pp. 281–294). New York: Springer.

Paulsen, J. S., Nance, M., Kim, J.-I., Carlozzi, N. E., Panegyres, P. K., Erwin, C. et al. (2013). A review of quality of life after predictive testing for and earlier identification of neurodegenerative diseases. *Progress in Neurobiology, 110,* 2–28. doi:10.1016/j.pneurobio.2013.08.003

Paulson, D., Bassett, R., Kitsmiller, E., Luther, K., & Conner, N. (in press). When employment and caregiving collide: Predictors of labor force participation in prospective and current caregivers. *Clinical Gerontologist*. doi:10.1080/07317115.2016.1198856

Pearlin, L. I., Mullan, J. T., Semple, S. J., & Skaff, M. M. (1990). Caregiving and the stress process: An overview of concepts and their measures. *The Gerontologist*, *30*, 583–594. doi:10.1093/geront/30.5.583

Penson, R. T. (2004). Bereavement across cultures. In R. J. Moore & D. Spiegel (Eds.), *Cancer, culture, and communication* (pp. 241–279). New York: Kluwer/Plenum.

Perkins, J. M., Subramanian, S. V., Smith, G. G., & Özaltin, E. (2016). Adult height, nutrition, and population health. *Nutrition Reviews*, *74*, 149–165. doi:10.1093/nutrit/nuv105. Retrieved from nutritionreviews.oxfordjournals.org/content/74/3/149.full.

Perls, T., & Terry, D. (2003). Genetics of exceptional longevity. *Experimental Gerontology*, *38*, 725–730. doi:10.1016/S0531-5565(03)00098-6

Perrone, K. M., Tschopp, K. M., Snyder, E. R., Boo, J. N., & Hyatt, C. (2010). A longitudinal examination of career expectations and outcomes of academically talented students 10 and 20 years post-high school graduation. *Journal of Career Development*, *36*, 291–309. doi:10.1177/0894845309359347

Perrone, K. M., Tschopp, M. K., Snyder, E. R., Boo, J. N., & Hyatt, C. (2010). A longitudinal examination of career expectations and outcomes of academically talented students 10 and 20 years post-high school graduation. *Journal of Career Development*, *36*, 291–309. doi: 10.1177/0894845309359347

Peterson, B. E., & Stewart, A. J. (1996). Antecedents and contexts of generativity motivation at midlife. *Psychology and Aging*, *11*, 21–33. doi:10.1037/0882-7974.11.1.21

Pettinato, J. (2013). Financing long-term care. In A. E. McDonnell (Ed.), *Managing geriatric health services* (pp. 147–172). Burlington, MA: Jones & Bartlett Learning.

Pew Research Center. (2015). *Median age in years, by sex, race and ethnicity: 2013*. Retrieved from www.pewhispanic.org/2016/04/19/statistical-portrait-of-hispanics-in-the-united-states/ph_2015–03_statistical-portrait-of-hispanics-in-the-united-states-2013_current-09/.

Pfeiffer, E. (2013). *Winning strategies for successful aging*. New Haven, CT: Yale University Press.

Piaget, J. (1970). Piaget's theory. In P. H. Mussen (Ed.), *Carmichael's manual of child psychology* (3rd ed., Vol. *1*, pp. 703–732). New York: Wiley.

Piaget, J. (1972). Intellectual evolution from adolescence to adulthood. *Human Development*, *15*, 1–12. doi:10.1159/000271225

Piaget, J. (1980). *Les formes et les mentaires de la dialectique*. Paris: Gallimard.

Piazza, J. R., Charles, S. T., & Luong, G. (2015). One size fits all? Applying theoretical predictions about age and emotional experiences to people with functional disabilities. *Psychology and Aging*, *30*, 930–939. doi:10.1037/pag0000045

Pienta, A. M., Hayward, M. D., & Jenkins, K. R. (2000). Health consequences of marriage for the retirement years. *Journal of Family Issues*, *21*, 559–586. doi:10.1177/019251300021005003

Pineda-Pardo, J. A., Martinez, K., Román, F. J., & Colom, R. (2016). Structural efficiencies within a parieto-frontal network and cognitive differences. *Intelligence*, *54*, 105–116. doi:10.1016/j.intell.2015.12.002

Pini, L., Pievani, M., Bocchetta, M., Altomare, D., Bosco, P., Cavedo, E. et al. (2016). Brain atrophy in Alzheimer's disease and aging. *Ageing Research Reviews*, *30*, 25–48. doi:10.1016/j.arr.2016.01.002

Pinto, K. M., & Coltrane, S. (2009). Division of labor in Mexican origin and Anglo families: Structure and culture. *Sex Roles*, *60*, 482–495. doi:10.1007/s11199-008-9549-5

Pioneer Network. (2016). *Mission, vision, values*. Retrieved from pioneernetwork.net/AboutUs/Values/.

Piquet, B. J. (2007). That's what friends are for. *Dissertation Abstracts International. Section B. Sciences and Engineering*, *67*(7-B), 4114.

Platt, M. L., Seyfarth, R. M., & Cheyney, D. L. (2016). Adaptations for social cognition in the primate brain. *Philospical Transactions of the Royal Society B*, *371*. doi:10.1098/rstb.2015.0096

Plonsky, L., & Oswald, F. L. (2012). How to do a meta-analysis. In A. Mackey & S. M. Gass (Eds.), *Research methods in second language acquisition: A practical guide* (pp. 275–295). New York: Wiley.

Poldrack, R. A. (2012). The future of fMRI in cognitive neuroscience. *NeuroImage*, *62*, 1216–1220. doi:10.1016/j.neuroimage.2011.08.007

Polivka, L. (2010). Neoliberalism and the new politics of aging and retirement security. In J. C. Cavanaugh & C. K. Cavanaugh (Eds.), *Aging in America: Vol. 3: Societal Issues* (pp. 161–202). Santa Barbara, CA: ABC-CLIO.

Polivka, L. & Luo, B. (2015). The neoliberal political economy and erosion of retirement security. *The Gerontologist*, *55*, 183–190. doi:10.1083/geront/gnv006

Polivka, L., & Rill, L. (2016). Assisted living. In S. K. Whitbourne (Ed.), *Encyclopedia of adulthood and aging* (Vol. 1, pp. 90–95). Malden, MA: Wiley-Blackwell. doi:10.1002/9781118521373.wbeaa109

Polku, H., Mikkola, T. M., Rantakokko, M., Portegijis, E., Törmäkangas, T., Rantanen, T. et al. (in press). Hearing and quality of life among community-dwelling older adults. *Journals of Gerontology: Psychological Sciences*. doi:10.1093/geronb/gbw045

Poole, J., Ward, J., DeLuca, E., Shildrick, M., Abbey, S., Mauthner, O. et al. (2016). Grief and loss for patient before and after heart transplant. *Heart & Lung*, *45*, 193–198. doi:10.1016/j.hrtlng.2016.01.006

Pope, T. M. (2017). Certified patient decision aids: Solving persistent problems with informed consent law. *Journal of Law, Medicine, & Ethics*, *45*, 12–40. doi:10.1177/1073110517703097

Popenoe, D. (2009). Cohabitation, marriage, and child wellbeing: A cross-national perspective. *Society: Social science and Public Policy*, *46*, 429–436. doi:10.1007/s12115-009-9242-5

Popham, L. E., & Hess, T. M. (2016). Stereotype threat. In S. K. Whitbourne (Ed.), *The encyclopedia of adulthood and aging* (pp. 1354–1358). Malden, MA: Wiley.

Porter, K. E., Brennan-Ing, M., Chang, S. C., dickey, l. m., Singh, A. A., Bower, K. L. et al. (2016). Providing competent and affirming services for transgender and gender nonconforming older adults. *Clinical Gerontologist*, *39*, 366–388. doi:10.1080/07317115.2016.1203383

Portnoy, A., Rana, P., Zimmerman, C., & Rodin, G. (2015). The use of palliative sedation to treat existential suffering: A reconsideration. In P. Taboada (Ed.), *Sedation at the end-of-life: An interdisciplinary approach* (pp. 41–54). New York: Springer. doi:10.1007/978-94-017-9106-9_4

Potočnik, K., Tordera, N., & Peiró, J. M. (2013). Truly satisfied with your retirement or just resigned? Pathways toward different patterns of retirement satisfaction. *Journal of Applied Gerontology*, *32*, 164–187. doi:10.1177/0733464811405988

Powell, B., Hamilton, L., Manago, B., & Cheng, S. (2016). Implications of changing family forms for children. *Annual Review of Sociology*, *42*, 301–322. doi:11.1146/annurev-soc-081715-074444

Power, T. L., & Smith, S. M. (2008). Predictors of fear of death and self-mortality: An Atlantic Canadian perspective. *Death Studies*, *32*, 252–272. doi:10.1080/07481180701880935

Pratt, H. D. (2010). Perspectives from a non-traditional mentor. In C. A. Rayburn, F. L. Denmark, M. E. Reuder, & A.M. Austria, (Eds.), *A handbook for women mentors: Transcending barriers of stereotype, race, and ethnicity* (pp. 223–232). Santa Barbara, CA: ABC-CLIO.

Pratt, S. I., Bartels, S. J., Mueser, K. T., & Forester, B. (2008). Helping older people experience success: An integrated model of psychosocial rehabilitation and health care management for older adults with serious mental illness. *American Journal of Psychiatric Rehabilitation*, *11*, 41–60. doi:10.1080/15487760701853193

Prebble, S. C., Addis, D. R., & Tippett, L. J. (2013). Autobiographical memory and sense of self. *Psychological Bulletin*, *139*, 815–840. doi:10.1037/a0030146

Priaulx, N. (2013). The troubled identity of the bioethicist. *Health Care Analysis*, *21*, 6–19. doi:10.1007/ s10728-012-0229-9

Price, V. (2016). Women in non-traditional work fields. In N. A. Naples, r. c. hoogland, M. Wickramasing, & W. C. A. Wong (Eds.), *The Wiley Blackwell encyclopedia of gender and sexuality studies*. Malden, MA: Wiley.

Prince-Paul, M., & Daly, B. J. (2016). Ethical considerations in palliative care. In N. Coyle (ed.), *Legal and ethical aspects of care* (pp. 1–28). New York: Oxford University Press.

Proctor, H. (2016). Personal construct psychology, society, and culture: A review. In D. A. Winter & N. Reed (Eds.), *The Wiley handbook of personal construct psychology* (pp. 139–153). Malden, MA: Wiley.

Proulx, C. M. (2016). Marital trajectories. In S. K. Whitbourne (Ed.), *The encyclopedia of adulthood and aging* (pp. 842–845). New York: Wiley.

Ptak, R. (2012). The frontoparietal attention network of the human brain: Action, saliency, and a priority map of the environment. *Neuroscientist*, *18*, 502–515. doi:10.1177/1073858411409051

Purser, J. L., Feng, Q., Yi, Z., & Hoenig, H. (2012). A new classification of function and disability in China: Subtypes based on performance-based and self-reported measures. *Journal of Aging and Health*, *24*, 779–798. doi:10.1177/0898264312444310

Pynoos, J. Caraviello, R., & Cicero, C. (2010). Housing in an aging America. In J. C. Cavanaugh & C. K. Cavanaugh (Eds.), *Aging in America: Vol. 3: Societal issues* (pp. 129–159). Santa Barbara, CA: Praeger Perspectives.

Queen, T. L., Berg, C. A., & Lowrance, W. (2015). A framework for decision making in couples across adulthood. In T. M. Hess, J. Strough, & C. E. Löckenhoff (Eds.), *Aging and decision making: Empirical and applied perspectives* (pp. 371–392). San Diego, CA: Academic Press.

Quéniart, A., & Charpentier, M. (2013). Initiate, bequeath, and remember: Older women's transmission role within the family. *Journal of Women and Aging*, *25*, 45–65. doi:10.1080/08952841.2012.720181

Quinn, J. F., & Cahill, K. E. (2016). The new world of retirement income security in America. *American Psychologist*, *71*, 321–333. doi:10.1037/a0040276

Quinn, K. (2016). Older adults and social media: Foreshadowing challenges of the future? In P. G. Nixon, R. Rawal, & A. Funk (Eds.), *Digital media usage across the life course* (pp. 132–145). New York: Routledge.

Quirin, M., Loktyushin, A., Arndt, J., Küstermann, E., Lo, Y.-Y., Kuhl, J. et al. (2012). Existential neuroscience: A functional magnetic resonance imaging investigation of neural responses to reminders of one's mortality. *Social Cognitive and*

Affective Neuroscience, 7, 193–198. doi:10.1093/scan/nsq106

Quirin, M., Loktyushin, A., Arndt, J., Küstermann, E., Lo, Y.-Y., Kuhl, J. et al. (2012). Existential neuroscience: A functional magnetic resonance imaging investigation of neural responses to reminders of one's mortality. *Social Cognitive and Affective Neuroscience, 7*, 193–198. doi: 10.1093/scan/nsq106

Radloff, L.S. (1977). The CES-D scale: A self-report depression scale for research in the general population. *Applied Psychological Measurement, 1*, 385–401. doi:10.1177/014662167700100306

Raji, C. A., Merrill, D. A., Eyre, H., Mallam, S., Torosyan, N., Erickson, K. I. et al. (2016). Longitudinal relationships between caloric expenditure and gray matter in the Cardiovascular Health Study. *Journal of Alzheimer's Disease, 52*, 719–729. doi:10.3233/JAD-160057, Retrieved from content.iospress.com/articles/journal-of-alzheimers-disease/jad160057.

Raju, S. S. (2011). *Studies on ageing in India: A review*. New Delhi: United Nations Population Fund. Retrieved from www.isec.ac.in/BKPAI%20Working%20paper%202.pdf.

Ramos-Zúñiga, R. (2015). Challenge of the translational neuroscience. *World Journal of Neurology, 5*, 102–106. doi.5316/wjn.v5.i4.102

Randall, G. K., Martin, P., Bishop, A. J., Johnson, M. A., & Poon. L. W. (2012). Social resources and change in functional health comparing three age groups. *International Journal of Aging and Human Development, 75*, 1–29. doi:10.2190/AG.75.1.c

Rape, Abuse, and Incest National Network. (2016). *Statistics*. Retrieved from www.rainn.org/statistics.

Raschick, M., & Ingersoll-Dayton, B. (2004). The costs and rewards of caregiving among aging spouses and adult children. *Family Relations: Interdisciplinary Journal of Applied Family Studies, 53*, 317–325. doi:10.1111/j.0022-2445.2004.0008.x

Rattan, S. I. S. (2012). Biogerontology: From here to where? The Lord Cohen Medal lecture—2011. *Biogerontology, 13*, 83–91. doi:10.1007/s10522-011-9354-3

Rattan, S. I. S., Kryzch, V., Schnebert, S., Perrier, E., & Nizard, C. (2013). Hormesis-based anti-aging products: A case study of a novel cosmetic. *Dose-Response, 11*, 99–108. doi:10.2203/dose-response.11-054. Rattan. Retrieved from dose-response.metapress.com/media/p3d6qpmvyp7ud5tpulft/contributions/l/4/5/4/l45443612h506376.pdf.

Ready, R. E., Carvalho, J. O., & Åkerstedt, A. M. (2012). Evaluative organization of the self-concept in younger, midlife, and older adults. *Research on Aging, 34*, 56–79. doi:10.1177/0164027511415244

Rebok, G., W., Ball, K., Guey, L. T., Jones, R. N., Kim, H.-Y., King, J. W. et al. (2014). Ten-year effects of the ACTIVE cognitive training trial on cognition and everyday functioning in older adults. *Journal of the American Geriatrics Society, 62*, 16–24. doi:10.1111/jgs.12607. Retrieved from www.ncbi.nlm.nih.gov/pmc/articles/PMC4055506/.

Redzanowski, U., & Glück, J. (2013). Who knows who is wise? Self and peer ratings of wisdom. *Journal of Gerontology: Psychological Sciences, 68*, 391–394. doi:10.1093/geronb/ gbs079

Reed, A. E., & Carstensen, L. L. (2012). The theory behind the age-related positivity effect. *Frontiers in Psychology*. doi: 10.3389/ fpsyg.2012.00339

Reed, R. G., & Raison, C. L. (2016). Stress and the immune system. In C. Esser (Ed.), *Environmental influences on the immune system* (pp. 97–126). New York: Springer. doi:10.1007/978-3-7091-1890-0_5

Reinke, B. J., Holmes, D. S., & Harris, R. L. (1985). The timing of psychosocial change in women's lives: The years 25 to 45. *Journal of Personality and Social Psychology, 48*, 1353–1364. doi:10.1037/0022-3514.48.5.1353

Remedios, J. D., Chasteen, A. L., & Packer, D. J. (2010). Sunny side up: The reliance on positive age stereotypes in descriptions of future older selves. *Self and Identity, 9*, 257–275. doi:10.1080/15298860903054175

Ren, Q., & Treiman, D. J. (2014). *Living arrangements of the elderly in China and consequences for their emotional well-being*. Population Studies Center Research Report 14-814, University of Michigan. Retrieved from www.psc.isr.umich.edu/pubs/pdf/rr14-814.pdf.

Rendeiro, C., Rhodes, J. S., & Spencer, J. P. E. (2015). The mechanisms of faction of flavonoids in the brain: Direct *versus* indirect effects. *Neurochemistry International, 89*, 126–139. doi:10.1016/j.neuint.2015.08.002

Renshaw, K. D., Rodrigues, C., & Jones, D. H. (2008). Psychological symptoms and marital satisfaction in spouses of operation Iraqi freedom veterans: Relationships with spouses' perceptions of veterans' experiences and symptoms. *Journal of Family Psychology, 22*, 586–594. doi:10.1037/0893-3200.22.3.586

Repetti, R., & Wangi, S-w.,(2017). Effects of job stress on family relationships. *Current Opinion in Psychology, 13*, 15–18. doi:10.1017/j.copsyc.2016.03.010

Reuter-Lorenz, P. A. (2002). New visions of the aging mind and brain. *Trends in Cognitive Sciences, 6* (9), 394–400. doi:10.1016/S1364–6613(02)01957-5

Reuter-Lorenz, P. A., & Cappell, K. A. (2008). Neurocognitive aging and the compensation hypothesis. *Current Directions in Psychological Science, 17*, 177–182. doi:10.1111/j.1467-8721.2008.00570.x

Reuter-Lorenz, P. A., & Mikels, J. A. (2006). The aging mind and brain: Implications of enduring plasticity for behavioral and cultural change. In P. B. Baltes, P. A. Reuter-Lorenz, & F. Rösler (Eds.), *Lifespan development and the brain: The perspective of biocultural co-constructivism* (pp. 255–276). New York: Cambridge University Press.

Reuter-Lorenz, P. A., & Park, D. C. (2014). How does it STAC up? Revisiting the Scaffolding Theory of Aging and Cognition. *Neuropsychology Review, 24*, 355–370. doi:10.1007/s11065-014-9270-9

Revenson, T. A., Griva, K., Luszczynska, A., Morrison, V., Panagopoulou, E., Vilchinsky, N. et al. (2016). *Caregiving in the illness context*. New York: Palgrave Macmillan.

Rich, K. L. (2013). Introduction to bioethics and ethical decision making. In J. B. Butts & K. L. Rich (Eds.), *Nursing ethics: Across the curriculum and into practice* (3rd ed., pp. 31–68). Burlington, MA: Jones & Bartlett Learning.

Rickard, A. P., Chatfield, M. D., Powell, J. J., Stephen, A. M., & Richards, M. (2012). Dietary iron is associated with memory in midlife: Longitudinal cohort study. *Journal of Pharmacy and Nutritional Sciences, 2*, 57–62. Retrieved from lifescienceglobal.com/pms/index.php/jpans/article/view/238/pdf.

Ridings, C., & Gefen, D. (2004). Virtual community attraction: Why people hang out online. *Journal of Computer-Mediated Communication, 10*. doi:10.1111/j.1083-6101.2004.tb00229.x. Retrieved from onlinelibrary.wiley.com/doi/10.1111/j.1083-6101.2004.tb00229.x/full.

Riediger, M., Freund, A. M., & Baltes, P. B. (2005). Managing life through personal goals: Intergoal facilitation and intensity of goal pursuit in younger and older adulthood. *Journals of Gerontology: Psychological Sciences, 60B*, P84–P91. doi:10.1093/ geronb/60.2.P84

Rijken, A. J. (2009). *Happy families, high fertility?: Childbearing choices in the context of family and partner relationships*. Dissertation submitted in partial fulfillment of the doctor of philosophy degree, University of Utrecht.

Rijken, A. J., & Knijn, T. (2009). Couples' decisions to have a first child: Comparing pathways to early and late parenthood. *Demographic Research, 21*, 765–802. doi:10.4054/DemRes.2009.21.26. Retrieved from core.ac.uk/download/pdf/6405965.pdf.

Riley, L. D., & Bowen, C. (2005). The sandwich generation: Challenges and coping strategies of multigenerational family. *Counseling & Therapy for Couples & Families, 13*, 52–58. doi:10.1177/1066480704270099

Ripp, J., Jones, E., & Zhang, M. (2016). Common functional problems. In J. L. Hayashi & B. Leff (Eds.), *Geriatric home-based medical care* (pp. 151–172). New York: Springer. doi:10.1007/978-3-319-23365-9_8

Rippe, J. M. (2013). *Lifestyle medicine* (2nd ed.). Boca Raton, FL: CRC Press.

Rippe, J. M. (2016). Lifestyle medicine: Continued growth and evolution. *American Journal of Lifestyle Medicine, 10*, 288–289. doi:10.1177/1559827616639894

Rizzuto, T. E., Cherry, K. E., & LeDoux, J. A. (2012). The aging process and cognitive capabilities. In J. W. Hedge & W. C. Borman (Eds.), *The Oxford handbook of work and aging* (pp. 236–255). New York: Oxford University Press.

Robert, L., Labat-Robert, J., & Robert, A. A. (2012). Physiology of skin aging. *Clinics in Plastic Surgery, 39*, 1–8. doi:10.1016/j.cps.2011.09.006

Roberto, K. A. (2016). The complexities of elder abuse. *American Psychologist, 71*, 302–311. doi:10.1037/a0040259

Roberto, K. A., & Jarrott, S. E. (2008). Family caregivers of older adults: A life span perspective. *Family Relations, 57*, 100–111. doi:10.1111/j.1741-3729.2007.00486.x

Roberts, B. W., & DelVecchio, W. F. (2000). The rank-order consistency of personality traits from childhood to old age: A quantitative review of longitudinal studies. *Psychological Bulletin, 126*, 3–25. doi:10.1037/0033-2909.126.1.3

Roberts, B. W., Walton, K., Bogg, T., & Caspi, A. (2006). De-investment in work and non-normative personality trait change in young adulthood. *European Journal of Personality, 20*, 461–474. doi:10.1002/per.607

Roberts, P., & Newton, P. M. (1987). Levinsonian studies of women's adult development. *Psychology and Aging, 2*, 154–163. doi:10.1037/0882-7974.2.2.154

Robinaugh, D. J., & McNally, R. J. (2013). Remembering the past and envisioning the future in bereaved adults with and without complicated grief. *Clinical Psychological Science, 1*, 290–300. doi:10.1177/2167702613476027

Robinson, A., Lea, E., Hemmings, L., Vosper, G., McCann, D., Weeding, F. et al. (2012). Seeking respite: Issues around the use of day respite care for the carers of people with dementia. *Ageing and Society, 32*, 196–218. doi:10.1017/S0144686X11000195

Robinson, O. C., & Stell, A. J. (2015). Later-life crisis: Towards a holistic model. *Journal of Adult Development, 22*, 38–49. doi:10.1007/s10804-014-9199-5

Robinson-Wood, T., & Weber, A. (2016). Deconstructing multiple oppressions among LGBT older adults. In D. A. Harley & P. B. Teaster (Eds.), *Handbook of LGBT elders* (pp. 65–81). New York: Springer.

Robson, S. M., Hansson, R. O., Abalos, A., & Booth, M. (2006). Successful aging: Criteria for aging well in the workplace. *Journal of Career Development, 33*, 156–177. doi:10.1177/0894845306292533

Rockwell, J. (2012). From person-centered to relational care: Expanding the focus in residential care facilities. *Journal of Gerontological Social Work, 55*, 233–248. doi:10.1080/0163 4372.2011.639438

Rockwood, K. (2016). Conceptual models of frailty: Accumulation of deficits. . *Canadian Journal* of *Cardiology, 32,* 1046–1050. doi:10.1016/j.cjca.2016.03.020

Rocque, G. B., & Cleary, J. F. (2013). Palliative care reduces morbidity and mortality in cancer. *Nature Reviews Clinical Oncology, 10,* 80–89. doi:10.1038/nrclinonc.2012.211

Rodin, J., & Langer, E. J. (1977). Long-term effects of a control-relevant intervention with the institutionalized aged. *Journal of Personality and Social Psychology, 35,* 897–902.

Rodrigue, K. M., Kennedy, K. M., Devous, M. D., Sr., Rieck, J. R., Hebrank, A. C., Diaz-Arrastia, R. et al. (2012). β-amyloid burden in healthy aging: Regional distribution and cognitive consequences. *Neurology, 78,* 387–395. doi:10.1212/WNL.0b013e318245d295

Rodriguez, J. J., Noristani, H. N., & Verkhratsky, A. (2012). The serotonergic system in ageing and Alzheimer's disease. *Progress in Neurobiology, 99,* 15–41. doi:10.1016/j.pneurobio.2012.06.010

Roediger, H. L., III, Wixted, J. H., & DeSoto, K. A. (2012). The curious complexity between confidence and accuracy in reports from memory. In L. Nadel & W. P. Sinnott-Armstrong (Eds.), *Memory and law* (pp. 84–118). New York: Oxford University Press.

Rohmann, E., Führer, A., & Bierhoff, H.-W. (2016). Relationship satisfaction across European cultures: The role of love styles. *Cross-Cultural Research, 50,* 178–211. doi:10.1177/1069397116630950

Rokach, R., Cohen, O., & Dreman, S. (2004). Triggers and fuses in late divorce: The role of short term crises vs. ongoing frustration on marital break-up. *Journal of Divorce & Remarriage, 40,* 41–60. doi:10.1300/ J087v40n03_03

Romeijn, N., Raymann, R. J. E. M., Most, E., Te Lindert, B., Van Der Meijden, W. P., Fronczek, R. et al. (2012). Sleep, vigilance, and thermosensitivity. *Pflügers Archiv—European Journal of Physiology, 463,* 169–176. doi:10.1007/s00424-011-1042-2

Rose, D. M., & Gordon, R. (2010). Retention practices for engineering and technical professionals in an Australian public agency. *Australian Journal of Public Administration, 69,* 314–325. doi:10.1111/j.1467-8500.2010.00693.x

Rosellini, A. J., Heeringa, S. G., Stein, M. B., Ursano, R. J., Chiu, W. T., Colpe, L. J. et al. (2015). Lifetime prevalence of DSM-IV mental disorders among new soldiers in the U.S. Army: Results from the Army Study to Assess Risk and Resilience in Servicemembers (Army STARRS). *Depression and Anxiety, 32,* 13–24. doi:10.1002/da.22316

Rosenbaum, J. L., Smith, J. R., & Zollfrank, B. C. C. (2011). Neonatal end-of-life support care. *Perinatal and Neonatal Nursing, 25,* 61–69. doi:10.1097 / JPN.0b013e318209e1d2.

Rosenberg, S. D., Rosenberg, H. J., & Farrell, M. P. (1999). Midlife crisis revisited. In S. L. Willis & J. D. Reid (Eds.), *Life in the middle: Psychological and social development in middle age* (pp. 47–70). San Diego, CA: Academic Press.

Rosenblatt, P. C. (1996). Grief that does not end. In D. Klass, P. R. Silverman, & S. L. Nickman (Eds.), *Continuing bonds: New understandings of grief* (pp. 45–58). Washington, DC: Taylor & Francis.

Rosenfield, S., & Mouzon, D. (2013). Gender and mental health. In C. S. Aneshensel, J. C. Phelan, & A. Bieman (Eds.), *Handbook of the sociology of mental health* (pp. 277–296). New York: Springer.

Rosi, A., Cavallini, E., Bottiroll, S., Bianco, F., & Lecce, S. (2016). Promoting theory of mind in older adults: Does age play a role? *Aging & Mental Health, 20,* 22–28. doi:10.1080/13607863.2015.1049118

Ross, N. A., Garner, R., Bernier, J., Feeny, D. H., Kaplan, M. S., McFarland, B. et al. (2012). Trajectories of health-related quality of life by socioeconomic status in a nationally representative Canadian cohort. *Journal of Epidemiology and Community Health, 66,* 593–598. doi:10.1136/jech.2010.115378

Rosso, B. D., Dekas, K. H., & Wrzesniewski, A. (2010). On the meaning of work: A theoretical integration and review. *Research in Organizational Behavior, 30,* 91–127. doi:10.1016/j.riob.2010.09.001

Rostila, M., Saarela, J., Kawachi, I., & Hjern, A. (2015). Testing the anniversary reaction: Causal effects of bereavement in a nationwide follow-up study from Sweden. *Psychiatric Epidemiology, 30,* 239–247. doi:10.1007/s10654-015-9989-5

Roszko, E. (2010). Commemoration and the state: Memory and legitimacy in Vietnam. *Sojourn: Journal of Social Issues in Southeast Asia, 25,* 1–28.. doi:10.1353/soj.0.0041

Rowe, G. (2011). *Determinants of working memory performance.* Dissertation presented to the Department of Psychology, University of Toronto. Retrieved from tspace.library.utoronto.ca/handle/1807/26515.

Rowe, M. M., & Sherlock, H. (2005). Stress and verbal abuse in nursing: Do burned out nurses eat their young? *Journal of Nursing Management, 13,* 242–248. doi:10.1111/j.1365-2834.2004.00533.x

Rowles, G. D. (2006). Commentary: A house is not a home: But can it become one? In H. W. Wahl et al. (Eds.), *The many faces of health, competence and well-being in old age* (pp. 25–32). New York: Springer.

Rowles, G. D., & Watkins, J. F. (2003). History, habit, heart, and hearth: On making spaces into places. In K. W. Schaie, H.-W. Wahl, H. Mollenkopf, & F. Oswald (Eds.), *Aging independently: Living arrangements and mobility* (pp. 77–96). New York: Springer.

Roxburgh, S. (2002). Racing through life. The distribution of time pressures by roles and roles resources among full-time workers. *Journal of Family and Economic Issues, 23,* 121–145. doi:10.1023/A:1015734516575

Roy, A., Punhani, S., & Shi, L. (2012). *Living longer: Why and how it affects us all?* Retrieved from doc.research-and-analytics.csfb.com/docView?language=ENG&source=ulg&format=PDF&document_id=804497550&serialid=hq62DgWSWwwUFH7wTbvN1lgs%2Fnev%2BhAHymGbTUrFJ1Y%3D.

Rozin, P., & Royzman, E. B. (2001). Negativity bias, negativity dominance, and contagion. *Personality and Social Psychology Review, 5,* 296–320. doi:10.1207/ S15327957PSPR0504_2

Rubin, S. S., & Malkinson, R. (2001). Parental response to child loss across the life cycle: Clinical and research perspectives. In M. S. Stroebe, R. O. Hansson, W. Stroebe, & H. Schut (Eds.), *Handbook of bereavement research: Consequences, coping, and care* (pp. 169–197). Washington, DC: American Psychological Association.

Rubio, J., Dumitrache, C., Cordon-Pozo, E., & Rubio-Herrara, R. (2016). Coping: Impact of gender and stressful life events in middle and old age. *Clinical Gerontologist, 39,* 468–488. doi:10.1080/07317115 .2015.1132290

Ruiz, M. E., Phillips, L. R., Kim, H., & Woods, D. L. (2016). Older Latinos: Applying the ethnocultural gerontological nursing model. *Journal of Transcultural Nursing, 27,* 8–17. doi:10.1177/1043659615569539

Ruppanner, L., & Maume, D. J. (2016). Shorter work hours and work-to-family interference: Surprising findings from 32 countries. *Social Forces, 95,* 693–720. doi:10.1093/sf/sow057

Rutherford, A., Markopoulos, G., Bruno, D., & Brady-Van den Bos, M. (2012). Long-term memory: Encoding to retrieval. In N. Braisby & A. Gellatly (Eds.), *Cognitive psychology* (pp. 229–265). New York: Oxford University Press.

Ryan, E. B., Giles, H., Bartolucci, G., & Henwood, K. (1986). Psycholinguistic and social psychological components of communication by and with the elderly. *Language and Communication, 6,* 1–24. doi:10.1016/0271-5309(86)90002-9

Ryan, E. B., Meredith, S. D., MacLean, M. J., & Orange, J. B. (1995). Changing the way we talk with elders: Promoting health using the communication enhancement model. *International Journal of Aging and Human Development, 41,* 89–107. doi:10.2190/FP05-FM8V-0Y9F-53FX

Ryan, M. K., Haslam, S. A., & Kulich, C. (2010). Politics and the glass cliff: Evidence that women are preferentially selected to contest hard-to-win seats. *Psychology of Women Quarterly, 34,* 56–64. doi:10.1111/j.1471-6402.2009.01541.x

Ryan, M. K., Haslam, S. A., Morgenroth, T., Rink, F., Stoker, J., & Peters, K. (2016). Getting on top of the glass cliff: Reviewing a decade of evidence, explanations, and impact. *The Leadership Quarterly, 27,* 446–455. doi:10.1016/j.leaqua.2015.10.008

Ryan, S. (2014) Psychological effects of living with rheumatoid arthritis. *Nursing Standard, 29,* 52–59. Retrieved from journals.rcni.com/doi/pdfplus/10.7748/ns.29.13.52.e9484.

Rye, M. S., Folck, C. D., Heim, T. A., Olszewski, B. T., & Traina, E. (2004). Forgiveness of an ex-spouse: How does it relate to mental health following a divorce? *Journal of Divorce & Remarriage, 41,* 31–51. doi:10.1300/ J087v41n03_02

Saavedra, C., Iglesias, J., & Olivares, E. I. (2012).Event-related potentials elicited by face identity processing in elderly adults with cognitive impairment. *Experimental Aging Research, 38,* 220–245. doi:10.1080/036107 3X.2012.660057

Sacks, O. (2015, February 19). My own life: Oliver Sacks on learning he has terminal cancer. *New York Times,* A25. Retrieved from www.nytimes.com/2015/02/19/opinion/oliver-sacks-on-learning-he-has-terminal-cancer.html?_r=0.

Sadeh, T., Ozubko, J. D., Winocur, G., & Moscovitch, M. (2014). How we forget may depend on how we remember. *Trends in Cognitive Sciences, 18,* 26–36. doi:10.1016/j.tics.2013.10.008

SAE International. (2014). *Taxonomy and definitions for terms related to on-road motor vehicle automated driving systems.* Retrieved from www.sae.org/misc/pdfs/automated_driving.pdf.

Sakaki, M., Niki, K., & Mather, M. (2012). Beyond arousal and valence: The importance of the biological versus social relevance of emotional stimuli. *Cognitive, Affective, and Behavioral Neuroscience, 12,* 115–139. doi:10.3758/s13415-011-0062-x

Sakraida, T. J. (2005).Divorce transition differences of midlife women. *Issues in Mental Health Nursing, 26,* 225–249. doi:10.1080/01612840590901699

Sala Frigerio, C., & De Strooper, B. (2016). Alzheimer's disease mechanisms and emerging roads to novel therapeutics. *Annual Review of Neuroscience, 39,* 57–79. doi:10.1146/annurev-neuro-070815-014015

Salai, L. K. (2013). Late-life psychosis. In M. D. Miller & L. K. Salai (Eds.), *Geriatric psychiatry* (pp. 237–251). New York: Oxford University Press.

Salomaa, R. (2014). Coaching of key talents in multinational companies. In A. Al Ariss (Ed.), *Global talent management* (pp. 43–63). New York: Springer.

Salovey, P., & Mayer, J. D. (1990). *Emotional intelligence. Imagination, Cognition, and Personality, 9,* 185–211. doi:10.2190/DUGG-P24E-52WK-6CDG

Salthouse, T. A. (1996). The processing speed theory of adult age differences in cognition. *Psychological Review, 103,* 403–428. doi:10.1037/0033-295X.103.3.403

Salthouse, T. A. (2014). Why are there different age relations in cross-sectional and longitudinal comparisons of cognitive functioning? *Current*

Directions in Psychological Science, 23, 252–256. doi:10.1177/0963721414535212

Samanta, T. (2017). Bridging the gap: Theory and research in social gerontology. In T. Samanta (Ed.), *Cross-cultural and cross-disciplinary perspectives in social gerontology* (pp. 3–22). New York: Springer.

Samieri, C., Maillard, P., Crivello, F., Proust-Lima, C., Peuchant, E., Helmer, C. et al. (2012). Plasma long-chain omega-3 fatty acids and atrophy of the medial temporal lobe. *Neurology, 79,* 642–650. doi:10.1212/WNL.0b013e318264e394

Sánchez-González, D., & Rodríguez-Rodríguez, V. (2016). Introduction to environmental gerontology in Latin America and Europe. In D. Sánchez-González & V. Rodríguez-Rodríguez (Eds.), *Environmental gerontology in Latin America and Europe* (pp. 1–7). New York: Springer. doi:10.1007/978-3-319-21419-1_1

Sandler, I. N., Wolchik, S. A. Ayers, T. S., Tein, J.-Y., & Luecken, L. (2013). Family bereavement program (FBP) approach to promoting resilience following the death of a parent. *Family Science, 4,* 87–94. doi:10.1080/19424620.2013.821763

Sandler, I. N., Wolchik, S. A., & Ayers, T. S. (200). Resilience rather than recovery: A contextual framework on adaptation following bereavement. *Death Studies, 32,* 59–73. doi:10.1080/07481180701741343

Sandrini, M., Manenti, R., Brambilla, M., Cobelli, C., Cohen, L. G., & Cotelli, M. (2016). Older adults get episodic memory boosting from noninvasive stimulation of prefrontal cortex during learning. *Neurobiology of Aging, 39,* 210–216. doi:10.1016/j.neurobiolaging.2015.12.010

Santos, L. E., Beckman, D., & Ferreira, S. T. (2016). Microglial dysfunction connects depression and Alzheimer's disease. *Brain, Behavior, and Immunity, 55,* 151–165. doi:10.1016/j.bbi.2015.11.011

Santos-Lozano, A., Santamarina, A., Pareja-Galeano, H., Sanchis-Gomez, F., Fiuza-Luces, C., Cristi-Montero, C. et al. (2016). The genetics of exceptional longevity: Insights from centenarians. *Maturitas, 90,* 49–57. doi:10.1016/j.maturitas.2016.05.006

Sargent, L. D., Lee, M. D., Martin, B., & Zikic, J. (2013). Reinventing retirement: New Pathways, new arrangements, new meanings. *Human Relations, 66,* 3–21. doi:10.1177/0018726712465658

Sasson, E., Doniger, G. M., Pasternak, O., Tarrasch, R., & Assaf, Y. (2012). Structural correlates of cognitive domains in normal aging with diffusion tensor imaging. *Brain Structure and Function, 217,* 503–515. doi:10.1007/s00429-011-0344-7

Šatienė, S. (2015). Learning in later life: The perspective of successful aging. *Applied Research in Health and Social Sciences: Interface and Interaction, 12,* 11–23. doi:10.1515/arhss-2015-0003

Savela, S., Saijonmaa, O., Strandberg, T. E., Koistinen, P., Strandberg, A. Y., Tilvis, R. S. et al. (2013). Physical activity in midlife and telomere length measured in old age. *Experimental Gerontology, 48,* 81–84. doi:10.1016/j.exger.2012.02.003

Savic, I., Perski, A., & Osika, W. (in press). MRI shows that exhaustion syndrome due to chronic occupational stress is associated with partially reversible cerebral changes. *Cerebral Cortex.* doi:10.1093/cercor/bhw413

Savickas, M. L. (2013). Career construction theory and practice. In S. D. Brown & R. W. Lent (Eds.), *Career development and counseling: Putting theory and research to work* (pp. 147–183). New York: Wiley.

Savundranayagam, M. Y., Sibalija, J., & Scotchmer, E. (2016). Resident reactions to person-centered communication by long-term care staff. *American Journal of Alzheimer's Disease & Other Disorders, 31,* 530–537. doi:10.1177/1533317515622291

Sbarra, D. A. (2015). Divorce and health: Current trends and future directions. *Psychosomatic Medicine, 77,* 227–236. doi:10.1097/0000000000000168

Schaie, K. W. (1994). The course of adult intellectual development. *American Psychologist, 49,* 304–313.

Schaie, K. W. (1996). Intellectual functioning in adulthood. In J. E. Birren & K. W. Schaie (Eds.), *Handbook of the psychology of aging* (4th ed., pp. 266–286). San Diego, CA: Academic Press.

Schaie, K. W. (2005). *Developmental influences on adult intelligence: The Seattle longitudinal study.* New York: Oxford University Press.

Schaie, K. W. (2008). A lifespan developmental perspective of psychological aging. In K. Laidlaw & B. G. Knight (Eds.), *Handbook of emotional disorders in late life: Assessment and treatment* (pp. 3–32). Oxford, UK: Oxford University Press.

Schaie, K. W. (2011). Historical influences on aging and behavior. In K. W. Schaie & S. L. Willis (Eds.), *Handbook of the psychology of aging* (7th ed., pp. 41–55). Burlington, MA: Academic Press.

Schaie, K. W., & Willis, S. L. (1999). Theories of everyday competence and aging. In V. L. Bengtson & K. W. Schaie (Eds.), *Handbook of theories of aging* (pp. 174–195). New York: Springer.

Schaie, K. W., & Willis, S. L. (2015). History of cognitive aging research. In N. A. Prachana (Ed.), *Encyclopedia of geropsychology* (pp. 1–19). Singapore: Springer Singapore.

Schaie, K. W., & Zanjani, F. (2006). Intellectual development across adulthood. In C. Hoare (Ed.), *Oxford handbook of adult development and learning* (pp. 99–122). New York: Oxford University Press.

Schaie, K. W., Maitland, S. B., Willis, S. L., & Intrieri, R. L. (1998). Longitudinal invariance of adult psychometric ability factor structures across seven years. *Psychology and Aging, 13,* 8–20. doi:10.1037/0882-7974.13.1.8

Schaie, K. W., Plomin, R., Willis, S. L., Gruber-Baldini, A., & Dutta, R. (1992). Natural cohorts: Family similarity in adult cognition. In T. Sonderegger (Ed.), *Psychology and aging: Nebraska symposium on motivation,* 1991 (pp. 205–243). Lincoln: University of Nebraska Press.

Scharlach, A. E., & Lehning, A. J. (2016). *Creating aging-friendly communities.* New York: Oxford University Press.

Scheibe, S., & Carstensen, L. L. (2010). Emotional aging: Current and future trends. *Journal of Gerontology: Psychological Sciences, 65B,* 133–144. doi:10.1093/geronb/gbp132

Scheibe, S., Kunzmann, U., & Baltes, P. B. (2007). Wisdom, life longings, and optimal development. In J. A. Blackburn & C. N. Dulmus (Eds.), *Handbook of gerontology: Evidence-based approaches to theory, practice, and policy* (pp. 117–142). Hoboken, NJ: Wiley.

Scheidt, R. J., & Schwarz, B. (2010). Environmental gerontology: A sampler of issues and application. In J. C. Cavanaugh & C. K. Cavanaugh (Eds.), *Aging in America: Vol. 1: Psychological aspects* (pp. 156–176). Santa Barbara, CA: Praeger Perspectives.

Schmidt, M., Arjomand-Wölkart, K., Birkhäuser, M. H., Genazzani, A. R., Gruber, D. M., Huber, J. et al. (2016). Consensus: Soy isoflavones as a first-line approach to the treatment of menopausal vasomotor complaints. *Gynecological Endocrinology,* 2016, 427–430. doi:10.3109/09513590.2016.1152240

Schmitt, D. P., Alcalay, L., Allensworth, M., Allik, J., Ault, L., Austers, I. et al. (2004). Patterns and universals of adult romantic attachment across 62 cultural regions: Are models of self and of other pancultural constructs? *Journal of Cross-Cultural Psychology, 35,* 367–402. doi:10.1177/0022022104266105

Schneider, J. (2013). The death of an adult child: Contemporary psychoanalytic models of mourning. In S. Arbiser & G. Saragnano (Eds.), *On Freud's inhibitions, symptoms, and anxiety* (pp. 219–230). London: Karnac Books.

Schoklitsch, A., & Bauman, U. (2012). Generativity and aging: A promising future research topic? *Journal of Aging Studies, 26,* 262–272. doi:10.1016/jaging.2012.01.002.

Schooler, K. K. (1982). Response of the elderly to environment: A stress-theoretical perspective. In M. P. Lawton, P. G. Windley, & T. O. Byerts (Eds.), *Aging and the environment: Theoretical approaches* (pp. 80–96). New York: Springer.

Schott, W. (2010). *Going back part-time: Federal leave legislation and women's return to work.* Retrieved from paa2010.princeton.edu/papers/101198.

Schoulte, J. (2011). Bereavement among African Americans and Latino/a Americans. *Journal of Mental Health Counseling, 33,* 11–20. doi:10.17744/mehc.33.1.r4971657p7176307

Schultz, D. P., & Schultz, S. E. (2017). *Theories of personality* (11th ed.). Boston: Cengage Learning.

Schulz, D. J., & Enslin, C. (2014). The female executive's perspective on career planning and advancement in organizations. *Sage Open.* doi:10.1172/2158244014558040

Schulz, R., & Moryzc, R. (2013). Psychosocial actors, health, and quality of life. In M. D. Miller & L. K. Salai (Eds.), *Geriatric psychiatry* (pp. 343–371). New York: Oxford University Press.

Schulz-Helk, R. J., Poole, J. H., Dahdah, M. N., Sullivan, C., Date, E. S., Salerno, R. M. et al. (2016). Long-term outcomes after moderate-to-severe traumatic brain injury among military veterans: Seccusses and challenges. *Brain Injury, 30,* 271–279. doi:10.3109/02699052.2015.1113567

Schwab, A. K., & Greitemeyer, T. (2015). The world's biggest salad bowl: Facebook connecting cultures. *Journal of Applied Social Psychology, 45,* 243–252. doi:10.1111/jasp.12291

Schwartz, B. (2015) *Why we work.* New York: TED Books.

Schwarz, B. (2013). Environmental gerontology: What now? In R. J. Scheidt & B. Schwarz (Eds.), *Environmental gerontology: What next?* (pp. 7–22). New York: Routledge.

Schwarzer, R. (2008). Modeling health behavior change: How to predict and modify the adoption and maintenance of health behaviors. *Applied Psychology, 57,* 1–29. doi:10.1111/j.1464-0597.2007.00325.x

Schwerdtfeger, A., & Friedrich-Mai, P. (2009). Social interaction moderates the relationship between depressive mood and heart rate variability: Evidence from an ambulatory monitoring study. *Health Psychology, 28,* 501–509. doi:10.1037/a0014664

Scullin, M. K., Bugg, J. M., & McDaniel, M. A. (2012). Whoops, I did it again: Commission errors in prospective memory. *Psychology and Aging, 27,* 46–53. doi:10.1037/a0026112

Seaman, P. M. (2012). Time for my life now: Early boomer women's anticipation of volunteering in retirement. *The Gerontologist, 52,* 245–254. doi:10.1093/geront/gns001

Seene, T. and Kaasik, P. (2015) Age-associated changes in skeletal muscle regeneration: Effect of exercise. *Advances in Aging Research, 4,* 230–241. doi:10.4236/aar.2015.46025

Seene, T., Kaasik, P., & Riso, E.-M. (2012). Review on aging, unloading and reloading: Changes in skeletal muscle quantity and quality. *Archives of Gerontology and Geriatrics, 54,* 374–380. doi:10.1016/j.archger.2011.05.002.

Segal, D. L., Qualls, S. H., & Smyer, M. A. (2011). *Aging and mental health* (2nd ed.). Malden, MA: Wiley-Blackwell.

Selkoe, D. J. (2016). The amyloid hypothesis of Alzheimer's disease at 25 years. *EMBO*

References

Molecular Medicine, 8, 595–608. doi:10.15252/emmm.201606210

Sengupta, M., Decker, S. L., Harris-Kojetin, L., & Jones, A. (2012). Racial differences in dementia care among nursing home residents. *Journal of Aging and Health, 24,* 711–731. doi:10.1177/0898264311432311

Sergi, G., Bano, G., Pizzato, S., Veronese, N., & Manzato, E. (2017). Taste loss in the elderly: Possible implications for dietary habits. *Critical Reviews in Food Science and Nutrition, 57,* 3684–3689. doi:10.1080/10408398.2016.1160208

Seward, R. R., & Stanley-Stevens, L. (2014). Fathers, fathering, and fatherhood across cultures. In H. Selin (Ed.), *Parenting across cultures* (pp. 459–474). New York: Springer.

Seychell, A. (2016). *Keeping your happy marriage: Tips for dealing with marriage issues.* Retrieved from positivepsychologyprogram.com/marriage-fulfillment-lifelong-relationship/.

Seyda, B. A., & Fitzsimons, A. M. (2010). Infant deaths. In C. A. Corr & D. A. Balk (Eds.), *Children's encounters with death, bereavement, and coping* (pp. 83–107). New York: Springer.

Shanafelt, T. D., Mungo, M., Schmitgen, J., Storz, K. A., Reeves, D., Hayes, S. N. et al. (2016). Longitudinal study evluating the association between physician burnout and changes in professional work effort. *Mayo Clinic Proceedings, 91,* 422–431. doi:10.1016/j.mayocp.2016.02.001

Shao, J., Li, D., Zhang, D., Zhang, L., Zhang, Q., & Qi, X. (2013). Birth cohort changes in the depressive symptoms of Chinese older adults: A cross-temporal meta-analysis. *International Journal of Geriatric Psychiatry, 28,* 1101–1108. doi:10.1002/gps.3942

Sharma, A., & Sharma, V. (2012). The psycho-cultural analysis of sex discrimination. *Advances in Asian Social Science, 2,* 411–414. Retrieved from www.worldsciencepublisher.org/journals/index.php/AASS/article/viewFile/380/362.

Sharma, T., Bamford, M., & Dodman, D. (2015). Person-centered care: An overview of reviews. *Contemporary Nurse, 51,* 107–120. doi:10.1080/10376178.2016.1150192

Sharp, D. J., Fleminger, S., & Powell, J. (2016). Traumatic brain injury. In M. Husain & J. M. Schott (Eds.), *Oxford textbook of cognitive neurology and dementia* (pp. 435–452). New York: Oxford University Press.

Shaw, S. S. (2007). Losing a parent twice. *American Journal of Alzheimer's Disease and Other Dementias, 21,* 389–390. doi:10.1177/1533317506292860

Shayshon, B., & Popper-Giveon, A. (in press). "These are not the realities I imagined": An inquiry into the lost hopes and aspirations of beginning teachers. *Cambridge Journal of Education.* doi:10.1080/0305764X.2016.1214238

Shega, J. W., Dale, W., Andrew, M., Paice, J., Rockwood, K., & Weiner, D. K. (2012). Persistent pain and frailty: A case for homeostenosis. *Journal of the American Geriatrics Society, 60,* 113–117. doi:10.1111/j.1532-5415.2011.03769.x

Sheldon, S., & Levine, B. (2016). The role of the hippocampus in memory and mental construction. *Annals of the New York Academy of Sciences, 1369,* 76–92. doi:10.1111/nyas.13006

Shelton, J. T., & Christopher, E. A. (2016). A fresh pair of eyes on prospective memory monitoring. *Cognitive Psychology, 44,* 837–845. doi:10.3758/s13421-016-0601-3

Shen, H. (2016, May 20). Why women earn less: Just two factors explain post-PhD pay gap. *Nature.* doi:10.1038/nature.2016.19950

Sherwin, S. (2011). Looking backwards, looking forward: Hope for *Bioethics'* next twenty-five years. *Bioethics, 25,* 75–82. doi:10.1111/j.1467-8519.2010.01866.x.

Sheu, H., Lent, R. W., Brown, S. D., Miller, M. J., Hennessy, K. D., & Duffy, R. D. (2010). Testing the choice model of social cognitive career theory across Holland themes: A meta-analytic path analysis. *Journal of Vocational Behavior, 76,* 252–264. doi:10.1016/j.jvb.2009.10.015

Shimamura, A. P. (2014). Remembering the past: Neural substrates underlying episodic encoding and retrieval. *Current Directions in Psychological Science, 23,* 257–263. doi:10.3758/s13415-016-0427-2

Shivapour, S. K., Nguyen, C. M., Cole, C. A., & Denburg, N. L. (2012). Effects of age, sex, and neuropsychological performance on financial decision-making. *Frontiers in Neuroscience, 6.* doi:10.3389/fnins.2012.00082

Shoji, K., Cieslak, R., Smoktunowicz, E., Rogala, A., Benight, C. C., & Luszczynska, A. (2016). Associations between job burnout and self-efficacy: A meta-analysis. *Anxiety, Stress, & Coping, 29,* 367–386. doi:10.1080/10615806.2015.1058369

Shonkoff, J. P., Garner, A. S., the Committee on Psychosocial Aspects of Child and Family Health, Committee on Early Childhood, Adoption, and Dependent Care, and Section on Developmental and Behavioral Pediatrics et al. (2012). The lifelong effects of early childhood adversity and toxic stress. *Pediatrics, 129,* e232-e246. doi:10.1542/peds.2011–2668

Shore, J. C., Gelber, M. W., Koch, L. M., & Sower, E. (2016). Anticipatory grief: An evidence-based approach. *Journal of Hospice & Palliative Nursing, 18,* 15–19. doi:10.1097/NJH.0000000000000208

Shors, T. J., & Millon, E. M. (2016). Sexual trauma and the female brain. *Frontiers in Neuroendocrinology, 41,* 87–98. doi:10.1016/j.yfrne.2016.04.001

Shum, C. K., Wai, M., Chan, Y. W., Yiu, D., Pang, W. S., Kwok, W. Y. et al. (2016). A quality improvement project to improve and reduce the use of hand mitt restraints in nursing home residents. *Journal of Post-Acute and Long-Term Care Medicine, 17,* 272–273. doi:10.1016/j.jamda.2015.12.006

Silva, A. R. (2016). HIV prevention and screening in older adults. In G. Guaraldi, J. Falutz, C. Mussi, & A. R. Silva (Eds.), *Managing the older adult patient with HIV* (pp. 117–122). New York: Springer. doi:10.1007/978-3-319-20131-3_8

Silva, L. C. R., de Araújo, A. L., Fernandes, J. R., Matias, M. de S. T., Silva, P. R., Duarte, A. J. S. et al. (2016). Moderate and intense exercise lifestyles attenuate the effects of aging on telomere length and the survival and composition of T cell subpopulations. *AGE, 38,* 24. doi:10.1007/s11357-016-9879-0

Silver, M. P. (2016). An inquiry into self-identification with retirement. *Journal of Women & Aging, 28,* 477–488. doi:10.1080/08952841.2015.1018068

Simons, B. S., Foltz, P. A., Chalupa, R. L., Hylden, C. M., Dowd, T. C., & Johnson, A. E. (2016). Burnout in U.S. military orthopaedic residents and staff physicians. *Military Medicine, 181,* 835–838. doi:10.7205/MILMED-D-15-00325

Simonton, D. K. (2006). Creative genius, knowledge, and reason: The lives and works of eminent creators. In J. C. Kaufman & J. Baer (Eds.), *Creativity and reason in cognitive development* (pp. 43–59). New York: Cambridge University Press.

Simonton, D. K. (2012). Creative productivity and aging. In S. K. Whitbourne & M. J. Sliwinski (Eds.), *The Wiley-Blackwell handbook of adulthood and aging* (pp. 477–496). Oxford, UK: Wiley-Blackwell.

Simonton, D. K. (in press). Defining creativity: Don't we also need to define what is *not* creative? *Journal of Creative Behavior.* doi:10.1002/jocb.137

Simpson, T., Camfield, D., Pipingas, A., Macpherson, H., & Stough, C. (2012). Improved processing speed: Online computer-based cognitive training in older adults. *Educational Gerontology, 38,* 445–458. doi:10.108 0/03601277.2011.559858

Sinclair, R. R., Sears, L. E., Zajack, M., & Probst, T. (2010). A multilevel model of economic stress and employee well-being. In J. Houdmont & S. Leka (Eds.), *Contemporary occupational health psychology: Global perspectives on research and practice* (Vol. 1, pp. 1–20). Malden, MA: Wiley-Blackwell.

Singh, J. A., Saag, K G., Bridges, S. L., Jr., Akl, E. A., Bannuru, R. R., Sullivan, M. C. et al. (2016). 2015 American College of Rheumatology Guideline for the treatment of rheumatoid arthritis. *Arthritis & Rheumatology, 68,* 1–26. doi:10.1002/art.39480 Retrieved from onlinelibrary.wiley.com/doi/10.1002/art.39480/full.

Singh, M., Kaur, M., Chadha, N., & Silakari, O. (2016). Hybrids: A new paradigm to treat Alzheimer's disease. *Molecular Diversity, 20,* 271–297. doi:10.1007/s11030-015-9628-9

Sinnott, J. D. (2014). *Adult development: Cognitive aspects of thriving close relationships.* New York: Oxford University Press.

Skarin, F., Olsson, L. E., Roos, I., & Friman, M. (2017). The household as an instrumental and affective trigger in intervention programs for travel behavior change. *Travel Behaviour and Society, 6,* 83–89. doi:10.1016/j.tbs.2016.08.001

Skevington, S. M., & McCrate, F. M. (2012).Expecting a good quality of life in health: Assessing people with diverse diseases using the WHOQOL-BREF. *Health Expectations, 15,* 49–62. doi:10.1111/j.1369-7625.2010.00650.x

Skinner, T. R., Scott, I. A., & Martin, J. H. (2016). Diagnostic errors in older patients: A systematic review of incidence and potential causes in seven prevalent diseases. *International Journal of General Medicine, 9,* 137–146. doi:10.2147/IJGM.S96741

Skouteris, H., McNaught, S., & Dissanayake, C. (2007). Mothers' transition back to work and infants' transition to child care: Does work-based child care make a difference? *Child Care in Practice, 13,* 33–47. doi:10.1080/13575270601103432

Slaats, E., (2017). The future of living. In J. van Hoof, G. Demiris, & E. J. M. Wouters (Eds.), *Handbook of smart homes, health care and well-being* (pp. 443–455). New York: Springer.

Slater, C. L. (2003). Generativity versus stagnation: An elaboration of Erikson's adult stage of human development. *Journal of Adult Development, 10,* 53–65. doi:10.1023/A:1020790820868

Slough, C., Masters, S. C., Hurley, R. A., & Taber, K. H. (2016). Clinical positron emission tomography (PET) neuroimaging: Advantages and limitations as a diagnostic tool. *Journal of Neuropsychiatry and Clinical Neurosciences, 28,* A4–71. doi:10.1176/appi.neuropsych.16030044

Smith, D. T., Mouzon, D. M., & Elliott, M. (in press). Reviewing the assumptions about men's mental health: An exploration of the gender binary. *American Journal of Men's Health.* doi:10.1177/1557988316630953

Smith, L. (1992). The tyranny of America's old. *Fortune, 125*(1), 68–72.

Smith, M. D. (2016). *Dr. Ann McKee: We have no idea what percentage of NFL players develop CTE.* Retrieved from profootballtalk.nbcsports.com/2016/03/28/dr-ann-mckee-we-have-no-idea-what-percentage-of-nfl-players-develop-cte/.

Smith, P. J., & Blumenthal, J. A. (2016). Dietary factors and cognitive decline. *Journal of Prevention of Alzheimer's Disease, 3,* 53–64. doi:10.14283/jpad.2015.71

Smith, T. C., & Smith, B. (2016). Consistency in physical activity and increase in mental health in elderly over a decade: Are we achieving better population health? *AIMS Medical Science, 3,* 147–161. doi:10.3934/medsci.2016.1.147. Retrieved from www.aimspress.com/article/10.3934/medsci.2016.1.147/fulltext.html.

Smith, W. J., Howard, J. T., & Harrington, K. V. (2005). Essential formal mentor characteristics and functions in governmental and non-governmental organizations from the program administrator's and the mentor's perspective. *Public Personnel Management, 34*, 31–58. Retrieved from crawl.prod.proquest.com.s3.amazonaws.com/fpcache/22bb207a33be85506e74f5ce0a29ab16.pdf?AWSAccessKeyId=AKIAJF7V7KNV2KKY2NUQ&Expires=1476718615&Signature=HVvte0f06r8kyrYY72ekZutsk9M%3D.

Smith-Howell, E. R., Hickman, S. E., Meghani, S. H., Perkins, S. M., & Rawl, S. M. (2016). End-of-life decision making and communication of bereaved family members of African Americans with serious illness. *Journal of Palliative Medicine, 19*, 174–182. doi:10.1089/jpm.2015.0314

Smits, S. J., & Bowden, D. E. (2013). Leveraging psychological assets from the development and maintenance of leadership capabilities. *International Leadership Journal, 5*, 3–26. Retrieved from cf-test.innersync.com/documents/ILJ_Winter_2013.pdf#page=4.

Smyke, A. T., Zeanah, C. H. Fox, N. A., Nelson, C. A., & Guthrie, D. (2010). Placement in foster care enhances quality of attachment among young institutionalized children. *Child Development, 81*, 212–223. doi:10.1111/j.1467-8624.2009.01390.x

Smyth, A. C., & Naveh-Benjamin, M. (2016). Can dryad explain age-related associative memory deficits? *Psychology and Aging, 31*, 1–13. doi:10.1037/a0039071

Sneed, J. R., & Whitbourne, S. K. (2003). Identity processing and self-consciousness in middle and later adulthood. *Journals of Gerontology: Psychological Sciences, 58B*, P313-P319.

Sneed, J. R., & Whitbourne, S. K. (2005). Models of the aging self. *Journal of Social Issues, 61*, 375–388. doi:10.1111/j.1540-4560.2005.00411.x

Social Security and Medicare Boards of Trustees. (2016). *A summary of the 2016 annual reports.* Retrieved from www.ssa.gov/oact/trsum/.

Spangler, A., & Payne, K. K. (2014). *Marital duration at divorce, 2012.* Retrieved from www.bgsu.edu/content/dam/BGSU/college-of-arts-and-sciences/NCFMR/documents/FP/FP-14-11-marital-duration-2012.pdf.

Spaniol, J. (2016). Item and source memory. In S. K. Whitbourne (Ed.), *The encyclopedia of adulthood and aging* (pp. 694–699). Malden, MA: Wiley.

Spaniol, J., & Grady, C. (2012). Aging and the neural correlates of source memory: Over-recruitment and functional reorganization. *Neurobiology of Aging, 33*, 425.e3-425.e18. doi:10.1016/j.neurobiolaging.2010.10.005

Spector, P. E., Allen, T. D., Poelmans, S., Cooper, C. L., Bernin, P., Hart, P. et al. (2005). An international comparative study of work-family stress and occupational strain. In S. A. Y. Poelmans (Ed.), *Work and family: An international research perspective* (pp. 71–84). Mahwah, NJ: Erlbaum.

Sperling, R. A., Aisen, P. S., Beckett, L. A., Dennett, D. A., Craft, S., Fagan, A. M. et al. (2011). Toward defining the preclinical stages of Alzheimer's disease: Recommendations from the National Institute on Aging—Alzheimer's Association workgroups on diagnositc guidelines for Alzheimer's disease. *Alzheimer's and Dementia: Journal of the Alzheimer's Assocation, 7*, 280–292. doi:10.1016/jalz.2011.03.003

Spiro, A., III, & Brady, C. B. (2008). Integrating health into cognitive aging research and theory: Quo vadis? In S. M. Hofer & D. F. Alwin (Eds.), *Handbook of cognitive aging: Interdisciplinary perspectives* (pp. 260–283). Greenwich, CT: Sage.

Spivak, I. M., Mikhelson, V. M., & Spivak, D. L. (2016). Telomere length, telomerase activity, stress, and aging. *Advances in Gerontology, 6*, 29–35. doi:10.1134/S2079057016010136

Sritharan, R., Heilpern, K., Wilbur, C. J., & Gawronski, B. (2010). I think I like you: Spontaneous and deliberate evaluations of potential romantic partners in an online dating context. *European Journal of Social Psychology, 40*, 1062–1077. doi:10.1002/ejsp.703

Srivastava, S., John, O. P., Gosling, S. D., & Potter, J. (2003). Development of personality in early and middle adulthood: Set like plaster or persistent change? *Journal of Personality and Social Psychology, 84*, 1041–1053. doi:10.1037/0022-3514.84.5.1041

Stafford, L., Kline, S. L., & Rankin, C. T. (2004). Married individuals, cohabiters, and cohabiters who marry: A longitudinal study of relational and individual well-being. *Journal of Social & Personal Relationships, 21*, 231–248. doi:10.1177/0265407504041385

Stalp, M. C., & Conti, R. (2011). Serious leisure in the home: Professional quilters negotiate family space. *Gender, Work and Organization, 18*, 399–414. doi:10.1111/j.1468-0432.2009.0044.x

Stanley, J. T., & Isaacowitz, D. M. (2012). Socioemotional perspectives on adult development. In S. K. Whitbourne & M. J. Sliwinski (Eds.), *The Wiley-Blackwell handbook of adulthood and aging* (pp. 237–253). Oxford, UK: Wiley-Blackwell.

Staudinger, U. (2015). Images of aging: Outside and inside perspectives. *Annual Review of Gerontology and Geriatrics, 35*, 187–209. doi:10.1891/0198-8794.35.187

Staudinger, U. M., & Glück, J. (2011). Psychological wisdom research: Commonalities and differences in a growing field. *Annual Review of Psychology, 62*, 215–241. doi:10.1146/annurev.psych.121208.131659

Staudinger, U. M., Dörner, J., & Mickler, C. (2005). Wisdom and personality. In R. J. Sternberg & J. Jordan (Eds.), *A handbook of wisdom: Psychological perspectives* (pp. 191–219). New York: Cambridge University Press.

Steck, A., & Steck, B. (2016). *Brain and mind: Subjective experience and scientific objectivity.* New York: Springer.

Stefaniak, J., & O'Brien, J. (2016). Imaging of neuroinflammation in dementia: A review. *Journal of Neurology, Neurosurgery & Psychiatry, 87*, 21–28. doi:10.1136/jnnp-2015-311336

Steffens, D. C., & Potter, G. G. (2008). Geriatric depression and cognitive impairment. *Psychological Medicine, 38*, 163–175.

Stein, R., Blanchard-Fields, F., & Hertzog, C. (2002). The effects of age-stereotype priming on the memory performance of older adults. *Experimental Aging Research, 28*, 169–191. doi:10.1080/03610730252800184

Stein-Morrow, E. L., & Miller, L. M. S. (2009). Aging, self-regulation, and learning from text. *Psychology of Learning and Motivation, 51*, 255–296. doi:10.1016/S0079-7421(09)1008-0

Stephan, Y., Sutin, A. R., Caudroit, J., & Terracciano, A. (2016). Subjective age and changes in memory in older adults. *Journal of Gerontology: Psychological Sciences, 71*, 675–683. doi:10.1093/geronb/gbv010

Stern, Y. (2017). An approach to studying the neural correlates of reserve. *Brain Imaging and Behavior, 11*, 410–416. doi:10.1007/s11682-016-9566-x

Sternberg, R. J. (1985). *Beyond IQ: A triarchic theory of human intelligence.* New York: Cambridge University Press.

Sternberg, R. J. (2006). A duplex theory of love. In R. J. Sternberg & K. Weis (Eds.), *The new psychology of love* (pp. 184–199). New Haven, CT: Yale University Press.

Sternberg, R. J. (2016). The gift that keeps on giving—But for how long? *Journal of Intelligence, 4*, 4. doi:10.3390/jintelligence4010004

Sternberg, R. J., & Sternberg, K. (2017). *Cognitive psychology* (7th ed.). Boston: Cengage Learning.

Sternberg, R. J., Jarvin, L., & Grigorenko, E. L. (2010). *Explorations in giftedness.* New York: Cambridge University Press.

Sterns, H. L., & Chang, B. (2010). Workforce issues and retirement. In J. C. Cavanaugh & C. K. Cavanaugh (Eds.), *Aging in America: Vol. 3: Societal issues* (pp. 81–105). Santa Barbara, CA: ABC-CLIO.

Sterns, H. L., & Huyck, M. H. (2001). The role of work in midlife. In M. E. Lachman (Ed.), *Handbook of midlife development* (pp. 447–486). New York: Wiley.

Steuerle, C. E., & Quakenbush, C. (2015). *Social Security and Medicare lifetime benefits and taxes.* Retrieved from www.urban.org/research/publication/social-security-and-medicare-lifetime-benefits-and-taxes/view/full_report

Stewart, J. S., Goad Oliver, E., Cravens, K. S., & Oishi, S. (2017). Managing millennials: Embracing generational differences. *Business Horizons, 60*, 45–54. doi:10.1016/j.bushor.2016.08.011

Stillman, C. M., You, X., Seaman, K. L., Vaidya, C. J., Howard, J. H., Jr., & Howard, D. V. (2016). Task-related functional connectivity of the caudate mediates the association between trait mindfulness and implicit learning in older adults. *Cognitive, Affective, & Behavioral Neuroscience, 16*, 736–753. doi:10.3758/s13415-016-0427-2

Stojnov, D. (2013). Stereotypes that help define who we are. *Journal of Constructivist Psychology, 26*, 21–29. doi:10.1080/10720537.201 3.732530

Stokes, J. (2016). The influence of intergenerational relationships on marital quality following the death of a parent in adulthood. *Journal of Social and Personal Relationships, 33*, 3–22. doi:10.1177/0265407514558962

Stoltz, K. B. (2016). Midlife adults: At 40, the eyes had it, now at 50, the career does! When career vision begins to blur. In W. K. Killam, S. Degges-White, & R. E. Michel (Eds.), *Career counseling interventions: Practice with diverse clients* (pp. 59–66). New York: Springer.

Stoner, S., O'Riley, A., & Edelstein, B. (2010). Assessment of mental health. In J. C. Cavanaugh & C. K. Cavanaugh (Eds.), *Aging in America: Volume 2: Physical and mental health* (pp. 141–170). Santa Barbara, CA: ABC-CLIO.

Stoner, S., O'Riley, A., & Edelstein, B. (2010). Assessment of mental health. In J. C. Cavanaugh & C. K. Cavanaugh (Eds.), *Aging in America: Volume 2: Physical and mental health* (pp. 141–170). Santa Barbara, CA: ABC-CLIO.

Stoner, S., O'Riley, A., & Edelstein, B. (2010). Assessment of mental health. In J. C. Cavanaugh & C. K. Cavanaugh (Eds.), *Aging in America: Volume 2: Physical and mental health* (pp. 141–170). Santa Barbara, CA: ABC-CLIO.

Štrac, D. Š., Pivac, N., & Mück-Šeler, D. (2016). The serotonergic system and cognitive function. *Translational Neuroscience, 7*, 35–49. doi:10.1515/tnsci-2016-0007 Retrieved from www.degruyter.com/view/j/tnsci.2016.7.issue-1/tnsci-2016-0007/tnsci-2016-0007.xml.

Strawbridge, W. J., Shema, S. J., Balfour, J. L., Higby, H. R., & Kaplan, G. A. (1998). Antecedents of frailty over three decades in an older cohort. *Journal of Gerontology: Social Sciences, 53B*, S9–S16. doi:10.1093/geronb/53B.1.S9

Street, D., & Burge, S. W. (2012). Residential context, social relationships, and subjective well-being in assisted living. *Research on Aging, 34*, 365–394. doi:10.1177/0164027511423928

Strinic, V. (2015). Arguments in support and against euthanasia. *British Journal of Medicine & Medical Research, 9*, 1–12. doi:10.9734/BJMMR/2015/19151

Stroebe, M. S., & Archer, J. (2013). Origins of modern ideas on love and loss: Contrasting forerunners of attachment theory. *Review of General Psychology, 17*, 28–39. doi:10.1037/a0030030

Stroebe, M., Finkenauer, C., Wijngaards-de Meij, L., Schut, H., van den Bout, J., & Stroebe, W. (2013). Partner-oriented self-regulation among bereaved parents: The costs of holding in grief for the partner's sake. *Psychological Science.* doi:10.1177/0956797612457383

Stroebe, M., Schut, H., & Boerner, K. (2010). Continuing bonds in adaptation to bereavement: Toward theoretical integration. *Clinical Psychology Review, 30,* 259–268. doi:10.1016/j.cpr.2009.11.007

Stroebe, M., Schut, H., & Stroebe, W. (2005). Attachment in coping with bereavement: A theoretical integration. *Review of General Psychology, 9,* 48–66. doi:10.1037/1089-2680.9.1.48

Stroebe, W., Abakoumkin, G., & Stroebe, M. (2010). Beyond depression: Yearning for the loss of a loved one. *OMEGA: Journal of Death and Dying, 61,* 85–101. doi:10.2190/OM.61.2.a

Strough, J., & Margrett, J. (2002). Overview of the special section on collaborative cognition in later adulthood. *International Journal of Behavioral Development, 26,* 2–5. doi:10.1080/01650250143000300

Strough, J., Berg, C. A., & Sansone, C. (1996). Goals for solving everyday problems across the interpersonal concerns. *Developmental Psychology, 32,* 1106–1115. doi:10.1037/0012-1649.32.6.1106

Strough, J., Cheng, S., & Swenson, L. M. (2002). Preferences for collaborative and individual everyday problem solving in later adulthood. *International Journal of Behavioral Development, 26,* 26–35. doi:10.1080/01650250143000337

Strough, J., de Bruin, W. B., & Peters, E. (2015). New perspectives for motivating better decisions in older adults. *Frontiers in Psychology, 6.* doi:10.3389/fpsyg.2015.00783 Retrieved from www.ncbi.nlm.nih.gov/pmc/articles/PMC4475788/

Suchy, Y. (2016). *Executive functioning: A comprehensive guide for clinical practice.* New York: Oxford University Press.

Sugimoto-Matsuda, J. J., & Guerrero, A. P. S. (2016). Violence and abuse. In D. Alicata, N. Jacobs, A. Guerrero, & M. Piasecki (Eds.), *Problem-based behavioral science and psychiatry* (pp. 113–133). New York: Springer.

Sugiura, M. (2016). Functional neuroimaging of normal aging: Declining brain, adapting brain. *Ageing Research Reviews, 30,* 61–72. doi:10.1016/j.arr.2016.006

Suja, C., Shuhaib, B., Khathoom, H., & Simi, K. (2016). A review on dietary antioxidants. *Research Journal of Pharmacy and Technology, 9*(2), 196–202. doi:10.5958/0974-360X.2016.00035.4

Sullivan, L., & Meschede, T. (2016). Race, gender, and senior economic well-being: How financial vulnerability over the life course shapes retirement for older women of color. *Public Policy & Aging Report, 26,* 58–62. doi:10.1093/ppar/prw001

Sumowski, J. F., Rocca, M. A., Leavitt, V. M., Riccitelli, G., Sandry, J., DeLuca, J. et al. (2016). Searching for the neural bases of reserve against memory decline: Intellectual enrichment linked to larger hippocampal volume in multiple sclerosis. *European Journal of Neurology, 23,* 39–44. doi:10.1111/ene.12662

Sumter, S. R., Vandenbosch, L., & Ligtenberg, L. (2017). Love me Tinder: Untangling emerging adults' motivations for using the dating application Tinder. *Telematics and Informatics, 34,* 67–78.

Sun, F., & Xiao, J. J. (2012). Perceived social policy fairness and subjective wellbeing: Evidence from China. *Social Indicators Research, 107,* 171–186.

Suo, C., Singh, M. F., Gates, N., Wen, W., Sachev, P., Brodaty, H. et al. (2016). Therapeutically relevant structural and functional mechanisms triggered by physical and cognitive exercise. *Molecular Psychiatry, 21,* 1633–1642. doi:10.1038/mp.2016.19

Swanson, D. A., & Sanford, D. A. (2012). Socio-economic status and life expectancy in the United States, 1990–2010. *Population Review, 51.* Retrieved from muse.jhu.edu/journals/population_review/v051/51.2.swanson.html

Swindell, R. (2012). Successful ageing and international approaches to later-life learning. In G. Boulton-Lewis & M. Tam (Eds.), *Active ageing, active learning* (pp. 35–63). New York: Springer

Tach, L., & Halpern-Meekin, S. (2009). How does premarital cohabitation affect trajectories of marital quality? *Journal of Marriage and the Family, 71,* 298–317. doi:10.1111/j.1741-3737.2009.00600.x

Talamini, L. M., & Gorree, E. (2012). Aging memories: Differential decay of episodic memory components. *Learning and Memory, 19,* 239–246. doi:10.1101/lm.024281.111

Talbot, L. A., Morrell, C. H., Fleg, J. L., & Metter, E. J. (2007). Changes in leisure time physical activity and risk of all-cause mortality in men and women: The Baltimore longitudinal study of aging. *Preventive Medicine, 45,* 169–176. doi:10.1016/j.ypmed.2007.05.014

Tam, K.-P. (2013). Existential motive underlying cosmetic surgery: A terror management analysis. *Journal of Applied Social Psychology, 43,* 947–955. doi:10.1111/jasp.12059

Tamayo, G. J., Broxson, A., Munsell, M., & Cohen, M. Z. (2010). Caring for the caregiver. *Oncology Nursing Forum, 37,* E50–E57. doi:10.1188/10.ONF.E50-E57

Tang, F., Morrow-Howell, N., & Choi, E. (2010). Why do older adult volunteers stop volunteering? *Ageing and Society, 30,* 859–878. doi:10.1017/S0144686X10000140

Tang, P.-L., Chiou, C.-P., Lin, H.-S., Wang, C., & Liand, S.-L. (2011). Correlates of death anxiety among Taiwanese cancer patients. *Cancer Nursing, 34,* 286–292. doi:10.1097/NCC.0b013e31820254c6

Tanner, J. L., & J. J. Arnett. (2009). The emergence of emerging adulthood: The new life stage between adolescence and young adulthood. In A. Furlong (Ed.), *Handbook of youth and young adulthood: New perspectives and agendas* (pp. 39–45). London: Routledge.

Tauber, S. C., Staszewski, O., Prinz, M., Nolte, K., & Bunkowski, S. (2016). HIV encephalopathy: Glial activation and hippocampal neuronal apoptosis, but limited neural repair. *HIV Medicine, 17,* 143–151. doi:10.1111/hiv.12288

Tauber, S. K., & Dunlosky, J. (2016). A brief history of metamemory research and handbook overview. In J. Dunlosky & S. K. Tauber (Eds.), *The Oxford handbook of metamemory* (pp. 7–21). New York: Oxford University Press.

Taylor, J. L., O'Hara, R., Mumenthaler, M. S., Rosen, A. C., & Yesavage, J. A. (2005). Cognitive ability, expertise, and age differences in following air-traffic control instructions. *Psychology and Aging, 20,* 117–133. doi:10.1037/0882-7974.20.1.117

Taylor, R. J., Chatters, L. M., & Levin, J. (2004). *Religion in the lives of African Americans.* Thousand Oaks, CA: Sage.

Taylor, S. (2015). *Health psychology* (9th ed.). New York: McGraw-Hill.

Taylor, S. E. (2006). Tend and befriend: Biobehavioral bases of affiliation under stress. *Current Directions in Psychological Science, 15,* 273–277. doi:10.1111/j.1467-8721.2006.00451.x

Teiga-Mocigemba, S., Klauer, K. C., & Sherman, J. W. (2010). A practical guide to implicit association tests and related tasks. In B. Gawronski & B. K. Payne (Eds.), *Handbook of implicit social cognition: Measurement, theory, and applications* (pp. 117–139). New York: Guilford.

Terkel, S. (1974). *Working.* New York: Pantheon.

The Commonwealth Fund. (2015). *U.S. health care from a global perspective: Spending, use of services, prices, and health in 13 countries.* Retrieved from www.commonwealthfund.org/publications/issue-briefs/2015/oct/us-health-care-from-a-global-perspective

The Green House Project. (2016a). *History.* Retrieved from www.thegreenhouseproject.org/about/history

The Green House Project. (2016b). *Discover.* Retrieved from www.thegreenhouseproject.org/about/discover

Therborn, G. (2010). Families in global perspective. In A. Giddens & P. W. Sutton (Eds.), *Sociology: Introductory readings* (3rd ed., pp. 119–124). Malden, MA: Polity Press.

Thomas, A. G., Dennis, A., Bandettini, P. A., & Johansen-Berg, H. (2012). The effects of aerobic activity on brain structure. *Frontier in Psychology, 3.* doi:10.3389/fpsyg.2012.00086. Retrieved from www.ncbi.nlm.nih.gov/pmc/articles/PMC3311131/

Thomas, A. K., Lee, M., & Hughes, G. (2016). Introspecting on the elusive: The uncanny state of the feeling of knowing. In J. Dunlosky & S. K. Tauber (Eds.), *The Oxford handbook of metamemory* (pp. 81–94). New York: Oxford University Press.

Thomas, F. (2008). Remarriage after spousal death: Options facing widows and implications for livelihood security. *Gender and Development, 16,* 73–83. doi:10.1080/13552070701876235

Thomas, M. D., Guihan, M., & Mambourg, F. (2011). What do potential residents need to know about assisted living facility type? The trade-off between autonomy and help with more complex needs. *Journal of Housing for the elderly, 25,* 109–124. doi:10.1080/02763893.2011.571108

Thomas, M. L., Bangen, K. J., Ardelt, M., & Jeste, D. V. (2017). Development of a 12-item Abbreviated Three-Dimensional Wisdom Scale (3D-WS-12). *Assessment, 24,* 71–82. doi:10.1177/107319115595714

Thomas, R. C., & Hasher, L. (2006). The influence of emotional valence on age differences in early processing and memory. *Psychology and Aging, 21,* 821–825. doi:10.1037/0882-7974.21.4.821

Thomas, R. C., & Hasher, L. (2012). Reflections of distraction in memory: Transfer of previous distraction improves recall in younger and older adults. *Journal of Experimental Psychology: Learning, Memory, and Cognition, 38,* 30–39. doi:10.1037/a0024882

Thompson, G. E., Cameron, R. E., & Fuller-Thompson, E. (2013). Walking the red road: the role of First Nations grandparents in promoting cultural well-being. *International Journal of Aging and Human development, 76,* 55–78. doi:10.2190/AG.76.1.c

Thornton, W. J. L., & Dumke, H. A. (2005). Age differences in everyday problem-solving and decision-making effectiveness: A meta-analytic review. *Psychology and Aging, 20,* 85–99. doi:10.1037/0882-7974.20.1.85

Thornton, W. L., Paterson, T. S. E., & Yeung, S. E. (2013). Age differences in everyday problem solving: The role of problem context. *International Journal of Behavioral Development, 37,* 13–20. doi:10.1177/0165025412454028

Tobin, D. J. (2017). Introduction to skin aging. *Journal of Tissue Viability, 26,* 37–46. doi:10.1016/j.jtv.2016.03.022

Tolkko, T. (2016). Becoming an expert by experience: An analysis of service users' learning process. *Social Work in Mental Health, 14,* 292–312. doi:10.1080/15332985.2015.1038411

Tong, C., & Kram, K. E. (2013). The efficacy of mentoring—the benefits for mentees, mentors, and organizations. In J. Passmore, D. B. Peterson, & T. Freire (Eds.), *The Wiley-Blackwell handbook of coaching and mentoring* (pp. 217–242). Oxford, UK: Wiley-Blackwell.

Torges, C. M., Stewart, A. J., & Duncan, L. E. (2008). Achieving ego integrity: Personality development in late midlife. *Journal of Research in Personality, 42,* 1004–1019. doi:10.1016/j.jrp.2008.02.006

Toril, P., Reales, J. M., Mayas, J., & Ballesteros, S. (2016). Video game training enhances visuospatial working memory and episodic memory in older adults. *Frontiers in Human Neuroscience, 10,* 206. doi:10.3389/fnhum.2016.00206 Retrieved from www.ncbi.nlm.nih.gov/pmc/articles/PMC4859063/

Torres, L., Lindstrom, K., Hannah, L., & Webb, F. (2016). Exploring barriers among primary care providers in referring patients to hospice. *Journal of Hospice & Palliative Nursing, 18,* 167–172. doi:10.1097/NJH.0000000000000233

Tremblay, F., & Master, S. (2016). Touch in aging. In T. Prescott, E. Ahissar, & E. Izhikevich (Eds.), *Scholarpedia of touch* (pp. 351–361). New York: Springer. doi:10.2991/978-94-6239-133-8_29

Trevisan, L. A. (2014). Elderly alcohol use disorders: Epidemiology, screening, and assessment issues. *Psychiatric Times.* Retrieved from www.psychiatrictimes.com/alcohol-abuse/elderly-alcohol-use-disorders-epidemiology-screening-and-assessment-issues.

Tromp, D., Dufour, A., Lithfous, S., Pebayle, T., & Després, O. (2015). Episodic memory in normal aging and Alzheimer's disease: Insights from imaging and behavioral studies. *Aging Research Reviews, 24 (Part B),* 232–262. doi:10.1016/j.arr.2015.08.066

Troutman, M., Nies, M. A., & Mavellia, H. (2011). Perceptions of successful aging in Black older adults. *Journal of Psychosocial Nursing and Mental Health Services, 49,* 28–34. doi:10.3928/02793695-20101201-01

Truxillo, D. M., Cadiz, D. M., & Hammer, L. B. (2015). Supporting the aging workforce: A review and recommendations for workplace intervention research. *Organizational Psychology and Organizational Behavior, 2,* 351–381. doi:10.1146/annurev-orgpsych-032414-111435

Truxillo, D. M., McCune, E. A., Bertolino, M., & Fraccaroli, F. (2012). Perceptions of older versus younger workers in terms of Big Five facets, proactive personality, cognitive ability, and job performance. *Journal of Applied Social psychology, 42,* 2607–2639. doi:10.1111/j.1559-1816.2012.00954.x

Trzesniewski, K., H., & Donnellan, M. B. (2010). Rethinking "Generation Me": A study of cohort effects from 1976–2006. *Perspective on Psychological Science, 5,* 58–75. doi:10.1177/1745691609356789

Tsang, W. W. N., & Fu, A. S. Sn. (2016). Virtual reality exercise to improve balance control in older adults at risk of falling. *Hong Kong Medical Journal, 22,* 19–22. Retrieved from www.hkmj.org/system/files/hkm1602sp2p19.pdf.

Tsuno, N., & Homma, J. A. (2009). Aging in Asia—The Japan experience. *Ageing International, 34,* 1–14. doi:10.1007/s12126-009-9032-9

Tu, M. C.-H. (2006). *Culture and job satisfaction: A comparative study between Taiwanese and Filipino caregivers working in Taiwan's long-term care industry.* Unpublished dissertation, Nova Southeastern University.

U. S. Food and Drug Administration. (2015). *Medicines and you: A guide for older adults.* Retrieved from: www.fda.gov/drugs/resourcesforyou/ucm163959.htm.

U.S. Department of Agriculture. (2014). *Expenditures on children by families, 2013.* Retrieved from www.cnpp.usda.gov/sites/default/files/expenditures_on_children_by_families/crc2013.pdf.

U.S. Department of Health and Human Services. (1991). *Healthy people 2000: National health promotion and disease prevention.* Publication No. PHS 91-50212. Washington, DC: US Government Printing Office.

U.S. Department of Labor Women's Bureau. (2016a). *Data and statistics.* Retrieved from www.dol.gov/wb/stats/stats_data.htm.

U.S. Department of Labor Women's Bureau. (2016b). *Women's earnings by race and ethnicity as a percentage of white, non-Hispanic men's earnings, March 1987–2014.* Retrieved from www.dol.gov/wb/stats/earnings_race_ethnic_percent_white_nonhisp_mens_earn_87_14_txt.htm.

U.S. Department of Labor. (2016) *Nontraditional occupations.* Retrieved from www.dol.gov/wb/stats/Nontraditional%20Occupations.pdf.

Ukraintseva, S. V., Yashin, A., Arbeev, K. G., Kulminski, A., Akushevich, I., Wu, D. et al. (2016). Puzzling role of genetic risk factors in human longevity: "Risk alleles" as prolongevity variants. *Biogerontology, 17,* 109–127. doi:10.1007/s10522-015-9600-1

Uleman, J. S., & Kressel, L. M. (2013). A brief history of theory and research on impression formation. In D. E. Carlston (Ed.), *The Oxford handbook of social cognition* (pp. 53–73). New York: Oxford University Press.

Uleman, J. S., & Saribay, S. A. (2012). Initial impressions of others. In K. Deaux & M. Snyder (Eds.), *The Oxford handbook of personality and social psychology* (pp. 337–366). New York: Oxford University Press.

Utz, R.L., & Pascoe, A. (2016). Bereavement/widowhood. In S. K. Whitbourne (Ed.), *Encyclopedia of adulthood and aging* (Vol. 1, pp. 118–121). Malden, MA: Wiley-Blackwell.

Vaandrager, L., & Kennedy, L. (2017). The application of salutogenesis in communities and neighborhoods. In M. B. Mittelmark, S. Sagy, M. Eriksson, G. F. Bauer, J. M. Pelikan, B. Lindström et al. (Eds.), *The handbook of salutogenesis* (pp. 159–170). New York: Springer.

Vagelatos, N. T., & Eslick, G. D. (2013). Type 2 diabetes as a risk factor for Alzheimer's disease: The confounders, interactions, and neuropathology associated with this relationship. *Epidemiologic Reviews, 35,* 152–160. doi:10.1093/epirev/mxs012

Valiathan, R., Ashman, M., & Asthana, D. (2016). Effects of ageing on the immune system: Infants to elderly. *Scandinavian Journal of Immunology, 83,* 255–266. doi:10.1111/sji.12413

Vallerand, R. J. (2008). On the psychology of passion: In search of what makes people's lives most worth living. *Canadian Psychology, 49,* 1–13. doi:10.1037/0708-5591.49.1.1

Vallerand, R. J. (2015). *The psychology of passion: A dualistic model.* New York: Oxford University Press.

Vallerand, R. J., Paquet, Y., Philippe, F. L., & Charest, J. (2010). On the role of passion for work in burnout: A process model. *Journal of Personality, 78,* 289–312. doi:10.1111/j.1467-6494.2009.00616.x

van den Wijngaart, M. A. G., Vernooij-Dassen, M. J. F. J., & Felling, A. J. A. (2007). The influence of stressors, appraisal and personal conditions on the burden of spousal caregivers of persons with dementia. *Aging & Mental Health, 11,* 626–636. doi:10.1080/13607860701368463

van der Geest, S. (2004). Dying peacefully: Considering good death and bad death in Kwahu-Tafo, Ghana. *Social Science and Medicine, 58,* 899–911. doi:10.1016/j.socscimed.2003.10.041

van der Pas, S., & Koopman-Boyden, P. (2010). Leisure and recreation activities and wellbeing among midlife New Zealanders. In C. Waldegrave & P. Koopman-Boyden (Eds.), *Midlife New Zealanders aged 40–64 in 2008: Enhancing well-being in an aging society* (pp. 111–128). Hamilton, New Zealand: Family Centre Social Policy Research Unit, Lower Hutt, Wellington and the Population Studies Centre, University of Waikato. Retrieved from www.familycentre.org.nz/Publications/PDF's/EWAS_M2.pdf.

van Impe, A., Coxon, J. P., Goble, D. J., Doumas, M., & Swinnen, S. P. (2012). White matter fractional anisotropy predicts balance performance in older adults. *Neurobiology of Aging, 33,* 1900–1912. doi:10.1016/j.neurobiolaging.2011.06.013

van Klaveren, C., van den Brink, H. M., & van Praag, B. (2013). Intrahousehold work timing: The effect on joint activities and the demand for child care. *European Sociological Review, 29,* 1–18. doi:10.1093/esr/jcr035

van Muijden, J., Band, G. P. H., & Hommel, B. (2012). Online games training aging brains: Limited transfer to cognitive control functions. *Frontiers in Human Neuroscience, 6.* doi:10.3389/fnhum.2012.00221 Retrieved from www.ncbi.nlm.nih.gov/pmc/articles/PMC3421963/.

van Wanrooy, B. (2013). Couple strategies: Negotiating working time over the life course. In A. Evans, & J. Baxter (Eds.), *Negotiating the life course: Stability and change in life pathways* (pp. 175–190). New York: Springer.

Vansteenkiste, S., Deschacht, N., & Sels, L. (2015). Why are unemployed aged fifty and over less likely to find a job? A decomposition analysis. *Journal of Vocational Behavior, 90,* 55–65. doi:10.1016/j.jvb.2015.07.004

Varkal, M. D., Yalvac, D., Tufan, F., Turan, S., Cengiz, M., & Emul, M. (2013). Metacognitive differences between elderly and adult outpatients with generalized anxiety disorder. *European Geriatric Medicine, 4,* 150–153. doi:10.1016/j.eurger.2012.12.001

Verbrugge, L. M. (1994). Disability in late life. In R. P. Abeles, H. C. Gift, & M. G. Ory (Eds.), *Aging and quality of life* (pp. 79–98). New York: Springer.

Verbrugge, L. M. (2005). Flies without wings. In J. R. Carey, J.-M. Robine, J. P. Michel, & Y. Christen (Eds.), *Longevity and frailty* (pp. 67–81). New York: Springer.

Verbrugge, L. M., & Jette, A. M. (1994). The disablement process. *Social Science and Medicine, 38,* 1–14. doi: 10.1016/0277-9536(94)90294-1

Verbrugge, L. M., Brown, D. C., Zajacova, A. (2017). Disability rises gradually for a cohort of older Americans, *Journals of Gerontology: Psychological Sciences, 72,* 151–161. doi:10.1093/geronb/gbw002

Vicente, R., Mausset-Bonnefont, A. L., Jorgensen, C., Louis-Plence, P., & Brondello, J. M. (2016). Cellular senescence impact on immune cell fate and function. *Aging Cell, 15,* 400–406. doi:10.1111/acel.12455

Voelkle, M. C., Ebner, N. C., Lindenberger, U., & Riediger, M. (2012). Let me guess how old you are: Effects of age, gender, and facial expression on perceptions of age. *Psychology and Aging, 27,* 265–277. doi:10.1037/a0025065

Volpe, U., Fiorillo, A., Jovanovic, N., & Bhugra, D. (2016). Mentoring and career coaching. In A. Fiorillo, U. Volpe, & D. Bhugra (Eds.), *Psychiatry in practice: Education, experience, and expertise* (pp. 83–95). New York: Oxford University Press.

von Hippel, W., & Henry, J. D. (2012). Social cognitive aging. In S. T. Fiske & C. N. Macrae (Eds.), *The SAGE handbook of social cognition* (pp. 390–410). Thousand Oaks, CA: Sage Publications.

Wahl, H.-W. (2015). Theories of environmental influences on aging and behavior. In N. A. Pachana (Ed.), *Encyclopedia of geropsychology* (pp. 1–8). New York: Springer. doi:10.1007/978-981-287-080-3_132-1

Wahl, H.-W., Heyl, V., & Schilling, O. (2012). Robustness of personality and affect relations under chronic conditions: The case of age-related vision and hearing impairment. Journal of *Gerontology: Psychological Sciences, 67,* 687–696. doi:10.1093/geronb/gbs002

Waites, C. (2009). Building on strengths: Intergenerational practice with African-American families. *Social Work, 54,* 278–287. doi:10.1093/sw/54.3.278

Walhovd, K. B., Westerhausen, R., de Lange, A.-M. G., Bråthen, A. C. S., Grydeland, H., Engvig, A. et al. (2016). Premises of plasticity—And the loneliness of the medial temporal lobe. *NeuroImage, 131,* 48–54. doi:10.1016/j.neuroimage.2015.10.060

Walker, A. C., & Balk, D. E. (2007). Bereavement rituals in the Muscogee Creek tribe. *Death Studies, 31,* 633–652. doi:10.1080/07481180701405188

References

Walker, L. E. A. (1984). *The battered woman syndrome.* New York: Springer.

Walter, S., Beltrán-Sánchez, H., Regidor, E., Gomez-Martin, C., del-Barrio, J. L., Gil-del-Miguel, A. et al. (2016). No evidence of morbidity compression in Spain: A time series study based on national hospitalization records. *International Journal of Public Health, 61,* 729–738. doi:10.1007/s00038-016-0829-5

Walther, A. N. (1991). *Divorce hangover.* New York: Pocket Books.

Wang, M., & Chen, Y. (2006). Age differences in attitude change: Influence of cognitive resources and motivation on responses to argument quantity. *Psychology and Aging, 21,* 581–589. doi:10.1037/0882-7974.21.3.581

Wang, S-W., & Repetti, R. L. (2016). Who gives to whom? Testing the support gap hypothesis with naturalistic observations of couple interactions. *Journal of Family Psychology, 30,* 492–502. doi:10.1037/fam0000196

Wang, T.-J., Chern, H.-L., & Chiou, Y.-E. (2005). A theoretical model for preventing osteoarthritis-related disability. *Rehabilitation Nursing, 30,* 62–67. doi:10.1002/j.2048-7940.2005. tb00361.x

Wang, W. (2015). *The link between a college education and a lasting marriage.* Retrieved from www.pewresearch.org/fact-tank/2015/12/04/education-and-marriage/.

Wang, W.-C., & Giovanello, K. S. (2016). The role of medial temporal lobe regions in incidental and intentional retrieval of item and relational information in aging. *Hippocampus, 26,* 693–699. doi:10.1002/hipo.22578

Wanzer, S. H., & Glenmullen, J. (2007). *To die well: Your right to comfort, calm, and choice in the last days of life.* Cambridge, MA: Da Capo Press.

Waring, J. D., Addis, D. R., & Kensinger, E. A. (2013). Effects of aging on neural connectivity underlying selective memory for emotional scenes. *Neurobiology of Aging, 34,* 451–467. doi:10.1016/j.neurobiolaging.2012.03.011

Warner, D. F., & Adams, S. A. (2016). Physical disability and increased loneliness among married older adults: The role of changing social norms. *Society and Mental Health, 6,* 106–128. doi:10.1177/2156869315616257

Warner, S. C., & Valdes, A. M. (2016). The genetics of osteoarthritis: A review. *Journal of Functional Morphology and Kinesiology, 1,* 140–153. doi:10.3390/jfmk1010140

Warr, P., Butcher, V., & Robertson, I. (2004). Activity and psychological well-being in older people. *Aging & Mental Health, 8,* 172–183. doi:10.1080/13607860410001649662

Warren, D. E., Duff, M., Magnotta, V., Capizzano, A. A., Cassell, M. D., & Tranel, D. (2012). Long-term neuropsychological, neuroanatomical, and life outcome in hippocampal amnesia. *The Clinical Neuropsychologist, 26,* 335–369. doi:10.1080/13854046. 2012.655781

Watson, R. W. (2013). *Frisky 60s flower children are still making love not war.* Retrieved from www.psychologytoday.com/blog/love-and-gratitude/201302/frisky-60s-flower-children-are-still-making-love-not-war.

Wayland, S., Maple, M., McKay, K., & Glassock, G. (2016). Holding onto hope: A review of the literature exploring missing persons, hope and ambiguous loss. *Death Studies, 40,* 54–60. doi:10.1080/07481187.2015.1068245

Weaver, D. A. (2010). Widows and Social Security. *Social Security Bulletin, 70,* 89–109. Retrieved from www.ssa.gov/policy/docs/ssb/v70n3/v70n3p89.html.

WebMD. (2016). *What is emphysema?* Retrieved from www.webmd.com/lung/copd/what-is-emphysema.

Webster-Marketon, J., & Glaser, R. (2008). Stress hormones and immune function. *Cellular Immunology, 252,* 16–26. doi:10.1016/j.cellimm.2007.09.006

Wechsler, D. (1958). *The measurement and appraisal of adult intelligence* (4th ed.). Baltimore: Williams & Wilkins.

Ween, M., Hodge, G., Reynolds, P., & Hodge, S. (2016). The new kid on the block: E-cigarettes can cause damage to airway cells and cause airway macrophage dysfunction. *American Journal of Respiratory and Critical Care Medicine, 193,* A1194. doi:10.1164/ajrccm-conference.2016.193.1_MeetingAbstracts.A1194

Weger, H., Jr. (2016). Cross-sex friendships. In C. R. Berger, M. E. Roloff, S. R. Wilson, J. P. Dillard, J. Caughlin, & D. Solomon (Eds), *The international encyclopedia of interpersonal communication.* New York, NY: Wiley. doi:10.1002/9781118540190.wbeic131

Wegman, L. A., Hoffman, B. J., Carter, N. T., Twenge, J. M., & Guenole, N. (in press). Placing job characteristics in context: Cross-temporal meta-analysis of changes in job characteristics since 1975. *Journal of Management.* doi:10.1177/149206316654545

Weiss, D. (in press). On the inevitability of aging: Essentialist beliefs moderate the impact of negative age stereotypes on older adults' memory performance and physiological reactivity. *Journal of Gerontology: Psychological Sciences.* doi:10.1093/geronb/gbw087

Weiss, D., & Lang, F. R. (2012). "They" are old but "I" feel younger: Age-group dissociation as a self-protective strategy in old age. *Psychology and Aging, 27,* 153–163. doi:10.1037/a0024887

Weiss, D., Job, V., Mathias, M., Grah, S., & Freund, A. M. (2016). The end (is not) near: Aging, essentialism, and future time perspective. *Developmental Psychology, 52,* 996–1009. doi:10.1037/dev0000115

Weiss, L. A., Westerhof, G. J., & Bohlmeijer, E. T. (2016). Can we increase psychological well-being? The effects of interventions on psychological well-being: A meta-analysis of randomized controlled trials. *PLOS ONE.* doi:10.1371/journa.pone.0158092. Retrieved from journals.plos.org/plosone/article?id=10.1371/journal.pone.0158092.

Wentura, D., & Brandtstädter, J. (2003). Age stereotypes in younger and older women: Analyses of accommodative shifts with a sentence-priming task. *Experimental Psychology, 50,* 16–26. doi:10.1027/1618–3169.50.1.16

Werner, T. L., & Shannon C. S. (20130. Doing more with less: Women's leisure during their partners' military deployment. *Leisure Sciences, 35,* 63–80. doi:10.1080/01490400.201 3.739897

West, R. L., & Strickland-Hughes, C. M. (2016). Memory training for older adults: A review with recommendations for clinicians. In D. Bruno (Ed.), *The preservation of memory* (pp. 152–168). New York: Routledge.

Westerhof, G. J., Bohlmeijer, E., & Webster, J. D. (2010). Reminiscence and mental health: A review of recent progress in theory, research and interventions. *Ageing and Society, 30,* 697–721. doi:10.1017/s0144686x09990328

Westrate, N. M., Ferrari, M., & Ardelt, M. (2016). The many faces of wisdom: An investigation of cultural-historical wisdom exemplars reveals practical, philosophical, and benevolent prototypes. *Personality and Social Psychology Bulletin, 42,* 662–676. doi:10.1177/0146167216638075

Wettstein, R. M. (2013). Legal issues geriatric psychiatrists should understand. In M. D. Miller & L. K. Salai (Eds.), *Geriatric psychiatry* (pp. 55–77). New York: Oxford University Press.

Whalley, L. J. (2015). *Understanding brain aging and dementia: A lifecourse approach.* New York: Columbia University Press.

Whitbourne, S. K. (1986). The psychological construction of the life span. In J. E. Birren & K. W. Schaie (Eds.), *Handbook of the psychology of aging* (pp. 594–618). New York: Van Nostrand Reinhold.

Whitbourne, S. K. (1987). Personality development in adulthood and old age: Relationships among identity style, health, and well-being. In K. W. Schaie (Ed.), *Annual review of gerontology and geriatrics* (Vol. 7, pp. 189–216). New York: Springer.

Whitbourne, S. K. (2010). *The search for fulfillment: Revolutionary new research that reveals the secret to long-term happiness.* New York: Ballantine Books.

Whitbourne, S. K., Culgin, S., & Cassidy, E. (1995). Evaluation of infantilizing intonation and content of speech directed at the aged. *International Journal of Aging and Human Development, 41,* 109–116. doi:10.2190/J9XE-2GB6-H49GMR7V

White, H., & Venkatesh, B. (2016). Traumatic brain injury. In M. Smith, G. Citerio, & W. A. Kofke (Eds.), *Oxford textbook of neurocritical care* (pp. 210–224). New York: Oxford University Press.

White, M. L., Peters, R., & Schim, S. M. (2011). Spirituality and spiritual self-care: Expanding self-care deficit nursing theory. *Nursing Science Quarterly, 24,* 48–56. doi:10.1177/0894318410389059

Whited, C., Keeler, J., Scearce, L., & Cohen, S. (2016). The aging voice. In M. S. Benninger, T. Murry, & M. M. Johns III (Eds.), *The performer's voice* (2nd ed., pp. 89–102). San Diego, CA: Plural Publishing.

Whitty, M. T., & Buchanan, T. (2009). Looking for love in so many places: Characteristics of online daters and speed daters. *Interpersona: An International Journal on Personal Relationships, 3*(Suppl. 2), 63–86. doi:10.5964/ijpr.v3isupp2.76 Retrieved from interpersona.psychopen.eu/article/view/76/pdf.

Wickrama, K. A. S., O'Neal, C. W., & Lorenz, F. O. (2013). Marital functioning form middle to later years: A life course-stress process framework. *Journal of Family Theory and Review, 5,* 15–34. doi:10.1111/jftr.12000

Wiebe, S. T., Cassoff, J., & Gruber, R. (2012). Sleep patterns and the risk for unipolar depression: A review. *Nature and Science of Sleep, 4,* 63–71. doi:10.2147/NSS.S23490. Available at www.dovepress.com/sleep-patterns-and-the-risk-for-unipolar-depression-a-review-peer-reviewed-article-NSS.

Wijdicks, E. F. M., Varelas, P. N., Gronseth, G. S., & Greer, D. M. (2010). Evidence-based guideline update: Determining brain death in adults. Report of the Quality Standards Subcommittee of the American Academy of Neurology. *Neurology, 74,* 1911–1918. doi:10.1212/WNL.0b013e3181e242a8

Wiles, J. L., & Jayasinha, R. (2013). Care for place: The contributions older people make to their communities. *Journal of Aging Studies, 27,* 93–101. doi:10.1016/j.jaging.2012.12.001

Willander, J., & Larsson, M. (2006). Smell your way back to childhood: Autobiographical odor memory. *Psychonomic Bulletin and Review, 13,* 240–244. doi:10.3758/BF03193837

Williams, C. N., Perkhounkova, Y., Herman, R., & Bossen, A. (2017). A communication intervention to reduce resistiveness in dementia care: A cluster randomized controlled trial. *The Gerontologist, 57,* 707–718. doi:10.1093/geront/gnw047

Williams, J. C., Phillips, K. W., & Hall, E. V. (2014). *Double jeopardy? Gender bias against women of color in science.* Retrieved from www.uchastings.edu/news/articles/2015/01/double-jeopardy-report.pdf.

Williams, S. A. (2005). Jealousy in the cross-sex friendship. *Journal of Loss & Trauma, 10,* 471–485. doi:10.1080/15325020500193937

Willis, S. L. (1991). Cognition and everyday competence. In K. W. Schaie (Ed.), *Annual review of gerontology and geriatrics* (Vol. 11, pp. 80–109). New York: Springer.

Willis, S. L., & Boron, J. B. (2008). Midlife cognition: The association of personality with cognition and risk of cognitive impairment. In S. M. Hofer & D. F. Alwin (Eds.), *Handbook of cognitive aging: Interdisciplinary perspectives* (pp. 647–660). Greenwich, CT: Sage.

Willis, S. L., & Schaie, K. W. (2009). Cognitive training and plasticity: Theoretical perspective and methodological consequences. *Restorative Neurology and Neuroscience, 27*, 375–389. doi:10.3233/RNN-2009-0527

Willis, S. L., Blieszner, R., & Baltes, P. B. (1981). Intellectual training research in aging: Modification of performance on the fluid ability of figural relations. *Journal of Educational Psychology, 73*, 41–50. doi:10.1016/0193-3973(81)90005-8

Winecoff, A., LaBar, K. S. Madden, D. J., Cabeza, R., & Huettel, S. A. (2011). Cognitive and neural contributions to emotion regulation in aging. *Social Cognitive and Affective Neuroscience, 6*, 165–176. doi:10.1093/scan/nsq030

Winslow, M., & Meldrum, M. (2013). A history of hospice and palliative care. In S. Lutz, E. Chow, & P. Hoskin (Eds.), *Radiation oncology in palliative cancer care* (pp. 63–71). New York: Wiley.

Winter, L., & Parks, S. M. (2012). Elders' preferences for life-prolonging treatment and their proxies' substituted judgment: Influence of the elders' current health. *Journal of Aging and Health, 24*, 1157–1178. doi:10.1177/0898264312454572

Wise, D. (2017). *Social security programs and retirement around the world.* Chicago: University of Chicago Press.

Witko, T. M. (2006). A framework for working with American Indian parents. In T. M. Witko (Ed.), *Mental health care for urban Indians: Clinical insights from Native practitioners* (pp. 155–171). Washington, DC: American Psychological Association.

Witten, T. M. (2016). The intersectional challenges of aging and of being a gender non-conforming adult. *Generations, 40*, 63–70.

Wloch E. G., Kuh D., & Cooper R. (2016). Is the hierarchy of loss in functional ability evident in midlife? Findings from a British birth cohort. *PLOS ONE, 11*, e0155815. doi:10.1371/journal.pone.0155815. Retrieved from journals.plos.org/plosone/article?id=10.1371/journal.pone.0155815.

Wojtunik-Kulesza, K. A., Oniszczuk, A., Oniszczuk, T., & Waksmundzka-Hajnos, M. (2016). The influence of common free radicals and antioxidants on development of Alzheimer's disease. *Biomedicine & Pharmacotherapy, 78*, 39–49. doi: 10.1016/j.biopha.2015.12.024

Wolinsky, F. D., & Tierney, W. M. (1998). Self-rated health and adverse health outcomes: An exploration and refinement of the trajectory hypothesis. *Journals of Gerontology: Social Sciences, 53B*, S336–S340. doi:10.1093/geronb/53B.6.S336

Women's Health Research Institute. (2016). *How hormone depletion affects you.* Retrieved from menopause.northwestern.edu/content/how-hormone-depletion-affects-you.

WomensHealth.gov. (2010). *Menopause basics.* Retrieved from www.omenshealth.gov/menopause/menopause-basics/index.html.

Wong, F. K. Y., & Yeung, S. M. (2015). Effects of a 4-week transitional care programme for discharged stroke survivors in Hong Kong: A randomised controlled trial. *Health and Social Care in the Community, 23*, 619–631. doi:10.1111/hsc.12477

Wong, P. T. P. (2015). *The meaning hypothesis of living a good life: Virtue, happiness and meaning.* Retrieved from www.drpaulwong.com/the-meaning-hypothesis-of-living-a-good-life-virtue-happiness-and-meaning/.

Wood, S., & Kisley, M. A. (2006). The negativity bias is eliminated in older adults: Age-related reduction in event-related brain potentials associated with evaluative categorization. *Psychology and Aging, 21*, 815–820. doi:10.1037/0882-7974.21.4.815

Woodbridge, S. (2008). Sustaining families in the 21st century: The role of grandparents. *International Journal of Environmental, Cultural, Economic and Social Sustainability.* Retrieved from www98.griffith.edu.au/dspace/bitstream/10072/27417/1/50932_1.pdf.

Woodward, A. T., Taylor, R. J., Abelson, J. M., & Matusko, N. (2013). Major depressive disorder among older African Americans, Caribbean blacks, and non-Hispanic whites: Secondary analysis of the National Survey of American Life. *Depression and Anxiety, 30*, 589–597. doi:10.1002/da.22041

Worden, W. (1991). *Grief counseling and grief therapy: A handbook for the mental health practitioner* (2nd ed.). New York: Springer.

World Health Organization. (2012). *Seniors and disabilities.* Retrieved from new.paho.org/hq/index.php?option=com_content&view=article&id=7316%3Aseniors-a-disabilities-april-2012&catid=4684%3Afch-hldisabilities-and-rehabilitation&Itemid=936&lang=en.

World Health Organization. (2013). *Responding to intimate partner violence and sexual violence against women.* Retrieved from www.who.int/reproductivehealth/publications/violence/9789241548595/en/.

World Health Organization. (2015). *10 facts on dementia.* Retrieved from www.who.int/features/factfiles/dementia/en/.

Wrenn, R. L. (1999). The grieving college student. In J. D. Davidson & K. J. Doka (Eds.), *Living with grief: At work, at school, at worship* (pp. 131–141). Levittown, PA: Brunner/Mazel.

Wrzus, C., & Roberts, B. W. (2017). Processes of personality development in adulthood: The TESSERA framework. *Personality and Social Psychology Review, 21*, 253–277. doi:10.1177/1088868316652279

Wu, L., & Zhao, L. (2016). ApoE2 and Alzheimer's disease: Time to take a closer look. *Neural Regeneration Research, 11*, 412–413. doi:10.4103/1673-5374.179044

Wurtele, S. K., & Maruyama, L. (2013). Changing students' stereotypes of older adults. *Teaching of Psychology, 40*, 59–61. doi:10.1177/0098628312465867

Wyatt, A. (2016). Resident advocates, diversity, and resident-centered care. In R. Perley (Ed.), *Managing the long-term care facility: Practical approaches to providing quality care* (pp. 69–97). San Francisco, CA: Jossey-Bass.

Xu, X., Zhu, F., O'Campo, P., Koenig, M. A., Mock, V., & Campbell, J. (2005). Prevalence of and risk factors for intimate partner violence in China. *American Journal of Public Health, 95*, 78–85. doi:10.2105/AJPH.2003.023978

Yaakobi, E. (2015). Desire to work as a death anxiety buffer mechanism. *Experimental Psychology, 62*, 110–122. doi:10.1027/1618-3169/a000278

Yaffe, K., Peltz, C. B., Ewing, S. K., McCulloch, C. E., Cummings, S. R., Cauley, J A. et al. (2016). Long-term cognitive trajectories and mortality in older women. *Journal of Gerontology: Medical Sciences, 71*, 1074–1080. doi:10.1093/Gerona/glw003

Yamasaki, T., Horie, S., Ohyagi, Y., Tanaka, E., Nakamura, N., Goto, Y. et al. (2016). A potential VEP biomarker for mild cognitive impairment: Evidence from selective visual deficit of higher-level dorsal pathway. *Journal of Alzheimer's Disease, 53*, 661–676. doi:10.3233/JAD-150939

Yang, T., Yang, X. Y., Cottrell, R. R., Wu, D., Jiang, S., & Anderson, J. G. (2016). Violent injuries and regional correlates among women in China: Results from 21 cities study in China. *The European Journal of Public Health, 26*, 513–517. doi:10.1093/eurpub/ckv193

Yang, Z., Bishai, D., & Harman, J. (2008). Convergence of body mass with aging: The longitudinal interrelationship of health, weight, and survival. *Economics & Human Biology, 6*, 469–481. doi:10.1016/j. ehb.2008.06.006

Yarwood, A., Huizinga, T. W. J., & Worthington, J. (2016). The genetics of rheumatoid arthritis: Risk and protection in different stages of the evolution of RA. *Rheumatology, 55*, 1990209. doi:10.1093/rheumatology/keu323

Yates, F. A. (1966) *The art of memory.* Chicago: University of Chicago Press.

Ybarra, O., & Park, D. C. (2002). Disconfirmation of person expectations by older and younger adults: Implications for social vigilance. *Journals of Gerontology: Psychological Sciences, 57B*, P435–P443. doi:10.1093/geronb/57.5.P435

Ybarra, O., Winkielman, P., Yeh, I., Burnstein, E., & Kavanagh, L. (2011). Friends (and sometimes enemies) with cognitive benefits: What types of social interactions boost executive functioning? *Social Psychological and Personality Science, 2*, 253–261. doi:10.1177/1948550610386808

Yesavage, J. A., Brink, T. L., Rose, T. L., Lum, O., Huang, V., Adey, M. et al. (1983). Development and validation of a geriatric depression screening scale: A preliminary report. *Journal of Psychiatric Research, 17*, 37–49. doi:10.1016/0022-3956(82)90033-4

Yin, D. (2016). The essential mechanisms of aging: What have we learnt in ten years? *Current Topics in Medicinal Chemistry, 16*, 503–510.

Yin, X., & Wang, R. (2016). Simulation of dopamine modulation-based memory model. *Neurocomputing, 194*, 241–245. doi:10.1016/j.neucom.2016.01.077

Yngvesson, B. (2010). *Belonging in an adopted world: Race, identity, and transnational adoption.* Chicago: University of Chicago Press.

Yoon, S. M. (2005). The characteristics and needs of Asian-American grandparent caregivers: A study of Chinese-American and Korean-American grandparents in New York City. *Journal of Gerontological Social Work, 44*, 75–94. doi:10.1300/J083v44n03_06

Yu, F. (2016). Behavioral management in long-term care. In S K. Whitbourne (Ed.), *The encyclopedia of adulthood and aging* (pp. 113–118). Malden, MA: Wiley-Blackwell.

Yuen, H. K., & Vogtle, L. K. (2016). Multi-morbidity, disability and adaptation strategies among community-dwelling adults aged 75 years and older. *Disability and Health Journal, 9*, 593–599. doi:10.1016/j.dhjo.2016.03.004

Zabriskie, R. B., & Kay, T. (2013). Positive leisure science: Leisure in family contexts. In T. Freire (Ed.), *Positive leisure science* (pp. 81–99). New York: Springer.

Zahodne, L. B., Glymour, M. M., Sparks, C., Bontempo, D., Dixon, R. A., MacDonald, S. W. S. et al. (2011). Education does not slow cognitive decline with aging: 12-year evidence form the Victoria Longitudinal Study. *Journal of the International Neuropsychological Society, 17*, 1039–1046. doi:10.1017/ S1355617711001044

Zarit, S. H., & Reamy, A. M. (2013). Future directions in family and professional caregiving for the elderly. *Gerontology, 59*, 152–158. doi:10.1159/000342242

Zarit, S. H., & Zarit, J. M. (2007). *Mental disorders in older adults: Fundamentals of assessment and treatment* (2nd ed.). New York: Guilford.

Zaval, L., Li, Y., Johnson, E. J., & Weber, E. U. (2015). Complementary contributions of fluid and crystallized intelligence to decision making across the life span. In T. M. Hess, J. Strough, and C. E. Lockenhoff (Eds.), *Aging and decision making: Empirical and applied perspectives* (pp. 149–168). New York: Academic Press.

Zelinski, E. M., & Kennison. R. F., Watts, A., & Lewis, K. L. (2009). Convergence between longitudinal and cross-sectional studies: Cohort matters. In C. Hertzog & H. Bosworth (Eds.), *Aging and cognition: Research methodologies and empirical advances* (pp. 101–118). Washington DC: American Psychological Association.

Zeng, Y., Gu, D., & George, L. K. (2011). Association of religious participation with mortality among Chinese old adults. *Research on Aging, 33*, 51–83. doi:10.1177/0164027510383584

Zetumer, S., Young, I., Shear, M. K., Skritskaya, N., Lebowitz, B., Simon, N. et al. (2015). The impact of losing a child on the clinical presentation of complicated grief. *Journal of Affective Disorders, 170*, 15–21. doi:10.1016/j.jad.2014.08.021

Zhan, H. J. (2006). Joy and sorrow: Explaining Chinese caregivers' reward and stress. *Journal of Aging Studies, 20*, 27–38. doi:10.1016/j.aging.2005.01.002

Zheng, Z., Shemmassian, S., Wijekoon, C., Kim, W., Bookheimer, S. Y., & Pouratian, N. (2014). DTI correlates of distinct cognitive impairments in Parkinson's disease. *Human Brain Mapping, 35*, 1325–1333. doi:10.1002/hbm.22256

Zhu, B., Caldwell, M., & Song, B. (2016). Development of stem cell-based therapies for Parkinson's disease. *International Journal of Neuroscience, 126*, 955–962. doi:10.3109/00207454.2016.1148034

Zhu, W., Chen, Q., Tang, C., Cao, G., Hou, Y., & Qiu, J. (2016). Brain structure links everyday creativity to creative achievement. *Brain and Cognition, 103*, 70–76. doi:10.1016/j.bandc.2015.09.008

Ziaei, M., & Fisher, H. (2016). Emotion and aging: The impact of emotion on attention, memory, and face recognition in late adulthood. In J. R. Absher & J. Cloutier (Eds.), *Neuroimaging personality, social cognition, and character* (pp. 259–278). San Diego, CA: Elsevier.

Ziegler, M., Cengia, A., Mussel, P., & Gerstorf, D. (2015). Openness as a buffer against cognitive decline: The Openness-Fluid-Crystallized-Intelligence (OFCI) model applied to late adulthood. *Psychology and Aging, 30*, 573–588. doi:10.1037/a0039493

Zimprich, D., & Martin, M. (2002). Can longitudinal changes in processing speed explain longitudinal age change in fluid intelligence? *Psychology and Aging, 17*, 690–695. doi:10.1037/0882-7974.17.4.690

Zimprich, D., & Martin, M. (2009). A multilevel factor analysis perspective on intellectual development in old age. In C. Hertzog & H. Bosworth (Eds.), *Aging and cognition: Research methodologies and empirical advances* (pp. 53–76). Washington DC: American Psychological Association.

Zogg, J. B., Woods, S. P., Sauceda, J. A., Wiebe, J. S., & Simoni, J. M. (2012). The role of prospective memory in medication adherence: A review of an emerging literature. *Journal of Behavioral Medicine, 35*, 47–62. doi:10.1007/s10865-011-9341-9

Zurlo, K. A., & Beach, C. M. (2013). Racial disparities in depression care among older adults: Can the perspectives of clinicians and patients be reconciled? *Current Translational Geriatrics and Experimental Gerontology Reports, 2*, 24–30. doi:10.1007/s13670-012-0036-z

Name Index

Aasland, O. G., 344
Abakoumkin, G., 393
Abbott, G., 341
Aberson, C. L., 309
Abraham, A., 209
Abrams, D., 344, 364
Abrams, R., 395
Abutalebi, J., 38
Achor, S., 344
Adams, C., 238
Adams, R. B., Jr., 224
Adams, R. G., 309, 310
Adams, S. A., 116
Adamy, J., 377
Addis, D. R., 41, 168
Addo, F. R., 317
Adhikari, K., 62
Adler, L. L., 314
Adler, R. A., 64, 65
Afendulis, C. C., 152
Afilalo, J., 119, 120
Agrigoroaei, S., 176
Ai, A. L., 264
Aichele, S., 196
Aisenbrey, S., 355
Ajrouch, K. J., 363, 365, 366
Akashi, J., 383
Åkerstedt, A. M., 262
Akincilar, S. C., 58–59
Aksoy, S., 375
Al-Attar, A., 96
Alavi, M. V., 68, 69
Al-Bar, M. A., 374
Albert, M. S., 290
Albuquerque, S., 394
Alden, D. L., 383
Aldwin, C. M., 61, 62, 66, 73, 128, 275, 408, 409, 410
Alegría, M., 279
Alexander, P. A., 37
Alhurani, R. E., 63
Alias, F., 374, 375
Alkadry, M. G., 356
Allaire, J. C., 133, 206, 237, 409
Allemand, M., 248
Allen, K. R., 332
Allen, R. S., 150
Allexandre, D., 346
Alley, J. L., 333
Almeida, J., 328
Alper, J., 329
Alspach, J. G., 386
Altgassen, M., 176
Amato, P. R., 324
Amoyal, N., 196
Anand, A., 285
Andersen, E., 151
Andersen, S. L., 117
Anderson, E. R., 328
Anderson, F. T., 167
Anderson, V. D., 327
Anderson, W. A., 310
Ando, S., 36
Andreassi, J. K., 358
Andreoletti, C., 196
Andrews-Hanna, J. R., 48
Aneshensel, C. S., 295

Angel, J. L., 363
Angel, R. J., 363
Angelou, M., 244
Anglin, J., 163
Ansari, Z., 287
Ansberry, C., 310
Anstey, K. J., 176
Antenucci, V., 173
Antheunis, M. L., 309
Anticevic, A., 204
Antonovsky, A., 409
Antonucci, T. C., 275, 363
Aponte, M., 343
Arango-Muñoz, S., 237
Arbeev, K. G., 60
Archer, J., 388, 389, 391
Ardelt, M., 209, 210, 211, 264
Arena, J. E., 178
Arizmendi, B., 393
Armstrong, P. I., 342
Arnett, J. J., 11, 257, 308
Artazcoz, L., 353
Artistico, D., 207
Arvanitakis, Z., 178
Aryee, S., 356, 358
Ashman, M., 99
Aslan, A., 160–161
Asoodeh, M. H., 320
Asp, E., 228
Assanangkornchai, S., 389
Astell-Burt, T., 196
Asthana, D., 99
Astone, N. M., 317
Atchley, R., 265
Attig, T., 387, 388, 394
Austin, J. T., 205
Awa, W. L., 346
Awadi, M. A., 385
Ayalon, L., 221
Ayers, T. S., 391
Aziz, T., 314

Bachman, B., 345
Bäckman, L., 36
Baddeley, A., 282
Bade, B. K., 103
Badham, S. P., 171
Badham, S. R., 171
Bagbey Darian, C. D., 387, 388, 389, 391, 392
Baggetta, P., 37
Bagnall, A.-M., 346
Bahn, R. S., 344
Bailey, H., 166
Baker, J. C., 294
Baker, L. A., 334
Baldi, R. A., 358
Baldridge, D. C., 343
Balistreri, C. R., 94
Balk, D. E., 373
Baltes, B. B., 232
Baltes, P. B., 4, 9, 13, 49, 98, 186, 187, 188, 189, 194, 195, 209, 210, 217, 231, 232, 410
Bambra, C., 353
Bamford, M., 144
Band, G. P. H., 161

Bangerter, L. R., 152
Barber, L. K., 341
Barber, S. J., 228
Barbey, A. K., 224
Barch, D. M., 204
Bargh, J. A., 219
Barja, G., 93
Barlow, M., 235, 236, 408, 409
Barneo, J. L., 49
Barnes, J. N., 414
Barnett, A. E., 331
Bar-Tal, Y., 233
Bartkowiak, G., 364
Bartlett, D. B., 414
Barton, C., 292
Barzilai, N., 58
Basten, U., 193
Bastida, E., 264
Bastos, A., 324
Batt, M. E., 415
Battista, R. N., 108
Baucom, B. R., 323
Bauer, G. F., 409
Baum, C. L., II, 355
Bauman, U., 255
Baumann, A., 375
Baumeister, R. F., 262
Bavishi, A., 101
Bayl-Smith, P. H., 344
Beach, C. M., 280
Beach, S. R. H., 321
Beanland, V., 161
Beason-Held, L. L., 292
Beatty, C., 228, 229
Beaty, R. E., 48
Beausaert, S., 352
Beavers, T., 70
Beck, A. T., 281, 282, 284
Beck, V., 365
Beckes, L., 309
Bedir, A., 375
Belser, A., 130
Beltrán-Sánchez, H., 117
Benjamins, M. R., 98
Bennett, K. M., 132, 321, 325
Benyamini, Y., 97
Berg, C. A., 187, 206, 207, 322, 386
Bergdahl, E., 379
Bergdahl, J., 105
Berger, R. G., 60
Berglund, P., 274
Bergman-Evans, B., 151
Bergsma, A., 211
Berk, R. A., 344
Berlin, L. J., 327
Bermejo-Toro, L., 345
Bernadotte, A., 58, 60
Berns, N., 388
Bernstein, L., 100
Berntsen, D., 169
Berry, J. M., 176
Besedeš, T., 205
Better Balance, A, 330
Bever, L., 376
Bhattarai, P., 410
Bhutta, M., 71

Bialystok, E., 171
Bian, F., 329
Biblarz, T. J., 329
Bidwell, M., 344
Bieman-Copland, S., 410
Bierhoff, H.-W., 314
Biesele, M., 14
Bietti, L. M., 237
Biggs, S., 351
Binet, A., 190
Binstock, R. H., 405
Birditt, K. S., 238
Birren, J. E., 10, 273
Bishai, D., 63
Blachford, D., 329
Blachnio, A., 310
Blackhall, L. J., 384
Blackstone, A., 327
Blanchard, C. M., 361
Blanchard-Fields, F., 42, 206, 207, 216, 220, 222, 227, 228, 229, 230, 231, 232, 358
Blatteis, C. M., 83–84
Blazer, D. G., 97
Bleiszner, R., 308, 309
Blieszner, R., 49, 308, 309, 310
Bligh, M. C., 345
Blom, M. M., 295
Blümel, J. E., 80
Blumenthal, H., 333, 334
Blumenthal, J. A., 50
Blume-Peytavi, U., 61
Bluntschli, J. R., 381
Bochenska, K., 293
Böckerman, P., 344
Boden, M. T., 224
Boehm, S. A., 349
Boerner, K., 389
Bohlmeijer, E., 253
Bohlmeijer, E. T., 253
Boisgontier, M. P., 73
Bolkan, C., 245
Boller, A.-M., 293
Bolton, J. M., 394
Bonanno, G. A., 388, 389, 390, 391
Bondmass, M. D., 389
Booker, J. A., 210
Booth, A. L., 98
Borbély, A. A., 281
Bordere, T. C., 389
Börjesson, M., 415
Boron, J. B., 196
Bos, H. M., 329
Bosch, S. J., 410
Boschma, J., 363
Bosco, A., 345
Bosman, E. A., 207
Boss, P., 393
Bosshard, G., 375
Boswell, G., 264
Boswell, J., 84
Botwinick, J., 186
Bouazzaoui, B., 220
Bourgeois, M. S., 174
Bourke, P., 160, 162
Bowden, D. E., 343

Bowen, C. E., 248
Bowers, B., 152
Bowlus, A. J., 195
Bowman, G. L., 50
Boyczuk, A. M., 321, 330
Boyle, J. M., Jr., 375
Boyle, P. J., 325
Boywitt, C. D., 170
Bradbury, T. N., 320, 324, 326
Brady, C. B., 196
Brady-Smith, C., 327
Brancucci, A., 193, 194
Brandburg, G. L., 144, 146
Brandtstädter, J., 218, 234, 235, 236
Bratkovich, K. L., 390
Brehmer, Y., 165, 172
Brendel, R. W., 386
Brenn, T., 325
Brennan, A. A., 237
Brett, C. E., 98
Brissette, I., 309
Brizzee, K. R., 70
Brodaty, H., 290
Bromell, L., 309
Brookdale, 142
Brooks-Gunn, J., 327
Brown, C., 84
Brown, D. C., 116, 119
Brown, J. E., 180
Brown, J. W., 366
Brown, S. D., 341–342
Bruce, M., 151
Brysiewicz, P., 389
Buchanan, T., 312
Budgeon, S., 316
Bueter, K., 145
Bugental, D., 147, 219
Bugg, J. M., 168
Buhl, H., 330
Bui, E., 390
Burge, S. W., 140
Burger, A., 352, 353
Burgio, L., 293
Burke, B. L., 381
Burnette, D., 333
Burrows, L., 219
Burton, A. E., 69
Bustos, M. L. C., 373
Butcher, V., 361
Butters, M. A., 414
Cabeza, R., 32, 39, 40, 46
Cacciatore, J., 389
Cacioppo, J. T., 262
Cadigan, R. O., 145
Cadiz, D. M., 217
Cagney, K. A., 309
Cahill, E., 332
Cahill, K. E., 362, 363, 364
Cairney, J., 104
Calamia, M., 221
Caldwell, M., 49
Camberis, A. L., 327
Cameron, R. E., 334
Camp, C. J., 12, 173, 174, 294–295
Camp, T. G., 333

Campbell, J., 101
Campbell, K., 312
Campbell, K. L., 45
Campinha-Bacote, J., 343
Cândea, D. M., 197
Cansino, S., 170
Cantarella, A., 132
Cantor, N., 251, 261
Capaldi, D. M., 324
Capistrant, B., 331
Cappeliez, P., 322
Cappell, K. A., 46
Caramagno, J., 275
Caravitello, R., 98
Carlander, I., 379
Carlo, G., 328
Carnelley, K., 361
Carney, K. O., 150
Carr, A., 285, 298, 299
Carr, D., 310, 325
Carroll, N., 98
Carstensen, L. L., 42, 205, 231, 232, 233, 236, 262, 310, 311
Carvalho, J. O., 262
Carver, C. S., 309
Casey, V. A., 169
Casillas, G., 405
Casper, W. J., 316
Caspi, A., 248
Cassano, J., 410
Cassel, C. K., 379
Cassidy, B. S., 224
Cassidy, E., 147
Cassoff, J., 281
Castel, A. D., 175
Castro, M., 177
Cavallaro, F., 147, 149
Cavallini, E., 221
Cavanaugh, J. C., 17, 59, 175, 176, 251, 257, 322, 331, 415
Cervone, D., 207
Chamsi-Pasha, H., 374
Chan, M. Y., 172
Chan, S. W-C., 265
Chandler, E. M., 383
Chang, B., 364
Chang, J. E., 388
Chang, S.-S., 354
Chang, T.-S., 310
Chapman, B., 320
Charchar, F. J., 59
Charles, S. T., 232, 233, 262, 310
Charlton, B., 379
Charness, N., 207
Charpentier, M., 238
Charras, K., 145
Chartier, E., 219
Chasteen, A. L., 263
Chatters, L. M., 264
Chaudhari, A., 58
Cheadle, J., 324
Chee, F. Y. T., 147–148
Chen, J., 97
Chen, M., 219
Chen, Y., 206, 224, 228, 230
Chenery, H. J., 149
Cheng, E., 361
Cheng, S., 237
Cherko, M., 71
Chern, H.-L., 118
Cherry, K. E., 161, 221
Chesson, B., 394
Cheuk, G., 71
Cheung, C. K., 351

Chew-Graham, C. A., 277, 278, 280, 281, 299
Cheyney, D. L., 41
Chi, M. T. H., 207
Chiao, C.-Y., 322
ChildStats.gov, 327
Chiou, Y.-E., 118
Chipperfield, J. G., 234
Chirgwin, S., 343
Chisholm-Burns, M. A., 114, 115
Chiu, H. F. K., 290
Choi, E., 366
Choi, H. S., 160, 362
Choi, M., 334
Chong, S., 290
Chonody, J. M., 217
Chou, S.-C., 146
Christ-Crain, M., 82
Christensen, A., 323
Christensen, A. J., 115
Christopher, E. A., 176
Chui, H., 133
Chun, S., 361
Ciani, E., 363
Cicero, C., 98
Cicirelli, V. G., 379, 381
Cinnirella, M., 10
Cirelli, C., 84
Ciscato, E., 318
Clare, L., 196, 299
Cleary, J. F., 384
Clevinger, A. M., 169
Coan, J. A., 309
Coates, B. A., 323
Coats, A. H., 227
Cohen, F., 353
Cohen, L. W., 152
Cohen, M. D., 264
Cohen, O., 321
Cohen, S., 101, 102, 104
Cohen-Mansfield, J., 363
Colcombe, S., 171
Coleman, J., 365
Coleman, M., 329
Coles, R. L., 327
Collardeau, F., 325
Collins, H. M., 161
Collins, K., 46
Collins, W. A., 311
Colom, R., 224
Colombel, F., 170, 176
Coltrane, S., 356
Coman, A., 238
Commons, M. L., 201
Compton, W. C., 332
Connidis, I. A., 321, 322
Connolly, A., 150
Connors, M. H., 196
Constantin, L. P., 358
Constantinidis, C., 49
Conti, R., 361
Conway, E. R., 149
Cook, D. A., 344
Cook, D. J., 410
Coombs, M. A., 388
Coon, D. W., 318
Cooper, A. M., 196
Cooper, R., 119
Copen, C. E., 317
Copley, S. J., 79
Corbett, B. A., 359
Cordes, C. L., 345
Corkin, S., 233
Cornwall, A., 348

Corpuz, R., 147, 219
Corr, C. A., 380, 382
Corr, D. M., 380, 382
Cortina, L. M., 351
Costa, P. T., Jr., 246, 247
Cotman, C. W., 50
Cotton, S. R., 310
Counts, D., 373
Cowl, A., 196
Cox, C. B., 334
Coyle, C. E., 196
Craik, F. I. M., 165, 171
Cram, B., 356
Crane, P. K., 292
Cready, C. M., 132
Crisp, R. J., 219, 220
Cristina, T. J. N., 97
Criter, R. E., 73
Crosby, L., 324
Cross, S., 262–263
Crown, J. S., 321
Crown, W., 405
Croy, I., 74
Cubanski, J., 405
Cuddy, A. J. C., 218
Cukier, H. N., 291
Culgin, S., 147
Cummings, K., 387, 388, 389
Cundiff, N. L., 349
Cunnane, S. C., 51
Cunningham, W., 10
Cunningham, W. R., 191
Curtin, N., 258
Curtis, J. R., 383
Curtis, R., 329
Curtis, R. G., 234

da Costa, J. F., 352
Dabelko-Schoeny, H., 135
Dadgari, A., 137
Dahlin, E., 49
Dai, B., 361
Dalton, C., 130
Dalton, D. S., 71
Daly, B. J., 383
Damian, R. I., 208
Damico, A., 405
D'Angelo, D., 379
Dannar, P. R., 343
Davidson, R. J., 265
Davies, L., 317
Davies, P. G., 97
Davis, A., 69, 70, 71
Davis, B. W., 149
Davis, S. R., 334
Davis, S. W., 46
Davy, C., 98
Dawadi, P. N., 410
de Bloom, J., 361
De Bloom, J., 361
de Bruin, W. B., 205
de Cabo, R., 114
De Jong Gierveld, J., 310
De la Monte, S., 292
de Magalhaes, J. P., 60
De Paula Couto, M. C. P., 218
de Pommereau, I., 365
De Rango, F., 94
De Strooper, B., 286, 287, 291
de Vries, B., 309
De Witt-Hoblit, I., 12

DeAndrea, D. C., 309
Deane, G., 330
Deary, I. J., 248
Debast, I., 245, 248
DeCarli, C., 46
DeFrain, J., 389
Dekas, K. H., 341
DeKosky, S. T., 287
Delgado, M., 275
DeLiema, M., 316
DelVecchio, W. F., 248
Demir, M., 309
Demiray, B., 169
Demler, O., 274
Denckla, C. A., 309
Deng, C.-P., 342
Denham, J., 59
Denney, N. W., 205, 206
Dennis, N. A., 32, 46
DePaulo, B. M., 316
DePaulo, M. B., 316
Deschacht, N., 351
DeSilver, D., 364
Desmond, N., 328
DeSoto, K. A., 169
Desrocher, M., 169
Dey, S., 320
Di Battista, A. M., 291
Di Domenico, S., 193, 194
Di Fabio, A., 341
di Masi, M. N., 345
Di Masso, A., 361
Diaz, A., 327
DiBello, K. K., 389
Dickens, B. M., 375
Diehl, M., 133, 206, 256, 257
Diersch, N., 208
DiGilio, D. A., 412
Dik, B., 341
Dillavou, E. D., 62
Dillaway, H., 80
Dilworth-Anderson, P., 264
Dirk, J., 160
Dishman, R. K., 409
Dismukes, R. K., 167
Dissanayake, C., 356
Dixon, J., 361
Dixon, P., 327
Dixon, R., 19
Dixon, R. A., 195, 237
Dobson, A. J., 120
Dodman, D., 144
Doerwald, F., 224, 311
Doets, E. L., 73
Dommaraju, P., 314
Donnellan, M. B., 343
Donnellan, W. J., 132
Dörner, J., 248
Doss, B. D., 329
Doubeni, C. A., 94
Doyle, K. O., Jr., 190
Dreman, S., 321
Drossel, C., 294
Drury, L., 344, 364
Duarte, A., 170
DuBois, P. H., 190
Dufour, A., 72
Dugan, E., 196
Dulas, M. R., 170
Duncan, L. E., 257
Dunkley, L., 318
Dunlop, W. L., 259
Dunlosky, J., 166, 175, 176
Dunn, T. R., 256

Dunsmore, J. C., 210
Dupuis, S., 329
Durmysheva, Y., 208
Durst, D., 329
Dutta, D., 59
Dutton, W. H., 312
Duval-Tsioles, D., 325
Duzel, E., 50

Earle, S., 394
Earles, J. L., 161
Ebberwein, C. A., 354
Ebersole, P., 64, 99
Ebner, N. C., 232
Echt, K. V., 275
Eddleston, K. A., 343
Edelstein, B., 177, 276, 278
Edelstein, B. A., 177, 276
Edwards, M. R., 358
Ehlert, U., 101
Ehrenberg, M., 325
Eifert, E. K., 295
Einstein, G. O., 161, 167
Eisma, M. C., 390
Ekerdt, D. J., 136, 139, 143
El Haber, N., 63
Elliott, M., 275
Ellis, J. W., 334
Elmendorf, D., 405
Elrod, N. M., 37
Elshourbagy, S. A. M., 410
Emery, L., 227
Emsell, L., 37
Engelberg, A., 316
English, T., 205, 232, 233, 310
Ennis, G. E., 205
Enns, J. T., 237
Enslin, C., 343
Epel, E., 59
Erber, J. T., 218
Erickson, K. I., 50, 414
Ericsson, K. A., 207, 209, 210
Erikson, E. H., 210, 248, 252–256, 258, 259, 343
Eslick, G. D., 292
Eslinger, J. G., 334
Estes, Z., 171
Etezadi, S., 211
Evans, D. G. R., 109
Evans, G. D., 327
Evertsson, M., 355
Eynard, C., 145

Faber, A. J., 325
Fabius, C. D., 333
Facal, D., 165
Fairchild, K. M., 294
Fairlie, H., 405
Fajgenbaum, D., 394
Fallon, E., 196
Fang, C., 224
Fänge, A. M., 129
Farrell, M. P., 257
Farris, D. N., 330, 331
Faubion, S. S., 80
Faucher, E. H., 381
Fauth, E. B., 118
Fein, E., 312
Feinberg, M., 324
Feldman, K., 330
Felix, L., 135
Felling, A. J. A., 322
Feltz, A., 383
Femia, E. E., 118
Feng, J., 160

Name Index

Feng, X., 196
Feng, Z., 325
Fernández-Alcántara, M., 393
Ferrari, M., 210
Ferrarini, T., 356
Ferrucci, L., 117
Festini, S. B., 36, 46, 160, 164, 165, 166
Fiebach, C. J., 193
Field, M. J., 379
Fields, N. L., 135
Figueiredo, B., 324
Fincham, F. D., 321
Fingerman, K. L., 330
Finkbeiner, N. W. B., 178
Finucane, T. E., 150
Fiori, K. L., 309
Fischer-Shofty, M., 101
Fisher, H., 41
Fisher, J., 294
Fisher, J. E., 129
Fiske, S. T., 3, 218, 224
Fitzgerald, J. M., 169
Fitzgerald, M., 224
Fitzsimons, A. M., 394
Fitzwater, E. L., 298
Fjell, A. M., 37
Flap, H., 312
Flegal, K. E., 167
Fleminger, S., 178, 179
Fletcher, P. C., 321, 330
Flores, R. A., 209
Flynn, E., 19
Fogarty, K., 327
Folkman, S., 102, 103, 132
Ford, J. H., 41
Formosa, M., 208
Fossati, P., 41
Foster, B. P., 352
Fouad, N. A., 341, 342
Fowler, K. L., 382
Fox, M. D., 375
Franceschi, K. A., 395
Frank, D. J., 206
Frank, M. G., 105
Frank, N., 329
Franses, P. H., 208
Frase, P., 358
Frazier, L. D., 263
Fredriksen-Goldsen, K. I., 318
Freitas, A. A., 60
Freund, A. M., 169, 232, 236
Fried, L. P., 117, 232
Friedemann-Sánchez, G., 331
Friederici, A. D., 162
Friedman, E. M., 331
Friedman, M. C., 116
Friedrich-Mai, P., 359
Friesen, S., 140, 324
Frith, C. D., 222, 224
Frith, U., 222, 224
Froehlich, D. E., 352
Frohlinger, C., 349
Fruhauf, C. A., 332, 333
Fu, A. S., 73
Fuentes, A., 169
Führer, A., 314
Fuligni, A. J., 328
Fuller-Thompson, E., 334
Fullerton, C. S., 394

Galichon, A., 318
Gallagher-Thompson, D., 293
Gallen, C. L., 43, 45, 46
Gamaldo, A. A., 206

Gamba, F., 387
Gamble, W. C., 327
Gandy, S., 287
Ganong, L., 329
Gans, D., 331
Ganzini, L., 375
Garcia, J. R., 312
Gardiner, P. A., 120
Garrard, E., 375
Garrido, M. M., 377
Gassaway, L., 318
Gatz, M., 278, 412
Gaudron, J.-P., 359
Gefen, D., 309
George, L. K., 265
Gerolimatos, L. A., 177, 276
Gervais, S. J., 347
Geurts, S., 361
Geurts, S. A. E., 361
Ghanim, D., 314
Gharaveis, A., 410
Ghisletta, P., 176, 196
Ghitza, Y., 216
Ghosh, D., 320
Ghosh, S., 331
Gibbs, N. R., 405
Giblin, S., 299
Gibran, K., 312, 341
Gibson, J. M., 69
Gibson, R. C., 275
Giele, J. Z., 404
Gilbert, D. T., 228, 229
Gilbert, K., 341
Gildengers, A. G., 414
Gilding, M., 310
Gill, D. P., 410
Gillick, M. R., 145, 150
Gilliver, M., 70
Gilmer, D. F., 61, 62, 66, 73, 275, 408, 409, 410
Gilson, L. L., 343
Gino, F., 373, 387
Giordano, P. C., 312, 314
Giovanello, K. S., 38, 46, 166, 170
Gire, J., 373, 379, 389
Gitlin, L. N., 98
Givertz, M., 320
Gladwell, M., 209, 210
Glaser, R., 105
Glass, B. D., 205
Glasser, M. F., 30
Glenmullen, J., 382, 383
Glück, J., 210, 211
Godfrey, D., 318
Godyń, J., 292
Golant, S. M., 129, 135
Gold, J. M., 325
Goldenberg, J. L., 381
Goldstein, E. G., 256
Goleman, D., 224
Golkar, A., 345
Gonyea, J. G., 332, 333
Gonza, G., 352, 353
Goodheart, C. D., 279
Goodkind, D., 403
Goodsell, T. L., 316
Gordijn, B., 410
Gordon, L., 102
Gordon, R., 352
Gordon, T. A., 388
Gornick, J. C., 358
Gorree, E., 168
Gostin, L. O., 377
Gottman, J. M., 323–324

Gould, C. E., 177, 178, 276, 277
Gould, S. J., 236
Gousse, M., 318
Govoni, S., 36
Grabowski, D. C., 152
Grady, C., 33, 42, 43, 44, 45, 48
Grady, C. L., 171
Grafman, J., 224
Graham, E. K., 245, 248, 258
Granacher, U., 73
Granbom, M., 129, 137, 140
Grawitch, M. J., 341
Gray, J. D., 37
Green, D. W., 38
Green, E. E., 176
Greenberg, D. L., 169
Greenberg, J., 381
Greene, S. M., 328
Greenfield, E. A., 310, 325, 365
Greenlund, K. J., 178
Greer, D. M., 374
Greitemeyer, T., 309
Gretebeck, R. J., 120
Greving, K. A., 321
Grey, R., 172
Griffin, B., 344
Griffin, M. L., 345
Grigorenko, E. L., 187
Groger, L., 146
Groh, A., 129
Groome, D., 167, 169, 170
Grossman, I., 210
Grossman, M., 37
Groth-Marnat, G., 276, 278
Gruber, M., 73
Gruber, R., 281
Gruenewald, T. L., 255
Gruhn, D., 203
Grühn, D., 248, 257, 258
Grunow, D., 355
Gu, D., 265
Gu, X., 204
Gubernskaya, Z., 327
Gudmundsdottir, M., 80
Guergova, S., 72
Guerrero, A. P. S., 314
Guihan, M., 139
Guilford, J. P., 246
Guitton, M. J., 312
Gunes, S., 82
Gunnell, D., 354
Guo, J., 254, 255, 259
Gutchess, A. H., 42, 224, 262
Gutierrez, H. C., 205

Haber, D., 412, 413
Habes, M., 36
Haier, R. J., 43, 193
Hains, C.-A. M., 375, 383
Håkansson, P., 310
Hales, S., 379, 388
Haley, W. E., 322, 331, 388
Hall, E. V., 343
Hall, J. A., 308, 311
Hall, S. S., 320
Halpern-Meekin, S., 317
Hambrick, D. Z., 207, 210
Hamilton, R. K. B., 204
Hammar, M., 415
Hammer, L. B., 217, 355
Hampstead, B. M., 41
Hansal, A., 320
Hansen, J.-I. C., 359
Hansen, S. R., 312
Hareven, T. K., 330

Harley, D. A., 318
Harman, J., 63
Harrington, K. J., 94, 108
Harrington, K. V., 343
Harris, D. L., 387, 388, 395
Harris, R. L., 256
Harrison, K., 299
Harry, B. B., 38
Hart, H. M., 255
Hartman, H., 349
Hartung, P. J., 341, 342
Harwood, J., 149
Haslam, C., 174
Haslam, S. A., 349
Hassan, Z., 316, 317
Hasher, L., 161, 232
Hasselmo, K., 309
Havaldar, R., 62, 63
Have, H., 410
Haworth, J., 351
Hawton, K., 275
Hay, E. L., 133
Hayakawa, T., 292
Hayflick, L., 58, 59, 93, 95
Hayslip, B., 196
Hayslip, B., Jr., 217, 333, 334
Hayward, M. D., 322
Hayward, R. D., 264
He, W., 403
He, W. L., 116
Healey, M. L., 37
Health.gov, 415
Heathcote, D., 163
Heckhausen, J., 235, 236, 408, 409
Hedgepath, A., 366
Hegewisch, A., 349
Hehman, J. A., 147, 219
Heilman, K. M., 209
Heinsinger, N. M., 291
Helbert, M., 99
Helson, R., 248, 249
Hemer, S. R., 373
Henderson, S., 310
Hendricks, A. A. J., 248
Hendriks, G.-J., 299
Hendry, M., 376
Henkens, K., 363, 364
Henkin, R. I., 74
Henrie, J. A., 381
Henrikson, C. R., 406
Henry, J. D., 220, 227
Heo, J., 361
Heppner, R. S., 349
Herbert, C. E., 206
Hernández, B., 361
Hernández, V., 345
Herrenbrueck, L., 312
Hersh, E. D., 216
Hershey, D. A., 205, 363, 364
Hertzog, C., 19, 162, 164, 165, 166, 175, 176, 195, 196, 220, 222, 359
Hess, P., 64, 99
Hess, T. M., 171, 205, 223, 225, 226, 227, 231
Heyl, V., 69, 71, 132
Hiatt, K., 384
Hiatt Racer, K., 204
Hickson, L., 71
Higgins, J. P., 116
Hilger, K., 193
Hill, B., 361
Hill, P. L., 249
Hill, R. T., 356

Hill, T. J., 295
Hills, L., 255
Hills, W. E., 333
Hillsdon, M., 360
Hilton, A., 150
Hilty, D. M., 359
Hinton, A., 343
Hipp, L., 356
Hirokawa, K., 99
Hirst, W., 238
Hirve, S., 97
Hitchcock, R., 14
Hodder, K. I., 174
Hodes, G. E., 281
Hofer, S. M., 193, 206
Hoffman, E., 332, 333
Hofhuis, J., 349
Holland, J. M., 341, 389
Holland, K. J., 351
Hollandis, C., 38
Hollwich, M., 134–135
Holmes, M. L., 73
Holton, E. F., III, 208
Holtzer, R., 162
Hom, P. W., 344
Homma, A., 328
Homma, M., 358
Hommel, B., 161
Honaker, J. A., 73
Honda-Howard, M., 358
Hooker, K., 245, 251, 258, 260, 261, 263
Hoon, T. C., 60
Hopthrow, T., 230
Horhota, M., 216, 222, 229, 230
Horn, J., 207
Horn, J. L., 192, 193, 194, 206
Horwitz, B. N., 312
Horwood, S., 161
Hostetler, A. J., 408
Howard, D. V., 163
Howard, J. H., Jr., 163
Howard, J. T., 343
Howard, L. W., 345
Howe, A. L., 138
Howe, D., 329
Hsiao, C.-Y., 322
Hsiao, W.-H., 310
Hsu, A., 112, 293
Hsu, H.-C., 262
Huang, A. J., 112, 293
Hubbard, R. R., 328
Huettel, S. A., 39, 40
Huffman, K. M., 414
Hughes, G., 164
Huizinga, T. W. J., 65
Hulbert-Williams, N. J., 375, 383
Hull, T. H., 317
Hülür, G., 176
Hummel, T., 74
Hummert, M. L., 217, 219, 221
Hunsberger, J. G., 49
Hunt, J. B., 224
Hunt, J. M., 343
Hunter, C. E. A., 174, 294
Hunter, D., 209
Husain, M., 177
Huxhold, O., 234
Huyck, M. H., 256, 257
Hwang, M. J., 349
Hyer, L., 331, 334

Ibrahim, R., 316, 317
Idler, E. L., 97
Igarashi, H., 128, 321, 395

Name Index

Igarashi, K. M., 287
Iglesias, J., 34
Imoscopi, A., 74
Ingersoll-Dayton, B., 322
Inoue, M., 386
Intlekofer, K. A., 50
Intuit, 340
Irwin, N., 340
Isaacowitz, D. M., 42, 227, 231, 232, 233
Ismail, Z., 288
Iwarsson, S., 129, 137
Izumi, S., 386

Jack, C. R., Jr., 290
Jackson, J. B., 321
Jackson, J. S., 275
Jackson, K., 331
Jackson, M. A., 364
Jackson, P. A., 37, 38
Jacobs, J., 287
Jacoby, L. L., 170
Jäger, H. R., 297
Jagust, W., 160
Jainer, A. K., 282
James, J. B., 362, 363, 404
Jamoulle, M., 412, 413
Jan, Y.-K., 83, 84
Janicki-Deverts, D., 104
Janssen, I., 415
Jarrott, S. E., 295, 296
Jarvin, L., 187
Jaspal, R., 10
Jayasinha, R., 366
Jefferson, A., 296
Jencks, C., 328
Jenkins, J. A., 151
Jenkins, K. R., 322
Jenny, G. J., 409
Jeon, H.-A., 162
Jeste, D. V., 278–279, 285
Jette, A. M., 116, 117, 118, 119, 120, 412, 413
Jiang, W., 352
Jiang, Z., 70
Jiménez, M. P., 117
Jin, R., 274
Johansson, B., 118
Johnson, B., 362
Johnson, H. A., 361
Johnson, J. A., 115
Johnson, M. D., 312, 317
Johnson, M. K., 33, 170
Johnson, M. M., 152
Johnson, R. W., 404
Johnson, T. L., 161
Johnson, W., 46, 248
Johnston, K. E., 329
Joiner, T., 375
Jolie, A., 109
Jonas, E., 381
Jones, A. E., 138
Jones, B. F., 208, 317
Jones, B. K., 255
Jones, D. H., 321
Jones, E., 137
Jones, M. R., 112
Jones, R., 198
Jones, R. N., 133, 172
Jonsson, C., 291
Jopp, D., 359
Jopp, D. S., 359
Jorge, M. P., 80
Josselson, R., 343

Joyner, M. J., 414
Juang, L., 9, 10
Juffer, F., 329
Jung, R. E., 43, 209
Justice, L., 341

Kaasik, P., 63
Kahana, B., 130, 131
Kahana, E., 130, 131
Kalanithi, L., 325
Kalish, E., 317
Kalish, K., 278
Kalish, R. A., 378, 381
Kalmijn, M., 312
Kalokerinos, E. K., 227
Kam, P. K., 351
Kan, D., 358
Kaneshiro, S., 332
Kao, H., 138
Kaplan, S., 374
Kapoor, U., 347
Kapp, M. B., 151, 152
Karasu, S. R., 321
Karasu, T. B., 321
Karel, M. J., 278
Karim, S., 98, 299
Karney, B. R., 320, 321, 324
Karp, N., 384
Kasl, S. V., 221
Kassim, P. N. J., 374, 375
Kastenbaum, R., 379, 380
Kasuya, H., 62
Kaszniak, A. W., 393
Kaufman, D. A. S., 46
Kaufman, J., 312
Kaufman, J. C., 208
Kaur, M., 287
Kavé, G., 171
Kay, T., 361
Kazanis, I., 49
Kazdin, A. E., 279
Kegan, R., 261
Keinan, G., 233
Keith, C. M., 46
Kelley, K., 244
Kelley-Moore, J., 131
Kelly, M., 294–295
Kennedy, H. P., 80
Kennedy, L., 409
Kensinger, E. A., 41, 42, 233, 262
Kepple, A. L., 150
Kersting, A., 388
Kessler, R. C., 102, 273, 274
Ketelaar, T., 311
Khalil, D. N., 108
Kiang, L., 328
Kiaye, R. E., 349
Kievit, R. A., 193, 194
Kikuchi, Y., 99
Killett, A., 146, 151
Kim, H. K., 324
Kim, H.-J., 318
Kim, P., 101
Kim, S., 205
Kimbler, K. J., 161, 237
King, A., 318
King, P. M., 201, 202
King, S. V., 333
Kingston, A., 119
Kinicki, A. J., 344
Kinney, J. M., 103, 322
Kinsella, G. J., 174, 294
Kinsella, K., 95

Kippen, R., 320
Kirkpatrick, L. A., 311
Kirmayer, L. J., 280
Kirwan, C. B., 38
Kisley, M. A., 232
Kitchener, K. S., 201, 202
Kite, E., 98
Kivett, V. R., 333
Klackl, J., 381
Klauer, K. C., 219
Kleiber, D. A., 361, 365
Kliegel, M., 167
Kliegl, R., 49
Kline, S. L., 317
Klingberg, T., 49
Klug, M. G., 143
Kluger, J., 172
Knee, D. O., 383, 384
Knijn, T., 326
Knowles, M. S., 208
Ko, H.-J., 245, 262, 263
Koenig, B. L., 311
Kojima, G., 120
Kojola, E., 362, 363
Kolb, D. M., 349
Koller, S. H., 218
Komaromy, C., 394
Kompier, M. A. J., 361
Koopman-Boyden, P., 359, 360
Koppel, J., 169
Kornadt, A. E., 223, 224
Koss, C., 136, 139, 143
Kotre, J. N., 254
Kotter-Grühn, D., 223, 224, 262
Kowal, P., 403
Kowalski, S. D., 389
Kozbelt, A., 208
Kram, K. E., 344
Kramer, A. F., 171
Kramer, H. J., 37
Kratzer, J. M. W., 312
Krause, N., 104, 211, 264
Kremer, S., 73
Kremer-Sadlik, T., 356, 358
Kressel, L. M., 227, 228
Kriewitz, K., 362
Kronbichler, M., 381
Krause, N., 104, 211, 264
Kuczmarska, A., 285
Kuh, D., 119
Kuhlmann, B. G., 170
Kuiper, J., 195–196
Kulich, C., 349
Kulik, L., 320, 321, 322
Kumar, D. K. V., 292
Kunda, Z., 219
Kunkle, F., 137
Kunz, J. A., 209
Kunzmann, U., 209
Kurdek, L. A., 318
Kurpiers, L. A., 95
Kwon, S., 143
Kyllonen, P. C., 195
Kyulo, N. L., 169

LaBar, K. S., 39, 40
Labat-Robert, J., 61
Labouvie-Vief, G., 201, 203, 252, 256, 257, 261–262
Lachman, M. E., 176, 196, 234, 236, 245, 248, 256, 257, 258

Ladin, K., 279
Lagattuta, K. H., 37
Lahey, J. N., 351
Lahti, J., 360, 361
Lai, C. K. Y., 293
Lai, D. W. L., 331
Lamanna, M. A., 321
Lambert-Pandraud, E., 205
Lamela, D., 324
Lamkin, J., 321
Lampkin-Hunter, T., 329
Lamson, A., 321
Landis, M., 321, 324
Landrine, H., 98
Lane, E., 296
Lane, R. D., 232
Lang, F. R., 223, 410
Langer, E., 220
Langer, E. J., 144, 220
Langer, N., 194
Langlais, M. R., 328, 329
Lanzl, R. G., 394
Lapersonne, E., 205
Larsen, L. M., 116
Larson, C., 138
Larsson, M., 169
Laurent, G., 205
Laurent, H. K., 101
Lavner, J. A., 321, 324, 326
Law, L. L. F., 196
Lawton, L. E., 356
Lawton, M. P., 98, 128, 129, 130
Layne, L., 394
Lazarov, O., 38
Lazarus, R. S., 102, 103, 132
Le Couteur, D. G., 114
Leah, V., 294
LeanIn.org, 349, 355, 356, 358
Lebo, P. B., 109
Lee, E.-K. O., 264
Lee, E.-Y., 296
Lee, K. H., 42
Lee, K. S., 331, 373
Lee, M., 164
Lee, M.-D., 331
Lee, P. C. B., 352
Lee, R. E., 14
Lee, S. A., 287, 334
Lee, T.-S., 290
Lee, Y.-M., 178
Leeuwen, K. van, 147
Lefkowitz, E. S., 263
Lehning, A. J., 128, 129, 135, 136, 140
Leichtentritt, R. D., 394
Lemaire, P., 171
Lemieux, A., 200, 201
Lent, R. W., 341–342
Leon, G. R., 248
LeRoux, H., 129
Leshikar, E. D., 224, 227
Lesnoff-Caravaglia, G., 409
Leuty, M. E., 359
Levenson, R. W., 323
Levin, J., 264
Levine, A. D., 318
Levine, B., 38
Levine, I. S., 311
Levinger, G., 309
Levinson, D., 256
Levinson, D. J., 256
Levinson, J. D., 256

Levkovitz, Y., 101
Levy, B. R., 101, 218, 220–221
Levy, C. R., 119
Levy, S. R., 66, 218
Lewin, K., 128
Lewinsohn, P. M., 284
Lewis, C., 19
Lewis, D. C., 333
Lewis, J. L., 129
Lewis, J. R., 373
Lewis, M., 321
Lewis, M. M., 375
Lewis, S., 351
Lewis-Fernández, R., 280
Li, C. M., 72
Li, F., 73
Li, J., 361, 393
Li, K. Z. H., 161, 231
Liao, D. H., 255
Liao, F., 83, 84
Lichtenberg, P., 205, 316
Lieber, J., 394
Lieberman, M. D., 41
Light, L. L., 164, 165, 166
Ligtenberg, L., 312
Li-Korotky, H.-S., 72
Lilgendahl, J. P., 259
Lillyman, S., 151
Limb, G. E., 333
Lindbergh, C. A., 409
Linden, D. E. J., 31, 32
Lindenberger, U., 4, 187
Lindgren, L., 105
Lindley, R. I., 117
Ling, K. H., 60
Lipp, I., 194
Lippke, S., 414
Lips, H. M., 366
Lips-Wiersma, M., 341
Litz, B., 388
Liu, C.-C., 291
Liu, G., 132
Livingston, G., 324
Lo, M., 314
Loaiza, V., 163, 164
Loaiza, V. M., 163
Löckenhoff, C. E., 205
Loe, M., 219
Logan, R. D., 254
Loken, E., 263
Lomanowska, A. M., 312
Long, M. V., 248
Longest, K. C., 97
Lonial, S., 352
Looi, C. Y., 198
López Turley, R. N., 328
Lord, K., 143
Lorenz, F. O., 364
Loretto, W., 362, 363
Lötsch, J., 74
Lou, V. W. Q., 132, 133
Lourenço, J. S., 161
Lövdén, M., 198
Lowrance, W., 386
Luca, M., 275
Lucas, H. D., 175
Lucero-Liu, A. A., 328
Ludke, R. L., 384
Luhmann, M., 389
Luk, G., 171
Luo, B., 406
Luo, S., 312
Luong, G., 233
Lustig, C., 167

Name Index

Luszcz, M. A., 176
Luszczynska, A., 414
Luthans, F., 344
Lutz, A., 265
Luxenberg, S., 317

Maatz, L., 366
Macdonald, J. L., 66, 218
Mace, J. H., 169
Maciejewski, P. K., 389
Mackenzie, P., 60
MacLean, M. J., 148
MacLullich, A. M. J., 285
Macnamara, B. N., 210
Madden, D. J., 37, 39, 40
Magai, C., 311
Mahady, G. B., 80
Malhi, G. S., 284
Malkinson, R., 394
Malone, M. L., 294
Malone, P. S., 228, 229
Mälzer, J. N., 100
Mambourg, F., 139
Mancini, A. D., 388
Mandemakers, J. J., 354
Manji, H., 297, 298
Mankus, A. M., 224
Mantler, J., 353
Manuti, A., 345
Manzoni, G. M., 409
Maple, M., 394
Marcia, J., 343
Margrett, J., 237
Margrett, J. A., 161
Markland, A. D., 112
Marks, N. F., 365
Markus, H., 262–263
Marquardt, G., 145
Marques-Aleixo, I., 171
Marsh, K., 344
Marshall, J. C., 45
Marsiske, M., 198
Marson, D., 32
Martens, A., 381
Martin, J. H., 288
Martin, M., 195, 248
Martin, S. P., 317
Martin-Uzzi, M., 325
Martyr, A., 196
Maruna, S., 255
Maruyama, L., 217
Mash, H. B. H., 394
Mask, L., 361
Master, S., 72
Masunaga, H., 207
Masunari, N., 63
Materstvedt, L. J., 375
Mather, M., 36, 41, 101, 228, 232, 233, 262
Matsumoto, D., 9, 10
Mattis, J., 84
Matz-Costa, C., 362
Maume, D. J., 358
Mavellia, H., 264
Maxfield, M., 379
Mayer, J. D., 224
Maylor, E. A., 161, 171
Mayo Clinic, 76, 109, 285, 414, 417
Mazerolle, M., 171
McAdams, D. P., 245, 251, 254, 255, 258, 259, 260, 261
McCabe, D. P., 163
McCarty, W. P., 345

McClinton, B. E., 362
McCloskey, M. S., 42
McCoyd, J. L. M., 325, 389, 394, 395
McCrae, R. R., 246, 247
McCrate, F. M., 98
McCrory, P., 179
McCullough, B. M., 310
McDaniel, M. A., 167, 168
McEwen, B. S., 37, 38, 41
McGarry, K., 325
McGillivray, S., 175
McGinty, T., 377
McGuire, L. C., 173
McKay, B., 105
McKee, A. C., 179
McKee, K. J., 415
McKee-Ryan, F., 352, 353, 354
McKhann, G. M., 290
McKinney, B. C., 281
McLachlan, A. J., 114
McLanahan, S., 328
McLean, K. C., 259
McLymont, R., 347
McNally, R. J., 390
McNaught, S., 356
McNulty, M., 285, 298, 299
Meade, S. M., 237
Medart, P., 70
Medicare.gov, 407
MedlinePlus, 80
Mehta, K. K., 264
Meijer, A. M., 321, 326
Meilaender, G., 375
Meiser, T., 170
Mejía, S., 245, 263
Meldrum, M., 383
Meléndez, J. C., 104
Meletti, S., 38
Menaker, R., 344
Ménard, C., 281
Mendez-Luck, C. A., 332
Menkin, J. A., 221
Menon, U., 257
Merakangas, K., 274
Mercado-Crespo, M. C., 280
Mercer, J. T., 173
Mercer, V., 294
Meredith, S. D., 148
Merriam, S. B., 256
Mertens, A., 410
Merz, E.-M., 310
Merz, M. Y., 383
Meschede, T., 363
MetLife, 138
Meyer, B. J. F., 205
Meyer, J. F., 328
Meza-Kubo, V., 133
Michaelian, K., 237
Michel, A., 345
Mickler, C., 248
Middlebrooks, C. D., 175
Midlarsky, E., 130
Miedema, M. D., 63
Mienaltowski, A., 207, 216, 230
Miething, A., 308
Mikels, J. A., 46, 205, 231, 232
Mikhelson, V. M., 58, 59
Miles, E., 220
Miller, A. C., 374, 375
Miller, K. I., 331
Miller, K. J., 172
Miller, L. M. S., 238
Miller, L. S., 409

Miller, M. N., 12
Miller, V. M., 80
Milligan, C., 379
Millon, E. M., 233
Minnotte, K. L., 319
Miranda, J., 275
Mishra, G. D., 120
Mitchell, B. A., 331
Mitchell, K. J., 233
Mitteldorf, J., 60
Mittelmark, M. B., 409
Moak, G. S., 281
Modra, L., 150
Moeller, J. R., 375, 382
Moen, P., 343, 362, 363, 364
Mohanty, P., 164
Mohlman, J., 147, 149
Mohr, C., 46
Mojon, D. S., 68
Mojon-Azzi, S. M., 68, 69
Mok, R. M., 160
Molenberghs, P., 222
Molin, P., 290
Monahan, A., 362, 363
Monden, C. W. S., 354
Montesanto, A., 94
Moon, P. J., 384
Moorman, S. M., 310, 325, 386
Morán, A. L., 133
Morcom, A. M., 46, 162, 163, 164, 165, 166
Morfei, M. Z., 263
Morgan, S., 144
Mori, H., 195
Morrell, R. W., 275
Morris, J. A., 41
Morris, J. N., 198
Morris, W. L., 316
Morrissey, T. W., 356
Morrow, D. G., 237
Morrow-Howell, N., 366
Morycz, R., 309
Môttus, R., 248, 249
Motzek, T., 145
Mouras, H., 203
Mouzon, D., 275
Mouzon, D. M., 275
Moye, A. M., 386
Moye, J., 386
Moyer, A. M., 80, 81
Mozaffarian, D., 75, 76
Mrayyan, M. T., 385
Mroczek, D. K., 249
Muck-Šeler, D., 36
Muehlbauer, T., 73
Mueller, M. L., 175
Mühlig-Versen, A., 248
Mullen, C. M., 331
Muller, E. D., 388
Munoz, R. T., 375
Muntaner, C., 275
Murayama, K., 161
Musson, G., 344
Mutchler, J. E., 334
Mwanyangala, M. A., 262

Nabe, C. M., 380
Nadel, L., 232
Naef, R., 389
Nagaratnam, K., 71
Nagaratnam, N., 71
Nagl, M., 388
Nahemow, L., 128, 129, 130
Napolitano, C. M., 232

Narciso, I., 394
Nasca, C., 37
Nash, J. F., 61
Nash, M. I., 38
Nashiro, K., 170, 228
Naveh-Benjamin, M., 164, 170
Nawijn, J., 361
Nayernouri, T., 375
Neal, M. B., 355
Neese, R. M., 390
Neft, N., 318
Nehamas, A., 308
Neimeyer, R. A., 389
Neisser, U., 159, 169
Nelson, T. D., 3, 218, 221, 223
Neugarten, B. L., 333
Nevalainen, N., 36
Neville, C., 138
Newman, A., 383
Newman, B. M., 7
Newman, J. P., 204
Newman, P. R., 7
Newsom, J. T., 332
Newton, N. J., 255, 257, 258
Newton, P. M., 256
Ng, J. W., 132, 133
Ng, R., 363
Ngan, R. M. H., 351
Nichols, L. O., 293
Nicolas, G., 291
Nielsen, M. K., 388
Nies, M. A., 264
Nigro, N., 82
Niki, K., 233
Nikolaidis, A., 43
Nimrod, G., 359
Ning, W. H., 60
Nishijima, T., 49
Nokes, T. J., 237
Nordin, S., 74
Noristani, H. N., 36
Norris, D. R., 353
Norström, T., 356
North, M. S., 3
Norton, M. I., 218, 373, 387
Nosek, M., 80
Nuzum, D., 394
Nurius, P., 262
Nuzum, D., 394
Nyberg, L., 105, 160, 173
Nylenna, M., 344

Obhi, H. K., 217
O'Brien, B. J., 59
O'Brien, J., 292
O'Brien, L. T., 217, 221
Oburu, P. O., 334
Ochs, E., 356, 358
O'Connor, M.-F., 393
O'Dell, C. D., 295
Oedekoven, C. S. H., 166
Oh, D. H., 275
Ohnsman, A., 411
Okonski, B., 394
Old, S., 170
O'Leary, K. D., 314, 315
Olivares, E. I., 34
Oliveira, B. S., 59
Oliveira, T. C., 352
Olson, B. D., 251, 255
Omori, M., 356
O'Neal, C. W., 364
O'Neill, K., 390
Oosterman, J. M., 163
Opdebeeck, C., 196

Operskalski, J. T., 224
Orange, J. B., 148
Ordy, J. M., 70
Orel, N. A., 318, 332
Oren, S., 174, 294
O'Riley, A., 177, 276
Orlova, N. S., 406
O'Rourke, N., 322
Orthel-Clark, H., 309
Ortiz-Walters, R., 343
Osika, W., 345
Osman, M., 205
Ossher, L., 167
Östgren, C. J., 415
Oswald, A. J., 262
Oswald, F. L., 21, 210
Oudekerk, B. A., 311
Owen, C. J., 330

Paccagnella, M., 195
Packer, D. J., 263
Paech, J., 414
Paggi, M. E., 359, 361
Palkovitz, R., 327
Palm, G., 327
Palmer, A. M., 206
Palmer, B. W., 278–279, 285
Palmérus, K., 334
Palmore, E. B., 60
Panay, N., 81
Papa, A., 388, 390
Pardal, R., 49
Park, C. L., 264
Park, D. C., 44, 46–47, 48, 160, 164, 165, 166, 227
Park, J., 332
Park, Y. C., 381
Park, Y. H., 178
Park, Y.-H., 138
Parker, L. D., 322
Parkes, C. M., 379
Parkman, A. M., 321
Parks, S. M., 150
Parrella, N., 408, 409, 414
Parris, B. A., 228
Pasccle, A., 36
Pascoe, A., 391
Passalacqua, S. A., 149
Passarino, G., 94
Pasupathi, M., 259
Paterson, S. E., 408
Paterson, T. S. E., 409
Patry, D. A., 361
Patterson, A. V., 254
Paul, R., 296
Paulsen, J. S., 291
Paulson, D., 345
Pearce, K. A., 206
Pearlin, L. I., 331
Pearson, F., 329
Pegg, S., 361
Peiró, J. M., 363
Peng, Y., 224
Penson, R. T., 373
Pereira, M., 394
Perkins, J. M., 62, 63
Perls, T., 96
Perlstein, W. M., 46
Perrone, K. M., 342
Perski, A., 345
Peters, E., 205
Peters, H. E., 317
Peters, R., 264
Peterson, B. E., 257

Pettinato, J., 142
Pezzuti, L., 207
Pfeiffer, E., 235, 236
Phillips, D. R., 95
Phillips, J. L., 410
Phillips, K. W., 343
Piaget, J., 199–201, 260, 261
Piazza, J. R., 233
Pienta, A. M., 322
Pilli, S. C., 62
Pine, K., 19
Pineda-Pardo, J. A., 43, 44, 193, 194
Pini, L., 36, 37
Pinto, K. M., 356
Piquet, B. J., 311
Pivac, N., 36
Platt, M. L., 41
Plaumann, M., 346
Plonsky, L., 21
Poldrack, R. A., 31
Polivka, L., 139, 140, 405, 406
Polku, H., 71
Poon, L. W., 248
Pope, T. M., 380
Popenoe, D., 317
Popham, L. E., 171
Popper-Giveon, A., 343
Porter, K. E., 318
Portnoy, A., 385
Potočnik, K., 363
Potter, G. G., 74
Powell, B., 328
Powell, J., 178, 179
Power, T. L., 381
Prager, I. G., 218
Pratt, H. D., 343
Pratt, S. I., 300
Prebble, S. C., 168
Priaulx, N., 374
Price, J., 176
Price, V., 347
Prieto-Ursúa, M., 345
Prigerson, H. G., 393
Prince-Paul, M., 383
Proctor, H., 219
Proulx, C. M., 320, 321, 322
Ptak, R., 160
Pullen, S. M., 225, 226
Punhani, S., 96
Purandare, N., 150
Purser, J. L., 118
Pushkar, D., 211
Putti, B. B., 62
Pynoos, J., 98, 128
Pyszczynski, T., 381

Quakenbush, C., 407
Qualls, S. H., 273
Queen, T. L., 205, 386
Quéniart, A., 238
Quinn, J. F., 362, 363, 364
Quinn, K., 310
Quirin, M., 381

Raab, G. M., 325
Rabbitt, P., 196
Rabinstein, A. A., 178
Radloff, L. S., 281
Raison, C. L., 100
Raji, C. A., 171
Raju, S. S., 265
Ramakumar, S., 327
Ramos-Zúñiga, R., 50

Randall, G. K., 277
Rankin, C. T., 317
Raschick, M., 322
Ratneshwar, S., 164
Rattan, S. I. S., 60, 93
Ray, M., 277, 278, 280, 281, 299
Ready, R. E., 262
Reamy, A. M., 151, 152
Rebeck, G. W., 291
Rebok, G. W., 133, 198, 199
Redzanowski, U., 210
Reed, A. E., 232, 233, 310
Reed, R. G., 100
Regev, I., 363
Reinhold, S., 279
Reinke, B. J., 256
Remedios, J. D., 263
Ren, Q., 6
Rendeiro, C., 180
Renner, V. J., 273
Renshaw, K. D., 321
Repetti, R., 358
Repetti, R. L., 358
Repovs, G., 204
Reuter-Lorenz, P., 44, 46–47, 48
Revenson, T. A., 322
Reynolds, D., 378
Rhoades, G. K., 329
Rhodes, J. S., 180
Rhodes, M. G., 163
Rhodes, R., 152
Rich, K. L., 150
Rickard, A. P., 180
Ridings, C., 309
Rieder, M., 232
Riedmann, A., 321
Rijken, A. J., 326
Rill, L., 139, 140
Ripp, J., 137
Rippe, J. M., 413
Riso, E.-M., 63
Ritter, J. O., 236
Rizzuto, T. E., 161
Robert, A. A., 61
Robert, L., 61
Roberto, K. A., 295, 296, 308, 309, 310, 316, 332
Roberts, A. E., 377
Roberts, B. W., 248, 249, 250
Roberts, P., 256
Robertson, I., 361
Robinaugh, D. J., 390
Robinson, A., 138
Robinson, C., 195
Robinson, O. C., 257
Robinson-Wood, T., 318
Robson, S. M., 344
Röcke, C., 234
Rockwell, J., 151
Rockwood, K., 119, 120, 290
Rocque, G. B., 384
Rodin, J., 144
Rodrigue, K. M., 160
Rodrigues, C., 321
Rodriguez, J. J., 36
Rodríguez-Rodríguez, V., 134, 135
Roediger, H. L., III, 169
Roehling, P., 343
Rohmann, E., 314
Rokach, R., 321
Romeijn, N., 84

Rose, D. M., 352
Rose, N. S., 165
Rosellini, A. J., 273
Rosenbaum, J. L., 394
Rosenberg, H. J., 257
Rosenberg, S. D., 257
Rosenblatt, P. C., 389
Rosenfield, S., 275
Rosi, A., 37
Rosinski, P., 341
Rosnick, C., 234
Ross, N. A., 120
Rosso, B. D., 341
Rosta, J., 341
Rostila, M., 389
Roszko, E., 373
Rothberg, S. T., 218
Rothermund, K., 223
Rounds, J., 342
Rowe, G., 163
Rowe, M. M., 345
Rowles, G. D., 135
Roxburgh, S., 355
Roy, A., 96
Royzman, E. B., 232
Rozin, P., 232
Rubin, S. S., 394
Rubio, J., 104
Rudolph, C. W., 232
Ruhm, C. J., 355
Ruiz, M. E., 143
Ruppanner, L., 358
Ruscher, J. B., 361
Russo, S. J., 281
Rutherford, A., 164
Rutledge, M. S., 406
Ryan, E. B., 146, 148, 410
Ryan, M. K., 349
Ryan, S., 66
Rye, M. S., 324

Saavedra, C., 34
Sabatino, C. P., 386
Sacks, O., 45
Sadeh, T., 168
Sakaki, M., 233
Sakraida, T. J., 324
Sala Frigerio, C., 286, 287, 291
Salai, L. K., 299
Salomaa, R., 341
Salovey, P., 224
Salthouse, T. A., 34, 160, 195
Samanta, T., 408
Samieri, C., 51
Sampson, E. L., 150
Sánchez-González, D., 134, 135
Sandler, I. N., 391
Sandoval, K., 333
Sandrini, M., 166
Sanford, D. A., 94
Sansone, C., 207
Santilli, S., 341, 342
Santos-Lozano, A., 94
Sargent, L. D., 362, 363
Saribay, S. A., 227, 228
Sasson, E., 177
Šatienė, S., 196
Sauceda, J. A., 167
Savci, E., 329
Savela, S., 59
Savic, I., 345
Savickas, M. L., 341
Savundranayagam, M. Y., 149

Sbarra, D. A., 309, 324
Schacter, D. L., 166, 170
Schaie, K. W., 22–23, 24, 34, 133, 186, 188, 194, 195, 196, 198, 206
Scharlach, A. E., 128, 129, 135, 136, 140
Scheibe, S., 42, 209
Scheidt, R. J., 134, 135, 136, 139, 140
Scheier, M. F., 309
Schilling, O., 69
Schim, S. M., 264
Schmidt, M., 80
Schmiedek, F., 160
Schmitt, D. P., 312, 313, 314
Schneider, J., 394
Schneider, S., 312
Schoeni, R. F., 325
Schoklitsch, A., 255
Schooler, K. K., 132
Schott, J. M., 177
Schott, W., 355
Schoulte, J., 389
Schultz, D. P., 245, 248
Schultz, S. E., 245, 248
Schulz, A. R., 100
Schulz, D. J., 343
Schulz, R., 235, 309, 408
Schulz-Helk, R. J., 178
Schut, H., 379, 389, 392
Schüz, B., 415
Schwab, A. K., 309
Schwartz, B., 341
Schwarz, B., 134, 135, 136, 139, 140
Schwarzer, R., 414
Schwerdtfeger, A., 359
Scotchmer, E., 149
Scott, I. A., 288
Scullin, M. K., 167, 168
Seaman, P. M., 366
Seay, R., 207
Seefeldt, D. A., 294
Seeman, T. E., 255
Seene, T., 63
Segal, D. L., 273, 274, 275, 278, 279, 280, 281, 282, 298, 299, 301
Segers, M., 352
Segrin, C., 320
Sehgal, A., 84
Selkoe, D. J., 291, 292
Sels, L., 351
Seltzer, J. A., 331
Sendtner, M., 50
Sengupta, M., 145
Seponski, D. M., 333
Sergi, G., 74
Seward, R. R., 329
Seychell, A., 321
Seyda, B. A., 394
Seyfarth, R. M., 41
Shafer, K., 333
Shamay-Tsoory, S. G., 101
Shanafelt, T. D., 345
Shannon, C. S., 361
Shao, J., 279
Sharma, A., 347
Sharma, I., 144, 146
Sharma, V., 347
Sharp, D. J., 178, 179
Sharpe, T., 264
Shastri, T., 352

Shaw, R. L., 69
Shaw, S. S., 395
Shayshon, B., 343
Shega, J. W., 112
Sheiner, L., 405
Sheldon, S., 38
Shelton, J. T., 176
Shen, H., 366
Sherlock, H., 345
Sherman, J. W., 219
Sherry, A., 219
Sherwin, S., 374
Sheu, H., 341
Shi, L., 96
Shimamura, A. P., 164, 165, 166
Shiner, R., 248
Shivapour, S. K., 205
Shoemaker, C., 309
Shoji, K., 345
Shonkoff, J. P., 105
Shore, J. C., 388
Shors, T. J., 233
Shrira, A., 233
Shum, C. K., 145
Shweder, R. A., 257
Sibalija, J., 149
Sibille, E., 281
Siegle, G. J., 42
Silva, A. R., 100
Silva, L. C. R., 59
Silver, M. P., 362, 363
Silver, N., 323
Simoni, J. M., 167
Simons, B. S., 345
Simonton, D. K., 208, 210
Simpson, T., 197
Sinclair, R. R., 352
Sinclair, S., 316
Singh, A. M., 349
Singh, J. A., 65
Singh, M., 287
Sinnott, J. D., 201
Skarin, F., 409
Skevington, S. M., 98
Skinner, T. R., 288
Skogan, W. G., 345
Skouteris, H., 356
Skrajner, M. J., 294–295
Slaats, E., 410
Slade, M. D., 221
Slater, C. L., 254
Slaug, B., 129
Slough, C., 33
Small, J., 174, 294
Smith, B., 278
Smith, D. M., 198
Smith, D. T., 275, 356
Smith, G. E., 177
Smith, J. R., 394
Smith, L., 405
Smith, M. D., 179
Smith, P. J., 50
Smith, S. M., 381
Smith, T. C., 278
Smith, W. J., 343
Smith-Howell, E. R., 384
Smits, S. J., 343
Smucker, D. R., 384
Smyer, M. A., 273, 278, 362, 412
Smyke, A., 329
Smyth, A. C., 170
Sneed, J. R., 260

Name Index

Son, C. V., 386
Song, B., 49
Soulsby, L. K., 132
Sousa-Poza, A., 68
Soya, H., 49
Spaniol, J., 44, 170
Speaks, S. Z., 359
Spector, P. E., 358
Spencer, J. P. E., 180
Spencer, S. J., 219
Sperling, R. A., 290
Spiers, J., 151
Spiro, A., 196, 249
Spivak, D. L., 59
Spivak, I. M., 58, 59
Sprang, G., 334
Sritharan, R., 312
Srivastava, S., 248
Stafford, L., 317
Stalp, M. C., 361
Stanley, J. T., 233
Stanley-Stevens, L., 329
Staszewski, O., 297
Staudinger, U. M., 4, 187, 209, 210, 211, 248, 249
Steck, A., 387, 388, 389
Steck, B., 387, 388, 389
Stefaniak, J., 292
Steffens, D. C., 74
Stein, R., 220
Stein-Morrow, E. L., 238
Stell, A. J., 257
Stephan, Y., 176
Stern, Y., 412
Sternberg, K., 162, 163
Sternberg, R. J., 162, 163, 187, 189, 190, 279, 311
Sterns, H. L., 256, 257, 364
Steuerle, C. E., 407
Stevens Aubrey, J., 312
Stewart, A. J., 257, 258
Stewart, J. S., 343
Stewart, M. D., 327
Stewart, S. D., 321
Stillman, C. M., 163
Stockdale, M. S., 349
Stojnov, D., 219
Stokes, J., 395
Stoltz, K. B., 352
Stoner, S., 177, 178, 276
Štrac, D. Š., 36
Strathearn, L., 101
Strawbridge, W. J., 120
Street, D., 140
Strickland-Hughes, C. M., 172, 175, 176
Strinic, V., 375
Stroebe, M. S., 379, 388, 389, 391, 392, 393, 394
Stroebe, W., 379, 393
Strough, J., 205, 207, 237
Styles, E., 160, 162
Subramanian, S. V., 117
Suchy, F. J., 115
Sugimoto-Matsuda, J. J., 314
Sugiura, M., 31, 32, 33, 41, 43, 44, 45, 48
Suja, C., 60
Sullivan, L., 363
Sumowski, J. F., 38
Sumter, S. R., 312
Sun, F., 265
Suo, C., 414
Suskind, A. M., 112, 293

Sutton, J., 237
Swain, J. E., 101
Swanson, D. A., 94
Swanson, R. A., 208
Swenson, L. M., 237
Swift, H. J., 344, 364
Swindell, 2R., 208
Szuchman, L. T., 218

Tach, L., 317
Tae, Y.-S., 143
Talamini, L. M., 168
Talbot, L. A., 361
Tam, K.-P., 381
Tamayo, G. J., 331
Tang, F., 366
Tang, P.-L., 381
Tanji, J., 415
Tanner, J. L., 257
Tanner, P. R., 61
Tauber, S. C., 297
Tauber, S. K., 175
Taylor, E. M., 224
Taylor, J. L., 207
Taylor, R. J., 264
Taylor, S., 97
Taylor, S. E., 101, 218, 224
Teiga-Mocigemba, S., 219
Tergaonkar, V., 58–59
Terkel, S., 340, 345
Terry, J., 96
Thai, J., 84
Therborn, G., 317
Thiede, K. W., 175
Thiel, A., 100
Thoits, P. A., 97
Thomas, A. G., 49
Thomas, A. K., 164
Thomas, F., 324
Thomas, M. D., 139
Thomas, M. L., 211
Thomas, R. C., 161, 232
Thompson, C. L., 388
Thompson, G. E., 334
Thompson, J., 383
Thompson, R. J., 224
Thornton, W. J. L., 206
Thornton, W. L., 409
Thuell, S., 380
Tierney, W. M., 97
Tilse, C., 138
Tippett, L. J., 168
Tobin, D. J., 61, 62
Tolkko, T., 208
Tomolillo, C., 309
Tong, C., 344
Tordera, N., 363
Torges, C. M., 257
Toril, P., 161
Torres, L., 384
Torres-Aleman, I., 49
Tournier, J.-D., 37
Tower, L. E., 356
Towne, T. J., 207
Treiman, D. J., 6
Tremblay, F., 72
Trevisan, L. A., 301
Tromp, D., 165
Troutman, M., 264, 363
Truxillo, D. M., 217
Trzesniewski, K. H., 343
Tsang, W. W. N., 73
Tsuno, N., 328
Tu, M. C.-H., 344

Tulkin, D. O., 356
Turner, R. N., 219

Ukraintseva, S. V., 60
Uleman, J. S., 227, 228
Ultsch, A., 74
Unal, B., 58–59
Unverzagt, F. W., 198
Ursano, R. J., 394
Utsuyama, M., 99
Utz, R. L., 391

Vaandrager, L., 409
Vagelatos, N. T., 292
Valdes, A. M., 65
Valiathan, R., 99
Vallerand, R. J., 345, 346
van den Brink, H. M., 358
van den Wijngaart, M. A. G., 322
van den Wittenboer, G. L. H., 321, 326
van der Geest, S., 373
van der Pas, S., 359, 360
van der Rijt, P. G. A., 349
van Dulmen, M., 311
Van Hecke, W., 37
van Impe, A., 73
van Klaveren, C., 358
van Muijden, J., 161
van Praag, B., 359
van Praag, H., 50
van Wanrooy, B., 358
Vandenbosch, L., 312
Vansteenkiste, S., 351
Varkal, M. D., 298
Vautier, S., 359
Veiga, J. F., 343
Venkatesh, B., 178, 179
Verbrugge, L. M., 116, 117, 118, 119, 120, 412
Verghese, A., 379
Verkhratsky, A., 36
Vernooij-Dassen, M. J. F. J., 322
Viatour, G., 145
Vicente, R., 99
Vickerstaff, S., 362, 363
Vlug, M., 349
Voelkle, M. C., 217
Vogtle, L. K., 137
Volpe, U., 343, 344
von Hippel, W., 220, 227
Vormittag, K., 408, 409, 414
Vukman, S. N., 263

Wahl, H.-W., 69, 71, 132, 135, 136, 137
Waites, C., 333
Walhovd, K. B., 198
Walker, A. C., 373
Walker, L. E. A., 314
Walter, C. A., 325, 389, 394, 395
Walter, S., 117
Walter, U., 346
Walters, E., 274
Walther, A. N., 324
Wang, M., 228
Wang, R., 36
Wang, S-W., 358
Wang, T.-J., 118
Wang, W., 323
Wang, W.-C., 38, 46, 166, 170

Wangi, S-w., 358
Wanzer, S. H., 382, 383
Waring, J. D., 41
Warner, D. F., 116
Warner, M. E., 356
Warner, S. C., 65
Warr, P., 361
Warren, D. E., 178
Watkins, J. F., 135
Watson, R. W., 82
Wayland, S., 393
Weaver, D. A., 325
Weber, A., 318
Webster, J. D., 253
Webster, N. J., 363
Webster-Marketon, J., 105
Wechsler, D., 186
Ween, M., 79
Weger, H., Jr., 311
Wegman, L. A., 348
Weinstein, K. K., 333
Weintraub, J. R., 343
Weiss, D., 221, 223, 224
Weiss, L. A., 253
Wentura, D., 218
Werner, T. L., 361
Werth, J. L., Jr., 375
West, R. L., 172, 175, 176
Westerhof, G. J., 253
Westphal, M., 388
Westrate, N. M., 210
Wettstein, R. M., 386
Whalley, L. J., 35
Whitbourne, S. K., 17, 147, 258, 259–260
White, H., 178, 179
White, M., 321
White, M. L., 264
Whited, C., 62
Whitty, M. T., 312
Wickrama, K. A. S., 364
Wiebe, J. S., 167
Wiebe, S. T., 281
Wijdicks, E. F. M., 374
Wilber, K. H., 316
Wiles, J. L., 366
Wilkinson, S., 375
Willander, J., 169
Willerton, C., 174, 294
Williams, C. N., 147, 149
Williams, J., 349
Williams, J. C., 343
Williams, S. A., 311
Willis, S. L., 49, 133, 196, 198, 206, 409
Windsor, T. D., 234
Winecoff, A., 38, 39, 40, 262
Wink, P., 264
Winslow, M., 383
Winston, A., 297
Winter, L., 150
Wise, D., 362
Witko, M. L., 327
Witmer, H., 310
Witten, T. M., 318
Wixted, J. H., 169
Wloch, E. G., 119
Wojtunik-Kulesza, K. A., 59
Wolchik, S. A., 391
Wolinsky, F. D., 97
Wong, F. K. Y., 138
Wong, P. T. P., 390
Wood, E., 384

Wood, S., 232
Woodhead, E. L., 217
Woods, S. P., 167
Woodward, A. T., 273, 275
Worden, W., 387
Worthington, J., 65
Wortman, C. B., 390
Wrenn, R. L., 394
Wright, A. J., 276, 278
Wright, S., 341
Wrosch, C., 235, 408
Wrzesniewski, A., 341
Wrzus, C., 249, 250
Wu, A. Y., 406
Wu, H.-S., 322
Wu, L., 291
Wu, S., 262
Wu, Z., 97
Wurtele, S. K., 217
Wyatt, A., 144, 152

Xiao, J. J, 265
Xu, X., 314

Yaakobi, E., 379
Yaffe, K., 37
Yamasaki, T., 34
Yang, T., 314
Yang, Z., 63
Yarwood, A., 65
Yashin, A. I., 60
Yates, F. A., 172
Yates, P. J., 174
Ybarra, O., 227
Yesavage, J. A., 281
Yeung, S. E., 409
Yeung, S. M., 138
Yin, D., 58
Yin, X., 36
Yngvesson, B., 329
Yoder, L. H., 144
Yon, Y., 316
Yoon, S. M., 334
Ytterstad, E., 325
Yu, F., 145
Yu, X., 320
Yu, X., 358
Yuen, H. K., 137

Zabriskie, R. B., 361
Zahodne, L. B., 196
Zajacova, A., 116, 119
Zanjani, F., 22, 23
Zarit, J. M., 273, 280, 299
Zarit, S. H., 118, 151, 152, 273, 280, 299
Zaval, L., 205, 206
Zeisel, J., 173
Zelinski, E. M., 195
Zeng, Y., 265
Zetumer, S., 394
Zhan, H. J., 331
Zhang, B., 361
Zhang, G., 312
Zhang, J., 130
Zhang, M., 137
Zhao, L., 291
Zheng, Z., 297
Zhu, B., 49, 209
Ziaei, M., 41
Ziegler, M., 196
Zimprich, D., 195, 248
Zogg, J. B., 115, 167
Zurlo, K. A., 280

Glossary/Subject Index

Note: Page numbers in bold indicate glossary terms, those with f indicate figures, and those with t indicate tables.

AARP, 82, 334, 362
Abandonment, 315
Absorption The time needed for a medication to enter a patient's bloodstream, 114, **124**
Abusive relationship A relationship that one partner displays aggressive behavior toward the other partner, 314, **337**
Acamprosate (Campral), 302
AccessoryDwellings.org, 137, 138
Accommodation Changing one's thought to better approximate the world of experience. (ii) Readjustments of goals and aspirations as a way to lessen or neutralize the effects of negative self-evaluations in key domains, 200, **214**, 235, **242**
Acetylcholine, 36
Activation imaging approach Attempts to directly link functional brain activity with cognitive behavioral data, 33, **54**
Active euthanasia The deliberate ending of someone's life, 375, **399**
Active life expectancy The age to which one can expect to live independently, 93–94, **124**
Activities of daily living (ADLs) Basic self-care tasks such as eating, bathing, toileting, walking, and dressing, 119–120, 119t, **124**
Acuity, 69
Acute diseases Conditions that develop over a short period of time and cause a rapid change in health, 100–101, **124**
Adaptation, 68
Adaptation level In Lawton and Nahemow's model, the point at which competence and environmental press are in balance, 129, 130, **155**
Administration on Aging (AoA), 412
Adult day care Designed to provide support, companionship, and certain services during the day, 138, **155**
Adult development
  core issues in, 11–14
  culture and, 9–10
  ethnicity and, 9–10
  forces of, 8–9
  issues in studying, 7–14
  neuroscience and, 33–42
  perspectives on, 3–7
  research methods, 15–24
Advance directives, 150
Aerobic exercise Exercise that places moderate stress on the heart by maintaining a pulse rate between 60% and 90% of the person's maximum heart rate, 414, **420**

Affordable Health Care Act, 142–143, 334, 377, 396, 407
African Americans. *See also* Race and ethnicity
  obesity rates, 417
  poverty rates and, 405
Age-based double standard When an individual attributes an older person's failure in memory as more serious than a memory failure observed in a young adult, 218, **242**
Age discrimination Denying a job or a promotion to a person solely on the basis of age, 351, **370**
Age Discrimination in Employment Act, 351
Age effects One of the three fundamental effects examined in developmental research, along with cohort and time-of-measurement effects, which reflects the influence of time-dependent processes on development, 17, 18t, **27**
Ageism The untrue assumption that chronological age is the main determinant of human characteristics and that one age is better than another, 3, **27**
Age-related macular degeneration (AMD), 68–69
Aging
  antiaging interventions, 60–61
  culture and, 9–10
  demographics of, 4–7, 5f
  ethnicity and, 9–10
  issues in studying, 7–14
  meaning of, 10–11
  mental health and, 275
  myths about, 3
  neuroscience and, 33–42
  perspectives on, 3–7
  in place, 135–136
  research methods, 15–24
  sleep and, 84
  stereotypes about, 3
Agreeableness, 247
AIDS dementia complex (ADC), 297–298
AIDS.gov, 100
Alcohol-related dementia, 297
Alcohol use disorder (AUD) A drinking pattern that results in significant and recurrent consequences that reflect loss of reliable control over alcohol use, 300–302, 300t, **306**
  diagnosis of, 300t
  medications for, 301–302
Ali, Muhammad, 297
Alienation Situation in which workers feel what they are doing is meaningless and their efforts are devalued, or when they do not see the connection between what they do and the final product, 345, **370**
Alzheimer's Association, 285, 286, 287, 288, 289, 290, 295, 302
Alzheimer's disease An irreversible form of dementia characterized by progressive

declines in cognitive and bodily functions, eventually resulting in death; it accounts for about 70% of all cases of dementia, 285–296, **306**
  behavioral interventions, 292–294
  caring for patients at home, 295–298
  cause of, 291–292
  diagnosis of, 288, 289f, 290
  genetic factors in, 291–292, 304
  medications for, 292
  neurological changes in, 286–287, 286f
  progression of, through brain, 288f
  symptoms of, 287–288
Ambiguous loss Refers to situations of loss in which there is no resolution or closure, 392–393, **399**
American Academy of Dermatology, 61
American Academy of Neurology, 374
American Academy of Ophthalmology, 69
American Academy of Pain Medicine, 384
American Bar Association, 150
American Cancer Society, 61, 82, 106, 107, 108, 111
American College of Rheumatology, 65
American Diabetes Association, 106
American Geriatrics Society Ethics Committee, 150
American Heart Association, 76, 78, 79, 417
American Lung Association, 79
American Medical Association, 279
American Psychiatric Association, 284
American Psychological Association, 21, 150, 278, 279
American Society for Reproductive Medicine, 81
American Stroke Association, 77
Amygdala The region of the brain, located in the medial-temporal lobe, believed to play a key role in emotion, 35, **54**
Analog hearing aid, 72t
Angelina Jolie effect, 109
Angelou, Maya, 244
Angina pectoris A painful condition caused by temporary constriction of blood flow to the heart, 76, **89**
Anniversary reaction Changes in behavior related to feelings of sadness on the anniversary date of a loss, 389, **399**
Antiaging interventions, 60–61
Anticipatory grief Grief experienced during the period before an expected death occurs that supposedly serves to buffer the impact of the loss when it does come and to facilitate recovery, 388, **399**
Antigens, 99
Antioxidants, 60
Antioxidants Compounds that protect cells from the harmful effects of free radicals, 30, **54**
Anxiety disorders, 298–299
  diagnosis, 298–299
  symptoms of, 298
  treating, 299

Appearance, 61–63
  body build, 62–63
  hair, 62
  psychological implications, 66–67
  skin, 61–62
  voice, 62
Aristotle, 11
Arnett, Donna K., 78
Arthritis
  osteoarthritis, 65–66, 66f, 67t
  rheumatoid, 65–66, 66f, 67t
Arthroplasty, 66
Assessment, 276–279
  developmental issues in therapy, 278–279
  factors influencing, 277–278
  methods, 278
  Mini Mental Status Exam, 276–277, 277t
  multidimensional, areas of, 276–277
  scales, for depression, 281
Assimilation Using currently available knowledge to make sense out of incoming information, 199–200, **214**
Assimilative activities Exercises that prevent or alleviate losses in domains that are personally relevant for self-esteem and identity, 235, **242**
Assisted living facilities Housing options for older adults that provide a supportive living arrangement for people who need assistance with personal care (such as bathing or taking medications) but are not so impaired physically or cognitively they need 24-hour care, 139–140, **155**
Assortative mating A theory that people find partners based on their similarity to each other, 312, **337**
Atherosclerosis A process by which fat is deposited on the walls of arteries, 77, 77f, **89**
  cerebrovascular accident, 77–78
  hypertension, 78
  hypotension, 78–79
Attention, 160–162
  automatic processing, 162
  basics of, 160
  effortful processing, 162
  processing resources, 160–162
  speed of processing, 160
Attentional resources, 161–162
Attributional biases, 229–231, 230f
Australian Government Department of Social Services, 133
Autobiographical memory Remembering information and events from your own life, 168–169, **183**
Autoimmunity The process by which the immune system begins attacking the body, 100, **124**
Automatic processing Processes that are fast, reliable, and insensitive to increased cognitive demands, 162, **183**
Autonomic nervous system The nerves in the body outside the brain and spinal column, 83–84, **89**
  body temperature, regulating, 83–84
  psychological implications, 84
  sleep and aging, 84

Average longevity The length of time it takes for half of all people born in a certain year to die, 92–94, 92–97, 93f, **124**
  environmental factors in, 94–95
  ethnic differences in, 95
  gender differences in, 95–96
  genetic factors in, 94
  international differences in, 96–97
Axon A structure of the neuron that contains neurofibers, 34, **54**

Baby boomers, 6, 9, 18, 402, 403, 405–406, 407
Backup care Emergency care for dependent children or adults so the employee does not need to lose a day of work, 356, **370**
Balance, 63, 73
Battered woman syndrome A situation in which a woman believes she cannot leave an abusive relationship and where she may even go so far as to kill her abuser, 314, **337**
Becker, Bob, 57
Behavior therapy A type of psychotherapy that focuses on and attempts to alter current behavior. Underlying causes of the problem may not be addressed, 284, **306**
Bell, Alexander Graham, 94
Benign prostatic hyperplasia (BPH), 111
Bereavement The state or condition caused by loss through death, 387, **399**
Bergoglio, Jorge Mario, 2
Berry, Halle, 69
Beta-amyloid A type of protein involved in the formation of neuritic plaques both in normal aging and in Alzheimer's disease, 287, **306**
Beta-amyloid cascade hypothesis The process that beta-amyloid deposits create neuritic plaques, that in turn lead to neurofibrillary tangles, that cause neuronal death and, when this occurs severely enough, Alzheimer's disease, 291–292, **306**
Bin Laden, Osama, 169
Bioethics Study of the interface between human values and technological advances in health and life sciences, 374–375, **399**
Biological age, 11
Biological forces One of four basic forces of development that includes all genetic and health-related factors, 8, 8f, **27**
Biological theories, of age related changes, 57–61
  cellular theories, 58–60
  forces of adult development and, 60–61
  genetic programming theories, 60
  metabolic theories, 58
Biopsychosocial framework Way of organizing the biological, psychological, and sociocultural forces on human development, 8–9, 8f, **27**
B-lymphocytes, 99
Body build, 62–63
Body mass index (BMI) A ratio of body weight and height that is related to total body fat, 417, 418f, **420**
Body temperature, regulating, 83–84
Bones, 63–65, 67t
  calcium and vitamin D intakes, recommended, 65t
  osteoporosis, 64–65, 64f, 67t

Brain, 33–42. *See also* Brain structures
  age-related changes in, 35–42
  default network of, 48
  neurons and, 34, 35
  neurotransmitters and, 34, 35–36
  organization of, 34–35, 34–35f
  plasticity and, 48–51
Brain structures
  age-related changes in, 36–42
  linking with emotion, 38–41
  linking with executive functioning, 37
  linking with memory, 37–38
  linking with social-emotional cognition, 41–42
  major, 34–35, 35f
  prefrontal cortex and, 35, 42
  Theory of Mind and, 37–42
BRCA1, 108, 111
BRCA2, 108, 111
Breast cancer, 107, 108, 109, 110t
Bronchodilators, 79
Bureau of Labor Statistics, 323, 354, 355
Burnout The depletion of a person's energy and motivation, the loss of occupational idealism, and the feeling of being exploited, 345–346, 346f, **370**
Bush, George H. W., 216
Bush, George W., 169

Calcium intake, recommended, 65t
Calment, Jeanne, 91, 93
Cancer, 106–108
  Angelina Jolie effect and, 109
  breast, 107, 108, 109, 110t
  cervical, 107, 110t
  colorectal, 107, 110t
  early detection of, ACS guidelines for, 110–111t
  genetics and, 108, 109
  incidence and mortality rates, 107t
  lung, 107, 110t
  prostate, 106, 107, 108, 110–111t, 111–112
Cancer Genome Anatomy Program (CGAP), 108
Cardiovascular diseases, 75–79
  angina pectoris, 76
  congestive heart failure, 76
  myocardial infarction, 76
Cardiovascular system, 75–79, 76f
  atherosclerosis, 77–79, 77f
  cardiovascular diseases, 75–76
Career construction theory Posits people build careers through their own actions that result from the interface of their own personal characteristics and the social context, 341, **370**
Career plateauing Situation occurring when there is a lack of challenge in the job or promotional opportunity in the organization or when a person decides not to seek advancement, 352, **370**
Carville, James, 216
Case study An intensive investigation of individual people, 17, **27**
Cataracts Opaque spots on the lens of the eye, 68, **89**
Causal attributions Explanations people construct to explain their behavior, that can be situational, dispositional, or interactive, 229, **242**
Cavanaugh, John, 272

Cell-mediated immunity, 99
Cellular theories, 58–60
Census Bureau, 6, 316, 317, 318, 319
Centers for Disease Control and Prevention, 77, 85, 100, 101, 384, 408, 412, 417, 418
Centers for Medicare and Medicaid Services, 141, 143–144, 145, 146, 152, 407
Cerebellum The part of the brain that is associated with motor functioning and balance equilibrium, 35, **54**
Cerebral cortex The outermost part of the brain consisting of two hemispheres (left and right), 34, **54**
Cerebrovascular accident (CVA) An interruption of the blood flow in the brain, 77–79, **89**
Cervical cancer, 107, 110t
Chronic diseases Conditions that last a longer period of time (at least 3 months) and may be accompanied by residual functional impairment that necessitates long-term management, 100–101, 105–113, **124**. *See also* Cancer
  common, 106–112
  diabetes mellitus, 106
  general issues in, 105–106
  incontinence, 108, 109, 112
  pain management, 112–113
Chronic obstructive pulmonary disease (COPD) A family of age-related lung diseases that block the passage of air and cause abnormalities inside the lungs, 79, **89**
Chronic traumatic encephalopathy (CTE), 179
Chronological age, 11
Circadian rhythms, 84
Climacteric The transition during which a woman's reproductive capacity ends and ovulation stops, 80, **89**
Clinical death Lack of heartbeat and respiration, 374, **399**
Clinton, Bill, 69, 216
Clinton, Hillary Rodham, 2, 225, 266
Cochlear implant, 72t
Cognitive behavior therapy, 283t, 284–285
Cognitive behavior therapy A type of psychotherapy aimed at altering the way people think as a cure for some forms of psychopathology, especially depression. delirium A disorder characterized by a disturbance of consciousness and a change in cognition that develop over a short period of time, 284–285, **306**
Cognitive processes A structural component of personality that acts jointly with life narratives to create natural interactions between a storyteller and listener, processes central in organizing life stories, 245, **268**
Cognitive reserve Factors that provide flexibility in responding and adapting to changes in the environment, 171, **183**
Cognitive-structural approach An approach to intelligence that emphasizes the ways people conceptualize problems and focuses on modes or styles of thinking, 189, **214**
Cognitive style as processing goal, 233
Cognitive style A trait-like pattern of behavior one uses when approaching a problem-solving situation, 233, **242**

Cohabitation Living with another person as part of a committed, intimate, sexual relationship, 317–318, **337**
Cohort A group of people born at the same point in time or within a specific time span, 9, **28**
Cohort effects One of the three basic influences examined in developmental research, along with age and time-of-measurement effects, which reflects differences caused by experiences and circumstances unique to the historical-time in which one lives, 17–18, 18t, **28**
Colbert, Stephen, 69
Collaborative cognition Cognitive performance that results from the interaction of two or more individuals, 237–238, **242**
Collagen, 59
Colorectal cancer, 107, 110t
Commonwealth Fund, The, 152
Community options, 133–140
  adult daycare, 138
  aging in place, 135–136
  assisted living, 139–140
  congregate housing, 138–139
  deciding on best option, 136
  home modification, 136–138
Compensation-Related Utilization of Neural Circuits Hypothesis (CRUNCH) model A model that describes how the aging brain adapts to neurological decline by recruiting additional neural circuits (in comparison to younger adults) to perform tasks adequately, 46, **54**
Compensatory changes Changes that allow older adults to adapt to the inevitable behavioral decline resulting from changes in specific areas of the brain, 33, **54**
Competence In the Lawton and Nahemow model, the theoretical upper limit of a person's ability to function, 128–130, **155**
  age stereotypes and perceived competence, 217–218
  person–environment interactions and, 128–130, 129f, 132–133
  social, 236–238
  technology to maintain and enhance, 410–411
  theoretical themes and everyday competence, 132–133
Complicated grief Expression of grief that is distinguished from depression and from normal grief in terms of separation distress and traumatic distress, 393, **399**
Compression of morbidity The situation in which the average age when one becomes disabled for the first time is postponed, causing the time between the onset of disability and death to be compressed into a shorter period of time, 117, **124**
Concrete operational period, 200
Concussions and athletes, 178–179
Confounding Any situation in which one cannot determine which of two or more effects is responsible for the behaviors being observed, 18, **28**
Congestive heart failure A condition occurring when cardiac output and the ability of the heart to contract severely decline, making

the heart enlarge, increasing pressure to the veins, and making the body swell, 76, **89**
Congregate housing, 138–139
Conscientiousness, 247
Continuity–discontinuity controversy The debate over whether a particular developmental phenomenon represents smooth progression over time (continuity) or a series of abrupt shifts (discontinuity), 13, **28**
Coping In the stress and coping paradigm, any attempt to deal with stress, 103, **124**
  person–environment interactions and, 132
Corpus callosum A thick bundle of neurons that connects the left and right hemispheres of the cerebral cortex, 34, **54**
Corrective adaptations Actions taken in response to stressors and can be facilitated by internal and external resources, 130–132, 131f, **155**
Correlational study An investigation in which the strength of association between variables is examined, 17, **28**
Correspondence bias The tendency to draw inferences about older people's dispositions from behavior that can be fully explained through situational factors, 229, **242**
Cosby, Bill, 351
Council for Adult and Experiential Learning, 208
Council on Contemporary Families, 325
Couple-forming behavior, 312
Creativity, 208–209, 209f, 210
Cross-linking Random interaction between proteins that produce molecules that make the body stiffer, 59, **89**
Cross-sectional study A developmental research design in which people of different ages and cohorts are observed at one time of measurement to obtain information about age differences, 18–19, 19t, 22–23, **28**
Cruzan, Nancy, 375
Crystallized intelligence Knowledge acquired through life experience and education in a particular culture, 192t, 193, 194f, **214**
Culture, 9–10. *See also* Race and ethnicity
  activities of daily living and, 119
  adoption and, 329
  caregiving and, 334
  cohabitation and, 317–318
  couple-forming behavior and, 312
  death and dying and, 373–374, 375
  grandparenthood and, 332–334
  grief processing and, 387, 389, 393, 396
  job satisfaction and, 344–346
  leisure activities and, 361
  normative history-graded influences and, 9
  nursing home residents and, 141, 141f
  partner abuse and, 314
  romantic relationships and, 313
  suicide and, 375
  wisdom and, 209
  work-family conflict and, 358

Dalai Lama, 2, 186
Data and Safety Monitoring Board (DSMB), 81
Death and dying, 372–396
  contextual theory of, 380
  dealing with one's own death, 379–380

death anxiety, 380–382
do not resuscitate order, 386
end-of-life issues, 382–386
ethical issues, 374–377
euthanasia, 375
final scenario, 382–383
grieving process, 386–396 (*See also* Grief)
healthcare power of attorney, 385–386
hospice, 383–385
Kübler-Ross's theory, 379–380
legal and medical definitions of, 374
life-course approach to, 378–379
life-sustaining care, 377
living will, 385–386
patient self-determination and competency evaluation, 386
physician-assisted suicide, 375–377
self-reflective exercise on, 378
social policy implications, 396
sociocultural definitions of, 373–374
Death anxiety People's anxiety or even fear of death and dying, 380–382, **399**
Death with Dignity Act, 376
Decision making, 205
Default network of the brain The regions of the brain that are most active at rest, 48, **54**
Defense and Veterans Brain Injury Center, 178
Delirium A disorder characterized by a disturbance of consciousness and a change in cognition that develop over a short period of time, 285, **306**
Dementia A family of diseases characterized by cognitive decline. Alzheimer's disease is the most common form, 285–298, **306**
  AIDS dementia complex, 297–298
  alcohol-related dementia, 297
  Alzheimer's disease, 285–296
  caring for patients at home, 295–298
  dementia with Lewy bodies, 296
  Huntington's disease, 297
  Parkinson's disease, 296–297
  training persons with, to be group leaders, 294–295
  vascular dementia, 296
Dementia with Lewy bodies, 296
Demographers People who study population trends, 4, **28**
Demographics
  of aging, 4–7, 5f
  trends in, 402–407
Dendrites A structural feature of a neuron that acts like antennas to receive signals from other nearby neurons, 34, **54**
DeNiro, Robert, 45
Dependency ratio The ratio of the number of people under age 15 and over age 64 in a country to the number of people between 15 and 64, 403–404, 403f, **420**
Dependent care dilemma, 355–356
  effects on workers, 355–356
  employed caregivers, 355
  employer responses and, 356
  Family and Medical Leave Act, 355
  household chores, 356
Dependent life expectancy The age to which one can expect to live with assistance, 93–94, **124**

Dependent variable Behaviors or outcomes measured in an experiment, 16–17, **28**
Depression, 279–285
  age at diagnosis, 279
  assessment scales, 281
  causes of, 281–282
  ethnic groups and, 279–280, 280f
  symptoms and characteristics of, 280–281
  treatment of, 282–285, 283t
Descartes, René, 11
Designer drugs, 94
Designs for studying development, 17–21, 22–23
Developmental coach Individual who helps a person focus on his or her goals, motivations, and aspirations to help the person achieve focus and apply them appropriately, 343, **370**
Developmental forces. *See* Forces of adult development
Diabetes mellitus A disease that occurs when the pancreas produces insufficient insulin, 106, **124**
Diabetic retinopathy, 69, 106
Diastolic pressure, 78
Diaz, Dan, 376–377
Differential reinforcement of incompatible behavior (DRI), 294
Diffusion tensor imaging (DTI) A type of magnetic resonance imaging that measures the diffusion of water molecules in tissue to study connections of neural pathways in the brain, 36–37, **54**
Digital hearing aid, 72t
Disability The effects of chronic conditions on people's ability to engage in activities that are necessary, expected, and personally desired in their society, 116–118, 118f, 118t, **124**
  of AHEAD living cohort by gender, 119f
  causes of, 120
  compression of morbidity and, 117
  exacerbators, 117, 118
  global differences in, 120
  model of, 116–118, 118f
  risk factors, 117
  socioeconomic factors in, 120
Disease prevention, 412–413, 413t
  issues in, 412–413
  types of, 412–413, 413t
Diseases, 100–101
Disenfranchised grief A loss that appears insignificant to others but is highly consequential to the person who suffers the loss, 395, **399**
Dispositional attribution An explanation for someone's behavior that resides within the actor, 229, 230f, **242**
Dispositional trait A relatively stable, enduring aspect of personality, 245–250, **268**
  across adulthood, 247–249
  conclusions about, 249
  five-factor model, 246–247
  TESSERA model and, 249, 250f
Disulfiram (Antabuse), 301
Diversity of older adults, 6–7. *See also* Culture
Divided attention The ability to pay attention and successfully perform more than one task at a time, 161, **183**

Divorce, 322–324
  effects of, 324
  rates, 323f
  reasons for, 323–324
Docility When people allow the situation to dictate the options they have and exert little control, 129, **156**
Docosahexaenoic acid (DHA), 51
Donne, John, 395
Do not resuscitate (DNR) order A medical order that means cardiopulmonary resuscitation (CPR) is not started should one's heart and breathing stop, 386, **399**
Dopamine A neurotransmitter associated with higher-level cognitive functioning, 36, **54**
Dopaminergic system Neuronal systems that use dopamine as their major neurotransmitter, 36, **54**
Dornenburg, Noreen and Mary, 310
Drug excretion The process of eliminating medications, usually through the kidneys in urine, but also through sweat, feces, and saliva, 114, **124**
Drug holiday, 65
Drug metabolism The process of getting rid of medications in the bloodstream, partly in the liver, 114, **124**
Dual process model (DPM) View of coping with bereavement that integrates loss-oriented stressors and restoration-oriented stressors, 391, 392f, **399**
Duerson, Dave, 179
Dysphoria Feeling down or blue, marked by extreme sadness; the major symptom of depression, 280, **306**

Echo boomers, 9
Ecology of aging Also called environmental psychology, a field of study that seeks to understand the dynamic relations between older adults and the environments they inhabit, 133–140, **156**
Eden Alternative, 151
Effortful processing It requires all of the available attentional capacity when processing information, 162, **183**
Ego development The fundamental changes in the ways our thoughts, values, morals, and goals are organized. Transitions from one stage to another depend on both internal biological changes and external social changes to which the person must adapt, 248, **268**
Eicosapentaenoic acid (EPA), 51
E-I-E-I-O model of memory, 173, 173t
Elder Justice Act, 334–335
Electroconvulsive therapy (ECT), 283t, 284
Emerging adulthood A period when individuals are not adolescents but are not yet fully adults, 11, **28**
Emotional intelligence People's ability to recognize their own and others' emotions, to correctly identify and appropriately tell the difference between emotions, and use this information to guide their thinking and behavior, 224, **242**
Emotion-focused coping A style of coping that involves dealing with one's feelings about the stressful event, 103, **124**

Emotions
    linking with structural changes in brain, 38–41
    logic and, integrating, 203–204
    as processing goal, 232–233
    well-being and, 262
Emphysema Most serious form of COPD characterized by the destruction of the membranes around the air sacs in the lungs, 79, **89**
Employment in late life, 364–365, 364f. *See also* Occupational development; Occupational selection; Work
Encoding The process of getting information into the memory system, 162, 165–166, **183**
End-of-life issues Issues pertaining to the management of the final phase of life, after-death disposition of the body, memorial services, and distribution of assets, 382–386, **399**
    competency evaluation and, 386
    do not resuscitate order, 386
    final scenario, creating, 382–383
    healthcare power of attorney, 385–386
    hospice option, 383–385
    living will, 385–386
    making intentions known, 385–386
    Patient Self-Determination Act and, 386
Environmental press In the Lawton and Nahemow model, the demands put on a person by the environment, 128–130, 129f, **156**
Epigenetic principle In Erikson's theory, the notion that development is guided by an underlying plan in which certain issues have their own particular times of importance, 252, 253, **268**
Episodic memory The general class of memory having to do with the conscious recollection of information from a specific event or point in time, 164, 165, 171, **184**
Equal Employment Opportunity Commission, 351
Equality Act of 2010, 351
Equality and Human Rights Commission, 351
Erikson's stages of psychosocial development, 252–256, 252t
Ethics
    in death and dying, 374–377
    in research methods, 21, 24
European Association of Palliative Care, 375
Euthanasia The practice of ending life for reasons of mercy, 375, **399**
Everyday competence A person's potential ability to perform a wide range of activities considered essential for independent living, 132–133, **156**
Exacerbators Situations that makes a situation worse than it was originally, 117, **124**
Exchange theory A theory of relationships based on the idea each partner contributes something to the relationship the other would be hard-pressed to provide, 320, **337**
Executive functions Include the ability to make and carry out plans, switch between tasks, and maintain attention and focus, 35, **54**
    linking with structural changes in brain, 37

Exercise, 414–415
    brain aging and, 49, 50
    memory and, 171
Experimental design, 16–17
Experiment A study in which participants are randomly assigned to experimental and control groups and in which an independent variable is manipulated to observe its effects on a dependent variable so that cause-and-effect relations can be established, 16–17, **28**
Expertise, 207–208
Explicit memory The conscious and intentional recollection of information, 163–164, **184**
Exploitation, 315
Extended family The most common family form globally in which grandparents and other relatives live with parents and children, 326, **337**
External aids Memory aids that rely on environmental resources, 173–174, 173t, **184**
Extraversion, 247
Eyes. *See* Vision

Factor analysis, 191
Factor The interrelations among performances on similar tests of psychometric intelligence, 191, **214**
False memory When one remembers items or events that did not occur, 170, **184**
Familism Refers to the idea the well-being of the family takes precedence over the concerns of individual family members, 328, **337**
Family and Medical Leave Act (FMLA), 330, 355
Family and work, 355–358
    dependent care dilemma, 355–356
    multiple roles, 356, 357f
    work-family conflict, 358
Family dynamics, 326–334
    grandparenthood, 332–334
    midlife issues, 330–332
    parental role, 326–330
Federal Interagency Forum on Aging Related Statistics, 404
Female reproductive system, 80–82
Filial obligation The feeling that, as an adult child, one must care for one's parents, 331, **337**
Final scenario Making choices known about how one does and does not want one's life to end, 382–383, **399**
Five-factor model A model of dispositional traits with the dimensions of neuroticism, extraversion, openness to experience, agreeableness–antagonism, and conscientiousness–undirectedness, 246–247, **268**
Flashbulb memories Memories for personally traumatic or unexpected events, 169, **184**
Fluid intelligence Abilities that make one a flexible and adaptive thinker, that allow one to draw inferences, and allow one to understand the relations among concepts independent of acquired knowledge and experience, 192, 192t, 193, 194f, **214**
Forces of adult development, 8–9
    biological forces, 8
    biological theories and, 60–61

    biopsychosocial framework for organizing, 8–9, 8f
    interrelations among, 9
    life-cycle forces, 8
    nonnormative influences and, 9
    normative age-graded influences and, 9
    normative history-graded influences and, 9
    psychological forces, 8
    sociocultural forces, 8
Foreman, George, 57, 60
Formal operational period, 200–201
Four-component model Model of grief that understanding grief is based on (1) the context of the loss; (2) continuation of subjective meaning associated with loss; (3) changing representations of the lost relationship over time; and (4) the role of coping and emotion regulation processes, 389–390, **399**
Fox, Michael J., 297
Frail older adults Older adults who have physical disabilities, are very ill, and may have cognitive or psychological disorders and need assistance with everyday tasks, 119, **125**
Francis, Pope, 2, 11, 12
Free radicals Substances that can damage cells, including brain cells, and play a role in cancer and other diseases as we grow older. (ii) Unstable chemicals produced randomly in normal metabolism that are thought to cause aging, 30, **54**, 59–60, **89**
Freud, Sigmund, 244, 251
Friendships, 308–311
    in adulthood, 309–310
    developmental aspects of, 310–311
    men's, women's, and cross-sex friendships, 311
    socioemotional selectivity and, 311
Functional health status How well a person is functioning in daily life, 119–120, **125**
    causes of, 120
    determining, 119–120
    socioeconomic factors in, 120
Functional incontinence A type of incontinence usually caused when the urinary tract is intact but due to physical disability or cognitive impairment the person is unaware of the need to urinate, 112, **125**
Functional neuroimaging Provides an indication of brain activity but not high anatomical detail, 31–32, **54**

Gay Men's Health Crisis, 100
Gender differences
    in average longevity, 95–96
    in hearing loss, 70f
    in mental health, 275–276
    in occupational selection a, 346–351
    in retirement, 363
Gender discrimination Denying a job to someone solely on the basis of whether the person is a man or a woman, 349, **370**
Generation X, 9, 403, 406
Generation Y, 9
Generativity, 254–255
Genetic factors
    in Alzheimer's disease, 291–292, 304
    in average longevity, 94
    in cancer, 108, 109

Genetic programming theories, 60
Genworth Financial, 140, 142
Gerontological Society of America, 149
Gerontology The study of aging from maturity through old age, 3, **28**
Glass ceiling The level to which a woman may rise in an organization but beyond which she may not go, 349, **370**
Glass cliff A situation in which a woman's leadership position in an organization is precarious, 349, **370**
Glaucoma A disease in the eye caused by improper drainage of fluid in the eye resulting in internal damage and progressive loss of vision, 68, **89**
Grandparenthood, 332–334
Green House project, 151–152
Gregory II, Pope, 12
Grief The sorrow, hurt, anger, guilt, confusion, and other feelings that arise after suffering a loss, 387–392, **399**
  adult developmental aspects of, 393–395
  ambiguous loss and, 392–393
  complicated or prolonged, 393
  coping with, 389–392
  death of child, 394
  death of parent, 395
  deliberate grief avoidance and, 390–391, 391f
  disenfranchised, 395
  dual process model and, 391, 392f
  four-component model and, 389–390
  model of adaptive grieving dynamics and, 391–392, 392f
  process, 387–388
  reactions, 388–389
  risk factors in, 388
  in young adulthood, 393–394
Grief work as rumination hypothesis An approach that not only rejects the necessity of grief processing for recovery from loss but views extensive grief processing as a form of rumination that may actually increase distress, 390, **400**
Grief work The psychological side of coming to terms with bereavement, 388–389, **399**
Grieving process, 386–396. *See also* Grief
Guilford-Zimmerman Temperament Survey (GZTS), 247

Hair, 62
Hayflick, Leonard, 58
Hayflick limit, 58
Healthcare power of attorney A document in which an individual appoints someone to act as his or her agent for healthcare decisions, 385–386, **400**
Health promotion, 409–410
Health-related quality of life Includes all of the aspects of life that are affected by changes in one's health status, 98, **125**
Health The absence of acute and chronic physical or mental disease and impairments, 97–98, 97–121, **125**
  chronic conditions and, 105–113
  defining, 97–98
  disability and, 116–118, 118f
  diseases and, 100–101
  functional health status and, 119–120

immune system and, 98–100
medications and, 113–116
memory and, 178
quality of life, 98
social policy implications, 121
stress and, 101–105
Healthy aging Involves avoiding disease, being engaged with life, and maintaining high cognitive and physical functioning, 408–418, **420**
  competence and, 410–411
  defined, 408–409
  disease prevention and, 412–413, 413t
  health promotion and, 409–410
  lifestyle factors and, 414–418
  quality of life and, 409–410
Hearing, 69–72
  aids for hearing loss, 72t
  gender differences in hearing loss, 70f
  presbycusis, 70–71
  quality of life among community-dwelling and, 71
Heart attack. *See* Myocardial infarction (MI)
Helpguide.org, 355
Hemispheric Asymmetry Reduction in OLDer adults (HAROLD) model A model that explains the empirical findings of reduced lateralization in prefrontal lobe activity in older adults (that is, the reduced ability of older adults to separate cognitive processing in different parts of the prefrontal cortex), 46, **54**
Henry J. Kaiser Family Foundation, 386
Hierarchy of loss Sequence of the loss of functional abilities, 119, **125**
High-density lipoproteins (HDLs) Help keep arteries clear and break down LDLs, 417, **420**
Hippocampus Located in the medial-temporal lobe, this part of the brain plays a major role in memory and learning, 35, **54**
Historical context, 4
HIV/AIDS, 100
Hollwich, Matthias, 134–135
Home modification, 136–138
Homogamy The notion similar interests and values are important in forming strong, lasting, interpersonal relationships, 319–320, **337**
Hospice An approach to assisting dying people that emphasizes pain management, or palliative care, and death with dignity, 383–385, **400**
Hospice Foundation of America, 384
HOXB13, 108, 111
HPC1, 108
HPV, 110t
Human Connectome Project, 30
Hunter Imagination Questionnaire (HIQ), 209
Huntington's disease, 297
Huntington's Disease Society of America, 297
Hyde, William, 94
Hypertension A disease in which one's blood pressure is too high, 78, **89**
Hypotension, 78–79

Illness The presence of a physical or mental disease or impairment, 97–98, 97–121, **125**
  chronic conditions and, 105–113
  defining, 97–98
  disability and, 116–118, 118f

diseases and, 100–101
functional health status and, 119–120
immune system and, 98–100
medications and, 113–116
quality of life, 98
social policy implications, 121
stress and, 101–105
Immune system, 98–100
  aging process of, 99f
  autoimmunity and, 100
  HIV/AIDS, 100
  psychoneuroimmunology and, 100
Immunizing mechanisms Control strategies that alter the effects of self-discrepant evidence, 235, **242**
Immunoglobulins, 99
Implicit memory The effortless and unconscious recollection of information, 163–164, **184**
Implicit stereotyping Stereotyped beliefs that affect your judgments of individuals without your being aware of it (i.e, the process is unconscious), 219, **242**
Impression formation The way people combine the components of another person's personality and come up with an integrated perception of the person, 224–227, 226f, **242**
Incontinence The loss of the ability to control the elimination of urine and feces on an occasional or consistent basis, 108, 109, 112, **125**
Independent variable The variable manipulated in an experiment, 16–17, **28**
Infantilization or elderspeak Also called secondary baby talk, a type of speech that involves the unwarranted use of a person's first name, terms of endearment, simplified expressions, short imperatives, an assumption that the recipient has no memory, and cajoling as a means of demanding compliance, 147–149, **156**
Information-processing model The study of how people take in stimuli from their environment and transform them into memories; the approach is based on a computer metaphor, 159–160, **184**
Inhibitory loss, 160–161
Instrumental activities of daily living (IADLs) Actions that entail some intellectual competence and planning, 119–120, 119t, **125**
Intelligence, 186–211. *See also* Thinking
  cognitive-structural approach and, 189
  crystallized, 192t, 193, 194f
  defining, 187–189
  developmental trends in, 190–199
  in everyday life, 187
  factor, 191
  fluid, 192, 192t, 193, 194f
  lifelong learning and, 208
  life-span view and, 187–189, 188f
  mechanics of, 188, 188f
  multidimensional, 187–188
  pragmatic, 188, 188f
  primary mental abilities and, 191–192, 191f
  psychometric approach and, 189
  qualitative differences in adults' thinking and, 199–204
  research approaches to, 189
  social policy implications, 211
  structure of, 190–191

Interindividual variability An acknowledgment adults differ in the direction of their intellectual development, 188, **214**
Internal aids Memory aids that rely on mental processes, 173, 173t, 174, **184**
International differences in average longevity, 96–97
International Labour Organization, 351

Jackson, Michael, 169
Jagger, Mick, 2
James, William, 244
Jarmul, Champa, 365
Jarmul, David, 365
Job satisfaction The positive feeling that results from an appraisal of one' work, 344–346, **370**
Joints, 65–66, 66f, 67t
  osteoarthritis, 65–66, 66f, 67t
  rheumatoid arthritis, 65–66, 66f, 67t
Jolie, Angelina, 108, 109
Jung, Carl, 244, 251–252, 256
Jung's theory, 251–252

Kaiser Family Foundation, 407
Kelley, Ken, 244
Kennedy, John F., 366
Kinkeeper The person who gathers family members together for celebrations and keeps them in touch with each other, 330, **337**
Knowledge accessibility, 227–228
Kowalek, Stephanie, 210
Kronos Early Estrogen Prevention Study (KEEPS), 81
!Kung tribe, 10, 14

Labeling theory Argues that when we confront an age-related stereotype, older adults are more likely to integrate it into their self-perception, 223, **242**
Latinos. *See also* Race and ethnicity
  obesity rates, 417
  poverty rates and, 405
Leisure A discretionary activity that includes simple relaxation, activities for enjoyment, and creative pursuits, 359–366, **370**
  consequences of, 361–362
  developmental changes in, 360
  long-term effects of, 360
  types of, 359–360
Lewis, John, 2
Lewy Body Dementia Association, 296
LGBTQ, 318
Life-cycle forces One of the four basic forces of development that reflects differences in how the same event or combination of biological, psychological, and sociocultural forces affects people at different points in their lives, 8, 8f, **28**
Lifelong learning, 208
Life narrative The aspects of personality that pull everything together, those integrative aspects that give a person an identity or sense of self, 245, 258–265, **268**
Life-Space Mobility in Old Age (LISPE) project, 71

Life-span construct In Whitbourne's theory of identity, the way people build a view of who they are, 259, **268**
Life-span development, 4, 12, 254, 273, 274, 408
Life-span perspective A view of the human life span that divides it into two phases: childhood/adolescence and young/middle/late adulthood, 4, **28**, 408, 410
Lifestyle factors, 414–418
  exercise, 414–415
  nutrition, 415–417, 418f
Life transitions, theories based on, 256–257
Lilly Ledbetter Fair Pay Act, 366
Limbic system A set of brain structures involved with emotion, motivation, and long-term memory, among other functions, 35, **54**
Living will A document in which a person states his or her wishes about life support and other treatments, 385–386, **400**
Locke, John, 11
Longevity, 91–97. *See also* **Average longevity**
  active life expectancy, 93–94
  dependent life expectancy, 93–94
  maximum, 93
  test, 92
Longitudinal study A developmental research design that measures one cohort over two or more times of measurement to examine age changes, 19–20, 19t, 22–23, **28**
LongTermCare.gov, 141
Long-term memory The aspects of memory involved in remembering rather extensive amounts of information over relatively long periods of time, 164–165, **184**
Lorayne, Harry, 172
Love relationships, 311–314
  falling in love, 312–314
  romantic attachment around the world, 313, 313f
  through adulthood, 311–312
Low-density lipoproteins (LDLs) Cause fatty deposits to accumulate in arteries, impeding blood flow, 417, **420**
Lung cancer, 107, 110t

Male reproductive system, 82
Mandela, Nelson, 373
Marital adjustment The degree spouses accommodate each other over a certain period of time, 319, **338**
Marital quality The subjective evaluation of the couple's relationship on a number of different dimensions, 319, **338**
Marital satisfaction A global assessment of one's marriage, 319, **338**
Marital success An umbrella term referring to any marital outcome, 319–320, **338**
Marriage, 318–322
  caring for spouse/partner, 322
  early years of, 321
  happiness in, 320–321
  median age at first marriage, 319f
  at midlife, 321
  older couples, 321–322
  remarriage, 324–325
  successful, 319–320
  vulnerability-stress-adaptation model and, 320–321, 320f

Married singles Married couples who have grown apart but continue to live together, 321, **338**
Mastery, 104
Matalin, Mary, 216
Maximum longevity The maximum length of time an organism can live—roughly 120 years for humans, 93, **125**
Maynard, Brittany, 376–377
McAdams's life story model, 259
McKee, Ann, 179
Meaning-mission fit Alignment between people's personal intentions and their company's mission, 341, **370**
Measurement in research, 15–16
Mechanics of intelligence The aspect of intelligence that concerns the neurophysiological architecture of the mind, 188, 188f, **214**
Medicare, 407
Medications, 113–116
  absorption of, 114
  adherence to medication regimens, 115–116, 115t
  for alcohol use disorder, 301–302
  for Alzheimer's disease, 292
  for anxiety disorders, 299
  for depression, 282–283, 283t
  designer drugs, 94
  drug excretion and, 114
  drug metabolism and, 114
  memory drugs, 174–175, 174t
  patient-by-treatment context interactive framework, 115, 116f
  patterns of use, 113–114
  polypharmacy and, 115
  for schizophrenia, 300
  side effects and interactions, 114–115
Medigap policies, 407
Memory
  aging, normal *vs.* abnormal, 177–178
  autobiographical, 168–169
  drugs, 174–175, 174t
  E-I-E-I-O model of, 173, 173t
  encoding and, 162, 165–166
  episodic, 164, 165, 171
  explicit, 163–164
  external aids for, 173–174, 173t
  false, 170
  flashbulb, 169
  implicit, 163–164
  information-processing model and, 159–160
  internal aids for, 173, 173t, 174
  long-term, 164–165
  mental health and, 178
  metamemory, 175–176
  monitoring, 175–176
  multilingualism and, 171
  negative stereotypes and, 171
  nutrition and, 180
  physical health and, 178
  preserving, 171
  prospective, 167–168, 167f
  rehearsal and, 163
  retrieval and, 162, 166
  self-efficacy, 176
  self-evaluations, 175
  semantic, 164–165, 171
  sensory, 159–160

social context of, 238
social policy implications, 180
source, 170
storage and, 162
structural changes in brain linked with, 37–38
testing, clinical issues and, 177–180
training memory skills, 172–175
transient global amnesia and, 178
working, 162–163
Memory monitoring The awareness of what we are doing in memory right now, 175–176, **184**
Memory self-efficacy The belief in one's ability to perform a specific memory task, 176, **184**
Menopausal hormone therapy (MHT) Low doses of estrogen, which is often combined with progestin (synthetic form of progesterone) taken to counter the effects of declining estrogen levels, 80–82, **89**
Menopause The cessation of the release of eggs by the ovaries, 80, **89**
Mental health, 273–303
aging and, 275
alcohol use disorder, 300–302, 300t
anxiety disorders, 298–299
assessment, 276–279
defining, 273
dementia, 285–298
depression, 279–285
ethnicity and, 275
gender and, 275–276
memory and, 178
psychotic disorders, 299–300
social policy implications, 302–303
Mental status exam A short screening test that assesses mental competence, usually used as a brief indicator of dementia or other serious cognitive impairment, 276–277, 277t, **306**
Mentor A person who is part teacher, sponsor, model, and counselor who facilitates on-the-job learning to help a new hire do the work required in his or her present role and to prepare for future roles, 343–344, **370**
Meta-analysis A technique that allows researchers to synthesize the results of many studies to estimate relations between variables, 21, **28**
Metabolic theories, 58
Metabolism How much energy the body needs, 415, **420**
Metamemory Memory about how memory works and what one believes to be true about it, 175–176, **184**
Microgenetic study A special type of longitudinal design in which participants are tested repeatedly over a span of days or weeks, typically with the aim of observing change directly as it occurs, 19–20, **28**
Middle-aged adults
aging parents of, 331–332
midlife crisis and, 256–257
midlife issues and, 330–332
as parents, 330–331
Midlife correction Reevaluating one's roles and dreams and making the necessary corrections, 257, **268**
Midlife crisis, 256–257

Midlife issues, 330–332
Millennials, 9, 403
Million Women Study, 81
Mini Mental Status Exam (MMSE), 276–277, 277t
Miranda, Lin-Manuel, 210
Mobility, 63–66
balance, 63
bones, 63–65, 67t
joints, 65–66, 66f, 67t
muscles, 63
psychological implications, 66–67
Model of adaptive grieving dynamics (MAGD) A model of grief based on two pairs of adaptive grieving dynamics: lamenting/heartening, and integrating/tempering, 391, 392, 392f, **400**
Modern Maturity sexuality study (AARP), 82
Monoamine oxidase (MAO) inhibitors, 283
Monocytes, 99
Morricone, Ennio, 2
Motivation, 231–233
Mourning The ways in which we express our grief, 387, **400**
Multidimensional The notion intelligence consists of many dimensions, 187–188, **214**
Multidirectionality The distinct patterns of change in abilities over the life span, with these patterns being different for different abilities, 4, 188, **214**
Multilingualism, 171
Multiple causation, 4
Muscles, 63
Myocardial infarction (MI) Also called heart attack, a result of a blockage in blood supply to the heart, 76, **89**

Naltrexone, 301
National Academy of Social Insurance, 406
National Adult Day Services Association, 138, 295
National Adult Protective Services Association, 335
National Alliance for Caregiving & AARP, 331
National Association for the Education of Young Children, 355
National Cancer Institute, 108, 111, 112
National Center for Assisted Living, 139, 140
National Center for Health Statistics, 92, 93, 95, 106, 109, 120, 327, 328, 372
National Center for State Courts, 315
National Comprehensive Cancer Network, 111
National Council on Aging, 73
National Council on Alcoholism and Drug Dependence, 301
National Eye Institute, 69
National Health Interview Survey, 85
National Heart, Lung and Blood Institute, 77, 81
National Institute of Arthritis and Musculoskeletal and Skin Diseases, 65, 67
National Institutes of Health, 16, 21, 60–61, 99
National Institute of Mental Health, 279, 280, 282, 284, 298, 300
National Institute of Neurological Disorders and Stroke, 297
National Institute on Aging, 75, 76, 120, 286, 287, 290

National Institute on Alcohol Abuse and Alcoholism, 300, 301
National Osteoporosis Foundation, 64, 65
National Women's Law Center, 350
Natural killer (NK) cells, 99
Nature–nurture issue A debate over the relative influence of genetics and the environment on development, 12, **28**
Negative life events and mastery, 104
Negativity bias Weighing negative information more heavily than positive information in a social judgment, 226–227, 226f, **242**
Neglect, 315
Neural efficiency hypothesis States intelligent people process information more efficiently, showing weaker neural activations in a smaller number of areas than less intelligent people, 194, **214**
Neural stem cells (Also known as neural progenitors or neural precursor cells) are cells in the brain and spinal cord (the central nervous system, CNS) that are thought to give rise to the broad array of specialized cells of the CNS, including both neurons and glial cells, 49, 50, **54**
Neuroanatomy The study of the structure of the brain, 34, **54**
Neuro-correlational approach An approach that attempts to relate measures of cognitive performance to measures of brain structure or functioning, 32–33, **54**
Neurofibers Structures in the neuron that carry information inside the neuron from the dendrites to the terminal branches, 34, **54**
Neuroimaging A set of techniques in which pictures of the brain are taken in various ways to provide understanding of both normal and abnormal cognitive aging, 31–32, **54**
functional, 31–32
structural, 31
Neurons A brain cell, 34, 34f, 35, **54**
age-related changes in, 35
Neuropsychological approach Compares brain functioning of healthy older adults with adults displaying various pathological disorders in the brain, 32, **54**
Neuroscience research, 42–48
compensating for changes in brain, 44–45
CRUNCH model, 46
HAROLD model, 46
Parieto-Frontal Integration Theory, 43–44
PASA model, 46
STAC-r model, 46–48, 47f
Neuroscience The study of the brain, 30–51, **54**. *See also* Brain
activation imaging approach in, 33
adult development and aging and, 33–42
compensatory changes and, 33
neuro-correlational approach in, 32–33
neuroimaging techniques, 31–32
neuropsychological approach in, 32
perspectives, 32–33
plasticity and, 48–51
research, 42–48
social policy implications, 51
Neuroticism, 246–247

Neurotransmitters Chemicals that carry information signals between neurons across the synapse, 34, 35–36, **54**
  acetylcholine, 36
  age-related changes in, 35–36
  dopamine, 36
  serotonin, 36
NIHSeniorHealth.gov, 142, 280
Non-health-related quality of life Refers to things in the environment, such as entertainment, economic resources, arts, and so on that can affect our overall experience and enjoyment in life, 98, **125**
Nonnormative influences Random events that are important to an individual but do not happen to most people, 9, **28**
Norepinephrine and dopamine reuptake inhibitors (NDRIs), 282, 283
Normative age-graded influences Experiences caused by biological, psychological, and sociocultural forces that are closely related to a person's age, 9, **28**
Normative history-graded influences Events that most people in a specific culture experience at the same time, 9, **28**
North American Menopause Society, 81
NotAlone.gov, 314
Nuclear family Form of family consisting only of parent(s) and child(ren), 326, **338**
Nursing homes, 140–152
  characteristics of, 143–144
  communicating with residents in, 146–149, 148f
  decision-making capacity in, 150–151
  Eden Alternative, 151
  Green House project, 151–152
  individual choices in, 150–151
  long-term care in, 142–143
  minority residents, 141, 141f
  misconceptions about, 141
  new directions for, 151–152
  Pioneer Network, 152
  resident satisfaction in, 145–146, 146f
  social activities and interaction in, 145
  special care units, 144–145
  staff training required at, 145
  typical resident of, 143
Nutrition, 415–417, 418f
  brain aging and, 50–51
  memory and, 180
Nyad, Diana, 2

Obama, Barack, 272, 308, 314, 334, 366, 375, 405
Obama, Michelle, 308
Obesity, 417, 418t
Object permanence, 200
Occupational development, 342–344
  ethnicity and, 349
  expectations, 342–343
  mentors and coaches, 343–344
  women and, 347–349, 348f
Occupational selection, 340–366
  age discrimination, 351
  employment in late life, 364–365, 364f
  gender and, 346–351
  glass ceiling, 349
  job satisfaction, 344–346

  leisure activities, 359–366
  meaning of work, 340–341
  occupational choice, 341–342
  retirement, 362–364
  salary discrimination, 350, 350f
  sexual harassment, 350–351
  social policy implications, 366
  volunteering, 365–366
  women and, 347–349
Occupational transitions, 351–354
  occupational insecurity, 352–353
  retraining workers, 352
  unemployment, 353–354, 354f
OECD, 356, 357
Older Americans Act, 405, 412
Openness to experience, 247
Optimally exercised ability The ability a normal, healthy adult would demonstrate under the best conditions of training or practice, 206, **214**
Osteoarthritis A form of arthritis marked by gradual onset and progression of pain and swelling, caused primarily by overuse of a joint, 65–66, 66f, 67t, **89**
Osteoporosis A degenerative bone disease more common in women in which bone tissue deteriorates severely to produce honeycomb-like bone tissue, 64–65, 64f, 67t, **89**
Overflow incontinence A type of incontinence usually caused by improper contraction of the kidneys, causing the bladder to become over distended, 112, **125**
Overweight, 417, 418t

Pain management, 112–113
PALB2, 108
Palliative care Care that is focused on providing relief from pain and other symptoms of disease at any point during the disease process, 383, **400**
Parental role, 326–330
  costs of raising a child, 326f
  deciding to have children, 326–327
  ethnic diversity and, 327–328
  of middle-aged adults, 330–331
  single parents, 328–329, 328f
  step-, foster-, adoptive, and same-sex couple parenting, 329
  support for, 329–330
Parieto-Frontal Integration Theory (P-FIT) A theory that proposes that intelligence comes from a distributed and integrated network of neurons in the parietal and frontal areas of the brain, 43–44, **54**
Parkinson's disease, 296–297
Parkinson's Disease Foundation, 297
Parks, Rosa, 271
Passion A strong inclination toward an activity that individuals like (or even love), that they value (and thus find important), and in which they invest time and energy, 345–346, 346f, **370**
Passive euthanasia Allowing a person to die by withholding available treatment, 375, **400**
Patient-by-treatment context interactive framework, 115, 116f
Patient Protection and Affordable Care Act, 142–143, 334, 377, 396, 407

Patient Self-Determination Act (PSDA), 150, 386
Patronizing speech Inappropriate speech to older adults based on stereotypes of incompetence and dependence, 147, **156**
Pausch, Randy, 377
Perceived age, 11
Perimenopause The time of transition from regular menstruation to menopause, 80, **89**
Persistent vegetative state Situation in which a person's cortical functioning ceases while brainstem activity continues, 374, **400**
Personal concerns Things that are important to people, their goals, and their major concerns in life, 245, 250–257, **268**
  conclusions about, 257
  Erikson's theory and, 252–256, 252t
  Jung's theory and, 251–252
  theories based on life transitions, 256–257
Personal control The belief that what one does has an influence on the outcome of an event, 234–235, 234–236, **242**
  multidimensionality of, 234–235
  primary, criticisms regarding, 236
  strategies for, 235–236
Personal goals, 231–232
Personality, 244–266
  dispositional traits, 245–250
  five-factor model, 246–247
  McAdams's life story model, 259
  personal concerns and qualitative stages, 250–257
  possible selves, 262–263
  self-concept, 261–262
  Six Foci Model of Personality, 260–261, 260f
  social policy implications, 265–266
  spiritual support, 264–265
  well-being, 262
  Whitbourne's identity theory, 259–260, 260f
Personality adjustment Involves developmental changes in terms of their adaptive value and functionality such as functioning effectively within society and how personality contributes to everyday life running smoothly, 248, **269**
Personality growth Refers to ideal end states such as increased self-transcendence, wisdom, and integrity, 248, **269**
Person–environment interactions The interface between people and the world they live in that forms the basis for development, meaning behavior is a function of both the person and the environment, 128–153, **156**
  adaptation level and, 129, 130
  community options, 133–140
  competence and, 128–130, 129f, 132–133
  coping and, 132
  corrective adaptations and, 130–132, 131f
  describing, 128–133
  environmental press and, 128–130
  nursing homes, 140–152
  preventive adaptations and, 130–132, 131f
  social policy implications, 152–153
  stress and, 132
Pew Research Center, 6, 317, 324
Physical abuse, 315
Physical changes, 57–85
  appearance, 61–63
  autonomic nervous system, 83–84
  biological theories, 57–61

mobility, 63–66
reproductive system, 80–82
sensory systems, 67–74
social policy implications, 85
vital functions, 75–79
Physical limitations (PLIM) Activities that reflect functional limitations such as walking a block or sitting for about two hours, 119–120, 119t, **125**
Physician-assisted suicide Process in which physicians provide dying patients with a fatal dose of medication the patient self-administers, 375–377, **400**
Piaget's theory, 199–201
    accommodation, 200
    assimilation, 199–200
    concrete operational period, 200
    formal operational period, 200–201
    preoperational period, 200
    sensorimotor period, 200
Pioneer Network, 152
Plasticity Involves the interaction between the brain and the environment and is mostly used to describe the effects of experience on the structure and functions of the neural system. (ii) The belief that capacity is not fixed, but can be learned or improved with practice. (iii) The range of functioning within an individual and the conditions under which a person's abilities can be modified within a specific age range, 4, 13, **28**, 48–51, **55**, 188, **214**
    defined, 49
    exercise and, 49, 50
    nutrition and, 50–51
Plato, 11
Plummer, Christopher, 2
Political debates, 405–406
Polymorphonuclear neutrophil leukocytes, 99
Polypharmacy The use of multiple medications, 115, **125**
Population pyramid Graphic technique for illustrating population trends, 4–6, 5f, **28**
Positivity effect When an individual remembers more positive information relative to negative information. (ii) The tendency to attend to and process positive information over negative information, 42, **55**, 232, **242**
Possible selves Aspects of the self-concept involving oneself in the future in both positive and negative ways, 262–263, **269**
Posterior-Anterior Shift in Aging (PASA) model Model of cognitive aging reflecting from occipital to frontal processing that is thought to reflect age-related compensation, 46, **55**
Postformal thought Thinking characterized by a recognition that truth varies across situations, solutions must be realistic to be reasonable, ambiguity and contradiction are the rule rather than the exception, and emotion and subjective factors play a role in thinking, 201, **214**
Poverty rates, 404–405, 404f
Pragmatic intelligence The component of intelligence that concerns acquired bodies of knowledge available from and embedded within culture, 188, 188f, **214**

Prefrontal cortex Part of the frontal lobe that is involved in executive functioning, 35, 42, **55**
Preoperational period, 200
Presbycusis A normative age-related loss of the ability to hear high-pitched tones, 70–71, **89**
Presbyopia The normative age-related loss of the ability to focus on nearby objects, usually resulting in the need for corrective lenses, 68, **89**
Preventive adaptations Actions that avoid stressors and increase or build social resources, 130–132, 131f, **156**
Primary aging The normal, disease-free development during adulthood, 10, **28**
Primary appraisal First step in the stress and coping paradigm in which events are categorized into three groups based on the significance they have for our well-being—irrelevant, benign or positive, and stressful, 102–103, **125**
Primary control The act of bringing the environment into line with one's own desires and goals, similar to Brandtstädter's assimilative activities, 235–236, 235f, **242**
Primary mental abilities Independent abilities within psychometric intelligence based on different combinations of standardized intelligence tests, 191–192, 191f, **214**
Primary prevention Any intervention that prevents a disease or condition from occurring, 412, 413t, **420**
Prince, 372
Proactivity When people choose new behaviors to meet new desires or needs and exert control over their lives, 129, **156**
Problem-focused coping A style of coping that attempts to tackle a problem head-on, 103, **125**
Problem solving, 205–207
Processing resources The amount of attention one has to apply to a particular situation, 160–162, **184**
    attentional resources, 161–162
    inhibitory loss, 160–161
Prospective memory Process involving remembering to remember something in the future, 167–168, 167f, **184**
Prostate cancer, 106, 107, 108, 110–111t, 111–112
Psychological age, 11
Psychological forces One of the four basic forces of development that includes all internal perceptual, cognitive, emotional, and personality factors, 8, 8f, **28**
Psychometric approach An approach to intelligence involving defining it as performance on standardized tests, 189, **214**
Psychoneuroimmunology The study of the relations between psychological, neurological, and immunological systems that raise or lower our susceptibility to and ability to recover from disease, 100, **125**
Psychopathology
    defining, 273
    multidimensional life-span approach to, 274–275
Psychotherapy, 283t, 284
Psychotic disorders, 299–300

Quality of life, 98
Quality of life A person's well-being and life satisfaction, 409–410, **420**
Quaternary prevention Efforts specifically aimed at improving the functional capacities of people who have chronic conditions and avoiding overmedication, 413, 413t, **420**

Race and ethnicity. *See also* African Americans; Latinos
    average longevity and, 95
    chronological age and, 11
    culture and, 9–10
    demographic trends, 404
    depression and, 279–280, 280f
    diabetes mellitus, 106
    diversity and, 6
    diversity of older adults, 6–7, 7f
    ethnic identity and, 10
    healthy aging and, 404, 408, 409, 412, 417
    mental health and, 275
    nursing home residents and, 141, 141f
    occupational development and, 349
    parental roles and, 327–328
    research and, 16
    retirement and, 363
    sociocultural forces and, 8
    terms referring to, 10
Rape, Abuse, and Incest National Network, 314
Reagan, Ronald, 271
Reality shock Situation in which what one learns in the classroom does not always transfer directly into the "real world" and does not represent all a person needs to know, 343, **370**
Reappraisal In the stress and coping paradigm, this step involves making a new primary or secondary appraisal resulting from changes in the situation, 102–103, **125**
Recall Process of remembering information without the help of hints or cues, 165, **184**
Recognition Process of remembering information by selecting previously learned information from among several items, 165, **184**
Reflective judgment Thinking that involves how people reason through dilemmas involving current affairs, religion, science, and the like, 201–202, 202t, **214**
Rehearsal Process by which information is held in working memory, either by repeating items over and over or by making meaningful connections between the information in working memory and information, 163, **184**
Relationships, 308–335
    cohabitation, 317–318
    divorce, 322–324
    family dynamics, 326–334
    friendships, 308–311
    LGBTQ, 318
    love relationships, 311–314
    marriage, 318–322
    remarriage, 324–325
    singlehood, 316–317
    social policy implications, 334–335
    violence in, 314–316, 315t
    widowhood, 325–326

Reliability The ability of a measure to produce the same value when used repeatedly to measure the identical phenomenon over time, 15, **28**
Remarriage, 324–325
Repetitive transcranial magnetic stimulation (rTMS), 284
Representative sampling, 16
Reproductive system, 80–82
 female reproductive system, 80–82
 male reproductive system, 82
 psychological implications, 82
Research designs, 17–21, 22–23
 age effects and, 17, 18t
 case studies, 17
 cohort effects and, 17–18, 18t
 correlational, 17
 cross-sectional, 18–19, 19t, 22–23
 experimental, 16–17
 general, 16–17
 longitudinal, 19–20, 19t, 22–23
 sequential, 20–21, 20t
 time-of-measurement effects and, 18, 18t
Research measurements, 15–16
 reliability of, 15
 representative sampling, 16
 sampling behavior with tasks, 16
 self-reports, 16
 systematic observation, 15
 validity of, 15
Research methods, 15–24. *See also* Neuroscience research; Research designs; Research measurements
 designs for studying development, 17–21, 22–23
 ethics in, 21, 24
 findings from different studies, integrating, 21
 general designs for, 16–17
 intelligence and, 189
 measurement, 15–16
 social policy implications, 24
Resilience theory Argues that confronting a negative stereotype results in a rejection of that view in favor of a more positive self-perception, 223, **242**
Respiratory diseases, 79
Respiratory system, 79
Retinal changes, 68–69
Retirement, 362–364
Retrieval The process of getting information back out of memory, 162, 166, **184**
Rheumatoid arthritis A destructive form of arthritis that develops slowly and involves different joints and more swelling than osteoarthritis, 65–66, 66f, 67t, **89**
Richardson, Natasha, 179
Risk factors Long-standing behaviors or conditions that increase one's chances of functional limitation or disability, 117, **125**
Rivera, Diego, 210
RNASEL, 111
Roosevelt, Franklin, 406

Sacks, Oliver, 45
SAE International, 411
Salutogenesis An approach that emphasizes factors that support and promote health, rather than factors that cause disease, 409, **420**

Sampling behavior with tasks, 16
Sandberg, Sheryl, 350
Sanders, Bernie, 2, 203, 266
Sandwich generation Middle-aged adults caught between the competing demands of two generations: their parents and their children, 330, **338**
Sarcopenia, 119
Saunders, Cicely, 383
Scaffolding Theory of Cognitive Aging-Revised (STAC-r) A model based on the idea that age-related changes in one's ability to function reflect a life-long process of compensating for cognitive decline by recruiting additional brain areas and takes life-course factors that enhance or deplete neural resources into account, 46–48, 47f, **55**
Schiavo, Terri, 396
Schizophrenia, 299–300
Secondary aging Developmental changes that are related to disease, lifestyle, and other environmental changes that are not inevitable, 10, **28**
Secondary appraisal In the stress and coping paradigm, an assessment of our perceived ability to cope with harm, threat, or challenge, 102–103, **125**
Secondary control The act of bringing oneself in line with the environment, similar to Brandtstädter's accommodative activities, 235–236, 235f, **242**
Secondary mental abilities Broad-ranging skills composed of several primary mental abilities, 191–193, 191f, 192–193t, **214**
Secondary prevention Instituted early after a condition has begun (but may not yet have been diagnosed) and before significant impairments have occurred, 413, 413t, **420**
Selection, optimization, and compensation (SOC) model, 98, 409, 410
Selective serotonin reuptake inhibitors (SSRIs), 282
Self-concept The organized, coherent, integrated pattern of self-perceptions, 261–262, **269**
Self-neglect, 316
Self-perception of aging Refers to individuals' perceptions of their own age and aging, 222–223, **242**
Self-reports People's answers to questions about a topic of interest, 16, **28**
Semantic memory Learning and remembering the meaning of words and concepts that are not tied to specific occurrences of events in time, 164–165, 171, **184**
Sensorimotor period, 200
Sensory memory A very brief and almost identical representation of the stimuli that exists in the observable environment, 159–160, **184**
Sensory systems, 67–74
 balance, 73
 hearing, 69–72
 smell, 74
 somesthesia, 72, 73
 taste, 73–74
 vision, 68–69

Separation distress Expression of complicated or prolonged grief disorder that includes preoccupation with the deceased to the point it interferes with everyday functioning, upsetting memories of the deceased, longing and searching for the deceased, and isolation following the loss, 393, **400**
Sequential designs Types of developmental research designs involving combinations of cross-sectional and longitudinal designs, 20–21, 20t, **28**
Serotonin, 36
Serotonin reuptake inhibitors (SRIs), 299
Serotonin reuptake inhibitors (SSRIs), 282, 299
Sex, Romance, and Relationships (AARP) study, 82
Sex in America study (AARP), 82
Singlehood, 316–317
Situational attribution An explanation for someone's behavior that is external to the actor, 229, **242**
Six Foci Model of Personality, 260–261, 260f
Skin, 61–62
Sleep and aging, 84
Smell, 74
Social beliefs, 221–223
 age differences in, 222
 self-perception and, 222, 223
Social cognition, 216–238
 motivation and social processing goals, 231–233
 personal control, 234–236
 social judgment processes, 224–231
 social knowledge structures and beliefs, 221–223
 social policy implications, 238
 social situations and social competence, 236–238
 stereotypes and, 217–221
Social cognitive career theory (SCCT) Proposes career choice is a result of the application of Bandura's social cognitive theory, especially the concept of self-efficacy, 341–342, 342f, **370**
Social-emotional cognition, linking with structural changes in brain, 41–42
Social judgment processes, 224–231
 attributional biases and, 229–231, 230f
 emotional intelligence and, 224
 impression formation and, 224–227, 226f
 knowledge accessibility and, 227–228
 processing capacity explanation for age differences in, 228
Social knowledge A cognitive structure that represents one's general knowledge about a given social concept or domain, 227–228, **242**
 structures and beliefs, 221–223
Social policy implications
 death and dying, 396
 health and illness, 121
 intelligence, 211
 memory, 180
 mental health, 302–303
 neuroscience, 51
 occupational selection and development, 366
 personality, 265–266
 person–environment interactions, 152–153
 physical changes, 85
 relationships, 334–335

research methods, 24
social cognition, 238
Social processing goals, 231–233
   cognitive style, 233
   emotion, 232–233
Social Security, 406, 407
Social Security and Medicare Boards of Trustees, 405, 406, 407
Social situations and social competence, 236–238
   collaborative cognition, 237–238
   social context of memory, 238
Society for Automotive Engineers (SAE), 411, 411f
Sociocultural age, 11
Sociocultural forces One of the four basic forces of development that include interpersonal, societal, cultural, and ethnic factors, 8, 8f, **28**
Socioemotional selectivity A theory of relationships that argues social contact is motivated by a variety of goals, including information seeking, self-concept, and emotional regulation, 311, **338**
Somesthesia, 72, 73
Source judgments Process of accessing knowledge wherein one attempts to determine where one obtained a particular piece of information, 228, **242**
Source memory The ability to remember the source of a familiar event as well as the ability to determine if an event was imagined or actually experienced, 170, **184**
Spaced retrieval, 174
Spaced retrieval A behavioral, implicit-internal memory intervention used in early- and middle-stage dementia, 294, **306**
Speed of processing How quickly and efficiently the early steps in information processing are completed, 160, **184**
Spiritual support Includes seeking pastoral care, participating in organized and nonorganized religious activities, and expressing faith in a God who cares for people as a key factor in understanding how older adults cope, 264–265, **269**
Stability–change issue A debate over the degree to which people remain the same over time as opposed to being different, 12–13, **28**
State processes A structural component of personality that acts with dispositional traits to create transient, short-term changes in emotion, mood, hunger, anxiety, and the like, 245, **269**
Statins, 417
Stereotypes Beliefs about characteristics, attributes, and behaviors of members of certain groups, 217–221, **242**
   activation of, 218–220
   age stereotypes and perceived competence, 217–218
   cognitive performance and, 220–221
   content of, 217–218
   negative, memory and, 171
   stereotype threat and, 220–221
Stereotype threat An evoked fear of being judged in accordance with a negative stereotype about a group to which an individual belongs, 220, **242**

Storage The manner in which information is represented and kept in memory, 162, **184**
Straine, Trish, 394
Strategies Various techniques that make learning or remembering easier and that increase the efficiency of storage, 165–166, **184**
Stress, 101–105
   appraisal and, 102–103
   coping and, 103
   effects of, on health, 105
   mastery and, 104
   person–environment interactions and, 132
   as physiological response, 101
   stress and coping paradigm and, 102, 103–104
   transactional model of, 102, 102f
Stress and coping paradigm A model that views stress, not as an environmental stimulus or as a response, but as the interaction of a thinking person and an event, 102, **125**
Stress incontinence A type of incontinence that happens when pressure in the abdomen exceeds the ability to resist urinary flow, 109, **125**
Stroke. See Cerebrovascular accident (CVA)
Structural neuroimaging A set of techniques that provides highly detailed images of anatomical features in the brain, 31, **55**
Structure of intelligence The organization of interrelated intellectual abilities, 190–191, **214**
Subjective well-being An evaluation of one's life that is associated with positive feelings, 262, **269**
Summit, Pat, 271, 272
Sundowning The phenomenon when people with Alzheimer's disease show an increase in symptoms later in the day, 287, **306**
Supplemental Poverty Measure (SPM), 404f, 405
Swanson, Gunhild, 60
Synapse The gap between neurons across which neurotransmitters travel, 34, **55**
Systematic observation A type of measurement involving watching people and carefully recording what they say or do, 15, **28**
Systolic pressure, 78

Taste, 73–74
Technology, 410–411
Telomerase An enzyme needed in DNA replication to fully reproduce the telomeres when cells divide, 58, **89**
Telomeres, Tips of the chromosomes that shorten with each cell replication, 58–59, 59f, **89**
Terminal branches The endpoints in a neuron that help transmit signals across the synapse, 34, **55**
Terminal decline The gradual decline in cognitive function that occurs relatively near death, 196, **214**
Terror management theory Addresses the issue of why people engage in certain behaviors to achieve particular psychological states based on their deeply rooted concerns about mortality, 381, **400**
Tertiary aging Rapid losses occurring shortly before death, 10–11, **28**

Tertiary prevention Involves efforts to avoid the development of complications or secondary chronic conditions, manage the pain associated with the primary chronic condition, and sustain life through medical intervention, 413, 413t, **420**
Thanatology The study of death, dying, grief, bereavement, and social attitudes toward these issues, 372, **400**
Theory of Mind (ToM) The ability that helps us understand that other people have beliefs, desires, ideas, feelings, intentions, and viewpoints that are different from our own, 37–42, **55**
Thinking, 199–211
   creativity, 208–209, 209f, 210
   decision making, 205
   emotion and logic, integrating, 203–204
   expertise, 207–208
   logic, integrating, 203–204
   Piaget's theory and, 199–201
   postformal thought, 201
   problem solving, 205–207
   qualitative differences in, 199–204
   reflective judgment, 201–202, 202t
   wisdom, 209, 210–211
Thomas, Bill and Jude Meyers, 151
Time-of-measurement effects One of the three fundamental effects examined in developmental research, along with age and cohort effects, which result from the time at which the data are collected, 18, 18t, **28**
T-lymphocytes, 99
Torres, Dara, 57, 60
Trait Any distinguishable, relatively enduring way in which one individual differs from others, 246, **269**
Trait theories of personality that assume little change occurs across adulthood, 246–250, **269**
Transactional model of stress, 102, 102f
Transgender and gender nonconforming (TGNC), 318
Transient global amnesia (TGA) Temporary experience of a complete memory loss and disorientation in time, 178, **184**
Traumatic brain injury (TBI), 178–179
Traumatic distress Expression of complicated or prolonged grief disorder that includes feeling disbelief about the death, mistrust, anger, and detachment from others as a result of the death, feeling shocked by the death, and the experience of physical presence of the deceased, 393, **400**
Triggering situations, Expectancy, States/State Expressions, and Reactions (TESSERA) model, 249, 250f
Trump, Donald J, 2, 225, 266
Type 1 diabetes A type of diabetes that tends to develop earlier in life and requires the use of insulin; also called insulin dependent diabetes, 106, **125**
Type 2 diabetes A type of diabetes that tends to develop in adulthood and is effectively managed through diet, 106, **125**

Underweight, 417, 418t
Unemployment, 353–354, 354f

Unexercised ability The ability a normal, healthy adult would exhibit without practice or training, 206, **214**

Universal *versus* context-specific development controversy A debate over whether there is a single pathway of development, or several, 14, **28**

Urge incontinence A type of incontinence usually caused by a central nervous system problem after a stroke or urinary tract infection in which people feel the urge to urinate but cannot get to a toilet quickly enough, 109, 112, **125**

U.S. Department of Agriculture, 327, 415–416
U.S. Department of Health and Human Services, 101
U.S. Department of Labor, 346–347, 354
U.S. Department of Labor Women's Bureau, 346, 349, 350
U.S. Food and Drug Administration, 113, 114, 174, 292, 301

Vacco v. Quill, 376
Vaginal dryness, 81, 82
Vagus nerve stimulation (VNS), 284
Validity The degree to which an instrument measures what it is supposed to measure, 15, **28**
Vascular dementia A form of dementia caused by a series of small strokes, 296, **306**
Violence Against Women Act, 335
Violence in relationships, 314–316, 315t
 abusive relationships, 314
 battered woman syndrome, 314
 continuum of progressive behaviors, 315t
 elder abuse, neglect, and exploitation, 315–316
Vision, 68–69
 acuity, 69
 adaptation, 68
 age-related macular degeneration, 68–69
 cataracts, 68
 diabetic retinopathy, 69
 glaucoma, 68
 presbyopia, 68
 psychological effects of, 69
 retinal changes, 68–69
 structural changes in eye, 68
Vital functions, 75–79
 cardiovascular system, 75–79, 76f
 respiratory system, 79
Vitamin D intake, recommended, 65t
Voice, 62
Volunteering, 365–366
Vulnerability-stress-adaptation model A model that sees marital quality as a dynamic process resulting from the couple's ability to handle stressful events in the context of their particular vulnerabilities and resources, 320–321, 320f, **338**

Washington v. Glucksberg, 376
WebMD, 79
Well-being, 261–262
 emotion and, 262
 subjective, 262
Whitbourne's identity theory, 259–260, 260f
White matter hyperintensities (WMH) Abnormalities in the brain often found in older adults; correlated with cognitive decline, 36, **55**
White matter Neurons that are covered by myelin that serve to transmit information from one part of the cerebral cortex to another or from the cerebral cortex to other parts of the brain, 36, **55**
Whole-brain death Death that is declared only when the deceased meets certain criteria established revised in 2010, 374, **400**

Widowhood, 325–326
Williams, Robin, 45, 271, 296
Winehouse, Amy, 372
Wisdom, 209, 210–211
Wittgenstein, Ludwig, 11
Women's Health Initiative (WHI), 81
Women's Health Research Institute, 80, 81
WomensHealth.gov, 80
Work. *See also* Employment in late life; Occupational development; Occupational selection
 family and, 355–358
 meaning of, 340–341
Work–family conflict The feeling of being pulled in multiple directions by incompatible demands from job and family, 358, **370**
Working memory Refers to the processes and structures involved in holding information in mind and simultaneously using that information, sometimes in conjunction with incoming information, to solve a problem, make a decision, or learn new information, 162–163, **184**
World Health Organization, 120, 285, 314

Yellen, Janet, 2
Young, Malcolm, 271

Zaslow, Jeff, 377
Zone of maximum comfort In competence–environmental press theory, the area where slight decreases in environmental press occur, 129, **156**
Zone of maximum performance potential In competence–environmental press theory, the area where increases in press tend to improve performance, 129, **156**